EIGHTH EDITION

THE ENDURING VISION

A History of the American People

Paul S. Boyer
University of Wisconsin

Clifford E. Clark, Jr.
Carleton College

Karen Halttunen
University of Southern California

Joseph F. Kett
University of Virginia

Neal Salisbury
Smith College

Harvard Sitkoff
University of New Hampshire

Nancy Woloch
Barnard College

WADSWORTH
CENGAGE Learning

Australia • Brazil • Japan • Korea • Mexico • Singapore • Spain • United Kingdom • United States

The Enduring Vision: A History of the American People, Volume II: Since 1865, Eighth Edition

Paul S. Boyer, Clifford E. Clark, Jr., Karen Halttunen, Joseph F. Kett, Neal Salisbury, Harvard Sitkoff, and Nancy Woloch

Senior Publisher: Suzanne Jeans

Senior Sponsoring Editor: Ann West

Senior Development Editor: Tonya Lobato

Assistant Editor: Megan Chrisman

Editorial Assistant: Kati Coleman

Managing Media Editor: Lisa Ciccolo

Executive Brand Manager: Melissa Larmon

Marketing Coordinator: Lorreen Towle

Senior Content Project Manager: Jane Lee

Senior Art Director: Cate Rickard Barr

Manufacturing Planner: Sandee Milewski

Senior Rights Acquisition Specialist: Jennifer Meyer Dare

Production Service: Integra

Text Designer: Diane Beasley

Cover Designer: Sarah Bishins, Sarah B Design

Cover Image Researcher: Anthony L. Saizon

Cover Image: An aerial view of the North Meadow and Reservoir in Central Park, Manhattan, New York City, New York. Credit: MICHAEL S. YAMASHITA/National Geographic Stock

Compositor: Integra

For product information and technology assistance, contact us at **Cengage Learning Customer & Sales Support, 1-800-354-9706**

For permission to use material from this text or product, submit all requests online at **www.cengage.com/permissions**. Further permissions questions can be emailed to **permissionrequest@cengage.com**.

Library of Congress Control Number: 2012946001

Student Edition:
ISBN-13: 978-1-133-94522-2
ISBN-10: 1-133-94522-8

Wadsworth
20 Channel Center Street
Boston, MA 02210
USA

Cengage Learning is a leading provider of customized learning solutions with office locations around the globe, including Singapore, the United Kingdom, Australia, Mexico, Brazil, and Japan. Locate your local office at **international.cengage.com/region**

Cengage Learning products are represented in Canada by Nelson Education, Ltd.

For your course and learning solutions, visit **www.cengage.com**.

Purchase any of our products at your local college store or at our preferred online store **www.cengagebrain.com**.

Instructors: Please visit **login.cengage.com** and log in to access instructor-specific resources.

Printed in the United States of America
1 2 3 4 5 6 7 16 15 14 13 12

In March 2012, shortly after completing his revisions to *The Enduring Vision*, our colleague Paul Boyer died, leaving both the text's authors and the editors at Cengage Learning deeply regretting our loss. Paul was a distinguished cultural and intellectual historian of the twentieth-century United States who served as a quiet leader on *The Enduring Vision* team ever since its inception more than 25 years ago. For every successive edition, he worked tirelessly to bring the textbook up to date, not only by adding recent events, but often overhauling the final chapters of the text from the new perspective generated by those recent events. He was a gentle and generous colleague, and we dedicate this Eighth Edition to him with gratitude and affection.

BRIEF CONTENTS

CONTENTS

SPECIAL FEATURES

MAPS

FIGURES

TABLES

PREFACE

The history of the United States has been shaped by an *enduring vision,* a shared commitment to a set of beliefs and values—including individual freedom, social equality, the rule of law, and openness to diversity—that run like threads through the lives of the American people. Those powerful beliefs and values express the people's collective determination to give meaning to America. Over the course of U.S. history, even when those values have been violated, that central vision of America has endured. *The Enduring Vision,* Eighth Edition, continues its authors' commitment, first undertaken more than 25 years ago, to convey the strength of that enduring vision over centuries of often destabilizing change.

Over the past 50 years, the discipline of history itself has changed dramatically, moving from an earlier focus on national political narrative toward a rich and complex array of approaches—such as social, cultural, environmental, and global history. *The Enduring Vision* aims to integrate the best recent scholarship in all fields of American history without abandoning a clear political and chronological framework. In keeping with our central theme, our primary emphasis from the First Edition to this new Eighth Edition has been social and cultural history, the fields that have shaped the authors' own teaching and scholarship. We are attentive to the lived historical experiences of women, African Americans, Hispanic Americans, Asian Americans, and American Indians—that is, of men and women of all ethnic groups, regions, and social classes who make up the American mosaic. It was in their daily lives, their lived experience of American history, that the enduring vision of America was articulated—and it was their actions that put those visionary values to the test.

The Enduring Vision is designed for both college classrooms and Advanced Placement courses in U.S. history. Though it offers an appropriately complex treatment of the American past, it requires no prerequisite knowledge from students. Our approach is not only comprehensive, but readable, lively, and illuminating. *The Enduring Vision* is also attentive to the process of historical learning. Recent research on history education has emphasized the crucial importance of teaching students the fundamental skills of historical thinking, such as addressing both continuity and change over time, using evidence to construct and test their own hypotheses, understanding past events in their own contexts, and coming to terms with the contingency of history. *The Enduring Vision* is especially effective in helping students understand the connections between particular historical events and larger trends and developments.

Newer Approaches to the American Past

This new Eighth Edition of *The Enduring Vision* sustains the emphasis on social and cultural history that was established in the First Edition. Religious history remains an important focus, from the spiritual values of pre-Columbian communities to the political activism of contemporary conservative Christian groups. Family history and the history of education receive serious attention. Visual culture—paintings, photographs, cartoons, and other illustrations—is investigated through all chapters in the volume. To help history come alive for our students, the Eighth Edition continues our practice of using **large-type quote displays** to highlight the words of people—both ordinary and famous—directly involved in the historical developments under discussion. To enhance our emphasis on social and cultural history, we also open each chapter with a **biographical vignette** of a single American life—millworker Harriet Jane Robinson, pro-slavery defender Edmund Ruffin, civil-rights activist Martin Luther King, Jr.—to introduce students to central themes of the chapter and remind us that history always involves the choices and actions of individual women and men.

Environmental History

From the first edition on, *The Enduring Vision* has also paid close attention to the environmental history of America's past, because it is clear that geography, land, and landscape have played an important role throughout human history. *The Enduring Vision's* unique **Prologue** on the American Land solidly establishes those themes early on, and our extensive coverage of environmental history, the land, and the West is fully integrated into the narrative and treated analytically—not simply "tacked on" to a traditional account. We seek to encourage students' spatial thinking about historical developments by offering a **map program** rich in information, easy to read, and visually appealing. And our primary source feature, **Going to the Source** (described in more detail later), offers a number of primary sources involving the land, including excerpts from Meriwether Lewis's Journal, Thoreau's essay "Walking," and a Dust Bowl diary.

Global History

In response to newer developments in the history discipline, recent editions of *The Enduring Vision* have underscored the global context of American history. We continue to engage with new literature on global history throughout the narrative, and in the special feature **Beyond America—Global Interactions** first introduced in the Sixth Edition. From the origins of agriculture ten millennia ago to the global impact of environmental changes today, we have emphasized how all facets of our historical experience emerge with fresh new clarity when viewed within a broader world framework.

Histories of Technology and Medicine

Students show a particular fascination with the histories of technology and medicine. In our popular **Technology & Culture** feature, and throughout the text, we continue to highlight the historical importance of new inventions and technological innovations. In addition to discussing the applications of science and technology, we note the often unanticipated cultural, social, and political consequences of such innovations—from new hunting implements developed by Paleo-Indians to contemporary breakthroughs in information processing. Medicine and disease receive extensive coverage, and we look at the epidemics brought by European explorers and settlers as well as today's AIDS crisis, bioethics debates, and controversies over health-care financing.

Organization and Special Features of *The Enduring Vision*

The general organization of the text is chronological, with individual chapters conforming to important historical periods. In keeping with our emphasis on social and cultural history, some chapters take a more thematic approach, overlapping chronologically with those that precede and follow them, thus introducing students to a more sophisticated understanding of the different levels—political, cultural, economic, social—of historical periodization.

Pedagogical Structure

Within each chapter, we offer a number of features designed to help students grasp its structure and purpose. The **opening vignette** focuses biographically on a single individual's experience and introduces students to the broader developments, themes, and historical problems that will be addressed in that chapter. The chapter opener also includes an **outline** that lists both the major headings and the subheads of the chapter. Then the student is presented with **focus questions** corresponding to the major sections of the chapter—questions designed to help students read the chapter actively rather than passively. **Chronologies** appear near the beginning of each chapter to provide an overview of key events. The chapter **conclusion** addresses and answers the focus questions, providing students with an opportunity to review what they've read.

As a further pedagogical aid, each chapter includes **key terms** that appear in boldface in the text where first introduced

and grouped at the end of the chapter. Key terms also appear in boldface in the index and are defined in an alphabetical glossary on *The Enduring Vision* website. In addition, an annotated, up-to-date list of core readings offers guidance for those wishing to explore a particular topic in depth.

Special Features

Every chapter of *The Enduring Vision* provides students with either a **Beyond America—Global Interactions** feature or a **Technology & Culture** feature. **Beyond America—Global Interactions** offers provocative, in-depth discussions of America's place in world history, focusing on such global developments as the origins and spread of agriculture, slave emancipation in the Atlantic World, and global climate change. **Technology & Culture** provides fascinating insight into such subjects as sugar production in the Americas, guns and gun culture, and the interstate highway system. Both features address important developments in U.S. history from the perspective of major new approaches to the past, with an intensity of detail geared to engaging students' curiosity and analytic engagement.

Every chapter of *The Enduring Vision* also includes a primary source feature, **Going to the Source**, first introduced in the Seventh Edition. Its pedagogical purpose is not only to bring history alive for our students, but to offer opportunities for their direct engagement in historical interpretation and analysis. **Going to the Source** offers a rich selection of primary sources, drawing on speeches, diaries, letters, and other materials created by Americans who lived through and helped shape the great events and historical changes of successive periods. In selecting documents, we focused especially, but not exclusively, on environmental themes. A brief introduction places each selection in context, and focus questions suggest assignment and discussion possibilities. The voices captured in **Going to the Source** include both prominent historical figures (from Christopher Columbus to Barack Obama) and lesser-known men and women (such as the Cherokee named Swimmer who explained the place of human beings in the natural world to an early anthropologist, and North Dakota farm girl Anna Marie Low who endured the terrible dust storms of the 1930s).

New to the Eighth Edition of *The Enduring Vision*

This edition of *The Enduring Vision* brings the work fully up to date, incorporating major developments and scholarship since the Seventh Edition went to press. In our chapter revisions, we have introduced new material and new visual images, tightened and clarified lines of argument, and responded to reviewers' suggestions for strengthening our work.

For the Eighth Edition of *The Enduring Vision*, we have carefully assessed the coverage, interpretations, and analytic framework of each chapter to incorporate the latest scholarship and emerging themes. This process is reflected both in our textual revisions and in the new works of scholarship cited in the end-of-chapter bibliographies. A chapter-by-chapter glimpse of some of the changes highlights new content and up-to-the-minute scholarship.

Chapter 1 elaborates on recently uncovered evidence pertaining to the earliest known humans in the Americas. **Chapter 2** provides a stronger emphasis on the Atlantic world as central to the major developments discussed there. In **Chapter 3**, the discussion of the transition from indentured servitude to slavery has been refined. The chapter also clarifies the distinctiveness of the Middle Colonies as a colonial region. **Chapter 4** offers added discussion of the rise of the Comanches as the dominant power challenging Spain on the southern Plains and in the Southwest, and new details on the War of Jenkins' Ear.

Chapter 5 now includes reference to the French uprising against Spanish rule in Louisiana, offers new details on the Sugar Act, and elaborates on the involvement of women in resistance to the British. **Chapter 6** provides additional information on the motives, backgrounds, and postwar fates of Loyalists. It also offers a new **Going to the Source** feature consisting of key sections of the Northwest Ordinance of 1787. **Chapter 7** provides new material on the impact in the United States of the black uprising in Saint Domingue, which resulted in the overthrow of French rule and the independence of the republic of Haiti.

Chapter 8 sharpens the distinction between mainstream National Republicans and strict Jeffersonians or Old Republicans. **Chapter 9** has been fully revised for clarity and condensed in length. **Chapter 10** clarifies the rise of the Whig opposition, explains the grassroots origins of the woman's rights movement, and offers a new **Going to the Source** feature: "The Declaration of Sentiments" issued by the Seneca Falls Convention in 1848. **Chapter 11** sharpens the distinction between the cultures of classicism and romanticism and explains the link between the romantic view of nature and the environmental devastation brought by the commercial and industrial revolutions.

Chapter 12 has been fully revised for clarity and includes a new **Going to the Source** feature: former slave Henry Bibb's account of slave religion and resistance and his decision to escape to freedom. **Chapter 14** now explains why the Lower South seceded from the Union before Lincoln was placed in office. **Chapter 15** revisits Lincoln's stance on slavery and explores the British response to the Civil War.

Chapter 17 includes new material on Chinese prostitution and Chinese laborers. **Chapter 18** elaborates on the treatment of child labor and offers new discussion of discrimination against the physically disabled. **Chapter 19** now explores the connection between intercollegiate sports and business leadership and provides new treatment of women writers. **Chapter 20** expands its coverage of racial lynching and the emergence of Black Populism. **Chapter 21** now defines "Social Gospel," expands its treatment of the 1912 Socialist party platform, explains in a more nuanced fashion the relationship between Progressivism and the New Deal, and offers a new **Going to the Source** feature about violence at a shirtwaist workers' strike.

Chapter 22 expands on the larger significance of U.S. involvements in Latin America and the effects of World War I on African American expectations of equality and includes a new **Going to the Source** feature describing the effects of the 1918 influenza epidemic. **Chapter 23** enhances the treatment of women voting in 1920, the rise of African American political consciousness in the 1920s, and the international protest over the Sacco-Vanzetti case. It also offers a new **Going to the Source** feature: a memoir of a young woman's movie-going memories from the 1920s. **Chapter 24** clarifies the overall themes of the New Deal; underscores on the role of the Civilian Conservation Corps in heightening environmental awareness; and emphasizes the interconnectedness of political, social, and cultural history in the 1930s. **Chapter 25** expands discussion of the dropping of the A-bombs in Japan.

Chapter 26 now includes sections on demobilization, the GI Bill of Rights, and the beginnings of the postwar economic boom. **Chapters 27 and 28** offer expanded discussions of the civil-rights movement. **Chapter 29** expands the treatment of feminism and Martin Luther King's concept of "a revolution of values."

Chapter 30 offers updated statistics on welfare and unemployment; more nuanced treatment of the term "conservative revolution"; and a brand new, more interpretive, conclusion. **Chapter 31** brings *The Enduring Vision* up to date with new material on the Obama presidency; health-care reform; economic recession; congressional gridlock; the Tea Party and Occupy Wall Street movements; the presidential campaign of 2012; and recent developments in Afghanistan, Pakistan, and Iran. It also offers a new chapter opener built around the housing foreclosure crisis.

Supplementary Resources for *The Enduring Vision,* Eighth Edition

The Enduring Vision, Eighth Edition, offers a wide array of supplements to help students master the material and to guide instructors in setting up and managing their courses. For more information on viewing or ordering these materials, please consult your sales representative.

For Students:

- **Companion Website for *The Enduring Vision*** features an assortment of resources and tools to help students master the subject matter. The Companion Website includes a glossary, flashcards, tutorial quizzes, and additional suggested readings.

- Cengage Learning's **History CourseMate** brings course concepts to life with interactive learning, study, and exam preparation tools that support the textbook. History CourseMate includes an integrated eBook; interactive teaching and learning tools, including quizzes, flashcards, and videos; as well as EngagementTracker, a first-of-its-kind tool that monitors student engagement in the course. Learn more at www.cengagebrain.com.

- The interactive multimedia **CL eBook** links out to rich media assets such as video and MP3 chapter summaries. Through this eBook, students can also access self-test quizzes, chapter outlines, focus questions, chronology exercises, essay questions (for which the answers can be e-mailed to their instructors), primary source documents with critical thinking questions, and interactive (zoomable) maps. Available at www.cengagebrain.com.

For Instructors:

- **Companion Website for *The Enduring Vision*, Eighth Edition,** offers instructors access to all of the features of the **Student Companion Website,** plus access to all the instructor resources, including the **Instructor's Resource Manual** as well as **PowerPoint® slides for lecture—and testing materials.** The IRM includes chapter themes, lecture suggestions, instructional suggestions, print and nonprint resources, and document set activities.

- **PowerLecture** with **ExamView** and **JoinIn** for *The Enduring Vision,* Eighth Edition [ISBN: 9781285056678]. This dual-platform, all-in-one multimedia resource includes the **Instructor's Resource Manual; Test Bank** (with short answer, multiple-choice, and essay questions); **Microsoft® PowerPoint®** slides of lecture outlines and images and maps from the text that can be used as offered, or customized by importing personal lecture slides or other material; and **JoinIn® PowerPoint®** slides with clicker content. Also included is **ExamView,** an easy-to-use assessment and tutorial system that allows instructors to create, deliver, and customize tests in minutes. Instructors can build tests with as many as 250 questions using up to 12 question types, and using ExamView's complete word-processing capabilities, they can enter an unlimited number of new questions or edit existing ones.

Additional Supplements

- *Rand McNally Atlas of American History,* 2/e [ISBN: 9780618842018], is available for packaging with this text. This comprehensive atlas features more than 80 maps, with new content covering global perspectives, including events in the Middle East from 1945 to 2005, as well as population trends in the United States and around the world. Additional maps document voyages of discovery; the settling of the colonies; major U.S. military engagements, including the American Revolution and World Wars I and II; and sources of immigrations, ethnic populations and patterns of economic change.

- Aplia™ is an online interactive learning solution that improves comprehension and outcomes by increasing student effort and engagement. Founded by a professor to enhance his own courses, Aplia provides automatically graded assignments with detailed, immediate explanations on every question. The interactive assignments have been developed to address the major concepts covered in *The Enduring Vision* and are designed to promote critical thinking and engage students more fully in their learning. Question types include questions built around animated maps, primary sources such as newspaper extracts, or imagined scenarios—like engaging in a conversation with Benjamin Franklin or finding a diary and being asked to fill in some blank words; more in-depth primary source question sets that address a major topic with a number of related primary sources and questions promote deeper analysis of historical evidence. Images, video clips, and audio clips are incorporated in many of the questions. Students get immediate feedback on their work (not only what they got right or wrong, but why), and they can choose to see another set of related questions if they want to practice further. A searchable eBook is available inside the course as well so that students can easily reference it as they are working. Map-reading and writing tutorials are available as well to get students off to a good start. Aplia's simple-to-use course management interface allows instructors to post announcements, upload course materials, host student discussions, e-mail students, and manage the gradebook; personalized support from a knowledgeable and friendly support team also offers assistance in customizing assignments to the instructor's course schedule. To learn more, ask your Cengage Learning sales representative to provide a demo—or view a specific demo for this book, at www.aplia.com.

- **CourseReader** is an online collection of primary and secondary sources that lets you create a customized electronic reader in minutes. With an easy-to-use interface and assessment tool, you can choose exactly what your students will be assigned—simply search or browse Cengage Learning's extensive document database to preview and select your customized collection of readings. In addition to print sources of all types (letters, diary entries, speeches, newspaper accounts, etc.), the collection includes a growing number of images and video and audio clips. Each primary source document includes a descriptive headnote that puts the reading into context and is further supported by both critical thinking and multiple-choice questions designed to reinforce key points. For more information visit www.cengage.com/coursereader.

- *Enduring Voices* Document Set. A two-volume document collection, ***Enduring Voices,*** can be packaged with the text. [Volume 1 ISBN: 9780395960844; Volume 2 ISBN: 9780395960868].

- **Other United States History Readers**. Wadsworth, Cengage Learning publishes a wide variety of primary and secondary source readers that could be used to complement this text. These include collections focusing on cultural history, political documents, social history essays, biography, and readers with specific methods of primary source analysis. Contact your Wadsworth, Cengage Learning sales representative for more details about the readers that would work best for you and your students.

Acknowledgments

In undertaking this major revision of our textbook, we have drawn on our own scholarly work and teaching experience. We have also kept abreast of new work of historical interpretation, as reported by our U.S. history colleagues in their books, scholarly articles, and papers at historical meetings. We list much of this new work in the books cited at the close of each chapter and in the Additional Bibliographies on *The Enduring Vision* website. We are much indebted to all these colleagues.

We have also benefited from the comments and suggestions of instructors who have adopted *The Enduring Vision;* from colleagues and students who have written us about specific details; and from the following scholars and teachers who offered systematic evaluations of specific chapters. Their perceptive comments have been most helpful in the revision process.

Robert Berta, *Northern Kentucky University*

Troy Bickham, *Texas A&M University*

Michael Brattain, *Georgia State University*

Kim Brinck-Johnsen, *University of New Hampshire*

Roger Bromert, *Southwestern Oklahoma State University*

Michael Colomaio, *Alfred State College*

Scott Cook, *Motlow State Community College*

Frank Delao, *Midland College*

Kristen Foster, *Marquette University*

Frederick B. Gates, *Southwestern Oklahoma State University*

Gary Henkel, *St. Petersburg College*

Stephanie Holyfield, *University of Delaware*

George Jarrett, *Cerritos College*

Steven Kite, *Fort Hays State University*

Michael Krenn, *Appalachian State University*

Lisa Lane, *MiraCosta College*

John Leiby, *Paradise Valley Community College*

Mary Linehan, *University of Texas at Tyler*

Edith MacDonald, *University of Central Florida*

Archie McDonald, *Stephen F. Austin State University*

Steven Miller, *Goshen College*

Rick Moser, *Texas A&M University—Commerce*

Earl Mulderink, *Southern Utah University*

Son Nguyen, *Los Angeles Harbor College*

Uraina Pack, *Clarion University*

Christopher Phelps, *Ohio State University*

Gerald Pierce, *Southern Polytechnic State University*

Steven Reiss, *Northeastern Illinois University*

Donald Rogers, *Central Connecticut State University*

Michael Smith, *Ithaca College*

Steve Stein, *University of Memphis*

Patricia Thompson, *University of Texas at San Antonio*

John Ulloa, *City College of San Francisco* and *Skyline College*

Paul Vandermeer, *Arizona State University*

Keith Volanto, *Collin County Community College*

William Whisenhunt, *College of DuPage*

Paul C. Young, *Utica College*

Michael Zartler, *Suffolk County Community College*

In addition, Clifford Clark would like to acknowledge the research assistance of David B. Hirsch.

Finally, we salute the skilled professionals at Wadsworth/Cengage Learning Company whose expertise and enthusiastic commitment to this new Eighth Edition guided us through every stage and helped sustain our own determination to make this the best book we could possibly write. Ann West, Senior Sponsoring Editor, presided over our initial planning meeting with good nature and wise suggestions, and has been a reassuring presence throughout. Development Editor Tonya Lobato managed the day-to-day challenges of keeping us all on track. Pembroke Herbert brought her creative skills to bear in seeking out fresh and powerful visual images for the work. Senior Content Project Manager Jane Lee ably shepherded the work through the crucial stages of production, while Assistant Editor Megan Chrisman oversaw the increasingly important Web-based resources. Charlotte Miller brought a wealth of cartographic experience to upgrading the *Enduring Vision*'s map program.

Paul S. Boyer
Clifford E. Clark, Jr.
Karen Halttunen
Joseph F. Kett
Neal Salisbury
Harvard Sitkoff
Nancy Woloch

ABOUT THE AUTHORS

PAUL S. BOYER was the Merle Curti Professor of History at the University of Wisconsin, Madison. He earned his Ph.D. from Harvard University. He was also a visiting professor at the University of California, Los Angeles; Northwestern University; and the College of William and Mary. An editor of *Notable American Women, 1607–1950* (1971), he also co-authored *Salem Possessed: The Social Origins of Witchcraft* (1974), for which, with Stephen Nissenbaum, he received the John H. Dunning Prize of the American Historical Association. His other works include *Urban Masses and Moral Order in America, 1820–1920* (1978), *By The Bomb's Early Light: American Thought and Culture at the Dawn of the Atomic Age* (1985), *When Time Shall Be No More: Prophecy Belief in Modern American Culture* (1992), and *Promises to Keep: The United States Since World War II* (third edition, 2005). He was also editor-in-chief of the *Oxford Companion to United States History* (2001). His articles and essays appeared in the *American Quarterly, New Republic,* and other journals.

CLIFFORD E. CLARK, Jr., M.A. and A.D. Hulings Professor of American Studies and professor of history at Carleton College, earned his Ph.D. from Harvard University. He has served as both the chair of the History Department and director of the American Studies program at Carleton. Clark is the author of *Henry Ward Beecher: Spokesman for a Middle-Class America* (1978), *The American Family Home, 1800–1960* (1986), *The Intellectual and Cultural History of Anglo-America Since 1789* in the *General History of the Americas Series,* and, with Carol Zellie, *Northfield: The History and Architecture of a Community* (1997). He also has edited and contributed to *Minnesota in a Century of Change: The State and Its People Since 1900* (1989). A past member of the Council of the American Studies Association, Clark is active in the fields of material culture studies and historic preservation, and he serves on the Northfield, Minnesota, Historical Preservation Commission.

KAREN HALTTUNEN, professor of history at the University of Southern California, earned her Ph.D. from Yale University. Her works include *Confidence Men and Painted Women: A Study of Middle-Class Culture in America, 1830–1870* (1982) and *Murder Most Foul: The Killer and the American Gothic Imagination* (1998). She edited *The Blackwell Companion to American Cultural History* (2008) and co-edited, with Lewis Perry, *Moral Problems in American Life: New Essays on Cultural History* (1998). As president of the American Studies Association and as vice-president of the Teaching Division of the American Historical Association, she has actively promoted K–16 collaboration in teaching history. She has held fellowships from the Guggenheim and Mellon Foundations, the National Endowment for the Humanities, the Huntington Library, and the National Humanities Center and has been principal investigator on several Teaching American History grants from the Department of Education.

JOSEPH F. KETT, James Madison Professor of History at the University of Virginia, received his Ph.D. from Harvard University. His works include *The Formation of the American Medical Profession: The Role of Institutions, 1780–1860* (1968), *Rites of Passage: Adolescence in America, 1790–Present* (1977), *The Pursuit of Knowledge under Difficulties: From Self-Improvement to Adult Education in America, 1750–1990* (1994), and *The New Dictionary of Cultural Literacy* (2002), of which he is co-author. A forthcoming book, *Merit: The History of a Founding Ideal from the American Revolution to the Twenty-First Century,* will be released in early 2013. As the former History Department chair at Virginia, he also has participated on the Panel on Youth of the President's Science Advisory Committee, has served on the Board of Editors of the *History of Education Quarterly,* and is a past member of the Council of the American Studies Association.

NEAL SALISBURY, Barbara Richmond 1940 Professor Emeritus in the Social Sciences (History), at Smith College, received his Ph.D. from the University of California, Los Angeles. He is the author of *Manitou and Providence: Indians, Europeans, and the Making of New England, 1500–1643* (1982), editor of *The Sovereignty and Goodness of God,* by Mary Rowlandson (1997), and co-editor, with Philip J. Deloria, of *The Companion to American Indian History* (2002). With R. David Edmunds and Frederick E. Hoxie, he has written *The People: A History of Native America* (2007). He has contributed numerous articles to journals and edited collections and co-edits a book series, Cambridge Studies in North American Indian History. He is active in the fields of colonial and Native American history and has served as president of the American Society for Ethnohistory and on the Council of the Omohundro Institute of Early American History and Culture.

HARVARD SITKOFF, Emeritus Professor of History at the University of New Hampshire, earned his Ph.D. from Columbia University. He is the author of *A New Deal for Blacks* (Thirtieth Anniversary Edition, 2009), *The Struggle for Black Equality* (Twenty-Fifth Anniversary Edition, 2008), *King: Pilgrimage to the Mountaintop* (2008), *Toward Freedom Land, The Long Struggle for Racial Equality in America* (2010), and *Postwar America: A Student Companion* (2000); co-author of the National Park Service's *Racial Desegregation in Public Education in the United States* (2000), and *The World War II Homefront* (2003); and editor of *Fifty Years Later: The New Deal Reevaluated* (1984), *A History of Our Time* (2012), and *Perspectives on Modern America: Making Sense of the Twentieth Century* (2001). His articles have appeared in the *American Quarterly, Journal of American History,* and *Journal of Southern History,* among others. A frequent lecturer at universities abroad, he has been awarded the Fulbright Commission's John Adams Professorship of American Civilization in the Netherlands and the Mary Ball Washington Professorship of American History in Ireland.

NANCY WOLOCH received her Ph.D. from Indiana University. She is the author of *Women and the American Experience* (fifth edition, 2011), editor of *Early American Women: A Documentary History, 1600–1900* (third edition, 2013), and co-author, with Walter LaFeber and Richard Polenberg, of *The American Century: A History of the United States Since the 1890s* (seventh edition, 2013). She is also the author of *Muller v. Oregon: A Brief History with Documents* (1996). She teaches American History and American Studies at Barnard College, Columbia University.

PROLOGUE
Enduring Vision, Enduring Land

IN THE VISION THAT Americans have shared, the American land has been central. For the Native Americans who spread over the land thousands of years ago, for the Europeans who began to arrive in the sixteenth century, and for the later immigrants who poured in by the tens of millions from all parts of the world, North America was a haven for new beginnings. If life was hard elsewhere, it would be better here. Once here, the immigrants continued to be lured by the land. If times were tough in the East, they would be better in the West. New Englanders migrated to Ohio; Ohioans migrated to Kansas; Kansans migrated to California. For Africans, the migration to America was forced and brutal. But after the Civil War, newly freed African Americans embraced the vision and dreamed of traveling to a Promised Land of new opportunities. Interviewed in 1938, a former Texas slave recalled a verse that he and other blacks had sung when emancipated:

> *I got my ticket,*
>
> *Leaving the thicket,*
>
> *And I'm a-heading for the Golden Shore!*

For most of America's history, its peoples have celebrated the land—its beauty, its diversity, and its ability to sustain and even enrich those who tapped its resources. But within this shared vision have been deep-seated tensions. Even Native Americans—who regarded the land and other natural phenomena as spiritual—sometimes depleted the resources on which they depended. Europeans, considering "nature" a force to be mastered, were even less restrained. The very abundance of America's natural resources led them to think of these resources as infinitely available and exploitable. In moving from one place to another, some sought to escape starvation or oppression, while others pursued wealth despite the environmental consequences. Regardless of their motives, migrants often left behind a land bereft of wild animals, its fertility depleted by intensive farming, its waters dammed and polluted or dried up altogether. If the land today remains part of Americans' vision, it is because they realize its vulnerability, rather than its immunity, to irreversible degradation at the hands of people and their technology.

To comprehend fully Americans' relationship with the land, we must know the land itself. The North American landscape, as encountered by its human inhabitants, formed over at least 3 billion years, culminating in the last Ice Age. From the earliest peopling to more recent waves of immigration, the continent's physical characteristics have shaped human affairs, including cycles of intensive agriculture and industrialization; the rise of cities; the course of politics; and even the basic themes of American literature, art, and music. Geology, geography, and environment are among the fundamental building blocks of human history.

The Continent and Its Regions

Differences in climate, physical features, soils and minerals, and organic life are the basis of America's geographic diversity (see Maps P.1, P.2, and P.3). As each region's human inhabitants utilized available resources, geographic diversity contributed to a diversity of regional cultures, first among Native Americans and then among the immigrant peoples who spread across America after 1492. Taken together, the variety of these resources would also contribute to the rise to wealth and global preeminence of the United States.

The West

With its extreme climate and profuse wildlife, Alaska recalls the land that North America's earliest peoples encountered (see Chapter 1). Alaska's far north is a treeless tundra of grasses, lichens, and stunted shrubs. This region, the Arctic, appears as a stark wilderness in winter and is reborn in fleeting summers of colorful flowers and returning birds. In contrast, the subarctic of central Alaska is a heavily forested country known as taiga. Here rises North America's highest peak, 20,320-foot Mt. McKinley. Average temperatures in the subarctic range from the fifties above zero Fahrenheit in summer to well below zero in the long, dark winters, and the soil is permanently frozen except during summer surface thaws and where, ominously, global warming is having an effect.

The Pacific coastal region is in some ways a world apart. Vegetation and animal life, isolated from the rest of the continent by mountains and deserts, include many species unfamiliar farther east. Warm, wet westerly winds blowing off the Pacific create a climate more uniformly temperate than anywhere else in North America. From Anchorage to south of San Francisco Bay, winters are cool, humid, and foggy, and the coast's dense forest cover includes the largest living organisms on Earth—the giant redwood trees. Along the southern California coast, winds and currents generate a warmer, Mediterranean climate, and vegetation includes a heavy growth of shrubs and short trees, scattered stands of oak, and grasses able to endure prolonged seasonal drought.

MAP P.1 **NORTH AMERICAN CLIMATIC REGIONS** America's variety of mostly temperate climates is key to its environmental and economic diversity. © Cengage Learning. All rights reserved. No distribution allowed without express authorization.

To the east of the coastal region, the rugged Sierra Nevada, Cascade, and coastal ranges stretch the length of Washington, Oregon, and California. Their majestic peaks trap abundant Pacific Ocean moisture carried eastward by gigantic clockwise air currents. Between the ranges nestle flat, fertile valleys that have been major agricultural centers in recent times.

Still farther east lies the Great Basin, encompassing Nevada, western Utah, southern Idaho, and eastern Oregon. The few streams here have no outlet to the ocean. A remnant of an inland sea that once held glacial meltwater survives in Utah's Great Salt Lake. Today, however, the Great Basin is dry and severely eroded, a cold desert rich in minerals and imposing in its austere grandeur and lonely emptiness. North of the basin, the Columbia and Snake Rivers, which drain the plateau country of Idaho and eastern Washington and Oregon, provide plentiful water for farming.

Western North America's "backbone" is the Rocky Mountains. The Rockies form part of the immense mountain system that reaches from Alaska to the

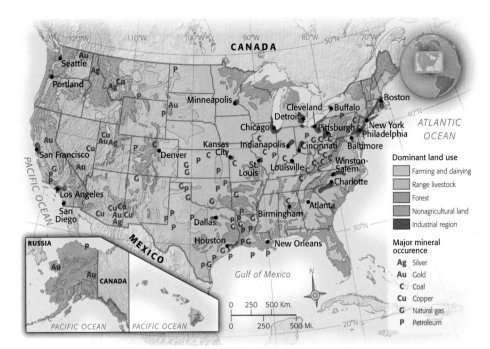

MAP P.2 LAND USE AND MAJOR MINERAL RESOURCES IN THE UNITED STATES The land has been central to America's industrial as well as agricultural productivity. © Cengage Learning. All rights reserved. No distribution allowed without express authorization.

MAP P.3 NATURAL VEGETATION OF THE UNITED STATES The current distribution of plant life came about only after the last Ice Age ended, ca. 10,000 B.C.E., and Earth's climate warmed. © Cengage Learning. All rights reserved. No distribution allowed without express authorization.

Andes of South America. Beyond the front range of the Rockies lies the Continental Divide, separating the rivers flowing eastward into the Atlantic from those draining westward into the Pacific. The climate and vegetation of the Rocky Mountain high country resemble those of the Arctic and subarctic regions.

Arizona, southern Utah, western New Mexico, and southeastern California form America's southwestern desert. The climate is arid, searingly hot on summer days and cold on winter nights. Adapted to these conditions, many plants and animals that thrive here could not survive elsewhere. Dust storms, cloudbursts, and flash floods have everywhere carved, abraded, and twisted the rocky landscape. The most monumental example is the Grand Canyon, where the Colorado River has been cutting down to Precambrian bedrock for 20 million years. In the face of such tremendous natural forces, human activity might well seem paltry and transitory. Yet it was in the Southwest that Native Americans cultivated the first crops in what is now the continental United States.

CARIBOU AND THE TRANS-ALASKA PIPELINE This scene from the open tundra of Alaska points to the uneasy co-existence between wildlife and the human pursuit of fossil fuels. *(Hugh Rose/Accent Alaska.com)*

The Heartland

North America's heartland comprises the area extending between the Rockies and the Appalachians. This vast region forms one of the world's largest drainage systems. From here, the Great Lakes empty into the North Atlantic through the St. Lawrence River, and the Mississippi-Missouri-Ohio river network flows southward into the Gulf of Mexico. By transporting peoples and goods, the heartland's network of waterways has supported commerce and communication for centuries, before—as well as since—the arrival of Europeans.

The mighty Mississippi—the "Great River" to the Ojibwe Indians and one of the world's longest rivers—has changed course many times. Southward from its junction with the Ohio River, the Mississippi meanders constantly, depositing rich sediments throughout its broad, ancient floodplain. It has carried so much silt over the millennia that its lower stretches flow above the surrounding valley, which it periodically floods when its high banks (levees) are breached. Only the Ozark Plateau and Ouachita Mountains remain exposed, forming the hill country of southern Missouri, north-central Arkansas, and eastern Oklahoma.

Below New Orleans, the Mississippi empties into the Gulf of Mexico through an enormous delta with an intricate network of grassy swamps known as bayous. The Mississippi Delta offers rich farm soil capable of supporting a large population. Swarming with waterfowl, insects, alligators, and marine plants and animals, this environment has nurtured a distinctive way of life for the Indian, white, and black peoples who have inhabited it.

North of the Ohio and Missouri Rivers, themselves products of glacial runoff, Ice Age glaciation distributed glacial debris. Spread even farther by wind and rivers, this fine-ground glacial dust slowly created the fertile farm soil of the Midwest. Glaciers also dug out the five Great Lakes (Superior, Michigan, Huron, Erie, and Ontario), collectively the world's largest body of fresh water. Water flowing from Lake Erie to the lower elevation of Lake Ontario created Niagara Falls, a testimony like the Grand Canyon to the way that water can shape a beautiful landscape.

Most of the heartland's eastern and northern sectors were once heavily forested while thick, tallgrass prairie covered Illinois, parts of adjoining states, and much of the Missouri and middle Arkansas river basins. Beyond the Missouri, the prairie gave way to short-grass steppe—the Great Plains, cold in winter, blazing hot in summer, and often dry. The great distances that separate the heartland's prairies and Great Plains from the moderating effects of the oceans

DEVASTATION FROM HURRICANE KATRINA, 2005 Businesses destroyed by Katrina in Gulfport, Mississippi.
(© Bettmann/Corbis)

continue to make this region's annual temperature range the most extreme in North America. As one moves westward, elevations rise gradually; trees grow only along streambeds; long droughts alternate with violent thunderstorms and tornadoes; and water and wood are ever scarcer.

During the nineteenth and twentieth centuries, much of this forested, grassy world became open farming country. Gone are the flocks of migratory birds that once darkened the daytime skies of the plains; gone are the free-roaming bison. Forests now only fringe the heartland: in the lake country of northern Minnesota and Wisconsin, on Michigan's upper peninsula, and across the hilly uplands of the Appalachians, southern Indiana, and the Ozarks. The settlers who largely displaced the region's Native Americans plowed up prairie grass and cut down trees. Destruction of the forest and grassy cover made the heartland both a "breadbasket" for the world market and, during intervals of drought, a bleak "dust bowl." With farming now in decline, the heartland's future is uncertain.

The Atlantic Seaboard

The eastern edge of the heartland is formed by the Appalachian Mountains, which over the course of 210 million years have been ground down to gentle ridges paralleling one another southwest to northeast. Between the ridges lie fertile valleys such as Virginia's Shenandoah. The Appalachian hill country's wealth is in thick timber and mineral beds—particularly coal deposits—whose heavy exploitation since the nineteenth century has accelerated destructive soil erosion in this softly beautiful, mountainous land.

Descending gently from the Appalachians' eastern slope is the Piedmont region. In this broad, rolling upland extending from Alabama to Maryland, the rich, red soil has been ravaged in modern times by excessive cotton and tobacco cultivation. The Piedmont's modern piney-woods cover constitutes "secondary growth," replacing the sturdy hardwood trees that Native Americans and pioneering whites and blacks once knew. The northward extension of the Piedmont from Pennsylvania to New England has more broadleaf vegetation and a harsher winter climate, and was shaped by glacial activity. The terrain in upstate New York and New England comprises hills contoured by advancing and retreating ice, and numerous lakes scoured out by glaciers. Belts of rocky debris remain, and in many places granite boulders shoulder their way up through the soil. Though picturesque, the land is the despair of anyone who has tried to plow it.

The character of the Atlantic coastal plain varies strikingly from south to north. At the tip of the

ABANDONED "RUST BELT" FACTORY The American landscape is littered with reminders that large-scale factory production has ended or been diminished in many industries. *(Dennis Brack/Black Star/Stockphoto.com)*

Florida peninsula in the extreme south, the climate and vegetation are subtropical. The southern coastal lands running north from Florida to Chesapeake Bay and the mouth of the Delaware River compose the tidewater region. This is a wide, rather flat lowland, heavily wooded with a mixture of broadleaf and coniferous forests, ribboned with numerous small rivers, occasionally swampy, and often miserably hot and humid in summer. North of Delaware Bay, the coastal lowlands narrow and flatten to form the New Jersey pine barrens, Long Island, and Cape Cod—all created by the deposit of glacial debris. Here the climate is noticeably milder than in the interior. North of Massachusetts Bay, the land beyond the immediate shoreline becomes increasingly mountainous.

North America's true eastern edge is not the coastline but the offshore continental shelf, whose relatively shallow waters extend as far as 250 miles into the Atlantic before plunging deeply. Along the rocky Canadian and Maine coasts, where at the end of the Ice Age the rising ocean half-covered glaciated mountains and valleys, oceangoing craft may find numerous small anchorages. South of Massachusetts Bay, the Atlantic shore and the Gulf of Mexico coastline form a shoreline of sandy beaches and long barrier islands paralleling the mainland. Tropical storms boiling up from the open seas regularly lash North America's Atlantic shores, and at all times brisk winds make coastal navigation treacherous.

For millions, the Atlantic coastal region of North America offered a welcome. Ancient Indian hunters and more recent European colonists alike found its climate and its abundance of food sources alluring. Offshore, well within their reach, lay such productive fishing grounds as the Grand Banks, off Newfoundland, and Cape Cod's coastal bays where cool-water upwellings on the continental shelf had lured swarms of fish and crustaceans. "The abundance of sea-fish are almost beyond believing," wrote a breathless English settler in 1630, "and sure I should scarce have believed it, except I had seen it with my own eyes."

A Legacy and a Challenge

North America's fertile soil, extensive forests, and rich mineral resources long nourished visions of limitless natural abundance that would yield untold wealth to its human inhabitants. Such visions have contributed to the acceleration of population growth, intensive agriculture, industrialization, urbanization, and hunger for material goods—processes that are exhausting resources, polluting the environment, and raising temperatures to the point of endangering human health and well-being.

In searching for ways to avoid environmental catastrophe, Americans would do well to recall the Native American legacy. Although Indians often wasted, and occasionally exhausted, a region's resources to their detriment, their practices generally encouraged the renewal of plants, animals, and soil over time. Underlying these practices were Indians' beliefs that they were spiritually related to the land and all living beings that shared it. In recapturing the sense that they are intimately related to the land they inhabit, rather than alien to it, future American generations could revitalize the enduring vision of those who came before them.

THE ENDURING
VISION

Reconstruction and Resistance, 1865–1877

KATIE ROWE IN 1937 *(Library of Congress)*

"I NEVER FORGET de day we was set free," former slave Katie Rowe recalled. "Dat morning we all go to de cotton field early. After a while de old horn blow up at de overseer's house, and we all stop and listen, 'cause it de wrong time of day for de horn." Later that day, after several more blasts of the horn, a stranger "with a big broad hat lak de Yankees wore" addressed the slaves. "'Today you is free, just lak I is,' de man say," Katie Rowe declared. "'You is your own bosses now.'" The date was June 4, 1865.

Born at midcentury, Katie Rowe grew up on a cotton plantation with two hundred slaves near Washington, Arkansas. The slaves had "hard traveling" on her plantation, she told an interviewer in 1937. The owner, Dr. Isaac Jones, lived in town, and an overseer ran the place harshly. Dr. Jones was harsh, too. When Union and Confederate forces clashed nearby in 1862 at Pea Ridge, Arkansas, Dr. Jones announced that the enemy would never liberate his slaves because he would shoot them first ("line you up on de bank of Bois d' Arc Creek and free you wid my shotgun"). Soon after, an explosion of the boiler of his steam-powered cotton gin incinerated Dr. Jones. "Later in de war Yankees come in all around and camp, and de overseer git sweet as honey in de comb," Katie Rowe observed. "But we know dey soon be gone."

Emancipation in June 1865 brought an era of transition for the former slaves. "None of us know whar to go," Katie Rowe remembered, "so we all stay and he [the overseer] split up de fields and show us which part we got to work in, and we go on lak we was … but dey ain't no horn after dat day." Still, the labor system proved unsatisfactory. The overseer charged the former slaves "half de crop for de quarter and all de mules and tools and grub," Katie Rowe noted. His replacement offered better arrangements: "[W]e all got something left over after dat first go-out." But new changes occurred. The next year the former owner's heirs sold the plantation, "and we scatter off." With her mother, teenage Katie Rowe left for Little Rock to "do work in de town."

Katie eventually married Billy Rowe, a Cherokee, and moved with him to Oklahoma. Interviewed decades later in Tulsa, Oklahoma, where she lived with her youngest daughter, Katie Rowe recalled the days of "hard traveling" and the joyful moment when slavery ended. "It was the fourth day of June in 1865 that I begins to live," Katie Rowe declared. "I know we living in a better world. … I sho' thank de good Lawd I got to see it."

For the nation, as for Katie Rowe, the end of the Civil War was an instant of uncharted possibilities and a time of unresolved conflicts. While former slaves exulted

THE DEVASTATED SOUTH After the Civil War, parts of the devastated Confederacy resembled a wasteland. Homes, crops, and railroads had been destroyed; farming and business had come to a standstill; and uprooted southerners wandered about. Here, ruins of homes in Baton Rouge, Louisiana. *(Louisiana and Lower Mississippi Valley Collection, C-31 LSU Libraries, Louisiana State University)*

16

over freedom, the postwar mood of ex-Confederates was often as grim as the wasted southern landscape. Unable to face "southern Yankeedom," some planters considered emigrating to the American West or to Europe, Mexico, or Brazil, and a few thousand did. The morale of the vanquished rarely concerns the victors, but the Civil War was a special case, for the Union had sought not merely military triumph but the return of national unity. The federal government in 1865 therefore faced unprecedented questions.

First, how could the Union be restored and the defeated South reintegrated into the nation? Would the Confederate states be treated as conquered territories, or would they quickly rejoin the Union with the same rights as other states? Who would set the standards for readmission—Congress or the president? Most important, what would happen to the more than 3.5 million former slaves? The future of the freedmen constituted the crucial issue of the postwar era, for emancipation had set in motion a profound upheaval. Before the war, slavery had determined the South's social, economic, and political structure. What would replace it? The end of the Civil War, in short, posed two problems that had to be solved simultaneously: how to readmit the South to the Union and how to define the status of free blacks in American society.

Between 1865 and 1877, the nation met these challenges, but not without discord and strife. Conflict prevailed in the halls of Congress as legislators debated plans to readmit the South to the Union; in the former Confederacy, where defeated southerners and newly freed former slaves faced an era of turbulence; and in the postwar North, where economic and political clashes arose. By 1877, ex-Confederate resistance had largely foiled northern plans for the postwar South. Indeed, the crises of Reconstruction—the restoration of the former Confederate states to the Union—reshaped the legacy of the Civil War.

Reconstruction Politics, 1865–1868

At the end of the Civil War, President Johnson might have exiled, imprisoned, or executed Confederate leaders and imposed martial law indefinitely. Demobilized Confederate soldiers might have continued armed resistance to federal occupation forces. Freed slaves might have taken revenge on former owners and other white southerners. But none of this occurred. Instead, intense *political* conflict dominated the immediate postwar years. National politics produced new constitutional amendments, a presidential impeachment, and some of the most ambitious domestic legislation ever enacted by Congress, the Reconstruction Acts of 1867–1868. The major outcome of Reconstruction politics was the enfranchisement of black men, a development that few—black or white—had expected when Lee surrendered.

In 1865, only a small group of politicians supported black suffrage. All were Radical Republicans, a minority faction that had emerged during the war. Led by Senator **Charles Sumner** of Massachusetts and Congressman **Thaddeus Stevens** of Pennsylvania, the Radicals had clamored for the abolition of slavery and a demanding reconstruction policy. But the Radicals, outnumbered in Congress by other Republicans and opposed by the Democratic minority, faced long odds. Still, they managed to win broad Republican support for parts of their Reconstruction program, including black male enfranchisement. Just as civil war had led to emancipation, a goal once supported by only a minority of Americans, so Reconstruction policy became bound to black suffrage, a momentous change that originally had only narrow political backing.

Lincoln's Plan

Conflict over Reconstruction began even before the war ended. In December 1863, President Lincoln issued the Proclamation of Amnesty and Reconstruction, which enabled southern states to rejoin the Union if at least 10 percent of those who had cast ballots in the election of 1860 would take an oath of allegiance to the Union and accept emancipation. This minority could then create a loyal state government. Lincoln's plan excluded some southerners from oath-taking, such as Confederate officials and military officers; they would have to apply for presidential pardons. Also excluded were

FOCUS Questions

- How did Radical Republicans gain control of Reconstruction politics?
- What impact did federal Reconstruction policy have on the former Confederacy and on ex-Confederates?
- How did the newly freed slaves reshape their lives after emancipation?
- What political and economic problems arose in the North during the era of Reconstruction?
- What factors contributed to the end of Reconstruction in 1877?

CHRONOLOGY 1863–1879

1863	President Abraham Lincoln issues Proclamation of Amnesty and Reconstruction.
1864	Wade-Davis bill passed by Congress and pocket-vetoed by Lincoln.
1865	Freedmen's Bureau established.
	Civil War ends.
	Lincoln assassinated.
	Andrew Johnson becomes president.
	Johnson issues Proclamation of Amnesty and Reconstruction.
	Ex-Confederate states hold constitutional conventions (May–December).
	Black conventions begin in the ex-Confederate states.
	Thirteenth Amendment added to the Constitution.
	Presidential Reconstruction completed.
1866	Congress enacts the Civil Rights Act of 1866 and the Supplementary Freedmen's Bureau Act over Johnson's vetoes.
	Ku Klux Klan founded in Tennessee.
	Tennessee readmitted to the Union.
	Race riots in southern cities.
	Republicans win congressional elections.
	American Equal Rights Association formed.
1867	Reconstruction Act of 1867.
	William Seward negotiates the purchase of Alaska.
	Constitutional conventions meet in the ex-Confederate states.
	Howard University founded.
1868	President Johnson is impeached, tried, and acquitted. Omnibus Act.
	Fourteenth Amendment added to the Constitution.
	Ulysses S. Grant elected president.
1869	Transcontinental railroad completed.
1870	Congress readmits the four remaining southern states to the Union.
	Fifteenth Amendment added to the Constitution.
	Enforcement Act of 1870.
1871	Second Enforcement Act.
	Ku Klux Klan Act.
1872	Liberal Republican party formed.
	Amnesty Act.
	Alabama claims settled.
	Grant reelected president.
1873	Panic of 1873 begins (September–October), setting off a five-year depression.
1874	Democrats gain control of the House of Representatives.
1875	Civil Rights Act of 1875. Specie Resumption Act.
1876	Disputed presidential election: Rutherford B. Hayes versus Samuel J. Tilden.
1877	Electoral commission decides election in favor of Hayes.
	The last Republican-controlled governments overthrown in Florida, Louisiana, and South Carolina.
1879	"Exodus" movement spreads through several southern states.

blacks, who had not been voters in 1860. Lincoln hoped to undermine the Confederacy by fostering pro-Union governments within it and to build a southern Republican party.

Radical Republicans in Congress, however, envisioned a slower readmission process that would bar even more ex-Confederates from political life. The Wade-Davis bill, passed by Congress in July 1864, provided that a military governor would rule each former Confederate state; after at least half the eligible voters took an oath of allegiance to the Union, delegates could be elected to a state convention that would repeal secession and abolish slavery. To qualify as a voter or delegate, a southerner would have to take a second, "ironclad" oath, swearing that he had never voluntarily supported the Confederacy. Like the 10 percent plan, the congressional plan did not provide for black suffrage, a measure then supported by only some Radicals. Unlike Lincoln's plan, however, the Wade-Davis scheme would have delayed the readmission process almost indefinitely.

Claiming he did not want to bind himself to any single restoration policy, Lincoln pocket-vetoed the Wade-Davis bill (failed to sign the bill within ten days of the adjournment of Congress). The bill's sponsors, Senator Benjamin Wade of Ohio and Congressman Henry Winter Davis of Maryland, blasted Lincoln's act. By the war's end, the president and Congress had reached an impasse. Arkansas, Louisiana, Tennessee, and parts of Virginia under Union army control moved toward readmission under variants of Lincoln's plan. But Congress refused to seat their delegates, as it had a right to do. What Lincoln's ultimate policy would have been remains unknown. But after his assassination, on April 14, 1865, Radical Republicans turned with hope toward his successor, **Andrew Johnson** of Tennessee.

> "Treason is a crime and must be made odious."

Presidential Reconstruction

The only southern senator to remain in Congress when his state seceded, Andrew Johnson had served as military governor of Tennessee from 1862 to 1864. Defying the Confederate stand, he had declared that "treason is a crime and must be made odious." Above all, Johnson had long sought the destruction of the planter aristocracy. A self-educated man of humble North Carolina origins, Johnson had moved to Greenville, Tennessee, in 1826. He had entered politics in the 1830s as a spokesman for non-slave-owning whites and rose rapidly from local official to congressman to governor to senator. Once the owner of eight slaves, Johnson reversed his position on slavery during the war. When emancipation became Union policy, he supported it. But Johnson neither adopted abolitionist ideals nor challenged racist sentiments. He hoped mainly that the fall of slavery would injure southern aristocrats. Johnson, in short, had his own political agenda, which, as Republicans would soon learn, did not duplicate theirs. Moreover, he was a lifelong Democrat who had been added to the Republican, or National Union, ticket in 1864 to broaden its appeal and who had become president by accident.

> "What can be hatched from such an egg but another rebellion?"

In May 1865, with Congress out of session, Johnson shocked Republicans by announcing his own program to bring back into the Union the seven southern states still without reconstruction governments—Alabama, Florida, Georgia, Mississippi, North Carolina, South Carolina, and Texas. Almost all southerners who took an oath of allegiance would receive a pardon and amnesty; all their property except slaves would be restored. Oath takers could elect delegates to state conventions, which would provide for regular elections. Each state convention, Johnson later added, would have to proclaim secession illegal, repudiate state debts incurred under the Confederacy, and ratify the Thirteenth Amendment, which abolished slavery. (Proposed by an enthusiastic wartime Congress early in 1865, the amendment would be ratified in December of that year.) As under Lincoln's plan, Confederate civil and military officers would still be disqualified, as would well-off ex-Confederates—those with taxable property worth $20,000 or more. This purge of the plantation aristocracy, Johnson said, would benefit "humble men, the peasantry and yeomen of the South, who have been decoyed … into rebellion." Poorer whites would now be in control.

Presidential Reconstruction took effect in the summer of 1865, but with unforeseen consequences. Disqualified Southerners applied in droves for pardons, which Johnson handed out liberally—some thirteen thousand of them. Johnson also dropped plans to punish treason. By the end of 1865, all seven states had created new civil governments that,

RADICAL REPUBLICAN LEADERS Charles Sumner, left, senator from Massachusetts, and Thaddeus Stevens, congressman from Pennsylvania, led the Radical Republican faction in Congress. *(Library of Congress)*

in effect, restored the status quo from before the war. Confederate army officers and large planters assumed state offices. Former Confederate generals and officials—including Alexander Stephens of Georgia, the former Confederate vice president—won election to Congress. Some states refused to ratify the Thirteenth Amendment or to repudiate their Confederate debts.

Most infuriating to Radical Republicans, all seven states took steps to ensure a landless, dependent black labor force: they passed **"black codes"** to replace the slave codes, state laws that had regulated slavery. Because Johnson's plan assured the ratification of the Thirteenth Amendment, all states guaranteed the freedmen some basic rights—to marry, own property, make contracts, and testify in court against other blacks—but the codes harshly restricted freedmen's behavior. Some established racial segregation in public places; most prohibited racial intermarriage, jury service by blacks, and court testimony by blacks against whites. All codes included provisions that effectively barred former slaves from leaving the plantations. South Carolina required special licenses for blacks who wished to enter nonagricultural employment. Mississippi prohibited blacks from buying and selling farmland. Most states required annual contracts between landowners and black agricultural workers; blacks without contracts risked arrest as vagrants and involuntary servitude.

The black codes left freedmen no longer slaves but not really liberated either. In practice, many clauses in the codes never took effect: the Union army and federal agents suspended the enforcement of racially discriminatory provisions of the new laws. But the black codes revealed white southern intentions. They showed what "home rule" would have been like without federal interference.

Many northerners denounced what they saw as southern defiance. "What can be hatched from such an egg but another rebellion?" asked a Boston newspaper. Republicans in Congress agreed. When Congress convened in December 1865, it refused to seat delegates of ex-Confederate states. Establishing the Joint (House-Senate) Committee on Reconstruction, Republicans prepared to dismantle the black codes and lock ex-Confederates out of power.

Congress Versus Johnson

Southern blacks' status now became the major issue in Congress. Radical Republicans like Congressman Thaddeus Stevens—who hoped to impose black suffrage on the former Confederacy and delay southern readmission—were still a minority in Congress. Conservative Republicans, who favored Johnson's plan, formed a minority too, as did the Democrats, who also supported the president. Moderate Republicans, the largest congressional bloc, agreed with Radicals that Johnson's plan was too feeble, but they wanted to avoid a dispute with the president. None of the four congressional blocs could claim the two-thirds majority needed to overturn a presidential veto. But ineptly, Johnson alienated a majority of moderates and pushed them into the Radicals' arms.

Two proposals to invalidate the black codes, drafted by a moderate Republican, Senator Lyman Trumbull of Illinois, won wide Republican support. Congress first voted to continue the Freedmen's Bureau, started in March 1865, whose term was ending (See Freedmen's Bureau, Chapter 15, p. 447). This federal agency, headed by former Union general O.O. Howard and staffed mainly by army officers, provided relief, rations, and medical care; built schools for freed blacks; put them to work on abandoned or confiscated lands; and tried to protect their rights as laborers. Congress extended the bureau's life for three years and gave it new power to run special military courts, to settle labor disputes, and to invalidate labor contracts forced on freedmen by the black codes. In February 1866, Johnson vetoed the Supplementary Freedmen's Bureau bill. The Constitution, he declared, did not sanction military trials of civilians in peacetime, nor did it support a system to care for "indigent persons."

In March 1866, Congress passed a second measure proposed by Trumbull, a bill that made blacks U.S. citizens with the same civil rights as other citizens and authorized federal intervention in the states to ensure black rights in court. Johnson vetoed the civil rights bill also. He argued that it would "operate in favor of the colored and against the white race." In April, Congress overrode his veto; the **Civil Rights Act of 1866** was the first major law ever passed over a presidential veto. In July, Congress enacted the Supplementary Freedmen's Bureau Act over Johnson's veto as well. Johnson's vetoes puzzled many Republicans because the new laws did not undercut presidential Reconstruction. The president insisted, however, that both bills were illegitimate because southerners had been shut out of the Congress that passed them. Johnson won support in the South and from northern Democrats. But he had alienated moderate Republicans, who now joined Radicals to oppose him. Johnson had lost "every friend he has," one moderate declared.

Some historians view Andrew Johnson as a political incompetent who, at this crucial juncture, bungled both his readmission scheme and his political future. Others contend he was merely trying to forge a centrist coalition. In either case, Johnson underestimated the possibility of Republican unity.

Once united, the Republicans took their next step: the passage of a constitutional amendment to prevent the Supreme Court from invalidating the new Civil Rights Act and block Democrats in Congress from repealing it.

The Fourteenth Amendment, 1866

In April 1866, Congress adopted the **Fourteenth Amendment,** proposed by the Joint Committee on Reconstruction. To protect blacks' rights, the amendment declared in its first clause that all persons born or naturalized in the United States were citizens of the nation and of their states and that no state could abridge their rights without due process of law or deny them equal protection of the law. This section nullified the *Dred Scott* decision of 1857, which had denied that blacks were citizens. Second, the amendment guaranteed that if a state denied suffrage to any of its male citizens, its representation in Congress would be proportionally reduced. This clause did not ensure black suffrage, but it threatened to deprive southern states of some legislators if black men were denied the vote. This was the first time that the word *male* was written into the Constitution; to the women's rights advocates, woman suffrage seemed a yet more distant prospect. Third, the amendment disqualified from state and national office *all* prewar officeholders—civil and military, state and federal—who had supported the Confederacy, unless Congress removed their disqualifications by a two-thirds vote. In so providing, Congress sought to invalidate Johnson's wholesale distribution of amnesties and pardons. Finally, the amendment repudiated the Confederate debt and maintained the validity of the federal debt.

> Johnson had lost "every friend he has," one moderate declared.

The most ambitious step Congress had yet taken, the Fourteenth Amendment revealed growing Republican receptivity to Radical demands, including black male enfranchisement. The amendment's passage created a firestorm. Abolitionists decried the second clause as a "swindle" because it did not explicitly ensure black suffrage. Southerners and northern Democrats condemned the third clause as vengeful. Southern legislatures, except for Tennessee's, refused to ratify the amendment, and President Johnson denounced it. His defiance solidified the new alliance between moderate and Radical Republicans, and turned the congressional elections of 1866 into a referendum on the Fourteenth Amendment.

Over the summer, Johnson set off on a whistle-stop train tour from Washington to St. Louis and

KING ANDREW This Thomas Nast cartoon, published in *Harper's Weekly* just before the 1866 congressional elections, conveyed Republican antipathy to Andrew Johnson. The president is depicted as an autocratic tyrant. Radical Republican Thaddeus Stevens, upper right, has his head on the block and is about to lose it. The Republic sits in chains. *(Harper's Weekly, 1866)*

Chicago and back. But this innovative campaign tactic—the "swing around the circle," as Johnson called it—failed. Humorless and defensive, the president made fresh enemies and doomed his hope of sinking the Fourteenth Amendment, which Moderate and Radical Republicans defended.

Republicans carried the congressional elections of 1866 in a landslide, winning almost two-thirds of the House and four-fifths of the Senate. They had secured a mandate for the Fourteenth Amendment and their own Reconstruction program, even if the president vetoed every part of it.

Congressional Reconstruction, 1866–1867

Congressional debate over reconstructing the South began in December 1866 and lasted three months. Radical Republican leaders called for black suffrage, federal support for public schools, confiscation of

Confederate estates, and an extended period of military occupation in the South. Moderate Republicans accepted parts of the plan. In February 1867, after complex legislative maneuvers, Congress passed the **Reconstruction Act of 1867**. Johnson vetoed the law, and on March 2, Congress passed it over his veto. Later that year and in 1868, Congress passed three further Reconstruction acts, all enacted over presidential vetoes, to refine and enforce the first (see Table 16.1).

The Reconstruction Act of 1867 invalidated the state governments formed under the Lincoln and Johnson plans. Only Tennessee, which had ratified the Fourteenth Amendment and had been readmitted to the Union, escaped further reconstruction. The new law divided the other ten former Confederate states into five temporary military districts, each run by a Union general (see Map 16.1). Voters—all black men, plus those white men who had not been disqualified by the Fourteenth Amendment—could elect delegates to a state convention that would write a new state constitution granting black suffrage. When eligible voters ratified the new constitution, elections could be held for state officers. Once Congress approved the state constitution, once the state legislature ratified the Fourteenth Amendment, and once the amendment became part of the federal Constitution, Congress would readmit the state into the Union.

The Reconstruction Act of 1867 was far more radical than the Johnson program because it enfranchised blacks and disfranchised many ex-Confederates. It fulfilled a central goal of the Radical Republicans: to delay the readmission of former Confederate states

TABLE 16.1 Major Reconstruction Legislation

Law and Date of Congressional Passage	Provisions	Purpose
Civil Rights Act of 1866 (April 1866)*	Declared blacks citizens and guaranteed them equal protection of the laws.	To invalidate the black codes.
Supplementary Freedmen's Bureau Act (July 1866)*	Extended the life of the Freedmen's Aid Bureau and expanded its powers.	To invalidate the black codes.
Reconstruction Act of 1867 (March 1867)*	Invalidated state governments formed under Lincoln and Johnson. Divided the former Confederacy into five military districts. Set forth requirements for readmission of ex-Confederate states to the Union.	To replace presidential Reconstruction with a more stringent plan.
Supplementary Reconstruction Acts		To enforce the First Reconstruction Act.
Second Reconstruction Act (March 1867)*	Required military commanders to initiate voter enrollment.	
Third Reconstruction Act (July 1867)*	Expanded military commanders' powers.	
Fourth Reconstruction Act (March 1868)*	Provided that a majority of voters, however few, could put a new state constitution into force.	
Army Appropriations Act (March 1867)*	Declared in a rider that only the general of the army could issue military orders.	To prevent President Johnson from obstructing Reconstruction.
Tenure of Office Act (March 1867)*	Prohibited the president from removing any federal official without the Senate's consent.	To prevent President Johnson from obstructing Reconstruction.
Omnibus Act (June 1868)†	Readmitted seven ex-Confederate states to the Union.	To restore the Union, under the term of the First Reconstruction Act.
Enforcement Act of 1870 (May 1870)‡	Provided for the protection of black voters.	To enforce the Fifteenth Amendment.
Second Enforcement Act (February 1871)	Provided for federal supervision of southern elections.	To enforce the Fifteenth Amendment.
Third Enforcement Act (Ku Klux Klan Act) (April 1871)	Strengthened sanctions against those who impeded black suffrage.	To combat the Ku Klux Klan and enforce the Fourteenth Amendment.
Amnesty Act (May 1872)	Restored the franchise to almost all ex-Confederates.	Effort by Grant Republicans to deprive Liberal Republicans of campaign issue.
Civil Rights Act of 1875 (March 1875)§	Outlawed racial segregation in transportation and public accommodations and prevented exclusion of blacks from jury service.	To honor the late senator Charles Sumner.

* Passed over Johnson's veto.

† Georgia was soon returned to military rule. The last four states were readmitted in 1870.

‡ Sections of the law declared unconstitutional in 1876.

§ Invalidated by the Supreme Court in 1883.

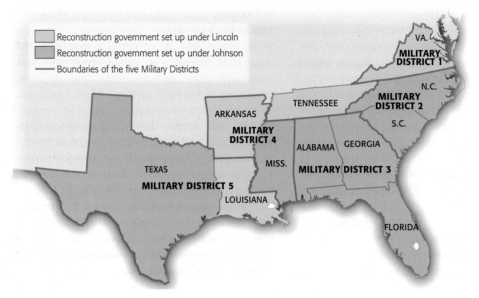

VA.

MILITARY DISTRICT 1

N.C.

MILITARY DISTRICT 2

TENNESSEE

S.C.

ARKANSAS

MILITARY DISTRICT 4

ALABAMA   GEORGIA

TEXAS

MILITARY DISTRICT 5

MISS.

MILITARY DISTRICT 3

LOUISIANA

FLORIDA

MAP 16.1   THE RECONSTRUCTION OF THE SOUTH The Reconstruction Act of 1867 divided the former Confederate states, except Tennessee, into five military districts and set forth the steps by which new state governments could be created.

until Republican governments could be established and thereby prevent an immediate rebel resurgence. But the new law was not as harsh toward ex-Confederates as it might have been. It provided for only temporary military rule; it did not prosecute Confederate leaders for treason, permanently bar them from politics, or provide for confiscation or redistribution of property.

During the congressional debates, Radical Republican congressman Thaddeus Stevens had argued for the confiscation of large Confederate estates to "humble the proud traitors" and to provide for former slaves. He had proposed subdividing such confiscated property into forty-acre tracts to be distributed among the freedmen and selling the rest, some 90 percent of it, to pay off war debts. Stevens's land-reform bill won Radical support but never made progress; most Republicans held property rights sacred. Tampering with such rights in the South, they feared, would jeopardize those rights in the North. Moreover, Stevens's proposal would alienate southern ex-Whigs, aggrieve other white southerners and thereby endanger the rest of Reconstruction. Thus land reform never came about. The "radical" Reconstruction acts were a compromise.

Congressional Reconstruction took effect in the spring of 1867, but Johnson, as Commander in Chief, impeded its enforcement by replacing pro-Radical military officers with conservative ones. Republicans seethed. More suspicious than ever, congressional moderates and Radicals again joined forces to block Johnson from further obstructing Reconstruction.

The Impeachment Crisis, 1867–1868

In March 1867, Republicans in Congress passed two laws to curb presidential power. The **Tenure of Office Act** barred the president from removing civil officers without Senate consent. Cabinet members, the law stated, were to hold office "during the term of the president by whom they may have been appointed" and could be fired only with the Senate's approval. The goal was to bar Johnson from dismissing Secretary of War Edwin M. Stanton, a Radical ally. The other law, a rider to an army appropriations bill, barred the president from issuing military orders except through the commanding general, Ulysses S. Grant, who could not be removed without the Senate's consent.

The Radicals' enmity toward Johnson, however, went further: they now sought grounds on which to impeach him. The House Judiciary Committee could at first find no valid charges against Johnson. But the president again rescued his foes by providing the charges they needed.

In August 1867, with Congress out of session, Johnson suspended Secretary of War Stanton and replaced him with General Grant. In early 1868, the reconvened Senate refused to approve Stanton's suspension, and Grant, sensing the Republican mood, vacated the office. Johnson then removed Stanton and replaced him with another general. Johnson's defiance forced Republican moderates, who had at first resisted impeachment, into yet another alliance with the Radicals: the president had "thrown down the gauntlet," a moderate charged. The House approved eleven charges of impeachment, nine based on violation of the Tenure of Office Act. The other charges accused Johnson of ignoring "the high duties of office," seeking to disgrace Congress, and not enforcing the Reconstruction acts.

Johnson's trial in the Senate, which began in March 1868, riveted public attention for eleven weeks. Seven congressmen, including leading Radical Republicans, served as prosecutors or "managers." Johnson's lawyers maintained that he was merely seeking a court test by violating the Tenure of Office Act, which he thought was unconstitutional. They also contended, somewhat inconsistently, that the law did not protect Secretary Stanton, an appointee of Lincoln, not Johnson. Finally, they asserted, Johnson was guilty of no crime indictable in a regular court.

The congressional "managers" countered that impeachment was a political process, not a criminal trial, and that Johnson's "abuse of discretionary power" constituted an impeachable offense. Although Senate opinion split along party lines, some Republicans wavered, fearful that removal of a president would destroy the balance of power among the three branches of the federal government. They also distrusted Radical Republican Benjamin Wade, the president pro tempore of the Senate, who, because there was no vice president, would become president if Johnson were thrown out.

Late in May 1868, the Senate voted against Johnson 35 to 19, one vote short of the two-thirds majority needed for conviction. Despite intense pressure, seven Republicans had risked political suicide and sided with the twelve Senate Democrats against removal. In so doing, they set a precedent: their vote discouraged impeachment on political grounds for decades to come. But the anti-Johnson forces had also achieved their goal: Andrew Johnson had no future as president. Serving out the rest of his term, Johnson returned to Tennessee, where he was reelected to the Senate five years later. Republicans in Congress, meanwhile, pursued their last major Reconstruction objective: to guarantee black male suffrage.

The Fifteenth Amendment and the Question of Woman Suffrage, 1869–1870

Black suffrage was the linchpin of congressional Reconstruction. Only with the black vote could Republicans secure control of the ex-Confederate states. The Reconstruction Act of 1867 had forced southern states to enfranchise black men in order to reenter the Union, but much of the North rejected black suffrage. Congressional Republicans therefore had two aims. The **Fifteenth Amendment,** proposed by Congress in 1869, sought to protect black suffrage in the South against future repeal by Congress or the states and to enfranchise northern and border-state blacks, who would presumably vote Republican. The amendment prohibited the denial of suffrage by the states to any citizen on account of "race, color, or previous condition of servitude."

Democrats argued that the proposed amendment violated states' rights by denying each state leverage over who would vote. But Democrats did not control enough states to defeat the amendment, and it was ratified in 1870. Four ex-Confederate states—Mississippi, Virginia, Georgia, and Texas—that had delayed the Reconstruction process were therefore forced to approve the Fifteenth Amendment, as well as the Fourteenth, in order to rejoin the Union. Some southerners appreciated the new amendment's omissions: as a Richmond newspaper pointed out, it had "loopholes through which a coach and four horses can be driven." What were these loopholes? The Fifteenth Amendment neither guaranteed black office holding nor prohibited voting restrictions such as property requirements and literacy tests. Such restrictions might be used—and ultimately were used—to deny blacks the vote.

The debate over black suffrage drew new participants into the political fray. In 1866, when Congress debated the Fourteenth Amendment, women's rights advocates tried to join forces with abolitionist allies in the American Equal Rights Association, which (they hoped) would promote both black suffrage and woman suffrage. Most Radical Republicans, however, did not want to be saddled with the woman-suffrage plank; they feared it would impede their primary goal, black enfranchisement.

This defection provoked disputes among women's rights advocates. Some argued that black suffrage would pave the way for the women's vote and that black men deserved priority. "If the elective franchise is not extended to the Negro, he is dead," explained Frederick Douglass, a longtime women's rights supporter. "Woman has a thousand ways by which she can attach herself to the ruling power of the land that we have not." But women's rights leaders Elizabeth Cady Stanton and **Susan B. Anthony** disagreed. In their view, the Fourteenth Amendment had disabled women by including the word *male*, and the Fifteenth Amendment failed to remedy this injustice. Instead, Stanton contended, the amendment established an "aristocracy of sex" and increased women's disadvantages.

The battle over black suffrage and the Fifteenth Amendment split women's rights advocates into two rival suffrage associations, formed in 1869. The Boston-based American Woman Suffrage

ANTHONY AND STANTON, CA. 1870 Women's rights advocates Susan B. Anthony (left) and Elizabeth Cady Stanton began to promote woman suffrage when the issue of black suffrage arose in 1866. They subsequently assailed the proposed Fifteenth Amendment for excluding women. "[I]n proportion as you multiply the rulers, the condition of the politically estranged is more hopeless and degraded," Stanton declared at a woman suffrage convention By the end of the 1860s, activists had formed two competing suffragist organizations. *(Schlesinger Library, Radcliffe Institute, Harvard University/ The Bridgeman Art Library)*

> "If the elective franchise is not extended to the Negro, he is dead. Woman has a thousand ways by which she can attach herself to the ruling power of the land that we have not."

Association, endorsed by reformers such as Julia Ward Howe and Lucy Stone, retained an alliance with male abolitionists and campaigned for woman suffrage in the states. The New York–based and more radical National Woman Suffrage Association, led by Stanton and Anthony, condemned its former male allies and promoted a federal woman suffrage amendment.

Throughout the 1870s, the rival woman suffrage associations vied for constituents. In 1869 and 1870, independent of the suffrage movement, two territories, Wyoming and Utah, enfranchised women. But suffragists failed to sway legislators elsewhere. When Susan B. Anthony mobilized about seventy women to vote nationwide in 1872, she was indicted, convicted, and fined. One woman who tried to vote, Missouri suffragist Virginia Minor, brought suit with her husband against the registrar who had excluded her. The Minors claimed that the Fourteenth Amendment enfranchised women. In *Minor* v. *Happersett* (1875), however, the Supreme Court declared that a state could constitutionally deny women the vote. Divided and rebuffed, woman suffrage advocates braced for a long struggle.

By 1870, when the Fifteenth Amendment was ratified, Congress could look back on five years of achievement. Since the start of 1865, three constitutional amendments had strengthened American democracy: the Thirteenth Amendment abolished slavery, the Fourteenth expanded civil rights, and the Fifteenth barred the denial of suffrage on the basis of race (see Table 16.2). Congress had also readmitted the former Confederate states into the Union. But after 1868, congressional momentum slowed, and the theater of action shifted to the South, where tumultuous change occurred.

Reconstruction Governments

During the unstable years of Presidential Reconstruction, 1865–1867, the southern states had to create new governments, revive the war-torn economy, and face the impact of emancipation. Crises abounded. War costs had devastated southern wealth, cities and factories lay in rubble, plantation labor systems disintegrated, and racial tensions flared. Beginning in 1865, freedmen organized black conventions, political meetings at which they

TABLE 16.2 The Reconstruction Amendments

Amendment and Date of Congressional Passage	Provisions	Ratification
Thirteenth (January 1865)	Prohibited slavery in the United States.	December 1865.
Fourteenth (June 1866)	Defined citizenship to include all persons born or naturalized in the United States. Provided proportional loss of congressional representation for any state that denied suffrage to any of its male citizens. Disqualified prewar officeholders who supported the Confederacy from state or national office. Repudiated the Confederate debt.	July 1868, after Congress made ratification a prerequisite for readmission of ex-Confederate states to the Union.
Fifteenth (February 1869)	Prohibited the denial of suffrage because of race, color, or previous condition of servitude.	March 1870; ratification required of Virginia, Texas, Mississippi, and Georgia for readmission to the Union.

protested ill treatment and demanded equal rights. A climate of violence prevailed. Race riots erupted in major southern cities, such as Memphis in May 1866 and New Orleans two months later. Even when Congress imposed military rule, ex-Confederates did not feel defeated. "Having reached bottom, there is hope now that we may rise again," a South Carolina planter wrote in his diary.

Congressional Reconstruction, supervised by federal troops, took effect in the spring of 1867. The Johnson regimes were dismantled, state constitutional conventions met, and voters elected new state governments, which Republicans dominated. In 1868, most former Confederate states rejoined the Union, and two years later, the last four states—Virginia, Mississippi, Georgia, and Texas—followed.

But Republican rule was very brief, lasting less than a decade in all southern states, far less in most of them, and on average under five years. Opposition from southern Democrats, the landowning elite, thousands of vigilantes, and, indeed, most white voters proved insurmountable. Still, the governments formed under Congressional Reconstruction were unique, because black men, including exslaves, participated in them. In no other society where slaves had been liberated—neither Haiti, where slaves had revolted in the 1790s, nor the British Caribbean islands, where Parliament had ended slavery in 1833—had freedmen gained democratic political rights.

A New Electorate

The Reconstruction laws of 1867–1868 transformed the southern electorate by temporarily disfranchising 10 to 15 percent of potential white voters and by enfranchising more than seven hundred thousand freedmen. Outnumbering white voters by one hundred thousand, blacks held voting majorities in five states.

The new electorate provided a base for the Republican Party, which had never existed in the South. To scornful Democrats, southern Republicans comprised three types of scoundrels: northern "carpetbaggers," who had allegedly come south seeking wealth and power (with so few possessions that they could be stuffed into traveling bags made of carpet material); southern "scalawags," predominantly poor and ignorant whites, who sought to profit from Republican rule; and hordes of uneducated freedmen, who were ready prey for Republican manipulators. Although the "carpetbag" and "scalawag" labels were derogatory and the stereotypes they conveyed inaccurate, they remain in use as a form of shorthand. Crossing class and racial lines, the hastily established Republican Party was in fact a loose coalition of diverse factions with often contradictory goals.

To northerners who moved south after the Civil War, the former Confederacy was an undeveloped region, ripe with possibility. The carpetbaggers' ranks included many former Union soldiers who hoped to buy land, open factories, build railroads, or simply enjoy the warmer climate. Albion Tourgee, a young lawyer who had served with the New York and Ohio volunteers, for example, relocated in North Carolina after the war to improve his health; there he worked as a journalist, politician, and Republican judge. Perhaps no more than twenty thousand northern migrants like Tourgee—including veterans, missionaries, teachers, and Freedmen's Bureau agents—headed south immediately after the war, and many soon returned north. But those who remained held almost one out of three state offices and wielded disproportionate political power.

Scalawags, white southerners who supported the Republicans, included some entrepreneurs who applauded party policies such as the national banking system and high protective tariffs as well as some prosperous planters, former Whigs who had opposed secession. Their numbers included a few prominent politicians, among them James Orr of South Carolina and Mississippi's governor James Alcorn, who became Republicans in order to retain influence and limit Republican radicalism. Most scalawags, however, were small farmers from the mountain regions of North Carolina, Georgia, Alabama, and Arkansas. Former Unionists who had owned no slaves and felt no loyalty toward the landowning elite, they sought to improve their economic position. Unlike carpetbaggers, they lacked commitment to black rights or black suffrage; most came from regions with few blacks and cared little whether blacks voted or not. Scalawags held the most political offices during Reconstruction, but they proved the least stable element of the southern Republican coalition: eventually, many drifted back to the Democratic fold.

> "We'd walk fifteen miles in wartime to find out about the battle," a Georgia freedman declared. "We can walk fifteen miles and more to find how to vote."

Freedmen, the backbone of southern Republicanism, provided eight out of ten Republican votes. Republican rule lasted longest in states with the largest black populations—South Carolina, Mississippi, Alabama, and Louisiana. Introduced to politics in the black conventions of 1865–1867, the freedmen sought land, education, civil rights, and political equality, and they remained loyal Republicans. As an elderly freedman announced at a Georgia political convention in 1867, "We know our friends." Although Reconstruction governments depended on African

American votes, freedmen held at most one in five political offices. Blacks served in all southern legislatures but constituted a majority only in the legislature of South Carolina, whose population was more than 60 percent black. In the House of Representatives, a mere 6 percent of southern members were black, and almost half of these came from South Carolina. No blacks became governor, and only two—Hiram Revels and Blanche K. Bruce, both of Mississippi—served in the U.S. Senate. (Still, the same number of African Americans served in the Senate throughout the entire twentieth century.)

Black officeholders on the state level formed a political elite. They often differed from black voters in background, education, and wealth. A disproportionate number were literate blacks who had been free before the Civil War. In the South Carolina legislature, most black members, unlike their constituents, came from large towns and cities; many had spent time in the North; and some were well-off property owners or even former slave owners. Color differences were evident, too: 43 percent of South Carolina's black state legislators were mulattos (mixed race), compared to only 7 percent of the state's black population.

Black officials and black voters often had different priorities. Most freedmen cared mainly about their economic future, especially about acquiring land; black officeholders cared most about attaining equal rights. Still, both groups shared high expectations and prized enfranchisement. "We'd walk fifteen miles in wartime to find out about the battle," a Georgia freedman declared. "We can walk fifteen miles and more to find how to vote."

REPUBLICANS IN THE SOUTH CAROLINA LEGISLATURE, CA. 1868
Only in South Carolina did blacks comprise a majority in the legislature and dominate the legislative process during Reconstruction. This photographic collage of "Radical" legislators, black and white, suggests the extent of black representation. "Now is the black man's day," declared a black politician. "[N]ow is *our time.*" A northern reporter, in contrast, saw in the legislature "the spectacle of a society suddenly turned upside down." In 1874, African Americans won the majority of seats in South Carolina's state senate as well. *(Museum of the Confederacy)*

Republican Rule

Large numbers of blacks participated in American government for the first time in the state constitutional conventions of 1867–1868. The South Carolina convention had a black majority, and in Louisiana half the delegates were freedmen. The conventions forged democratic changes in their state constitutions. Delegates abolished property qualifications for office holding, made many appointive offices elective, and redistricted state legislatures more equitably. All states established universal manhood suffrage.

But no state instituted land reform. When proposals for land confiscation and redistribution arose at the state conventions, they fell to defeat, as they had in Congress. Hoping to attract northern investment to the reconstructed South, southern Republicans hesitated to threaten property rights or to adopt land-reform measures that northern Republicans had rejected. South Carolina did set up a commission to buy land and make it available to freedmen, and several states changed their tax structures to force uncultivated land onto the market, but in no case was ex-Confederate land confiscated.

Once civil power shifted from the federal army to the new state governments, Republican regimes began ambitious programs of public works. They built roads, bridges, and public buildings; approved railroad bonds; and funded institutions to care for orphans, the insane, and the disabled. They also expanded state bureaucracies, raised pay for state employees, and formed state militia, in which blacks were often heavily represented. Finally, they created public-school systems, almost nonexistent in the South until then.

These changes cost millions, and taxes skyrocketed. State legislatures increased poll taxes or "head" taxes (levies on individuals); enacted luxury, sales, and occupation taxes; and imposed new property

ELECTIONEERING AT THE SOUTH A candidate for public office addresses a political meeting in the late 1860s. Such meetings attracted entire communities of freed people. Black women, though un-enfranchised, often attended political rallies and other events (as shown). They may have viewed the decision involved in voting as a household choice and the franchise as a collective possession. *(The Granger Collection, New York)*

taxes. Before the war, southern states had taxed property in slaves but had barely taxed landed property. Now state governments assessed even small farmers' holdings; propertied planters felt overburdened. Although northern tax rates still exceeded southern rates, southern landowners resented the new levies. In their view, Reconstruction punished the propertied, already beset by labor problems and falling land values, in order to finance the vast expenditures of Republican legislators.

To Reconstruction's foes, Republican rule was wasteful and corrupt, the "most stupendous system of organized robbery in history." A state like Mississippi, which had an honest government, provided little basis for such charges. But critics could justifiably point to Louisiana, where the governor pocketed thousands of dollars of state funds and corruption permeated all government transactions (as indeed it had before the war). Or they could cite South Carolina, where bribery ran rampant. Besides government officials who took bribes, postwar profiteers included the railroad promoters who doled them out. Not all were Republicans. Nor did

the Republican regimes in the South hold a monopoly on corruption. After the war, bribery pervaded government transactions North and South, and far more money changed hands in the North. But critics assailed Republican rule for additional reasons.

Counterattacks

Ex-Confederates spoke with dread about black enfranchisement and the "horror of Negro domination." As soon as congressional Reconstruction took effect, former Confederates campaigned to undermine it. Democratic newspapers assailed delegates to North Carolina's constitutional convention as an "Ethiopian minstrelsy" and called Louisiana's constitution "the work of ignorant Negroes cooperating with a gang of white adventurers."

Democrats delayed mobilization until southern states were readmitted to the Union and then swung into action. At first, they sought to win black votes; but when that failed, they tried other tactics. In 1868–1869, Georgia Democrats challenged the eligibility of black legislators and expelled them from office. In response, the federal government reestablished military rule in Georgia, but determined Democrats still undercut Republican power. In every southern state, they contested elections, backed dissident Republican factions, elected some Democratic legislators, and lured scalawags away from the Republican Party.

Vigilante efforts to reduce black votes bolstered the Democrats' campaigns to win white ones. Antagonism toward free blacks, long a motif in southern life, resurged after the war. In 1865, Freedmen's Bureau agents itemized outrages against blacks, including shooting, murder, rape, arson, and "inhuman beating." Vigilante groups sprang up spontaneously in all parts of the former Confederacy under names like moderators, regulators, and, in Louisiana, Knights of the White Camelia. One group rose to dominance. In the spring of 1866, six young Confederate war veterans in Tennessee formed a social club, the **Ku Klux Klan,** distinguished by elaborate rituals, hooded costumes, and secret passwords. By the election of 1868, when

black men could first vote, Klan dens had spread to all southern states. Klansmen embarked on night raids to intimidate black voters. No longer a social club, the Ku Klux Klan was now a terrorist movement and a violent arm of the Democratic Party.

The Klan sought to suppress black voting, reestablish white supremacy, and topple Reconstruction governments. Its members attacked Freedmen's Bureau officials, white Republicans, black militia units, economically successful blacks, and black voters. Concentrated in areas where black and white populations were most evenly balanced and racial tensions greatest, Klan dens adapted their tactics and timing to local conditions. In Mississippi, the Klan targeted black schools; in Alabama, it concentrated on Republican officeholders. In Arkansas, terror reigned in 1868; in Georgia and Florida, Klan strength surged in 1870. Some Democrats denounced Klan members as "cutthroats and riff-raff." But Klansmen included prominent ex-Confederates, among them General Nathan Bedford Forrest, the leader of the 1864 Fort Pillow massacre, in which Confederate

THE KU KLUX KLAN Disguised in long white robes and hoods, Ku Klux Klansmen sometimes claimed to be the ghosts of Confederate soldiers. The Klan, which spread rapidly after 1867, sought to end Republican rule, restore white supremacy, and obliterate, in one southern editor's words, "the preposterous and wicked dogma of Negro equality." *(Tennessee State Archives/Picture Research Consultants & Archives)*

troops who captured a Union garrison in Tennessee murdered black soldiers who had surrendered. Vigilantism united southern whites of different social classes and drew on Confederate veterans' energy. In areas where the Klan was inactive, other vigilante groups took its place.

Republican legislatures passed laws to outlaw vigilantism, but as state militia could not enforce them, state officials sought federal help. Between May 1870 and February 1871, Congress passed three **Enforcement Acts,** each progressively more stringent. The First Enforcement Act protected black voters, but witnesses to violations were afraid to testify against vigilantes, and local juries refused to convict them. The Second Enforcement Act provided for federal supervision of southern elections, and the Third Enforcement Act, or Ku Klux Klan Act, strengthened punishments for those who prevented blacks from voting. It also empowered the president to use federal troops to enforce the law and to suspend the writ of *habeas corpus* in areas that he declared in insurrection. (The writ of *habeas corpus* is a court order requiring that the detainer of a prisoner bring that person to court and show cause for his or her detention.) The Ku Klux Klan Act generated thousands of arrests; most terrorists, however, escaped conviction.

By 1872, the federal government had effectively suppressed the Klan, but vigilantism had served its purpose. Only a large military presence in the South could have protected black rights, and the government in Washington never provided it. Instead, federal power in the former Confederacy diminished. President Grant steadily reduced troop levels in the South; Congress allowed the Freedmen's Bureau to die in 1869; and the Enforcement acts became dead letters. White southerners, a Georgia politician told congressional investigators in 1871, could not discard "a feeling of bitterness, a feeling that the Negro is a sort of instinctual enemy of ours." The battle over Reconstruction was in essence a battle over the implications of emancipation, and it had begun as soon as the war ended.

The Impact of Emancipation

"The master he says we are all free," a South Carolina slave declared in 1865. "But it don't mean we is white. And it don't mean we is equal." Emancipated slaves faced daunting handicaps. They had no property, tools, or capital; they possessed meager skills; and more than 95 percent were illiterate. Still, the exhilaration of freedom was overwhelming, as slaves realized, "Now I am for myself" and "All that I make is my own." Emancipation gave them the right to their own labor and a new sense of autonomy.

Under Reconstruction, they sought to cast off white control and shed the vestiges of slavery.

Confronting Freedom

For former slaves, liberty meant mobility. Some moved out of slave quarters and set up dwellings elsewhere on their plantations; others left their plantations entirely. Landowners found that one freed slave after another vanished, with house servants and artisans leading the way. "I have never in my life met with such ingratitude," one South Carolina mistress exclaimed when a former slave ran off. Field workers, who had less contact with whites, were more likely to stay behind. Still, flight remained tempting. "The moment they see an opportunity to improve themselves, they will move on," diarist Mary Chesnut observed.

Emancipation stirred waves of migration within the former Confederacy. Some freed slaves left the Upper South for the Deep South and the Southwest— Florida, Mississippi, Arkansas, and Texas—where planters desperately needed labor and paid higher wages. More left the countryside for towns and cities. Urban black populations sometimes doubled or tripled after emancipation; the number of blacks in small rural towns grew as well. Many migrants eventually returned to their old locales, but they tended to settle on neighboring plantations rather than with former owners. Freedom was the major goal. "I's wants to be a free man … and nobody say nuffin to me, nor order me roun,'" an Alabama freedman told a northern journalist.

> "The master he says we are all free. But it don't mean we is white. And it don't mean we is equal."

Efforts to find lost family members prompted much movement. "They had a passion, not so much for wandering as for getting together," a Freedmen's Bureau official commented. Parents sought children who had been sold; husbands and wives who had been separated by sale, or who lived on different plantations, reunited; and family members sought extended networks of kin. The Freedmen's Bureau helped former slaves get information about missing relatives and travel to find them. Bureau agents also tried to resolve conflicts that arose when spouses who had been separated under slavery married other people.

Reunification efforts often failed. Some fugitive slaves had died during the war or were untraceable. Other exslaves had formed new relationships and could not revive old ones. Still, success stories abounded. "I'se hunted an' hunted till I track you up here," one freedman told his wife, whom he found in a refugee camp twenty years after their separation

FORMER SLAVES ON PLANTATION IN WARREN COUNTY, MISSISSIPPI Emancipation brought the possibility of movement. Some freed people on big plantations (like this one in Warren County, Mississippi) remained where they were; some moved off to find work on other plantations; and others gravitated toward towns and cities. "If I stay here I'll never know I'm free," a valued cook told her former owner. "They all want to go to the cities," a South Carolina planter observed. "The fields have no attractions." *(Old Court House Museum, Vicksburg, Mississippi)*

by sale. Once reunited, freed blacks quickly legalized unions formed under slavery, sometimes in mass ceremonies of up to seventy couples. Legal marriage affected family life. Men asserted themselves as household heads; wives of able-bodied men often withdrew from the labor force to care for homes and families. "When I married my wife, I married her to wait on me and she has got all she can do right here for me and the children," a Tennessee freedman explained.

Black women's desire for domestic life caused labor shortages. Before the war, at least half of field workers had been women; in 1866, a southern journal claimed, men performed almost all the field labor. Still, by Reconstruction's end, many black women had returned to agricultural work as part of sharecropper families. Others took paid work in cities, as laundresses, cooks, and domestic servants. (White women often sought employment, too, because the war had incapacitated many white breadwinners, reduced the supply of future husbands, and left families impoverished.) However, former slaves continued to view stable, independent domestic life—especially the right to bring up their own children—as a major blessing of freedom. In 1870, eight out of ten black families in the cotton-producing South were two-parent families, about the same proportion as among whites.

African American Institutions

Freed blacks' desire for independence also fostered growth of black churches. In the late 1860s, some freedmen congregated at churches operated by northern missionaries; others withdrew from white-run churches and formed their own. The African Methodist Episcopal church, founded by Philadelphia blacks in the 1790s, gained thousands of new southern members. Negro Baptist churches sprouted everywhere, often growing out of plantation "praise meetings," religious gatherings organized by slaves.

Black churches offered a fervent, participatory experience. They also provided relief, raised funds for schools, and supported Republican policies. Black ministers assumed leading political roles, first in the black conventions of 1865–1866 and later in Reconstruction governments. After southern Democrats excluded most freedmen from political life at Reconstruction's end, ministers remained the main pillars of authority in black communities.

Black schools played a crucial role for freedmen, too; exslaves eagerly sought literacy for themselves and, above all, for their children. At emancipation, blacks organized their own schools, which the Freedmen's Bureau soon supervised. Northern philanthropic societies paid the wages of instructors, about half of them women. "Our work is just as much missionary work as if we were in India or China," a Sea Islands teacher commented. In 1869, the bureau reported more than four thousand black schools in the former Confederacy. Within three years, each southern state had a public school system, at least in principle, generally with separate schools for blacks and whites. Advanced schools for blacks opened to train tradespeople, teachers, and ministers. The Freedmen's Bureau and northern organizations like the American Missionary Association helped found Howard, Atlanta, and Fisk universities (1866–1867) and Hampton Institute (1868).

However, black education remained limited. Few rural blacks could reach freedmen's schools located in towns. Underfunded black public schools, similarly inaccessible to most rural black children, held classes only for short seasons and sometimes drew vigilante attacks. At the end of Reconstruction, more than 80 percent of the black population was still illiterate, though literacy rose steadily among youngsters (see Table 16.3).

School segregation and other forms of racial separation were taken for granted. Some black codes of

TABLE 16.3 Percentage of Persons Unable to Write, by Age Group, 1870–1890, in South Carolina, Georgia, Alabama, Mississippi, and Louisiana

Age Group	1870	1880	1890
10–14			
Black	78.9	74.1	49.2
White	33.2	34.5	18.7
15–20			
Black	85.3	73.0	54.1
White	24.2	21.0	14.3
Over 20			
Black	90.4	82.3	75.5
White	19.8	17.9	17.1

Source: *Roger Ransom and Richard Sutch,* One Kind of Freedom. *(Cambridge: Cambridge University Press, 1978), 30.*

1865–1866 had segregated public-transportation and public accommodations. Even after the invalidation of the codes, the custom of segregation continued on streetcars, steamboats, and trains as well as in churches, theaters, inns, and restaurants. In 1870, Senator Charles Sumner of Massachusetts, a steadfast Radical, began promoting a bill to desegregate

HAMPTON INSTITUTE Founded in 1868, Hampton Institute in southeastern Virginia welcomed newly freed African Americans to vocational programs in agriculture, teacher training, and homemaking. These students, photographed at the school's entrance around 1870, were among Hampton's first classes. *(Archival and Museum Collection, Hampton University)*

schools, transportation facilities, juries, and public accommodations. After Sumner's death in 1874, Congress honored him by a new law, the **Civil Rights Act of 1875,** which included his proposals, save for the controversial school-integration provision. But in 1883, in the *Civil Rights Cases*, the Supreme Court invalidated the law; the Fourteenth Amendment did not prohibit discrimination by individuals, the Court ruled, only that perpetrated by the state.

White southerners rejected the prospect of racial integration, which they insisted would lead to racial amalgamation. "If we have social equality, we shall have intermarriage," one white southerner contended, "and if we have intermarriage, we shall degenerate." Urban blacks sometimes challenged segregation practices; black legislators promoted bills to desegregate public transit; and some black officeholders decried all forms of racial separatism. "The sooner we as a people forget our sable complexion," said a Mobile official, "the better it will be for us as a race." But most freed blacks were less interested in "social equality," in the sense of interracial mingling, than in black liberty and community. The new postwar elite—teachers, ministers, and politicians—served black constituencies and therefore had a vested interest in separate black institutions. Rural blacks, too, widely preferred all-black institutions. They had little desire to mix with whites. On the contrary, they sought freedom from white control. Above all, they wanted to secure personal independence by acquiring land.

Land, Labor, and Sharecropping

"The sole ambition of the freedman," a New Englander wrote from South Carolina in 1865, "appears to be to become the owner of a little piece of land, there to erect a humble home, and to dwell in peace and security, at his own free will and pleasure." Indeed, to freed blacks everywhere, landownership signified economic independence; "forty acres and a mule" (a phrase that originated in 1864 when Union general William T. Sherman set aside land on the South Carolina Sea Islands for black settlement) promised emancipation from plantation labor, white domination, and cotton, the "slave crop."

> "You must begin at the bottom of the ladder and climb up."

But freedmen's visions of landownership failed to materialize, for, as we have seen, neither Congress nor the southern states imposed large-scale land reform. Some freedmen obtained land with the help of the Union army or the Freedmen's Bureau, and black soldiers sometimes pooled resources to buy land, as on the Sea Islands of South Carolina and Georgia. In 1866, Congress passed the Southern Homestead Act, which set aside 44 million acres of public land in five southern states for freedmen and loyal whites. This acreage contained poor soil, and few former slaves had the resources to survive even until their first harvest. About four thousand blacks resettled on homesteads under the law, but most were unable to establish farms (poor whites fared little better.) By Reconstruction's end, only a small minority of former slaves owned working farms. In Georgia in 1876, for instance, blacks controlled a mere 1.3 percent of total acreage. Without large-scale land reform, obstacles to black landownership remained overwhelming.

What were these obstacles? First, most freedmen lacked the capital to buy land and the equipment needed to work it. Furthermore, white southerners generally opposed selling land to blacks. Most important, planters sought to preserve a black labor force. Freedmen, they insisted, would work only under coercion, and not at all if the possibility of landownership arose. As soon as the war ended, the white South took steps to ensure that black labor would remain available on plantations.

During Presidential Reconstruction, southern state legislatures had tried to curb black mobility and preserve a captive labor force through the black codes. Under labor contracts in effect in 1865–1866, freedmen received wages, housing, food, and clothing in exchange for fieldwork. With cash scarce, wages usually took the form of a very small share of the crop, often one-eighth or less, divided among the entire plantation work force. Freedmen's Bureau agents promoted the new labor system; they saw black wage labor as an interim arrangement that would lead to economic independence. "You must begin at the bottom of the ladder and climb up," Freedmen's Bureau head O.O. Howard exhorted a group of Louisiana freedmen in 1865.

But freedmen disliked the new wage system, especially the use of gang labor, which resembled the work pattern under slavery. Planters had complaints, too. In some regions the black labor force had shrunk to half its prewar size or less, due to the migration of freedmen and to black women's withdrawal from fieldwork. Once united in defense of slavery, planters now competed for black workers. But the freedmen, whom planters often scorned as lazy or inefficient, did not intend to work as long or as hard as they had labored under slavery. One planter claimed that workers accomplished only "two-fifths of what they did under the old system." As productivity fell, so did land values. Plummeting cotton prices and poor harvests compounded planters' woes. By 1867, an agricultural impasse had been reached: landowners lacked labor, and freedmen lacked land. But free blacks, unlike slaves, had the right to enter into contracts—or to refuse to do so—and thereby gained some leverage.

Planters and freedmen began experimenting with new labor schemes, including the division of plantations into small tenancies (see Map 16.2). **Sharecropping,** the most widespread arrangement, evolved as a compromise. Under the sharecropping system, landowners subdivided large plantations into farms of thirty to fifty acres, which they rented to freedmen under annual leases for a share of the crop, usually half. Freedmen preferred sharecropping to wage labor because it represented a step toward independence. Household heads could use the labor of family members. Moreover, a half-share of the crop far exceeded the fraction that freedmen had received as wages under the black codes. Planters often spoke of sharecropping as a concession, but they benefited, too. They retained power over tenants, because annual leases did not have to be renewed; they could expel undesirable tenants at the end of the year. Planters also shared the risk of planting with tenants: if a crop failed, both suffered the loss. Most important, planters retained control of their land and in some cases extended their holdings. The most productive land, therefore, remained in the hands of a small group of owners, as before the war. Sharecropping forced planters to relinquish daily control over the labor of freedmen but helped to preserve the planter elite (see Going to the Source).

Sharecropping arrangements varied widely. On sugar and rice plantations, the wage system continued; strong markets for those crops enabled planters to pay workers in cash—cash that cotton planters lacked. Some freedmen remained independent renters. Some landowners leased areas to white tenants, who then subcontracted with black labor. But by the end of the 1860s, sharecropping prevailed in the cotton South, and continued to expand. A severe depression in 1873 drove many black renters into sharecropping. Thousands of independent white farmers became sharecroppers as well. Stung by wartime losses and by the dismal postwar economy, they sank into debt and lost their land to creditors. Many backcountry residents, no longer able to get by on subsistence farming, shifted to cash crops like cotton and suffered the same fate. At Reconstruction's end, one-third of white farmers in Mississippi, for instance, were sharecroppers.

By 1880, 80 percent of the land in the cotton-producing states had been subdivided into tenancies, most of it farmed by sharecroppers, white and black (see Map 16.3, page 492). Indeed, white sharecroppers now outnumbered black ones, although a higher proportion of southern blacks, about 75 percent, were involved in the system. Changes in marketing and finance, meanwhile, made the sharecroppers' lot increasingly precarious.

Toward a Crop-Lien Economy

Before the Civil War, planters had depended on factors, or middlemen, who sold them supplies, extended credit, and marketed their crops through urban merchants. These long-distance credit arrangements were backed by the high value and liquidity of slave property. When slavery ended, the factorage system collapsed. The postwar South, with hundreds of thousands of tenants and sharecroppers, needed a far more localized credit network.

Into the gap stepped the rural merchants (often themselves planters), who advanced supplies to tenants and sharecroppers on credit and sold their crops to wholesalers or textile manufacturers. Because renters had no property to use as collateral, the merchants secured their loans with a lien, or claim, on each farmer's next crop. Exorbitant interest rates of 50 percent or more quickly forced many tenants and sharecroppers into a cycle of indebtedness. Owing part of the crop to a landowner for rent, a sharecropper also owed a rural merchant a large sum (perhaps amounting to the rest of his crop, or more) for supplies. Illiterate tenants who lost track of their financial arrangements often fell prey to unscrupulous merchants. "A man that didn't know how to count would always lose," an Arkansas freedman later explained. Once a tenant's debts or alleged debts exceeded the value of his crop, he was tied to the land, to cotton, and to sharecropping.

By Reconstruction's end, sharecropping and crop liens had transformed southern agriculture. They bound the region to staple production and prevented crop diversification. Despite plunging cotton prices, creditors—landowners and merchants—insisted that tenants raise only easily marketable cash crops. Short of capital, planters could no longer invest in new equipment or improve their land by crop rotation and contour plowing. Soil depletion, land erosion, and agricultural backwardness soon locked much of the South into a cycle of poverty.

Trapped in perpetual debt, tenant farmers became the chief victims of the new agricultural order. Raising cotton for distant markets, for prices over which they had no control, remained the only survival route open to poor farmers, regardless of race. But low income from cotton locked them into sharecropping and crop liens, from which escape was difficult. African American tenants saw their political rights dwindle, too. As one southern regime after another returned to Democratic control, freedmen could look for protection to neither state governments nor the federal government; northern politicians were preoccupied with their own problems (see Beyond America).

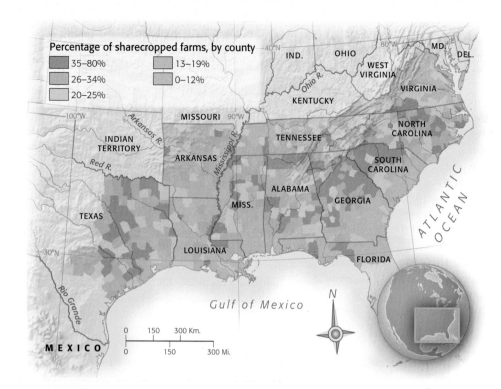

Percentage of sharecropped farms, by county

- 35–80%
- 26–34%
- 20–25%
- 13–19%
- 0–12%

Gulf of Mexico

MAP 16.3 SOUTHERN SHARECROPPING, 1880 The depressed economy of the late 1870s caused poverty and debt, increased tenancy among white farmers, and forced many renters, black and white, into sharecropping. By 1880, the sharecropping system pervaded most southern counties, with the highest concentrations in the cotton belt from South Carolina to eastern Texas. Sharecropping was most common, in short, in areas that had once had large numbers of slaves.

Source: U.S. Census Office, Tenth Census, 1880, *Report of the Production of Agriculture* (Washington, DC: Government Printing Office, 1883), Table 5.

New Concerns in the North, 1868–1876

The nomination of Ulysses S. Grant for president in 1868 launched a chaotic era in national politics. Grant's two terms in office saw political scandals, a party revolt, massive depression, and steady retreat from Reconstruction policies. By the mid-1870s, northern voters cared more about the economic climate, unemployment, labor unrest, and currency problems than about the "southern question." Responsive to the shift in popular mood, Republicans became eager to end sectional conflict and turned their backs on the freedmen of the South.

SHARECROPPERS DURING RECONSTRUCTION

By the end of the 1870s, about three out of four African Americans in the cotton-producing states had become sharecroppers. Here, sharecroppers pick cotton in Aiken, South Carolina. (*© Collection of the New York Historical Society*)

Grantism

Republicans had good reason to bypass party leaders and nominate the popular Grant. A war hero, Grant was endorsed by Union veterans and widely admired throughout the North. To oppose Grant, the Democrats nominated New York governor Horatio Seymour, arch-critic of the Lincoln administration in wartime and now a foe of Reconstruction. Grant ran on personal popularity more than issues. Although he carried all but eight states, the popular vote was close; in the South, newly enfranchised freedmen provided Grant's margin of victory.

A strong leader in war, Grant proved a passive president. Although he lacked Johnson's instinct for disaster, he had little political skill. Many of his cabinet appointees were mediocre if not unscrupulous; scandals plagued his administration. In 1869, financier Jay Gould and his partner Jim Fisk tried to corner the gold market with the help of Grant's brother-in-law, a New York speculator. When gold prices tumbled, investors were ruined and Grant's reputation suffered. Then, before the president's first term ended, his vice president, Schuyler Colfax, was found to be linked to the Crédit Mobilier, a fraudulent scheme to skim off the profits of the Union Pacific Railroad. Discredited, Colfax was dropped from the Grant ticket in 1872.

More trouble lay ahead. Grant's private secretary, Orville Babcock, was unmasked in 1875 after taking money from the "whiskey ring," distillers who bribed federal agents to avoid paying millions in taxes. In 1876, voters learned that Grant's secretary of war, William E. Belknap, had taken bribes to sell lucrative Indian trading posts in Oklahoma. Impeached and disgraced, Belknap resigned.

Although uninvolved in the scandals, Grant defended his subordinates. To his critics, "Grantism" came to stand for fraud, bribery, and political corruption—evils that spread far beyond Washington. In Pennsylvania, for example, the Standard Oil Company and the Pennsylvania Railroad controlled the legislature. Urban politics also provided rich opportunities for graft and swindles. The New York City press revealed in 1872 that Democratic boss William M. Tweed, the leader of Tammany Hall, led a ring that had looted the city treasury and collected millions in kickbacks and payoffs. When Mark Twain and coauthor Charles Dudley Warner published their satiric novel *The Gilded Age* (1873), readers recognized the book's speculators, self-promoters, and opportunists as familiar types in public life. (The term "Gilded Age" was subsequently used to refer to the decades from the 1870s to the 1890s.)

BOSS TWEED Thomas Nast's cartoons in *Harper's Weekly* helped topple New York Democratic boss William M. Tweed, who, with his associates, embodied corruption on a large scale. The Tweed Ring had granted lucrative franchises to companies they controlled, padded construction bills, practiced graft and extortion, and exploited every opportunity to plunder the city's funds. *(Brown Brothers and Harper's Weekly, 1871)*

Grant had some success in foreign policy. In 1872, his administration engineered the settlement of the *Alabama* claims with Britain. To compensate for damage done by Confederate-owned but British-built ships, an international tribunal awarded the United States $15.5 million. But Grant's administration faltered when it tried to add nonadjacent territory to the United States. In 1867, Johnson's secretary of state, William H. Seward, had negotiated a treaty in which the United States bought Alaska from Russia at the bargain price of $7.2 million. Although the press mocked "Seward's Ice Box," the purchase kindled expansionists' hopes. In 1870, Grant decided to annex the eastern half of the Caribbean island of Santo Domingo (today called the Dominican Republic); the territory had been passed back and forth since the late eighteenth century among France, Spain, and Haiti. Annexation, Grant believed, would promote Caribbean trade and provide a haven for persecuted southern blacks. American speculators anticipated windfalls from land sales, commerce, and mining. But Congress disliked Grant's plan. Senator Charles Sumner denounced it as an imperialist "dance of blood." The Senate rejected the annexation treaty and further diminished Grant's reputation.

As the 1872 election approached, dissident Republicans voiced fears that "Grantism" at home and abroad would ruin the party. The dissidents took action. Led by a combination of former Radicals and other Republicans left out of Grant's "Great Barbecue" (a disparaging reference to profiteers who feasted at the public trough), the president's critics formed their own party, the **Liberal Republicans.**

"Anything to Beat Grant."

The Liberals' Revolt

The Liberal Republican revolt split the Republican Party and undermined support for Republican southern policy. (The label "liberal" then meant support for economic doctrines such as free trade, the gold standard, and the law of supply and demand.) Denouncing "Grantism" and "spoilsmen" (political hacks who gained party office), Liberals urged civil service reform to bring the "best men" into government. Rejecting the "regular" Republicans' high-tariff policy, they espoused free trade. Most important, Liberals decried "bayonet rule" in the South. Even some one-time Radicals claimed that Reconstruction had achieved its goal: blacks had been enfranchised and could now fend for themselves. Corruption in government, North and South, posed greater danger than Confederate resurgence, Liberals claimed. In the South, they said, corrupt Republican regimes remained in power because the

"best men"—the most capable politicians—were ex-Confederates barred from office holding.

For president, the new party nominated *New York Tribune* editor Horace Greeley, who had inconsistently supported both a stringent reconstruction policy and leniency toward former rebels. The Democrats endorsed Greeley, too; their slogan was "Anything to Beat Grant." Horace Greeley campaigned so diligently that he worked himself to death making speeches from the back of a train, and died a few weeks after the election.

Grant, who won 56 percent of the popular vote, carried all the northern states and most of the sixteen southern and border states. But division among Republicans affected Reconstruction. To deprive the Liberals of a campaign issue, Grant Republicans in Congress, the "regulars," passed the Amnesty Act, which allowed most ex-Confederate officials to hold office. A flood of private amnesty acts followed. In Grant's second term, Republican desires to discard the "southern question" mounted as depression gripped the nation.

The Panic of 1873

The postwar years brought accelerated industrialization, rapid economic growth, and frantic speculation. Investors rushed to profit from rising prices, new markets, high tariffs, and seemingly boundless opportunities. Railroads led the speculative boom. In May 1869, railroad executives drove a golden spike into the ground at Promontory Point, Utah, joining the Union Pacific and Central Pacific lines. By 1873, almost four hundred railroad corporations crisscrossed the Northeast, consuming tons of coal and miles of steel rail from the mines and mills of Pennsylvania and neighboring states. Transforming the economy, the railroad boom led entrepreneurs to overspeculate, with drastic results.

Philadelphia banker Jay Cooke, who had helped finance the Union effort with his wartime bond campaign, had taken over a new transcontinental line, the Northern Pacific, in 1869. Northern Pacific securities sold briskly for several years, but in 1873 the line's construction costs outran bond sales. In September, Cooke defaulted on his obligations, and his bank, the largest in the nation, shut down. A financial panic began; other firms collapsed, as did the stock market. The Panic of 1873 triggered a five-year depression. Banks closed, farm prices plummeted, steel furnaces stood idle, and one out of four railroads failed. Within two years, eighteen thousand businesses went bankrupt; 3 million were unemployed by 1878. Wage cuts struck those still employed; labor protests mounted; and industrial violence spread. The depression of the 1870s revealed that conflicts born of industrialization had replaced sectional divisions.

The depression also fed a dispute over currency that had begun in 1865. During the Civil War, Americans had used greenbacks, a paper currency not backed by a specific weight in gold. To stabilize the postwar currency, "sound money" supporters demanded withdrawal of greenbacks from circulation. Their opponents, "easy money" advocates, such as farmers and manufacturers dependent on easy credit, wanted an expanding currency (more greenbacks). Once depression began, demands for such "easy money" rose. The issue divided both major parties and was compounded by another one: how to repay the federal debt.

In wartime, the Union government had borrowed what were then astronomical sums, mainly by selling war bonds. Bondholders wanted repayment in coin, gold or silver, even though many had paid for bonds in greenbacks. To pacify bondholders, Senator John Sherman of Ohio and other Republicans pressed for the Public Credit Act of 1869, which promised repayment in coin. With investors reassured, Sherman guided legislation through Congress that swapped the old short-term bonds for new ones payable over the next generation. In 1872, another bill in effect defined "coin" as "gold coin" by dropping the silver dollar from the official coinage. Through a feat of compromise, which placated investors and debtors, Sherman preserved the public credit and Republican unity. His Specie Resumption Act of 1875 promised to put the nation on the gold standard in 1879.

But Sherman's measures did not satisfy the Democrats, who gained control of the House in 1875. Many Democrats and some Republicans demanded restoration of the silver dollar in order to expand the currency and relieve the depression. These "free-silver" advocates secured passage of the Bland-Allison Act of 1878, which partially restored silver coinage. In 1876, other expansionists formed the **Greenback Party,** which adopted the debtors' cause and fought to keep greenbacks in circulation, though with little success. As the depression receded in 1879, the clamor for "easy money" subsided, only to resurge in the 1890s. The controversial "money question" of the 1870s, never resolved, gave politicians and voters another reason to forget about the South.

Reconstruction and the Constitution

The Supreme Court of the 1870s also played a role in weakening northern support for Reconstruction. In wartime, few cases of note had reached the Court. After the war, however, constitutional questions arose.

First, would the Court support congressional laws to protect freedmen's rights? The decision in *Ex parte* Milligan (1866) suggested not. In *Milligan*, the Court declared that a military commission

established by the president or Congress could not try civilians in areas remote from war where the civil courts were functioning. Thus, special military courts to enforce the Supplementary Freedmen's Bureau Act were doomed. Second, would the Court sabotage the congressional Reconstruction plan, as Republicans feared? In *Texas* v. *White* (1869), the Court ruled that although the Union was indissoluble and secession was legally impossible, the process of Reconstruction was still constitutional. It was grounded in Congress's power to ensure each state a republican form of government and to recognize the legitimate government in any state.

But in the 1870s, the Court backed away from Reconstruction. In the **slaughterhouse cases** of 1873, the Supreme Court chipped away at the Fourteenth Amendment. The cases involved a business monopoly, not freedmen's rights, but provided an opportunity to interpret the amendment narrowly. In 1869, the Louisiana legislature had granted a monopoly over the New Orleans slaughterhouse business to one firm and closed down all other slaughterhouses in the interest of public health. The excluded butchers brought suit. The state had deprived them of their lawful occupation without due process of law, they claimed; such action violated the Fourteenth Amendment, which guaranteed that no state could "abridge the privileges or immunities" of U.S. citizens. The Supreme Court upheld the Louisiana legislature by issuing a doctrine of "dual citizenship." The Fourteenth Amendment, declared the Court, protected only the rights of *national* citizenship, such as the right of interstate travel, but not those rights that fell to citizens through *state* citizenship. The *Slaughterhouse* decision vitiated the intent of the Fourteenth Amendment—to secure freedmen's rights against state encroachment.

The Supreme Court again backed away from Reconstruction in two cases in 1876 involving the Enforcement Act of 1870, enacted to protect black suffrage. In *United States* v. *Reese* and *United States* v. *Cruikshank*, the Supreme Court undercut the act's effectiveness. Continuing its retreat from Reconstruction, the Supreme Court in 1883 invalidated both the Civil Rights Act of 1875 and the Ku Klux Klan Act of 1871. These decisions cumulatively dismantled the Reconstruction policies that Republicans had sponsored after the war and confirmed rising northern sentiment that Reconstruction's egalitarian goals could not be enforced.

Republicans in Retreat

The Republicans did not reject Reconstruction suddenly but rather disengaged from it gradually, a process that began with Grant's election to the presidency in 1868. Not an architect of Reconstruction policy, Grant defended it. But he believed in decentralized government and hesitated to assert federal authority in local and state affairs.

In the 1870s, as northern military force shrank in the South, Republican idealism waned in the North. The Liberal Republican revolt of 1872 eroded what remained of radicalism. Among "regular" Republicans, who backed Grant, many held ambivalent views. Commercial and industrial interests now dominated both wings of the party, and few Republicans wished to rekindle sectional strife. After the Democrats won the House in 1874, support for Reconstruction became a political liability.

By 1875, the Radical Republicans, so prominent in the 1860s, had vanished. Chase, Stevens, and Sumner were dead. Other Radicals had lost office or conviction. "Waving the Bloody Shirt"—defaming Democratic opponents by reviving wartime animosity—now seemed counterproductive. Republican leaders reported that voters were "sick of carpetbag government" and tiring of both the "southern question" and the "Negro question." It seemed pointless to continue the unpopular and expensive policy of military intervention in the South to prop up Republican regimes that even President Grant found corrupt. Finally, few Republicans shared the egalitarian spirit that had animated Stevens and Sumner. Politics aside, Republican leaders and voters generally agreed with southern Democrats that blacks, although worthy of freedom, were inferior to whites. To insist on black equality would be thankless, divisive, politically suicidal—and would quash any hope of reunion between the regions. The Republicans' retreat from Reconstruction set the stage for its demise in 1877.

> "We are in a very hot political contest just now, with a good prospect of turning out the carpetbag thieves by whom we have been robbed for the past six to ten years."

Reconstruction Abandoned, 1876–1877

"We are in a very hot political contest just now," a Mississippi planter wrote to his daughter in 1875, "with a good prospect of turning out the carpetbag thieves by whom we have been robbed for the past six to ten years." Similar contests raged through the South in the 1870s, as the white resentment grew and Democratic influence surged. By the end of 1872, the Democrats had regained power in Tennessee, Virginia, Georgia, and North Carolina. Within three years, they won control in Texas, Alabama, Arkansas, and Mississippi (see Table 16.4). By 1876, Republican rule survived in only three states—South Carolina, Florida, and Louisiana. Democratic victories in state elections of 1876 and political bargaining in Washington in 1877 abruptly ended what little remained of Reconstruction.

"Redeeming" the South

Republican collapse in the South accelerated after 1872. Congressional amnesty enabled

TABLE 16.4 The Duration of Republican Rule in the Ex-Confederate States

Former Confederate States	Readmission to the Union Under Congressional Reconstruction	Democrats (Conservatives) Gain Control	Duration of Republican Rule
Alabama	June 25, 1868	November 14, 1874	6½ years
Arkansas	June 22, 1868	November 10, 1874	6½ years
Florida	June 25, 1868	January 2, 1877	8½ years
Georgia	July 15, 1870	November 1, 1871	1 year
Louisiana	June 25, 1868	January 2, 1877	6½ years
Mississippi	February 23, 1870	November 3, 1875	6½ years
North Carolina	June 25, 1868	November 3, 1870	2 years
South Carolina	June 25, 1868	November 12, 1876	8 years
Tennessee	July 24, 1866*	October 4, 1869	3 years
Texas	March 30, 1870	January 14, 1873	3 years
Virginia	January 26, 1870	October 5, 1869†	0 years

Source: *John Hope Franklin,* Reconstruction After the Civil War *(Chicago: University of Chicago Press, 1962), 231.*

* Admitted before start of congressional Reconstruction
† Democrats gained control before readmission.

ex-Confederate officials to regain office; divisions among the Republicans weakened their party's grip on the southern electorate; and attrition diminished Republican ranks. Carpetbaggers returned North or became Democrats. Scalawags deserted in even larger numbers. Tired of northern interference and finding "home rule" by Democrats a possibility, Scalawags concluded that staying Republican meant going down with a sinking ship. Scalawag defections ruined Republican prospects. Unable to win new white votes or retain the old ones, the always-fragile Republican coalition crumbled.

Meanwhile, Democrats mobilized once-apathetic white voters. The resurrected southern Democratic party was divided: businessmen who envisioned an industrialized "New South" opposed an agrarian faction called the Bourbons—the old planter elite. But Democrats shared one goal: to oust Republicans from office. Tactics varied by state. Alabama Democrats won by promising to cut taxes and by getting out the white vote. In Louisiana, the "White League," a vigilante organization formed in 1874, undermined Republicans. Intimidation also proved effective in Mississippi, where violent incidents—like the 1874 slaughter in Vicksburg of about three hundred blacks by rampaging whites—terrorized black voters. In 1875, the "Mississippi plan" took effect: local Democratic clubs armed their members, who dispersed Republican meetings, patrolled voter-registration places, and marched through black areas. "The Republicans are paralyzed through fear and will not act," the anguished carpetbag governor of Mississippi wrote to his wife. "Why should I fight a hopeless battle?" In 1876, South Carolina's "Rifle Clubs" and "Red Shirts," armed groups that threatened Republicans, continued the scare tactics that had worked so well in Mississippi.

Intimidation did not completely squelch black voting, but Democrats deprived Republicans of enough black votes to win state elections. In some counties, they encouraged freedmen to vote Democratic at supervised polls where voters publicly placed a card with a party label in a box. In other instances, economic pressure impeded black suffrage. Labor contracts included clauses barring attendance at political meetings; planters used eviction threats to keep sharecroppers in line. Together, intimidation and economic pressure succeeded.

"Redemption," the word Democrats used to describe their return to power, brought sweeping changes. Some states called constitutional conventions to reverse Republican policies. All cut back expenses, wiped out social programs, lowered taxes, and revised their tax systems to relieve landowners

of large burdens. State courts limited the rights of tenants and sharecroppers. Most important, the Democrats, or "redeemers," used the law to ensure a stable black labor force. Legislatures restored vagrancy laws, revised crop-lien statutes to make landowners' claims superior to those of merchants, and rewrote criminal law. Local ordinances in heavily black counties often restricted hunting, fishing, gun carrying, and ownership of dogs and thereby curtailed freedmen's everyday activities. States passed severe laws against trespassing and theft; stealing livestock or wrongly taking part of a crop became grand larceny with a penalty of up to five years at hard labor. By Reconstruction's end, black convict labor was commonplace.

For the freedmen, whose aspirations rose under Republican rule, redemption was devastating. The new laws, Tennessee blacks contended at an 1875 convention, would impose "a condition of servitude scarcely less degrading than that endured before the late civil war." In the late 1870s, as the political climate grew more oppressive, an "exodus" movement spread through Mississippi, Tennessee, Texas, and Louisiana. Some African Americans became homesteaders in Kansas. After an outbreak of "Kansas fever" in 1879, four thousand **exodusters** from Mississippi and Louisiana joined about ten thousand who had reached Kansas earlier in the decade. But the vast majority of freedmen, devoid of resources, had no migration options or escape route. Mass movement of southern blacks to the North and Midwest would not gain momentum until the twentieth century.

The Election of 1876

By the autumn of 1876, with redemption almost complete, both parties sought to discard the heritage of animosity left by the war and Reconstruction. Republicans nominated Rutherford B. Hayes, three times Ohio's governor, for president. Untainted by the Grant-era scandals and popular with all factions in his party, Hayes presented himself as a "moderate" on southern policy. He favored "home rule" in the South and a guarantee of civil and political rights for all—two contradictory goals. The Democrats nominated Governor Samuel J. Tilden of New York, a millionaire corporate lawyer and political reformer, known for his assaults on the Tweed Ring that had plundered New York City's treasury. Both candidates favored sound money, endorsed civil-service reform, and decried corruption, an irony since the 1876 election would be extremely corrupt.

Tilden won the popular vote by a 3 percent margin and seemed destined to capture the 185

THE WHITE LEAGUE Alabama's White League, formed in 1874, strove to oust Republicans from office by intimidating black voters. To political cartoonist Thomas Nast in *Harper's Weekly,* such vigilante tactics suggested an alliance between the White League and the outlawed Ku Klux Klan. *(Harper's Weekly, October 24, 1874)*

electoral votes needed for victory (see Map 16.4). But the Republicans challenged the pro-Tilden returns from South Carolina, Florida, and Louisiana. If they could deprive the Democrats of these nineteen electoral votes, Hayes would triumph. The Democrats, who needed only one of the disputed electoral votes for victory, challenged (on a technicality) the validity of Oregon's single electoral vote, which the Republicans had won. Twenty electoral votes, therefore, were in contention. But Republicans still controlled the electoral machinery in the three unredeemed southern states, where they threw out enough Democratic ballots to declare Hayes the winner.

The nation now faced an unprecedented dilemma. Each party claimed victory in the contested states, and each accused the other of fraud. In fact, both sets of southern results involved fraud: the Republicans had discarded legitimate Democratic ballots, and the Democrats had illegally prevented freedmen from voting. In January 1877, Congress created a special electoral commission—seven Democrats, seven Republicans, and one independent—to decide which party would get the contested electoral votes. When the independent

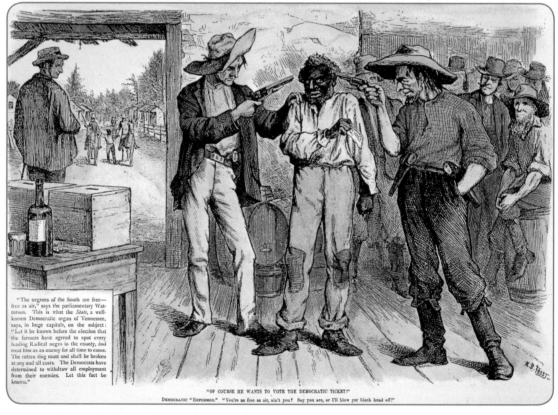

In another *Harper's Weekly* cartoon, published during the presidential campaign of 1876, White League vigilantes allied with Democrats assail a black voter in the polling place. Their goal: to topple the last Republican governments in the South. "You're free as air, ain't you?" declares one of the armed assailants. "Say you are or I'll blow your head off." *(The Granger Collection, New York)*

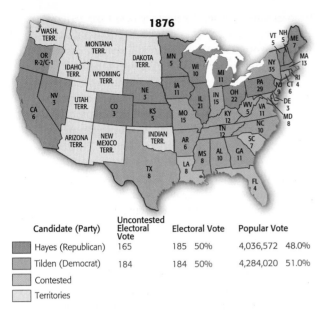

1876

Candidate (Party)	Uncontested Electoral Vote	Electoral Vote		Popular Vote	
■ Hayes (Republican)	165	185	50%	4,036,572	48.0%
■ Tilden (Democrat)	184	184	50%	4,284,020	51.0%
□ Contested					
□ Territories					

MAP 16.4 THE DISPUTED ELECTION OF 1876 Congress resolved the contested electoral vote of 1876 in favor of Republican Rutherford B. Hayes.

resigned, Congress replaced him with a Republican, and the commission gave Hayes the election by a vote of 8 to 7.

Congress now had to certify the new electoral vote. But Democrats controlled the House, and some threatened to obstruct debate and delay approval of the electoral vote. Had they done so, the nation would have lacked a president on inauguration day, March 4. Room for compromise remained, for many southern Democrats accepted Hayes's election: former scalawags with commercial interests still favored Republican financial policies; railroad investors expected Republican support for a southern transcontinental line. Other southerners did not mind conceding the presidency as long as the new Republican administration would leave the South alone. Republican leaders, although sure of eventual triumph, were willing to bargain as well, for candidate Hayes desired not merely victory but southern approval.

Informal negotiations ensued, at which politicians exchanged promises. Ohio Republicans and southern Democrats, who met at a Washington hotel, agreed that if Hayes won the election, he would remove federal troops from South Carolina and Louisiana, and Democrats could gain control of those states. In other bargaining sessions, southern politicians asked for federal patronage, federal aid to railroads, and federal support for internal improvements. In return, they promised to drop

> "When you turned us loose, you turned us loose to the sky, to the storm, to the whirlwind, and worst of all … to the wrath of our infuriated masters."

Ho for Kansas!

Brethren, Friends, & Fellow Citizens:
I feel thankful to inform you that the
REAL ESTATE
AND
Homestead Association,
Will Leave Here the
15th of April, 1878,
In pursuit of Homes in the Southwestern
Lands of America, at Transportation
Rates, cheaper than ever
was known before.
For full information inquire of
Benj. Singleton, better known as old Pap,
NO. 5 NORTH FRONT STREET.
Beware of Speculators and Adventurers, as it is a dangerous thing
to fall in their hands.
Nashville, Tenn., March 18, 1878.

THE EXODUS TO KANSAS Benjamin "Pap" Singleton, a one-time fugitive slave from Tennessee, returned there to promote the "exodus" movement of the late 1870s. Forming a real estate company, Singleton traveled the South recruiting parties of freed people who were disillusioned with the outcome of Reconstruction. These "exodusters," awaiting a Mississippi River boat, looked forward to political equality, freedom from violence, and homesteads in Kansas. *(Library of Congress)*

the filibuster, to accept Hayes as president, and to treat freedmen fairly. With the threatened filibuster broken, Congress ratified Hayes's election. Once in office, Hayes fulfilled some of the promises his Republican colleagues had made. He appointed a former Confederate as postmaster general and ordered federal troops who guarded the South Carolina and Louisiana statehouses back to their barracks. Federal soldiers remained in the South after 1877 but no longer served a political function. Democrats, meanwhile, took over state governments in Louisiana, South Carolina, and Florida. When Republican rule toppled in these states, the era of Reconstruction finally ended.

But some of the bargains struck in the **Compromise of 1877,** such as Democratic promises to treat southern blacks fairly, were forgotten, as were Hayes's pledges to ensure freedmen's rights. "When you turned us loose, you turned us loose to the sky, to the storm, to the whirlwind, and worst of all … to the wrath of our infuriated masters," Frederick Douglass had charged at the Republican convention in 1876. "The question now is, do you mean to make good to us the promises in your Constitution?" The answer provided by the 1876 election and the 1877 Compromise was "No."

CONCLUSION

Between 1865 and 1877, the nation experienced a series of political crises. In Washington, conflict between President Johnson and Congress led to a stringent Republican plan for restoring the South, a plan that included the radical provision of black male enfranchisement. President Johnson ineptly abetted the triumph of his foes by his defiant stance, which drove moderate Republicans into an alliance against him with Radical Republicans. In the ex-Confederate states, Republicans took over and reorganized state governments. A new electorate, in which recently freed African Americans were prominent, endorsed Republican policies. Rebuilding the South cost millions, and state expenditures soared. Objections to taxes, resentment of black suffrage, and fear of "Negro domination" spurred counterattacks on African Americans by former Confederates.

Emancipation reshaped black communities where former slaves sought new identities as free people. African Americans reconstituted their families; created black institutions, such as churches and schools; and participated in government for the first time in American history. They also took part in the transformation of southern agriculture. By Reconstruction's end, a new labor system, sharecropping, replaced slavery. Begun as a compromise between freedmen and landowners, sharecropping soon trapped African Americans and other tenant farmers in a cycle of debt; black political rights waned as well as Republicans lost control of the southern states.

The North, meanwhile, hurtled headlong into an era of industrial growth, labor unrest, and financial crises. The political scandals of the Grant administration and the impact of depression after the Panic of 1873 diverted northern attention from the South. By the mid-1870s, northern politicians were ready to discard the Reconstruction policies that Congress had imposed a decade before. Simultaneously, the southern states returned to Democratic rule, as Republican regimes toppled one by one. Reconstruction's final collapse in 1877 reflected not only a waning of northern resolve but a successful ex-Confederate campaign of violence, intimidation, and protest that had started in the 1860s. By 1877, resistance had trumped Reconstruction.

Reconstruction's end gratified both political parties. Although unable to retain a southern constituency, the Republican Party no longer faced the unpopular "southern question." The Democrats, now empowered in the former Confederacy, remained entrenched there for over a century. To be sure, the South was tied to sharecropping and economic backwardness as securely as it had once been tied to slavery. But "home rule" was firmly in place. Reconstruction's end also signified a triumph for nationalism and reunion. As the nation applauded reconciliation of South and North, Reconstruction's reputation sank. Looking back on the 1860s and 1870s, most late-nineteenth-century Americans dismissed the congressional effort to reconstruct the South as a fiasco—a tragic interlude of "radical rule" or "black reconstruction" fashioned by carpetbaggers, scalawags, and Radical Republicans.

With the hindsight of a century, historians continued to regard Reconstruction as a failure, though of a different kind. No longer viewed as a misguided scheme that collapsed because of radical excess, Reconstruction is now widely seen as a democratic experiment that did not go far enough. Historians cite two main causes. First, Congress did not promote freedmen's independence through land reform; without property of their own, southern blacks lacked the economic power to defend their interests as free citizens. Property ownership, however, does not necessarily ensure political rights nor invariably provide economic security. Considering the depressed state of postwar southern agriculture, the freedmen's fate as independent farmers would likely have been perilous. Thus the land-reform question remains a subject of debate. A second cause of Reconstruction's collapse evokes less dispute: the federal government neglected to back congressional Reconstruction with military force. Given the choice between protecting blacks' rights at whatever cost and promoting reunion, the government opted for reunion. As a result, the nation's adjustment to the consequences of emancipation would continue into the twentieth century.

The Reconstruction era left some significant legacies, including the Fourteenth and Fifteenth amendments. Although neither amendment would be used to protect minority rights for almost a century, they remain monuments to the democratic zeal that swept Congress in the 1860s. The aspirations and achievements of Reconstruction also left an indelible mark on black citizens. After Reconstruction, many Americans turned to their economic futures—to railroads, factories, and mills, and to the exploitation of the country's bountiful natural resources.

KEY TERMS

Charles Sumner (p. 470)

Thaddeus Stevens (p. 470)

Andrew Johnson (p. 471)

Presidential Reconstruction (p. 472)

"black codes" (p. 473)

Civil Rights Act of 1866 (p. 473)

Fourteenth Amendment (p. 474)

Reconstruction Act of 1867 (p. 475)

Tenure of Office Act (p. 476)

Fifteenth Amendment (p. 477)

Susan B. Anthony (p. 477)

Ku Klux Klan (p. 482)

Enforcement Acts (p. 483)

Civil Rights Act of 1875 (p. 486)

sharecropping (p. 487)

Liberal Republicans (p. 494)

Greenback Party (p. 495)

slaughterhouse cases (p. 495)

"exodusters" (p. 497)

Compromise of 1877 (p. 500)

FOR FURTHER REFERENCE

David W. Blight, *Race and Reunion: The Civil War in American Memory* (2001). Explores competing views on the significance of the Civil War in the Reconstruction era and the decades that followed.

Garrett Epps, *Democracy Reborn: The Fourteenth Amendment and the Fight for Civil Rights in Post-Civil War America* (2006). Examines the struggle to protect citizenship for African Americans.

Carol F. Faulkner, *Women's Radical Reconstruction: The Freedmen's Aid Movement* (2004). A study of abolitionist teachers and women's rights advocates, their impact on federal policy, and their interactions with former slaves

Eric Foner, *Reconstruction: America's Unfinished Revolution, 1863–1877* (1988). A thorough exploration of Reconstruction that draws on recent scholarship and stresses the centrality of the black experience.

Steven Hahn, *A Nation Under Our Feet: Black Political Struggles in the Rural South from Slavery to the Great Migration* (2003). How African American communities shaped politics during and after Reconstruction.

Tera W. Hunter, *To,' Joy My Freedom: Southern Black Women's Lives and Labors After the Civil War* (1997). Explores the experience of women workers in Atlanta from Reconstruction into the twentieth century.

Peter Kolchin, *A Sphinx on the American Land: The Nineteenth-Century South in Comparative Perspective* (2003). Includes a comparative approach to emancipation and its impact.

Nicholas Lemann, *Redemption: The Last Battle of the Civil War* (2006). Explores the role of ex-Confederate resistance in Reconstruction's demise.

Leon Litwack, *Been in the Storm So Long: The Aftermath of Slavery* (1979). A comprehensive study of the black response to emancipation in 1865–1866.

Heather Cox Richardson, *The Death of Reconstruction: Race, Labor, and Politics in the Post-Civil War North, 1865–1901* (2001). Explores northern disenchantment with Reconstruction policies and the dwindling of northern support for freed blacks in the South.

Christopher M. Span, *From Cotton Field to Schoolhouse: African American Education in Mississippi, 1862–1875* (2009). Conflict over black aspiration shapes the start of schooling for African Americans.

Visit the CourseMate website at **www.cengagebrain.com** for additional study tools and review materials for this chapter.

The Transformation of the Trans-Mississippi West, 1860–1900

BUFFALO BIRD WOMAN *(Minnesota Historical Society)*

"THE BUFFALOES AND

the black-tail deer are gone, and our Indian ways are almost gone," reminisced Maxidiwiac (mah-chee-dee-WEE-ahsh), or Buffalo Bird Woman, in 1920. A Hidatsa Indian born about 1843 in present-day North Dakota, she found the changes overwhelming. "Sometimes I find it hard to believe I ever lived them [her Indian ways]," she continued. "My little son grew up in the white man's school. He can read books, and he owns cattle and has a farm. He is a leader among our Hidatsa people, helping teach them to follow the white man's road … But for me, I cannot forget our old ways. Often in summer I rise at daybreak and steal out to the cornfields; and as I hoe the corn I sing to it, as we did when I was young." In her own lifetime, Buffalo Bird Woman had moved from a traditional native existence into the modern world. She could not help but ponder how the native customs that she had learned as a girl had changed in so short a time.

President Jefferson's emissaries Meriwether Lewis and William Clark had wintered among the Hidatsas in 1804 and had been impressed by their horsemanship and hunting ability. Decimated by smallpox and by attacks from the Dakota Sioux, the Hidatsas in the 1840s had joined with two neighboring tribes, the Mandan and Arikara, to build a new village called Like-A-Fishhook. Initially, the new settlement prospered. But after the Civil War, as white settlers crowded onto their lands, Buffalo Bird Woman and her tribe were pressured by a nearby military garrison into signing away more and more of their territory. In 1870, the same year Buffalo Bird Woman's only son, Goodbird, was born, the federal government created the Fort Berthold Indian reservation nearby. Forced by the federal government to scatter onto small farms, Buffalo Bird Woman and her tribe in 1885 abandoned their village. Interviewed in 1906 by an anthropologist at her son's North Dakota ranch, she was able to tell the remarkable story of her life.

Buffalo Bird Woman's experience was all too common. The displacement of native peoples and the attack on their cultures was a recurring feature around the world, as white Europeans seized native lands. Like the British conquest of the Kikuyu in Kenya and of the Aborigines in Australia, the settlement of the trans-Mississippi West began

FIRE CANOE AT FORT BERTHOLD, BY WILLIAM DE LA MONTAGNE CARY Indians at Like-A-Fishook village on the Missouri watch the arrival of a steamboat that will supply the nearby military fort. *(Gilcrease Museum, Tulsa, Oklahoma)*

with the removal of native peoples. This wrenching and brutal relocation of the Indians onto reservations opened up vast tracts of land for the exploitation of their natural resources.

In the North-American trans-Mississippi West, miners, farmers, land speculators, and railroad developers in the 1850s flooded onto the fertile prairies of Iowa, Minnesota, and Kansas, carving the land into farms and communities. Then, in the 1860s, drawn by the earlier discovery of gold in the Rocky Mountains, settlers swarmed onto the Great Plains and the semiarid regions beyond them. Scarcely a decade later, the trans-Mississippi West became a contested terrain as Native peoples fought to protect their homeland from these newcomers.

The transformation of the West left a mixed legacy. Although many white families prospered, the rapid development of the land and its resources threatened not only the Native Americans, but the environment, and sometimes the settlers themselves. Unscrupulous westerners exploited white, Native American, Chinese, and Mexican laborers alike. Hunters slaughtered millions of bison for their hides, miners skinned the mountainsides in search of minerals, and farmers plowed up the prairie sod to build farms, even in areas where limited rainfall made farming problematic.

Although westerners attributed their economic achievements to American self-reliance, the development of the trans-Mississippi West depended heavily on the federal government. The government sent troops to subjugate the Indians, distributed farmland through the Homestead Act (1862), and subsidized the transcontinental railroad lines.

Eastern banks and foreign capitalists provided investment capital and eased access to international markets. In their scramble for new economic opportunities, many Americans chose to view the destruction of the Indian ways of life as the necessary price of civilization and progress.

Native Americans and the Trans-Mississippi West

No aspect of the transformation of the West was more visible and dramatic than the destruction of traditional Indian ways of life. Even before the newcomers poured onto the Great Plains at mid-century, Indian life in the trans-Mississippi West had changed considerably. In the Southwest, the Navajos had gradually given up migratory life in favor of settled agriculture. To the north, the Cheyenne and the Lakota Sioux, pushed out of the Great Lakes region by white settlement, had moved onto the Great Plains and had driven their enemies, the Pawnees and the Crows, farther west. These and other nomadic warrior tribes, dispersed in small bands, had followed the bison herds.

When whites invaded their territory at mid-century, these Indians resisted. Caught between a stampede of miners and settlers who took their land and the federal government that sought to force them onto reservations, Native Americans fought back. By the 1890s, confinement on reservations had become the fate of almost every Indian nation. Undaunted, Native Americans struggled to preserve their customs and rebuild their numbers.

The Plains Indians

The Indians of the Great Plains inhabited three major subregions. The northern Plains, from the Dakotas and Montana southward to Nebraska, were home to large tribes, most notably the Lakota, as well as Flatheads, Blackfeet, Assiniboins, northern Cheyennes, Arapahos, Crows, Hidatsas, and Mandans. Some of these were allies, but others were bitter enemies frequently at war. In the Central Plains, the so-called Five Civilized Tribes, driven there from the Southeast in the 1830s, pursued an agricultural life in the Indian Territory (present-day Oklahoma). Farther west, the Pawnees of Nebraska maintained the older, more settled tradition characteristic of Plains river valley culture before the introduction of horses. On the southern Plains of western Kansas, Colorado, eastern New Mexico, and Texas, the Comanches, Kiowas, Cheyennes, southern Arapahos, and Apaches maintained a migratory life appropriate to the arid environment.

FOCUS Questions

- How was Indian life on the Great Plains transformed in the second half of the nineteenth century?
- What roles did the federal government, the army, and the railroads play in the re-settlement of the West?
- How did ranchers and settlers displace Spanish-speaking Americans in the Southwest?
- How was the Wild West image of cowboys and Indians created?
- What discoveries and developments prompted the establishment of national parks?

CHRONOLOGY 1860–1900

1862	Homestead Act.
	Morrill Anti-Bigamy Act.
	Pacific Railroad Act.
1864	Nevada admitted to the Union.
	Massacre of Cheyennes at Sand Creek, Colorado.
	George Perkins Marsh, *Man and Nature*.
1867	Joseph McCoy organizes cattle drives to Abilene, Kansas.
	New Indian policy of smaller reservations adopted.
	Medicine Lodge Treaty.
	Purchase of Alaska.
1868	Fort Laramie Treaty.
1869	Board of Indian Commissioners established to reform Indian reservation life.
	Wyoming gives women the vote.
1872	Yellowstone National Park established.
1873	Panic allows speculators to purchase thousands of acres in the Red River valley of North Dakota cheaply.
	Timber Culture Act.
	Biggest strike on Nevada's Comstock Lode.
1874	Invention of barbed wire.
	Gold discovered in the Black Hills of South Dakota.
	Red River War.
1875	John Wesley Powell, *The Exploration of the Colorado River*.

1876	Colorado admitted to the Union, gives women the right to vote in school elections.
	Little Bighorn massacre.
1877	Desert Land Act.
1878	Timber and Stone Act.
	John Wesley Powell, *Report on the Lands of the Arid Regions of the United States*.
1879	*United States* v. *Reynolds*.
1881	Helen Hunt Jackson, *A Century of Dishonor*.
1883	Women's National Indian Rights Association founded.
	William ("Buffalo Bill") Cody organizes Wild West Show.
1884	Helen Hunt Jackson, *Ramona*.
1886	Severe drought on the Plains destroys cattle and grain.
1887	Dawes Severalty Act.
	Edmunds-Tucker Act.
1888	White Caps raid ranches in northern New Mexico.
1889	Oklahoma Territory opened for settlement.
1890	Ghost Dance movement spreads to the Black Hills.
	Massacre of Teton Sioux at Wounded Knee, South Dakota.
1892	John Muir organizes Sierra Club.
1898	Curtis Act.

Considerable diversity flourished among the Plains peoples, and customs varied even within subdivisions of the same tribe. For example, the easternmost branch of the great Sioux Nation, the Dakota Sioux of Minnesota who inhabited the wooded edge of the prairie, led a semisedentary life based on small-scale agriculture and bison hunting. In contrast, many Plains tribes—not only the Lakota Sioux, but also the Blackfeet, Crows, and Cheyennes—using horses obtained from the Spanish, roamed the High Plains to the west, and followed the bison migrations.

For all the **Plains Indians,** life revolved around extended family ties and tribal cooperation. Children were raised without physical punishment and were taught to treat each adult clan member with the respect accorded to relatives. Families and clans joined forces to hunt and farm and reached decisions by consensus.

Sioux religion, which provided the cement for village and camp life, was complex. The Lakota Sioux thought of life as a series of circles. Living within the daily cycles of the sun and moon, Lakotas were born into a circle of relatives, which broadened to the band, the tribe, the Sioux Nation, and on to animals and plants. The Lakotas also believed in a hierarchy of spirits whose help could be invoked in ceremonies like the Sun Dance. To gain access to spiritual power, or to fulfill vows made on behalf of their relatives' well-being, young men would "sacrifice" themselves by forgoing food and water, dancing until exhausted, and suffering self-torture. For example, some suspended themselves from poles or cut pieces of their flesh and placed them at the foot of the Sun Dance pole. Painter George Catlin, who recorded Great Plains Indian life before the Civil War, described such a ceremony: "Several of them, seeing me making sketches, beckoned me to look at their faces, which I watched through all this horrid operation, without being able to detect anything but the pleasantest smiles as they looked me in the eye, while I could hear the knife rip through the flesh."

INDIAN MOTHER AND SON, CA. 1890s Indian children were taught to ride horses at an early age. Horses were a form of wealth for migratory Plains peoples and made hunting buffalo (depicted on the tipi) considerably easier. *(Library of Congress)*

> "I watched through all this horrid operation, without being able to detect anything but the pleasantest smiles as they looked me in the eye, while I could hear the knife rip through the flesh."

On the semiarid High Plains, where rainfall averaged less than twenty inches a year, both the bison and the Native peoples adapted to the environment. The huge bison herds, which at their peak contained an estimated 30 million animals, broke into small groups in the winter and dispersed into river valleys. In the summer, they returned to the High Plains to mate and feed on the nutritious short grasses. Like the bison, the Indians dispersed across the landscape to minimize their impact on the land, wintering in the river valleys

and returning to the High Plains in summer. When their horses consumed the grasses near their camps, they moved. Hunting bison not only supplied the Native peoples with food, clothing, and tipi covers, but also created a valuable trading commodity, buffalo robes. To benefit from this trade, Indians themselves, as the nineteenth century progressed, increased their harvest of animals.

The movement of miners and settlers onto the eastern High Plains in the 1850s eroded the habitat and threatened the Native American way of life. Pioneers occupied the river valley sites, where the buffalo had wintered, and exhausted the grasses. In the 1860s, the whites began systematically to hunt the animals, often with Indian help, to supply eastern markets with carriage robes and industrial belting. **William F. "Buffalo Bill" Cody,** a famous scout, killed thousands of bison in 1867–1868 to feed railroad construction crews. Army commanders also encouraged the slaughter of buffalo to undermine Indian resistance. Inconceivable carnage resulted. Between 1872 and 1875, hunters killed 9 million buffalo, taking only the skin and leaving the carcasses to rot. By the 1880s, the once-thundering herds had been reduced to a few thousand animals, and the Native American way of life dependent on the buffalo had been ruined.

The Assault on Nomadic Indian Life

In the 1850s, Indians faced the onslaught of thousands of miners lured by the discovery of gold and silver in the Rocky Mountains. To remove the Indians, the federal government abandoned its previous position, which had treated much of the West as a vast Indian reserve, and introduced a system of smaller tribal reservations where the Indians were to be concentrated, by force if necessary.

Some Native Americans, like the Pueblos of the Southwest (who had adapted to Spanish colonial life), the Crows of Montana, and the Hidatsas of North Dakota, adjusted peacefully. Others, among them the Navajos of Arizona and New Mexico and the eastern Dakota Sioux, opposed the new policy to no avail. By 1860, eight western reservations had been established.

Significant segments of the remaining tribes on the Great Plains, more than a hundred thousand people, fought against removal. Between 1860 and 1890, the western Sioux, Cheyennes, Arapahos, Kiowas, and Comanches on the Great Plains; the Nez Percés and Bannocks in the northern Rockies; and the Apaches in the Southwest—faced the U.S. army in a series of final battles for the West (see Map 17.1).

Misunderstandings, unfulfilled promises, brutality, and butchery marked the conflict. Near Sand Creek, Colorado, in 1864, soldiers from the local militia destroyed Cheyenne and Arapaho camps. The Indians retaliated with a flurry of attacks on travelers. The governor, in a panic, authorized Colorado's white citizenry to seek out and kill hostile Indians on sight. He then activated a regiment of troops under Colonel John M. Chivington, a Methodist minister. At dawn on November 29, under orders to "remember the murdered women and children on the Platte [River]," Chivington's troops massacred a peaceful band of Indians, including terrified women and children, camped at Sand Creek.

This massacre and others rekindled public debate over federal Indian policy. In response, in 1867 Congress sent a peace commission to end the fighting and set aside two large land reserves—one north of Nebraska, the other south of Kansas. There, it was hoped, the tribes would take up farming and

BUFFALO SKULLS AT THE MICHIGAN CARBON WORKS, 1895 Once the vast herds of bison had been decimated, resourceful entrepreneurs, such as those pictured here, collected the skulls and sold them for industrial use. In all, nearly 2 million tons of bones were processed. *(Detroit Public Library, Burton Historical Collection)*

convert to Christianity. Behind the federal government's persuasion lay the threat of force. Any Native Americans who refused to relocate, warned Commissioner of Indian Affairs Ely S. Parker, himself a Seneca Indian, "would be subject wholly to the control and supervision of military authorities, [and] . . . treated as friendly or hostile as circumstances might justify."

At first, the plan appeared to work. Representatives of sixty-eight thousand southern Kiowas, Comanches, Cheyennes, and Arapahos signed the Medicine Lodge Treaty of 1867 and pledged to live in present-day Oklahoma. The following year, scattered bands of Sioux, representing nearly fifty-four thousand northern Plains Indians, signed the **Fort Laramie Treaty** and agreed to move to reservations on the so-called Great Sioux Reserve in the western part of what is now South Dakota in return for money and provisions.

But Indian dissatisfaction with the treaties ran deep. As a Sioux chief, Spotted Tail, told the commissioners, "We do not want to live like the white man. . . . The Great Spirit gave us hunting grounds, gave us the buffalo, the elk, the deer, and the antelope. Our fathers have taught us to hunt and live on the Plains, and we are contented." Rejecting the new system, many bands of Indians refused to move to the reservations or to remain on them once there.

> "It is inconsistent with our civilization and with common sense to allow the Indian to roam over a country as fine as that around the Black Hills, preventing its development in order that he may shoot game and scalp his neighbors."

In August 1868, war parties of defiant Cheyennes, Arapahos, and Sioux raided settlements in Kansas and Colorado, burning homes and killing whites. In retaliation, army troops attacked Indians, even peaceful ones, who refused confinement. That autumn, Lieutenant Colonel George Armstrong Custer's raiding party struck a sleeping Cheyenne village, killing more than a hundred warriors, shooting more than eight hundred horses, and taking fifty-three women and children prisoner. Other hostile Cheyennes and Arapahos were pursued, captured, and returned to the reservations.

In 1869, spurred on by Christian reformers, Congress established a Board of Indian Commissioners drawn from the major Protestant denominations to reform reservation abuses. But the new and inexperienced church-appointed Indian agents quickly encountered problems. Indians left the reservations in large numbers and agents were unable to restrain scheming whites who fraudulently purchased reservation lands from those who remained. Frustrated by the manipulation of Indian treaties and irritated by the ineptness of the Indian agents, Congress in 1871 abolished treaty making and replaced treaties with executive orders and acts of Congress. In the 1880s, the federal government ignored the churches' nominations for Indian agents and made its own appointments.

Caught in the sticky web of an ambiguous and deceptive federal policy, defiant Native Americans struck back in the 1870s. On the southern Plains, Kiowa, Comanche, and Cheyenne raids in the Texas Panhandle in 1874 set off the so-called Red River War. In a fierce winter campaign, regular army troops slaughtered Cheyenne fugitives near the Sappa River in Kansas. The exile of seventy-four "ringleaders" to reservations in Florida thus ended Native American independence on the southern Plains. In the Southwest, in present-day Arizona and New Mexico, the Apaches fought an intermittent

MAP 17.1 **MAJOR INDIAN BATTLES IN THE WEST** Although they were never recognized as such in the popular press, the battles between the Native Americans and the U.S. army on the Great Plains amounted to an undeclared war.

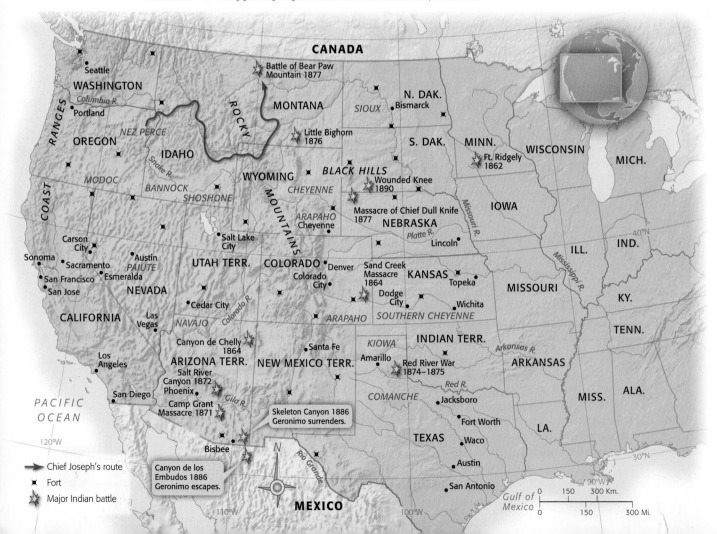

guerrilla war until their leader, Geronimo, surrendered in 1886.

Custer's Last Stand, 1876

Of all the acts of Indian resistance against the new reservation policy, none aroused more passion or caused more bloodshed than the battles waged by the western Sioux tribes in the Dakotas, Montana, and Wyoming. The 1868 Treaty of Fort Laramie had set aside the Great Sioux Reserve "in perpetuity." But not all the Sioux bands had signed the treaty.

By 1873, Chief Red Cloud's Oglala band and Chief Spotted Tail's Brulé band had managed to remain on their traditional lands. To protect their hunting grounds, they raided encroaching non-Indian settlements in Nebraska and Wyoming, intimidated federal agents and harassed anyone who ventured onto their lands.

Nontreaty Sioux found a powerful leader in the Lakota Sioux chief and holy man **Sitting Bull.** Broad-shouldered and powerfully built, Sitting Bull led by example and had considerable fighting experience. "You are fools," he told the reservation Indians, "to make yourselves slaves to a piece of fat bacon, some hard-tack, and a little sugar and coffee."

Pressured by would-be settlers and developers, General William Tecumseh Sherman in 1874 sent a force under Colonel George Armstrong Custer into the Black Hills of South Dakota, near the western edge of the Great Sioux Reserve. Lean and mustachioed, the thirty-four-year-old Custer had been a celebrity since his days as an impetuous young Civil War officer.

Custer's mission was to extract concessions from the Sioux. In November 1875, negotiations to buy the Black Hills had broken down because the Indians' asking price was deemed too high. Custer now sought to drive the Indians out of the Black Hills. Indians still outside the reservations after January 31, 1876, the government announced, would be hunted down and taken in by force.

In June 1876, leading 600 troops of the Seventh Cavalry, Custer proceeded to the Little Bighorn River area of present-day Montana, a hub of Indian resistance. On the morning of June 25, underestimating the Indian enemy and unwisely dividing his force, Custer, with 209 men, recklessly advanced against Cheyenne and Sioux warriors led by Chief Sitting Bull, who had encamped along the Little Bighorn. Custer and his outnumbered troops were wiped out.

Americans reeled from this unexpected Indian victory. Newspaper columnists groped to assess the meaning of "Custer's last stand." Some questioned the wisdom of current federal policy toward the Indians. Most, however, endorsed the federal government's determination to quash the Native American rebellion. "It is inconsistent with our civilization and with common sense," trumpeted a writer in the *New York*

DULL KNIFE (LEFT) AND SITTING BULL "I don't want a white man over me," Sitting Bull insisted. "I want to have the white man with me, but not to be my chief. I ask this because I want to do right by my people …" *(National Anthropological Archives, Smithsonian Institution, Washington, DC, and Library of Congress)*

Herald, "to allow the Indian to roam over a country as fine as that around the Black Hills, preventing its development in order that he may shoot game and scalp his neighbors. That can never be."

Defeat at Little Bighorn made the army more determined. In Montana, troops harassed various Sioux bands for more than five years, attacking Indian camps in the dead of winter and destroying all supplies. Even Sitting Bull, who had led his band to Canada to escape the army, surrendered in 1881 for lack of provisions. The slaughter of the buffalo had wiped out his tribe's major food source.

Similar measures were used elsewhere in the West. Chief Dull Knife led some 150 survivors, including men, women, and children, north in September 1878 to join the Sioux. But the army chased them down and imprisoned them in Fort Robinson, Nebraska. When the army denied their request to stay nearer to their traditional northern lands, tribal leaders refused to cooperate. The post commander then withheld all food, water, and fuel. On a frigid night in January 1879, Dull Knife and his followers, in a desperate escape attempt, shot the guards and broke for freedom. Soldiers chased the Indians and gunned down half of them in the snow, including women and children as well as Dull Knife himself. The *Atlanta Constitution* condemned the incident as "a dastardly outrage upon humanity and a lasting disgrace to our boasted civilization." Although sporadic Indian resistance continued until the end of the century, these brutal tactics had sapped the Indians' will to resist.

"Saving" the Indians

A growing number of Americans were outraged by the federal government's flagrant violation of its Indian treaties. The Women's National Indian Rights Association, founded in 1883, and other groups took up the cause. **Helen Hunt Jackson** published *A Century of Dishonor* in 1881 to rally public opinion against the government's broken treaty obligations. "It makes little difference … where one opens the record of the history of the Indians," she wrote; "every page and every year has its dark stain."

To encourage Indians to abandon nomadic life, reformers like Jackson advocated the creation of Indian boarding schools, much like those established for emancipated slaves. Richard Henry Pratt, a retired military officer, opened such a school in Carlisle, Pennsylvania, in 1879. Pratt believed that the Indians' customs and languages had halted their progress toward white civilization. His motto therefore became "Kill the Indian and save the man." Modeled after Carlisle, other Indian boarding schools taught farming, carpentry, dressmaking, and nursing.

Despite the reformers' best efforts, the attempt to stamp out Indian identity in the boarding schools often backfired. Forming friendships with Indians from many different tribes, boarding school students forged their own sense of Indian identity. As Mitch Walking Elk, a Cheyenne-Arapaho-Hopi student at the Phoenix Indian School, put it, "They put me in the boarding school and they cut off all my hair, gave me an education, but the Apache's still in there."

> "It makes little difference … where one opens the record of the history of the Indians; every page and every year has its dark stain."

In addition to their advocacy of boarding schools, well-intentioned humanitarians concluded that the Indians' interests would be best served by breaking up the reservations, ending recognition of tribal governments, and gradually giving them the rights of citizens. In short, they proposed to eliminate the "Indian problem" by eliminating the Indians as a culturally distinct entity. Inspired by this vision, they supported the **Dawes Severalty Act**, passed in 1887 (see Map 17.2).

The Dawes Act sought to turn Indians into landowners and farmers. The law emphasized severalty, or the treatment of Indians as individuals rather than as tribal members, and called for the distribution of 160 acres of reservation land for farming, or 320 acres for grazing, to each head of an Indian family who accepted the law's provisions (see Going to the Source). The remaining reservation lands were to be sold to speculators and settlers. To prevent unscrupulous people taking the lands granted to individual Indians, the government would hold each tribal member's property in trust for twenty-five years and make them U.S. citizens.

The Dawes Act did not specify a timetable for the breakup of the reservations. Few allotments were made to the Indians until the 1890s. The act proved to be a boon to speculators, who evaded its safeguards and obtained the Indians' best land. Much of what remained in Indian hands was too dry and gravelly for farming. In the twentieth century, ironically, periodic droughts and the fragile, arid High Plains landscape would push many white farmers back off the land.

Although some Native Americans who received land under the Dawes Act prospered enough to expand their holdings, countless others struggled just to survive. Hunting restrictions on the former reservation lands prevented many Indians from supplementing their limited farm yields. Alcoholism, a continuing problem exacerbated by the prevalence of whiskey as a trade item (and by the boredom that resulted from the disruption of hunting and other traditional pursuits), became more prevalent as Native Americans strove to adapt to the constraints of reservation life (see Table 17.1).

The Ghost Dance and the End of Indian Resistance on the Great Plains, 1890

Living conditions for the Sioux worsened in the late 1880s. The federal government reduced their meat rations and restricted hunting. When disease killed a third of their cattle, they became desperate. The Sioux, who still numbered almost twenty-five thousand, turned to Wovoka, a new visionary prophet popular among the Great Basin Indians in Nevada. Wovoka foresaw a catastrophic event that would bring the return of dead relatives, the restoration of the bison herds, and the renewal of traditional life. Some versions of his vision included the destruction of European Americans and their removal from Indian lands. To bring on this new day, the prophet preached a return to traditional ethics, and taught his followers a cycle of ritual songs and dance steps known as the **Ghost Dance.**

In the fall of 1890, as the Ghost Dance movement spread among the Sioux in the Dakota Territory, Indian officials grew alarmed. The local reservation agent decided that Chief Sitting Bull, whose cabin on the reservation had become a rallying point for the Ghost Dance movement, must be arrested. On a freezing, drizzly December morning, he dispatched Indian policemen from the agency to take Sitting Bull into custody. When the chief was pulled from his cabin, shots rang out, and Sitting Bull was mortally wounded. As bullets whizzed by, Sitting Bull's horse began to perform the tricks it remembered from its days in the Wild West show. Observers were terrified, convinced that the spirit of the dead chief had entered his horse.

Two weeks later, one of the bloodiest episodes of Indian–white strife on the Plains occurred. On December 29, as the Seventh Cavalry was rounding up 340 starving and freezing Sioux at **Wounded Knee,** South Dakota, a shot was fired. The soldiers

MAP 17.2 WESTERN INDIAN RESERVATIONS, 1890 Native American reservations were almost invariably located on poor-quality lands. Consequently, when the Dawes Severalty Act broke up the reservations into 160-acre farming tracts, many of the semiarid divisions would not support cultivation.

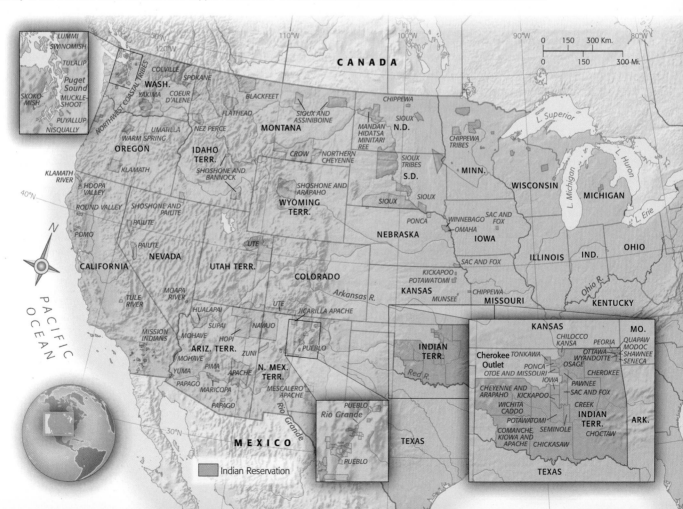

The Board of Indian Commissioners and the Dawes Act

From 1869, the Christian reformers who served on the Board of Indian Commissioners sought to improve Indian life. They persistently supported the goal, later written into the General Allotment Act (The Dawes Act, 1887), of breaking up the reservations, allotting 160 acres to each head of family, and making Indians landowner citizens of the United States. The Dawes Act corrected a glaring problem: the inability of Indians, who were not citizens, to contest in U.S. courts the fraudulent seizure of their lands. Nevertheless, by 1934, the Dawes Act had reduced Indian landholdings by nearly 65 percent.

One of the difficulties we have steadily encountered is the want of titles to land in severalty. No white man nor Indian can be expected to devote his energies to the improvement and cultivation of land to which he has no valid and sure title. … The Board, painfully conscious of this truth, has spared no labors to correct the evil, by urging the bestowment of titles to homesteads with a proper limitation of the right of alienation, to such Indians as desire to avail themselves of this privilege. …

In many cases the government has failed to protect Indians even in the exclusive occupancy of lands, pledged to them under treaty stipulations. Gradually have these sacred barriers been broken down, until the onward sweeping tide of emigration has overrun them altogether, despoiling them of their homes and possessions. If this inevitable fate awaits them, let at least partial justice be done by the conferring of titles to a portion of the land which has been solemnly set apart for their use under existing treaties. …

Colorado is rapidly filling up with a busy, active, and enterprising population. It is as evident to every reflecting mind that civilization and barbarism cannot long live side by side as it was to President Lincoln that the country could not long remain "half slave and half free." There is the same "irrepressible conflict" between civilization and barbarism as between freedom and slavery. Barbarism must yield to and accept civilization, flee before it, or sooner or later be overborne by it. As friends of the Indians, our efforts are directed to induce them to accept civilization while as loyal citizens we use what influence we have to induce the government to be just, patient, kind, and even generous to this weak and ignorant race. …

We may moralize over the natural rights of the Indian as much as we please, but after all they have their limit. His right to the soil is only possessory. He has no title in fee. If he will cultivate it and use it as civilized men use their possessions, it will or should be well with him; but it is evident that no 12,000,000 acres of the public domain, whose hills are full of ores, and whose valleys are waiting for diligent hands to "dress and keep them," in obedience to the divine command, can long be kept simply as a park, in which wild beasts are hunted by wilder men. This Anglo-Saxon race will not allow the car of civilization to stop long at any line of latitude or longitude on our broad domain. If the Indian in his wildness plants himself on the track, he must inevitably be crushed by it. But when he sets his face and his heart towards civilization, … then it becomes alike the interest and the duty both of the government and the people to afford all needed aid.

Source: Eleventh Annual Report of the Board of Indian Commissioners, 1879 *(Washington, DC: U.S. Government Printing Office, 1880), pp. 5, 11, 12.*

QUESTIONS

1. Why did reformers draw a parallel between the treatment of slaves and Indians?
2. Why did the Indian Commissioners link the rights of citizenship to the reduction of tribal lands?

TABLE 17.1 Nineteenth-Century Federal Indian Policy

Law or Treaty	Provisions	Purpose
Bill for the Removal of Indians, 1830.	Payment to move to the Indian Territory (Oklahoma), land allotments, and supplies.	To move the Cherokees from Georgia and open their lands to settlers.
Numerous treaties with various tribes, 1830s–1860s.	Payment of debts, supplies, and yearly subsidies (annuities).	Removal to vaguely specified lands west of the Mississippi River.
Fort Laramie Treaty, 1868. Included Sioux, Crows, northern Cheyennes, and northern Arapahos but not Sitting Bull's band.	Created the Great Sioux Reserve west of the Missouri River in South Dakota. Provided livestock and farm implements.	Part of a new reservation policy to "insure civilization for the Indians and peace and safety for the whites."
Establishment of the Board of Indian Commissioners in 1869.	Church denominations could appoint Indian agents.	To clean up corrupt reservation management.
The U.S. unilaterally ends all treaty-making in 1871.	Executive orders or bilateral agreements ratified by both houses of Congress now establish or modify reservations.	Of the 162 Indian reservations in 1890, 56 were created by executive order.
General Allotment Act (Dawes Act), 1887.	Divided tribally held reservation lands into small allotments for families and individuals. Sold off "surplus."	Designed to destroy tribal organization and assimilate Indians.
Curtis Act, 1898.	Abolished the Indian Territory in Oklahoma.	Passed to undercut tribal power.

Source: Francis Paul Prucha, American Indian Treaties *(Berkeley: University of California Press, 1994).*

WOUNDED KNEE, PINE RIDGE RESERVATION, SOUTH DAKOTA, 1890 Thrown into an open trench, the frozen bodies of the Sioux slaughtered at Wounded Knee were a grim reminder that the U.S. army would brook no opposition to its control of Indian reservations. *(Denver Public Library, Western History Division)*

responded with cannon fire. Within minutes three hundred Indians, including seven infants, were slaughtered. Three days later, a baby who had miraculously survived was found wrapped in a blanket under the snow. She wore a buckskin cap on which a beadwork American flag had been embroidered. Brigadier General L.W. Colby, who adopted the baby, named her Marguerite, but the Indians called her Lost Bird.

As the frozen corpses at Wounded Knee were dumped into mass graves, a generation of Indian–white conflict on the Great Plains shuddered to a close. Lost Bird, with her poignantly patriotic beadwork cap, highlights the irony of the Plains Indians' response to white expansion. Many Natives did try to adapt to non-Indian ways, and some succeeded fully. Goodbird, the son of Buffalo Bird Woman, became a Congregational minister, a prosperous farmer, and a leader of the Hidatsa tribe. He carefully blended his traditional Indian religious beliefs with Christianity. Others struggled with poverty. Driven onto reservations, many Indians became

dependent on governmental support. By 1900, the Plains Indian population had shrunk from nearly a quarter-million to just over a hundred thousand. Nevertheless, the population began to increase slowly after 1900. Against overwhelming odds, the pride, religious traditions, and cultural identities of the Plains Indians survived all efforts at eradication.

Unlike the nomadic western Sioux, the more settled Navajos of the Southwest adjusted more successfully to the reservation system, preserving traditional ways and adapting to their new locations. By 1900, the Navajos had tripled their reservation land, dramatically increased their numbers and their herds, and carved out for themselves a distinct place in Arizona and New Mexico.

In the name of civilization and progress, whites after the Civil War had forced Indians off their lands in an effort that involved a mixture of sincere (if misguided) benevolence, coercion wrapped in an aura of legality, and outbursts of naked violence. Many Americans felt only contempt for Indians and greed for their land. Others had tried to uplift and Christianize the natives. Both groups, however, were blind to the value of Native American life and traditions. And both were unsuccessful in their attempts to shatter proud peoples and their ancient cultures.

Re-Settling the West

The successive defeats of the Native Americans and their removal to reservations opened a vast territory for settlement. In the 1840s, when nearly a quarter-million Americans had trudged overland to Oregon and California, they had typically endured a six-to eight-month trip in ox-drawn wagons. After 1870, railroad expansion made the trip faster and considerably easier. In the next three decades, more land was parceled out into farms than in the previous 250 years of American history combined, and agricultural production doubled.

The First Transcontinental Railroad

Passed in 1862, the Pacific Railroad Act authorized the construction of a new transcontinental link. The act provided grants of land and other subsidies to the railroads for each mile of track laid, which made them the largest landholders in the West. More than any other factor, the expansion of these railroads accelerated the transformation of everyday life west of the Mississippi.

Building the railroad took backbreaking work. Searching for inexpensive labor, the railroads turned to immigrants. The Central Pacific employed Chinese workers to chip and blast rail bed out of

GENERAL COLBY AND HIS ADOPTED DAUGHTER In keeping with his missionary mission, Brigadier General L.W. Colby, commander of the Nebraska National Guard, proudly holds his adopted Indian daughter, whose parents had been killed in the bloody massacre. *(National Anthropological Archives, Smithsonian Institution, Washington, D.C. GN 031198)*

RUSSIAN IMMIGRANTS IN NEBRASKA, CA. 1890 Lured by railroad land agents who promised cheap farm land, immigrants like these Russians who did not speak English faced daunting challenges. *(Nebraska State Historical Society)*

solid rock in the Sierra Nevada. The railroad preferred the Chinese because they worked hard for low wages, did not drink, and furnished their own food and tents. Nearly twelve thousand Chinese graded the roadbed while Irish, Mexican American, and black workers put down the track (See Table 17.2.)

On May 10, 1869, Americans celebrated the completion of the first railroad spanning North America.

TABLE 17.2 The African American and Chinese Population in Western States and Territories, 1880–1900

State or Territory	Blacks		Chinese	
	1880	1900	1880	1900
Arizona Territory	155	1,846	1,630	1,419
California	6,018	11,045	75,132	45,753
Colorado	2,435	8,570	612	599
Idaho	53	293	3,379	1,467
Kansas	43,107	52,003	19	39
Montana	346	1,523	1,765	1,739
Nebraska	2,385	6,269	18	180
Nevada	488	134	5,416	1,352
New Mexico Territory	1,015	1,610	57	341
North Dakota	113	286	NA	32
Oklahoma Indian Territory	NA	56,684*	NA	31
Oregon	487	1,105	9,510	10,397
South Dakota	288	465	NA	165
Texas	393,384	620,722	136	836
Utah	232	672	510	572
Washington	325	2,514	3,186	3,629

Combined total for Indian and Oklahoma territories.

Source: U.S. Bureau of the Census, Negro Population in the United States, 1790–1915 *(Washington, DC: U.S. Government Printing Office, 1918), 43, 44; Michael Doran, "Population Statistics of Nineteenth Century Indian Territory," Chronicles of Oklahoma 53:4 (Winter 1975), 501; and The Tenth Census, 1880, Population, and Twelfth Census, 1900, Population (Washington, DC: U.S. Government Printing Office, 1883 & 1901).*

As the two sets of tracks—the Union Pacific's, stretching westward from Omaha, Nebraska, and the Central Pacific's, reaching eastward from Sacramento, California—met at Promontory Point, Utah, beaming officials drove in a final ceremonial golden spike. The nation's vast midsection was now far more accessible than it had ever been.

The railroads sped up western development. In the battles against Native Americans, the army shipped horses and men west in the dead of winter to attack the Indians when they were most vulnerable. From the same trains, hunters gained quick access to the bison ranges and increased their harvest of the animals. Once Indian resistance had been crushed, the railroads hastened the arrival of new settlers and later shipped their cattle and grain to eastern urban markets. Railroads even supplied special detectives to support local police in towns along their lines.

Settlers and the Railroad

During the decade after the passage of the Pacific Railroad Act, Congress awarded the railroads 170 million acres, worth more than half a billion dollars. By 1893, Minnesota and Washington had also deeded to railroad companies a quarter of their state lands. As mighty landowners, the railroads had a unique opportunity to shape settlement in the region—and to reap enormous profits (see Map 17.3).

The railroads set up land sales offices and sent agents to the East Coast to recruit settlers. While the agents glorified the West as a new Garden of Eden, the land bureaus offered prospective buyers long-term loans and free transportation. Acknowledging that life on the Great Plains could be lonely, the promoters advised young men to bring their wives (because "maidens are scarce") and to emigrate as entire families and with friends.

One unintended consequence of these land promotions was to make land available to single women, or "girl homesteaders" as they were known

> The promoters advised young men to bring their wives (because "maidens are scarce").

MAP 17.3 **TRANSCONTINENTAL RAILROADS AND FEDERAL LAND GRANTS, 1850–1900** Despite the laissez-faire ideology that argued against government interference in business, federal and state governments heavily subsidized American railroads and gave them millions of acres of land. © Cengage Learning. All rights reserved. No distribution allowed without express authorization.

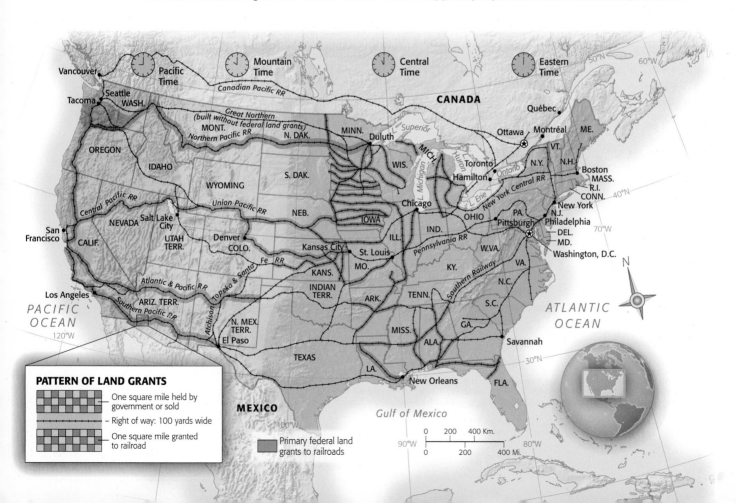

JERRY SHORES FAMILY BY SOLOMON D. BUTCHER, CUSTER NEBRASKA, 1887 Seated proudly in front of their sod house and barn, the two generations of this black family were part of the more than six thousand blacks who had moved to Nebraska by 1900. *(Nebraska State Historical Society)*

at the time. In Wyoming, single women made up more than 18 percent of the claimants. Women filed 10 to 20 percent of the claims in Colorado, sometimes as individuals and sometimes to add to family holdings.

In addition to the millions of American migrants, the railroads helped bring nearly 2.2 million foreign-born settlers to the trans-Mississippi West between 1870 and 1900. Some agents recruited whole villages of Germans to relocate to the North Dakota plains. Irish laborers hired to lay track could be found in every town along the rail lines. By 1905, the Santa Fe Railroad alone had transported sixty thousand Russian Mennonites to the fertile Kansas plains where black pioneers called exodusters had preceded them in the 1870s (see Chapter 16).

The railroads influenced agriculture as well. To ensure repayment of money owed to them, the railroads urged farmers to specialize in cash crops—wheat on the northern Plains, corn in Iowa and Kansas, cotton in Texas. Although these crops initially brought in high revenues, many farmers grew dependent on income from a single crop and became vulnerable to fluctuating market forces.

Homesteading on the Great Plains

Liberalized land laws pulled settlers westward. The 1862 Homestead Act reflected the Republican Party's belief that free land would promote economic opportunity. It offered 160 acres of land to anyone who would pay a ten-dollar registration fee, live on the land for five years, and cultivate it. Although nearly four hundred thousand families

claimed land under its provisions between 1860 and 1900, the law did not function as Congress had envisioned. Unscrupulous speculators filed false claims for the choicest locations, and railroads acquired huge landholdings. Only one acre in every nine went to the pioneers for whom it was intended.

The 160-acre limit specified by the Homestead Act created a second problem. On the rich soils of Iowa or in the fertile lands in Oregon, and Washington, a 160-acre farm was ample, but in the drier areas west of the hundredth meridian, a farmer needed more land. In 1873, to rectify this problem, Congress passed the Timber Culture Act, which gave homesteaders an additional 160 acres if they planted trees on 40 acres. Congress enacted the Desert Land Act in 1877, which made 640 acres available at $1.25 an acre, and the Timber and Stone Act of 1878, which permitted the purchase of up to 160 acres of forest land for $2.50 an acre. However, these measures were abused by grasping speculators, lumber-company representatives, and cattle ranchers. Yet, even though families did not receive as much land as Congress had intended, federal laws kept alive the dream of the West as a place for new beginnings.

In addition to problems caused by insufficient rainfall in many regions, almost all settlers faced difficult psychological adjustments to frontier life. The first years of settlement were the most difficult. Toiling to build a house, plant the first crop, and dig a well, the pioneers put in an average of sixty-eight hours of backbreaking work a week in isolated surroundings. Howard Ruede, a Pennsylvania printer who migrated to Kansas to farm, wrote home in 1877 complaining about the mosquitoes and bedbugs infesting his house, which was cut out of thick grass sod and dug into the ground. He and countless others saw their shining vision of idyllic farm life quickly dim. For blacks who emigrated from the South to Kansas and other parts of the Plains after the Civil War, prejudice compounded the burdens of adjusting to a different life.

Many women found adaptation to Plains frontier life especially difficult. At least initially, some were enchanted by the landscape. But far more were struck by the "horrible tribes of Mosquitoes," the violent drenching summer thunderstorms with hailstones as "big as hen's eggs" and blinding winter blizzards, and the crude sod huts that served as their early homes because of the scarcity of timber. One woman burst into tears upon first seeing her new sod house. The young bride angrily informed her husband that her father had built a better house for his hogs.

The high transience rate on the Great Plains in these years reflected the difficulty that newcomers faced in adjusting. Nearly half of those who staked homestead claims in Kansas between 1862 and

1890 gave up and moved on. However, in places like Minnesota and the Pacific Northwest that were populated by Germans, Norwegians, and other immigrants with a tradition of family prosperity tied to continuous landownership, the persistence rate (or percentage of people staying for a decade or more) could be considerably higher.

Many who weathered the lean early years came to identify deeply with the land. Within a decade, the typical Plains family that had "stuck it out" had moved into a new wood-framed house and had fixed up the front parlor. Women worked particularly hard on these farms and took pride in their accomplishments. "Just done the chores," wrote one woman to a friend. "I went fence mending and getting out cattle … and came in after sundown. I fed my White Leghorns [chickens] and then sat on the step to read over your letter. I forgot my wet feet and shoes full of gravel and giggled joyously."

New Farms, New Markets

Farmers on the Plains took advantage of advances in farm mechanization and the development of improved strains of wheat and corn to boost production dramatically. Efficient steel plows; specially designed wheat planters; and improved grain binders, threshers, and windmills enabled the typical Great Plains farmer of the late nineteenth century to increase the land's yield tenfold.

Barbed wire, patented in 1874, was another crucial invention that permitted farmers to keep roving livestock out of their crops. But fencing the land touched off violent clashes between farmers and cattle ranchers, who demanded the right to let their herds roam freely until the roundup. Generally, the farmers won.

New machinery together with increased demand for wheat, milk, and other farm products created the impression that farming was entering a period of unparalleled prosperity. But few fully understood the perils of pursuing agriculture as a livelihood. The cost of the land, horses, machinery, and seed needed to start up a farm could exceed twelve hundred dollars, far more than the annual earnings of the average industrial worker. Faced with substantial mortgage payments, many farmers had to specialize in a crop such as wheat or corn that would fetch high prices. This specialization made them dependent on the railroads for shipping and put them at the mercy of the international grain market's shifting prices.

Far from being an independent producer, the western grain grower competed in a complex world market economy. High demand could bring prosperity, but when world overproduction forced grain prices down, the heavily indebted grower faced ruin. Confronted with these realities, many Plains farmers quickly abandoned the illusion of frontier independence and easy wealth.

Unpredictable rainfall and weather conditions further exacerbated homesteaders' difficulties west of the hundredth meridian, where rainfall averaged less than twenty inches a year. Farmers compensated through "dry farming"—plowing deeply to stimulate the capillary action of the soils and harrowing lightly to raise a covering of dirt that would retain precious moisture after a rainfall. They also built windmills and diverted creeks for irrigation. But the onset of unusually dry years in the 1870s, together with grasshopper infestations and the major economic depression that struck the United States between 1873 and 1878 (see Chapter 16), made the plight of some midwesterners desperate.

Building a Society and Achieving Statehood

Despite the hardships, many remote farm settlements blossomed into thriving communities. Churches and Sunday schools became humming centers of social activity as well as of worship. Neighbors readily lent a hand to the farmer whose barn had burned or whose family was sick. Cooperation was a practical necessity and a form of insurance in a rugged environment where everyone was vulnerable to instant misfortune or even disaster.

When the population increased, local boosters lobbied to turn the territory into a state. Achieving statehood required the residents of the territory to petition Congress to pass an enabling act and then to elect delegates for a state constitutional convention. Once the state constitution had been drawn up and ratified by popular vote, the territory applied to Congress for admission as a state.

Under these procedures, Kansas entered the Union in 1861, followed by Nevada in 1864, Nebraska in 1867, and Colorado in 1876. Not until 1889 did North Dakota, South Dakota, Montana, and Washington gain statehood. Wyoming and Idaho followed the next year, and Utah in 1896. Oklahoma's admission in 1907 and Arizona's and New Mexico's in 1912 completed the process of creating states in the trans-Mississippi West (see Map 17.4).

"I went fence mending and getting out cattle … and came in after sundown. I fed my White Leghorns [chickens] and then sat on the step to read over your letter. I forgot my wet feet and shoes full of gravel and giggled joyously."

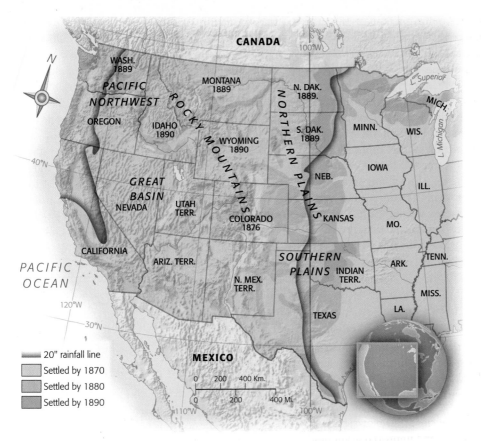

MAP 17.4 THE SETTLEMENT OF THE TRANS-MISSISSIPPI WEST, 1860–1890 The West was not settled by a movement of peoples gradually creeping westward from the East. Rather, settlers first occupied California and the Midwest and then filled up the nation's vast interior.

Although generally socially conservative, the new state governments supported woman suffrage. As territories became states, pioneer women battled for the vote. Seven western states held referenda on this issue between 1870 and 1910. Success came first in the Wyoming Territory, where men outnumbered women six to one. The tiny legislature enfranchised women in 1869 in the hope that it would attract women, families, and economic growth. The Utah Territory followed in 1870 and reaffirmed its support for woman suffrage when it became a state. Nebraska in 1867 and Colorado in 1876 permitted women to vote in school elections. Although these successes were significant, by 1910 only four states—Idaho, Wyoming, Utah, and Colorado—had granted women full voting rights.

The Spread of Mormonism

In 1847, members of the Church of Jesus Christ of Latter-day Saints—known as Mormons—had escaped persecution by moving to the Great Salt Lake Valley. Led by Brigham Young, their prophet-president, and a Council of Twelve Apostles, they sought to create the independent country of Deseret. Their faith emphasized self-sufficiency and commitment to family. In the next two decades, recruitment in Great Britain and the Scandinavian countries boosted their numbers to more than 100,000. These Mormon communities increasingly conflicted with non-Mormons and with the U.S. government, which disapproved of the church's involvement in politics, its communal business practices, and its support of polygamy or plural marriage.

The Mormons tried to be economically independent. In 1869, they developed their own railroad branches connecting Salt Lake City and Ogden to the Central Pacific Railroad and set up Zion's Cooperative Mercantile Institution to control wholesale and retail activities. They asked all Mormons to abstain from coffee, tea, and alcohol, and established their own People's Party to mobilize the Mormon vote.

But a series of federal acts and court decisions, starting with the Morrill Anti-Bigamy Act in 1862, challenged the authority of their church and their practice of polygamy. In *United States* v. *Reynolds* (1879), the Supreme Court declared plural marriages unlawful and held that freedom of religion did not protect religious practices. Then, in 1887, the **Edmunds-Tucker Act** dissolved the church corporation, limited the church's assets to $50,000, abolished women's right to vote, and put its properties and funds into receivership (control by the courts).

In response, in 1890 the church president publicly announced the official end of polygamy. A year later, the Mormons dissolved their People's Party. The church supported the application for statehood, which was granted in 1896. Confiscated church properties were returned, voting rights were restored, and jailed polygamists were pardoned, but the balance between sacred and secular had permanently shifted. Mormon settlements would continue in the twentieth century to draw new members and influence development in western communities.

Southwestern Lands

The annexation of Texas in 1845 and the Treaty of Guadalupe Hidalgo that had ended the Mexican-American War in 1848 ceded to the United States an immense territory, part of which became Texas, California, Arizona, and New Mexico. At the time, Mexicans had controlled vast expanses of the Southwest, maintaining their own churches, large ranching operations, and trade with the Indians. Although the United States had pledged to protect the property of Mexicans who remained on American soil, over the next three decades American ranchers and settlers forced much of the Spanish-speaking population off the land. Mexicans who stayed in the region adapted to the new Anglo society with varying degrees of success.

In Texas, the struggle for independence from Mexico had left a legacy of bitterness and misunderstanding. After 1848, Texas cotton planters confiscated Mexican lands and began a racist campaign that labeled Mexicans as nonwhite. Angered by their loss of land and discriminatory treatment, Mexican bandits retaliated by raiding American communities. Tensions peaked in 1859 when Juan Cortina, a Mexican rancher, attacked the Anglo border community of Brownsville, Texas, and freed all the prisoners in jail. Cortina battled the U.S. army for years until the Mexican government, fearing a U.S. invasion, imprisoned him in 1875.

Mexican Americans in California in the 1850s and 1860s faced similar pressures. A cycle of flood and drought, together with a slumping cattle industry, had ruined many of the large southern California ranches owned by the *californios*, Spanish-speaking descendants of the original Spanish settlers. The collapse of the ranch economy forced many of them to retreat into segregated urban neighborhoods called barrios. Spanish-surnamed citizens made up nearly half the 2,640 residents of Santa Barbara, California, in 1870; ten years later, after an influx of new settlers, they comprised barely a quarter of the population.

In many western states, Mexicans, Native Americans, and Chinese experienced similar patterns of racial discrimination, manipulation, and exclusion. At first, the number of new "Anglos" was small. As the number of whites increased, they identified minority racial, cultural, and language differences as marks of inferiority. White state legislators passed laws that made ownership of property difficult for non-Anglos. Relegated to a migratory labor force, non-Anglos were tagged as shiftless and irresponsible. Yet their labor made possible increased prosperity for the farmers, railroads, and households that hired them.

The cultural adaptation of Spanish-speaking Americans to Anglo society initially unfolded more smoothly in Arizona and New Mexico, where Spanish settlement had been sparse and a small class of wealthy Mexican landowners had long dominated a poor, illiterate peasantry. Moreover, since the 1820s, well-to-do Mexicans in Tucson, Arizona, had educated their children in the United States and formed trading partnerships and business alliances with Americans. One of the most successful was Estevan Ochoa, who began a long-distance freight business in 1859 with a U.S. partner and then expanded it into a lucrative merchandising, mining, and sheep-raising operation.

> Juan Cortina, a Mexican rancher, attacked the Anglo border community of Brownsville, Texas, and freed all the prisoners in jail.

The success of men such as Ochoa, who became mayor of Tucson, helped moderate American settlers' antagonistic attitudes. So, too, did the work of popular writers like Helen Hunt Jackson, who sentimentalized the colonial Spanish past. Jackson's 1884 romance *Ramona*, a tale of the doomed love of a Hispanicized mixed-blood (Irish-Indian) woman set on a California ranch overwhelmed by the onrushing tide of Anglo civilization, was enormously popular. Jackson's novel also appealed to upper-class Mexican Americans known as *Nuevomexicanos* who traced their lineage back to the Spanish conquest.

Still, conflicts over property persisted in Arizona and New Mexico. In the 1880s, Mexican American ranchers organized themselves into a self-protection vigilante group called Las Gorras Blancas (the

SANTA FE PLAZA, NEW MEXICO, IN THE 1880s, BY FRANCIS X. GROSSHENNEY After the railroad went through in 1878, Santa Fe became a popular tourist attraction known for its historic adobe buildings. Although the town retained a large Spanish-speaking population with their own newspaper, by the 1880s American and German immigrants monopolized most positions in business, government, the professions, and the skilled trades. *(Courtesy Museum of New Mexico, Neg. No. 37916)*

White Caps). In 1888, they tore up railroad tracks and attacked both Anglo newcomers and those upper-class Hispanics who had fenced acreage previously considered public grazing land. But this vigilante action did not stop the Anglo-dominated corporate ranchers from steadily increasing their land holdings. In towns and cities, discrimination limited the economic opportunities for Mexican American businessmen and the Spanish-speaking population as a whole became more impoverished. Even in Tucson, where the Mexican American elite enjoyed considerable economic and political success, 80 percent of the Mexican Americans in the work force were laborers in 1880, taking jobs as butchers, barbers, cowboys, and railroad workers.

As increasing numbers of Mexican American men were forced to search for seasonal migrant work, women took responsibility for holding families and communities together. Women managed the households and fostered group identification by maintaining traditional customs, kinship ties, and allegiance to the Catholic Church. They tended garden plots and traded food, soap, and produce with other women, generally stabilizing the community in times of drought or persecution by Anglos.

Violence and discrimination against Spanish-speaking citizens of the Southwest escalated in the 1890s, a time of rising racism in the United States. Rioters in Beeville and Laredo, Texas, in 1894 and 1899 attacked and beat up Mexican Americans. Whites increasingly labeled Mexican Americans as violent and lazy. For Spanish-speaking citizens, the battle for fair treatment and respect would continue into the twentieth century.

Exploiting the Western Landscape

The displacement of Mexican American and Native peoples from their lands opened the way for the exploitation of the natural environment in the trans-Mississippi West. Between 1860 and 1900, a generation of Americans sought to strike it rich. Although the mining, ranching, and farming "bonanzas" promised unheard-of wealth, they set in motion a boom-and-bust economy in which some succeeded but others went bankrupt or barely survived.

The Mining Frontier

In the half-century that began with the California gold rush in 1849, a series of mining booms swept from the Southwest northward into Canada and Alaska. In 1853, Henry Comstock, an illiterate prospector, stumbled on the rich **Comstock Lode** along Nevada's Carson River. Later in the same decade, prospectors swarmed into the Rocky Mountains and uncovered deep veins of gold and silver near present-day Denver. Over the next five decades, gold was discovered in Idaho, Montana, Wyoming, South Dakota, and, in 1896, in the Canadian Klondike. Although the popular press clearly exaggerated reports of miners scooping up gold by the panful, by 1900 more than a billion dollars' worth of gold had been mined in California alone.

The early discoveries of "placer" gold, panned from streams, attracted a young male population thirsting for wealth and reinforced the myth of mining country as "a poor man's paradise" (see Map 17.5). In contrast to the Great Plains, where ethnic groups recreated their own ethnic enclaves, western mining camps became ethnic melting pots. In the California census of 1860, more than thirty-three thousand Irish and thirty-four thousand Chinese had staked out early claims.

Although a few prospectors became fabulously wealthy, the experience of Henry Comstock, who sold out one claim for eleven thousand dollars and another for two mules, was more typical. Because the larger gold and silver deposits lay embedded in veins of quartz deep within the earth, extracting them required huge investments in expensive equipment. Deep shafts had to be blasted into the rock. Once lifted to the surface, the rock had to be crushed and flushed with mercury or cyanide to collect the silver, which was then smelted into ingots. No sooner had the major discoveries been made, therefore, than large mining companies backed by eastern or British capital bought them out and took them over.

Life in the new mining towns was vibrant but unpredictable. Men outnumbered women three to one. Money quickly earned was even more rapidly lost. During the heyday of the Comstock Lode in the 1860s and 1870s, Virginia City, Nevada, erupted in an orgy of speculation and building. Started as a shantytown in 1859, it swelled by 1873 into a thriving metropolis of twenty thousand people complete

MAP 17.5 THE MINING AND CATTLE FRONTIERS, 1860–1890 The western mining and ranching bonanzas lured thousands of Americans hoping to get rich quick. © Cengage Learning. All rights reserved. No distribution allowed without express authorization.

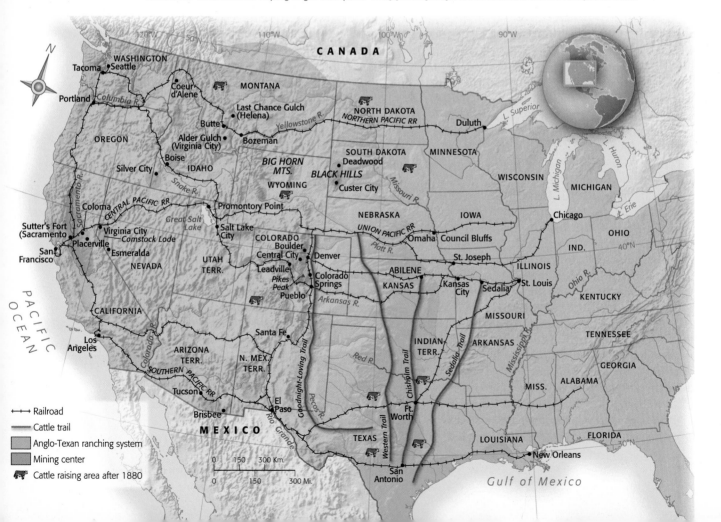

with elaborate mansions, a six-story hotel, an opera house, 131 saloons, four banks, its own Chinatown, and uncounted brothels. Of the 138 prostitutes noted in the 1870 census, 43 were Chinese women who worked as sexual slaves.

The boom-and-bust cycle evident in Virginia City was repeated in towns across the West. Mark Twain captured the thrill of the mining "stampedes" in *Roughing It* (1872). "Every few days," wrote Twain, "news would come of the discovery of a brand-new mining region: immediately the papers would teem with accounts of its richness, and away the surplus population would scamper to take possession. By the time I was fairly inoculated with the disease, 'Esmeralda' had just had a run and 'Humboldt' was beginning to shriek for attention. 'Humboldt! Humboldt!' was the new cry, and straightway Humboldt, the newest of the new, the richest of the rich, the most marvelous of the marvelous discoveries in silver-land, was occupying two columns of the public prints to 'Esmeralda's' one."

The gold rush mania also spurred the growth of settlement in Alaska. Small strikes there in 1869, two years after the United States had purchased the territory from Russia, brought the first prospectors. More miners arrived in the 1880s. But it was the discovery of gold in the Canadian Klondike in 1897 that brought thousands of prospectors into the area and eventually enabled Alaska to establish its own territorial government in 1912.

Word of new ore deposits like the ones in Alaska lured transient populations salivating to get rich. Miners typically earned about $2,000 a year at a time when teachers made $450 to $650 and domestic help $250 to $350. But the work was extremely dangerous. One journalist commented that "no premature explosion of blasts, crushing in of timbers, caving of earth or rock—no accident of any kind is so much feared…or is more terrible than a great fire in a large mine. It is hell. …" One out of eighty miners died annually in the 1870s. Most prospectors earned only enough to go elsewhere, perhaps buy some land, and try again. Nevertheless, the production of millions of ounces of gold and silver stimulated the economy, lured foreign investors, and helped usher the United States into the mainstream of the world economy.

Progress came at a high cost to the environment. Hydraulic mining—which used water cannons to dislodge minerals—polluted rivers, turned creeks brown, and flushed millions of tons of silt into valleys. The scarred landscape that remained was

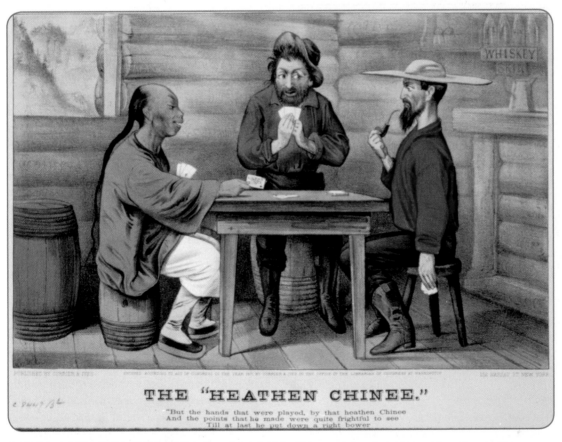

THE "HEATHEN CHINEE."
"But the hands that were played, by that heathen Chinee
And the points that he made were quite frightful to see
Till at last he put down a right bower

CURRIER & IVES, CARD GAME, 1875 In the mining districts, Chinese workers loved to gamble and were often stereotyped as being dishonest. *(Library of Congress)*

> "Every few days, news would come of the discovery of a brand-new mining region: immediately the papers would teem with accounts of its richness, and away the surplus population would scamper to take possession."

littered with rock and gravel filled with traces of mercury and cyanide, and nothing would grow on it. Smelters spewed dense smoke containing lead, arsenic, and other carcinogenic chemicals, often sickening those who lived nearby. The devastation is still evident today.

Cowboys and the Cattle Frontier

The feverish growth of open-range cattle ranching paralleled the expansion of the mining frontier

NAT LOVE Although Nat Love, pictured here with his Winchester rifle, personified the rugged, tough cowboy, when the railroads undercut the cattle-drive business, Love became a Pullman sleeping car porter. In 1907 he published his memoires detailing his colorful career. *(Library of Congress)*

during the 1860s and 1870s. In this case, astute businessmen and railroad entrepreneurs, eager to fund their new investments in miles of track, promoted cattle herding as the new route to fame and fortune. The cowboy, once scorned as a ne'er-do-well and drifter, was now glorified as a man of rough-hewn integrity and self-reliant strength.

In 1868, Joseph G. McCoy, a young cattle dealer from Springfield, Illinois, shrewdly combined organizational and promotional skills to turn the cattle industry into a new money-maker. With the forced relocation of the Plains Indians onto reservations and the extension of the railroads into Kansas after the Civil War, McCoy realized that cattle dealers could now amass enormous fortunes by raising steers cheaply in Texas and bringing them north for shipment to eastern urban markets (see Map 17.5).

McCoy built a new stockyard in Abilene, Kansas. By guaranteeing to transport his steers in railcars to hungry eastern markets, he obtained a five-dollar kickback from the railroads on each cattle car shipped. To make the overland cattle drives from Texas to Abilene easier, McCoy also helped survey and shorten the Chisholm Trail in Kansas. Finally, in a clever feat of showmanship, he organized the first Wild West show, sending four Texas cowboys to St. Louis and Chicago, where they staged roping and riding exhibitions that attracted enthusiastic crowds. At the end of his first year in business, thirty-five thousand steers were sold in Abilene; the following year the number more than doubled.

The great **cattle drives** of the 1860s and 1870s turned into a bonanza for herd owners. Steers purchased in Texas at nine dollars a head could be sold in Abilene, after deducting four dollars in trail expenses, for twenty-eight dollars. A herd of two thousand head could thus bring a tidy thirty-thousand-dollar profit. But the cattlemen, like the grain growers farther north on the Great Plains, lived at the mercy of high interest rates and an unstable market. During the financial panic of 1873, cattle drovers fell into bankruptcy by the hundreds.

Little of the money made by the large-scale cattle ranchers found its way into the pockets of the cowboys themselves. The typical cowpunchers who drove herds through the dirt and dust from southern Texas to Abilene earned a mere thirty dollars a month, about the same as common laborers. They also braved the gangs of cattle thieves that operated along the trails. The most notorious of the cattle rustlers, William H. Bonney, better known as Billy the Kid, may have murdered as many as eleven men before he was killed by a sheriff in 1881 at the age of twenty-one. The long hours, low pay, and hazardous work discouraged older ranch hands from applying. Most cowboys were men in their teens and twenties who worked for a year or two and then pursued different livelihoods.

Of the estimated 35,000 to 55,000 men who rode the trails in these years, nearly one-fifth were black or Mexican. Barred by discrimination from many other trades, blacks enjoyed the freedom of life on the trail. Although they were excluded from the position of trail boss, they distinguished themselves as resourceful and shrewd cowpunchers. **Nat Love,** the son of Tennessee slaves, left for Kansas after the Civil War to work for Texas cattle companies. As chief brander, he moved through Texas and Arizona "dancing, drinking, and shooting up the town." On July 4, 1876, when the Black Hills gold rush was in full swing, Love delivered three thousand head of cattle to a point near the hills and rode into Deadwood to celebrate. Local miners and gamblers had raised prize money for roping and shooting contests, and Nat Love won both, as well as a new title, Deadwood Dick.

Close relationships sometimes developed between black and white cowboys. Shortly before Charles Goodnight, a white pioneer trailblazer, died in 1929, he recalled of the black cowboy Bose Ikard, a former slave, that "he was my detective, banker, and everything else in Colorado, New Mexico, and the other wild country I was in. The nearest and only bank was at Denver, and when we carried money I gave it to Bose." Goodnight revealed much about the economic situation of blacks on the Plains, however, when he added that "a thief would…never think of looking in a Negro's bed for money."

The cattle bonanza, which peaked between 1880 and 1885, produced more than 4.5 million head of cattle for eastern markets (see Beyond America). Prices began to sag as early as 1882, however, and many ranchers plunged heavily into debt. In 1885 and 1886, two of the coldest and snowiest winters on record combined with summer droughts and Texas fever to destroy nearly 90 percent of the cattle in some regions, pushing thousands of ranchers into bankruptcy. The cattle industry lived on, but railroad expansion brought the days of the open range and the great cattle drives to an end. As had the mining frontier, the cattle frontier left behind memories of individual daring, towering fortunes for some, and hard times for many.

Cattle Towns and Prostitutes

One legacy of the cattle boom was the growth of cities like Abilene, Kansas, which shipped steers to Chicago and eastern markets. Like other cattle towns, Abilene went through an early period of violence that saw cowboys pulling down the walls of the jail as it was being built. But the town quickly established a police force to maintain law and order. City ordinances forbade carrying firearms and regulated saloons, gambling, and prostitution. James B. "Wild Bill" Hickok served as town marshal in 1871. Dime novelists described him as "a veritable terror to bad men on the border," but during his term as Abilene's lawman, Hickok killed just two men, one of them by mistake. Transient, unruly types certainly gave a distinctive flavor to cattle towns like Abilene, Wichita, and Dodge City, but the overall homicide rates there were not unusually high.

If cattle towns were neither as violent nor as lawless as legend would have it, they did still experience a lively business in prostitution, as did most cities at this time. Given the large numbers of unattached young men and numerous saloons (Abilene, in the 1870s, with a permanent population of five hundred, had thirty-two drinking establishments), prostitution thrived. Prostitutes came from all social classes and from as far away as China, Ireland, Germany, and Mexico. Some became prostitutes as an escape from domestic violence or because of economic hardship. Others, like the Chinese, were forced into the trade. All prostitutes risked venereal disease, physical abuse, and drug and alcohol addiction.

> "A thief would … never think of looking in a Negro's bed for money."

As western towns became more settled, the numbers of women in other occupations increased. Some found work as cooks or laundresses on ranches. Others married merchants, doctors, and businessmen. Although few of the first generation rode the range, their daughters became increasingly involved in the everyday work of ranching and became proficient riders themselves.

Bonanza Farms

Like the gold rushes and cattle bonanzas, the wheat boom of the 1870s and 1880s started small but rapidly attracted large capital investments that produced the nation's first agribusinesses. The boom in the Dakota Territory began during the Panic of 1873, when the Northern Pacific Railroad began exchanging land for its depreciated bonds. Speculators purchased more than three hundred thousand acres in the fertile Red River Valley of North Dakota for between fifty cents and a dollar an acre.

Operating singly or in groups, the speculators established factory-like ten-thousand-acre farms, each run by a hired manager, and invested heavily in labor and equipment. On the Cass-Cheney-Dalrymple farm near Fargo, North Dakota, fifty

GLOBAL INTERACTIONS

Cattle-Raising in the Americas

Nineteenth-century dime novels and Wild West Shows celebrated cowboys as quintessentially American—independent, self-reliant, tough, and occasionally violent. Driving herds of cattle north from Texas to Kansas, the cowboys, who rode the open range from the end of the Civil War through the mid-1880s, appeared to be the unique product of the American West. From a more global perspective, however, North American cowboys shared much in common with the Mexican *vaqueros* and Argentinian *gauchos.* Like their counterparts in Latin and South America, they drew on a long tradition of cattle herding that had begun centuries earlier in Africa, England, and Spain.

Spanish conquistadors and English colonists brought to the New World their practice of raising beef cattle on the open range rather than in fixed enclosures. In sixteenth-century Mexico, African slaves often joined mixed-bloods of Spanish and Indian ancestry to brand and tend cattle. On the rich grasslands of Argentina, horsemen first hunted wild cattle that had escaped earlier settlements. Later, after the Indians were driven off the open range, these horsemen, now called *gauchos*, tended cattle on large ranches.

Gauchos and cowboys were colorful characters, usually young men, often from lower-class backgrounds. The English naturalist, Charles Darwin, visiting Argentina in 1833, described them as "generally tall and handsome, but with a proud and dissolute expression of countenance. They frequently wear their mustaches, and long black hair curling down their backs. With their brightly-colored garments, great

ARGENTINE GAUCHOS Ostriches provided gauchos with meat as well as extra income from the sale of feathers used to decorate women's hats. *(From Picturesque Illustrations of Buenos Ayres and Montevideo, London, 1820)*

ARIZONA COWBOY, BY FREDERIC REMINGTON, 1901 In his paintings and sculptures, Remington captured the popular image of the quintessential American cowboy: a tough, fearless, expert horseman. *(Library of Congress)*

spurs clanking about their heels, and knives stuck as daggers (and often so used) at their waists, they look a very different race of men from what might be expected from their name of Gauchos, or simple countrymen." Like cowboys, they busted broncos, taming the wild horses to accept riders, and rounded up strays. They also hunted wild ostriches, whose feathers fetched high prices in Europe. As in North America, some gauchos became bandits, which added to their romantic appeal.

Gauchos and cowboys, like other cattle herders around the world, whether Russian Cossacks, South African Dutch farmers, or Canadian cowhands, were often skilled horsemen. American cowboys drew on both Anglo and Hispanic traditions. Unlike the gauchos in Argentina who used *bolas*, an Indian invention of three balls connected by rawhide thongs, to entangle a steer's feet and immobilize it, American cowboys used the Hispanic *lariat to* rope the necks of their cattle and place them in a corral. Like British herders who used dogs, American cowboys taught their horses to maneuver quickly and sharply to keep the herd in line or to cut out a steer to be branded. Like their counterparts in Canada, they organized rodeos to show off their riding and lassoing skills.

Although horses were universally used to herd cattle throughout the Americas, each open-range cattle-raising region had its own distinctive features. In California, where the open-range cattle boom peaked in the decade after 1848, Hispanic cowhands used rawhide lassos, which they looped around the saddle horn to immobilize steers, and wore the Spanish great-rowel spurs over soft shoes. Because Anglo-Texans adapted British cattle-herding practices that used abrupt turns to cut a steer from the herd, they modified the traditional Spanish saddle by adding a second belt to hold it more securely on the horse, and adopted the pointed-toe, high-heeled riding boot to hold it in the stirrup during these tight turns. Cattle-raisers on the Great Plains, while following many Texas cowboy practices, added river irrigation to grow hay fields to help tide their herds over the harsh winters. Canadian cattlemen, in contrast, employed acculturated Indians as cowhands and sometimes followed British practices and used collie dogs as well as horses to help herd cattle.

By the end of the nineteenth century, the cattle booms in both North and South America that depended on open-range grazing practices had passed. By maximizing herd size and fertility, cattlemen had inadvertently destroyed perennial grasses, damaged the landscape, and in some cases caused desertification. Farmers and sheep-raisers competed for grazing land and fenced off access to many ranges. At the same time, the extension of railroad lines made it possible to ship cattle directly from ranches to urban areas, a practice that fundamentally changed the livestock industry. In both North and South America, large-scale ranchers took control of cattle-raising and kept wages low. British investment syndicates, for example, purchased large ranches in Texas and Wyoming where they raised immense herds for eastern urban markets.

Not surprisingly, the idealization and romanticization of the cowboy that occurred after open-range grazing had disappeared in North America produced similar celebrations of gauchos and *vaqueros* in Argentina and Mexico. In all three areas, the reality was different. The colorful cowhands who had stirred the popular imagination as symbols of a freer, more independent way of life had been reduced to seasonal laborers with little chance of advancement.

QUESTIONS FOR ANALYSIS

- What traditions shaped open-range ranching in the Americas?
- What was the popular mythic image of the cowboy, the *vaquero*, and the gaucho?
- What was the environmental impact of open-range grazing?

or sixty plows rumbled across the flat landscape on a typical spring day. Northern Pacific president George W. Cass, who had invested fifty thousand dollars for land and equipment, paid all his expenses plus the cost of the ten thousand acres with his first harvest alone.

The publicity generated by the tremendous success of a few large investors like Cass led to an unprecedented wheat boom in the Red River Valley in 1880. Eastern banking syndicates and small farmers alike rushed to buy land. North Dakota's population tripled in the 1880s. Wheat production skyrocketed to almost 29 million bushels by the end of the decade. But the profits soon evaporated. By 1890, some Red River Valley farmers were destitute.

The wheat boom collapsed for a variety of reasons. Overproduction, high investment costs, too little or too much rain, excessive reliance on one crop, and depressed grain prices on the international market all undercut farmers' earnings. Large-scale farmers who had invested in hopes of getting rich felt lucky just to survive. Oliver Dalrymple lamented in 1889 that "it seems as if the time has come when there is no money in wheat raising."

Large-scale farms proved most successful in California's Central Valley. Using canals and other irrigation systems to water their crops, farmers by the mid-1880s were growing higher-priced specialty crops and had created new cooperative marketing associations for cherries, apricots, grapes, and oranges. By 1900, led by California citrus growers, who used the "Sunkist" trademark for their oranges, large-scale agribusinesses in California were shipping a variety of fruits and vegetables in refrigerated train cars to midwestern and eastern markets.

The Oklahoma Land Rush, 1889

As farmers in the Dakotas and Minnesota were enduring poor harvests and falling prices, would-be homesteaders greedily eyed the Indian Territory, as present-day Oklahoma was then known. The federal government, considering much of this land virtually worthless, had reserved it for the Five Civilized Tribes since the 1830s. These tribes (except for some Cherokees) had sided with the Confederacy during the Civil War. Although Washington had already punished them by settling other tribes on lands in the western part of the territory, land-hungry whites demanded even more land.

In 1889, over the Native Americans' protests, Congress transferred to the federally owned public domain nearly 2 million acres in the central part of the Oklahoma Territory that had not been specifically assigned to any Indian tribe. At noon on April 22, 1889, thousands of men stampeded into the new lands to stake out homesteads. (Other settlers, the so-called Sooners, had illegally arrived earlier and were already plowing the fields.) Before nightfall, tent communities had risen at Oklahoma City and Guthrie near stations on the Santa Fe Railroad. Nine weeks later, six thousand homestead claims had been filed. In the next decade, the Dawes Severalty Act broke up the Indian reservations into individual allotments and opened the surplus to non-Indian settlement (see Map 17.6).

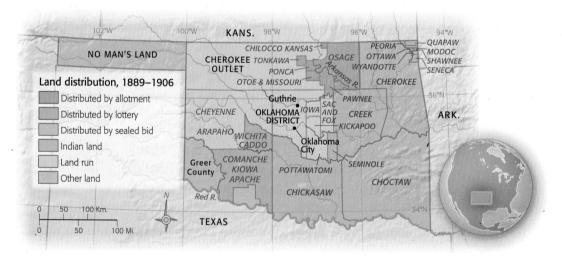

MAP 17.6 THE OKLAHOMA LAND RUSH, 1889–1906 Lands in Oklahoma not settled by "Sooners" were sold by lotteries, allotments, and sealed-bid auctions. By 1907, the major reservations had been broken up, and each Native American family had been given a small farm.

The **Curtis Act** in 1898 dissolved the Indian Territory and abolished tribal governments.

The Oklahoma land rush demonstrated the continuing power of the frontier myth, which tied "free" land to the ideal of economic opportunity. Most Oklahoma farmers survived because they had obtained fertile land in an area where the normal rainfall was thirty inches, ten inches more than in the semiarid regions farther west. Still, within two generations a combination of exploitative farming, poor land management, and sporadic drought would place Oklahoma at the desolate center of the dust bowl in the 1930s (covered in Chapter 24).

The West of Myth and Legend

In 1893, four years after the last major tract of western Indian land, the Oklahoma Territory, was opened to non-Indian settlement, a young Wisconsin historian, Frederick Jackson Turner, delivered a lecture entitled "The Significance of the Frontier in American History." "[T]he frontier has gone," declared Turner, "and with its going has closed the first period of American history." Although Turner's assertion that the frontier was closed was based on a Census Bureau announcement, it was inaccurate (more western land would be settled in the twentieth century than in the nineteenth). But his linking of economic opportunity with the transformation of the trans-Mississippi West caught the popular imagination and launched a new school of historical inquiry into the effects of the frontier on U.S. history.

Scholars now recognize that many parts of Turner's "frontier thesis," particularly its ethnocentric omission of Native Americans' claims to the land, were inaccurate. Yet his idealized view of the West did reflect ideas popular among his contemporaries in the 1890s. A legendary West had taken deep root in the American imagination. In the nineteenth century, this mythic West was a product of novels, songs, and paintings. In the twentieth century, it would be perpetuated by movies, radio programs, and television shows. The legend merits attention, for its evolution is fascinating and its influence has been far-reaching.

The American Adam and the Dime-Novel Hero

Late-nineteenth-century writers presented the frontiersman as a kind of mythic American Adam—simple, virtuous, and innocent—untainted by a corrupt social order. For example, at the end of Mark Twain's *Huckleberry Finn*, Huck rejects the constraints of settled society as represented by Aunt Sally and heads west with the declaration, "I reckon I got to light out for the territory ahead of the rest, because Aunt Sally she's going to adopt me and sivilize me, and I can't stand it. I been there before." In this version of the legend, the West is a place of adventure where one can escape from society and its pressures.

But even as this conception of the myth was being popularized, another powerful theme had emerged as well. The authors of the dime novels of the 1860s and 1870s offered the image of the western frontiersman as a new masculine ideal, the tough guy who fights for truth and honor. In *Buffalo Bill: King of the Border Men* (1869), a dime novel loosely based on real-life William F. "Buffalo Bill" Cody, Edward Judson (who published under the name Ned Buntline) created an idealized hero who is a powerful moral force as he drives off treacherous Indians and rounds up villainous cattle rustlers.

> "[T]he frontier has gone, and with its going has closed the first period of American history."

Cody himself, playing upon the public fascination with cowboys, organized his own **Wild West Show** in 1883. In the show, which toured the East Coast and Europe, cowboys engaged in mock battles with Indians, reinforcing the dime-novel image of the West as an arena of moral encounter where virtue always triumphed.

Revitalizing the Frontier Legend

Eastern writers and artists eagerly embraced both versions of the myth—the West as a place of escape from society and the West as a stage on which the moral conflicts confronting society were played out. Three young members of the eastern establishment, Theodore Roosevelt, Frederic Remington, and Owen Wister, spent much time in the West in the 1880s, and each was intensely affected by the adventure.

Each man found precisely what he was looking for. The frontier that Roosevelt glorified in such books as *The Winning of the West* (four volumes, 1889–1896), and that Remington portrayed in his statues and paintings, was a stark physical and moral environment that stripped away all social artifice and tested each individual's character. Drawing on a popular version of English scientist

GRAND CANYON OF THE YELLOWSTONE, BY THOMAS MORAN Dazzled by the monumental beauty of the West, painters portrayed natural wonders such as Yellowstone as one of God's works. In the process, they stimulated a new popular interest in preserving the spectacular features of the land. *(Smithsonian American Art Museum, Washington, DC/ Art Resource, NY)*

Charles Darwin's evolutionary theory, which characterized life as a struggle in which only the fittest survived, Roosevelt and Remington exalted the disappearing frontier as the proving ground for a new kind of virile manhood and the last outpost of an honest and true social order.

This version of the frontier myth reached its apogee in **Owen Wister's** popular novel *The Virginian* (1902). In Wister's tale, the elemental environment of the Great Plains produces individuals like his unnamed cowboy hero, "the Virginian," an honest, strong, and compassionate man, quick to help the weak and fight the wicked. The Virginian sums up his own moral code in describing his view of God's justice: "He plays a square game with us." For Wister, as for Roosevelt and Remington, the cowboy was the Christian knight on the Plains, indifferent to material gain as he pursued justice and attacked evil.

Needless to say, the western myth was far removed from the reality of the West. Critics delighted in pointing out that not one scene in *The Virginian* showed the hard physical labor of the cattle range. The idealized version of the West also glossed over the darker underside of frontier expansion—the brutalities of Indian warfare, the racist discrimination against Mexican Americans and blacks, the risks of commercial agriculture and cattle-raising, and the boom-and-bust mentality rooted in the exploitation of natural resources.

Further, the myth obscured the complex links between the settlement of the frontier and the emergence of the United States as a major industrialized nation increasingly tied to a global economy. Eastern and foreign capitalists controlled large-scale mining, cattle, and agricultural operations in the West. The technical know-how of industrial America underlay the marvels of western agricultural productivity. Without the railroad, that quintessential symbol of the new industrial order, the transformation of the West would have been far slower.

Beginning a National Parks Movement

Despite its one-sided and idealized vision, Owen Wister's celebration of the western experience reinforced a growing recognition that many unique features of the western landscape were being threatened by overeager entrepreneurs. One important byproduct of the western legend was a surge of public support for creating national parks and the beginning of an organized conservation movement.

Those who went west in the 1860s and 1870s to map its rugged terrain were often awed by the natural beauty of the landscape. Major **John Wesley Powell,** the one-armed veteran of the Civil War who charted the Colorado River through the Grand Canyon in 1869, waxed euphoric about its towering rock formations and powerful cataracts. "The river turns sharply to the east, and seems enclosed by a wall, set with a million brilliant gems ... On coming nearer, we find fountains bursting from the rock, high overhead, and the spray in the sunshine forms the gems which bedeck the way."

In his important study, *Report on the Lands of the Arid Regions of the United States* (1878), Powell argued that settlers needed to readjust their expectations about the use of water in the dry terrain west of the hundredth meridian. He urged Congress to establish governmental control of watersheds, irrigation, and public lands, a request that went largely unheeded.

Around the time Powell was educating Congress about the arid nature of the far West, a group of adventurers led by General Henry D. Washburn visited the hot springs and geysers near the Yellowstone River in northwestern Wyoming and eastern Montana. They were stunned by what they saw. Wrote one of the party, "[A]mid the canyon and falls, the boiling springs and sulphur mountain, and, above all, the mud volcano and the geysers of the Yellowstone, your memory becomes filled and clogged with objects new in experience, wonderful in extent, and possessing unlimited grandeur and beauty." Overwhelmed by the view, the Washburn explorers abandoned their plan to claim the area for the Northern Pacific Railroad and instead petitioned Congress to protect it from settlement, occupancy, and sale. Congress responded in 1872 by creating **Yellowstone National Park** to "provide for the preservation ... for all time, [of] mineral deposits, natural curiosities, or wonders within said park ... in their natural condition." In doing so, they excluded the Native Americans who had long considered the area a prime hunting range.

These first steps to conserve a few of the West's unique natural sites reflected the beginning of a changed awareness of the environment. In his influential study *Man and Nature* in 1864, **George Perkins Marsh,** an architect and politician from Vermont, attacked the view that nature existed to be tamed and conquered. Cautioning Americans to curb their destructive use of the landscape, he warned the public to change its ways. "Man," he wrote, "is everywhere a disturbing agent. Wherever he plants his foot, the harmonies of nature are turned to discords."

Marsh's plea for conservation found its most eloquent support in the work of **John Muir,** a Scottish immigrant who had grown up in Wisconsin. In 1869, Muir traveled to San Francisco and quickly fell in love with the redwood forests. For the next forty years, he tramped the rugged mountains of the West and campaigned for their preservation. A romantic at heart, he struggled to experience the wilderness at its most elemental level. Once trekking high in the Rockies during a summer storm, he climbed the tallest pine he could find and swayed back and forth in the raging wind.

Muir became the late nineteenth century's most articulate publicist for wilderness protection. "Climb the mountains and get their good tidings," he advised city dwellers. "Nature's peace will flow into you as the sunshine into the trees." Muir's spirited campaign to protect the wilderness contributed strongly to the establishment of Yosemite National Park in 1890. Two years later, he became president of the Sierra Club, an organization created to encourage the enjoyment and protection of the wilderness in the mountain regions of the Pacific coast.

The precedent established by the creation of Yellowstone National Park remained ambiguous well into the twentieth century. Other parks that preserved the high rugged landforms of the West were often chosen because Congress viewed the sites as worthless for other purposes (see Map 30.2). Awareness of the need for biological conservation would not emerge until later in the twentieth century (as discussed in Chapter 21).

Ironically, despite the crusades of Muir, Powell, and Marsh to educate the public about conservation, the campaign for wilderness preservation reaffirmed the image of the West as a unique region whose magnificent landscape produced tough individuals of superior ability. Overlooking the senseless violence and ruthless exploitation of the land, contemporary writers, historians, and publicists proclaimed that the settlement of the final frontier marked a new stage in the history of civilization, and they kept alive the legend of the western frontier as a seedbed of American virtues.

CONCLUSION

The image of the mythic West has long obscured the transformation of people and landscape that took place there in the second half of the nineteenth century. Precisely because industrialization, urbanization, and immigration were altering the rest of the nation in unsettling ways (covered in Chapters 18 and 19), many Americans embraced the legend of the West as a visionary, uncomplicated, untainted Eden of social simplicity and moral clarity. The mythic West represented what the entire society had once been like (or so Americans chose to believe), before the advent of cities, factories, and masses of immigrants.

But the mythic view of the frontier West obscured the dark side of expansion onto the Great Plains and beyond. Under the banner of economic opportunity and individual achievement, nineteenth-century Americans used the army to subdue the Indians, undermine their traditional way of life, and drive them onto reservations. They also ruthlessly exploited the region's vast natural resources. In less than three decades, they killed off the enormous buffalo herds, tore up the prairie sod, and littered parts of the landscape with mining debris.

Despite the promise of the Homestead Act, which offered 160 acres of free land to those who would settle on it for five years, much of the best land in the West had been given to railroads to encourage their expansion. Speculators purchased other prime locations. Homesteaders were often forced to settle on poorer-quality tracts in areas where rainfall was marginal. In many places, large business enterprises in mining, ranching, and agribusiness, financed by eastern and European bankers, shoved aside the small entrepreneur and took control of the choicest natural resources.

Nevertheless, the settlement of the vast continental interior did reinforce the popular image of the United States as a land of unprecedented economic opportunity and as a seedbed for democracy. The founding of new towns, the creation of new territorial and state governments, and the interaction of peoples of different races and ethnicities tested these ideas and, with time, forced their rethinking. The exclusion of blacks, Indians, and Spanish-speaking Americans belied the voiced commitment to an open society, but the increasing willingness to give women the vote in many of the new western states would spread within the next two decades.

Although the persisting mythic view of the West hid the more ruthless and destructive features of western expansionism, settling the interior territories and exploiting their extensive physical resources gave birth to the conservation movement and a reassessment of traditional American views of the environment. By the turn of the century, the West's thriving farms, ranches, mines, and cities would help make the United States into one of the world's most prosperous nations.

KEY TERMS

Plains Indians   (p. 505)

William F. "Buffalo Bill" Cody   (p. 506)

Fort Laramie Treaty   (p. 507)

Sitting Bull   (p. 509)

Helen Hunt Jackson   (p. 510)

Dawes Severalty Act   (p. 510)

Ghost Dance   (p. 511)

Wounded Knee   (p. 511)

Edmunds-Tucker Act   (p. 520)

White Caps   (p. 521)

Comstock Lode   (p. 522)

cattle drives   (p. 524)

Nat Love   (p. 525)

Curtis Act   (p. 529)

Wild West Show   (p. 529)

Owen Wister   (p. 530)

John Wesley Powell   (p. 531)

Yellowstone National Park   (p. 531)

George Perkins Marsh   (p. 531)

John Muir   (p. 531)

FOR FURTHER REFERENCE

Jean H. Baker, ed., *Votes for Women: The Struggle for Suffrage Revisited* (2002). A new examination of the complex factors that shaped woman suffrage in the West and elsewhere.

Ned Blackhawk, Violence *Over the Land: Indians and Empires in the Early American West* (2006). A study of the impact of conquest and colonialism on the Great Basin's native peoples.

John M. Nieto-Phillips, *The Language of Blood: The Making of Spanish-American Identity in New Mexico, 1880s–1930s* (2004). A thoughtful analysis of the politics behind the creation of the Spanish-American ethnic identity.

Jeffrey Ostler, *The Plains Sioux and U.S. Colonialism from Lewis and Clark to Wounded Knee* (2004). A provocative study that places the Plains Indian removal in the context of the conquest of native peoples worldwide.

Jean Pfaelzer, *Driven Out: The Forgotten War Against Chinese Americans* (2007). A fine analysis of the persistent violence and discrimination directed against Chinese immigrants in the nineteenth century.

Glenda Riley, *Taking Land, Breaking Land: Women Colonizing the American West and Kenya, 1840–1940* (2003). An insightful examination of women's experiences on the American and African frontiers.

Elliott West, *The Contested Plains: Indians, Goldseekers, and the Rush to Colorado* (1998). An excellent analysis of the environmental factors that shaped the competition among Indians and settlers on the central Great Plains.

Elliot West, *The Last Indian War: The Nez Perce Story* (2009). A perceptive account that places the Nez Perce war in the larger context of the Civil War and Reconstruction.

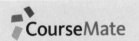

Visit the CourseMate website at **www.cengagebrain.com** for additional study tools and review materials for this chapter.

> "The sufferings of the working classes are daily increasing, Famine has broken into the home of many of us, and is at the door of all."

in countless small industries also introduced new technologies and innovative advertising campaigns to swell production and increase sales. By 1900, new enterprises both large and small, supported by investment bankers and using a nationwide railroad distribution system, offered a vast array of goods for national and international markets.

This stunning industrial growth came at a high cost. New manufacturing processes transformed the nature of work, undercut skilled labor, and created mind-numbing, assembly-line routines. Large-scale manufacturing companies often polluted the environment, spewing noxious smoke into the air and dumping toxic waste into nearby rivers. The challenges of new business practices made the American economy difficult to control. Rather than smoothly rolling forward, it lurched between booms and busts in business cycles that produced labor unrest and crippling depressions in 1873–1879 and 1893–1897.

FOCUS Questions

- What innovations in technology and business drove increases in industrial production after 1865, and what was their social and environmental impact?

- How did Carnegie, Rockefeller, and other corporate leaders consolidate control over their industries?

- Why did the South's experience with industrialization differ from that of the North and the Midwest?

- How did the changing nature of work affect factory workers' lives, and how did they respond?

- How did corporations undercut labor's bargaining power in the 1890s?

The Rise of Corporate America

In the early nineteenth century, the corporate form of business organization had been used to raise large amounts of start-up capital for transportation

enterprises such as turnpikes and canals. By selling stocks and bonds to raise money, the corporation separated the company's managers, who guided its day-to-day operation, from its owners. After the Civil War, American business leaders pioneered new forms of corporate organization that combined innovative technologies, creative management structures, and limited liability should the enterprise fail. The rise of the giant corporation is a story of risk-taking and innovation as well as of conspiracy and corruption.

The Character of Industrial Change

Six features dominated the world of large-scale manufacturing after the Civil War: (1) the exploitation of immense coal deposits as a source of cheap energy; (2) the rapid spread of technological innovation in transportation, communication, and factory systems; (3) the demand for workers who could be driven and controlled; (4) the constant pressure on firms to compete tooth-and-nail by cutting costs, eliminating rivals, and creating monopolies; (5) the relentless drop in prices (a stark contrast to the inflation of other eras); and (6) the failure of the money supply to keep pace with productivity, a development that drove up interest rates and restricted the availability of credit.

All six factors were closely related. The great coal deposits in Pennsylvania, West Virginia, and Kentucky provided cheap energy to fuel railroad and factory growth. New technologies stimulated productivity and catalyzed breathtaking industrial expansion. Technological innovation enabled manufacturers to cut costs and hire unskilled labor. Cost cutting enabled firms to undersell one another, destroy weaker competitors, and consolidate themselves into more efficient and more ruthless firms. At least until the mid-1890s, cheap energy, immigrant labor, new technology, and fierce competition forced down overall price levels.

But almost everyone struggled terribly during the depression years, when the government did nothing to relieve distress. "The sufferings of the working classes are daily increasing," wrote a Philadelphia worker in 1874. "Famine has broken into the home of many of us, and is at the door of all." Above all, business leaders' unflagging drive to reduce costs both created colossal fortunes at the top of the economic ladder and forced millions of wage earners to live near the subsistence level.

Out of the new industrial system poured clouds of haze and soot, as well as the first tantalizing trickle of what would become an avalanche of consumer goods. In turn, mounting demands for consumer

1859	First oil well drilled in Titusville, Pennsylvania.	**1886**	American Federation of Labor (AFL) formed. Haymarket riot in Chicago.	
1866	National Labor Union founded.	**1887**	Interstate Commerce Act establishes Interstate Commerce Commission.	
1869	Transcontinental railroad completed. Knights of Labor organized.	**1888**	Edward Bellamy, *Looking Backward.*	
1870	John D. Rockefeller establishes Standard Oil Company.	**1889**	Andrew Carnegie, "The Gospel of Wealth."	
1873	Panic of 1873 triggers a depression lasting until 1879.	**1890**	Sherman Anti-Trust Act. United Mine Workers formed.	
1876	Alexander Graham Bell patents the telephone.	**1892**	Standard Oil of New Jersey and General Electric formed. Homestead Strike. Columbian Exposition in Chicago. Miners strike at Coeur d'Alene, Idaho.	
1877	Edison invents phonograph. Railway workers stage first nationwide strike.			
1879	Henry George, *Progress* and *Poverty.* Edison perfects incandescent lamp.	**1893**	Panic of 1893 triggers a depression lasting until 1897.	
1882	Standard Oil Trust established. Edison opens first electric power station in New York City. Chinese Exclusion Act.	**1894**	Pullman Palace Car workers strike.	
		1901	J. Pierpont Morgan organizes United States Steel.	
1883	William Graham Sumner, *What Social Classes Owe to Each Other.* Lester Frank Ward, *Dynamic Sociology.*			

goods stimulated heavy industry's production of capital goods—machines to boost farm and factory output even further. Together with the railroads, the corporations that manufactured capital goods, refined petroleum, and made steel became driving forces in the nation's economic growth (see Figure 18.1).

Railroad Innovations

Competition among the capitalists who headed American heavy industry was most intense among the nation's railroads. By 1900, 193,000 miles of railroad track crisscrossed the United States—more than in all of Europe including Russia. Taking

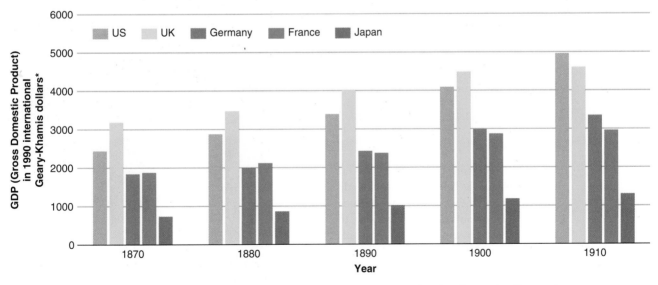

* 1990 international Geary-Khamis dollars represent the monetary values of the output of the final goods and services produced in a country in one year converted into 1990 dollars at the exchange rate which would pertain if the goods and services had the same prices in all countries (purchasing power parity). See the statistical definition at the UN site: http://unstats.un.org/unsd/methods/icp/ipc7_htm.htm.

FIGURE 18.1 LATE NINETEENTH-CENTURY ECONOMIC GROWTH IN GLOBAL PERSPECTIVE

advantage of enormous government land subsidies, these rail lines connected every state in the Union, opened up an immense new internal market, and pioneered new forms of large-scale corporate enterprise. They created national distribution systems, and perfected new management structures.

Railroad entrepreneurs such as Collis P. Huntington of the Central Pacific Railroad, **Jay Gould** of the Union Pacific, and James J. Hill of the Northern Pacific faced enormous financial and organizational problems. To raise the staggering sums necessary for laying track and building engines, railroads obtained generous land and loan subsidies from federal, state, and local governments (see Chapter 17). At the same time, they borrowed heavily by selling stocks and bonds to the public. Bond holders earned a fixed rate of interest; stockholders received dividends only when the company earned a profit. By 1900, the yearly interest repayments required by the combined debt of all U.S. railroads (which stood at an astounding $5.1 billion—nearly five times that of the federal government) cut heavily into their earnings.

In addition to raising substantial capital, the railroads created new systems for collecting and using information. To coordinate the complex flow of cars across the country, they relied on the magnetic telegraph, invented in 1837. To improve efficiency, they set up clearly defined, hierarchical organizational structures and divided their lines into separate divisions, each with its own superintendent. Elaborate accounting systems documented the cost of every operation for each division, from coal consumption to the repair of engines and cars. Using these reports, railroad officials could set rates and accurately predict profits as early as the 1860s, a time when most businesses had no idea of their total profit until they closed their books at year's end. Railroad management innovations thus became a model for many other businesses seeking a national market.

Consolidating the Railroad Industry

The expansion and consolidation of railroading reflected both the ingenuity and the dishonesty flourishing on the corporate management scene. Despite their organizational innovations, the industry remained chaotic in the 1870s. Hundreds of small companies used different standards for track width and engine size. Financed by large eastern and British banks, Huntington, Gould, and others devoured these smaller lines to create large, integrated track networks. In the Northeast, four major trunk lines were completed. West of the Mississippi, five great companies controlled most of the track by 1893.

Huntington, Gould, and the other corporate leaders who reorganized and expanded the railroad industry in the 1870s and 1880s often were depicted by their contemporaries as villains and robber barons who manipulated stock markets to line their own pockets. Newspaper publisher Joseph Pulitzer called Jay Gould, the short, secretive president of the Union Pacific, "one of the most sinister figures that have ever flitted batlike across the vision of the American people." Historians agree that many were indeed corrupt pirates, but note that others were shrewd innovators. Indeed, some of their ideas were startling in their originality and inventiveness.

ABUSIVE MONOPOLY POWER This *Puck* cartoon depicts financiers Jay Gould (left) and Cornelius Vanderbilt (right) and suggests that their manipulation of markets and their ownership of railroads, telegraph companies, and newspapers is powerful enough to strangle Uncle Sam. *(Frank Wood Historical Collections)*

The massive railroad systems created by these entrepreneurs became the largest business enterprises in the world. As they consolidated small railroads into a few interlocking systems, these masterminds standardized all basic equipment and facilities, from engines and cars to automatic couplers, air brakes, and signal systems. In 1883, independently of the federal government, the railroads corrected scheduling problems by dividing the country into four time zones (see Map 17.3). In May 1886, all railroads shifted simultaneously to the new standard 4'8½" gauge track. Finally, cooperative billing arrangements enabled the railroads to ship cars from other roads at uniform rates nationwide.

But the systemization and consolidation of the railroads had its costs. Heavy indebtedness, over-extended systems, and crooked business practices forced the railroads to compete recklessly with each other for traffic. They cut rates for large shippers, showered free passes on politicians, and granted substantial rebates and kickbacks to favored clients while ignoring worker safety. None of these tactics, however, shored up the railroads' precarious financial position. Ruthless competition and fraudulent business practices drove some overbuilt lines into bankruptcy.

Stung by exorbitant rates and secret kickbacks, farmers and small business owners turned to state governments for help. In the 1870s, midwestern state legislatures responded by outlawing rate discrimination. Initially upheld by the Supreme Court, these and other decisions were negated in the 1880s when the Court ruled that states could not regulate interstate commerce. In response in 1887, Congress passed the **Interstate Commerce Act.** A five-member Interstate Commerce Commission (ICC) was established to oversee the practices of interstate railroads. The law banned monopolistic activity like pooling, rebates, and discriminatory short-distance rates.

The railroads challenged the commission's rulings in the federal courts. Of the sixteen cases brought to the Supreme Court before 1905, the justices found in favor of the railroads in all but one, essentially nullifying the ICC's regulatory clout. The Hepburn Act (covered in Chapter 21), passed in 1906, strengthened the ICC by finally empowering it to set rates.

The railroads' vicious competition weakened in 1893 when a national depression forced a number of roads into the hands of **J. Pierpont Morgan** and other investment bankers. Morgan, a massively built man with piercing eyes and a commanding presence, took over the weakened systems, reorganized their administration, refinanced their debts, and built intersystem alliances. By 1906, under the bankers' centralized management, seven giant networks controlled two-thirds of the nation's rail mileage.

Applying the Lessons of the Railroads to Steel

The close connections between railroad expansion, which absorbed millions of tons of steel for tracks, and the growth of corporate organization and management are well illustrated in the career of **Andrew Carnegie.** Born in Scotland, Carnegie immigrated to America in 1848 at the age of twelve. His first job as a bobbin boy in a Pittsburgh textile mill paid only $1.20 a week. The following year, Carnegie became a Western Union messenger boy. Taking over when the telegraph operators wanted a break, he soon became the city's fastest telegraph operator and gained an insider's view of the operations of every major Pittsburgh business.

Carnegie's big break came in 1852 when Tom Scott, superintendent of the Pennsylvania Railroad's western division, hired him as his secretary and personal telegrapher. Later promoted to division chief, Carnegie cut costs while more than doubling the road's mileage. Having invested his earnings in the railroads, by 1868 Carnegie was earning more than $56,000 a year from his investments, a substantial fortune in that era.

In the early 1870s, Carnegie built his own steel mill to produce high-grade steel rails using a new technology named after its English inventor, Henry Bessemer, which shot a blast of air through an enormous crucible of molten iron to burn off carbon and impurities. Combining this new technology with the cost-analysis approach learned from his railroad experience, Carnegie became the first steelmaker to know the actual production cost of each ton of steel.

Carnegie's philosophy was deceptively simple: "Watch the costs, and the profits will take care of themselves." Using rigorous cost accounting and limiting wage increases to his workers, he lowered his production costs and prices below those of his competitors. When these tactics did not drive them out of business, he asked for favors from his railroad-president friends and gave "commissions" to railroad purchasing agents to win business.

As output climbed, Carnegie discovered the benefits of **vertical integration,** that is, controlling all aspects of manufacturing from the mining and smelting of ore to the selling of steel rails. Carnegie Steel thus became the classic example of how sophisticated new technology could be combined with innovative management (and brutally low wages) to create a mass-production system

> "So much oil is produced that it is impossible to care for it, and thousands of barrels are running into the creek; the surface of the river is covered with oil for miles."

that could dramatically increase production and slash consumer prices (see Figure 18.2).

The management of daily operations by his close associates left Carnegie free to pursue philanthropic activities. While still in his early thirties, Carnegie donated money to charitable projects. In his lifetime, he gave more than $300 million to libraries, universities, and international-peace causes.

By 1900, Carnegie Steel, employing twenty thousand people, had become the world's largest industrial corporation. Carnegie's competitors, worried about his domination of the market, decided to buy him out. In 1901, J. Pierpont Morgan purchased Carnegie's companies and set up the United States Steel Corporation, the first business capitalized at more than $1 billion. The corporation, made up of two hundred member companies employing 168,000 people, marked a new scale in industrial enterprise.

A systematic self-publicist, Carnegie portrayed his success as the result of self-discipline and hard

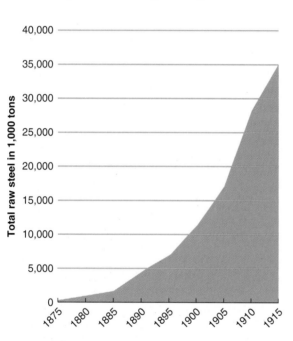

FIGURE 18.2 IRON AND STEEL PRODUCTION, 1875–1915
New technologies, improved plant organization, economies of scale, and the vertical integration of production brought a dramatic spurt in iron and steel production. *Note:* short ton = 2,000 pounds.

Source: *Historical Statistics of the United States*

ANDREW CARNEGIE Although his contemporaries called him "the world's richest man," Andrew Carnegie was careful to deflect criticism by focusing on his philanthropic and educational activities. *(Library of Congress)*

Andrew Carnegie Sums Up the Cost Savings of Vertical Integration

The eighth wonder of the world is this: two pounds of iron-stone purchased on the shores of Lake Superior and transported to Pittsburgh;

two pounds of coal mined in Connellsville and manufactured into coke and brought to Pittsburgh;

one half pound of limestone mined east of the Alleghenies and brought to Pittsburgh;

a little manganese ore,

mined in Virginia and brought to Pittsburgh.

And these four and one half pounds of material manufactured into one pound of solid steel and sold for one cent.

That's all that need be said about the steel business.

Source: *Harold C. Livesay,* Andrew Carnegie and the Rise of Big Business *(Boston: Little, Brown, 1975), 189.*

work. The full story was more complex. Carnegie did not mention his uncanny ability to see the larger picture, his cleverness in hiring talented associates who would drive themselves (and the company's factory workers) mercilessly, his ingenuity in transferring organizational systems and cost accounting methods from railroads to steel, and his callousness in keeping wages as low as possible. To a public unaware of corporate management techniques, however, Carnegie's success gave credence to the idea that anyone might rise from rags to riches.

The Trust: Creating New Forms of Corporate Organization

Between 1870 and 1900, the same fierce competition that had stimulated consolidation in the railroad and steel industries (see Table 18.1) also swept the oil, salt, sugar, tobacco, and meat-packing industries. Like steel, these highly competitive businesses required large capital investments. Entrepreneurs in each industry therefore raced to reduce costs, lower prices, and drive their rivals out of the market.

The evolution of the oil industry illustrates the process by which new corporate structures evolved. After Edwin L. Drake drilled the first successful petroleum (or "crude-oil") well in 1859 near Titusville, Pennsylvania, competitors rushed into the business. Petroleum was distilled into oil, which soon replaced animal tallow as the major lubricant, and into kerosene, which became the leading fuel for household and public lighting.

By the 1870s, the landscape near Pittsburgh and Cleveland, the sites of the first discoveries, was littered with rickety drilling rigs, assorted collection tanks, and ramshackle refineries. Oil spills were a constant problem. "So much oil is produced," reported one Pennsylvania newspaper in 1861, "that it is impossible to care for it, and thousands of barrels are running into the creek; the surface of the river is covered with oil for miles."

TABLE 18.1 Industrial Consolidation: Iron and Steel Firms, 1870 and 1900

	1870	1900
Number of firms	808	669
Number of employees	78,000	272,000
Output (tons)	3,200,000	29,500,000
Capital invested	$121,000,000	$590,000,000

Source: *Robert L. Heilbroner and Aaron Singer,* The Economic Transformation of America: 1600 to Present, *2nd ed. (San Diego: Harcourt Brace Jovanovich, 1984), 92.*

In this rush for riches, **John D. Rockefeller,** a young Cleveland merchant, gradually achieved dominance. Like Andrew Carnegie, the solemn Rockefeller had a passion for cost cutting and efficiency. In one case, he insisted a manager find 750 missing barrel stoppers. He realized that in a mass-production enterprise, small changes could save thousands of dollars.

Rockefeller resembled Carnegie, too, in his ability to understand the inner workings of an entire industry and the benefits of vertical integration. The firm that controlled the shipment of oil between the well and the refinery and between the refinery and the retailers, he realized, could dominate the industry. In 1872, he purchased his own tanker cars and obtained not only a 10 percent rebate from the railroads for hauling his oil but also a kickback on his competitors' shipments. When new pipeline technology became available, Rockefeller set up his own massive interregional pipeline network.

Like Carnegie, Rockefeller aggressively forced out his competitors. If local refineries rejected his offers to buy them out, he priced his products below cost and strangled their businesses. When rival firms teamed up against him, Rockefeller set up a pool—an agreement among several companies— that established production quotas and fixed prices. By 1879, Rockefeller had seized control of 90 percent of the country's oil-refining capacity.

In 1882, Rockefeller decided to eliminate competition by establishing a new form of corporate organization, the **Standard Oil Trust.** In place of the "pool" or verbal agreement among companies to control prices and markets, which lacked legal status, the trust created an umbrella corporation that ran them all. To implement his trust, Rockefeller and his associates persuaded the stockholders of forty companies to exchange their stock for trust certificates. Under this arrangement, stockholders retained their share of the trust's profits while enabling the trust to control production. Within three years, the Standard Oil Trust had consolidated crude-oil buying throughout its member firms and slashed the number of refineries in half. In this way, Rockefeller integrated the petroleum industry both vertically, by controlling every function from production to local retailing, and horizontally, by merging the competing oil companies into one giant system.

While Standard Oil justified its trust organization by pointing to the public usefulness of inexpensive heating and cooking fuels, other monopolies did not provide such benefits. James B. "Buck" Duke's American Tobacco trust, for example, targeted youths with trading cards and prizes to persuade them to smoke cigarettes. For addictive products such as cigarettes, targeting children became a means for ensuring continuous use. To gain access to even bigger markets, Duke purchased controlling interests in tobacco companies in England and Japan.

Taking a leaf from Duke and Rockefeller's book, companies in the copper, sugar, whiskey, lead, and other industries established their own trust arrangements. By limiting the number of competitors, the trusts created an *oligopoly*, the market condition that exists when a small number of sellers can greatly influence prices. But their unscrupulous tactics, semimonopolistic control, and sky-high earnings provoked a public outcry. Both major political parties denounced them in the presidential election of 1888.

Fearful that the trusts would stamp out all competition, Congress, under the leadership of Senator John Sherman of Ohio, passed the **Sherman Anti-Trust Act** in 1890. The Sherman Act outlawed trusts and any other monopolies that fixed prices in restraint of trade and slapped violators with fines of up to $5,000 and a year in jail. But the act failed to define clearly either *trust* or *restraint of trade*. The government prosecuted only eighteen antitrust suits between 1890 and 1904. When Standard Oil's structure was challenged in 1892, its lawyers simply reorganized the trust as an enormous holding company. Unlike a trust, which literally owned other businesses, a holding company simply owned a controlling share of the stock of one or more firms. The new board of directors for Standard Oil (New Jersey), the new holding company, made more money than ever.

The Supreme Court further hamstrung congressional antitrust efforts by interpreting the Sherman Act in ways sympathetic to big business. In 1895, for example, the federal government brought suit against the sugar trust in *United States* v. *E.C. Knight Company*, arguing that by controlling more than 90 percent of all U.S. sugar refining, it operated in illegal restraint of trade. Asserting that manufacturing was not interstate commerce and ignoring the company's vast distribution network that enabled it to dominate the market, the Court threw out the suit. Thus vindicated, corporate mergers and consolidations surged ahead at the turn of the century. By 1900, these mammoth firms accounted for nearly two-fifths of the capital invested in the nation's manufacturing sector.

Stimulating Economic Growth

Large-scale corporate enterprise did not alone account for the colossal growth of the U.S. economy in the late nineteenth-century. Other factors proved equally important, including new inventions, specialty production, and innovations in advertising and marketing. In fact, the resourcefulness of small enterprises, which combined innovative technology with new methods of advertising and merchandising, enabled many sectors of the economy to grow dramatically by adapting quickly to changing fashions and consumer preferences.

BASEBALL TRADING CARD To encourage boys and young men to smoke cigarettes, the American Tobacco Company included in the cigarette package collectable cards with pictures of baseball heroes such as Ty Cobb. *(Library of Congress)*

The Triumph of Technology

New inventions not only streamlined the manufacture of traditional products but also stimulated consumer demand by creating entirely new product lines. The development of a safe, practical way to generate electricity, for example, made possible a vast number of electrical motors, household appliances, and lighting systems.

Many of the major inventions that stimulated industrial output and underlay mass production in these years were largely hidden from public view. Few Americans had heard of the improved technologies that facilitated bottle making and glassmaking, canning, flour milling, match production, and petroleum refining. Fewer still knew much about the refrigerated railcars that enabled Gustavus Swift's company to slaughter beef in Chicago and ship it east.

The inventions people did see were the ones that changed the patterns of everyday life: the sewing machine, mass-produced by the Singer Sewing Machine Company beginning in the 1860s; the telephone, developed by Alexander Graham Bell in 1876; and the light bulb, perfected by **Thomas A. Edison** in 1879.

These new inventions eased household drudgery and reshaped social interactions. The sewing machine, which relieved the tedium of sewing apparel by hand, expanded personal wardrobes. The spread of telephones—by 1900, the Bell Telephone Company had installed almost eight hundred thousand in the United States—not only transformed communication but also undermined social conventions for polite behavior that had been premised on face-to-face or written exchanges. The light bulb, by freeing people from dependence on daylight, made it possible to shop after work.

In the eyes of many, Thomas A. Edison epitomized the inventive impulse and the capacity for creating new consumer products. Born in 1847 in Milan, Ohio, Edison, like Andrew Carnegie, had little formal education and worked in the telegraphic industry. A born salesman and self-promoter, Edison shared Carnegie's vision of a large, interconnected industrial system resting on a foundation of technological innovation (see Technology and Culture).

Edison's first major invention, a stock-quotation printer, in 1868 earned enough money to finance Edison's first "invention factory" in Newark, New Jersey, a research facility he moved to nearby Menlo Park in 1876. Assembling a staff that included university-trained scientists, Edison boastfully predicted "a minor invention every ten days, and a big one every six months."

Buoyed by the success and popularity of his invention in 1877 of a phonograph, or "sound writer" (*phono*: "sound"; *graph*: "writer"), Edison set out to develop a new filament for incandescent light

THOMAS EDISON'S LABORATORIES IN MENLO PARK, NEW JERSEY, CA. 1881 Always a self-promoter, Edison used this depiction of his "invention factory" to suggest that his development of a durable light bulb in 1879 would have an impact on life around the globe. (*U.S. Department of the Interior, National Park Service, Edison National Historic Site*)

Electricity

Of all the technological achievements of the nineteenth century, none seemed more inspiring or mysterious than the ability to generate electricity. Using Alessandro Volta's discovery that chemical reactions in batteries produced a weak electric current, Samuel F.B. Morse had used batteries to power his telegraph in 1837. Alexander Graham Bell followed suit with his telephone in 1876. But higher voltages were needed to run lighting systems and motors. Michael Faraday in England and Joseph Henry in America discovered in 1831 that a rotating magnet surrounded by a conducting wire would produce a continuous flow of electric current. After the Civil War, American inventors used this discovery to develop powerful generators to run incandescent lights (1879), to power motors to run trolley cars (1888), and to drive machines in factories. For many Americans, the ability to harness electricity marked the subjugation of nature and indicated the progress of American civilization.

Nowhere did the knowledge of electricity seem more impressive than its promise to reveal the secrets of the human body. X-rays, discovered in 1895 by the German physicist Wilhelm Roentgen and developed into a practical hospital machine a year later by Thomas Edison, enabled doctors to see inside the body. Physicians discovered that the workings of the nervous system and the brain itself depended on electrical impulses. It was no accident that Edison was known as the "wizard of Menlo Park," where his research laboratory was located.

The spread of electric lighting illustrates how technological advances pushed innovation. Thomas Edison's vision went far beyond the development of a practical light bulb. He conceived of an interrelated system of power plants, transmission lines, and light fixtures, all to be produced by companies he had established. Edison's system of direct current lighting (DC—which flowed in only one direction in the wires) required that users be located near power plants. But in 1886, George Westinghouse set up a competing company that used the Italian inventor Nikola Tesla's discovery that alternating current (AC—which cycled back and forth within the wires) could send high voltage electricity efficiently over long distances. Competition between the two systems was finally resolved in 1896 when Edison's successor company, General Electric, agreed to share its patents with the Westinghouse Company. With electric current now standardized as 110 volts AC at

CREATION OF THE EDISON SYSTEM, MENLO PARK *Frank Leslie's Weekly* in 1880 illustrated Thomas Edison's process of making electric light bulbs using glass-blowers and vacuum machines in his Menlo Park laboratory. *(Library of Congress)*

60 Hertz (60 cycles per second), dozens of other inventors developed electric motors, spotlights, electric signs, water pumps, elevators, and household appliances—all drawing power from the same power grid. Only twenty years after the first power station had been built, electrification had started to transform everyday life.

By 1898, when the city of London had sixty-two different utilities that produced thirty-two different voltage levels, American companies had created a unified national electrical system with standardized voltages, and the United States had established itself as a world leader in electrical technology. The remarkable achievements of the American electrical industry resulted from a combination of factors. Skilled inventors such as Edison, Westinghouse, and Frank Sprague, who developed electric motors for trolley and subway cars, were critical. But the efforts might never have made it out of the laboratories without financiers, such as J.P. Morgan and Henry Villard, who funded the enormous investment in electric generators, power plants, and transmission lines. A third factor was the independence of large corporations like General Electric and Westinghouse, which were able to operate nationally and avoid conflicting state regulations.

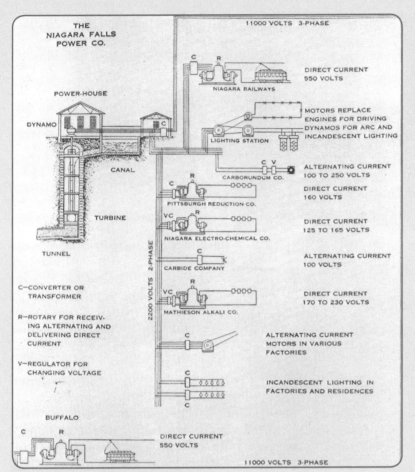

THE NIAGARA FALLS POWER COMPANY As this diagram of the power station at Niagara Falls reveals, the early transmission of electric power was closely tied to large manufacturers who had the funds to support large investments in generating equipment and power lines. *(From Adams, Niagara Power)*

Operating as regional monopolies, these corporations standardized voltage, alternating current, and electrical fixtures nationwide. Finally, the pooling of patents was crucial. The American patent system, by granting inventors property rights in their inventions and by publicly identifying how the discoveries worked, stimulated technological innovation in general.

At first, electricity was very expensive, and the general public could not afford the cost of wiring homes. Still, even confined to the public sphere, the establishment of a national electrical system was one of the greatest technological innovations of the century. Electric streetcars and subways, public lighting systems, and electric elevators transformed urban America, allowing the construction of skyscrapers and the quick transportation of millions of people. The electrification of factories extended the workday into the night and made work safer. In the following decades, electrification made possible the invention of lighting systems, fans, washing machines, and a host of other devices to ease the drudgery of everyday life.

In the twentieth century, some shortcomings in Americans' love affair with electricity became obvious. In the early years, urban electrification accentuated the differences between city and country life. After World War II, massive power failures showed that the centralization of power distribution systems, first constructed as private monopolies between 1880 and 1932, made them vulnerable to failure when a subsystem problem cascaded throughout the network. The private ownership of power companies, now called utility companies, has enabled them at times to inflate energy prices for their own profit. Most electrical power in the United States today is produced from coal, a nonrenewable resource that also produces acid rain and air pollution. Nevertheless, the creation of a national system of electrical power generation paved the way for remarkable innovations—from lighting to televisions and computers—that remain today closely tied to America's sense of progress and material advancement.

QUESTIONS FOR ANALYSIS

- Why did the early electrical inventions seem to mark the subjugation of nature?
- What technological breakthroughs paved the way for the widespread use of electricity for street lighting and transportation?
- Why did the standardization and consolidation of the electric industry take place more quickly in the United States than in England?

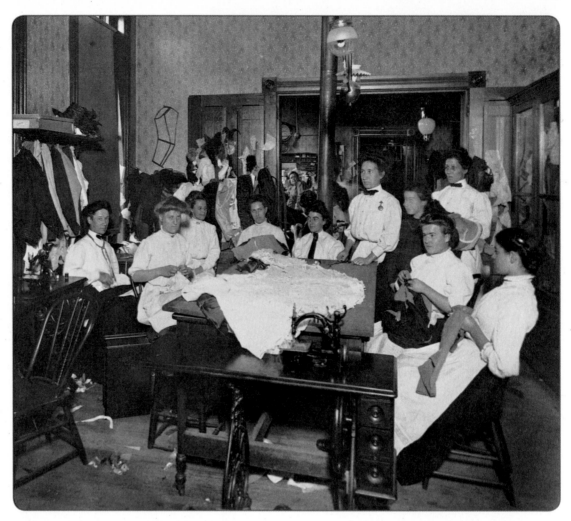

SKILLED WOMEN DRESSMAKERS, 1890 As these dressmakers in Mary Malloy's shop in St. Paul, Minnesota, indicate, industrialization did not displace all skilled workers. In this case, handwork and machine work continued together. Women's dressmaking persisted as a skilled occupation into the 1890s and gave women entrepreneurs an opportunity to run their own businesses. *(© Minnesota Historical Society/Corbis)*

bulbs. Characteristically, he announced his plans for an electricity-generation process before he perfected his inventions and then worked feverishly, testing hundreds of materials before he found a carbon filament that would glow dependably in a vacuum.

Edison realized that practical electrical lighting had to be part of a complete system containing generators, voltage regulators, electric meters, and insulated wiring and that the system needed to be easy to install and repair. It also had to be cheaper and more convenient than kerosene or natural gas lighting, its main competitors. In 1882, having built this system with the support of banker J. Pierpont Morgan, the Edison Illuminating Company opened a power plant in the heart of New York City's financial district, furnishing lighting for eighty-five buildings.

In the following years, Edison and his researchers pumped out invention after invention, including the mimeograph machine, the microphone, the motion picture camera and film, and the storage battery. By the time of his death in 1931, he had patented 1,093 inventions and amassed an estate worth more than $6 million. Yet Edison's greatest achievement remained his laboratory at Menlo Park. A model for the industrial research labs later established by Kodak, General Electric, and Du Pont, Edison's laboratory demonstrated that the systematic use of science in support of industrial technology paid large dividends. Invention had become big business.

Specialized Production

Along with inventors, manufacturers of custom and specialized products such as machinery, jewelry, furniture, and women's clothes dramatically expanded economic output. Using skilled labor, these companies crafted one-of-a-kind or small batches of articles that ranged in size from large steam engines and machine tools to silverware, furniture, and custom-made dresses. Keenly attuned to innovations in technology and design, they constantly created new products tailored to the needs of individual buyers.

Small dressmaking shops run by women were typical of flexible specialization displayed by small batch processors. Until the turn of the twentieth century, when ready-to-wear clothes came to dominate the market, most women's apparel was custom produced in small shops run by female proprietors. Unlike the tenement sweatshops that produced men's shirts and pants, dressmakers and milliners (a term derived from fancy goods vendors in sixteenth-and seventeenth-century Milan, Italy) paid good wages to highly skilled seamstresses. The small size of the shops together with the skill of the workers enabled them to shift styles quickly to follow the latest fashions.

Thus, alongside of the increasingly rationalized and bureaucratic big businesses like steel and oil in the late nineteenth century, American productivity was also stimulated by small producers who provided a variety of goods that supplemented the bulk-manufactured staples of everyday life.

Advertising and Marketing

As small and large factories alike spewed out an amazing array of new products, business leaders often discovered that their output exceeded what the market could absorb. This was particularly true for mass-produced consumer goods such as matches, flour, soap, and canned foods. Not surprisingly, these industries were trailblazers in developing advertising and marketing techniques. Strategies for whetting consumer demand and for differentiating one product from another represented a critical component of industrial expansion in the post–Civil War era.

Through the use of brand names, trademarks, guarantees, slogans, endorsements, and other gimmicks, manufacturers built demand for their products and won enduring consumer loyalty. Americans bought Ivory Soap, first made in 1879 by Procter and Gamble of Cincinnati, because of the absurdly precise but impressive pledge that it was "99 and 44/100ths percent pure."

Other manufacturers won consumer loyalty through the development of unique products. In the 1880s, George Eastman developed a paper-based photographic film as an alternative to the fragile glass plates then in use and sold this film loaded into an inexpensive camera. Consumers returned the

The Girl with the White Cap.

HEINZ KETCHUP ADVERTISEMENT, CA. 1900 To sell its products in a mass market, H J Heinz company in Pittsburgh developed the brand name "57 Varieties" for its ketchup, pickles, and other condiments. The "girl with the white cap" was meant to symbolize the purity of its food processing. *(Library & Archives Division, Historical Society of Western Pennsylvania, Pittsburgh, PA)*

camera to his Rochester factory where, for a charge of ten dollars, the film was developed and printed, the camera reloaded, and everything shipped back. In marketing a new technology, Eastman had revolutionized an industry and democratized a visual medium previously confined to a few.

Social and Environmental Costs and Benefits

By 1900, the chaos of early industrial competition, when thousands of companies had struggled to enter a national market, had given way to the most productive economy in the world, supported by a legion of small, specialized companies and dominated by a few enormous ones. An industrial transformation that had originated in railroading and expanded to steel and petroleum had spread to every nook and cranny of American business and raised the United States to a position of world leadership.

The vast expansion of economic output brought social benefits in the form of labor-saving products, lower prices, and advances in transportation and communications. The benefits and liabilities sometimes seemed inextricably interconnected. The sewing machine, for example, created thousands of new factory jobs, made available a wider variety of clothing, and eased the lives of millions of housewives. At the same time, it encouraged avaricious entrepreneurs to operate sweatshops in which the immigrant poor—often vulnerable young women—toiled long hours for pitifully low wages (discussed further in Chapter 21).

For those who fell by the wayside in this era of spectacular economic growth, the cost could be measured in bankrupted companies and shattered dreams. John D. Rockefeller put things with characteristic bluntness when he said he wanted "only the big ones, only those who have already proved they can do a big business" in the Standard Oil Trust. "As for the others, unfortunately they will have to die."

The cost was high, too, for millions of American workers, immigrant and native-born alike. The vast expansion of new products was built on the backs of an army of laborers who were paid subsistence wages and who could be fired on a moment's notice when hard times or new technologies made them expendable.

Industrial growth often devastated the environment as well. Rivers fouled by oil or chemical waste, skies filled with clouds of soot, and a landscape littered with reeking garbage and toxic materials bore mute witness to the relentless drive for efficiency and profit.

> Rockefeller said he wanted "only the big ones, only those who have already proved they can do a big business. As for the others, unfortunately they will have to die."

Whatever the final balance sheet of social gains and costs, one thing was clear: the United States had muscled its way onto the world stage as an industrial titan. The ambition and drive of countless inventors, financiers, managerial innovators, and marketing wizards had combined to lay the groundwork for a new social and economic order in the twentieth century.

The New South

The South entered the industrial era far more slowly than the Northeast. As late as 1900, total southern cotton-mill output, for example, remained little more than half that of the mills within a thirty-mile radius of Providence, Rhode Island. Moreover, the South's $509 average per capita income was less than half that of northerners.

The reasons for the South's late economic blossoming are not hard to discern. The Civil War's physical devastation, racism, the scarcity

INDUSTRIAL POLLUTION Although some Americans celebrated factory smoke as a sign of industrial growth, those who lived downwind, such as the longshoreman in this Thomas Nast cartoon, often suffered from respiratory diseases and other ailments. For him as well as for other Americans, the price of industrial progress often was pollution. (© Bettmann/Corbis)

of southern towns and cities, lack of capital, illiteracy, northern control of financial markets and patents, and a low rate of technological innovation crippled efforts by southern business leaders to promote industrialization. Economic progress was also impeded by the myth of the Lost Cause, which, through its nostalgic portrayal of pre–Civil War society, perpetuated an image of the South as traditional and unchanging. As a result, southern industrialization inched forward haltingly and was shaped in distinctive ways.

Obstacles to Economic Development

Much of the South's difficulty in industrializing arose from its lack of capital and the devastation of the Civil War. So many southern banks failed during the Civil War that by 1865 the South, with more than a quarter of the nation's population, possessed just 2 percent of its banks. The federal government policies added to the banking problem by requiring anyone wishing to start a bank to have $50,000 in capital. Few southerners could meet this standard.

With banks in short supply, country merchants and storekeepers became bankers by default, lending supplies rather than cash to local farmers in return for a lien, or mortgage, on their crops (see Chapter 16). The burden of paying these liens trapped farmers on their own land and created a shortage of the labor needed for industrial expansion.

The shift from planting corn to specializing in either cotton or tobacco made small southern farmers particularly vulnerable to the fluctuations of commercial agriculture. When the price of cotton tumbled in national and international markets from eleven cents per pound in 1875 to less than five cents in 1894, well under the cost of production, many southern farmers grew desperate.

The South's chronic shortage of funds affected the economy in indirect ways as well, by limiting the resources available for education. During Reconstruction, northern philanthropists together with the Freedmen's Bureau, the American Missionary Association, and other relief agencies had begun a modest expansion of public schooling for both blacks and whites. But Georgia and many other southern states operated segregated schools and refused to tax property for school support until 1889. As a result, school attendance remained low, severely limiting the number of educated people able to staff technical and managerial positions in business and industry.

Southern states, like those in the North, often contributed the modest funds they had to war veterans' pensions. In this way, southern state governments built a white patronage system for Confederate veterans and helped reinforce southerners' idealization of the old Confederacy—the South's Lost Cause. As late as 1911, veterans' pensions in Georgia ate up 22 percent of the state's entire budget, leaving little for economic or educational development.

The New South Creed and Southern Industrialization

Despite these obstacles, energetic southern newspaper editors such as **Henry W. Grady** of the *Atlanta Constitution* and Henry Watterson of the *Louisville Courier Journal* championed the doctrine that became known as the New South creed. The South's rich coal and timber resources and cheap labor, they proclaimed in their papers, made it a natural site for industrial development.

The movement to industrialize the South gained momentum in the 1880s. To attract northern capital, southern states offered tax exemptions for new businesses, set up industrial and agricultural expositions, and leased prison convicts to serve as cheap labor. Florida, Texas, and other states gave huge tracts of lands to railroads, whose expansion in turn stimulated the birth of new towns and villages. Other states sold forest and mineral rights on nearly 6 million acres of federal lands to speculators, mostly from the North, who significantly expanded the production of iron, sulfur, coal, and lumber.

Following the lead of their northern counterparts, the southern iron and steel industries expanded as well. Birmingham, Alabama, founded in 1871 in a region blessed with rich deposits of coal, limestone, and iron ore, grew in less than three decades to a bustling city with noisy railroad yards and roaring blast furnaces. By 1900, it was the nation's largest pig-iron shipper. In these same years, Chattanooga, Tennessee, housed nine furnaces, seventeen foundries, and numerous machine shops.

As large-scale recruiters of black workers, the southern iron and steel mills contributed to the migration of blacks to the cities. By 1900, 20 percent of the southern black population was urban. Many urban blacks toiled as domestics or in similar menial capacities, but others entered the industrial work force. Southern industry reflected the patterns of racial segregation in southern life. Tobacco companies used black workers, particularly women, to clean the tobacco leaves while white women, at a different location, ran the machines that made cigarettes. The burgeoning textile mills were lily-white. In the iron and steel industry, blacks, who comprised 60 percent of the unskilled work force by 1900, had practically no chance of advancement. Nevertheless, in a rare reversal of the usual pattern, southern blacks in the iron and steel industry had a higher skill level and on average earned more than did southern white textile workers.

Black miners were also recruited by the West Virginia coal industry that lured them with free transportation, high wages, and company housing. The coal boom at first forced companies to pay similar wages to blacks and whites, and they initially joined biracial labor unions. But the depression of 1893 weakened the unions and workers became increasingly confined to separate jobs.

Southern segregation, while restricting black employment in many ways, opened up new opportunities for black barbers, doctors, and businessmen to work with black customers. Nevertheless, economic opportunities for blacks remained severely limited. In lumbering, which was the South's largest industry, large numbers of blacks worked in the turpentine industry, collecting sap from trees. In good times, wages could be better than those offered to farm laborers, but during economic downturns workers were laid off or confined to work camps by vagrancy laws and armed guards.

The Southern Mill Economy

Unlike the urban-based southern iron and steel industry, the textile mills that mushroomed in the southern countryside in the 1880s often became catalysts for the formation of new towns and villages. In these mill towns, country ways and values suffused the new industrial workplace.

The cotton-mill economy grew largely in the Piedmont, the highland country stretching from central Virginia to northern Georgia and Alabama. The Piedmont had long been the South's backcountry, a land of subsistence farming and limited roads. But postwar railroad construction sparked a period of intense town building and textile-mill expansion. By 1920, the South was the nation's leading textile-mill center. Augusta, Georgia, with 2,800 mill workers, became known as the Lowell of the South, named after the mill town in Massachusetts where industrialization had flourished earlier. The expansion of the textile industry nurtured promoters' visions of a new, more prosperous, industrialized South.

Sharecroppers and tenant farmers at first hailed the new cotton mills as a way out of rural poverty. But appearances were deceptive. The chief cotton-mill promoters were drawn from the same ranks of merchants, lawyers, doctors, and bankers who had profited from the commercialization of southern agriculture (and from the misfortunes of poor black and white tenant farmers and sharecroppers trapped in the new system). Cotton-mill entrepreneurs shamelessly exploited their workers, paying just seven to eleven cents an hour, 30 percent to 50 percent less than what comparable mill workers in New England were paid.

The mills dominated most Piedmont textile communities. The mill operator not only built and owned the workers' housing and the company store but also supported the village church, financed the local elementary school, and pried into the morals and behavior of the mill hands. To prevent workers from moving from one mill to another, the mill owner usually paid them just once a month, often in scrip—a certificate redeemable only in goods from the company store. Since few families had enough money to get through a month, they often overspent and fell behind in their payments. The charges were deducted from workers' wages the following month. In this way, the mill drew workers and their families into a cycle of indebtedness very much like that faced by sharecroppers and tenant farmers.

To help make ends meet, mill workers kept their own garden patches and raised chickens, cows, and pigs. Southern mill hands thus brought communal farm values, long associated with large farm families and nurtured through cooperative planting and harvesting, into the mills themselves. Although they had to adapt to machine-paced work and received barely enough pay to live on, the working poor in the mill districts, like their prewar counterparts in the North, eased the shift from rural to village-industrial life by embracing a cooperative country ethic.

As northern cotton mills did before the Civil War, southern textile companies exploited the cheap rural labor around them, settling transplanted farm people in paternalistic company-run villages. Using these tactics, the industry underwent a period of steady growth.

The Southern Industrial Lag

Industrialization progressed at a slower rate in the South than in the North and depended on outside financing, technology, and expertise. The late-nineteenth-century southern economy remained essentially in a colonial status, dominated by northern industries and financial syndicates. U.S. Steel, for example, controlled the Birmingham foundries and in 1900 priced Birmingham steel according to the "Pittsburgh plus" formula based on the price of Pittsburgh steel, plus the freight costs of shipping from Pittsburgh. As a result, southerners paid higher prices for steel than northerners, despite cheaper production costs.

An array of factors thus combined to retard industrialization in the South. Banking regulations requiring large reserves, scarce capital, wartime debts, lack of industrial experience, a segregated labor force, discrimination against blacks, and control by profit-hungry northern enterprises all hampered the region's economic development. Dragged down by a poorly educated white population and by a largely unskilled black population, southern industry languished. Not until after the turn of the century did southern industry undergo the restructuring and consolidation that had occurred in northern business enterprise two decades earlier.

As in the North, industrialization brought significant environmental damage, including polluted rivers and streams, decimated forests, grimy coal-mining towns, and soot-infested steel-making cities. Although Henry Grady's vision of a New South may have inspired many southerners to

> To prevent workers from moving from one mill to another, the mill owner usually paid them just once a month, often in scrip—a certificate redeemable only in goods from the company store.

work toward industrialization, economic growth in the South, limited as it was by outside forces, progressed in its own distinctly regional way.

Factories and the Work Force

Industrialization proceeded unevenly nationwide, and most late-nineteenth-century Americans still worked in small shops. But as the century unfolded, large factories with armies of workers sprang onto the industrial scene. The pattern of change was evident. Between 1860 and 1900, the number of industrial workers jumped from 885,000 to 3.2 million, and the trend toward large-scale production became unmistakable.

From Workshop to Factory

The transition to a factory economy came not as an earthquake but rather as a series of seismic jolts varying in strength and duration. Whether they occurred quickly or slowly, however, the changes in factory production had a profound impact on artisans and unskilled laborers alike, because they involved a fundamental restructuring of work habits and a new emphasis on workplace discipline. The impact of these changes can be seen by examining the boot and shoe industry. As late as the 1840s, most shoes were custom-made by skilled artisans who worked in small, independent shops. Shoemakers were aristocrats in the world of labor. Taught in an apprentice system, they took pride in their work and controlled the quality of their products.

A distinctive working-class culture subdivided along ethnic lines evolved among these shoemakers. Foreign-born English, German, and Irish workers set up ethnic trade organizations and joined affiliated benevolent associations. Bound together by religious and ethnic ties, they observed weddings and funerals according to old-country traditions, relaxed together at the local saloon after work, and helped one another weather accidents or sicknesses.

As early as the 1850s, even before the widespread use of machinery, changes in the ready-made shoe trade had eroded the status of skilled labor. The manufacturing process was broken down into a sequence of repetitive, easily mastered tasks. Thus, instead of crafting a pair of shoes from start to finish, each team member specialized in only one part of the process, such as attaching the heel or polishing the leather.

In the 1880s, shoe factories became larger and more mechanized, and traditional skills largely vanished. Shoe companies replaced skilled operatives with lower-paid, less-skilled women and children. By 1890, women made up more than 35 percent of the work force. Like the laborer whose machine nailed heels on forty-eight hundred shoes a day, even "skilled" workers in the new factories found themselves performing numbingly repetitive tasks.

The Hardships of Industrial Labor

The expansion of the factory system spawned an unprecedented demand for unskilled labor. By the 1880s, nearly one-third of the 750,000 workers employed in the railroad and steel industries, for example, were common laborers.

In the construction trades and the garment-making industries, unskilled laborers were hired under the so-called contract system by a subcontractor who took responsibility for employee relations. These common workers were seasonal help, hired in times of need and laid off in slack periods. The steel industry employed them to shovel ore in the yards and to move ingots inside the mills. The foremen drove the gangs hard; in the Pittsburgh area, the workers called the foremen "pushers."

Notoriously transient, unskilled laborers drifted from city to city and from industry to industry. In the late 1870s, unskilled laborers earned $1.30 a day, while bricklayers and blacksmiths earned more than $3. Only unskilled southern mill workers, whose wages averaged a meager eighty-four cents a day, earned less.

Unskilled and skilled workers alike worked up to twelve-hour shifts and faced grave hazards to their health and safety. Children were the most vulnerable. In the coal mines and cotton mills, child laborers typically entered the work force at age eight or nine. In the cotton mills, children could be injured by the unprotected pulley belts that powered the machines or develop brown lung disease, a crippling illness caused by breathing in cotton dust. In the coal industry, where children were commonly employed to remove pieces of slate from the conveyor belts, the cloud of coal dust that swirled around them gave them black lung disease—a disorder that leads to emphysema and heart failure.

In addition to facing these workplace hazards, working children often fell behind in their schooling. Pressured by families that needed additional

"Wherever the heat is most insupportable, the flames most scorching, the smoke and soot most choking, there we are certain to find compatriots bent and wasted in toil."

income and by the desire to have some spending money of their own, many children forged work permits and their birth certificates to avoid the compulsory schooling laws (see Chapter 19) to enter the mills and the mines. This lack of education, plus the physical trauma to their bodies, would often exclude them from better-paying jobs as adults.

For adult workers, the railroad industry was one of the most perilous. In 1889, the first year the Interstate Commerce Commission compiled reliable statistics, almost two thousand rail workers were killed on the job and more than twenty thousand injured.

Those who were maimed and disfigured by industrial accidents were further ostracized when San Francisco, Chicago, and other cities passed ordinances in the 1880s that removed "unsightly beggars" from the streets. The overall effect of these laws was to make those handicapped by industrial accidents invisible to the general population at large and to hamstring efforts to force companies to adopt more effective safety regulations.

Disabled workers and widows received minimal financial aid from employers. Until the 1890s, the courts considered employer negligence one of the normal risks borne by employees. Railroad and factory owners fought the adoption of state safety and health standards on the grounds that the cost would be excessive. For sickness and accident benefits, workers joined fraternal organizations and ethnic clubs, part of whose monthly dues benefited those in need. But in most cases, the amounts set aside were too low to be of much help. When a worker was killed or maimed in an accident, the family had to rely on relatives or friends for support.

Immigrant Labor

As we shall see in more detail in Chapter 19, factory owners turned to unskilled immigrants for the muscle they needed in dangerous and undesirable jobs. Poverty-stricken French Canadians filled the most menial positions in northeastern textile mills. On the West Coast, Chinese immigrants performed the dirtiest and most physically demanding jobs in mining, canning, and railroad construction.

Writing home in the 1890s, eastern European immigrants described the hazardous and draining work in the steel mills. "Wherever the heat is most insupportable, the flames most scorching, the smoke and soot most choking, there we are certain to find compatriots bent and wasted in toil," reported one Hungarian. Yet those immigrants disposed to live frugally in a boardinghouse and to

work an eighty-four-hour week could save fifteen dollars a month, far more than they could have earned in their homeland.

Although most immigrants worked hard, few adjusted easily to the fast pace of the factory. Factory operations were relentless, dictated by the unvarying speed of the machines. A brochure used by the International Harvester Corporation to teach English to its Polish workers promoted the "proper" values. Lesson I read:

I hear the whistle. I must hurry.
I hear the five minute whistle.
It is time to go into the shop.
I take my check from the gate board and hang it on the department board.
I change my clothes and get ready to work.
The starting whistle blows.
I eat my lunch.
It is forbidden to eat until then.
The whistle blows at five minutes of starting time.
I get ready to go to work.
I work until the whistle blows to quit.
I leave my place nice and clean.
I put all my clothes in the locker.
I must go home.

As this "lesson" reveals, factory work tied the immigrants to a rigid timetable very different from the pace of farm life.

When immigrant workers resisted the tempo of factory work, drank on the job, or took unexcused absences, employers used a variety of tactics to enforce discipline. Some sponsored temperance societies and Sunday schools to teach punctuality and sobriety. Others cut wages and put workers on the piecework system, paying them only for the items produced. Employers sometimes also provided low-cost housing to gain leverage against work stoppages; if workers went on strike, the boss could simply evict them.

In the case of immigrants from southern Europe whose skin colors were often darker than northern Europeans', employers asserted that the workers were nonwhite and thus did not deserve the same compensation as native-born Americans. Because the concept of "whiteness" in the United States bestowed a sense of privilege and the automatic extension of the rights of citizenship, Irish, Greek, Italian, Jewish, and a host of other immigrants, although of the Caucasian race, were also considered nonwhite. Rather than a fixed category based on biological differences, the concept of race was thus used to justify the harsh treatment of foreign-born labor.

TEXTILE WORKERS Young children like this one often were used in the textile mills because their small fingers could tie together broken threads more easily than those of adults. *(Library of Congress)*

Women and Work in Industrial America

Women's work experiences, like those of men, were shaped by marital status, social class, and race. Upper-class white married women widely accepted an ideology of "separate spheres" (as discussed in Chapter 19) and remained at home, raised children, and looked after the household. The well-to-do hired maids and cooks to ease their burdens.

Working-class married women, in contrast, often had to contribute to the financial support of the family. In fact, working for wages at home by sewing, button-making, taking in boarders, or doing laundry had predated industrialization. In the late nineteenth century, unscrupulous urban entrepreneurs exploited this captive work force.

In the clothing industry, manufacturers hired out finishing tasks to lower-class married women and their children, who labored long hours in crowded apartments.

Young, working-class single women often viewed factory work as an opportunity. In 1870, 13 percent of all women worked outside the home, the majority as cooks, maids, cleaning ladies, and laundresses. But most working women intensely disliked the long hours, low pay, and social stigma of being a "servant." When jobs in industry expanded in the last quarter of the century, growing numbers of single white women abandoned domestic employment for better-paying work in the textile, food-processing, and garment industries. Discrimination barred black working women from following this path. Between 1870 and 1900, the number of women of

PENNSYLVANIA CHILD SLATE PICKERS Child slate pickers risked having fingers torn off, developing black lung disease, and falling into the machinery where they could be crushed to death. *(Library of Congress)*

all races working outside the home nearly tripled. By the turn of the century, women made up 17 percent of the country's labor force.

A variety of factors propelled the rise in the employment of single women. Changes in agriculture prompted many young farmwomen to seek

WOMEN IN THE WORKPLACE The women in this photograph are testing their typing skills at a civil service exam in Chicago in the 1890s. The expansion of banking, insurance, and a variety of other businesses opened up new career opportunities for women as secretaries, stenographers, and typists. *(Chicago Historical Society)*

employment in the industrial sector (discussed further in Chapter 19), and immigrant parents often sent their daughters to the factories to supplement meager family incomes. Plant managers welcomed young immigrant women as a ready source of inexpensive unskilled labor. But factory owners treated them as temporary help and kept their wages low. In 1890, young women operating sewing machines earned as little as four dollars for seventy hours of work while their male counterparts made eight.

Despite their paltry wages, long hours, and often unpleasant working conditions, many young women relished earning their own income and joined the work force in increasing numbers. Although the financial support these working women contributed to their families was significant, few working women were paid enough to provide homes for themselves. Rather than fostering their independence, industrial work tied them more deeply to a family economy that depended on their earnings.

When the typewriter and the telephone came into general use in the 1890s, office work provided new employment opportunities, and women with high school educations moved into clerical and secretarial jobs earlier filled by men. They were attracted by the clean, safe working conditions and relatively good pay. First-rate typists could earn six to eight dollars a week, which compared favorably with factory wages. Office work carried higher prestige and generally was steadier than work in the factory or shop.

> "I live in a tenement house, three stories up, where the water comes in through the roof, and I cannot better myself."

Despite the growing number of women workers, the late-nineteenth-century popular press portrayed women's work outside the home as temporary. Few people even considered the possibility that a woman could attain local or even national prominence in the emerging corporate order.

Hard Work and the Gospel of Success

Although women were generally excluded from the equation, influential opinion molders in these years preached that any man could achieve success in the new industrial era. In *Ragged Dick* (1867) and scores of later tales, **Horatio Alger,** a Unitarian minister turned dime novelist, recounted the adventures of poor but honest lads who rose through initiative and self-discipline.

Some critics did not accept this belief. In an 1871 essay, Mark Twain chided the public for its naïveté and suggested that business success was more likely to come to those who lied and cheated. In testimony given in 1883 before a Senate committee investigating labor conditions, a New Yorker named Thomas B. McGuire dolefully recounted how he had been forced out of the horse-cart business by larger, better financed concerns. Declared McGuire, "I live in a tenement house, three stories up, where the water comes in through the roof, and I cannot better myself. … Why? Simply because this present system … is all for the privileged classes, nothing for the man who produces the wealth." Only with starting capital of $10,000—then a large sum—said McGuire, could the independent entrepreneur hope to compete with the large companies.

What are the facts? Studies of nearly two hundred of the largest corporations reveal that few workers rose from poverty to colossal wealth. Ninety-five percent of the industrial leaders came from middle- and upper-class backgrounds. The best chance for native-born working-class Americans to get ahead was to master a skill and to rise to the top in a small company. Although only a few reaped immense fortunes, many improved their standard of living.

The different fates of immigrant workers in San Francisco show the possibilities and perils of moving up within the working class. In the 1860s, the Irish-born Donahue brothers grew wealthy from the Union Iron Works they had founded, where six hundred men built heavy equipment for the mining industry. In contrast, the nearly fifteen thousand Chinese workers who returned to the city after the Central Pacific's rail line was completed in 1869 were consigned by prejudice to work in cigar, textile, and other light-industry factories. Even successful Chinese entrepreneurs faced discrimination. When a Chinese merchant, Mr. Yung, refused to sell out to the wealthy Charles Crocker, a dry-goods merchant turned railroad entrepreneur who was building a mansion on Nob Hill, Crocker built a thirty-foot-high "spite fence" around Yung's house so that it would be completely sealed from view.

Thus, while some skilled workers became owners of their own companies, the opportunities

SHOEWORKERS Shoeworkers pose near their machines in Haverhill, Massachusetts, ca. 1880. For them as well as for others, work became increasingly repetitive and routinized. *(Courtesy of the Trustees of the Haverhill Public Library, Special Collections Department)*

for advancement for unskilled immigrant workers were considerably more limited. Some did move to semiskilled or skilled positions. Yet most immigrants, particularly the Irish, Italians, and Chinese, moved far more slowly than the sons of middle- and upper-class Americans who began with greater educational advantages and family financial backing. The upward mobility possible for such unskilled workers was generally mobility within the working class. Immigrants who got ahead in the late nineteenth century went from rags to respectability, not rags to riches.

One positive economic trend in these years was the rise in real wages, representing gains in actual buying power. Average real wages climbed 31 percent for unskilled workers and 74 percent for skilled workers between 1860 and 1900. Overall gains in purchasing power, however, often were undercut by injuries and unemployment during slack times or economic slumps. The position of unskilled immigrant laborers was particularly shaky. Even during a prosperous year like 1890, one out of every five nonagricultural workers was unemployed at least one month of the year. During the depressions of the 1870s and 1890s, wage cuts, extended layoffs, and irregular employment pushed those at the bottom of the industrial work force to the brink of starvation.

Thus, the overall picture of late-nineteenth-century economic mobility is complex. At the top of the scale, a mere 10 percent of American families owned 73 percent of the nation's wealth in 1890, while less than half of industrial laborers earned more than the five-hundred dollar poverty line annually. In between the very rich and the very poor, skilled immigrants and small shopkeepers improved their economic position significantly. So although the standard of living for millions of Americans rose, the gap between the poor and the well-off remained a yawning abyss.

Labor Unions and Industrial Conflict

Aware that the growth of large corporations gave industrial leaders unprecedented power to control the workplace, labor leaders searched for ways to create broad-based, national organizations that could protect their members. But this drive to create a nationwide labor movement faced many problems. Employers deliberately accentuated ethnic and racial divisions within the work force to hamper unionizing efforts. Skilled crafts workers, moreover, felt little kinship with low-paid common laborers. Divided into different trades, they often saw little

reason to work together. Thus, unionization efforts moved forward slowly and experienced setbacks.

Two groups, the National Labor Union and the Knights of Labor, struggled to build a mass labor movement that would unite skilled and unskilled workers regardless of their specialties. After impressive initial growth, however, both efforts collapsed. Far more effective was the American Federation of Labor (AFL), which represented skilled workers in powerful independent craft unions. The AFL survived and grew, but it represented only a small portion of the total labor force.

With unions weak, labor unrest during economic downturns reached crisis proportions. When pay rates were cut or working conditions became intolerable, laborers walked off the job without union authorization. These actions, called **wildcat strikes** often exploded into violence. The labor crisis of the 1890s, with its strikes and bloodshed, would reshape the legal environment, increase the demand for state regulation, and eventually contribute to a movement for progressive reform.

Organizing Workers

From the eighteenth century on, skilled workers had organized local trade unions to fight wage reductions and provide benefits for their members in times of illness or accident. But the effectiveness of these organizations was limited. The challenge that labor leaders faced in the postwar period was how to boost the unions' clout. Some believed this goal could be achieved by forming one big association that would transcend craft lines and pull in the mass of unskilled workers.

Inspired by this vision of a nationwide labor association, William H. Sylvis, president of the Iron Molders' International Union, an organization of iron-foundry workers, in 1866 called a convention in Baltimore to form a new organization, the **National Labor Union** (NLU). Reflecting the pre–Civil War idealism, the NLU endorsed the eight-hour-day movement, which insisted that labor deserved eight hours for work, eight hours for sleep, and eight hours for personal affairs. Leaders also called for an end to convict labor, for the establishment of a federal department of labor, and for currency and banking reform. To push wage scales higher, they endorsed immigration restriction, especially of Chinese migrants, whom native-born workers blamed for undercutting prevailing wage levels. The NLU under Sylvis's leadership supported the cause of working women and elected a woman as one of its national officers. It urged black workers to organize as well, though in racially separate unions.

Chinese Labor

Despite the protests of white workers who believed that Chinese laborers undercut their wages, business leaders in the 1870s like Charles Crocker, president of the Central Pacific Railroad, argued that the Chinese should be imported to work in the U.S. Although he supported Chinese immigration, Crocker tried to evict a Chinese man who lived near his mansion in San Francisco. The following testimony by Crocker about his Chinese workers was published in an 1881 book by the former U.S. ambassador to China in opposition to the Chinese Exclusion Act that passed the following year.

Q. Do you or do you not believe that Chinese immigration to this country has the same tendency to degrade free white labor as that of Negro slavery in the South?

A. No, sir; because it is not servile labor.

Q. It is not?

A. It is not; it is free labor; just as free as yours or mine. You cannot control a Chinaman unless you pay him for it. You cannot make a contract with him, or his friend, or supposed master, and get his labor unless you pay for it, and pay him for it. ...

Q. When you employed Chinamen, did you employ the individual Chinaman, or did you employ some man to furnish you with a certain number of Chinamen?

A. On any road where we employed them for labor, we always procured them through the house of Sisson, Wallace & Co., here. That house furnished us with Chinamen. They gathered them, one at a time, two, three, four of them in a place, and got them together to make what is called a gang, and each gang is numbered.

Q. Just like mules?

A. Well, sir, we cannot distinguish Chinamen by names very well.

Q. Like mules?

A. Not like mules, but like men. We have treated them like men, and they have treated us like men, and they are men, good and true men. ... We have a foreman, and he keeps the account with the gang, and credits them. ... When the pay day comes, the gang is paid for all the labor of the gang, and then they divide it among themselves.

Q. Does the same thing obtain with the white men?

A. No, sir; we get the individual names of the white men.

Q. You do not pay the individual Chinaman when he works for you?

A. We pay the head-man of the gang.

Q. Some head-man?

A. He is a laborer among them.

Q. You do not pay them in the same manner that you pay white men?

A. In the same manner, except that we cannot keep the names of the Chinamen; it is impossible. We should not know Ah Sin, Ah You, Kong Won, and all such names. We cannot keep their names in the same way, because it is a difficult language. You understand the difficulty. It is not done in that way because they are slaves.

Q. Is it not a kind of servile labor?

A. Not a bit. I give you my word of honor, under oath here, that I do not believe there is a Chinese slave in this State, except it may be a prostitute. I hear of that, but I do not know anything about it. It will be seen from this evidence that the Central Pacific Railroad Company have not imported, through the six companies, or through a wealthy Chinese, or through any one else, any contract-laborers to work on the railroad in question, or on any of the roads controlled by them.

Source: *George F. Seward,* Chinese Immigration in its Social and Economical Aspects *(New York, Charles Scribners Sons, 1881), pp. 140–142.*

QUESTIONS

1. Why does the questioner link Chinese workers to slaves or mules?
2. Why does he focus on how they were paid?
3. What kinds of bias do the questions display?

When Sylvis's own union failed to win a strike in 1867 to improve wages, Sylvis turned to national political reform. He invited a number of reformers to the 1868 NLU convention, including woman suffrage advocates Susan B. Anthony and Elizabeth Cady Stanton, who, according to a reporter, made "no mean impression on the bearded delegates." But when Sylvis suddenly died in 1869, the NLU faded quickly. After a brief incarnation in 1872 as the National Labor Reform party, it vanished from the scene.

The dream of a labor movement that combined skilled and unskilled workers lived on in a new organization, the Noble and Holy Order of the **Knights of Labor,** founded in 1869. Led by Uriah H. Stephens, head of the Garment Cutters of Philadelphia, the Knights welcomed all wage earners. The Knights demanded equal pay for women, an end to child labor and convict labor, and the cooperative employer–employee ownership of factories, mines, and other businesses. At a time when no federal income tax existed, they called for a progressive tax on all earnings, graduated so that higher-income earners would pay more.

The Knights grew slowly at first. But membership rocketed in the 1880s after the eloquent Terence V. Powderly replaced Stephens as the organization's head. In the early 1880s, the Knights of Labor reflected both its idealistic origins and Powderly's collaborative vision. Powderly opposed strikes, which he considered "a relic of barbarism," and organized producer and consumer cooperatives. A teetotaler, he also urged temperance upon the membership. Powderly advocated the admission of blacks into local Knights of Labor assemblies, although he recognized the strength of racism and allowed southern local assemblies to be segregated. Under his leadership, the Knights welcomed women members; by 1886, women organizers had recruited thousands of workers, and women made up an estimated 10 percent of the union's membership.

> "The Wabash victory is with the Knights, no such victory has ever before been secured in this or any other country."

Powderly supported restrictions on immigration and a total ban on Chinese immigration. In 1877, San Francisco workers demonstrating for an eight-hour workday, destroyed twenty-five Chinese-run laundries and terrorized the local Chinese population. In 1880, both major party platforms included anti-Chinese immigration plans. Two years later, Congress passed the Chinese Exclusion Act, placing a ten-year moratorium on Chinese immigration. The ban was extended in 1902 and not repealed until 1943.

Powderly's greatest triumph came in 1885. In that year, when Jay Gould tried to get rid of the Knights of Labor on his Wabash railroad by firing active union members, Powderly and his executive board instructed all Knights on the Wabash line to walk off the job. This action crippled the Wabash's operations. To the nation's amazement, Gould met with Powderly and canceled his campaign against the Knights of Labor. "The Wabash victory is with the Knights," declared a St. Louis newspaper; "no such victory has ever before been secured in this or any other country."

Membership in the Knights of Labor soared. By 1886, more than seven hundred thousand workers were organized in nearly six thousand locals. Turning to political action that fall, the Knights mounted campaigns in nearly two hundred towns and cities nationwide, electing several mayors and judges (Powderly himself had served as mayor of Scranton since 1878). They secured passage of state laws banning convict labor and federal laws against the importation of foreign contract labor. Business executives warned that the Knights could cripple the economy and take over the country if they chose.

But the organization's strength soon waned. Workers became disillusioned when a series of unauthorized strikes failed in 1886. By the late 1880s, the Knights of Labor was a shadow of its former self.

As the Knights of Labor declined, another national labor organization, pursuing more immediate and practical goals, was gaining strength. The skilled craft unions had long been uncomfortable with labor organizations like the Knights that welcomed skilled and unskilled alike. They were also concerned that the Knights' broad reform goals would undercut their own commitment to better wages and protecting the interests of their particular crafts. The break came in May 1886 when the craft unions left the Knights of Labor to form the **American Federation of Labor** (AFL).

The AFL replaced the Knights' grand visions with practical tactics aimed at bread-and-butter issues. **Samuel Gompers,** the immigrant cigar maker who became head of the AFL in 1886 and led it until his death in 1924, believed in "trade unionism, pure and simple." For Gompers, higher wages were the necessary base to enable working class families to live decently, with respect and dignity. The stocky, mustachioed labor leader argued that labor, to stand up to the corporations, would have to harness the bargaining power of skilled workers, whom employers could not easily replace, and concentrate on the practical goals of raising wages and reducing hours.

THE FIRST LABOR DAY PARADE, 1882 Thousands of workers, led by the Knights of Labor, marched in the first Labor Day Parade in New York. As the numerous American flags in this contemporary illustration suggest, the workers believed that labor deserved substantial credit for building the American nation. *(Granger Collection)*

A master tactician, Gompers believed the trend toward large-scale industrial organization necessitated a comparable degree of organization by labor. He also recognized, however, that the skilled craft unions that made up the AFL retained a strong sense of independence. To persuade crafts workers from the various trades to join forces without violating their sense of craft autonomy, Gompers organized the AFL as a federation of trade unions, each retaining control of its own members but all linked by an executive council that coordinated strategy during boycotts and strike actions. "We want to make the trade union movement under the AFL as distinct as the billows, yet one as the sea," he told a national convention.

Focusing the federation's efforts on short-term improvements in wages and hours, Gompers at first sidestepped divisive political issues. The new organization's platform did, however, demand an eight-hour workday, employers' liability for workers' injuries, and mine safety laws. Although women participated in many craft unions, the AFL did little to recruit women workers after 1894 because Gompers and others believed that women workers undercut men's wages. By 1904, under Gompers's careful tutelage, the AFL had grown to more than 1.6 million strong.

Although the unions held up an ideal toward which many might strive, labor organizations before 1900 remained weak. Less than 5 percent of the work force joined union ranks. Split between skilled artisans and common laborers, separated along ethnic and religious lines, and divided over tactics, the unions battled with only occasional effectiveness against the growing power of corporate enterprise. Lacking financial resources, they typically watched from the sidelines when unorganized workers launched wildcat strikes that sometimes turned violent.

Strikes and Labor Unrest

Americans lived with a high level of violence from the nation's beginnings, and the nineteenth century—with its international and civil wars, urban riots, and Indian-white conflict—was no exception. Terrible labor clashes toward the end of the century were part of this continuing pattern, but they nevertheless shocked and dismayed contemporaries. From 1881 to 1905, close to thirty-seven thousand strikes erupted, in which nearly 7 million workers participated.

The first major wave of strikes began in 1873 when a Wall Street crash triggered a stock-market

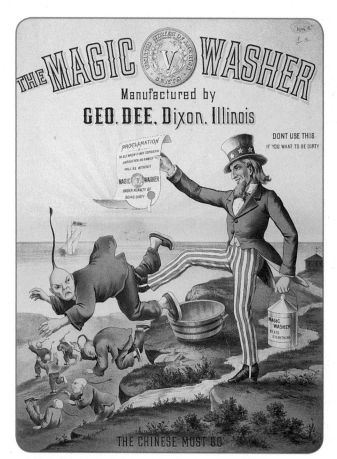

ETHNIC AND RACIAL HATRED Conservative business owners used racist advertising such as this trade card stigmatizing Chinese laundry workers to promote their own products and to associate their company with patriotism. *(Library of Congress)*

PINKERTONS SURRENDER AT THE HOMESTEAD STEEL STRIKE, 1892 After a gun battle, Pinkerton security forces surrender to strikers at the Homestead, Pennsylvania, steel works. Companies cited worker violence such as this as justification for government suppression of labor unrest. *(Granger Collection)*

panic and a major depression. Six thousand businesses closed the following year, and many more cut wages and laid off workers. Striking Pennsylvania coal miners were fired and evicted from their homes. The tension turned deadly in 1877 during a wildcat railroad strike. Ignited by wage reductions on the Baltimore and Ohio Railroad in July, the strike exploded up and down the railroad lines, spreading to New York, Pittsburgh, St. Louis, Kansas City, Chicago, and San Francisco. Rioters in Pittsburgh torched Union Depot. By the time newly installed president Rutherford B. Hayes had called out the troops and quelled the strike two weeks later, nearly one hundred people had died, and two-thirds of the nation's railroads stood idle.

> "If the club of the policeman, knocking out the brains of the rioter, will answer, then well and good, [but if not] then bullets and bayonets … constitute the one remedy."

The railroad strike stunned middle-class America. The religious press responded hysterically. "If the club of the policeman, knocking out the brains of the rioter, will answer, then well and good," declared one Congregationalist journal, "[but if not] then bullets and bayonets … constitute the one remedy." The same middle-class Americans who worried about Jay Gould and the corporate abuse of power grew terrified of mob violence.

Employers capitalized on the public hysteria to crack down on labor. Many required their workers to sign "yellow dog" contracts in which they promised not to strike or join a union. Some hired Pinkerton agents, a private police force, to defend their factories and, when necessary, turned to the federal government and the U.S. army to suppress labor unrest.

Although the economy recovered, more strikes and violence followed in the 1880s. On May 1, 1886, 340,000 workers walked off their jobs in support of the campaign for an eight-hour workday.

Three days later, Chicago police shot and killed four strikers at the McCormick Harvester plant. At a protest rally the next evening in the city's Haymarket Square, someone threw a bomb, killing or fatally wounding seven policemen. In response, the police fired wildly into the crowd and killed four demonstrators.

Public reaction was immediate. Business leaders and middle-class citizens lashed out at labor activists and particularly at the sponsors of the Haymarket meeting, most of whom were associated with a German-language anarchist newspaper that advocated the violent overthrow of capitalism. Eight men were arrested. Although no evidence connected them directly to the bomb throwing, all were convicted of murder, and four were executed. One committed suicide in prison. In Haymarket's aftermath, still more Americans became convinced that the nation was in the grip of a deadly foreign conspiracy, and animosity toward labor unions intensified.

Confrontations between capital and labor became particularly violent in the West. When the Mine Owners' Protective Association cut wages at work sites along Idaho's Coeur d'Alene River in 1892, the miners, who were skilled dynamiters, blew up a mill and captured the guards sent to defend it. Mine owners responded by mustering the Idaho National Guard to round up the men and cripple their union.

Back east that same year, armed conflict broke out during the **Homestead Strike** at the Carnegie Steel Company plant in Homestead, Pennsylvania. To destroy the union, managers had cut wages and locked out the workers. When workers fired on the armed men from the Pinkerton Detective Agency who came to protect the plant, a battle broke out. Seven union members and three Pinkertons died. A week later the governor sent National Guardsmen to restore order. The union crushed, the mills resumed full operation a month later.

The most systematic use of troops to smash union power came in 1894 during a strike against the Pullman Palace Car Company. In 1880 George Pullman, a manufacturer of elegant dining and sleeping cars for the nation's railroads, had constructed a factory and town, called Pullman, ten miles south of Chicago. The carefully planned community provided solid brick houses for the workers, beautiful parks and playgrounds, and even its own sewage-treatment plant. Pullman also closely policed workers' activities, outlawed saloons, and insisted that his properties turn a profit.

When the depression of 1893 hit, Pullman slashed workers' wages without reducing their rents. In reaction, thousands of workers joined the newly formed American Railway Union and went on strike. They were led by a fiery young organizer, **Eugene V. Debs,** who vowed "to strip the mask of hypocrisy from the pretended philanthropist and show him to the world as an oppressor of labor." Union members working for the nation's largest railroads refused to switch Pullman cars, paralyzing rail traffic in and out of Chicago, one of the nation's premier rail hubs.

In response, the General Managers' Association, an organization of top railroad executives, set out to break the union. The General Managers imported strikebreakers from among jobless easterners and asked U.S. attorney general Richard Olney, who sat on the board of directors of three major railroad networks, for a federal injunction (court order) against the strikers for allegedly refusing to move railroad cars carrying U.S. mail.

In fact, union members had volunteered to switch mail cars onto any trains that did not carry Pullman cars, and it was the railroads' managers who were delaying the mail by refusing to send their trains without the full complement of cars. Nevertheless, Olney, supported by President Grover Cleveland and citing the Sherman Anti-Trust Act, secured an injunction against the leaders of the American Railway Union for restraint of commerce. When the union refused to order its members back to work, Debs was arrested, and federal troops poured in. During the ensuing riot, workers burned seven hundred freight cars, thirteen people died, and fifty-three were wounded. By July 18, the strike had been crushed.

By playing upon a popular identification of strikers with anarchism and violence, crafty corporate leaders persuaded state and federal officials to cripple organized labor's ability to bargain with business. When the Supreme Court (in the 1895 case *In re Debs*) upheld Debs's prison sentence and legalized the use of injunctions against labor unions, the judicial system gave business a potent new weapon with which to restrain labor organizers.

Yet organizers persisted. In 1897, the feisty Irish-born Mary Harris Jones, known as **Mother Jones,** persuaded coal miners in Pennsylvania to join the United Mine Workers of America, a union founded seven years earlier. She staged parades of children, invited workers' wives to stockpile food, and dramatized the importance of militant mothers fighting for their families. Her efforts were successful. Wage reductions were restored because no large companies dominated the industry and the owners needed to restore production.

Despite the achievements of the United Mine Workers, whose members had climbed to three hundred thousand by 1900, the successive attempts

MOTHER JONES Tough, fearless Mary Harris Jones, better known as "Mother Jones," supported coal mine strikes in West Virginia and Pennsylvania. At one strike, she led a group of fifty-seven little girls carrying placards that read: "Our Papas Aren't Scared." *(Library of Congress)*

"If the United States, like the countries of the Old World, are also to grow vast crops of poor, desperate, dissatisfied, nomadic, miserably-waged populations, ... then our republican experiment, notwithstanding all its surface-successes, is at heart an unhealthy failure."

by the National Labor Union, Knights of Labor, American Federation of Labor, and American Railway Union to build a national working class labor movement achieved only limited success. Aggressive employer associations and conservative state and local officials hamstrung their efforts. In sharp contrast to Great Britain and Germany, where state officials often mediated disputes between labor and capital, federal and state officials in the United States increasingly sided with manufacturers. Ineffective in the political arena, blocked by state officials, divided by ethnic differences, harassed by employers, and frustrated by court decisions, American unions failed to expand their base of support. Post–Civil War labor turmoil had sapped the vitality of organized labor and given it a negative public image that it would not shed until the 1930s.

Social Thinkers Probe for Alternatives

Widespread industrial violence was particularly unsettling when examined in the context of working-class poverty. In 1879, after observing three men rummaging through garbage to find food, the poet and journalist Walt Whitman wrote, "If the United States, like the countries of the Old World, are also to grow vast crops of poor, desperate, dissatisfied, nomadic, miserably-waged populations, such as we see looming upon us of late years … then our republican experiment, notwithstanding all its surface-successes, is at heart an unhealthy failure." Whitman's bleak speculation was part of a general public debate over the social meaning of the new industrial order. At stake was a larger issue: should government become the mechanism for helping the poor and regulating big business?

Defenders of capitalism preached the laissez-faire ("hands-off") argument, insisting that government should never attempt to control business. They buttressed their case by citing Scottish economist Adam Smith, who had argued in *The Wealth of Nations* (1776) that self-interest acted as an "invisible hand" in the marketplace, automatically regulating the supply of and demand for goods and services. In "The Gospel of Wealth," an influential essay published in 1889, Andrew Carnegie justified laissez-faire by applying the evolutionary theories of British social scientist Herbert Spencer to human society. "The law of competition," Carnegie argued, "may be sometimes hard for the individual, [but] it is best for the race, because it insures the survival of the fittest in every department."

Tough-minded Yale professor **William Graham Sumner** shared Carnegie's disapproval of government interference. His combative book *What Social Classes Owe to Each Other* (1883) applied the evolutionary theories of British naturalist Charles Darwin to human society. In an early statement of what became known as **Social Darwinism,** Sumner asserted that inexorable natural laws controlled the social order: "A drunkard in the gutter is just where he ought to be … The law of survival of the fittest was not made by man, and it cannot be abrogated by man. We can only, by interfering with it, produce the survival of the unfittest." The state, declared Sumner, owed its citizens nothing but law, order, and basic political rights.

"A drunkard in the gutter is just where he ought to be … The law of survival of the fittest was not made by man, and it cannot be abrogated by man."

Sumner's argument did not go unchallenged. In *Dynamic Sociology* (1883), Lester Frank Ward, a geologist, argued that contrary to Sumner's claim, the supposed "laws" of nature could be circumvented by human will. Just as scientists had applied their knowledge to breeding superior livestock, government experts could use the power of the state to regulate big business, protect society's weaker members, and prevent the heedless exploitation of natural resources.

Other social theorists offered more utopian solutions to the problems of poverty and social unrest. Henry George, a self-taught San Francisco newspaper editor and economic theorist, proposed to solve the nation's uneven distribution of wealth through what he called the single tax. In *Progress and Poverty* (1879), he noted that speculators reaped huge profits from the rising price of land that they neither developed nor improved. By taxing this "unearned increment," the government could obtain the funds necessary to ameliorate the misery caused by industrialization. The result would bring the benefits of socialism—a state controlled economic system that distributed resources according to need—without socialism's great disadvantage, the stifling of individual initiative. George's program was so popular that he lectured around the country and only narrowly missed being elected mayor of New York in 1886.

The vision of a harmonious industrialized society was vividly expressed in the utopian novel *Looking Backward* (1888) by Massachusetts newspaper editor Edward Bellamy. Cast as a glimpse into the future, Bellamy's novel tells of Julian West, who falls asleep in 1888 and awakens in the year 2000 to find a nation without poverty or strife. In this future world, West learns, a completely centralized, state-run economy and a new religion of solidarity have combined to create a society in which everyone works for the common welfare. Bellamy's vision of a conflict-free society where all share equally in industrialization's benefits so inspired middle-class Americans fearful of corporate power and working-class violence that nearly five hundred local Bellamyite organizations, called Nationalist clubs, sprang up to try to turn his dream into reality.

Ward, George, and Bellamy did not deny the benefits of the existing industrial order; they simply sought to humanize it. These utopian reformers envisioned a harmonious society whose members all worked together.

Marxist socialists advanced a different view. Elaborated by German philosopher and radical agitator Karl Marx (1818–1883) in *Das Kapital* (1867) and other works, **Marxism** rested on the labor theory of value: a proposition (which Adam Smith had also accepted) that the labor required to produce a commodity was the only true measure of that commodity's value. Any profit made by the capitalist employer was "surplus value" appropriated from the exploited workers. As competition among capitalists increased, Marx predicted, wages would decline to starvation levels, and more and more capitalists would be driven out of business. Society would be divided between a shrinking bourgeoisie (capitalists, merchants, and middle-class professionals) and an impoverished proletariat (the workers). The proletariat would then revolt and seize control of the state and of the economy. Although Marx viewed class struggle as the essence of modern history, his eyes were also fixed on the shining vision of the communist millennium that the revolution would eventually usher in—a classless utopia in which the state would "wither away" and all exploitation would cease. To lead the working class in its showdown with capitalism, Marx and his collaborator Friedrich Engels helped found socialist parties in Europe, whose strength grew steadily, beginning in the 1870s.

Despite Marx's keen interest in the United States, Marxism proved to have little appeal in late-nineteenth-century America other than for a tiny group of primarily German-born immigrants. The Marxist-oriented Socialist Labor Party (1877) had attracted only about fifteen hundred members by 1890. More alarming to the public at large was the handful of anarchists, again mostly immigrants, who rejected Marxist discipline and preached the destruction of capitalism, the violent overthrow of the state, and the immediate introduction of a stateless utopia. In 1892, Alexander Berkman, a Russian immigrant anarchist, attempted to assassinate Henry Clay Frick, the manager of Andrew Carnegie's Homestead Steel Works. Entering Frick's office with a pistol, Berkman shot him in the neck and then tried to stab him. A carpenter working in Frick's office overpowered the assailant. Rather than igniting a workers' insurrection that would usher in a new social order as he had hoped, Berkman came away with a long prison sentence. His act confirmed the business stereotype of "labor agitators" as lawless and violent.

CONCLUSION

By 1900, industrialization had propelled the United States into the forefront of the world's major powers, lowered the cost of goods through mass production, generated thousands of jobs, and produced a wide range of new consumer products. Using accounting systems first developed by the railroads and sophisticated new technologies, national corporations had pioneered innovative systems for distributing and marketing their goods. In the steel and oil industries, Andrew Carnegie and John D. Rockefeller had vertically integrated their companies, controlling production from the raw materials to the finished product. Through systematic cost cutting and ruthless underselling of their competitors, they had gained control of most of their industry and lowered prices.

Despite these advantages, most Americans recognized that industrialization's cost was high. The rise of the giant corporations had been achieved through savage competition, exploited workers, shady business practices, polluted factory sites, and the collapse of an economic order built on craft skills. In the South in particular, the devastation of the Civil War and the control of banking and raw materials by northern capitalists encouraged industrialists to adopt a paternalistic, family-oriented approach in the cotton mills and to pay exceedingly low wages.

Outbursts of labor violence, the growth of urban slums, and grinding poverty showed starkly that all was not well in industrial America. Although the Knights of Labor and the American Federation of Labor attempted to organize workers nationally, the labor movement could not control spontaneous wildcat strikes and violence. In response, company owners appealed to government authorities to arrest strikers, obtain court injunctions against union actions, and cripple the ability of labor leaders to expand their organizations.

As a result, Americans remained profoundly ambivalent about the new industrial order. Caught between their desire for the higher standard of living that industrialization made possible and their fears of capitalist power and social chaos, Americans of the 1880s and 1890s sought strategies that would preserve the benefits while eliminating corruption. Efforts to regulate railroads at the state level and such national measures as the Interstate Commerce Act and the Sherman Anti-Trust Act, as well as the fervor with which the ideas of a utopian theorist like Edward Bellamy were embraced, represented early manifestations of this impulse. In the Progressive Era of the early twentieth century, Americans would redouble their efforts to formulate political and social responses to the nation's economic transformation after the Civil War.

KEY TERMS

Jay Gould   (p. 538)

Interstate Commerce Act   (p. 539)

J. Pierpont Morgan   (p. 539)

Andrew Carnegie   (p. 539)

vertical integration   (p. 539)

John D. Rockefeller   (p. 541)

Standard Oil Trust   (p. 541)

Sherman Anti-Trust Act   (p. 542)

Thomas A. Edison   (p. 543)

Henry W. Grady   (p. 549)

Horatio Alger   (p. 554)

wildcat strikes   (p. 556)

National Labor Union   (p. 556)

Knights of Labor   (p. 558)

American Federation of Labor
    (p. 558)

Samuel Gompers   (p. 558)

Homestead Strike   (p. 561)

Eugene V. Debs   (p. 561)

Mother Jones   (p. 561)

William Graham Sumner   (p. 562)

Social Darwinism   (p. 562)

Marxism   (p. 563)

FOR FURTHER REFERENCE

Edward L. Ayers, *The Promise of the New South: Life After Reconstruction* (1992). A comprehensive overview of economic and social change in the post–Civil War South.

Alice Kessler-Harris, *Gendering Labor* (2007). Thoughtful essays on women's roles in labor history.

James D. Schmidt, *Industrial Violence and the Legal Origins of Child Labor* (2010). An important study of the complex forces that opposed child labor laws.

Richard Schneirov, Shelton Stromquist, and Nick Salvatore, eds., *The Pullman Strike and the Crisis of the 1890s: Essays on Labor and Politics* (1999). Surveys the impact of the Pullman strike on politics, the role of the state, and the public controversy over governmental regulation of corporate activity.

Susan M. Schweik, *The Ugly Laws: Disability in Public* (2009). An important study of discriminatory laws directed at people with physical handicaps.

Philip Scranton, *Endless Novelty: Specialty Production and American Industrialization, 1865–1925* (1997). A useful corrective to the argument that large corporations alone account for American economic growth in the post–Civil War era.

T.J. Stiles, *The First Tycoon: The Epic Life of Cornelius Vanderbilt* (2009). An innovative reconstruction of Vanderbilt's secretive life through the use of court records.

Joel A. Tarr, *The Search for the Ultimate Sink: Urban Pollution in Historical Perspective* (1996). An important study of the environmental problems created by industrialization.

Kim Voss, *The Making of American Exceptionalism: The Knights of Labor and Class Formation in the Nineteenth Century* (1993). A comparative analysis of American labor's attempts to mobilize workers in the face of business opposition.

Richard White, *Railroaded: The Transcontinentals and the Making of Modern America* (2011). Argues that the transcontinental railroads' achievements were not worth the corruption and social costs they entailed.

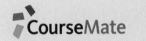

Immigration, Urbanization, and Everyday Life, 1860–1900

SCOTT JOPLIN *(Granger Collection)*

ON A SWELTERING DAY IN AUGUST 1899, Scott Joplin, a young black pianist, signed an unusual contract with his music publisher in Sedalia, Missouri. Instead of receiving the usual one-time fee for his new piano composition, "Maple Leaf Rag," Joplin would earn one cent for every copy sold. The contract signaled a new era in the popular music industry. Over the next two decades, "Maple Leaf Rag" would sell more than half a million copies a year and make Joplin the king of ragtime, the syncopated dance music that had become a national sensation.

Scott Joplin's rise from unknown saloon piano player to renowned composer sheds light not only on the extraordinary expansion of the entertainment industry at the turn of the nineteenth century but also on the class and racial tensions that pervaded popular culture. Joplin published more than seventy-five songs or piano rags before 1917, but his success was undercut by white competitors who stereotyped his compositions as "Negro music" and "Coon songs." His publishers refused to accept his classical compositions, including his opera "Treemonisha." Opera was considered a high art form for the upper classes; blacks, even those with Joplin's talent, could not enter the field. Scott Joplin died in 1917, an admired leader in the entertainment industry whose full genius would not be recognized for another half century. As Joplin's experience revealed, racial discrimination could reinforce the barriers of social class.

Many Americans faced similar difficulties in moving up the economic ladder and adjusting to the changes in popular culture taking place at the turn of the century. American society was slowly shifting from a rural producer economy that stressed work and thrift to an urban consumer economy that emphasized new forms of entertainment, leisure activities, and material possessions.

Many middle-class Americans now enjoyed unheard-of levels of comfort and convenience. Industrialization had opened up new jobs and destroyed older ones, rearranging the occupational structure, altering the distribution of income within society, and sharpening class divisions. These changes, together with the expansion of salaried, white-collar occupations such as teaching and accounting, created new expectations for family life and fostered growing class awareness.

Nowhere were class divisions more visible than in the cities crowded with immigrants where the working class created its own vigorous culture of dance halls, saloons, vaudeville theaters, and amusement parks. Middle-class reformers who strove to remake this working-class culture into their own image of propriety were soon frustrated. In the long run, the culture of the masses would prove more influential in shaping modern America.

BACKYARD BASEBALL, BOSTON, 1906, BY LEWIS HINE Often idealized as a rural pastime, baseball at the turn of the century became immensely popular in cities where professional teams turned the sport into entertainment for the masses. *(Courtesy of George Eastman House, International Museum of Photography and Film)*

The New American City

Everyday life was transformed most visibly in cities. During the late nineteenth century, American cities grew spectacularly (see Table 19.1). Between 1870 and 1900, New Orleans's population increased by nearly 50 percent, Buffalo's tripled, and Chicago's increased more than fivefold. At the start of the new century, Philadelphia, New York, and Chicago all had more than a million residents, and 40 percent of all Americans lived in cities. (In the census, cities were defined as having more than twenty-five hundred inhabitants.) In 1900, New York's 3.4 million

inhabitants almost equaled the nation's entire 1850 urban population.

This spectacular urban growth, fueled by migration from the countryside and the arrival of nearly 11 million immigrants between 1870 and 1900, stimulated economic development. Like the frontier, the city symbolized opportunity for all comers.

The city's unprecedented scale and diversity threatened traditional expectations about community life and social stability. Rural America had been a place of face-to-face personal relations. In contrast, the city was a seething caldron where immigrant groups contended with one another and with native-born Americans for jobs, power, and influence. Moreover, the same rapid growth that energized manufacturing and production strained city services, generated terrible housing and sanitation problems, and accentuated class differences.

Native-born Americans complained about the noise, stench, and congestion of this transformed cityscape. They fretted about the newcomers' squalid tenements, fondness for drink, and strange customs. When native-born reformers set about cleaning up the city, they sought not only to improve the physical environment but also to destroy the distinctive customs that made immigrant culture different from their own. The late nineteenth century thus witnessed an intense struggle to control the city and benefit from its economic and cultural potential. The stakes were high, for America was increasingly becoming an urban nation.

Migrants and Immigrants

The concentration of urban industries produced demands for thousands of new workers. The promise of good wages and a broad range of jobs (labeled by historians as "pull factors") drew men and women from the countryside. So great was the migration from rural areas, especially New England, that some farm communities vanished from the map.

Young farmwomen led the exodus to the cities. With the growing mechanization of farming in the late nineteenth century, farming was increasingly male work. Rising sales of factory-produced goods through nationally distributed mail-order catalogs reduced the need for rural women's labor. So young farmwomen flocked to the cities, where they competed for jobs with immigrant, black, and city-born white women.

From 1860 to 1890, the prospect of a better life also attracted nearly 10 million northern European immigrants to American cities. Their numbers included nearly 3 million Germans, 2 million English, Scottish, and Welsh immigrants, and almost 1.5 million Irish. By 1900 more than eight hundred

TABLE 19.1 Urban Growth: 1870–1900

City	1870 Population	1900 Population	Percent Increase
Boston	250,525	560,892	123.88
Chicago	298,977	1,698,575	468.12
Cincinnati	216,239	325,902	50.71
Los Angeles	5,728	102,479	1,689.08
Milwaukee	71,440	285,315	299.37
New Orleans	191,418	287,104	49.98
New York	1,478,103	3,437,202	132.54
Philadelphia	647,022	1,293,697	99.94
Pittsburgh	86,076	321,616	273.64
Portland	8,293	90,426	990.38
Richmond	51,038	85,050	66.64
San Francisco	149,473	342,782	129.32
Seattle	1,107	237,194	21,326.73

Source: *Thirteenth Census of the United States (Washington, DC: U.S. Government Printing Office, 1913).*

CHRONOLOGY 1860–1900

1865	Vassar College founded.
1869	First intercollegiate football game.
1872	Anthony Comstock founds New York Society for the Suppression of Vice.
1873	John Wanamaker opens his Philadelphia department store.
1875	Smith and Wellesley colleges founded.
1876	National League of baseball organized.
1880	William Booth's followers establish an American branch of the Salvation Army.
1881	Josephine Shaw Lowell founds New York Charity Organization Society (COS).
1884	Mark Twain, *Huckleberry Finn.*
1885	Stanford University founded.

1889	Jane Addams and Ellen Gates Starr open Hull House.
1891	University of Chicago founded. Basketball invented at Springfield College, Massachusetts.
1892	Ellis Island Immigration Center opened. General Federation of Women's Clubs organized.
1895	Coney Island amusement parks open in Brooklyn, New York.
1899	Scott Joplin, "Maple Leaf Rag." Kate Chopin, *The Awakening.* Thorstein Veblen, *The Theory of the Leisure Class.*
1900	Theodore Dreiser, *Sister Carrie.* National Association of Colored Women's Clubs organized.
1910	Angel Island Immigration Center opens in San Francisco.

thousand French-Canadians had entered the New England mills, and close to a million Scandinavian newcomers had put down roots in the rich farmlands of Wisconsin and Minnesota. On the West Coast, despite the Chinese Exclusion Act of 1882 (see Chapter 18), more than eighty-one thousand Chinese remained in California and nearby states in 1900.

In the 1890s, these earlier immigrants from northern and western Europe were joined by swelling numbers of **"new immigrants"**—Italians, Slavs, Greeks, and Jews from southern and eastern Europe, Armenians from the Middle East, and in Hawaii, Japanese from Asia (see Map 19.1). In the next three decades, these new immigrants, many from peasant backgrounds, would boost America's

MAP 19.1 ASIAN AND EUROPEAN IMMIGRANTS LIVING IN THE WESTERN HEMISPHERE AND HAWAII IN 1900

Migration in the nineteenth century was a global phenomenon.

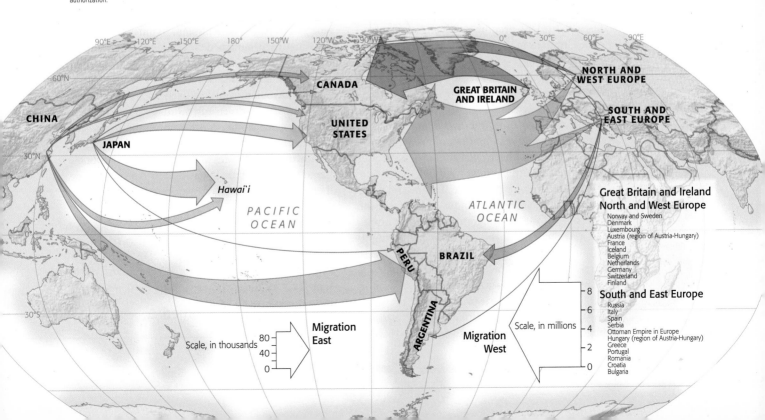

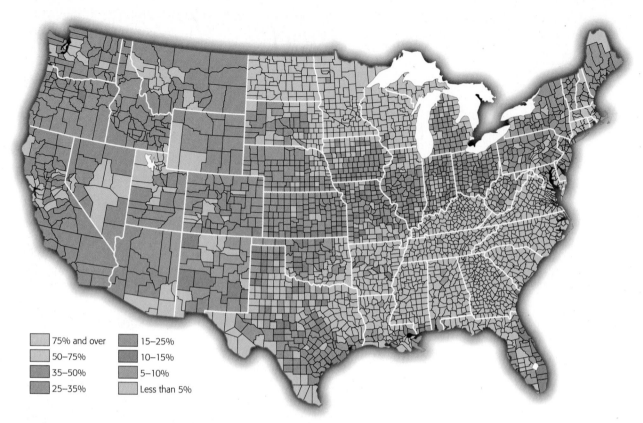

75% and over	15–25%
50–75%	10–15%
35–50%	5–10%
25–35%	Less than 5%

MAP 19.2 **PERCENT OF FOREIGN-BORN WHITES AND NATIVE WHITES OF FOREIGN OR MIXED PARENTAGE IN TOTAL POPULATION, BY COUNTIES, 1910** As this map indicates, new immigrants rarely settled in the South.

Source: *D. W. Meinig,* The Shaping of America—A Geographical Perspective of 500 Years of History. *Yale University Press, Volume 3.*

foreign-born population by more than 18 million (see Map 19.2).

The overwhelming majority of immigrants settled in cities in the northeastern and north-central states, with the Irish predominating in New England and the Germans in the Midwest. The effect of their numbers was staggering. In 1890, New York City (including Brooklyn, still a legally separate municipality) contained twice as many Irish as Dublin, as many Germans as Hamburg, half as many Italians as Naples, and 2½ times the Jewish population of Warsaw. That same year, four out of five people living in New York had been born abroad or were children of foreign-born parents.

Overpopulation, crop failure, famine, religious persecution, violence, or industrial depression drove some of these immigrants from their homelands. (Historians call these reasons for immigration "push factors.") At the same time, the promise of high wages (a "pull factor") lured more than one hundred thousand Japanese laborers to Hawaii in the 1890s to work on sugar plantations.

A large number of immigrants were single young men. Birger Osland, an eighteen-year-old Norwegian, explained his reasons for leaving to a friend: "as I now probably have a foundation upon which I can build my own further education, I have come to feel that the most sensible thing I can do is to emigrate to America." Although significant numbers of young men remained in the United States after they had become successful, large numbers, especially Italians and Chinese, returned home as well.

Single women were less likely to come on their own, but Irish women often did so and sent their earnings back home. Most commonly, wives and children waited in the old country until the family breadwinner had secured a job and saved enough money to pay for their passage to America. They then endured a cramped steamship journey noted for its poor food, lack of privacy, and rudimentary sanitary facilities. Immigrants arrived tired, fearful, and in some cases sick.

> "I have come to feel that the most sensible thing I can do is to emigrate to America."

Further complications awaited the travelers when they reached their destination, most often New York City or San Francisco. Customs officials inspected the newcomers for physical handicaps and contagious diseases. After 1892, those with "loathsome" infections such as leprosy, trachoma (a contagious viral disease of the eye), or sexually transmitted diseases were refused admittance and deported. Immigrants who passed the physical examination then had their names recorded. If a customs inspector had difficulty pronouncing a foreign name, he often Anglicized it. One German Jew became flustered when asked for his name and mumbled, "Schon vergessen [already forgotten]," meaning that he could not recall it. The inspector, who did not understand German, wrote "Sean Ferguson" on the man's roster. In this manner, many immigrants ended up with Americanized names.

In 1892, the federal government built a new immigration facility on **Ellis Island** in New York harbor. Angel Island in San Francisco Bay on the West Coast served a similar purpose after 1910. At the immigrant processing centers, America's newest residents exchanged foreign currency for U.S. dollars and purchased railroad tickets. Outside the facility, immigrants were hounded by tavernkeepers, peddlers, and porters who tried to exploit them. "When you land in America," wrote one Swedish resident to friends back home, "you will find many who will offer their services, but beware of them because there are so many rascals who make it their business to cheat the immigrants."

Those who arrived with sufficient cash, including many German artisans and Scandinavian farmers, commonly traveled west to Chicago and the rolling prairies beyond. Most of the Irish, and later the Italians remained in eastern cities like Boston, New York, and Philadelphia. The Irish and Italians who did go west typically made the trip in stages, moving from job to job on the railroad and canal systems.

Adjusting to an Urban Society

In the cities, immigrants clustered together with compatriots who had arrived earlier to ease the stress of adjusting to a new life. (Historians call this tendency "chain migration.") If a map of New York City's streets and neighborhoods were colored in by nationality, Jacob Riis observed in 1890, it "would show more stripes than on the skin of a zebra, and more colors than any rainbow." Between the West Side Irish and the East Side German neighborhoods, the streets of Manhattan teemed with Poles, Hungarians, Russians, Italians, and Chinese.

Within the cities, some immigrant groups adjusted more easily than others. Ethnic groups

FAMILY LOOKING FOR LOST BAGGAGE, ELLIS ISLAND, 1905
In this photograph, Lewis Hine, the celebrated photographer, captures the fear that immigrants experienced if they lost any of their possessions. *(Courtesy of George Eastman House, International Museum of Photography and Film)*

that formed a substantial percentage of a city's population had a major advantage. The Irish, for example, who by the 1880s made up nearly 16 percent of New York's population, 8 percent of Chicago's, and 17 percent of Boston's, facilitated Irish immigrants' entry into the American mainstream by dominating Democratic Party politics and controlling the hierarchy of the Catholic church in all three cities.

The domination of urban institutions by one immigrant group, however, often made adjustment to American society more difficult for others. In cities like Milwaukee, Germans excluded Poles from desirable jobs. Elsewhere, English and German dominance of the building trades enabled those nationalities to limit the numbers of Italians hired.

The experience of being discriminated against helped create a common ethnic identity for many groups. Groups of immigrants forged a sense of ethnic distinctiveness as Irish Americans, German Americans, or Jewish Americans that helped them

Slums and Ghettos

Every major city had its share of rundown, overcrowded slum neighborhoods. Generally clustered within walking distance of manufacturing districts, slums developed when landlords subdivided long, narrow buildings with few windows, called tenements, and packed in many residents. The poorer the renters, the worse the slum. Slums became ghettos when laws, prejudice, and community pressure prevented the tenement inhabitants from renting elsewhere. During the 1890s, Italians in New York, blacks in Philadelphia and Chicago, Mexican Americans in Los Angeles, and Chinese in San Francisco increasingly became locked in segregated ghettos.

Life in the slums was particularly difficult for children. Whooping cough (pertussis), measles, and scarlet fever took a fearful toll, and infant mortality skyrocketed. In one immigrant ward in Chicago in 1900, 20 percent of infants died in their first year of life.

> A map of New York City, colored in by nationality, "would show more stripes than on the skin of a zebra, and more colors than any rainbow."

Because tenements often bordered industrial districts, residents had to put up with the noise, pollution, and foul odors of tanneries, foundries, factories, and packing houses. Coal-fired steam engines and apartment house furnaces produced vast quantities of soot and dust that tinged the atmosphere a hazy gray and coated buildings with a grimy patina.

Most immigrants stayed in the shabbiest tenements only until they could afford better housing. Blacks, in contrast, were trapped in segregated districts. Driven out of the skilled trades and excluded from most factory work, blacks took menial jobs whose low pay left them little income for housing (see Chapter 18). Racist city-dwellers used high rents, real-estate covenants (agreements not to rent or sell to blacks), and neighborhood pressure to exclude them from areas inhabited by whites. Because the numbers of northern urban blacks in 1890 remained relatively small—for example, they composed only 1.2 percent of Cleveland's population and 1.3 percent of Chicago's—they could not overcome whites' campaigns to shut them out. Instead, wealthy black entrepreneurs established their own churches and charitable organizations in the black neighborhoods where they lived.

CHINATOWN, SAN FRANCISCO As evident in this photograph at the turn of the century, Chinese immigrants often lived in separate enclaves called "chinatowns." *(Picture Research Consultants & Archives)*

compete for political power and move into mainstream society.

Not all immigrants intended to remain in the United States. Expecting only a brief stay, some made little effort to learn English or understand American customs. Of the Italians who immigrated to New York before 1914, nearly 50 percent went back to Italy. Although the rate of return migration was greatest among Chinese and Italians, significant numbers of other nationalities returned to their homelands as well.

As the number of foreigners in U.S. cities ballooned toward the turn of the century, all immigrant groups faced increasing hostility from white native-born Americans who disliked the newcomers' social customs and worried about their growing influence. Fearing the loss of the privileges and status that were associated with their white skin color, native-born whites often stigmatized immigrants as racially different and inferior. Only gradually, and with much effort, did Irish, Jews, Slavs, and Italians come to be considered "white."

Fashionable Avenues and Suburbs

The same cities that harbored slums, filth, suffering, and violence also boasted of neighborhoods of dazzling opulence with the latest lighting and plumbing technologies (see Technology and Culture). The wealthy built monumental residences along thoroughfares radiating from the city centers, among them Commonwealth Avenue in Boston, Euclid Avenue in Cleveland, and Summit Avenue in St. Paul (see Going to the Source).

In the 1870s and 1880s, city-dwellers began moving to nearby suburbs. Promoters of the suburban ideal contrasted the rolling lawns and stately houses on the city's periphery with the teeming streets, noisy saloons, and mounds of garbage and horse excrement downtown. Soon, most major cities could boast of their own stylish suburbs.

Middle-class city-dwellers followed the precedents set by the wealthy. Skilled artisans, shopkeepers, clerks, accountants, and sales personnel moved either to new developments at the city's edge or to outlying suburban communities (although those at the lower fringe of the middle class typically rented apartments in neighborhoods closer to the city center). Lawyers, doctors, small businessmen, and other professionals moved farther out along the main thoroughfares served by the street railway, where they purchased homes on large lots.

In time, a pattern of informal residential segregation by income took shape in the cities and suburbs. Built for families of a particular income level, certain neighborhoods and suburbs developed remarkably similar standards for lot size and house design. Two-story houses with front porches, set back thirty feet from the sidewalk, became the norm in many suburbs. Commuters who rode the new street railways out from the city center could identify the social class of the suburban dwellers along the way as readily as a geologist might distinguish different strata on a washed-out riverbank.

By 1900, whirring trolley cars and hissing steam powered trains had burst the boundaries of the compact midcentury city. As they expanded, cities often annexed contingent suburbs. Within this enlarged city, sharp dissimilarities in building height and neighborhood quality set off business sectors from fashionable residential avenues and differentiated squalid manufacturing districts from parklike suburban subdivisions. Musing about urban America in 1902, James F. Muirhead, a popular Scottish guidebook author, wrote that New York and other U.S. cities reminded him of "a lady in a ball costume, with diamonds in her ears, and her toes out at her boots." To Muirhead, urban America had become a "land of contrasts" in which the separation of various social groups and the increasingly dissimilar living conditions for rich and poor had heightened ethnic, racial, and class divisions. Along with the physical change in American cities, in short, had come a new awareness of class and cultural disparities.

> A Scottish guidebook author wrote that U.S. cities reminded him of "a lady in a ball costume, with diamonds in her ears, and her toes out at her boots."

Middle- and Upper-Class Society and Culture

Spared the struggle for survival that confronted most Americans after the Civil War, society's middle and upper ranks faced a different challenge: how to rationalize their enjoyment of the products of the emerging consumer society. To justify the position of society's wealthier members, ministers such as Brooklyn preacher Henry Ward Beecher and advice-book writers appealed to **Victorian morality,** a set of social ideas embraced by the privileged classes of England and America during the long reign (1837–1901) of Britain's Queen Victoria.

E.L. Godkin, the editor of *The Nation*, Phillips Brooks, minister to Boston's Trinity Church, and other proponents of Victorian morality argued that the financial success of the middle and upper classes arose from their superior talent, intelligence, morality, and self-control. They also extended the antebellum ideal of separate spheres by arguing that women were the driving force for moral improvement. While men were expected to engage in self-disciplined, "manly" dedication to the new industrial order, women would provide the gentle, elevating influence that would lead society in its upward march. A network of institutions, from elegant department stores and hotels to elite colleges and universities, reinforced the privileged position of these groups.

Manners and Morals

Several fundamental assumptions shaped the Victorian worldview. First, human nature was malleable: people could improve themselves. Second, work had social value: working hard not only developed self-discipline but also helped advance

Flush Toilets and the Invention of the Nineteenth-Century Bathroom

The development of a system of indoor plumbing was typical of the technological breakthroughs that simplified everyday life in the late nineteenth century. In the 1860s, only about 5 percent of American houses had running water. Most Americans used chamber pots or outhouses that emptied into slimy, smelly cesspools. Two decades later, indoor plumbing standards had been established in most major U.S. cities, and wealthier urban Americans used flush toilets connected to municipal sewer systems.

The driving force for change came from outbreaks of cholera, typhoid, and yellow fever, diseases spread by polluted water, that periodically terrorized American cities. Building on the discovery of germs by Louis Pasteur and Robert Koch, sanitary reformers established stringent metropolitan health laws, created state boards of health, and mandated the licensing of plumbers and the inspection of their work. By the turn of the century, George E. Waring, Jr., a prominent sanitary engineer, could confidently declare that "Plumbing, as we know it, is essentially and almost exclusively an American Institution."

The decision to adopt a water-based system for the removal of human wastes depended on a series of inventions. First, municipal water systems had to be built with reservoirs, pumps, and water towers to provide water to the pipes that supplied buildings. A sewage system of interconnected pipes was also necessary to remove and process wastes. Machines to manufacture lead, cast-iron, and glazed stoneware pipes had to be created, as did a uniform system of pipe threads and melted lead joints to create a reliable standardized system for connecting them. Finally, a porcelain toilet with a built-in gas trap was needed because the bacteria in feces produce methane or sewer gas. (A trap is a U-shaped joint in which the water at the low part of the U prevents gas from seeping back into the bathroom. The gas vents through a pipe in the roof.)

Despite its usefulness, the new technology was not rapidly adopted. In 1890, only 24 percent of American dwellings had running water. As late as 1897, more than 90 percent of the families in tenements had no baths and had to wash in hallway sinks or courtyard hydrants. By 1920, 80 percent of American houses, particularly those in rural areas, still lacked indoor flush toilets. The reason was simple: indoor plumbing was expensive and depended on the availability of water and sewer systems. Adding indoor plumbing increased the price of a new house by 20 percent.

Advertisers did their best to increase demand. They skillfully used the findings of science to advocate new standards of cleanliness or "hygiene," as it was called, which they associated with upper-class principles of respectability and decorum. Bathing and hand washing were touted as symbols of upper-class refinement.

Indoor plumbing not only reinforced higher standards for personal hygiene; it also enmeshed the homeowner in a web of local and state regulations. As sewage and water systems expanded to cover larger constituencies, political control moved from local to state and sometimes national arenas. Once largely independent, the homeowner now had to deal with water and power companies that often functioned regionally.

The adoption of strict sanitation systems and the use of indoor plumbing did achieve their intended result: they

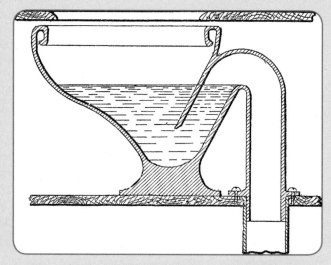

TOILET Porcelain toilets were designed for easy cleaning. They contained a trap that sealed the connection to the sewer with a U-shaped drain that prevented sewer gas from seeping back into the house. *(House Drainage and Sanitary Plumbing by William Paul Gerhard, 1882. Miriam and Ira D. Wallach Division of Art, Prints and Photographs, The New York Public Library. Astor, Lenox and Tilden Foundations.)*

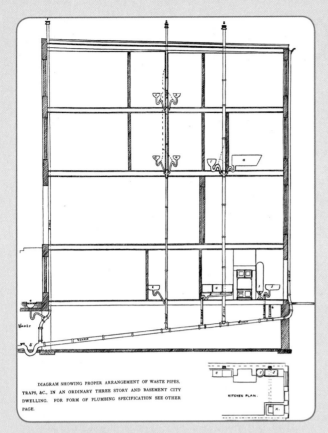

DIAGRAM SHOWING PROPER ARRANGEMENT OF WASTE PIPES, TRAPS, &C., IN AN ORDINARY THREE STORY AND BASEMENT CITY DWELLING. FOR FORM OF PLUMBING SPECIFICATION SEE OTHER PAGE.

KITCHEN PLAN.

PLUMBING DESIGN An architectural design shows the proper arrangement of waste pipes and traps in a three-story and basement city dwelling. *(Avery Architectural and Fine Arts Library, Columbia University)*

dramatically reduced the spread of disease. But the advances had unintended consequences. Indoor plumbing encouraged the phenomenal waste of water. A single faulty toilet could easily leak a hundred gallons of water a day. Not until the 1990s with the development of new low-water-usage toilets, which could save between 18,000 and 26,400 gallons of water a year, would new standards be established to reduce the use of water, an increasingly precious natural resource.

QUESTION FOR ANALYSIS

- Why does the successful introduction of new technologies often involve a system of inventions rather than a single invention?

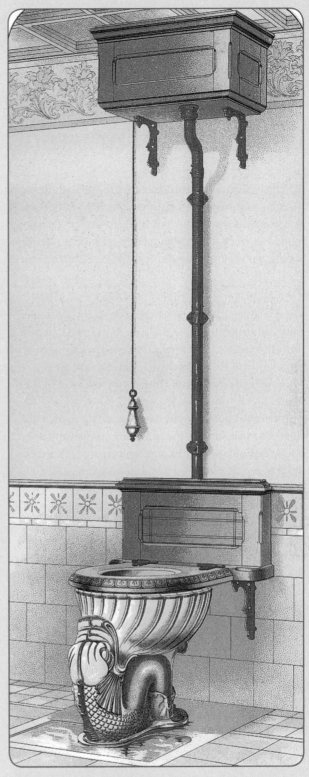

ARTISTIC TOILET DESIGN By elevating the water tank for the toilet and hiding it in a wooden box, designers solved the problem of low water pressure and eased the acceptance of the new technology. The additional pressure when the water dropped that distance ensured that the contents of the toilet bowl would be effectively flushed. *(House Drainage and Sanitary Plumbing by William Paul Gerhard, 1882. Miriam and Ira D. Wallach Division of Art, Prints and Photographs, The New York Public Library. Astor, Lenox and Tilden Foundations.)*

Frederick Law Olmsted and the Redesign of the Urban Environment

No changes to the urban landscape in the late nineteenth century were more dramatic than the filling-in of Back Bay in Boston. Between 1857 and 1900, special gravel trains ran round the clock, raising the ground level by an average of twenty feet in the 450-acre tidal basin. But filling the tidal flats left open the question of what to do with the Muddy River, whose noxious, sewage-soiled waters emptied into the Charles River basin. In 1881, landscape architect Frederick Law Olmsted, who had designed Central Park in New York in the 1850s, offered the following plan.

The tidal part of Muddy River above the basin now under construction has the usual character of a salt creek winding through a valley. ... The city is rapidly advancing in compact blocks towards the region, and public convenience will, before many years, require a more comprehensive treatment of it.

It usually happens when a town is building up on both sides of a small water-course and valley that the sanitary and other disadvantages of the low ground prevent it from being much occupied, except in a way damaging to the value of the adjoining properties. In ... time, the stream and valley and the uses to which they are put, come to be regarded as a nuisance, and radical measures, such as the construction of a great underground channel, and the filling up of the alley, are urged as the only adequate remedy. The cost of these, and the local disturbance they make, excite opposition to them; their complete beneficial operation is long-delayed. Though necessary, therefore, to public health and to convenience of general transit through the district, the result in the increased tax-bearing capacity of the locality is no compensation for the required outlay.

As an alternative to such a possible course the policy now suggested for Muddy River would look to the preservation of the present channel with certain modifications and improvements adapted to make it permanently attractive and wholesome, and an element of constantly increasing advantage to the neighborhood. ... The indirect course of the parkway, following the river bank, would prevent its being much used for purposes of heavy transportation. It would thus, without offensive exclusiveness or special police regulation, be left free to be used as a pleasure route. ...

... the result would be a chain of pleasant waters, ... all of natural and in some degree picturesque outline, with banks wooded and easily furnished with verdure and foliage throughout ...

Taken in connection with the mall upon Commonwealth Avenue, the Public Garden and the Common, the parkway would complete a pleasure-route from the heart of the city a distance of six miles into its suburbs. These older pleasure-grounds, which continuing to serve equally well all their present purposes, would, by becoming part of an extended system, acquire increased importance and value. They could have a larger use, be more effective as appliances for public health, and every dollar expended for their maintenance would return a larger dividend."

Sources: Olmsted, Frederick Law. Edited by Charles E. Beveridge, Carolyn F. Hoffman, and Kenneth Hawkins. Tina Hummel, Assistant Editor. *The Papers of Frederick Law Olmsted: Parks, Politics, and Patronage,* 1874–1882 (Vol. 7). pp. 518, 520–21. © 2007 The Johns Hopkins University Press. Reprinted with permission of The Johns Hopkins University Press.

QUESTIONS

1. What problems does Olmsted's plan for a connected park system solve?
2. In what ways does Olmsted's argument that the preservation of nature will pay for itself foreshadow features of the modern environmental movement?

the progress of the nation. Finally, good manners and the cultivation of literature and art ennobled society. Although these genteel assumptions were sometimes ignored, they were held up as universal standards.

Victorian morality stressed the importance of manners and social rituals. Middle- and upper-class families in the 1870s and 1880s increasingly defined their own social standing in terms not only of income but also of behavior. Good manners, including knowledge of dining and entertaining etiquette, and good posture became important marks of status.

In her popular advice book, *The American Woman's Home* (1869), Catharine Beecher (the sister of Henry Ward Beecher) displayed the typical Victorian self-consciousness about proper manners. The following dinner-table behaviors, she said, should be avoided by those of "good breeding":

Reaching over another person's plate; standing up to reach distant articles, instead of asking to have them passed … using the table-cloth instead of napkins; eating fast, and in a noisy manner; putting large pieces in the mouth; … [and] picking the teeth at the table.

For Beecher and other molders of manners, meals became important rituals that differentiated the social classes. The elaborate china and silver that wealthy families exclusively possessed also provided telltale clues to a family's level of refinement and sophistication.

The Victorian code—with its emphasis on morals, manners, and proper behavior—thus heightened the sense of class differences and created visible distinctions among social groups. Victorian Americans made bold claims about their interest in helping others improve themselves. More often than not, however, their self-righteous, intensely moralistic outlook simply widened the gap that income disparities had already opened.

The Cult of Domesticity

Victorian views on morality and culture, coupled with the need to make decisions about a mountain of domestic products, had a subtle but important effect on middle-class expectations about women's role within the home. From the 1840s on, architects, clergymen, and other promoters of the so-called cult of domesticity had idealized the home as "the woman's sphere." They praised the home as a protected retreat where women could express their maternal gifts, including sensitivity toward children and an aptitude for religion. "The home is the

wife's province," asserted one writer; "it is her natural field of labor … to govern and direct its interior management."

During the 1880s and 1890s, Victorian advocates of the cult of domesticity added a new obligation to foster an artistic environment that would nurture her family's cultural improvement. Houses became statements of cultural aspiration with front parlors cluttered with artwork and curiosities. Excluded from the world of business and commerce, many middle- and upper-class women directed their energies to decorating their homes, seeking to make the home, as one advice book suggested, "a place of repose, a refuge from the excitement and distractions of outside … provided with every attainable means of rest and recreation."

Not all middle-class women pursued this domestic ideal. For some, housework and family responsibilities overwhelmed the concern for artistic accomplishment. For others, the artistic ideal was not to their taste. Sixteen-year-old Mary Putnam complained privately to a friend that she played the piano because of "an abstract general idea … of a father coming home regularly tired at night (from the plow, I believe the usual legend runs), and being solaced by the brilliant yet touching performance of a sweet only daughter upon the piano." She then confessed that she detested the piano. In the 1880s and 1890s, as middle- and upper-class women sought other outlets for their creative energies in settlement-house work, social reform, and women's club activities, the older domestic ideal began to unravel.

Department Stores

Although Victorian social thought justified the privileges of the well-to-do, many people found it difficult to shake the thriftiness of their early years and accept the new preoccupation with accumulation and display. To lure these consumers, merchandisers in the 1880s stressed the high quality and low cost of the objects they sold, encouraging Americans to loosen their purse strings and enjoy prosperity without reservations. This argument particularly appealed to women who, to provide for their families, now had to shop for soap, canned foods, and other products formerly made at home.

Department stores set the standard for consumption. In the final quarter of the nineteenth century, Rowland H. Macy in New York, John Wanamaker in Philadelphia, and Marshall Field in Chicago built giant department stores that transformed the shopping experience for their middle- and upper-class patrons. The stores advertised "rock-bottom" prices and engaged in price wars. To avoid

The Transformation of Higher Education

At a time when relatively few Americans had even a high school education and only 4 percent of the nation's eighteen- to twenty-one-year-olds were enrolled in institutions of higher learning, colleges and universities represented another stronghold of the business and professional elite.

Wealthy capitalists gained status and a measure of immortality by endowing colleges and universities. Leland Stanford and his wife, Jane Lathrop Stanford, launched Stanford University in 1885 with a bequest of $24 million; John D. Rockefeller donated $34 million to the University of Chicago in 1891. Industrialists and businessmen dominated the boards of trustees of most educational institutions.

Not only the classroom experience but also social contacts and athletic activities—especially football—prepared affluent young men for later responsibilities in business and the professions. Adapted by American college students in the 1860s from English rugby, football became an elite sport played by college teams. But the game, initially played without pads or helmets, was marred by violence. In 1905, eighteen students died of playing-field injuries. Many college presidents dismissed football as a dangerous waste of time and money. In 1873, when the University of Michigan challenged Cornell to a game in Ann Arbor, Cornell's president Andrew D. White huffily telegraphed back, "I will not permit thirty men to travel four hundred miles merely to agitate a bag of wind."

But eager alumni and coaches strongly defended the new sport. Some—among them Henry Lee Higginson, the Civil War veteran and Boston banker who gave Harvard "Soldiers' Field" stadium as a memorial to those who had died in battle—praised football as a character-building sport. Others, including famed Yale coach Walter Camp, insisted that football could function as a surrogate frontier experience in an increasingly urbanized society. By 1900, collegiate football had become a popular fall ritual, and team captains were campus heroes. At a time when businesses stressed teamwork and played down individuality, football suggested that intercollegiate sports forged manhood by emphasizing vision, integrity, and leadership.

More than 150 new colleges and universities were founded between 1880 and 1900, and enrollments more than doubled. While wealthy capitalists endowed some institutions, others,

TRADE CARD, CA. 1880 For middle- and upper-class Victorian families, the front parlor, with its elaborate curtains and artwork, reflected the domestic ideal. Like the sleeping dog in the picture, pets were seen as appropriate means for teaching children kindness, compassion, and discipline. *(Picture Research Consultants & Archives)*

keeping their stock too long, they held giant end-of-the-season sales at drastically marked-down prices.

Department stores made shopping an exciting activity. Rapid turnover of merchandise created a sense of constant novelty. With stained-glass skylights, marble staircases, sparkling chandeliers, and plush carpets, the large urban department store functioned as a workplace for the lower classes and as a social club for comfortably fixed women. For those who could afford it, shopping became an adventure, a form of entertainment, and a way to affirm their place in society.

"The home is the wife's province, it is her natural field of labor ... to govern and direct its interior management."

JUST BEFORE THE CHRISTMAS HOLIDAYS—SATURDAY AFTERNOON ON SIXTH AVENUE, IN THE HEART OF THE WEST-SIDE SHOPPING DISTRICT, NEW YORK CITY.

SATURDAY ON SIXTH AVENUE, 1897 Large department stores, located on fashionable city avenues, turned shopping into a social activity that telegraphed one's social status. To return home, the wealthy took horse-drawn cabs rather than the elevated trains. *(© Collection of the New York Historical Society)*

such as the state universities in the South and Midwest, were financed largely through public funds generated from public land sales under the Morrill Land Grant Act (1862). Many colleges were also founded and funded by religious denominations.

Following the precedent set by Oberlin College in 1836, coeducational private colleges and public universities in the Midwest enrolled increasing numbers of women. In the East, Columbia, Brown, and Harvard universities admitted women to the affiliated but separate institutions of Barnard (1889), Pembroke (1891), and Radcliffe (1894), respectively. Some colleges—Mount Holyoke (1837), Vassar (1865), Wellesley and Smith (1875), and Bryn Mawr (1884)—were founded solely for women. The generation of women educated at female institutions in the late nineteenth century developed the self-confidence to break with the Victorian ideal of passive womanhood and to compete with men by displaying strength, aggressiveness, and

intelligence—popularly considered male attributes. Nationally, the percentage of colleges admitting women jumped from 30 percent to 71 percent between 1880 and 1900. By the turn of the century, women made up more than one-third of the total college-student population.

At the university level, innovative presidents such as Cornell's Andrew D. White and Harvard's Charles W. Eliot, influenced by new discoveries in science and medicine, shifted the focus of higher education. In the 1850s, most physicians had attended medical school for only two sixteen-week terms. They typically received their degrees without ever having visited a hospital or examined a patient. The Civil War exposed the abysmal state of American medical knowledge. Twice as many soldiers died from infections as from wounds. Doctors were so poorly trained and ignorant about sanitation that they often infected soldiers' injuries when they probed wounds with hands wiped on pus-stained aprons. "The ignorance and general incompetency of the average graduate of American medical schools, at the time when he receives the degree which turns him loose upon the community," wrote Eliot in 1870, "is something horrible to contemplate."

In the 1880s and 1890s, leading medical professors, many of whom had studied in France and Germany, began restructuring American medical education. Using the experimental method developed by German scientists, they insisted that all medical students be trained in biology, chemistry, and physics, including working in a laboratory. Although medical school reform improved health care in some areas, it also effectively shut out African American and poor women who could not afford the tuition. New educational and professional standards, similarly, were established for architects, engineers, and lawyers.

These changes were part of a larger transformation in higher education, the rise of a new kind of institution, the **research university.** Unlike the best of the mid-nineteenth-century colleges, which focused on teaching Latin and Greek, theology, logic, and mathematics, the new research universities offered courses in a wide variety of subject areas, established professional schools, and encouraged faculty members to pursue basic research. At Cornell University, President Andrew D. White's objective was to create an environment "where any person can find instruction in any study." At Cornell, the University of Wisconsin at Madison, Johns Hopkins, Harvard, and other institutions, this new conception of higher education laid the groundwork for

CHEMISTRY CLASS, SMITH COLLEGE, 1889 Thanks to their education in science at colleges and universities, increasing numbers of women in the 1890s became physicians. Nevertheless, most medical schools refused to appoint women doctors to their teaching staffs. *(Sophia Smith Collection, Smith College)*

the central role that America's universities would play in the intellectual, cultural, and scientific life of the twentieth century.

Reforming the Working Class

The contrast between the affluent world of the college educated middle and upper classes and the gritty lives of the working class was most graphically on display in the nation's growing urban centers, where immigrant newcomers reshaped political and social institutions to meet their own needs. If fancy department stores and elegant hotels furnished new social spaces for the middle and upper classes, saloons became the poor man's club, and dance halls became single women's home away from home. While the rich and the wellborn looked suspiciously at lower-class recreational activities and sought to force the poor to change their ways, working-class Americans, the immigrant newcomers in particular, fought to preserve their own distinctive way of life. Indeed, the late nineteenth century witnessed an ongoing battle to eradicate social drinking and curb lower-class recreational activities.

> "The ignorance and general incompetency of the average graduate of American medical schools … is something horrible to contemplate."

Battling Poverty

Stunned by the levels of poverty and suffering in the expanding industrial cities, middle-class city leaders sought comprehensive solutions for relieving poverty. Jacob Riis and the first generation of reformers believed that immigrants' lack of self-discipline and their unsanitary living conditions caused their problems. Consequently, Riis and his peers focused on moral improvement and exposing squalid tenement housing. Only later would Jane Addams, Florence Kelley, and other settlement-house workers examine the crippling impact of low wages and dangerous working conditions. Although many reformers genuinely sympathized with the suffering of the lower classes, the humanitarians often turned their campaigns to help the destitute into missions to Americanize the immigrants and eliminate customs that they perceived as offensive and self-destructive.

Poverty-relief workers first targeted their efforts at the young, who were thought to be most malleable. Energized by the religious revivals of the 1830s and 1840s, Protestant reformers started charitable societies to help transient youths and abandoned street children. In 1843, Robert M. Hartley, a former employee of the New York Temperance Society, organized the New York Association for Improving the Condition of the Poor to help poor families.

Hartley's voluntaristic approach was supplemented by the more coercive tactics of Charles Loring Brace, who founded the New York Children's Aid Society in 1853. Brace admired "these little traders of the city … battling for a hard living in the snow and mud of the street" but worried that they might join the city's "dangerous classes." Brace established dormitories, reading rooms, and workshops where the boys could learn practical skills; he also swept orphaned children off the streets, shipped them to the country, and placed them with families to work as farm hands.

Where Brace's Children's Aid Society gave adolescents an alternative to living in the slums, the Young Men's Christian Association (YMCA), founded in England in 1841 and exported to America ten years later, provided housing and wholesome recreation for country boys who had migrated to the city. The Young Women's Christian Association (YWCA) similarly provided housing and a day nursery for young women and their children. Both organizations subjected their members to curfews and expelled them for drinking and other forbidden behavior.

By 1900, more than fifteen hundred YMCAs and YWCAs served as havens for nearly a quarter-million young men and women. But YMCA and

ORPHAN TRAIN ON THE ATCHISON, TOPEKA & SANTA FE RAILROAD LINE, CA. 1900 From the 1850s to the 1920s, the Children's Aid Society placed more than two hundred and fifty thousand orphans such as these with foster families in the western United States. Families who wished to adopt an orphan needed recommendations from their pastor and a justice of the peace. *(Santa Fe Collection, Kansas State Historical Society)*

YWCA leaders reached only a small portion of the young adult population. Although charity workers made some progress in their efforts to aid youth, the strategy was too narrowly focused to stem the rising tide of urban problems.

New Approaches to Social Reform

The inability of the Children's Aid Society, YMCA, YWCA, and other relief organizations to cope with the explosive growth of the urban poor in the 1870s and 1880s convinced reformers to search for new allies in the fight against poverty. One effective agency was the **Salvation Army.** A church established along pseudomilitary lines in England in 1865 by Methodist minister "General" William Booth, the Salvation Army sent uniformed volunteers to the United States in 1880 to provide food, shelter, and temporary employment for families. Its members ran soup kitchens and day nurseries and dispatched its "slum brigades" to carry the message of morality to the immigrant poor. The army's strategy was simple. Attract the poor with marching bands and lively preaching; follow up with offers of food, assistance, and employment; and then teach them the solid middle-class virtues of temperance, hard work, and self-discipline.

The New York Charity Organization Society (COS), founded in 1882 by **Josephine Shaw Lowell,** implemented a similar approach to poor relief. To make aid to the poor more efficient, Lowell and the COS leaders divided New York City into districts, compiled files on all aid recipients, and sent "friendly visitors," who were trained, salaried women, into the tenements to counsel families on how to improve their lives. Convinced that moral deficiencies lay at the root of poverty and that the "promiscuous charity" of overlapping church welfare agencies undermined the desire to work, the COS tried to foster self-sufficiency in its charges. In 1891, Lowell helped found the Consumers' League of New York, which encouraged women to buy only from manufacturers who paid fair wages and maintained decent working conditions.

Although the COS did coordinate relief efforts and developed helpful statistics on the extent of poverty, critics justly accused the society of seeking more to control the poor than to alleviate their suffering. One of the manuals, for example, stressed the importance of introducing "messy housekeepers" to the "pleasures of a cheery, well-ordered home." Unable to see slum problems from the vantage point of the poor, they failed, for the most part, in their underlying objective: to convert the poor to their own standards of morality and decorum.

The Moral-Purity Campaign

While Josephine Shaw Lowell and other like-minded social disciplinarians worked to eradicate urban poverty, other reformers pushed for tougher measures against sin and immorality. In 1872, **Anthony Comstock,** a pious young dry-goods clerk, founded the New York Society for the Suppression of Vice. The organization demanded that municipal authorities close down gambling and lottery operations and censor obscene publications.

Nothing symbolized the contested terrain between middle- and lower-class culture better than the fight over prostitution. Considered socially degenerate by some and a source of recreation by others, prostitution both exploited women and offered them a steady income and a measure of personal freedom. After the Civil War, the number of brothels expanded rapidly. In the 1880s, saloons and cabarets hired prostitutes of their own. Even though immigrant women do not appear to have made up the majority of big-city prostitutes, reformers often labeled them as the major source of the problem.

In 1892, brothels, along with gambling dens and saloons, became targets for the reform efforts of New York Presbyterian minister Charles Parkhurst. Blaming the "slimy, oozy soil of Tammany Hall" (the Democratic organization that dominated New York City politics, discussed in the next chapter) and the New York City police—"the dirtiest, crookedest, and ugliest lot of men ever combined in semi-military array outside of Japan and Turkey"— for the city's rampant evils, he organized the City Vigilance League to clean up the city. Two years later, a nonpartisan Committee of Seventy elected a new mayor who pressured city officials to enforce the laws against prostitution, gambling, and Sunday liquor sales.

The purity campaign lasted scarcely three years. The reform coalition quickly fell apart. New York City's population was too large, and its ethnic constituencies too diverse, for middle- and upper-class reformers to curb all the illegal activities flourishing within the sprawling metropolis.

The Social Gospel

In the 1870s and 1880s, a handful of Protestant ministers took a different approach to helping impoverished city dwellers. Led by William S. Rainsford, the Irish-born minister of New York City's Saint George's Episcopal Church, they pioneered the development of the so-called institutional church movement by insisting that large downtown churches in once-elite districts that had been overrun by immigrants provide their new neighbors with social services as well as a place to worship. With the financial help of J. Pierpont Morgan, a warden of his church, Rainsford organized a boys' club, built church recreational facilities for the destitute on the Lower East Side, and established an industrial training program.

Other Protestant ministers, led by Washington Gladden, a Congregational clergyman in Columbus, Ohio, launched the **Social Gospel** movement in the 1870s. Gladden insisted that true Christianity commits men and women to fight social injustice wherever it exists. Thus, in response to the wave of violent strikes in 1877, he urged church leaders to mediate the conflict between business and labor. Their attempt to do so was unsuccessful.

If Gladden set the tone for the Social Gospel, Walter Rauschenbusch, a minister at a German Baptist church in New York's notorious "Hell's Kitchen" neighborhood, articulated the movement's central philosophy. Educated in Germany, Rauschenbusch argued that a truly Christian society would unite all churches, reorganize the industrial system, and work for international peace. Rauschenbusch's appeal for Christian unity led to the formation of the Federal Council of Churches in 1908, but his other goals were never achieved. Although the Social Gospel attracted only a handful of Protestants, their earnest voices blended with a growing chorus of critics bemoaning the nation's urban woes.

"They're like the rest, a bunch of people planning for us and deciding what is good for us without consulting us."

The Settlement-House Movement

In the 1880s, a younger generation of charity workers led by **Jane Addams** developed a new weapon against destitution: the settlement house. Like the Social Gospelers, these reformers recognized that the hardships of slum life were often beyond the individual's control. Living in the poor neighborhoods where they worked, they could see firsthand "the struggle for existence, which is so much harsher among people near the edge of pauperism."

The youngest daughter of a successful Illinois businessman, Jane Addams purchased a dilapidated mansion on Chicago's south side in 1889 and opened it as Hull House. Putting the middle-class ideal of true womanhood into action, Addams turned Hull House into a social center for immigrants. She invited them to plays; sponsored art projects; held classes in English, civics, cooking, and dressmaking; and encouraged them to preserve their traditional crafts. She set up a kindergarten, a laundry, an employment bureau, and a day nursery for working mothers. Hull House also sponsored recreational and athletic programs and dispensed legal aid and health care.

In the hope of upgrading the filthy and overcrowded housing in its environs, Addams and her coworkers conducted surveys of city housing conditions and pressured politicians to enforce sanitation regulations. For a time, demonstrating her principle of direct engagement with the lives of the poor, Addams even served as garbage inspector for her local ward.

By 1895, at least fifty settlement houses had opened in cities around the nation. Settlement-house leaders trained a generation of young college students, mostly women, many of whom would later serve as state and local government officials. **Florence Kelley,** for example, who had worked at Hull House, became the chief factory inspector for Illinois in 1893. For Kelley as for other female settlement workers, settlement houses functioned as a supportive sisterhood of reform. Many settlement-house veterans would later draw on their experience to play an influential role in the regulatory movements of the Progressive Era (covered in Chapter 21). Through their sympathetic attitudes toward the immigrants and their systematic publication of data about factory and slum conditions, settlement-house workers gave Americans renewed hope that urban problems could be overcome.

In their attempt to promote class cooperation and social harmony, however, settlement houses had mixed success. Although many immigrants appreciated the settlement houses' resources and activities, they believed that the reformers had little interest in helping them gain political power. Settlement-house workers did tend to overlook immigrant organizations and their leaders. In 1894, Hull House attracted two thousand visitors per week, but this was only a fraction of the more than seventy thousand people who lived within six blocks of the building. "They're like the rest," complained one immigrant, "a bunch of people planning for us and deciding what is good for us without consulting us or taking us into their confidence."

Working-Class Leisure in the Immigrant City

In colonial America, preachers had warned against leisure and idleness as temptations to sin. In the rural culture of the early nineteenth century, the unremitting routines of farm labor left little time for relaxation. Family picnics, horse races, county fairs, revival meetings, and Fourth of July and Christmas celebrations had provided occasional permissible

GARBAGE BOX, FIRST WARD, CHICAGO, CA. 1900 Lacking space for recreation, immigrant children played atop garbage boxes in crowded alleys. Concerned for their health, Jane Addams wrote that "this slaughter of the innocents, this infliction of suffering on the newborn, is so gratuitous and so unfair, that it is only a question of time until an outraged sense of justice shall be aroused on behalf of these children." *(Chicago Historical Society)*

diversions. But most Americans continued to view leisure activities skeptically. Henry Clay Work's popular song "My Grandfather's Clock" (1876), which praised the ancient timepiece for "wasting no time" and working "ninety years, without slumbering," bore witness to the tenacity of this deep-seated reverence for work and suspicion of play.

As urban populations shot up after the Civil War, striking new patterns of leisure and amusement emerged, most notably among the urban working class. After spending long hours in factories, in mills, behind department-store counters, or as domestic servants in the homes of the wealthy, working-class Americans craved relaxation and diversion. They thronged the streets, patronized saloons and dance halls, cheered at boxing matches and baseball games, and organized group picnics and holiday celebrations. As amusement parks, vaudeville theaters, sporting clubs, and racetracks provided further outlets for workers' need for entertainment, leisure became a big business catering to a mass public rather than to a wealthy elite.

For millions of working-class Americans, leisure time took on increasing importance as factory work became routinized and impersonal. Although many recreational activities involved both men and women, others attracted one gender in particular. Saloons offered an intensely male environment where patrons could share good stories, discuss and bet on sporting events, and momentarily put aside pressures of job and family. Young working women preferred to share confidences with friends in informal social clubs, tried out new fashions in street promenading, and found excitement in neighborhood dance halls and amusement parks.

Streets, Saloons, and Boxing Matches

No segment of the population had a greater need for amusement and recreation than the urban working class. Hours of tedious, highly disciplined, and physically exhausting labor left workers tired and thirsting for excitement and escape from their cramped housing quarters. In 1889, a banner carried by a carpenters' union summed up their wishes: "EIGHT HOURS FOR WORK, EIGHT HOURS FOR REST, AND EIGHT HOURS FOR WHAT WE WILL."

City streets provided recreation that anyone could afford. Relaxing after a day's work, shop girls and laborers clustered on busy corners, watching shouting pushcart peddlers and listening

> "EIGHT HOURS FOR WORK, EIGHT HOURS FOR REST, AND EIGHT HOURS FOR WHAT WE WILL."

to organ grinders and street musicians play familiar melodies. For a penny or a nickel, they could buy bagels, baked potatoes, soda, and other foods and drinks. In the summer, when the heat and humidity in tenement apartments reached unbearable levels, the streets became a hive of neighborhood social life. One immigrant fondly recalled his boyhood on the streets of New York's Lower East Side: "Something was always happening, and our attention was continually being shifted from one excitement to another."

The streets were open to all, but other leisure institutions drew mainly a male clientele. For example, in cities with a strong German immigrant presence like Baltimore, Milwaukee, and Cincinnati, gymnastic clubs (called *Turnverein*) and singing societies (*Gesangverein*) provided both companionship and the opportunity to perpetuate old-world cultural traditions.

For workmen of all ethnic backgrounds, saloons offered companionship, conviviality, and five-cent beer, often with a free lunch thrown in. New York City had an estimated ten thousand saloons by 1900 and Denver nearly five hundred. As neighborhood gathering places, saloons reinforced group identity and became centers for immigrant politics. Saloonkeepers, who often doubled as local ward bosses and turned out the vote in their neighborhoods, performed small services for their patrons, including finding jobs and writing letters for illiterate immigrants. Sports memorabilia and pictures of prominent prizefighters adorned saloon walls. With their rich mahogany bars, etched glass, shiny brass rails, and elegant mirrors, saloons provided patrons with a taste of luxury. Although working-class women rarely joined their husbands at the saloon, they might send a son or daughter to the corner pub to fetch a "growler"—a large tin pail of beer.

The conventions of saloon culture thus stood in marked contrast to both the socially isolating routines of factory labor and the increasingly private and family-centered social life of the middle class. Nevertheless, it would be a mistake to view the old-time saloon through a haze of sentimental nostalgia. Prostitution and crime flourished in the rougher saloons. Moreover, drunken husbands sometimes beat their wives and children, squandered their limited income, and lost their jobs. The pervasiveness of alcoholism was devastating. Temperance reformers, in their attack on saloons, targeted a widespread social problem.

The Rise of Professional Sports

Contrary to the prevailing myth, schoolboy Abner Doubleday did not invent baseball in Cooperstown, New York, in 1839. As an English game called

SALOON INTERIOR Neighborhood saloons were places where friends could get together. In his novel *Sister Carrie,* Theodore Dreiser admiringly described "the long bar … [with its] blaze of lights, polished woodwork, colored and cut glassware and many fancy bottles." *(Library of Congress)*

rounders, the pastime had existed in one form or another since the seventeenth century. If Americans did not create baseball, they did turn it into a major professional sport. In 1845, the first organized baseball team, the New York Knickerbockers, was formed. In the 1860s, rules were codified and the sport assumed its modern form. Overhand pitches replaced underhand tosses. Fielders wore gloves, games were standardized at nine innings, and bases were spaced ninety feet apart.

In that same decade, promoters organized professional clubs and began to charge admission and compete for players. The Cincinnati Red Stockings, the first team to put its players under contract for the whole season, gained fame in 1869 by touring the country and ending the season with fifty-seven wins and no losses. Team owners organized the National League in 1876, took control from the players by requiring them to sign contracts that barred them from playing for rival organizations, and limited each city to one professional team. Soon the owners were filling baseball parks with crowds of ten to twelve thousand fans and earning enormous profits. By the 1890s, baseball had become big business.

Although baseball attracted a national following from all social levels, the working class particularly took the sport to heart. The most profitable teams were those in major industrial cities with a large working-class population. Workers avidly followed their team's progress. Many saloons reported scores on blackboards and an estimated 50 percent of players worked in saloons in the off-season or became saloon owners when they retired from the game.

If baseball helped build solidarity among some ethnic groups, it also fostered discrimination against blacks. Although at least fifty-five blacks played on integrated teams between 1883 and 1898, the refusal of the Chicago White Stockings in 1887 to play a team with George Stovey, a star black pitcher, marked a turning point. That same year, Colored baseball clubs opened in six cities. Increasingly thereafter, blacks were banned from playing on professional teams.

Newspapers thrived on baseball. Joseph Pulitzer introduced the first separate sports page when he bought the *New York World* in 1883, and much of the sporting news in the *World* and other papers was devoted to baseball. Fans who cheered the

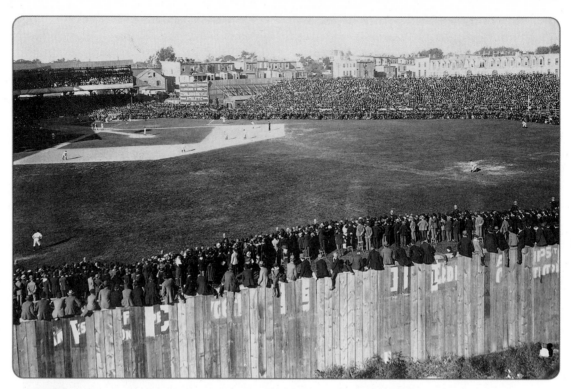

BALTIMORE, 1897 An overflow crowd watches the Baltimore Orioles play the Boston Beaneaters. Nestled in among the row houses, urban stadiums like this one drew huge crowds. *(Library of Congress)*

hometown team provided cities with a shared sports loyalty that reduced ethnic, class, and religious differences, but drinking and gambling continued to plague the game.

Although no organized sport attracted as large a following as baseball, horse racing and boxing contests drew big crowds of spectators and bettors. Louisville's Kentucky Derby became an important social event for the rich, but professional boxing aroused more passionate devotion among laborers. Bare-knuckled prizefighting became a testing ground where men could demonstrate their toughness and physical prowess.

For many working-class Americans, heavyweight fighter **John L. Sullivan,** "the Boston Strong Boy" personified these traits. Of Irish immigrant stock, Sullivan began boxing in 1877 at the age of nineteen. His first professional fight came in 1880 when he knocked out John Donaldson, "the Champion of the West," in a Cincinnati beer hall. With his massive physique, handlebar mustache, and arrogant swagger, Sullivan was enormously popular among immigrants. Barnstorming across the country, he vanquished a succession of local strongmen, invariably wearing his trademark green tights with an American flag wrapped around his middle. Yet, Sullivan refused to fight blacks, supposedly in deference to the wishes of his fans. This policy conveniently

allowed him to avoid facing the finest boxer of the 1880s, the Australian black, Peter Jackson.

Sullivan loved drink and high living, and by the end of the 1880s he was sadly out of shape. But when the editor of the *Police Gazette,* a sensational tabloid, designed a new heavyweight championship belt—allegedly containing two hundred ounces of silver and encrusted with diamonds and pure gold—and awarded it to Sullivan's rival Jake Kilrain, the champion had to defend himself. The two met on a sweltering, hundred-degree day in New Orleans in July 1889 for the last bare-knuckles championship match. After seventy-five short but grueling rounds, Kilrain's managers threw in the towel. Newspapers around the nation banner-headlined the story. Contemptuously returning the championship belt to the *Police Gazette* after having had it appraised at $175, Sullivan went on the road to star in a melodrama written specifically for him. Playing the role of a blacksmith, he (in the words of

> "His colors are the Stars and Stripes, / He also wears the green, / And he's the grandest slugger that / The ring has ever seen."

a recent historian of bare-knuckles boxing) "pounded an anvil, beat a bully, and mutilated his lines." But his fans did not care; he was one of them, and they adored him. As one admirer wrote,

His colors are the Stars and Stripes,
He also wears the green,
And he's the grandest slugger that
The ring has ever seen.

Vaudeville, Amusement Parks, and Dance Halls

In contrast to the male preserve of saloons and prizefights, the world of vaudeville, amusement parks, and neighborhood dance halls welcomed all comers regardless of gender. Some of them proved particularly congenial to working-class women.

Vaudeville evolved out of antebellum minstrel shows that featured white singers made up as blacks. The shows typically opened with a trained animal routine or a dance number, followed by a musical interlude. Comic skits then ridiculed the trials of urban life, satirizing police and municipal ineptitude, poking fun at immigrant accents, and mining a rich vein of broad ethnic humor and stereotypes. Black-face skits were sometimes included. After a highbrow operatic aria and acts by ventriloquists, pantomimes, and magicians, the program ended with a "flash" finale such as flying-trapeze artists swinging against a black background. By the 1880s, vaudeville was drawing larger crowds than any other form of theater.

The white working class's fascination with vaudeville's blackface acts has been the subject of considerable recent scrutiny by historians. Some have interpreted it as a way for the white working class to mock middle-class ideals. By pretending to act like the popular stereotypes of blacks, white working-class youths could challenge traditional family structures, the virtue of sexual self-denial, and adult expectations about working hard. In this view, popular culture was making fun of the ideals of thrift and propriety being promoted in marketplace and domestic ideology. Other historians have argued that blackface buffoonery, with its grotesque, demeaning caricatures of African Americans, reinforced prejudice against blacks and restricted their escape from lower-class status. Paradoxically, therefore, the popularity of blackface vaudeville acts reinforced white racial solidarity and strengthened the expanding wall separating whites and African Americans.

FOR THE HEAVY-WEIGHT CHAMPIONSHIP OF THE WORLD.

John Lawrence Sullivan, the Champion, and James J. Corbett, the Adonis of the Fistic Arena, Who Are to Battle September 7th Next For a Purse and Stakes of $25,000 and the Big Fellow's Title.

WORLD'S HEAVYWEIGHT BOXING CHAMPIONSHIP, 1892 In dethroning ring champion John L. Sullivan, "Gentleman Jim" Corbett demonstrated that speed and finesse were more than a match for brute strength. *(Courtesy Ford Archives)*

Where vaudeville offered psychological escape from the stresses of working-class life, amusement parks provided physical escape. New York's Coney Island, a section of Brooklyn's oceanfront, evolved into a resort for the masses in the 1870s. At Coney Island, young couples went dancing, rode through the dark Tunnel of Love, sped down the dizzying roller coaster in Steeplechase Park, or watched belly dancers in the carnival sideshows. Customers were encouraged to surrender to the spirit of play, forget the demands of the industrial world, and lose themselves in fantasy.

By the end of the nineteenth century, New York City had well over three hundred thousand female wage earners, most of them young, unmarried women working as seamstresses, laundresses, typists, domestic servants, and department-store clerks. For this army of low-paid young working women and their counterparts in other cities, amusement parks exerted a powerful lure. Here, they could meet friends, spend time with young men beyond the watchful eyes of their parents, show off their new dresses, and try out the latest dance steps. As a twenty-year-old German immigrant woman who worked as a servant in a wealthy household observed,

I have heard some of the high people with whom I have been living say that Coney Island is not tony. The trouble is that these high people don't know how to dance. I have to laugh when I see them at their balls and parties. If only I could get out on the floor and show them how—they would be astonished.

For such women, the brightly decorated dance pavilion, the exciting music, and the spell of a warm summer night could seem a magical release from the drudgery of daily life.

Ragtime

Nothing could illustrate more sharply the differences between middle- and working-class culture than the contrasting styles of popular music they favored. The middle class preferred hymns or songs that conveyed a moral lesson. The working class delighted in ragtime, which originated in the 1880s with black musicians in the saloons and brothels of the South and Midwest and was played strictly for entertainment.

Ragtime developed out of the rich tradition of sacred and secular songs through which African Americans had long eased the burdens of their lives. Like spirituals, ragtime used syncopated rhythms and complex harmonies, but it blended these with marching-band musical structures to create a distinctive style. A favorite of "honky-tonk" piano players, ragtime was introduced to the broader public in the 1890s and became a national sensation.

The reasons for the sudden ragtime craze were complex. Inventive, playful, with catchy syncopations and an infectious rhythm in the bass clef, the music displayed an originality that had an appeal all its own. Part of ragtime's popularity also came from its origin in brothels and its association with blacks, who were widely stereotyped in the 1890s as sexual, sensual, and uninhibited by the rigid Victorian social conventions that restricted whites. The "wild" and complex rhythms of ragtime were widely interpreted to be a freer and more "natural" expression of elemental feelings about love and sex.

Ragtime's great popularity proved a mixed blessing for blacks. It testified to the achievements of brilliant composers like Scott Joplin, helped break down the barriers faced by blacks in the music industry, and contributed to a spreading rebellion against the repressiveness of Victorian standards. But ragtime simply confirmed some whites' stereotype of blacks as primitive and sensual, a bias that underlay the racism of the period and helped justify segregation and discrimination.

Cultures in Conflict

Even within the elite and middle classes, Victorian morality and genteel cultural standards were never totally accepted. As the century ended, increasing numbers of people questioned these beliefs. Women stood at the center of the era's cultural turbulence. Thwarted by a restrictive code of feminine propriety, they made their dissatisfactions heard. The rise of women's clubs, the growth of women's colleges, and even the 1890s bicycle fad testified to the emergence of what some began to call the "new woman."

At the same time, a widening chasm divided the well-to-do from urban working-class immigrants. In no period of American history have class conflicts—cultural as well as economic—been more open and raw. As middle-class leaders nervously eyed the sometimes disorderly culture of city streets, saloons, boxing clubs, dance halls, and amusement parks, they saw a challenge to their own cultural and social values. Some middle-class reformers promoted the public school as a way to impose middle-class values on the urban masses. Others battled urban "vice" and "immorality." But ultimately it

> Mark Twain declared that he was through with "literature and all that bosh."

was the polite mores of the middle class, not urban working-class culture, that proved more vulnerable. By 1900, the Victorian social and moral ethos was crumbling on every front.

The Genteel Tradition and Its Critics

What was this genteel culture that aroused such opposition? In the 1870s and 1880s, a group of upper-class writers and magazine editors, led by Harvard art history professor Charles Eliot Norton and New York editors Richard Watson Gilder of *The Century* magazine and E.L. Godkin of *The Nation,* codified Victorian standards for literature and the arts. They campaigned to improve American taste in interior furnishings, textiles, ceramics, wallpaper, and books. By fashioning rigorous criteria for excellence in writing and design, they hoped to create a coherent national artistic culture. Nevertheless, at the start, they relied on women writers such as Helen Hunt Jackson (see Chapter 17), who often questioned their patriarchal views.

In the 1880s, Norton, Godkin, and Gilder, joined by the editors of other highbrow periodicals such as the *Atlantic Monthly* and *North American Review,* set up new guidelines for serious literature. They lectured the middle class about the value of high culture and the insights to be gained from painting and music. They censored their own publications to remove all sexual allusions, disrespectful treatments of Christianity, and unhappy endings. Expanding their combined circulation to nearly two hundred thousand copies, Godkin and the other editors of "quality" periodicals created an important forum for serious writing. Novelists Henry James, who published virtually all of his work in the *Atlantic,* and William Dean Howells, who served as editor of the same magazine, helped lead this elite literary establishment. James believed that "it is art that makes life. … [There is] no substitute whatever for [its] force and beauty …"

This interest in art for art's sake paralleled a broader crusade called the "aesthetic movement," led in England by William Morris, Oscar Wilde, and other art critics, who sought to bring art into every facet of life. In America, Candace Wheeler and other reformers made its influence felt through the work of architects, jewelers, and interior decorators.

Although the magazines initially provided an important forum for new writers, their editors' elitism and desire to control the nation's literary standards soon aroused opposition. Samuel Langhorne Clemens, better known as **Mark Twain,** spoke for many young writers when he declared that he was through with "literature and all that bosh." Attacking aristocratic literary conventions, Twain and

MARK TWAIN Twain not only broke from highbred literary standards but also created unique personal style through his studied poses and distinctive attire. *(North Wind Picture Archives)*

other authors who shared his concerns explored new forms of fiction and worked to broaden its appeal to the general public.

These efforts to chart new directions for American literature rested on fundamental changes taking place in the publishing industry. To compete with elite periodicals costing twenty-five to thirty-five cents, new magazines like *Ladies' Home Journal, Cosmopolitan,* and *McClure's* lowered their prices to a dime or fifteen cents and tripled or quadrupled their circulation. Supporting themselves through advertising, these magazines encouraged new trends in fiction while mass-marketing new products. Their editors sought writers who could provide accurate depictions of the "whirlpool of real life" and create a new civic consciousness to heal the class divisions of American society.

Some of these authors have been called regionalists because they captured the distinctive dialect and details of local life in their environs. In *The Country of the Pointed Firs* (1896), for example, Sarah Orne Jewett wrote of the New England village life that she knew in South Berwick, Maine. Others, most notably William Dean Howells, have been called realists because of their focus on the truthful depiction of the commonplace, especially in urban areas. Still others have been categorized as naturalists because their novels and stories deny free will and stress the ways in which life's outcomes are determined by economic and psychological forces. Stephen Crane's *Maggie: A Girl of the Streets* (1892), a bleak story of an innocent girl's exploitation and ultimate suicide in an urban slum, is generally considered the first naturalistic American novel. Yet, in practice, these categories are imprecise and often overlap. What many of these writers shared was a skepticism about literary conventions and an intense desire to understand the society around them and portray it in words.

The careers of Mark Twain and Theodore Dreiser highlight the changes in the publishing industry and the evolution of new forms of writing. Both authors grew up in the Midwest, outside the East Coast literary establishment. Twain was born near Hannibal, Missouri, in 1835, and Dreiser in Terre Haute, Indiana, in 1871. As young men, both worked as newspaper reporters and traveled widely. Both learned from direct and sometimes bitter experience about the greed, speculation, and fraud that figured centrally in Gilded Age life.

Of the two, Twain more incessantly sought a mass-market audience. With his drooping mustache, white hair, and white suits, Twain turned himself into a media personality, lecturing from coast to coast, founding his own publishing house, and using door-to-door salesmen to sell his books. The name Mark Twain became his trademark, identifying him to readers as a literary celebrity much as the labels Coca-Cola and Ivory Soap won instant consumer recognition. Although Dreiser possessed neither Twain's flamboyant personality nor his instinct for salesmanship, he, too, learned to crank out articles.

Drawing on their own experiences, Twain and Dreiser wrote about the human impact of the wrenching social changes taking place around them: the flow of people to the cities and the relentless scramble for power, wealth, and fame. In *The Adventures of Huckleberry Finn* (1884), Twain tells a story of two runaways, the rebellious Huck and the slave Jim, drifting down the Mississippi in search of freedom. Their physical journey, which contrasts idyllic life on the raft with the tawdry, fraudulent world of small riverfront towns, is a journey of identity that brings with it a deeper understanding of contemporary American society.

Dreiser's *Sister Carrie* (1900) also tells of a journey. In this case, the main character, Carrie Meeber, an innocent girl on her way from her Wisconsin farm home to Chicago, is seduced by a traveling salesman and then moves in with the married proprietor of a fancy saloon. Driven by her desire for expensive department-store clothes and lavish entertainment, Carrie is an opportunist incapable of feeling guilt. She follows her married lover to New York, knowing that he has stolen the receipts from his saloon, abandons him when his money runs out, and pursues her own career in the theater.

Twain and Dreiser broke decisively with the genteel tradition's emphasis on manners and decorum. *Century* magazine readers complained that *Huckleberry Finn* was coarse and "destitute of a single redeeming quality." The publisher of *Sister Carrie* was so repelled by Dreiser's novel that he printed only a thousand copies (to fulfill the legal terms of his contract) and then stored them in a warehouse, refusing to promote them.

Growing numbers of scholars and critics similarly challenged the self-serving certitudes of Victorian mores, including assumptions that moral worth and economic standing were closely linked and that the status quo of the 1870s and 1880s represented a social order decreed by God and nature alike. Whereas Henry George, Lester Ward, and Edward Bellamy elaborated their visions of a cooperative and harmonious society (see Chapter 18), economist Thorstein Veblen in *The Theory of the Leisure Class* (1899) offered a caustic critique of the lifestyles of the new capitalist elite. Raised in a Norwegian farm community in Minnesota, Veblen looked at the captains of industry and their families with a jaundiced eye, documenting their "conspicuous consumption" of expensive products and lamenting the widening gap between "those who worked without profit" and "those who profited without working."

> Veblen lamented the widening gap between "those who worked without profit" and "those who profited without working."

Within the new discipline of sociology, Annie MacLean exposed the exploitation of department-store clerks, Walter Wyckoff uncovered the hand-to-mouth existence of unskilled laborers, and W.E.B. Du Bois documented the suffering and hardships faced by blacks in Philadelphia. The publication of these social scientists' writings, coupled with the economic depression and seething labor agitation of the 1890s, made it increasingly difficult for turn-of-the-century middle-class Americans to accept the smug, self-satisfied belief in progress and gentility that had been a hallmark of the Victorian outlook.

Modernism in Architecture and Painting

The challenge to the genteel tradition also found strong support among architects and painters. By the 1890s Chicago architects William Holabird, John Wellborn Root, and others had tired of copying European designs. Breaking with established architects such as Richard Morris Hunt, the designer of French châteaux for New York's Fifth Avenue, these Chicago architects followed the lead of Louis Sullivan, who argued that a building's form should follow its function. In their view, banks should look like the financial institutions they were, not like Greek temples. Striving to create functional American design standards, the Chicago architects looked for inspiration to the future—to **modernism**—not to the past.

The Chicago architect **Frank Lloyd Wright** designed "prairie-school" houses that represented a typical modernist break with past styles. Wright scorned the three-story Victorian house with its large attic and basement. His designs, which featured broad, sheltering roofs and horizontal silhouettes, used interconnecting rooms to create a sense of spaciousness.

The call of modernism, with its rejection of Victorian refinement, influenced late-nineteenth-century American painting as well. The watercolors of Winslow Homer, a magazine illustrator during the Civil War, revealed nature as brutally tough and unsentimental. In Homer's grim, elemental seascapes, lone men struggle against massive waves that constantly threaten to overwhelm them. Thomas Eakins's canvases of swimmers, boxers, and rowers (such as his well-known *Champion Single Sculls,* painted in 1871) similarly captured moments of vigorous physical exertion

in everyday life. While Mary Cassatt shared Eakins's interest in everyday life, she often took as her subject the bond between mother and child, as in her painting *The Bath* (ca. 1891). After studying at the Pennsylvania Academy of Fine Arts, she moved to Paris in 1874, where she worked closely with French Impressionist painters such as Monet and Degas.

The revolt by architects and painters against Victorian standards was symptomatic of a larger shift in middle-class thought. This shift resulted from fundamental economic changes that had spawned a far more complex social environment than that of the past. As Protestant minister Josiah Strong perceptively observed in 1898, the transition from muscle to mechanical power had "separated, as by an impassable gulf, the simple, homespun, individualistic world of the … past, from the complex, closely associated life of the present." The increasingly evident gap between rural or small-town life—a world of quiet parlors and flickering kerosene lamps—and life in the big, glittering, electrified cities of iron and glass made nineteenth-century Americans acutely aware of differences in upbringing and wealth. Given the disparities between rich and poor, between rural and urban, and between native-born Americans and recent immigrants, it is no wonder that pious Victorian platitudes about proper manners and graceful arts seemed out of touch with the new social realities.

Distrusting the idealistic Victorian assumptions about social progress, middle-class journalists, novelists, artists, and politicians nevertheless remained divided over how to replace them. Not until the Progressive Era would social reformers draw on a new expertise in social research and an enlarged conception of the federal government's regulatory power to break sharply with their Victorian predecessors' social outlook.

From Victorian Lady to New Woman

Although middle-class women figured importantly in the revolt against Victorian refinement, their role was complex and ambiguous. Dissatisfaction with the cult of domesticity did not necessarily lead to open rebellion. Many women, although chafing against the constraints of deference and the assumption that they should limit their activities to the home, remained committed to playing a nurturing role within the family. In fact, early advocates of a "widened sphere" for women often fused the traditional Victorian ideal of womanhood with a firm commitment to political action.

> Josiah Strong observed that the transition from muscle to mechanical power had "separated, as by an impassable gulf, the simple, homespun, individualistic world of the … past, from the complex, closely associated life of the present."

RIDE A CRAWFORD
allowed women to ge
young women and m
parents. *(Library of C*

middle-cla
could reas
social worl
tory worke
hours a we
the ideal r
many wom
control ove
as their pri

pediatrician Joseph Mayer Rice, who toured thirty-six cities and interviewed twelve hundred teachers in 1892, scornfully criticized an educational establishment that stressed singsong memorization and prisonlike discipline.

Rice's biting attack on public education overlooked the real advances in reading and mathematics made in the previous two decades. Nationally, despite the influx of immigrants, the illiteracy rate in English for individuals ten years and older dropped from 17 percent in 1880 to 13 percent in 1890, largely because of the expansion of urban educational facilities. American high schools were also coeducational, and girls made up the majority of the students by 1900. But Rice was on target in assailing many teachers' rigid emphasis on silence, docility, and unquestioning obedience to the rules. When a Chicago school inspector found a thirteen-year-old boy huddled in the basement of a stockyard building and ordered him back to school, the weeping boy blurted out, "[T]hey hits ye if yer don't learn, and they hits ye if ye whisper, and they hits ye if ye have string in yer pocket, and they hits ye if yer seat squeaks, and they hits ye if ye don't stan' up in time, and they hits ye if yer late, and they hits ye if ye ferget the page."

By the 1880s, several different groups found themselves in opposition to centralized urban public school bureaucracies. Although many working-class families valued education, those who depended on their children's meager wages for survival resisted the attempt to force their sons and daughters to attend school past the elementary grades. Although some immigrant families made great sacrifices to enable their children to get an education, many withdrew their offspring from school as soon as they had learned the rudiments of reading and writing, and sent them to work.

Furthermore, Catholic immigrants objected to the overwhelmingly Protestant orientation of the public schools. Distressed by the use of the King James translation of the Bible and by the schools'

ELEMENTARY CLASS PHOTOGRAPH, LOWER EAST SIDE, NEW YORK Dressed in native costumes, these elementary school students posed with their teacher, costumed as the Statute of Liberty, to indicate the diversity of their immigrant backgrounds. *(Picture Research Consultants & Archives)*

failure to observe saints' days, Catholics set up separate parochial school systems. In response, Republican politicians, resentful of Catholic immigrants' overwhelming preference for the Democratic Party, tried unsuccessfully to pass a constitutional amendment cutting off all public aid to church-related schools in 1875. Catholics in turn denounced federal aid to public schools as intended "to suppress Catholic education, gradually extinguish Catholicity in this country, and to form one homogeneous American people after the New England Evangelical type."

At the other end of the social scale, upper-class parents who did not wish to send their children to immigrant-thronged public schools enrolled their daughters in female seminaries such as Chatham Hall in Chatham, Virginia, and their sons in private academies and boarding schools like St. Paul's in Concord, New Hampshire. The proliferation of private and parochial schools, together with the controversies over compulsory education, school funding, and classroom decorum, reveals the extent to which public education had become mired in ethnic and class differences. Unlike Germany and Japan, which created national education systems in the late nineteenth century, the United States, reflecting its social heterogeneity, maintained a system of locally run public and private institutions that allowed each segment of society to retain some influence over the schools attended by its own children. Amid the disputes, school enrollments dramatically expanded. In 1870, fewer than seventy-two thousand students were attending the nation's 1,026 high schools. By 1900, the number of high schools had jumped to more than five thousand and the number of students to more than half a million.

CONCLUSION

By the 1890s, class conflict was evident in practically every area of city life, from mealtime manners to popular entertainment and recreation. As new immigrants flooded the tenements and spilled out onto neighborhood streets, it became impossible for native-born Americans to ignore their strange religious and social customs. Ethnic differences were compounded by class differences. Often poor and from peasant or working-class backgrounds, the immigrants from southern and eastern Europe took unskilled jobs and worked for subsistence-level wages. The slums and tenements in which they lived had high rates of disease. Middle- and upper-class Americans often responded by moving to fashionable avenues or suburbs and by stigmatizing them as nonwhite and racially inferior.

To distinguish themselves from these newcomers, native-born Americans stressed their commitment to Victorian morality, with its emphasis on manners, decorum, and self-control. Although never fully accepted even among the well-to-do, these Victorian ideals were meant to apply new standards for society. Lavish department stores and artistically designed houses reflected the middle- and upper-class faith that the consumption of material goods indicated good taste.

To raise standards, the prosperous classes expanded the number of high schools and created a new research university system for training educators, lawyers, doctors, and other professionals. As defenders of the new Victorian morality, educated middle- and upper-class women were expected to become the protectors of the home. Some members of the upper classes also tried to address the problems of poverty and congestion in the inner city. While Jacob Riis, Jane Addams, and other reformers worked to improve overcrowded housing and dangerous working conditions, Anthony Comstock and less sympathetic reformers attacked immigrant values and cultures in an effort to uplift and Americanize them.

Nowhere was the conflict between the social classes more evident than in the controversy over leisure entertainment. Caught up in the material benefits of a prospering industrial society, middle- and upper-class Americans battled against what they deemed "indecent" lower-class behavior in all its forms, from dancing to ragtime, gambling, and prizefighting to playing baseball on Sunday and visiting bawdy boardwalk sideshows. Even public parks became arenas of class conflict. Whereas the elite favored large, impeccably groomed urban parks that would serve as models of orderliness and propriety, working people fought for parks where they could picnic, play ball, drink beer, and escape the stifling heat of tenement apartments.

Although the well-to-do classes often appeared to have the upper hand in these clashes, significant disagreements about moral standards surfaced early within their own ranks. Critics, among them Charlotte Perkins Gilman, faulted middle-class society for its obsession with polite manners, empty social rituals, and restrictions on the occupations open to women.

By 1900, the contest for power between the elite classes and the largely immigrant working class was heading toward a partial resolution. As Victorian morality eroded, undermined by dissension from within and opposition from without, new standards emerged that blended elements of earlier positions. For example, new rules regulated behavior in the boxing ring and on the baseball field. Still, it was immigrant heroes who captured the popular imagination. The elite vision of sport as a vehicle for instilling self-discipline and self-control was transformed into a new commitment to sports as spectacle and entertainment. Sports had become big business and an important part of the new consumerism.

Similar patterns of compromise and change took place in other arenas. Vaudeville houses, attacked by the affluent for their risqué performances, evolved into the nation's first movie theaters. Ragtime music, with its syncopated rhythms, gave rise to jazz. In short, the dashing, disreputable, and raucous working-class culture of the late-nineteenth-century city can be seen as the seedbed of twentieth-century mass culture. And everywhere popular culture became increasingly dominated by commercial interests that capitalized on the disposable income created by the nation's explosive urban and industrial growth.

KEY TERMS

Scott Joplin   (p. 567)

"new immigrants"   (p. 569)

Ellis Island   (p. 571)

Victorian morality   (p. 573)

department stores   (p. 577)

research university   (p. 579)

Salvation Army   (p. 581)

Josephine Shaw Lowell   (p. 581)

Anthony Comstock   (p. 581)

Social Gospel   (p. 582)

Jane Addams   (p. 582)

Florence Kelley   (p. 583)

John L. Sullivan   (p. 586)

Mark Twain   (p. 589)

modernism   (p. 591)

Frank Lloyd Wright   (p. 591)

Frances Willard   (p. 592)

Charlotte Perkins Gilman
   (p. 592)

Kate Chopin   (p. 592)

FOR FURTHER REFERENCE

Tom Buk-Swienty, *The Other Half: The Life of Jacob Riis and the World of Immigrant America* (2008). A fascinating look into the world of investigative journalism, immigration, and photography.

Malcolm Campbell, *Ireland's New World: Immigrants, Politics, and Society in the United States and Australia, 1815–1922* (2008). A comparative view of Irish immigration in a transnational context.

Daniel A. Clark, *Creating the College Man: American Mass Magazines and Middle-Class Manhood* (2010). An insightful look at how a collegiate education became considered essential for business and professional advancement.

Janet Floyd, Alison Easton, R.J. Ellis, and Lindsey Traub, *Becoming Visible: Women's Presence in Late Nineteenth-Century America* (2010). Interdisciplinary essays on women's complex engagement with American society.

Elliot Gorn and Warren Goldstein, *A Brief History of American Sports* (1993). A skillful analysis of the effect of urbanization, industrialization, and commercialization on American sports.

Richard B. McKensie, ed., *Home Away from Home: The Forgotten History of Orphanages* (2009). A balanced assessment of the successes and drawbacks of the orphanage movement.

Mark J. Noonan, *Reading the Century Monthly Magazine: American Literature and Culture, 1870–1893* (2010). A careful analysis of the ways in which a major periodical tried to shape middle-class values and reading habits.

Carl Smith, *Urban Disorder and the Shape of Belief: The Great Chicago Fire, the Haymarket Bomb, and the Model Town of Pullman* (1995). An innovative study of the ways in which the nineteenth-century responses to urban disorders shaped contemporary perceptions about city life.

Peter Stearns, *Schools and Students in Industrial Society: Japan and the West, 1870–1940* (1998). Stearns's comparative examination of high school education in Europe, the United States, and Japan highlights the distinctive features of American education.

Olivier Zunz, *Making America Corporate, 1879–1920* (1990). A pioneering exploration of corporate capitalism's effect on the creation of a consumer culture.

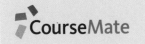

Visit the CourseMate website at **www.cengagebrain.com** for additional study tools and review materials for this chapter.

Politics and Expansion in an Industrializing Age,

1877–1900

PRESIDENT JAMES A. GARFIELD
(National Portrait Gallery, Smithsonian Institution/Art Resource, NY)

JULY 2, 1881, was a muggy summer day in Washington, DC, and President James A. Garfield was leaving town for a visit to western Massachusetts. At 9:30 A.M., as he strolled through the railroad station, shots rang out. Garfield fell, a bullet in his back. The shooter, Charles Guiteau, immediately surrendered.

At first, doctors thought the president would recover. But Garfield, a veteran who had seen the long-term effects of gunshot wounds, knew better. "I am a dead man," he told them. His doctors tried everything. But as the doctors probed the wound with bare hands and unsterilized instruments, blood poisoning set in. On September 19, Garfield died.

The nation mourned. An Ohio farm boy, Will Boyer, was shocked to hear the news from another farmer as he walked along a country road. Garfield embodied the American dream of the self-made man. Born in a log cabin in Ohio (he was the last log-cabin president), he had worked his way through Williams College, preached in the Disciples of Christ Church, taught at Hiram College, practiced law, and won election to the Ohio senate. He fought in the Civil War, went to Congress in 1863, and was elected president in 1880. As for Guiteau, the jury rejected his insanity plea, and in June 1882 he was hanged.

An ambitious, well-meaning man, Garfield also embodied a political generation that seemed more preoccupied with the spoils of office than with the problems of ordinary people. In Congress, Garfield had been tainted by the 1872 Crédit Mobilier scandal and other corruption charges. His presidential nomination in 1880 had resulted from a split in the Republican Party between two rival factions, the Stalwarts and the Half-Breeds, that vied with each other over the distribution of patronage jobs.

The obscure Guiteau, a loyal party member who had supported Garfield, expected to be rewarded with a high diplomatic post. When this failed to materialize, his delusionary mental state worsened. Viewing Garfield's death as "a political necessity," he believed the public would hail him as a hero. (Indeed, he had selected as his gun a .44-caliber "British Bulldog" pistol because it would look good in a museum.)

While contemporary critics like Henry Adams viewed Garfield's assassination as an example of the absurdity of late-nineteenth-century politics—a time, Adams sneered, of "little but damaged reputations"—historians today see it as a sign of how closely contested political battles were. The phenomenal expansion of large corporations, the settlement of the trans-Mississippi West, and the surge in urban growth put intense pressure on the political process. At stake was not only the government's proper role in the stimulation and regulation of America's explosive industrial growth but also the thorny issues of how to assimilate new immigrants, control chaotic urban life, gain access to new markets, and encourage territorial expansion.

THE POLITICS OF INDUSTRIALIZATION As this cartoon in *Puck* attests, many Americans in the late nineteenth century believed that high tariffs on imported goods could lead to strikes and the formation of monopolies. *(Frank Wood Historical Collections)*

These intense debates over economic and social policy involved nothing less than contending visions of how industrial growth should or should not be regulated and who should benefit financially. The struggle to control economic expansion reached its peak in the 1890s when a new third party, the Populists, joined with the Democrats to challenge corporate control of the economy. The leading symbol of this challenge became the campaign for "free silver"—backing currency with silver reserves as well as gold. Representing the opposite position, the Republican Party's support for high tariffs and the gold standard represented a commitment to encouraging the growth of large corporations, to freeing industry to expand without regulation, and to developing new markets.

From the mid-1870s to the mid-1890s, power had seesawed back and forth between the political parties. No party was able to control the political process. But in 1896, the election of President William F. McKinley ushered in a generation of Republican domination of national politics. Elected in a campaign focused on the restoration of prosperity, McKinley stumbled into war with Spain, substantially increased U.S. territory, and established new outposts from which American corporations could gain access to overseas markets.

FOCUS Questions

- How did political parties build coalitions out of their diverse ethnic and regional constituencies?
- What factors prompted the rise of the Grange and the Farmers' Alliance movements?
- Why did William Jennings Bryan fail to win the presidency in 1896?
- Why did the United States go to war with Spain and become an imperial power?

Party Politics in an Era of Upheaval, 1877–1884

Between 1877 and 1894, four presidents squeezed into office by the narrowest of margins, control of the House of Representatives changed hands five times, and seven new western states were admitted into the Union. Competition between political parties was intense. No one party could muster a working majority.

To meet these challenges, party leaders sought desperately to cement the loyalty of their followers. While the Democrats rebuilt their strength in the South, Republicans struggled to maintain the loyalties of the working class and to increase their support from business. At the municipal level, political machines worked to recruit immigrants and other newcomers in the rapidly expanding cities.

Contested Political Visions

In the late nineteenth century, more than 80 percent of eligible white males often voted, and in hard-fought elections, the percentage rose to 95 percent. Voter participation a century later would equal scarcely half that level.

Higher voter turnout resulted in part from the attempts of the major parties to navigate the stormy economy created by postwar industrial and geographic expansion, the influx of millions of immigrants, and the explosive growth of cities. As voter turnout shot up, however, political parties sidestepped issues such as taxation of corporations, support for those injured in factory accidents, and poverty relief. Nor was the American labor movement, unlike its counterpart in Europe, able to organize itself effectively as a political force. Except for the Interstate Commerce Act of 1887 and the largely symbolic Sherman Anti-Trust Act of 1890, Washington generally ignored the social consequences of industrialization.

How can we explain this refusal to address economic concerns and, at the same time, account for the enormous popular support for parties? The answer lies in the political ideology of the period and the three major symbolic and economic issues that preoccupied lawmakers nationally: the tariff, the money supply, and civil-service reform.

Political parties in the late nineteenth century energized voters not only by appealing to economic self interest, as was evident in support for industrialization and pensions for Civil War veterans and their widows but also by linking their programs to deeply held beliefs about the nature of the family and the proper role of government. Republicans justified their support for the tariff and defended their commitment to Union widows' pensions as a protection for the family home. Democrats countered, using metaphors of the seduction and rape of white women by outsiders and labeling Republican programs as classic examples of the perils of using excessive government force. High tariffs imperiled the family and threatened economic disaster. With respect to

CHRONOLOGY 1877–1902

1869	Boss William M. Tweed gains control of New York's Tammany Hall political machine.
1878	Congress requires U.S. Treasury to purchase silver.
1880	James Garfield elected president.
1881	Assassination of Garfield; Chester A. Arthur becomes president.
1883	Pendleton Civil Service Act.
1884	Grover Cleveland elected president.
1886	*Wabash* v. *Illinois*.
1887	Interstate Commerce Act.
1888	Benjamin Harrison elected president.
1889	National Farmers' Alliance formed.
1890	Sherman Silver Purchase Act. Sherman Anti-Trust Act. McKinley Tariff pushes tariffs to all-time high.

1893	Panic of 1893; depression of 1893–1897 begins. Repeal of the Sherman Silver Purchase Act.
1894	Coxey's "army" marches on Washington. Pullman strike. Wilson-Gorman Tariff.
1895	Supreme Court declares federal income tax unconstitutional.
1896	Free-silver forces capture Democratic Party and nominate William Jennings Bryan. William McKinley elected president.
1898	Acquisition of Hawai'i. Spanish-American War.
1898–1902	Guerrilla uprising in Philippines.
1900	Currency Act officially places United States on gold standard.
1901	Platt Amendment retains U.S. role in Cuba. Regular Army Nursing Corps founded.
1902	Philippine Government Act.

both parties, men, in particular, associated loyalty to party with a sense of masculinity.

Despite their differences over the tariff and monetary policy, neither Republicans nor Democrats believed that the national government had any right to regulate corporations or to protect the social welfare of workers. Neither party therefore courted the labor union vote. Many members of both parties embraced the doctrine of **laissez-faire**—the belief that unregulated competition represented the best path to progress. According to this view, the federal government should promote economic development but not regulate industry.

Rather than looking to Washington, people turned to local or state authorities. On the Great Plains, angry farmers demanded that their state legislatures regulate railroad rates. In the cities, immigrant groups, organized by political bosses, battled for control of municipal governments and local contracts. In response, native-born reformers attempted to oust the organizations in power and clean up corruption. Meanwhile, city and state governments vied with each other for control. Cities often could not change their system of government, alter their tax structure, or regulate municipal utilities without state approval. When Chicago wanted to issue permits to street popcorn vendors, for example, the Illinois legislature had to pass a special act.

Both parties, in the North and the South, practiced fraud by rigging elections, throwing out opposition votes, and paying for "floaters" who moved from precinct to precinct to vote. Each also expressed moral outrage at the other's illegal behavior.

By linking economic policy to family values, both parties reinforced the appeal of their platforms and encouraged the participation of women in the political process. Although most women could not vote, they played an active role in politics. Frances Willard and her followers in the Woman's Christian Temperance Union (WCTU), for example, helped create a Prohibition and Home Protection Party in the 1880s. A decade later, western women Populists won full suffrage in Colorado, Idaho, and Utah.

Patterns of Party Strength

In the 1870s and 1880s, each party had its own ideological appeal and centers of regional strength. The Democrats ruled the South, southern sections of border states like Ohio, and northern cities with large immigrant populations. They campaigned for minimal government expenditures, opposed tariff increases, and generally attacked what they considered to be "governmental interference in the economy." In addition, Democrats staunchly defended their immigrant followers. On the state and local levels, they fiercely opposed prohibition, supported parochial schools, and rejected requirements that immigrant children attend only those schools that taught in English.

The Republicans reigned in rural and small town New England, Pennsylvania, and the upper

Midwest and drew support from the **Grand Army of the Republic** (GAR), a social and political lobbying organization of northern Civil War veterans. They often "waved the bloody shirt," reminding voters that their party had led the nation during the Civil War. "The Democratic Party," wrote one Republican, "may be described as a common sewer and loathsome receptacle, into which is emptied every element of treason North and South." To emphasize their patriotism, the Republicans ran a series of former Union army generals for president and voted generous veterans' benefits.

State and local party leaders managed campaigns. They chose the candidates, raised money, organized rallies, and—if their candidate won—distributed public jobs to party workers. Bosses like the former saloonkeepers "Big Jim" Pendergast of Kansas City, a Democrat, and George B. Cox of Cincinnati, a Republican, turned out the vote by taking care of constituents, handing out municipal jobs, and financing campaigns with "contributions" extracted from city employees.

Although issues of governmental authority dominated on the federal level, family tradition, ethnic ties, religious affiliation, and local issues often determined an individual's vote. Outside the South, ethnicity and religion were the most reliable predictors of party affiliation. Catholics, especially Irish Catholics, and Americans of German ancestry tended to vote Democratic. Old-stock Protestant northerners, in contrast, voted Republican. Among immigrant groups, most British-born Protestants and 80 percent of Swedish and Norwegian Lutherans voted Republican, as did African Americans, North and South. Although intolerant of racial differences, the Democrats were generally more accepting of religious diversity than were the Republicans.

Political battles often centered on cultural differences, most notably, prohibition. Irish whiskey drinkers, German beer drinkers, and Italian wine drinkers were equally outraged by antiliquor legislation. State and local prohibition proposals always aroused passionate voter interest.

> "The Democratic Party may be described as a common sewer and loathsome receptacle, into which is emptied every element of treason North and South."

Political Bosses and Machine Politics

The swelling numbers of urban dwellers gave rise to a new kind of politician, the "boss," who listened to his urban constituents and lobbied on their behalf. The boss presided over the city's "machine"—an unofficial political organization designed to keep a particular party or faction in office. Whether

"TRAMP, TRAMP, TRAMP" THE BOYS ARE MARCHING, GAR REUNION POSTER, 1888. In addition to their nostalgic annual reunions, Union army veterans, organized as the Grand Army of the Republic, were a potent force in Republican Party politics, lobbying for pensions and other benefits. *(Library of Congress)*

officially serving as mayor or not, the boss, assisted by local ward or precinct captains, wielded enormous influence in city government. Often a former saloonkeeper or labor leader, the boss knew his constituents well.

For better or worse, the **political machine** was America's unique contribution to municipal government in an era of pell-mell urban growth. Typified by Tammany Hall, the Democratic organization that dominated New York City politics from the 1830s to the 1930s, machines emerged in Baltimore, Philadelphia, Atlanta, San Francisco, and a host of other cities after the Civil War.

By the turn of the century, many cities had experienced machine rule. Working through the local ward captains to turn out voters, the machine rode herd on the tangle of municipal bureaucracies, controlling who was hired for the police and fire departments. It rewarded its friends and punished its enemies through its control of taxes, licenses, and inspections. The machine gave tax breaks to favored contractors in return for large payoffs and slipped them insider information about upcoming street and sewer projects.

At the neighborhood level, the ward boss often acted as a welfare agent, helping the needy. To spend three dollars to pay a fine for a juvenile offense meant a lot to the poor, but it was small change to a boss who raked in millions from public-utility contracts and land deals. While the machine helped alleviate some suffering, it entangled urban social services with corrupt politics and often prevented city government from responding to the real problems of the city's neediest inhabitants.

Under New York City's boss, **William "Magear" Tweed,** the Tammany Hall machine revealed the slimy depths to which extortion and contract padding could sink. Between 1869 and 1871, Tweed gave $50,000 to the poor and $2,250,000 to schools, orphanages, and hospitals. In these same years, his machine dispensed sixty thousand patronage positions and pumped up the city's debt by $70 million through graft.

By the turn of the century, the bosses were facing well-organized assaults on their power, led by an urban elite whose members sought to restore "good government." In this atmosphere, the bosses increasingly forged alliances with civic organizations and reform leagues. The results, although never entirely satisfactory to anyone involved, paved the way for new sewage and transportation systems, expanded parklands, and improved public services—a record of considerable accomplishment, given the magnitude of the problems created by urban growth.

Regulating the Money Supply

In the 1870s, the debate over monetary policy—the question of how much money should be in circulation—was part of a larger struggle over how wealth and power should be distributed in post–Civil War America. The debate was shaped by Americans' almost superstitious reverence for gold and silver. Many believed that only gold or silver, or certificates exchangeable for these metals, were trustworthy. Reflecting this notion, all the federally issued currency in circulation in 1860 consisted of gold or silver coins or U.S. Treasury notes redeemable for gold or silver. (Currency from some sixteen hundred state banks also circulated, worsening a chaotic monetary situation.) During the Civil War, the federal government issued "greenbacks," paper money not backed by gold or silver.

Bankers and creditors also believed that economic stability required a strictly limited currency supply. Debtors, in contrast, favored expanding the money supply to make it easier for them to pay off their debts. The monetary debate thus focused on a specific question: should the Civil War paper "greenbacks" currently in circulation be retained or eliminated, leaving only a currency backed by gold? The hard times associated with the Panic of 1873 sharpened this dispute.

The Greenback Party (founded 1877) advocated an expanded money supply and other measures to benefit workers and farmers. In the 1878 midterm elections, with the support of labor organizations angered by the government's hostility toward the labor unrest of 1877, Greenback candidates won fourteen seats in Congress.

As prosperity returned and the Greenback party faded, the debate became focused on the controversy over the coinage of silver. In 1873, Congress instructed the U.S. mint to cease making silver coins. Silver had been "demonetized." But new discoveries in Nevada (see Chapter 17) vastly increased the silver supply, and debtor groups, hoping to lower interest rates on borrowed money, now demanded that the government resume the coinage of silver.

Backed by the silver-mine owners, silver forces won a partial victory in 1878, when Congress required the treasury to buy and mint up to $4 million worth of silver each month. But the treasury, dominated by monetary conservatives, sabotaged the law's intent by refusing to circulate the silver dollars that it minted.

Frustrated silver advocates tried a new approach in the **Sherman Silver Purchase Act** of 1890. This measure instructed the treasury to buy 4.5 million ounces of silver monthly and issue treasury notes,

TABLE 20.1 Major Currency Legislation, 1873–1900

Law	Provisions	Purpose
Coinage Act of 1873	Demonetized silver by ending the minting of silver dollars.	To make gold the only backing for U.S. currency.
Brand-Allison Silver Act of 1878 Sherman Silver Purchase Act of 1890	Authorized the treasury to mint $2–4 million in silver coins each month. Required the treasury to purchase 4.5 million ounces of silver per month at the prevailing market price.	To expand the money in circulation by remonetizing silver. To placate silver inflationists without sacrificing the dominance of gold.
Repeal of the Sherman Purchase Act (1893)	Ended the government purchase of silver.	To protect the gold standard for currency.
Currency Act of 1900	Set aside a gold reserve that could be legally exchanged for paper currency.	To place the U.S. currency on an internationally accepted monetary basis.

Source: Gretchen Ritter, *Goldbugs and Greenbacks* (Cambridge: Cambridge University Press, 2005), Appendix B.

redeemable in gold or silver, equivalent to the cost of these purchases. The monetary supply slightly increased, but the government paid far less for its monthly purchases and therefore issued fewer treasury notes. The controversy over silver dragged on (see Table 20.1).

Civil-Service Reform

A parallel controversy to the debate over the distribution of wealth and power raged over political appointments. For decades, successful candidates in national, state, and local elections had rewarded supporters with jobs ranging from cabinet seats to lowly municipal posts. Defenders claimed that this system was a democratic means of filling government positions. Critics called it a corrupt spoils system after the old expression, "To the victor belong the spoils."

For years, a small but influential group of upper-class reformers, including Missouri senator Carl Schurz and editor E.L. Godkin of *The Nation*, had campaigned for a professional civil service based on merit. Well-educated and wealthy, these reformers favored a civil service staffed by "gentlemen." The reformers had a point. A professional civil service was needed to remove corruption and manage complex government affairs.

Elected through the compromise that ended Reconstruction (see Chapter 16), Republican president Rutherford B. Hayes cautiously embraced the civil-service cause. In 1877, he launched an investigation of the corruption-riddled New York City customs office and fired two high officials. One, Chester A. Arthur, had played a key role in passing out jobs.

"To the victor belong the spoils."

When Congressman James A. Garfield won the 1880 Republican presidential nomination, the delegates, to appease the opposing New York faction, chose Chester A. Arthur, the loyalist Hayes had recently fired, as Garfield's running mate. Because Garfield enjoyed excellent health, the choice of the totally unqualified Arthur seemed safe.

The Democrats nominated a career army officer from Pennsylvania, Winfield Scott Hancock, and the Greenbackers gave the nod to Congressman James B. Weaver of Iowa. Garfield's managers stressed his Civil War record and his log-cabin birth. By a razor-thin margin, Garfield edged out Hancock; Weaver trailed far behind.

Garfield's assassination in 1881 by the crazed office-seeker Charles Guiteau brought to the White House Vice President Arthur, the very symbol of patronage corruption, and gave a powerful emotional thrust to the reform cause. Civil-service reformers portrayed the fallen president as a spoils-system martyr. In 1883, Congress enacted a civil-service law introduced by Senator George Pendleton of Ohio (Garfield's home state) and drafted by the Civil Service Reform League that had been created two years earlier. The **Pendleton Civil Service Act** set up a commission to prepare competitive examinations and establish standards of merit for a variety of federal jobs; it also forbade political candidates to solicit contributions from government workers.

Although the Pendleton Act initially covered only about 12 percent of federal employees, subsequent presidents gradually expanded the number of positions. By the 1890s, the act had opened up new positions for women, who now held nearly a third of the jobs as federal clerks in government agencies. The creation of a professional civil service thus helped bring the federal government in step with the modernizing trends transforming society.

WHERE IS THE DIFFERENCE?

"WHERE IS THE DIFFERENCE?" 1894 By equating criminal payoffs to the police with corporate contributions to senators, this cartoon in *Puck* magazine suggests that corruption pervades society and needs to be stopped. *(Granger Collection)*

As for Chester A. Arthur, his performance surprised those who had expected an utter disaster. Arthur supported civil-service reform and proved quite independent. Fed up with the feuding Republicans, in 1882 the voters gave the Democrats a strong majority in the House of Representatives. In 1884, for the first time since 1856, they would put a Democrat in the White House: Grover Cleveland.

Politics of Privilege, Politics of Exclusion, 1884–1892

The stalemate between the two major parties in their battle to control the standards for economic growth continued under President Cleveland, a Democrat, and President Harrison, a Republican. Both presidents challenged powerful interests and faced stiff opposition. Cleveland alienated strong lobbies by calling for cuts in the tariff and in veterans' pensions. In 1888, business and veterans' groups rallied to defeat Cleveland and elect Benjamin Harrison of Indiana, a former Civil War general, in one of the most corrupt campaigns in American history. Harrison alienated voters by passing a high tariff and an expanded pension law that increased the number of pensioners by 43 percent.

Responding to major party fraud and inattention to the needs of rural Americans, farmers mounted protests and began to organize. While the Grange and Farmers' Alliance movements condemned the monopolistic practices of grain and cotton buyers in the post-Reconstruction South, the white majority consolidated their political power by denying the region's black citizens their most basic rights.

A Democrat in the White House: Grover Cleveland, 1885–1889

At a tumultuous Chicago convention in 1884, the Republicans nominated their best-known leader, James G. Blaine. A gifted orator, Blaine spoke for the younger, more dynamic wing of the Republican Party eager to promote economic development and reinvigorate foreign policy.

But Blaine had been stained by the revelation that he, as Speaker of the House, had offered political favors to a railroad company in exchange for stock. For reformers, Blaine epitomized the hated patronage system. To E.L. Godkin, he "wallowed in spoils like a rhinoceros in an African pool."

85

Sensing Blaine's vulnerability, the Democrats chose a sharply contrasting nominee, Grover Cleveland of New York. In a meteoric rise from reform mayor of Buffalo to governor, Cleveland had fought the bosses and spoils men. The shrewdness of the Democrats' choice became apparent when Godkin, Carl Schurz, and other Republican reformers bolted to Cleveland. They were promptly nicknamed **Mugwumps,** an Algonquian term for a renegade chief.

Unfortunately, Cleveland as a youth had fathered an illegitimate child. Although he admitted the indiscretion, Republicans still jeered at rallies: "Ma, Ma, where's my pa?" Cleveland also faced opposition from Tammany Hall, the New York City Democratic machine that he had fought as governor. If Tammany's immigrant voters stayed home on election day, Cleveland could lose his own state. But, in October, a New York City clergyman denounced the Democrats as the party of "Rum, Romanism, and Rebellion." Blaine failed to immediately repudiate the remark. The Cleveland campaign managers widely publicized this triple insult to Catholics, to patriotic Democrats, and to drinkers. This blunder and the Mugwumps' defection allowed Cleveland to carry New York State by twelve hundred votes, and with it the election.

Once in office, Cleveland embraced the belief that government must not meddle in the economy and opposed any public regulation of corporations. He also rejected providing any governmental help for those in need. Vetoing a bill that would have given seeds to drought stricken farmers in Texas, he warned that people should not expect the government to solve their problems.

One public matter did arouse Cleveland's energies: the tariff. Because it brought in revenue in the era before a federal income tax, the tariff functioned as a protection for special interests and a source of government income. But which imported goods should be subject to duties, and how much? Opinions differed radically. Producers of such commodities as coal, hides, timber, and wool demanded tariff protection against foreign competition as did many manufacturers. Other businesses, however, while seeking protection for their finished products, wanted low tariffs on the raw materials they required. Massachusetts shoe manufacturers, for example, urged high duties on imported shoes but low duties on imported hides. Most farmers, by contrast, hated all tariffs for making it hard to sell American farm products abroad.

> To E.L. Godkin, Blaine "wallowed in spoils like a rhinoceros in an African pool."

Cleveland's call for lower tariffs arose from his concern that high tariffs created huge federal budget surpluses, which tempted legislators to distribute the money in the form of veterans' pensions or expensive public-works programs in their home districts, commonly called pork-barrel projects. With his horror of paternalistic government, Cleveland viewed the budget surplus as a corrupting influence. Although the Democratic campaign of 1888 gave little attention to the issue, Cleveland's talk of lowering the tariff angered many corporate leaders.

Cleveland stirred up another hornet's nest by opposing the routine payment of veterans' disability pensions. No one opposed pensions for the deserving, but fraudulent claims had proliferated. Unlike his predecessors, Cleveland investigated these claims and rejected many of them. He also vetoed a bill that would have pensioned all disabled veterans whether or not their injuries occurred in military service. The pension list should be an honor roll, he stressed, not a refuge for fraud.

Big Business Strikes Back; Benjamin Harrison, 1889–1893

By 1888, influential interest groups had concluded that Cleveland must go. The Republicans turned to Benjamin Harrison of Indiana. A corporation lawyer and former senator, Harrison was so aloof that some ridiculed him as the human iceberg. To avoid alienating voters, Harrison argued that a high tariff would ensure business prosperity, decent wages for workers, and a healthy home market for farmers.

The Republicans amassed a $4 million campaign fund from worried business leaders to purchase posters, buttons, and votes. Despite voter fraud, Cleveland received almost a hundred thousand more votes than Harrison. But Harrison carried the key states of Indiana and New York and won the Electoral College vote. The Republicans held the Senate and regained the House. Once in office, Harrison swiftly rewarded his supporters. He appointed as commissioner of pensions a GAR official who, on taking office, declared "God help the surplus!" The pension rolls soon ballooned from 676,000 to nearly a million (see Figure 20.1). This massive pension system (which was coupled with medical care in a network of veterans' hospitals) became America's first large-scale public welfare program. In 1890, the triumphant Republicans also enacted the McKinley Tariff, which pushed rates to an all-time high.

Rarely has the federal government been so subservient to entrenched economic interests and so out of touch with the plight of the disadvantaged as during the 1880s. But inaction bred discontent. In

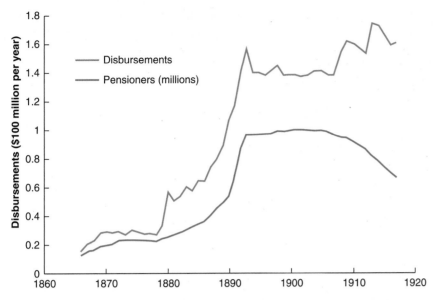

FIGURE 20.1 CIVIL WAR PENSIONS AND PENSIONERS, 1866–1917 The pension system for Union army veterans represented a major federal welfare program in the late nineteenth and early twentieth centuries. Because of corruption, the cost of pensions increased even though the actual number of veterans declined. © Cengage Learning. All rights reserved. No distribution allowed without express authorization.

Source: William H. Glasson, *Federal Military Pensions in the United States* (New York: Oxford University Press, 1918), 273.

the election of 1890, the Democrats gained sixty-six congressional seats and won control of the House of Representatives. Farmers, too, turned to politics and swung into action.

Agrarian Protest and the Rise of the People's Party

Great Plains farming had long been a risky venture. Between 1873 and 1877, terrible grasshopper infestations had consumed nearly half the midwestern wheat crop. As production rose, prices fell. Wheat tumbled from $2.95 a bushel in 1866 to $1.06 in 1880 (see Figure 20.2). Farmers who had borrowed heavily to finance homesteads went bankrupt or barely survived. One struggling Minnesota farmer wrote the governor in 1874, "[W]e can see nothing but starvation in the future if relief does not come."

> "[W]e can see nothing but starvation in the future if relief does not come."

Midwestern farmers in 1867, under the leadership of Oliver H. Kelley, a Department of Agriculture clerk, formed the **Grange,** or "Patrons of Husbandry." In the next decade, membership soared to more than 1.5 million. Offering information, emotional support, and fellowship, the Grange urged farmers to "buy less and produce more, in order to make our farms more self-sustaining." They negotiated special discounts with farm-machinery dealers and set up "cash-only" cooperative stores and grain-storage elevators to cut out the "middlemen"—the bankers, grain brokers, and merchants who made money at the farmers' expense.

Grangers focused their wrath on railroads, which routinely gave discounts to large shippers, bribed state legislators, and charged higher rates for short runs than for long hauls. Stung by these practices, Grangers in Illinois, Wisconsin, Minnesota, and Iowa lobbied state legislatures in 1874 to pass laws fixing maximum rates for freight shipments.

The railroads appealed these "Granger laws" to the Supreme Court, but in *Munn* v. *Illinois* (1877) the Court rejected the railroads' appeal and upheld an Illinois law setting maximum grain storage rates. The regulation of grain elevators, declared the Court's majority, was legitimate under the federal Constitution's acknowledgment of the right of states to exercise police powers. When the Court in *Wabash* v. *Illinois* (1886) modified this position by prohibiting states from regulating interstate railroad rates, Congress passed the Interstate Commerce Act (1887), reaffirming the federal government's power to oversee railroad activities and establishing a new agency, the Interstate Commerce Commission (ICC), to do just that. Although the commission failed to curb the railroads' monopolistic practices,

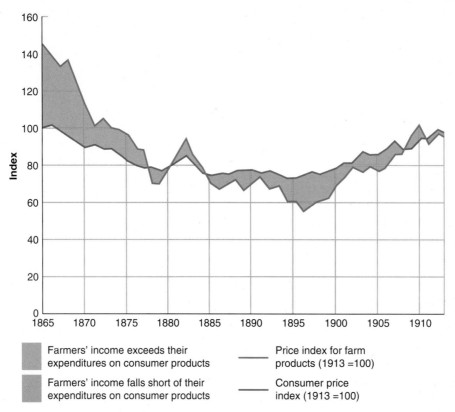

Index

| 1865 | 1870 | 1875 | 1880 | 1885 | 1890 | 1895 | 1900 | 1905 | 1910 |

■ Farmers' income exceeds their
expenditures on consumer products

■ Farmers' income falls short of their
expenditures on consumer products

—— Price index for farm
products (1913 =100)

—— Consumer price
index (1913 =100)

FIGURE 20.2 CONSUMER PRICES AND FARM-PRODUCT PRICES, 1865–1913 From 1865 to 1895, the prices that farmers received for their crops gradually declined. Even when they increased after 1895, farmers had difficulty making ends meet. As cycles of drought and debt battered Great Plains wheat growers, a Kansas farmer wrote, "At the age of 52, after a long life of toil, economy, and self-denial, I find myself and family virtually paupers." © Cengage Learning. All rights reserved. No distribution allowed without express authorization.

it did establish the principle of federal regulation of interstate transportation.

Despite promising beginnings, the Grange movement soon faltered. In 1878, the railroads, which had lost their battle on the national level, lobbied state legislatures and won repeal of most of the state-regulation laws. The cash-only cooperative stores closed because most farmers had little cash. The Grange ideal of financial independence from banks and merchants proved unrealistic because conditions on the Plains made it impossible to farm without borrowing money. When the prices of corn, wheat, and cotton briefly revived after 1878, many farmers deserted the movement. The Grange lived on as a social and educational institution, but it had lost its appeal because it was unable to improve its members' financial position.

The problems that drove farmers to form the Grange prompted southern and midwestern farmers to form the alliance movement. The **Farmers' Alliance** began in Texas in the 1870s as small planters, trapped by the crop lien system, mortgaged future harvests to cover current expenses. Mired in

debt, about a third of southern farmers gave up their land and became tenants or sharecroppers by 1900.

In 1887, Texan Charles W. Macune, a self-trained lawyer and a physician, assumed leadership of the Alliance movement. By 1889, Macune had merged several regional organizations into the National Farmers' Alliance and Industrial Union, or Southern Alliance. A parallel black organization, the National Colored Farmers' Alliance, had meanwhile emerged in Arkansas and spread to other southern states.

As they attended alliance rallies and picnics, read the alliance newspaper, and listened to alliance speakers, hard-hit farm families became increasingly aware of their political potential. An Arkansas member wrote in 1889, "Reform never begins with the leaders, it comes from the people." By 1890, the Southern Alliance claimed 3 million members. An additional 1.2 million joined the National Colored Farmers' Alliance.

Meanwhile, Alliance fever had spread to the Great Plains. In the drought-plagued years of 1880 and 1881, alliances sprang up in Kansas, Nebraska,

Iowa, and Minnesota. Membership grew when insects destroyed much of the wheat crop and increases in world production drove down prices for agricultural products. Under these conditions, many settlers returned East. "In God we trusted, in Kansas we busted," some scrawled on their wagons. Western Kansas lost 50 percent of its population between 1888 and 1892. Others hung on, and the Northwestern Alliance grew rapidly. By 1890, the Kansas Alliance claimed 130,000 members, followed closely by alliances in Nebraska, the Dakotas, and Minnesota. What had begun as a desperate attempt to save their farms had now turned into a massive political campaign to change the American political and economic system.

Alliance members at first tried to create a biracial movement. Southern Alliance leaders Tom Watson of Georgia and Leonidas Polk of North Carolina urged southern farmers, black and white, to act together. For a time, this message of racial cooperation in the interest of reform offered promise. But Alliance members also shared the "separate but equal" philosophy of their "New South" counterparts that combined progressive reform with the separation of races (see Chapter 18).

Women joined the alliance leadership as well. Mary E. Lease, a Wichita lawyer, burst on the scene in 1890 as a fiery alliance orator. Other women, veterans of the Granger or prohibition cause, founded the National Women's Alliance (NWA) in 1891. Declared the NWA, "Put 1,000 women lecturers in the field and revolution is here." By no coincidence, a strong feminist strain pervades Ignatius Donnelly's *The Golden Bottle* (1892), a novel portraying the agrarian reformers' social vision (see Going to the Source).

As the movement swelled, the opposition turned nasty. When Jerry Simpson, an Alliance rancher from Kansas, mentioned the silk stockings of a conservative politician in his district and noted that he had no such finery, a hostile newspaper editor labeled him "Sockless Jerry" Simpson, the nickname he carried to his grave. When Mary Lease advised Kansas to "raise less corn and more hell," another editor sneered: "[Kansas] has started to raise hell, as Mrs. Lease advised, and [the state] seems to have an overproduction. But that doesn't matter. Kansas never did believe in diversified crops."

All this activity helped shape a new political agenda. In 1889, the Southern and Northwestern Alliances loosely merged and lined up candidates

16 TO 1: THE SPEECH THAT WON THE NOMINATION AT THE NATIONAL DEMOCRATIC CONVENTION IN CHICAGO, 1896 Shown with his family, a farmer, and a blacksmith, William Jennings Bryan is depicted as focusing on the free coinage of silver to gold at the rate of sixteen to one, which oversimplified the demands of the Populist Party, including a graduated income tax, postal savings banks, and governmental ownership of the railroads. *(Library of Congress)*

in the 1890 midterm elections. Alliance candidates focused on government action on behalf of farmers and workers, including tariff reduction, a graduated income tax, public ownership of the railroads, federal funding for irrigation research, a ban on landownership by foreigners, and "the free and unlimited coinage of silver."

The 1890 elections revealed the strength of agrarian protest. Southern Democrats who endorsed

Women in Politics

In this article, written for the *Arena* magazine in 1892, Annie L. Diggs, a Populist orator and editor from Kansas, identifies twenty-five prominent women speakers and editors who played important roles nationally in the Farmers' Alliance and the Populist Party. In 1892, the Populists in Kansas elected the governor and a majority in the state senate only to be stymied by a Republican majority in the state house.

Farm life for women is a treadmill. ... The worn and weary treadmillers are anxious, troubled. ... Instead of mythologic lore, they read "Seven Financial Conspiracies," "Looking Backward," "Progress and Poverty." Alas! Of this last word they know much and fear more – fear for their children's future. The [women] ... turn with all the fierceness of their primal mother-nature to protect their younglings from devouring, devastating plutocracy.

The great political victory of the people of Kansas would not have been won without the help of the women of the Alliance. Women who never dreamed of becoming public speakers grew eloquent in their zeal and fervor. ...

Before this question of the salvation of the imperiled homes of the nation, all other questions, whether of "prohibition" or "suffrage" pale into relative inconsequence. For where shall temperance or high thought of franchise be taught to children, by whose breath the world is saved, if sacred hearth fires shall go out? The overtopping, all-embracing moral question of the age is this for which the Alliance came. Upon such great ethical foundations is the labor movement today building itself. How could women do otherwise than be in it?

Easily first among Kansas women who rose to prominence as a platform speaker for the political party which grew out of the Alliance is Mrs. Mary E. Lease. ... Seldom, if ever, was a woman so vilified and so misrepresented by malignant newspaper attacks. A woman of other quality would have sunk under the avalanche. She was quite competent to cope with all that was visited upon her. Indeed, the abuse did her much service. The people loved her for the enemies she made.

Already the story of the wondrous part she has played in the people's struggle for justice has reached other countries. ...

In the to-be-written history of this great epoch, Mrs. Mary E. Lease will have a most conspicuous place.

Consider this Kansas record, oh supercilious sneerer at "strong-minded" women. Most of these women have opened their mouths and spake before many people. ... All these heretical things they have done, and yet are the womanliest, gentlest of women, the best of homekeepers, the loyalist of wives, the carefulest of mothers. ...

Thus splendidly do the *facts* about women in politics refute the frivolous *theories* of timorous or hostile objectors. The women prominent as active, responsible factors in the political arena are those who are characterized by strong common sense, high ideals, and lofty patriotism. When such as these cast ballot throughout the nation,

"Then shall their voice of sovereign choice
Swell the deep bass of duty done,
And strike the key of time to be
When God and man shall speak as one."

Source: Annie L. Diggs, "The Women in the Alliance Movement," *The Arena*, July 1892, No. XXXII, pp. 160–180.

QUESTIONS

1. How does Diggs justify women's participation in politics?
2. What roles do traditional ideas about women's responsibilities play in her argument?
3. What ideals shaped Populist religiosity?

alliance goals won four governorships and control of eight state legislatures. On the Great Plains, alliance-endorsed candidates controlled the Kansas and Nebraska legislatures and gained the balance of power in Minnesota and South Dakota. Three alliance-backed senators, together with some fifty congressmen (including Watson and Simpson), went to Washington as angry winds from the hinterlands buffeted the political system.

Shared economic grievances soon overcame the regional differences, which had threatened to divide the movement. Southern Alliance leaders who initially opposed endorsing a third party, fearing it would weaken the southern Democratic Party, the bastion of white supremacy, eventually adopted the third-party idea. In February 1892, alliance leaders organized the People's Party of the United States, generally called the **Populist Party.** At the party convention in Omaha, Nebraska, that August, cheering delegates nominated for president the former Civil War general and Greenback nominee James B. Weaver of Iowa. Courting the South, they chose as Weaver's running mate the Virginian James Field, who had lost a leg fighting for the Confederacy.

The Populist platform called for the direct popular election of senators and other electoral reforms. It also endorsed a **subtreasury plan** devised by alliance leader Charles Macune by which farmers could store their nonperishable commodities in government warehouses, receive low-interest loans using the crops as collateral, and then sell the stored commodities when market prices rose. Their model was the postal service, an efficient, centralized, large-scale organization that worked for the public good. Ignatius Donnelly's ringing preamble pronounced the nation on "the verge of moral, political, and material ruin" and called for a return of the government "to the hands of 'the plain people' with which class it originated."

"Raise less corn and more hell."

African Americans After Reconstruction

As the Populists organized, a group of citizens with profound grievances suffered renewed oppression. With the end of Reconstruction in 1877 and the restoration of power to white elites (see Chapter 16), southern white opinion demanded an end to the hated "Negro rule," and local Democratic Party officials pursued this objective. Suppressing the black vote became a major goal. Intimidation, terror, and vote fraud kept blacks from the polls or forced them to vote Democratic. Mississippi amended its state constitution in 1890 to exclude most black voters, and other southern states soon followed suit.

Because the Fifteenth Amendment (1870) guaranteed all male citizens' right to vote, white southerners used indirect means such as literacy tests (a test of the ability to read), poll taxes (a tax paid to vote), and property requirements (which restricted the right to vote to those who owned property) to disfranchise blacks. To protect illiterate whites, the so-called grandfather clause exempted from these electoral requirements anyone with an ancestor who had voted in 1860. Although black disfranchisement proceeded erratically over the South, by the early twentieth century it was essentially complete.

Disfranchisement was only one part of the system of white supremacy. In a parallel development, state after state passed laws imposing strict racial segregation in many realms of life (to be discussed in Chapter 21). African American caterers, barbers, bricklayers, and other artisans lost their white clientele. Blacks who went to prison—sometimes for minor offenses—faced the convict-lease system, which cotton planters, railroad builders, and other employers used to "lease" prison gangs and force them to work under slave-labor conditions.

The convict-lease system enforced the racial hierarchy and played an important economic role as industrialization and agricultural change came to the South. The system brought income to hard-pressed state governments and provided factories, railroads, and large-scale farms with predictable, controllable, cheap labor. The system also intimidated free laborers and discouraged foreign immigrants from going South. Thousands died under this brutal convict-labor system, which continued into the early decades of the twentieth century.

Lynching became the ultimate enforcer of southern white supremacy. Through the 1880s and 1890s, about a hundred blacks were lynched annually in the United States, mainly in the South. The stated reasons, often the rape of a white woman, frequently arose from rumor and unsubstantiated accusations. The charge of "attempted rape," as the black journalist Ida B. Wells pointed out to a national audience, could cover a wide range of behaviors unacceptable to whites, such as questioning authority or talking back.

The lynch mob demonstrated whites' absolute power. In the South, more than 80 percent of the lynchings involved black victims. Lynchings most commonly occurred in the Cotton Belt, and they tended to rise at times of economic distress.

By no coincidence, lynching peaked in 1892 as many poor blacks embraced the Colored Farmers' Alliance and rallied to the Populist Party banner. Fifteen black Populists were killed in Georgia alone, it has been estimated, during that year's bitter campaign. Ironically, the photographs that reinforced racial terror and flaunted the disregard for law became the basis for reformers' proof of the brutality of the tactic.

The relationship between southern agrarian protest and white racism was complex. African American farm organizations had developed independently from their white counterparts. Some Populists, like Georgia's Tom Watson, sought to build an interracial movement with them. Watson denounced lynching and the convict-lease system. When a black Populist leader pursued by a lynch mob took refuge in his house during the 1892 campaign, Watson summoned two thousand armed white Populists to defend him. But most white Populists clung to racism. The white ruling elite, eager to drive a wedge in the protest movement, inflamed lower-class white racism.

On balance, the rise of southern agrarian protest deepened racial hatred and ultimately worsened blacks' situation. Meanwhile, the federal government stood aside. A generation of northern politicians paid lip service to egalitarian principles but failed to apply them to African Americans.

The Supreme Court similarly abandoned African Americans. The Court ripped gaping holes in the Fourteenth Amendment (1868), which granted blacks citizenship and the equal protection of the law, and in the Civil Rights Act of 1875, which outlawed racial discrimination on juries, in public places, and on railroads and streetcars. In the *Civil Rights Cases* (1883), the Court declared the Civil Rights Act of 1875 unconstitutional. The Fourteenth Amendment protected citizens only from governmental infringement of their civil rights, the justices ruled, not from acts by private citizens such as railroad conductors. In ***Plessy v. Ferguson* (1896)**, the justices upheld a Louisiana law requiring segregated railroad cars. Racial segregation was constitutional, the Court held, if equal facilities were made available to each race. With the Supreme Court's blessing, the South segregated its public school system, ignoring the caveat that such separate facilities must be equal. White children studied in nicer buildings, used newer equipment, and were taught by better-paid teachers. Not until 1954 did the Court overturn the "separate but equal" doctrine. Rounding out their dismal record, in 1898 the justices upheld the poll tax and literacy tests by which southern states had disfranchised blacks.

Few northerners protested the South's white supremacist society. Until the North condemned lynching outright, declared the aged abolitionist Frederick Douglass in 1892, "it will remain equally involved with the South in this common crime." The restoration of sectional harmony, in short, came at a high price: acquiescence by the North in the utter debasement of the South's African American citizenry. Further, the separatist principle endorsed in *Plessy* had a negative impact, affecting blacks nationwide, Mexicans in Texas, Asians in California, and other groups.

> Until the North condemned lynching outright, declared Douglass, "it will remain equally involved with the South in this common crime."

LYNCHING AT CLANTON, ALABAMA, AUGUST 1891 Reprinted in Ida B. Wells's *A Red Record*, this photograph is typical of many taken where the white audience faces the camera near the body of the victim. Such photographs were meant to intimidate any blacks who challenged white supremacy. *(Chicago Historical Society)*

Blacks responded to their plight in various ways. The nation's foremost black leader from the 1890s to his death in 1915 was **Booker T. Washington.** Born in slavery in Virginia in 1856, Washington attended a freedman's school in Hampton, Virginia, and in 1881 organized a black state vocational school in Alabama that eventually became Tuskegee University. Although Washington secretly contributed to lawyers who challenged segregation, he publicly urged accommodation to a racist society. In a widely publicized address in Atlanta in 1895, he insisted that the first task of America's blacks must be to acquire useful skills such as farming and carpentry. Once blacks proved their economic value, he predicted, racism would fade; meanwhile, they must patiently accept their lot. This was a position later challenged by W.E.B. Du Bois (covered in Chapter 21). Washington lectured widely, and his autobiography, *Up from Slavery* (1901), recounted his rise from poverty thanks to honesty, hard work, and kindly patrons—themes familiar to a generation reared on Horatio Alger's self-help books.

Other blacks responded resourcefully to racism. Black churches provided emotional support, as did black fraternal lodges like the Knights of Pythias. Some African Americans started businesses to serve their community. Two black-owned banks, in Richmond and Washington, DC, were chartered in 1888. The North Carolina Mutual Insurance Company, organized in 1898 by John Merrick, a prosperous Durham barber, evolved into a major enterprise. Bishop Henry M. Turner of the African Methodist Episcopal church urged blacks to return to Africa and build a great Christian nation.

Meanwhile, African American protest never wholly died out. Frederick Douglass urged that blacks press for full equality. Blacks should meet violence with violence, insisted militant New York black leader T. Thomas Fortune. But for others, the solution was to leave the South. In 1879, several thousand moved to Kansas (see Chapter 16). Some ten thousand migrated to Chicago between 1870 and 1890. Blacks who moved north, however, soon found that public opinion sanctioned many forms of de facto discrimination.

The rise of the so-called solid South, firmly established on racist foundations, had important political implications. For one thing, it made a mockery of the two-party system. For years, the only meaningful election south of the Potomac was the Democratic primary. Only in the 1960s, in the wake of sweeping social and economic changes, would a genuine two-party system emerge there. The large bloc of southern Democrats selected to Congress each year, accumulating seniority and power, exerted a great and often reactionary influence on public policy. Finally, southern Democrats wielded enormous clout in the national party. No Democratic contender for national office who was unacceptable to them stood a chance.

Above all, the caste system that evolved in the post-Reconstruction South shaped the consciousness of those caught up in it, white and black alike. White novelist Lillian Smith described her girlhood in turn-of-the-century Florida and Georgia: "From the day I was born, I began to learn my lessons. . . . I learned it is possible to be a Christian and a white southerner simultaneously; to be a gentlewoman and an arrogant callous creature at the same moment; to pray at night and ride a Jim Crow car the next morning; … to glow when the word democracy was used, and to practice slavery from morning to night."

The 1890s: Politics in a Depression Decade

Discontent with the major parties, which had smoldered during the 1870s and 1880s, burst into flames in the 1890s. As banks failed and railroads went bankrupt, the nation slid into a grinding depression. The crises of the 1890s laid bare the paralysis of the federal government—dominated by a business elite—when confronted by the new social realities of factories, urban slums, immigrant workers, and desperate farmers. In response, irate farmers, laborers, and their supporters joined a new party, the Populists, to change the system. But in 1896, in the aftermath of the massive depression, the Republicans built a coalition strong enough to control Congress and the presidency for the next fifteen years.

1892: Populists Challenge the Status Quo

In July 1892, the same month that the Populists adopted their party platform, thirteen people died in a gun battle between strikers and strikebreakers at the Homestead steel plant near Pittsburgh, and President Harrison sent federal troops to Coeur d'Alene, Idaho, where a silver-mine strike had turned violent. Events seemed to justify the platform's warnings of chaos ahead.

Ignoring the escalating unrest, both major parties launched campaigns for the White House that replayed the1888 contest. The Republicans renominated Harrison. The Democrats turned again to Grover Cleveland, who in four years out of office had made clear his growing conservatism and his opposition to the Populists. But this time Cleveland won by more than 360,000 votes, a decisive margin in this era of close elections. A public reaction against labor violence and the McKinley Tariff hurt Harrison, while Cleveland's support for the gold standard won business support.

Meanwhile, a solid showing by Populist candidates sparked great hopes for the future. James B. Weaver got more than a million votes—8.5 percent of the total—and the Populists elected five senators, ten congressmen, and three governors. The new party carried Kansas and registered some appeal in the West and in Georgia, Alabama, and Texas, where the alliance movement had taken deep root. But the party's strength was spotty. It made no dent in New England, the urban East, or the traditionally Republican farm regions of the Midwest. It even failed to show broad strength in the upper Great Plains. "Beaten! Whipped! Smashed!" moaned Minnesota Populist Ignatius Donnelly in his diary.

Throughout most of the South, racism, ingrained Democratic loyalty, distaste for a ticket headed by a former Union general, and widespread voter fraud kept the Populist vote under 25 percent. This failure killed the prospects for interracial agrarian reform. After 1892, as Populism began to revive in the South and Midwest, many southern politicians seeking to appeal to poor whites—including a disillusioned Tom Watson—stayed within the Democratic fold and laced their populism with racism.

> "Beaten! Whipped! Smashed!" moaned Minnesota Populist Ignatius Donnelly.

POPULIST ORATOR, MARY E. LEASE An Irish immigrant who became a resident of Kansas in 1873 and was admitted to the bar in 1885, Lease toured the country in the 1890s speaking on behalf of oppressed farmers and asserting women's right to participate in politics. (Granger Collection)

Capitalism in Crisis: The Depression of 1893–1897

Cleveland soon confronted a major crisis, an economic collapse in the railroad industry that quickly spread. Trouble flared up in February 1893 when the Philadelphia and Reading Railroad failed. This bankruptcy came at a time of weakened confidence in the gold standard, the government's pledge to redeem paper money for gold on demand.

Confidence had ebbed when, in response to the collapse of a leading London investment bank in 1890, British investors had sold millions of dollars' worth of stock in American railroads and converted their dollars to gold, draining U.S. gold reserves. Moreover, Congress's lavish veterans' benefits during the Harrison administration had reduced government resources just as tariff revenues were dropping because of the high McKinley Tariff. Finally, the 1890 Sherman Silver Purchase Act's requirement that the government pay for its monthly silver purchases with treasury certificates redeemable for either silver or gold had further drained gold reserves.

Between January 1892 and March 1893, when Cleveland took office, the gold reserve had fallen sharply to around $100 million, the minimum considered necessary to support the dollar. This decline alarmed those who viewed the gold standard as the only sure evidence of the government's financial stability.

The collapse of a railroad thus triggered the **Panic of 1893.** Fear fed on itself as alarmed investors converted their stock holdings to gold. Stock prices fell in May and June; gold reserves sank; by the end of the year, seventy-four railroads and more than fifteen thousand commercial institutions, including six hundred banks, had failed. Just as the railroad boom had spurred the industrial prosperity of the 1880s, so had the railroad crisis of the early 1890s battered the entire economy. The Panic of 1893 started a full-scale depression and set off four years of hard times.

The crisis took a heavy human toll. Industrial unemployment soared into the 20 to 25 percent range, leaving millions of factory workers with no money to feed their families and heat their homes. Recent immigrants faced disaster. Jobless men tramped the streets and rode freight trains from city to city seeking work.

The unusually harsh winters of 1893 and 1894 made matters worse. In New York City, where the crisis quickly swamped local relief agencies, a minister reported actual starvation. Rural America, already hard-hit by declining agricultural prices, faced ruin. Farm prices dropped by more than 20 percent between 1890 and 1896. Corn plummeted from fifty cents to twenty-one cents a bushel; wheat, from eighty-four cents to fifty-one cents. Cotton sold for five cents a pound in 1894.

Some desperate Americans turned to protest. In Chicago, workers at the Pullman factory reacted to successive wage cuts by walking off the job in June 1894 (see Chapter 18). In Massillon, Ohio, self-taught monetary expert Jacob Coxey proposed as a solution to unemployment a $500 million public-works program funded with paper money not backed by gold but simply designated "legal tender" (just as it is today). A man of action as well as ideas, Coxey organized a march on Washington to lobby for his scheme. Thousands joined him en route, and several hundred reached Washington in late April 1894. Police arrested Coxey and other leaders when they attempted to enter the Capitol grounds, and his "army" broke up. Although some considered Coxey eccentric, his proposal closely resembled programs that the government would adopt during the depression of the 1930s.

> A church magazine demanded that troops put "a pitiless stop" to outbreaks of unrest.

As unrest intensified, fear clutched middle-class Americans. A church magazine demanded that troops put "a pitiless stop" to outbreaks of unrest. To some observers, a bloody upheaval seemed imminent.

Business Leaders Respond

In the face of suffering and turmoil, Cleveland refused to intervene. Boom-and-bust economic cycles were inevitable, he insisted. The government could do nothing. Missing the larger picture, Cleveland focused on a single issue: the gold standard. In August 1893 he persuaded Congress to repeal the Sherman Silver Purchase Act, which he blamed for the run on gold.

Nevertheless, the gold drain continued. In early 1895, with the gold reserve down to $41 million, Cleveland turned to Wall Street. Bankers J.P. Morgan and August Belmont agreed to lend the government $62 million in exchange for U.S. bonds at a special discount. With this loan, the government purchased gold to replenish its reserve. Meanwhile, Morgan and Belmont resold the bonds for a substantial profit. This deal with the bankers did help restore confidence in the government's economic stability but it confirmed radicals' suspicions of an unholy alliance between Washington and Wall Street.

COXEY'S ARMY Detractors characterized Coxey's "army" of unemployed as "never do wells," but this photograph of Jacob Coxey's "Commonwealth of Christ Army" entering Washington, DC, in 1894 indicates that it was led by more well-to-do Americans making a statement about the government's responsibility to help those hurt by the depression. *(Library of Congress)*

As the battle over the tariff made clear, corporate interests held the whip hand. Although Cleveland favored tariff reform, the Congress of 1893–1895 (despite its Democratic majorities) generally yielded to high-tariff lobbyists. The Wilson-Gorman Tariff of 1894 lowered duties somewhat, but made so many concessions to protectionist interests that Cleveland disgustedly allowed it to become law without his signature.

Hinting at changes ahead, the Wilson-Gorman Tariff imposed a modest income tax of 2 percent on all income over $4,000 (about $40,000 in purchasing power today). But in *Pollock* v. *Farmers' Loan & Trust Co.* (1895), the Supreme Court narrowly ruled the law unconstitutional, arguing that the federal government could impose such a direct tax on personal property only if it were apportioned according to the population of each state. Whether one looked at the executive, the legislature, or the judiciary, Washington's subordination to financial interests seemed absolute.

Cleveland's policies split the Democratic Party. Farm leaders and silver Democrats condemned his opposition to the Sherman Silver Purchase Act. This split in the Democratic ranks affected the elections of 1894 and 1896 and reshaped politics as the century ended.

The depression also helped reorient social thought. Middle-class charitable workers, long convinced that individual character flaws caused poverty, now realized—as socialists proclaimed and as the poor well knew—that even sober and hard-working people could succumb to economic forces beyond their control. Laissez-faire ideology weakened too, as many depression-worn Americans adopted a broadened view of the government's role in dealing with the social consequences of industrialization. The depression, in short, not only brought suffering; it also taught lessons.

Silver Advocates Capture the Democratic Party

Republican gains in the 1894 midterm election revealed the depth of revulsion against Cleveland and the Democrats, who were blamed for the hard times. The Republicans gained control of Congress and several key states. Populist candidates won nearly 1.5 million votes, 40 percent more than their 1892 total. Most Populist gains occurred in the South.

The serious economic divisions that split Americans in the mid-1890s focused on a symbolic issue: free silver. Cleveland's rigid defense of the gold standard forced his opponents into an equally exaggerated obsession with silver, obscuring the genuine issues that divided rich and poor, creditor and debtor, and farmer and city dweller. Conservatives tirelessly upheld the gold standard while agrarian radicals, urged on and sometimes financed by western silver-mine owners, extolled silver as a universal cure-all.

Each side had a point. Gold advocates recognized that a nation's paper money must be based on more than a government's ability to run printing presses and that uncontrolled inflation could be catastrophic. The silver advocates knew from experience how tight-money policies depressed prices and devastated farmers. Unfortunately, these underlying realities were rarely expressed clearly.

At the 1896 Democratic convention in Chicago, western and southern delegates adopted a platform including a demand for the free and unlimited coinage of silver at the ratio to gold of sixteen to one, in effect repudiating the Cleveland administration. **William Jennings Bryan** of Nebraska, an ardent advocate of free silver, captured the nomination. Only thirty-six years old, the young lawyer had already served two terms in Congress championing western agrarian interests.

Joining Christian imagery with economic analysis, Bryan delivered his major convention speech in the debate over the platform. With his booming voice carrying his words to the upper gallery of the convention hall, Bryan praised farmers as the nation's bedrock. The wildly cheering delegates had identified their candidate even before he reached his rousing conclusion—"You shall not press down upon the brow of labor this crown of thorns, you shall not crucify mankind upon a cross of gold!"

The silverites' capture of the Democratic Party presented a dilemma to the Populists. They, too, advocated free silver, but only as one reform among many. To back Bryan would be to abandon the broad Populist program. Furthermore, fusion with the Democrats could destroy their influence as a third party. Yet the Populist leaders recognized that a separate Populist ticket would likely siphon votes from Bryan and ensure a Republican victory. Reluctantly, the Populists endorsed Bryan, while preserving a shred of independence (and confusing voters) by naming their own vice-presidential candidate, Tom Watson of Georgia. The Populists were learning the difficulty of organizing an independent political movement in a nation wedded to the two-party system.

> "[Y]ou shall not crucify mankind upon a cross of gold!"

The Republicans, meanwhile, had nominated former governor William McKinley, who as an Ohio congressman had given his name to the McKinley Tariff of 1890. The Republican platform embraced the high protective tariff and endorsed the gold standard.

1896: Republicans Triumphant

Bryan tried to sustain the momentum of the Chicago convention. Crisscrossing the nation by train, he delivered his free-silver campaign speech to hundreds of audiences in twenty-nine states. One skeptical editor compared him to Nebraska's notoriously shallow Platte River: six inches deep and a mile wide at the mouth.

McKinley's campaign was shrewdly managed by Mark Hanna, a Cleveland industrialist. Dignified and aloof, McKinley could not match Bryan's popular touch. Accordingly, Hanna built the campaign not around the candidate but around posters, pamphlets, and newspaper editorials. These publications warned of the dangers of free silver, caricatured Bryan as a rabid radical, and portrayed McKinley and the gold standard as twin pillars of prosperity.

Drawing on an enormous war chest, Hanna spent lavishly. J.P. Morgan and John D. Rockefeller together contributed half a million dollars, far more than Bryan's total campaign contributions. Like Benjamin Harrison in 1888, McKinley stayed

WOMEN BRYAN SUPPORTERS Although women could not vote in national elections in the 1890s, they actively participated in political campaigns. These women worked to turn out the vote for William Jennings Bryan. *(© David J. & Janice L. Frent Collection/Corbis)*

home in Canton, Ohio, emerging from time to time to read speeches to visiting delegations. Carefully orchestrated by Hanna, McKinley's deceptively bucolic "front-porch" campaign involved elaborate organization. All told, 750,000 people trekked to Canton that summer.

On election day, McKinley beat Bryan by more than six hundred thousand votes (see Map 20.1). He swept the Northeast and the Midwest and even carried three farm states beyond the Mississippi—Iowa, Minnesota, and North Dakota—as well as California and Oregon. Bryan's strength was limited to the South and the sparsely settled Great Plains and mountain states. The Republicans retained control of Congress.

Why did Bryan lose despite the depression and the protest spirit abroad in the land? Certainly, Republicans' cash reserves, influence on the East Coast press, and scare tactics played a role. But Bryan's candidacy carried its own liabilities. His

core constituency, while passionately loyal, was limited. Seduced by free silver and Bryan's oratory, the Democrats had upheld a platform and a candidate with little appeal for factory workers, the urban middle class, or the settled family farmers of the midwestern corn belt. Urban voters, realizing that higher farm prices, a major free-silver goal, also meant higher food prices, went heavily for McKinley. Bryan's weakness in urban America reflected cultural differences as well. To urban Catholics and Jews, this moralistic, teetotaling Nebraskan thundering like a Protestant revival preacher seemed utterly alien.

The McKinley administration quickly translated its conservative platform into law. The Dingley Tariff (1897) pushed rates to all-time high levels, and the Currency Act of 1900 officially committed the United States to the gold standard. With returning prosperity, rising farm prices after 1897, and the discovery of gold in Alaska and elsewhere, these

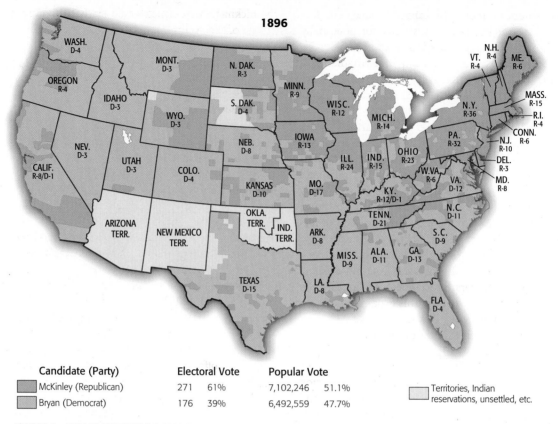

1896

Candidate (Party)	Electoral Vote		Popular Vote	
McKinley (Republican)	271	61%	7,102,246	51.1%
Bryan (Democrat)	176	39%	6,492,559	47.7%

Territories, Indian reservations, unsettled, etc.

MAP 20.1 THE ELECTION OF 1896 Republicans won the election by carrying the urban vote. © Cengage Learning. All rights reserved. No distribution allowed without express authorization.

measures aroused little protest. Bryan won renomination in 1900, but the fervor of 1896 was missing. The Republican campaign theme of prosperity easily won McKinley a second term.

The elections of 1894 and 1896 produced a Republican majority that, except for Woodrow Wilson's two presidential terms (1913–1921), would dominate national politics until the election of Franklin D. Roosevelt in 1932. Bryan's defeat and the Republicans' emergence as the party of prosperity killed the Populist Party and drove the Democrats back to their regional base in the South. But although populism collapsed, a new reform movement called progressivism was emerging. Many of the Populists' reform proposals would be enacted into law in the progressive years.

Expansionist Stirrings and War with Spain, 1878–1901

The same corporate elite that dominated late-nineteenth century domestic politics influenced U.S. foreign policy as well, contributing to surging expansionist pressures. Not only business

leaders but politicians, statesmen, and editorial writers insisted that national greatness required that America match Europe's imperial expansion. Fanned by sensationalistic newspaper coverage of a Cuban struggle for independence and by elite calls for greater American international assertiveness, war between the United States and Spain broke out in 1898.

Roots of Expansionist Sentiment

Ever since the first European settlers colonized North America's Atlantic coast, the newcomers had been an expansionist people. By the 1840s, the push westward had acquired a name: Manifest Destiny. Directed inward after 1865 toward the re-settlement of the trans-Mississippi West (see Chapter 17), this impulse turned outward in the 1880s as Americans followed the example set by Great Britain, France, Belgium, Italy, Germany, and Japan, which were busily collecting colonies from North Africa to the Pacific islands. National greatness, it appeared, demanded an empire.

Many business leaders believed that continued domestic prosperity required overseas markets.

As American industrial capacity expanded, foreign markets offered a safety valve for potentially explosive pressures in the U.S. economy. Secretary of State James Blaine warned in 1890 that U.S. productivity was outrunning "the demands of the home market" and insisted that American business must look abroad.

Advocates of a stronger navy further fueled the expansionist mood. In *The Influence of Sea Power upon History* (1890), **Alfred Thayer Mahan** equated sea power with national greatness and urged a U.S. naval buildup. Because a strong navy required bases abroad, Mahan and other naval advocates supported the movement to acquire foreign territories, especially Pacific islands with good harbors. Military strategy, in this case and others, often masked the desire for access to new markets.

Religious leaders proclaimed America's mission to spread Christianity. This expansionist argument sometimes took on a racist tinge. As Josiah Strong put it in his 1885 work *Our Country*, "God is training the Anglo-Saxon race for its mission"—a mission of Christianizing and civilizing the world's "weaker races" (see Beyond America).

> "God is training the Anglo-Saxon race for its mission."

A group of Republican expansionists, led by Senator Henry Cabot Lodge of Massachusetts, diplomat John Hay, and Theodore Roosevelt of New York, preached imperial greatness and military might. "I should welcome almost any war," declared Roosevelt in 1897; "…this country needs one." Advocates of expansionism, like Roosevelt and Lodge, built upon the Social Darwinist rhetoric of the day and argued that war, as a vehicle for natural selection, would test and refurbish American manhood, restore chivalry and honor, and create a new generation of civic-minded Americans. This gendered appeal to renew American masculinity both counterbalanced concerns about women's political activism and helped forge the disparate arguments for expansionism into a simpler, more visceral plea for international engagement that had a broad appeal.

A series of diplomatic skirmishes between 1885 and 1895 revealed the newly assertive American mood and paved the way for the war that Roosevelt desired. In the mid-1880s, quarrels between the United States and Great Britain over fishing rights in the North Atlantic and in the Bering Sea off Alaska reawakened Americans' latent anti-British feelings as well as the old dream of acquiring Canada. A poem published in the *Detroit News* (adapted from an English music-hall song) supplied the nickname that critics would apply to the promoters of expansion—jingoists:

We do not want to fight,
But, by jingo, if we do,
We'll scoop in all the fishing grounds
And the whole dominion too!

The fishing-rights dispute was resolved in 1898, but by then attention had shifted to Latin America. In 1891, as civil war raged in Chile, U.S. officials seized a Chilean vessel that was attempting to buy guns in San Diego. Soon after, a mob in Valparaiso, Chile, killed two unarmed sailors on shore leave. President Harrison practically called for war. Only when Chile apologized and paid an indemnity was the incident closed.

Another Latin American conflict arose from a boundary dispute between Venezuela and British Guiana in 1895 (see Map 20.2). The disagreement worsened after gold was discovered in the contested territory. When the British rejected a U.S. arbitration offer and condescendingly insisted that America's revered Monroe Doctrine had no standing in international law, a livid Grover Cleveland asked Congress to set up a commission to settle the disputed boundary even without Britain's approval. As patriotic fervor pulsed through the nation, the British in 1897 accepted the commission's findings.

Pacific Expansion

Meanwhile, the U.S. navy focused on the Samoan Islands in the South Pacific, where it sought access to the port of Pago Pago as a refueling station. Britain and Germany had ambitions in Samoa as well, and in March 1889 the United States and Germany narrowly avoided a naval clash when a hurricane wrecked both fleets. Secretary of State Blaine's wife wrote to one of their children, "Your father is now looking up Samoa on the map." Once he found it, negotiations began, and the United States, Great Britain, and Germany established a three-way "protectorate" over the islands.

Attention had by that time shifted to the Hawaiian Islands, which had both strategic and economic significance for the United States (see Map 20.2). New England trading vessels had visited **Hawai'i** as early as the 1790s, and Yankee missionaries had come in the 1820s. By the 1860s American-owned sugar plantations worked by Chinese and Japanese laborers dotted the islands. Under an 1887 treaty (negotiated after the planters had forcibly imposed a new constitution on Hawai'i's native ruler, Kala-kaua), the United States built a naval base at Pearl Harbor, near Honolulu. American economic dominance

GLOBAL INTERACTIONS

Missionaries to the World

In 1885, twenty-two-year-old Elaine Goodale from Massachusetts secured a commission from an Episcopal bishop to be a "lady missionary" and open a day school for Sioux Indians in the newly formed Dakota Territory. While she taught school there during the next seven years, Goodale learned the Dakota Sioux language, became the federal supervisor of education in the territory, and married Charles Eastman (Ohiyesa), an Indian who had attended Dartmouth College and received his medical degree from Boston University.

American women did not confine their missionary work to North America. Nancy Jones, the child of runaway slaves, was educated at Fisk University and became the first African American missionary in Southern Rhodesia (present-day Zimbabwe). In 1883, Baptists sent six black couples as missionaries to West Africa. In the late nineteenth century, thousands of American and European women served as Christian missionaries not only in Africa and the American West, but also in the Middle East, India, China, Japan, Australia, the Philippines, and the Hawaiian Islands.

American women's missionary experiences were similar to those of women from England, Belgium, France, and

ELAINE GOODALE, WHITE RIVER MISSION, SOUTH DAKOTA, 1887 Elaine Goodale, age twenty-four, to the left of the doorway in this photograph, taught Dakota Indians at this mission school. *(Private Collection)*

Germany. The growth of missionary work was closely associated with Western imperialism. The relationship between missionary work and imperialism was complex. An examination of the lives of missionaries like Goodale and Jones reveals a paradox: on the one hand missionaries encouraged education, Christianization, and the inculcation of Western values that supported imperialism; on the other hand, women working alone in a foreign land gained a degree of independence and social responsibility that often led them to criticize imperial policy and become an advocate for native peoples.

Why did thousands of women become missionaries? Many women signed up out of an

PROTESTANT MISSIONARY EXPANSION IN EAST ASIA, TO 1910

- Guangzhou, only point of missionary activity in China, 1838
- Treaty port opened to missionaries, 1842–1864
- Other major center of missionary activity, by 1910

Shenyang · Beijing · Tianjin · KOREA · Pyongyang · Seoul · Shenyang

Huang He R. (Yellow R.) · Yellow Sea (East Sea) · Sea of Japan (East Sea) · Sapporo

CHINA · Chengdu · Yangzi R. · Nanjing · Wuhan · Chongqing · Shanghai · Hangzhou · JAPAN · Kyoto · Kobe · Tokyo · Nagoya · Osaka

Ava · Xi R. · Fuzhou · Xiamen · Taiwan · PACIFIC OCEAN

Guangzhou · Hong Kong · South China Sea

0 250 500 Km. / 0 250 500 Mi. / Inset same scale as main map

idealistic urge to help poor, "pagan," malnourished, uneducated women and girls. They believed the racist theories of the time that nonwhites were members of inferior races, with debased social values and ignorant religious beliefs. Missionaries took on a role similar to that of settlement-house workers: teaching reading and writing, improving household sanitation and personal hygiene, and instilling Western religious beliefs and moral standards.

Women missionaries, whether they came from Europe or the United States, opposed polygamy, child marriage, and hard physical labor for women and girls. Both Catholic and Protestant missionaries from the United States and Great Britain taught their charges in English, believing that native languages were inferior and that women were the primary source of morality. In Mozambique, Portuguese nuns instructed girls in how to sew and wear their clothes in the latest European styles. In China, missionary magazines with titles like *The Heathen Woman's Friend*, taught that cleanliness was the true sign of civilization. Female missionaries, both single and married, hoped to train their converts to be good wives for Christian men. In their view, good Christians made good colonial subjects, an attitude that historians have called "domestic imperialism."

Working alone or with little supervision in a foreign territory gave female missionaries a measure of independence and personal authority. Service as missionary teachers elevated their social status and opened up travel opportunities that would not have been available at home. Goodale accompanied a Sioux hunting party on horseback west to Yellowstone Park, sleeping in a tipi and learning native traditions and customs. Other American women traveled by canoe along rivers through China and Africa. Travel was often quite dangerous, and many women were injured or suffered from diseases such as malaria, dysentery, or typhoid fever.

Some women missionaries became doctors and founded hospitals. The British doctor Edith Pechey ran a hospital for women and children in Bombay, India (now called Mumbai). American Methodist missionaries in China helped one of their best students, Mary Stone (Shi Meiyu), attend the University of Michigan medical school in 1896 and return home to work as a physician. Other missionaries, whether Protestant teachers or Catholic nuns, ran boarding schools and set up orphanages.

Although a few missionaries adopted native customs and dress, and even married native men, most upheld European and American middle-class values. They taught their women

EVA SWIFT IN INDIA By dressing in a Western manner, missionaries such as Eva Swift, here pictured teaching in India, reinforced the assumption that Western standards were superior to native ones. *(United Theological College)*

charges that modesty, humility, and service were Christian virtues and emphasized the superiority of Western culture and institutions.

If most women missionaries came to change, not to be changed, some, like Goodale, were transformed by the experience. Introduced to the "strange new world of an Indian reservation," she later wrote, "We found it, rather, two distinct worlds existing side by side, now in dramatic opposition, now intimately mixed." Four years later, after some of the bleeding survivors of the Wounded Knee massacre escaped to her schoolhouse, she wrote to the New York newspapers attacking "the indiscriminate slaughter of the unarmed and helpless."

Overall, American women missionaries left a mixed legacy. Their perception of native societies as backward and barbaric encouraged colonial intervention and subjugation. But their experiences empowered the women missionaries, encouraged the creation of medical and educational institutions, and at times fostered a critique of colonialism itself.

QUESTIONS FOR ANALYSIS

- What was the relationship between women missionaries and imperialism?
- Why did women become missionaries?
- Why did the experiences of some missionaries change their view of native peoples?

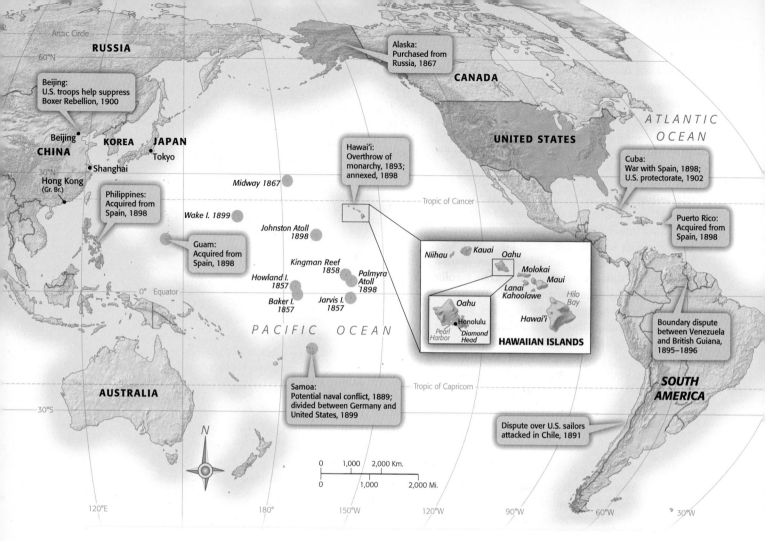

MAP 20.2 **U.S. TERRITORIAL EXPANSION IN THE LATE NINETEENTH CENTURY** The major U.S. territorial expansion abroad came in a short burst of activity in the late 1890s, when newspapers and some politicians urged Americans to acquire strategic ports and coaling stations abroad. © Cengage Learning. All rights reserved. No distribution allowed without express authorization.

and the influx of foreigners angered Hawaiians. In 1891, they welcomed Liliuokalani, a strong-willed woman hostile to Americans, to the Hawaiian throne.

Meanwhile, in 1890, the framers of the McKinley Tariff, pressured by domestic sugar growers, eliminated the duty-free status enjoyed by Hawaiian sugar. In January 1893, facing ruin as Hawai'i's wholesale sugar prices plunged 40 percent, the planters deposed Queen Liliuokalani, proclaimed the independent Republic of Hawai'i, and requested U.S. annexation. The U.S. State Department's representative in Hawai'i cabled Washington, "The Hawaiian pear is now fully ripe, and this is the golden hour for the United States to pluck it." But the grab for Hawai'i troubled Grover Cleveland, who sent a representative to investigate the situation. This representative's report questioned whether the Hawaiian people actually desired annexation.

Cleveland's scruples infuriated expansionists. When William McKinley succeeded Cleveland in 1897, the acquisition of Hawai'i was pushed forward by sugar companies that had similar investments in Cuba. In 1898, Congress proclaimed Hawai'i an American territory. Sixty-one years later, it joined the Union as the fiftieth state.

Crisis over Cuba

Many of the same expansionists who had argued for the annexation of Hawai'i turned their attention in 1898 to the Spanish colony of Cuba, ninety miles off Florida, where in 1895 an anti-Spanish rebellion had broken out. This revolt, organized by the Cuban writer José Martí and other Cuban exiles in New York City, won little support from U.S. business, which had $50 million invested in Cuba and annually imported $100 million worth of sugar and other products from the island.

Nor did the rebels initially secure the backing of Washington, which urged Spain to grant Cuba a degree of autonomy.

But the rebels' cause aroused popular sympathy in the United States. This support increased with revelations that the Spanish commander in Cuba, Valeriano Weyler, was herding vast numbers of Cubans into squalid camps. Malnutrition and disease turned these camps into hellholes in which perhaps two hundred thousand Cubans died.

Fueling American anger was the sensationalized reporting of two competing New York City newspapers, William Randolph Hearst's *Journal* and Joseph Pulitzer's *World*. The *Journal*'s color comic strip, "The Yellow Kid," provided a name for Hearst's debased editorial approach: yellow journalism. The Hungarian immigrant Pulitzer normally had higher standards, but in the cutthroat battle for readers, Pulitzer's *World* matched the *Journal*'s sensationalism. Both editors exploited the Cuban crisis. Headlines turned rumor into fact, and feature stories detailed "Butcher" Weyler's atrocities. When a young Cuban woman was jailed for resisting a rape attempt by a Spanish officer, a Hearst reporter helped the woman escape and brought her triumphantly to New York.

In 1897, a new, more liberal Spanish government sought a peaceful resolution of the Cuban crisis. But Hearst and Pulitzer continued to inflame the public. On February 8, 1898, Hearst's *Journal* published a private letter by Spain's minister to the United States that described McKinley as "weak" and "a bidder for the admiration of the crowd." Irritation over this incident turned to outrage when on February 15 an explosion sank the U.S. battleship *Maine* in Havana harbor and killed 266 crewmen. Scholarly opinion about what caused the explosion is still divided, but a careful review of the evidence in 1998 concluded that a mine most likely set off the ammunition explosion that sank the ship. Newspaper headlines at the time blamed the same cause and war spirit flared high.

> It had been, Hay wrote Roosevelt, "a splendid little war."

Despite further Spanish concessions, McKinley sent a war message to Congress on April 11, and legislators enacted a joint resolution recognizing Cuba's independence and authorizing force to expel the Spanish. The Teller Amendment, introduced by Senator Henry M. Teller of Colorado, renounced any U.S. interest in "sovereignty, jurisdiction, or control" in Cuba and pledged that America would leave the island alone once independence was assured.

The Spanish-American War, 1898

The war with Spain involved only a few days of actual combat. The first action came on May 1, 1898, when a U.S. fleet commanded by George Dewey steamed into Manila Bay in the Philippines and destroyed or captured all ten Spanish ships anchored there, at the cost of 1 American and 381 Spanish lives (see Map 20.3). In mid-August, U.S. troops occupied the capital, Manila.

In Cuba, the fighting centered on the military stronghold of Santiago on the southeastern coast. On May 19, a Spanish battle fleet of seven aging vessels sailed into the Santiago harbor, where five U.S. battleships and two cruisers blockaded them (see Map 20.4). On July 1, in the war's only significant land action, American troops seized three strongly defended Spanish garrisons overlooking Santiago on El Caney Hill, Kettleman's Hill, and San Juan Hill. Theodore Roosevelt led the volunteer "Rough Riders" unit in the capture of San Juan Hill and became a war hero. Emphasizing his toughness and sense of honor, Roosevelt would later use his war experience to reaffirm the aptitude of men like himself for political leadership.

On July 3, the Spanish attempted to break through the American blockade to the open sea. The U.S. navy fired and sank their archaic vessels. Spain lost 474 men in this gallant but doomed defense. Americans might have found a cautionary lesson in this sorry end to four hundred years of Spanish rule in the New World, but few had time for somber musings. The *Washington Post* observed, "A new consciousness seems to have come upon us—the consciousness of strength—and with it a new appetite, the yearning to show our strength." Secretary of State John Hay was more succinct. It had been, he wrote Roosevelt, "a splendid little war."

Many who served in Cuba found the war far from splendid. Ill-trained and poorly equipped, the troops went into summer combat wearing heavy woolen uniforms. The army also lacked adequate medical support. When **Clara Barton,** president of the American Association for Red Cross, visited Santiago, she found wounded soldiers lying in the rain, unable to eat the hardtack rations. Under her leadership, 1,000 trained nurses worked with the medical corps. Despite the efforts of these nurses and doctors, 379 American soldiers died in combat and more than 5,000 succumbed to food poisoning, yellow fever, malaria, and other diseases during and after the war.

Several thousand black troops fought in Cuba. Some, such as the Twenty-fourth Infantry and Tenth Cavalry, were seasoned regular army "buffalo

WE LEAVE THE TRENCHES, **BY CHARLES JOHNSON POST, AUGUST 8, 1898** Weakened by disease and clad in their wool uniforms, American soldiers prepare to leave Cuba. Their initial enthusiasm for the Spanish-American War had been dampened by spoiled food and sickness. *(U.S. Army Center of Military History)*

soldiers" transferred from bases in the West. Others were volunteers from various states. At assembly points in Georgia, and then at the embarkation port of Tampa, Florida, these troops encountered the racism of a Jim Crow society. Tampa restaurants and bars refused them service; Tampa whites disparaged them. On June 6, after weeks of racist treatment, some black troops exploded in riotous rage, storming into restaurants, bars, and other establishments that had barred them. White troops from Georgia restored order. Although white and black troops sailed to Cuba on the same transport ships (actually, hastily converted freighters), the ships themselves were segregated, with black troops often confined to the lowest quarters in the stifling heat, denied permission to mingle on deck with the other units, and in other ways discriminated against.

Despite the racism, African Americans served with distinction once they reached Cuba. Black troops played key roles in the taking of both San Juan Hill and El Caney Hill. Of the total U.S. troops involved in the latter action, some 15 percent were black.

The Spanish sought an armistice on July 17. In the peace treaty signed that December in Paris, Spain recognized Cuba's independence and, after a U.S. payment of $20 million, ceded the Philippines, Puerto Rico, and the Pacific island of Guam to the United States. Americans now possessed an island empire stretching from the Caribbean to the Pacific.

From 1898 to 1902, the U.S. army governed Cuba under the command of General Leonard Wood. Wood's administration improved public health, education, and sanitation but nevertheless violated the spirit of the 1898 Teller Amendment. The troops eventually withdrew, though under conditions that limited Cuban sovereignty. The 1901 **Platt Amendment,** attached to an army appropriations bill offered by a Connecticut senator at the request of the War Department, authorized American withdrawal only after Cuba agreed not to make any treaty with a foreign power limiting its independence and not to borrow beyond its means. The United States also reserved the right to intervene in Cuba when it saw fit and to maintain a naval base there, a policy resented by the Cubans. With U.S. troops still occupying the island, the Cuban

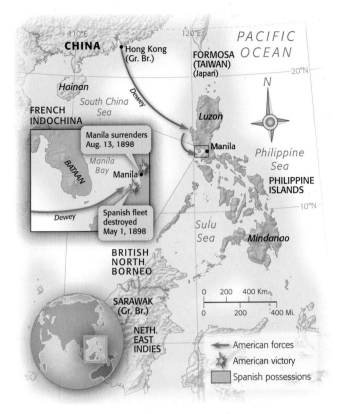

MAP 20.3 DEWEY'S ROUTE IN THE PHILIPPINES, 1898 Admiral Dewey's prompt defeat of the Spanish fleet made it evident that naval plans for this attack had been drawn up even before war had been declared. © Cengage Learning. All rights reserved. No distribution allowed without express authorization.

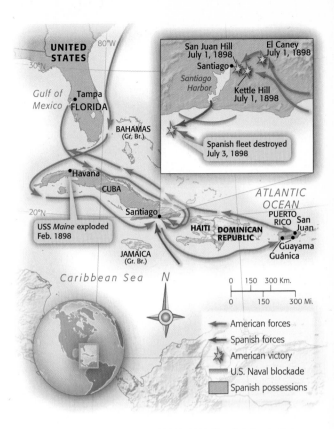

MAP 20.4 THE CUBAN CAMPAIGN, 1898 The fighting in Cuba lasted only 113 days. © Cengage Learning. All rights reserved. No distribution allowed without express authorization.

constitutional convention of 1901 accepted the Platt Amendment, which remained in force until 1934. Under its terms the United States established a naval base at Guantánamo Bay, near Santiago de Cuba, which it still maintains. U.S. investments in Cuba, some $50 million in 1898, soared to half a billion dollars by 1920.

Critics of Empire

Some Americans, who had opposed imperialism for more than a decade, were dismayed by the victories of the expansionists in Cuba and the Philippines. Although few in number, the critics, like the Mugwumps who had challenged the spoils system, were influential. Indeed, some of them, like Carl Schurz and E.L. Godkin, were former Mugwumps. Other anti-imperialists included William Jennings Bryan, settlement-house founder Jane Addams, novelist Mark Twain, and Harvard philosopher William James. Steel king Andrew Carnegie gave thousands of dollars to the cause. In 1898, these critics of empire formed the **Anti-Imperialist League.**

For the United States to rule other peoples, the anti-imperialists believed, was to violate the principles of the Declaration of Independence and the Constitution. As one of them wrote, "Dewey took Manila with the loss of one man—and all our institutions." The military fever that accompanied expansionism also dismayed the anti-imperialists. Some labor leaders feared that imperial expansion would lead to competition from cheap foreign labor and products.

In February 1899, the anti-imperialists failed by one vote to prevent Senate ratification of the peace treaty with Spain. McKinley's overwhelming reelection victory in 1900 and the defeat of expansionist critic William Jennings Bryan eroded the anti-imperialists' cause. Nevertheless, at a time of jingoistic rhetoric and militaristic posturing, they had upheld an older and more traditional vision of America.

Guerrilla War in the Philippines, 1898–1902

Events in the Philippines confirmed the worst fears of the anti-imperialists. When the war ended, President McKinley was faced with the urgent problem of what to do about this group of Pacific islands that had a population of more than 5 million people.

AFRICAN AMERICAN SOLDIERS OF THE TENTH U.S. CAVALRY IN CUBA, JULY 1898 These men posed shortly after the capture of San Juan Hill. Black troops, known as buffalo soldiers, played an important role in the Spanish-American War, but they were subject to harassment and discrimination. *(National Archives)*

At the war's outset, few Americans knew that the Philippines belonged to Spain or even where they were. Without a map, McKinley later confessed, "I could not have told where those darn islands were within two thousand miles."

But the victory over Spain whetted the appetite for expansion. To the U.S. business community, the Philippines offered a steppingstone to the China market. McKinley, reflecting the prevailing mood as always, reasoned that the Filipinos were unready for self-government and would be gobbled up if set adrift in a world of imperial rivalries. McKinley further persuaded himself that American rule would enormously benefit the Filipinos, whom he called "our little brown brothers." A devout Methodist, he explained that America's mission was "to educate the Filipinos, and to uplift and civilize and Christianize them, and by God's grace do the very best we could by them." (In fact, most Filipinos were already Catholic, a legacy of centuries of Spanish rule.) Having prayerfully reached his decision, McKinley instructed the American peace negotiators in Paris to insist on U.S. acquisition of the Philippines.

"Uplifting" the Filipinos required a struggle. In 1896 young **Emilio Aguinaldo** had organized a Filipino independence movement to drive out Spain. In 1898, with arms supplied by George Dewey, Aguinaldo's forces had captured most of Luzon, the Philippines' main island. When the Spanish surrendered, Aguinaldo proclaimed Filipino independence and drafted a democratic constitution. Feeling betrayed when the peace treaty ceded his country to the United States, Aguinaldo ordered his rebel force to attack Manila, the American base of operations. Seventy thousand more U.S. troops were shipped to the Philippines; by the end of 1899, the initial Filipino resistance had been crushed.

These hostilities became the opening phase of a long guerrilla conflict. Before it ended, more than 125,000 American men had served in the Philippines, and four thousand had been killed. As many as twenty thousand Filipino independence fighters died. As in the later Vietnam and Iraq wars, casualties and suffering ravaged the civilian population as well. Historians estimate that at least 200,000 civilians died in the conflict. Aguinaldo was captured in March 1901, but large-scale guerrilla fighting continued through the summer of 1902.

In 1902, a special Senate committee heard testimony from veterans of the Philippines war about

> "I could not have told where those darn islands were within two thousand miles."

the execution of prisoners, the torture of suspects, and the burning of villages. The humanitarian mood of 1898, when Americans had rushed to save Cuba from the cruel Spaniards, seemed remote indeed. In retrospect, the American troops' ambivalent attitudes about the peoples of the Philippines, while deplorable, are not hard to understand. Despite America's self-image as a beacon of liberty and a savior of the world's peoples, many Americans in the 1880s and 1890s had been deeply troubled by the new immigrants from southern and eastern Europe and had expressed concerns over "backward" and "useless" races. As American nationalism was reformulated in this cauldron of immigration, imperialism, and the "winning of the West," racist attitudes about Native peoples and foreigners intermixed with rhetorical pleas for supervision and stewardship. In the process, as was evident in the treatment of American Indians (see Chapter 17), well-meaning paternalism often degenerated into deadly domination.

> Samuel Gompers warned that "an inundation of Mongolians" might steal jobs from white labor.

The subjugation of the Philippines followed years of expansionism that proclaimed America's debut on the world stage and underscored the global reach of U.S. capitalism. Nevertheless, most Americans remained ambivalent about the acquisition of territory. While anti-imperialist Mark Twain could acidly condemn "the Blessings of Civilization Trust," labor leader Samuel Gompers warned that "an inundation of Mongolians" might steal jobs from white labor. From the debate over the annexation of Hawai'i in 1898 to the end of the war against Philippine independence in 1902, white Americans recoiled from making these "barbarian peoples" a part of the United States. Not fit to manage their own affairs, Cuban, Puerto Rican, Hawaiian, and Filipino peoples were placed in a protective status that denied their independence and kept them under U.S. control.

To stabilize relations in the Philippines, Congress passed the Philippine Government Act in 1902, which vested authority in a governor general to be appointed by the president. The act also provided for an elected Filipino assembly and promised eventual self-government. Progress toward this goal inched forward, with intervals of semi military rule. In 1946, nearly half a century after Admiral Dewey's guns had boomed in Manila Bay, independence finally came to the Philippines.

CONCLUSION

By 1900 immigration, the settlement of the frontier West, and rapid industrial expansion had pushed America to the forefront of the world economy and had sparked a major realignment in American politics. After nearly two decades of hard-fought elections in which political control had seesawed back and forth between the major parties, the Republicans now held power.

It had been difficult to achieve political dominance. The dynamic growth of the American economy, together with rapid urbanization and a massive influx of immigrants, had strained the political process. As the parties struggled to define their vision of the proper role of government in stimulating economic development, they were forced to deal with ethnic, cultural, and racial issues that included prohibition, church schools, and segregation. All this was further complicated by the Democratic Party's attempt to throw off the limits imposed by Reconstruction and gain political control of the South.

On the national level, both parties built a loyal following by linking their positions to deeply held beliefs about the family and the proper role of government. Republicans justified their support for the tariff and soldiers' pensions in terms of patriotic protection of the family. Democrats countered that a high-tariff policy was indicative of precisely the kind of excessive governmental force that would destroy family life. On the local level, both parties secured loyal voters by stressing ethnic and cultural issues. Democrats, often as political bosses and urban machines, courted the new immigrants, while Republicans catered to rural and small-town native-born Americans in the Northeast and Midwest. Political bosses gave immigrants a foothold in the political process but their participation often came at the high cost of inflated contracts and corruption that siphoned millions of dollars from the public treasury.

In the competition for new voters, the needs of rural Americans were often overlooked. Caught between declining prices for grain and cotton, and high railroad and bank rates, farmers struggled to survive. Their precarious position was further strained by years of drought, insect infestation, and overspecialization in one crop. In desperation, farmers turned first to the Grange and Farmers' Alliance movements and then to the Populist Party for help. In the South, after first courting black farmers, members of the Farmers' Alliance and later the Populists joined with Democrats to disfranchise black voters. Using lynching and intimidation, Democrats seized control of southern politics.

In the face of these threats, the Republican Party in 1896 raised huge sums from big business to turn back the Populist challenge and take control of national politics. The fusion of the Populists and Democrats behind William Jennings Bryan and the silver issue created problems of its own. Although he carried the South and almost all the Midwest, the teetotaling Bryan had little appeal for urban workers and the middle class, who believed that a monetary policy based on free silver promised only inflation and higher prices. McKinley won by playing down moral reforms such as prohibition and emphasizing patriotism and fiscal responsibility. Republicans won over the urban-industrial core of the nation—the Northeast and much of the Midwest. They would control the House of Representatives for twenty-eight out of the thirty-six years from 1894 to 1930.

McKinley's administration was drawn by events in Cuba and jingoistic advocates within his own party into the Spanish-American War and the subsequent acquisition of Hawai'i, Samoa, Guam, the Philippines, and Cuba. Although the Republicans preferred the term "expansionism" to "imperialism," the move to acquire new bases for access to global markets fit the party's probusiness stance. But expansion into the Pacific created its own obstacles when the United States became involved in a guerrilla war with Philippine nationalists. Facing mounting criticism at home, the expansionists adopted the Teller and Platt amendments, which foreshadowed eventual disengagement from the acquisition of foreign territory.

Notwithstanding these foreign interventions, the fundamental question of late-nineteenth century American politics persisted: could a government designed for the needs of a small agrarian society serve an industrialized nation of factories and immigrant-crowded cities? The answer was by no means clear. Although issues such as patronage, the tariff, veterans' benefits, and monetary policy had enabled the industrial system to grow dramatically, the needs of farmers, workers, and immigrant Americans had largely been ignored. The Republicans successfully carried the field in 1896, but Populists and other critics who argued that government should play an assertive role in solving social and economic problems would help shape the political environment of the progressive movement.

KEY TERMS

laissez-faire   (p. 601)

Grand Army of the Republic
   (p. 602)

political machine   (p. 603)

William "Magear" Tweed   (p. 603)

Sherman Silver Purchase Act
   (p. 603)

Pendleton Civil Service Act   (p. 604)

Mugwumps   (p. 606)

Grange   (p. 607)

Farmers' Alliance   (p. 608)

Populist Party   (p. 611)

subtreasury plan   (p. 611)

lynching   (p. 611)

Plessy v. *Ferguson*   (1896)   (p. 612)

Booker T. Washington   (p. 613)

Panic of 1893   (p. 614)

William Jennings Bryan   (p. 616)

Alfred Thayer Mahan   (p. 619)

Hawai'i   (p. 619)

Clara Barton   (p. 623)

Platt Amendment   (p. 624)

Anti-Imperialist League   (p. 625)

Emilio Aguinaldo   (p. 626)

FOR FURTHER REFERENCE

Omar Ali, *In the Lion's Mouth: Black Populism in the New South* (2010). An innovative study of the independent black farmers' movements in the South.

Richard F. Bensel, *The Political Economy of American Industrialization, 1877–1900* (2000). An astute analysis, based on a close reading of party platforms, of the connections among the tariff, monetary policy, veterans' benefits, and industrial expansion.

Rebecca Edwards, *Angels in the Machinery: Gender in American Party Politics from the Civil War to the Progressive Era* (1997). An innovative exploration of women's role in the political process and in the formation of political ideology.

William James Hull Hoffer, *To Enlarge the Machinery of Government: Congressional Debates and the Growth of the American State, 1858–1891* (2007). An important analysis of the growth of government intervention in daily life through its support of civil service, education, and law enforcement.

Matthew F. Jacobson, *Barbarian Virtues: The United States Encounters Foreign Peoples at Home and Abroad, 1877–1900* (2000). An innovative study of the interconnections between politics, racism, and American economic development.

Amy Kaplan, *The Anarchy of Empire in the Making of U.S. Culture* (2002). An important study of how imperial expansion was shaped by and reshaped domestic ideas of race and gender.

Michael Perman, *Struggle for Mastery: Disfranchisement in the South, 1888–1908* (2001). An important examination of the Democratic Party's systematic disfranchisement of black voters.

David M. Pletcher, *The Diplomacy of Trade and Investment: American Economic Expansion in the Hemisphere, 1865–1900* (1998). An astute analysis of the direct and indirect governmental support for trade expansionism in the late nineteenth century.

Charles Postel, *The Populist Vision* (2007). A new look at the Populist reform ideals emphasizing both their strengths and their weaknesses.

Amy L. Wood, *Lynching and Spectacle: Witnessing Racial Violence in America* (2009). A careful analysis of the social and symbolic impact of lynching.

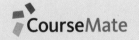

The Progressive Era,

1900–1917

YOUNG FEMALE GARMENT WORKER, 1915, PHOTOGRAPHED BY LEWIS W. HINE *(Granger Collection)*

IT WAS LATE SATURDAY AFTERNOON ON MARCH 25, 1911, but at the Triangle Shirtwaist factory in New York City, hundreds of young women and a few men remained at work. In the eighth- and ninth-floor workrooms, the clatter of sewing machines filled the air. Suddenly fire broke out, quickly turning the upper floors into an inferno. Panicked workers found some of the doors locked. Crushes of people jammed against doors that opened inward (a fire-law violation).

A few escaped. Young Pauline Grossman crawled to safety across a narrow alleyway when three male employees formed a human bridge. As others tried to cross, however, the weight became too great, and all fell to their deaths. Dozens leaped from the windows to certain death below.

Immigrant parents searched all night for their daughters; newspaper reporters could hear "a dozen pet names in Italian and Yiddish rising in shrill agony above the deeper moan of the throng." Sunday's headlines summed up the grim count: 141 dead.

The horrifying Triangle fire underscored what many citizens had long recognized. Industrialization, for all its benefits, had taken a heavy toll on American life. Many factory workers and slum-dwellers endured a desperate cycle of poverty, exhausting labor, and early death.

Industrialization, urban growth, and the rise of great corporations affected all Americans. A new middle class of white-collar workers and urban professionals gained political influence. Middle-class women, joining clubs and reform organizations, focused attention on urgent social issues.

These developments produced a wave of reform that came to be called the progressive movement. Historians once portrayed this movement as a triumph of "the people" over evil corporations. More recent historians have complicated this picture, noting the role of special-interest groups (including big business) in promoting specific reforms, as well as the movement's racist, anti-immigrant, and coercive social-control aspects.

The progressive movement was a response to vast changes that had overwhelmed an older America. Whatever their specific agendas, all progressives grappled with the new America of corporations, factories, cities, and immigrants. In contrast to the rural Populists, progressives concentrated on the social effects of the new urban-industrial order.

Emerging in the 1890s at the city and state levels, an array of organizations, many led by women, pursued varied reform objectives. As journalists, novelists, religious leaders, and politicians joined in, these grassroots efforts evolved into a national

MULBERRY STREET ON NEW YORK CITY'S LOWER EAST SIDE, AROUND 1900 *(Library of Congress)*

THE TRIANGLE FIRE The bodies of Triangle Shirtwaist factory workers lie on the sidewalk after they jumped from the burning building. *(Brown Brothers)*

movement. By 1917, when reform gave way to war, America's political and social landscape had been transformed. New laws, organizations, and regulatory agencies had arisen to address the consequences of urbanization, industrial expansion, and corporate growth. The progressives could be maddeningly moralistic. They had their blind spots (especially on such subjects as immigration and race), and their reforms didn't always work as planned. But, on balance, their achievements left a powerful legacy.

FOCUS Questions

- How did intellectuals, novelists, and journalists inspire the progressive movement?
- How did state and local progressives seek to reform cities and the new industrial order?
- How did progressives try to control morality, and how did they view immigrants and blacks?
- What strategies did African Americans, women, and industrial workers use to improve their lot?
- As progressivism became a national movement, what issues proved most important?

Progressives and Their Ideas

As the twentieth century dawned, groups across the nation grappled with the problems of the new urban-industrial order. Workers protested unsafe and exhausting jobs. Experts investigated social conditions. Women's clubs embraced reform. Intellectuals challenged the ideological foundations of a business-dominated social order, and journalists exposed municipal corruption and industrialism's human toll. Throughout America, activists worked to make government more democratic, improve conditions in cities and factories, and curb corporate power.

Historians have grouped all these efforts under a single label: "the progressive movement." In fact, "progressivism" was less a single movement than a spirit of discontent with the status quo and an exciting sense of new social possibilities. International in scope, this spirit found many outlets and addressed many issues (see Beyond America).

The Many Faces of Progressivism

Who were the progressives, and what reforms did they pursue? The social changes of the era provide clues to the answers. Along with immigration, a growing middle class transformed U.S. cities. From the men and women of this class—mostly white, native-born Protestants—came many of the progressive movement's leaders and supporters.

From 1900 to 1920, the white-collar work force jumped from 5.1 million to 10.5 million—more than double the growth rate of the labor force as a whole. This burgeoning white-collar class included corporate executives and small-business owners; secretaries, accountants, and sales clerks; civil engineers and people in advertising; and professionals such as lawyers, physicians, and teachers. New professional groups arose, from the American Association of University Professors (1915) to the American Association of Advertising Agencies (1917). For many middle-class Americans, membership in a national professional society provided a sense of identity that might earlier have come from neighborhood, church, or political party. Ambitious, well educated, and valuing social stability, the members of this new middle class were eager to make their influence felt.

For middle-class women, the city offered both opportunities and frustrations. Young unmarried women often became schoolteachers, secretaries, typists, clerks, and telephone operators. The number of women in such white-collar jobs, as well as

1900	International Ladies' Garment Workers' Union (ILGWU) founded.
	Socialist Party of America organized.
	Theodore Dreiser, *Sister Carrie*.
	Carrie Chapman Catt becomes president of the National American Woman Suffrage Association (NAWSA).
1901	Assassination of McKinley; Theodore Roosevelt becomes president.
	J.P. Morgan forms United States Steel Company.
1902	Jane Addams, *Democracy and Social Ethics*.
1903	W.E.B. Du Bois, *The Souls of Black Folk*.
	Wright brothers' flight.
1904	Theodore Roosevelt elected president in his own right.
	Lincoln Steffens, *The Shame of the Cities*.
1905	Industrial Workers of the World (IWW) organized.
1906	Upton Sinclair, *The Jungle*.
1907	William James, *Pragmatism*.
1908	William Howard Taft elected president. Model T Ford introduced.
1909	Ballinger-Pinchot controversy.
	National Association for the Advancement of Colored People (NAACP) founded.
1909 (*Cont.*)	Herbert Croly, *The Promise of American Life*.
	Daniel Burnham, *Plan of Chicago*.
1910	Insurgents curb power of House Speaker Joseph Cannon.
1911	Triangle Shirtwaist Company fire.
1912	Republican Party split; Progressive (Bull Moose) Party founded.
	Woodrow Wilson elected president.
	International Opium Treaty.
1913	Sixteenth Amendment (Congress empowered to tax incomes).
	Seventeenth Amendment (direct election of U.S. senators).
1914	American Social Hygiene Association founded.
	Narcotics Act (Harrison Act).
1915	D.W. Griffith, *The Birth of a Nation*.
1916	John Dewey, *Democracy and Education*.
	Margaret Sanger opens nation's first birth-control clinic in Brooklyn, New York.
	National Park Service created.
	Louis Brandeis appointed to Supreme Court.
1919	Eighteenth Amendment (national prohibition).
1920	Nineteenth Amendment (woman suffrage).

the ranks of college-educated women, more than tripled from 1900 to 1920.

But for middle-class married women caring for homes and children, city life could bring stress and loneliness. The divorce rate rose from one in twelve marriages in 1900 to one in nine by 1916. As we shall see, middle-class women joined female white-collar workers and college graduates in leading a revived women's movement. Cultural commentators wrote nervously of the "New Woman."

This urban middle class rallied to the banner of reform. The initial reform impetus came not from political parties but from women's clubs, settlement houses, and groups with names like the Playground Association of America, the National Child Labor Committee, and the American League for Civic Improvement. In this era of organizations, the reform movement, too, drew strength from organized interest groups.

The native-born middle class, while central to progressivism, sometimes found allies in promoting reform. On issues affecting factory workers and slum dwellers, the urban-immigrant political machines—and workers themselves—often took the initiative. After the 1911 Triangle fire, New York's machine politicians joined with middle-class reformers and union officials to push for protective legislation. Some corporate leaders promoted business regulations that served their interests.

What, then, was progressivism? Fundamentally, it was a broad-based response to industrialization and its social byproducts: immigration, urban growth, growing corporate power, and widening class divisions. In contrast to populism, it enlisted many more city-dwellers, journalists, academics, and social theorists. Finally, most progressives were *reformers*, not radicals. They wished to make the new urban-industrial order more humane, not overturn it entirely.

But what specific remedies were required? Reaching different answers to this key question, progressive reformers embraced causes that sometimes overlapped, sometimes diverged. Many demanded stricter business regulation, from local transit companies to the almighty trusts. Others focused on protecting workers and the urban poor.

GLOBAL INTERACTIONS

Progressive Reformers Worldwide Share Ideas and Strategies

Progressive reform was not an American invention. U.S. progressives drew ideas from continental Europe, the British Isles, Canada, and even faraway Australia and New Zealand. Sometimes, the exchange flowed in the other direction, as reformers abroad found inspiration in America.

Industrialization and urbanization had transformed other societies as well. The smoky factory cities of Manchester and Birmingham in England, Glasgow in Scotland, Liège in Belgium, and Düsseldorf and Essen in Germany's coal-rich Ruhr Valley all experienced the same social problems as did U.S. industrial cities like Pittsburgh, Chicago, and Cleveland. The grinding poverty of London's East End was as notorious as that of New York's Lower East Side.

The shocked response to these conditions crossed national boundaries as well. Jacob Riis's grim account of life in New York's immigrant wards, *How the Other Half Lives* (1890), echoed the Rev. Andrew Mearns's polemic *The Bitter Cry of Outcast London* (1883). William T. Stead's sensational 1885 exposé of prostitution in London, "The Maiden Tribute of Modern Babylon," helped inspire the American antiprostitution

A POOR FAMILY IN LONDON'S EAST END, 1912 Grim urban slum conditions were a reality in Europe and Great Britain no less than in the United States, spurring reform efforts on both sides of the Atlantic. *(Hulton Archive/Getty Images)*

crusade. The sociological studies of poverty in Chicago, Pittsburgh, Philadelphia, and other cities undertaken by American investigators drew inspiration from Charles Booth's massive survey of London poverty. Beginning in 1886, Booth and his collaborators had painstakingly studied conditions in London's slums. Their handwritten data eventually filled twelve thousand notebook pages. Booth published detailed maps showing the economic situation street by street, first in the East End (1887) and eventually in the entire city (1902–1903).

Efforts to solve the problems of the new urban-industrial order crossed national boundaries, giving rise to a transnational reform movement. The breadth and diversity of this movement was showcased at the Paris Exposition of 1900 in a Musée Social (Social Museum) featuring exhibits of many nations' reform innovations.

As early as the 1880s, Germany's conservative Chancellor Otto von Bismarck, trying to keep the socialists from power, instituted a remarkable series of reforms, including a ban on child labor; maximum working hours; and illness, accident, and old-age insurance for workers. Britain's Liberal party, in power in 1906–1914, introduced minimum-wage laws, unemployment insurance, and a health-insurance program on the German model. In France, a coalition of reform parties established a maximum working day, a progressive income tax (one with higher rates for wealthier taxpayers), and a program of medical aid for the elderly poor. Denmark adopted an old-age pension system. Not all the reforms were state sponsored; some relied on voluntary philanthropy. For example, the first settlement house, Toynbee Hall, was started in London in 1884 by the Anglican clergyman Samuel Augustus Barnett and others. While Australia introduced an ambitious program of water-resource planning to promote agricultural development in its vast interior, New Zealand's trailblazing reforms included woman suffrage, arbitration courts to resolve labor disputes, and programs enabling small farmers to lease public lands.

American reformers followed these developments carefully. Jane Addams visited Toynbee Hall repeatedly in the 1880s. In 1900, the muckraking U.S. journalist Henry

Demarest Lloyd praised New Zealand as "the political brain of the modern world." American students in German and Swiss universities and the London School of Economics (founded by socialists in 1895) encountered challenges to the laissez-faire doctrine that prevailed back home. The federal government's Bureau of Labor Statistics collected data on European social and labor conditions and labor-related issues to give government officials and legislators a comparative perspective on issues of concern in America. For the same reason, reform-minded labor historian John R. Commons at the University of Wisconsin plastered his graduate-seminar room with charts showing labor laws around the world. American Social Gospel leaders kept in close touch with like-minded clergy in England and elsewhere. Experiments with publicly owned electric power companies in the Canadian province of Ontario offered a model for municipal reformers who were proposing this innovation in Cleveland and other U.S. cities.

Transatlantic conferences and delegations furthered the exchange of reform strategies. In 1910, ten Americans attended an International Congress on Unemployment in Paris, while twenty-eight Americans came to Vienna for an International Housing Congress. The National Civic Federation sent fifteen experts to England and Scotland in 1906 to study new ideas in urban reform. A delegation from the Bureau of Municipal Research spent several months in Frankfurt in 1912 learning about administrative innovations in that city. In 1911, a sociology professor at the City College of New York offered social workers a package tour, including visits to London settlement houses, planned cities elsewhere in England, workers' cooperatives in Belgium, and infant nurseries in Paris.

Reformers committed to causes such as world peace or women's rights often joined forces with kindred spirits abroad.

"ENFRANCHISED!" This cartoon commemorated Australia's adoption of woman suffrage in 1902. American woman-suffrage advocates closely followed developments elsewhere and borrowed tactics and strategies from abroad for their campaigns. *(National Library of Australia)*

The birth-control advocate Margaret Sanger, pacifist Jane Addams, and woman-suffrage leader Alice Paul all maintained close contact with activists elsewhere who shared their commitments. The introduction of woman suffrage in New Zealand (1893) and Australia (1902) energized the U.S. suffrage movement.

Housing reformers and city planners cultivated international ties as well. The New York State Tenement House Law of 1901, a key reform measure, owed much to the groundbreaking work of English housing reformers. Daniel Burnham's 1909 *Plan of Chicago* (discussed later in this chapter) drew inspiration from classical Athens and Rome; Renaissance Florence and Siena; Georges Haussmann's great Paris boulevards of the mid-nineteenth century; and Vienna's Ringstrasse, itself inspired by the Paris model.

Magazines contributed to the global flow of reform ideas. The muckraking journalist Ray Stannard Baker reported on reforms in Germany for *McClure's* magazine in 1900, providing a broader context for the magazine's articles on reform in the United States. Not to be outdone, *Everybody's* magazine sent Charles E. Russell around the world in 1905 to investigate reform initiatives in England, Switzerland, Germany, Australia, New Zealand, and elsewhere.

Reform-minded foreigners also visited the United States to report on the juvenile court system, the playground movement, innovative public schools, and other progressive developments. One English progressive visiting Madison, Wisconsin, in 1911 praised the university's role in promoting reform legislation. "The State has been practically governed by the University ...," he wrote. "[E]very question is threshed out in class before it is threshed out by the legislature." The Kansas editor William Allen White, recalling the Progressive Era in his 1946 autobiography, marveled at the movement's transnational character: "We were parts, one of another,...the United States and Europe. Something was welding us into one social and economic whole with local political variations, [but]...all fighting [for] a common cause."

American progressivism, in short, was simply one manifestation of a larger effort to cope with the social impact of rapid industrialization and urban growth. Through a dense network of publications, conferences, and personal ties, reformers of many nations kept in touch, shared strategies, and drew on a vast storehouse of ideas as they addressed the problems and circumstances of their societies.

QUESTION FOR ANALYSIS

- What early twentieth-century reforms transcended national boundaries, and how did reformers in different countries share ideas and strategies?

Still others championed reform of municipal government. Some, fearful of urban disorder, favored immigration restriction or social-control strategies to regulate city-dwellers' behavior. All this contributed to the mosaic of progressive reform.

Progressives believed that most social problems could be solved through study and organized effort. They respected science and expert knowledge. Scientific and technological expertise had produced the new industrial order, so such expertise could surely also correct the social problems spawned by industrialism. Progressives marshaled research data, surveys, and statistics to support their various causes.

Some historians have portrayed progressivism as an organizational stage that all modernizing societies pass through. This perspective is useful, provided we remember that it was not an automatic process unfolding independently of human will. Persistent journalists, activist workers, and passionate reformers all played a role. Human emotion—whether indignation over child labor, suspicion of corporate power, or raw political ambition—drove the movement forward.

Intellectuals Offer New Social Views

A group of innovative social thinkers provided progressivism's underlying ideas. As we have seen, some Gilded Age intellectuals had argued that Charles Darwin's theory of evolution justified unrestrained economic competition. In the 1880s and 1890s, sociologist Lester Ward, utopian novelist Edward Bellamy, and Social Gospel advocates (a liberal religious movement that advocated applying Christian principles to the problems of the new urban-industrial order) had all attacked this harsh version of Social Darwinism (see Chapters 18 and 19). This attack intensified after 1900.

Economist Thorstein Veblen, a Norwegian American from Minnesota, satirized America's newly rich capitalists in *The Theory of the Leisure Class* (1899). Dissecting their lifestyle the way an anthropologist might study an exotic tribe, he argued that they built mansions, threw elaborate parties, and otherwise engaged in "conspicuous consumption" to flaunt their wealth and assert their claims to superiority.

The Harvard philosopher William James argued in *Pragmatism* (1907) that truth emerges not from abstract theorizing but from the experience of coping with life's realities through practical action. James's philosophy of pragmatism deepened reformers' skepticism toward the older generation's

entrenched ideas and strengthened their belief in the necessity of social change.

Herbert Croly, the son of reform-minded New York journalists, shared this faith that new ideas could transform society. In *The Promise of American Life* (1909), Croly called for an activist government of the kind advocated by Alexander Hamilton, the first secretary of the treasury. But rather than serving the interests of the business class, as Hamilton had proposed, he argued that government should promote the welfare of all. In 1914, Croly founded the *New Republic* magazine to promote progressive ideas.

The settlement-house leader Jane Addams, in *Democracy and Social Ethics* (1902) and other books, rejected the claim that unrestrained competition ensured social progress. Instead, she argued, in a complex industrial society, each individual's well-being depends on the well-being of all. Addams urged middle-class Americans to recognize their common interests with the laboring masses and to demand better conditions in factories and immigrant slums. Teaching by example, Addams made her Chicago social settlement, Hull House, a center of social activism and legislative-reform initiatives.

With public-school enrollments growing rapidly, the educational reformer John Dewey saw schools as potent engines of social change. In his model school at the University of Chicago, Dewey encouraged pupils to work collaboratively and to interact with one another. The ideal school, he said in *Democracy and Education* (1916), would be an "embryonic community" where children would learn to live as members of a social group.

Oliver Wendell Holmes, Jr., a law professor, focused on changing judicial thinking. In *The Common Law* (1881), Holmes had criticized judges who interpreted the law rigidly to protect corporate interests and had insisted that law must evolve as society changes. Appointed to the U.S. Supreme Court in 1902, Holmes often dissented from the conservative Court majority. As the new social thinking took hold, the courts slowly grew more open to reform legislation.

Novelists, Journalists, and Artists Spotlight Social Problems

While reform-minded intellectuals reoriented American social thought, novelists and journalists chronicled corporate wrongdoing, municipal corruption, slum conditions, and industrial abuses.

In his novel *The Octopus* (1901), Frank Norris of San Francisco portrayed the struggle between California railroad barons and the state's wheat

WOMEN ENTER THE LABOR FORCE Young female workers take an exercise break at the National Cash Register Company in Dayton, Ohio, around 1900. From schools and hospitals to corporate offices and crowded sweatshops, women poured into the workforce in the early twentieth century. *(From the NCR Archive at Dayton History)*

growers. Though writing fiction, Norris accurately described the railroad owners' bribery, intimidation, rate manipulation, and other tactics.

Theodore Dreiser's novel *The Financier* (1912) featured a hard-driving business tycoon lacking a social conscience. Dreiser modeled his story on the scandal-ridden career of an actual railway financier. Such works encouraged skepticism toward the industrial elite and stimulated pressures for tougher business regulation.

Mass magazines such as *McClure's* and *Collier's* stirred reform energies with articles exposing urban political corruption and corporate wrongdoing. President Theodore Roosevelt criticized the authors as **"muckrakers"** publicizing the worst in American life, but the label became a badge of honor. Journalist Lincoln Steffens began the exposé vogue in 1902 with a *McClure's* article documenting municipal corruption in St. Louis.

Some investigative journalists worked as factory laborers or lived in slum tenements. One described her experiences working in a Massachusetts shoe factory where the caustic dyes rotted workers' fingernails. The British immigrant John Spargo researched his 1906 book about child labor, *The Bitter Cry of the Children,* by visiting mines in Pennsylvania and West Virginia and attempting to do the work that young boys performed for ten hours a day, picking out slate and other refuse from coal in cramped workspaces filled with choking coal dust.

The muckrakers awakened middle-class readers to conditions in industrial America. Some magazine exposés later appeared as books, including Lincoln Steffens's *The Shame of the Cities* (1904), Ida Tarbell's damning *History of the Standard Oil Company* (1904), and David Graham Phillips's *The Treason of the Senate* (1906).

Artists and photographers played a role as well. A group of New York painters dubbed the Ashcan School portrayed the harshness as well as the vitality of slum life. The photographer Lewis Hine, working for the National Child Labor Committee, captured haunting images of child workers with stunted bodies and worn expressions.

JOHN SLOAN, *SUNDAY, WOMEN DRYING THEIR HAIR* An artist of the so-called Ashcan School, Sloan lived in New York's Greenwich Village and painted scenes of immigrant and working-class life. His work conveys not only the harsh conditions endured by the urban poor, but also scenes of sociability and relaxation. *(© Addison Gallery of American Art, Phillips Academy, Andover, Massachusetts. All Rights Reserved.)*

Grassroots Progressivism

Middle-class citizens not only read about the problems of urban-industrial America, they observed these problems firsthand in their own communities. In fact, the progressive movement began with grassroots campaigns to end urban political corruption, regulate corporate behavior, and improve conditions in factories and slums. Eventually, these local efforts came together in a powerful national movement.

Reforming Local Politics

Beginning in the 1890s, middle-class reformers battled corrupt city governments that provided services and jobs to immigrants, but often at the price of graft and rigged elections (see Chapter 19). In New York City, Protestant clergy battled Tammany Hall, the city's entrenched Democratic organization.

In San Francisco, a courageous newspaper editor led a 1907 crusade against the city's corrupt boss. When the original prosecutor was gunned down in court, attorney Hiram Johnson took his place, winning convictions against the boss and his cronies. Full of reform zeal—one observer called him "a volcano in perpetual eruption"—Johnson rode his newly won fame to the California governorship and the U.S. Senate.

In Toledo, Ohio, a colorful figure named Samuel M. ("Golden Rule") Jones led the reform crusade. A businessman converted to the Social Gospel, Jones introduced profit sharing in his factory, and as mayor he established playgrounds, free kindergartens, and lodging houses for homeless transients.

Urban political reformers soon began to probe the roots of municipal misgovernment, including the private monopolies that ran municipal water, gas, electricity, and transit systems. Reformers passed laws regulating the rates these utilities could charge and curbing their political influence. (Some even advocated public ownership of these companies.)

> One observer called Hiram Johnson "a volcano in perpetual eruption."

Reflecting the Progressive Era's regard for expertise and efficiency, some municipal reformers advocated substituting professional city managers for mayors, and councils chosen in citywide elections for aldermen elected on a ward-by-ward basis. Dayton, Ohio, adopted a city-manager system after a ruinous flood in 1913. Supposedly above politics, these experts were expected to run the city like an efficient business. Milwaukee set up a Citizens' Bureau of Municipal Efficiency to streamline city-government operations.

Municipal reform attracted different groups, depending on the issue. The native-born middle class, led by clergymen, editors, and other opinion molders, provided the initial impetus and core support. Business interests often pushed for citywide elections and the city-manager system, because these changes reduced immigrants' political clout and increased the influence of the corporate elite. Reforms that promised improved services or better conditions for ordinary city-dwellers won support from immigrants and political bosses who realized that the old, informal system of patronage could no longer meet constituents' needs.

The electoral-reform movement soon spread to the state level. By 1910, for example, all states had replaced the old system of voting, involving pre-printed ballots bearing the names of specific candidates, with the secret ballot, which made it harder to rig elections. The direct primary, introduced in Wisconsin in 1903, enabled rank-and-file voters rather than party bosses to select their parties' candidates for public office.

Hoping to trim the political power of corporate interests, some western states inaugurated the *initiative, referendum,* and *recall.* By an initiative, voters can instruct the legislature to consider a specific bill. In a referendum, citizens can actually enact a law or express their views on a proposed measure. By a recall petition, voters can remove a public official from office if they muster enough signatures to trigger a special election.

RESCUING VICTIMS OF THE 1913 DAYTON FLOOD. This devastating natural disaster, which took more than 360 lives, left 65,000 people homeless, and caused millions in property damage, led Dayton to adopt the city-manager form of government, favored by efficiency-minded reformers *(Library of Congress)*

While these reforms aimed to democratize voting, party leaders and interest groups soon learned to manipulate the new electoral machinery. Ironically, the new procedures may have weakened party loyalty and reduced voter interest. Voter-participation rates dropped steeply in these years, while political activity by organized interest groups increased.

Regulating Business, Protecting Workers

The corporate consolidation that produced giants like Carnegie Steel and Standard Oil (see Chapter 18) continued after 1900. The United States Steel Company created by J.P. Morgan in 1901 controlled 80 percent of all U.S. steel production. A year later, Morgan combined six competing companies into the International Harvester Company, which dominated the farm-implement business. The General Motors Company, formed in 1908 by William C. Durant with backing from the DuPont Corporation, brought various independent automobile manufacturers, from the inexpensive Chevrolet to the luxury Cadillac, under one corporate umbrella.

Many workers benefited from this corporate growth. Industrial workers' average annual real wages (defined in terms of actual purchasing power) rose from $487 in 1900 to $687 by 1915. In railroading and other unionized industries, wages climbed still higher. But even with the cost of living far lower than today, such wages barely supported a family and provided little cushion for emergencies.

To survive, entire families went to work. Two-thirds of young immigrant women entered the labor force in the early 1900s, working as factory help or domestics or in small business establishments.

Even children worked. In 1910, the nonfarm labor force included some 1.6 million children aged ten to fifteen employed in factories, mills, tenement sweatshops, and street trades such as shoe shining and newspaper vending (see Table 21.1). The total may have been higher, because many "women workers" listed in the census were in fact young girls. One investigator found a girl of five working nights in a South Carolina textile mill.

Work was long and hazardous. Despite the eight-hour movement of the 1880s, in 1900 the average worker still toiled 9½ hours a day. Some southern textile mills required workdays of twelve or thirteen hours. In one typical year (1907), 4,534 railroad workers and more than 3,000 miners were killed on the job. Few workers enjoyed vacations or retirement benefits.

Workers accustomed to the rhythms of farm labor faced the discipline of the factory. Efficiency experts used time-and-motion studies to increase production. In *Principles of Scientific Management* (1911), Frederick W. Taylor explained how to increase output by standardizing job routines and rewarding the fastest workers. "Efficiency" became a popular catchword, but workers resented the pressures to speed up.

Americans concerned about the social implications of industrialization deplored unregulated corporate power and the hazards facing industrial workers. The drive to regulate big business, inherited from the populists, became an important component of progressivism. Because corporations had benefited from government policies such as high protective tariffs and railroad subsidies, reformers reasoned, they should also be subject to government regulation.

Wisconsin, under Governor **Robert** ("Fighting Bob") **La Follette,** took the lead in regulating railroads, mines, and other businesses. As a Republican congressman, La Follette had feuded with the state's conservative party leadership, and in 1900 he won the governorship as an independent. Challenging powerful corporate interests, La Follette and his administration adopted the direct-primary system, set up a railroad regulatory commission, increased corporate taxes, and limited campaign spending. Reflecting progressivism's faith in experts, La Follette consulted reform-minded professors at the University of Wisconsin and set up a legislative reference library to help lawmakers draft bills. La Follette's reforms gained national attention as the "Wisconsin Idea."

If electoral reform and corporate regulation represented the brain of progressivism, the impulse to improve conditions for workers represented its heart. This movement, too, began at the local and state level. By 1907, for example, thirty states had outlawed child labor. A 1903 Oregon law limited women in industry to a ten-hour workday.

Campaigns for industrial safety and better working conditions won support from some big-city political bosses. A leader of Tammany Hall, New York City's Democratic organization, headed the Triangle fire investigation. Thanks to his committee's efforts, New York passed fifty-six worker-protection laws, including required fire-safety inspections. By 1914, twenty-five states had made employers liable for job-related injuries or deaths.

Florence Kelley of Hull House, the daughter of a conservative Republican congressman, spearheaded the drive to remedy industrial abuses. In 1893, after investigating conditions in factories and sweatshops, Kelley persuaded the Illinois legislature to outlaw child labor and limit working hours for women. In 1899, she became head of the National Consumers' League, which mobilized consumer pressure for improved factory conditions. Campaigning for a federal child-labor law, Kelley asked, "Why are…wild game in the national parks, buffalo, [and] migratory birds all found suitable for federal protection, but not children?"

TABLE 21.1 Children in the Labor Force,* 1880–1930

	1880	1890	1900	1910	1920	1930
	6.6	8.3	9.6	10.8	12.5	14.3
Total number of children employed (in millions)	1.1	1.5	1.7	1.6	1.4	0.7
Percentage of children employed	6.8	18.1	18.2	15.0	11.3	4.7

Source: The Statistical History of the United States from Colonial Times to the Present (*Stamford, CT: Fairfield Publishers, 1965*).

*Nonagricultural workers.

TRAIN WRECK IN EVANS CITY, PENNSYLVANIA, AROUND 1900–1910 In a dangerous era for industrial laborers, railroad workers faced special hazards, with frequent crashes and thousands of injuries and deaths each year. This dark underside of industrialization spurred Progressive Era campaigns for stricter safety standards and compensation for job-related injuries or fatalities. *(William B. Becker Collection/ American Museum of Photography)*

Like many progressive reforms, the crusade for workplace safety relied on expert research. The bacteriologist Alice Hamilton, a pioneer in the new field of "industrial hygiene," reported on lead poisoning among industrial workers in 1910. Later, as an investigator for the U.S. Bureau of Labor, Hamilton publicized other work-related medical hazards.

Workers themselves, who well understood the hazards of their jobs, provided further pressure for reform. For example, when the granite industry introduced new power drills that created a fine dust that workers inhaled, the *Granite Cutters' Journal* called them "widow makers." Sure enough, investigators soon linked the dust to a deadly lung disease, silicosis.

Making Cities More Livable

By 1920, the U.S. urban population passed the 50 percent mark, and sixty-eight cities boasted more than a hundred thousand inhabitants. New York City grew by 2.2 million from 1900 to 1920, Chicago by 1 million. America had become an urban nation.

Political corruption was only one of many urban problems. As factories and businesses attracted a tide of immigrants and job-seekers from rural and small-town America, many cities became congested human warehouses, lacking adequate parks, public-health resources, recreational facilities, and basic municipal services. As the reform spirit spread, the urban crisis loomed large.

Extending the achievements of Frederick Law Olmsted and others (see Chapter 19), reformers campaigned for parks, boulevards, and street lights; opposed unsightly billboards and overhead electrical wires; and advocated city planning and beautification projects. Daniel Burnham, chief architect of the 1893 Chicago world's fair, led a successful 1906 effort to revive a plan for Washington, DC, first proposed in 1791.

Burnham's 1909 *Plan of Chicago* offered a vision of a city both more efficient and more beautiful. He recommended wide boulevards, lakefront parks and museum, statuary and fountains, and a majestic domed city hall and vast civic plaza. Chicago spent more than $300 million on projects reflecting his ideas. Many urban planners shared Burnham's faith that more beautiful cities and imposing public buildings would produce orderly, law-abiding citizens.

The municipal reform impulse also included such practical goals as decent housing and better garbage collection and street cleaning. Providing a model for other cities and states, the New York legislature imposed strict health and safety regulations on tenements in 1911.

With the discovery in the 1880s that germs cause cholera, typhoid fever, and other diseases, municipal hygiene became a high priority. Reformers distributed public-health information, promoted school vaccination programs, and called for safer water and sewer systems and the regulation of food and milk suppliers. When Mary Mallon, an Irish-immigrant cook in New York, was found to be a healthy carrier of the typhoid bacillus in 1907, she was confined by the city health authorities and demonized in the press as "Typhoid Mary."

> "Why are . . . wild game in the national parks, buffalo, [and] migratory birds all found suitable for federal protection, but not children?"

These efforts bore fruit. From 1900 to 1920, U.S. infant mortality (defined as death in the first year of life), as well as death rates from tuberculosis, typhoid fever, and other infectious or communicable diseases, all fell sharply.

Urban reformers shared the era's heightened environmental consciousness (see Chapter 17). Factory chimneys belching smoke had once inspired pride, but by the early 1900s physicians had linked factory smoke to respiratory problems, and civic reformers were deploring the soot and smoke spewing from coal-fueled factory steam boilers.

The antismoke campaign combined expertise with activism. Civil engineers formed the Smoke Prevention Association in 1906, and researchers at the University of Pittsburgh—one of the nation's smokiest cities with its steel mills—documented the hazards and costs of air pollution. Chicago merchant Marshall Field declared that the "soot tax" he paid to clean his buildings' exteriors exceeded his real-estate taxes. As women's clubs and other civic groups embraced the cause, many cities passed smoke-abatement laws.

Success proved elusive, however, as railroads and corporations fought back in the courts. With coal still providing 70 percent of the nation's energy as late as 1920, cities remained smoky. Not until years later, with the shift to other energy sources, did municipal air pollution significantly diminish.

Progressivism and Social Control

The reform zeal of white, native-born, middle-class progressives sprang from their confidence that they knew what was best for society. While municipal corruption, unsafe factories, and corporate abuses captured their attention, so, too, did issues of personal behavior, particularly immigrant behavior. The problems they addressed deserved attention, but their moralistic rhetoric and coercive remedies also betrayed an impulse to impose their own moral standards by force of law.

Urban Amusements; Urban Moral Control

Despite the slums, dangerous factories, and other problems, early-twentieth-century cities also offered fun and diversion with their department stores, vaudeville, music halls, and amusement parks (see Chapter 19). While some vaudeville owners sought respectability, bawdy routines full of sexual innuendo delighted working-class audiences.

Amusement parks offered families escape from tenements, and gave female workers an opportunity to socialize with friends, meet young men, and

THE PRICE OF INDUSTRIALIZATION Smoke and pollutants pour from a Pittsburgh steel mill in 1890. "Hell with the lid off" was one observer's description of the city in these years. *(© Bettmann/Corbis)*

LUNA PARK, SURF AVENUE, BY NIGHT, CONEY ISLAND, N. Y.

CONEY ISLAND, LUNA PARK ENTRANCE, 1912 Electric street lights, illuminated buildings, and the headlights of automobiles and streetcars added to the excitement of early-twentieth-century urban nightlife. *(Picture Research Consultants & Archives)*

show off new outfits. New York City's amusement park, Coney Island, a subway ride from the city, attracted several million visitors a year by 1914.

With electrification, streetcar rides and evening strolls on well-lit downtown streets became leisure activities in themselves. Orville and Wilbur Wright's successful airplane flight in 1903 and the introduction of Henry Ford's Model T in 1908, transforming the automobile from a toy of the rich to a vehicle for the masses, foretold exciting changes ahead, with cities central to the action.

Jaunty music-hall songs added to the vibrancy of city life. The blues, rooted in the chants of southern black sharecroppers, reached a broader public with such songs as W.C. Handy's classic "St. Louis Blues" (1914). Ragtime, another import from the black South (see Chapter 19), enjoyed great popularity in early-twentieth-century urban America. Both the black composer Scott Joplin, with such works as "Maple Leaf Rag" (1899), and the white composer Irving Berlin, with his hit tune "Alexander's Rag-Time Band" (1911), contributed to this vogue.

These years also brought a new entertainment medium—the movies. Initially a part of vaudeville shows, movies soon migrated to five-cent halls called "nickelodeons" in immigrant neighborhoods. At first featuring brief comic sequences like *The Sneeze* or *The Kiss,* movies began to tell stories with *The Great Train Robbery* (1903). *A Fool There Was* (1914), with its daring line, "Kiss me, my fool!,"

made Theda Bara (really Theodosia Goodman of Cincinnati) the first female star. The British music-hall performer Charlie Chaplin immigrated to America and appeared in some sixty short comedies between 1914 and 1917. Like amusement parks, the movies allowed immigrant youth to briefly escape parental supervision. As a New York garment worker recalled, "The one place I was allowed to go by myself was the movies. My parents wouldn't let me go anywhere else."

The diversions that eased city life for the poor worried middle-class reformers. Fearful of immorality and disorder, they campaigned to regulate amusement parks, dance halls, and the darkened nickelodeons, which they saw as moral hazards. Several states and cities set up film censorship boards, and the Supreme Court upheld such measures in 1915.

Building on the moral-purity crusade of the Woman's Christian Temperance Union (WCTU) and other groups (see Chapter 19), reformers also targeted prostitution, a major urban problem. Male procurers lured young women into prostitution and then took a share of their income. Women's paltry wages for factory work or domestic service made this more-lucrative occupation tempting. Why "get up at 6:30 . . . and work in a close stuffy room . . . until dark for $6 or $7 a week," reasoned one prostitute, when an afternoon with a man could bring in more.

Adopting the usual progressive approach, investigators gathered statistics on what they called "the social evil." The American Social Hygiene Association (1914), financed by John D. Rockefeller, Jr., sponsored research on sexually transmitted diseases, paid for "vice investigations" in major cities, and drafted antiprostitution laws.

As prostitution came to symbolize urban America's larger moral dangers, a "white slave" hysteria took hold. Novels, films, and magazine articles warned of kidnapped farm girls forced into urban brothels. The Mann Act (1910) made it illegal to transport a woman across a state line "for immoral purposes." Amid much fanfare, reformers shut down the red-light districts of New Orleans, Chicago, and other cities.

Racism, anti-immigrant prejudice, and anxieties about changing sexual mores all fueled the antiprostitution crusade. Authorities employed the new legislation to pry into private sexual behavior. Blackmailers entrapped men into Mann Act violations. In 1913, the African American boxer Jack Johnson, the heavyweight champion, was convicted under the Mann Act for crossing a state line with a (white) woman for "immoral purposes." Johnson went abroad to escape imprisonment.

Battling Alcohol and Drugs

Temperance had long been part of America's reform agenda, but reformers' objectives changed in the Progressive Era. Earlier campaigns had urged individuals to give up drink. By contrast, the **Anti-Saloon League** (ASL), founded in 1895, called for a total ban on the sale of alcoholic beverages. In typical Progressive fashion, full-time professionals ran the ASL, with Protestant ministers staffing state committees. ASL publications offered statistics documenting alcohol's role in many social problems. As churches and temperance groups worked for prohibition at the municipal, county, and state levels, the ASL moved to its larger goal: national prohibition.

Alcohol abuse did indeed contribute to domestic violence, health problems, and workplace injuries. But like the antiprostitution crusade, the prohibition campaign became a symbolic battleground pitting native-born citizens against immigrants. The ASL embodied Protestant America's impulse to control the immigrant city.

> One prominent sociologist described recent immigrants as "low-browed, big-faced persons of obviously low mentality."

Reformers also targeted drug abuse—and for good reason. Physicians, patent-medicine peddlers, and legitimate drug companies freely prescribed or sold opium (derived from poppies) and its derivatives morphine and heroin. Cocaine, extracted from coca leaves, was an ingredient of Coca-Cola until about 1900.

Amid mounting reform pressure, Congress passed the Harrison Act in 1914, banning the distribution of heroin, morphine, cocaine, and other addictive drugs except by licensed physicians or pharmacists. Like progressives' environmental concerns, this campaign anticipated an issue that remains important today. But this reform, too, had racist undertones. Antidrug crusaders luridly described Chinese "opium dens" and warned that "drug-crazed Negroes" imperiled white womanhood.

Immigration Restriction and Eugenics

While many new city-dwellers came from farms and small towns, immigration remained the main source of urban growth. More than 17 million newcomers arrived from 1900 to 1917 (many passing through New York's immigration center, Ellis Island), and most settled in cities (see Figure 21.1). As in the 1890s (see Chapter 19), the influx came mainly from southern and eastern Europe, but more than two hundred thousand Japanese arrived between 1900 and 1920. An estimated forty thousand Chinese entered in these years, despite the 1882 Chinese Exclusion Act (see Chapter 18), which remained in force until 1943. Thousands of Mexicans came as well, many seeking railroad work.

The dismay that middle-class Americans felt about urban slum conditions stimulated support not only for protective legislation but also for immigration restriction. If the immigrant city bred social problems, some concluded, immigrants should be excluded. Prominent Bostonians formed the Immigration Restriction League in 1894. The American Federation of Labor, fearing job competition, also endorsed restriction.

Like most Progressive Era reformers, immigration-restriction advocates tried to document their case. A 1911 congressional report allegedly proved the new immigrants' innate degeneracy. One prominent sociologist described the newcomers as "low-browed, big-faced persons of obviously low mentality."

Led by Massachusetts senator Henry Cabot Lodge, Congress passed literacy-test bills in 1896, 1913, and 1915, only to see them vetoed. These measures would have excluded immigrants over sixteen years old who could not read either English or their native language, thus discriminating against persons lacking formal education. In 1917, Lodge's bill became law over President Woodrow Wilson's veto.

Anti-immigrant fears helped fuel the eugenics movement. Eugenics is the control of reproduction to alter a plant or animal species, and some U.S.

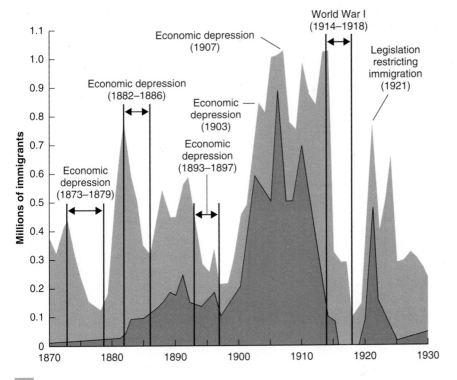

eugenicists believed that human society could be improved by this means. Leading eugenicists urged immigration restriction to protect America from "inferior" genetic stock.

In *The Passing of the Great Race* (1916), Madison Grant, a prominent progressive and eugenics advocate, used bogus data to denounce immigrants from southern and eastern Europe, especially Jews. He also viewed African Americans as inferior. Anticipating the program of Adolf Hitler in the 1930s (covered in Chapter 25), Grant called for racial segregation, immigration restriction, and the forced sterilization of the "unfit," including "worthless race types." The vogue of eugenics gave "scientific" respectability to racism and anti-immigrant sentiment.

Inspired by eugenics, many states legalized the sterilization of criminals, sex offenders, and persons adjudged mentally deficient. In the 1927 case *Buck v. Bell,* the Supreme Court upheld such laws.

Racism and Progressivism

Progressivism arose at a time of intense racism in America as well of major African American population movements. These realities are crucial to understanding the movement.

In 1900, the nation's 10 million blacks lived mostly in the rural South as sharecroppers and tenant farmers. As devastating floods and the cotton boll weevil, which spread from Mexico in the 1890s, worsened their lot, many southern blacks left the land. By 1910, more than 20 percent of blacks lived in cities, mostly in the South, but many in the North. Black men in the cities took jobs in factories, docks, and railroads or became carpenters, plasterers, or bricklayers. Many black women became domestic servants, seamstresses, or workers in laundries and tobacco factories. By 1910, 54 percent of America's black women held jobs.

Across the South, legally enforced racism peaked after 1900. Local "Jim Crow" laws segregated streetcars, schools, parks, and even cemeteries. The facilities for blacks, including the schools, were invariably inferior. Many southern cities imposed residential segregation by law until the Supreme Court restricted it in 1917. Most labor unions excluded black workers. Disfranchised and trapped in a cycle of poverty, poor education, and discrimination, southern blacks faced bleak prospects.

Fleeing such conditions, two hundred thousand blacks migrated north between 1890 and 1910. Wartime job opportunities drew still more in 1917–1918 (see Chapter 22), and by 1920, 1.4 million African Americans lived in the North, mostly in cities. Here, too, racism worsened after 1890 as hard times and immigration heightened social

Le Petit Journal

SUPPLÉMENT ILLUSTRÉ

DIMANCHE 7 OCTOBRE 1906

LES « LYNCHAGES » AUX ÉTATS-UNIS
Massacre de nègres à Atlanta (Georgie)

THE 1906 ATLANTA RACE RIOT The brutality of this outbreak attracted horrified attention even in Europe, as this cover illustration from a French periodical makes clear. *(Le Petit Journal, 1906/Picture Research Consultants & Archives)*

Smoldering racism sometimes exploded in violence. Antiblack rioters in Atlanta in 1906 murdered twenty-five blacks and burned many black homes. From 1900 to 1920, an average of about seventy-five lynchings occurred yearly. Blacks whose assertive behavior or economic aspirations angered whites were especially vulnerable. Some lynchings involved brutal sadism, with large crowds on hand, mutilated bodies, and graphic photo postcards sold later. Authorities rarely intervened. At a 1916 lynching in Texas, the mayor warned the mob not to damage the hanging tree, on city property.

In such times, African Americans developed strong institutions. Black churches proved a bulwark of support. Working mothers, drawing on strategies dating to slavery days, relied on relatives and neighbors for child care. A handful of black higher-education institutions carried on against heavy odds. John Hope, who became president of Atlanta's Morehouse College in 1906, assembled a distinguished faculty, championed African American education, and fought segregation. His sister Jane (Hope) Lyons was dean of women at nearby Spelman College.

Urban black communities included black-owned insurance companies and banks, and a small elite of entrepreneurs, teachers, and ministers. Although major-league baseball excluded blacks, a thriving Negro League attracted African American fans.

In this racist age, progressives compiled a mixed racial record. Lillian Wald, director of a New York City settlement house, protested racial injustice. Muckraker Ray Stannard Baker documented racism in *Following the Color Line* (1908). Settlement-house worker Mary White Ovington helped found the National Association for the Advancement of Colored People (discussed in the next section) and wrote *Half a Man* (1911), which discussed racism's psychological toll.

But most progressives viewed African Americans, like immigrants, not as potential allies but as part of the problem. They generally supported or tolerated segregated schools and housing; restrictions on black voting rights; moral oversight of black communities; and, at best, paternalistic efforts to "uplift" this supposedly childlike people. Viciously racist southern politicians like Mississippi governor James K. Vardaman and South Carolina senator Ben Tillman also supported progressive reforms. Southern woman-suffrage leaders argued that enfranchising women would strengthen white supremacy.

At the national level, President Theodore Roosevelt's racial record was marginally better than that of other politicians in this racist age. He appointed a black to head the Charleston customs house, despite white opposition, and closed a Mississippi post office rather than yield to demands

tensions. (Immigrants, competing with blacks for jobs and housing, sometimes exhibited intense racial prejudice.) Segregation, though not imposed by law, was enforced by custom and sometimes by violence. Blacks lived in run-down "colored districts," attended dilapidated schools, and worked at the lowest-paying jobs.

Their ballots—usually cast for the party of Lincoln—brought little political influence. The only black politicians tolerated by Republican Party leaders distributed low-level patronage jobs and otherwise kept silent. African Americans in the segregated army faced hostility from white soldiers and from nearby civilians. Even the movies preached racism. D.W. Griffith's *The Birth of a Nation* (1915) disparaged blacks and glorified the Ku Klux Klan.

THE BIRTH OF A NATION (1915) D.W. Griffith's epic film glorified the racist Ku Klux Klan. President Woodrow Wilson called it "history written with lightning." *(Picture Research Consultants & Archives)*

to dismiss the black postmistress. In a symbolically important gesture, he dined with Booker T. Washington at the White House. In 1906, however, he approved the dishonorable discharge of an entire regiment of black soldiers in Brownsville, Texas, because some members of the unit, goaded by racist taunts, had killed a local civilian. The "Brownsville Incident" incensed African Americans. (In 1972, after most of the men were dead, Congress reversed the dishonorable discharges.)

Under President Woodrow Wilson, racism became rampant in Washington. A southerner, Wilson displayed at best a patronizing attitude toward blacks, praised the racist movie *The Birth of a Nation,* and allowed southerners in his cabinet and in Congress to impose rigid segregation on all levels of the government.

Blacks, Women, and Workers Organize

Progressivism's organizational strategy also proved useful for groups facing discrimination or exploitation. African Americans, middle-class women, and wage workers all organized to address their grievances and improve their situation.

African American Leaders Organize Against Racism

With racism on the rise, Booker T. Washington's self-help message (see Chapter 20) seemed increasingly unrealistic, particularly to northern blacks. Washington's themes would appeal to later generations of African Americans, but in the early twentieth century, blacks confronting segregation, lynching, and blatant racism tired of his cautious approach. In 1902, William Monroe Trotter, editor of the *Boston Guardian,* a black newspaper, called Washington's go-slow policies "a fatal blow...to the Negro's political rights and liberty."

Another opponent was the black activist **Ida Wells-Barnett.** Moving to Chicago from Memphis in 1892 after a white mob destroyed her offices, Wells-Barnett mounted a national antilynching campaign, in contrast to Booker T. Washington's public silence on the subject. Documenting the grim facts in *A Red Record* (1895), she toured the United States and Great Britain lecturing against lynching and other racial abuses.

Booker T. Washington's principal black critic was **W.E.B. Du Bois** (1868–1963). After earning a Ph.D. in history from Harvard in 1895, Du Bois taught at Ohio's Wilberforce College, the University of Pennsylvania, and Atlanta University. In *The Souls of Black Folk* (1903), Du Bois rejected Washington's call for patience and his exclusive emphasis on manual skills. Instead, Du Bois demanded full racial equality, including equal educational opportunities, and urged resistance to all forms of racism.

In 1905, under Du Bois's leadership, blacks committed to battling racism held a conference at Niagara Falls. For the next few years, participants in the "Niagara Movement" met annually. Meanwhile, white reformers led by newspaper publisher Oswald Garrison Villard, grandson of abolitionist William Lloyd Garrison, had also grown dissatisfied with Washington's cautiousness. In 1909, Villard and his allies joined with Du Bois and other blacks from the Niagara Movement to form the **National Association for the Advancement of Colored People** (NAACP). This new organization called for sustained activism, including legal challenges, to achieve political equality for blacks and full integration into American life. Attracting the urban black middle class, the NAACP by 1914 had six thousand members in fifty branches.

A NEW BLACK LEADERSHIP Ida Wells-Barnett, Chicago-based crusader against lynching, and W.E.B. Du Bois, outspoken critic of Booker T. Washington and author of the classic *The Souls of Black Folk*. The challenge, wrote Du Bois, was to find a way "to be both a Negro and an American." *(Schomburg Center for Research in Black Culture, New York Public Library/Art Resource, NY; Special Collections and Archives, W.E.B. Du Bois Library, University of Massachusetts Amherst)*

Revival of the Woman-Suffrage Movement

As late as 1910, women could vote in only four western states: Wyoming, Utah, Colorado, and Idaho. But women's active role in progressive reform movements revitalized the suffrage cause. A vigorous suffrage movement in Great Britain reverberated in America as well. Like progressivism itself, this revived campaign had grassroots origins. A 1915 suffrage campaign in New York State, though unsuccessful, underscored the new momentum.

Developments in California illustrate both the movement's new momentum and its limitations. In the early 1900s, California's women's clubs shifted from their earlier cultural and domestic focus to reform, especially on city-government and public-school issues. In the process, many women activists concluded that full citizenship meant the right to vote. While working with labor leaders and male progressives, they nevertheless insisted on the unique role of "organized womanhood" in building a better society. Success came in 1911 when California voters approved woman suffrage.

But "organized womanhood" had its limits. Elite and middle-class women, mainly based in Los Angeles and San Francisco, led the campaign. Working-class and farm women played a small role, while African American, Mexican American, and Asian American women were almost totally excluded.

New leaders translated the state-level momentum into a revitalized national movement. In 1900, **Carrie Chapman Catt** of Iowa succeeded Susan B. Anthony as president of the National American Woman Suffrage Association (NAWSA). Under Catt, NAWSA adopted the so-called Winning Plan: grassroots organization with tight central coordination, focused on state-level campaigns.

Emulating the new urban consumer culture, suffragists ran newspaper ads, festooned posters and banners with catchy slogans, paraded in open cars, arranged photo opportunities for the media, and distributed fans and other items emblazoned with the suffrage message. Gradually, state after state fell into the suffrage column (see Map 21.1).

As in California (and like progressive organizations generally), NAWSA's membership remained largely white, native-born, and middle-class. Some upper-class women opposed the reform. Women already enjoyed behind-the-scenes influence, they argued; invading the male realm of electoral politics would tarnish their moral and spiritual role.

Not all suffragists accepted Catt's strategy. Alice Paul, influenced by the British suffragists' militant tactics, rejected NAWSA's state-by-state approach. In 1913, Paul founded the Congressional Union for Woman Suffrage, renamed the National Woman's Party in 1917, to pressure Congress to enact a woman-suffrage constitutional amendment. Targeting "the party in power"—in this case, the Democrats—Paul and her followers in the 1916

Full voting rights for women with effective date

Women voting in primaries

Women voting in presidential elections

No voting by women

MAP 21.1 WOMAN SUFFRAGE BEFORE THE NINETEENTH AMENDMENT Beginning with Wyoming in 1869, woman suffrage made steady gains in western states before 1920. Farther east, key victories came in New York (1917) and Michigan (1918). But much of the East remained an anti-woman-suffrage bastion throughout the period.

election opposed President Woodrow Wilson and congressional Democrats who had failed to endorse a suffrage amendment. In 1917–1918, with the United States at war, the suffrage cause prevailed in New York and Michigan (see Map 21.1) and advanced toward final success (further discussed in Chapter 22).

Enlarging the "Woman's Sphere"

The suffrage cause did not exhaust women's energies in the Progressive Era. Women's clubs, settlement-house residents, and individual activists like Florence Kelley, Alice Hamilton, and Ida Wells-Barnett promoted an array of reforms. These included the campaigns to bring playgrounds and day nurseries to the slums, abolish child labor, and ban unsafe foods and quack remedies. As Jane Addams observed, women's concern for their own families' welfare could also draw them into political activism in an industrial age when hazards came from outside the home as well as inside.

Cultural assumptions about "woman's sphere" weakened as women invaded many fronts. Katherine Bement Davis served as New York City's commissioner of corrections. Emma Goldman crisscrossed the country lecturing on politics, feminism, and modern drama while coediting a radical monthly, *Mother Earth*. A vanguard of women in higher education included the chemist Ellen Richards of the Massachusetts Institute

of Technology and Marion Talbot, first dean of women at the University of Chicago.

In *Women and Economics* (1898) and other works, Charlotte Perkins Gilman explored the cultural roots of gender roles and linked women's subordinate status to their economic dependence on men. Confining women to the domestic sphere, Gilman argued, was an evolutionary throwback that had become outdated and inefficient. She advocated gender equality in the workplace; the collectivization of cooking and other domestic tasks; and state-run child-care centers. In the utopian novel *Herland* (1915), Gilman wittily critiqued patriarchal assumptions by injecting three naïve young men into an exclusively female society.

Some reformers challenged laws banning the distribution of contraceptives and birth-control information. Although countless women, particularly the poor, suffered from frequent pregnancies, artificial contraception was widely denounced as immoral. In 1914, **Margaret Sanger** of New York, whose mother had died after bearing eleven children, began her crusade for birth control, a term she coined. When her journal *The Woman Rebel* faced prosecution on obscenity charges, Sanger fled to England. Returning in 1916, she opened the nation's first birth-control clinic in Brooklyn; launched *The Birth Control Review*; and

PARADING FOR WOMAN SUFFRAGE Suffrage leaders built support for the cause by using modern advertising and publicity techniques, including automobiles festooned with flags, bunting, banners, posters, and—in this case—smiling little girls. *(Library of Congress)*

founded the American Birth Control League, forerunner of today's Planned Parenthood Federation.

Meanwhile, another New Yorker, Mary Ware Dennett, had also emerged as an advocate of birth control and sex education. While Sanger championed direct action to promote the cause, Dennett urged lobbying efforts to change the law. Sanger insisted that only physicians should supply contraceptives; Dennett argued for widespread distribution. These differences, plus personal rivalries, divided the movement.

The birth-control and sex-education movements stand as important legacies of progressivism. At the time, however, conservatives and religious leaders bitterly opposed them. Dennett's frank 1919 informational pamphlet for youth, *The Sex Side of Life*, was long banned as obscene. Not until 1965 did the Supreme Court fully legalize the dissemination of contraceptive materials and information.

Workers Organize; Socialism Advances

In this age of organization, labor unions continued to expand. In 1900–1920, the American Federation of Labor (AFL) grew from 625,000 to 4 million members. This still represented only about 20 percent of the industrial work force. With recent immigrants hungry for jobs, union activities posed risks. The boss could always fire an "agitator" and hire a newcomer. Judicial hostility also retarded unionization. In the 1908 *Danbury Hatters* case, for example, the Supreme Court ruled that boycotts in support of strikes were a "conspiracy in restraint of trade," and thus a violation of the Sherman Anti-Trust Act. The AFL's strength remained in the traditional skilled trades, not in the factories, mills, and sweatshops where most immigrants and women worked.

A few unions did try to reach these laborers. The International Ladies' Garment Workers' Union (ILGWU), founded in 1900 by immigrant workers in New York City's needle trades, conducted successful strikes in 1909 and after the 1911 Triangle fire. The 1909 strike began when young Clara Lemlich jumped up as speechmaking droned on at a union meeting and passionately called for a strike. Some picketers lost

> The Supreme Court ruled that boycotts in support of strikes were a "conspiracy in restraint of trade."

PROTESTING CHILD LABOR Carrying American flags and wearing banners proclaiming "Abolish Child Slavery" in English and Yiddish, these young marchers in a 1909 New York City May Day parade urged an end to the employment of children in factories and street occupations. *(Library of Congress)*

A Violent Encounter at a 1909 Shirtwaist Workers' Strike

Before the tragic 1911 fire at the Triangle shirtwaist factory in New York, shirtwaist workers had organized a union and gone on strike for better wages and working conditions. This vivid account describes a confrontation between strikers and special police hired by the factory owners.

POLICE MISHANDLE GIRL STRIKE PICKETS
New York Times, December 10, 1909

Officers of the striking Shirt Waist Makers' Union are anxious to obtain a judicial interpretation of the rights of pickets. ... The representatives of the union believe that pickets have the right to approach strikebreakers and persuade them peacefully to stop work. The agents of the employers, and as the girls say, the police ... prevent the strikers from accosting the workers.

Miss Henrietta Mercy of 58 West 115th Street called at THE TIMES office last night to relate her experiences as a picket yesterday. Miss Mercy is not herself a striker, but the private secretary of a woman of wealth. She is a sister of Dr. Anna Mercy of 182 West Houston Street, and is herself a graduate of the Normal College. She wore a tailor-made coat with a fur turban and stole. She showed a TIMES reporter a torn sleeve in her waist which she said had been ripped by the roughness of policemen.

[S]aid Miss Mercy last night, "I am deeply interested in the girl workers of the east side. As secretary of the East Side Equal Rights League, I went out yesterday afternoon as a volunteer picket with Lena Cohen ... a striker.

"There were about a dozen of us picketing a shirt waist factory at Greene and Grand Streets. We girls walked peacefully up and down in pairs. ... We had no intention of creating any violence. All we wished to do was to speak to the [strikebreaking] girls kindly. ...

"As the girls got ready to come out of the factory [that is, the workers who had not joined the strike], between twenty and thirty special policemen employed by the factory as guards for the workers, formed a double line on the sidewalk. ... They hurled themselves upon us and threw us off the sidewalk onto the pavement. ... [S]ome of the girls fell on the stones. We tried to get back on the sidewalk and they shoved, elbowed and even kicked some of us to keep us in the street.

"I managed to break through the line. A uniformed policeman picked me up and pinned me against the wall. ... The special policemen seized the other girls and pinned them against the wall till the strike-breakers had passed by. I said to the policeman who held me: 'You are supposed to be impartial. All we want to do is talk to these girls and you have no right to hold us against our will. It's our privilege to talk to them if they want to.' He replied: 'You can walk and talk all you want to, after they're gone. But keep still now, or I'll run you in.'

"I got free after the girls [from the factory] got away and started to run after them. ... One of the special policemen seized me and threw me against a hydrant. I narrowly missed having my skull fractured. I picked myself up, and managed to reach the uptown stairs [of the elevated train station], where several of the strike-breakers had gone.

"The special policemen followed and nearly pulled the clothes off me to keep me from going up the stairs. They called me the most vile and insulting names, and finally dragged me from the stairs. I was weak from struggling and mad with shame when I reached my sister's office in Houston Street with my clothing all disarranged and my waist torn. I believe that I should have been badly injured if a crowd had not gathered and shamed the men."

Source: *The New York Times*, December 10, 1909.

QUESTIONS

1. The strikers wanted to persuade the non-strikers to join them. What arguments might each side have used if the police had permitted them to talk to each other?

2. Why, do you think, did the *New York Times* reporter provide so much information about Henrietta Mercy's education, expensive clothing, and employment by "a woman of wealth"?

their jobs or endured police beatings, but the strikers did win higher wages and improved working conditions.

Another union that targeted the most exploited workers was the **Industrial Workers of the World (IWW)**, nicknamed the Wobblies, founded in Chicago in 1905. The IWW's leader was William "Big Bill" Haywood, a Utah-born miner who in 1905 was acquitted of complicity in the assassination of an antilabor former governor of Idaho. IWW membership peaked at around thirty thousand, mostly western miners, lumbermen, fruit pickers, and itinerant laborers. It captured the imagination of young cultural rebels in New York City's Greenwich Village, where Haywood, a compelling orator, often visited.

The IWW led strikes of Nevada gold miners, Minnesota iron miners, and timber workers in the Northwest. Its victory in a bitter 1912 textile strike in Massachusetts owed much to Elizabeth Gurley Flynn, a fiery Irish American orator who publicized the cause. With an exaggerated reputation for violence, the IWW faced government harassment, especially during World War I, and by 1920 its strength was broken.

Other workers, along with some middle-class Americans, turned to socialism. All socialists foresaw capitalism's collapse and advocated public ownership of factories, utilities, railroads, and communications systems, but they differed on how to achieve these goals. The revolutionary ideology of German social theorist Karl Marx won a few converts, but the vision of democratic socialism achieved at the ballot box proved more appealing. In 1900 democratic socialists formed the Socialist Party of America (SPA). Members included Morris Hillquit, a New York City labor organizer; Victor Berger, leader of Milwaukee's German socialists; and **Eugene V. Debs,** the Indiana labor leader. Debs, a popular orator, ran for president five times between 1900 and 1920. Many Greenwich Village cultural rebels embraced socialism and supported the radical magazine *The Masses,* founded in 1911.

By 1912, SPA membership stood at 118,000, but many more voted the Socialist ticket. Debs received more than 900,000 votes for president that year, and the Socialists elected a congressman (Berger) and many municipal officials (see also the later section, "The Four-Way Election of 1912").The party published more than three hundred newspapers, including foreign-languages papers targeting immigrants.

IWW JOURNALISM On April 28,1917, three weeks after the United States entered World War I, the IWW periodical *Solidarity* pictured a heroic IWW worker battling an array of evils, including "militarism." *(© Bettmann/Corbis)*

National Progressivism, Phase I: Roosevelt and Taft, 1901–1913

By around 1905, local and state reform activities were coalescing into a national movement. In 1906, Wisconsin governor Robert La Follette was elected a U.S. senator. Five years earlier, progressivism had found its first national leader, **Theodore Roosevelt,** nicknamed "TR."

Self-righteous, jingoistic, verbose—but also brilliant, politically savvy, and endlessly interesting—Roosevelt became president in 1901 and made the White House a cauldron of activism. Orchestrating public opinion, Roosevelt pursued his goals—labor mediation, consumer protection, corporate regulation, natural-resource conservation, and engagement abroad.

TR's activist approach permanently enlarged the powers of the presidency. His handpicked successor, William Howard Taft, proved politically inept, however, and controversy marked his administration. With the Republicans divided, the Democrat Woodrow Wilson, espousing a somewhat different reform vision, won the presidency in 1912.

Roosevelt's Path to the White House

On September 6, 1901, in Buffalo, anarchist Leon Czolgosz shot William McKinley. At first recovery seemed likely, and Vice President Theodore Roosevelt continued a hiking trip in New York's Adirondack Mountains. But on September 14, McKinley died. At age forty-two, Theodore Roosevelt became president.

Many Republican leaders shuddered at the thought of what one called "that damned cowboy" in the White House. Roosevelt did, indeed, display traits associated with the West. The son of an aristocratic New York family of Dutch origins, he overcame a sickly childhood through bodybuilding exercises and summers in Wyoming to become a model of physical fitness. When his young wife died in 1884, he stoically carried on. Two years on a Dakota ranch deepened his enthusiasm for what he termed "the strenuous life."

Although his social peers scorned politics, Roosevelt served as a state assemblyman, New York City police commissioner, and a U.S. civil-service commissioner. In 1898, fresh from his Cuban exploits, he was elected New York's governor. Two years later, the state's Republican boss, eager to be rid of him, arranged for Roosevelt's nomination as vice president.

As with everything he did, TR found the presidency energizing. "I have been President emphatically…," he boasted. "I believe in a strong executive." He enjoyed public life and loved the limelight. "When Theodore attends a wedding he wants to be the bride," his daughter observed, "and when he attends a funeral he wants to be the corpse." With his toothy grin, machine-gun speech, and amazing energy, he dominated the political landscape. When he refused to shoot a bear cub on a hunting trip, a shrewd toy maker marketed a cuddly new product, the Teddy Bear.

> "I have been President emphatically. ... I believe in a strong executive."

Labor Disputes, Trustbusting, Railroad Regulation

Events soon tested the new president's political skills. In May 1902, the United Mine Workers Union (UMW) called a strike to gain not only higher wages and shorter hours but also recognition as a union. The mine owners resisted, and in October, with winter looming, TR acted. Summoning the two sides to the White House and threatening to seize the mines, he forced them to accept arbitration. The arbitration commission granted the miners a 10 percent wage increase and reduced their working day from ten to nine hours.

TR's approach to labor disputes differed from that of his predecessors, who typically sided with management, sometimes using troops as strikebreakers. Though not consistently prolabor, he defended workers' right to organize. When a mine owner insisted that the miners' welfare should be left to those "whom God in his infinite wisdom has given control of the [country's] property interests," Roosevelt derided such "arrogant stupidity."

With his elite background, TR neither feared nor much liked business tycoons. The prospect of spending time with "big-money men," he once wrote, "fills me with frank horror." While believing that corporations contributed to national greatness, he also embraced the progressive conviction that they must be regulated. A strict moralist, he held corporations, like individuals, to a high standard.

Yet as a political realist, Roosevelt also understood that many Washington politicians abhorred his views—among them Senator Nelson Aldrich of Rhode Island, a wily defender of business interests. Roosevelt's progressive impulses thus remained in tension with his grasp of power realities in capitalist America.

Another test came when J.P. Morgan in 1901 formed the United States Steel Company, the nation's first billion-dollar business. As public distrust of big corporations deepened, TR dashed to the head of the parade. His 1902 State of the Union message called for breaking up business monopolies, or "trustbusting." Roosevelt's attorney general soon sued the Northern Securities Company, a giant holding company recently created by Morgan and other tycoons to control railroading in the Northwest, for violating the Sherman Anti-Trust Act. On a speaking tour in the summer of 1902, TR called for a "square deal" for all Americans and denounced special treatment for capitalists. "We don't wish to destroy corporations," he said, "but we do wish to make them…serve the public good." In 1904, a divided Supreme Court ordered the Northern Securities Company dissolved.

The Roosevelt administration filed more than forty antitrust lawsuits. In two key rulings in 1911, the Supreme Court ordered the breakup of the Standard Oil Company and the reorganization of the American Tobacco Company to make it less monopolistic.

As the 1904 election neared, Roosevelt made peace with Morgan and other business magnates. The GOP convention that nominated Roosevelt adopted a probusiness platform, stimulating $2 million in corporate contributions. The Democrats, meanwhile, eager to erase the taint of radicalism lingering from the 1890s, embraced the gold standard and nominated a conservative New York judge.

Winning easily, Roosevelt turned to a major goal: railroad regulation. He now saw corporate regulation as more effective than trustbusting, and this shift underlay the 1906 **Hepburn Act.** This law empowered the Interstate Commerce Commission to set maximum railroad rates and to examine railroads' financial records. It also curtailed the railroads' practice of distributing free passes to ministers and other shapers of public opinion.

The Hepburn Act displayed TR's political skills. In a key compromise with Senator Aldrich and other conservatives, he agreed to delay tariff reform in return for railroad regulation. Although failing to fully satisfy reformers, the Hepburn Act did expand the government's regulatory powers.

Consumer Protection

Of all progressive reforms, the campaign against unsafe food, drugs, and medicine proved especially popular. Upton Sinclair's *The Jungle* (1906) graphically described conditions in some meatpacking plants. Wrote Sinclair in one vivid passage, "[A] man could run his hand over these piles of meat and sweep off handfuls of dried dung of rats. These rats were nuisances, and the packers would put poisoned bread out for them, they would die, and then rats, bread, and meat would go into the hoppers

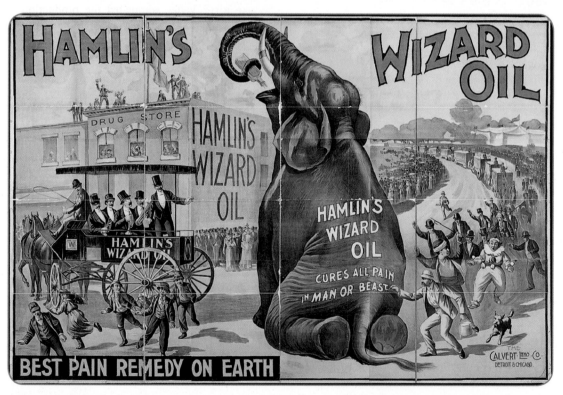

PATENT MEDICINES Progressive Era reformers targeted unregulated and often dangerous nostrums. Hamlin's Wizard Oil, a pain remedy marketed by traveling shows and musical groups, contained alcohol, ammonia, chloroform, and turpentine, among other ingredients. *(Chicago Historical Society)*

together." (The socialist Sinclair also detailed the exploitation of immigrant workers, but this message proved less potent. "I aimed at the nation's heart, but hit it in the stomach," he later lamented.) As women's organizations and consumer groups rallied public opinion, an Agriculture Department chemist, Harvey W. Wiley, helped shape the proposed legislation. Other muckrakers exposed useless or dangerous patent medicines laced with cocaine, opium, or alcohol. One tonic "for treatment of the alcohol habit" contained 26.5 percent alcohol. Peddlers of these nostrums freely claimed that they could cure cancer, grow hair, and restore sexual vigor.

Sensing the public mood, Roosevelt supported the **Pure Food and Drug Act** and the Meat Inspection Act, both passed in 1906. The former outlawed the sale of adulterated foods or drugs and required accurate ingredient labels; the latter imposed strict sanitary rules on meatpackers and set up a federal meat-inspection system. Reputable food processors, meatpackers, and medicinal companies, eager to regain public confidence, supported these measures.

Environmentalism: Progressive Style

Environmental concerns loomed large for Theodore Roosevelt. Describing conservation in his first State of the Union message as America's "most vital internal question," he highlighted an issue that still reverberates.

By 1900, decades of expansion and urban-industrial growth had taken a heavy toll on the land. In the West, mining and timber interests, farmers, ranchers, sheep growers, and preservationists advanced competing land-use claims. While business interests and boosters preached exploitation of the West's resources, and agricultural groups sought government aid for irrigation projects, John Muir's Sierra Club (founded in San Francisco in 1892) urged wilderness preservation. Under a law passed in 1891, Presidents Harrison and Cleveland had set aside some 35 million acres of public lands as national forests.

In the early twentieth century, amid spreading cities and factories, a wilderness vogue swept America. Popular writers evoked the tang of the campfire and the lure of the primitive. Summer camps, as well as the Boy Scouts (founded in 1910) and Girl Scouts (1912), gave city children a taste of wilderness living. Socially prominent easterners embraced the cause.

Between the wilderness enthusiasts and the developers stood government experts like Gifford Pinchot who saw the public domain as a resource to be managed wisely. Appointed by TR in 1905 to head the new U.S. Forest Service, Pinchot stressed not preservation but conservation—the planned use of forest lands for public and commercial purposes.

Wilderness advocates welcomed Pinchot's opposition to mindless exploitation, but worried that the multiple-use approach would despoil wilderness areas. "[T]rees are for human use," conceded a Sierra Club member, but added that these uses included "the spiritual wealth of us all, as well as … the material wealth of some."

At heart Roosevelt was a preservationist. In 1903, he spent a blissful few days camping in Yosemite National Park with John Muir. He once compared "the destruction of a species" to the loss of "all the works of some great writer." But TR the politician backed the conservationists' call for planned development. He supported the **National Reclamation Act** (1902), which designated the money from public-land sales for water management in arid western regions, and set up the Reclamation Service to construct dams and irrigation projects.

This measure (also known as the **Newlands Act** for its sponsor, a Nevada congressman) ranks with the Northwest Ordinance of 1787 for promoting the settlement and productivity of a vast continental region—this one between the Rockies and the Pacific. Arizona's Roosevelt Dam spurred the growth of Phoenix; dams and waterways in Idaho's Snake River Valley stimulated the production of potatoes and other commodities on hitherto barren acres. The law required farmers who benefited from these projects to repay the construction costs, creating a federal fund for further projects. The Newlands Act and other measures of these years transformed the West from a series of isolated "island settlements" into a thriving, interconnected region.

The competition for scarce water resources in the West sparked bitter political battles. The Los Angeles basin, for example, with 40 percent of California's population in 1900, found itself with only 2 percent of the state's surface water. In 1907, the city derailed a Reclamation Service project intended for the farmers of California's Owens Valley, more than 230 miles to the north, and diverted the precious water to Los Angeles.

Meanwhile, President Roosevelt, embracing Pinchot's multiple-use land-management program, set aside 200 million acres of public land (85 million of them in Alaska) as national forests, mineral reserves, and waterpower sites. But the national-forest provisions provoked corporate opposition, and in 1907 Congress revoked the president's authority to create national forests in six timber-rich western states. Before signing the bill, Roosevelt designated 16 million more acres in the six states as

> Roosevelt once compared "the destruction of a species" to the loss of "all the works of some great writer."

national forests. TR also created fifty-three wildlife reserves, sixteen national monuments, and five new national parks. Congress established the National Park Service in 1916 to manage them.

In 1908, Gifford Pinchot organized a White House conservation conference for the nation's governors. There, experts discussed the utilitarian benefits of resource management. John Muir and other wilderness preservationists were not invited. But the struggle between wilderness purists and multiple-use advocates went on. Rallying support through magazine articles, preservationist groups and women's organizations saved a large grove of California's giant redwoods and a lovely stretch of the Maine coastline from logging.

The Sierra Club lost a battle to save the Hetch Hetchy Valley in Yosemite National Park when Congress in 1913 approved a dam on the Tuolumne River to provide water and hydroelectric power for San Francisco, 150 miles away. (Other opponents of the dam were less interested in preserving Hetch Hetchy as a wilderness than in developing it for tourism.) While the preservationists lost this battle, the controversy focused attention on environmental issues, as Americans for the first time weighed the aesthetic implications of a major public-works project.

Taft in the White House, 1909–1913

Roosevelt had pledged not to seek a third term, and as the 1908 election approached, the Republican Party's most conservative leaders regained control. They nominated TR's choice, Secretary of War **William Howard Taft,** for president but selected a conservative vice-presidential nominee and adopted a deeply conservative platform. The Democrats, meanwhile, nominated William Jennings Bryan for a third time. The Democratic platform called for a lower tariff, denounced the trusts, and embraced the cause of labor.

With Roosevelt's endorsement, Taft coasted to victory. But Bryan bested the Democrats' 1904 vote total by 1.3 million, and progressive Republican state candidates outran the national ticket. Overall, the outcome suggested a lull in the reform movement, not its end.

Republican conservatives welcomed Roosevelt's departure to hunt big game in Africa. Quipped Senator Aldrich, "Let every lion do its duty." But even an ocean away, TR's presence remained vivid.

"When I am addressed as 'Mr. President,'" Taft wrote him, "I turn to see whether you are not at my elbow."

Taft, from a prominent Ohio political family, differed from TR in many respects. Whereas TR kept in fighting trim, Taft was obese. Roosevelt had installed a boxing ring in the White House; Taft preferred golf. TR loved speechmaking and battling evildoers; Taft disliked controversy. His happiest days would come later, as chief justice of the United States.

Pledged to support TR's program, Taft backed the Mann-Elkins Act (1910), which beefed up the Interstate Commerce Commission's regulatory authority and extended it to telephone and telegraph companies. Taft's administration actually prosecuted more antitrust cases than had Roosevelt's, but with little publicity. To the public, TR remained the mighty trustbuster.

The reform spotlight, meanwhile, shifted to Congress, where a group of reform-minded Republicans, nicknamed the Insurgents, including Senators La Follette and Albert Beveridge of Indiana and Congressman George Norris of Nebraska, had challenged their party's conservative congressional leadership. In 1909, the Insurgents and Taft fought a bruising battle over the tariff. Taft first backed the Insurgents' call for a lower tariff. But when high-tariff advocates in Congress pushed through a measure raising duties on hundreds of items, Taft not only signed it but praised it extravagantly, infuriating the Insurgents.

The Insurgents next set their sights on House Speaker Joseph G. Cannon of Illinois, a reactionary Republican who prevented most reform bills from even reaching a vote. In March 1910, the Insurgents joined with the Democrats to trim Cannon's power by removing him from the pivotal Rules Committee. This directly challenged Taft, who supported Cannon.

The so-called Ballinger-Pinchot controversy widened the rift. Taft's interior secretary, Richard Ballinger, was a Seattle lawyer who favored unregulated private development of natural resources. In one of several decisions galling to conservationists, Ballinger in 1909 approved the sale of several million acres of coal-rich public lands in Alaska to a Seattle business consortium that promptly resold it to J.P. Morgan and other financiers. When an Interior Department official protested, he was fired. In true muckraking style, he went public, blasting Ballinger in a *Collier's* magazine article. When Gifford Pinchot of the Forest Service also criticized Ballinger, he too got the ax. TR's supporters seethed.

Upon Roosevelt's return to America in June 1910, Pinchot met the boat. Openly breaking with Taft, Roosevelt campaigned for Insurgent candidates in that year's midterm elections. On August 31,

PRESIDENT THEODORE ROOSEVELT AND FRIENDS COMMUNE WITH NATURE, 1903 Dwarfed by an ancient sequoia, the Grizzly Giant, in the Mariposa Grove of California's Yosemite National Park, TR's party includes California governor George Pardee (third from left), the naturalist and Sierra Club founder John Muir (fourth from right) and the presidents of Columbia University (third from right) and the University of California (far right). The Grizzly Giant still stands and remains a favorite with tourists. *(The Yosemite Museum, Yosemite National Park)*

in a speech at Osawatomie, Kansas, before a cheering throng of 30,000, Roosevelt borrowed a term from Herbert Croly's *The Promise of American Life,* and proposed a "New Nationalism" that would powerfully engage the federal government in reform. Declared the former president: "This new Nationalism regards the executive power as the steward of public welfare. It demands of the judiciary that it shall be interested primarily in human welfare rather than in property, just as it demands that the representative body shall represent all the people rather than any one class or section of the people." Particularly alarming conservatives, he endorsed the radical idea of reversing by popular vote judicial rulings that struck down reform laws favored by progressives.[1]

The Democrats captured the House in 1910, a coalition of Democrats and Insurgent Republicans controlled the Senate, and TR increasingly sounded like a presidential candidate.

---

[1] More than a century later, in December 2011, President Barack Obama deliberately chose Osawatomie, with its echoes of Theodore Roosevelt's "New Nationalism" address, for a major speech outlining the themes of his 2012 presidential campaign.

The Four-Way Election of 1912

In February 1912, Roosevelt announced his candidacy for the Republican nomination. But Taft wanted a second term. Roosevelt generally walloped Taft in the Republican state primaries and conventions. Taft controlled the party machinery, however, and the Republican convention in Chicago disqualified many of Roosevelt's hard-won delegates. Outraged, TR's backers walked out and formed the **Progressive Party.** What had been a general term for a broad reform movement now became the official name of a political party. Riding an emotional high, the cheering delegates nominated their hero, with California senator Hiram Johnson as his running mate.

"I feel fit as a bull moose," Roosevelt trumpeted, giving his organization its nickname, the Bull Moose Party. The convention platform endorsed most reform causes of the day, including lower tariffs, woman suffrage, business regulation, the abolition of child labor, the eight-hour workday, workers' compensation, the direct primary, and the popular election of senators. The new party attracted a diverse following, united mainly by affection for Roosevelt.

THEODORE ROOSEVELT ON THE CAMPAIGN TRAIL, 1912 With a characteristic fist-pumping gesture, TR delivers a speech from the rear of a railroad car. *(© Bettman/Corbis).*

Meanwhile, the reform spirit had also infused the Democratic Party. In New Jersey in 1910, voters had elected a political novice, **Woodrow Wilson**, as governor. A "Wilson for President" boom soon arose, and at the Democratic convention in Baltimore, Wilson won the nomination, defeating several established party leaders.

In the campaign, Taft more or less gave up, satisfied to have denied Roosevelt the nomination and kept his party safe for conservatism. The Socialist

candidate Eugene Debs proposed the "collective ownership and democratic control" of large industries, major financial institutions, and transportation and communications systems. The Socialist platform included many other reforms, some of which would later be realized, including woman suffrage, a shorter work week, a graduated income tax, and a federal "bureau of health." TR preached his New Nationalism: corporations must be regulated in the public interest, the welfare of workers and consumers safeguarded, and the environment protected.

Wilson, by contrast, called his political vision the "New Freedom." Warning that corporations were choking off opportunity for ordinary Americans, he nostalgically evoked an era of small government, small businesses, and free competition. "The history of liberty," he said, "is the history of the limitation of governmental power, not the increase of it."

Roosevelt outpolled Taft by 630,000 votes, but the Republicans' split proved costly (see Map 21.2). Wilson easily won the presidency, and the Democrats took both houses of Congress. More than 900,000 voters opted for Debs and socialism.

The 1912 election linked the Democrats firmly with reform (except on the issue of race)—a link that Franklin D. Roosevelt would strengthen in the 1930s. TR's third-party campaign demonstrated the continued appeal of reform among many grassroots Republicans. Debs's nearly 1 million votes, about 6 percent of the total, revealed socialism's appeal and the depths of discontent with the status quo, particularly among urban immigrant workers.

Several recent scholars (see books by Gould and Milkis in "For Further Reference") have noted how the 1912 presidential contest anticipated future political trends. It involved party primaries, continuous campaigning, celebrity endorsements, and the new mass medium: film. TR's campaign, bypassing the party establishment, focused on his personal appeal and, targeting voters directly, in some ways foreshadowed the campaigns of Jimmy Carter in 1976 and Barack Obama in 2008 (see Chapters 29 and 31). In another modern touch, as the campaign unfolded, a sports event distracted public attention: the 1912 World Series, in which the Boston Red Sox narrowly edged out the New York Giants.

National Progressivism, Phase II: Woodrow Wilson, 1913–1917

The son and grandson of Presbyterian ministers, Wilson grew up in Virginia and Georgia in a churchly atmosphere that shaped his oratorical style

1912

Candidate (Party)	Electoral Vote		Popular Vote	
Wilson (Democrat)	435	82.0%	6,296,547	41.9%
Roosevelt (Progressive)	88	16.5%	4,118,571	27.4%
Taft (Republican)	8	1.5%	3,486,720	23.2%
Debs (Socialist)	0		900,672	6.1%

MAP 21.2   THE ELECTION OF 1912

and moral outlook. Despite a learning disability (probably dyslexia), he graduated from Princeton and earned a Ph.D. in political science from Johns Hopkins University. Joining Princeton's faculty, he became its president in 1902. A rigid unwillingness to compromise cost him faculty support, and in 1910 Wilson resigned to enter politics. Three years later, he was president of the United States.

Impressive in bearing, with piercing gray eyes, Wilson was an eloquent orator. But the idealism that inspired people could also alienate them. At his best, he excelled at political deal-making. "He can walk on dead leaves and make no more noise than a tiger," declared one awed politician. But under pressure, he could retreat into a fortress of absolute certitude. As president, all these facets of his personality would come into play.

> "[Wilson] can walk on dead leaves and make no more noise than a tiger."

The progressive movement gained fresh momentum in Wilson's first term (see Table 21.2). Under his leadership, Congress enacted an array of reform measures. Despite the nostalgia for simpler times in his campaign rhetoric, he proved ready to address the problems of the new corporate order.

Tariff and Banking Reform

Lowering tariff rates—long a goal of southern and agrarian Democrats—headed Wilson's agenda. Many progressives agreed that high protective tariffs increased corporate profits at the public's expense. Breaking a precedent dating from Thomas Jefferson's presidency, Wilson appeared personally before Congress in April 1913 to read his tariff message. A low-tariff bill quickly passed the House but bogged down in the Senate. Showing his flair for drama, Wilson denounced the lobbyists flooding into Washington. His censure led to a Senate investigation of lobbyists and of senators who profited from high tariffs. Stung by the publicity, the Senate slashed tariff rates even more than the House had done. The Underwood-Simmons Tariff reduced rates an average of 15 percent.

Wilson again addressed Congress in June, this time calling for banking and currency reform. The nation's banking system clearly needed overhauling. Totally decentralized, it lacked a strong central institution, a "lender of last resort" to help banks survive fiscal crises. A financial panic in 1907, when many banks had failed, remained a vivid memory.

No consensus existed on specifics, however. Many reformers wanted a publicly controlled central banking system. But the nation's bankers, whose Senate spokesman was Nelson Aldrich, favored a privately controlled central bank similar to the Bank of England. The large banks of New York City advocated a strong central bank, preferably privately owned, so they could better compete with London banks in international finance. Others, including influential Virginia congressman Carter Glass, opposed any central banking authority, public or private.

No banking expert, Wilson did insist that the monetary system ultimately be publicly controlled. As the bargaining unfolded, Wilson's behind-the-scenes role proved crucial. The result was the **Federal Reserve Act** (1913). This compromise measure created twelve regional Federal Reserve banks under mixed public/private control. Each could issue U.S. dollars, called Federal Reserve notes, to the banks in its district to make loans to corporations and individual borrowers. Overall control of the system was shared by the heads of the twelve regional banks and the members of a Washington-based Federal Reserve Board, appointed by the president for fourteen-year terms.

The Federal Reserve Act stands as Wilson's greatest legislative achievement. Initially, the Federal Reserve Board's authority was diffuse, but eventually "the Fed" grew into the strong central monetary institution it remains today, setting interest rates and adopting fiscal policies to prevent financial panics, promote economic growth, and combat inflation.

Regulating Business; Aiding Workers and Farmers

In 1914, Wilson and Congress turned to that perennial progressive cause, business regulation. The two laws that resulted sought a common goal, but embodied different approaches.

The Federal Trade Commission Act took an administrative approach. This law created a new "watchdog" agency, the **Federal Trade Commission** (FTC), with power to investigate violations of federal regulations, require regular reports from corporations, and issue cease-and-desist orders (subject to judicial review) when it found unfair methods of competition.

The Clayton Antitrust Act, by contrast, took a legal approach. It listed corporate activities that could lead to federal lawsuits. The Sherman Act of 1890, although outlawing business practices in restraint of trade, had been vague about details. The Clayton Act spelled out specific illegal practices, such as selling at a loss to undercut competitors.

Because Wilson appointed some conservatives with big-business links to the FTC, this agency

TABLE 21.2 Progressive Era Legislation, Supreme Court Rulings, and Constitutional Amendments

Legislation

	Act	Provisions
1902	National Reclamation Act	Funds dams and irrigation projects in the West.
1906	Hepburn Act	Regulates railroad rates and other practices.
	Pure Food and Drug Act	Imposes strict labeling requirements for food processors and pharmaceutical companies.
	Meat Inspection Act	Requires federal inspection of packinghouses.
	Antiquities Act	Protects archaeological sites in Southwest.
1909	Payne-Aldrich Tariff	Raises tariffs, deepens Republican split.
1910	Mann Act	Antiprostitution measure; prohibits transporting a woman across state lines for "immoral purposes."
	Mann-Elkins Act	Strengthens powers of Interstate Commerce Commission.
1913	Underwood-Simmons Tariff	Lowers tariff rates; Wilson plays key role.
	Federal Reserve Act	Restructures U.S. money and banking system.
1914	Federal Trade Commission Act	Creates FTC as federal watchdog agency over corporations.
	Clayton Antitrust Act	Specifies illegal business practices.
	Narcotics Act (Harrison Act)	Forbids distribution of addictive drugs except by physicians and pharmacists.
1916	Federal Farm Loan Act	Enables farmers to secure low-interest federal loans.
	Keating-Owen Act	Bans products manufactured by child labor from interstate commerce.
	Adamson Act	Establishes eight-hour workday for interstate railway workers.
	Workmen's Compensation Act	Provides accident and injury protection for federal workers.

Court Rulings

	Court Case	Significance
1904	*Northern Securities* case	Upholds antitrust suit against Northern Securities Company, a railroad conglomerate.
1905	*Lochner* v. *New York*	Overturns New York law setting maximum working hours for bakery workers.
1908	*Muller* v. *Oregon*	Upholds Oregon law setting maximum working hours for female laundry and factory workers.
1911	*Standard Oil Co.* v. *U.S.*	Orders dissolution of Standard Oil.
1927	*Buck* v. *Bell*	Upholds Virginia sterilization law.

Constitutional Amendments

	Amendment	Provisions
1913	Sixteenth Amendment	Gives Congress authority to impose income tax.
	Seventeenth Amendment	Requires the direct election of U.S. senators by voters.
1919	Eighteenth Amendment	Prohibits the manufacture and sale of intoxicating liquors.
1920	Nineteenth Amendment	Grants women the vote.

initially proved ineffective. But under the Clayton Act, the Wilson administration filed antitrust suits against nearly a hundred corporations.

Leading a party long identified with workers, Wilson supported labor unions and workers' right to organize. He also endorsed a Clayton Act clause exempting strikes, boycotts, and picketing from the antitrust laws' prohibition of actions in restraint of trade.

In 1916 (an election year), Wilson and congressional Democrats enacted three important worker-protection laws. The Keating-Owen Act barred from interstate commerce products manufactured by child labor. (This law was declared unconstitutional in 1918, as was a similar law enacted in 1919.) The Adamson Act established an eight-hour day for interstate railway workers. The Workmen's Compensation Act provided accident and injury protection to federal workers. As we have seen, however, Wilson's sympathies for the underdog stopped at the color line.

Other 1916 laws helped farmers. The Federal Farm Loan Act and the Federal Warehouse Act enabled farmers, using land or crops as collateral, to get low-interest federal loans. The Federal Highway Act, providing funds for highway programs, benefited not only the new automobile industry but also farmers plagued by bad roads.

UNDERAGE FACTORY WORKER A young worker in a glass factory in Alexandria, Virginia, on the outskirts of Washington, DC. The photographer, Lewis Hine, wrote of such child laborers: "I have heard their tragic stories ... and seen their fruitless struggles in the industrial game where the odds are all against them." *(Library of Congress)*

Progressivism and the Constitution

The probusiness bias of the courts weakened a bit in the Progressive Era. In *Muller* v. *Oregon* (1908), the Supreme Court upheld an Oregon law limiting female laundry and factory workers to a ten-hour workday. Defending this law's constitutionality, Boston attorney **Louis Brandeis** not only cited legal precedent, but offered economic, medical, and sociological evidence documenting the ways long hours harmed women workers. While making an exception based on gender, the Court continued to hold (as it had in the 1905 case *Lochner* v. *New York*) that in general such worker-protection laws violated the due-process clause of the Fourteenth Amendment. Nevertheless, *Muller* v. *Oregon* marked an advance in making the legal system more responsive to new social realities.

In 1916, Woodrow Wilson nominated Brandeis to the Supreme Court. Disapproving of Brandeis's innovative approach to the law, the conservative American Bar Association protested, as did Republican congressional leaders and other prominent conservative voices. Anti-Semites opposed Brandeis because he was a Jew. But Wilson stood firm, and Brandeis won Senate confirmation.

These years also produced four Constitutional amendments, the first since 1870. The Sixteenth (ratified in 1913) empowered Congress to tax incomes, thus ending a long legal battle. A Civil War income tax had been phased out in 1872. Congress had again imposed an income tax as part of an 1894 tariff act, but the Supreme Court had promptly denounced it as "communistic" and ruled it unconstitutional. With the constitutional issue resolved, Congress in 1913 imposed a graduated federal income tax with a maximum rate of 7 percent on incomes greater than five hundred thousand dollars. Income-tax revenues helped pay for the government's expanded regulatory duties under various progressive reform measures.

The Seventeenth Amendment (1913) provided for the direct election of U.S. senators by the voters, rather than their selection by state legislatures, as described in Article I of the Constitution. This reform, earlier advocated by the Populists, sought to make the Senate less subject to corporate influence and more responsive to the popular will.

The Eighteenth Amendment (1919) prohibited the manufacture, sale, or importation of "intoxicating liquors." The Nineteenth (1920) granted women the vote. This remarkable wave of amendments

WARREN HARDING RUNS FOR THE U.S. SENATE, 1914 From 1788 until 1914, senators were chosen by their state legislatures. The Seventeenth Amendment, ratified in 1913, provided for the direct popular election of senators. In the 1914 election, senatorial candidates for the first time campaigned for votes from the electorate at large. Ohio voters that year received this postcard promoting the Republican Party's senatorial candidate, Warren G. Harding, a Marion, Ohio, newspaper editor. Harding won, and in 1920 he was elected President of the United States. *(Collection of Janice L. and David J. Frent)*

underscored the Progressive Movement's profound impact on the political landscape.

1916: Wilson Edges Out Hughes

As Wilson won renomination in 1916, the Republicans turned to Charles Evans Hughes, a Supreme Court justice and former New York governor. Progressive Party loyalists again courted Theodore Roosevelt. But TR, now obsessed with the war in Europe (covered in the next chapter), told them to endorse Hughes, which they did, effectively removing the Progressive Party from the contest.

With the Republicans more or less reunited, the election was extremely close. War-related issues loomed large. Wilson won the popular vote, but the Electoral College outcome remained in doubt for several weeks as the California tally seesawed back and forth. Ultimately, Wilson carried the state by fewer than four thousand votes and, with it, the election.

The progressive movement lost momentum as attention turned from reform to war. Final success for the prohibition and woman-suffrage campaigns came in 1919–1920, and Congress enacted a few reform measures in the 1920s. But, overall, the movement faded as America marched to war in 1917.

CONCLUSION

What we call the progressive movement began as preachers, novelists, journalists, photographers, and painters highlighted appalling conditions in America's cities and factories. Intellectuals offered ideas for reform through the creative use of government.

At the local and state level, reform-minded politicians, together with a host of reform organizations, worked to combat political corruption, make cities safer and more beautiful, regulate corporations, and improve conditions for workers.

Progressivism had its coercive side. Some reformers concentrated on regulating urban amusements and banning alcohol consumption. Racism and hostility to immigrants are part of the progressive legacy as well.

Progressivism crested as a national movement under presidents Theodore Roosevelt and Woodrow Wilson. These years saw advances in corporate regulation, environmental conservation, banking reform, and consumer and worker protection. Constitutional amendments granted Congress the power to tax incomes and provided for the direct election of senators, woman suffrage, and national prohibition of alcohol—all aspects of the progressive impulse.

Along with specific laws, progressivism's legacy included an enlarged view of government's role in society. Progressives expanded the meaning of democracy and challenged the cynical view of government as a tool of the rich and powerful. They did not seek "big government" for its own sake. Rather, they recognized that in an industrial age of great cities and concentrated corporate power, government, too, must grow to serve the public interest and protect society's more vulnerable members.

This ideal sometimes faltered in practice. Reform laws and regulatory agencies often fell short of their purpose as bureaucratic routine set in. Reforms designed to promote the public good sometimes mainly benefited special interests. Corporations proved adept at manipulating the new regulatory state to their own advantage.

Still, the Progressive Era stands as a time when American politics seriously confronted the social upheavals caused by industrialization. It was also an era when Americans learned to think of government as an arena of possibility where public issues and social problems could be thrashed out. The next great reform movement, the New Deal of the 1930s, would build on progressivism's legacy while shedding its moralistic social-control features and broadening its white, native-born, Protestant, middle-class limitations.

KEY TERMS

"Muckrakers" (p. 637)

Robert La Follette (p. 640)

Anti-Saloon League (p. 644)

Ida Wells-Barnett (p. 647)

W.E.B. Du Bois (p. 647)

National Association for the Advancement of Colored People (p. 647)

Carrie Chapman Catt (p. 648)

Margaret Sanger (p. 649)

Industrial Workers of the World (p. 652)

Eugene V. Debs (p. 652)

Theodore Roosevelt (p. 653)

Hepburn Act (p. 654)

Pure Food and Drug Act (p. 655)

National Reclamation Act (Newlands Act) (p. 655)

William Howard Taft (p. 656)

Progressive Party (p. 657)

Woodrow Wilson (p. 658)

Federal Reserve Act (p. 659)

Federal Trade Commission (p. 659)

Louis Brandeis (p. 661)

FOR FURTHER REFERENCE

Douglas Brinkley, *The Wilderness Warrior: Theodore Roosevelt and the Crusade for America* (2009). A vividly written account of the origins, achievements, and occasional failures of TR's environmental vision.

Leon Fink, *Progressive Intellectuals and the Dilemmas of Democratic Commitment* (1997). Insightful exploration of the tensions between democratic theory and the Progressive Era focus on expertise and specialized knowledge.

Richard A. Greenwald, *The Triangle Fire* (2005). Documents how middle-class experts, reformers, and machine politicians forged a new "urban liberalism" in response to the tragedy.

Louis L. Gould, *Four Hats in the Ring: The 1912 Election and the Birth of Modern American Politics* (2008). Gould closely examines the personalities, ideology, rhetoric, and strategies of the four contending presidential candidates in 1912, a campaign he sees as foreshadowing the course of modern American politics.

Gayle Gullett, *Becoming Citizens: The Emergence and Development of the California Woman's Movement, 1880–1911* (2000). Illuminating case study of the movement in a key state.

Patricia G. Harrison, *Connecting Links: The British and American Woman Suffrage Movements, 1900–1914* (2000). Examines the web of relationships and associations linking the woman-suffrage campaigns in the two nations and the disruption of those relations when World War I began in 1914.

Michael McGerr, *A Fierce Discontent: The Rise and Fall of the Progressive Movement in America* (2005). Well written and readable, this challenging new interpretation stresses the movement's ambitious goals, middle-class roots and ideological perspective, and ultimate failure amid the reactionary climate of World War I and its aftermath.

Sidney M. Milkis, *Theodore Roosevelt, the Progressive Party, and the Transformation of American Democracy* (2009). Explores how TR, especially in the 1912 presidential campaign, recast American politics through his appeal to a mass electorate, his vision of presidential leadership, and his articulation of a democratic response to the new corporate order.

David Montgomery, *The Fall of the House of Labor: The Workplace, the State, and American Labor Activism, 1865–1925* (1989). A classic study tracing the first great wave of U.S. labor activism and the response of the state, focusing on the experience of workers themselves in a changing corporate and industrial environment.

Daniel T. Rodgers, *Atlantic Crossings: Social Politics in a Progressive Age* (1998). A superb history positioning American progressivism in a transnational context.

Jacqueline Van Voris, *Carrie Chapman Catt: A Public Life* (1996). A comprehensive biography tracing Catt's key role in the woman-suffrage campaign's final stage and her later peace activism.

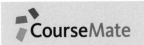

Visit the CourseMate website at **www.cengagebrain.com** for additional study tools and review materials for this chapter.

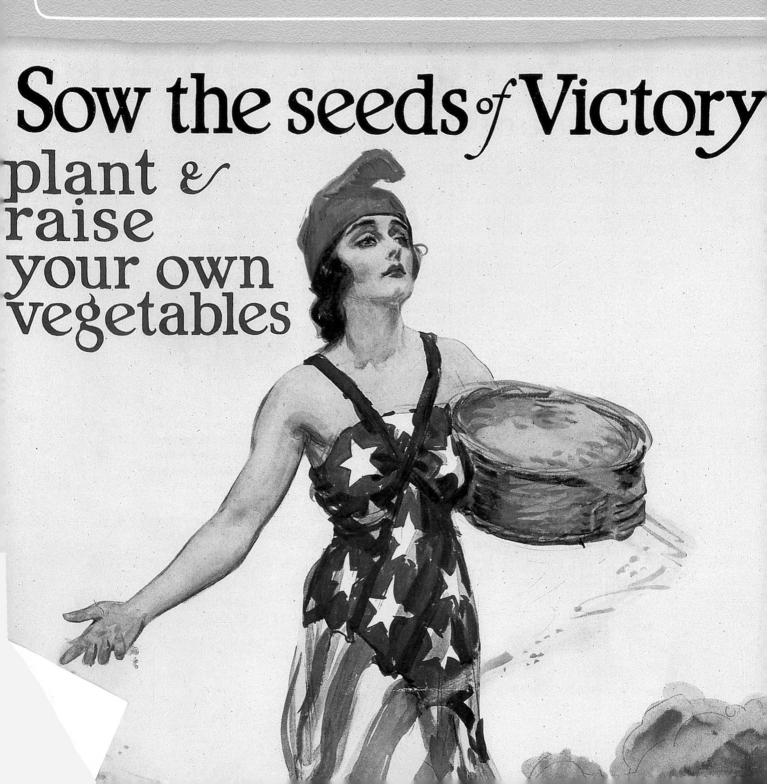

Sow the seeds of Victory
plant &
raise
your own
vegetables

JANE ADDAMS IN 1914 *(© Bettmann/ Corbis)*

IT WAS APRIL 6, 1917, and Jane Addams was troubled. By overwhelming margins, Congress had just declared war on Germany. Deeply patriotic, Addams also believed in peace and deplored her nation's decision for war. As the founder of Hull House, a Chicago settlement house, Addams had worked to overcome tensions among different ethnic groups. In *Newer Ideals of Peace* (1907), she had insisted that the multiethnic "internationalism" of America's immigrant neighborhoods proved that national and ethnic hostilities could be overcome. Addams had also observed how war spirit could inflame a people. During the Spanish-American War, she had watched Chicago children play at killing "Spaniards."

When Europe went to war in 1914, Addams worked to end the conflict. A founder of the Woman's Peace Party in 1915, she attended an International Congress of Women that urged the warring nations to submit their differences to arbitration. Addams met with President Wilson in a futile effort to enlist his support for arbitration.

Now America had entered the war, and Addams had to take a stand. Deepening her dilemma, many of her friends, including John Dewey, were lining up behind Wilson. Theodore Roosevelt, whose 1912 presidential campaign Addams had enthusiastically supported, was beating the drums for war.

Despite the pressures, Addams heeded her conscience and opposed the war. The reaction was swift. Editorial writers who had praised her settlement-house work now denounced her. For years after, the American Legion and other patriotic organizations attacked Addams for her "disloyalty" in 1917. She described her wartime isolation in *Peace and Bread in Time of War* (1922).

Addams did not sit out the war on the sidelines, however. She gave speeches across America urging increased food production to aid refugees and other war victims. In 1919, after the war ended, she was elected first president of the Women's International League for Peace and Freedom. In 1931, she won the Nobel Peace Prize. During the 1960s, some opponents of the Vietnam War found inspiration in her example.

Addams's experience underscores how deeply World War I affected America. Whether they donned uniforms, worked on farms or in factories, or simply experienced U.S. life in wartime, the war touched all Americans. Beyond its immediate effects, the war had long-lasting social, economic, and political ramifications.

WORLD WAR I POSTER URGING FOOD CONSERVATION, BY THE ILLUSTRATOR JAMES MONTGOMERY FLAGG Home-front propaganda played a key role in mobilizing Americans in support of the war effort in 1917–1918. *(Library of Congress)*

Well before 1917, events abroad gripped the attention of Washington, the media, and ordinary Americans. From this perspective, World War I was one episode in a larger process of deepening U.S. global involvement. By 1900 America had become an industrial powerhouse seeking foreign markets and raw materials, and these widening economic interests brought a new level of international engagement. This expanded world role, with important home-front ramifications, has continued to shape American history to the present. These broader involvements around the world, culminating in World War I, are the focus of this chapter.

FOCUS Questions

- What goals underlay America's early-twentieth-century involvements in Asia and Latin America?
- Considering both immediate and long-term factors, why did the United States go to war in 1917?
- How did Washington mobilize the nation for war, and what role did U.S. troops play in the war?
- What was the war's economic, political, and social impact on the American home front?
- How did the League of Nations begin, and why did the Senate reject U.S. membership in the League?

Defining America's World Role, 1902–1914

The annexation of Hawaii, the Spanish-American War, the occupation of the Philippines, and other developments in the 1890s (see Chapter 20) reflected a desire to assert American power as European nations built colonial empires; to protect and extend U.S. business investments abroad, especially in Asia and Latin America; and to impose American standards of good government beyond the nation's borders. This process continued after 1900.

Both economic and ideological considerations shaped America's dealings with Asian and Latin American nations in these years. U.S. policymakers wanted to expand corporate America's access to foreign markets and raw materials. But they also believed that other societies would benefit by adopting the principles of democracy, individual freedom, and the rule of law. Sometimes economic motives predominated, sometimes ideological, and often both.

The "Open Door": Competing for the China Market

As the U.S. campaign to suppress the Philippines insurrection dragged on, the China market beckoned. Proclaimed Indiana senator Albert J. Beveridge in 1898, "American factories are making more than the American people can use; American soil is producing more than they can consume… [T]he trade of the world must and shall be ours."

Textile producers dreamed of clothing China's millions; investors envisioned railroad construction. As China's 250-year-old Manchu Qing empire faltered, U.S. business people watched carefully. In 1896, a consortium of New York capitalists formed a company to promote trade and railroad investment in China.

But other nations were also eyeing the China market. Some pressured the weak Manchu rulers to give them exclusive trading and development rights in designated regions, or "spheres of influence." In 1896, Russia won both the right to build a railway across the Chinese province of Manchuria and a long-term lease on much of the region. In 1897, Germany secured a ninety-nine-year lease on a Chinese port as well as mining and railroad rights in the adjacent province. The British won concessions as well.

In 1899, U.S. Secretary of State John Hay asked the major European powers to ensure American trading rights in China by opening the ports in their spheres of influence to all countries. The nations gave noncommittal answers, but Hay blithely announced their acceptance of the principle of an "Open Door" to American business in China.

Hay's Open Door note showed how commercial considerations were increasingly influencing American foreign policy. It reflected a form of economic expansionism historians have called "informal empire." The U.S. government did not seek Chinese territory, but it did want access to Chinese markets for American businesses.

As Hay pursued this effort, a more urgent threat emerged. For years, antiforeign feeling had simmered in China, fanned by the aged Qing Dynasty empress, who hated the West's growing influence. In 1899, an antiforeign secret society known as the Harmonious Righteous Fists (called "Boxers" by Western journalists) killed thousands of foreigners and Chinese Christians. In June 1900, the Boxers

CHRONOLOGY 1899–1920

1899	First U.S. Open Door note seeking access to China market.
	Boxer Rebellion erupts in China.
1900	Second U.S. Open Door note.
1904	President Theodore Roosevelt proclaims "Roosevelt Corollary" to Monroe Doctrine.
1905	Roosevelt mediates the end of the Russo-Japanese War.
1906	At the request of Roosevelt, San Francisco ends segregation of Asian schoolchildren.
	Panama Canal construction begins.
1911	U.S.-backed revolution in Nicaragua.
1912	U.S. Marines occupy Nicaragua.
1914	U.S. troops occupy Veracruz, Mexico.
	Panama Canal opens.
	World War I begins.
	President Wilson proclaims American neutrality.
1915	U.S. Marines occupy Haiti and the Dominican Republic.
	Woman's Peace Party organized.
	British liner *Lusitania* sunk by German U-boat.
	Wilson permits U.S. bank loans to Allies.
1916	U.S. punitive expedition invades Mexico, seeking Pancho Villa.
	Germany pledges not to attack merchant ships without warning.
	Wilson reelected.
1917	U.S. troops withdraw from Mexico.
	Germany resumes unrestricted U-boat warfare; United States declares war. Selective Service Act sets up national draft.
	War Industries Board, Committee on Public Information, and Food Administration created.
	Espionage Act passed.

1917 (Cont.)	War Risk Insurance Act authorizes payments to servicemen's dependents.
	NAACP march in New York City protests upsurge in lynchings.
	Bolsheviks seize power in Russia; Russia leaves the war.
	New York State passes woman-suffrage referendum.
	U.S. government operates the nation's railroads.
	Striking miners forcibly expelled from Bisbee, Arizona.
1918	Wilson outlines Fourteen Points.
	Sedition Amendment passed.
	Global influenza pandemic takes heavy toll in United States.
	National War Labor Board created.
	American forces see action at Château-Thierry, Belleau Wood, St. Mihiel, and Meuse-Argonne campaign.
	Republicans win control of both houses of Congress (November 5).
	Armistice signed (November 11).
1919	Eighteenth Amendment added to the Constitution (prohibition).
	Peace treaty, including League of Nations covenant, signed at Versailles.
	Supreme Court upholds silencing of war critics in *Schenck* v. *United States*.
	Upsurge of lynchings; racial violence in Chicago.
	Wilson suffers paralyzing stroke.
	Versailles treaty, with League covenant, rejected by Senate.
1920	"Red raids" organized by Justice Department.
	Nineteenth Amendment added to the Constitution (woman suffrage).
	Warren G. Harding elected president.

occupied Beijing (Peking), the Chinese capital, and besieged the foreign legations. Twenty-five hundred U.S. soldiers joined an international army that marched on Beijing, quashed the **Boxer Rebellion,** and rescued the threatened legations.

The Boxers' defeat further weakened China's government. Fearing that the regime's collapse would allow European powers to carve up China, Hay issued a second, more important, series of **Open Door notes** in 1900. He reaffirmed the principle of open trade in China for all nations and announced America's determination to preserve China's territorial and administrative integrity. In

the 1930s, when Japanese expansionism menaced China, Hay's policy helped shape the American response.

Along with U.S. economic expansion in China came missionary activity. American Protestant missionaries had come to Hawaii in the 1820s, and by 1900 some five thousand U.S. missionaries were active in China, Africa, India, and elsewhere. While proclaiming their religious message, the missionaries also blazed the way for U.S. economic expansion. As a U.S. diplomat in China wrote in 1895: "Missionaries are the pioneers for American trade and commerce. ... The missionary, inspired by holy zeal, goes everywhere, and by degrees foreign trade and commerce follow."

The Panama Canal: Hardball Diplomacy

Traders had long dreamed of a canal across the forty-mile-wide ribbon of land joining North and South America to eliminate the hazardous voyage around South America. In 1879, a French company secured permission from Colombia to build a canal across Panama, then part of Colombia (see Map 22.1). But mismanagement and yellow fever doomed the project, and by 1888 it was bankrupt. Seeking to recoup its losses, the French company offered its assets, including the concession from Colombia, to the United States for $109 million.

America was in an expansionist mood. In 1902, after the French lowered their price to $40 million, Congress authorized President Theodore Roosevelt to accept the offer. The following year, Secretary of State Hay signed an agreement with a Colombian diplomat granting the United States a ninety-nine-year lease on the proposed canal for a down payment of $10 million and an annual fee of $250,000. But the Colombian senate, seeking a better deal, rejected the agreement. An outraged Roosevelt privately denounced the Colombians as "greedy little anthropoids."

"Missionaries are the pioneers for American trade and commerce."

Determined to have his canal, Roosevelt found a willing collaborator in Philippe Bunau-Varilla, an official of the bankrupt French company. Dismayed that his company might lose its $40 million, Bunau-Varilla organized a "revolution" in Panama from a New York hotel room. While his wife stitched a flag, he wrote a declaration of independence and a constitution for the new nation. When the "revolution" occurred as scheduled on November 3, 1903, a U.S. warship hovered offshore. Proclaiming Panama's independence, Bunau-Varilla appointed himself its first ambassador to the United States. John Hay quickly recognized the newly hatched nation and signed a treaty with Bunau-Varilla granting the United States a ten-mile-wide strip of land across Panama "in perpetuity" (that is, forever) on the terms earlier rejected by Colombia. Theodore Roosevelt later summed up the episode: "I took the Canal Zone, and let Congress debate, and while the debate goes on, the canal does also."

The U.S. canal builders' first challenge was the yellow fever that had haunted the French. Dr. Walter Reed of the Army Medical Corps led this effort. Earlier, in Cuba, Reed had used volunteer U.S. experimental subjects (including himself) to prove that mosquitoes breeding in stagnant water spread the yellow fever virus. In Panama, Reed's drainage projects eradicated the disease-bearing mosquito—a remarkable public-health achievement. Construction began in 1906, and in 1914 the first ship sailed through the **Panama Canal.** In 1921, implicitly conceding the dubious methods used to acquire the Canal Zone, the U.S. Senate voted a payment of $25 million to Colombia. But the ill feeling generated by Theodore Roosevelt's actions, combined with other instances of U.S. interventionism, would long shadow U.S.-Latin American relations.

☐☐ VISITS THE PANAMA CANAL CONSTRUCTION SITE, 1906 President ☐☐☐sevelt played a key role in securing the strip of land on which ☐☐☐ilt. Here, he proudly poses in a steam shovel used in the ☐☐☐ject. *(Theodore Roosevelt Collection, Harvard College Library)*

Roosevelt and Taft Assert U.S. Power in Latin America and Asia

Other, less-familiar episodes further underscored Washington's growing readiness to assert U.S. power and protect U.S. business interests in Latin America (see Map 22.1) and Asia. In 1902, German, British, and Italian warships blockaded and bombarded the ports of Venezuela, which had defaulted on its debts to European investors. The standoff ended when President Theodore Roosevelt pressed all sides to settle the dispute through arbitration.

A second crisis flared in 1904 when several European nations threatened to invade the Dominican Republic, a Caribbean island nation that had also defaulted on its debts. Roosevelt reacted swiftly. If any nation intervened, he believed, it should be the United States. "Chronic wrongdoing" by any Latin American nation, he declared that December, would justify U.S. intervention.

This pronouncement has been called "the Roosevelt Corollary" to the 1823 Monroe Doctrine, which had warned European powers against meddling in Latin America. Now Roosevelt asserted that "wrongdoing" (a word he left undefined) gave the United States the right to step in. Suiting actions to words, the Roosevelt administration took over the Dominican Republic's customs service for two years and managed its foreign debt. Roosevelt once summed up his foreign-policy approach by quoting what he said was an African proverb, "Speak softly and carry a big stick."

The foreign policy of the Taft administration (1909–1913) focused on advancing American commercial interests, a policy some called "dollar diplomacy." A U.S.-backed revolution in mineral-rich Nicaragua in 1911 brought to power Adolfo Díaz, an officer of an American corporation that controlled several Nicaraguan gold mines. Washington, fearing growing British influence in Nicaragua, also worried that Germany or Japan might build a canal across Nicaragua to rival the Panama Canal. American bankers lent Díaz's government $1.5 million, in exchange for control of Nicaragua's national bank, customs service, and railroad. When a revolt against Díaz broke out in 1912, Taft sent marines to protect the bankers' investment. Except for one brief interval, they remained until 1933. Overall, these early twentieth-century U.S. involvements

> "Speak softly and carry a big stick."

MAP 22.1 **U.S. HEGEMONY IN THE CARIBBEAN AND LATIN AMERICA, 1900–1941** Through many interventions, territorial acquisitions, and robust economic expansion, the United States became the predominant power in Latin America in the early twentieth century. Acting on Theodore Roosevelt's assertion of a U.S. right to combat "wrongdoing" in Latin America and the Caribbean, the United States dispatched troops to the region, where they met nationalist opposition. © Cengage Learning. All rights reserved. No distribution allowed without express authorization.

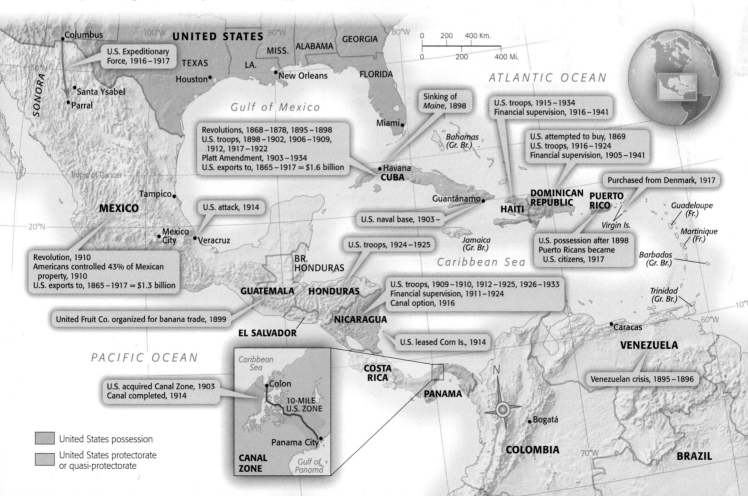

in Latin America served America's expanding corporate interests and warned off other foreign powers, while planting the seeds of future hostility and resentments.

In Asia, too, Roosevelt and Taft sought to project U.S. power and advance American business interests. In 1900, exploiting the turmoil caused by the Boxer uprising, Russia occupied Manchuria and began building railroads. This alarmed the Japanese, who also had designs on Manchuria and nearby Korea. Japan and Russia went to war in 1904 after a surprise Japanese attack destroyed Russian ships in a Manchurian port. As Japan completely dominated Russia, an Asian power for the first time checked Western imperialist expansion.

Roosevelt, while pleased to see Russian expansionism challenged, believed that a Japanese victory would disrupt the Asian balance of power and threaten America's position in the Philippines. Accordingly, he invited Japan and Russia to a peace conference at Portsmouth, New Hampshire. In September 1905, the two rivals signed a peace treaty. Russia recognized Japan's rule in Korea and made other territorial concessions. After this outcome, curbing Japanese expansionism—peacefully, if possible—became America's major objective in Asia. For his role in ending the war, Roosevelt received the Nobel Peace Prize.

In 1906, U.S.-Japanese relations soured when the San Francisco school board assigned all Asian children to segregated schools. When Japan angrily protested, Roosevelt summoned the school board to Washington and persuaded them to reverse this discriminatory policy. In return, in 1908 the administration negotiated a "gentlemen's agreement" with Japan by which Tokyo voluntarily halted Japanese emigration to America. Racist attitudes and discriminatory laws against Japanese in California continued to poison U.S.-Japanese relations, however.

While Californians warned of the "yellow peril," Japanese journalists, eyeing America's military strength and involvement in Asia, spoke of a "white peril." In 1907, Roosevelt ordered sixteen gleaming U.S. battleships on a "training operation" to Japan. Although officially friendly in intent, this "Great White Fleet" underscored America's naval might.

President Taft's policies in Asia extended the focus on dollar diplomacy, which in this case meant promoting U.S. commercial interests in China— the goal Secretary of State Hay had sought with his Open Door notes. A plan for a U.S.-financed railroad in Manchuria failed, however. Not only did U.S. bankers find the project too risky, but Russia and Japan signed a treaty carving up Manchuria for commercial purposes, freezing out the Americans.

Wilson and Latin America

Taking office in 1913, Woodrow Wilson criticized his Republican predecessors' expansionist policies. The United States, he pledged, would "never again seek one additional foot of territory by conquest." But he, too, soon intervened in Latin America. In 1915, after upheavals in Haiti and the Dominican Republic (two small nations sharing the Caribbean island of Santo Domingo), Wilson sent in U.S. marines, who brutally suppressed Haitians who resisted. A Haitian constitution favorable to U.S. commercial interests was overwhelmingly ratified in a 1918 vote supervised by the marines. The marines occupied the Dominican Republic until 1924 and Haiti until 1934 (see Map 22.1).

Events in Mexico triggered Wilson's most serious crisis in Latin America. Mexico had won independence from Spain in 1820, but the nation remained divided between a landowning elite and an impoverished peasantry. In 1911, rebels led by the democratic reformer Francisco Madero had ended the thirty-year rule of President Porfirio Díaz, a defender of the wealthy elite. Early in 1913, just as Wilson took office, Mexican troops loyal to General Victoriano Huerta, a full-blooded Indian, overthrew and murdered Madero.

Wilson's response focused on protecting the forty thousand U.S. citizens who had settled in Mexico under Díaz's regime and safeguarding the U.S. investors who had poured some $2 billion into Mexican oil wells and other ventures. Reversing the long-standing U.S. practice of recognizing all governments, Wilson refused to recognize Huerta's "government of butchers." Authorizing arms sales to General Venustiano Carranza, Huerta's rival, Wilson ordered the port of Veracruz blockaded to prevent a shipment of German arms from reaching Huerta (see Map 22.1). Announced Wilson: "I am going to teach the South American republics to elect good men." In April 1914, seven thousand U.S. troops occupied Veracruz and battled Huerta's forces. Sixty-five Americans and approximately five hundred Mexicans were killed or wounded. Bowing to U.S. might, Huerta abdicated; Carranza took power; and the troops withdrew.

But turmoil continued. In January 1916, a bandit chieftain in northern Mexico, Pancho Villa, murdered sixteen U.S. mining engineers. Soon after, Villa's gang burned the town of Columbus,

> "I am going to teach the South American republics to elect good men."

WOODROW ON TOAST.

President Woodrow Wilson, U.S.A. "IF YOU DON'T TAKE CARE, I SHALL HAVE TO TREAT YOU THE SAME WAY AS EUROPE TREATS THE TURK."
Mexico. "AND HOW'S THAT?"
President Woodrow Wilson. "WELL, I SHALL HAVE TO—TO GO ON WAGGING MY FINGER AT YOU."

WOODROW WILSON INSTRUCTS MEXICO IN GOOD BEHAVIOR. This 1913 cartoon from a London humor magazine captured Wilson's moralistic tone toward other nations, and the resentments it aroused. *(© Bettmann/Corbis)*

viewing with patronizing condescension the "backward" peoples they encountered in the process.

Meanwhile, a crisis unfolding in Europe challenged Wilson's dream of an American-based world order.

War in Europe, 1914–1917

When war engulfed Europe in 1914, most Americans wished only to remain aloof, and President Wilson proclaimed U.S. neutrality. But by April 1917, economic considerations, cultural ties, visions of a world remade in America's image, and German violations of Wilson's definition of neutral rights all combined to suck America into the maelstrom.

The Coming of War

Although western Europe was at peace through much of the nineteenth century, a series of ominous developments raised warning flags. In a short, sharp war in 1870–1871, an alliance of German states handed France a humiliating defeat. In the aftermath, Germany emerged as a powerful united nation ruled by Kaiser Wilhelm II. With many Germans convinced that Germany had lagged in the race for empire, Berlin pursued modernization, expansion, and military power. Germany, Austria-Hungary, and Italy signed a military-defense treaty in 1882. France, Great Britain, and Russia signed similar treaties in 1904 and 1907.

Meanwhile, the once-powerful Ottoman Empire, centered in Turkey, was weakening, leaving in its wake such newly independent nations as Romania, Bulgaria, and Serbia. Serbian patriots dreamed of expanding their boundaries to include Serbs living in neighboring Bosnia-Herzegovina. Serbia's ally Russia supported these ambitions. The Austro-Hungarian empire, based in Vienna, had other ideas. In 1908, Austria-Hungary annexed (took over) Bosnia-Herzegovina, alarming Russia and Serbia.

In this volatile atmosphere, Archduke Franz Ferdinand of Austria visited Bosnia's capital, Sarajevo, in June 1914. As Ferdinand and his wife

New Mexico, and killed nineteen inhabitants. Enraged Americans demanded action. Wilson dispatched a punitive expedition under General **John J. Pershing.** When Villa eluded Pershing and brazenly staged another cross-border raid into Texas, Wilson ordered 150,000 National Guardsmen to the border— a massive response that stirred anti-American feelings among Mexico's poor, for whom Villa was a folk hero. Villa ended his raids in 1920 when the Mexican government gave him a large land grant, but he was soon assassinated.

These involvements in Asia and Latin America illuminate the basic U.S. foreign-policy goal: to achieve a global order that would embrace American political values and welcome American business. These goals reflected the worldview of the white, male, native-born foreign-policy elite. Confident of their ethnic, gender, and class status, they promoted U.S. political and corporate interests abroad, while

rode in an open car, a young Bosnian Serb gunned them down. This act pushed a continent already poised for war over the precipice. Austria declared war on Serbia. Russia, aligned with Serbia by a secret treaty, mobilized for war. Austria's ally Germany declared war on Russia and France. Great Britain, linked by treaty to Russia and France, declared war on Germany.

Thus began what contemporaries called the Great War, now known as World War I. On one side were Great Britain, Russia, and France, called the Allies. On the other were the Central Powers: Germany and Austria-Hungary. (Italy, despite its alliance with the Central Powers, joined the Allies in 1915.)

The Perils of Neutrality

President Wilson urged Americans to remain neutral "in thought as well as in action." Most citizens fervently agreed. A popular song summed up the mood: "I Didn't Raise My Boy to Be a Soldier." Carrie Chapman Catt and other feminists joined Jane Addams in forming the Woman's Peace Party. In New York City, fifteen hundred women marched to protest the war.

> Wilson urged Americans to remain neutral "in thought as well as in action."

Neutrality proved difficult, however. Many Americans had ancestral ties to England. Schoolbooks stressed the English origins of American institutions. The English language itself—the language of Shakespeare, Dickens, and the King James Bible— deepened the bond. British propaganda subtly stressed such links.

Many German Americans, by contrast, sympathized with Germany, as did some Scandinavian immigrants. Irish Americans speculated that a German victory might free Ireland from British rule. Despite these cultural and ethnic cross-currents, however, most Americans initially supported Wilson's commitment to neutrality.

Yet in 1917, America went to war. What caused this turnabout? Fundamentally, Wilson's vision of a peaceful, democratic, and capitalist world order conflicted with his neutrality. Such an international system would be impossible, he believed, if Germany won the war. Even an Allied victory would not ensure a transformed world order, Wilson became convinced, without a U.S. role in the postwar settlement. To shape the peace, America must fight the war.

These underlying ideas influenced Wilson's handling of the war's most troubling immediate challenge: neutral nations' rights. When the war began, Britain intercepted U.S. merchant ships bound for Germany, insisting that their cargo might aid Germany's war effort. Wilson protested, especially when Britain, exploiting its naval advantage, declared the North Sea a war zone; planted it with explosive mines; and blockaded all German ports, choking off Germany's imports, including food.

But Germany, not England, ultimately pushed the United States into war. If Britannia ruled the waves, Germany controlled the ocean depths with its torpedo-equipped submarines, or U-boats. In February 1915, Berlin proclaimed the waters around Great Britain a war zone and warned off all ships. Wilson quickly responded: Germany would be held to "strict accountability" for any loss of U.S. vessels or lives.

On May 1, 1915, in a small ad in U.S. newspapers, the German embassy cautioned Americans against travel on British or French vessels. Six days later, a U-boat sank the British liner *Lusitania* off Ireland, killing 1,198 people, including 128 Americans. (The *Lusitania,* historians later discovered, was secretly carrying munitions destined for England.)

In three stern notes to Germany, Wilson demanded that Berlin stop unrestricted submarine warfare and pay reparations for the U.S. deaths in the *Lusitania* sinking. Publicly, he insisted that the United States could persuade the belligerents to recognize the principle of neutral rights without going to war. "There is such a thing as a man being too proud to fight," he said.

The *Lusitania* disaster exposed deep divisions in U.S. public opinion. Many Americans, now ready for war, ridiculed Wilson's "too proud to fight" speech. Theodore Roosevelt denounced the president's "abject cowardice." The National Security League, a lobby of bankers and industrialists, promoted stepped-up U.S. arms production and organized "preparedness" parades in major cities. By late 1915, Wilson himself called for a military buildup.

Lurid British propaganda (much of it false or exaggerated) screamed of atrocities committed by "the Huns" (a derogatory term for Germans). Intercepted German messages relating to espionage in U.S. factories further discredited the German cause.

Others, however, deplored the drift toward war. Some progressives warned that war fever was eroding support for reforms. The war, Jane Addams lamented, had destroyed the international movements to reduce infant mortality and improve care for the aged. Late in 1915, automaker Henry Ford chartered a vessel to take a group of pacifists to Scandinavia to persuade the belligerents to end the war by Christmas.

Divisions surfaced even within the Wilson administration. Secretary of State William Jennings Bryan, believing Wilson's *Lusitania* notes too hostile,

THE SINKING OF THE CUNARD LINER *LUSITANIA*, MAY 7, 1915, OFF THE IRISH COAST The destruction of the *Lusitania* by a German U-boat, portrayed here in an illustration from an English newspaper, took nearly 1,200 lives, including 128 Americans. This event outraged U.S. public opinion and led to a build-up in military preparedness. But as President Wilson pursued diplomatic exchanges with Germany, nearly two more years would pass before the United States entered the war. *(Granger Collection)*

resigned in June 1915. Under Bryan's weak successor, Robert Lansing, Wilson himself shaped U.S. policy.

Early in 1916, some Congressmen, seeking to avoid more *Lusitania*-type crises, introduced a bill to ban Americans from sailing on belligerents' ships. President Wilson successfully opposed it, however, insisting that the principle of neutral rights must be upheld.

For a time, Wilson's conciliatory approach seemed to work. Germany ordered its U-boats to spare passenger ships and offered compensation for the Americans lost in the *Lusitania* sinking. In March 1916, however, a U-boat sank a French passenger ship in the English Channel, injuring several Americans. When Wilson threatened to break diplomatic relations—a step toward war—Berlin pledged not to attack merchant vessels without warning, provided that Great Britain, too, observed "the rules of international law." Ignoring this qualification, Wilson announced Germany's acceptance of American demands, and the crisis eased.

Meanwhile, U.S. banks' support for the Allies eroded the principle of neutrality. Early in the war, Secretary of State Bryan had rejected banker J.P. Morgan's request to extend loans to France. Such loans, said Bryan, would violate "the true spirit of neutrality." But economic considerations undermined this policy. In August 1915, Treasury Secretary William G. McAdoo warned Wilson that Allied purchases of American munitions and farm products were essential "[t]o maintain our prosperity." Only substantial loans to England, agreed Secretary of State Lansing, could prevent serious domestic economic problems, including "unrest…among the laboring classes." The neutrality principle must not "stand in the way of our national interests," warned Lansing.

Swayed by such arguments and personally sympathetic to the Allies, Wilson permitted Morgan's bank to lend $500 million to the British and French governments. By April 1917, U.S. banks had lent the Allies $2.3 billion, in contrast to $27 million to Germany.

The land war, meanwhile, had settled into a grim stalemate. A September 1914 German drive into France bogged down along the Marne River. The two sides then dug in, constructing trenches across France from the English Channel to the Swiss border. For more than three years, this line scarcely changed. A German offensive in February 1916 began with the capture of two forts near the town of Verdun and ended that June when the French recaptured the same two forts, now nothing but rubble, at a horrendous cost in human life. Trench warfare became a nightmare of mud, rats, artillery bursts, and random death.

The war dominated the 1916 presidential election, which pitted Wilson against Republican Charles Evans Hughes, a former New York governor. Somewhat confusingly, Hughes criticized Wilson's lack of aggressiveness while rebuking him for policies that risked war. Theodore Roosevelt campaigned more for war than for the Republican ticket. The only difference between Wilson and the bearded Hughes, Roosevelt jeered, was a shave. While Hughes did well among Irish Americans and German Americans, Wilson eked out a narrow victory, aided by women voters in western states that had adopted woman suffrage. The Democrats' winning campaign slogan, "He kept us out of war," revealed the strength of popular peace sentiment as late as November 1916.

"He kept us out of war."

The United States Enters the War

In February 1917, Germany resumed unrestricted submarine warfare. Even if the United States declared war as a result, German strategists believed, the U-boat campaign could bring victory before American troops reached the front.

Events now rushed forward. Wilson broke diplomatic relations on February 3. During February and March, U-boats sank five American ships. A coded telegram from German foreign secretary Arthur Zimmermann to Germany's ambassador to Mexico, intercepted by the British, promised that if Mexico declared war on the United States, Germany would help restore Mexico's "lost territories" of Texas, Arizona, and New Mexico. The "Zimmermann telegram" further inflamed the war spirit in America.

Events in Russia also helped create favorable conditions for America's entry into the war. In March 1917, Russian peasants, industrial workers, intellectuals inspired by Western liberal values, and communist revolutionaries joined in an uprising that overthrew the country's repressive czarist government. A provisional government under the liberal Alexander Kerensky briefly seemed to promise a democratic Russia, making it easier for President Wilson to portray the war as a battle for democracy.

On April 2, before a joint session of Congress, Wilson called for a declaration of war. Applause rang out as Wilson described his vision of America's role in creating a postwar international order to make the world "safe for democracy." After a short debate, the Senate voted 82 to 6 for war. The House agreed, 373 to 50. German violation of U.S. neutrality, reinforced by American ideological commitments, cultural affinities, and economic considerations had propelled the nation into the war. British propaganda and the "preparedness" campaign mounted by U.S. financial and corporate interests had played a role as well.

Mobilizing at Home, Fighting in France, 1917–1918

Compared to its effects on Europe, the war only grazed America. Russia suffered heavily. France, Great Britain, and Germany fought for more than four years; the United States, for nineteen months. Their armies suffered casualties of 70 percent or more; the U.S. casualty rate was 8 percent. The fighting left parts of France and Belgium brutally scarred; North America was physically untouched. Nevertheless, the war profoundly affected America. It changed not only those who participated in it directly but also the home front and the nation's government and economy.

Raising, Training, and Testing an Army

April 1917 found America's military woefully unprepared. The regular army consisted of 120,000 men, few with combat experience, and an aging officer corps, plus eighty thousand National Guard members. Ammunition reserves were paltry. The War Department was a jungle of jealous bureaucrats, one of whom hoarded thousands of typewriters as the war approached.

While army chief-of-staff Peyton C. March brought order to the bureaucracy, Wilson's secretary of war, Newton D. Baker, a former mayor of Cleveland, concentrated on raising an army. The **Selective Service Act** of May 1917 required all men between twenty-one and thirty (later expanded to eighteen through forty-five) to register with local draft boards. Mindful of the Civil War draft riots, Baker planned the draft-registration day, June 5, 1917, as a "festive and patriotic occasion."

By the war's end, more than 24 million men had registered, of whom nearly 3 million were drafted. Volunteers and National Guardsmen swelled the total to 4.3 million. Training camps gave combat instruction and introduced recruits to military discipline. Volunteer organizations built morale through shows, games, and recreational activities. The American Library Association contributed books. YMCA volunteers offered classes in literacy, French slang, and Bible study. Women volunteers in communities near military camps opened

WHIPPING UP WAR ENTHUSIASM IN THE HEARTLAND In Denver, automobiles carrying young army recruits parade through the city. In reality, many Americans opposed U.S. entry into the war. *(Denver Public Library, Western History Division)*

"Hostess Houses" to give homesick recruits a touch of domesticity.

The War Department closely monitored recruits' off-duty behavior. The **Commission on Training Camp Activities** presented films, lectures, and posters on the dangers of alcohol and prostitution. Any soldier disabled by venereal (sexually transmitted) disease, one poster warned, "is a Traitor!" Officers confined trainees to camp until nearby towns closed brothels and saloons.

Recruits also underwent intelligence testing. Psychologists eager to demonstrate the usefulness of their new field claimed that measuring recruits' "intelligence quotient" (IQ) could help win the war by identifying potential officers and those qualified for more specialized assignments.

When many recruits received very low scores, editorial writers reacted with alarm. In fact, the results mostly revealed recruits' lack of formal education and the tests' cultural biases. One question asked whether *mauve* was a drink, a color, a fabric, or a food. The testing also reinforced racial and ethnic stereotypes: native-born recruits of northern European origins scored highest, African Americans and recent immigrants lowest.

In short, the training camps not only turned civilians into soldiers but also reinforced the Progressive Era's moral-control campaigns (see Chapter 21) and signaled changes ahead, including a vogue for standardized testing.

Some twelve thousand Native Americans served in the **American Expeditionary Force** (AEF). While some reformers eager to preserve Indian culture argued for all-Indian units, military officials integrated Native Americans into the general army. The wartime experience, some observers predicted, would hasten Indians' assimilation into mainstream American life.

Some blacks resisted the draft, especially in the South (as discussed later in this chapter), but most followed W.E.B. Du Bois's advice urging African Americans to "close ranks" and support the war. More than 260,000 blacks volunteered or were drafted, and some 50,000 went to France. Racism pervaded the military, as it did American society. The navy assigned blacks only to menial positions, and the marines excluded them altogether.

Black troops in some camps endured abuse. One racist senator from Mississippi warned that the sight of "arrogant, strutting" black soldiers would trigger race riots. Tensions exploded in Houston in August 1917 when black soldiers stationed at nearby Camp Logan, goaded by abuse, seized weapons, marched into town, and fatally shot sixteen whites. After court-martial trials, nineteen black soldiers were hanged and sixty-one sentenced to life imprisonment.

Organizing the Economy for War

World War I helped shape modern America. The war furthered such key later developments as an expanded government role in the economy; the growth of new professional and managerial elites; and the spread of mass production, corporate consolidation, and product standardization.

The war led to unprecedented government economic oversight and corporate regulation, long advocated by Populists and progressives. In 1916, Congress created an advisory body, the Council of National Defense, to oversee the government's military preparedness program. After war was declared, this council set up the **War Industries Board** (WIB) to coordinate military purchasing and ensure production efficiency. President Wilson reorganized the WIB in March 1918 and put the Wall Street financier Bernard Baruch in charge. Under Baruch, the WIB allocated raw materials, established production priorities, and induced competing companies to standardize and coordinate their products and processes to save scarce commodities.

With congressional authorization, Wilson set up two more new agencies, the Fuel Administration and the Food Administration. The Fuel Administration controlled coal output, regulated fuel prices and consumption, and introduced daylight-saving time—an idea first proposed by Benjamin Franklin. The Food Administration, headed by Herbert Hoover, oversaw the production and allocation of wheat, meat, and sugar to ensure supplies for the army as well as for the desperately food-short Allies. Born in poverty in Iowa, Hoover had prospered as a mining engineer in Asia. He was organizing food relief in Belgium when Wilson brought him back to Washington.

These agencies relied on voluntary cooperation, reinforced by government propaganda. Food Administration posters and ads urged Americans to conserve food. Housewives signed pledges to observe "Meatless Monday" and "Wheatless Wednesday." Slogans such as "Serve Beans by All Means" promoted substitutes for scarce commodities.

Harriot Stanton Blatch, daughter of woman's-rights pioneer Elizabeth Cady Stanton, headed the Food Administration's Speakers' Bureau, which spread the administration's conservation message. Blatch also organized the Woman's Land Army, which recruited women to replace male farm workers.

In all, nearly five thousand government boards supervised home-front activities. These included the National War Labor Board, which resolved labor-management disputes that jeopardized production, and the Railroad Administration, headed by Treasury Secretary William McAdoo. When a railroad tie-up during the winter of 1917–1918 threatened the flow of supplies to Europe, the Railroad Administration stepped in and soon transformed the thousands of miles of track operated by competing companies into an efficient national system.

American business, much criticized by progressive reformers, utilized the war emergency to improve its image. Corporate executives ran regulatory agencies. Factory owners distributed prowar

> Housewives signed pledges to observe "Meatless Monday" and "Wheatless Wednesday."

A RECRUITMENT POSTER TARGETING AFRICAN AMERICANS In this poster, Abraham Lincoln looks down approvingly as black soldiers battle the German foe. In reality, most black troops were restricted to noncombat roles. *(Library of Congress)*

propaganda to workers. Trade associations coordinated war production.

The war hastened the process of corporate consolidation and economic integration. In place of trustbusting, the government now encouraged cooperation and mergers among businesses. "Instead of punishing companies for acting in concert," one magazine observed, "the government is now in some cases forcing them to unite."

> "Instead of punishing companies for acting in concert," one magazine observed, "the government is now in some cases forcing them to unite."

Overall, the war was good for business. Despite wartime tax increases, profits soared. After-tax profits in the copper industry, for example, jumped from 12 percent in 1913 to 24 percent in 1917.

The old laissez-faire suspicion of government, already weakened, eroded further in 1917–1918. The wartime regulatory agencies disappeared quickly after the war, but their influence lingered. In the 1930s, when the nation faced a different crisis, the government activism of World War I would be remembered (as discussed in Chapter 24).

With the American Expeditionary Force in France

As the U.S. military mobilized for combat, Allied prospects looked bleak. German U-boats were battering Allied shipping. French troops mutinied in the spring of 1917 after suffering ghastly casualties. Later that year, the Italian army suffered a disastrous defeat at Caporetto near the Austrian border, and a British offensive along the French-Belgian border gained only four miles at a cost of many thousands killed and wounded. A breakthrough in military technology came in November 1917 when the British mobilized three hundred tanks along a six-mile section of the front near Cambrai, France, shattering the German defenses. Still the stalemate continued.

Russia, ill-prepared for war, had suffered devastating setbacks as well, contributing to the revolutionary upheaval. The communist faction of the revolution, the Bolsheviks (Russian for "majority"), gained strength when its top leaders, including Vladimir Lenin and Leon Trotsky, returned from exile abroad. On November 6, 1917 (October 24 by the Russian calendar), a Bolshevik coup overthrew Alexander Kerensky's provisional government and effectively removed Russia from the war. Early in 1918, the Bolsheviks signed an armistice with Germany, the Treaty of Brest-Litovsk, freeing thousands of German troops on the Russian front for fighting in France.

In these desperate circumstances, U.S. aid to the Allies initially consisted of munitions and convoys to protect Allied ships. The first U.S. troops, designated as the Allied Expeditionary Force (AEF), reached France in October 1917. Eventually about 2 million American soldiers served in France under General John J. Pershing. A West Point graduate and commander of the 1916 expedition against Pancho Villa, Pershing was an iron-willed officer with a ramrod bearing, steely eyes, and trim mustache. The death of his wife and three of their children in a fire in 1915 had further hardened him. (Ironically, Pershing was of German origin; his family name had been Pfoersching.)

Most men of the AEF at first found the war a great adventure. Plucked from towns and farms, they sailed for Europe on crowded freighters or, for a lucky few, captured German passenger liners. Once in France, railroad freight cars marked "HOMMES 40, CHEVAUX 8" (forty men, eight horses) took them to the front. Then began the routine of marching, training—and waiting.

The African Americans with the AEF worked mainly as mess-boys (mealtime aides), laborers, and stevedores (ship-cargo handlers). Although discriminatory, the latter assignments vitally aided the war effort. Sometimes working twenty-four hours nonstop, black stevedores efficiently unloaded supply ships. Some whites of the AEF pressed the French to treat African Americans as inferiors, but most ignored this advice and related to blacks without prejudice. This eye-opening experience would remain with black veterans after the war.

While most African American troops served behind the front lines, regiments of the all-black 92nd and 93rd infantry divisions saw action under French command in the Second Battle of the Marne and the Meuse-Argonne campaign near the war's end. France awarded the Croix de Guerre, a military honor, to the entire 369th infantry regiment, nicknamed the "Harlem Hellfighters," and gave several hundred black U.S. soldiers individual decorations for bravery. German propaganda leaflets described U.S. racism and urged African American soldiers to defect, but none did. Only in death was the AEF integrated, however: graves in military cemeteries were not racially segregated.

In the air, a scant fifteen years after the Wright brothers' first flight, German and Allied planes dropped bombs, reported on troop movements, and engaged in deadly aerial dogfights (see Going to the Source). Germany's legendary "Red Baron," Manfred von Richthofen, downed eighty Allied planes before his luck ran out in April 1918. As early as 1916, American volunteers joined a French air unit known as the Lafayette Escadrille (squadron). The U.S. Army's air corps was established early in 1918. America's output of planes lagged, however, despite pressure from Secretary of War Baker—a rare war-production failure.

Continuing the military's policy of close moral oversight, AEF officials warned troops of the danger of venereal disease. "A German bullet is cleaner than a whore" declared one poster. When the French government offered to provide prostitutes for the AEF (as was the French practice), Newton Baker exclaimed, "For God's sake, don't show this to the President, or he'll stop the war."

> "A German bullet is cleaner than a whore."

The YMCA, Red Cross, and Salvation Army, including many female volunteers, provided a touch of home. Some 16,500 U.S. women served directly in the AEF as nurses, telephone operators, canteen workers, and secretaries.

In March 1918, when Germany launched a major offensive, the Allies created a unified command under French general Ferdinand Foch. Some Americans participated in the fighting around Amiens and Armentières that slowed the German advance.

The French and British wanted to continue this pattern of absorbing the Americans into existing units. But for both military and political reasons (including ensuring a strong U.S. voice at the peace table), Pershing and his superiors in Washington insisted that the AEF fight in "distinct and separate" units. Pershing, favoring aggressive combat in traditional battle settings, abhorred the defensive mentality ingrained by three years of trench warfare.

The Germans' spring offensive resumed in May along the Aisne River, where they broke through to the Marne and faced a nearly open route to Paris, fifty miles away. On June 4, as the French government prepared to evacuate, American forces arrived in strength. Parts of three U.S. divisions and a marine brigade helped stop the Germans at the town of Château-Thierry and nearby Belleau Wood. (An AEF division at full strength consisted of twenty-seven thousand men and one thousand officers, plus twelve thousand support troops.)

The German offensive had punched several deep holes (called salients) in the Allied line. With the help of some eighty-five thousand American troops, the Allies at enormous cost halted a German attack on the cathedral city of Rheims between two of these salients (see Map 22.2). This battle proved to be the war's turning point.

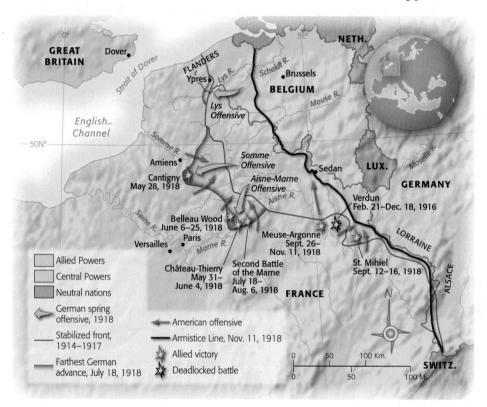

MAP 22.2 THE UNITED STATES ON THE WESTERN FRONT, 1918 American troops first saw action in the campaign to throw back Germany's spring 1918 offensive in the Somme and Aisne-Marne sectors. The next heavy American engagement came that autumn as part of the Allies' Meuse-Argonne offensive, which ended the war. © Cengage Learning. All rights reserved. No distribution allowed without express authorization.

American soldiers now endured the filth, vermin, and dysentery familiar to veterans of the trenches. Many would never forget the terror of combat. As shells streaked overhead, one recalled, "We simply lay and trembled from sheer nervous tension." Some collapsed emotionally and were hospitalized for "shell shock."

Deadly poison gas (first used by the Germans in 1915) often hung in the air, and rats scurried in the mud. "We are not men anymore, just savage beasts," wrote a young American. Death came in many forms, and without ceremony. Bodies, packs, rifles, photos of loved ones, and letters from home sank indiscriminately into the all-consuming mud. Worsening the horror, thousands of men on both sides died of influenza, in a pandemic that began in the war zone and quickly spread (as discussed later in this chapter).

Religious and ethical principles faded as men struggled to survive. "Love of thy neighbor is forgotten," recalled one, with "all the falsities of a sheltered civilization." The war's brutality would shape the literature of the 1920s as writers such as Ernest Hemingway stripped away the illusions obscuring the reality of mass slaughter.

Turning the Tide

The Allied counteroffensive began in July 1918. About 270,000 U.S. soldiers joined the drive to push the Germans back from the Marne. Rain pelted down as the AEF moved into position. One wrote in his diary, "Trucks, artillery, infantry columns, cavalry, wagons, caissons, mud, MUD, utter confusion." Another 100,000 AEF troops joined a parallel British counterattack in the Somme region.

In early September, as fighting continued on all fronts, Foch authorized an AEF campaign to close a German salient around the town of St. Mihiel on the Meuse River, 150 miles east of Paris (see Map 22.2). Pershing assembled nearly five hundred thousand American and one hundred thousand French soldiers. Shelling of German positions began at 1:00 A.M. on September 11. Recorded an American in his diary, "[I]n one instant the entire front...was a sheet of flame, while the heavy artillery made the earth quake." Within four days, the salient was closed. Although some German units had already withdrawn, St. Mihiel still cost seven thousand U.S. casualties.

THE FOG OF WAR. U.S. TROOPS ON THE WESTERN FRONT, JUNE 26, 1918 The reality of combat differed from the idealized images offered in home-front propaganda. As the war's final stage began, these American soldiers attacked entrenched German positions in Alsace, a disputed region along the French-German border near Switzerland (see Map 22.2). They are firing a 37-mm machine gun, a weapon of deadly accuracy with a maximum range of a mile and a half. *(National Archives)*

In late September, 1.2 million Americans joined the struggle to drive the Germans from the Meuse River and the Argonne Forest north of Verdun. The AEF was assigned to cut the Sedan-Mezières Railroad, a vital German supply route protected by three long, heavily fortified trenches, called Stellungen. The fighting was long and fierce but the AEF at last overran the dreaded Stellungen. In early November the Sedan-Mezières Railroad was cut. The AEF had fulfilled its assignment, at a cost of 26,277 dead.

The successful Meuse-Argonne offensive ended the war. On November 11, 1918, Germany surrendered.

Promoting the War and Suppressing Dissent

In their own way, the war's domestic effects matched the battlefield in importance. Spurred by government propaganda, patriotic fervor gripped America. The war fever, in turn, encouraged ideological conformity and smothered dissent. Fueling the repressive spirit, government authorities and private vigilante groups hounded socialists, pacifists, and other dissidents, trampling citizens' constitutional rights.

Advertising the War

President Wilson viewed home front support as crucial to military success. "It is not an army we must shape and train for war, it is a nation," he declared. The administration drew on the new professions of advertising and public relations to pursue this goal. Treasury Secretary William McAdoo orchestrated government bond drives, called Liberty Loans, that financed about two-thirds of the war's $35.5 billion cost.

Posters exhorted citizens to "Fight or Buy Bonds." Liberty Loan parades featured flags, banners, and marching bands. Charlie Chaplin and other movie stars promoted the cause. Schoolchildren purchased "thrift stamps" convertible into war bonds.

Patriotic war songs reached millions through phonograph recordings (see Technology and Culture). Beneath the ballyhoo ran a note of coercion. Only "a friend of Germany," McAdoo warned, would refuse to buy bonds.

The balance of the government's war costs came from taxes. Under authority granted by the recently ratified Sixteenth Amendment, Congress imposed wartime income taxes that reached 70 percent at the top level. War-profits taxes, excise taxes on liquor

and luxuries, and increased estate taxes also helped finance the war.

Journalist George Creel headed the government's wartime propaganda agency, the **Committee on Public Information** (CPI). While claiming merely to report facts, Creel's committee in reality publicized the government's version of events and discredited all who questioned that version. One CPI division distributed posters drawn by leading illustrators. Another wrote propaganda releases that appeared in the press as "news" with no indication of their source. Popular magazines published CPI ads warning of spies, saboteurs, and anyone who "spreads pessimistic stories" or "cries for peace." Theaters screened CPI films bearing such titles as *The Kaiser: The Beast of Berlin*. All this propaganda played upon basic fears that the German enemy posed a direct threat to home, family, and cherished American values.

The CPI poured foreign-language pamphlets into immigrant neighborhoods and supplied prowar editorials to the foreign-language press. At a CPI event at Mount Vernon on July 4, 1918, an

"SAVE YOUR CHILD" POSTER U.S. government propaganda in World War I (like that of other warring nations) appealed to basic emotions, urging support for the war as a way to protect home and family. *(© Bettmann/Corbis)*

Irish-born tenor sang "The Battle Hymn of the Republic" while immigrants from thirty-three nations filed reverently past George Washington's tomb. CPI posters in factories attacked the socialists' charge that this was a capitalists' war. Samuel Gompers of the American Federation of Labor headed a prowar "Alliance for Labor and Democracy" with CPI funding. CPI volunteers called "Four-Minute Men" gave prowar pep talks to movie audiences.

Teachers, writers, editors, and religious leaders overwhelmingly supported the war. These custodians of culture saw the conflict as a struggle to defend threatened values. Historians wrote essays contrasting German brutality with the Allies' ideals. In *The Marne* (1918), expatriate American writer Edith Wharton expressed her love for France. The popular war poems of Alan Seeger, who volunteered to fight for France and died in action in 1916, portrayed the conflict as a noble crusade. An artillery barrage was for him "the magnificent orchestra of war."

> For poet Seeger, an artillery barrage was "the magnificent orchestra of war."

Progressive reformers who had applauded Wilson's domestic program now cheered his war. Herbert Croly, Walter Lippmann, and others associated with the *New Republic* magazine zealously backed the war. In gratitude, administration officials regularly briefed them on the government's war policies.

The educator John Dewey endorsed the war in a series of *New Republic* essays. Progressive intellectuals must accept reality and shape it toward positive social goals, he wrote, not withdraw in self-righteous isolation. The war, he went on, presented exciting "social possibilities." The government's wartime activism could be channeled to reform purposes when peace returned. Internationally, America's participation in the war would transform an imperialistic struggle into a global democratic crusade.

Wartime Intolerance and Dissent

Responding to the propaganda, some Americans lashed out at all things German. Reports of sabotage by German agents, including mysterious fires at munitions plants in New Jersey and Pennsylvania, fanned the flames of fear. Libraries banished German books; towns with German names changed them. An Iowa politician charged that "90 percent of all the men and women who teach the German language are traitors." Some restaurant menus replaced

"A GERMAN IN AMERICA; AN AMERICAN IN NO MAN'S LAND" This March 1918 cartoon in the *New York Herald* attacked Karl Muck, the German conductor of the Boston Symphony Orchestra, when the orchestra performed in New York. Muck was arrested soon after and imprisoned for the rest of the war. Propaganda like this helped whip up anti-German hysteria on the home front. *(W.A. Rogers, New York Herald, 1918)*

hamburgers with "liberty sandwiches." The Boston Symphony Orchestra dismissed its German-born conductor. The Philadelphia Orchestra banned all German music since Brahms. A popular evangelist, Billy Sunday, proclaimed, "If you turn hell upside down you will find 'Made in Germany' stamped on the bottom."

The zealots also targeted American citizens suspected of pro-German or antiwar sentiments. Some were forced to kiss the flag or recite the Pledge of Allegiance. An Ohio woman accused of disloyalty was wrapped in a flag, marched to a bank, and compelled to buy a war bond. A Cincinnati mob horsewhipped a pacifist minister. Theodore Roosevelt branded antiwar Senator Robert La Follette "an unhung traitor." Columbia University fired two antiwar professors.

In Bisbee, Arizona, in July 1917, two thousand armed vigilantes calling themselves the Citizens Protective League forced twelve hundred striking copper miners, some of whom belonged to the

The Phonograph, Popular Music, and Home-Front Morale in World War I

Today's iPods, compact discs, MTV videos, and Internet music websites all trace their ancestry to technologies developed in the late nineteenth century. Along with the movies and national magazines, recorded music laid the groundwork for an American mass culture in the early twentieth century and helped build support for the U.S. war effort in 1917–1918.

As early as 1859, the Frenchman Leon Scott had developed the "vibrograph," which captured the variations of the human voice on a rotating wax-covered drum. But it was Thomas Edison who in 1877 developed a machine that could reproduce recorded sound. (Historians differ over whether the first recorded words were "Halloo" in July or "Mary had a little lamb" in December.) The following year, Edison patented a "phonograph" utilizing cylinders wrapped in tin foil. (Wax-coated cylinders soon proved superior.) The first known recorded musical performance was by an eleven-year-old pianist, Josef Hoffmann, in Edison's laboratory in New Jersey in 1887.

Unlike today's digital sound reproduction, phonographic recording is a mechanical process. The sound is first converted to electrical impulses, which in turn create slight variations in circular grooves on a rotating master disk, from which records are manufactured. When a record is played, a stylus, or needle, attached to a tone arm senses the variations and changes them back into electrical signals that are converted into sound and amplified by a loudspeaker.

The new technology became commercially available in 1890 when the Columbia Phonograph Company published a catalog of cylinder recordings. By 1894, Emile Berliner's U.S. Gramophone Company was selling around a thousand phonographs and some twenty-five thousand records a year, including hymns, classical works, and popular songs. The United States Marine Band conducted by John Philip Sousa was an early favorite. The first commercial jazz record, "Livery Stable Blues," appeared in 1917, recorded by a white

THOMAS A. EDISON CONTEMPLATES AN EARLY CYLINDER PHONOGRAPH Emile Berliner patented a new technique of recording on disks in 1887, and disks quickly replaced cylinders. Berliner also developed a technique for mass-producing hard-rubber records from a zinc master disk. *(U.S. Department of the Interior, National Park Service, Edison National Historic Site)*

New Orleans group called the Original Dixieland Jass [sic] Band. The Sears Roebuck catalog, widely distributed across America in the early twentieth century, offered "talking machines" on which buyers could play commercially produced records or make their own recordings.

In 1900, Eldridge Johnson bought Emile Berliner's company and formed the Victor Talking Machine Company. Johnson's Victrola, a handsome cabinet-style phonograph, proved so popular that "Victrola" became a generic name for all record players. Sales were boosted by Victor's trademark, a fox terrier named "Nipper" sitting in rapt attention before a Victrola beneath the caption "His Master's Voice." The earliest phonographs had amplified the sound by a large and unsightly external speaker horn. The Victrola concealed the horn inside the cabinet, making the unit more attractive for the living room or parlor. The "volume control" had two settings: open the cabinet doors to increase the volume, close them to reduce it.

Early Victrolas were expensive, ranging from $75 for the basic table model to luxury floor models. Despite the prices, annual sales reached 573,000 by 1917. Although electric-powered Victrolas became available in 1913, most buyers preferred the hand-cranked model well into the 1920s.

The American home front during World War I resonated to the sound of patriotic music blaring from thousands of Victrolas and phonographs produced by rival companies. War songs ranged from the sentimental, such as the waltz "Till We Meet Again," to novelty numbers, including "Oo-La-La Wee, Wee"; the tongue-twister "Sister Susie's Sewing Shirts for Soldiers"; and Irving Berlin's comic soldier's lament "Oh! How I Hate to Get Up in the Morning."

Other songs were rousingly patriotic, such as "America, I Love You" and George M. Cohan's 1917 hit "Over There," which became the war's unofficial anthem. The famed Italian tenor Enrico Caruso recorded it and in September 1918 performed it live before a huge audience in New York's Central Park. With many Americans opposed to U.S. intervention, prowar songs like "Over There" played an important propaganda role.

In the nineteenth century, new songs had been introduced by music-hall performers and then sold in sheet-music form, allowing families and social groups to sing them at home around the piano. Sheet music remained popular, but by 1917–1918, the mechanical reproduction of popular music was spreading through the culture.

By the war's end, American popular music was firmly linked to the recording technology pioneered by Edison, Berliner, Johnson, and others. With the coming of radio in the 1920s, recordings of classical music and popular songs could reach a mass audience simultaneously.

By the middle of the twentieth century, phonographs and phonograph records, incorporating many technological advances, played a huge role in American popular culture, accounting for millions of dollars in annual sales.

QUESTIONS FOR ANALYSIS

- What key technical developments made it possible for the phonograph to evolve from a laboratory novelty into a major commercial product?
- How did popular songs spread by phonograph recordings help build support for American participation in World War I?

WORLD WAR I SOLDIERS LISTEN TO A SPECIAL "ARMY AND NAVY MODEL" EDISON PHONOGRAPH "Since the beginning of the war," declared the Edison Company, "there has welled up from the trenches in Europe a great cry for music." *(Library of Congress)*

A FAN ADVERTISING VICTROLA RECORDS AND PHONOGRAPHS *(Collection of Paul Boyer)*

MILWAUKEE SOCIALIST LEADER VICTOR BERGER OPPOSES WAR PROFITEERS AND THE SUPPRESSION OF FREE SPEECH Elected to Congress in 1918, Berger was denied a seat because of his conviction under the wartime Espionage Act. The Supreme Court reversed the conviction in 1921, and Berger served in Congress from 1923 to 1929. *(Wisconsin Historical Society [WHi-1901])*

antiwar Industrial Workers of the World (IWW), onto a freight train that dumped them in the New Mexico desert without food, water, or shelter. Without doubt, declared Theodore Roosevelt, "the men deported from Bisbee were bent on destruction and murder."

In Collinsville, Illinois, in April 1918, a mob lynched a German American coal miner, Robert Prager. When a jury freed the ringleaders, a jury member shouted, "Nobody can say we aren't loyal now." The *Washington Post* condemned the lynching but saw it as evidence of a "wholesome awakening" in the American heartland. President Wilson criticized Prager's murder when the German press publicized it, but the administration's strident attacks on radicals and war critics created the climate that led to such actions. In a June 1917 speech urging home-front vigilance, Wilson declared ominously: "Woe be to the man or group of men that seeks to stand in our way." A New York newspaper, advising direct action against war opponents, added: "You do not require any official authority. . . . [T]he only badge you need is your patriotic fervor."

Despite the persecution, many Americans persisted in opposing the war. Some had sentimental or ancestral ties to Germany. Others were religious pacifists, including Quakers, Mennonites, and Jehovah's Witnesses. Montana Congresswoman Jeannette Rankin, a pacifist and the first woman elected to Congress, opposed the declaration of war. "I want to stand by my country," she declared, "but I cannot vote for war."

Of some sixty-five thousand men who registered as conscientious objectors (COs), twenty-one thousand were drafted. Assigned to noncombat duty on military bases, these COs often experienced harsh treatment. Those who rejected this alternative went to prison. Woodrow Wilson scorned the pacifists. "[M]y heart is with them, but my mind has contempt for them," he declared; "I want peace, but I know how to get it, and they do not."

Socialist leaders such as Eugene Debs and Victor Berger denounced the war as a capitalist struggle for markets, with the soldiers as cannon fodder. The government's decision for war, they insisted, reflected Wall Street's desire to protect its loans to England and France. Other socialists supported the war, however, dividing the party.

The war split the women's movement as well. Some leaders joined Jane Addams in opposition, others endorsed the war while keeping their own goals in view. Carrie Chapman Catt, president of the National American Woman Suffrage Association (NAWSA), had helped start the Woman's Peace Party in 1915. But she supported U.S. entry into the war in 1917, sharing to some extent Wilson's vision of a more liberal postwar world order. Catt continued to fight for woman suffrage, however, as NAWSA's "number one war job." For this, some superpatriots accused her of disloyalty.

Draft resistance extended beyond the ranks of conscientious objectors. An estimated 2.4 to 3.6 million young men failed to register. Others who did register either did not appear when drafted or deserted from training camp. The rural South saw high levels of draft resistance. The urban elites who

A New York newspaper advised direct action against war opponents: "You do not require any official authority. ...[T]he only badge you need is your patriotic fervor."

ran the draft boards were more inclined to excuse young men of their own class from service than poor farmers, white or black, fueling class resentment. In June 1918, a truck carrying soldiers pursuing draft evaders in rural Georgia crashed when a bridge collapsed, killing three. Investigators found that the bridge had been deliberately sabotaged.

African Americans had added reasons to oppose the draft. Of southern blacks who registered, one-third were drafted, in contrast to only one-quarter of whites. White draft boards justified this by arguing that black families could more easily spare a male breadwinner. As an Alabama board observed: "[I]t requires more for a white man and his wife to live than it does a negro man and his wife, due to their respective stations in life." But racial bias worked in complex ways: some southern whites, fearful of arming black men even for military service, favored drafting only whites.

One war critic, Randolph Bourne, a young journalist, rejected John Dewey's argument that reformers could direct the war to their own purposes. "If the war is too strong for you to prevent," he asked, "how is it going to be weak enough for you to...mould to your liberal purposes?" Many pro-war intellectuals eventually agreed. By 1919, Dewey conceded that the war, far from promoting reform, had encouraged reaction and intolerance. Bourne did not live to see his vindication, however. He died of influenza in 1918, aged thirty-two.

Suppressing Dissent by Law

Wartime intolerance surfaced in federal laws and official actions. The **Espionage Act** of June 1917 set fines and prison sentences for a variety of loosely defined antiwar activities. The **Sedition Amendment** (May 1918) imposed stiff penalties on anyone convicted of using "disloyal, profane...or abusive language" about the government, the Constitution, the flag, or the military.

Wilson's attorney general, Thomas W. Gregory, used these laws to suppress dissent. Opponents of the war, proclaimed Gregory, should expect no mercy "from an outraged people and an avenging government." Under the federal legislation and similar state laws, authorities arrested some fifteen hundred pacifists, socialists, IWW leaders, and other war critics. One socialist, Rose Pastor Stokes, received a ten-year prison sentence (later commuted) for telling an audience, "I am for the people, and the government is for the profiteers."

Socialist leader Eugene V. Debs, arrested in June 1918 for a speech in Canton, Ohio, discussing the war's economic causes, was convicted by a jury of violating the Espionage Act and sentenced to ten years in prison. At his sentencing he declared: "[W]hile there is a lower class, I am in it; while there is a criminal element, I am of it; while there is a soul in prison, I am not free."

Under the Espionage Act, Postmaster General Albert S. Burleson banned socialist periodicals, including *The Masses*. In January 1919 Congressman-elect Victor Berger was convicted for publishing antiwar articles in his socialist newspaper, the *Milwaukee Leader*. Socialist Norman Thomas complained that Burleson "didn't know socialism from rheumatism," and Upton Sinclair protested to President Wilson that no one of Burleson's "childish ignorance" should wield such power. Still, Wilson did little to restrain the Postmaster General's excesses.

A patriotic organization called the American Protective League and local "Councils of Defense" claiming vague governmental authority further enforced ideological conformity. A group called "Boy Spies of America" recruited young patriots. The 1917 takeover in Russia by Bolsheviks who believed in a one-party state and preached the overthrow of capitalism deepened suspicion of domestic radicals. Could the United States itself fall to communism, some fearful Americans wondered.

> "If the war is too strong for you to prevent, how is it going to be weak enough for you to . . . mould to your liberal purposes?"

In three 1919 decisions, the U.S. Supreme Court upheld the Espionage Act convictions of war critics despite the First Amendment guarantee of free speech. In *Schenck* v. *United States,* Justice Oliver Wendell Holmes, Jr., writing for a unanimous court, justified such repression in cases where a person's speech posed a "clear and present danger" to the nation. When the war ended, Wilson vetoed a bill repealing the Espionage Act, increasing the likelihood that the miasma of conformity and suspicion would linger into the postwar era.

Economic and Social Trends in Wartime America

In many diverse ways, the war affected the lives of millions of Americans, including industrial workers, farmers, women, and blacks. Another of the war's byproducts, a deadly influenza pandemic, took a grievous toll. Some Progressive Era reforms advanced, but overall the war weakened the reform movement.

Boom Times in Industry and Agriculture

World War I benefited the U.S. economy. From 1914 to 1918, factory output grew by more than one-third. Even with many men in uniform, the civilian work force expanded by 1.3 million between 1916 and 1918, thanks to new jobs in shipbuilding, munitions, steel, and other war-related industries. Prices rose, but so did wages. Even unskilled workers enjoyed wartime wage increases averaging nearly 20 percent. Samuel Gompers urged a moratorium on strikes. Some IWW members and maverick AFL locals ignored this advice, but with the economy booming, most workers observed the no-strike request.

The war's social impact took many forms. Job seekers pouring into industrial centers strained housing, schools, and municipal services. Consumption of cigarettes, which soldiers and workers could carry in their shirt pockets more easily than pipes or cigars, more than tripled. Reflecting wartime prosperity, automobile production jumped from 460,000 in 1914 to 1.8 million in 1917, then dipped briefly in 1918 as steel went for military production.

Farmers profited, too. With European farm production disrupted, U.S. agricultural prices, including cotton, corn, and other commodities, more than doubled between 1913 and 1918, and farmers' real income rose significantly. This agricultural boom proved a mixed blessing, however. Farmers who borrowed heavily to expand production faced a credit squeeze when farm prices fell after the war. In the 1920s and 1930s, hard-pressed farmers would look back to the war years as a golden age of prosperity.

Blacks Migrate Northward amid New Activist Energies

An estimated half-million African Americans moved north during the war, and most settled in cities. Each day, fresh arrivals poured into Philadelphia,

AN AFRICAN AMERICAN FAMILY ARRIVES IN CHICAGO, 1912 Seeking a better life, African Americans moved North in great numbers in the early twentieth century. Among the newcomers was Fraser Robinson, Jr., grandfather of Michelle Obama, the future first lady, who came to Chicago from South Carolina. *(Miriam and Ira D. Wallach Division of Art, Prints and Photographs, The New York Public Library. Astor, Lenox and Tilden Foundations)*

New York, Detroit, and Pittsburgh. Chicago's black population grew from forty-four thousand in 1910 to 110,000 in 1920, Cleveland's from eight thousand to thirty-four thousand.

With European immigration choked off by the war, booming industries hired more black workers. Some companies sent agents south to recruit black workers. African American newspapers like the *Chicago Defender* spread the word, as did letters and word-of-mouth reports. One southern black, newly settled near Chicago, wrote home, "Nothing here but money, and it is not hard to get." A Pittsburgh newcomer presented a more balanced picture: "They give you big money for what you do, but they charge you big things for what you get." As economic opportunity beckoned, impoverished southern blacks welcomed the prospect of securing jobs in a region where racism seemed less oppressive. By 1920, 1.5 million African Americans were working in northern factories and other urban-based jobs.

This vast population movement had profound social ramifications. Churches and storefront missions sprang up to serve deeply religious migrants from the South. As organizers for the National Association for the Advancement of Colored People built a national network of local branches, membership surged from 9,000 before the war to nearly 100,000 by the early 1920s. NAACP leaders pointed to African American support for the war to buttress their demand for equality.

The war profoundly affected African Americans' political consciousness as well. As Adriane Lentz-Smith argues in *Freedom Struggles: African Americans and World War I* (2009), blacks who served in the military and those who supported the war at home became convinced that their patriotic involvement would hasten the day when they would achieve full equality and the full rights of citizenship.

The struggle against racism faltered in the 1920s amid a white racist backlash, but the population movements and heightened race consciousness of the war years laid the groundwork for the civil-rights movement that lay ahead. The concentration of blacks in New York City set the stage for the Harlem Renaissance, a cultural flowering of the 1920s (covered in Chapter 23).

Still, African American newcomers in northern cities faced severe challenges. White workers resented the labor competition, and white homeowners lashed out as blacks moved into "their" neighborhoods. Tensions exploded on July 2, 1917, in East St. Louis, Illinois, home to thousands of recently arrived southern blacks. In a coordinated attack, a white mob torched black homes and shot the fleeing residents. At least thirty-nine blacks died, including a two-year-old who was shot and thrown into a burning house.

A few weeks later, an NAACP silent march down New York's Fifth Avenue protested racist violence. One banner echoed Wilson's phrase justifying U.S. involvement in the war: "Mr. President, Why Not Make AMERICA Safe for Democracy?"

A banner in an NAACP march read, "Mr. President, Why Not Make AMERICA Safe for Democracy?"

Women in Wartime

From one perspective, World War I seems a uniquely male experience. Male politicians led their nations into war. Male officers ordered other men into battle. Yet war touches all of society, not just half of it. The war affected women differently, but still profoundly.

Feminist leaders like Carrie Chapman Catt hoped that the war would lead to full equality and greater opportunity for women. For a time, these goals seemed attainable. In addition to the women holding AEF clerical positions and in wartime volunteer agencies, about 1 million women worked in industry. Thousands more held other jobs, from streetcar conductors to bricklayers. "Out of...repression into opportunity is the meaning of the war to thousands of women," wrote Florence Thorne of the American Federation of Labor in 1917.

A key victory for the woman-suffrage movement came in November 1917 when New York voters amended the state constitution to permit women to vote. In Washington, members of Alice Paul's National Woman's Party (see Chapter 21) picketed the White House and posted banners criticizing President Wilson for opposing woman suffrage at home while championing democracy abroad. Several protesters were jailed and force-fed when they went on a hunger strike. Pressured by all wings of the suffrage movement, Wilson declared that women's war service had earned them the right to vote. In 1919, barraged by pro-suffrage petitions, the House and Senate overwhelmingly passed the **Nineteenth Amendment** granting women the vote. Ratification soon followed.

Beyond this victory, however, the war did little to better women's status permanently. Relatively few women entered the work force for the first time in 1917–1918; most simply moved to better-paying jobs. But even in these jobs, most earned less than the men they replaced. As for the women in the AEF, the War Department refused their requests for military rank and benefits.

At the war's end, many women lost their jobs to returning veterans. The New York labor federation advised, "The same patriotism which induced women to enter industry during the war should induce them to vacate their positions after the war." Male streetcar workers in Cleveland went on strike to force women conductors off the job. In 1920, the percentage of U.S. women in the paid labor force was actually slightly lower than it had been in 1910.

Public-Health Crisis: The 1918 Influenza Pandemic

Along with the war's other effects, the nation in 1918 reeled under an outbreak of influenza (or "flu"), a highly contagious viral infection. The **influenza pandemic**, spread by a particularly deadly strain of the virus, killed an estimated 50 to 100 million people worldwide. Despite public-health advances, medical science had few weapons against influenza in 1918 (see Figure 22.1).

Originating in Africa, the virus spread from battlefields in France to U.S. military camps, striking Fort Riley, Kansas, in March 1918 and quickly advancing to other bases and the urban population. In September, a health official visiting Camp Devens in Massachusetts wrote, "I saw hundreds of young stalwart men in uniform coming into…the hospital. …The faces wore a bluish cast, a cough brought up blood-stained sputum. In the morning, the dead bodies are stacked about the morgue like cord-wood."

The flu hit the cities hard. After a September Liberty Loan rally in Philadelphia, doctors reported 635 new influenza cases. Many cities forbade public gatherings. In the worst month, October, influenza killed 195,000 Americans. The total U.S. death toll reached about 550,000, over six times the number of AEF battle deaths in France.

The development of a flu vaccine in the 1940s and of antibiotics to control influenza's secondary infections reduced the severity of later outbreaks, but flu pandemics remain a threat. In 2004, using tissue preserved from two U.S. soldiers who had died of influenza in 1918 and from the frozen corpse of another victim buried in the Alaska tundra, scientists successfully synthesized the 1918 virus for research purposes.

The War and Progressivism

The war had mixed effects on Progressive Era reform movements. It strengthened progressivism's coercive, moral-control aspect, including the drive to prohibit alcohol consumption. Pointing out the German origins of large breweries such as Pabst, Schlitz, and Anheuser-Busch, prohibitionists hinted that beer was a German plot to undermine American fitness. With food conservation a high priority, they stressed the wastefulness of using grain to make liquor. The **Eighteenth Amendment**

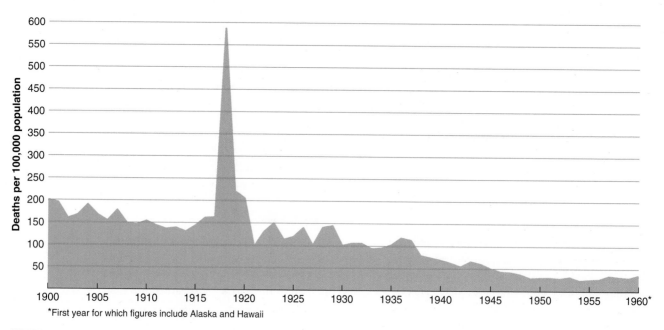

*First year for which figures include Alaska and Hawaii

FIGURE 22.1 U.S. DEATH RATE FROM INFLUENZA AND PNEUMONIA, 1900–1960 This chart shows the devastating toll of the 1918 influenza epidemic, as well as the gradual decline of influenza mortality thanks to the discovery of antibiotics that combat the secondary infections that are often fatal.

Source: *Historical Statistics of the United States: Colonial Times to 1970 (1975), vol. I, p. 58.* Note: Number of deaths per 100,000 population.

A U.S. Navy Admiral Copes with the Influenza Pandemic

The U.S.S. *Pittsburgh,* an armored cruiser and flagship of Rear Admiral William B. Caperton, with a crew of 829, patrolled in the South Atlantic during World War I under the command of Captain George Bradshaw. In October 1918, with the *Pittsburgh* anchored at Rio de Janeiro, Brazil, officers and crew suddenly had to cope with the influenza pandemic. Caperton's later account vividly conveys the terror of the outbreak, both on shipboard and in the city.

On the fourth of October we had noted that the so called Spanish influenza, which had passed thru Europe, had made its appearance in Brazil. ... On the arrival in Rio of the SS *Dannemara* from Lisbon and Dakar, Africa, the ship reported four deaths from the disease ... [but] the local health authorities ... made no effort to quarantine the vessel. ... By the seventh the *Pittsburgh* reported a few cases and the disease was incapacitating hundreds daily in Rio de Janeiro. ... By the 9th, 92 cases had made their appearance on board and hundreds ashore were dying. ... On the 14th of October 644 cases had been admitted to the [*Pittsburgh's*] sick list. ... The Commanding Officer [Captain Bradshaw] ... and two members of my staff were sick, while the disease raged unabated in Rio where conditions defied description.

The [Navy] Department directed me to ... proceed to Bahia, ... [b]ut the prescribed cruise ... was an impossibility. ... Conditions in the ship were rapidly becoming worse. More than half of the hospital corps were ill, ... [a]nd the drizzle and the rain which had set in ... continued fitfully, rendering it difficult to find room for the cots of the sick who had been kept on deck in the open, during the good weather. Ashore people died like flies, and many lay in the streets for two or three days waiting interment. ... By the 18th, twelve of the 48 pneumonia cases had died in the *Pittsburgh.* Further caskets could not be obtained ashore, at any price, and the burial of our men became an urgent necessity. ... On the 21st of October 16 bodies were taken from the *Pittsburgh* and landed for burial in the Sao Francisco Xavier Cemetery. Notwithstanding the previous arrangement with cemetery authorities for the opening of 20 graves, the funeral cortege arrived at the cemetery and found no graves prepared ... and we were finally compelled to dig the graves for our own dead shipmates.

Conditions in the cemetery beggared description. Eight hundred bodies in all states of decomposition, and lying about in the cemetery, were awaiting burial. Thousands of buzzards swarmed overhead. In the city itself there were no longer medicines, or wood for coffins and very little food. Rich and poor alike were stricken. In the big public hospital ... hundreds of naked bodies lay thrown upon each other like cord wood. ...

The ship had been unable to secure milk or fresh eggs and no chickens could be obtained in the market at any price. ... The American women of Rio de Janeiro immediately offered their assistance and soon an adequate supply of fresh milk, eggs and chickens was available for the sick at the hospital, while sweaters and pajamas were sent off to the ship for the hundreds still in the throes of the disease. By the 24th, 654 men were on the [sick] list. ... The army ... gave us one hundred beds in the hospital and the *Pittsburgh* transferred cooks and sufficient hospital corpsmen to care for the contingent ashore. The Rio Light and Power Company generously loaned us all manner of kitchen ware, glassware, ranges, mosquito netting, bed screens and other necessities for use in the hospital. ... By the 31st of October there had been 58 fatal cases, but great improvement was shown throughout the ship and many men were returned to duty. Ashore, ... the streets of Rio de Janeiro, generally gay and vivid with movement and color, were deserted and motionless. ... [N]ow and then some poor native with a miniature coffin on his head and followed by a sorrowful family trudged drearily to the nearest cemetery with his loved load. ... [T]here was hardly a family ashore where the hand of death had not left its trace.

Source: *William B. Caperton, "History of Flag Career of Rear Admiral William B. Caperton, U.S. Navy ...," pp. 377–382, National Archives and Records Administration, Washington DC, Record Group 45. Online at www.history.navy.mil/library/online/influenza_caper.htm.*

QUESTIONS

1. According to Caperton's narrative, how did the influenza pandemic first reach Rio de Janeiro?
2. How did the U.S. women of Rio de Janeiro assist the *Pittsburgh* crewmen suffering from influenza?

establishing national prohibition, which passed Congress in December 1917, was widely seen as a war measure. Ratified in 1919, it went into effect on January 1, 1920.

As we have seen, the war also strengthened the Progressive Era antiprostitution campaign. Congress appropriated $4 million to combat venereal disease among soldiers and war workers. The War Department closed red-light districts near military bases, including New Orleans's famed Storyville. (As Storyville's jazz musicians moved northward, jazz reached a national audience.) In San Antonio, a major military hub, an antiprostitution leader reflected the war mood when he declared, "We propose to fight vice…with the cold steel of the law, and to drive in the steel from the point to the hilt until the law's supremacy is acknowledged."

In the wartime climate of "vigilance," the antiprostitution drive expanded to a broader policing of morals. Female lecturers for the Commission on Training Camp Activities urged unmarried young women to practice chastity. "Do Your Bit to Keep Him Fit" one pamphlet advised. Wartime "protective bureaus" in major cities monitored women's behavior. In Boston, female social workers hid in the Common after dark to apprehend young women dating soldiers from nearby bases.

All this moral-reform activity convinced some that traditional codes of sexual behavior, weakening

before the war, had been restored. One antiprostitution crusader exulted, "Young men of today…are nearer perfection in conduct, morals, and ideals than any similar generation. …Their minds have been raised to ideals that would never have been attained save by the heroism of…the World War."

Labor reforms advanced as well. The Railroad Administration and the **War Labor Board** (WLB), spurred by progressives, encouraged workers to join unions and guaranteed unions' right to bargain with management. The WLB also pressured factory owners to introduce the eight-hour workday, end child labor, and open their plants to safety and sanitation inspectors. Under these favorable conditions, union membership rose from 2.7 million in 1916 to more than 5 million by 1920. Several state legislatures, eager to advance the war effort, passed wage-and-hour laws and other measures benefiting factory workers.

The **Bureau of War Risk Insurance** (BWRI), created in 1917 to aid soldiers' families, established a precedent of government help for families at risk. As Julia Lathrop, head of the Federal Children's Bureau, observed, "The least a democratic nation can do, which sends men into war, is to… [care for] the families." By the war's end, more than two million families were receiving regular BWRI checks.

Overall, however, at least in the short run, the war weakened the Progressive Era's powerful

BATTLING INFLUENZA, 1918 Red Cross workers like these in Philadelphia and other public-health professionals mobilized to combat a deadly epidemic that claimed more than half a million American lives. *(Courtesy American Red Cross)*

social-justice impulse. While the war brought stricter regulation of the economy—a key progressive goal—business interests often dominated the regulatory agencies, and these agencies were quickly dismantled after the war. The government's repression of radicals and antiwar dissenters fractured the fragile coalition of left-leaning progressives, women's groups, trade unionists, socialists, and politicians that had supported the prewar reforms, and ushered in a decade of reaction. The 1918 midterm election signaled the shift, as the Democrats lost both houses of Congress to a deeply conservative Republican Party.

> "Everything for which America has fought has been accomplished," Wilson proclaimed.

Nevertheless, taking a longer view, reform energies, after diminishing in the 1920s, would reemerge in the depression decade of the 1930s (covered in Chapter 24). As Franklin D. Roosevelt's New Deal took shape, the memory of such World War I agencies as the War Industries Board, the War Labor Board, and the Bureau of War Risk Insurance provided ideas and inspiration.

Joyous Armistice, Bitter Aftermath, 1918–1920

The euphoria that greeted the November 1918 armistice proved short lived. Having defined America's war aims in lofty terms, Woodrow Wilson dominated the 1919 peace conference but failed in his most cherished objective—American membership in the League of Nations. Amid a sour climate of racism and intolerance, the voters in 1920 repudiated Wilsonian idealism and internationalism and elected a conservative Republican as president.

Wilson's Fourteen Points; The Armistice

President Wilson took America to war determined to put his personal stamp on the peace. He and his reform-minded supporters believed that U.S. participation could transform a sordid squabble for power and empire into a crusade for a transformed world order. Wilson recruited a group of advisers to translate his vision into specific war aims. The need for such a statement grew urgent after the Bolsheviks, having seized power in Russia, published the self-serving secret treaties negotiated by European powers before the war.

Addressing Congress in January 1918, Wilson summed up U.S. war aims in fourteen points. Eight of these promised the subject peoples of the Austro-Hungarian and Ottoman empires the right of self-determination—that is, the freedom to choose their own political futures. A ninth point insisted that imperial disputes should consider the interests of the colonized peoples. The remaining five points offered Wilson's larger postwar vision: a world of free navigation, free trade, reduced armaments, openly negotiated treaties, and "a general association of nations" to resolve conflicts peacefully. The **Fourteen Points** solidified American support for the war, especially among liberals. They seemed proof that America was fighting for noble motives, not selfish aims.

In early October 1918, facing defeat, Germany proposed an armistice based on Wilson's Fourteen Points. The British and French hesitated, but when Wilson threatened to negotiate a separate peace, they agreed. Meanwhile, in Berlin, Kaiser Wilhelm II had abdicated and a German republic had been proclaimed.

In the early morning of November 11, 1918, the Allied commander Marshal Foch and his German counterparts signed an armistice ending hostilities at 11:00 A.M. Rockets burst over the front that night, not in anger but in relief and celebration. In America, cheering throngs (some wearing masks against the influenza epidemic) filled the streets. "Everything for which America has fought has been accomplished," Wilson proclaimed.

As troop ships ferried the soldiers home, Captain Harry Truman of Missouri described his feelings in a letter to his fiancée:

I've never seen anything that looks so good as the Liberty Lady in New York Harbor…[T]he men…have been in so many hard places that it takes something real to give them a thrill, but when the band…played "Home Sweet Home" there were not many dry eyes. The hardest of hard-boiled cookies even had to blow his nose a time or two.

The Versailles Peace Conference, 1919

Unwisely, Wilson decided to lead the U.S. delegation to the peace conference himself. The strain of long bargaining sessions would take its toll on his frail nerves. Wilson compounded his mistake by naming only one Republican to the delegation, an elderly diplomat with little influence in the party. Selecting more prominent Republicans might have spared Wilson future grief. The Democrats' loss of Congress in 1918 offered a further ill omen.

Nevertheless, crowds cheered and ships' whistles blared on December 4, 1918, as the *George Washington,* a converted German liner, left New York, bearing Wilson to Europe—the first sitting U.S. president to go abroad. The giddy mood continued when Wilson reached Europe. Shouts of "Voodrow Veelson" rang out as he rode up the Champs-Élysées, Paris's ceremonial boulevard. In England, children spread flowers in his path. The euphoria faded once the peace conference began at the palace of Versailles near Paris, where, 136 years before, diplomats had signed the treaty ending the Revolutionary War. Joining Wilson were the other Allied heads of state: Italy's Vittorio Orlando; France's aged and cynical Georges Clemenceau; and England's David Lloyd George, whom Wilson called "slippery as an eel." Japan participated as well.

The French and British came to the **Versailles Peace Conference** determined to punish Germany for their nations' wartime losses. Their vengeful, vindictive agenda bore little relation to Wilson's liberal vision. As Clemenceau remarked, "God gave us the Ten Commandments and we broke them. Mr. Wilson has given us the Fourteen Points. We shall see."

Reflecting this toxic climate, the peace treaty the sullen German delegation signed was harshly punitive. Germany was disarmed, stripped of its colonies, forced to admit sole blame for the war, and saddled with staggering reparation payments. France regained border provinces lost to Germany in 1871 and took control for fifteen years of Germany's coal-rich Saar Basin. The treaty demilitarized Germany's western border and transferred a slice of eastern Germany to Poland. These provisions cost Germany one-tenth of its population and one-eighth of its territory. The treaty gave Italy a slice of Austria that contained two hundred thousand German-speaking inhabitants. These harsh terms, bitterly resented in Germany, planted the seeds of World War II.

Some provisions did reflect Wilson's themes of democracy and self-determination. Germany's former colonies went to the various Allies under a "mandate" or trusteeship system that in theory promised eventual independence. The treaty also recognized the independence of Poland and the Baltic states of Estonia, Latvia, and Lithuania (seized by Germany in its 1918 peace treaty with Bolshevik Russia). Separate treaties provided for the independence of Czechoslovakia and Yugoslavia, new nations carved from the Austro-Hungarian and Ottoman empires.

Palestine, a part of the Ottoman Empire, went to Great Britain under a mandate arrangement. In 1917, after gaining military control of Palestine, the British had issued the Balfour Declaration supporting a Jewish "national home" in the region while also acknowledging the rights of the non-Jewish Palestinians.

But the statesmen of Versailles ignored the aspirations of colonized peoples in Asia and Africa—people like Ho Chi Minh. A young Vietnamese nationalist who would later lead his nation, Ho tried unsuccessfully to secure Vietnamese independence from France.

Nor did the peacemakers come to terms with revolutionary Russia. Indeed, in August 1918 a fourteen-nation Allied army, including some seven thousand U.S. troops, had landed at Russian ports, ostensibly to protect Allied war equipment. In fact, the aim was to overthrow the new Bolshevik regime, whose communist ideology terrified European and American leaders. President Wilson, having welcomed the liberal Russian revolution of March 1917, viewed the Bolshevik coup and Russia's withdrawal from the war as a betrayal of his hopes for a democratic Russia. Not until 1933 would the United States recognize the Soviet Union.

The Fight over the League of Nations

Dismayed by the treaty's vindictive features, Wilson focused on his one shining achievement at Versailles—a treaty provision, or covenant, creating a new international organization, the **League of Nations.** The League covenant embodied Wilson's vision of a new world order of peace and justice.

But Wilson's League faced major hurdles. A warning shot came in February 1919 when thirty-nine Republican senators and senators-elect, including powerful Henry Cabot Lodge, signed a letter rejecting the League in its present form. To reject the League covenant, Wilson retorted defiantly, would destroy the Versailles treaty's "whole vital structure."

When Wilson sent the treaty to the Senate for ratification in July 1919, Lodge bottled it up in the Foreign Relations Committee. To rally popular opinion, Wilson left Washington in September for a national speaking tour. Covering more than nine thousand miles by train, Wilson defended the League before large and friendly audiences. People wept as he described his visits to American war cemeteries in France and sketched his vision of a new world order.

But the trip exhausted Wilson, and on September 25 he collapsed in Colorado. His train sped back to Washington, where on October 2, he suffered a severe stroke. Wilson spent the rest of his term mostly in bed or in a wheelchair, a reclusive invalid,

THE VICTORIOUS ALLIED LEADERS IN PARIS, DECEMBER 1918 Seated, left to right: Vittorio Orlando (Italy), David Lloyd George (Great Britain), Georges Clemenceau (France), and Woodrow Wilson. The peace conference revealed deep divisions among the Allies, as Wilson promoted his visionary new world order, including a League of Nations, and the European powers pursued their own interests and imposed harsh terms on defeated Germany. *(Granger Collection)*

his fragile emotions betraying him into tearful outbursts and irrational, self-defeating actions. He broke with close advisers, refused to see the British ambassador, and dismissed Secretary of State Lansing, accusing him of disloyalty. In January 1920, he rejected his physician's advice to resign.

Wilson's first wife had died in 1914. His strong-willed second wife, Edith Galt, played a crucial behind-the-scenes role during this crisis. She concealed Wilson's condition from the public, controlled his access to information, and decided who could see him, barring cabinet members, diplomats, and congressional leaders. When one leader seeking a meeting urged Mrs. Wilson to consider "the welfare of the country," she snapped, "I am not thinking of the country now, I am thinking of my husband." (The Twenty-fifth Amendment,

addressing issues of presidential disability, was not adopted until 1967.)

Against this grim backdrop, the League drama unfolded. On September 10, 1919, the Foreign Relations Committee at last sent the treaty to the Senate, but with a series of amendments. The Senate split into three groups. First were Democrats who supported the treaty without changes, including U.S. membership in the League of Nations. Second were Republican "Irreconcilables," led by Hiram Johnson of California, Wisconsin's Robert La Follette, and Idaho's William Borah, who opposed the League absolutely. Intensely nationalistic, they feared that League membership would restrict U.S. freedom of action and entangle America with corrupt foreign powers. Finally, a group of Republican "Reservationists," led by Lodge, demanded amendments as a condition of their support. The Reservationists especially objected to Article 10 of the League covenant, which pledged each member nation to defend the independence and territorial integrity of all other members. This provision, they believed, limited America's sovereignty and infringed on Congress's constitutional power to declare war.

Had Wilson compromised, the Senate would probably have ratified the Versailles treaty, including the League covenant, with amendments. But Wilson, ill and unyielding, instructed Senate Democrats to reject the Foreign Relations Committee's version of the treaty, which now included Lodge's reservations. Although international-law specialists argued that these reservations would not prevent U.S. participation in the League, Wilson stood firm.

Despite Wilson's speaking tour, the public did not rally behind the League, thanks in part to the reactionary mood his own administration had helped create. As the *Nation* magazine observed, "If [Wilson] loses his great fight for humanity, it will be because he was deliberately silent when freedom of speech and the right of conscience were struck down in America."

On November 19, 1919, pro-League Democrats, obeying Wilson's instructions, and anti-League Irreconcilables joined forces to defeat the proposed measure that included Lodge's reservations. A second vote in March 1920 produced the same result. The United States would not join the forty-four nations who in January 1920 launched the League of Nations, the forerunner of the United Nations. What might have been Wilson's crowning achievement had turned to ashes.

Racism and Red Scare, 1919–1920

The war's strident patriotism left a bitter aftertaste. The years 1919–1920 brought new racial violence and anti-radical hysteria. Seventy-six blacks were lynched in 1919, the worst toll in fifteen years. The victims included ten veterans, several still in uniform. In Omaha, a mob inflamed by sensational newspaper stories seized a black prisoner from the courthouse, hanged him from a lamppost, dragged his body through the streets, and burned it. Henry Fonda, a future film actor, witnessed the lynching as a fourteen-year-old. "It was the most horrendous sight I'd ever seen," he later recalled.

The worst violence exploded in Chicago, where simmering racial tension erupted on a hot afternoon in July 1919. When a black youth swimming at a Lake Michigan beach drowned after whites had pelted him with stones, black neighborhoods erupted in fury. A thirteen-day reign of terror

followed as white and black marauders engaged in random attacks and arson. Black gangs stabbed an Italian peddler; white gangs pulled blacks from streetcars and shot or whipped them. The outbreak left fifteen whites and twenty-three blacks dead, more than five hundred injured, and more than a thousand families, mostly black, homeless.

Wartime antiradicalism crested in a postwar Red Scare. (Communists were called "reds" because of the red flag favored by revolutionary organizations.) A rash of strikes in 1919 deepened overwrought fears of a communist takeover in America. When the IWW and other unions called a general strike in Seattle, the panicky mayor accused the strikers of seeking to "duplicate the anarchy of Russia" and called for federal troops to maintain order. Anxiety crackled again in April, when various public officials received packages containing bombs. One severely injured a senator's maid; another damaged the home of Attorney General A. Mitchell Palmer. When 350,000 steelworkers went on strike in September, mill owners ran newspaper ads denouncing the leaders as "Red agitators."

Antiradical paranoia also infected politics. In 1919, the House of Representatives refused to seat

"REFUSING TO GIVE THE LADY A SEAT" In this newspaper cartoon published during the Senate battle over U.S. membership in the League of Nations, three Republican opponents of the League—William Borah of Idaho, Henry Cabot Lodge of Massachusetts, and Hiram Johnson of California—stubbornly refuse to give a seat to an angelic female passenger symbolizing peace. *(Library of Congress)*

CHICAGO RACE RIOT, 1919 This graphic photo vividly conveys the horrifying reality of the racial violence that struck Chicago in July 1919. *(Chicago History Museum)*

Milwaukee socialist Victor Berger, recently indicted under the Espionage Act. Milwaukee voters promptly reelected him, but the House stood firm. The New York legislature expelled several socialist members. The Justice Department set up an antiradical division under young J. Edgar Hoover, future head of the Federal Bureau of Investigation, who ordered the arrest of hundreds of suspected communists and radicals. In December 1919, the government deported 249 Russian-born aliens, including Emma Goldman, a prominent lecturer and birth-control advocate.

On January 2, 1920, in a Justice Department dragnet coordinated by Wilson's politically ambitious Attorney General, A. Mitchell Palmer, federal marshals and local police raided the homes of suspected radicals and the headquarters of radical organizations in thirty-two cities. Without search warrants or arrest warrants, they arrested more than four thousand persons (some 550 were eventually deported) and seized a horde of papers. Boston police paraded arrested persons through the streets in handcuffs and chains and jammed them into unsanitary cells without formal charges or the opportunity to post bail.

Gripped by anticommunist hysteria, Palmer luridly described the menace he believed his raids had averted: "The blaze of revolution was sweeping over every American institution of law and order…eating its way into the homes of the American workman, its sharp tongues of revolutionary heat…licking at the altars of the churches, leaping into the belfry of the school bell, crawling into the sacred corners of American homes…burning up the foundations of society."

The hysteria soon subsided. When a bomb exploded in New York City's financial district in September 1920, killing thirty-eight people, most Americans saw the deed as the work of an isolated fanatic, not evidence of approaching revolution.

The Election of 1920

As the 1920 election approached, the invalid Wilson, lost in fantasy, considered seeking a third term, but was dissuaded. Few heeded his call to make the election a "solemn referendum" on the League. "The bitterness toward Wilson is everywhere…," wrote a Democratic campaign worker; "he hasn't a friend."

The Democratic convention in San Francisco nominated James M. Cox, the mildly progressive governor of Ohio. As Cox's running mate they chose the young assistant secretary of the navy, Franklin D. Roosevelt, who possessed a potent political name.

The confident Republicans, meeting in Chicago, nominated Senator **Warren G. Harding** of Ohio, an amiable politician of little distinction. As one GOP leader observed, "There ain't any first raters this year. …We got a lot of second raters, and Harding is the best of the second raters." For vice president, they chose Massachusetts governor Calvin Coolidge, who had won attention in 1919 with his denunciation of a Boston policemen's strike.

Harding's vacuous campaign speeches reminded one critic of "an army of pompous phrases moving over the landscape in search of an idea." But many voters welcomed his reassuring promise of a return to "normalcy," and he won in a landslide. Nearly a million citizens defiantly voted for socialist Eugene Debs, still imprisoned for his earlier antiwar speeches (see Table 22.1).

TABLE 22.1 The Election of 1920

Candidates	Parties	Electoral Vote	Popular Vote	Percentage Popular Votes
WARREN G. HARDING	Republican	404	16,143,407	60.4
James M. Cox	Democrat	127	9,130,328	34.2
Eugene V. Debs	Socialist		919,799	3.4
P.P. Christensen	Farmer-Labor		265,411	1.0

The election dashed all hope for American entry into the League of Nations. Senator Lodge expressed grim satisfaction that the voters had ripped "Wilsonism" up by the roots. The sense of high purpose Wilson had evoked in April 1917 seemed remote indeed as Americans turned to a new president and a new era.

CONCLUSION

The early twentieth century saw intensifying U.S. involvement abroad. Focused initially on Latin America and Asia, this new globalism arose from a desire to export American values, promote U.S. business interests internationally, and extend the power of a newly confident, industrialized nation.

After initial neutrality, the nation's 1917 decision to enter the European war on the Allied side reflected a combination of cultural ties, economic interests, concern for neutral rights, and President Wilson's dream of a transformed world order emerging from the carnage.

By conservative estimates, World War I cost 10 million dead. Included in this toll were 112,000 American soldiers—forty-nine thousand in battle and sixty-three thousand from disease, mostly influenza. The toll of dead and injured reflected new technologies of warfare, from U-boat torpedoes and primitive aerial bombs to tanks, poison gas, and deadlier machine guns. The Allies won, but Wilson's visionary hopes, including American membership in the new League of Nations, went unrealized.

The war had far-reaching social, political, and economic effects. It advanced some reforms, notably woman suffrage and the campaigns against prostitution and alcohol. As war measures, the government expanded its regulatory power over corporations and took steps to ensure workers' well-being and right to organize. These initiatives offered models that would prove influential in the future.

But in a larger sense, the war undermined progressivism's openness to new ideas, its larger commitment to social justice, and its humanitarian concern for society's most vulnerable members. As government propaganda encouraged ideological conformity and fear of radicalism, the reform impulse withered. The reactionary climate intensified in the early postwar era.

The war at least temporarily improved the economic prospects of many workers, farmers, blacks, and women, and enhanced the standing of the corporate executives, psychologists, public-relations specialists, and other professionals who contributed their expertise to the cause. Internationally, despite the wrangles that kept America out of the League of Nations, the conflict underscored America's new status as a world power, and left the nation's businesses and financial institutions poised for global expansion.

Some of these changes endured; others proved fleeting. Cumulatively, however, their effect was profound. The nation that celebrated the armistice in November 1918 was very different from the one that Woodrow Wilson had solemnly taken into battle only nineteen months earlier.

KEY TERMS

Boxer Rebellion   (p. 667)
Open Door notes   (p. 667)
Panama Canal   (p. 668)
John J. Pershing   (p. 671)
Selective Service Act   (p. 674)
Commission on Training Camp
    Activities   (p. 675)
American Expeditionary Force
    (p. 675)

War Industries Board   (p. 676)
Committee on Public
    Information   (p. 680)
Espionage Act   (p. 685)
Sedition Amendment   (p. 685)
Nineteenth Amendment   (p. 687)
influenza pandemic   (p. 688)
Eighteenth Amendment   (p. 688)
War Labor Board   (p. 690)

Bureau of War Risk Insurance
    (p. 690)
Fourteen Points   (p. 691)
Versailles Peace Conference
    (p. 692)
League of Nations   (p. 692)
Warren G. Harding   (p. 695)

FOR FURTHER REFERENCE

Ernest Freeberg, *Democracy's Prisoner: Eugene V. Debs, the Great War, and the Right to Dissent* (2008). Uses Debs's imprisonment to illuminate larger controversies over the First Amendment and the postwar Red Scare.

Mark Ethan Grotelueschen, *The AEF Way of War: The American Army and Combat in World War I* (2007). Examines the U.S. Army's outdated battle doctrines and how these evolved during actual combat in France.

Robert E. Hannigan, *The New World Power: American Foreign Policy, 1898–1917* (2002). This work analyzes the values and world view of U.S. policymakers in a period of deepening global involvement.

Pearl James, ed., *Picture This: World War I Posters and Visual Culture* (2009). Illuminating transnational essays closely examining U.S., German, British, French, and Russian wartime propaganda posters.

David M. Kennedy, *Over Here: The First World War and American Society* (1980). Deeply researched interpretive history of the wartime home front.

Gina Bari Kolata, *Flu: The Story of the Great Influenza Pandemic of 1918 and the Search for the Virus That Caused It* (1999). Fascinating account by a *New York Times* science writer.

Adriane Lentz-Smith *Freedom Struggles: African Americans and World War I* (2009). Documents African Americans' wartime activism and rising expectations, the white racist reaction, and the after-effects of these developments.

Alexander Missal, *Seaway to the Future: American Social Visions and the Construction of the Panama Canal* (2008). Original study of the social and cultural meanings American writers and journalists found in the canal project.

David S. Patterson, *The Search for Negotiated Peace: Women's Activism and Citizens' Diplomacy in World War I* (2009). Documents women's international peace activism and the divisions that arose among U.S. woman-suffrage leaders.

Gerald E. Shenk, *"Work or Fight!": Race, Gender, and the Draft in World War I* (2006). This in-depth examination of four draft boards' records documents how local economic interests and prevailing assumptions about race, class, and gender influenced their rulings.

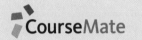

Visit the CourseMate website at **www.cengagebrain.com** for additional study tools and review materials for this chapter.

Coping with Change,

1920–1929

RUDOLPH VALENTINO IN *THE FOUR HORSEMEN OF THE APOCALYPSE* *(Granger Collection)*

AMONG THE MANY IMMIGRANTS arriving at Ellis Island in 1913 was the eighteen-year-old son of a veterinarian from a southern Italian village: Rodolfo Alfonso Raffaello Piero Filiberto Guglielmi di Valentina d'Antoguolla. After working as a gardener and dance instructor, he joined a touring operetta company that soon went bankrupt. Adrift in San Francisco, he met an actor who encouraged him to move to Hollywood, America's emerging movie capital. Shortening his name to "Rudolph Valentino," he appeared in fifteen short films in 1919–1920.

Stardom came in 1921 with *The Sheik* and *The Four Horsemen of the Apocalypse.* Appearing in romantic melodramas such as *Blood and Sand* (1922), *Monsieur Beaucaire* (1924), and *The Son of the Sheik* (1926), Valentino reigned as Hollywood's most popular male actor. With his good looks, swarthy skin, and piercing dark eyes, he exuded sex appeal, rousing fantasies of erotic adventures in female viewers. In this era of silent films, his poor English posed no problem. Movie magazines chronicled his two marriages and an affair with a famous actress, Pola Negri.

In August 1926, at thirty-one, Valentino died in New York after surgery for a perforated ulcer. Lines of female fans stretched for blocks around the funeral home. Pola Negri collapsed at the coffin. For several years thereafter, a veiled woman in black appeared each year on the anniversary of his death to place flowers at his grave in Hollywood. In a meteoric seven-year career, an unknown immigrant had become one of the brightest celebrities of a celebrity-obsessed decade. The popularity of the movies and their larger-than-life stars was only one novelty in a turbulent era that brought a Niagara of new consumer goods, a gushing flood of automobiles, and a babble of sound from millions of radios and phonographs. The decade also saw changing cultural values, creativity in the arts, and bitter social conflicts. With good reason, it soon acquired a nickname, "the Roaring Twenties."

Many features of contemporary American life may be traced to the 1920s. Indeed, this decade marks the dawn of the modern era. This chapter explores how different groups of Americans responded to technological, social, and cultural changes that could be both exciting and threatening.

A PLEASURE-MAD DECADE A 1925 railroad poster advertises the Lake Michigan beaches near Chicago. *(Chicago Historical Society)*

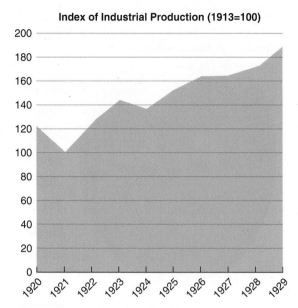

FIGURE 23.1 ECONOMIC EXPANSION, 1920–1929 After a brief postwar downturn, the American economy surged in the 1920s. © Cengage Learning. All rights reserved. No distribution allowed without express authorization.

Source: *U.S. Department of Commerce,* Long-Term Economic Growth *(Washington, DC: U.S. Government Printing Office, October 1966), 169.*

A New Economic Order

Fueled by new products and new ways of producing and selling goods, the economy surged in the 1920s. Not everyone benefited, and farmers suffered severe economic woes. Still, the overall picture appeared rosy. These economic changes influenced the decade's political, social, and cultural climate, as Americans confronted a changing society.

Booming Business, Ailing Agriculture

Recession struck in 1920 as Washington canceled wartime defense contracts and veterans reentered the job market. Recovery came by 1922, however, and for the next few years the nonfarm economy hummed as the gross national product (GNP) grew by 43 percent from 1922 to 1929 (see Figure 23.1).

New consumer goods, including electrical products, fed the prosperity. By the mid-1920s, with more than 60 percent of the nation's homes electrified, new appliances, from refrigerators to fans, filled the stores. The manufacture and marketing of such appliances, as well as the construction of hydroelectric generating plants, provided a massive economic stimulus.

The automobile helped fuel the boom. Introduced before the war (see Chapter 21), automobiles spread like wildfire in the 1920s. By 1930, some 60 percent of U.S. families owned cars (see Figure 23.2). Ford

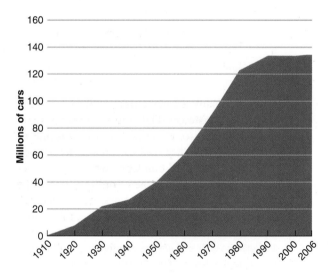

FIGURE 23.2 THE AUTOMOBILE AGE: PASSENGER CARS REGISTERED IN THE UNITED STATES, 1910–2006 From a plaything for the rich, the automobile emerged after 1920 as the basic mode of transportation for the masses. The number leveled off after 1990, as many people switched to sports utility vehicles (SUVs) and light trucks, which are not included in these statistics. © Cengage Learning. All rights reserved. No distribution allowed without express authorization.

Sources: Historical Statistics of the United States, Colonial Times to 1970 *(Washington, DC: U.S. Government Printing Office, 1975), 716;* Statistical Abstract of the United States, 1980–2009 *(Washington, DC: U.S. Government Printing Office).*

CHRONOLOGY 1920–1929

1920–1921	Postwar recession.
1920	Warren G. Harding elected president.
	League of Women Voters founded.
	Radio station KDKA, Pittsburgh, broadcasts election returns.
	Sinclair Lewis, *Main Street*.
1921	Economic boom begins; agriculture remains depressed.
	Sheppard-Towner Act.
	Shuffle Along, all-black musical review.
1921–1922	Washington Naval Arms Conference.
1922	Supreme Court declares child-labor law unconstitutional.
	Fordney-McCumber Tariff restores high rates.
	Herbert Hoover, *American Individualism*.
1923	Harding dies; Calvin Coolidge becomes president.
	Teapot Dome scandals investigated.
	National Origins Act (immigration restriction).
1924	Calvin Coolidge elected president.
1925	Scopes Trial.
	Ku Klux Klan scandal in Indiana.
1925 (Cont.)	Alain Locke, *The New Negro*.
	DuBose Heyward, *Porgy*.
	F. Scott Fitzgerald, *The Great Gatsby*.
1926	Book-of-the-Month Club founded.
	National Broadcasting Company founded.
	Langston Hughes, *The Weary Blues*.
	U.S. Marines intervene in Nicaragua.
1927	*The Jazz Singer*, first sound movie.
	Coolidge vetoes the McNary-Haugen farm bill.
	Henry Ford introduces the Model A.
	Ford apologizes for anti-Semitic publications.
	Execution of Sacco and Vanzetti.
	Charles A. Lindbergh's transatlantic flight.
	Marcus Garvey deported.
	Mississippi River flood.
1928	Herbert Hoover elected president.
1929	Federal Farm Board created.
	Sheppard-Towner program terminated.
	Textile strike in Gastonia, North Carolina.
	Ernest Hemingway, *A Farewell to Arms*.
	Claude McKay, *Home to Harlem*.

Motor Company led the market until mid-decade, when General Motors (GM) spurted ahead by touting comfort and color (Ford's Model T came only in black). GM's lowest-priced car, named for French automotive designer Louis Chevrolet, proved especially popular. In 1927 **Henry Ford** introduced the stylish Model A in various colors. By the decade's end, the automobile industry accounted for about 9 percent of all manufacturing wages and had stimulated such industries as rubber, gasoline and motor oil, advertising, and highway construction.

The stock market reflected the prevailing prosperity, and then far outran it, as a speculative frenzy gripped Wall Street (covered in Chapter 24).

To supply overseas markets, Ford, GM, and other corporations built production facilities abroad. U.S. meatpackers built plants in Argentina; Anaconda Copper bought Chile's biggest copper mine; the mammoth United Fruit Company established plants across Latin America. But true economic globalization lay far ahead. Economic nationalism prevailed in the 1920s, as the industrialized nations, including the United States, erected high tariff barriers. The Fordney-McCumber Tariff (1922) and the Smoot-Hawley Tariff (1930) pushed U.S. tariffs to all-time highs, helping domestic manufacturers but stifling foreign trade.

While prosperity lifted overall wages, workers benefited unequally, reflecting regional variations and discriminatory employment practices. Unskilled workers in the South earned about 40 percent less per hour than those in the North. Textile corporations moved south seeking lower wage rates, devastating New England mill towns. African Americans, women workers, Mexican Americans, and recent immigrants clustered at the bottom of the wage scale. For farmers, wartime prosperity gave way to hard times. Grain prices plummeted as government purchases for the army dwindled and America's high tariffs depressed agricultural exports. As tractors and other new machinery boosted farm production, the resulting surpluses further weakened prices. Farmers who had bought land and equipment on credit during the war felt the squeeze as payments came due.

New Modes of Producing, Managing, and Selling

Productivity increased in the 1920s as new assembly-line techniques boosted industrial workers' per capita output. At Ford plants near Detroit, workers stood in place and performed repetitive tasks as chains conveyed the vehicles past them.

Assembly-line work influenced employees' behavior. Managers discouraged individual initiative and even distracting conversation. Ford employees learned to speak without moving their lips and adopted an expressionless mask that some called "Fordization of the face." Job satisfaction diminished. Assembly-line labor did not foster the pride that came from farming or mastering a craft. Nor did it offer much prospect of advancement. In Muncie, Indiana, factories employing more than four thousand workers announced only ten openings for foremen in 1924–1925.

U.S. mass-production methods had a global impact. *Fordism* became a synonym worldwide for assembly-line manufacturing. In Russia, which purchased twenty-five thousand Ford tractors in the 1920s, people "ascribed a magical quality to the name of Ford," a visitor reported.

Business consolidation, spurred by the war, continued. By the late 1920s, more than a thousand companies a year vanished through merger. Corporate giants dominated the major industries. By 1930, one hundred corporations controlled nearly half the nation's business. Without actually merging, companies that made similar products formed trade associations to set prices and product specifications.

As U.S. capitalism matured, management structures evolved. Corporations set up separate divisions for product development, market research, economic forecasting, employee relations, and so on, each under a professional manager.

The shift to a consumer economy affected wage policies. Rather than paying the lowest wages possible, business leaders now realized that higher wages increased consumers' buying power. Henry Ford had led the way in 1914 by paying his workers five dollars a day, well above the average for factory workers. Other companies soon followed suit.

New systems for distributing goods emerged. Automobiles reached consumers through dealer networks. By 1926, nearly ten thousand Ford dealerships dotted the nation. Chain stores accounted for about 25 percent of retail sales by 1930. The A&P grocery chain boasted 17,500 stores. Department stores grew more inviting, with remodeled interiors and attractive displays. Air conditioning, a recent invention, made department stores (as well as movie theaters and restaurants) welcome havens on summer days.

Advertising and credit sales further stimulated the consumer economy. In 1929, corporations spent nearly $2 billion on radio, billboard, newspaper, and magazine ads, and advertising companies employed some six hundred thousand people. Advertisers used celebrity endorsements, promises of social success, and threats of social embarrassment. Beneath a picture of a sad young woman, a Listerine mouthwash ad proclaimed: "She was a beautiful girl and talented too. … Yet in the one pursuit … foremost in the mind of every girl and woman—marriage—she was a failure." Her problem was "halitosis," or bad breath. The remedy, of course, was Listerine, and lots of it.

Portraying a fantasy world of elegance, pleasure, and limitless abundance, ads aroused desires that the advertisers promised to fulfill. One critic in 1925 described the advertisers' "dream world":

[S]miling faces, shining teeth, schoolgirl complexions, cornless feet, perfect fitting [underwear], distinguished collars, wrinkleless pants, odorless breath, regularized bowels, … charging motors, punctureless tires, perfect busts, shimmering shanks, self-washing dishes, backs behind which the moon was meant to rise.

"HONEY, WHERE DID YOU PARK THE CAR?" Hundreds of identical Fords jam Nantasket Beach near Boston on a Fourth of July in the early 1920s. (*Archive/Getty Images*)

Advertisers even defined America's essential meaning in terms of its abundance of material goods. Buying more products, they claimed, fulfilled the "pursuit of happiness" promised in the Declaration of Independence and was thus the duty of all good citizens.

A few critics challenged the advertisers' cultural dominance. In *Your Money's Worth* (1927), Stuart Chase and F.J. Schlink punctured advertisers' exaggerated claims. The *Consumers' Research Bulletin,* launched by Chase and Schlink in 1929, tested products and reported the results to consumers.

Easy credit further lubricated the economy. Earlier, credit had typically involved pawnbrokers, bank loans, or informal arrangements between buyers and sellers. Now retailers routinely offered credit plans for big-ticket items such as automobiles, furniture, and refrigerators.

Business values saturated 1920s' culture. "America stands for one idea: Business," proclaimed the *Independent* magazine in 1921; "Thru business, ... the human race is finally to be redeemed." Presidents Harding and Coolidge praised corporate America and magazines profiled business tycoons. A 1923 opinion poll ranked Henry Ford as a leading presidential prospect. In *The Man Nobody Knows* (1925), ad man Bruce Barton described Jesus Christ as a managerial genius who "picked up twelve men from the bottom ranks of business and forged them into an organization that conquered the world."

> "America stands for one idea: Business."

Although the number of working women as a proportion of the total female population held steady in the 1920s at about 24 percent, male workers dominated the auto plants and other assembly-line factories. Women who did enter the workplace faced wage discrimination. In 1929, for example, a male trimmer in the meatpacking industry received fifty-two cents an hour; a female trimmer, thirty-seven cents. Most women workers, especially recent immigrants and members of minority groups, held low-paying, unskilled positions. By 1930, however, some 2 million women were employed in corporate offices as secretaries, rarely at higher ranks. Indeed, office-space arrangements often segregated male managers and female clerks.

Nearly fifty thousand women received college degrees in 1930, almost triple the 1920 figure. Of these female graduates who joined the work force, many entered such traditional "women's professions" as nursing, librarianship, and school teaching. With medical schools limiting the number of women students to 5 percent of their total enrollment, the number of women physicians actually declined from 1910 to 1930. A handful of women, however, following the lead of Progressive Era trailblazers, pursued postgraduate education to become faculty members in colleges and universities.

Marginalized in the workplace, women were courted as consumers. In the decade's advertising, glamorous women smiled behind the steering wheel, swooned over new appliances, and smoked cigarettes in romantic settings. (One ad man promoted cigarettes for women as "torches of freedom.") In the advertisers' dream world, housework became an exciting challenge. As one ad put it, "Men are judged ... according to their power to delegate work. Similarly the wise woman delegates to electricity all that electricity can do."

> "Men are judged ... according to their power to delegate work. Similarly the wise woman delegates to electricity all that electricity can do."

Struggling Labor Unions in a Business Age

Organized labor struggled in the 1920s. Union membership fell from 5 million to 3.4 million in the decade. Several factors underlay this decline. Despite inequities and regional variations, overall wage rates rose, reducing the incentive to join a union. Further, the movement's strength lay in traditional crafts and older industries like printing, railroading, mining, and construction, not in the new mass-production factories.

Management hostility further weakened organized labor. Henry Ford hired thugs to intimidate union organizers. In 1929, anti-union violence flared in North Carolina, where textile workers faced low wages, long hours, and appalling work conditions. In Marion, deputy sheriffs shot and killed six striking workers. In Gastonia, the communist-led National Textile Workers Union organized the strike. The mill's absentee owners refused to negotiate and evicted strikers from their company-owned homes. When armed thugs in league with the owners raided an encampment of strikers, the police chief was shot, possibly by one of his own deputies. In the end, these strikes failed, and the textile industry remained nonunion.

As wartime antiradical sentiments persisted, opponents of labor unions often smeared them with the "communist" label, whether accurate or not. The antiunion campaign took subtler forms

Blue Bird Electric Clothes Washer, 1920

THE EXCITING NEW WORLD OF ELECTRIC APPLIANCES In this 1920 ad, a bride contemplates the thrill of owning her very own electric washing machine. Pay only "a few dollars" down, the ad promised, and the balance "in convenient monthly sums." *(Picture Research Consultants & Archives)*

as well. Manufacturers' associations renamed the nonunion shop the "open shop" and dubbed it the "American Plan" of labor relations. Some corporations provided cafeterias and recreational facilities. Corporate publicists praised "welfare capitalism" (the term for this anti-union strategy) as evidence of employers' benevolent concern for their workers.

The weakening of the union movement hit women workers hard. By 1929, the proportion of women workers belonging to unions fell to a minuscule 3 percent.

Black membership in labor unions stood at only about eighty-two thousand by 1929, mostly miners, dockworkers, and railroad porters. The American Federation of Labor officially prohibited racial discrimination, but most AFL unions in fact barred African Americans. Corporations often hired jobless blacks as strikebreakers, increasing organized labor's hostility toward them.

Standpat Politics in a Decade of Change

With Republicans in control of Congress and the White House, politics reflected the decade's business orientation. Unsettled by rapid social change, voters turned to conservative candidates who seemed to represent stability and traditional values. In this climate, would-be reformers and exploited groups had few political options.

The Evolving Presidency: Scandals and Public-Relations Manipulation

While white southerners and urban immigrants remained heavily Democratic, the Republican Party continued to attract northern farmers, businesspeople, many white-collar workers and professionals, and some skilled blue-collar workers. The GOP also benefited from the antiradical mood that fueled the early postwar Red Scare (see Chapter 22) and the anti-union campaign. Exploiting such fears, the Republican-led New York legislature set up a committee to investigate "seditious activities" and required loyalty oaths of public-school teachers.

With Republican progressives having bolted to Theodore Roosevelt in 1912, GOP conservatives controlled the 1920 convention and nominated Ohio Senator **Warren G. Harding** for president. As a young newspaper editor, Harding had married the local banker's daughter, who helped manage his 1914 Senate campaign. A genial backslapper, he enjoyed good liquor, a good poker game, and at least one long-term extramarital affair. In the election, Harding swamped his Democratic opponent James

M. Cox. After the stresses of war and Wilson's moralizing, voters welcomed Harding's bland oratory.

Harding made some notable cabinet selections: Henry C. Wallace, the editor of an Iowa farm periodical, as secretary of agriculture; **Charles Evans Hughes,** former New York governor and 1916 presidential candidate, secretary of state; and **Andrew Mellon,** a Pittsburgh financier, treasury secretary. **Herbert Hoover,** the wartime food czar, became secretary of commerce.

Harding also made some disastrous appointments: his political manager, Harry Daugherty, as attorney general; a Senate pal, Albert Fall of New Mexico, as secretary of the interior; a wartime draft dodger, Charles Forbes, as Veterans' Bureau head. Such men set the low ethical tone of Harding's presidency. By 1922, Washington rumor hinted at corruption in high places. "I have no trouble with my enemies," Harding told an associate; "[b]ut … my goddamn friends … keep me walking the floor nights." In summer 1923, vacationing in the West, Harding suffered a heart attack and died in a San Francisco hotel.

> "I have no trouble with my enemies," Harding told an associate; "[b]ut … my goddamn friends … keep me walking the floor nights."

A 1924 Senate investigation exposed the scandals. Charles Forbes, convicted of stealing Veterans' Bureau funds, evaded prison by fleeing abroad. The bureau's top lawyer committed suicide, as did an aide to Attorney General Daugherty accused of influence peddling. Daugherty himself narrowly escaped conviction in two criminal trials. Interior Secretary Fall went to jail for leasing government oil reserves, one in Teapot Dome, Wyoming, to oilmen in return for a $400,000 bribe. Like "Watergate" in the 1970s, **"Teapot Dome"** became a shorthand label for a tangle of scandals.

With Harding's death, Vice President **Calvin Coolidge,** on vacation in Vermont, took the presidential oath by lantern light from his father, a local magistrate. After entering local politics in Massachusetts, Coolidge had been elected Massachusetts governor in 1918 and secured the Republican vice-presidential nomination in 1920.

Coolidge's image as "Silent Cal," a Yankee embodiment of old-fashioned virtues, was carefully crafted. The advertising executive Bruce Barton, an early master of political image-making, guided Coolidge's bid for national office in 1919–1920. Having persuaded a Boston publisher to issue a book of Coolidge's speeches, Barton sent autographed copies to key GOP convention delegates. Barton planted pro-Coolidge articles in

PRESIDENT HARDING WITH LADDIE, JUNE 1922 As politicians learned the arts of publicity, posed scenes like this became more common. *(Library of Congress)*

magazines and in other ways marketed his candidate just as advertisers were marketing soap, socks, and cereal. The very name *Calvin Coolidge*, he wrote in a *Collier's* magazine article building brand recognition, "seems cut from granite; one could almost strike sparks with such a name, like a flint." Targeting newly enfranchised women, Barton composed a "Message to Women" published under Coolidge's name in *Woman's Home Companion*.

Long before Franklin D. Roosevelt's "fireside chats" of the 1930s (covered in Chapter 24), Bruce Barton understood the political potential of radio. He advised Coolidge to speak conversationally in his radio addresses, avoiding earlier politicians' spread-eagle oratory. Wrote an admirer of Barton: "No man is his equal in [analyzing] the middle-class mind and directing an appeal to it."

Republican Policy Making in a Probusiness Era

While Coolidge raised the ethical tone of the White House, the probusiness policies, symbolized by high tariffs, continued. Prodded by Treasury Secretary Mellon, Congress lowered income-tax rates for the wealthy from their high wartime levels. Lower tax rates for the well-to-do, Mellon argued, would actually increase revenues by reducing the incentive to seek tax shelters. He also contended that tax cuts for high-income earners encouraged business investment and thus benefited everyone. In the same probusiness spirit, the Supreme Court under Chief Justice William Howard Taft (appointed by Harding in 1921) overturned a federal ban on child labor passed in 1919.

While promoting corporate interests, Coolidge opposed government assistance for other Americans. This position faced a test in 1927 when torrential spring rains caused severe flooding on the Mississippi River. Soil erosion resulting from poor farming practices worsened the flood conditions, as did ill-considered engineering projects aimed at draining the river's natural floodplain for development purposes. One official described the river as "writh[ing] like an imprisoned snake" within its artificial confines. From Cairo, Illinois, to the Gulf of Mexico, water poured over towns and farms, flooding twenty-seven thousand square miles. Hundreds died, and the toll of the homeless, including many African Americans, reached several hundred thousand. Disease spread in makeshift refugee camps. Floodwaters swept over New Orleans's low-lying black neighborhoods.

President Coolidge rejected calls to aid the victims. The government had no duty to protect citizens "against the hazards of the elements," he declared. Coolidge did, however, sign the Flood Control Act of 1928 funding levee construction along the Mississippi.

Another test of Coolidge's antigovernment ideology came when hard-pressed farmers rallied behind the **McNary-Haugen Bill,** a price-support plan under which the government would purchase the surplus of six basic farm commodities—cotton, corn, rice, hogs, tobacco, and wheat—at their average price in 1909–1914 (when farm prices were high). The government would then sell these surpluses abroad at market prices and recover the difference, if any, through a tax on domestic sales of these commodities. Coolidge twice vetoed the McNary-Haugen bill, warning of "the tyranny of bureaucratic regulation and control." The government must not favor a single interest group, he argued—even though corporations had long benefited from high tariffs and other measures. These vetoes led many angry farmers to vote Democratic in 1928. In the 1930s, New Deal planners would draw upon the McNary-Haugen approach in shaping farm policy (as discussed in Chapter 24).

> The government had no duty to protect citizens "against the hazards of the elements," Coolidge declared.

Independent Internationalism

The Harding and Coolidge administrations continued to oppose U.S. membership in the League of Nations. Coolidge did support U.S. membership in the new International Court of Justice (the World Court), but the Republican-controlled Congress imposed unacceptable reservations, and the United States did not join.

Backing away from Woodrow Wilson's idealistic view of America's global destiny, the Republican administrations of the 1920s pursued foreign policies that served America's economic interests—an approach historians have called "independent internationalism." Despite postwar Europe's battered economies, Washington demanded repayment of $22 billion in Allied war debts and German reparation payments. A study commission in 1924 reduced these claims, but high U.S. tariffs and Europe's economic problems, including runaway inflation in Germany, made repayment of even the lower claims unrealistic. When Adolf Hitler took power in Germany in 1933 (covered in Chapter 25), he repudiated all reparations payments.

The Republican administrations worked to protect U.S. corporate interests in Latin America. In Mexico, the U.S. State Department vigorously opposed the efforts of a new revolutionary government to regain control of oilfields earlier granted to U.S. companies and to restrict landholding by foreign interests. In Nicaragua, President Coolidge in 1926 sent U.S. Marines to put down an insurrection against the country's president, Adolfo Diàz, who had close ties to a U.S.-owned gold-mining company.

One notable diplomatic achievement was the **Washington Naval Arms Conference.** After the war ended, the United States, Great Britain, and Japan edged toward a dangerous (and costly) naval-arms race. In 1921, Secretary of State Hughes called a Washington conference to address the problem. He startled the delegates by outlining a specific ratio of warships among the world's naval powers. Great Britain, Japan, Italy, and France accepted Hughes's plan, and agreed to halt battleship construction for ten years. The United States and Japan also pledged to respect each other's territorial holdings in the Pacific. Although this treaty ultimately failed to prevent World War II, it did represent an early arms-control effort.

Another U.S. peace initiative was mainly symbolic. In 1928, the United States and France, eventually joined by sixty other nations, signed the Kellogg-Briand Pact renouncing aggression and outlawing war. Lacking enforcement mechanisms, this high-sounding document accomplished little.

Progressive Stirrings, Democratic Party Divisions

The reform spirit survived in Congress. The **Sheppard-Towner Act** (1921) funded rural prenatal and baby-care centers staffed by public-health nurses. The Federal Radio Commission, created by Congress in 1927, extended the regulatory principle to this new industry. A reform-minded Nebraska senator, George Norris, prevented the Coolidge administration from selling a wartime federal hydroelectric plant to Henry Ford at bargain prices. In the 1930s, this Alabama plant would become part of the Tennessee Valley Authority, a key New Deal agency.

In the 1922 midterm election, labor and farm groups joined forces to defeat some conservative

THE 1927 MISSISSIPPI RIVER FLOOD A few of the 700,000 people displaced by the raging waters of the Mississippi await rescue, their partially submerged homes in the background. President Calvin Coolidge resisted calls for federal aid. *(Special Collections Research Center, University of Chicago Library)*

Republicans. In 1924, this alliance revived the Progressive Party and nominated Senator Robert La Follette for president. The Socialist Party and the American Federation of Labor endorsed La Follette.

The 1924 Democratic convention in New York City split between urban and rural wings. By one vote, the delegates defeated a resolution condemning the **Ku Klux Klan** (discussed later in this chapter). While the party's Protestant southern wing favored former Treasury Secretary William G. McAdoo, the big-city delegates championed New York's Catholic governor **Alfred E. Smith,** of Irish, German, and Italian immigrant origins. This split mirrored deep divisions in the nation. After 102 ballots, the exhausted delegates nominated an obscure New York corporation lawyer, John W. Davis.

Calvin Coolidge, aided by media adviser Barton, easily won the Republican nomination. The GOP platform praised the high protective tariff and urged tax cuts and reduced government spending. Amid general prosperity, Coolidge polled about twice Davis's total. La Follette's 4.8 million votes cut into the Democratic total, contributing to Coolidge's landslide victory.

Women and Politics in the 1920s: Achievements and Setbacks

With the ratification of the Nineteenth Amendment in August 1920, the long struggle for women's suffrage succeeded at last, and women streamed to the polls for the first time in a national election that November. (Charlotte Woodward, a youthful signer of the "Declaration of Sentiments" at the 1848 Women's Rights Convention in Seneca Falls, New York, survived to see women vote in 1920.) Suffrage advocates had long predicted that this reform would transform politics, and this hope survived briefly after the war. Polling places shifted from saloons to schools and churches. Carrie Chapman Catt and other suffrage leaders founded the nonpartisan **League of Women Voters** in 1920 to educate voters on issues and research civic issues. The 1920 major-party platforms endorsed several measures proposed by the League. The **Women's Joint Congressional Committee** (WJCC), a coalition of activist groups, lobbied for child-labor laws, protection of women workers, maternal health care, and federal support for education. The WJCC played a key role in passage of the

LEADERS OF THE LEAGUE OF WOMEN VOTERS VISIT THE WHITE HOUSE With the passage of the Nineteenth Amendment in 1920, both parties courted women voters. What does the dress of these women suggest about the social class status of the League of Women Voters? *(© Bettmann/Corbis)*

Sheppard-Towner Act and in congressional enactment of a constitutional amendment banning child labor in 1924.

As former suffragists scattered across the political spectrum, however, the movement lost focus. The League of Women Voters, drawing mainly white middle-class and professional women, played a role in the formation of the WJCC, but otherwise gradually abandoned feminist activism. Alice Paul's National Woman's Party proposed a constitutional amendment guaranteeing women equal rights, but other reformers argued that it could jeopardize laws protecting women workers. Politically active African American women battled racial discrimination rather than addressing feminist issues; Hispanic women in the Southwest focused on labor-union organizing.

The reactionary political climate intensified this retreat from feminist activism. Patriotic groups accused Jane Addams and other woman's-rights leaders of communist sympathies. Younger women, bombarded by ads defining liberation in terms of consumption, rejected the prewar feminists' civic engagement. One in 1927 criticized earlier suffragists' lack of "feminine charm" and

their "constant clamor about equal rights."

The reforms backed by women's groups proved short-lived. The Supreme Court struck down child-labor and women's-protective laws. Few states ratified the constitutional amendment banning child labor, as critics accused its supporters, including the WJCC, of undermining the free-enterprise system. The Sheppard-Towner Act, denounced by the American Medical Association for weakening physicians' monopoly of health care, expired in 1929.

> One young woman criticized earlier suffragists' lack of "feminine charm" and their "constant clamor about equal rights."

Mass Society, Mass Culture

Amid this conservative political climate, major transformations were reshaping society. Assembly lines, advertising, new consumer products, and innovations in mass entertainment and corporate organization all fueled the ferment. While some welcomed these changes, others recoiled in fear.

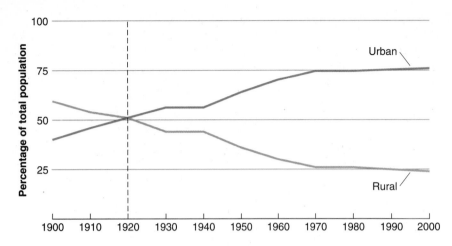

FIGURE 23.3 THE URBAN AND RURAL POPULATION OF THE UNITED STATES, 1900–2000 The urbanization of America in the twentieth century had profound political, economic, and social consequences.

Source: Census Bureau, Historical Statistics of the United States, *updated by relevant* Statistical Abstracts of the United States, and U.S. Department of Transportation, Federal Highway Administration.

Cities, Cars, Consumer Goods

In the 1920 census, the urban population (defined as persons living in communities of twenty-five hundred or more) surpassed the rural (see Figure 23.3). The United States had become an urban nation.

Urbanization affected different groups in different ways. African Americans migrated cityward in massive numbers, especially after the 1927 Mississippi River floods. By 1930, more than 40 percent of the nation's 12 million blacks lived in cities, 2 million of them in urban centers of the North and West (see Figure 23.4). The first black congressman since Reconstruction, Oscar De Priest of Chicago, won election in 1928.

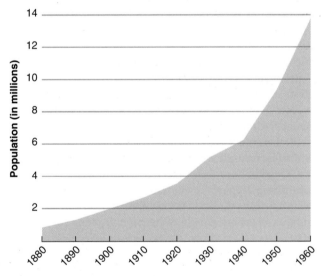

FIGURE 23.4 THE AFRICAN AMERICAN URBAN POPULATION, 1880–1960 (IN MILLIONS) The increase in America's urban black population from under 1 million in 1880 to nearly 14 million by 1960 represents one of the great rural-urban migrations of modern history. © Cengage Learning. All rights reserved. No distribution allowed without express authorization.

Source: Historical Statistics of the United States, Colonial Times to 1970 (Washington, DC: Bureau of the Census, 1975), vol. I, p. 12.

For many women, city life meant eased housework thanks to laborsaving appliances. Store-bought clothes replaced hand-sewn apparel. Home baking and canning declined as bakeries and supermarkets proliferated.

For social impact, nothing matched the automobile. In *Middletown* (1929), a study of Muncie, Indiana, Robert and Helen Lynd reported one resident's comment: "Why ... do you need to study what's changing this country? I can tell you ... in just four letters: A-U-T-O."

The A-U-T-O's social impact proved decidedly mixed, including traffic jams, parking problems, and highway fatalities (more than twenty-six thousand in 1924). In some ways, the automobile brought families together. As family vacations became more common, tourist cabins and roadside restaurants sprang up. But the automobile also eroded family cohesion and parental authority. Young people could borrow the car to catch a movie, attend a distant dance, or park in a secluded lovers' lane.

Middle- and upper-class women welcomed the automobile. They could now drive to work, attend meetings, visit friends, and gain a sense of independence. Stereotypes of feminine delicacy faded as women mastered this new technology. As an automotive magazine editorialized in 1927, "[E]very time a woman learns to drive, ... it is a threat to yesterday's order of things."

Automobiles offered farm families easier access to neighbors and to the city, lessening rural isolation. The automobile's country cousin, the tractor, increased productivity and reduced the physical demands of farming. Yet increased productivity did not always mean increased profits. And as farmers bought automobiles, tractors, and other mechanized equipment on credit, the rural debt crisis worsened.

Ads celebrated the freedom automobiles offered, in contrast to the fixed routes and schedules of trains and streetcars. Yet the automobile and other forms of motor transport also further standardized American life. Buses carried children to consolidated schools. Neighborhood grocery stores declined as people drove to supermarkets served by trucks bringing commercial foods from distant facilities. With the automobile came the first suburban shopping center (in Kansas City) and the first fast-food chain (A & W Root Beer).

Even at $300 or $400, and despite a thriving used-car market, automobiles remained too expensive for many. The "automobile suburbs" that sprang up beyond the streetcar lines attracted mainly the well-to-do, widening class divisions in American society.

Soaring Energy Consumption and Environmental Threats

Electrification and the spread of motorized vehicles impacted America's natural resources and the environment. Electrical generating plants consumed growing quantities of coal. In 1929, U.S. refineries used more than a billion barrels of petroleum to meet the gasoline and oil demands of the nation's 20 million cars.

Rising gasoline consumption underlay Washington's efforts to ensure U.S. access to Mexican oil and triggered feverish competition in the oilfields of Texas and Oklahoma. The natural gas found with petroleum seemed so abundant that it was simply burned off. In short, heavy fossil-fuel consumption, though small by later standards, already characterized America in the 1920s.

The wilderness that had inspired nineteenth-century artists and writers became more accessible as cars and improved roads gave easier access to national parks and once-pristine regions. While this development broadened the constituency for wilderness preservation, it also subjected the nation's parks and wilderness areas to heavy pressures as vacationers came to expect service stations, restaurants, hotels, and other amenities. Worried by such contradictions, Secretary of Commerce Herbert Hoover in 1924 called a National Conference on Outdoor Recreation to consider ways to balance wilderness preservation and the decade's vacation-minded leisure culture.

The Sierra Club and other groups battled to protect wilderness and wildlife. In 1923, the Izaak Walton League, serving fishing enthusiasts, persuaded Congress to halt a development scheme to drain wetlands on the upper Mississippi. Instead, Congress declared this beautiful waterway a wildlife preserve.

For too long, wrote preservationist Aldo Leopold, "a stump was our symbol of progress."

For too long, wrote preservationist Aldo Leopold in 1925, "a stump was our symbol of progress." However, few Americans in the expansive 1920s worried about the environmental issues that would occupy future generations.

Mass-Produced Entertainment

Prosperity and workplace drudgery stimulated leisure activities in the 1920s. In their free hours, Americans sought the fulfillment their jobs often failed to provide.

Mass-circulation magazines proliferated. By 1922, ten U.S. magazines boasted circulation of more than 2.5 million. The *Saturday Evening Post*, with its Norman Rockwell covers and fiction featuring small-town life, specialized in nostalgia. *Reader's Digest,* founded in 1921 by DeWitt and Lila Wallace, offered condensed versions of articles first published elsewhere. A journalistic equivalent of the Model T, the *Digest* offered standardized fare for mass consumption.

Book publishers expanded their market by selling through department stores or directly to the public via the Book-of-the-Month Club (founded 1926). While some criticized such mass-market ventures for debasing literary taste, they did help sustain a common national culture in an increasingly diverse society.

Radio and the movies similarly offered standardized cultural fare. The radio era began on November 2, 1920, when Pittsburgh station KDKA reported Warren Harding's election. In 1922, New York's WEAF began a regular news program, and a Newark station broadcast the World Series (the New York Giants beat the Yankees). Hundreds of new stations soon began operations, as radio fever gripped America.

In 1926, three corporations—General Electric, Westinghouse, and the Radio Corporation of America—formed the first radio network, the National Broadcasting Company (NBC). The Columbia Broadcasting System (CBS) soon followed. Testing popular taste through market research, the networks soon ruled broadcasting. Americans everywhere laughed at the same jokes, heard the same news, and absorbed the same commercials.

Some public-policy commentators advocated preserving radio as an educational and cultural medium, free of advertising, but commercial sponsorship soon won out. The first network comedy show, *Amos 'n Andy* (1928), enriched its sponsor, Pepsodent toothpaste. White actors played the black characters on the program, which softened the realities of a racist society with stereotyped caricatures of African American life.

The movies migrated from the nickelodeons of the immigrant wards to elegant uptown pleasure palaces and reached all social classes. Los Angeles and its nearby suburb Hollywood, with abundant sunlight ideal for filming, replaced New York as the nation's film capital. In 1922, facing protests about sexually suggestive movies, industry moguls named Postmaster General Will Hays, a former head of the Republican National Committee, to police movie morals. While enforcing a code of standards, Hays also promoted Hollywood films.

Despite charges of immorality, movies often reinforced conservative values. *The Ten Commandments* (1923), directed by Cecil B. De Mille (the son of an Episcopal clergyman), cautioned against breaking moral taboos. "America's sweetheart," Mary Pickford, with her look of frail vulnerability, played innocent girls in need of protection, reinforcing traditional gender stereotypes that many young women were challenging. (Pickford herself sometimes played plucky young women facing danger courageously, and in real life she shrewdly managed her career and financial interests.)

Technical innovations kept moviegoers coming. Al Jolson's *The Jazz Singer* (1927) introduced sound. Walt Disney's cartoon *Steamboat Willy* (1928) not only introduced Mickey Mouse but also showed the potential of animation. By 1930, with weekly attendance approaching 80 million, the corporate giants Metro-Goldwyn-Mayer, Warner Brothers, and Columbia, relying on formulaic plots and typecast stars, produced most films. As U.S. business expanded abroad, Hollywood, too, sought overseas markets.

Like advertising, the movies created a dream world only loosely tethered to reality. One ad promised "all the adventure, …romance, …[and] excitement you lack in your daily life." These mass-produced fantasies shaped behavior and values, especially of the young. Hollywood, observed novelist John Dos Passos, offered a "great bargain sale of five-and-ten-cent lusts and dreams." Along with department stores, mass magazines, and advertising, the movies, too, stimulated consumption with alluring images of the good life, opening new vistas of consumer abundance (see Going to the Source).

> Hollywood offered a "great bargain sale of five-and-ten-cent lusts and dreams."

RADIO: THE EARLY YEARS In 1925, to promote the Ringling Brothers Barnum & Bailey Circus, radio station WJZ in New York City offered an hour-long broadcast of circus sounds, including the bellowing of Dolly, a two-year-old elephant. *(Library of Congress)*

A College Student Recalls Her Movie-Going Experiences in the 1920s

In the early 1930s, sociologist Herbert Blumer asked more than 1,500 young people to write their "motion-picture autobiographies." Here are excerpts from the recollections of a twenty-two year old young woman.

[T]he first time that I went to a movie ... must have been when I was very young, because I cannot recall the event.... At fifteen I liked the stories of modern youth; the gorgeous clothes and settings fascinated me. My first favorite was Norma Talmadge ... in a picture where she wore ruffly hoop-skirts which greatly attracted me.... I like Joan Crawford because she is so modern, so young, and so vivacious! Billie Dove is so beautifully beautiful that she just gets under your skin.... Sue Carol is cute 'n' peppy. Louise Brooks has her assets, those being legs and a clever hair-cut. Norma Shearer wears the kind of clothes I like and is a clever actress.

The day-dreams instigated by the movies consist of clothes, ideas on furnishings, and manners. I don't day-dream much, ... [but] it is hard for any girl not to imagine herself cuddled up in some voluptuous ermine wrap, etc.

I'm always at the mercy of the actor at a movie. I feel nearly every emotion he portrays.... Movies do change my moods, but they never last long. I'm off on something else before I know it. If I see a dull or morose show, it sort of deadens me and the vim and vigor dies out 'til the movie is forgotten....

Goodness knows, you learn plenty about love from the movies.... You meet the flapper, the good girl, 'n' all the feminine types and their little tricks of the trade. We pick up their snappy comebacks which are most handy when dispensing with an unwanted suitor, a too ardent one, too backward one, etc. ...

I can remember when we all nudged one another and giggled at the last close-up in a movie. I recall [one] ... close-up when the boyfriend squeezes your arm and looks soulfully at you. Oh, it's lotsa fun! No, I never fell in love with my movie idol ... [or wrote] them idiotic letters as some girls I've known do. I have imagined playing with a movie hero many times, though, ... while I'm watching the picture. I forget about it when I'm outside the theater. Buddy Rodgers and Rudy Valentino have kissed me oodles of times, but they don't know it. God bless 'em!"

Yes, love scenes have thrilled me and have made me more receptive to love. I was going with a fellow whom I liked as a playmate, so to speak; he was a little younger than me and he liked me a great deal. We went to the movie [*Adoration*, 1928]—Billie Dove in it..., Antonio Moreno was the lead, and there were some lovely scenes which just got me all hot 'n' bothered. After the movie we went for a ride 'n' parked along the lake; it was a gorgeous night. Well, I just melted (as it were) in his arms, making him believe I loved him, which I didn't. I sort of came to, but I promised to go steady with him. I went with him till I couldn't bear the sight of him. ... I've wished many times that we'd never seen that movie. Another thing not exactly on the subject, but important, I began smoking after watching Dolores Costello, I believe it was, smoke, which hasn't added any joy to my parents' lives.

Source: Herbert Blumer, *Movies and Conduct* (New York, 1933), excerpts in Robert Sklar, ed., *The Plastic Age, 1917–1930* (New York, 1970), pp. 44–47.

QUESTIONS

1. As this young woman discusses her favorite film actresses, what traits does she single out for admiration?
2. On the basis of this memoir, in what ways did the movies most significantly influence young people's behavior and values in the 1920s?

The 1920s mass culture was a byproduct of urbanization. Even when advertisers, radio programmers, filmmakers, and magazine editors nostalgically evoked rural or small-town life, they did so from big-city offices and studios.

For all its influence, the new mass culture penetrated society unevenly. It had less impact in rural America and met resistance among evangelical Christians suspicious of worldly amusements. Mexican Americans preserved traditional festivals and leisure activities despite the "Americanization" efforts of non-Hispanic priests and well-intentioned outsiders. Working-class African Americans flocked to concerts by performers outside the mass-culture mainstream like blues singers Bessie Smith and Gertrude "Ma" Rainey. Black-oriented "race records" catered to this specialized market.

BILLIE DOVE, SILENT-MOVIE STAR. This scene is from Dove's 1928 film *Night Watch* with Donald Reed, the same year she made *Adoration* with Antonio Moreno, mentioned by the young women whose movie memories appear in Going to the Source. Such torrid scenes help explain why moralists and religious leaders of the 1920s found the movies so alarming. *(© Bettmann/Corbis)*

Along with network shows, radio stations also broadcast farm reports, local news, church services, community announcements, and ethnic or regional music. Similarly, neighborhood movie theaters provided opportunities for socializing and for exuberant responses to the film. The *Chicago Defender,* voice of the city's black middle class, deplored the raucousness of movie theaters in black neighborhoods, where "during a death scene … you are likely to hear the orchestra jazzing away." Despite the new mass culture, cultural diversity survived in the 1920s.

Celebrity Culture

Professional sports and media-promoted spectacles provided diversion as well. In 1921, Atlantic City promoters launched a bathing-beauty contest they grandly called the Miss America Pageant. Celebrities dominated professional sports: Babe Ruth of the New York Yankees, who hit sixty home runs in 1927; Ty Cobb, the Detroit Tigers' manager, whose earlier record of 4,191 hits still inspired awe; prizefighters Jack Dempsey and Gene Tunney, whose two heavyweight fights drew massive radio audiences. Ruth was a coarse, heavy-drinking womanizer; Cobb, a foul-tempered racist. Yet the alchemy of publicity transformed them into heroes with contrived nicknames: "the Sultan of Swat" (Ruth) and "the Georgia Peach" (Cobb).

This celebrity culture illuminates the stresses facing ordinary Americans in these years of social change. For young women uncertain about society's shifting expectations, beauty pageants offered one ideal to which they could aspire. For men confronting unsettling developments from feminism to Fordism, the exploits of sports heroes like Dempsey or Ruth could restore damaged self-esteem.

Celebrity worship crested in the response to **Charles Lindbergh,** a daredevil stunt pilot who flew solo across the Atlantic in his small single-engine plane, *The Spirit of St. Louis,* on May 20–21, 1927. A Minnesotan of Swedish ancestry, Lindbergh had entered a $25,000 prize competition offered by a New York hotel for the first nonstop New York-to-Paris flight. His success gripped the public's imagination. In New York, thousands cheered a ticker-tape parade. Radio, newspapers, magazines, and movie newsreels offered saturation coverage.

An instant celebrity, Lindbergh became a blank screen onto which people projected their hopes, fears, and ideologies. President Coolidge praised the flight as a triumph of U.S. business and corporate technology. Many editorial writers, by contrast, saw Lindbergh as proof that despite standardization and mechanization, the individual still counted. Others praised this native-born midwesterner of

THE ROMANCE OF THE MOVIES The 1927 film *Wings,* starring twenty-two year old Clara Bow, told of two World War I flying aces in love with the same young woman. It won the first Academy Award for best picture. *(Collection of Hershenson-Allen Archives)*

Scandinavian roots as more authentically American than the recent immigrants crowding the cities.

Overall, the new mass media had mixed social effects. Certainly, they promoted cultural standardization and uniformity of thought. But mass magazines, radio, and movies also helped forge a national culture and introduced new viewpoints and ways of behaving. Implicitly they conveyed a potent message: a person's immediate surroundings need not limit his or her horizons. If the larger world they opened for Americans was often superficial or tawdry, it could also be exciting and liberating.

Cultural Ferment and Creativity

American life in the 1920s involved more than politics, assembly lines, and celebrity worship. Young people savored the postwar moment as engrained pieties and traditional ways faced challenges. As writers, artists, and musicians embraced the modernist spirit of cultural innovation, African Americans created a cultural flowering known as the Harlem Renaissance.

The Jazz Age and the Postwar Crisis of Values

The war's disillusioned aftermath sharpened the cultural restlessness already bubbling in prewar America. The year 1918, wrote Randolph Bourne, marked "a sudden … stop at the end of an intellectual era." Poet Ezra Pound hammered the same point in 1920. America had marched to war, he wrote, to save "a botched civilization; … an old bitch gone in the teeth."

The postwar cultural ferment, summed up in the phrase "the Jazz Age," took many forms. Some young people—especially affluent college students—boisterously assailed middle-class standards of behavior. Grabbing the freedom offered by the automobile, they threw parties, drank bootleg liquor, and flocked to jazz clubs. Asked her favorite activity, a California college student replied, "I adore dancing; who doesn't?" Urged by advertisers, many young women defied prevailing taboos and took up cigarettes. For some, smoking became a feminist issue. As one female college student reasonably asked, "Why [should] men … be permitted to smoke while girls are expelled for doing it?"

Young people also discussed sex more freely. Sigmund Freud, the Viennese physician who explored the sexual aspects of human psychology, enjoyed a popular vogue in the 1920s. Despite much talk about sex and charges of rampant immorality, however, the 1920s' "sexual revolution" is hard to pin down. Premarital intercourse remained exceptional and widely disapproved, especially for women.

What *can* be documented are changing courtship patterns. "Courting" had once been a formal prelude to marriage. The 1920s brought the more casual practice of "dating," whereby young people gained social confidence and a degree of sexual experience without necessarily contemplating marriage. Wrote novelist F. Scott Fitzgerald, "None of the Victorian mothers had any idea how casually their daughters were accustomed to be kissed." A Methodist bishop denounced new dances that brought "the bodies of men and women in unusual relation to each other." The 1920s saw greater erotic freedom, but within bounds, as most young people drew a clear line between permissible and taboo behavior.

For women, these changes in some ways proved liberating. Female sexuality was more openly acknowledged. Skirt lengths crept up; makeup became more acceptable; and the elaborate armor of petticoats

> A Methodist bishop denounced new dances that brought "the bodies of men and women in unusual relation to each other."

and corsets fell away. The awesome matronly bosom mysteriously deflated as a more boyish figure became the fashion ideal.

An enduring twenties stereotype is "the flapper," the sophisticated, pleasure-mad young woman. (The term originated with a magazine illustration of a fashionable young lady whose rubber rain boots were open and flapping.) In the nineteenth century, the idealized woman on her moral pedestal had symbolized an elaborate complex of cultural ideals. The flapper, with her bobbed hair, defiant cigarette, lipstick, and short skirt, although a journalistic creation, similarly epitomized youthful rejection of entrenched stereotypes (see Beyond America).

In some ways, however, 1920s' mass culture thwarted full gender equality nearly as effectively as had earlier Victorian stereotypes. Many young women, while rejecting older taboos, now molded their appearance according to standards dictated by fashion magazines. Advertisers and movies encouraged women to pursue a "glamorous" lifestyle by purchasing new fashions, cosmetics, silk stockings, and other consumer accessories. Further, the traditional double standard, which held women to a stricter behavior code, remained in force. Young men could boast of sexual exploits, but young women who "went all the way" or were reputed to be "fast" risked damaged reputations.

Around 1922, according to F. Scott Fitzgerald, adults embraced the rebelliousness of the young. As middle-aged Americans "discovered that young liquor will take the place of young blood," he wrote, "the orgy began." But such sweeping cultural generalizations can mislead. During the years of Fitzgerald's alleged national orgy, the divorce rate remained constant, and many conservative, religious Americans clung to traditional standards, rejecting alcohol and wild parties. Many farmers, industrial workers, blacks, Hispanics, and recent immigrants found economic concerns more pressing than the latest fads.

The "Jazz Age" was partially a media and literary creation. Fitzgerald's romanticized novel about affluent postwar youth, *This Side of Paradise* (1920), spawned many imitators. With his movie-idol good looks, Fitzgerald not only wrote about the Jazz Age but lived it. Yet if the Jazz Age stereotype obscured the complexity of the 1920s, it did capture a part of the postwar scene, especially the raucous new mass culture and the hedonism and materialism of the well-to-do as they basked in the era's prosperity.

Alienated Writers

Like Fitzgerald, many young writers found the decade's cultural turbulence energizing. Rejecting the old order's moralistic pieties, they also disliked the business pieties of the new order. In *Main Street* (1920), novelist Sinclair Lewis satirized the smugness and cultural barrenness of Gopher Prairie, a fictional midwestern town based on his native Sauk Centre, Minnesota. In *Babbitt* (1922), Lewis skewered a mythic larger city, Zenith, and the protagonist George F. Babbitt, a real-estate agent trapped in middle-class conformity.

H.L. Mencken, a journalist and critic, in 1924 launched the iconoclastic *American Mercury* magazine, an instant success with alienated intellectuals and college youth. Mencken championed writers like Lewis and Theodore Dreiser while ridiculing politicians, small-town America, Protestant fundamentalism, and the middle-class "Booboisie." His essays on Harding, Coolidge, and

F. SCOTT FITZGERALD AND HIS WIFE ZELDA While Fitzgerald chronicled the 1920s in his fiction, he and Zelda lived the high life in New York, Paris, and the French Riviera. *(Stock Montage)*

Bryan remain classics of political satire. Asked why he stayed in America, Mencken replied, "Why do people visit zoos?"

For the novelist Ernest Hemingway, seriously wounded in 1918 while a Red Cross volunteer on the Italian front, World War I was a watershed experience. In 1926, now an expatriate in Paris, Hemingway published *The Sun Also Rises,* portraying a group of American and English young people, variously damaged by the war, as they drift around Spain. His *A Farewell to Arms* (1929), loosely based on his own experiences, depicts the war's futility and politicians' empty rhetoric. In one passage, the narrator says,

I was always embarrassed by the words sacred, glorious, and sacrifice and the expression in vain. We ... had read them, on proclamations that were slapped up ... over other proclamations, now for a long time, and I had seen nothing sacred, and the things that were glorious had no glory and the sacrifices were like the stockyards at Chicago if nothing was done with the meat except to bury it.

Although writers like Hemingway and Lewis blasted wartime hypocrisy and postwar vulgarity, they remained American at heart, striving to create a more authentic national culture. Even Fitzgerald, himself caught up in Jazz Age excesses, was fundamentally a moralist. His masterpiece, *The Great Gatsby* (1925), portrayed not only the party-filled lives of the decade's moneyed class, but also their superficiality, selfishness, and heedless disregard for the less fortunate.

Architects, Painters, and Musicians Confront Modern America

A burst of architectural creativity transformed the urban skyline in the 1920s. By 1930, New York City boasted four buildings more than fifty stories tall. Work on the 102-story Empire State Building, long the world's tallest building, began that year. The skyscraper, proclaimed one writer, "epitomizes ... American civilization." Cultural critic Lewis Mumford, by contrast, in *Sticks and Stones* (1924) and other works, deplored urban America's skyscrapers and automobile-clogged streets. Mumford preferred smaller communities and regional cultures to the congested cities and mass culture of 1920s' America.

The decade's leading painters took America—real or imagined—as their subject. While Thomas Hart Benton evoked a past of cowboys, pioneers, and riverboat gamblers, Edward Hopper portrayed faded towns and lonely cities of the present. Hopper's painting *Sunday* (1926), picturing a man slumped on the curb of an empty street of abandoned stores, conveyed both the bleakness and potential beauty of urban America.

The painter and photographer Charles Sheeler found inspiration in factories, including Henry Ford's plant near Detroit. The Italian immigrant Joseph Stella captured New York's vitality in such paintings as *The Bridge* (1926), an abstract representation of the Brooklyn Bridge. Wisconsin's Georgia O'Keeffe, who moved to New York City in 1918, evoked the allure of the metropolis in her paintings of the later 1920s.

The decade's creative ferment inspired composers as well. Ruth Crawford Seeger arranged American folksongs for the poet Carl Sandburg's *American Song-bag* (1927). Carl Ruggles set a Walt Whitman poem to music in 1923. And Frederick Converse's ambitious 1927 tone poem about the automobile, "Flivver Ten Million," featured such episodes as "May Night by the Roadside" and "The Collision."

Of all the musical innovations, jazz best captured the modernist spirit. The Original Dixieland Jass Band—white musicians imitating New Orleans' black jazz bands—had debuted in New York City in 1917, launching a vogue that spread by live performances, radio, and recordings. The white bandleader Paul Whiteman offered watered-down "jazz" versions of standard tunes, and white composers embraced jazz as well. George Gershwin's *Rhapsody in Blue* (1924) and *An American in Paris* (1928) revealed strong jazz influences.

Meanwhile, black musicians preserved authentic jazz and explored its potential. The 1920s recordings of trumpeter Louis Armstrong and his band decisively influenced the future of jazz. While the composer and bandleader Duke Ellington mesmerized audiences at Harlem's Cotton Club, Fletcher Henderson's band, featuring singer Ethel Waters and saxophonist Coleman Hawkins, held forth at New York's Roseland Ballroom. Pianists Fats Waller, Ferdinand "Jelly Roll" Morton, and Earl Hines demonstrated that instrument's jazz potential. Although much of 1920s' popular culture faded quickly, jazz endured.

The Harlem Renaissance

Jazz was only one of many black contributions to 1920s' American culture. The social upheavals of these years energized African American cultural

GLOBAL INTERACTIONS

The "New Woman" in the 1920s

In 1922, the French writer Victor Margueritte published *La Garçonne,* a novel about a young woman who pursues a series of relationships with other men after her fiancé betrays her. The novel created a scandal. Even the title unsettled readers: blurring gender distinctions, it gave a feminine twist to "garçon," the word for boy. The French were not alone in worrying about gender issues in the 1920s. Throughout the Western world, the behavior, dress, and even hairstyles of what journalists called the "New Woman" drew nervous scrutiny.

FRENCH TENNIS STAR SUZANNE LENGLEN AT ENGLAND'S WIMBLEDON STADIUM IN THE EARLY 1920S With her short tennis outfits and fondness for sipping brandy between sets, Lenglen offered one version of the international "New Woman" of the 1920s. *(© Bettmann/Corbis)*

In part, the "New Woman" phenomenon involved politics and feminist activism. The Netherlands granted women the vote in 1917, Canada in 1918, Austria in 1919, the United States in 1920, and so on. In some European parliaments, women comprised up to 10 percent of the members in the 1920s. In England, the American-born heiress Nancy Astor, having married into the British nobility, became in 1919 the first woman elected to the House of Commons, three years after Jeannette Rankin's pathbreaking election to the U.S. House of Representatives.

Most Mexican states adopted woman suffrage in the 1920s, and in 1927 the government affirmed women's equal rights. During the Mexican Revolution (1915–1919), the young activist Hermila Galindo had published a feminist journal, *Mujer Moderna (Modern Woman).* In the 1920s, organizations such as the Consejo Feminista de Mexico (Feminist Council of Mexico) pursued the cause despite opposition from Catholic leaders and a strong tradition of *machismo,* or male dominance.

Facing a conservative backlash at home, some 1920s' women's-rights advocates turned to the League of Nations. The British feminist Vera Brittain declared: "The time has now come … to obtain by international agreement what national legislation has failed to accomplish." The American Alice Paul joined with British feminists to promote a League of Nations treaty upholding women's rights worldwide. Although the effort failed, the League's successor, the United Nations, created a Commission on Women in 1946. Other causes embraced by women's organizations, including world peace, similarly transcended national boundaries. The Women's International League for Peace and Freedom drew delegates from as far away as China to its conferences.

The birth-control cause, led in the United States by Margaret Sanger, attracted broader support as well, though with mixed results. While contraceptives became more accessible in England, religious opposition kept them illegal in Spain and Italy. In Germany and France, government campaigns to replace wartime population losses by increasing the birthrate retarded the movement.

The "New Woman" phenomenon involved not only feminist activism but also young women's career and lifestyle choices. This social process, too, flowed across national borders. The Paris fashion designer Coco Chanel shaped women's fashions from Vienna to Vancouver. Her gender-bending designs featured slim, knee-length outfits patterned on men's suits.

The so-called flapper look spread across Europe and the Americas thanks to movies, fashion journals, and women's magazines. A Mexico City newspaper in 1924 advertised a movie called *La Esposa Flapper (The Flapper Wife)*. A Danish woman, recalling her 1920s' girlhood, wrote: "I grew up on a farm … far from anywhere, but of course we knew what was in style. We saw it in pictures and magazines and movies." One influence on her was doubtless the 1926 "Miss Denmark" competition, in which the winner, Edith Jørgensen, met the press in a short, sleeveless dress; silk stockings; and high-heeled shoes.

The "New Woman" image involved behavior as well as fashions. In many countries, young women of the 1920s became secretaries, university students, and department-store clerks—career choices that implied independence and at least a postponement of marriage and domesticity. Many also embraced the permissive climate of the era, from movies and casual dating to cigarettes and alcohol. As the writer Elisabeth de Gramont summed up her youth in 1920s' France: "We all wanted to forget the war; while eminent men were discussing its consequences, we were dancing."

WOMEN ATHLETES AT THE 1928 OLYMPIC GAMES IN AMSTERDAM
Runners from (l. to r.) Canada, the Netherlands, and New Zealand in the final lap of the 100-meter relay. The Canadian, Myrtle Cook, won the gold medal for her team. A Toronto ticker-tape parade honoring Canada's female track-and-field team, dubbed "the Matchless Six," drew an estimated 100,000 people. *(© Bettmann/Corbis)*

In Europe and England, as in the United States, the subject of sex, including homosexuality and lesbianism, was more freely discussed. *The Well of Loneliness,* a 1928 novel about a love affair between two women by the English writer Radclyffe Hall, attracted censors' attention, but became a best seller in the process.

The sports world welcomed young women, including the tennis stars Helen Moody of the United States and Suzanne Lenglen of France, known equally for her brilliant play and her revealing outfits. Despite protests from the Vatican, the 1928 Olympic Games in Amsterdam for the first time included female athletes.

The "New Woman" movement had limits. In Italy and Spain, where Catholic influence was strong and fewer women had access to movies and popular magazines, traditional ways persisted. An Italian bishop even denied communion to women with bobbed hair. Under the dictator Benito Mussolini, who came to power in 1922, Italy discouraged feminism and celebrated motherhood with an annual parade in Rome honoring the (married) women who had borne the most children.

Despite such exceptions, changes in women's lives pervaded the Western world, upsetting conservatives in many countries. A German government radio program launched in 1924, *Schule der Frau* (Woman's School), featured recipes and homemaking tips to encourage domesticity among German women. In France, the gender debate became a way of discussing a broader postwar cultural crisis. Commentators dismayed by the disorienting changes of the 1920s pinpointed shifting gender roles as a cause. In abandoning her traditional role, they warned, "the modern woman" threatened the social order itself.

In Canada, a businessman wrote the *Montreal Herald* in 1921 complaining of his secretary's "peek-a-boo" blouse." [W]hy is she not satisfied to reserve for her own boudoir the display of her feminine charms [?]" he grumbled. A 1926 column in the same paper disapprovingly described a typical evening scene as young people enjoyed the freedom and anonymity of downtown Montreal: "[A] stenographer waiting for her girlfriend, a saleslady keeping a tryst with her fellow … a young sheik waits for a dance-hungry jazz baby."

Such alarmed commentary pervaded the 1920s, as observers in many countries confronted that unsettling creature, the "New Woman."

QUESTIONS FOR ANALYSIS

- What did 1920s' commentators mean by the "New Woman"?
- Why did so many find the changes in female dress and behavior disturbing?

life, especially in New York City's Harlem. Once an elite white suburb, Harlem attracted many African Americans during and after World War I, and by 1930 most of New York's 327,000 blacks lived within its boundaries. This concentration, plus the proximity of Broadway theaters, record companies, book publishers, and the NAACP's national headquarters, all contributed to the Harlem Renaissance.

This cultural flowering took varied forms. The Mississippi-born black composer William Grant Still, moving to Harlem in 1922, produced many works, including *Afro American Symphony* (1931). Painter Aaron Douglas and sculptor Augusta Savage explored the visual arts. Savage, moving from Florida to Harlem in 1921, opened a studio and later an art school.

The 1921 Broadway hit *Shuffle Along* launched a series of popular all-black musicals. Film-maker Oscar Micheaux featured black actors and black story lines. The multi-talented Paul Robeson gave vocal concerts; made films; and appeared on Broadway in Eugene O'Neill's *The Emperor Jones* and other plays.

Poet Langston Hughes incorporated African themes and southern black traditions in *The Weary Blues* (1926), and the Jamaican-born poet and novelist Claude McKay evoked Harlem's vibrant, sometimes sinister, nightlife in *Home to Harlem* (1928). In *Cane* (1923), Jean Toomer used poetry, drama, and fictional vignettes to convey the world of the rural black South. Novelist Nella Larsen, from the Danish West Indies, told of a mulatto woman's struggles in *Quicksand* (1928). In *The New Negro* (1925), Alain Locke, a philosophy professor at Howard University, assembled essays, poems, short stories, and artworks to document Harlem's cultural riches.

The white cultural establishment took notice. Book publishers and magazine editors courted black writers. Broadway producers mounted black shows. Whites jammed Harlem's jazz clubs. The 1929 Hollywood film *Hallelujah*, featuring an all-black cast, romanticized plantation life and dramatized the city's dangers. DuBose Heyward's 1925 novel *Porgy* (adapted for the stage by Heyward and his wife Dorothy) drew inspiration from Charleston's African American community. George Gershwin's musical version, *Porgy and Bess,* premiered in 1935.

The Harlem Renaissance resonated internationally. Jazz won fans in Europe. Langston Hughes and Claude McKay found readers in Africa, Latin America, and Europe. The dancer and singer Josephine Baker, after debuting in Harlem, moved to Paris in 1925, where her highly erotic performances created a sensation.

With white support came misunderstanding and attempts at control. Rebellious young whites romanticized Harlem nightlife, ignoring the community's social problems. Some whites idealized black culture for its spiritual or "primitive" qualities. When Langston Hughes's poems addressed the gritty realities of black life in America, his wealthy white patron angrily withdrew her support. Wrote Hughes: "[S]he felt that [Negroes] were America's great link with the primitive. … But unfortunately I did not feel the rhythms of the primitive surging through me … I was not Africa. I was Chicago and Kansas City and Broadway and Harlem."

LANGSTON HUGHES, POET OF THE HARLEM RENAISSANCE. Hughes was part of the African American cultural and political awakening of the 1920s that foreshadowed changes ahead. *(© Bettmann/Corbis)*

"[U]nfortunately I did not feel the rhythms of the primitive surging through me … I was not Africa. I was Chicago and Kansas City and Broadway and Harlem."

The exuberance of the Harlem Renaissance faded as hard times hit in the 1930s. Nevertheless, future black writers, artists, musicians, and performers would owe a great debt to their predecessors of the 1920s. With this cultural awakening came a heightened political consciousness, mobilized by such groups as the National Association for the Advancement of Colored People, the National Urban League, and the National Association of Colored Women. As historian Clare Corbould argues in *Becoming African Americans: Black Public Life in Harlem, 1919–1939* (2009), this sharpened political awareness involved tensions between integrationist and separatist impulses—tensions that W.E.B. Du Bois had expressed in a famous essay in *The Souls of Black Folk* (1903) on the "double consciousness" of African Americans.

A Society in Conflict

The social changes and tensions of the 1920s produced a fierce backlash. While Congress restricted immigration, highly publicized trials in Massachusetts and Tennessee cast a harsh spotlight on the nation's divisions. Millions of whites embraced the bigotry of a revived Ku Klux Klan, and many newly urbanized African Americans rallied to Marcus Garvey, a magnetic black leader with a riveting message of racial pride. Prohibition stirred further controversy in this conflict-ridden decade.

Immigration Restriction

Fed by wartime super-patriotism and xenophobia, the impulse to remake America into a nation of like-minded, culturally homogeneous people revived in the 1920s.

The **National Origins Act** (1924) restricted annual immigration from any foreign country to 2 percent of the number of persons of that "national origin" in the United States in 1890. The great influx of southern and eastern Europeans had come later, so this provision clearly aimed to reduce immigration from these regions. As Calvin Coolidge observed on signing the law, "America must be kept American."

In 1929, Congress changed the base year for determining "national origins" to 1920, but even under this formula, Poland's annual quota stood at a mere 6,524; Italy's at 5,802; and Hungary's, 869. This quota system, which survived to 1965, represented a counterattack by native-born Protestant America against the immigrant cities. Total immigration fell from 1.2 million in 1914 to 280,000 in 1929. The law excluded Asians and South Asians entirely.

Court rulings underscored the nativist message. In *Ozawa* v. *United States* (1922), the U.S. Supreme Court denied citizenship to a Japanese-born university student. In 1923, the Supreme Court upheld a California law limiting Japanese immigrants' right to own or lease farmland.

Needed Workers/Unwelcome Aliens: Hispanic Newcomers

Extremely restrictive otherwise, the 1924 law did not limit immigration from the Western Hemisphere. Accordingly, immigration from Latin America (as well as from French Canada) soared. Poverty and political turmoil propelled thousands of Mexicans northward. By 1930, at least 2 million Mexican-born immigrants lived in the United States, mostly in the Southwest. California's Mexican American population surged from 90,000 to nearly 360,000 in the 1920s.

Many of these immigrants worked in low-paid migratory agricultural jobs. Mexican labor sustained California's citrus industry. Cooperatives such as the Southern California Fruit Growers

FROM GROVE TO CONSUMER: THE CALIFORNIA CITRUS INDUSTRY IN THE 1920s The photo shows Mexican workers at a citrus grove in southern California's Orange County. The idealized scene of a mother and child with Valencia oranges is from a crate label used by an Orange County citrus grower. *(Courtesy of the Local History Collection, Orange Public Library, Orange, CA; Private Collection)*

Exchange (which used the brand name "Sunkist") hired itinerant workers on a seasonal basis, provided substandard housing in isolated settlements, and fought the migrants' attempts to form labor unions.

Other Mexican immigrants settled in cities. Migrants to the Midwest worked not only in agriculture but also in the automobile, steel, and railroad industries. Retaining deep ties to "México Lindo" (Beautiful Mexico), they formed local support networks and cultural institutions. The Mexican American community was divided, however, between recent arrivals and earlier immigrants who had become U.S. citizens. The strongest Mexican American organization in the 1920s, the League of United Latin-American Citizens, ignored the migrant laborers of the Southwest.

Though deeply religious, Mexican Americans found little support from the U.S. Catholic Church. Earlier, European Catholic immigrants had attended ethnic parishes and worshiped in their own languages, but church policy had changed by the 1920s. In parishes with non-Hispanic priests, Spanish-speaking Mexican newcomers encountered pressure to abandon their language and traditions.

In the larger society, Mexican immigrants faced ambivalent attitudes. Their labor was needed, but their presence angered nativists eager to preserve a "white" and Protestant nation. Would-be immigrants confronted strict literacy and financial tests, and in 1929 Congress made it a criminal offense to cross the border without following required immigration procedures. The flow continued, however, as an estimated one hundred thousand Mexicans arrived annually, legally and clandestinely, to fill the U.S. labor market's pressing demands.

Nativism, Antiradicalism, and the Sacco-Vanzetti Case

The anti-immigration movement reflected deep ethnic, racial, and religious prejudice in 1920s' America. Anti-Semitic propaganda filled Henry Ford's weekly newspaper, the *Dearborn Independent*, distributed through Ford dealerships and mailed free to schools and libraries. The anti-Semitic articles were reprinted in pamphlets called *The International Jew*. Sued for defamation by a Jewish attorney, Ford in 1927 issued an evasive apology blaming subordinates.

Ethnic and antiradical prejudices pervaded the **Sacco-Vanzetti Case,** a Massachusetts murder case that began in April 1920, when robbers shot and killed a paymaster and guard at a South Braintree, Massachusetts, shoe factory. In 1921, a jury convicted two Italian immigrants, Nicola Sacco and Bartolomeo Vanzetti, of the crime. After many appeals and a review by a blue-ribbon panel of notables, they were electrocuted on August 23, 1927.

These bare facts hardly convey the passions the case aroused. Sacco and Vanzetti were anarchists, and the prosecution harped on their radicalism. The judge barely concealed his hostility to the pair, whom he privately called "those anarchist bastards." While conservatives supported the verdict, liberals and socialists protested. On the night of the electrocution, novelist John Dos

> Privately the judge called Sacco and Vanzetti "those anarchist bastards."

Passos wrote a bitter poem that ended: *All right you have won you will kill the brave men our friends tonight...all right we are two nations.*

Later research on Boston's anarchist community and ballistics tests on Sacco's gun pointed to their guilt. But the prejudices that tainted the trial remain indisputable, as does the case's symbolic importance in exposing the deep fault lines in 1920s' American society. Indeed, the case stirred global protests, as radical groups in Europe and elsewhere made it an international cause célèbre.

Fundamentalism and the Scopes Trial

An equally famous case in Tennessee highlighted another front in the decade's cultural wars: the growing prestige of science. While "individually powerless," wrote the Harvard philosopher Alfred North Whitehead in *Science and the Modern World* (1925), scientists were "ultimately the rulers of the world." Many Americans welcomed the advance of science, but some religious believers found it threatening. Their fears had deepened as scholars had subjected the Bible to critical scrutiny, psychologists and sociologists had studied supernatural belief systems as expressions of human emotional needs, and biologists had embraced the naturalistic explanation for the variety of life forms on earth advanced in Charles Darwin's *Origin of Species* (1859).

While liberal Protestants had generally accepted these findings, evangelical believers had resisted. This gave rise to a movement called **fundamentalism,** after *The Fundamentals,* a series of tracts published in 1909–1914. Fundamentalists insisted on the Bible's inerrancy and literal truth, including the Genesis account of Creation.

In the early 1920s, fundamentalists targeted Darwin's theory of evolution. Many state legislatures considered barring public schools from teaching evolution, and several southern states enacted such laws. Texas governor Miriam "Ma" Ferguson personally censored textbooks that discussed evolution. "I am a Christian mother," she declared, "and I am not going to let that kind of rot go into Texas textbooks." Former Democratic presidential candidate William Jennings Bryan endorsed the antievolution cause.

> "I am a Christian mother," declared the governor, "and I am not going to let that kind of rot go into Texas textbooks."

In 1925, when Tennessee's legislature outlawed the teaching of evolution in the state's public schools, the American Civil Liberties Union (ACLU) offered to defend any teacher willing to challenge this law. A high-school teacher in Dayton, Tennessee, John T. Scopes, encouraged by local businessmen and civic boosters, accepted the offer. After summarizing Darwin's theory to a science class, Scopes was arrested. Famed criminal lawyer Clarence Darrow headed the defense, while Bryan assisted the prosecution. Journalists poured into Dayton; a Chicago radio station broadcast the proceedings; and the **Scopes Trial** became a media sensation.

Cross-examined by Darrow, Bryan embraced the biblical version of creation and dismissed evolutionary theory. Although the jury found Scopes guilty (in a decision later reversed on a technicality), the trial exposed Fundamentalism to ridicule. When Bryan died of a heart attack soon after, H.L. Mencken wrote a scathing column contemptuously dismissing him and his fundamentalist admirers.

The Scopes Trial exposed the anxieties felt by many Americans. Bryan shrewdly appealed to citizens fearful of cultural forces beyond their control. Let parents and local communities decide what children are taught, he pled, evoking memories of his 1896 populist campaign defending common folk against the rich and powerful (see Chapter 20). Despite the setback in Dayton, Fundamentalism survived. Mainstream Protestant denominations grew more liberal, but many local congregations, radio preachers, Bible schools, new denominations, and flamboyant evangelists like Billy Sunday upheld the traditional faith. Southern and western states continued to pass antievolution laws, and textbook publishers modified their treatment of evolution to appease local school boards.

In Los Angeles, the charismatic Aimee Semple McPherson filled her cavernous Angelus Temple and reached thousands more by radio. Her followers, mainly transplanted midwesterners, embraced her fundamentalist theology while enjoying her theatrical sermons. (She once used a gigantic electric scoreboard to illustrate the triumph of good over evil.) At her death in 1944, her International Church of the Foursquare Gospel had more than six hundred branches in the United States and abroad.

The Ku Klux Klan

The tensions gripping American society of the 1920s also bubbled up in the form of a resurrected Ku Klux Klan (KKK). The original Klan of the Reconstruction South had eventually faded (see Chapter 16), but in 1915 hooded men gathered at Stone Mountain, Georgia, revived it. D.W. Griffith's glorification of the original Klan in his 1915 movie *The Birth of a Nation* provided further fuel.

In 1920, two Atlanta entrepreneurs plotted a national campaign to profit from the appeal of the Klan's ritual and its nativist, white-supremacist ideology. Their wildly successful scheme involved a ten-dollar membership fee divided among the salesman (called the Kleagle), the local sales manager (King Kleagle), the district sales manager (Grand Goblin), the state leader (Grand Dragon), and national leader (Imperial Wizard)—with a rake-off to themselves. The sale of Klan robes, masks, horse blankets, and bottled Chattahoochee River water (used in initiation rites) added to the take.

Preaching "100 percent Americanism," the Klan demonized blacks, Catholics, Jews, aliens, and, in some cases, women suspected of violating sexual taboos. Membership estimates for the KKK and its women's auxiliary in the early 1920s range as high as 5 million. From its southern base, the Klan spread through the Midwest and across the country from Long Island to the West Coast. The white working class and lower middle class in cities with native-born Protestant majorities proved especially receptive. In 1922, Imperial Wizard Hiram Wesley Evans admitted the Klan's image as a haven of "hicks" and "rubes" and urged college graduates to support the great cause.

Although the Klan was basically a money-making scam riddled with corrupt and cynical leaders, observers commented on the ordinariness of the typical members. (Evans, a Texas dentist, called himself "the most average man in America.") The Klan's litany of enemies and its promise to restore the nation's lost purity—racial, ethnic, religious, and moral—appealed to economically marginal Protestants disoriented by a new social order of giant corporations, mass media, rebellious youth, and immigrant-filled cities. The rituals, parades, and night-time cross burnings added a jolt of drama and excitement to life's everyday routines.

But if individual Klan members seemed more needy than sinister, the Klan as a mass movement was menacing. Some KKK groups employed threats, beatings, and lynching in their quest to purify America. In several states, the Klan won political power. Oklahoma's Klan-controlled legislature impeached and removed an anti-Klan governor. The Oregon Klan elected a governor and enacted legislation requiring all children to attend

THE KU KLUX KLAN IN WASHINGTON, DC In a brazen display of power, the Ku Klux Klan organized a march in the nation's capital in 1926. By this time, the Klan was already in decline. *(Library of Congress)*

public school, an attempt to destroy the state's Catholic schools.

The Klan collapsed with shocking suddenness. In March 1925, Indiana's Grand Dragon, David Stephenson, brutally raped his young secretary, who swallowed poison and died several weeks later. In prison, Stephenson revealed sordid details of political corruption. Its moral pretensions in shreds, the KKK faded. When civil-rights activism surged in the 1950s, however, the Klan would again rear its head.

The Garvey Movement

Among African Americans who had fled southern rural poverty and racism only to experience discrimination and racism in the urban North, the 1920s produced a different kind of mass movement, led by **Marcus Garvey** and his Universal Negro Improvement Association (UNIA). Born in Jamaica in 1887, the son of a stonemason, Garvey founded UNIA in 1914 and soon after moved to Harlem. In a white-dominated society, Garvey glorified all things black. Urging black economic solidarity and capitalist enterprise as the lever of racial advance, he founded UNIA grocery stores and other businesses. Summoning blacks to return to "Motherland Africa," he established the Black Star Steamship Line to help them get there.

An estimated eighty thousand blacks joined UNIA, and thousands more felt the lure of Garvey's oratory, the excitement of UNIA parades and uniforms, and the appeal of economic self-sufficiency and a glorious future in Africa. Although centered in New York and other northern cities, the movement had chapters across the South as well. Garvey's popularity unsettled established black church leaders and roused opposition from the NAACP, which saw the African American future in America, not Africa, and advocated racial integration rather than separation. W.E.B. Du Bois was among Garvey's sharpest critics.

The movement also highlighted social tensions in Harlem, where two streams of the African diaspora, one from the Caribbean, the other from the American South, converged. The resulting economic and political rivalry sharpened resistance to the UNIA, with its Jamaican founder and Caribbean leadership.

In 1923, a federal court convicted Garvey of fraud in the management of his Black Star Steamship Line. He was deported in 1927, and the UNIA collapsed. But this first mass movement in black America had revealed the social aspirations and activist potential of African Americans in the urban North. "In a world where black is despised," commented an African American newspaper after Garvey's fall, "he taught his followers that black is beautiful." Garvey is honored in his native island as a heroic forerunner of Jamaican independence from British Colonial rule.

The NAACP, meanwhile, remained active even in a decade of rampant racism. In some 300 branches nationwide, members kept the civil-rights cause alive and patiently laid the groundwork for legal challenges to segregation.

> "In a world where black is despised, [Garvey] taught his followers that black is beautiful."

Prohibition: Cultures in Conflict

A bitter controversy over alcohol deepened the fissures in American society. As noted in Chapter 21, the Progressive Era **prohibition** campaign was both a legitimate effort to address social problems associated with alcohol abuse and a symbolic crusade by native-born Protestants to control the immigrant cities. These tensions persisted in the 1920s. When the Eighteenth Amendment took effect in 1920, prohibitionists rejoiced. Saloons closed, liquor advertising vanished, and arrests for drunkenness declined. Yet prohibition gradually lost support, and in 1933 it ended.

What went wrong? Essentially, prohibition's failure illustrates the difficulty in a democracy of enforcing a widely opposed law. The Volstead Act, the 1919 prohibition law, was underfunded and weakly enforced, especially in antiprohibition areas. New York, for example, repealed its prohibition-enforcement law as early as 1923. Would-be drinkers grew bolder as enforcement faltered. For many young people, alcohol's illegality increased its appeal. Challenging prohibition, declared one college student, represented "the natural reaction of youth to rules and regulations."

Rum-runners smuggled liquor from Canada and the West Indies, and every city harbored speakeasies selling alcoholic drinks. People concocted home brew, shady entrepreneurs sold flavored industrial-grade alcohol, and sacramental wine sales soared. By 1929, alcohol consumption reached about 70 percent of prewar levels.

Organized crime helped circumvent the law. Chicago, where gangsters battled to control the liquor business, witnessed 550 gangland killings in the 1920s. Speakeasies controlled by Chicago gangster Al Capone generated annual profits of $60 million. Although not typical, Chicago's crime wave underscored prohibition's failure. A reform designed to improve public morality was turning citizens into lawbreakers and mobsters into celebrities.

A UNIA PARADE IN NEW YORK'S HARLEM, 1924 Marcus Garvey's Universal Negro Improvement Association attracted many African Americans in the 1920s. The banner reads: "THE NEW NEGRO HAS NO FEAR." *(Photographs and Prints Division, Schomburg Center for Research in Black Culture, The New York Public Library. Astor, Lenox and Tilden Foundations)*

Prohibition, too, became a battleground in the decade's cultural wars. The "drys"—usually native-born Protestants—praised it. The "wets"—liberals, Jazz Age rebels, big-city immigrants—condemned it as moralistic meddling. At one college, the student newspaper suggested a campus distillery as the senior class gift.

Prohibition influenced the 1928 presidential campaign. While Democratic candidate Al Smith advocated repeal of the Eighteenth Amendment, Republican Herbert Hoover praised it as "a great social and economic experiment, noble in motive and far-reaching in purpose." Once elected, Hoover appointed a commission to study the issue. Its confusing 1931 report admitted prohibition's failure, but urged its retention. A journalist parodied the findings:

> "Prohibition is an awful flop. / We like it. … It don't prohibit worth a dime, / Nevertheless we're for it."

Prohibition is an awful flop.
We like it.
It can't stop what it's meant to stop.
We like it.
It's left a trail of graft and slime,
It's filled our land with vice and crime,
It don't prohibit worth a dime,
Nevertheless we're for it.

The Eighteenth Amendment was finally repealed in 1933, a relic of another age.

Hoover at the Helm

Herbert Hoover, elected president in 1928, appeared well fitted to sustain the nation's prosperity. No standpat conservative like Harding and Coolidge, he brought to the White House a social and political philosophy that reflected his engineering background. He seemed the ideal president for the new technological age.

The Election of 1928

A Hollywood casting agent could not have chosen two individuals who better personified America's divisions than the 1928 presidential candidates, Al Smith and Herbert Hoover.

The Democratic Party's urban-immigrant wing had gained strength since the deadlocked 1924 convention, and New York governor Al Smith easily won the nomination. A Catholic and a wet, Smith exuded the flavor of immigrant New York. Originally a machine politician and basically conservative, he had impressed reformers by backing social-welfare measures. His key advisers included several reform-minded women, notably Frances Perkins, head of the state industrial board.

Herbert Hoover won the Republican nomination after Coolidge chose not to run. Some conservative party leaders mistrusted the brilliant but aloof Hoover, who had never held elective office and had spent much of his adult life abroad. Born in Iowa and orphaned in boyhood, Hoover had put himself through Stanford University and made a fortune as a mining engineer in China and Australia. After his tour as wartime food administrator, he had served as secretary of commerce since 1921.

Disdaining conventional campaigning, Hoover instead issued "tons of reports on dull subjects" (as H.L. Mencken complained) and read radio speeches in a droning monotone that obscured the originality of his ideas. (Some Hoover strategists did make use of sound film to promote his cause.) Smith, by contrast, campaigned spiritedly across the nation. This may have hurt him, however, because his big-city wise-cracking and New York accent put off many voters.

The effect of Smith's Catholicism remains debatable. Hoover urged tolerance, and Smith himself denied any conflict between his religion and the duties of the presidency. His candidacy energized Catholic voters, but anti-Catholic prejudice also played a role. Rumors circulated that Smith would follow the Vatican's orders if he won. (A postelection joke had Smith sending the pope a one-word telegram, "Unpack."). The decisive issue was probably not popery but prosperity. Republican orators pointed to the booming economy and warned of "soup kitchens instead of busy factories" if Smith won. In his nomination-acceptance speech, Hoover grandly predicted "the final triumph over poverty."

Hoover won in a landslide, grabbing 58 percent of the vote and even making deep inroads in the Democratic South (see Map 23.1). However, the outcome also hinted at an emerging political realignment (see Table 23.1). Smith did well among hard-pressed midwestern farmers angered by Coolidge's insensitivity to their plight. In northern cities, Catholic and Jewish wards voted heavily Democratic. Smith carried the nation's twelve largest cities, all of which had gone Republican in 1924. Should prosperity falter, the Republican Party faced trouble.

> Hoover grandly predicted "the final triumph over poverty."

THE POLITICAL USES OF THE NEW MEDIA Exploiting the latest in film technology, the 1928 Republican presidential campaign used sound motion pictures to promote Herbert Hoover's candidacy. *(Herbert Hoover Presidential Library)*

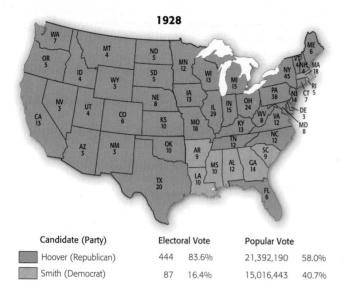

1928

Candidate (Party)	Electoral Vote		Popular Vote	
Hoover (Republican)	444	83.6%	21,392,190	58.0%
Smith (Democrat)	87	16.4%	15,016,443	40.7%

MAP 23.1 **THE ELECTION OF 1928** Although Hoover won every state but Massachusetts and six Deep South states, Smith's 1928 vote in the midwestern farm belt and the nation's largest cities showed significant gains for the Democratic Party over 1924. © Cengage Learning. All rights reserved. No distribution allowed without express authorization.

TABLE 23.1 **Presidential Voting by Selected Groups in Chicago, 1924, 1928, and 1932**

	Percent Democratic		
	1924	1928	1932
Blacks	10	23	21
Czechoslovaks	40	73	83
Germans	14	58	69
Italians	31	63	64
Jews	19	60	77
Lithuanians	48	77	84
Poles	35	71	80
Swedes	15	34	51
Yugoslavs	20	54	67

Source: John M. Allswang, *A House for All Peoples: Ethnic Politics in Chicago, 1890–1936* (Lexington: University Press of Kentucky, 1971).

Herbert Hoover's Social Thought

Admirers dubbed Hoover "the Great Engineer." Although a self-made man, he did not uncritically praise the capitalist system. His Quaker background, humanitarian activities, engineering experience, and Republican loyalties combined to produce a unique social outlook, summed up in his 1922 book *American Individualism.*

Like Theodore Roosevelt (whom he had supported in 1912), Hoover opposed untrammeled free-market competition. Rational economic development, he insisted, demanded corporate cooperation in resource allocation, product standardization, and other areas. The economy, in short, should operate like an efficient machine. Believing in ethical business behavior, Hoover welcomed the growth of welfare capitalism. But above all, he advocated *voluntarism.* The efficient, socially responsible economic order he envisioned must arise from the voluntary action of capitalist leaders, not government coercion or labor-management power struggles.

Putting his philosophy into practice, Hoover as secretary of commerce had convened more than 250 conferences where business leaders discussed issues of common concern. He urged higher wages to increase consumer purchasing power, and in 1923 he persuaded the steel industry to adopt an eight-hour workday as an efficiency measure. During the 1927 Mississippi River floods, as President Coolidge did nothing, Hoover had visited the stricken area to mobilize private relief efforts.

A conservationist, Hoover as secretary of commerce had pushed for planned use of water resources and programs to combat the pollution of rivers and lakes. In 1922, he negotiated a compact among western states to share Colorado River water. This agreement opened the way for a dam on the Colorado to provide hydroelectric power, control flooding, and supply water for irrigation. Construction of Hoover Dam began in 1930. (In an act of petty politics, Democrats changed the name to Boulder Dam in 1933, but Congress later restored the original name.)

Hoover's ideology had limitations. He showed more enthusiasm for cooperation among capitalists than among consumers or workers. His belief that capitalists would voluntarily embrace ethical behavior and pursue the general good reflected an exaggerated faith in the power of altruism in business decision making. His opposition to government economic intervention would prove disastrous when such intervention became urgently necessary.

Still, Hoover's presidency began promisingly. He created various commissions to gather data on recent social trends. At his urging, Congress created a Federal Farm Board to promote cooperative marketing. This, he hoped, would raise farm prices while preserving the voluntarist principle. Meanwhile, however, an economic crisis was approaching that would overwhelm and ultimately destroy his presidency.

CONCLUSION

Repudiating the Wilsonian vision of America's postwar world role, the Republican administrations of the 1920s pursued a nationalistic foreign policy aimed at collecting war debts and protecting U.S. corporate interests in Latin America. The 1921 Washington Naval Arms Conference, though ultimately unsuccessful, represents the one diplomatic initiative of note in these years.

At home, the Twenties brought new entertainment media, consumer products, marketing strategies, and mass-production techniques. While enjoying widespread (if uneven) prosperity, Americans grappled with massive technological and social changes. Like jet-lagged travelers, they struggled to adapt to the new order. Skyscrapers, radio, automobiles, movies, and electrical appliances—all familiar today—were exciting novelties for this generation.

While the Harding and Coolidge administrations celebrated the corporate order and pursued probusiness policies, society seethed in ferment. Ironically, the same stresses that sparked social conflict also stimulated cultural creativity. Jazz Age youth; Mexican immigrants seeking a better life; native-born advocates of immigration restriction, prohibition, and Fundamentalism; white Protestant KKK members; blacks who rallied to Marcus Garvey; the artists and writers of the Harlem Renaissance; and the musicians, painters, and novelists who revitalized American culture were all, in their different ways, responding to the promise and uncertainties of modernity.

KEY TERMS

Henry Ford   (p. 701)

Warren G. Harding   (p. 705)

Charles Evans Hughes   (p. 705)

Andrew Mellon   (p. 705)

Herbert Hoover   (p. 705)

Teapot Dome   (p. 705)

Calvin Coolidge   (p. 705)

McNary-Haugen Bill   (p. 707)

Washington Naval Arms
  Conference   (p. 707)

Sheppard-Towner Act   (p. 707)

Ku Klux Klan   (p. 708)

Alfred E. Smith   (p. 708)

League of Women Voters   (p. 708)

Women's Joint Congressional
  Committee   (p. 708)

Charles Lindbergh   (p. 714)

H.L. Mencken   (p. 716)

National Origins Act   (p. 721)

Sacco-Vanzetti Case   (p. 722)

fundamentalism   (p. 723)

Scopes Trial   (p. 723)

Marcus Garvey   (p. 725)

prohibition   (p. 725)

FOR FURTHER REFERENCE

Kendrick A. Clements, *The Life of Herbert Hoover: Imperfect Visionary, 1918–1928* (2010). Part of a multi-volume biography, focused on Hoover's efforts to achieve a modern, standardized socioeconomic order by voluntarist means.

Clare Corbould, *Becoming African Americans: Black Public Life in Harlem, 1919–1939* (2009). Illuminating study of how the cultural flowering of the Harlem Renaissance and a network of new organizations shaped African American political identity.

Ellis W. Hawley, *The Great War and the Search for a Modern Order* (1979). An economic study that traces the emergence (and collapse in 1929) of the first mass-consumption society.

Thomas Kessner, *The Flight of the Century: Charles Lindbergh and the Rise of American Aviation* (2010). Explores the cultural context of Lindbergh's surge to celebrity status and his role in popularizing aviation.

Edward J. Larson, *Summer for the Gods: The Scopes Trial and America's Continuing Debate over Science and Religion* (1997). Authoritative narrative of a famous trial and its aftermath, with attention to the larger issues at stake.

Angela J. Latham, *Posing a Threat: Flappers, Chorus Girls, and Other Brazen Performers in the American 1920s* (2000). An examination of the cultural uneasiness caused by changing standards of female behavior in the 1920s.

Thomas R. Pegram, *One Hundred Percent American: The Rebirth and Decline of the Ku Klux Klan in the 1920s* (2011). A well-written overview, with attention to conflicts and tensions within the Klan.

Matthew Avery Sutton, *Aimee Semple McPherson and the Resurrection of Christian America* (2007). Examines McPherson's colorful career for what it reveals about the religious trends, gender issues, mass culture, and politics of her era.

Moshik Temkin, *The Sacco-Vanzetti Affair: America on Trial* (2009). Valuable study of the coalition of organizations that focused international attention on the case and shaped attitudes toward the U.S. justice system.

Jan Doolittle Wilson, *The Women's Joint Congressional Committee and the Politics of Maternalism, 1920–1930* (2007). A well-researched study of a lobbying organization that promoted issues of particular interest to women.

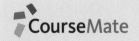 CourseMate   Visit the CourseMate website at **www.cengagebrain.com** for additional study tools and review materials for this chapter.

The Great Depression and the New Deal, 1929–1939

FRANKLIN D. ROOSEVELT SAILING AT CAMPOBELLO ISLAND, MAINE, 1916 *(FDR Library)*

RUGGED CAMPOBELLO ISLAND, lying off Eastport, Maine, was sunlit that August afternoon in 1921. A small sailboat bobbed in the waters off the island. At the helm, with several of his children, was thirty-nine-year-old **Franklin Delano Roosevelt.** Assistant secretary of the navy during World War I, Roosevelt had been the Democratic Party's vice-presidential candidate in 1920. But all this was far from his mind now. He loved sailing, and he loved Campobello Island.

The idyllic afternoon took an ominous turn when Roosevelt spotted a fire. Beaching the boat, he and the children frantically beat back the flames. The exertion left Roosevelt unusually fatigued. The next morning his left leg dragged, and soon both legs became paralyzed. He had suffered an attack of poliomyelitis (infantile paralysis), a viral infection that most often struck children but sometimes adults as well. Except for a cumbersome shuffle with crutches and heavy metal braces, he would never walk again.

This illness changed the lives of both Franklin Roosevelt and his wife, **Eleanor Roosevelt.** To Franklin, it seemed the end of his career. But he endured endless therapy and gradually reentered politics. In 1928, laboriously mounting the podium at the Democratic National Convention, he nominated his friend Al Smith for president. That fall, he himself was elected governor of New York.

Roosevelt's disability, although mostly concealed by the media, profoundly shaped his personality. Somewhat superficial and even arrogant before 1921, this privileged only child became, through his ordeal, more understanding of the disadvantaged and far more determined. "If you had spent two years in bed trying to wiggle your big toe," he once said, "after that everything else would seem easy!"

Along with child-rearing duties, Eleanor Roosevelt at first devoted herself to her husband's care. But she also encouraged his return to politics, resisting his domineering mother's efforts to turn him into an invalid at the family home at Hyde Park, New York. Already involved with social issues, Eleanor now became active in the New York Democratic Party and edited its newsletter for women. Painfully shy, she forced herself to make public speeches.

The Roosevelts would soon need the qualities of character they had acquired. Elected president in 1932 amid the worst depression in U.S. history, Franklin Roosevelt dominated U.S. politics until his death in 1945. The early years of Roosevelt's long presidency, the era of the so-called New Deal, spawned a dizzying array of laws, agencies, and programs. But certain patterns do emerge. In what some label the First New Deal (1933–1935), the dual themes were relief and recovery through a united national effort. In 1935, challenged politically from both the left and right, Roosevelt charted a more

PRESIDENT FRANKLIN D. ROOSEVELT This idealized painting captures the exuberance FDR projected and the hope his optimism inspired. *(FDR Library)*

radical course. The so-called Second New Deal (1935 and after) placed less emphasis on unity and more on business regulation and on policies benefiting workers, small farmers, sharecroppers, migrant laborers, and others at the lower end of the scale.

The New Deal involved countless programs, agencies, and sometimes squabbling officials. But in the public mind, it meant Roosevelt. Loved by some and reviled by others, Roosevelt was a consummate politician whose administration set the national agenda for a generation.

This chapter develops two themes. The first is the New Deal's expansive view of the government's role in promoting economic and social welfare. The second is the response of the American people to the Depression. From factory workers, urban blacks, and Hispanic migrant laborers to moviemakers, artists, writers, and photographers, diverse groups met the crisis with resourcefulness, creativity, and organized social action.

FOCUS Questions

- What caused the Great Depression, and how did President Hoover respond?
- What strategy guided the early New Deal, and what problems and challenges arose in 1934–1935?
- What key measures and setbacks marked the course of the New Deal from 1935 on?
- How did the depression and the New Deal affect specific social groups in the United States?
- What key developments shaped American culture in the 1930s?

Crash and Depression, 1929–1932

The prosperity of the 1920s ended in October 1929 with the stock market collapse. The Wall Street crash, and the economic problems that underlay it, launched a depression that hit every household. President Hoover struggled to respond, but his commitment to private initiative and his horror of direct federal intervention limited his effectiveness. In November 1932, voters turned to the Democratic Party and its leader, Franklin Roosevelt. This set the stage for a vast federal response to the economic and social crisis.

Black Thursday and the Onset of the Depression

Stock prices had risen through much of the 1920s, but 1928–1929 brought a frenzied upsurge as speculators plunged into the market. In 1925, the market value of all stocks had stood at about $27 billion; by October 1929, it hit $87 billion. With stockbrokers lending buyers up to 75 percent of a stock's cost, credit or "margin" buying spread. The income-tax cuts promoted by Treasury Secretary Andrew Mellon had increased the flow of money into the market. Upbeat statements also fed the boom. In March 1929, former president Calvin Coolidge declared stocks "cheap at current prices." "Investment trusts," akin to today's mutual funds, lured novices into the market. The construction industry faltered in 1928–1929, signaling a decline in the housing market and in business expansion.

The Federal Reserve Board tried to dampen speculation by raising interest rates and urging member banks to restrain their lending. But with speculators paying up to 20 percent interest to buy more stock, lending institutions continued to loan money freely—equivalent to dumping gasoline on a raging fire (see Figure 24.1).

The collapse came on October 24, 1929—"Black Thursday." As prices fell, some stocks found no buyers at all: they had become worthless. In the ensuing weeks, feeble upswings alternated with further plunges.

President Hoover, in the first of many optimistic statements, pronounced the economy "sound and prosperous." After a weak upswing early in 1930, the economy went into a long tailspin, producing a full-scale depression.

Economists probing the depression's underlying causes focus on structural problems that made 1920s' prosperity highly unstable. Agriculture remained depressed throughout the decade. In the industrial sector, wage increases lagged behind factory output, reducing consumer purchasing power. At the same time, assembly-line methods encouraged overproduction. By summer 1929, not only housing but also the automobile, textile, tire, and other industries were seriously overextended. Further, key industries such as railroads, steel, and textiles lagged technologically in the 1930s and could not attract the investment needed to stimulate recovery.

Some economists, called monetarists, also blame the Federal Reserve System's tight-money policies in the early 1930s. This policy, they argue, strangled any hope of recovery by reducing the capital available to businesses for investment and growth.

CHRONOLOGY 1929–1939

1929	Stock market crash; onset of depression.
1932	Reconstruction Finance Corporation.
	Veterans' bonus march.
	Franklin D. Roosevelt elected president.
1933	Repeal of Eighteenth Amendment.
	Civilian Conservation Corps (CCC).
	Federal Emergency Relief Act (FERA).
	Tennessee Valley Authority (TVA).
	Agricultural Adjustment Administration (AAA).
	National Recovery Administration (NRA).
	Public Works Administration (PWA).
1934	Securities and Exchange Commission (SEC).
	Taylor Grazing Act.
	Indian Reorganization Act.
1934–1936	Strikes by Mexican American agricultural workers in the West.
1935	Supreme Court declares NIRA unconstitutional.
	Works Progress Administration (WPA).
	Resettlement Administration.
	National Labor Relations Act (Wagner Act).
	Social Security Act.
	NAACP campaign for federal antilynching law.
	Huey Long assassinated.
	Revenue Act raises taxes on corporations and the wealthy.

1935 (Cont.)	Supreme Court reverses conviction of the "Scottsboro Boys."
	Harlem protests and riot.
1935–1939	Era of the Popular Front.
1936	Supreme Court declares AAA unconstitutional.
	Roosevelt wins landslide reelection victory.
	Autoworkers' sit-down strike against General Motors begins (December).
1937	Roosevelt's "court-packing" plan defeated.
	Farm Security Administration.
	GM, U.S. Steel, and Chrysler sign union contracts.
1934	Securities and Exchange Commission (SEC).
	Taylor Grazing Act.
	Indian Reorganization Act.
1937–1938	The "Roosevelt recession."
1938	Fair Labor Standards Act.
	Republicans gain heavily in midterm elections.
	Congress of Industrial Organizations (CIO) formed.
	Carnegie Hall concert by Benny Goodman Orchestra.
	Orson Welles's "War of the Worlds" radio broadcast.
1939	Hatch Act.
	Marian Anderson concert at Lincoln Memorial.
	John Steinbeck, *The Grapes of Wrath.*
1940	Ernest Hemingway, *For Whom the Bell Tolls.*

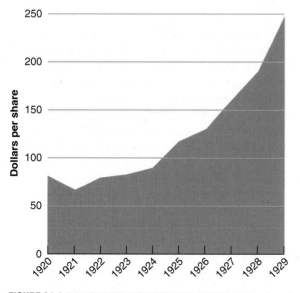
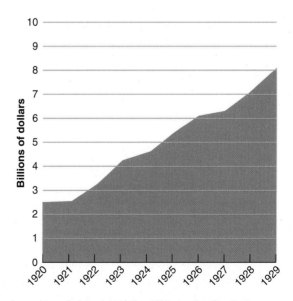

FIGURE 24.1 CONSUMER BORROWING IN THE 1920s Americans plunged heavily into debt in the 1920s to play the stock market and to buy their new Fords, Chevrolets, and consumer products. By 1929, their total debt stood at about $8 billion.

All analysts link the U.S. depression to a global economic crisis. European economies, struggling with war-debt payments and a severe trade imbalance with the United States, collapsed in 1931, crippling the U.S. export market.

The worsening depression devastated the U.S. economy. From 1929 to 1932, the gross national product dropped from $104 billion to $59 billion. Farm prices, already low, fell by nearly 60 percent. By early 1933 more than fifty-five hundred banks had closed, and unemployment stood at 25 percent, or nearly 13 million workers (see Figure 24.2). In some cities, the jobless rate surged far higher. Many who still had jobs faced cuts in pay and hours.

Hoover's Response

Historically, Americans had viewed depressions as similar to natural disasters: little could be done other than ride out the storm. President Hoover disagreed. Drawing upon his experience as U.S. food administrator in World War I and as secretary of commerce, Hoover initially responded boldly. But his belief in private initiative limited his options.

Viewing unemployment as a local issue, Hoover advised city and state officials to create public-works projects. In October 1930, he set up an Emergency Committee for Employment to coordinate voluntary relief efforts. In 1931, he persuaded the nation's largest banks to create a private lending agency to help smaller banks make business loans.

Despite these initiatives, public opinion turned against Hoover. In the 1930 midterm election, the Republicans lost the House of Representatives and gave up eight Senate seats. In 1931, dreading a budget deficit, Hoover called for a tax increase, further angering hard-pressed Americans. That same year, U.S. Steel and other big corporations slashed wages. The crisis swamped private charities and local welfare agencies. Philadelphia, with more than three hundred thousand jobless by 1932, cut weekly relief payments to $4.23 per family and then stopped them entirely.

In 1932, a presidential election year, Hoover swallowed his principles and took a bold step. In January, at Hoover's recommendation, Congress set up a new agency, the **Reconstruction Finance Corporation** (RFC), to make loans to banks and other lending institutions. By July, the RFC had pumped $1.2 billion into the economy. The RFC also granted $2 billion to state and local governments for job-creating public-works programs, and allocated $750 million for loans to struggling businesses.

Hoover supported these measures reluctantly, warning that they could lead to "socialism and collectivism." Blaming global forces for the depression, he argued that only international measures would help. His call for a moratorium on war-debt and reparations payments by European nations made sense, but seemed irrelevant to the plight of ordinary Americans. As Hoover predicted recovery "just around the corner," his unpopularity deepened.

> Hoover predicted recovery "just around the corner."

Mounting Discontent and Protest

An ominous mood spread as the jobless waited in breadlines, trudged the streets, and rode freight trains seeking work. Americans reared on the ethic of hard work and self-reliance found chronic unemployment deeply demoralizing.

The *New York Times* described "Hoover Valley"—a section of Central Park where jobless men lived in boxes and packing crates, keeping warm with layers of newspapers they bitterly called Hoover blankets. The suicide rate soared. In Youngstown, Ohio, a jobless father of ten whose family faced eviction jumped to his death from a bridge. Violence threatened in some cities when landlords evicted families unable to pay their rent.

Many farmers lost their lands because of tax delinquency, with Iowa and the Dakotas especially hard hit. At some forced farm auctions, neighbors bought the foreclosed farm for a trivial sum and returned it to the evicted family.

In 1931, midwestern farmers organized a movement called the Farmers' Holiday Association to force prices up by withholding grain and livestock from the market. Dairy farmers angered by low prices dumped milk in Iowa and Wisconsin.

The most alarming protest came from World War I veterans. In 1924, Congress had voted veterans a bonus stretched over a twenty-year period. In June 1932, some ten thousand veterans, many jobless, descended on Washington to lobby for immediate payment of these bonuses. When Congress refused, most of the "bonus marchers" went home, but about two thousand stayed on, building makeshift shelters. President Hoover called in the army.

On July 28, troops commanded by General Douglas MacArthur and armed with tear gas, tanks, and machine guns drove the veterans from

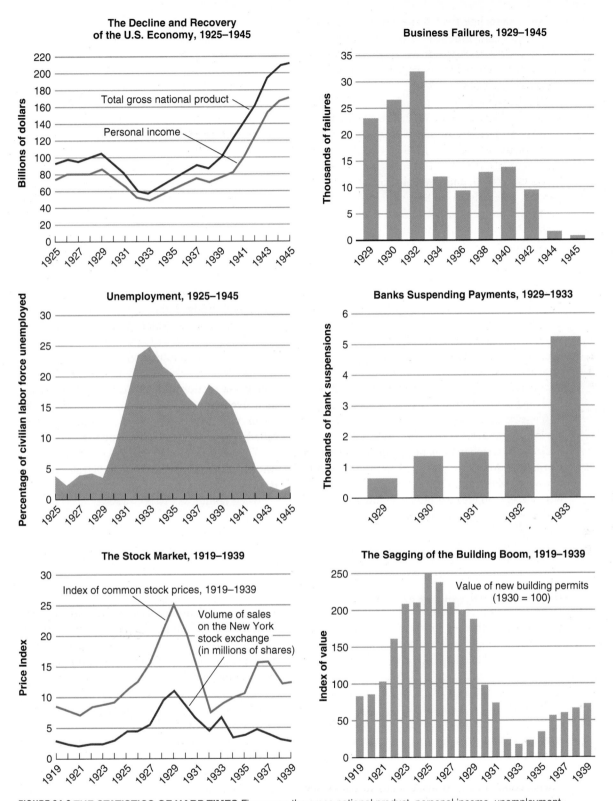

The Decline and Recovery of the U.S. Economy, 1925–1945

Total gross national product

Personal income

Business Failures, 1929–1945

Unemployment, 1925–1945

Banks Suspending Payments, 1929–1933

The Stock Market, 1919–1939

Index of common stock prices, 1919–1939

Volume of sales on the New York stock exchange (in millions of shares)

The Sagging of the Building Boom, 1919–1939

Value of new building permits (1930 = 100)

FIGURE 24.2 THE STATISTICS OF HARD TIMES Figures on the gross national product, personal income, unemployment, the stock market, and business failures all show the depression's shattering impact, with gradual and uneven improvement as the 1930s wore on. © Cengage Learning. All rights reserved. No distribution allowed without express authorization.

Sources: Thomas C. Cochran, *The Great Depression and World War II: 1929–1945* (Glenview, IL: Scott, Foresman, 1968); *Historical Statistics of the United States, Colonial Times to 1970* (Washington, DC: U.S. Government Printing Office, 1975).

BURNING SHANTIES OF BONUS MARCHERS, WASHINGTON, DC, JULY 1932 When President Herbert Hoover ordered the army to evict jobless veterans who had come to Washington seeking early payment of promised bonuses, it reinforced his public image as aloof and uncaring amid a worsening depression. *(© Bettmann/Corbis)*

their camp and burned their shelters. A journalist described the scene:

[The veterans and their families] wandered from street to street or sat in ragged groups, the men exhausted, the women with wet handkerchiefs laid over their smarting eyes, the children waking from sleep to cough and whimper from the tear gas in their lungs. ... Their shanties and tents had been burned, their personal property destroyed, except for the few belongings they could carry on their backs.

To many Americans, this action symbolized the administration's heartlessness.

American writers shared the despairing mood. In *The 42nd Parallel* (1930), John Dos Passos drew a grim picture of a depression-wracked nation. Says one character: "Everything you've wanted crumbles in your fingers as you grasp it." In *Young Lonigan* (1932), James T. Farrell portrayed the empty existence of a jobless Irish-immigrant youth in Chicago. Betrayed by the American dream, he aimlessly wanders the streets.

Some radical novelists openly attacked the capitalist system. The Communist Party encouraged such fiction through writers' clubs and contests for working-class writers. Jack Conroy's *The Disinherited* (1933) dealt with life in the Missouri coal fields, where his own father and brother had died in a mine disaster.

The Election of 1932

A gloomy 1932 Republican convention renominated Hoover. The Democrats gathered in Chicago, by contrast, scented victory. Their platform, crafted to erase the party divisions of the 1920s, appealed to urban voters with a call for repeal of prohibition, to farmers with support for aid programs, and to fiscal conservatives with demands for a balanced budget and spending cuts. Rejecting Al Smith, the party's

1928 candidate, the delegates nominated New York governor Franklin D. Roosevelt for president.

Despite a rousing acceptance speech pledging "a new deal for the American people," Roosevelt's campaign offered few specifics. He called for "bold persistent experimentation" and compassion for "the forgotten man at the bottom of the economic pyramid," yet he also attacked Hoover's "reckless" spending and insisted that "only as a last resort" should Washington play a larger depression-fighting role.

But Roosevelt exuded confidence, and above all he was not Hoover. On November 8, FDR and his running mate, Texas congressman John Nance Garner, received nearly 23 million votes, while Hoover received fewer than 16 million. Roosevelt carried every state but Pennsylvania and four in New England. Both houses of Congress went heavily Democratic.

How would Roosevelt use this impressive mandate? The nation waited.

The New Deal Takes Shape, 1933–1935

The Roosevelt years began in a whirl of activity. An array of emergency measures reflected three basic goals: industrial recovery through business-government cooperation and pump-priming federal spending; agricultural recovery through crop reduction; and short-term emergency relief. These programs conveyed the sense of an activist government addressing urgent national problems. Hovering over the bustle loomed a confident Franklin Roosevelt, cigarette holder jauntily tilted upward, a symbol of hope. By 1935, however, the New Deal faced problems, and opposition was building.

Roosevelt and His Circle

FDR's inaugural address exuded confidence and hope. "The only thing we have to fear," he intoned, "is fear itself." In an outpouring of support, half a million letters deluged the White House.

Roosevelt seemed an unlikely popular hero. Like his distant cousin Theodore, FDR was of the social elite, with merchants and landowners among his Dutch-immigrant ancestors. He attended Harvard College and Columbia Law School. But as a state senator and governor, he had backed the Democratic Party's urban-immigrant wing. When the depression hit, he had introduced innovative measures in New York, including unemployment insurance and a public-works program.

> "The only thing we have to fear is fear itself."

Intent on promoting recovery while preserving capitalism and democracy, Roosevelt encouraged competing proposals, compromised (or papered over) differences, and then backed the measures he sensed that Congress and the public would support.

Roosevelt brought to Washington a circle of advisers nicknamed the brain trust. It included Columbia University professor Rexford G. Tugwell and lawyer Adolph A. Berle. Shaped by the progressive reform tradition, Tugwell and Berle advocated federal economic planning and corporate regulation. But no single ideology or inner circle controlled the New Deal, for FDR sought a broad range of opinions.

Eleanor Roosevelt played a key role. A niece of Theodore Roosevelt, she had been active in settlement-house work and in Florence Kelley's National Consumers' League. Through her, FDR met reformers, social workers, and advocates of minority rights. Recalled Rexford Tugwell: "No one who ever saw Eleanor Roosevelt sit down facing her husband, and holding his eyes firmly, say to him 'Franklin, I think you should …,' or 'Franklin, surely you will not …' will ever forget the experience." Traveling ceaselessly, she was an astute observer for her wheelchair-bound husband. (A Washington newspaper once headlined "MRS. ROOSEVELT SPENDS NIGHT AT WHITE HOUSE.") In 1935, she began a newspaper column, "My Day."

Roosevelt's cabinet reflected the New Deal's diversity. Postmaster General James Farley distributed patronage jobs, managed his campaigns, and dealt with state and local Democratic leaders. Secretary of Labor Frances Perkins, the first woman cabinet member, had served as industrial commissioner of New York. Interior Secretary Harold Ickes had organized liberal Republicans for Roosevelt in 1932. Secretary of Agriculture Henry A. Wallace held the same post his father had occupied in the 1920s. Treasury Secretary Henry Morgenthau, Jr., FDR's neighbor and political ally, though a fiscal conservative, tolerated the spending necessary to finance New Deal antidepression programs.

Newcomers poured into Washington in 1933—former progressives, liberal-minded professors, bright young lawyers. They drafted bills, staffed government agencies, and debated recovery strategies. From this pressure-cooker environment emerged the laws, programs, and agencies gathered under a catch-all label: the New Deal.

While the "alphabet soup" of New Deal agencies can seem intimidating, it is important to keep the larger picture in mind. Reflecting a variety of approaches and shifting emphases, these programs, extending from 1933 to 1938, represented a remarkable and unprecedented level of government intervention in the economy, aimed at stimulating

ELEANOR ROOSEVELT VISITS A NURSERY SCHOOL IN DES MOINES OPERATED BY THE WORKS PROGRESS ADMINISTRATION, JUNE 1936 Intensely shy as a young woman, Mrs. Roosevelt played an active, influential, and highly visible role during her years as First Lady. *(FDR Library)*

recovery, regulating the financial industry, reducing glaring economic inequities, and helping those most hurt by the crisis.

The Hundred Days

Between March and June 1933, a period labeled the "Hundred Days," Congress enacted more than a dozen key measures (see Table 24.1). Drawing upon precedents from the Progressive Era, World War I, and the Hoover presidency, these measures expanded Washington's involvement in America's economic life.

FDR first addressed the banking crisis. As borrowers defaulted, depositors withdrew savings, and homeowners missed mortgage payments,

TABLE 24.1 Major Measures Enacted During the "Hundred Days" (March 9–June 16, 1933)

March 9	**Emergency Banking Act** Set up procedures for managing failed banks, and tightened regulations governing banking practices.
31	**Unemployment Relief Act** Created Civilian Conservation Corps (CCC) to provide jobs for young men in public works and conservation projects.
May 12	**Agricultural Adjustment Act** Created Agricultural Adjustment Administration to raise farm income by cutting production in basic commodities.
12	**Federal Emergency Relief Act** Appropriated $500 million for relief grants administered by the Federal Emergency Relief Administration (FERA).
18	**Tennessee Valley Authority Act** Created the Tennessee Valley Authority (TVA) to build dams on the Tennessee River system for power generation, flood and soil-erosion control, recreation.
27	**Federal Securities Act** Required full disclosure to investors of information relating to stock offerings, and registration of most stock offerings with the Federal Trade Commission.
June 13	**Home Owners' Refinancing Act** Appropriated $200 million to the Home Owners Loan Corporation (HOLC) to refinance mortgages for nonfarm homeowners.
16	**Farm Credit Act** Set up procedures to enable farmers to refinance their mortgages and secure loans for their production and marketing operations.
16	**Banking Act of 1933 (Federal Deposit Insurance Corporation)** Insured all bank deposits up to $5,000; extended powers of Federal Reserve Board to prevent stock speculation.
16	**National Industrial Recovery Act** Created the National Recovery Administration (NRA) to promote industrial and business recovery; appropriated $3.3 billion to the Public Works Administration (PWA) for major public-works projects to provide jobs and stimulate the economy.

thousands of banks had failed, undermining confidence in the system. On March 5, Roosevelt ordered all banks to close for four days. At the end of this so-called bank holiday, he proposed an Emergency Banking Act. This law and a later one permitted healthy banks to reopen, set up procedures for managing failed banks, increased government oversight of banking, and required banks to separate savings deposits from investment funds. Congress also created the Federal Deposit Insurance Corporation (FDIC) to insure bank deposits up to five thousand dollars. Launching a series of radio talks, the president assured Americans that they could again trust their banks.

Other measures addressed the urgent problem of relief for Americans struggling to survive. Two new agencies assisted those who were losing their homes. The Home Owners Loan Corporation (HOLC) helped city-dwellers refinance their mortgages. The Farm Credit Administration provided loans to rural Americans (see Figure 24.3).

Another early relief program, the **Civilian Conservation Corps** (CCC), employed jobless youths in government projects such as reforestation,

park maintenance, and erosion control. By 1935, half a million young men were earning thirty-five dollars a month in CCC camps—a godsend to desperate families. As Neil M. Maher argues in *Nature's New Deal: The Civilian Conservation Corps and the Roots of the American Environmental Movement* (2008), the CCC introduced many city youth to the American wilderness and helped keep environmental awareness alive in the 1930s (see also the later section "The Environment and the West").

The principal relief measure of the Hundred Days, the **Federal Emergency Relief Act,** appropriated $500 million for financially strapped state and local relief agencies. To head this program, FDR chose **Harry Hopkins,** the relief administrator in New York State, who soon emerged as a powerful New Deal figure.

While supplying immediate relief, the early New Deal also faced the larger challenge of promoting agricultural and industrial recovery. To push up low farm prices, the government advocated reduced production. As a first step, the government paid southern cotton planters to plow under much of their crop and midwestern farmers

CIVILIAN CONSERVATION CORPS WORKERS CUT FIREWOOD IN NEW HAMPSHIRE'S WHITE MOUNTAINS
While providing work for jobless urban youth and modest payments to their families, the CCC also heightened the nation's environmental awareness *(© Bettman/Corbis)*

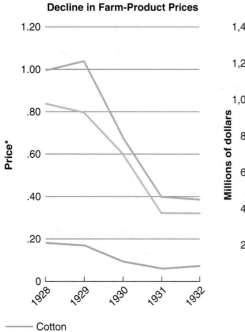

Decline in Farm-Product Prices

Cotton
Corn
Wheat

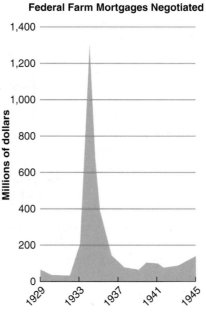

Federal Farm Mortgages Negotiated

FIGURE 24.3 AGRICULTURE DURING THE GREAT DEPRESSION The depression hit rural America with brutal ferocity, as the statistics on commodity prices and farm mortgages show. © Cengage Learning. All rights reserved. No distribution allowed without express authorization.

Source: Historical Statistics of the United States, Colonial Times to 1970 *(Washington, DC: Government Printing Office, 1975) pp. 491, 511, 517.*

*The graph shows the price per pound for cotton and the price per bushel for corn and wheat.

to slaughter some 6 million piglets and pregnant sows. Destroying crops and killing pigs amid widespread hunger proved a public-relations nightmare. Pursuing the same goal more systematically, in May 1933 Congress passed the Agricultural Adjustment Act. This law gave payments, called subsidies, to producers of the major farm commodities—including hogs, wheat, corn, cotton, and dairy products—in return for cutting production. A tax on grain mills and other food processors (a tax ultimately passed on to consumers) financed these subsidies. A new agency, the **Agricultural Adjustment Administration** (AAA), supervised the program.

The other key recovery measure of the Hundred Days, the National Industrial Recovery Act, appropriated $3.3 billion for large-scale public-works projects to provide jobs and stimulate the economy. The **Public Works Administration** (PWA), headed by Interior Secretary Harold Ickes, ran this program.

This law also created the **National Recovery Administration** (NRA). The NRA brought together business leaders to draft codes of "fair competition" for their industries. These codes set production limits, prescribed wages and working conditions, and forbade price cutting and unfair competitive practices. The aim was to promote recovery by breaking the cycle of wage cuts, falling prices, and layoffs. This approach revived the trade associations promoted by Washington during World War I (see Chapter 22). Indeed, the NRA's head, Hugh Johnson, had served with the War Industries Board of 1917–1918.

Dependent on voluntary support by business and the public, NRA officials used parades, billboards, magazine ads, and celebrity events to persuade people to patronize companies that subscribed to an NRA code. Such companies displayed the NRA symbol, a blue eagle, and its slogan, "We Do Our Part."

While the NRA sought economic recovery, some New Dealers also saw its reform potential. Pressured by Labor Secretary Frances Perkins, the NRA's textile-industry code banned child labor. And thanks to New York senator Robert Wagner, Section 7a of the National Industrial Recovery Act affirmed workers' right to organize unions.

The Reconstruction Finance Corporation, dating from the Hoover years, remained active, lending large sums to banks, insurance companies, and even new business ventures. The early New Deal thus had a strong probusiness tone. In his speeches of 1933–1935, FDR always included business in the "all-American team" working for recovery.

A few early measures, however, took a tougher approach to business. A post–1929 antibusiness

"WE DO OUR PART" Companies that cooperated with the National Recovery Administration displayed this banner. The NRA, a centerpiece of the early New Deal, soon ran into difficulties. *(Collection of Janice L. and David J. Frent)*

mood deepened when a Senate investigation revealed that none of the twenty partners of the powerful Morgan Bank had paid any income tax in 1931 or 1932. People jeered when the head of the New York Stock Exchange told a Senate committee considering regulatory measures, "You gentlemen are making a big mistake. The Exchange is a perfect institution."

> "You gentlemen are making a big mistake. The Exchange is a perfect institution."

Reflecting public support for tougher regulation, the Federal Securities Act of 1933 required corporations to inform the government fully on all stock offerings. This law also made executives personally liable for any misrepresentation of securities their companies issued.

The most innovative program of the Hundred Days, the **Tennessee Valley Authority** (TVA), had its origins in a government-built hydroelectric plant on the Tennessee River in Alabama that had powered a World War I munitions factory. In the 1920s, Senator George Norris of Nebraska had urged the use of this facility to supply electricity to nearby farmers.

Expanding Norris's idea, TVA advanced the economic and social development of the poverty-stricken Tennessee River Valley. While creating construction jobs, TVA dams brought electricity to the region, provided recreational facilities, and reduced flooding and soil erosion. Under director David Lilienthal, TVA proved one of the New Deal's most popular and enduring achievements.

The outpouring of laws and new agencies during the Hundred Days suggests both the dynamism and the confusion of the New Deal. How all these new programs would work in practice remained to be seen.

Problems and Controversies Plague the Early New Deal

As the depression persisted, several early New Deal programs, including the NRA and the AAA, faltered. The NRA's problems related partly to the personality of the hard-driving, hard-drinking Hugh Johnson, who left in 1934. But the trouble went deeper. As the unity spirit of the Hundred Days faded, corporate America resisted NRA regulation. Code violations increased. Small businesses complained as corporate trade associations used the codes to stifle competition and fix prices. The agency itself, meanwhile, became bogged down in drafting trivial codes. The shoulder-pad industry, for example, had its own code.

In May 1935, the Supreme Court unanimously ruled the NRA unconstitutional. The Court cited two reasons: first, the law gave the president regulatory powers that constitutionally belonged to Congress; second, the NRA regulated commerce inside states, violating the constitutional provision limiting federal regulation to *interstate* commerce. Few mourned. As a recovery measure, the NRA had failed.

The AAA, too, faced controversy. Farm prices did rise as production fell, and by 1937 overall farm income increased by 50 percent. But the AAA did not help farm laborers or migrant workers; indeed, its crop-reduction payments actually hurt southern tenants and sharecroppers, who faced eviction as cotton planters removed acreage from production.

Some victims of this process resisted. In 1934, the interracial Southern Tenant Farmers' Union, led by the Socialist Party, emerged in Arkansas. Declared one black sharecropper at the organizing meeting: "The same chain that holds my people holds your people too. ... [We should] get together and stay together." The landowners struck back, harassing union organizers.

While some New Dealers focused on raising total agricultural income, others took a more class-based approach and urged attention to the poorest farmers. Their cause was strengthened as a parching drought turned much of the Great Plains into a dust bowl (see Map 24.1). The rains failed in 1930, devastating wheat

> "The same chain that holds my people holds your people too. ... [We should] get together and stay together."

MAP 24.1 **THE DUST BOWL** From the Dakotas southward to the Mexican border, farmers in the Great Plains suffered from a lack of rainfall and severe soil erosion in the 1930s, worsening the hardships of the Great Depression. © Cengage Learning. All rights reserved. No distribution allowed without express authorization.

and livestock. In 1934, dust clouds darkened the skies over East Coast cities. As a dense dust cloud passed over Washington, DC, one legislator commented: "There goes Oklahoma." Through 1939, each summer brought a new scourge of dust (see Going to the Source).

Even night brought no relief. Recalled a Kansas woman, "A trip for water to rinse the grit from our lips, and then back to bed with washcloths over our noses. We try to lie still, because every turn stirs the dust on the blankets." Folk singer Woody Guthrie recalled his 1930s' boyhood in Oklahoma and Texas in a song called "The Great Dust Storm."

Battered by debt and drought, many families gave up. Nearly 3.5 million people left the Great Plains in the 1930s. Some migrated to nearby cities, further swamping relief rolls. Others packed their belongings into old cars and headed west. Though from various states, they all bore a derisive nickname, Okies. The plight of dust-bowl migrants further complicated New Deal agricultural planning.

Policy differences also plagued New Deal relief. Harry Hopkins argued for direct federal relief programs, rather than channeling funds through state and local agencies. Late in 1933, FDR named Hopkins to head a temporary agency, the Civil Works Administration (CWA). Through the winter the CWA funded short-term work projects for the jobless, but when spring came, FDR abolished it. Like his conservative critics, FDR feared creating a permanent welfare underclass. As local relief agencies ran out of money, however, further federal programs became inevitable.

Hopkins and Harold Ickes, head of the Public Works Administration, competed to control federal relief policy. Large-scale PWA projects did promote recovery, but the cautious Ickes micro-managed every proposal, leaving funds stalled in the pipeline. Hopkins, by contrast, wanted to put people to work, even at make-work projects like raking leaves and collecting litter, and get money circulating. Given the urgent crisis, Hopkins's approach proved more influential.

Despite problems and rivalries, the public works programs of the PWA and WPA not only created jobs but reshaped the nation's infrastructure and promoted economic development. With projects throughout the nation, these agencies built dams, public buildings, airports, highways, bridges, viaducts, dams, water utilities, and sewage-treatment plants. The military factories and war-workers' housing construction of World War II and the public housing and interstate highway system of the postwar era would all reflect the legacy of these New Deal agencies.

1934–1935: Challenges from Right and Left

Despite the New Deal's initiatives, hard times persisted. In 1934 national income rose about 25 percent above 1933 levels but remained far below that of 1929. Millions had been jobless for years. Rising frustration exploded in 1934 in nearly two thousand strikes, some communist-led. Conservatives, meanwhile, attacked the New Deal as socialistic. In 1934, several business leaders, joined by an embittered Al Smith, formed the anti–New Deal American Liberty League. Anti-Roosevelt jokes circulated among the rich, many of whom denounced him as a traitor to his class.

But the New Deal remained broadly popular, reflecting both its promise and FDR's political skills, enhanced by speechwriters and publicists. Pursuing his "national unity" theme, he exhorted Americans to join the battle for economic recovery just as they had united for war in 1917. Although Republican newspaper publishers remained hostile, FDR enjoyed good relations with the working press, and journalists responded with favorable stories.

Unlike Hoover, Roosevelt loved public appearances and took naturally to radio. Frances Perkins described his radio talks, nicknamed "fireside chats": "His head would nod and his hands would move in simple, natural, comfortable gestures. His face would smile and light up as though he were actually sitting … with [his listeners]."

> "His face would smile and light up as though he were actually sitting … with [his listeners]."

The 1934 midterm election ratified the New Deal's popularity. Reversing the usual pattern, the Democrats increased their congressional majorities. As for FDR, Kansas journalist William Allen White observed, "He's been all but crowned by the people."

Yet the political scene remained unstable. While conservatives criticized the New Deal for going too far, critics on the left attacked it for not going far enough and ridiculed Roosevelt's efforts to include big business in his "all-American team."

In 1934, socialist Upton Sinclair, famed for his 1906 muckraking exposé of the meatpacking Industry, *The Jungle*, won the Democratic nomination for governor of California. Sinclair's End Poverty in California (EPIC) program proposed to take over idle factories and run them cooperatively. Despite a barrage of vicious attack ads that anticipated a later era of U.S. politics, Sinclair garnered 37 percent of the vote.

Demagogues peddled various nostrums. The Detroit Catholic priest and radio spellbinder

Dust Bowl Diary: Life on the Great Plains in the 1930s

The dust storms of the 1930s on the Great Plains, one of the twentieth century's major ecological disasters, resulted from a severe drought plus decades of farming practices that had destroyed the prairie grasses holding the soil in place. These excerpts from the diary of Ann Marie Low, a young schoolteacher, convey the reality of the Dust Bowl as she experienced it on her parents' farm near Kensal, North Dakota.

April 25, 1934. Last weekend was the worst dust storm we ever had. ... [T]he air is just full of dirt coming, literally, for hundreds of miles. It sifts into everything. After we wash the dishes and put them away, so much dust sifts into the cupboard we must wash them again before the next meal. Clothes in the closets are covered with dust. ... Newspapers say the deaths of many babies and old people are attributed to breathing in so much dirt.

May 21, 1934. ... Saturday Dad, Bud [her brother], and I planted an acre of potatoes. There was so much dirt in the air I couldn't see Bud only a few feet in front of me. ... The newspapers report that on May 10 ... [an] estimated 12,000,000 tons of Plains soil was dumped on [Chicago].

May 30, 1934 [returning home after a week away]. The mess was incredible! Dirt had blown into the house all week and lay inches deep on everything. Every towel and curtain was just black. There wasn't a clean dish or cooking utensil. ... The cupboards had to be washed out to have a clean place to put them. ... [E]very towel, curtain, piece of bedding, and garment had to be taken outdoors to have as much dust as possible shaken out before washing. The cistern is dry, so I had to carry all the water we needed from the well. ... That evening Cap [her boyfriend] came to take me to the movie, as usual. Ixnay [No]. I'm sorry I snapped at Cap. It isn't his fault, or anyone's fault, but I was tired and cross. Life in what the newspapers call "the Dust Bowl" is becoming a gritty nightmare.

July 9, 1934 [After a movie, Ann and Cap talk of marriage, but the discussion soon turns to their bleak economic prospects.] [Cap] is really a handsome man, ... [but] suddenly I seemed to see what his face will be someday—a tombstone on which is written an epitaph of dead dreams. I shivered. [Cap said] "Oh sweetheart, you are cold. ... I'll take you home." I didn't tell him I wasn't shivering from cold.

August 1, 1934. As far as one can see are brown pastures and fields which, in the wind, just rise up and fill the air with dirt. It tortures animals and humans, makes housekeeping an everlasting drudgery, and ruins machinery. The crops are long since ruined. ... [A]ll subsoil moisture is gone. Fifteen feet down the ground is dry as dust. Trees are dying by the thousands. Cattle and horses are dying, some from starvation and some from dirt they eat on the grass.

July 11, 1936. Yesterday was 110° with a hot wind blowing. Today is the same. I'm writing this lying on the living room floor, dripping sweat and watching the dirt drift in the windows and across the floor. I've dusted this whole house twice today and won't do it again.

August 1, 1936. This is the worst summer yet. The fields are nothing but grasshoppers and dried-up Russian thistle. ... There is one dust storm after another. It is the most disheartening situation I have seen yet. Livestock and humans are really suffering. I don't know how we keep going. ...

Source: From Dust Bowl Diary *by Ann Marie Low by permission of the University of Nebraska Press. Copyright 1984 by the University of Nebraska Press.*

QUESTIONS

1. Along with their economic toll, what does this diary reveal about the dust storms' emotional and psychological impact?
2. What was Ann Marie Low's basic source of information for events outside her immediate community?

Charles Coughlin viciously attacked FDR, made anti-Semitic allusions, and called for nationalization of the banks. For a time, Coughlin's National Union of Social Justice attracted considerable support, mainly from the lower middle class.

Meanwhile, California doctor Francis Townsend proposed that the government pay all retired citizens two hundred dollars a month, requiring them to spend it within thirty days. This plan, Townsend insisted, would help the elderly, stimulate the economy, and create jobs by encouraging retirement. The scheme would have bankrupted the nation, but many older citizens rallied to Townsend's banner.

FDR's wiliest rival was Louisiana's Huey Long. A country lawyer elected governor in 1928, Long built highways, schools, and public housing while tolerating graft and political corruption. He roared into Washington as a senator in 1933, preaching his "Share Our Wealth" program: a 100 percent tax on all income over $1 million and appropriation of all fortunes over $5 million. Once this money was redistributed, Long promised, every family could live in comfort. By 1935, he boasted 7.5 million supporters. His 1935 book, *My First Days in the White House,* made clear his ultimate goal. Long

was assassinated that September, but his organization survived.

Battling back, Roosevelt regained the political high ground in 1935 with a fresh surge of legislation that rivaled that of the Hundred Days.

The New Deal Changes Course, 1935–1936

As the 1936 election neared, Roosevelt shelved the unity theme and championed the poor and the working class. His 1935 State of the Union address outlined six initiatives: expanded public-works programs, assistance to the rural poor, support for organized labor, benefits for retired workers and other at-risk groups, tougher business regulation, and heavier taxes on the well-to-do. These priorities translated into a bundle of reform measures some called "the Second New Deal" (see Table 24.2). FDR's landslide victory in 1936 solidified a new Democratic coalition. The New Deal also addressed environmental issues and launched public-works and power projects that stimulated economic development in the American West.

TABLE 24.2 Major Later New Deal Legislation (November 1933–1938)

Nov. 1933	**Civilian Works Administration** Short-term relief program, created public-works employment for the jobless during the winter of 1933–1934.
1934	**Civil Works Emergency Relief Act** Temporary public-works program, replaced by Works Progress Administration (WPA) in 1935. **Securities Exchange Act** Created Securities and Exchange Commission (SEC) to regulate stock trading activities. **National Housing Act** Created Federal Housing Administration (FHA) to insure loans by private lending agencies for upgrading farms and small businesses. **Indian Reorganization Act** Halted sale of tribal lands and enabled tribes to regain unallocated lands.
1935	**Emergency Relief Appropriations Act** Created Works Progress Administration (WPA) to provide public-works jobs for the unemployed. **National Labor Relations Act (Wagner Act)** Guaranteed unions' collective-bargaining rights and outlawed anti-union practices. **Revenue Act of 1935 (Wealth Tax Act)** Raised taxes on corporations and the wealthy. **Social Security Act** Launched a federal-state program of workers' pensions, unemployment insurance, and other welfare benefits. **Public Utilities Holding Company Act** Restricted gas and electric companies to one geographic region. **Rural Electrification Act** Provided for low-cost loans to utility companies and cooperatives to spread electric power to rural America.
1937	**Farm Tenancy Act** Created Farm Security Administration (FSA) to aid small farmers and tenant farmers. Replaced 1935 Resettlement Administration.
1938	**Fair Labor Standards Act** Banned child labor and set a national minimum wage.

Expanding Federal Relief

With unemployment still high, Congress passed the $5 billion Emergency Relief Appropriation Act in April 1935. Roosevelt swiftly set up the **Works Progress Administration** (WPA) under Harry Hopkins to funnel assistance directly to the jobless. Roosevelt insisted that the WPA provide work, not handouts. Over its eight-year life, the WPA employed more than 8 million Americans and constructed or improved vast numbers of bridges, roads, post offices, and other public facilities.

The WPA also assisted writers, performers, and artists. The Federal Writers' Project (FWP) employed jobless writers nationwide to produce state and city guides and histories of ethnic and immigrant groups. In the South, research teams recorded the reminiscences of former slaves. Sterling Brown, the FWP's "Negro Affairs editor," worked to include African American history and voices in FWP publications.

Under the WPA's Federal Music Project, unemployed musicians gave free concerts, often featuring American composers. Artists working for the Federal Arts Project designed posters, offered courses, and painted murals on public buildings.

The Federal Theatre Project (FTP) employed actors. One FTP project, the Living Newspaper, which dramatized current social issues, was criticized as New Deal propaganda. Nervous WPA officials canceled one FTP production, Marc Blitzstein's radical musical *The Cradle Will Rock* (1937), before the opening-night performance. The cast and audience defiantly walked to another theater, and the show went on.

Harold Ickes's Public Works Administration, after a slow start, eventually completed some thirty-four thousand major construction projects, from New York City's Lincoln Tunnel to the awesome Grand Coulee Dam on the Columbia River. The PWA employed thousands of jobless workers.

All this relief spending generated large federal budget deficits, cresting at $4.4 billion in 1936. According to British economist John Maynard Keynes, governments should deliberately use deficit spending during depressions to fund public-works programs, thereby increasing purchasing power and stimulating recovery. The New Deal approach, however, was not Keynesian. Because every dollar spent on relief programs was counterbalanced by taxation or government borrowing, the stimulus effect was nil. FDR saw deficits as an unwelcome necessity, not a positive good.

The New Deal's second phase more frankly targeted workers, the poor, and the disadvantaged. Social-justice advocates like Frances Perkins and

A FEDERAL MUSIC PROJECT EVENT IN NEW YORK'S CENTRAL PARK. Musicians employed by the New Deal's Federal Music Project (FMP) taught classes in addition to giving concerts. These young singers were participating in a children's music festival sponsored by the FMP. *(National Archives)*

Eleanor Roosevelt encouraged this class-based emphasis, but so did political calculations. Looking to 1936, FDR's political advisers feared that the followers of Coughlin, Townsend, and Long could siphon off enough votes to cost him the election.

The Second New Deal's agricultural policy addressed the plight of sharecroppers (a plight the AAA had helped create) and other poor farmers. The Resettlement Administration (1935) made loans to help tenant farmers buy their own farms and to enable displaced sharecroppers, tenants, and dust-bowl migrants to move to more productive areas.

The Resettlement Administration also funded two documentary films directed by Pare Lorenz. *The Plow That Broke the Plains* (1936) explained the farming practices that led to the dust bowl. *The River* (1938) dealt with the devastating effects of Mississippi River flooding, and the promise of New Deal flood-control projects. Lorenz's films rank among the outstanding cultural productions of the 1930s.

The Rural Electrification Administration, also started in 1935, made low-interest loans to utility companies and farmers' cooperatives to extend electricity to the 90 percent of rural America that still lacked it. By 1941, 40 percent of U.S. farms enjoyed electric power.

The agricultural-recovery program suffered a setback in January 1936 when the Supreme Court declared the Agricultural Adjustment Act unconstitutional. The processing tax that funded the AAA's subsidies, the Court held, was an illegal use of the government's tax power. To replace the AAA, Congress passed a soil-conservation act that paid farmers to plant grasses and legumes instead of soil-depleting crops such as wheat and cotton (which also happened to be the major surplus commodities).

Organized labor won a key victory in 1935, thanks to Senator Robert Wagner. During the New Deal's national-unity phase, FDR had criticized Wagner's campaign for a prolabor law as "special interest" legislation. But in 1935, when the Supreme Court outlawed the NIRA, including Section 7a protecting union members' rights, as unconstitutional, FDR called for a labor law that would survive court scrutiny. The **National Labor Relations Act** of July 1935 (the **Wagner Act**) guaranteed collective-bargaining rights and outlawed such management tactics as blacklisting union organizers. The law created the National Labor Relations Board (NLRB) to enforce the law and supervise shop elections. A wave of unionization soon followed (discussed later in this chapter).

The Second New Deal's more class-conscious thrust shaped other 1935 measures as well. The Banking Act strengthened the Federal Reserve Board's control over the nation's financial system. The Public Utilities Holding Company Act, targeting the sprawling public-utility empires of the 1920s, restricted gas and electric companies to one geographic region.

In 1935, too, Roosevelt called for steeper taxes on the rich to combat the "unjust concentration of wealth and economic power." Congress responded with a revenue act, also called the Wealth Tax Act, raising taxes on corporations and on the well-to-do. With its many loopholes, this law was not quite the "soak the rich" measure some believed, but it did express the Second New Deal's more radical spirit.

The Social Security Act of 1935; End of the Second New Deal

The **Social Security Act** of 1935 stands out for its long-range significance. Drafted by a committee chaired by Frances Perkins, this measure drew upon Progressive Era ideas and European social-welfare programs. It established a mixed federal-state system of workers' pensions, unemployment insurance, survivors' benefits for victims of industrial accidents, and aid for disabled persons and dependent mothers with children.

Taxes paid partly by employers and partly by workers (in the form of sums withheld from their paychecks) helped fund the program. This cut in take-home pay contributed to a recession in 1937. But it made sense politically because workers would resist any threat to a pension plan they had contributed to. As FDR put it, "With those taxes in there, no damned politician can ever scrap my social security program."

> "With those taxes in there, no damned politician can ever scrap my social security program."

The Social Security Act bypassed farmers, domestic workers, and the self-employed. But it established the principle of federal responsibility for social welfare and laid the foundation for future welfare programs.

As 1935 ended, the Second New Deal was complete. Although conservatives called it "anti-business," FDR insisted that he had saved capitalism through prudent reform. In earlier eras, the business class had dominated government, marginalizing other groups. Business interests remained influential in the 1930s, but the evolving New Deal also responded to other organized interest groups, including labor. And in 1935, with an election looming, New Deal strategists reached farther still, crafting legislation to aid sharecroppers, migrant workers, the disabled, the elderly, and others largely ignored by politicians of the past.

In the process, the New Deal enlarged the government's role in American life, as well as the power of the presidency. Building on precedents set by Theodore Roosevelt, FDR so dominated 1930s' politics that Americans now expected presidents to offer programs, address national issues, and shape the public debate. This decisively altered the power balance between the White House and Congress. Along with specific programs, the New Deal's importance thus also lay in how it enlarged the scope of the presidency and the social role of the state.

The 1936 Roosevelt Landslide and the New Democratic Coalition

FDR confidently faced the 1936 campaign. "There's one issue," he told an aide; "it's myself, and people must be either for me or against me."

The Republican candidate, Kansas governor Alfred Landon, a moderate fiscal conservative, proved an inept campaigner. ("Wherever I have gone in this country, I have found Americans," he revealed in one speech.) FDR, by contrast, responded zestfully when Republicans lambasted his alleged dictatorial ambitions or charged that the social security law would require all workers to wear metal dog tags. The forces of "selfishness and greed ... are united in their hatred for me," he declared at a tumultuous election-eve rally in New York City, "and I welcome their hatred."

In the greatest landslide since 1820, FDR carried every state but Maine and Vermont (see Table 24.3). Landon even lost Kansas. Pennsylvania went Democratic for the first time since 1856. The Democrats increased their majorities in Congress. Socialist Norman Thomas received less than 200,000 votes, the Communist Party's presidential candidate only about 80,000. The Union Party, a coalition of Coughlinites, Townsendites, and Huey Long supporters, seemingly so formidable in 1935, polled less than 900,000 votes.

The 1936 election signaled the emergence of a new Democratic coalition. Since Reconstruction, the Democrats had enjoyed three bases of support: the white South, parts of the West, and urban white ethnic voters. FDR retained these centers of strength. He rarely challenged state or local party leaders who produced the votes, whether or not they supported the New Deal.

Building on Al Smith's urban gains in 1928, FDR carried the nation's twelve largest cities in 1936. Aided by New Deal relief programs, many city-dwellers idolized Roosevelt. Cheering throngs greeted his visits to New York, Boston, or other cities. In filling New Deal positions, FDR often turned to the newer urban-immigrant groups, including Catholics and Jews.

Expanding the Democratic base, FDR also courted farmers and union members. Republican midwestern farmers, won over by the New Deal's agricultural program, voted accordingly. FDR decisively carried Iowa, a GOP bastion, in 1936. Union members, too, joined the Roosevelt bandwagon that year, and unions pumped money into Roosevelt's campaign chest (though far less than business gave the Republicans). Despite his early criticism of the Wagner bill, FDR's reputation as a "friend of labor" proved unassailable.

African Americans came aboard as well. Although most southern blacks remained disfranchised, northern blacks could vote, and as late as 1932, two-thirds of them voted Republican, the party of Lincoln. The New Deal caused a historic shift. In 1936, 76 percent of black voters supported FDR.

Economically, this shift made sense. New Deal relief programs greatly aided blacks. On racial-justice issues, however, the New Deal's record was mixed at best. Some NRA codes included racially discriminatory clauses, causing black activists to deride the agency as "Negroes Ruined Again." TVA and other New Deal agencies tolerated racial bias. Lynchings increased in the 1930s as some whites translated economic worries into racial violence, but Roosevelt kept aloof from an NAACP campaign to make lynching a federal crime. When southern Democratic senators killed such a bill in 1935, FDR, concerned about other legislative initiatives, did little. "[T]he Roosevelt administration [has] nothing for [blacks]," the NAACP concluded bitterly.

In limited ways, FDR did address racial issues. He cautiously tried to rid New Deal agencies of blatant racism. He appointed more than a hundred blacks to policy-level and judicial positions, including

TABLE 24.3 The Election of 1936

Candidate	Party	Electoral Vote	Popular Vote	Percentage of Popular Vote
Franklin D. Roosevelt	Democratic	523	27,752,869	60.8
Alfred M. Landon	Republican	8	16,674,665	36.5
William Lemke	Union	—	882,479	1.9

Eleanor Roosevelt's friend Mary McLeod Bethune as director of minority affairs in the National Youth Administration. Bethune, a Florida educator, led the so-called black cabinet that linked the administration and black organizations. Roosevelt's Supreme Court appointees opposed racial discrimination in cases involving housing, voting rights, and other issues.

The New Deal also supported racial justice in symbolic ways. In 1938, when the participants in a conference in Birmingham, Alabama, were segregated in compliance with local statutes, Mrs. Roosevelt placed her chair halfway between the white and black delegates. In 1939, when the Daughters of the American Revolution barred black contralto Marian Anderson from performing in Washington's Constitution Hall, Mrs. Roosevelt and Harold Ickes arranged an Easter concert by Anderson at the Lincoln Memorial. Even symbolic gestures outraged many southern whites. When a black minister delivered the invocation at the 1936 Democratic convention, a South Carolina senator noisily stalked out.

Led by Molly Dewson, head of the Democratic Party's women's division, the New Deal also courted women voters. In the 1936 campaign, fifteen thousand women volunteers distributed flyers describing New Deal programs. "[W]e did not make the old-fashioned plea that our nominee was charming," she recalled; "We appealed to [women's] intelligence."

Dewson did not promote a specifically feminist agenda. The New Deal's economic programs, she argued, benefited both sexes. FDR did, however, appoint the first woman cabinet member, the first woman ambassador, and a number of female federal judges. Through Dewson's efforts, the 1936 Democratic platform committee reflected a fifty-fifty gender balance.

Despite the New Deal's symbolic gestures and appointment of a few blacks and women, racial and gender discrimination pervaded U.S. society in the 1930s, and Roosevelt, grappling with the depression, did relatively little to change things. That challenge would await a later time.

The Environment and the West

Environmental issues loomed large in the New Deal. While still in the New York Senate, FDR had sought logging regulation to protect wildlife. As president, he strongly supported the Civilian Conservation Corps' program of planting trees, thinning forests, and building hiking trails.

Soil conservation had high priority. The 1930s' dust storms resulted not only from drought, but from overgrazing and poor farming practices. For decades, Great Plains' wheat farmers had used tractors, combines, and heavy-duty plows called "sodbusters" to uproot the native prairie grasses that anchored the soil. When the rains failed, as they do in this drought-prone region, little remained to hold the soil in place, and parching winds whipped up devastating dust storms. By the 1930s, 9 million acres of farmland had been lost to erosion in the Great Plains, the South, and elsewhere.

In response, the Department of Agriculture's Soil Conservation Service promoted contour plowing, crop rotation, and soil-strengthening grasses. The Taylor Grazing Act of 1934 restricted the grazing on public lands that had exacerbated the problem. TVA dams helped control the floods that worsened erosion in the Tennessee valley.

New Deal planners also promoted national-park development, including Olympic National Park in Washington, Virginia's Shenandoah National Park, and Kings Canyon National Park in California. The administration also created some 160 new national wildlife refuges. FDR even closed a Utah artillery range near a nesting site of the endangered trumpeter swan!

The wilderness-preservation movement gained momentum in the 1930s, supported by such groups as the Wilderness Society (1935), started by environmentalist Aldo Leopold and others, and the National Wildlife Federation (1936), funded by firearms makers eager to preserve hunting areas. Pressured by such groups, Congress began to set aside protected wilderness areas. Building on these beginnings, the United States by 2008 had 704 officially designated national wilderness areas, comprising 107 million acres.

By later standards, the New Deal's environmental record was spotty. The decade's massive hydroelectric projects, while providing rural families with electricity, had serious ecological consequences. The Grand Coulee Dam, for example, destroyed salmon spawning on much of the Columbia River's tributary system. Other dams disrupted fragile ecosystems and the livelihoods of local residents, particularly Native American communities, who depended on them.

Viewed in context, however, the New Deal's environmental record remains impressive. While coping with the depression, the Roosevelt administration also focused a level of attention on environmental issues that had not been seen since the Progressive Era and would not be seen again for a generation.

The New Deal impact on the West was profound, especially because the federal government owned a third or more of the land in eleven western states and much more in some states. New Deal agencies and laws such as the Soil Conservation Service, the Taylor Grazing Act, and the Farm Security Administration (discussed shortly) set new rules for western agriculture, from prairie wheat fields and cattle ranges to California citrus groves and truck farms dependent on migrant labor.

The PWA and WPA built many large projects in the West, including thousands of public buildings, from courthouses and post offices to tourist facilities such as beautiful Timberline Lodge on Oregon's Mount Hood. Federal assistance also upgraded the highways linking the West to the rest of America, such as Route 66 from Chicago to Los Angeles.

Above all, the PWA in the West built dams—not only Grand Coulee, but also Shasta on the Sacramento River, Bonneville on the Columbia, Glen Canyon on the Colorado, and others. The PWA completed Hoover Dam on the Colorado, authorized by Congress in 1928 (see Chapter 23), well ahead of schedule. Despite their ecological downside, these great undertakings—among the largest engineering projects in history—supplied electricity to vast regions while contributing to flood control, irrigation, and soil conservation. (Las Vegas owed its post–World War II emergence as a gambling and entertainment mecca to power from nearby Hoover Dam.)

A New Deal initiative especially important for the West was Harold Ickes's National Planning Board, later renamed the National Resources Planning Board. This agency, which extended Herbert Hoover's promotion of multi-state water-resource planning in the West, facilitated state and regional management of water, soil, timber, and minerals.

The New Deal's End Stage, 1937–1939

Buoyed by his 1936 victory, Roosevelt proposed a controversial restructuring of the Supreme Court. After losing this fight, FDR confronted a stubborn recession and resurgent conservative opposition. With a few measures in 1937–1938, the New Deal ended.

FDR and the Supreme Court

In 1937, four of the Supreme Court's nine elderly justices were archconservatives who abhorred the New Deal. Joined by more moderate colleagues, these conservatives had struck down the NRA, the AAA, and progressive state laws. Roosevelt feared

that the Social Security Act, the Wagner Act, and other key measures would meet a similar fate. Indeed, some corporate lawyers, convinced that the Social Security Act would be ruled unconstitutional, advised their clients to ignore it.

In February 1937, FDR proposed a bill that would have allowed him to appoint an additional Supreme Court member for each justice over age seventy, up to a total of six. Roosevelt blandly insisted that this would ease aging justices' heavy workload, but his political motivation was obvious.

Despite FDR's popularity, the press and public reacted with hostility. The Supreme Court's size, although unspecified in the Constitution, had held steady at nine since 1869, and thus seemed almost sacrosanct. Conservatives blasted FDR's "court-packing" scheme as a dangerous power grab. Even many Democrats disapproved. When the Senate voted down the scheme in July, FDR quietly dropped it.

But was this a defeat? Roosevelt's challenge to the Court, plus his 1936 electoral victory, sent powerful political signals that the justices heeded. In spring 1937, the Court upheld several New Deal measures, including the Wagner Act and a state minimum-wage law. Four conservative justices soon retired, enabling FDR to nominate successors of his choice and to create a judicial legacy that would long endure.

Overall, the New Deal era saw a fundamental shift in the Supreme Court's constitutional views. For decades, the court had interpreted very narrowly the Constitution's Commerce Clause (Article I, Sec. 8), which empowers the government to regulate business. After the 1930s, the court interpreted the Commerce Clause more broadly and proved much more receptive to business regulation and to the protection of individual rights as well as property rights.

The Roosevelt Recession

After a partial recovery, the economy dipped ominously in August 1937. Industrial production slumped. Unemployment again dominated the headlines. Federal policies that reduced consumer income contributed to this "Roosevelt recession." Social-security payroll taxes withdrew some $2 billion from circulation. The Federal Reserve Board had raised interest rates to forestall inflation, further contracting the money supply. FDR, meanwhile, concerned about mounting deficits, had cut back the New Deal relief programs.

Echoing Hoover, FDR assured his cabinet, "Everything will work out … if we just sit tight."

> "Everything will work out ... if we just sit tight."

Meanwhile, however, some advisers had embraced John Maynard Keynes's advocacy of deficit spending as the key to recovery. Aware that political rather than economic arguments carried more weight with FDR, they warned of a political backlash if conditions worsened. Convinced, FDR in April 1938 authorized new relief spending. By late 1938, unemployment had declined and industrial output increased. As late as 1939, however, more than 17 percent of the labor force remained jobless.

Final Measures; Growing Opposition

Preoccupied by the Supreme Court fight, the recession, and events abroad (covered in Chapter 25), FDR offered few domestic initiatives after 1936. Congress, however, enacted several significant measures.

In 1937, Congress created the **Farm Security Administration** (FSA), replacing the under-funded Resettlement Administration. The FSA made low-interest loans to help tenant farmers and sharecroppers become farm owners. However, the FSA often rejected the poorest farmers' loan applications as too risky, weakening the program's impact.

The FSA operated camps offering shelter and medical services to impoverished migrant farm workers. FSA nurses and home economists provided practical advice on hygiene and housekeeping to poor farm families. The FSA also commissioned photographers to record the lives of migrant workers, tenant farmers, and dust-bowl refugees. These FSA photographs, published in various periodicals, helped shape a gritty documentary style that pervaded 1930s' popular culture, including movies and Henry Luce's photo magazine *Life,* launched in 1936. Today, they comprise a haunting album of depression-era images.

Other measures set precedents for the future. The 1937 Housing Act appropriated $500 million for slum-clearance and public-housing projects that would vastly expand in the 1950s. The **Fair Labor Standards Act** of 1938 banned child labor and set a national minimum wage (initially forty cents an hour) and a maximum workweek of forty hours. This measure reflected not only humanitarianism but also some northern legislators' desire to undermine the competitive edge of the low-wage South. Despite many loopholes, the law helped exploited workers and underscored the government's role in regulating abusive workplace conditions.

In a final stab at raising farm income, the 1938 Agricultural Adjustment Act created a mechanism by which the government, in years of big harvests and low prices, would make loans to farmers and warehouse their surplus crops. When prices rose, farmers could sell these commodities and repay their loans. This complicated system set the framework of federal farm price support for decades.

Overall, New Deal farm policy produced mixed results. Large-scale growers benefited from government payments, but the cumbersome price-support mechanisms created many problems. The FSA assisted some tenants, sharecroppers, and small farmers (though often not the neediest), but did little to slow the long-term decline of family farms and the rise of agribusinesses. In reality, many small farmers dreamed of becoming large-scale commercial operators. Most did not succeed, however, and gradually left the land.

The New Deal's slower pace after 1935 also reflected the rise of an anti–New Deal congressional coalition of Republicans and conservative southern Democrats. In 1937, this coalition rejected FDR's proposal to reorganize the executive branch. The plan made administrative sense, but critics again warned darkly of FDR's dictatorial ambitions.

In 1938–1939, conservative legislators slashed relief appropriations, cut corporate taxes, and killed the WPA's Federal Theatre Project for its alleged radicalism. Meanwhile, the House Un-American Activities Committee (created in 1937) investigated New Deal agencies for communist infiltration. The 1939 Hatch Act, barring federal employees from electoral campaigning, reflected conservatives' suspicions that WPA staff members were doubling as campaign workers. Indeed, Harry Hopkins and other public-works officials well understood these programs' electoral value, and political calculations influenced the allocation of PWA and WPA funds.

Although FDR campaigned in the 1938 midterm elections, the Republicans gained in the House and Senate and won a net of thirteen governorships. In the Democratic primaries, Roosevelt opposed several anti-New Deal Democratic senators, but most defeated their pro–New Deal primary challengers and went on to win in November. Highlighting foreign affairs in his January 1939 State of the Union message, FDR proposed no new domestic measures and merely noted the need to "preserve our reforms." The New Deal was over.

A CAMERA'S-EYE VIEW OF DEPRESSION-ERA AMERICA This 1937 image by Dorothea Lange, a photographer with the Farm Security Administration, pictures migrants from the Texas dust bowl gathered at a roadside camp near Calipatria in southern California. *(Library of Congress)*

Social Change and Social Action in the 1930s

American life in the 1930s involved more than politics. The depression affected everyone, including the jobless and their families; working women; and all age groups. For industrial workers, African Americans, Hispanics, and Native Americans, the crisis brought hard times but also encouraged organized resistance to exploitation and brought new legislative initiatives.

In organizing our treatment of the 1930s, we have separated the decade's political developments and its social/cultural trends. In reality, of course, all these realities unfolded together. The social crisis and labor activism added urgency to the New Deal and helped drive its shifts of emphasis. New Deal agencies influenced the decade's culture, while the era's cultural products, in turn, shaped public perceptions of the meaning of the Depression and the New Deal for America.

The Depression's Psychological and Social Impact

The depression marked all who lived through it. Despite the New Deal, unemployment never fell below about 14 percent in the 1930s and was often considerably higher. A quarter of all farm families sought public or private assistance during the 1930s. Even the employed often had to take jobs below their level of training: college alumni pumped gas; business-school graduates sold furniture; a retired navy captain became a movie theater usher.

Psychologists described "unemployment shock": jobless persons who walked the streets seeking work and then lay awake at night worrying. When shoe soles wore out, cardboard or folded newspapers had to serve. Advertisements for mouthwashes, deodorants, and correspondence courses exploited feelings of shame and failure. Women's magazines described low-cost meals and other budget-trimming strategies. Habits of scrimping and saving acquired in the 1930s often survived into more affluent times. As Caroline Bird wrote in *The Invisible Scar* (1966), a social history of the 1930s, the depression for many boiled down to "a dull misery in the bones."

New York senator Robert Wagner called the working woman in the depression "the first orphan in the storm." Indeed, for the 25 percent of U.S. women employed in 1930, the depression brought difficult times. The female jobless rate exceeded 20 percent for much of the decade. Working women often took lower-paying jobs. Laid-off factory workers became waitresses. Jobless men competed with women even for such traditional "women's work" as library posts and school teaching.

Married women workers endured harsh criticism. Although most worked because of economic necessity, critics accused them of stealing men's jobs. Even Labor Secretary Frances Perkins urged married women to leave the labor market so more men could work. School boards fired married women teachers.

Women workers faced wage discrimination. In 1939, women teachers earned nearly 20 percent less than male teachers with comparable experience. Some NRA codes authorized lower pay for women. The minimum-wage provision of the Fair Labor Standards Act did not include the more than 2 million women who worked for wages in private households.

The late 1930s' unionization drive had mixed effects on women workers. Women employed in mass-production industries benefited, but the heavily female sectors of the labor force—textiles, sales, clerical and service work—resisted unionization. Male managers and even male union leaders opposed a campaign to unionize female clerical workers.

Despite the criticism, the percentage of married women in the work force increased in the 1930s from under 12 percent to nearly 16 percent. The depression may actually have hastened the long-term movement of women into the workplace as married women took jobs out of necessity. When her husband stopped looking for work in 1932, one working wife explained, "[At] twenty-eight, with two little girls, … I took a job as a salesclerk … , and worked through the Depression."

As this story suggests, the depression affected family life. The birthrate fell in the early thirties as married couples postponed a family, and as birth-control devices became more readily available. The

U.S. population in the 1930s grew by only 7 percent, in contrast to an average of 20 percent per decade from 1900 to 1930.

Family survival posed major challenges. Parents patched clothes, stretched food resources, and sought public assistance when necessary. In homes with a tradition of strong male authority, the husband's loss of a job could prove devastating. "I would rather turn on the gas and put an end to the whole family than let my wife support me," one man told a social investigator. Desertions increased, and the divorce rate spiked, hitting a then all-time high by 1940.

The depression spared neither old nor young. Bank failures wiped out the savings of older Americans. By 1935, a million citizens over sixty-five were on relief. One observer compared young people to runners waiting for a starting gun that never sounded. High-school enrollment increased

ANN BURLAK ENCOURAGES STRIKING FALL RIVER, MASSACHUSETTS, TEXTILE WORKERS, 1934 Burlak, a former millworker and Communist Party member nicknamed the "Red Flame," was an organizer for the National Textile Workers Union. *(© Bettmann/Corbis)*

as many youths, lacking job prospects, stayed in school. The marriage rate declined as anxious young people postponed this step. Commented Eleanor Roosevelt in 1934, "I have moments of real terror when I think we might be losing this generation."

Children found vacation plans canceled, birthdays with few presents, and mealtimes tense with anxious discussions. Depression-era children wrote sad letters to Eleanor Roosevelt. A Michigan high-school senior described her shame at lacking a graduation dress. "I give all I earn for food for the family," she explained. A thirteen-year-old Arkansas girl wrote, "I have to stay out of school because I have no books or clothes to ware."

Rediscovering traditional skills, depression-era families canned fruit and vegetables, painted their houses, and repaired their own cars. Many would later recall the 1930s as a time of simple, inexpensive pleasures and neighborly sharing of scant resources.

For the neediest—among them blacks, Hispanics, and southern sharecroppers—the depression imposed added misery on poverty-blighted lives. In *Native Son* (1940), novelist Richard Wright portrayed the desperate conditions in Chicago's black slums. Yet hope survived. Emotional resilience, habits of mutual aid, and survival skills honed over the years helped poor families cope. In New York's Harlem, a charismatic black religious leader calling himself Father Divine institutionalized this cooperative spirit by organizing kitchens that distributed free meals to the needy.

Industrial Workers Unionize

Of America's 7.7 million factory workers in 1930, most remained unorganized. Major industries such as steel, automobiles, and textiles had resisted workers' attempts to unionize. The conservative mood of the 1920s had further weakened the labor movement.

But with hard times and a favorable government climate, labor militancy surged in the 1930s. The Wagner Act's guarantee of workers' right to organize jolted the U.S. labor movement. The nation's major labor organization, the American Federation of Labor (AFL), had historically organized unions of skilled craftsmen rather than of all workers in a given industry (see Chapter 18). In the 1930s, that pattern changed. In November 1935, John L. Lewis of the United Mine Workers and Sidney Hillman of the Amalgamated Clothing Workers, frustrated by the AFL's slowness in organizing factory workers, started the Committee for Industrial Organization (CIO) within the AFL. CIO activists preached unionization in Pittsburgh steel mills, Detroit auto

plants, Akron rubber factories, and southern textile mills. Unlike the narrowly restrictive AFL unions, CIO unions welcomed all workers in a particular industry, regardless of race, gender, or skill level.

In 1936 a CIO-sponsored organizing committee announced a strike to unionize the steel industry. (In fact, John L. Lewis had already secretly negotiated a settlement with the head of U.S. Steel.) In March 1937, U.S. Steel recognized the union, raised wages, and introduced a forty-hour workweek. Other big steel companies followed suit, and soon four hundred thousand steelworkers were union members (see Figure 24.4).

Other CIO organizers targeted General Motors, an anti-union stronghold. Their leader was a red-headed young autoworker and labor activist, Walter Reuther. Reuther's German American father was a committed socialist, and when the depression hit, young Reuther rediscovered his radical roots. On December 30, 1936, employees at GM's plants in Flint, Michigan, stopped work and peacefully occupied the factories. This "sit-down" strategy (adopted so GM could not hire strikebreakers to keep the plants operating) paralyzed GM's production.

Although women workers did not participate in the plant occupation (to avoid gossip that might discredit the strike), they picketed outside. A Women's

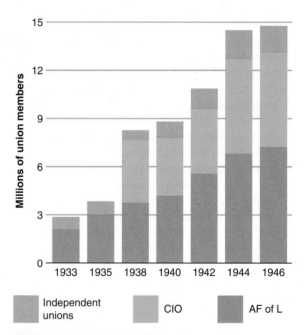

FIGURE 24.4 THE GROWTH OF LABOR UNION MEMBERSHIP, 1933–1946 The CIO's industrial unions grew rapidly with passage of the pro-union National Labor Relations Act in 1935. Union membership increased still more as war plants hired workers in the early 1940s.

Source: *Historical Statistics of the United States, Colonial Times to 1970 (1975), 176–177.*

Auxiliary led by strikers' families provided meals, set up a speakers' bureau, and organized marches.

GM sent spies to union meetings, called in police to harass the strikers, and threatened to fire them. A showdown with the police led to the formation of the Women's Emergency Brigade, whose members remained on twenty-four-hour alert for picket duty or to surround the plants in case of police raids.

GM asked President Roosevelt and Michigan's governor to send troops to expel the strikers, as Herbert Hoover had done with the bonus marchers. Both declined, however. Although the sit-down tactic troubled FDR, he refused to intervene.

On February 11, 1937, GM signed a contract recognizing the United Automobile Workers (UAW). Bearded workers who had vowed not to shave until victory was won streamed out of the plants. As Chrysler fell into line also, the UAW boasted more than four hundred thousand members. Unionization of the electrical and rubber industries advanced as well.

In 1938 the Committee for Industrial Organization broke with the AFL to become the **Congress of Industrial Organizations,** a 2-million-member association of industrial unions. In response, the AFL, too, began to adapt to the changed nature of the labor force. Overall, U.S. union membership shot from fewer than 3 million in 1933 to more than 8 million in 1941.

Some big corporations resisted. Henry Ford hated unions, and his tough lieutenant Harry Bennett organized a squad of union-busting thugs to fight the UAW. In 1937, Bennett's men viciously beat Walter Reuther and other UAW officials outside Ford's plant near Detroit. Not until 1941 did Ford finally yield to the union's pressure.

The Republic Steel Company, headed by a union hater named Tom Girdler, dug in as well. Even after the major steelmakers signed with the CIO, Republic and other smaller companies known collectively as "Little Steel" resisted. In May 1937, workers in twenty-seven Little Steel plants, including Republic's factory in Chicago, walked off the job. Anticipating the strike, Girdler had assembled an arsenal of guns and tear gas. On May 30, Memorial Day, a group of strikers approached more than 250 police guarding the factory. When someone threw a large stick at the police, they responded with gunfire that left four strikers dead and scores wounded. An investigative committee

> An investigative committee condemned the killings as "clearly avoidable."

condemned the killings as "clearly avoidable." In 1941, under growing pressure, the Little Steel companies, including Republic, finally accepted the CIO union.

Another holdout was the textile industry, with more than six hundred thousand low-paid workers, mostly in the South and 40 percent female. A unionizing effort in the 1920s had failed owing to mill owners' hostility (see Chapter 23). In 1934, the AFL-affiliated United Textile Workers launched a new drive. Some four hundred thousand textile workers went on strike, but again the mill owners fought back. Anti-union southern governors mobilized the National Guard. Several strikers were killed and thousands arrested. The strike failed, and the textile industry remained mostly nonunion as the decade ended.

Indeed, despite the unionization surge, more than three-quarters of the nonfarm labor force remained unorganized in 1940, including low-paid manual laborers; domestic workers; and employees in department stores, offices, restaurants, and laundries—categories that included many women, blacks, and recent immigrants. Nevertheless, the unionization of many industrial workers ranks among the decade's memorable developments.

Why did powerful corporations yield to unionization after years of resistance? Workers' militancy and union organizers' tactical skill were crucial. But so was a changed government climate. Historically, the government had helped corporations break strikes. Although this still happened in the 1930s, as in the textile-industry strike, the Roosevelt administration and state officials generally refused to play

LABOR ORGANIZING, 1930s STYLE Walter Reuther (left) and Richard Frankensteen of the United Auto Workers, after their beating by Ford Motor Company security guards, Detroit, May 1937. (*Archives of Labor and Urban Affairs/Wayne State University*)

the role of strikebreaker. New Deal labor laws made clear that Washington would no longer automatically back management in labor disputes. Once corporate managers realized this, unionization often followed.

Organized labor's successes in the later 1930s concealed some complex tensions. A core of activists, including communists and socialists, led the unionizing drive. Most rank-and-file workers were not political radicals, but once the CIO's militant minority showed the effectiveness of picket lines and sit-down strikes, workers signed up by the thousands. As they did, the radical organizers lost influence, and the unions became more conservative.

Black and Hispanic Americans Resist Racism and Exploitation

The depression stirred activism within the African American and Hispanic communities. Although black migration northward slowed in the 1930s, four hundred thousand southern blacks moved to northern cities in the decade. By 1940, nearly one-quarter of America's 12 million blacks lived in the urban North.

Rural or urban, life was hard. Black tenant farmers and sharecroppers often faced eviction. Although some black industrial workers benefited from the CIO's nondiscriminatory policy, workplace racism remained a fact of life.

More than one hundred blacks died by lynching in the 1930s, and other miscarriages of justice continued, especially in the South. In 1931, an all-white jury in Scottsboro, Alabama, sentenced eight black youths to death on highly suspect rape charges. In 1935, after heavy publicity and an aggressive defense, the Supreme Court ordered a new trial for the "Scottsboro Boys" because they had been denied legal counsel and blacks had been excluded from the jury. Five of the group were again convicted, however, and served long prison terms.

But rising activism signaled changes ahead. The NAACP battled in courts and legislatures for voting rights and against lynching and segregation. Under the banner "Don't Shop Where You Can't Work," black protesters picketed businesses that refused to hire blacks, particularly in black neighborhoods. In March 1935, hostility toward discriminatory white-owned businesses in Harlem, intensified by anger over racism and joblessness, ignited a riot that caused heavy property damage and left three dead.

The Communist Party publicized lynchings and racial discrimination, and supplied lawyers for the "Scottsboro

"Don't Shop Where You Can't Work."

Boys," as part of a depression-era recruitment effort in the black community. But despite a few notable recruits (including the novelist Richard Wright), few blacks joined the party.

Other groups also faced discrimination. California continued to restrict landownership by Japanese Americans. In 1934, Congress limited annual immigration from the Philippines to fifty, and offered free travel "home" for Filipinos long settled in the United States.

The more than 2 million Hispanic Americans confronted difficulties as well. Some were citizens with ancestral roots in the Southwest, but most were recent arrivals from Mexico or Caribbean islands such as Cuba and Puerto Rico (a U.S. holding whose residents are American citizens). While the Caribbean immigrants settled in East Coast cities, most Mexican newcomers worked as migratory agricultural laborers in the Southwest and elsewhere or in midwestern steel or meatpacking plants.

As the depression deepened, Mexican-born residents endured rising hostility. "Okies" fleeing the dust bowl competed for jobs with Hispanic farm workers. By 1937, more than half of Arizona's cotton workers were out-of-staters who had supplanted Mexican-born laborers. With their migratory work patterns disrupted, Mexican Americans poured into the barrios (Hispanic neighborhoods) of southwestern cities. Lacking work, half a million returned to Mexico in the 1930s. Many did so voluntarily, but immigration officials and local authorities repatriated others. Los Angeles welfare officials announced free one-way transportation to Mexico. The savings in relief payments, they calculated, would more than offset the cost of sending *repatriados* to Mexico. Though the plan was "voluntary," those who remained were denied relief payments or jobs with New Deal work programs. Under federal and local pressure, an estimated seventy thousand Mexicans left Los Angeles in 1931 alone.

Mexican American farm workers who remained endured appalling conditions and near-starvation wages. A wave of strikes (some led by Communist organizers) swept California. A labor organization called the Confederación de Uniones de Campesinos y Obreros Mexicanos (Confederation of Unions of Mexican Workers and Farm Laborers) emerged from a 1933 grape workers' strike. More strikes erupted in 1935–1936 from the celery fields and citrus groves around Los Angeles to the lettuce fields of the Salinas Valley.

Organizations like the citrus-growers' marketing cooperative Sunkist fought the unions, sometimes with violence. In October 1933, bullets ripped into a cotton pickers' union hall in Pixley, California, killing two men and wounding others. Resisting

A CARAVAN OF PICKETERS DURING A 1933 STRIKE OF COTTON WORKERS IN CORCORAN, CALIFORNIA Protesting low wages and appalling working conditions, agricultural workers from Mexico went on strike across California's rich San Joaquin Valley in the early 1930s. In some cases, Communist Party members helped organize these strikes. *(Library of Congress)*

intimidation, the strikers won a 20 percent pay increase. Striking cotton pickers and other Mexican American farm workers gained hard-fought victories as well. These strikes awakened at least some Americans to the plight of one of the nation's most exploited groups.

A New Deal for Native Americans

The 1930s also focused attention on the nation's 330,000 Native Americans, most of whom endured poverty, scant education, and poor health care. The 1887 Dawes Act (see Chapter 17) had dissolved the tribes as legal entities, allocated some tribal lands to individual Indians, and offered the rest for sale. By the 1930s, non-Indians held about two-thirds of the land that Indians had possessed in 1887. Indians had gained voting rights in 1924, but this did little to improve their lot.

In 1923, the reformer John Collier, who had lived among New Mexico's Pueblo Indians, founded the American Indian Defense Association to reverse the Dawes Act approach and to revitalize traditional Indian life. The National Council of American Indians, headed by Gertrude Bonnin, a Yankton Dakota Sioux, also pressed for reform.

Appointed commissioner of Indian affairs in 1933, Collier gathered funds from various New Deal agencies to construct schools, hospitals, and irrigation systems on reservations, and to preserve sites of cultural importance. The Civilian Conservation Corps employed twelve thousand Indian youths on projects on Indian lands.

Pursuing his vision, Collier drafted a bill to halt tribal land sales and restore the remaining unallocated lands to tribal control. Collier's bill also gave broad powers to tribal councils and required Indian schools to teach Native American history and handicrafts. Some Indian leaders criticized it as a plan to transform reservations into living museums and to isolate Native Americans from modern life. Some Indian property owners and entrepreneurs rejected the bill's tribalist assumptions. The bill did, indeed, reflect the idealism of well-meaning outsiders rather than the views of the nation's diverse Native American groups.

The **Indian Reorganization Act** of 1934, a compromise measure, halted tribal land sales and enabled tribes to regain title to unallocated lands. But Congress scaled back Collier's proposals for tribal self-government and dropped his proposals for renewing traditional tribal culture.

Of 258 tribes that voted on the law (a requirement for it to go into effect), 181 favored it, while 77 did not. America's largest tribal group, the 40,000-strong Navajo, voted no, largely because the law, to promote soil conservation, restricted grazing rights.

Indian policy remained contentious. But the law did recognize Indian interests and the value of cultural diversity. The restoration of tribes as legal entities laid the groundwork for later tribal business ventures as well as legal efforts to enforce long-ignored treaty rights (to be discussed in Chapter 30).

The American Cultural Scene in the 1930s

Radio and the movies offered escapist fare amid the hard times of the 1930s, though some films addressed depression-era realities. Novelists, artists, playwrights, and photographers tended toward a highly critical view of capitalist America when the depression first struck, as we have seen. As the decade went on, however, a more positive view of America emerged, reflecting both optimism about the New Deal and apprehension about events abroad.

Avenues of Escape: Radio and the Movies

The standardization of mass culture continued in the 1930s. Each evening, Americans turned to their radios for network news, musical programs, and comedy shows. Radio humor flourished as Americans battled hard times. Comedians like Jack Benny and the husband-and-wife team George Burns and Gracie Allen attracted millions.

So, too, did the fifteen-minute afternoon domestic dramas known as soap operas (for the soap companies that sponsored them). Despite their assembly-line quality, these programs won a devoted audience, consisting mostly of housewives. Identifying with the radio heroines' troubles, female listeners gained temporary escape from their own difficulties. As one put it, "I can get through the day better when I hear they have sorrows, too."

"I can get through the day better when I hear they have sorrows, too."

The movies, with their low-priced tickets, remained extremely popular. In 1939, 65 percent of Americans went to the movies at least once a week.

Films of the early 1930s like *I Am a Fugitive from a Chain Gang* (1932) captured the grimness of the early depression. The popular Marx Brothers movies reflected the uncertainty of the Hoover years, when the economy and the social order itself seemed on the verge of collapse. In comedies like *Animal Crackers* (1930) and *Duck Soup* (1933), these vaudeville troupers of German Jewish immigrant origins ridiculed authority and satirized the established order.

After Roosevelt took office, Warner Brothers studio (with close ties to the administration) made several topical films that presented the New Deal in a favorable light. These included *Wild Boys of the Road* (1933), about unemployed youth; *Massacre* (1934), on the mistreatment of Indians; and *Black Fury* (1935), dealing with striking coal miners.

Early thirties' gangster movies, inspired by real-life criminals like Al Capone, presented a different style of film realism. Films like *Little Caesar* (1930) and *The Public Enemy* (1931) offered gritty images of depression America: menacing streets, forbidding industrial sites, gunfights between rival gangs. (When civic groups protested the glorification of crime, Hollywood made the police and "G-men"—FBI agents—the heroes, while retaining the violence.) The movie gangsters played by Edward G. Robinson and James Cagney, variants of the Horatio Alger hero battling adversity, appealed to depression-era moviegoers.

Above all, Hollywood offered escape from depression-era realities. The publicist who claimed that the movies "literally laughed the big bad wolf of the depression out of the public mind" exaggerated, but cinema's escapist function in the 1930s is clear. Musicals such as *Gold Diggers of 1933* (with its theme song, "We're in the Money") offered dancing, music, and cheerful plots involving the triumph of pluck over adversity. In Frank Capra's *Mr. Deeds Goes to Town* (1936) and *Mr. Smith Goes to Washington* (1939), virtuous heroes representing "the people" vanquish entrenched interests. When color movies arrived in the late 1930s (see Technology and Culture), they seemed an omen of better times ahead.

African Americans appeared in 1930s' movies, if at all, mostly as stereotypes: the scatterbrained maid in *Gone with the Wind* (1939); the indulgent house servant played by tap dancer Bill Robinson and patronized by child star Shirley Temple in *The Little Colonel* (1935); the slow-witted "Stepin Fetchit" played in many movies by black actor Lincoln Perry.

In representing women, Hollywood offered mixed messages. While some 1930s' movie heroines found fulfillment in marriage and domesticity, other films challenged the stereotype. Joan Bennett played a strong-willed professional in *The Wedding Present* (1936). Katharine Hepburn portrayed independent-minded women in such films as *Spitfire* (1934) and *A Woman Rebels* (1936). Mae West, brassy and openly sexual, mocked conventional stereotypes in *I'm No Angel* (1933) and other 1930s hits.

The Later 1930s: Opposing Fascism; Reaffirming Traditional Values

The 1930s ended on a cautiously upbeat note. America had survived the depression. The social fabric remained whole; revolution had not come. As other societies collapsed into dictatorships, U.S. democracy endured. Writers, composers, and other cultural creators reflected the changed mood.

International developments and a domestic political movement known as the **Popular Front** influenced this shift. In the early 1930s, the U.S. Communist Party attacked Roosevelt and the New Deal. But in 1935, Russian dictator Joseph Stalin, fearing attack by Nazi Germany, called for a worldwide alliance, or Popular Front, against Adolf Hitler and his Italian fascist ally, Benito Mussolini. (Fascism is a form of government involving one-party rule, extreme nationalism, hostility to minority groups, and the suppression of dissent.) Parroting the new Soviet line, U.S. communists now praised FDR and summoned writers and intellectuals to the antifascist cause. Many noncommunists, alarmed by developments in Europe, responded.

The Spanish Civil War was the Popular Front's high-water mark. In July 1936, Spanish fascist general Francisco Franco began a military revolt against Spain's legally elected government, a coalition of left-wing parties. With aid from Hitler and Mussolini, Franco won backing from Spanish monarchists, landowners, industrialists, and the Catholic Church.

The Spanish Loyalists (that is, those loyal to Spain's elected government) won support from U.S. writers, artists, and intellectuals who backed the Popular Front, including the writer Ernest Hemingway, who visited Spain in 1936–1937. In contrast to his antiwar novels of the 1920s (see Chapter 23), Hemingway's *For Whom the Bell Tolls* (1940) told of a young American volunteer who dies while fighting with the Loyalists. For Hemingway, the Spanish Civil War offered a cause "in which you felt an absolute brotherhood with the others who were engaged in it."

The Popular Front collapsed in August 1939 when Stalin and Hitler signed a nonaggression pact. Overnight, enthusiasm for joining with communists under the "antifascism" banner faded. But while it lasted, the Popular Front influenced U.S. culture and alerted Americans to threatening events abroad.

The New Deal's programs for writers, artists, and musicians, as well as its turn leftward in 1935–1936, also contributed to the late 1930s' cultural shift. More positive views now replaced the cynical tone of the 1920s and early 1930s. In John Steinbeck's best-selling novel *The Grapes of Wrath* (1939), an uprooted dust-bowl family, the Joads, make their difficult way from Oklahoma to California along Route 66. Steinbeck stressed ordinary Americans' endurance, cooperation, and mutual support. As Ma Joad tells her son Tom, "They ain't gonna wipe us out. Why, we're the people—we go on." Made into a movie starring Henry Fonda, *The Grapes of Wrath* stands as a memorable cultural document of the later 1930s.

In 1936, journalist James Agee and photographer Walker Evans lived with Alabama sharecropper families while researching a magazine article. From this experience came Agee's masterpiece, *Let Us Now Praise Famous Men* (1941). Enhanced by Evans's photographs, Agee's work evoked the strength and decency of depression-era Americans.

On the stage, Thornton Wilder's *Our Town* (1938) lovingly portrayed early-twentieth-century life a New England town. William Saroyan's *The Time of Your Life* (1939) celebrated the foibles and virtues of a colorful group of patrons gathered in a San Francisco waterfront bar.

Composers, too, caught the spirit of cultural nationalism. In such works as *Billy the Kid* (1938), Aaron Copland drew upon American legends and folk melodies. George Gershwin's 1935 musical *Porgy and Bess,* based on DuBose and Dorothy Heyward's 1920s' novel and play (see Chapter 23), brought this portrayal of black life in Charleston, South Carolina, to a larger audience.

***LET US NOW PRAISE FAMOUS MEN* (1941)** Journalist James Agee and photographer Walker Evans created a memorable record of a month spent with Alabama sharecroppers in 1936. *(Photography Collection, Harry Ransom Humanities Research Center, The University of Texas at Austin General Libraries)*

October 1938, another European war loomed on the horizon.

The panic triggered by Orson Welles's Halloween prank quickly faded, but the anxieties aroused by the all-too-real dangers abroad only escalated. By the time the New York World's Fair offered its hopeful vision of the future, the actual world of 1939 looked bleak indeed.

CONCLUSION

The stock-market crash and the Great Depression exposed major weaknesses in the U.S. and world economies. These ranged from chronically low farm prices and uneven income distribution to trade barriers, a glut of consumer goods, and a constricted money supply. As the crisis deepened, President Hoover struggled to respond. In 1932, with Hoover discredited, Franklin D. Roosevelt and his promised "New Deal" brought a surge of hope.

Initially focusing on immediate economic relief and recovery, Roosevelt welcomed big business in his depression-fighting coalition. By 1935, however, the New Deal adopted a more class-based approach. FDR now addressed the plight of the poor, including sharecroppers and migrants; pursued business regulation and higher taxes for the wealthy; and championed such fundamental reforms as Social Security, centerpiece of the welfare state, and the Wagner Act, guaranteeing workers' right to unionize. His smashing reelection victory in 1936 solidified FDR's Democratic coalition, including the white South, farmers, urban ethnics, union members, and African Americans. By 1938, facing conservative opposition and menaces abroad, the New Deal's reformist energies faded.

The depression and the New Deal affected different groups in different ways. For citizens across the West and in the region served by TVA, public-works projects brought hydroelectric power and economic growth, while the New Deal also renewed attention to conservation and environmental issues. Women were told to stay home so jobless men could find work. Many resisted, however, and the female labor force expanded. For industrial workers, the decade's spirit of militance and favorable legislation brought a wave of strikes and unionization campaigns.

While African Americans benefited from New Deal relief programs, the Roosevelt administration failed to address lynching and racial discrimination. Mexican-born farm laborers, facing deportation threats, organized strikes demanding better wages and working conditions. For Native Americans, New Deal legislation restored tribes' legal status, laying the groundwork for future enterprises and treaty claims.

American culture in the 1930s reflected the decade's economic and social realities. While movies and radio offered diversion, writers, painters, and other cultural creators initially expressed disillusionment over capitalism's failure. But as New Deal programs inspired hope, and as foreign threats loomed, the later 1930s brought a more upbeat and affirmative cultural climate.

The New Deal has its downside. Some programs failed, and recovery proved elusive. Only in 1943, as war plants boomed, did full employment return. On racial issues, symbolic gestures substituted for genuine engagement. But the New Deal's achievements remain impressive, reflecting an unprecedented level of governmental engagement with social and economic issues. FDR and his administration reshaped the role of the presidency, the Supreme Court, the nation's political agenda, and citizens' expectations of government's role in meeting urgent public needs.

When a severe economic recession hit the United States in 2008, thoughts turned back to the Great Depression, seventy-five years earlier. The economic policies of the New Deal, and their relevance to the current crisis, were debated with fresh intensity, underscoring how profoundly the 1930s reshaped American thought about the role of government in the economy.

Looming over the decade is the larger-than-life image of Franklin D. Roosevelt. Neither saint nor superman, FDR could be devious, superficial, and cavalier about details. But for most Americans of the 1930s—and most historians since—his strengths outweighed his liabilities. His experimental approach served a suffering nation well. He once compared himself to a football quarterback, deciding which play to call after seeing how the last one worked out.

Above all, Roosevelt's optimism inspired a demoralized people. "We Americans of today ... " he told an audience of young people in 1939, "are characters in the living book of democracy. But we are also its author. It falls upon us now to say whether the chapters ... to come will tell a story of retreat or a story of continued advance."

KEY TERMS

Franklin Delano Roosevelt (p. 731)

Eleanor Roosevelt (p. 731)

Reconstruction Finance
Corporation (p. 734)

Frances Perkins (p. 737)

Harold Ickes (p. 737)

Civilian Conservation Corps
(p. 739)

Federal Emergency Relief Act
(p. 739)

Harry Hopkins (p. 739)

Agricultural Adjustment
Administration (p. 741)

Public Works Administration
(p. 741)

National Recovery
Administration (p. 741)

Tennessee Valley Authority (p. 741)

Works Progress Administration
(p. 746)

National Labor Relations Act
(Wagner Act) (p. 747)

Social Security Act (p. 747)

Farm Security Administration
(p. 751)

Fair Labor Standards Act (p. 751)

Congress of Industrial
Organizations (p. 755)

Indian Reorganization Act (p. 757)

Popular Front (p. 759)

FOR FURTHER REFERENCE

Lizabeth Cohen, *Making a New Deal: Industrial Workers in Chicago, 1919–1939* (1990). Influential, well-researched study of working-class and union culture.

Blanche D. Coll, *Safety Net: Welfare and Social Security, 1929–1979* (1995). Balanced, well-written history of the sources of the Social Security Act and its aftermath.

Susan Dunn, *Roosevelt's Purge: How FDR Fought to Change the Democratic Party* (2010). Well-researched account of Roosevelt's failed 1938 effort to transform his party into a truly progressive political force.

Timothy Egan, *The Worst Hard Time* (2005). A history of the dust bowl, stressing the unwise farming practices that contributed to this ecological disaster.

Lewis Erenberg, *Swingin' the Dream: Big Band Jazz and the Rebirth of American Culture* (1998). Stimulating interpretive study linking New Deal politics and popular music in the later 1930s.

David M. Kennedy, *Freedom from Fear: The American People in Depression and War* (1998). A sweeping synthesis, especially good on Washington politics and the Social Security Act.

Lauren Rebecca Sklaroff, *Black Culture and the New Deal: The Quest for Civil Rights in the Roosevelt Era* (2009). Illuminating study of the link between 1930s' black cultural expression and civil-rights activism and the New Deal's ambiguous role.

Jason Scott Smith, *Building New Deal Liberalism: The Political Economy of Public Works* (2006). Careful, archives-based study of public-works programs that strengthened the nation's infrastructure, promoted economic development, and won votes for FDR.

Nick Taylor, *America Made: The Enduring Legacy of the WPA; When FDR Put the Nation to Work* (2008). A readable narrative history, illuminated by personal vignettes, documenting the WPA's vast impact on the lives of millions.

Robert H. Zieger, *The CIO, 1935–1955* (1995). Valuable history of organized labor in the later New Deal, highlighting tensions between the leadership and the rank-and-file.

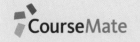 Visit the CourseMate website at **www.cengagebrain.com** for additional study tools and review materials for this chapter.

Americans and a World in Crisis, **1933–1945**

E.B. SLEDGE *(Private Collection)*

MOST AMERICANS AT THE TIME agreed that the United States fought a just war against aggressive Nazi Germany and Japan. As the years passed, particularly after the traumas of the Vietnam War and the economic setbacks of the 1970s, that war became remembered as the "Good War" fought by the "Greatest Generation." Unlike the nations of Asia and Europe, the United States suffered no invasion of its homeland, no bombing of its cities, no mass killing of its civilians. Indeed, the war lifted the United States out of the Great Depression, propelled many into the middle class, and gave unprecedented opportunities to millions of minorities and women. That "Good War," however, had little to do with E.B. Sledge's experience fighting in the South Pacific.

Born in 1923, Sledge had enjoyed a carefree boyhood of fishing and hunting in Mobile, Alabama, until the United States entered the Second World War. Filled with idealism and patriotism, he dropped out of school to join the marines and defend his country. His harrowing experiences drove him to write a wartime memoir of unrelenting horror, *With the Old Breed.* Describing the battles of Peleliu and Okinawa, Sledge depicts a brutal landscape of war without mercy, of kill or be killed, of prisoners tortured and the dead mutilated, of the most savage violence abetted by the most lethal technology of modern warfare.

On Peleliu, where Sledge's Company K reported 64 percent casualties in a campaign later deemed unnecessary, he witnessed helpless comrades being slaughtered. Unable to reclaim the bodies of fallen marines, he watched as buddies oozed into a wasteland of mud and excreta, land crabs feeding on them. He saw a fellow marine use a knife to try to extract the gold teeth of a wounded Japanese soldier. Frustrated in the attempt, the marine sliced open the prisoner's cheeks and continued to gouge and pry, unfazed by the man's thrashing and gurgling. On Okinawa's Half Moon Hill, he dreamed that the decomposed bodies of marines sprawled about him slowly rose, unblinkingly stared at him, and said, "It is over for us who are dead, but you must struggle, and will carry the memories all your life. People back home will wonder why you can't forget."

The wartime experiences of few Americans matched those of Sledge. Yet World War II fundamentally changed national institutions and transformed individual behavior. History's greatest armed conflict proved as much a turning point in American

OKINAWA, 1945 Wounded in the head, his hands clasped as if in prayer, a GI from the Seventh Infantry Division awaits evacuation from Rocky Crags in southern Okinawa. *(W. Eugene Smith/ TimeLife Pictures/Getty Images/Getty Images)*

personal lives as in world affairs. Gone were the high unemployment and low productivity of the Great Depression and the accompanying doubts about the vitality of American institutions and national purpose. Gone too was the world in which the United States played only a peripheral role. The war was a watershed, separating what had come before from what would become the dominant patterns of postwar life. The war destroyed certain traditional American ways and communities and created a new world order that left the United States at the pinnacle of its power and sowed the seeds of a postwar crisis. It was indeed, in Eleanor Roosevelt's words, "no ordinary time."

FOCUS Questions

- How did the American people and government respond to the international crises of the 1930s?
- How did war mobilization transform the American economy and government?
- What were the major aspects of Allied military strategy in Europe and Asia?
- What were the major effects of World War II on American minorities and women?
- What new issues did the U.S. government confront in defeating Germany and Japan in 1945?

The United States in a Menacing World, 1933–1939

Apart from improving relations with Latin America, the early administration of President Franklin D. Roosevelt (FDR) remained largely aloof from the crises in the world. Americans reacted ambivalently as Italy, Germany, and Japan grew more aggressive. Millions of Americans, determined not to stumble into war again, supported neutrality. Only a minority wanted the United States to help embattled democracies abroad. All the while, the world slid toward the precipice.

Nationalism and the Good Neighbor

President Roosevelt at first put American economic interests above all else and showed little interest in

international cooperation. He did, however, extend the internationalist approach of his predecessor in Latin America, where bitterness over "Yankee imperialism" ran high. FDR declared a **"Good Neighbor" policy,** renouncing any nation's right to intervene in the affairs of another. To that end, Roosevelt withdrew the last U.S. troops from Haiti and the Dominican Republic and terminated the Platt Amendment, which had given the United States its right to intervene in Cuba since 1901.

An economic crisis in Cuba in 1933 brought to power a leftist regime that the United States opposed. Instead of sending in the marines, as earlier administrations might have done, the United States provided indirect aid to a conservative revolt led by Fulgencio Batista in 1934 that overthrew the radical government. American economic assistance would then allow Batista to retain power until his overthrow by Fidel Castro in 1959. In Mexico, a reform government came to power in 1936 and promptly nationalized several oil companies owned by U.S. and British corporations. While insisting on fair compensation, the United States refrained from military intervention. The better relations fostered by FDR would help the United States achieve hemispheric solidarity in World War II, as well as later in the Cold War.

The Rise of Aggressive States in Europe and Asia

Meanwhile, powerful forces raged across much of the world. As early as 1922, economic and social unrest in Italy enabled **Benito Mussolini** to seize power. Dictator until 1943, Mussolini suppressed dissent, imposed one-party fascist rule, adopted anti-Semitic laws, and, hoping to recreate a Roman empire, invaded Ethiopia in 1935.

Borrowing the straight-armed Roman salute from Mussolini, **Adolf Hitler** and his National Socialist (Nazi) party in Germany gained broad support as a result of the depression, fear of communism, and resentment of the harsh Versailles treaty. In 1933, Hitler became Germany's chancellor. Crushing opponents and rivals, Hitler imposed a brutal dictatorship on Germany and began the pursuit of world domination he had proclaimed in his book *Mein Kampf* (*My Struggle*) (1923). He also instituted a program to purify the fatherland of Jews—whom he considered an "inferior race" responsible for Germany's defeat in World War I.

Violating the Versailles treaty, Hitler began rearming Germany in 1935. A year later, German troops reoccupied the Rhineland, a region between the Rhine River and France specifically

CHRONOLOGY 1933–1945

1931–1932	Japan invades Manchuria and creates a puppet government.
1933	Adolf Hitler becomes chancellor of Germany and assumes dictatorial powers.
1934–1936	Nye Committee investigations.
1935–1937	Neutrality Acts.
1937	Japan invades China.
1938	Germany annexes Austria; Munich Pact gives Sudetenland to Germany.
	Kristallnacht, night of Nazi terror against German and Austrian Jews.
1939	Nazi-Soviet Pact.
	Germany invades Poland; World War II begins.
1940	Germany conquers the Netherlands, Belgium, France, Denmark, Norway, and Luxembourg.
	Germany, Italy, and Japan sign the Tripartite Pact.
	Selective Service Act.
	Franklin Roosevelt elected to an unprecedented third term.
1941	Lend-Lease Act.
	Roosevelt establishes the Fair Employment Practices Commission (FEPC).
	Germany invades the Soviet Union.
	Japan attacks Pearl Harbor; the United States enters World War II.
	War Powers Act.

1942	Battles of Coral Sea and Midway halt Japanese offensive.
	Internment of Japanese Americans.
	Revenue Act expands graduated income-tax system.
	Allies invade North Africa (Operation TORCH).
	First successful atomic chain reaction.
	CORE founded.
1943	Soviet victory in Battle of Stalingrad.
	Coal miners strike; Smith-Connally War Labor Disputes Act.
	Detroit and Los Angeles race riots.
	Allied invasion of Italy.
	Roosevelt, Churchill, and Stalin meet in Tehran.
1944	Allied invasion of France (Operation Overlord).
	U.S. forces invade the Philippines.
	Roosevelt wins fourth term.
	Battle of the Bulge.
1945	Yalta Conference.
	Battles of Iwo Jima and Okinawa.
	Roosevelt dies; Harry S Truman becomes president.
	Germany surrenders.
	Truman, Churchill, and Stalin meet in Potsdam.
	United States drops atomic bombs on Hiroshima and Nagasaki; Japan surrenders.

demilitarized by the Versailles treaty. In 1938, as German tanks rolled into Vienna, Hitler proclaimed an *anschluss* (union) between Austria and Germany. London, Paris, and Washington murmured disapproval but took no action. An emboldened Hitler then claimed Germany's right to the Sudetenland, a part of neighboring Czechoslovakia containing 3 million ethnic Germans. British prime minister Neville Chamberlain and his French counterpart, insisting that their countries could not endure another war like that of 1914–1918, yielded to Hitler's demands in return for his assurance that Germany had no further territorial ambitions—a policy dubbed **appeasement**—at a conference in Munich in September 1938 (see Map 25.1).

In Japan, meanwhile, militarists gained control of the government and launched a fateful course of expansion, sending troops into the northern Chinese province of Manchuria in 1931. Japan then initiated a full-scale war against China in 1937 and soon controlled key parts of that nation (see Map 25.2).

The American Mood: No More War

The feeble American response reflected the people's belief that the decision to go to war in 1917 had been a mistake. This conviction was rooted in the nation's isolationist tradition—its wish to avoid military and political entanglements in Old World quarrels—as well as in its desire to have the government focus on the problems of the depression, not foreign affairs. Numerous popular books concluded that banking and corporate interests had dragged the United States into World War I. So did a 1934–1936 Senate investigation headed by Republican Gerald P. Nye of North Dakota, which maintained that war profiteers, whom it called "merchants of death," had tricked the United States into war for financial gain. A January 1937 poll showed that 70 percent of the people believed that the United States should have stayed out of the war.

By the mid-1930s, an overwhelming majority of Americans thought that the "mistake" of intervention must not be repeated. In 1935–1937, a series of

MAP 25.1 **EUROPEAN AGGRESSION BEFORE WORLD WAR II** Less than twenty years after the end of World War I, war again loomed in Europe as Hitler launched Germany on a course of military and territorial expansion. © Cengage Learning. All rights reserved. No distribution allowed without express authorization.

Neutrality Acts echoed the longing for peace. To prevent a repetition of 1917, these measures outlawed arms sales and loans to nations at war and forbade Americans to travel on the ships of belligerent powers. With the public firmly isolationist and some American companies, like IBM, with large financial investments in German industry, confrontation with fascism came solely in sports. At the 1936 Olympics in Berlin, African American track star Jesse Owens made a mockery of Nazi theories of racial superiority by winning four gold medals. In 1938, in a boxing match laden with symbolism, the black American Joe Louis knocked out German fighter Max Schmeling in the first round of their world heavyweight championship fight. Americans cheered—but still opposed any policies that might involve them in war.

The Gathering Storm: 1938–1939

On March 15, 1939, Nazi troops overran the rest of Czechoslovakia, violating the Munich accords. Five months after that, Hitler reached an agreement with Soviet Premier **Joseph Stalin** in the German-Soviet Nonaggression Pact that their nations would not fight one another and that they would divide Poland after Germany invaded it. No longer worried about waging war on two fronts, Hitler's troops attacked Poland. As expected, Britain and France declared war on Germany. World War II had begun.

Although isolationist sentiment remained strong in the United States, opinion began to shift. After the fall of Czechoslovakia, Roosevelt called for actions "short of war" to check fascism and asked Hitler and Mussolini to pledge no further aggression. A jeering Hitler ridiculed FDR's message, while in Rome Mussolini mocked Roosevelt's physical disability, joking that the president's paralysis must have reached his brain. Roosevelt, however, did more than send messages. In October 1938, he asked Congress for a $300 million military appropriation; in November, he instructed the Army Air Corps to plan for an annual production of 20,000 planes; in January 1939, he submitted a $1.3 billion defense budget. Hitler and

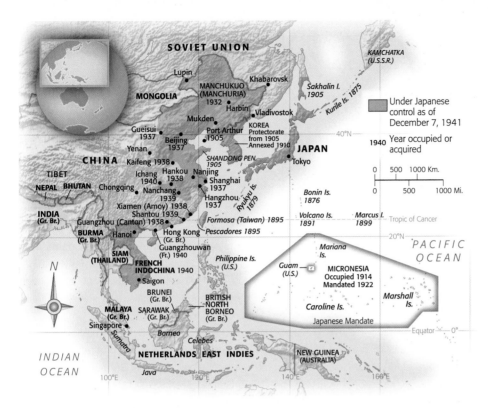

MAP 25.2 **JAPANESE EXPANSION BEFORE WORLD WAR II** Dominated by militarists, Japan pursued an expansionist policy in Asia in the 1930s, extending its sphere of economic and political influence. In July 1937, having already occupied the Chinese province of Manchuria, Japan attacked China proper. © Cengage Learning. All rights reserved. No distribution allowed without express authorization.

> Hitler and Mussolini, Roosevelt said, were "two madmen" who "respect force and force alone."

Hitler and the Nazis had translated their hatred of Jews into official policy. The Nuremberg Laws of 1935 stripped Jews of the rights of German citizenship and increased restrictions on Jews in all spheres of German educational, social, and economic life. This campaign of hatred reached a violent crescendo on November 9–10, 1938, when the Nazis unleashed *Kristallnacht* (Night of the Broken Glass), a frenzy of arson, destruction, and looting against Jews throughout Germany.

No longer could anyone mistake Hitler's malignant intent. Jews, who had been leaving Germany since 1933, streamed out by the hundreds of thousands, seeking haven. Between 1933 and 1938, sixty thousand fled to the United States (see Beyond America). Most Americans condemned the Jews'

Mussolini, he said, were "two madmen" who "respect force and force alone."

America and the Jewish Refugees

persecution, but only a minority favored admitting more refugees. Congress rejected all efforts to liberalize the immigration law, with its discriminatory quotas, and FDR did little to translate his sympathy for the Jews into effective policies.

The consequences of such attitudes became clear in June 1939, when the *St. Louis*, a German liner jammed with 950 Jewish refugees, asked permission to put its passengers ashore at Fort Lauderdale, Florida. Immigration officials refused this request and a Coast Guard cutter stood by to prevent possible attempts by refugees to jump off and swim ashore. The *St. Louis* turned slowly away from the lights of America and sailed back to Europe, where most of its passengers would die from Nazi brutality.

Into the Storm, 1939–1941

Following the lightning German victories in western Europe in spring 1940, President Roosevelt's policy of neutrality to keep America out of war gave way to a policy of economic intervention. He knew that extending increasing amounts of aid to those resisting aggression by the so-called Rome-Berlin-Tokyo Axis, as well as his toughening conduct toward Germany and Japan, could, as he said,

Refugees from Fascism: The Intellectual Migration to the United States

In line with Adolf Hitler's obsessive and virulent anti-Semitism, the Nazi government undertook a systematic campaign to deprive German Jews of their legal rights. In 1933, they were dismissed from government service and from the universities, where, although less than 1 percent of the German population, they constituted 12 percent of the professors. In 1935, the Nuremberg laws deprived Jews of the rights of citizenship; prohibited intermarriage with non-Jews; and excluded them from hospitals, theaters, museums, and athletic fields. In November 1938, Nazi gangs murdered scores of Jews, destroyed 267 synagogues, and vandalized thousands of Jewish businesses throughout Germany. In this pogrom, known as the Night of the Broken Glass *(Kristallnacht)*, for the many Jewish shop windows smashed by the brown shirts, the Nazis sent between twenty and thirty thousand Jews to concentration camps and ordered the rest to wear yellow Stars of David. Meanwhile, Hitler also stepped up his persecution of non-Jewish intellectuals, like Thomas Mann, who opposed his murderous regime.

Some Jews in central Europe (particularly Austria, Germany, and Hungary) saw the handwriting on the wall and sought to escape. Although most lacked the means to emigrate—being forbidden to bring their property out of the country with them—or found their way blocked by countries who refused to accept refugees, Nazi anti-Semitism and political repression led perhaps a half million immigrants, between 1933 and 1941, to seek safe haven in western Europe, Switzerland, or the United States—whose rigid numerical quotas on immigration blocked entry to most.

However, as the news of Nazi persecutions made its way out of Germany, various groups organized to find refuge for the many prominent artists, scholars, and scientists who were Jews or opponents of fascism. The British Academic Assistance Council and the American Emergency Committee in Aid of Displaced Foreign Scholars worked to obtain university positions in the United States for émigré scholars. To take a stand for academic freedom and add eminence to their faculty, the presidents of some American colleges formed the Emergency Committee in Aid of German Displaced Scholars. The New School for Social Research in New York hired

German émigrés to train American graduate students in its new University in Exile. Similarly, the Institute for Advanced Study at Princeton, North Carolina's Black Mountain College, and scores of other academic, artistic, and scientific institutions opened their doors to thousands of exiles.

Although the Nazis had sought to destroy what they sneered at as Jewish science and culture, they, as one refugee scholar wrote, "spread it all over the world. Only Germany would be the loser." The United States, given the extraordinary number and talents of the refugees it accepted, would be the big winner.

Because the Second World War was in no small part a struggle of opposing scientists, the intellectual migration weakened the Axis and strengthened the Allies. The most decisive impact of the émigré scientists came in the field of nuclear physics. Fearing the possibility that Hitler might develop atomic weapons, two refugee physicists, Leo Szilard (from Hungary) and Enrico Fermi (from Italy) convinced fellow refugee Albert Einstein to sign a letter to President Roosevelt warning about recent German discoveries in uranium fission. The result would eventually be the Manhattan Project, an Anglo American effort to produce atomic bombs. In it, scores of émigré scientists brought their different skills and intellectual traits to bear on the single objective of beating the Germans in building a super-bomb. The refugee scientists—Hans Bethe, James Franck, Edward Teller, and Eugene Wigner, among others—succeeded, and changed the world.

Mainly due to the efforts of the American Psychoanalytic Association and the Menninger Clinic in Topeka, Kansas, a lion's share of Europe's psychoanalytic teachers, therapists, and thinkers, among whom Jews predominated, also came to the United States in the 1930s and had a huge impact. Bruno Bettelheim, Erich Fromm, and other psychologists influenced by Sigmund Freud changed America's approach to mental illness, stressing the value of therapy. They influenced Americans to have greater tolerance for adolescent rebellious behavior, and convinced parents to pay attention to the psychological needs of the young. They also shaped attitudes toward crime and criminals—from punishment to rehabilitation; made public relations and sales experts more savvy

LAURA AND ENRICO FERMI ENRICO Fermi, pictured here with his Jewish wife, Laura, emigrated to the United States in 1938 to escape the anti-Semitic persecutions in Mussolini's Italy. Credited with designing the first manmade nuclear reactor, Fermi, along with his fellow émigrés, played an indispensable role in the development of the atomic bomb by the Manhattan Project. *(© Bettmann/Corbis)*

ALBERT EINSTEIN Leaving Germany for the United States in 1932, Nobel Prize physicist Albert Einstein, perhaps the greatest scientist of the twentieth century, aided many other Jews trying to flee persecution by the Nazis and helped alert President Roosevelt to the importance of developing an atomic bomb. *(© Bettmann/Corbis)*

about what motivates buyers; and popularized the notion that everyone has a right to self-fulfillment and happiness.

Significant changes similarly came in the social sciences and humanities. The leading lights among Austrian intellectuals, known as the Vienna Circle, advanced the school of logical positivism in American philosophy. Joseph Schumpeter and Ludwig von Mises changed the teaching of economics in the United States, much as Hannah Arendt, Theodor Adorno, and Herbert Marcuse influenced political thought. Virtually en masse, the many political and social scientists at the Institute for Social Research in Frankfurt escaped to the United States with the assistance of sympathetic Columbia University faculty. They would go on to make fundamental changes in sociology, emphasizing both a quantitative approach to studying social issues and a psychological approach to social phenomena, especially prejudice and discrimination.

Some of the brightest stars in the new American firmament were émigré artists. From Germany's Bauhaus school of design, furniture-maker Marcel Breuer and architects Walter Gropius and Ludwig Mies van der Rohe became the giants of postwar American design. Great musicians—the conductors Otto Klemperer, Erich Leinsdorf, Pierre Monteux, George Szell, and Bruno Walter; the composers Paul Hindemith, Darius Milhaud, and Arnold Schoenberg; and the pianists Artur Rubinstein, Rudolf Serkin, and Vladimir Horowitz, among many others—added luster to the concert stage and, as master teachers, influenced an entire generation of American musicians.

No other immigrant group in history had ever brought such gifts as these émigré artists and scholars brought to the United States in the 1930s. They found in the United States

the freedom of thought and freedom from fear that enabled them to pursue their talents and ideas. Despite the financial difficulties of the Great Depression, private American generosity provided the funds for many of the positions in colleges, laboratories, and music schools that enabled the refugees to earn a living. And most of the Americans they worked with welcomed them and judged them on their abilities rather than their religion or place of birth. The government, moreover, displayed unprecedented trust in these foreign-born, hiring scores of them for positions of responsibility in the atomic bomb project and other war work.

In return, most of these refugees quickly learned English, sought and obtained American citizenship, and left an indelible mark on American life. Summing up her account of these "illustrious immigrants," Laura Fermi, the wife of atomic scientist Enrico Fermi, who had fled Italy's anti-Semitism and fascism with her husband in 1938, wrote: "In making room for countless Europeans and saving many whose lives were threatened, America proved once more a land of opportunity and a haven to which the persecuted of the world might continue to look with confidence." In return, the United States would be more than repaid in full "in a currency compounded of prestige, knowledge, and a general enrichment of culture."

QUESTIONS FOR ANALYSIS

- What were the major contributions to American life made by the refugees in the Intellectual Migration?
- What steps did Americans take to welcome émigré scholars and artists and facilitate their profound impact on American life and thought?

ISOLATIONISM VERSUS INTERVENTIONISM In front of the White House in 1941, an American soldier grabs a sign from an isolationist picketing against the United States entering the war in Europe. A diverse group, isolationists ran the gamut from pacifists who opposed all wars, to progressives who feared the growth of business and centralized power that a war would bring, to ultra-rightists who sympathized with fascism and/or shared Hitler's anti-Semitism. *(Thomas McAvoy/TimeLife Pictures/Getty Images)*

"push" the United States into the crisis of worldwide war. Japan's attack on the U.S. fleet at Pearl Harbor would provide the push.

The European War

The war in Europe began on September 1, 1939, as Nazi armies poured into Poland and the *Luftwaffe* (German air force) devastated Polish cities. Two days later, Britain and France, honoring commitments to Poland, declared war on Germany. Although FDR invoked the Neutrality Acts, he would not ask Americans to be impartial in thought and deed.

Tailoring his actions to the public mood, which favored both preventing a Nazi victory and staying out of war, FDR persuaded Congress in November to amend the Neutrality Acts to allow the belligerents to purchase weapons from the United States if they paid cash and carried the arms away in their own ships. But "cash-and-carry" did not stop the Nazis. In spring 1940, Hitler unleashed a *blitzkrieg* (lightning war) against Denmark, Norway, the Netherlands, Belgium, and Luxembourg. The Nazi *wehrmacht* (war machine) swept all the way to the English Channel in a scant two months. In early June, the British evacuated most of their army at Dunkirk, and on June 22, France surrendered.

Hitler then took aim against Great Britain, terror-bombing British cities in hopes of forcing a surrender or, failing that, preparing the ground for a cross-channel invasion. With thousands of civilians killed or wounded and much of London in smoking ruins, British Prime Minister **Winston Churchill** pleaded for American aid. Many Americans, shocked at the use of German air power against British civilians, favored such aid. But a large minority opposed it as wasteful of materials needed for U.S. defenses or as a ruse to lure Americans into war.

From Isolation to Intervention

In the United States in 1940, news of the "Battle of Britain" competed with speculation about whether FDR would break with tradition and run for an unprecedented third term. Not until the eve of the Democrats' July convention did he reveal that, given the world crisis, he would consent to a "draft" from his party. The Axis threat clinched his renomination and similarly led the Republicans to nominate Wendell Willkie of Indiana, an all-out internationalist who championed greater aid to Britain.

Adroitly playing the role of a national leader too busy with defense and diplomacy to engage in partisan politics, Roosevelt appointed republicans Henry Stimson and Frank Knox as secretaries of war and the navy, respectively; signed the Selective Service and Training Act, the first peacetime draft in U.S. history; approved a dramatic increase in defense funding; and, in September, engineered a "destroyers-for-bases" swap with England, sending fifty vintage American ships to Britain in exchange for leases on British air and naval bases in the Western Hemisphere.

These moves infuriated isolationists, particularly the America First Committee. Largely financed by Henry Ford, and featuring Charles Lindbergh as its most popular speaker, the AFC insisted "Fortress America" could stand alone. But 55 percent of Americans, reassured by the president's promise never to "send an American boy to fight in a foreign war," voted him into a third term.

Roosevelt now called on the United States to become "the arsenal of democracy." He proposed a **"lend-lease"** program to allow the U.S. to lend or lease war materiel to any nation vital to America's security. While Roosevelt likened the plan to loaning a garden hose to a neighbor whose house was on fire, isolationist Senator Robert Taft compared it to chewing gum: after a neighbor uses it, "you don't want it back." Congress, however, approved lend-lease in March 1941, and supplies began to flow across the Atlantic. When Hitler's armies invaded the Soviet Union in June 1941, FDR

To defeat Hitler, FDR said, "I would hold hands with the Devil."

dispatched supplies to the Soviets, despite American hostility toward communism. To defeat Hitler, FDR said, "I would hold hands with the Devil."

To counter the menace of German submarines that threatened to choke the transatlantic supply line, Roosevelt in mid-1941 authorized the U.S. Navy to convoy British ships, with orders to destroy enemy ships if necessary. In August he met with Churchill aboard a warship off Newfoundland. They issued a statement, known as the **Atlantic Charter,** that condemned aggression, affirmed national self-determination, and endorsed the principles of collective security, free trade, and disarmament. After a German submarine fired at an American destroyer in September, Roosevelt authorized naval patrols to shoot on sight all Axis vessels operating in the western Atlantic. Now on a collision course with Germany, Roosevelt persuaded Congress in November to permit the arming of merchant ships and to allow the transport of lend-lease supplies to belligerent ports in war zones. Unprepared for a major war, America was nevertheless fighting a limited one, and full-scale war seemed imminent.

Pearl Harbor and the Coming of War

Hitler's triumphs in western Europe encouraged Japan to expand farther into Asia. Seeing Germany as America's primary threat, Roosevelt tried to apply enough pressure to deter Japanese aggression without provoking Tokyo to war before the United States had built the "two-ocean navy" authorized by Congress in 1940. "I simply have not got enough navy to go around," he told Harold Ickes in mid-1941, "and every episode in the Pacific means fewer ships in the Atlantic."

The Japanese, too, hoped to avoid war but would not compromise their desire to create the Greater East Asia Co-Prosperity Sphere (an empire embracing much of China, Southeast Asia, and the western Pacific). Japan saw the United States as blocking its legitimate rise to power, while Americans viewed Japan's talk of national aspirations as a smokescreen to cloak aggression. Decades of "yellow-peril" propaganda had hardened U.S. attitudes toward Japan, and even those who were isolationist toward Europe tended to be interventionist toward Asia.

The two nations became locked in a deadly dance. In 1940, believing that economic coercion would force the Japanese out of China, the United

DESTRUCTION ON PEARL HARBOR In the early morning of Sunday, December 7, 1941, Japanese airplanes launched from aircraft carriers attacked the United States fleet moored at Pearl Harbor, on Oahu Island, Hawaii. The surprise attack by the Japanese, which brought the United States into World War II, destroyed or damaged nineteen ships, including five battleships, and some three hundred planes and killed 2,335 American servicemen. It was "a date which live in infamy," Franklin Roosevelt told Congress and the nation as he asked for a declaration of war. It would unite the country for the war effort, as well as have long-range and far-reaching consequences for American foreign relations and for American attitudes toward the world. *(© Bettmann/Corbis)*

States ended a long-standing trade treaty with Japan and banned the sale of aviation fuel and scrap metal to the Japanese. Tokyo responded by occupying northern Indochina, a French colony, and signing the Tripartite Pact with Germany and Italy in September, creating a military alliance, the Berlin-Rome-Tokyo Axis, that required each government to help the others in the event of a U.S. attack.

When the Japanese then overran the rest of Indochina in July 1941, Roosevelt froze all Japanese assets in the United States and clamped a total embargo on trade with Japan. Tokyo had two choices: submit to the United States to gain a resumption of trade for vital resources or conquer new lands to obtain them. In October, expansionist war minister General Hideki Tojo became Japan's prime minister. Tojo set the first week in December as the deadline for a preemptive strike if the United States did not yield. By late November, U.S. intelligence—deciphering Japan's top diplomatic code—alerted the Roosevelt administration that war was imminent. Eleventh-hour negotiations under way in Washington made no headway, and warnings went out to all commanders in the Pacific advising that a Japanese attack was imminent. U.S. officials believed the Japanese would strike British or Dutch possessions or even the Philippines—but the Japanese gambled on a knockout punch, hoping to destroy the U.S. Pacific Fleet at Pearl Harbor and compel Roosevelt, preoccupied with Germany, to seek accommodation with Japan.

Waves of Japanese dive-bombers and torpedo planes thundered across Hawaii's island of Oahu Sunday morning, December 7, 1941, bombing ships at anchor in Pearl Harbor and strafing planes parked wingtip to wingtip at nearby air bases. In less than three hours, eight battleships, three light cruisers, and two destroyers had been sunk or crippled, and 360 aircraft destroyed or damaged. The attack killed more than twenty-four hundred Americans and opened the way for Japan's advance toward Australia. Americans had underestimated the resourcefulness, skill, and daring of the Japanese. At the same time, Japanese leaders erred in counting on a paralyzing blow at Pearl Harbor. That miscalculation assured an aroused and united nation determined to avenge the attack.

Roosevelt called December 7 a "date which will live in infamy." On December 8, Congress declared war on Japan. (The sole dissenter was Montana's Jeannette Rankin, who had also cast a nay vote against U.S. entry into World War I). Three days later, Hitler declared war on the "half Judaized and the other half Negrified" Americans, and Mussolini followed suit. Congress immediately reciprocated without a dissenting vote. America faced a global war that it was not ready to fight.

> Roosevelt called December 7 a "date which will live in infamy."

After Pearl Harbor, U-boats wreaked havoc in the North Atlantic and prowled the Caribbean and the East Coast of the United States. Every twenty-four hours, five more Allied vessels went to the bottom. By the end of 1942, U-boat "wolf packs" had destroyed more than a thousand Allied ships, offsetting the pace of American ship production. The United States was losing the battle of the Atlantic.

Additionally, the war news from Europe and Africa was, as Roosevelt admitted, "all bad." Hitler's rule covered an enormous swath of territory, from the outskirts of Moscow and Leningrad—a thousand miles deep into Russia—to the Pyrenees on the French-Spanish border, and from northern Norway to the Libyan desert. In North Africa, the German Afrika Korps swept toward the Suez Canal, the British oil lifeline. It seemed as if the Mediterranean would become an Axis sea and that Hitler would soon be in India to greet Tojo marching across Asia before the United States was ready to fight.

The Japanese inflicted defeat after defeat on Allied Pacific forces. Tojo followed Pearl Harbor with a rampage across the Pacific that put Guam, Wake Island, Hong Kong, Singapore, Burma, and the Netherlands East Indies under Japan's control by the end of April 1942. American forces in the Philippines, besieged for months on the island of Bataan, surrendered in May. Japan's rising sun flag blazed over hundreds of islands in the central and western Pacific and over the entire eastern perimeter of the Asian mainland from the border of Siberia to the border of India.

America Mobilizes for War

In December 1941, American armed forces numbered just 1.6 million, and war production accounted for only 15 percent of U.S. industrial output. Pearl Harbor changed everything. Congress passed a War Powers Act, granting the president unprecedented authority over all aspects of the war. Volunteers and draftees swelled the armed forces; by war's end, some 15 million men and nearly 350,000 women would serve. More would work in defense industries. Mobilization required unprecedented coordination of the American government, economy, and military. In 1942, those responsible for managing America's growing war machine moved into the world's largest building, the newly constructed Pentagon. Like the Pentagon, which was intended to house civilian agencies after the war, far-reaching domestic changes would also outlast the war and significantly alter American attitudes, behavior, and institutions.

Organizing for Victory

To direct the military engine, Roosevelt formed the Joint Chiefs of Staff, made up of representatives of the army, navy, and army air force. (Only a minor "corps" within the army as late as June 1941, the air force would grow more dramatically than any other branch of the service, achieve virtual autonomy, and play a vital role in combat strategy.) The changing nature of modern warfare also led to the creation of the Office of Strategic Services (OSS), forerunner of the Central Intelligence Agency, to conduct the espionage required for strategic planning.

Roosevelt established the **War Production Board** (WPB) to allocate materials, limit the production of civilian goods, and distribute contracts. The newly created War Manpower Commission (WMC) supervised the mobilization of men and women for the military, war industry, and agriculture; the National War Labor Board (NWLB) mediated disputes between management and labor; and the **Office of Price Administration** (OPA) imposed strict price controls to check inflation.

Although a Nazi commander had jeered, "The Americans can't build planes, only electric iceboxes and razor blades," the United States achieved a miracle of war production in 1942. Car makers retooled to produce planes and tanks; a pinball-machine maker converted to armor-piercing shells. By late 1942, 33 percent of the economy was committed to war production. Whole new industries appeared virtually overnight. With almost all of the nation's crude-rubber supply now in Japanese-controlled territory, the government built some fifty new synthetic-rubber plants. By the end of the war, the United States had become the world's largest exporter of synthetic rubber.

America also became the world's greatest weapons manufacturer, producing more war materiel by 1944 than its Axis enemies combined: 300,000 military aircraft, 86,000 tanks, 2.6 million machine guns, and 6 million tons of bombs. "To American production," Stalin would toast FDR and Churchill, "without which the war would have been lost." The United States also built more than five thousand cargo ships and eighty-six thousand warships. Henry J. Kaiser, who had supervised the construction of the Boulder Dam, introduced prefabrication to cut the time needed to build ships. In 1941, the construction of a Liberty-class merchant ship took six months; in 1943, less than two weeks. By 1945, Kaiser, dubbed "Sir Launchalot," was completing a cargo ship every day.

Such breakneck production had costs. The size and powers of the government expanded as defense spending zoomed from 9 percent of gross national product (GNP) in 1940 to 46 percent in 1945; the federal budget soared from $9 billion to $98 billion. Federal civilian employees mushroomed from 1.1 million to 3.8 million. The executive branch, directing the war effort, grew the most, and an alliance formed between the defense industry and the military. (A generation later, Americans would call these concentrations of power the "imperial presidency" and the "military-industrial complex.")

"Dr. New Deal," in FDR's words, gave way to "Dr. Win the War." Because the government sought the maximum production in the shortest time, it guaranteed profits, provided generous tax write-offs and subsidies, and suspended antitrust prosecutions. "If you are going to try to go to war in a capitalist country," said Secretary of War Stimson, "you have to let business make money out of the process or business won't work." Two-thirds of all war-production dollars went to the hundred largest firms, greatly accelerating trends toward economic concentration.

> "If you are going to try to go to war in a capitalist country, you have to let business make money out of the process or business won't work."

The War Economy

The United States spent more than $360 billion ($250 million a day) to defeat the Axis, ten times the cost of World War I. Wartime spending stimulated an industrial boom that transformed the nation from economic paralysis to record-shattering productivity and prosperity. It doubled U.S. industrial output and the per capita GNP, created 17 million new jobs, increased corporate after-tax profits by 70 percent, and raised the real wages or purchasing power of industrial workers by 50 percent (see Figure 25.1).

The federal government poured $40 billion into the West, making it an economic powerhouse, the center of massive aircraft and shipbuilding industries. California alone secured more than 10 percent of all federal funds; by 1945, nearly half the personal income in the state came from the federal government.

A dynamic Sun Belt, stretching from the coastal Southeast to the coastal Southwest, was the recipient of billions spent on military bases and the needs of the armed forces. The South's industrial capacity increased by 40 percent, and per capita income tripled. Boom times enabled hundreds of thousands of sharecroppers and farm tenants to leave the land for better-paying industrial jobs. While the South's farm population decreased by 20 percent in the 1940s, its urban population grew 36 percent.

Full employment, a longer workweek, larger paychecks, and the increased hiring of minorities, women, and the elderly brought a middle-class standard of living to millions of families. In California, the demand for workers in the shipyards and aircraft factories opened opportunities for thousands of Chinese Americans previously confined to menial jobs within their own

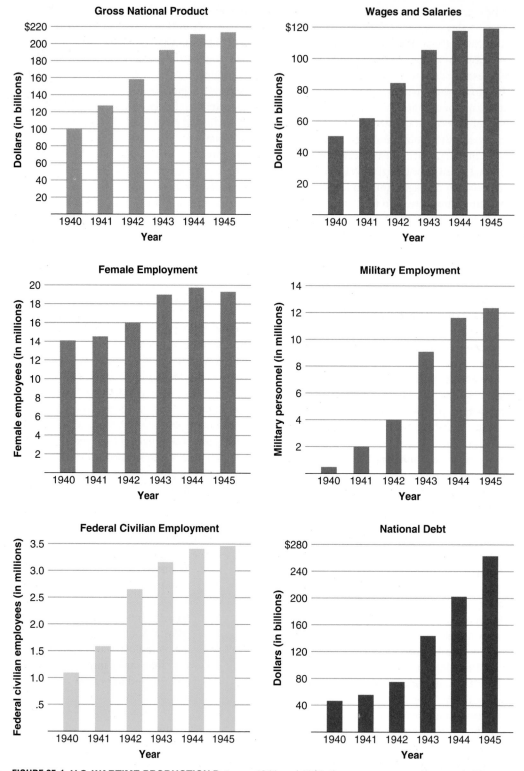

FIGURE 25.1 U.S. WARTIME PRODUCTION Between 1941 and 1945, the economy grew at a remarkable pace.

communities. In San Diego, 40 percent of retirees returned to work. Deafening factories hired the hearing-impaired, and aircraft plants employed dwarfs as inspectors because of their ability to crawl inside small spaces.

The war years produced the only significant shift toward greater equality in the distribution of income in the twentieth century. The earnings of the bottom fifth of all workers rose 68 percent, and those of the middle class doubled. The richest

5 percent, conversely, saw their share of total disposable income drop from 23 to 17 percent.

Large-scale commercial farmers prospered, benefiting from higher consumer prices and increased productivity thanks to improved fertilizers and more mechanization. As sharecroppers, tenants, and small farmers left the land for better-paying industrial jobs, the overall agricultural population fell by 17 percent. Farming became "agribusiness," and organized agriculture wielded power alongside organized labor, big government, and big business.

Organized labor grew mightier as union membership rose from 9 million to 14.8 million workers. Although the National War Labor Board attempted to limit wage increases to restrain inflation, salaries and wages more than doubled during the war, and unions negotiated unprecedented fringe benefits for workers, including paid vacation time and health and pension plans. Because most workers honored the "no-strike" pledge that they had given immediately after Pearl Harbor, less than one-tenth of 1 percent of wartime working hours was lost to wildcat strikes. Those strikes, however, cost the union movement: in 1943, Congress passed, over Roosevelt's veto, the Smith-Connally War Labor Disputes act, empowering the president to take over any facility where strikes threatened war production.

Far more than strikes, inflation threatened the wartime economy. The OPA constantly battled inflation—fueled by greater spending power combined with a scarcity of goods. Throughout 1942, prices climbed at a 2-percent-per-month clip, and at the year's end, Congress gave the president authority to freeze wages, prices, and rents. As the OPA clamped down, inflation slowed dramatically: consumer prices went up only 8 percent in the war's last two years.

The OPA also instituted rationing to combat inflation and conserve scarce materials. Under the slogan "Use it up, wear it out, make it do, or do without," the OPA rationed gasoline, coffee, sugar, butter, cheese, and meat. Americans endured "meatless Tuesdays" and cuffless trousers, ate sherbet instead of ice cream, and put up with imitation chocolate that tasted like soap and imitation soap that did not lather. Most Americans cheerfully formed carpools, planted victory gardens, and recycled paper and fats, while their children, known as "Uncle Sam's Scrappers" and "Tin-Can Colonels," scoured their neighborhoods for scrap metal.

Buying war bonds—"bullets in the bellies of Hitler's hordes!" said the Treasury Department—further curtailed inflation by decreasing consumer purchasing power, while giving civilians a sense of involvement in the distant war. Small investors bought $40 billion in "E" bonds, and wealthy individuals and corporations invested nearly twice that amount. Bond sales raised almost half the money needed to finance the war. Roosevelt sought to raise the rest by drastically increasing taxes. Congress refused the president much of what he sought. Still, the Revenue Act of 1942 raised the top income-tax rate from 60 percent to 94 percent and imposed income taxes on middle- and lower-income Americans for the first time. Beginning in 1943, the payroll-deduction system automatically withheld income taxes from wages and salaries. In 1945, the federal government collected nearly twenty times the tax revenue it had in 1940.

"A Wizard War"

Recognizing wartime scientific and technological developments, Winston Churchill dubbed World War II "a wizard war." Mathematicians went to work deciphering enemy codes, psychologists devised propaganda, and, as never before, the major combatants mobilized scientists into virtual armies of invention. In 1941, FDR created the Office of Scientific Research and Development (OSRD) for the development of new weapons and medicines. The OSRD spent more than $1 billion to produce improved radar and sonar, rocket weapons, and proximity fuses for mines and artillery shells. It also funded the development of jet aircraft and high-altitude bombsights. Other OSRD research hastened the development of the laser and insecticides, contributed to improved blood transfusions, and produced "miracle drugs," such as penicillin.

The demand for greater accuracy in artillery required the kind of rapid, detailed calculations that only computing machines could supply. By 1944, navy personnel in the basement of Harvard's physics laboratory were operating IBM's Mark I, a cumbersome device fifty-one feet long and eight feet high that weighed five tons and contained 760,000 parts. A second-generation computer, ENIAC (electronic numerical integrator and computer), soon reduced the time to multiply two tenth-place numbers from Mark I's three seconds to less than three-thousandths of a second.

Nothing saved the lives of more wounded servicemen than improvements in battlefield medical care. Military needs led to advances in heart and lung surgery and to the use of synthetic antimalarial drugs to substitute for scarce quinine. So-called miracle drugs, antibiotics to combat infections (which were a rarity on the eve of war), would be copiously produced. The use of DDT cleared many islands of malaria-carrying mosquitoes. Along with innovations like the Mobile Auxiliary Surgical

RITA HAYWORTH AIDS SCRAP DRIVE One of the many Hollywood stars who used their popularity to aid the war effort, actress Rita Hayworth displays her famous legs to urge Americans to donate scrap metals for the manufacture of military equipment. *(National Archives)*

the **Manhattan Project**—had employed more than 120,000 people and spent nearly $2 billion.

Just before dawn on July 16, 1945, a blinding fireball with "the brightness of several suns at midday" rose over the desert at Alamogordo, New Mexico, followed by a billowing mushroom cloud. Equivalent to twenty thousand tons of TNT, the blast from this first atomic explosion was felt a hundred miles away. "A few people laughed, a few people cried," recalled J. Robert Oppenheimer, the Manhattan Project's scientific director. "Most people were silent. I remembered the line from the Hindu scripture, the Bhagavad-Gita: 'Now I am become Death, the destroyer of worlds.'" The atomic age had dawned.

> "Now I am become Death, the destroyer of worlds."

Propaganda and Politics

People as well as science and machinery had to be mobilized. To sustain a spirit of unity, the Roosevelt administration carefully managed public opinion. The Office of Censorship, established in December 1941, examined all letters going overseas and worked with publishers and broadcasters to suppress information that might damage the war effort, such as details of troop movements. Fearful of demoralizing the public, the government banned, until late 1943, the publication of any pictures of American war dead; then, worried about an overconfident public, it prodded the media to show American servicemen killed by the enemy.

To shape public opinion, FDR created the Office of War Information (OWI) in June 1942. The OWI employed more than four thousand writers, artists, and advertising specialists to explain the war and to counter enemy propaganda. The OWI depicted the war as a moral struggle between good and evil—the enemy had to be destroyed, not merely defeated. Hollywood films highlighted the heroism and unity of the American forces, while inciting hatred of the enemy. Films about the war portrayed the Japanese, in particular, as treacherous and cruel, as beasts in the jungle, as "slant-eyed rats," while jukeboxes blared songs like "We're Gonna Have to Slap the Dirty Little Jap."

While the Roosevelt administration concentrated on the war, Republican critics seized the initiative in domestic politics. Full employment and high wages undermined the Democrats' class appeal, and many of the urban and working-class

Hospital (MASH), science helped save tens of thousands of soldiers' lives and improved the health of the nation as well. Life expectancy rose by three years during the war.

The atomic bomb project began in August 1939 when Albert Einstein, a Jewish refugee and Nobel Prize–winning physicist, warned Roosevelt that Nazi scientists were seeking to use atomic physics to construct an extraordinarily destructive weapon. In 1941, FDR launched a massive Anglo American secret program—the Soviets were excluded—to construct an atomic bomb. The next year, the participating physicists, both Americans and Europeans, achieved a controlled chain reaction under the University of Chicago football stadium and acquired the basic knowledge necessary to develop the bomb. By July 1945, this program—code-named

voters essential to the Roosevelt coalition were serving in the armed forces and did not vote in the 1942 elections. Republicans gained nine seats in the Senate and forty-six in the House. A coalition of conservative Republicans and southern Democrats held power and, resentful of the wartime expansion of executive authority and determined to curb labor unions and welfare spending, it abolished the CCC and the WPA and rebuffed attempts to extend the New Deal.

Despite the strength of the conservative coalition, the war expanded governmental and executive power enormously. As never before, Washington managed the economy, molded public opinion, funded scientific research, and influenced people's daily lives.

The Battlefront, 1942–1944

America's industrial might and Soviet manpower turned the tide of war, and diplomacy followed in its wake. Allied unity diminished as the Axis weakened; increasingly, the United States, Britain, and the Soviet Union each sought wartime strategies and postwar arrangements best suited to its own interests.

Liberating Europe

After Pearl Harbor, British and American officials agreed to concentrate on defeating Germany first and then Japan. But they differed on where to mount an attack. Stalin demanded a second front, an invasion of western Europe to force Hitler to transfer troops west and thus relieve pressure on the Russians, who faced the full fury of the Nazi armies. Churchill insisted on clearing the Mediterranean before invading France, and he wanted American aid in North Africa to protect the Suez Canal. Despite Soviet protests, Roosevelt gave in to Churchill, and American troops under General Dwight D. Eisenhower landed in Morocco and Algeria in November 1942 as part of "Operation Torch." Pushing eastward, they trapped the German and Italian armies being driven westward by the British, and in May 1943 some 260,000 German-Italian troops surrendered (see Figure 25.2).

Left alone to face two-thirds of the Nazi force, the Soviet Union hung on and, in the turning point of the European war, halted the German advance in the protracted Battle of Stalingrad (August 1942–January 1943). As the Russian snow turned red with blood (costing each side more battle deaths in half a year than the United States suffered in the entire

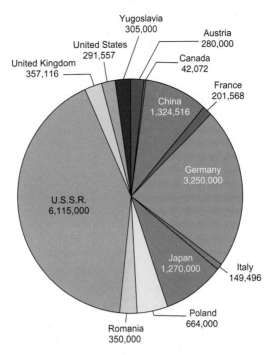

FIGURE 25.2 WORLD WAR II MILITARY DEATHS AND CASUALTIES © Cengage Learning. All rights reserved. No distribution allowed without express authorization.

war), and its hills became "white fields," strewn with human bones, Soviet forces saved Stalingrad, defended Moscow, and relieved besieged Leningrad (now St. Petersburg). The Red Army then went on the offensive along a thousand-mile front (see Map 25.3).

> As Russia's snow turned red with blood, its hills became "white fields," strewn with human bones.

Although Stalin renewed his plea for a second front, Churchill again objected, and Roosevelt again agreed to a British plan: the invasion of Sicily. In summer 1943, Anglo-American forces overran Sicily in less than a month, leading the Italian military to depose, and then execute, Mussolini, and to surrender to the Allies on September 8. As Allied forces moved up the Italian peninsula, German troops poured into Italy. Facing elite Nazi divisions in strong defensive positions, the Allies spent eight months inching their way 150 miles to Rome, and were still battling through northern Italy when the war in Europe ended in May 1945.

In 1943 and 1944, the United States and Britain turned the tide in the Atlantic and sent thousands of bombers over Germany. British and American air forces began round-the-clock bombardment, raining thousands of tons of bombs on German cities. In raids on Hamburg in July 1943, Allied

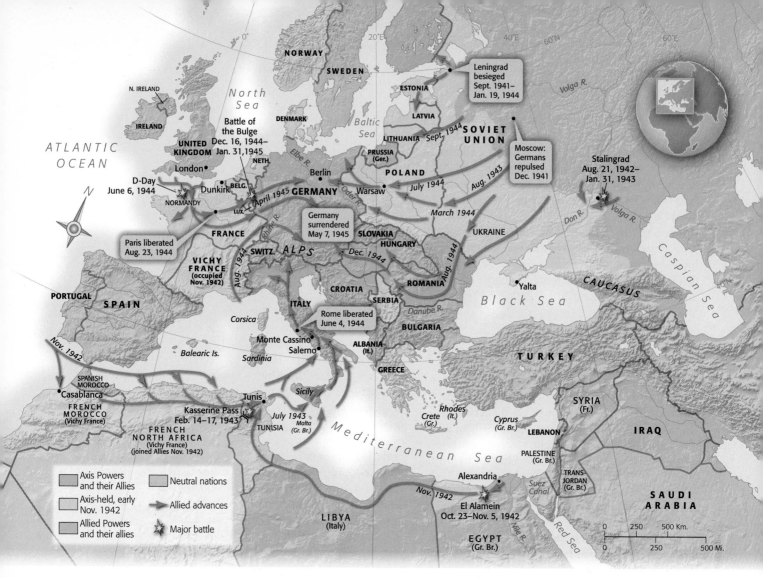

MAP 25.3 WORLD WAR II IN EUROPE AND AFRICA The momentous German defeats at Stalingrad and in Tunisia in early 1943 marked the turning point in the war against the Axis. By 1945, Allied conquest of Hitler's "thousand-year" Reich was imminent. © Cengage Learning. All rights reserved. No distribution allowed without express authorization.

planes dropping incendiary bombs created terrible firestorms, killing more than thirty-five thousand people and leveling the city, much as they had done earlier at Cologne and would do in February 1945 to Dresden, where some sixty thousand people died.

Meanwhile, in July 1943, the Red Army, eating U.S. rations, marching in American-made boots, and driving Dodge and Ford trucks, engaged the Germans at Kursk. With a million men actively engaged on each side in the largest pitched battle of the war, Soviet soldiers won decisively and forced a German retreat. Advancing swiftly, they drove the Germans out of Soviet territory by mid-1944 and plunged into Poland, where the Soviets set up a puppet government. Late summer and early fall saw Soviet troops seize Romania and Bulgaria and aid communist guerillas under Josip Broz Tito in liberating Yugoslavia.

As the Soviets swept across eastern Europe, Allied forces opened the long-promised second front. On June 6, 1944—D-Day—nearly 200,000 Allied troops in the largest armada ever assembled landed in Normandy in northwestern France. Within six weeks, another million Allied troops had crossed the channel and waded ashore. Under General Eisenhower, the Allies liberated Paris in August and reached the German border by the end of summer.

In mid-December, as the Allies prepared for a full-scale assault on the German heartland, Hitler desperately threw his last reserves against American positions. The **Battle of the Bulge**— named for the "bulge" eighty miles long and fifty miles wide that Hitler's troops drove into the Allies' line—raged for nearly a month, and when it ended American troops stood on the banks of the Rhine. It had cost the United States 55,000 soldiers dead or wounded and 18,000 taken prisoner. But the way to Germany lay open, and the end of the European war was in sight.

"FULL VICTORY—NOTHING ELSE!" Commander-in-Chief of Allied Expeditionary Force General Dwight D. ("Ike") Eisenhower gives the order of the day to U.S. paratroopers in England on the eve of D-Day. *(National Archives)*

War in the Pacific

The day after the Philippines fell to Japan in mid-May 1942, U.S. and Japanese fleets confronted each other in the Coral Sea off northeastern Australia, the first naval battle fought entirely from aircraft carriers. Both sides took heavy losses, but the Battle of the Coral Sea stopped the Japanese advance on Australia. Less than a month later, a Japanese armada turned toward Midway Island, the crucial American outpost between Hawaii and Japan. Because the U.S. Signal Corps had broken the Japanese naval code, Japan's plans were known. The Americans won a decisive victory, sinking four Japanese carriers and hundreds of enemy planes. The stunned Japanese could now only try to hold what they had already won.

On the offensive, U.S. marines waded ashore at Guadalcanal in the Solomon Islands in August 1942. Facing fierce resistance as well as tropical diseases like malaria, the Americans needed six months to take the island, a bitter preview of the battles to come. As the British moved from India to retake Burma, the United States began a two-pronged advance toward Japan in 1943. The army, under General Douglas MacArthur, advanced north on the islands between Australia and the Philippines, and the navy and marines, under Admiral Chester Nimitz, "island-hopped" across the central Pacific to seize strategic bases and put Tokyo in range of American bombers. In fall 1944 the navy annihilated what remained of the Japanese fleet at the battles of the Philippine Sea and Leyte Gulf, giving the United States control of Japan's air and shipping lanes and leaving the Japanese home islands open to invasion (see Map 25.4).

The Grand Alliance

President Roosevelt had two main goals for the war: the total defeat of the Axis at the least possible cost in American lives, and the establishment of a world order strong enough to ensure peace, open trade, and national self-determination in the postwar era. Aware that only a common enemy fused the Grand Alliance together, Roosevelt tried to promote harmony by concentrating on military victory and postponing divisive postwar matters.

Churchill and Stalin had other goals. Britain wanted to remain a world power and retain its imperial possessions. As Churchill said, he had "not become the King's First Minister to preside over the liquidation of the British Empire." The Soviet Union wanted a permanently weakened Germany and a sphere of influence (a region whose governments can be counted on to do a great power's bidding) in eastern Europe. To hold together this fragile alliance, FDR relied on personal diplomacy to mediate conflicts.

> Churchill said, "I have not become the King's First Minister to preside over the liquidation of the British Empire."

The first president to travel by plane while in office, Roosevelt arrived in Casablanca, Morocco's main port, in January 1943, where he and Churchill resolved to attack Italy before invading France and proclaimed that the war would continue until the "unconditional surrender" of the Axis. By so doing, they sought to reduce Soviet mistrust of the West, which had deepened with the postponement of the second front. Ten months later, in Cairo, Roosevelt met with Churchill and Jiang Jieshi (Chiang Kai-shek), the anticommunist head of the Chinese government. To keep China in the war, FDR promised the return of Manchuria and Taiwan to China and a "free and independent Korea." From Cairo, FDR and Churchill continued on to Tehran, Iran's capital, to meet with Stalin. Here they set the invasion of France for June 1944, and agreed to divide Germany into zones of occupation and to impose reparations on the Reich. Most importantly to Roosevelt, Stalin pledged to enter the war against Japan after Hitler's defeat.

Roosevelt then turned his attention to domestic politics. Increasing conservative sentiment in the nation led him to drop the liberal Henry A. Wallace from the ticket and accept Harry S Truman as his vice-presidential candidate. A moderate senator from Missouri, now dubbed "the new Missouri Compromise," Truman restored a semblance of

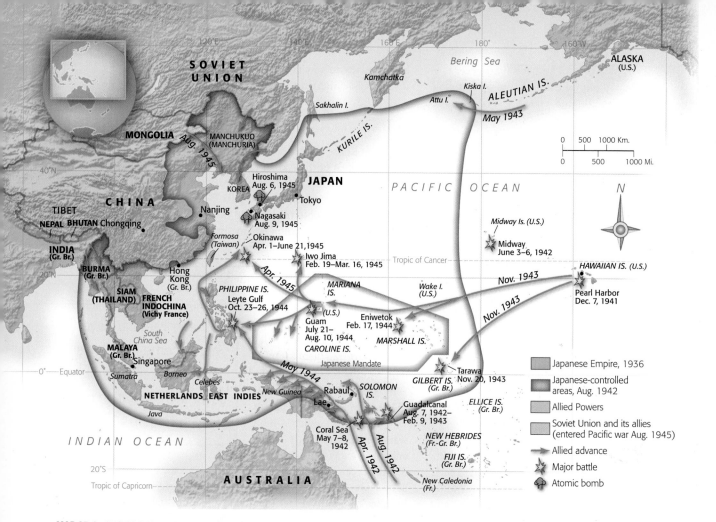

MAP 25.4 WORLD WAR II IN THE PACIFIC American ships and planes stemmed the Japanese offensive at the battles of the Coral Sea and Midway Island. Thereafter, the Japanese were on the defensive against American amphibious assaults and air strikes. © Cengage Learning. All rights reserved. No distribution allowed without express authorization.

unity to the Democrats for the 1944 campaign. To compete, the Republicans nominated moderate and noncontroversial New York governor Thomas E. Dewey. The campaign focused more on personalities than on issues, and the still-popular FDR defeated his dull GOP opponent, but with the narrowest margin since 1916—winning only 53 percent of the popular vote. A weary Roosevelt, secretly suffering from hypertension and heart disease, now directed his waning energies toward defeating the Axis and constructing an international peacekeeping system.

War and American Society

The crisis of war altered the most basic patterns of American life. Few families went untouched: more than 15 million Americans served in the armed forces (three out of every four men aged eighteen to thirty-two), an equal number moved to find jobs, and millions of women went to work outside the home. As well, the war opened some doors of opportunity for African Americans and other minorities,

although many remained closed. It heightened minority aspirations and widened cracks in the wall of white racist attitudes and policy, while maintaining much of America's racial caste system, thereby tilling the ground for future crises.

The GIs' War

Most servicemen griped about regimentation and were more interested in dry socks than in ideology. They knew little of the big strategies, and cared less. They fought because they were told to and wanted to stay alive. Reluctant recruits rather than professional warriors, most had few aims beyond returning to a safe, familiar United States.

But the GIs' war dragged on for almost four years, transforming them in the process. Millions who had never been far from home traveled to unfamiliar cities and remote lands, shedding their parochialism. Sharing tents and foxholes with men of different religions, ethnicities, and classes, they experienced a "melting pot" effect that freed them from some prewar prejudices.

Besides serving with people they had never previously encountered, more than a million GIs married overseas, broadening personal horizons and sowing the seeds of a more tolerant and diverse national culture. At the same time, many GIs became evermore distrustful of foreigners and outsiders and returned home obsessed with the flag as a symbol of patriotism.

Physical misery, chronic exhaustion, and, especially, intense combat took a heavy toll, leaving lasting psychological as well as physical wounds. Both American and Japanese troops saw the other in racist images, as animals to be exterminated, and brutality became as much the rule as the exception in "a war without mercy." Both sides machine-gunned hostile flyers in parachutes; both tortured and killed prisoners in cold blood; both mutilated enemy dead for souvenirs. In the fight against Germany, cruelties and atrocities also occurred, although on a lesser scale. A battalion of the second armored division calling itself "Roosevelt's Butchers" boasted that it shot all the German soldiers it captured. Some who served became cynical about human life; others, haunted by nightmares about the war, would long languish in veterans' hospitals.

The Home Front

Nothing transformed the social topography more than the vast internal migration of an already mobile people. About 15 million men moved because of military service, often accompanied by family members. Many other Americans moved to secure new economic opportunities, especially in the Pacific Coast states. Nearly a quarter of a million found jobs in the shipyards of the Bay area and at least as many in the aircraft industry that arose in the orange groves of southern California. More than one hundred thousand worked in the Puget Sound shipyards of Washington State and half as many in the nearby Boeing airplane plants. Others flocked to the world's largest magnesium plant in Henderson, Nevada, and to the Rocky Mountain Arsenal and Remington Rand arms plant outside Denver (see Map 25.5).

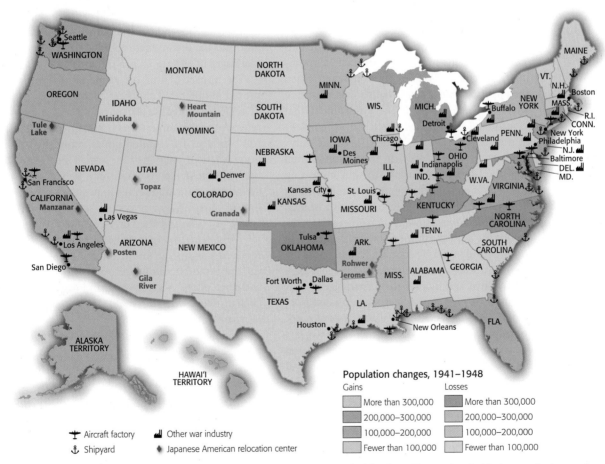

MAP 25.5   THE HOME FRONT, 1941–1945 War-related production finally ended the Great Depression, but it also required many Americans to move, especially to western states, where the jobs were. This map shows major war-related industries and the states that gained and lost populations. For Japanese Americans, relocation did not mean new jobs, but a loss of freedom as they were assigned to one of ten relocation centers across the country. © Cengage Learning. All rights reserved. No distribution allowed without express authorization.

War and American Society   **785**

At least 6 million people left farms to work in urban areas, including several million southern blacks and whites. They doubled Albuquerque's population and increased San Diego's some 90 percent. This mass uprooting of people from familiar settings made Americans both more cosmopolitan and lonelier. Some who moved far from their hometowns left behind their traditional values. Housing shortages left millions living in converted garages and trailer camps, even in cars. Some workers in Seattle lived in chicken coops. The swarms of migrants to Mobile, Alabama, attracted by a new aluminum plant, two massive shipyards, an air base, and an army supply depot, transformed a sleepy fishing village into a symbol of urban disorder.

Overcrowding and wartime separations strained family and community life. High rates of divorce, mental illness, family violence, and juvenile delinquency reflected the disruptions caused in part by the lack of privacy, the sense of impermanence, the absence of familiar settings, and the competition for scarce facilities. Few boom communities had the resources to supply their swollen populations with transportation, recreation, and social services. Urban blight and conflicts between newcomers and old-timers accelerated.

While military culture fostered a sexist mentality, emphasizing the differences between "femininity" and "masculinity," millions of American women donned pants, put their hair in bandannas, and went to work in defense plants. The government that previously had discouraged women from employment now proclaimed it was their "patriotic duty" to join the war effort. More than 6.5 million women entered the labor force during the war, increasing the number of employed women to 19 million. Less than a quarter of the labor force in 1940, women constituted well over a third of all workers in 1945.

Before the war, most female wage earners had been young and single. By contrast, 75 percent of the new women workers were married, 60 percent were over thirty-five, and more than 33 percent had children under the age of fourteen. They tended blast furnaces, operated cranes, greased locomotives, drove taxis, welded hulls, loaded shells, and worked in coke plants and rolling mills. On the Pacific Coast, more than one-third of all workers in aircraft and shipbuilding were women. **"Rosie the Riveter,"** holding a pneumatic gun in arms bulging with muscles, became the symbol of the woman war worker; she was, in the words of a popular song, "making history working for victory" (see Going to the Source).

Yet traditional attitudes and gender discrimination existed throughout the war. Many women workers were clustered in "women only" jobs, and women in manufacturing earned just 65 percent of what men earned for the same work. One popular advertisement pictured a woman in overalls about to leave for work. Her daughter asks, "Mother, when will you stay home again?" The woman responds: "Some jubilant day, mother will stay home again doing the job she likes—making a home for you and daddy when he gets back."

The stigma attached to working mothers also shaped government resistance to establishing child-care centers for women employed in defense. "A mother's primary duty is to her home and children," the Labor Department's Children's Bureau stated. "This duty is one she cannot lay aside, no matter what the emergency." Funds for federal child-care centers covered fewer than 10 percent of defense

"We're the Janes Who Make the Planes."

workers' children, and the young suffered. Terms like "eight-hour orphans" and "latch-key children" described unsupervised children forced to take care of themselves. Fueling fears that the employment of women outside the home would cause the family to disintegrate, juvenile delinquency increased five-fold, and the divorce rate zoomed from 16 per 100 marriages in 1940 to 27 per 100 in 1944.

The impact of war on women and the family proved multifaceted and even contradictory. As the divorce rate soared, so did marriage rates and birthrates. Although some women remained content to roll bandages for the Red Cross, more than three hundred thousand joined the armed forces and, for the first time in American history, were given regular military status and served in positions other than that of nurse. As members of the Women's Army Corps (WACs) and the Navy's Women Appointed for Volunteer Emergency Service (WAVES) they replaced men in such noncombat jobs as mechanics and radio operators and served as mapmakers and ferry pilots. About a thousand women became civilian pilots with the WASPs (Women's Airforce Service Pilots).

Overall, women gained a new sense of their potential. The war proved their capabilities and widened their world. Recalled one war wife whose returning husband did not like her independence, "He had left a shrinking violet and come home to a very strong oak tree." Some of these women were among the 350,000 teachers who took better-paying war work or joined the armed services, leaving schools badly understaffed. Students, too, abandoned school in record numbers. High school enrollments sank as the full-time employment of teenagers rose from 900,000 in 1940 to 3 million in 1944.

Women War Workers of Color

African American Fanny Christina Hill moved from Texas to Los Angeles in 1940, and found work as a live-in domestic, cleaning and cooking for a white family. In 1943, while her husband served in the military, she took a job with North American Aviation for sixty cents an hour.

Sometimes even if you're good, you just don't get the breaks if the color's not right. I could see where they made a difference in placing you in certain jobs. They had fifteen or twenty departments, but all the Negroes went to Department 17 because there was nothing but shooting and bucking rivets. You stood on one side of the panel and your partners stood on this side, and he would shoot the rivets with a gun and you'd buck them with the bar. That was about the size of it. I just didn't like it. I didn't think I could stay there with all this shooting and a'bucking and a'jumping and a'bumping. I stayed in it about two or three weeks and then I just decided I did *not* like that. I went and told my foreman and he didn't do anything about it, so I decided to leave. … I went over to the union and they told me what to do. I went back inside and they sent me to another department where you did bench work and I liked that much better. …

I must have stayed there nearly a year, and then they put me over in another department, "Plastics." … I worked over there until the end of the war. Well, not quite the end, because I got pregnant, and while I was off having the baby the war was over. …

When North American called me back, was I a happy soul! … So, from sixty cents an hour, when I first hired in there, up to one dollar. That wasn't traveling fast, but it was better than anything else because you had hours to work by and you had benefits and you come home at night with your family. So it was a good deal.

It made me live better. I really did. We always say that Lincoln took the bale off of the Negroes. … Well, my sister always said—that's why you can't interview her because she's so radical—"Hitler was the one that got us out of the white folks' kitchen."

Born in Mexico, Beatrice Morales Clifton was a married mother of four children when, over her husband's strenuous objections, she accepted a job offer from Lockheed in Los Angeles. Like Hill, she encountered resistance from male co-workers yet worked her way up to increasingly more skilled positions.

I felt proud of myself and felt good being that I had never done anything like that. I felt good that I could do something, and being that it was war, I felt that I was doing my part.

I went from 65 cents to $1.05. That was top pay. It felt good and, besides, it was my own money. I could do whatever I wanted with it because my husband, whatever he was giving to the house, he kept on paying it. I used to buy clothes for the kids; buy little things that they needed. I had a bank account and I had a little saving at home where I could get ahold of the money right away if I needed it. Julio never asked about it. He knew how much I made; I showed him. If there was something that had to be paid and I had the money and he didn't, well, I used some of my money.

Source: Sherna Berger Gluck, Rose the Riveter: Women, the War, and Social Change, *Twayne Publishers, 1987, pp. 37–42, 208–211. Reprinted by permission of the author.*

QUESTIONS

1. What effects did wartime employment have on these women's sense of themselves?
2. How might their wartime experiences have helped generate the civil rights and women's movements of the postwar era?

AFRICAN AMERICAN WOMEN WAR WORKERS Unlike the situation during the Great Depression, when women were expected to step aside in the job market to make way for unemployed men, the war brought increased opportunities for women in munitions plants and on assembly lines. Some 400,000 African American women left domestic work as servants in private homes for work in defense plants. "Hitler was the one," recalled one such defense worker, "that got us out of the white folk's kitchen." *(© Bettmann/Corbis)*

The loss of students to war production and the armed services forced colleges to admit large numbers of women and to contract themselves out to the armed forces. Nearly a million servicemen took college classes in science, engineering, and foreign languages. Harvard University awarded four military-training certificates for every academic degree it conferred. The chancellor of one branch of the University of California announced that his school was "no longer an academic tent with military sideshows. It is a military tent with academic sideshows." Higher education became more dependent on the federal government, and most universities sought increased federal contracts and subsidies. The universities in the West received some $100 billion from the Office of Scientific Research and Development, more money than had been spent on scientific research by all the western universities since their founding.

The war profoundly affected American culture. Spending on books and theater entertainment doubled. More than sixty million people (in a population of 135 million) attended movies weekly, and the film industry reached its zenith in 1945–1946. But as the war dragged on, people grew tired of war films, and Hollywood reemphasized romance and nostalgia with such stars as Katharine Hepburn and Judy Garland.

Similarly, popular music went from "Goodbye, Mama, I'm Off to Yokohama," the first hit of 1942,

to songs of lost love and loneliness, like "They're Either Too Young or Too Old." By 1945, bitterness pervaded lyrics, and songs like "Saturday Night Is the Loneliest Night of the Week" revealed impatience for the war's end.

In bookstores, nonfiction ruled the roost, and every newsmagazine increased its circulation. The Government Printing Office published Armed Services Editions, paperback reprints of classics and new releases; the nearly 350 million copies distributed free to soldiers sped up the American acceptance of quality paperbacks, which were introduced in 1939 by the Pocket Book Company. Wendell Willkie's *One World* (1943) became the fastest-selling title in publishing history to that time, with 1 million copies snapped up in two months. A vision of a world without military alliances and spheres of influence, this brief volume expressed hope that an international organization would extend peace and democracy through the postwar world. Most startlingly, Willkie attacked "our imperialisms at home." Unless the United States ended its own racism, he concluded, nonwhites around the globe would rebuff its claim to world leadership.

An avid interest in wartime news also spurred the major radio networks to increase their news programs from 4 percent to nearly 30 percent of broadcasting time, and enticed Americans to listen to the radio an average of 4½ hours a day. Daytime radio serials, like those featuring Dick Tracy tracking down Axis spies, reached the height of their popularity, as did juvenile comic books in which a platoon of new superheroes, including Captain America and Captain Marvel, saw action on the battlefield. Even Bugs Bunny donned a uniform to combat America's foes.

Racism and New Opportunities

Recognizing that the government needed the loyalty and labor of a united people, black leaders entered World War II determined to secure equal rights. In 1942, civil rights spokesmen insisted that African American support of the war hinged on America's commitment to racial justice. They demanded a *"Double V"* campaign to gain victory over racial discrimination at home as well as over the Axis abroad. Membership in the NAACP multiplied nearly ten times, reaching half a million in 1945. The association pressed for legislation outlawing the poll tax and lynching, decried discrimination in defense industries and the armed services, and sought to end black disfranchisement. Its campaign for voting rights gained momentum when the Supreme Court, in *Smith* v. *Allwright* (1944), ruled the Texas all-white primary unconstitutional. The decision

TUSKEGEE AIRMEN Although the great majority of African Americans in the army served in menial labor, noncombat, segregated units, black units performed admirably in combat when given the opportunity. The 99th Air Force Fighter squadron, known as the Tuskegee Airmen, gained high marks in action against the *Luftwaffe* and became one of the most highly respected fighter groups in the Army Air Corps. *(© Bettmann/Corbis)*

eliminated a bar that had existed in eight southern states, although these states promptly resorted to other devices to minimize voting by blacks.

A new civil-rights organization, the Congress of Racial Equality (CORE), was founded in 1942. Employing the same forms of nonviolent direct action that Mohandas Gandhi used in his campaign for India's independence, CORE sought to desegregate public facilities in northern cities.

Also proposing nonviolent direct action, **A. Philip Randolph,** president of the Brotherhood of Sleeping Car Porters, in 1941 called for a "thundering march" of one hundred thousand blacks on Washington if the president did not end discrimination in the armed services and the defense industry. FDR agreed to compromise.

In June 1941, Roosevelt issued Executive Order 8802, the first presidential directive on race since Reconstruction. It prohibited discriminatory employment practices by federal agencies and by all unions and companies engaged in war-related work and established the Fair Employment

Practices Commission (FEPC) to monitor compliance. Although the FEPC lacked effective enforcement powers, booming war production and a labor supply depleted by military service resulted in the employment of some 2 million African Americans in industry and two hundred thousand in the federal civil service. Between 1942 and 1945, the proportion of blacks in war production work rose from 3 to 9 percent. Black membership in labor unions doubled to 1.25 million, and the number of skilled and semiskilled black workers tripled. Formerly mired in low-paying domestic and farm jobs, nearly half a million black women found work in factories and the civil service. Overall, the average wage for African Americans increased from $457 to $1,976 a year, compared with a gain from $1,064 to $2,600 for whites.

About 1 million African Americans served in the armed forces. Wartime needs forced the military to end the policies of excluding blacks from the marines and coast guard, restricting them to jobs as mess boys in the navy, and confining them to noncombatant units in the army. From just five in 1940—three of them chaplains—the number of black officers grew to over seven thousand in 1945, including the Tuskegee Air Corps. The first class of five African American pilots, trained in Tuskegee, graduated in March 1942. They, and those that followed, manned both fighter planes and bombers. Their 332nd Fighter Group, commanded by West Point graduate Lt. Col. Ben Davis, Jr., the son of America's first black general, eventually flew more than fifteen hundred missions over Italy and the Mediterranean, earning numerous awards and making it a special source of pride for African Americans.

The great majority of blacks, however, served throughout the war in segregated service units commanded by white officers. This indignity, made worse by the failure of military authorities to protect black servicemen off the post and by the use of white military police to keep blacks "in their place," sparked rioting on army bases. At least fifty black soldiers died in racial conflicts during the war. "I used to sing gospel songs until I joined the Army," recalled blues-guitar great B.B. King, "then I sang the blues."

Violence within the military mirrored growing racial tensions on the home front. As blacks protested against discrimination, many whites resisted blacks' efforts to improve their economic and social status. Race riots erupted in 1943 in Harlem, Mobile, and Beaumont, Texas. The bloodiest melee exploded in Detroit that year when white mobs assaulted blacks caught riding on trolleys or sitting in movie theaters and blacks smashed and looted white-owned stores and shops. After thirty hours of racial beatings, shootings, and burning, twenty-five African Americans and nine whites lay dead, more than seven hundred had been injured, and more than $2 million of property had been destroyed. The fear of continued violence led to a greater emphasis on racial tolerance by liberal whites and to a reduction in the militancy of African American leaders.

Yet the war jolted the racial status quo in ways that laid the foundation for an eventual successful drive for black civil rights. The migration of hundreds of thousands of rural southern either to cities in the South or to the North and West transformed race into a national concern. It created a new attitude of independence in African Americans freed from the constraints of caste. As the growing numbers of blacks in northern cities began to vote, moreover, African Americans could hold a balance of power in close elections. This prompted politicians in both major parties to extend greater recognition to blacks and to pay more attention to civil-rights issues.

African American expectations of greater government concern for their rights also resulted from the new prominence of the United States as a major power in a predominantly nonwhite world. As Japanese propaganda appeals to the peoples of Asia and Latin America emphasized lynchings and race riots in the United States, Americans had to confront the peril that white racism posed to their national security. In addition, the horrors of Nazi racism discredited America's own white-supremacist attitudes and practices. A pluralist vision of American society now became part of official rhetoric—and of the liberal-left agenda. The contradiction between American ideals of freedom and equality and the actual state of African Americans became manifest. Swedish economist Gunnar Myrdal, in his massive study of race problems, *An American Dilemma* (1944), concluded that "not since Reconstruction had there been more reason to anticipate fundamental changes in American race relations ... there is bound to be a redefinition of the Negro's status as a result of this War." Returning black veterans, and African Americans who had served the nation on the home front, soon expected to gain all the rights enjoyed by whites.

War and Diversity

Wartime winds of change also brought new opportunities and difficulties to other minorities. More than twenty-five thousand Native Americans served in the armed forces, including 400 Navajo "code talkers" who confounded the Japanese by using their complex native language to relay messages between U.S. command centers. "Were it not for the Navajos, the Marines would never have taken Iwo Jima," one Signal Corps officer declared.

Another fifty thousand Indians left the reservation to work in defense industries, mainly on the West Coast. The Rosebud Reservation in South Dakota lost more than a quarter of its population to migration during the war. It was the first time most had lived in a non-Indian world, and the average income of Native American households tripled during the war. Such economic improvement encouraged many Indians to remain outside the reservation and to try to assimilate into mainstream life. But anti-Indian discrimination, particularly in smaller towns near reservations, such as Gallup, New Mexico, and Billings, Montana, forced many Native Americans back to their reservations, which had suffered severely from budget cuts during the war. Prodded by those who coveted Indian lands, lawmakers demanded that Indians be taken off the

> "I used to sing gospel songs until I joined the Army, then I sang the blues."

A "DOUBLE V" PROTEST As the mobilization for war lifted the pall of the depression for white workers, management and labor joined together to exclude African Americans from the benefits of the war boom. To protest, picketers rallied for defense jobs outside the Glenn Martin aircraft plant in Omaha, Nebraska. *(Schomburg Center for Research in Black Culture, New York Public Library/Art Resource, NY)*

backs of the taxpayers and "freed from the reservations" to fend for themselves." To mobilize against the campaign to end all reservations and trust protections, Native Americans organized the National Congress of American Indians in 1944.

To relieve labor shortages in agriculture, caused by conscription and the movement of rural workers to city factories, the U.S. government negotiated an agreement with Mexico in July 1942 to import *braceros*, or temporary workers. Classified as foreign laborers rather than as immigrants, an estimated two hundred thousand **braceros**, half of them in California, received short-term contracts promising adequate wages, medical care, and decent living conditions. But farm owners frequently violated the terms of these contracts and also encouraged an influx of illegal migrants from Mexico desperate for employment. Unable to complain about their working conditions without risking arrest and deportation, hundreds of thousands of Mexicans were exploited by agribusinesses in Arizona, California, and Texas. At the same time, tens of thousands of

Chicanos left agricultural work for jobs in factories, shipbuilding yards, and steel mills. By 1943, about half a million Chicanos were living in Los Angeles County, 10 percent of the total population. In New Mexico nearly 20 percent of Mexican American farm laborers escaped from rural poverty to urban jobs. Even as their occupational status and material conditions improved, most Mexican Americans remained in communities (*colonias*), segregated from the larger society and frequently harassed by the police.

Much of the hostility toward Mexican Americans focused on young gang members who wore "zoot suits"—a fashion that originated in Harlem and emphasized long, broad-shouldered jackets and pleated trousers tightly pegged at the ankles. Known as *pachucos*, zoot-suited Mexican Americans aroused the ire of servicemen stationed or on leave in Los Angeles who saw them as delinquents and draft dodgers. After a luridly publicized trial arising from a Mexican American gang fight at a swimming hole called Sleepy Lagoon, and newspaper headlines of a Chicano "crime wave," bands of sailors and soldiers rampaged through Los Angeles in early June 1943, stripping *pachucos*, cutting their long hair, and beating them. Military authorities looked the other way. City police intervened only to arrest Mexican Americans, and the city council made the wearing of a zoot suit a misdemeanor. Nothing was done about the substandard housing, disease, and racism Hispanics had to endure.

Unlike African Americans, however, more than 350,000 Mexican Americans served in the armed forces without segregation, and in all combat units. They volunteered in higher numbers than warranted by their percentage of the population and earned a disproportionate number of citations for distinguished service as well as seventeen Medals of Honor. Returning Mexican American GIs joined established antidiscrimination groups, like the League of United Latin American Citizens (LULAC), and organized their own associations, like the American GI Forum, to press for equal rights.

Thousands of gay men and lesbians who served in the armed forces also found new wartime opportunities. The military officially barred those they defined as "sexual perverts," but owing to the urgency of building a massive armed forces, just four to five thousand men out of eighteen million examined for induction were excluded because of homosexuality. For the vast majority of gays not excluded, being emancipated from traditional expectations and the close scrutiny of family and neighbors, and living in overwhelmingly all-male or all-female environments, brought freedom to meet like-minded gay men and women. Like other minorities, many gays saw the war as a chance to prove their worth under fire. Yet some suspected of being gay were dishonorably discharged, sent to psychiatric hospitals, or imprisoned in so-called queer stockades. In 1945, gay veterans established the Veteran's Benevolent Association, the first organization in the United States to combat discrimination against homosexuals.

The Internment of Japanese Americans

Far more than any other minority in the United States, Japanese Americans suffered grievously during the war. About thirty-seven thousand first-generation Japanese immigrants (Issei) and nearly seventy-five thousand native-born Japanese American citizens (Nisei) were interned in "relocation centers" guarded by military police—a tragic reminder of the fragility of civil liberties in wartime.

The **internment of Japanese Americans** reflected forty years of anti-Japanese sentiment on the West Coast, rooted in racial prejudice and economic rivalry. Nativist politicians and farmers who wanted Japanese American land had long decried the "yellow peril." Following the attack on Pearl Harbor they whipped up the rage of white Californians, aided by a government report falsely blaming Japanese Americans in Hawaii for aiding the Japanese naval force. Patriotic associations and many newspapers clamored for evacuating the Japanese Americans, as did the army general in charge of the Western Defense Command, who proclaimed, "A Jap is a Jap is a Jap. It makes no difference whether he is an American citizen or not. … I don't want any of them."

In February 1942, President Roosevelt gave in to the pressure and issued Executive Order 9066, authorizing the removal from military areas of anyone deemed a threat. Although not a single Japanese American was apprehended for espionage or sedition and neither the FBI nor military intelligence uncovered any evidence of disloyal behavior by Japanese Americans, the military ordered the eviction of all Nisei and Issei from the West Coast. Only Hawaii was excepted. Despite the far larger number of Hawaiians of Japanese ancestry, as well as of Japanese living in Hawaii, no internment policy was implemented there, and no sabotage occurred.

Forced to sell all they owned at whatever prices they could obtain, Japanese Americans lost an estimated $2 billion in property and possessions. Tagged with numbers rather than names, they were herded into barbed-wire-encircled detention camps in the most desolate parts of the West and Great Plains—places, wrote one historian, "where nobody had lived before and no one has lived since." Few protested the incarceration. Stating that it would not question government claims of military necessity during time of war, the Supreme Court upheld the constitutionality of the evacuation in the *Korematsu* case (1944). By then the hysteria had subsided, and the government had begun a program of gradual release, allowing some Nisei to attend college or take factory jobs (but not on the West Coast); about eighteen thousand served in the military. The 442nd regimental combat team, entirely Japanese American, became the most decorated unit in the military.

In 1982, a special government commission concluded in its report, *Personal Justice Denied*, that

> "A Jap's a Jap. It makes no difference whether he is an American citizen or not."

internment "was not justified by military necessity."
It blamed the Roosevelt administration's action
on "race prejudice, war hysteria, and a failure of
political leadership" and apologized to Japanese
Americans for "a grave injustice." In 1988, Congress
voted to pay twenty thousand dollars in compensation
to each of the nearly sixty-two thousand
surviving internees; in 1998, President Bill Clinton
further apologized for the injustice by giving the
nation's highest civilian honor, the Presidential
Medal of Freedom, to Fred Korematsu, who had
protested the evacuation decree all the way to the
Supreme Court.

Triumph and Tragedy, 1945

Spring and summer 1945 brought stunning changes
and new crises. In Europe, a new balance of power
emerged after the collapse of the Third Reich. In
Asia, continued Japanese reluctance to surrender
led to the use of atomic bombs. And in the United
States, a new president, Harry S Truman, presided
over both the end of World War II and the beginning
of the Cold War and the nuclear age.

The Yalta Conference

By the time Roosevelt, Churchill, and Stalin met
in the Soviet city of Yalta in February 1945, the
military situation favored the Soviet Union. The
Red Army had overrun Poland, Romania, and
Bulgaria; driven the Nazis out of Yugoslavia; penetrated
Austria, Hungary, and Czechoslovakia; and
was massed just fifty miles from Berlin. American
forces, in contrast, were still recovering from the
Battle of the Bulge and facing stiff resistance on the
route to Japan. The Joint Chiefs of Staff, contemplating
the awesome cost in American casualties of
invading Japan, insisted that Stalin's help was worth
almost any price. And Stalin was in a position to
make demands. The Soviet Union had suffered
most in the war against Germany, it already dominated
eastern Europe, and, knowing that the United
States did not want to fight a prolonged war against
Japan, Stalin had the luxury of deciding whether
and when to enter the Pacific war.

The **Yalta accords** reflected these realities. Stalin
again vowed to declare war on Japan "two or three
months" after Germany's surrender, and in return
Churchill and Roosevelt reneged on their arrangement
with Jiang Jieshi and promised the Soviet
Union concessions in Manchuria and the territories
it had lost in the Russo-Japanese War (1904)
(see Chapter 22). The Big Three delegated a final
settlement of the German reparations issue to a
postwar commission and left vague the matter of

YOUNG NISEI EVACUEES AT THE TURLOCK ASSEMBLY CENTER
Awaiting their turn for baggage inspection on May 2, 1942, these children
would be interned in remote "relocation centers" along with 37,000 first-
generation Japanese immigrants (Issei) and some 75,000 native-born
Japanese American (Nisei) citizens of the United States. Hastily uprooted
from their homes, farms, and stores, most lost all their property and personal
possessions and spent the war under armed guard. *(National Archives)*

partitioning Germany and its eventual reunification.
The conference also vaguely called for interim
governments in eastern Europe "broadly representative
of all democratic elements" and for eventual
freely elected permanent governments. On the matter
dearest to FDR's heart, the negotiators accepted
a plan for a new international organization and
agreed to a founding conference of the new United
Nations in San Francisco in April 1945.

Stalin proved adamant about the nature of the
postwar Polish government. Twice in the twentieth
century German troops had used Poland as a springboard
for invading Russia. Stalin would not expose
his land again, and after the Red Army had captured
Warsaw in January 1945, he installed a procommunist
regime and brutally subdued the anticommunist
Poles. Conservative critics would later charge
that FDR "gave away" eastern Europe. Actually, the
Soviet Union gained little it did not already control,
and short of going to war against the Soviets while
still battling Germany and Japan, FDR could only
hope that Stalin would keep his word.

Victory in Europe

As the Soviets prepared for their assault on Berlin, American troops crossed the Rhine at Remagen in March 1945 and encircled the Ruhr Valley, Germany's industrial heartland. Churchill now proposed a rapid thrust to Berlin. But Eisenhower and Roosevelt saw no point in risking high casualties to rush to an area of Germany already designated as the Soviet occupation zone. So Eisenhower advanced methodically along a broad front until the Americans met the Russians at the Elbe River on April 25. By then, the Red Army had taken Vienna and reached the suburbs of Berlin. On April 30, as Soviet troops approached his headquarters, Hitler committed suicide. Berlin fell to the Soviets on May 2, and on May 8 a new German government surrendered unconditionally.

Jubilant Americans celebrated Victory in Europe (V-E) Day less than a month after they had mourned the death of their president. On April 12, an exhausted President Roosevelt had abruptly clutched his head, moaned that he had a "terrific headache," and fell unconscious. A cerebral hemorrhage ended his life. As the nation grieved, Roosevelt's unprepared successor assumed the burden of ending the war and dealing with the Soviet Union.

> "I don't know whether you fellows ever had a load of hay or a bull fall on you, but last night the moon, the stars, and all the planets fell on me."

"I don't know whether you fellows ever had a load of hay or a bull fall on you," Harry Truman told reporters on his first full day in office, "but last night the moon, the stars, and all the planets fell on me." An unpretentious politician awed by his new responsibilities, Truman struggled to continue FDR's policies. But Roosevelt had made no effort to familiarize his vice president with world affairs. Perhaps sensing his own inadequacies, Truman adopted a tough pose toward adversaries. In office less than two weeks, he lashed out at Soviet ambassador V.M. Molotov that the United States was tired of waiting for the Russians to allow free elections in Poland, and he threatened to cut off lend-lease aid if the Soviet Union did not cooperate. The Truman administration then reduced U.S. economic assistance to the Soviets and stalled on their request for a $1 billion reconstruction loan. Simultaneously, Stalin strengthened his grip on eastern Europe, ignoring the promises he had made at Yalta.

The United States neither conceded the Soviet sphere of influence in eastern Europe nor tried to end it. Although Truman still sought Stalin's cooperation in establishing the United Nations and in defeating Japan, Soviet-American relations deteriorated. By June 1945, when the Allied countries succeeded in framing the United Nations Charter, hopes for a new international order had dimmed, and the United Nations emerged as a diplomatic battleground. Truman, Churchill, and Stalin met at Potsdam, Germany, from July 16 to August 2 to complete the postwar arrangements begun at Yalta. But the Allied leaders could barely agree to demilitarize Germany and to punish Nazi war criminals. Given the diplomatic impasse, only military power remained to determine the contours of the postwar world.

The Holocaust

When news of the **Holocaust**—the term later given to the Nazis' extermination of European Jewry—first leaked out in early 1942, many Americans discounted the reports. Not until November did the State Department admit knowledge of the massacres. A month later, the American broadcaster Edward R. Murrow, listened to nationwide, reported on the systematic killing of millions of Jews, "It is a picture of mass murder and moral depravity unequalled in the history of the world. It is a horror beyond what imagination can grasp. … There are no longer 'concentration camps'—we must speak now only of 'extermination camps.'"

Most Americans considered the annihilation of Europe's 6 million Jews beyond belief. There were no photographs to prove it, and, some argued, the atrocities attributed to the Germans in World War I had turned out to be false. So few took issue with the military's view that the way to liberate those enslaved by Hitler was by speedily winning the war. Pleas by American Jews for the Allies to bomb the death camps and the railroad tracks leading to them fell on deaf ears. In fall 1944, U.S. planes flying over Auschwitz in southern Poland bombed nearby factories but left the gas chambers and crematoria intact, in order, American officials explained, not to divert air power from more vital raids elsewhere. "How could it be," historian David Wyman has asked, "that Government officials knew that a place existed where 2,000 helpless human beings could be killed in less than an hour, knew that this occurred over and over again, and yet did not feel driven to search for some way to wipe such a scourge from the earth?"

How much could have been done remains uncertain. Still, the U.S. government never seriously considered rescue schemes or searched for a way to curtail the Nazis' "final solution" to the "Jewish question." Its feeble response was due to its overwhelming focus on winning the war as quickly as possible, congressional and public fears of an influx of destitute

THE HOLOCAUST When the extermination camps and forced labor camps in Germany and Poland were finally liberated in 1945, the vast majority of prisoners were dead or barely alive. After seeing the ghastly Ohrdruf camp, the first Nazi concentration camp liberated by the U.S. Army, General Eisenhower wanted every American unit not in combat on the front line "to see this place. We are told that the American soldier does not know what he is fighting for. Now, at least," Eisenhower said, "he will know what he is fighting against." *(© Bettmann/Corbis)*

Jews into the United States, Britain's wish to placate the Arabs by keeping Jewish settlers out of Palestine, and the fear of some Jewish American leaders that pressing the issue would increase anti-Semitism at home. Accordingly, the State Department assisted in saving the lives of just two hundred thousand Jews, while 6 million other Jews—75 percent of the European Jewish population—were gassed, shot, and incinerated. The internal investigation of its inaction was appropriately entitled "Report to the Secretary on the Acquiescence of This Government in the Murder of the Jews."

"The things I saw beggar description," wrote General Eisenhower after visiting the first death camp liberated by the U.S. army. He sent immediately for a delegation of congressional leaders and newspaper editors to make sure Americans would never forget the gas chambers and human ovens. Only after viewing the photographs and newsreels of corpses stacked like cordwood, boxcars heaped with the bones of dead prisoners, bulldozers shoving emaciated bodies into hastily dug ditches, and liberated, barely-alive living skeletons lying in their own filth, their vacant, sunken eyes staring through barbed wire, did most Americans see that the Holocaust was no myth.

The Atomic Bombs

Meanwhile, the war with Japan ground on. Early in 1945, an assault force of marines invaded Iwo Jima, 700 miles from Japan. In places termed the "Meat Grinder" and "Bloody Gorge," the marines savagely battled thousands of Japanese soldiers hidden in tunnels and behind concrete bunkers and pillboxes. Securing the five-square-mile island would cost the marines nearly twenty-seven thousand casualties—and one-third of all the marines killed in the Pacific. In June, American troops waded ashore on Okinawa, 350 miles from Japan and a key staging area for the planned U.S. invasion of the Japanese home islands. Death and destruction engulfed Okinawa as waves of Americans attacked nearly impregnable Japanese defenses head-on, repeating the bloody strategy of World War I. After eighty-three days of fighting on land and sea, twelve thousand Americans lay dead and three times as many wounded, a 35 percent casualty rate, higher than at Normandy.

The appalling rate of loss on Iwo Jima and Okinawa weighed on the minds of American strategists. The Japanese Cabinet showed no willingness to give up the war despite Japan's being blockaded and bombed daily (on March 9–10 a fleet of B-29s dropped napalm-and-magnesium bombs on Tokyo, burning sixteen square miles of the city to the ground and killing some eighty-four thousand). Japanese military leaders insisted on fighting to the bitter end; surrender was unthinkable. Japan possessed an army of more than 2 million—plus up to 4 million reservists and five thousand kamikaze aircraft—and the U.S. Joint Chiefs initially feared it might take eighteen more months of battle and more than a hundred thousand American casualties before victory could be achieved.

The successful detonation of history's first nuclear explosion at Alamagordo in mid-July gave Truman an alternative. On July 25, while meeting with Stalin and Churchill in Potsdam, Truman ordered the use of an atomic bomb if Japan did not surrender before August 3. The next day, in the **Potsdam Declaration,** he warned Japan to surrender unconditionally or face "prompt and utter destruction." Japan refused, and on August 6, a B-29 bomber named *Enola Gay* took off from the Marianas island of Tinian and dropped a uranium bomb on Hiroshima. It plunged the city into what Japanese novelist Masuji Ibuse termed "a hell of unspeakable torments." The 300,000-degree centigrade fireball incinerated houses and vaporized people. More than sixty thousand died immediately from the blast, and another seventy-five thousand died from burns and radiation poisoning by late 1945. On August 8, Stalin declared war on Japan, and U.S. planes dropped leaflets on Japan warning that

"A hell of unspeakable torments."

another bomb would be dropped if it did not surrender. Japan's military leaders still preferred death to surrender. The next day, at high noon, the *Bock's Car* flattened Nagasaki with a plutonium bomb, killing thirty-six thousand, and injuring more than sixty thousand. On August 14, Japan accepted the American terms of surrender, which implicitly permitted the emperor to retain his throne but subordinated him to the U.S. commander of the occupation forces. General MacArthur received Japan's surrender on the battleship *Missouri* on September 2, 1945. The war was over.

HIROSHIMA AFTER THE ATOMIC BOMB "Little Boy," the A-bomb dropped on Hiroshima on August 6, 1945, incinerated the industrial city, killing more than 60,000 Japanese immediately. Three days later, "Fat Man" destroyed Nagasaki, suddenly killing another 36,000. An editorial in the Japanese *Nippon Times* declared: "This is not war, this is not even murder, this is pure nihilism…a crime against God which strikes at the very basis of moral existence." *(© Bettmann/Corbis)*

While Americans at the time overwhelmingly backed the atomic bombings of Japan as the necessary way to end the war with the least cost in U.S. lives, many historians have subsequently questioned the necessity of using such a terrible weapon of mass destruction. Some believe that racist American attitudes toward the Japanese motivated the decision to drop the bombs. As war correspondent Ernie Pyle wrote, "The Japanese are looked upon as something inhuman and squirmy—like some people feel about cockroaches or mice." However, those involved in the Manhattan Project had regarded Germany as the target, and considering the ferocity of the Allied bombings of Hamburg and Dresden—which claimed more victims than Hiroshima and Nagasaki—there is little reason to assume that the Allies would not have dropped atomic bombs on Germany had they been available. By 1945, the Allies as well as the Axis had abandoned restraints on attacking civilians.

Other critics maintain that demonstrating the bomb's terrible destructiveness on an uninhabited island would have moved Japan to surrender. We will never know for sure. American scientists rejected a demonstration bombing because the United States had an atomic arsenal of only two bombs and they did not know whether the mechanism for detonating them in the air would work. Still others are persuaded that the president, aware of worsening relations between the United States and the USSR, ordered the atomic attack to scare the Russians into submission and end the Pacific war before Stalin could enter it and share in the postwar occupation of Japan. Referring to the Soviets, President Truman noted just before the atomic test at Alamogordo, "If it explodes, as I think it will, I'll certainly have a hammer on those boys." Truman's new secretary of state, James Byrnes, thought that the bomb would "make Russia more manageable" and would "put us in a position to dictate our own terms at the end of the war." Citing a U.S. intelligence survey that concluded that "Japan would have surrendered even if the atomic bombs had not been dropped, even if Russia had not entered the war, and even if no invasion had been planned or contemplated," critics charge that the bomb was used primarily to intimidate the Soviet Union rather than to secure victory over Japan.

In fact, no military or political leader advising Truman debated *not* using the bomb. The momentum behind the Manhattan Project was such that no one in power questioned the assumption that, once developed, the atomic weapon would be used. Secretary of War Stimson considered it "as legitimate as any other of the deadly explosive weapons of modern war." And given the ferocious Japanese resistance at Okinawa and Iwo Jima, and the likelihood of still greater bloodshed if an invasion of Japan became necessary, Truman saw no reason not to save American lives. As throughout the war, American leaders relied on production and technology to win the war with the minimum loss of American life. Every new weapon was put to use, the concept of "total war" easily accommodated the bombing of civilians, and the atomic bomb was one more item in an arsenal that had already wreaked enormous destruction on the Axis. In "Operation Thunderclap," the Allies had obliterated miles of German and Japanese cities, making no pretense of distinguishing military and civilian targets. The rules of war that had once stayed the use of weapons of mass destruction against enemy civilians no longer prevailed. Before Hiroshima, the United States had already crossed the callous threshold into mass murder from the air.

No member of the committee formed to advise Truman on the use of the bomb counseled that the United States should sacrifice American servicemen to lessen death and destruction in Japan, the nation that had unleashed a wanton, brutal attack on Pearl Harbor, or not use a weapon developed with $2 billion in taxpayer money, or not drop bombs that might force Stalin to be more reasonable. There seemed no good reason not to drop the bombs. To the vast majority of Americans, the atomic bomb was, in Churchill's words, simply "a miracle of deliverance" that saved Allied lives. So E.B. Sledge and his comrades in the First Marine Division, slated to take part in the first wave of the invasion of Japan's home islands, breathed "an indescribable sense of relief." Hearing the news of the atomic bombs and Japan's surrender, Sledge wrote, they sat in stunned silence:

We remembered our dead. So many dead. So many maimed. So many bright futures consigned to the ashes of the past. So many dreams lost in the madness that engulfed us. Except for a few widely scattered shouts of joy, the survivors of the abyss sat hollow-eyed and silent, trying to comprehend a world without war.

ATOMIC BOMBS BRING RELIEF AND JOY TO SOME These U.S. servicemen, like many others, hearing the news of the atomic bombs and the Japanese surrender, expressed their relief and joy that they would soon be safely coming home rather than having to participate in an invasion of Japan. *(AP Images)*

The atomic bombs ended the deadliest war in history. A truly global conflict, involving over half the world's peoples and some fifty nations, with armies ranging over continents and navies fighting on every ocean, the war affected women, men, and children as victims of civilian bombing campaigns, as war workers, as slave laborers and comfort women. Neither side gave much quarter in seeking to destroy the other's will and resources. Perhaps 60 million died—more than half of them civilians. The Soviet Union lost roughly 20 million people, China 15 million, Poland 6 million, Germany 4 million, and Japan 2 million. Much of Asia and Europe was rubble. Some three hundred thousand Americans died in combat, and, although physically unscathed, the United States had changed profoundly—for better and worse.

CONCLUSION

Most Americans, and their government, initially responded to the war clouds over Asia and Europe by reaffirming their isolationism. As one senator proclaimed, prior to the vote that defeated Roosevelt's effort to have the United States join the World Court, "To hell with Europe and the rest of those nations!" Not till the Japanese attack on the American fleet at Pearl Harbor, more than two years after the war in Europe had begun, did the United States enter the fray, and even then it waited until Hitler and Mussolini declared war on it before joining the armed struggle engulfing the world. Once engaged, the Americans rapidly went on a war footing. Mobilization transformed the scope and authority of the federal government, vastly expanding presidential powers. It ended the unemployment of the depression and made American industry more productive than it had ever been—and made most Americans more prosperous than they had ever been. It tilted the national economic balance toward the South Atlantic, Gulf, and Pacific coasts. It accelerated trends toward bigness in business, agriculture, and labor. It involved the military in the economy and education as never before.

To achieve an unconditional victory, with the least possible cost in American lives, Roosevelt concentrated on defeating Germany first yet delaying a second front in Europe until Soviet forces had routed the German army in eastern Europe. Meanwhile, half a world away, a two-pronged American offensive, across the central Pacific and north from Australia, brought Japan to the brink of defeat. On the home front, the war catalyzed vital changes in racial and social relations, causing fundamental challenges to long-held assumptions about the "place" for women and blacks. Both arenas intensified prejudices against minorities and women and also broadened educational and employment opportunities that widened their public spheres and heightened their expectations. Fighting and winning the greatest war in history, moreover, restored American faith in capitalism and democratic institutions. It was a vital coming-of-age experience for an entire generation that did much to give postwar American society a confident, "can-do" spirit, optimistic for the "American Century" that they knew lay ahead.

The awesome development and use of an atomic bomb bolstered that spirit and enabled the United States to defeat Japan promptly, to try to force the Soviets to be more manageable, and to avoid an invasion of the Japanese home islands costing untold thousands of American casualties. The mass destruction of the war and total defeat of the Axis, however, brought new crises to cloud the bright dawn of peace. The world's two superpowers—the United States and the USSR—soon squared off in a Cold War that would see the United States play a role in global affairs inconceivable to most Americans just five years before.

KEY TERMS

"Good Neighbor" policy   (p. 768)

Benito Mussolini   (p. 768)

Adolf Hitler   (p. 768)

appeasement   (p. 769)

Neutrality Acts   (p. 770)

Joseph Stalin   (p. 770)

Winston Churchill   (p. 774)

"lend-lease"   (p. 774)

Atlantic Charter   (p. 775)

War Production Board   (p. 777)

Office of Price Administration   (p. 777)

Manhattan Project   (p. 780)

Battle of the Bulge   (p. 782)

"Rosie the Riveter"   (p. 786)

A. Philip Randolph   (p. 789)

braceros   (p. 791)

internment of Japanese Americans   (p. 792)

Yalta accords   (p. 793)

Holocaust   (p. 794)

Potsdam Declaration   (p. 795)

FOR FURTHER REFERENCE

Luis Alvarez, *The Power of the Zoot: Youth Culture and Resistance during World War II* (2008). A lively account of youth and ethnicity during the war.

Max Arthur, ed., *Forgotten Voices of the Second World War: A New History of World War Two in the Words of the Men and Women Who Were There* (2004). A fascinating oral history.

Elizabeth Borgwardt, *A New Deal for the World: America's Vision for Human Rights* (2005). A major study of America's ideals in foreign policy.

Max Hastings, *Inferno: The World at War, 1939–1945* (2011). A magisterial history of the truly global nature of the war and an intimate account of its many consequences for everyday people.

Laura Hillenbrand, *Unbroken: A World War II Story of Survival, Resilience, and Redemption* (2010). An account of a downed Air Force lieutenant's extraordinary struggle to surmount all obstacles and survive the war.

Tetsuden Kashima, *Judgement Without Trial: Japanese-American Imprisonment During World War II* (2003). A critical examination of the wartime internment.

Todd Moye, *Freedom Flyers: The Tuskegee Airmen of World War II* (2010). The struggles and accomplishments of blacks in the Army Air Forces.

Margaret Paton-Walsh, *Our War Too: American Women Against the Axis* (2002). A solid introduction to the role of U.S. servicewomen in World War II.

Andrew J. Rotter, *Hiroshima: The World's Bomb* (2008). A balanced, insightful examination of the role of the atomic bombs.

E.B. Sledge, *With the Old Breed at Peleliu and Okinawa* (1990). A candid memoir of a marine's war in the Pacific.

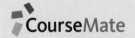

The Cold War Abroad and at Home, 1945–1960

ALGER HISS *(AP Images)*

WHITTAKER CHAMBERS *(AP Images)*

TESTIFYING BEFORE THE HOUSE Un-American Activities Committee in 1948, Whittaker Chambers, a repentant ex-communist and an editor of *Time* magazine, identified Alger Hiss as an underground member of a secret "communist cell" operating in Washington in the 1930s. The sad-faced, rumpled, often disheveled Chambers appeared a tortured Christian soul crusading to save the West from the atheistic Red peril. The elegant, handsome Hiss, in contrast, seemed the very symbol of the liberal establishment: Harvard Law School graduate, former New Dealer, State Department official who accompanied FDR to Yalta, and now president of the Carnegie Endowment for International Peace. Hiss categorically denied any communist affiliation and claimed not to know Chambers.

Most liberals saw Hiss as the victim of conservatives bent on tarnishing New Deal liberalism. Conversely, those suspicious of the Rooseveltian liberal tradition thought Hiss the personification of a communist-riddled Democratic administration. To conservatives, he symbolized every wrong turn the nation had taken since the start of the New Deal. Under rigorous questioning by freshman Republican congressman Richard Nixon of California, Hiss eventually admitted he knew Chambers but continued to deny having ever been a communist. Chambers, in front of reporters at his Maryland farm, then produced microfilms he had hidden inside a hollowed-out pumpkin. The so-called pumpkin papers appeared to be State Department documents that had been copied on a typewriter once owned by Hiss. Chambers claimed Hiss had stolen the documents in the late 1930s and passed them on to the Soviets.

***THE DAY THE COMMUNISTS TOOK OVER AMERICA* BY ISABEL MOORE** Books, magazines, TV, and Hollywood competed to combat the "Commie Menace." *(The Michael Barson Collection/ Past Perfect/Picture Research Consultants & Archives)*

Because the statute of limitations on espionage had expired, the Justice Department indicted Hiss for perjury. After the first perjury trial ended in deadlock, a second one convicted Hiss in January 1950, sentencing him to five years in federal prison. Although one could not tell truth from lies in the trial testimony, and the documents in question seemed insignificant, the conviction of Hiss fueled paranoia of a communist conspiracy. If distinguished officials such as Hiss had been disloyal, what other "fifth columnists" might be part of a diabolical Red underground in the United States, manipulating what America could, and could not, do in the world?

The Hiss case emboldened many committees, public and private, to broaden their anticommunist probes and encouraged many Republicans, particularly Nixon and Senator Joseph McCarthy, to press the communists-in-government issue hard. Once-reasonable concerns about American security now mushroomed into demagoguery and witch-hunts, the trampling of civil liberties, and suppression of dissent.

Such was the chief, and most chilling, domestic legacy of what came to be called the Cold War: a new form of international rivalry in which the United States and the Soviet Union avoided direct military conflict while using all their resources to thwart each other's objectives.

Hard on the heels of V-J Day, an uncompromising Truman squared off against an obsessive Stalin over the postwar fate of Eastern Europe. Abandoning its historic aloofness from events outside the Western Hemisphere, the United States plunged into a global struggle to contain the Soviet Union and stop communism. While the United States experienced dramatic changes, the conflict would persist through the 1950s and beyond. The United States in 1940 had no military alliances, a small defense budget, and limited troops; by 1960, it had built a massive military establishment, signed mutual-defense pacts with forty countries, directly intervened in the affairs of allies and enemies alike, erected military bases on every continent, and engaged the USSR in a seemingly unending nuclear-arms race.

Containing communism abroad profoundly changed America at home as well. It transformed the economy, shifted national priorities, expanded the powers of the executive branch, and spawned a second Red Scare that decimated the Left, stifled liberalism, and helped bring the Republicans to power. While the Democrats proved unable to expand the New Deal into such areas as civil rights, education, and health care, the Republicans failed to turn back the clock and repeal the New Deal. The politics of deadlock, inherited from the late 1930s, continued into the 1960s. Obsessed with communist spies and traitors, Americans increasingly looked to their own prosperity and family life for the joy and blessings denied them by the Cold War.

Anticommunism and Containment, 1946–1953

The "shotgun wedding" that joined the United States and the USSR in an alliance to defeat Hitler dissolved at war's end into a struggle to fill the power vacuums left by the defeat of the Axis, the exhaustion and bankruptcy of Western Europe, and the crumbling of colonial empires in Asia and Africa (see Map 26.1). As the two powers sought greater security, each feeding the other's fears, a cycle of misperception and misunderstanding, of distrust and animosity, resulted in the Cold War.

Polarization and Cold War

The destiny of Eastern Europe, especially Poland, stood at the heart of the strife between the United States and the USSR. Wanting to end the Soviet Union's vulnerability to invasions from the West, Stalin insisted on a demilitarized Germany and a buffer zone of nations friendly to Russia along its western flank. He considered a Soviet sphere of influence in Eastern Europe essential to Russian security, a just reward for bearing the brunt of the war against Germany, and no different than the American spheres of influence in Western Europe, Japan, and Latin America. Stalin also believed that Roosevelt and Churchill had implicitly accepted a Soviet zone in Eastern Europe at the Yalta Conference.

FOCUS Questions

- How did the policies of both the United States and Soviet Union lead to the start of the Cold War?

- What effect did the Cold War have on the domestic programs of Truman and Eisenhower?

- What domestic and international events led to the Second Red Scare?

- In what ways did Eisenhower continue—and change—Truman's foreign policy?

- What actions support the notion of Eisenhower as a centrist or moderate politician?

CHRONOLOGY 1945–1960

1946	George Kennan's "long telegram." Winston Churchill's "iron curtain" speech. Republicans win control of Congress.
1947	Truman Doctrine. Federal Employee Loyalty Program. Taft-Hartley Act. National Security Act. HUAC holds hearings on Hollywood.
1948	State of Israel founded. Berlin airlift. Congress approves Marshall Plan to aid Europe. Communist leaders put on trial under the Smith Act. Truman elected president.
1949	North Atlantic Treaty Organization (NATO) established. East and West Germany founded as separate nations. Communist victory in China; People's Republic of China established. Soviet Union detonates an atomic bomb.

1950	Soviet spy ring at Los Alamos uncovered. Joseph McCarthy launches anticommunist crusade. Korean War begins. McCarran Internal Security Act. Truman accepts NSC-68.
1951	Julius and Ethel Rosenberg convicted of espionage.
1952	First hydrogen bomb exploded. Dwight D. Eisenhower elected president.
1953	Korean War truce signed.
1954	Army-McCarthy hearings.
1956	Suez crisis. Eisenhower reelected.
1957	Eisenhower Doctrine announced.
1959	Fidel Castro comes to power in Cuba.
1960	U-2 incident.

With the Red Army occupying half of Europe at war's end, Stalin installed pro-Soviet puppet governments in Bulgaria, Hungary, and Romania and supported the establishment of communist regimes independent of Moscow in Albania and Yugoslavia. Ignoring the Yalta Declaration of Liberated Europe, Stalin barred free elections in Poland and brutally suppressed Polish democratic parties. Poland, he said, was "not only a question of honor for Russia, but one of life and death."

> Poland, Stalin said, was "not only a question of honor for Russia, but one of life and death."

Stalin's insistence on dominance in Eastern Europe collided with Truman's unwillingness to concede Soviet supremacy beyond Russia's borders. What Stalin saw as critical to Russian security Truman viewed as a violation of national self-determination, a betrayal of democracy, and a cover for communist aggression. He believed that accepting the "enforced sovietization" of Eastern Europe would betray American war aims and that appeasement of dictators only fed their appetite for aggressive expansion. Domestic political considerations also shaped Truman's response to Stalin. The chief executive feared that the Democrats would invite political disaster if he reneged on the Yalta agreements. The Democrats counted on winning most of the votes of the 6 million Polish Americans and millions of other Americans of Eastern European origin, who remained keenly interested in the fates of their homelands. The president resolved not to appear "soft on communism."

Combativeness fit the temperament of the feisty Truman. Eager to demonstrate his command, the president matched Stalin's intransigence on controlling Poland with his own demands for Polish democracy. Emboldened by America's monopoly of atomic weapons and its position as the world's economic superpower, he believed the United States could control the terms of the postwar settlement.

The Iron Curtain Descends

Truman's assertiveness inflamed Stalin's mistrust of the West and deepened Soviet obsession with its own security. The Soviet Union stepped up its confiscation of materials and factories from occupied territories and forced its satellite nations (countries under Soviet control) to close their doors to American trade and influence. In a February 1946 speech that the White House considered a "declaration of World War III," Stalin asserted that there could be no lasting peace with capitalism and vowed to overcome the American edge in weapons.

MAP 26.1   DECOLONIZATION IN AFRICA AND ASIA, 1947–1999 Following the Second World War, decolonization movements swept Africa and Asia, liberating many peoples from their colonial rulers. Achieving independence in the postwar international system dominated by the Cold War, most newly independent states became targets of both the United States and the Soviet Union, as each sought to advance its interests in these regions, usually by intervention, intrigue, or economic influence. The Cold War became a global phenomenon. At the same time, decolonization provided a powerful impetus to the struggle for black equality in the United States.   © Cengage Learning. All rights reserved. No distribution allowed without express authorization.

Legend (as shown on map):

1960 Year independence achieved

Former ruler

- Great Britain
- France
- Netherlands
- Italy
- Belgium
- Portugal
- United States
- Other

Country labels on map:

GREAT BRITAIN
PORTUGAL
SPAIN
FRANCE
ITALY
BELGIUM
NETHERLANDS
JAPAN

WESTERN SAHARA 1975 (Morocco) (From Spain)
MOROCCO 1956
ALGERIA 1962
TUNISIA 1957
MALTA 1964 (From Gr. Br.)
LIBYA 1951
CAPE VERDE 1975 (From Port.)
MAURITANIA 1960
MALI 1960
NIGER 1960
CHAD 1960
SENEGAL 1960
GAMBIA 1965
GUINEA-BISSAU 1974
GUINEA 1958
BURKINA FASO 1960
CÔTE D'IVOIRE 1960
GHANA 1957
TOGO 1960
BENIN 1960
NIGERIA 1960
SIERRA LEONE 1961
LIBERIA 1820s
EQUATORIAL GUINEA 1968 (From Spain)
SÃO TOMÉ AND PRÍNCIPE 1975 (From Port.)
CAMEROON 1960
GABON 1960
REPUBLIC OF CONGO 1960
CENTRAL AFRICAN REPUBLIC 1960
DEM. REP. OF CONGO 1960
ANGOLA 1975
NAMIBIA 1990 (From South Africa)
BOTSWANA 1966
SOUTH AFRICA (Republic 1961)
ZIMBABWE 1980
ZAMBIA 1964
MALAWI 1964
MOZAMBIQUE 1974
SWAZILAND 1968
LESOTHO 1966
MADAGASCAR 1960
MAURITIUS 1968 (From Gr. Br.)
COMOROS 1975 (From France)
SEYCHELLES 1976 (From Gr. Br.)
TANZANIA 1964
RWANDA 1962
BURUNDI 1962
UGANDA 1962
KENYA 1963
SOMALIA 1960
ETHIOPIA
DJIBOUTI 1977
ERITREA 1993 (From Ethiopia)
SUDAN 1956
EGYPT 1922
CYPRUS 1960
LEBANON 1944
ISRAEL 1948
SYRIA 1944
JORDAN 1946
IRAQ 1932
BAHRAIN 1971
QATAR 1971
UNITED ARAB EMIRATES 1971
KUWAIT 1961
OMAN 1971
P.D.R. OF YEMEN 1967
YEMEN (Unified 1990)
PAKISTAN 1947
INDIA 1947
MALDIVES 1975 (From Gr. Br.)
SRI LANKA (CEYLON) 1948
PAKISTAN 1947, BANGLADESH 1973
MYANMAR (BURMA) 1947
LAOS 1949
NORTH VIETNAM 1954
SOUTH VIETNAM 1954 (Unified 1975)
CAMBODIA 1953
MALAYSIA 1963
SINGAPORE 1965 (From Malaysia)
BRUNEI 1984 (From Gr. Br.)
PHILIPPINES 1946
INDONESIA 1949
TIMOR-LESTE 1999 (From Indonesia)
PAPUA NEW GUINEA 1975 (From Australia)
NORTH KOREA 1948
SOUTH KOREA 1948 (From Japan)
JAPAN

Water bodies:
ATLANTIC OCEAN
PACIFIC OCEAN
INDIAN OCEAN
Mediterranean Sea
Black Sea
Caspian Sea
Arabian Sea
Bay of Bengal

Scale: 0 1,000 2,000 Km. / 0 1,000 2,000 Mi.

Lines: Tropic of Cancer, Equator, Tropic of Capricorn

Two weeks later, **George F. Kennan,** an American diplomat in Moscow and leading student of Russian affairs, wired a telegram to the State Department describing Soviet expansionism as "like a toy automobile, wound up and headed in a given direction, stopping only when it meets some unanswerable force." The only way to deal with Soviet aggressiveness, Kennan asserted, was a "long-term, patient but firm and vigilant containment of Russian expansive tendencies." Truman, who had already insisted the time had come "to stop babying the Soviets" and "to get tough with Russia," accepted Kennan's advice. **Containment**—a policy uniting military, economic, and diplomatic strategies to curb, or "contain," any further Soviet communist expansion—became Washington gospel (see Beyond America).

In early March 1946, Truman accompanied Winston Churchill to Westminster College in Missouri, where the former British prime minister warned of a new threat to democracy. Stalin, he said, had drawn an "iron curtain" across the eastern half of Europe. To meet the threat of further Soviet aggression, Churchill called for an alliance of the English-speaking peoples and the maintenance of an Anglo-American monopoly of atomic weapons: "There is nothing the Communists admire so much as strength and nothing for which they have less respect than for military weakness."

As mutual hostility escalated, the Soviets and Americans rushed to develop doomsday weapons. In June, Truman submitted to the United Nations a plan for the United States to destroy its atomic arsenal if the Soviet Union stopped its work on nuclear weapons and submitted to UN inspections. As expected, the Soviets rejected the American proposal, and Congress established the Atomic Energy Commission (AEC) to spur both nuclear energy and, especially, nuclear weaponry. By 1950, one AEC adviser reckoned, the United States "had a stockpile capable of somewhat more than reproducing World War II in a single day."

Thus, less than a year after American and Soviet soldiers had jubilantly met at the Elbe River to celebrate Hitler's defeat, a Cold War emerged. It would be waged by economic pressure, nuclear intimidation, propaganda, subversion, and proxy wars (fought by governments and peoples allied to the principals rather than directly by the principals themselves). It would affect American life as decisively as any military engagement the nation had fought.

Containing Communism

On February 21, 1947, Britain informed the United States that it could no longer afford to assist Greece and Turkey in their struggles against communist insurgents in the eastern Mediterranean. The harsh European winter, the most severe in memory, heightened the sense of urgency in Washington. The economies of Western Europe had come to a near halt. Famine and tuberculosis plagued the continent. European colonies in Africa and Asia had risen in revolt. Cigarettes and candy bars circulated as currency in Germany, and the communist parties in France and Italy appeared ready to topple democratic coalition governments. Truman resolved to meet the challenge. But congressional leaders balked, agreeing to support the president only if he could "scare hell out of the country" to gain popular backing for meeting the Soviet threat.

Truman could and did. On March 12, 1947, addressing a joint session of Congress, he asked for $400 million in military assistance to Greece and Turkey while announcing the **Truman Doctrine.** Instead of mentioning that the aid would go to a right-wing, military-dominated Greek regime and an autocratic Turkey, the Truman Doctrine pictured the matter as a global struggle "between alternative ways of life," a holy war between God-fearing democracy and an atheistic communism that relied on "terror and oppression." Accordingly, the policy of the United States would be to support any free people "resisting attempted subjugation by armed minorities or by outside pressures." The Truman Doctrine and the funds appropriated by Congress helped the Greek monarchy to defeat the rebel movement and Turkey to stay out of the Soviet orbit. Moreover, this unilateral declaration proclaimed the nation's intention to be a global policeman—everywhere on guard against advances by the Soviet Union and its allies—and laid the foundation for American foreign policy for much of the next four decades.

> The United States must support free peoples everywhere "resisting attempted subjugation by armed minorities or by outside pressures."

To back up the new international initiative, Congress passed the **National Security Act of 1947,** unifying the armed forces under a single Department of Defense, creating the National Security Council (NSC) to advise the president on strategic matters, and establishing the Central Intelligence Agency (CIA) to gather information abroad and engage in covert activities in support of the nation's security. Congress also approved the administration's proposal for massive U.S. assistance for European recovery in 1947. Advocated by Secretary of State George C. Marshall, and thus called the **Marshall Plan,** the European Recovery Plan (ERP) aimed to combat the "hunger, poverty, desperation" that

Decolonization and the Cold War

Defeat in World War II forced Italy to relinquish Ethiopia, Libya, and Somalia and Japan to give up its colony of Korea, repeating a pattern established at the end of World War I. What few expected was that the victors, too, would rapidly lose their empires in Africa, the Middle East, and Asia. The war led to a massive overturning of colonial rule, as scores of independent nations emerged from the empires established in previous centuries. The emergence of a broad-based, assertive nationalism throughout the developing world created a new world order that exacerbated tensions between the United States and Soviet Union as the two superpowers competed for the resources and support of the new emerging nations. Decolonization created a power vacuum that both Moscow and Washington sought to fill, which guaranteed the Cold War would be global in scale and scope. Flashpoints ranged from Algeria to Korea, from Mozambique to Vietnam. The United States and the Soviet Union vigorously competed for the allegiance of the nonwhite peoples of the Third World, compelling every administration from Truman to Johnson to promote civil rights for African Americans as part of its mission of fighting world communism.

Exhausted by the war, and desperately needing to concentrate their energies on reconstruction, Britain, France, and other Allied nations were not eager to fight new wars against colonial peoples pressing for independence after 1945. The war weariness of the European powers encouraged Asian and African peoples to intensify their demands for independence. The Japanese defeats of British, Dutch, and French colonial armies had shattered assumptions of white superiority. Asians no longer regarded the humiliated Europeans with awe. In addition, the ideals of the United Nations, Allied propaganda, and the Atlantic Charter, which characterized World War II as a struggle for freedom and self-determination, intensified the desires for self-rule, especially among the many colonial peoples who had loyally fought alongside their masters. Although circumstances differed from place to place, decolonization—the relinquishing of colonial possessions by imperial powers—became an irresistible trend. In 1945, fifty-one nations signed the UN Charter; in the next two decades, seventy-one additional countries—nearly all of them former colonial territories—became members.

In Asia, the United States led the way in 1946, keeping its promise of postwar independence for the Philippines. Once Hindu and Muslim leaders agreed on a partition of British India into two nations, one constitutionally secular but dominated by Hindus, the other formally Muslim, independent India and Pakistan emerged in 1947. In 1948, Britain also granted autonomy to Burma (now Myanmar), Ceylon (now Sri Lanka), and the newly created Malay Federation (now Malaysia). The following year, the Dutch East Indies, colonized three and a half centuries earlier, became the independent republic of Indonesia—a nation of more than 100 million people of scores of religions and races, scattered over hundreds of islands.

France followed a bloodier path, however. It sought to regain the colonies in Southeast Asia it had lost to Japan in World War II. The result was a war against the Vietnamese nationalists led by Ho Chi Minh, and a civil war within Vietnam.

HO CHI MINH FIGHTING THE FRENCH, 1950 Following the Second World War, the communist organizer and revolutionary Ho Chi Minh led an almost decade-long nationalist struggle to end French colonialism in Indochina. *(AFP/Getty Images)*

After France finally withdrew in 1954, Vietnam would become the site of a major Cold War conflict between noncommunist South Vietnam and communist North Vietnam, and their respective allies.

In Africa, as well, France's determination to hold on to Algeria led to a bitter war in 1954, pursued with great brutality by both sides until Algeria won independence in 1962. The map and legal status of most of the area south of the Sahara, on the other hand, were transformed relatively peacefully in the 1950s and 1960s. The absence of protracted warfare between rulers and subjects enabled England and France to retain influence with their former colonies, limiting the involvement of both the United States and the Soviet Union in this region.

One area of the world critical for U.S. and Soviet interests—becoming a focal point of the Cold War—was the Middle East. Syria and Lebanon gained their independence from France in the course of the war. Britain surrendered its mandate over Jordan in 1946 and the oil-rich state of Kuwait in 1961. One legacy of colonialism, Palestine, however, absorbed much of the region's energies and the world's attention. With the Balfour Declaration of 1917, supported by the Allies at the Paris Peace Conference in 1919, Britain had committed itself to a Jewish homeland in Palestine. The United Nations voted to create both a Jewish and an Arab state, but the Palestinians and other Arab nations refused to accept a neighboring Jewish state. The consequence was decades of instability and war, as Israeli and Arab nationalist interests clashed in combination with the efforts of the United States and Soviet Union to control the flow of oil—the lifeblood of industrial nations. The Middle East was a Cold War powder keg.

Decolonization struggles became an integral part of the Cold War. To secure access to raw materials and markets, strategic military bases, supportive votes in the UN, and allies in armed conflicts, the United States and the Soviet Union each sought to seduce or coerce the countries emerging from colonial rule. Hoping to steer the colonial independence movements into its own orbit—long seen by the Soviets as an integral part of the communist fight against the capitalist West—the USSR supported them with advisers and weapons and proclaimed an ideology calling for the liberation of all oppressed peoples. It maintained close contacts with many nationalist leaders fighting for independence, like Ho Chi Minh, who was trained in Moscow and worked in communist movements in Europe and Asia before returning to his native Indochina. In turn, by 1954 the United States would be bearing three-fourths of the cost of France's war against the independence struggle of Ho Chi Minh and his followers. Viewing the Third World through the distorting lens of the Cold War, the United States would too often see the Kremlin as the force behind anticolonialism, elevate local struggles to global significance, and frequently confuse nationalism with communism. Access to markets and vital materials, the desire for prestige, and confidence that the American way was the best way—as well as anticommunism—led the United States to bid with money and flattery for the favor of many newly independent Third World countries such as Egypt, India, Pakistan, and the Philippines.

Both the American and Soviet conceptions of their own area of interest and activity grew steadily larger. As an Asian counterpart of the NATO military alliance, the United States formed the Southeast Asia Treaty Organization (SEATO) in 1954, and the following year organized the collective security pact, known as the Central Treaty Organization (CENTO), of Britain, Turkey, Pakistan, and Iran. Many in the Third World, however, sought a Third Way—nonalignment—beholden to neither the United States nor the USSR, and genuinely neutral in the Cold War. Resisting choosing sides, insisting on taking charge of their own destinies, some leaders of the new states—like India's Jawaharlal Nehru—skillfully manipulated Cold War antagonisms to their own advantage, flirting with one side to extract money and support from the other. In 1955, representatives of twenty-nine African and Asian nations who had been part of the colonial empires met in Bandung, Indonesia. They served notice on the United States and Soviet Union that their countries wanted to stay out of the Cold War. The conference claimed to speak for 65 percent of the world's population and declared that colonialism in all its manifestations was an evil that must be ended.

Using the international criticism of America's lynchings and racism to their advantage, African American leaders demanded civil-rights reforms. President Truman responded. Mindful of the effectiveness of Soviet propaganda denouncing American racial segregation and violence—and understanding that racism at home impeded the ability of the United States to espouse democracy abroad—he issued executive orders to desegregate the federal bureaucracy and the armed forces, appointed a commission to recommend measures to bolster the status of civil rights, and ordered the Justice Department to submit briefs in support of a range of desegregation cases winding through the federal court system. The campaign for African American civil rights, once a wholly domestic concern, became enmeshed in the Cold War effort of the United States to gain support in a decolonized world.

QUESTIONS FOR ANALYSIS
- In what ways did the Second World War spur decolonization?
- How and why did decolonization struggles and the newly independent states of the Third World become a major battleground in the Cold War?

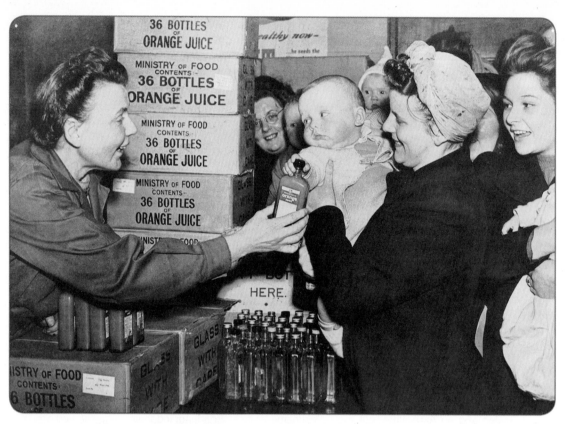

AMERICAN FOOD FOR A HUNGRY EUROPE Grateful English mothers line up for orange juice sent by the United States to assist Europeans devastated by the Second World War. *(National Archives)*

spawned communism. Truman correctly guessed that the Soviet Union and its satellites would refuse to take part in the plan, because of the controls linked to it, and accurately foresaw that Western European economic recovery would expand sales of American goods abroad and promote prosperity in the United States.

> "Prosperity Makes You Free."

Although denounced by the Left as a "Martial Plan" and by the Right as a "Share-the-American-Wealth Plan," the Marshall Plan helped Western Europe revive, prosper, and achieve an unprecedented unity. By 1952, industrial production had risen 200 percent in Western Europe, and the economic and social chaos that communists had exploited had been overcome in the sixteen nations that shared the $17 billion in aid. Not coincidentally, Western Europe had also become a major center of American trade and investment.

Confrontation in Germany

The Soviet Union reacted to the Truman Doctrine and the Marshall Plan by tightening its grip on Eastern Europe. Communist takeovers added Hungary and Czechoslovakia to the Soviet bloc in 1947 and 1948, and Stalin set his sights on Germany. The 1945 Potsdam Agreement had divided Germany into four separate zones (administered by France, Great Britain, the Soviet Union, and the United States) and created a joint four-power administration for Germany's capital, Berlin, which lay 110 miles within the Soviet-occupied eastern zone. As the Cold War intensified, the Western powers moved toward uniting their zones into an anti-Soviet West German state. Stalin responded in June 1948 by blocking all rail and highway traffic into Berlin.

Truman resolved neither to abandon Berlin nor to shoot his way into the city and possibly trigger World War III. Instead, he ordered a massive airlift of supplies to the city (the **Berlin airlift**). American cargo planes landed in West Berlin every three minutes around the clock, bringing the mountain of food and fuel necessary to provide the blockaded city with a precarious lifeline. In May 1949, the Soviets ended the blockade. Stalin's gambit had failed. The airlift highlighted American determination and technological prowess, revealed Stalin's readiness to use innocent people as pawns, and dramatically heightened anti-Soviet feeling in the West. Continuing fears of a Soviet attack on Western Europe and public support for "firmness and

THE BERLIN AIRLIFT, 1948 German children watching an American plane in "Operation Vittles" bring food and supplies to their beleaguered city. The airlift kept a city of 2 million people alive for nearly a year and made West Berlin a symbol of the West's resolve to contain the spread of Soviet communism. *(© Bettmann/Corbis)*

increased 'toughness' in relations with Russia" then led Truman to push for a rearmed West German state and an Atlantic collective security alliance.

In May 1949, the United States, Britain, and France ended their occupation of Germany and approved the creation of the Federal Republic of Germany (West Germany). A month earlier, ten Western Europe nations had signed the North Atlantic Treaty, establishing a military alliance with the United States and Canada in which "an armed attack against one or more of them … shall be considered an attack against them all." After overwhelming Senate approval, the United States officially joined the **North Atlantic Treaty Organization** (NATO), marking the formal end of America's long tradition of avoiding entangling alliances abroad.

Truman believed that if NATO had been in existence in 1914 and 1939, the world would have been spared two disastrous wars. Accordingly, he spurred Congress to authorize the deployment of U.S. troops in Europe and $1.3 billion for military assistance to NATO nations. The Soviet Union responded by creating the German Democratic Republic (East Germany) in 1949, exploding its own atomic bomb that same year, and forming in 1955 an Eastern bloc military alliance—the Warsaw Pact (see Map 26.2). The United States and Soviet Union had divided Europe into two armed camps.

The Cold War in Asia

Moscow-Washington hostility also carved Asia into contending camps. The Russians created a sphere of influence in Manchuria, the Americans denied Moscow a role in postwar Japan, and the two superpowers partitioned a helpless Korea.

As head of the U.S. occupation forces in Japan, General Douglas MacArthur oversaw that nation's transformation from an empire in ruins into a prosperous democracy. In 1952, the occupation ended, but a military security treaty allowed the United States to retain its Japanese bases and brought Japan under the American "nuclear umbrella." In further pursuit of containment, the United States helped crush a procommunist insurgency in the Philippines and aided French efforts to reestablish colonial rule in Indochina (Vietnam, Laos, and Cambodia), despite American declarations in favor of national self-determination and against imperialism.

In China, however, U.S. efforts to block communism failed. The Truman administration first tried to mediate the civil war between the nationalist government of Jiang Jieshi and the communist forces of **Mao Zedong.** Between 1945 and 1949, it also sent nearly $3 billion in aid to the nationalists. But American dollars could not prevent the surrender of Jiang's armies to Mao's forces or the collapse of the nationalists' corrupt regime, whose remnants fled to the island of Taiwan.

MAP 26.2 **THE POSTWAR DIVISION OF EUROPE, 1945–1989** The wartime dispute between the Soviet Union and the Western Allies over Poland's future hardened after World War II into a Cold War that split Europe into competing American and Russian spheres of influence. Across an "iron curtain," NATO countries faced the Warsaw Pact nations.

Mao's establishment of the communist People's Republic of China (PRC) shocked Americans. The most populous nation in the world, seen as a counterforce to communism and a market for American goods, had become "Red China." Although Truman blamed Jiang's defeat on his failure to reform China, most Americans were unconvinced. China's "fall" especially embittered conservatives who believed that America's interests lay in Asia, not Europe. Their pressure influenced the administration's refusal to recognize the PRC, block its admission to the United Nations, and proclaim Jiang's nationalist regime in Taiwan the legitimate government of China.

In September 1949, as the "Who lost China" debate raged, the president announced that the Soviet Union had exploded an atomic bomb. The loss of its nuclear monopoly shattered American illusions of invincibility. Combined with Mao's victory, it spawned an anticommunist hysteria and led to irrational searches for scapegoats and subversives to explain American setbacks in world affairs.

Ordinary Americans sought safety in civil defense. Public schools held air-raid drills, teaching students to "duck and cover"—dive under their desks and shield their eyes against atomic blasts. "We took the drills seriously," recalled novelist Annie Dillard; "surely Pittsburgh, which had the nation's steel, coke, and aluminum, would be the enemy's first target." Four million Americans volunteered to be Sky Watchers, looking for Soviet planes.

DUCK AND COVER At the height of the Korean War, President Truman created the Federal Civil Defense Administration, which sought to tell Americans how best to survive a nuclear attack. Much of their effort went into teaching students to duck and shield their eyes from an atomic blast. The Eisenhower administration later changed the emphasis of civil defense to the mass evacuation of populated areas. The policy, said one wag, had switched from "Duck and Cover" to "Run Like Hell." *(Picture Research Consultants & Archives)*

> "Surely Pittsburgh, which had the nation's steel, coke, and aluminum, would be the enemy's first target."

More than a million purchased or constructed their own family bomb shelters. Those who could not afford a bomb shelter were advised by the Federal Civil Defense Administration to "jump in any handy ditch or gutter … bury your face in your arms … never lose your head."

In January 1950, stung by charges that he was "soft on communism," Truman ordered the development of a fusion-based hydrogen bomb (H-bomb), a thousand times more destructive than an atomic bomb. In November 1952, the United States exploded its first H-bomb, completely vaporizing one of the Marshall Islands in the Pacific, carving a mile-long, 175-foot-deep crater in the ocean floor, and spilling radioactive dust over thousands of square miles. "You would swear the whole world was on fire," a sailor wrote home. Nine months later, the Soviets detonated their own H-bomb. The balance of terror escalated.

So, too, did nuclear-generated environmental and health problems. Nuclear tests left minimally protected U.S. soldiers and South Pacific islanders exposed to radiation, and radioactive debris from atomic tests contaminated vast areas of Colorado, Utah, Nevada, and Washington. Although the AEC insisted the fallout was harmless, many people exposed to radiation, as well as unborn children, would pay the cost of an out of control arms race poisoning the atmosphere.

In April 1950, a committee appointed by the president issued a sweeping analysis of U.S. defense policy. **National Security Paper 68 (NSC-68)** emphasized the Soviet Union's aggressive intentions, territorial greed, and military strength. To counter the Soviets' "design for world domination," NSC-68 urged massive increases in America's nuclear arsenal, vigorous covert action by the CIA, and open-ended increases in the defense budget to resist Communist expansion anywhere and everywhere. Secretary of State Acheson characterized NSC-68 as "the fundamental paper" defining American foreign policy into the foreseeable future. The United States now approached the Cold War as a military confrontation. By the end of 1950, Congress had tripled the defense budget of the self-proclaimed "world policeman."

The Korean War, 1950–1953

After World War II, the United States and Soviet Union temporarily divided Korea, which had been controlled by Japan since the Russo-Japanese War of 1904, at the thirty-eighth parallel. This line then solidified into a de facto border between the Soviet-backed Democratic People's Republic of Korea in the north and the American-supported Republic of Korea, or South Korea, each claiming the sole right to rule all of Korea.

On June 25, 1950, North Korean troops swept across the thirty-eighth parallel to attack South Korea (see Map 26.3). Truman decided to fight back, viewing the assault as Stalin's test of U.S. will and containment policy. "Korea is the Greece of the Far East," Truman maintained. "If we are tough enough now, if we stand up to them like we did in Greece … they won't take any next steps." Mindful of the failure of appeasement at Munich in 1938, he believed the communists were doing in Korea exactly what Hitler and the Japanese had done in the 1930s: "If this was allowed to go unchallenged," Truman observed, "it would mean a third world war."

Without consulting Congress, Truman ordered air and naval forces to Korea on June 27. That same day, he asked the United Nations to authorize action to repel the invasion. Because the Soviets were boycotting the Security Council to protest the UN's unwillingness to seat Mao's China, and could not use their veto power, Truman gained approval for a UN "police action" to restore South Korea's border. The Cold War had turned hot.

North Korean forces initially routed the outnumbered American and South Korean troops. Then, in mid-September, with UN forces cornered on the southeastern tip of the Korean peninsula, struggling to avoid being pushed into the sea, General Douglas MacArthur, the commander of the UN forces, executed a brilliant amphibious maneuver, landing his troops at Inchon, 150 miles behind North Korean lines. Within two weeks, UN forces drove the North Koreans back across the thirty-eighth parallel. Basking in victory, MacArthur persuaded Truman to let him go beyond the UN mandate to repel aggression and to cross the border to liberate all of Korea from communism.

As UN troops approached the Yalu River—the boundary between Korea and China—the Chinese, fearful of America's commitment to "liberate" China and return Jiang Jieshi to control, warned that they would not "sit back with folded hands and let the Americans come to the border." Dismissing the threat

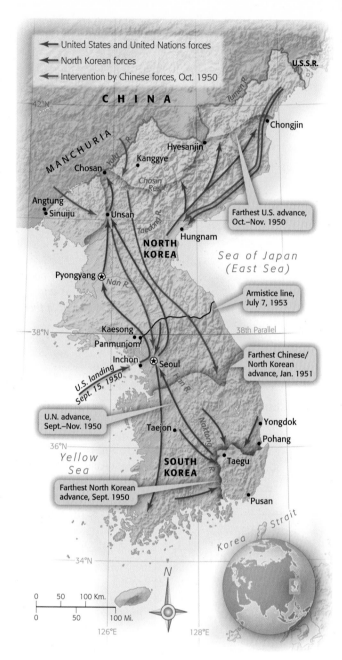

MAP 26.3 **THE KOREAN WAR, 1950–1953** The experience of fighting an undeclared war for the limited objective of containing communism confused the generation of Americans who had just fought an all-out war for the total defeat of the Axis. General MacArthur spoke for the many who were frustrated by the Korean conflict's mounting costs in blood and dollars: "There is no substitute for victory." © Cengage Learning. All rights reserved. No distribution allowed without express authorization.

as "hot air," MacArthur deployed his forces in a thin line below the river. On November 25, thirty-three Chinese divisions (about 300,000 men) counterattacked, driving MacArthur's forces back below the thirty-eighth parallel in what *Time* magazine called "the worst military setback the United States has

"There were bodies strewn all over the place. Hundreds of bodies frozen in the snow."

ever suffered." By March 1951, the fighting had deadlocked at roughly the original dividing line between the two Koreas. "We were eyeball to eyeball," recalled Bev Scott, one of the first black lieutenants to head a racially integrated infantry squad.

Just 20 meters of no man's land between us. We couldn't move at all in the daytime without getting shot at. ... It was like World War I. We lived in a maze of bunkers and deep trenches. ... There were bodies strewn all over the place. Hundreds of bodies frozen in the snow. We could see the arms and legs sticking up. Nobody could get their dead out of there.

Stalemated, Truman reversed course and sought a negotiated peace based on the original objective of restoring the integrity of South Korea. MacArthur rocked the boat, however, urging that he be allowed to seek total victory even at the risk of an all-out war with China. Truman refused: "We are trying to prevent a world war—not to start one." He sought a limited war for a limited objective: to hold the line in Korea. But MacArthur would not accept a stalemate. When he bluntly and repeatedly criticized Truman's limited war—the "appeasement of Communism"—the president fired the general to protect civilian control of the military. Public opinion, however, backed the general. To Americans accustomed to unconditional victory, the very idea of limited war was baffling. Mounting casualties for no apparent purpose at places named Heartbreak Ridge or Pork Chop Hill added anger to the mix. Despite warnings from the chairman of the Joint Chiefs of Staff that MacArthur's proposals would result in "the wrong war at the wrong place in the wrong time and with the wrong enemy," a growing number of Americans agreed with MacArthur that "There is no substitute for victory," and listened sympathetically to Republican charges that communist agents controlled American policy.

Truman, meanwhile, found himself bogged down in Korea, unable to win a victory or craft a peace. After two more years of fighting, the two sides reached an armistice in July 1953 that left Korea divided. The "limited" conflict cost the United States 54,246 lives (about 33,700 of them battlefield deaths), another 103,284 wounded, and some $54 billion. The Chinese lost 900,000 men, and the two Korean armies lost 800,000. As in World War II, massive U.S. "carpet bombing" killed at least a

A RACIALLY INTEGRATED UNIT IN THE KOREAN WAR The Korean War was the first war in U.S. history in which most soldiers fought in racially integrated units. President Truman ordered the integration of the armed forces in 1948, despite the opposition of many military officers, and the successful performance of African Americans in Korea accelerated acceptance of military integration. *(© Bettmann/Corbis)*

million civilians and left North Korea looking like a moonscape.

The **Korean War** had major consequences. It accelerated implementation of NSC-68 and the expansion of the containment doctrine into a global commitment. From 1950 to 1953, defense spending zoomed from $13 billion to $60 billion—from one-third to two-thirds of the entire federal budget—the U.S. army grew from half a million men to 3.6 million, and the American atomic stockpile mushroomed from 150 to 750 nuclear warheads. The United States acquired new bases around the world, committed itself to rearm West Germany, and joined a mutual-defense pact with Australia and New Zealand. Increased military aid flowed to Jiang Jieshi on Taiwan and to France's fight against communist insurgents in Indochina.

Truman's intervention in Korea preserved a precarious balance of power in Asia and stepped up the administration's commitment to the anticommunist struggle. Containment, originally advanced to justify U.S. aid to Greece and Turkey, had become the ideological foundation for a major war in Korea and, ominously, for a deepening U.S. involvement in Vietnam. Truman's actions enhanced the powers of an already powerful presidency and set a precedent for future undeclared wars. They also augmented an economic boom, accelerated the desegregation of the armed forces, and brought to fever pitch a period of xenophobia that rivaled the Red Scare of 1919.

The Truman Administration at Home, 1945–1952

The Cold War profoundly changed the United States for better and for worse. It weakened the nation's commitment to civil liberties while propelling research in medicine and science that, for the most part, made lives longer and better. It spurred more than a quarter of a century of economic growth and prosperity, the longest such period in American history. That, along with a vast expansion of higher education, enabled many Americans to become middle class, diminishing support for the expansion of the welfare state.

Demobilization and Reconversion

When the war ended, GIs and civilians alike wanted those who had served overseas "home alive in '45."

Troops demanding transport ships barraged Congress with threats of "no boats, no votes." On a single day in December 1945, sixty thousand postcards flooded the White House with the message "Bring the Boys Home by Christmas." Truman bowed to popular demand, and by 1948, American military strength had dropped from 12 million to just 1.5 million.

Returning veterans faced readjustment problems intensified by a soaring divorce rate and a drastic housing shortage. Many feared the return of mass unemployment and economic depression as war plants closed. Defense spending dropped from $76 billion in 1945 to under $20 billion in 1946, and more than a million defense jobs vanished.

Yet by the end of the decade, more women were working outside the home than during World War II. Most took jobs in traditional women's fields, especially office work and sales, to pay for family needs. Although the postwar economy created new

VETERANS AT PENNSYLVANIA STATE COLLEGE The Serviceman's Readjustment Act of 1944 (the so-called GI Bill), included among its various programs financial assistance for every veteran of the Second World War who sought further education. Some 8 million veterans would eventually study at technical institutes, trade schools, and universities. *(© Bettmann/Corbis)*

openings for women in the labor market, many public figures urged women to seek fulfillment at home. Popular culture romanticized married bliss and demonized career women as a threat to social stability.

The GI Bill of Rights

The Servicemen's Readjustment Act of 1944, commonly called the GI Bill of Rights or **GI Bill,** was designed to forestall the expected recession by easing veterans back into the work force and to reward the "soldier boys" for their wartime service. The GI Bill gave veterans priority for many jobs, occupational guidance, and if need be, fifty-two weeks of unemployment benefits. It also provided low-interest government loans to some 4 million returning GIs who were starting businesses or buying homes, helping to fuel a baby boom, suburbanization, and a record demand for new goods and services.

The government also promised to pay up to four years of further education or job training for veterans. Some Americans opposed it as opening the door to socialism, and some university administrators, fearing the influx of riffraff, echoed the complaint of the University of Chicago president that their colleges would become "educational hobo jungles." Yet, by 1946, flush with stipends of $65 a month—$90 for those with dependents—and up to $500 a year for tuition and books, 1.5 million veterans were attending college, spurring the creation of many new state and community colleges. By 1947, veterans made up more than half of all college students. Often married and the fathers of young children, they were generally less interested in knowledge than in a degree and a higher-paying job. Accommodating them, colleges offered accelerated programs and more vocational or career-oriented courses.

To make room for the millions of GIs pursuing higher education after the war, many colleges limited the percentage of women admitted or barred students from out of state. The percentage of female college graduates dropped from 40 percent in 1949 to 25 percent in 1950. By then, most women who might have been students were the working wives of the veterans who took advantage of the GI Bill to go college.

The GI Bill democratized higher education. By 1956, nearly 10 million veterans had used the GI Bill to enroll in vocational training programs and colleges (most the first in their families to do so). No longer a citadel of privilege, universities awarded twice as many degrees in 1950 as in 1940, propelling millions of veterans into the middle class. Two decades later, these more affluent and educated veterans expected their children to follow suit. Higher education became an accepted part of the American Dream.

The Economic Boom Begins

In addition to the assistance given returning servicemen, a 1945 tax cut of $6 billion spurred corporate investment in new factories and equipment and helped produce an economic boom (see Figure 26.1). Wartime savings and a pent-up demand for consumer goods further kindled postwar growth and prosperity. The men and women who had endured the Great Depression and Second World War craved the "good life" and had $140 billion in bank accounts and government bonds to purchase the advertised "all-electrified kitchen-of-the-future." Sales of homes, cars, and appliances skyrocketed. Scores of new products—televisions, high-fidelity phonographs, filter cigarettes, automatic transmissions, freezers, and air conditioners—became hallmarks of the middle-class lifestyle.

The Bretton Woods Agreement (1944) among the Allies had set the stage for the United States to become economic leader of the noncommunist world. It created several institutions to oversee international trade and finance: the International Monetary Fund (IMF) to stabilize exchange rates by valuing ("pegging") other currencies in relation to the U.S. dollar, the International Bank for Reconstruction and Development (World Bank)

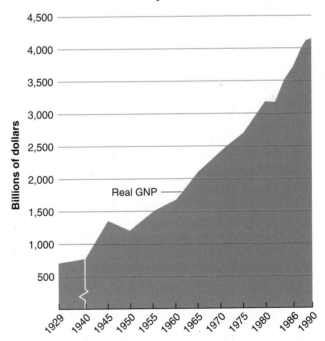

FIGURE 26.1 GROSS NATIONAL PRODUCT, 1929–1990 Following World War II, the United States achieved the highest living standard in world history. Between 1950 and 1970, the real GNP, which factors out inflation and reveals the actual amount of goods and services produced, steadily increased. However, in 1972, 1974–1975, 1980, and 1982, the real GNP declined. Note: Data shown in 1982 dollars.
© Cengage Learning. All rights reserved. No distribution allowed without express authorization.

Source: Economic Report of the President, 1991.

to help rebuild war-battered Asia and Europe, and the 1947 General Agreement on Tariffs and Trade (GATT) to break up closed trading blocs and expand international trade. Because Americans largely controlled and funded these economic institutions, they gave the United States an especially favorable position on the world stage.

With many nations in ruins, American firms could import raw materials cheaply; with little competition from other industrial countries, they could increase exports to record levels. U.S. economic dominance also resulted from wartime advances in science and technology, which significantly increased the productivity of American workers and led to revolutionary developments in such industries as electronics and plastics.

Truman's Domestic Program

Americans' hunger for the fruits of affluence left them with little appetite for extending the New Deal. Truman agreed. "I don't want any experiments," he confided. "The American people have been through a lot of experiments and they want a rest." His only major domestic accomplishment in the Seventy-ninth Congress was the **Employment Act of 1946.** It committed the federal government to ensuring economic growth and established the Council of Economic Advisers to confer with the president and formulate policies for maintaining employment, production, and purchasing power. Congress, however, gutted both the goal of full employment and the enhanced executive powers to achieve that objective.

> "I don't want any experiments. The American people have been through a lot of experiments and they want a rest."

Congressional eagerness to dismantle wartime controls worsened the nation's chief economic problem: inflation. Consumer demand outran the supply of goods, intensifying the pressure on prices. The Office of Price Administration (OPA) sought to hold the line by enforcing price controls, but food producers, manufacturers, and retailers opposed continuing wartime controls. While some consumers favored the OPA, others deplored it as an irksome relic of wartime regulations. In June 1946, Truman vetoed a bill that would have extended the OPA's life but deprived it of power, effectively ending all price controls. Food costs rose 16 percent within a week and the price of beef doubled. "PRICES SOAR, BUYERS SORE, STEERS JUMP OVER THE MOON," headlined the *New York Daily News*.

Congress then passed, and Truman signed, a second bill extending price controls in weakened form. Protesting any price controls, however, farmers and meat producers threatened to withhold food from the market. Knowing that "meatless voters are opposition voters," Truman lifted controls on food prices just before the 1946 midterm elections. When Democrats fared poorly anyway, Truman ended all price controls. By then, the consumer price index had jumped nearly 25 percent since the end of the war.

Sharp price rises and shrinking paychecks shorn of overtime goaded organized labor to demand higher wages. In 1946 alone, more than 4.5 million workers went on strike. When a United Mine Workers walkout paralyzed the economy for forty days, Truman ordered an army seizure of the mines. A week later, after Truman had pressured owners to grant most of the union's demands, the miners returned to work, only to walk out again six months later. Meanwhile, on the heels of the first mine workers settlement, railway engineers and trainmen announced they would shut down the nation's railroad system for the first time in history. "If you think I'm going to sit here and let you tie up this whole country," Truman shouted at the heads of the two unions, "you're crazy as hell." In May, he asked Congress for authority to draft workers who struck vital industries. Before he could finish his speech, the rail unions gave in, leaving the Senate to reject the president's proposal. Still, Truman's threat alienated labor leaders.

By the fall of 1946, Truman had angered most major interest groups. Less than a third of Americans polled approved of his performance. "To err is Truman," some gibed. Summing up the public discontent, Republicans asked, "Had enough?" In the 1946 elections, they captured twenty-five governorships and, for the first time since 1928, won control of Congress.

The public mood reflected more than just economic discontent. Under the surface, laughter at stores advertising atomic sales or bartenders mixing atomic cocktails ran a deep current of fear. An NBC radio program depicted a nuclear attack on Chicago in which most people died instantly. "Those few who escaped the blast, but not the gamma rays, died slowly after they had left the ruined city," intoned the narrator. "No attempt at identification of the bodies or burial ever took place. Chicago was simply closed." Schoolchildren wore dog tags in order to be identified after an atomic attack and practiced crawling under their desks and putting their hands over their heads to protect themselves from the bomb. There was much talk of urban dispersal—resettling people in small communities in the country's vast open spaces—and of how to protect oneself in a nuclear attack. The end of World War II had brought an uneasy peace.

The Eightieth Congress, 1947–1948

In 1946, Republicans won control of Congress for the first time since 1930. Many Republicans interpreted the election as a mandate to reverse the New Deal. As "Mr. Republican," Senator Robert A. Taft of Ohio, declared, "We have got to break with the corrupting idea that we can legislate prosperity, legislate equality, legislate opportunity." The Republican-controlled Congress defeated Democratic bills to raise the minimum wage and to provide federal funds for education and housing. Capitalizing on the national consensus for curbing labor union power generated by the waves of postwar strikes, Congress passed the **Taft-Hartley Act** (Labor-Management Relations Act) in 1947. It barred the closed shop—a workplace where all employees had to join the union; outlawed secondary boycotts—strikes against suppliers of a targeted business; required union officials to sign anticommunist loyalty oaths; and permitted the president to call a cooling-off period to delay strikes that might endanger national safety or health. The act weakened organizing drives in the nonunion South and West, hastening the relocation of labor-intensive industries, such as textiles, from the Northeast and Midwest to the Sunbelt, and it drove leftist leaders out of the CIO, weakening organized labor as a force for social justice.

> "We have got to break with the corrupting idea that we can legislate prosperity, legislate equality, legislate opportunity."

Truman gave in to union demands that he veto the "slave labor bill." Although Congress easily overrode the veto, Truman had taken a major step toward regaining organized labor's support and reforging FDR's New Deal coalition. Now playing the role of a staunch liberal New Dealer, Truman urged Congress to repeal Taft-Hartley and to provide federal aid to education and housing, national health insurance, and high farm-price supports. To woo ethnic voters of Eastern European descent, Truman railed against Soviet communism; and to court Jewish American voters, as well as express his deep sympathy toward Holocaust survivors, he overrode the objections of the State Department, which feared alienating the oil-rich Arab world,

and extended diplomatic recognition to the new state of Israel within hours of its establishment in May 1948.

Still, Truman's chances for victory dimmed as southern segregationists, alarmed by the president's support in 1948 for antilynching and anti-poll tax bills, bolted the Democrats and nominated Governor Strom Thurmond of South Carolina as the candidate of the States' Rights ("Dixiecrat") party, a significant step toward the eventual breakup of the Democratic political coalition of southern conservatives and northern liberals. Further diminishing Truman's chances, leftwing Democrats joined with communists to launch a new Progressive Party headed by former vice president Henry A. Wallace. To capitalize on Democratic divisions, Republicans tried to play it safe, nominating the moderate governor of New York, Thomas E. Dewey, for president, and Californian Earl Warren for vice president. Confident of victory, Dewey ran a complacent campaign designed to offend the fewest people. Truman, in contrast, campaigned aggressively, blasting the "no-good, do-nothing" Republicans as "gluttons of privilege." To shouts of "Give 'em hell, Harry," the president hammered away at the Republican-controlled Congress. Pollsters applauded Truman's spunk but predicted a Dewey victory.

Instead, the president won the biggest electoral upset in U.S. history (see Map 26.4). The Progressives and Dixiecrats, ironically, helped Truman. Their extremism kept most moderates safely in

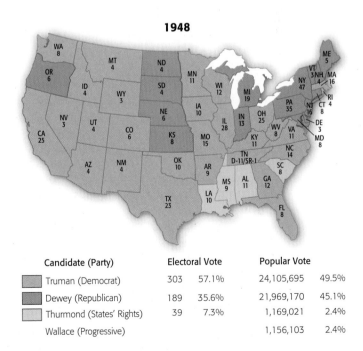

1948

Candidate (Party)	Electoral Vote		Popular Vote	
Truman (Democrat)	303	57.1%	24,105,695	49.5%
Dewey (Republican)	189	35.6%	21,969,170	45.1%
Thurmond (States' Rights)	39	7.3%	1,169,021	2.4%
Wallace (Progressive)			1,156,103	2.4%

MAP 26.4   THE ELECTION OF 1948 © Cengage Learning. All rights reserved. No distribution allowed without express authorization.

the Democratic fold. Most importantly, Truman succeeded as the defender of the New Deal against the party of Herbert Hoover and the depression. The Roosevelt coalition—organized labor, farmers, urban ethnics, blacks, and most white southerners—had held together one more time.

The Fair Deal

Despite his slim victory, Truman proposed in 1949 a vast liberal agenda—the **Fair Deal**—that included civil rights, national health-care legislation, and federal aid to education. Unlike New Deal liberalism, the Fair Deal counted on continual economic growth. An expanding economic pie would mean a bigger piece for most Americans (so they would not resent helping those left behind) and more tax revenue for the government (so it would have the funds to pay for more social-welfare programs).

With increasing prosperity sapping public enthusiasm for liberal initiatives, the bipartisan conservative coalition of northern Republicans and southern Democrats, which had largely controlled Congress since 1938, rejected the Fair Deal. While extending some existing programs, such as the minimum wage and social security, and authorizing the construction of 800,000 units of low-income housing, Congress would go no further. Special interest groups, such as the American Medical Association and the National Association of Manufacturers, lobbied extensively against what they called "creeping socialism," and by 1950, Truman again subordinated domestic issues to foreign policy.

The Politics of Anticommunism

As the Cold War worsened, some Americans concluded that the roots of the nation's difficulties abroad lay in domestic treason and subversion. How else could the communists have taken China and built an atomic bomb? Millions of fearful Americans enlisted in a crusade that equated dissent with disloyalty and blamed scapegoats for the nation's problems.

Similar intolerance had prevailed in the Red Scare of 1919–1920 (see Chapter 22), but the Second Red Scare lasted longer, affected more people, and had greater consequences. It took root in the creation of the House Committee on Un-American Activities—later called the House Un-American Activities Committee (HUAC)—in 1938 to ferret out fascists, but it quickly became a platform for right-wing denunciations of the New Deal as a communist plot. After World War II, mounting numbers of conservative Democrats and Republicans found it popular to climb aboard the anti-Red bandwagon.

The **Second Red Scare** influenced both governmental and personal actions. Millions of Americans were subjected to security investigations and loyalty oaths. Anticommunist extremism destroyed the Left, undermined labor militancy, and discredited liberalism. Any and all progressive initiatives—from health insurance to child-care centers to proposals for civil rights—were denounced as socialist or "soft on communism." Foreign and domestic anticommunist policies reinforced each other, spawning a "silent generation" of college students and prohibiting any dissent from America's cold war against the USSR.

Loyalty and Security

The U.S. Communist Party had claimed eighty thousand members during the Second World War, and no one knew how many occupied sensitive government positions. In mid-1945, a raid on the offices of a procommunist magazine revealed that classified documents had been given to it by government employees. Ten months later, the Canadian government exposed a spy network that had passed American military information and atomic secrets to the Soviets during the war. Moreover, recently disclosed Soviet documents, declassified after the fall of communism, revealed that the Russians had spies in the scientific community working on the atom bomb as well as highly placed Communists operating undercover in the federal government.

Republicans accused the Democratic administration of being "soft on communism," and in March 1947, a week after his Truman Doctrine speech defining the Cold War as a holy crusade between good and evil, the president issued Executive Order 9835 establishing the Federal Employee Loyalty Program to root out subversives in the government. It authorized the attorney general to prepare a list of "subversive" organizations and made association with such groups grounds for dismissal. The drive for security overran civil liberties because those suspected could neither face their accusers nor require investigators to reveal sources.

Mere criticism of American foreign policy could result in an accusation of disloyalty. People lost jobs because they liked foreign films, associated with radical friends, or favored the unionization of federal workers. "Of course the fact that a person believes in racial equality doesn't prove he's a communist," mused an Interior Department Loyalty Board chairman, "but it certainly makes you look twice, doesn't it?" Of the 4.7 million jobholders and applicants who underwent loyalty checks by 1952, 560 were fired or denied jobs, and several thousand resigned or withdrew their applications. Although Loyalty Board probes uncovered no evidence of espionage or subversion, it spread fear among government employees. The effect on free political debate was chilling. "If communists like apple pie and I do," claimed one federal worker, "I see no reason why I should stop eating it. But I would."

The Anticommunist Crusade

The very existence of a federal loyalty probe fed fears of domestic subversion. It promoted hysteria about communist infiltrators and legitimated a witch-hunt for subversives. College administrators cooperated with the FBI in spying on students and faculty, universities banned controversial speakers, and popular magazines featured articles like "Reds Are After Your Child." By the end of Truman's term, thirty-nine

"Reds Are After Your Child."

states had created loyalty programs. Few had any procedural safeguards. Schoolteachers, college professors, and state and city employees throughout the nation had to sign loyalty oaths or lose their jobs. No one knows how many were dismissed, denied tenure, or drifted away, leaving behind colleagues too frightened to speak out.

In 1947, blurring distinctions between dissent and disloyalty, between radicalism and subversion, the **House Un-American Activities Committee** (HUAC) held hearings to expose communist influence in American life. When some prominent film directors and screenwriters, dubbed the Hollywood Ten, refused to testify about past political associations, claiming the free-speech protections of the First Amendment, HUAC had them cited for contempt of Congress and sent to federal prison. The president of the Motion Picture Association announced that no one would be hired who failed to cooperate with HUAC. Blacklists in the motion picture industry and in radio broadcasting quickly followed. They barred the employment of those with a questionable past or those who had associated, however remotely, with others deemed "subversive"

THE RED MENACE, 1949 Although Hollywood generally avoided overtly political films, it released a few dozen explicitly anticommunist films in the postwar era. Depicting American communists as vicious hypocrites, if not hardened criminals, Hollywood's Cold War movies, like its blacklist, were an effort to protect its imperiled public image after HUAC's widely publicized investigation of the movie industry. *(The Michael Barson Collection/Past Perfect)*

The release of classified Soviet documents in the 1990s confirm that Hiss did pass secret information to the Soviets and that Julius Rosenberg, who described himself as a "soldier of Stalin," was part of a spy ring that gave the USSR data on America's atomic bomb project. Ethel Rosenberg, however, appears to have been merely "a lever" to pressure Julius into naming other spies.

By 1950, many Americans could not separate fact from fantasy regarding the communist threat. Only a conspiracy, it seemed, could explain U.S. setbacks. Frustrated by unexpected failure in the 1948 election, Republicans eagerly exploited the fearful mood, accusing the "Commiecrats" of selling out America.

In February 1950, Republican senator **Joseph R. McCarthy** of Wisconsin, desperate for an issue on which to run for reelection in 1952, boldly told a West Virginia audience that communists working in the State Department had betrayed America. "I have in my hand 205 cases of individuals," he asserted as he waved a laundry list, "who would appear to be either card carrying members or certainly loyal to the Communist Party, but who nevertheless are still helping to shape our foreign policy." Although McCarthy never released any names or proof, his senatorial stature and brazen style gave him a national forum. A Senate committee found

THE MANY MOODS OF JOE MCCARTHY With the war going badly in Korea in 1950, and communist advances in Eastern Europe and in China, the American public was genuinely frightened about the possibilities of internal subversion. McCarthy, as chairman of the Government Committee on Operations of the Senate, was in an ideal position to exploit this situation. And he did. His charges of treason in high places made him an instant celebrity, and the anticommunist witch-hunt that followed became known as McCarthyism. *(© Bettmann/Corbis)*

McCarthy's accusations "a fraud and a hoax," but he persisted. "McCarthyism" became a synonym for personal attacks on individuals by means of indiscriminate allegations and unsubstantiated charges.

As the Korean War dragged on, McCarthy's efforts to "root out the skunks" escalated. He ridiculed Secretary of State Dean Acheson as the "Red Dean" and charged George Marshall with having "aided and abetted a communist conspiracy so immense as to dwarf any previous such venture in the history of man." McCarthyism especially appealed to midwestern Republicans opposed to Democratic internationalism and restrictions on business. For them, anticommunism was a weapon of revenge against liberals—a means to regain the dominance that conservatism had once held. McCarthy also won a devoted following among blue-collar workers who felt that all true Americans detested "communists and queers" and among Catholic ethnics, who sought acceptance as "100 percent Americans" through a show of anticommunist zeal. Countless Americans also shared McCarthy's scorn for State Department liberals as the "bright young men who are born with silver spoons in their mouths." And McCarthy's conspiracy theory offered a simple answer to the perplexing questions of the Cold War: the fault is in Washington.

McCarthy's political power rested on both the Republican establishment and Democratic fears of antagonizing him. In the 1950 elections, when he helped Republicans defeat Democrats who had denounced him, McCarthy appeared invincible.

Over Truman's veto, Congress in 1950 adopted the **McCarran Internal Security Act,** which required organizations deemed communist by the attorney general to register with the Department of Justice. It also authorized the arrest and detention during a national emergency of "any person as to whom there is reason to believe might engage in acts of espionage or sabotage." The McCarran-Walter Immigration and Nationality Act of 1952, also adopted over Truman's veto, maintained the quota system that severely restricted immigration from southern and eastern Europe and from Asia, but did end Asian exclusion. The new law also strengthened the attorney general's authority to exclude or deport "undesirable" aliens suspected of homosexuality or communism.

The Election of 1952

In 1952, public apprehension about the loyalty of government employees combined with frustration over the Korean stalemate to sink Democratic hopes to their lowest level since the 1920s. Truman's approval rating plummeted to 23 percent, the lowest ever recorded by a president. Popular resentment of Truman's handling of the Korean War and revelations of bribery by his political associates gave the GOP ammunition for charging the Democrats with "plunder at home, and blunder abroad." Republicans campaigned on the "K1 C2" slogan—"Korea, Communism, and Corruption."

With Truman too unpopular to run for reelection, dispirited Democrats drafted Governor Adlai Stevenson of Illinois and, to appease southern white voters, nominated segregationist Senator John A. Sparkman of Alabama for vice president. But Stevenson could neither dissociate himself from Truman nor overcome the sentiment that twenty years of Democratic rule was enough.

> Nixon red-baited his opponent, Helen Gahagan Douglas, as "pink right down to her underwear."

Compounding Democratic woes, the GOP nominated the hugely popular war hero **Dwight D. Eisenhower** and chose as his running mate Richard Nixon, who had won a seat in the Senate in 1950 by red-baiting his opponent, Helen Gahagan Douglas, as "pink right down to her underwear."

Eisenhower and Nixon proved unbeatable. With a captivating grin and an unimpeachable record of public service, Eisenhower projected both personal warmth and the vigorous authority associated with military command. At the same time, Nixon kept public apprehensions at the boiling point. Accusing the Democrats of treason, he charged that the election of "Adlai the appeaser … who got a Ph.D. from Dean Acheson's College of Cowardly Communist Containment" would bring "more Alger Hisses, more atomic spies."

Less than two weeks before the election, Eisenhower dramatically pledged to "go to Korea" to end the stalemated war. It worked: 62.7 percent of those eligible to vote (compared to just 51.5 percent in 1948) turned out in 1952 and gave the Republican ticket 55 percent of the ballots. Ike cracked the Solid South, carrying thirty-nine states (and 442 electoral votes). Enough Republicans rode his coattails to give the GOP narrow control of both houses of Congress.

The Downfall of Joseph McCarthy

Although he despised Joseph McCarthy, Eisenhower thought it beneath his dignity to "get into the gutter with that guy." He also understood the usefulness of anticommunism as a GOP campaign issue. So Ike allowed McCarthy to grab plenty of rope in hopes that the demagogue would hang himself. He did.

In 1954, McCarthy accused Army officials of harboring communist spies; the military retaliated by charging McCarthy with using his influence to get preferential treatment for an aide who had been drafted. The resulting Army-McCarthy hearings—the first Senate hearings broadcast on the new medium of television—brought McCarthy down. Millions witnessed McCarthy's boorish behavior on television. His contemptuous combativeness repelled viewers. He behaved like the bad guy in a TV western, observed novelist John Steinbeck: "He had a stubble of a beard, he leered, he sneered, he had a nasty laugh. He bullied and shouted. He looked evil." When the hearings ended in June, the spell of the inquisitor had been broken. That December, the Senate voted 67 to 22 to censure McCarthy for contemptuous behavior. This powerful rebuke demolished McCarthy as a political force. In 1957, he died from an alcohol-related illness, ignored by the media that had made him powerful. But the fears he exploited lingered. Congress annually funded HUAC into the 1960s, and local governments continued to require loyalty oaths from teachers. Just to be safe, the Cincinnati Reds renamed their baseball team the "Redlegs."

McCarthyism also remained a rallying call of conservatives disenchanted with the postwar consensus. Young conservatives like William F. Buckley, Jr., and groups like the Christian Anti-Communist Crusade continued to claim that domestic communism was a major subversive threat. The John Birch Society denounced Eisenhower as a conscious agent of communism and equated liberalism with treason. Although few saw the conspiratorial dangers that the John Birch Society did, Barry Goldwater, George Wallace, and Ronald Reagan, among others, used its anticommunist, antigovernment rhetoric to advantage. Stressing victory over communism, rather than its containment, the "new conservatives" (or radical Right, as their opponents called them) criticized the "creeping socialism" of Eisenhower, advocated a return to traditional moral standards, and condemned the liberal rulings of the Supreme Court.

"Modern Republicanism"

Most Americans in the 1950s did not venture that far right. They voted for a president who would steer a moderate course, and they got what they wanted. Rarely in history has a president better fit the national mood than "Ike." Exhausted by a quarter-century of upheaval, Americans craved stability and peace. And Eisenhower delivered. He gave a people weary of partisanship a sense of unity; he set a quieter, less angry national mood; and he inspired confidence and comforted people in an anxious, demanding age.

Born on October 14, 1890, in Denison, Texas, Eisenhower grew up in Abilene, Kansas, in a poor, religious family. More athletic than studious, he graduated from the U.S. Military Academy at West Point in 1915. In directing the Allied invasion of North Africa in 1942 and of western Europe in 1944, he proved to be a skillful war planner and diplomatic executive. His approach to the presidency reflected his wartime leadership style. He concentrated on major matters, delegated authority, and worked to reconcile contending factions. His restrained view of presidential authority and his low-key style, combined with frequent fishing and golfing vacations, led Democrats to scoff at Eisenhower as a leader who "reigned but did not rule."

The image of passivity masked a "hidden-hand" presidency that enabled him to work successfully behind the scenes. More pragmatic than ideological, the president wished to reduce taxes, contain inflation, and when necessary, check downturns by stimulating the economy. After the Democrats retook Congress in 1954, Eisenhower supported extending social-security benefits, raising the minimum wage, adding 4 million workers to those eligible for unemployment benefits, and providing federally financed public housing for low-income families. He also approved construction of the St. Lawrence Seaway, linking the Great Lakes and the Atlantic Ocean, and creation of the Department of Health, Education, and Welfare. In 1956, Eisenhower backed the largest and most expensive public-works program in American history: the Interstate Highway Act, authorizing construction of a 41,000-mile system of expressways that would soon snake across America, accelerating suburban growth, heightening dependence on imported oil, and contributing to urban decay and air pollution.

Republicans renominated Ike by acclamation in 1956, and voters gave him a landslide victory over Democrat Adlai Stevenson. With the GOP crowing, "Everything's booming but the guns," the president won by the greatest popular majority since FDR's victory in 1936.

The Cold War Continues

Eisenhower essentially maintained Truman's containment policy. Stalin's death in 1953 and Eisenhower's veiled threat to use nuclear weapons broke the Korean stalemate. The armistice signed in July 1953 set the boundary between North and South Korea once again at the thirty-eighth parallel. Some Americans claimed that communist aggression had been thwarted and containment vindicated; others condemned the truce as peace without honor.

Ike and Dulles

Eager to ease Cold War hostilities, Eisenhower first had to quiet the GOP right wing's clamor to roll back the Red tide. To do so, he chose as his secretary of state **John Foster Dulles,** a rigid, humorless Presbyterian who advocated a holy war against "atheistic communism," including "instant, massive retaliation" with nuclear weapons. Dulles called for "liberation" of the captive peoples of Eastern Europe and for unleashing Jiang Jieshi against communist China. Believing that the Soviet Union understood only force, Dulles insisted on the necessity of "brinksmanship," the art of never backing down in a crisis—even at the risk of war.

Such saber rattling pleased the Right, but Eisenhower preferred conciliation, partly to keep the cost of containment at a manageable level and partly because he feared a nuclear war—the Soviet Union had tested its own hydrogen bomb in 1953. Eisenhower refused to translate Dulles's rhetoric into action. Aware of the limits of American power, the United States did nothing to check the Soviet interventions that crushed uprisings in East Germany (1953) and Hungary (1956). There would be no rolling back Red power in Eastern Europe.

As multimegaton thermonuclear weapons replaced atomic bombs in U.S. and Soviet arsenals, and both nations developed intercontinental ballistic missiles (ICBMs) to deliver such bombs, Eisenhower

"I LIKE IKE" The darling of his many moderate Republican supporters, Dwight D. Eisenhower had a natural talent for taking his case to the American people. At a typical campaign stop he would speak in simple, reassuring terms, introduce his wife Mamie, promise to clean up the "mess in Washington," and wave goodbye as the train pulled away to chants of "I Like Ike." (© Bettmann/Corbis)

worked to reduce the probability of mutual annihilation. He proposed "atoms for peace," whereby both superpowers would contribute fissionable materials to a new UN agency for use in industrial projects. In the absence of a positive Soviet response, the government constructed an electronic air defense system to provide early warning of a missile attack.

Work also began on commercial nuclear plants in the mid-1950s, promising electricity "too cheap to meter." However, most money continued to go for military nuclear research. Radioactive fallout from atomic tests, especially the 1954 U.S. tests that spread strontium-90 over a wide area, heightened world concern about the nuclear-arms race. In 1955, Eisenhower and Soviet leaders met in Geneva for the first East-West conference since World War II. Discussions produced no concrete plan for arms control, but mutual talk of "peaceful coexistence" led reporters to hail the "spirit of Geneva." In March 1958, Moscow suspended atmospheric tests of nuclear weapons, and the United States followed suit.

But the Cold War continued. Dulles negotiated mutual-defense pacts with forty-three nations and created SEATO in 1954, extending collective security agreements between the United States and Australia, New Zealand, Pakistan, the Philippines, and Thailand. Rather than trying to match the communists "man for man, gun for gun," Eisenhower's "New Look" defense program reduced conventional forces and emphasized nuclear weapons. Promising "more bang for the buck," it succeeded in reducing the defense budget yet spurred the Soviets to seek "more rubble for the ruble" by enlarging their nuclear stockpile.

Meanwhile, the focus of the Cold War shifted from Europe to the Third World, the largely nonwhite developing nations. There, the two superpowers waged war by proxy, using local guerrillas and military juntas. There, too, the CIA fought covert wars against those thought to imperil American interests.

CIA Covert Actions

Established in 1947 to conduct foreign intelligence gathering, the CIA soon began to carry out undercover operations to topple regimes friendly to communism. By 1957, half its personnel and 80 percent of its budget were devoted to "covert action." To woo influential foreign thinkers away from communism, the CIA also sponsored intellectual conferences and jazz concerts. It bankrolled anticommunist cultural events, subsidized magazines to publish articles supporting the United States, and recruited college students and businessmen traveling abroad as "fronts" in clandestine CIA activities.

In 1953, the CIA orchestrated a coup to overthrow the government of Iran. Fearing that the prime minister, who had nationalized the oil fields, might open oil-rich Iran to the Soviets, the CIA replaced him with the pro-American Shah Reza Pahlavi. The United States gained a loyal ally on the Soviet border, and Western oil companies prospered when the Shah made low-priced oil available to them. But Iranian hatred of America took root—a hostility that would haunt the United States into the twenty-first century.

The CIA also intervened in Philippine elections in 1953 to ensure a pro-American government. The following year, a CIA-supported band of mercenaries in Guatemala overthrew the elected communist-influenced regime, which had seized land from the American-owned United Fruit Company. The new pro-American government restored United Fruit's properties and trampled political opposition. "Our traditional ideas of international sportsmanship," Eisenhower noted privately in 1955, "are scarcely applicable in the morass in which the world now flounders."

> "Our traditional ideas of international sportsmanship are scarcely applicable in the morass in which the world now flounders."

Troubles in the Third World

In Indochina, viewed as a Cold War battleground, Eisenhower first followed Truman's course of providing France with large-scale military assistance to fight Vietnamese insurgents. When that failed, he pinned his hopes on the CIA-installed President Ngo Dinh Diem to keep South Vietnam an independent anticommunist nation tied to the United States. That policy, too, appeared to be faltering as he left office (to be further discussed in Chapter 28).

Eisenhower faced his greatest crisis, however, in the Middle East. In 1954, Gamal Abdel Nasser came to power in Egypt, determined to modernize his nation. To woo him, the United States offered financing for a dam at Aswan to harness the Nile River. But when Nasser purchased arms from Czechoslovakia, John Foster Dulles canceled the loan. Nasser retaliated by nationalizing the British-controlled Suez Canal.

Viewing the canal as the lifeline of its empire, Britain, in alliance with France, which feared Arab nationalism in their Algerian colony, and with Israel, which feared the Egyptian arms buildup, attacked Egypt in October 1956. Angered that America's three closest allies had not consulted him, and fearful that such military action would drive the Arab world and its precious oil to the Russians, Eisenhower forced his allies to withdraw their troops.

The **Suez crisis** had major consequences. It swelled Third World anti-Western sentiment, and the United States replaced Britain and France as the protector of Western interests in the Middle East. Determined to guarantee the flow of oil to the West, the president announced the **Eisenhower Doctrine** in 1957—a proclamation that the United States would send military aid and, if necessary, troops to any Middle Eastern nation threatened by "Communist aggression."

Such interventions intensified anti-American feelings in Third World nations. Angry crowds in Peru and Venezuela spat at Vice President Nixon and stoned his car in 1958. In 1959, Fidel Castro overturned a dictatorial regime in Cuba and confiscated American properties without compensation. He then established close economic and military ties with the Soviet Union. If the United States dared intervene, Soviet premier Nikita Khrushchev warned, he would defend Cuba with nuclear weapons. "The Monroe Doctrine has outlived its time," Khrushchev said.

> "The Monroe Doctrine has outlived its time."

A tougher blow came on May 1, 1960, two weeks before a scheduled summit conference between Eisenhower and Khrushchev, when Soviet air defenses shot down a U.S. spy plane far inside their border. Khrushchev displayed the captured CIA pilot and the photos taken of Soviet missile sites. Eisenhower refused to apologize, and the summit collapsed.

The Eisenhower Legacy

Just before leaving office, Eisenhower offered Americans a farewell and a warning. The demands of national security, he stated, had produced the "conjunction of an immense military establishment and a large arms industry." Swollen defense budgets had yoked American economic health to military expenditures, and military contracts had become the staff of life for research scholars, politicians, and America's largest corporations. This combination of interests, Eisenhower believed, exerted enormous leverage and threatened the traditional subordination of the military in American life. "We must guard against the acquisition of unwarranted influence ... by the **military-industrial complex**. The potential for the disastrous rise of misplaced power exists and will persist."

The president concluded that he had avoided war but that lasting peace was not in sight. Most scholars agreed. Eisenhower ended the Korean War, avoided direct intervention in Vietnam, initiated relaxing tensions with the Soviet Union, and suspended atmospheric nuclear testing. At the same time, he presided over an accelerating nuclear-arms race and a Cold War that encircled the globe. His domestic record was mixed as well. His acceptance of some progressive social-welfare measures angered the Republican Right, and liberal Democrats faulted his passivity toward McCarthyism. Still, Ike had given the majority of Americans what they most wanted—prosperity, reassurance, and a breathing spell in which to relish the comforts of life.

CONCLUSION

After nearly two decades of depression and war, the end of World War II meant the beginning of a new era of hope for most Americans. At the same time, an assertive United States, eager to protect and expand its influence and power in the world, sought to contain a Soviet Union obsessed with its own security and self-interest. Stalin's aggressive posture toward Eastern Europe and the Persian Gulf was met by an American policy of containment, in whose name the United States aided Greece and Turkey, established the Marshall Plan, airlifted supplies into Berlin for a year, approved the creation of the Federal Republic of Germany (West Germany), established NATO, implemented NSC-68, financed France's war in Vietnam, and went to war in Korea. The resulting stalemate would last for four decades, define American politics and society, transform the U.S. economy, and condition the thinking of a generation.

The Cold War obsession with communism, as well as postwar prosperity, weakened the appeal of liberal reform. In a political climate far more conservative than that of the 1930s, New Deal measures remained in place, but Truman's Fair Deal to assist the disadvantaged with new initiatives in education, health insurance, and civil rights failed. Anticommunist hysteria squashed the Left and narrowed the range of politically acceptable ideas. Most importantly, Truman's actions at home and abroad fed America's fear of communism, which grew with the president's responses to the Soviet detonation of an atomic bomb, the fall of China to the communists, the invasion of South Korea, and Truman's own loyalty probe to root out subversive government workers. Witch-hunts for communism in American life and the discovery of a Soviet atomic spy ring added to the paranoia. In this atmosphere, Truman's actions encouraged others to seek scapegoats for American failures abroad and legitimated conservative accusations that equated dissent with disloyalty.

As the Cold War continued throughout the 1950s, continuity would also mark the domestic and foreign policies of Truman's successor. Dwight Eisenhower, in the main, pursued a centrist course in domestic affairs. While tilting to the right in favoring private corporations, the Eisenhower administration left New Deal reforms in place, expanded existing social-welfare benefits, and employed Keynesian deficit spending to curtail economic recessions. The president made no effort to hamper labor unionization and proposed construction of a vast interstate highway system.

Eisenhower also followed Truman in his determination to contain communism abroad, while putting new emphasis on the need to avoid nuclear war and to fight communism in the Third World. Gaining short-term victories in local conflicts, often by clandestine means, Ike and Secretary of State Dulles largely ignored the nationalist yearnings and socioeconomic deprivations of local peoples and increasingly allied the United States with reactionary, repressive regimes.

KEY TERMS

George F. Kennan   (p. 805)

Containment   (p. 805)

Truman Doctrine   (p. 805)

National Security Act of 1947   (p. 805)

Marshall Plan   (p. 805)

Berlin airlift   (p. 808)

North Atlantic Treaty Organization   (p. 809)

Mao Zedong   (p. 809)

National Security Paper 68 (NSC-68)   (p. 811)

Korean War   (p. 813)

GI Bill   (p. 815)

Employment Act of 1946   (p. 816)

Taft-Hartley Act   (p. 817)

Fair Deal   (p. 818)

Second Red Scare   (p. 818)

House Un-American Activities Committee   (p. 819)

Alger Hiss and Whittaker Chambers   (p. 821)

Julius and Ethel Rosenberg   (p. 821)

Joseph R. McCarthy   (p. 822)

McCarran Internal Security Act   (p. 822)

Dwight D. Eisenhower   (p. 823)

John Foster Dulles   (p. 824)

Suez crisis   (p. 826)

Eisenhower Doctrine   (p. 826)

military-industrial complex   (p. 826)

FOR FURTHER REFERENCE

Brian Burnes, *Harry S Truman: His Life and Times* (2003). A lively account that avoids excessive nostalgia.

James Callanan, *Covert Action in the Cold War: U.S. Policy, Intelligence, and CIA Operations* (2010). A perceptive critique of U.S. covert actions from 1947 to 1963.

Richard M. Fried, *The Russians Are Coming! The Russians Are Coming! Pageantry and Patriotism in Cold-War America* (1999). A balanced introduction to some of the social consequences of the Cold War.

John Lewis Gaddis, *George F. Kennan: An American Life* (2011). A comprehensive and perceptive biography.

John Earl Haynes and Harvey Klehr, *Venona: Recoding Soviet Espionage in America* (1999). Soviet spying in the United States, as disclosed by recently declassified yet sometimes ambiguous evidence.

Edward Humes, *Over Here: How the GI Bill Transformed the American Dream* (2006). A comprehensive, thoughtful interpretation.

Robert J. McMahon, *Dean Acheson and the Creation of an American World Order* (2009). A brief, insightful study of this important strategist.

Jim Newton, *Eisenhower: The White House Years* (2011). A cogent narrative of the man and his era.

Paul G. Pierpaoli, Jr., *Truman and Korea* (1999), and Stanley Sandler, *The Korean War: No Victors, No Vanquished* (1999). Two indispensable accounts of the war.

Ellen Schrecker, *The Age of McCarthyism* (2001). A good collection of primary documents and critical survey of the excesses of domestic anticommunism.

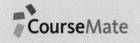

Visit the CourseMate website at **www.cengagebrain.com** for additional study tools and review materials for this chapter.

America at Midcentury,

1945–1961

JACKIE ROBINSON *(Photo File/MLB
Photos via Getty Images)*

**"WHEN JACKIE TOOK
THE FIELD,"** the Reverend
Jesse Jackson declared at Jack
Roosevelt Robinson's funeral in
1972, "something reminded us of
our birthright to be free." Indeed, as
no one else in the postwar period,
Jackie Robinson personified the
accelerating momentum of the
struggle against racial discrimination
that emerged from the Second World
War. Like other grandchildren of
slaves and children of sharecroppers,
Robinson moved from the Deep South to California. He lettered in four
sports at UCLA before serving in World War II. Refusing to accept
segregation on army buses—"Nobody's going to separate bullets
and label them 'for white troops' and 'for colored troops,'" he told an
officer—Robinson was tried and acquitted of insubordination in a court
martial. After being honorably discharged, Robinson briefly played in
the Negro Baseball League before accepting the 1945 offer of Branch
Rickey, general manager of the Brooklyn Dodgers organization, to play
for their farm club in Montreal. Although intensely proud of himself and
his race, Robinson agreed to Rickey's condition that he not respond to
the abuse he would face: "I want a ballplayer with enough guts not
to fight back." Robinson did not. Instead, he won the batting crown
of the International League in 1946, and joined the Brooklyn club
the following year—the first African American to play major league
baseball in the twentieth century.

It would not, however, be an easy trip around the bases to racial harmony. He endured
racist insults and beanballs (a record nine times that season, sixty-five times in seven
years), flying spikes and hate mail, even death threats, from fans and other players. But
his dazzling bat, feet, and glove, and his dignified courage, helped the Dodgers win the
pennant and Robinson was named Rookie of the Year. His success led the Cleveland
Indians to make Larry Doby the first black to play in the American League and eroded
the resistance to African Americans in collegiate sports.

"It was unquestioned gospel," feminist Betty Friedan would later write in *The Feminine Mystique*
(1963), that postwar women "could identify with nothing beyond the home—not politics, not art,
not science, not events large or small, war or peace, in the United States or the world, unless it
could be approached through female experience as a wife or mother or translated into domestic
detail." *(State Library and Archives of Florida)*

More than batting champion for 1949 and Most Valuable Player, Robinson became a symbol of progress in race relations and a spur to changes in national policy and institutional practices. His example led the Cleveland and Los Angeles franchises of the All-American Football Conference, and the Boston Celtics in the National Basketball Association, to follow the Dodgers' lead. Moreover, the popular press increasingly attacked prejudice, and more groups than ever before preached tolerance; various cities and states, particularly in the Northeast, passed laws against discrimination in employment and public accommodations; the Supreme Court chipped away at the judicial foundations of segregation; the Truman Administration proposed civil rights legislation; and antiracism took its place alongside bread-and-butter issues in the agenda of liberalism. Yet many changes came very slowly, if at all. The Boston Red Sox refused to integrate until 1959, and just as Robinson, following his retirement in 1957, never received an offer to return to the game in a management capacity, the coaches and front-office personnel of most sports clubs remained lily-white for decades. The struggle to end racism in America had taken root, but not yet flowered.

For most white Americans, however, economic growth and prosperity, and the Cold War, defined the postwar era. Many would remember it as "the good life," a time of affluence and suburbia. A new way of life, centered on family "togetherness" and consumption, became the American Dream. Yet

Americans also worried about the arms race, and the atmospheric nuclear testing that pumped strontium-90, a cancer-causing chemical that accumulates in the teeth and bone marrow of children, into the world's environment. Fewer middle-class whites paid much attention to racial discrimination or to critics who railed against mainstream values in the postwar years.

A time of fundamental changes and of portents of yet greater change, the period from 1945 to 1961 brought the advent of an automated and computerized postindustrial society, the incredible spread and influence of television, the baby boom, the growth of suburbs and the Sunbelt, high-speed interstate highways, and an enormous internal migration. Midcentury America encompassed booming prosperity and persistent poverty, civil-rights triumphs and rampant racism, consensus and alienation. Much like Jackie Robinson breaking the color line in major league baseball, it showcased what we were, and what we would become.

"Bring the Boys Home by Christmas"

Postwar Jitters

The immediate concerns of most Americans following V-J Day centered on "bringing the boys home" and avoiding a return to the Great Depression. The steep decline in defense spending and factory jobs caused many to fear demobilization and the reconversion to a peacetime economy. Strife between labor and management, as well as inflation and shortages, intensified the anxiety. But by 1947, consumer spending and the Cold War had begun to spur a quarter-century of economic growth and prosperity, the longest such period in American history.

The Affluent Society

In 1958, the economist John Kenneth Galbraith published *The Affluent Society*, a study of postwar America whose title reflected the broad-based prosperity that made the 1950s seem the fulfillment of the American Dream. By the end of the decade, about 60 percent of American families owned homes; 75 percent, cars; and 87 percent, at least one TV. The economy perfectly matched Eisenhower's pursuit of moderation. Government spending, a huge upsurge in productivity, and steadily increasing consumer demand pushed the gross national product (GNP) up 50 percent. The United States achieved the world's highest living standard ever. By 1960, the average worker's income, adjusted for

FOCUS Questions

- What were the main sources of the postwar economic expansion and affluence?
- What, if any, were the negative consequences of the era's preoccupation with economic growth and prosperity?
- What factors account for the growth of suburbia in postwar America, and how accurate is the image of 1950s suburban life as one of contentment, conservatism, and conformity?
- What actions by minorities and youth foretold the movements for social change to come in the 1960s?
- What innovative strategies were developed by the civil rights movement in this era, and what were the main reasons for the increasing success of the movement?

1944	Servicemen's Readjustment Act (GI Bill).
1946	ENIAC, the first electronic computer, begins operation.
1947	Levittown, New York, development started.
	Jackie Robinson breaks major league baseball's color line.
	President's Committee on Civil Rights issues *To Secure These Rights*.
1948	Bell Labs develops the transistor.
1950	*Asociación Nacional México-Americana* established.
1953	Earl Warren appointed chief justice.
	Operation Wetback begins.
1954	*Brown v. Board of Education of Topeka*.
	Father Knows Best begins on TV.
1955	Salk polio vaccine developed.
	AFL-CIO merger.

1955 (*Cont.*)	Elvis Presley ignites rock-n-roll.
	James Dean stars in *Rebel Without a Cause*.
	Montgomery bus boycott begins.
1956	Interstate Highway Act.
1957	Little Rock school-desegregation crisis.
	Soviet Union launches *Sputnik*.
	Peak of baby boom (4.3 million births).
	Southern Christian Leadership Conference founded.
1958	National Defense Education Act.
	National Aeronautics and Space Administration (NASA) founded.
1960	Sit-ins begin.
	Suburban population almost equals that of central city.
1961	Freedom Rides begin.

inflation, was 35 percent higher than in 1945. With just 6 percent of the world's population, the United States produced and consumed nearly half of everything made and sold on Earth.

The New Industrial Society

Federal spending constituted a major source of economic growth, nearly doubling in the 1950s to $180 billion. Just 1 percent of the GNP in 1929, federal expenditures reached 17 percent by the mid-1950s. These funds built roads and airports, financed home mortgages, supported farm prices, and provided stipends for education. More than half the federal budget—10 percent of the GNP—went to defense spending. These expenditures made the federal government the nation's main financier of scientific and technological research and development (R&D).

For the West, especially, it was as if World War II never ended. Politicians from both parties in California sought contracts for Lockheed, those from Texas labored for General Dynamics, and those from Washington State kept defense funds flowing to Boeing. By the late 1950s, California alone received half the space budget and a quarter of all major military contracts. By then, Denver had the largest number of federal employees outside Washington, DC; Albuquerque boasted more Ph.D. degrees per capita than any other U.S. city; and more than a third of workers in Los Angeles

depended on defense industries. Utah, once the Mormon dream of an agricultural utopia, received the nation's highest per capita expenditures on space and defense research. Government spending transformed the mythic West of rugged individualists into a West of bureaucrats, defense contractors, and scientists dependent on federal funds.

Science became a ward of the state, and government funding and control transformed both the U.S. military and industry. Financed by the Atomic Energy Commission (AEC) and utilizing navy scientists, the nation's first nuclear-power plant came on line in 1957. The chemical industry continued its wartime growth. As pesticides contaminated ground water supplies and plastics reduced landfill space, Americans—unaware of the hidden perils—marveled at vegetables covered with Saran Wrap and delighted in their Dacron suits, Acrilan socks, and Teflon-coated pans.

Electricity consumption tripled in the 1950s, and electronics became the fifth-largest American industry, as factories automated and consumers purchased all manner of electric appliances. Domestic oil production and foreign imports rose steeply, and by 1960 oil had replaced coal as the nation's main energy source. Hardly anyone paid attention when a physicist warned in 1953 that "adding 6 billion tons of carbon dioxide to the atmosphere each year is warming up the Earth."

Plentiful, cheap gasoline fed the growth of the automobile and aircraft industries. The nation's

THE GOOD LIFE, FORTIES-STYLE After the war, Americans grabbed for the good life, whether that meant jiving to a jukebox, trying some fast food at the first McDonald's in San Bernardino, California, or celebrating Thanksgiving—as this couple in Joliet, Illinois, does with their sixteen children. *(AP Images and © Bettmann/Corbis)*

Hardly anyone paid attention when a physicist warned in 1953 that "adding 6 billion tons of carbon dioxide to the atmosphere each year is warming up the Earth."

The Age of Computers

The computer was key to technological revolution. To decipher secret Axis codes, International Business Machines (IBM) in 1944 produced the third-largest industry in the 1950s, aerospace depended on defense spending and on federally funded research. The automobile industry, still the nation's industrial titan, also utilized technological R&D. Between 1945 and 1960, the industry halved the number of hours and workers required to produce a car.

Mark I calculator, a cumbersome device with five hundred miles of wiring. In late 1945, to improve artillery accuracy, the military devised ENIAC, the first electronic computer. Still unwieldy, with eighteen thousand vacuum tubes, ENIAC could perform five thousand calculations per second. Next came the development of operating instructions, or programs, that could be stored inside the computer's memory; the substitution of printed circuits for wires; and in 1948, at Bell Labs, the invention of tiny solid-state transistors that ended reliance on radio tubes.

Sales of electronic computers to industry rose from twenty in 1954 to more than a thousand in 1957 and more than two thousand in 1960. Major manufacturers used them to monitor production lines, track inventory, and ensure quality control. In government, computers were as indispensable to Pentagon strategists playing war games as they were to the Census Bureau and the Internal Revenue Service. By the mid-1960s, more than thirty thousand mainframe computers would be used by banks, hospitals, and universities. Further developments led to the first integrated circuits and to what would ultimately become the Internet.

The development of the high-technology complex known as Silicon Valley began in 1951 as Stanford University utilized its science and engineering faculties to design and produce products for the Fairchild Semiconductor and Hewlett-Packard companies. This relationship between universities and corporations became a model followed by other high-tech firms. Soon apricot and cherry orchards throughout the Santa Clara Valley gave way to industrial parks filled with computer firms and pharmaceutical laboratories. Similar developments would follow the military-fueled research complexes along Boston's Route 128, near Austin, Texas, and in North Carolina's Research Triangle.

The Costs of Bigness

Rapid technological advances accelerated the growth and power of big business. In 1950, twenty-two U.S. firms had assets of more than $1 billion; ten years later more than fifty did. By then, one-half of 1 percent of all companies earned more than half the total corporate income in the United States. The wealthiest became oligopolies, swallowing up weak competitors. Three television networks monopolized the nation's airwaves; three automobile and three aluminum companies produced more than 90 percent of America's cars and aluminum; and a handful of firms controlled the lion's share of assets and sales in steel, petroleum, chemicals, and electrical machinery. Corporations acquired overseas facilities to become "multinational" enterprises and formed "conglomerates" by merging companies in unrelated industries: International Telephone and Telegraph (ITT) branched out from

PRODUCTION LINE AT DOUGLAS AIRCRAFT COMPANY The Cold War stimulated an enormous boom in defense spending. By midcentury, more than half the federal budget, about 10 percent of the GNP, went to defense contractors like Douglas Aircraft, which helped the economy of the South and the West to flourish. *(© Bettmann/Corbis)*

communications into car rental, home building, motel chains, insurance, and more. Growth and consolidation meant greater bureaucratization. "Executives" replaced "capitalists." Success required conformity not creativity, teamwork not individuality. According to sociologist David Riesman's *The Lonely Crowd* (1950), the new "company people" were "other-directed," eager to follow the cues from their peers and not think innovatively or act independently. In the old nursery rhyme "This Little Pig Went to Market," Riesman noted, each pig went his own way. "Today, however, all little pigs go to market; none stay home; all have roast beef, if any do; and all say 'we-we.'"

Changes in American agriculture paralleled those in industry. Farming grew increasingly scientific and mechanized. Technology halved the work hours necessary to grow crops between 1945 and 1960, causing many farm families to migrate to cities. In 1956 alone, one-eleventh of the farm population left the land (see Figure 27.1). Meanwhile, heavily capitalized farm businesses, running "factories in the field," prospered by using more machines and chemicals.

Until the publication of Rachel Carson's *Silent Spring* in 1962, few Americans understood the extent to which fertilizers, herbicides, and pesticides poisoned the environment. Carson, a former researcher for the Fish and Wildlife Service (see page 832), dramatized the problems caused by use of the insecticide DDT and its spread through the food chain. Her depiction of a "silent spring" caused by the death of songbirds from DDT toxicity led many states to ban its use. The federal government followed suit. But the incentives for cultivating more land, and more marginal land, led to further ravages.

Blue-Collar Blues

Consolidation also transformed the labor movement. In 1955, the merger of the AFL and CIO

ENIAC, THE ELECTRONIC NUMERICAL INTEGRATOR AND COMPUTER The co-conceiver and designer of ENIAC, Dr. John W. Mauchly of the University of Pennsylvania's School of Electrical Engineering, publicly unveiled the first general-purpose electronic computer in February 1946. *(© Bettmann/Corbis)*

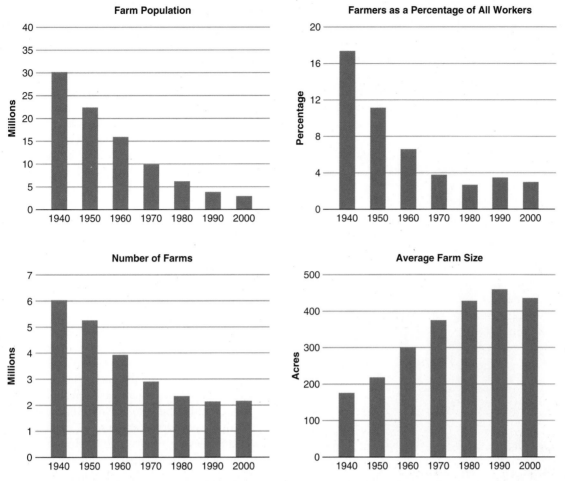

FIGURE 27.1 THE AMERICAN FARMER, 1940–2000 The postwar years saw a fundamental transformation of American agriculture. While the small family farmer joined the rural exodus to the cities, large farms prospered. © Cengage Learning. All rights reserved. No distribution allowed without express authorization.

Sources: *National Agricultural Statistics Service, U.S. Department of Agriculture; U.S. Bureau of the Census,* Statistical Abstract of the United States, *1991, 1992, 2001 (Washington, DC).*

brought 85 percent of union members into a single federation. Although labor leadership promised aggressive unionism, organized labor fell victim to its success at the bargaining table. Higher wages, shorter workweeks, paid vacations, health-care coverage, and automatic wage hikes tied to the cost of living led most workers to view themselves as middle class rather than the proletariat.

Further sapping labor militancy, by 1956, for the first time in U.S. history, white-collar employees outnumbered blue-collar workers. The office with hundreds of little cubicles superseded the assembly line as the dominant image of the American workplace. Employees in ties or skirts replaced those in blue-collar work shirts. Although most service jobs were as routinized as any factory job, few unions sought to woo white-collar workers. The percentage of the unionized labor force dropped from a high of 36 percent in 1953 to 31 percent in 1960, and kept falling.

Prosperity and the Suburbs

As real income (adjusted for inflation) rose, Americans spent less of their income on necessities and more on powered lawnmowers and air conditioners. They heaped their shopping carts with frozen, dehydrated, and fortified foods. When they lacked cash, they borrowed. In 1950, Diner's Club issued the first credit card; American Express followed in 1958. Installment buying, home mortgages, and auto loans tripled Americans' private indebtedness in the 1950s. In its effort to convince people to buy what they did not need, business spent more on advertising than the nation did on public schools.

Suburban America

Urged to "Buy Now, Pay Later," Americans purchased 58 million new cars during the 1950s.

RACHEL CARSON The mother of modern ecology, Carson exposed the dangers of pesticides to animal and human life in her 1962 best seller *Silent Spring,* an enormously influential work that helped redefine the way humans look at their place in nature. *(Alfred Eisenstaedt/TimeLife Pictures/Getty Images)*

Manufacturers enticed people to trade in and up by offering flashier models, two-tone color, tail fins, and extra-powerful engines—like Pontiac's 1955 "Sensational Strato-Streak V-8," which could go more than twice as fast as any speed limit. Seat belts remained an unadvertised extra-cost option. The consequences were increases in highway deaths, air pollution, oil consumption, and "autosclerosis"—clogged urban arteries.

Government policy as well as "auto mania" spurred white Americans' exodus to the suburbs (see Figure 27.2). Federal spending on highways skyrocketed from $79 million in 1946 to $2.6 billion in 1960, putting once-remote areas within "commuting distance" for city workers (see Technology and Culture). The income-tax code stimulated home sales by allowing deductions for home-mortgage interest payments and for property taxes. The Federal Housing Administration (FHA) and Veterans Administration (VA) offered low-interest loans; and both continued to deny loans to blacks who sought to buy homes in white neighborhoods. In 1960, suburbia was 98 percent white.

In 1947, some thirty miles from midtown Manhattan on Long Island, Alfred and William Levitt used the mass-production construction techniques they perfected during the war to construct standardized 720-square-foot houses as quickly as possible. All 17,000 looked alike. Deeds to the property prohibited picket fences, mandated regular lawn mowing, and specified when the wash could be hung to dry in the backyard. All the town streets curved at the same angle. A tree was planted every twenty-eight feet. The Levitts then built a second, larger Levittown in Bucks County, Pennsylvania, and a third in Willingboro, New Jersey.

Other contractors followed suit, and 85 percent of the 13 million new homes built in the 1950s were in the suburbs. In the greatest internal migration in the nation's history, some 20 million Americans moved to the suburbs in the decade—making the suburban population equal to that of the central cities. Many critics followed Lewis Mumford in decrying the "multitude of uniform, unidentifiable houses, lined up inflexibly, at uniform distances, on uniform roads, in a treeless, communal wasteland, inhabited by people of

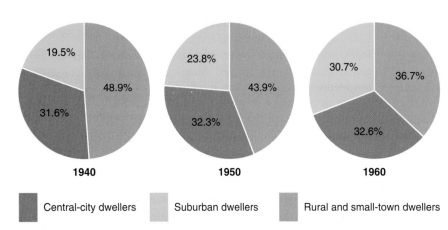

1940   **1950**   **1960**

■ Central-city dwellers   ■ Suburban dwellers   ■ Rural and small-town dwellers

FIGURE 27.2   URBAN, SUBURBAN, AND RURAL AMERICANS, 1940–1960 In the fifteen years following World War II, more than 40 million Americans migrated to the suburbs, where, as one father put it, "a kid could grow up with grass stains on his pants." Over the same period, fourteen of the fifteen largest U.S. cities lost population. © Cengage Learning. All rights reserved. No distribution allowed without express authorization.

Source: *Adapted from U.S. Bureau of the Census,* Current Censuses, *1930–1970 (Washington, DC: U.S. Government Printing Office).*

the same class, the same income, the same age group." Yet suburbia remained the American dream for most families longing for their own home, good schools, safe streets, and neighbors like themselves.

Americans also moved South and West, into the Sunbelt, lured by job opportunities, the climate, and the pace of life. California, where the population went from 9 to 19 million between 1945 and 1964, supplanted New York as the most populous state. Los Angeles boasted the highest per capita ownership of private homes and cars of any city. Initially designed to lure shoppers downtown, the highway system instead had become the road to a home in the suburbs (see Map 27.1).

Industry, too, headed south and west, drawn by low taxes, low energy costs, and anti-union right-to-work laws. Senior citizens headed to the easier climate. Both brought a conservative outlook. By 1980, the population of the **Sunbelt**, which stretched from the old Confederacy across Texas to southern California, exceeded that of the North and East. The political power of the Republican Party rose accordingly.

Consensus and Conservatism

Not everyone embraced the conformity of 1950s consumer culture. Intellectuals found an audience for their attack on "organization men" bent on getting ahead by going along and on "status seekers" pursuing external rewards to compensate for inner insecurities. Others, like Riesman, took aim at "other-directed" conformists and "an America of mass housing, mass markets, massive corporations, massive government, mass media, and massive boredom." Riesman described modern Americans as shaped by the opinions of their peers rather than by their own consciences. Some took aim at the consumerist middle class: "all items in a national supermarket—categorized, processed, labeled, priced, and readied for merchandising."

This criticism oversimplified reality. It ignored ethnic and class diversity, the acquisitiveness and

> "An America of mass housing, mass markets, massive corporations, massive government, mass media, and massive boredom."

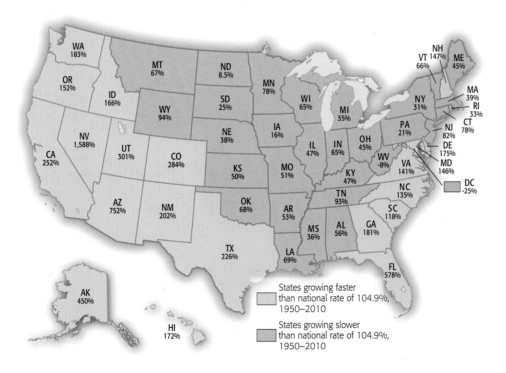

MAP 27.1 THE GROWTH OF THE SUNBELT, 1950–2010 Millions of Americans headed for warmer climates in the decades following World War II. Many from the Northeast and Upper Midwest, the regions hardest hit by the decline of jobs in established manufacturing industries, sought new employment opportunities, and many of the growing population of senior citizens sought the good life in the mushrooming number of "golden age" communities in Arizona, Florida, and southern California. © Cengage Learning. All rights reserved. No distribution allowed without express authorization.

Source: *D.W. Meinig,* The Shaping of America, *Vol. 4 (New Haven, CT: Yale University Press, 2004), p. 232.*

Technology & CULTURE

The Interstate Highway System

As a young captain after World War I, Dwight Eisenhower had been given the task of accompanying a convoy of army trucks across the country. The woefully inadequate state of the roads for military transport dismayed him then as much as he would later be impressed by the German autobahns that allowed Hitler to deploy troops around Germany with incredible speed. Not surprisingly, when he became president, he sought a transportation system that would facilitate the rapid movement of the military, as well as increase road safety and aid commerce. The arms race with the Soviet Union, moreover, necessitated a network of highways for evacuating cities in case of a nuclear attack—a change, according to the *Bulletin of the Atomic Scientists*, from "Duck and Cover" to "Run Like Hell."

In 1954, Eisenhower set up a high-powered commission to recommend a highway program that would cost as much as a war. He appointed an army general to head it to emphasize the connection between highways, national defense, and the concerns Americans had about their security. The next year,

with the entire federal budget at $71 billion, Eisenhower asked Congress for a $40 billion, forty-one-thousand-mile construction project, to be financed by government bonds. Conservative Republicans, fearful of increasing the federal debt, balked. So Ike switched to a financing plan based on new gasoline, tire, bus, and trucking taxes. The federal government would use the taxes to pay 90 percent of the construction costs in any state willing to come up with the other 10 percent.

Millions of suburbanites commuting to central cities loved the idea of new multilane highways. So did motorists dreaming of summer travel; the powerful coalition of automobile manufacturers, oil companies, asphalt firms, and truckers, who stood to benefit financially the most; and the many special interests in virtually every congressional district, including real-estate developers, shopping mall entrepreneurs, engineers, and construction industries. Indeed, the interstate highway bill promised something to almost everybody except the inner-city poor. It sailed through Congress in 1956,

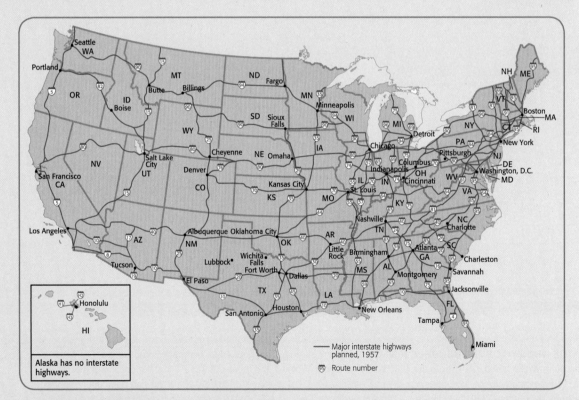

PROJECTED INTERSTATE HIGHWAY SYSTEM, 1957 Touted as the largest public works project in the history of the world, the Highway Act provided for the nation's first centrally planned transportation system and the construction of a national system of high-speed expressways.

BREAKING GROUND FOR I-70 IN MISSOURI More than a commuter's delight, the new expressways proved a boon for the automobile, concrete, oil, tire, and interstate trucking businesses, as well as providing steady work for construction firms. *(Missouri State Archives)*

winning by voice vote in the House and by an 89 to 1 margin in the Senate.

The largest and most expensive public-works scheme in American history, the interstate highway system was designed and built as a single project for the entire country, unlike the haphazard development of the canal and railroad networks. It required taking more land by eminent domain than had been taken in the entire history of road building in the United States. Expected increases in highway use, speed of travel, and weight of loads necessitated drastic changes in road engineering and materials. Utilizing the technological advances that had produced high-quality concrete and asphalt, diesel-powered roadbed graders, reinforced steel, and safely controlled explosives, construction crews built superhighways with standardized twelve-foot-wide lanes, ten-foot shoulders, and median strips of at least thirty-six feet in rural areas. Terrain in which a dirt trail was difficult to blaze was laced with cloverleaf intersections and some sixteen thousand exits and entrances. More than fifty thousand bridges, tunnels, and overpasses traversed swamps, rivers, and mountains. Road curves were banked for speeds of seventy miles per hour, with grades no greater than 3 percent and minimum sight distances of six hundred feet. The massive amounts of concrete poured, Ike later boasted, could have made "six sidewalks to the moon" or sixty Panama Canals.

The network of four-to-eight-lane roads linking cities and suburbs made it possible to drive from New York to San Francisco without encountering a stoplight. It more than fulfilled the initial hopes of most of its backers, enormously speeding the movement of goods and people across the country, invigorating the tourist industry, providing steady work for construction firms, enriching those who lived near the interstates and sold their lands to developers, and hastening suburban development.

The freeways that helped unify Americans by increasing the accessibility of once-distant regions also helped homogenize the nation with interchangeable shopping malls, motels, and fast-food chains. In 1955, Ray Kroc, who supplied the Multimixers for milk shakes to the original McDonald's drive-in in San Bernardino, California, began to franchise similar family restaurants beside highways, each serving the same standardized foods under the instantly recognizable logo of the golden arches. By century's end, McDonald's would be the world's largest private real-estate enterprise, as well as the largest food provider, serving more than 40 million meals daily in a hundred countries.

Moreover, the expressways boosted the interstate trucking business and hastened the decline of the nation's railroad lines and urban mass-transportation systems. The highways built to speed commuters into the central cities—"white men's roads through black men's bedrooms," said the National Urban League—often bulldozed minority neighborhoods out of existence or served as barriers between black and white neighborhoods. The beltways that lured increasingly more residents and businesses to suburbia eroded city tax bases, which in turn accelerated urban decay, triggering the urban crisis that then furthered suburban sprawl. The interstates had locked the United States into an ever-increasing reliance on cars and trucks, drastically increasing air pollution and American dependence on a constant supply of cheap and plentiful gasoline.

QUESTIONS FOR ANALYSIS

- Why did Congress authorize the construction of an interstate highway system?
- Describe some of the unintended consequences of the new highway system.

conformity of earlier generations, and the currents of dissent swirling beneath the surface. But it rightly spotlighted the elevation of comfort over challenge, and of private pleasures over public affairs. It was, in the main, a time of political passivity and preoccupation with personal gain.

Togetherness, the Baby Boom, and Domesticity

After years of separation and loss, Americans yearned for emotional security as well as material success, and looked to family for stability in an insecure world. In 1954, *McCall's* magazine coined the term *togetherness* to celebrate the "ideal" couple: the man and woman who centered their lives on home and children. Confident in continued economic prosperity, Americans in the 1950s tended to marry young, to have babies quickly, and to have more of them. The fertility rate (the number of births per thousand women), eighty in 1940, peaked at 123 in 1957, when an American baby was born every seven seconds. That year, the number of children per family had risen to 3.2, from 2.4 in 1945, and one-third of the population was under the age of 15.

New antibiotics subdued diphtheria and whooping cough, streptomycin drastically reduced tuberculosis, and the Salk and Sabin vaccines ended the dread of polio. The decline in childhood mortality helped raise American life expectancy from 65.9 years in 1945 to 70.9 years in 1970. Coupled with the "baby boom," it led to a 19 percent population spurt during the 1950s—a larger jump than in any previous decade.

The sheer size of the **baby-boom generation** (the 76 million Americans born between 1946 and 1964) ensured its impact and historical importance. Its needs and expectations at each stage of life would be as contorting as the digestion of a pig by a boa constrictor. First came the bulge in baby carriages; in the 1950s, school construction boomed; and in the 1960s, college enrollments soared. Then in the 1970s—as the baby boomers had their own families—home construction peaked. The 1980s and 1990s brought a surge in retirement investments, and the twenty-first century a preoccupation with health matters. In the 1950s, the baby boom also made child rearing a foremost concern, reinforcing the idea that women's place was in the home. No one did more to emphasize the necessity for women to be full-time mothers than **Dr. Benjamin Spock.** Only the Bible outsold his *Common Sense Book of Baby and Child Care* (1946) in the 1950s. Spock urged mothers not to work outside the home in order to create an atmosphere of warmth and intimacy for their children. Crying babies were to be comforted; breast-feeding came back into vogue.

The postwar emphasis on family togetherness renewed the ideal of domesticity in defining—and constraining—the role of women. Popular culture glorified marriage and parenthood, emphasizing a woman's role as a helpmate to her husband and a full-time mother to her children. Television mostly pictured women as at-home mothers, and Hollywood perpetuated the stereotype of career women as neurotic.

Education reinforced these notions. Girls were encouraged to study typing and cooking and cautioned not to "miss the boat" of marriage by pursuing higher education. "Men are not interested in college degrees but in the warmth and humanness of the girls they marry," stressed a textbook on the family. More men than women went to college in the 1950s, and only one-third of college women completed a degree.

> "Men are not interested in [women having] college degrees but in the warmth and humanness of the girls they marry."

Profound changes, however, were under way. By 1952, 2 million more women worked outside the home than had during the war; and by 1960, twice as many did as in 1940. In 1960, one-third of the labor force was female, and one out of three married women worked outside the home. Of all women workers that year, 60 percent were married, while 40 percent had school-age children.

Most women worked to augment family income, not to challenge stereotypes. Most held so-called "pink-collar" jobs in the service industry—secretary or clerk, waitress or hairdresser. Their median wage was less than half that for men. Yet many women, as during World War II, developed a heightened sense of expectations and empowerment as a result of employment. Transmitted to their daughters, their experience would fuel a feminist resurgence in the late 1960s.

Religion and Education

"Today in the U.S.," *Time* claimed in 1954, "the Christian faith is back in the center of things." Evangelist **Billy Graham,** Roman Catholic Bishop Fulton J. Sheen, and Protestant minister Norman Vincent Peale all had syndicated newspaper columns, best-selling books, and radio and television programs. Each promoted a potent mixture of religious salvation and aggressive anticommunism.

Hollywood religious extravaganzas were the biggest box-office hits of the 1950s, while television pronounced that "the family that prays together stays together." Congress added "under God" to the Pledge of Allegiance and required "IN GOD WE TRUST" to be put on all U.S. currency. While church membership doubled to 114 million between 1945 and 1960, the *intensity* of faith diminished for some, as mainstream churches downplayed sin and evil and preached Americanism and fellowship. Yet millions of others, alienated by the rapidity of social change and appalled at the secular hedonism of modern life, embraced evangelical fundamentalism, becoming "born again" Christians—a trend that would swell in the coming decades.

Similarly, education swelled in the 1950s yet seemed to many to be less rigorous than in earlier decades. The baby boom inflated primary school enrollment by 10 million (compared with 1 million in the 1940s). California opened a new school every week throughout the decade and still faced a classroom shortage. The proportion of college-age Americans in higher education climbed from 15 percent in 1940 to more than 40 percent by the early 1960s. "Progressive" educators promoted sociability and self-expression over science and history. The "well-rounded" student became more prized than the highly skilled or intelligent student. Surveys of college students found them conservative, conformist, and careerist—a "silent generation" seeking security and comfort.

Few university faculty challenged the reigning thought of the day or addressed the problems of those in need. Historians downplayed class conflicts and highlighted the pragmatism of most Americans. Consensus—the widely shared agreement on most matters of importance, especially respect for private property and equal opportunity—was frequently depicted as central to America's history and greatness.

Postwar Culture

American culture reflected both the spirit of prosperity and Cold War anxiety. Enjoying more leisure time and fatter paychecks, Americans spent one-seventh of the GNP on entertainment. Spectator sports boomed, new symphony halls opened, and book sales doubled.

With the opening of a major exhibit of abstract expressionists by the Museum of Modern Art in 1951, New York replaced Paris as the capital of the art world. Like the abstract canvases of Jackson Pollock and the cool jazz of trumpeter Miles Davis,

introspection and improvisation characterized the major novels of the era. Popular writers, like J.D. Salinger and John Updike, presented characters vaguely dissatisfied with jobs and home, longing for a more vital and authentic existence but incapable of decisive action. Southern, African American, and Jewish American writers turned out the decade's most vital fiction. William Faulkner continued his dense saga of Yoknapatawpha County, Mississippi, while Eudora Welty evoked southern small-town life in *The Ponder Heart* (1954). The black experience found memorable expression in James Baldwin's *Go Tell It on the Mountain* (1953) and Ralph Ellison's *Invisible Man* (1951). Bernard Malamud's *The Assistant* (1957) explored the Jewish immigrant world, and Philip Roth's *Goodbye Columbus* (1959) dissected the very different world of upwardly mobile Jews.

Hollywood reflected the diminished interest in political issues, churning out westerns, musicals, and costume spectacles. Most films about contemporary life portrayed Americans as one happy white, middle-class family. Minorities and the poor remained invisible, and women appeared largely as "dumb blondes" or cute helpmates. As TV viewing soared, movie attendance dropped 50 percent, and a fifth of the nation's theaters became bowling alleys or supermarkets by 1960.

The Television Culture

No cultural medium ever grew so huge so quickly as television. In 1946, one in 18,000 households had a TV set; by 1960, nine of ten households had at least one TV, and more Americans had televisions than had bathrooms (see Figure 27.3).

Business capitalized on the phenomenon. The three main radio networks—ABC, CBS, and NBC—gobbled up virtually every TV station in the country and, just as in radio, they profited by selling time to advertisers who wanted to reach the largest possible audiences. *TV Guide* soon outsold all other periodicals. First marketed in 1954, the TV dinner altered the nation's eating habits. When Walt Disney produced a show on Davy Crockett in 1955, stores could not keep up with the massive demand for "King of the Wild Frontier" coonskin caps. TV could sell anything.

Initially, TV showcased talent and creativity. Opera performances appeared in prime time, as did sophisticated dramas and political documentaries. Early situation comedies featured ethnic working-class families. But as the price of TV sets came down and the chill of McCarthyism spread, the networks' caution and appetite for a mass audience transformed TV into a celebration of conformity

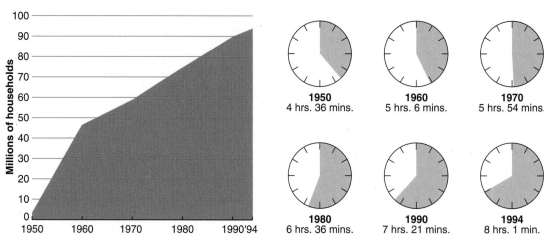

Households Owning Televisions

Average Daily Television Viewing

1950
4 hrs. 36 mins.

1960
5 hrs. 6 mins.

1970
5 hrs. 54 mins.

1980
6 hrs. 36 mins.

1990
7 hrs. 21 mins.

1994
8 hrs. 1 min.

FIGURE 27.3   THE TELEVISION REVOLUTION, 1950–1994 As televisions became commonplace in the 1950s, TV viewing altered the nature of American culture and politics.

and consumerism. Controversy went off the air. Most situation comedies portrayed perfectly coiffed moms who loved to vacuum in high heels, frisky yet obedient kids, and all-knowing dads. Even Lucille Ball and Desi Arnaz in *I Love Lucy*—which no network initially wanted because its all-American redhead was married to a Cuban—had a baby and left New York for suburbia.

Decrying TV's mediocrity in 1961, the head of the Federal Communications Commission called it "a vast wasteland." A steady parade of soaps, unsophisticated comedies, and violent westerns led others to call TV the "idiot box."

Measuring television's impact is difficult. Different people read the "texts" of TV (or of movies or books) in their own way and so receive their own messages from the medium. While TV bound some to the status quo, it raised expectations of others. It functioned both as a conservator and as a spur to change. In the main, however, television reflected existing values and institutions. It stimulated the desire to be included in American society, not to transform it. It spawned mass fads for Barbie dolls and hula hoops and spread the message of consumerism. It reinforced gender and racial stereotypes, rarely showing African Americans and Latinos—except in servile roles or prison scenes. It extolled male violence in fighting evil; it portrayed women as either zany madcaps or self-effacing moms.

Television also changed political life. Politicians could effectively appeal to the voters over the heads of party leaders, and appearance mattered more than content. At least 20 million watched Senator

> The head of the FCC called TV "a vast wasteland." Others called it the "idiot box."

THE BARBIE DOLL Based on a German-comic-strip-inspired blond bombshell doll named Bild-Lillie, the first Barbie doll made her debut in the United States in March 1959. She wore a black and white zebra-striped swimsuit, had a topknot ponytail, and was available as either a blonde or brunette. One of the very first products to have a marketing strategy based extensively on television advertising, Barbie would go on to become the best-selling doll ever—owning a wide range of vehicles, such as her pink Corvette convertible; having numerous careers, including flight attendant; and being able to speak a number of phrases, including "Will we ever have enough clothes?" and "I love shopping!" *(© Bettmann/Corbis)*

Joseph McCarthy bully and demean witnesses. Richard Nixon reached 58 million and saved his political career with his appeal in the "Checkers" speech, answering charges that he had received gifts and money from California businessmen. Eisenhower's pioneering use of brief "spot advertisements" clinched his smashing presidential victories. And in 1960, John F. Kennedy's "telegenic" image played a major role in his winning the presidency.

Overall, television helped produce a more national, homogenized culture, diminishing provincialism and regional differences. It vastly increased the cost of political campaigning while decreasing the content level of political discussion. And its overwhelming portrayal of a contented citizenry reinforced complacency and hid the reality of "the other America."

The Other America

"I am an invisible man," declared the African American narrator of Ralph Ellison's *Invisible Man*; "I am invisible, understand, simply because people refuse to see me." Indeed, few middle-class white Americans perceived the extent of social injustice in the United States. "White flight" from cities to suburbs physically separated races and classes. New expressways walled off ghettos and rural poverty from middle-class motorists speeding by. Popular culture focused on affluent Americans enjoying the "good life." But poverty and racial discrimination were rife and dire, and the struggles for social justice intensified.

Poverty and Urban Blight

Although the percentage of poor families (defined as a family of four with a yearly income of less than $3,000) declined from 34 percent in 1947 to 22 percent in 1960, 35 million Americans remained below the "poverty line." Eight million elderly had yearly incomes of less than $1,000. A third of the poor lived in depressed rural areas, where 2 million migrant farm workers experienced the most abject poverty. Observing a Texas migratory-labor camp in 1955, a journalist reported that 96 percent of the children had consumed no milk in the previous six months; eight out of ten adults had eaten no meat; and most slept "on the ground, in a cave, under a tree, or in a chicken house."

The bulk of the poor huddled in decaying inner-city slums. Displaced southern blacks and

MOTOROLA TV FAMILY AD The television set itself, so grandly advertised and displayed, was a symbol of postwar affluence, and both advertising and programming, which featured largely middle-class, consumption-oriented suburban families, stimulated the consumer culture. Overall, TV powerfully reinforced the conservative, celebratory values of everyday American life in the 1950s. *(Courtesy of Motorola Museum © 1955 Motorola, Inc/Picture Research Consultants & Archives)*

IN A KENTUCKY MINING TOWN Life was not the "nifty fifties" for many Americans. Nearly one in four lived below the poverty line, which was calculated by the federal government to be $2,973 for a family of four in 1959. The bottom 20 percent of Americans then owned only 0.05 percent of the nation's wealth. *(National Archives)*

Appalachian whites, Native Americans forced off reservations, and newly arrived Hispanics strained cities' inadequate facilities. Nearly two hundred thousand Mexican Americans were herded into San Antonio's Westside barrio. A local newspaper described them as living like cattle in a stockyard. As described by Michael Harrington in *The Other America: Poverty in the United States* (1962), the poor lived trapped in a vicious cycle of want and a culture of deprivation. Unable to afford good housing, a nutritious diet, and doctors, the poor got sick more often and for longer than more affluent Americans. Losing wages and finding it hard to hold steady jobs, they could not pay for the decent housing, good food, or doctors that would keep them from getting and staying sick. Children of the poor started school disadvantaged, quickly fell behind, and, lacking encouragement or expectation of success, dropped out. Living with neither hopes nor skills, the poor bequeathed a similar legacy to their children.

The pressing need for low-cost housing went unanswered. "Slum clearance" generally meant "Negro clearance," and "urban renewal" meant "poor removal," as developers razed low-income neighborhoods to put up parking garages and expensive housing. Bulldozers razed the Los Angeles barrio of Chavez Ravine to make way for Dodger Stadium. Landlords, realtors, and bankers deliberately excluded nonwhites from decent housing. Half of the housing in New York's Harlem predated 1900. A dozen people might share a tiny apartment with broken windows, faulty plumbing, and gaping holes in the walls. Harlem's rates of illegitimate births, infant deaths, narcotics use, and crime soared above the averages for the city and the nation. "Where flies and maggots breed, where the plumbing is stopped up and not repaired, where rats bite helpless infants," black social psychologist Kenneth Clark observed, "the conditions of life are brutal and inhuman."

Latinos and Latinas

High unemployment on the Caribbean island and the advent of direct air service to New York in 1945 brought a steady stream of Puerto Ricans to the city, where they could earn four times the average wage on the island. From seventy thousand in 1940 to a quarter of a million in 1950 and then nearly a million in 1960, El Barrio in New York City's East Harlem had a larger Puerto Rican population and more bodegas than San Juan.

In New York, Puerto Ricans suffered from inadequate housing, employment, and schools and from police harassment. Like countless earlier immigrants, they gained greater personal freedom in the United States while losing the security of a strong cultural tradition. Family frictions flared in the transition to unaccustomed ways. Parents felt upstaged by children who learned English and obtained jobs that were closed to older Puerto Ricans. The relationship between husbands and wives changed as women found readier access to jobs than did men. Yet, however much they tried to embrace American ways, many could not enjoy the promise of the American Dream because of their skin color and language. Increasingly, they turned to organizations like Antonia Pantoja's Puerto Rican Association for Community Affairs (PRACA), which sought to end discrimination against Puerto Ricans and *Nuyoricans*—their children born in New York City.

Mexican Americans suffered the same indignities. Most were underpaid and segregated from mainstream American life. The presence of countless "undocumented aliens" compounded their woes.

After World War II, new irrigation systems added 7.5 million acres to the agricultural lands of the Southwest, stimulating demand for cheap Mexican labor. In 1951, to stem the resulting tide of illegal Mexican immigrants, Congress reintroduced the wartime "temporary worker" program that brought in seasonal farm laborers (*braceros*). Many stayed without authorization, joining a growing number of Latinos who entered the country illegally.

During the 1953–1955 recession, the U.S. government deported some 3 million allegedly undocumented entrants during the Eisenhower administration's "Operation Wetback" (*wetback* being a term of derision for illegal Mexican immigrants who supposedly swam across the Rio Grande to enter the United States). Periodic roundups, however, did not stop the millions of Mexicans who continued to cross the poorly guarded border. The **bracero program** itself peaked in 1959, admitting 450,000 workers. Neither the *Asociación Nacional México-Americana* (founded in 1950) nor the older League of United Latin American Citizens (LULAC) could stop the exploitation or widespread violations of the rights of Mexican American citizens.

The Mexican American population of Los Angeles County doubled to more than six hundred thousand, and the *colonias* of Denver, El Paso, Phoenix, and San Antonio grew proportionally as large. The most rural of all major ethnic groups in 1940, 85 percent of Mexican Americans lived in urban areas by 1970. As service in World War II gave Hispanics an increased sense of their own American identity and of their claim on the rights of American citizens, urbanization provided better educational and employment opportunities. Unions like the United Cannery, Agricultural, Packing and Allied Workers of America brought higher wages and better working conditions for their Mexican American members. Middle-class organizations included LULAC, the Unity League, and the GI Forum (established in 1949 after a funeral parlor in Texas refused to bury a deceased Chicano veteran). These groups campaigned to end discrimination and segregation and won important court decisions that declared school segregation of Mexican Americans unconstitutional (*Mendez*, 1947, and *Delgado*, 1948) and ended their exclusion from Texas jury lists (*Hernandez*, 1954).

The mobilization of Hispanic voters led to the election of the first Mexican American mayor, in El Paso, in 1958. Latinos also took pride in baseball star Roberto Clemente and their growing numbers in the major leagues, in Nobel Prize winners like biologist Severo Ochoa, and in Anthony Quinn and other Hollywood stars. But the existence of millions of undocumented aliens and the continuation of the *bracero* program stigmatized all Hispanics. Their median income was less than two-thirds that of Anglos. At least a third lived in poverty.

Native Americans

Native Americans remained the poorest minority, with a death rate three times the national average. Unemployment rates on reservations during

MEXICAN FARM LABORERS BEING DEPORTED BACK TO MEXICO Following World War II, the U.S government continued to use the *bracero* program when it needed inexpensive laborers to do the arduous work in the hot agricultural fields of the Sunbelt and then deported millions of Mexicans when it no longer needed them, as in this photo taken during "Operation Wetback" in the recession of 1953–1955. *(© Bettmann/Corbis)*

the 1950s reached a staggering 70 to 86 percent for some tribes. Congress again changed course, moving away from New Deal efforts to reassert Indian sovereignty and cultural autonomy and back toward the goal of assimilation. Between 1954 and 1962, Congress terminated treaties and withdrew financial support from sixty-one reservations. Proponents claimed such measures would increase "Indian self-sufficiency," but this termination policy, which reduced federal services, sold off tribal lands, and pushed Indians off the reservations, was disastrous. First applied to the Menominees of Wisconsin and the Klamaths of Oregon, who owned valuable timberlands, it further impoverished the tribes and transferred more than 500,000 acres of Native American lands to non-Indians.

To lure Indians off the reservations and into urban areas, and to speed the sale of Indian lands to developers, the government established the Voluntary Relocation Program. It provided Native Americans with moving costs, assistance in finding housing and jobs, and living expenses until they

obtained work. "We're like wheat," said one Hopi woman who went to the city. "The wind blows, we bend over. . . . You can't stand up when there's wind."

By 1960, about sixty thousand Indians had been relocated to cities. Some became middle class, generally losing their Indian identity in the process; some ended up on state welfare rolls, living in rundown shantytowns and addicted to alcohol; and nearly a third returned to their reservations. The National Congress of American Indians vigorously opposed termination, and most tribal politicians advocated Indian sovereignty, treaty rights, federal trusteeship, and the special status of Indians.

The Civil Rights Movement

The integration of baseball in 1947, spearheaded by the brilliant Jackie Robinson, symbolized a new robustness in the fight against racial discrimination and segregation in the postwar era. The war had heightened African American expectations for racial equality, and demands included a permanent

Fair Employment Practices Commission (FEPC), the outlawing of lynching, and the right to vote.

The Politics of Race

Fearful of black assertiveness in seeking the vote and in mobilizing grassroots forces, as during the war, white racists accelerated their repression and violence. In 1946, whites killed several black veterans in Georgia for daring to vote and blinded a black soldier for failing to sit in the rear of a bus in South Carolina. In Columbia, Tennessee, also in 1946, a white riot against blacks who were insisting on their rights led to the arrest of seventy African Americans and the jailhouse lynching of two of the prisoners.

These events horrified President Truman. Aware of the importance to the Democratic party of the growing African American vote, Truman also realized how much white racism damaged U.S. relations with much of the world. Genuinely believing that every American should enjoy the full rights of citizenship, Truman established the **President's Committee on Civil Rights** in late 1946 to investigate race relations. The committee's report, *To Secure These Rights,* published in 1947, called for the eradication of racial discrimination and segregation and proposed antilynching and antipoll tax legislation and enactment of a permanent FEPC. Boldly, Truman sent a special message to Congress in February 1948 urging lawmakers to enact most of the committee's proposals. Although Truman's subsequent actions would fall short of his rhetoric, the president insisted on closing the gap between the nation's ideals and its racist practices, and he issued executive orders barring discrimination in federal employment and creating a committee to ensure "equality of treatment and opportunity" for all persons in the armed services.

Jim Crow in Court

During the Truman presidency, moreover, the Supreme Court declared segregation in interstate bus transportation unconstitutional (*Morgan* v. *Virginia,* 1946) and outlawed restrictive housing covenants that forbade the sale or rental of property to minorities (*Shelley* v. *Kraemer,* 1948). Soon thereafter, reflecting the growing determination of black Americans to demand their rights, the NAACP's chief attorney, Thurgood Marshall, abandoned the call for greater equality within "separate but equal" under which, for example, a county in South Carolina with segregated schools could, and did, provide $179 in public funds per white student but only $43 per black student. Instead, Marshall undertook a direct attack on segregation

itself. He pursued a strategy built on an earlier federal court ruling that had prohibited the segregation of Mexican American children in California schools as well as on decisions in 1950 in which the Supreme Court significantly narrowed the possibility of separate law school and graduate education ever being constitutional.

In May 1954, the new Chief Justice appointed by Eisenhower, **Earl Warren** (1953), speaking for a unanimous Court, reversed the "separate but equal" doctrine of *Plessy* v. *Ferguson* (see Chapter 20) in the landmark case of **Brown v. Board of Education of Topeka.** Overturning more than sixty years of legal segregation, the Supreme Court ruled that separate educational facilities for blacks and whites were "inherently unequal," denying black children the "equal protection of the laws" guaranteed by the Fourteenth Amendment, and thereby unconstitutional. A year later, however, the Court decreed that school desegregation should proceed "with all deliberate speed"—an oxymoron that implied gradualism.

In the border states, some African American and white students sat side by side for the first time in history. But in the South, where segregation was deeply entrenched in law and custom, politicians vowed resistance, and President Eisenhower refused to press them to comply: "I don't believe you can change the hearts of men with laws or decisions." Although not personally racist, Ike never publicly endorsed the *Brown* decision. He privately called his appointment of Earl Warren "the biggest damn fool mistake I ever made" and later told an aide that *Brown* had "set back progress in the south at least fifteen years."

Encouraged by the president's indecisiveness, White Citizens' Councils organized to defend segregation, and the Ku Klux Klan revived. Declaring *Brown* "null, void, and of no effect," southern legislatures adopted a strategy of "massive resistance" to thwart compliance with the law. They closed down or denied state aid to school systems that desegregated and enacted pupil-placement laws that permitted school boards to assign black and white children to different schools. In 1956, more than a hundred members of Congress signed the **Southern Manifesto,** denouncing *Brown,* and that year not a single African American attended school with whites in the Deep South, and few did so in the Upper South (see Going to the Source).

The Laws of the Land

Southern resistance reached a climax in September 1957. Although the Little Rock school board had accepted a federal court order to desegregate Central High School, Arkansas governor Orval

blacks in the freedom struggle and to arouse white America's conscience.

In the 1950s, racism still touched even the smallest details of daily life. In Montgomery, Alabama, black bus riders had to surrender their seats so that no white rider would stand. Although they were more than three-quarters of all passengers, African Americans had to pay their fares at the front of the bus, leave, and reenter through the back door, sit only in the rear, and then give up their seats to any standing white passengers.

On December 1, 1955, **Rosa Parks,** for many years an officer of the Montgomery NAACP and a veteran of protests in the 1930s and 1940s to secure dignity and proper treatment of black folks, refused to get up so that a white man could sit. "I was not tired physically," she later wrote. "No, the only tired I was, was tired of giving in." Her arrest sparked Jo Ann Robinson of the Women's Political Council, and other blacks who had been engaged in the freedom struggle in Montgomery, to propose a boycott of the buses—the beginning of the mass phase of the civil-rights movement. They founded the Montgomery Improvement Association (MIA) to organize the protest, and elected **Martin Luther King, Jr.,** a twenty-seven-year-old preacher, to lead the boycott. "There comes a time when people get tired," declared King, articulating the anger of Montgomery blacks, "tired of being segregated and humiliated; tired of being kicked about by the brutal feet of oppression." The time had come, he continued, to cease being patient "with anything less than freedom and justice." "My soul has been tired for a long time," an old woman told a minister who had stopped his car to offer her a ride; "now my feet are tired, and my soul is resting." Montgomery African Americans—inspired by earlier protests and by *Brown*—trudged the streets, organized car pools, and raised thousands of dollars to carry on the fight, and when city leaders would not budge, blacks persisted for more than a year until the Supreme Court ordered the buses desegregated.

The Montgomery bus boycott demonstrated African American strength and determination.

ROSA PARKS BEING BOOKED Rosa Parks's arrest for refusing to give up her seat to a white man and move to the back of the bus inspired Montgomery's black leaders to strike a blow for freedom—to call for a boycott of the city bus system in protest. The massive response by the city's black community sparked the nonviolent civil disobedience phase of the struggle against white supremacy. *(AP Images)*

It shattered the myth that African Americans approved of segregation and that only outside agitators opposed Jim Crow. It affirmed the possibility of social change and inspired further protests elsewhere in the South. It vaulted Dr. King, whose oratory simultaneously inspired black activism and touched white consciences, into the national spotlight. As no one before, King presented the case for black rights in a vocabulary that echoed both the Bible and the Founding Fathers.

King's philosophy of civil disobedience fused the spirit of Christianity with the strategy of achieving racial justice by nonviolent resistance. Casting aside the legalistic strategies of the NAACP, direct action gave every African American an opportunity to demonstrate the moral evil of racial discrimination. King's insistence on nonviolence also diminished the likelihood of bloodshed. Preaching that blacks must lay their bodies on the line to provoke crises that would force whites to confront their racism, King urged his followers to love their enemies. By so doing, he believed, blacks would convert their oppressors and bring "redemption and reconciliation." In 1957, King and a group of black ministers formed the Southern Christian Leadership Conference (SCLC) "to carry on nonviolent crusades against the evils of second-class citizenship." Yet more than on leaders, the movement's triumphs in the decade ahead would depend on the thousands of African Americans who marched, rallied, and demonstrated courageously in grassroots protest movements.

New Tactics for a New Decade

Foreshadowing the massive grassroots activism to come, four black college students in Greensboro, North Carolina, entered the local Woolworth's on February 1, 1960, and sat down at the whites-only lunch counter, defying segregation. "We don't serve colored here," the waitress replied when the freshmen ordered coffee and doughnuts. The blacks remained seated. They would not be moved.

Impatient yet hopeful, taught by teachers who urged them to believe in themselves and stand up for their rights, the students would not accept the inequality their parents had endured. They vowed to sit-in until they were served. Six months later, after prolonged sit-ins, boycotts, and demonstrations by hundreds of students, and after violent white resistance, Greensboro's civic leaders grudgingly allowed blacks to sit down at hitherto segregated restaurants and be served.

The courageous example of the Greensboro "coffee party" catalyzed similar sit-ins throughout the border states and Upper South. Black students

confronted humiliations and violence: they endured beatings, cigarette-burnings, tear-gassing, and jailing in their sit-ins to desegregate eating facilities, as well as in their "kneel-ins" in churches, "sleep-ins" in motel lobbies, "wade-ins" on restricted beaches, "read-ins" at public libraries, "play-ins" at city parks, and "watch-ins" at segregated movie theaters. Yet they stayed true to nonviolent principles and refused to retaliate.

The determination of the students transformed the struggle for racial equality. Their activism and commitment emboldened black adults and other youths to act. Their assertiveness desegregated facilities and generated a sense of self-esteem and strength. "I myself desegregated a lunch counter, not somebody else, not some big man, some powerful man, but little me," claimed a student. By year's end, nearly fifty thousand people had participated in demonstrations, desegregating lunch counters and other public facilities in 126 southern cities. Each victory convinced others that "nothing can stop us now."

Newly encouraged and emboldened, the Congress of Racial Equality (CORE), which had been founded in World War II, organized a "freedom ride" through the Deep South in spring 1961 to dramatize the flouting of federal court decisions banning segregation in interstate transportation facilities. It aroused white wrath. Mobs beat the Freedom Riders in Anniston, Alabama, burning their bus, and they mauled the protestors in Birmingham, making the **Freedom Rides** front-page news. A week later, scores of racist southerners in Montgomery beat Freedom Riders with bats and iron chains, generating international publicity and indignation, which ultimately forced the Interstate Commerce Commission to require the desegregation of all interstate carriers and terminals.

Many of the Freedom Riders were members of the **Student Nonviolent Coordinating Committee** (SNCC). Brought together by Ella Baker of SCLC, they followed her advice to form their own independent organization in April 1960, and to strive for "more than a hamburger," more than a seat in a restaurant, more than a place in the bus. SNCC (known as "Snick") stressed both nonviolent civil disobedience and the need to stimulate local activism and leadership. Within months, SNCC volunteers spread out into Mississippi, organizing voting-rights campaigns and sit-ins; in fall 1961, it chose Albany, Georgia, as the site of a campaign to desegregate public facilities and secure the vote. There, wily local authorities avoided the overt violence that had won the Freedom Riders national sympathy. The Albany movement collapsed; but the lesson of Albany, and of the Freedom Rides, had been learned: only the provocation of cruel, vicious white violence generated national publicity and forced the federal government to intervene to protect the rights of African Americans. The young activists who learned that lesson and how to use the media skillfully would chart the course of the 1960s.

Seeds of Disquiet

Late in the 1950s, apprehension ruffled the calm surface of American life. Questions about the nation's values and goals, periodic recessions, rising unemployment, and the growing national debt made Khrushchev's boast that "your grandchildren will live under communism" ring in American ears. The growing alienation of American youth and a technological breakthrough by the Soviet Union further diminished national pride.

> "Your grandchildren will live under communism."

Sputnik

On October 4, 1957, the Soviet Union launched the first artificial satellite, **Sputnik** ("Little Traveler"). Weighing 184 pounds and only twenty-two inches in diameter, *Sputnik* dashed the American myth of unquestioned technological superiority. When *Sputnik II*, carrying a dog, went into a more distant orbit on November 3, Democrats charged that Eisenhower had allowed a "technological Pearl Harbor."

The Eisenhower administration disparaged the Soviet achievement, but behind the scenes pushed to have the American Vanguard missile launch a satellite. On December 6, with millions watching on TV, Vanguard rose six feet in the air and exploded. Newspapers ridiculed America's "Flopnik."

Eisenhower did not laugh. He more than doubled the funds for missile development and established the Science Advisory Committee, whose recommendations led to the creation of the National Aeronautics and Space Administration (NASA) in July 1958. By decade's end, the United States had launched several space probes and successfully tested the Atlas intercontinental ballistic missile (ICBM).

Spurred by *Sputnik*, Americans embarked on a crash program to improve American education. The National Defense Education Act (1958) for the first time provided direct federal funding to higher education, especially to improve the teaching of the sciences, mathematics, and foreign languages. Far more funds went to university research to ensure national security. By 1960, the U.S. government was funneling $1.5 billion to universities, a hundred-fold increase over 1940, and nearly a third of scientists and engineers on university faculties worked full-time on government research, primarily defense projects. Some observers dubbed it the "military-industrial-educational complex."

A Different Beat

Few adults considered the implications of affluence for the young, or the consequences of having a teenage generation stay in school instead of working. Few pondered how the young would respond to growing up in an age when traditional values like thrift and self-denial had declining relevance or to maturing when young people had the leisure and money to shape their own subculture. Little attention was paid to the decline in the age of menarche (first menstruation) or the ways that the relatively new institution of junior high school affected the behavior of youth. Despite talk of family togetherness, busy fathers paid little attention to their children, and mothers sometimes spent more time chauffeuring their young than listening to them. Much of what adults knew about teenagers (a noun that first appeared in the 1940s but was not commonly used until the 1950s) they learned from the mass media, which focused on the sensational and the superficial.

Accounts of juvenile delinquency abounded, portraying high schools as war zones, city streets as jungles, and teenagers as zip-gun-armed hoodlums. In truth, teenage crime had barely increased. But male teenagers sporting black-leather motorcycle jackets, their hair slicked into "ducktails," aroused adult alarm.

As dismaying to parents, young Americans embraced rock-and-roll. In 1952, Cleveland radio host Alan Freed, having observed white teenagers dancing to rhythm-and-blues records by such black performers as Chuck Berry and Bo Diddley, started a new radio program, "Moondog's Rock and Roll Party," to play "race music." In 1954, Freed took the program to New York, creating a national craze for "rock-and-roll," the very term that had been used in blues songs for sexual intercourse.

Just as white musicians in the 1920s and 1930s had adapted black jazz for white audiences, white performers in the 1950s transformed the heavy beat and suggestive lyrics of rhythm-and-blues into "Top Ten" rock-and-roll. In 1954, Bill Haley and the Comets dropped the sexual allusions from Joe Turner's "Shake, Rattle, and Roll," added country-and-western guitar riffs, and had the first major white rock-and-roll hit. When

Haley performed "Rock Around the Clock" in *The Blackboard Jungle*, a 1955 film about juvenile delinquency, many parents linked rock-and-roll with crime. Red hunters saw it as a communist plot to corrupt youth. Segregationists claimed it was a ploy "to mix the races." Psychiatrists feared it was "a communicable disease." Churches condemned it as the "devil's music."

"If I could find a white man who had the Negro sound and the Negro feel," said Sam Phillips, the

"ELVIS THE PELVIS" IN 1956 That year Elvis Presley skyrocketed to rock-and-roll stardom. His rebellious sensuality, which caused girls to scream and faint, and boys to imitate his gyrating hips, reflected a hunger for more immediate and vital experiences than was considered "proper" in the 1950s. *(AP Images)*

> "If I could find a white man who had the Negro sound and the Negro feel, I could make a million dollars."

owner of Sun Records in Memphis, "I could make a million dollars." He made it by finding **Elvis Presley.** Born in Tupelo, Mississippi, Elvis melded the Pentecostal music of his boyhood with the powerful beat and sexual energy of rhythm-and-blues. In songs like "Hound Dog" and "All Shook Up" he transformed the bland pop music that youth found wanting into a proclamation of teenage "separateness." Presley's gyrating pelvis and bucking hips—exuding sexuality—shocked middle-class adults, but the more adults condemned rock-and-roll, the more teenagers relished its assault on mainstream values. Record sales tripled between 1954 and 1960, and Dick Clark's *American Bandstand* became the decade's biggest TV hit. The songs for black artists written by the Jewish songwriters Jerry Leiber and Mike Stoller, the rocking versions of Mexican folk music by East Los Angeles' Richie Valens (Valenzuela), and Little Richard dancing on his piano nourished the roots of the coming youth revolt.

Portents of Change

Teens cherished rock-and-roll for defying adult propriety. They elevated characters like James Dean in *Rebel Without a Cause* (1955) to cult status for rejecting society's mores. They delighted in *Mad* magazine's ridiculing of the phony and pretentious in middle-class America. They customized their cars to reject Detroit's standards. All were signs of their distinctiveness from the adult world.

Nonconformist writers known as the **Beats** expressed a more fundamental revolt against middle-class society. In Allen Ginsberg's *Howl* (1956) and Jack Kerouac's *On the Road* (1957), the Beats scorned the conformity, religion, family values, and materialism of "square" America. They romanticized society's outcasts—the mad ones, wrote Kerouac, "the ones who never yawn or say a commonplace thing, but burn, burn, burn like fabulous yellow roman candles exploding like spiders across the stars." They glorified uninhibited sexuality and spontaneity in the search for "It," the ultimate authentic experience.

The mass media scorned the Beats, as they did all dissenters. But some college youth admired their rejection of conformity. They read poetry and listened to jazz; some even protested capital punishment and demonstrated against the continuing investigations of the House Un-American Activities Committee. Others decried the nuclear-arms race. In 1958 and 1959, thousands participated in Youth Marches for Integrated Schools in Washington.

Together with the Beats and rock music, this vocal minority of the "silent generation" revealed the currents of agitation just beneath the surface calm of centrist conformity. They heralded a youth movement that would explode in the 1960s.

CONCLUSION

A far more complex era than that implied in the stereotype of the "nifty fifties," the decade encompassed contradictions. Although mightier than any nation had ever been and basking in a level of material comfort previously unknown in world history, many Americans felt uneasiness as the Cold War continued and prosperity brought unsettling changes.

The postwar era was one of unparalleled affluence for most Americans. New technologies that increased productivity and high levels of government spending spurred an economic boom. Prosperity further enriched the rich, transformed the working class into the middle class, and left the poor isolated on a remote island of deprivation and powerlessness in "the other America."

Overall, the postwar United States, with its burgeoning suburbia and cornucopia of consumerism, seemed the very model of contentment and complacency—what Americans considered the good life. Despite the criticism by the Beats and intellectuals of conservatism and conformity, despite the alienation and rebelliousness of young people questioning their parents' embrace of the status quo, most middle-class whites ignored the seeds of disquiet along with the inequities in American society. Enjoying their private pleasures, they rejected radicalism, condoned the income disparity and persistent prejudice minorities encountered, extolled a benign and optimistic religion, lauded mass culture, and idealized traditional gender roles, domesticity, and togetherness. Busy working and consuming, they left for a future decade the festering problems of hidden poverty, urban decay, and racial injustice.

Still, the cracks in the picture of a placid people widened. Unrest competed with consensus. Although racism remained omnipresent, the seeds of struggle, planted in the 1930s and World War II, flowered in new campaigns to end racial discrimination and segregation. In the courts, the NAACP ceased requesting that separate facilities be equal and instead insisted that true equality required desegregation. And in the streets, Martin Luther King, Jr., SNCC, and CORE employed the techniques of nonviolent civil disobedience to attack Jim Crow, bringing some gains and stimulating an insurgency that spurred further challenges to make the nation live up to its ideals.

KEY TERMS

Jackie Robinson   (p. 829)

Sunbelt   (p. 837)

baby-boom generation   (p. 840)

Dr. Benjamin Spock   (p. 840)

Billy Graham   (p. 840)

bracero program   (p. 845)

President's Committee on Civil Rights   (p. 847)

Earl Warren   (p. 847)

Brown v. *Board of Education of Topeka*   (p. 847)

Southern Manifesto   (p. 847)

Rosa Parks   (p. 850)

Martin Luther King, Jr.   (p. 850)

Freedom Rides   (p. 851)

Student Nonviolent Coordinating Committee   (p. 851)

Sputnik   (p. 852)

Elvis Presley   (p. 854)

Beats   (p. 854)

FOR FURTHER REFERENCE

Glenn C. Altschuler, *All Shook Up: How Rock 'n' Roll Changed America* (2003). A superb social history of the music and the major issues arising from it.

Roger Biles, *The Fate of Cities: Urban America and the Federal Government, 1945–2000* (2011). A judicious documentation of federal urban policies.

Gary R. Edgerton, *The Columbia History of American Television* (2007). A highly readable and balanced introduction.

James Gilbert, *Men in the Middle: Searching for Masculinity in the 1950s* (2005). A significant addition to the literature.

Elizabeth Jacoway, *Turn Away Thy Son: Little Rock, The Crisis That Shocked the Nation* (2007). A major study.

Stephen P. Miller, *Billy Graham and the Rise of the Republican South* (2009). A scholarly analysis of the relationship between evangelicalism and the new conservatism.

Mae Ngai, *Impossible Subjects: Illegal Aliens and the Making of Modern America* (2005). A probing discussion of a continuing issue in contemporary America.

Barbara Ransby, *Ella Baker and the Black Freedom Movement: A Radical Democratic Vision* (2003). A compelling biography of a leading light in the Movement.

Harvard Sitkoff, *The Struggle for Black Equality* (25th Anniversary Edition, 2008). A landmark history of the civil rights movement.

Jessica Weiss, *To Have and to Hold: Marriage, the Baby Boom, and Social Change* (2000). An incisive study that places the family patterns of the 1950s in historical perspective.

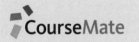

Liberalism, Civil Rights, and War in Vietnam,

1960–1975

MARTIN LUTHER KING, JR. *(AP Images)*

FACING THE NEARLY QUARTER of a million Americans who had come to Washington, DC, on August 28, 1963, to petition the government for civil rights, Martin Luther King, Jr., began by claiming that the appalling condition of African-Americans had barely changed in a century: "The life of the Negro is still sadly crippled by the manacles of segregation and the chains of discrimination. … One hundred years later, the Negro is still not free."

Blacks, King insisted, would not brook delay: "This sweltering summer of the Negro's legitimate discontent will not pass until there is an invigorating autumn of freedom and equality." There would be no tranquility in the nation until blacks were satisfied with their rights.

We can never be satisfied as long as our bodies, heavy with the fatigue of travel, cannot gain lodging in the motels of the highways and the hotels of the cities. We cannot be satisfied as long as the Negro's basic mobility is from a smaller ghetto to a larger one. We can never be satisfied as long as our children are stripped of their selfhood and robbed of their dignity by signs stating: "For Whites Only." We cannot be satisfied as long as the Negro in Mississippi cannot vote and the Negro in New York believes he has nothing for which to vote. No, no, we are not satisfied and we will not be satisfied until justice rolls down like the waters and righteousness like a mighty stream.

In less than fifteen minutes, King had tapped into both Christian and American symbolism to transform a masterful lobbying effort into the high-water mark of the black freedom struggle. Along with inspiring the enactment of the Civil Rights Act of 1964, which sounded the death knell for Jim Crow, and the Voting Rights Act of 1965, which enfranchised millions of southern blacks, King had helped redefine liberalism to embrace civil rights.

President John Kennedy launched the era with a promise to "pay any price, bear any burden" to win the Cold War and fulfill America's destiny as the last best hope of mankind. While his failures matched his successes both at home and abroad, JFK's rhetoric generated fervent hopes and lofty expectations. His assassination, at a time of peace and prosperity, would begin a long descent toward national disillusionment.

But first, his successor, Lyndon Johnson, brought forth the Great Society—the apex of liberalism, premised on the belief that an expanded state and democratic capitalism could end injustice and lift the economic and spiritual well-being of all. The Great Society promised health care for the aged and indigent, federal aid to education, urban

MARTIN LUTHER KING, JR. "I have a dream that one day this nation will rise up and live out the true meaning of its creed: 'We hold these truths to be self-evident, that all men are created equal.'" *(Frances Miller/Time Life Pictures/Getty Images)*

development, environmental safeguards, immigration that welcomed new Americans regardless of skin color or national origin, an end to racial discrimination and segregation, the enfranchisement of southern blacks, and an end to poverty.

But the liberal hope to enhance liberty and equality throughout the entire world crashed against defeat in Vietnam. African Americans and other minorities, demanding equality in fact as well as in law, became increasingly aggressive and less nonviolent. The racial strife of the "long hot summers," and the change from "Freedom Now" to "Black Power," splintered the movement and provoked a growing conservative reaction.

Much as Presidents Truman and Eisenhower did, their successors—JFK, LBJ, and Richard Nixon—all saw the need to preserve a non-Communist South Vietnam. The war they waged to thwart the spread of communism in Southeast Asia would cost America dearly in lives and dollars. It damaged the economy, fomented internal dissent, eroded public faith in elected officials, and transformed the brief era of triumphant liberalism into a time of discord and despair.

FOCUS Questions

- To what extent did the Kennedy administration's domestic record reflect its liberal rhetoric?

- What were the major successes and failures of the civil-rights movement from 1960 to 1968?

- How and why did the protest movements of minorities shift from the goals and tactics associated with Martin Luther King to those of Black Power?

- How did Lyndon Johnson's Great Society program exemplify the new liberalism of the 1960s?

- How and why did Kennedy, Johnson, and Nixon each deepen America's involvement in the war in Indochina?

The Kennedy Presidency, 1961–1963

Projecting an image of youthful vigor, **John F. Kennedy** personified the self-confident liberal who believed that an activist state could improve life at home and confront the communist challenge abroad. His wealthy father, Joseph P. Kennedy, seethed with ambition and instilled in his sons a passion to excel and to rule. Despite a severe back injury, John Kennedy served in the navy in World War II and came home a war hero. He then used his charm and his father's connections to win election in 1946 to the House of Representatives from a Boston district where he had never lived. Although Kennedy earned no distinction in Congress, Massachusetts voters sent him to the Senate in 1952 and overwhelmingly reelected him in 1958.

By then, Kennedy had a beautiful wife, Jacqueline, and a Pulitzer Prize for *Profiles in Courage* (1956), written largely by a staff member. Despite the obstacle of his Roman Catholic faith, he won a first-ballot victory at the 1960 Democratic convention. Just forty-two years old, he sounded the theme of a "New Frontier," to "get this country moving again."

A New Beginning

"All at once you had something exciting," recalled a University of Nebraska student. "You had a guy who had little kids and who

> "All at once you had something exciting."

liked to play football on his front lawn. Kennedy was talking about pumping new life into the nation and steering it in new directions." But most voters, middle aged and middle class, wanted the stability and security of Eisenhower's "middle way" promised by the Republican candidate, Vice President Richard M. Nixon. Although scorned by liberals for his McCarthyism, Nixon was better known and more experienced than Kennedy, identified with the still-popular Ike, and a Protestant.

Nixon fumbled his opportunity, agreeing to meet his challenger in televised debates. More than 70 million tuned in to the first televised debate between presidential candidates, a broadcast that secured the dominance of television in American politics. Nixon, sweating visibly, appeared haggard and insecure; in striking contrast, the tanned, telegenic Kennedy radiated confidence. Radio listeners judged the debate a draw, but the far more numerous television viewers declared Kennedy the victor. He shot up in the polls, and Nixon never recovered.

Kennedy also benefited from an economic recession in 1960 and from his choice of a southern Protestant, Senate Majority Leader Lyndon B. Johnson, as his running mate. Still, the election was the closest since 1884. Only 120,000 votes separated the two candidates. Kennedy's religion cost him

1960	John F. Kennedy elected president.
1961	Peace Corps and Alliance for Progress created.
	Bay of Pigs invasion.
	Berlin Wall erected.
1962	Cuban missile crisis.
1963	Civil-rights demonstrations in Birmingham.
	March on Washington.
	Test-Ban Treaty between the Soviet Union and the United States.
	Kennedy assassinated; Lyndon B. Johnson becomes president.
1964	Freedom Summer in Mississippi.
	Civil Rights Act.
	Gulf of Tonkin incident and resolution.
	Economic Opportunity Act initiates War on Poverty.
	Johnson elected president.
	Bombing of North Vietnam and Americanization of the war begin.
1965	Assassination of Malcolm X.
	Civil-rights march from Selma to Montgomery.

1965 (Cont.)	César Chávez's United Farm Workers strike in California.
	Teach-ins to question U.S. involvement in war in Vietnam begin.
	Voting Rights Act.
	Watts riot in Los Angeles.
1966	SNCC and CORE call for Black Power.
	Black Panthers formed.
	Massive antiwar demonstrations.
1967	Race riots in Newark, Detroit, and other cities.
1968	Vietnam peace talks open in Paris.
	Richard Nixon elected president.
1970	United States invades Cambodia.
1971	United States and South Vietnam invade Laos.
1973	Vietnamese cease-fire agreement signed.
1974	Indian Self-Determination Act.
1975	South Vietnam surrenders following North Vietnam's capture of Saigon.

millions of popular votes, but his capture of 80 percent of the Catholic vote in the closely contested midwestern and northeastern states delivered crucial Electoral College votes, enabling him to squeak to victory (see Map 28.1).

Kennedy's inauguration set the tone of a new era: "the torch has been passed to a new generation of Americans." In sharp contrast to Eisenhower's reliance on businessmen (see Chapter 27), Kennedy surrounded himself with liberal intellectuals. He seemed more a celebrity than a politician. He adorned his presidency with the trappings of culture and excellence, inviting distinguished artists to perform at the White House and studding his speeches with quotations from Emerson. Awed by his grace and taste—and his wit and wealth—the media extolled him as a vibrant leader and adoring husband. The public knew nothing of his fragile health, use of mood-altering drugs to alleviate pain, and extramarital affairs.

Kennedy's Domestic Record

Media images obscured Kennedy's lackluster domestic record. The conservative coalition of Republicans and southern Democrats that had stifled Truman's Fair Deal similarly doomed the New Frontier. Lacking the votes, JFK rarely pressed Congress for social legislation.

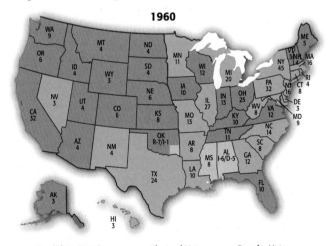

1960

Candidate (Party)	Electoral Vote		Popular Vote	
Kennedy (Democrat)	303	56.50%	34,226,731	49.7%
Nixon (Republican)	219	40.75%	34,108,157	49.5%
Byrd (Independent)	15	2.75%	501,643	0.7%

MAP 28.1   THE ELECTION OF 1960 © Cengage Learning. All rights reserved. No distribution allowed without express authorization.

Pressing for higher defense expenditures and investment incentives for private enterprise, JFK made stimulating economic growth his domestic priority. In 1961, he persuaded Congress to boost the defense budget by 20 percent. He vastly increased America's nuclear stockpile, strengthened the military's conventional forces, and established the Special Forces ("Green Berets") to engage in guerrilla warfare. By 1963, the defense budget reached its highest level as a percentage of total federal expenditures in the entire Cold War era. Kennedy also persuaded Congress to finance a "race to the moon," which Americans would win in 1969 at a cost of more than $25 billion. Most importantly, Kennedy took his liberal advisers' Keynesian advice to call for a huge cut in corporate taxes, which would greatly increase the deficit but would presumably provide capital for business to invest, stimulating the economy and thus increasing tax revenues.

When the Kennedy presidency ended tragically in November 1963, the proposed tax cut was bottled up in Congress. But Kennedy's spending on technology and the military had already doubled the 1960 rate of economic growth, and decreased inflation and unemployment, triggering the United States' longest uninterrupted economic expansion.

The boom would both cause further ecological damage and provide the affluence that enabled Americans to care about the environment. A growing concern for the environment would build on an older conservation movement, emphasizing the efficient use of resources, a preservation movement (focusing on preserving "wilderness"), and the fallout scare of the 1950s, which had raised questions about the biological well-being of the planet. The publication in 1962 of Rachel Carson's *Silent Spring* (see Chapter 27), documenting the hazards of pesticides, intensified concern. Additionally, postwar prosperity made many Americans less interested in increased production and more with the quality of life. In 1963, Congress passed a Clean Air Act, regulating automotive and industrial emissions. After decades of heedless pollution, Washington hesitantly began to address environmental problems.

Cold War Activism

Proclaiming in his inaugural address that "we shall pay any price, bear any burden, meet any hardship," to assure the "success of liberty," Kennedy launched a major military buildup and surrounded himself with Cold Warriors who shared his belief that American security depended on superior force and the willingness

> "We shall pay any price, bear any burden, meet any hardship."

to use it. He also increased economic assistance to Third World countries to counter the appeal of communism. The Peace Corps, created in 1961, exemplified the New Frontier's liberal anticommunism. By 1963, five thousand Peace Corps volunteers were serving two-year stints as teachers, sanitation engineers, crop specialists, and health workers in more than forty Third World nations.

In early 1961, a crisis flared in Laos, a tiny nation in Southeast Asia where a civil war between American-supported forces and Pathet Lao rebels seemed headed toward a communist triumph. In July 1962, Kennedy agreed to a face-saving compromise that restored a neutralist government but left communist forces dominant in the countryside.

Spring 1961 brought Kennedy's first major foreign-policy crisis. To turn back communism in the hemisphere, he approved a CIA plan, drawn up in the Eisenhower administration, to invade Cuba. In April, fifteen hundred anti-Castro exiles, "La Brigada," stormed Cuba's Bay of Pigs, expecting their arrival to trigger a general uprising to overthrow Fidel Castro. It was a fiasco. Deprived of air cover by Kennedy's desire to conceal U.S. involvement, the invaders had no chance against Castro's superior forces.

In July 1961, on the heels of the Bay of Pigs failure, Kennedy met with Soviet premier Nikita Khrushchev, who threatened war unless the West retreated from Berlin (see Chapter 26). A shaken Kennedy returned to the United States and declared the defense of West Berlin essential to the Free World. He doubled draft calls, mobilized reservists, and called for increased defense spending. The threat of nuclear war escalated until mid-August, when the Soviets constructed a wall to seal off East Berlin and end the exodus of brains and talent to the West. The Berlin Wall became a concrete symbol of communism's denial of personal freedom until it fell in 1989.

To the Brink of Nuclear War

In mid-October 1962, aerial photographs revealed that the Soviet Union had built bases for intermediate-range ballistic missiles (IRBMs) in Cuba, capable of striking U.S. soil. Smarting from the Bay of Pigs disaster, and believing his credibility at stake, Kennedy responded forcefully. He announced that the United States would "quarantine" Cuba—impose a naval blockade—to prevent delivery of more missiles and would dismantle by force the missiles already in Cuba if the Soviets did not do so.

The world held its breath. The two superpowers appeared on a collision course toward nuclear war. Soviet technicians worked feverishly to complete the missile launch pads, and Soviet missile-carrying

A PRESIDENT GREETS A FUTURE PRESIDENT At the White House on January 1, 1963, President John F. Kennedy greets a group of student leaders that includes a young Bill Clinton. *(Arnold Sachs/Hulton Archive/Getty Images)*

> "We're eyeball to eyeball. ... I think the other fellow just blinked."

ships steamed toward the blockade. U.S. B-52s armed with nuclear bombs took to the air, and nearly a quarter-million troops assembled in Florida to invade Cuba. Secretary of State Dean Rusk gulped, "We're eyeball to eyeball."

"I think the other fellow just blinked," a relieved Rusk remarked on October 25. Kennedy received a message from Khrushchev promising to remove the missiles if the United States pledged never to invade Cuba. As Kennedy prepared to respond

positively, a second, more belligerent message arrived from Khrushchev insisting that American missiles be withdrawn from Turkey as part of the deal. Hours later, an American U-2 reconnaissance plane was shot down over Cuba. Robert Kennedy then persuaded his brother to accept the first message and ignore the second one. The next morning Khrushchev pledged to remove the missiles in return for Kennedy's noninvasion promise. Less publicly, Kennedy subsequently removed U.S. missiles from Turkey.

Only after the end of the Cold War did the Russians disclose that Soviet forces in Cuba had possessed thirty-six nuclear warheads as well as nine tactical nuclear weapons for battlefield use and that Soviet field commanders had independent authority to use these weapons. Speaking in 1992, former secretary of defense Robert McNamara stated: "No one should believe that U.S. troops could have been attacked by tactical nuclear warheads without the U.S.'s responding with nuclear warheads. … And where would it have ended? In utter disaster."

Chastened by coming to the brink of nuclear war, Kennedy and Khrushchev installed a telephone "hot line" so that the two sides could communicate instantly in future crises and then agreed to a treaty outlawing atmospheric and undersea nuclear testing. These efforts signaled a new phase of the Cold War, later called détente, in which the superpowers moved from confrontation to negotiation. Concurrently, the **Cuban missile crisis** escalated the arms race by convincing both sides of the need for nuclear superiority.

The Thousand-Day Presidency

On November 22, 1963, during a trip to Texas to shore up the president's reelection chances, John and Jackie Kennedy rode in an open car along Dallas streets lined with cheering crowds. Shots rang out. The president slumped, dying, his skull and throat shattered. Soon after, aboard Air Force One, Lyndon B. Johnson was sworn in as president.

Grief and disbelief numbed the nation, as most Americans spent the next four days in front of TV sets staring at replays of the murder of accused assassin Lee Harvey Oswald; at the somber state funeral, with the small boy saluting his father's casket; at the grieving family lighting an eternal flame at Arlington National Cemetery. Few who watched would forget. Kennedy had helped make television central to American politics; now, in death, it made him the fallen hero-king of Camelot.

More admired in death than in life, JFK ranked as one of the very few "great" presidents, in the view of a public that associated him with a spirit of energy and innovation, with new beginnings. While Kennedy loyalists continue to stress his intelligence and ability to change, his detractors point to his lack of achievements, the discrepancy between his public image and his private philandering, his aggressive Cold War tactics, and his vast expansion of presidential powers.

Kennedy's rhetoric expressed the new liberalism, but he frequently compromised with conservatives and segregationists in Congress; economic expansion came from spending on missiles and the

JACK RUBY SHOOTING LEE HARVEY OSWALD Two days after Oswald's arrest for the assassination of President John Kennedy, as television cameras filmed his transfer to a different jail, Dallas nightclub owner Jack Ruby stepped from a crowd of onlookers and fatally shot Oswald. *(JACK BEERS/The Dallas Morning News)*

space race, not on social welfare. Partly because his own personal behavior made him beholden to FBI director J. Edgar Hoover, JFK allowed the agency to infringe on civil liberties, even as the CIA plotted with the Mafia to assassinate Fidel Castro. (Scholars are still trying to untangle the plots and policies that enmeshed the Kennedy brothers, Hoover, organized crime, and the national security agencies.)

Internationally, Kennedy left a mixed record. He signed the world's first nuclear-test-ban treaty, yet initiated a massive arms buildup. He compromised on Laos but deepened U.S. involvement in Vietnam. He came to question the need for confronting the Soviet Union yet insisted on U.S. global superiority and aggressively prosecuted the Cold War. However, JFK inspired Americans to expect greatness, aroused the poor and the powerless, and stimulated the young to activism. Dying during the calm before the storm, he left his successor soaring expectations at home and a deteriorating entanglement in Vietnam.

The Continuing Struggle for Black Equality, 1961–1968

Following the lunch-counter sit-ins and Freedom Rides, civil-rights activists eager to climb the next steps of racial justice pressed Kennedy to act. Yet the president continued to stall. Viewing civil rights as a thorny thicket to avoid, not as a moral issue, Kennedy feared it would split the Democratic Party, immobilize Congress in filibusters, and jeopardize his reelection. Yet the movement persisted until it had achieved de jure, or legal, equality; made protest respectable; and become an inspiration and model of activism for aggrieved others.

The African American Revolution

As television coverage of the struggle for racial equality brought mounting numbers of African Americans into the movement, civil-rights leaders beseeched Kennedy to intervene. They realized it would take decades of blood and bravery to dismantle segregation piecemeal; only comprehensive national legislation, backed by the power of the federal government, could guarantee full citizenship for African Americans. To achieve this goal, they needed a crisis that would outrage the conscience of the white majority and force the president's hand.

Determined to expose the violent extremism of southern racism and provoke a crisis, Martin Luther King launched nonviolent marches, sit-ins, and pray-ins in Birmingham, Alabama. In the most rigidly segregated big city in America, nicknamed "Bombingham" for the many past acts of violence against civil-rights protestors, few doubted Police Commissioner Eugene "Bull" Connor's pledge that "blood would run in the streets of Birmingham before it would be integrated."

When jailed for instigating a march that a local court had prohibited, King penned the "Letter from Birmingham Jail." It detailed the humiliations of racial discrimination and segregation, vindicated the nonviolent struggle against Jim Crow, and justified civil disobedience to protest unjust laws.

In May, thousands of schoolchildren, some only six years old, joined King's crusade. Connor lost his temper. He unleashed his men—armed with electric cattle prods, high-pressure water hoses, and snarling attack dogs—on the nonviolent youthful demonstrators. The ferocity of Connor's attacks, caught on camera and television, horrified the world.

"The civil-rights movement should thank God for Bull Connor," JFK remarked. "He's helped it as much as Abraham Lincoln." Connor's vicious tactics seared the nation's conscience and pushed Kennedy to help negotiate a settlement that ended the demonstrations in return for desegregating stores and

> Bull Connor pledged that "blood would run in the streets of Birmingham before it would be integrated."

BIRMINGHAM, 1963 The ferocious attempts by local authorities, led by Eugene "Bull" Connor, to repel nonviolent black protesters with fire hoses (capable of 100 pounds of water pressure per square inch), electric cattle prods, and snarling, biting police dogs—shown nightly on TV—made white supremacy an object of revulsion throughout most of the country and forced the Kennedy administration to intervene to end the crisis. *(AP Images)*

hiring black workers. By mid-1963, the rallying cry "Freedom Now!" reverberated across the nation as the protests grew. Increasingly concerned about America's image abroad as well as the "fires of frustration and discord" raging at home, Kennedy feared that if the government did not act, blacks would turn to violence. When Governor George Wallace refused to allow two black students to enter the University of Alabama in June 1963, Kennedy forced Wallace—who had pledged "Segregation now! Segregation tomorrow! Segregation forever!"—to capitulate to a court desegregation order.

On June 11, the president went on television to define civil rights as "a moral issue" and to declare that "race has no place in American life or law." A week later, Kennedy proposed a bill outlawing segregation in public facilities and authorizing the federal government to withhold funds from programs that discriminated. As the bill bogged down in Congress, civil-rights adherents planned to march on Washington to muster support for the legislation.

The March on Washington, 1963

The idea for a March on Washington had originally been proposed by A. Philip Randolph in 1941 to protest discrimination against blacks in the defense mobilization (see Chapter 25). Twenty-two years later, a quarter of a million people, including fifty thousand whites, converged on Washington, DC. After a long, sweltering day of speeches and songs, Martin Luther King took the podium to remind Americans that the hopes generated by the Emancipation Proclamation had still not been fulfilled and to reiterate his dream of true brotherhood, in which blacks would be an integral, equal part of American society, not embittered opponents of it.

With one of the greatest American speeches ever, portrayed at the beginning of this chapter, King turned a political rally into a historic event (see Beyond America). But not even that quelled the rage of white racists. In September, the Ku Klux Klan bombing of a black church in Birmingham killed four girls attending Sunday school. (Not until 2002 was the last of the four main suspects brought to justice.) And southern obstructionism still kept the civil-rights bill stymied in Congress.

Civil Rights at High Tide

Kennedy's assassination, however, brought to the White House a southerner, Lyndon Johnson, who knew he had to prove himself on the race issue or the liberals "would get me. ... I had to produce a civil rights bill that was even stronger than the one they'd have gotten if Kennedy had lived."

The resulting **Civil Rights Act of 1964**—the most significant civil-rights law in U.S. history—banned racial discrimination and segregation in public accommodations, outlawed bias in federally funded programs, granted the federal government new powers to fight school segregation, and created the Equal Employment Opportunity Commission (EEOC) to enforce the ban on job discrimination.

The Civil Rights Act did not, however, address the right to vote. So CORE and SNCC activists, believing the ballot held the key to power for southern blacks, mounted a major campaign to register black voters. They organized the Mississippi Freedom Summer Project of 1964 to focus on the state most hostile to black rights. Although 42 percent of Mississippi's population, blacks comprised only 5 percent of the registered voters. A thousand college-student volunteers assisted blacks in registering to vote and in organizing "Freedom Schools" that taught black history and emphasized African American self-worth. Harassed by Mississippi law-enforcement officials and Ku Klux Klansmen, the volunteers endured the firebombing of black churches and of movement headquarters, as well as arrests and even murders.

To show that blacks wanted to vote, the civil-rights workers enrolled nearly sixty thousand disfranchised African Americans in the Mississippi Freedom Democratic Party (MFDP). In August 1964, they took their case to the national Democratic convention, seeking to be seated as the proper delegation. "I was beaten till I was exhausted," Fannie Lou Hamer, the twentieth child of poor sharecroppers, told the convention. "All of this on account we wanted to register, to become first class citizens. If the Freedom Democratic party is not seated now, I question America." Despite her testimony, the MFDP was not seated. The disillusioned members of the MFDP, rejecting Johnson's compromise offer of two open delegate seats as a "token" gesture, then walked out of the convention.

Still determined to win a strong voting-rights law, however, King and the SCLC organized mass protests in Selma, Alabama, in March 1965. Blacks were half the population of Dallas County, where Selma was located, but only 1 percent were registered to vote.

King knew he again had to create a crisis to pressure Congress to act. He masterfully provoked Selma's county sheriff, Jim Clark, into brutally beating and arresting thousands of black protestors.

When civil-rights activists sought to march from Selma to Montgomery, to petition Governor George Wallace, Alabama state police stormed into the

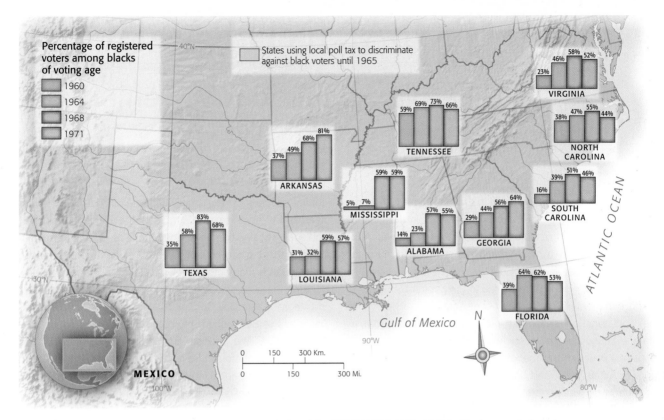

MAP 28.2 VOTER REGISTRATION OF AFRICAN AMERICANS IN THE SOUTH, 1960–1971 As blacks overwhelmingly registered to vote as Democrats, some former segregationist politicians, among them George Wallace, started to court the black vote, and many southern whites began to cast their ballots for Republicans, inaugurating an era of real two-party competition in the South. © Cengage Learning. All rights reserved. No distribution allowed without express authorization.

defenseless marchers, who were clubbed, shocked with cattle prods, and tear-gassed. Showcased on TV, the spectacle provoked national outrage and support for a voting rights bill.

Signed by the president in August 1965, the **Voting Rights Act** invalidated the use of any test or device to deny the vote and authorized federal examiners to register voters in states that had disfranchised blacks. The law dramatically expanded black suffrage, boosting the number of registered black voters in the South from 1 million in 1964 to 3.1 million in 1968, and transformed southern politics (see Map 28.2).

The number of blacks holding office in the South swelled from fewer than two dozen in 1964 to nearly twelve hundred in 1972, including half the seats on Selma's city council and the first two African Americans elected to Congress from the former Confederacy since the nineteenth century. Electoral success brought jobs for African Americans, contracts for black businesses, and improvements in facilities and services in black neighborhoods. Most importantly, as Fannie Lou Hamer recalled, when African Americans could not vote, "white folks would drive past your house in a pickup truck with guns hanging up on the back and give you hate stares. … Those same people now call me Mrs. Hamer."

Fire in the Streets

The civil-rights movement changed, but did not revolutionize race relations. It ended de jure racial discrimination and segregation, broke the white monopoly on political power in the South, and galvanized a new black sense of self-esteem. It raised hopes for the possibility of greater change and legitimated protest. But its inability to move beyond opportunity to achievement, to gain equality as a result, not just a right, underscored the limitations of liberal change, especially in the urban ghetto. The movement did little to change the deplorable economic conditions of many African Americans, and the anger bubbling below the surface boiled over.

On August 11, 1965, five days after the signing of the Voting Rights Act, a scuffle between white

> "White folks would drive past your house in a pickup truck with guns hanging up on the back and give you hate stares … Those same people now call me Mrs. Hamer."

The Black Freedom Movement

Most often discussed as an event in African American history and as a catalyst for other social movements in the United States, the Black Freedom Movement, in its origins and consequences, was a global phenomenon. It owed much to the ideological battle of the Cold War, when race became a national security issue, threatening to undermine U.S. claims of the superiority of democracy over communism. Although the Cold War led civil rights proponents to shrink from a broader critique of the American economic and political system, they counted on America's need to appeal to people of color in Africa, Asia, and Latin America to gain governmental support for black rights. In turn, Washington was eager to counter Communist propaganda that emphasized American racism and keen to maintain its stature as the "leader of the free world." The federal government began to view civil rights for African Americans as integral to its foreign policy mission.

For example, America's alleged mission to de-nazify and democratize West Germany took place amid separate, sub-standard accommodations for African American soldiers,

commanded almost exclusively by white officers, in the former heartland of Aryanism. Embarrassed, the Truman administration desegregated the military and broke precedent by submitting friend of the court briefs on behalf of the African American plaintiffs in the momentous *Brown* v. *Board of Education* cases. John Kennedy reversed course and submitted a civil-rights bill to Congress after Bull Connors's televised fire-hosing of demonstrators in Birmingham prompted international condemnation. Similarly, the criticism from abroad following violence against demonstrators in Selma helped push Lyndon Johnson to propose voting-rights legislation far sooner than he wished.

The movement also owed much to India's independence activist Mohandas Gandhi and to Africans struggling for their freedom and independence. Various African American leaders had avidly followed Gandhi's struggle against British colonialism, and Martin Luther King, Jr., as he led the Montgomery Bus Boycott, promoted the techniques and philosophy of Gandhian nonviolent civil disobedience. Often referred to in the press as "the American Gandhi," King made the strategy of nonviolent direct action his own, rooting his own Southern Christian Leadership Conference in Gandhian precepts of love, nonviolence, and reconciliation. His lead prompted activists in SNCC and CORE to apply Gandhian tactics in their own endeavors to end southern racism.

King had closely followed South African Albert Lutuli's efforts to make Gandhian nonviolence the keynote of the African National Congress struggle against apartheid, and like other African Americans, he had been persuaded by African anticolonialists such as Kenya's Tom Mboya and Ghana's Kwame Nkrumah that they were all part of a worldwide struggle by black people to control their own destiny. Seventeen African nations achieved independence between January and November 1960, and another seventeen freed themselves from colonial bondage by 1963. It

STUDENT PROTESTORS IN PARIS, MAY 1968 After the University Chancellor called in the police to arrest student protestors at the Sorbonne, continuing demonstrations and street battles with the police catalyzed the largest general strike in French history. *(Image by © Jacques Haillot/Apis/Sygma/Corbis)*

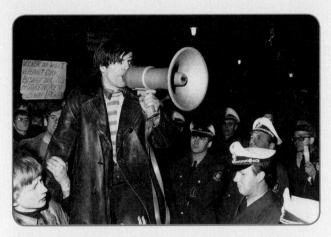

RUDI ("THE RED") DUTSCHKE One of the leaders of the West German SDS, Dutschke borrowed heavily from the U.S. antiwar movement and SNCC in his advocacy of militant direct action. *(AP Images)*

was an embarrassment to some: "All of Africa will be free before we can get a lousy cup of coffee," sneered black author James Baldwin. It was an inspiration to others: "We could hardly miss the lesson for ourselves," said SNCC's John Lewis. "They were getting their freedom, and we still didn't have ours in what we believed was a free country."

Soon after, it would be the black freedom struggle in the United States that would inspire the oppressed around the globe. In South Africa, Steve Biko's Students' Organization patterned itself on SNCC, Bishop Desmond Tutu repeatedly quoted Martin Luther King, and the Black Consciousness movement owed much to the American Black Power movement. To protest discrimination, Australian aborigines conducted Freedom Rides, and called them that. The leaders who freed Surinam from Dutch rule in 1975 credited the African American civil-rights campaigns for their tactics and motivation. The New Beginning Movement in Trinidad adopted the ideology and language of late-1960s African American militancy.

Trinidad, and most other Caribbean nations, also appropriated the protest music of African Americans. Songs such as the Impressions' "Keep on Pushing," Nina Simone's "Mississippi Goddam," and James Brown's "Say It Loud—I'm Black and I'm Proud," along with many others, carried specifically African American notions of dissent and self-esteem.

In Canada, the civil rights movement to the south raised the awareness and sense of liberation among that nation's 100,000 blacks. They too railed against the term "Negro" and condemned the disparities in income, health, occupation, and education between white and black Canadians. Young Native Canadian militants, criticizing the "Uncle Tomahawks" among their own people, assumed the leadership of organizations like the National Indian Brotherhood to promote the betterment of Indians and the recognition of aboriginal rights.

Much like the segregation of buses in Montgomery, a specific local irritant spawned a more pervasive movement in Northern Ireland. In May 1963—when the black struggle in the United States was headline news around the world—a group of young Catholic housewives in Dungannon organized to protest discrimination in the allocation of public housing. Amid talk of a march on the town like the proposed March on Washington, the local Catholic newspaper insisted that the Catholic minority in Northern Ireland were "white negroes."

Catholic protests against similar discrimination in the Springtown area of Derry led to sit-ins at the local council chamber. The demonstrators sang American civil rights songs and vowed to fight for their rights "as the Blacks in America were fighting." The Derry civil rights protests attracted new participants, particularly youths, who supplied unsuspected reservoirs of energy and initiative. In 1964 some university students set up the Working Committee on Civil Rights in Northern Ireland, the first Irish organization to use the term "civil rights" in its name. The various protest organizations soon engaged together in direct-action civil disobedience to protest discrimination and demand constitutional equality.

By 1968, the banners at mass protests in Northern Ireland invariably included "Civil Rights," the sit-ins included singing "We Shall Overcome," and police reaction included violence that inevitably fueled the discontent. In October 1968, a Belfast to Derry march modeled on the Selma to Montgomery march produced a baton charge by the Royal Ulster Constabulary analogous to the Alabama State Police charge on black marchers.

Moreover, as in the United States, the endless television replays of police attacking peaceful demonstrators sparked dissatisfaction with the slow pace of reform. Increasingly, the Catholic minority engaged in provocative street marches likely to bring violence in full view of the media. And as in the United States, it worked. The Northern Ireland and United Kingdom governments implemented a series of reforms, including universal adult suffrage for local council elections and a Fair Employment Act and Equal Opportunities Commission.

The civil-rights movement in Northern Ireland had brought change—but not enough. And again as in the United States, that shortcoming triggered a generational and ideological conflict. Young Irish militants, like their African American counterparts, demanded a far more radical transformation than their moderate elders. As one, Bernadette Devlin, admitted in her autobiography: "What we really wanted to do was pull the carpet off the floor to show the dirt that was under it." Yet as increasingly combative, less politically sophisticated youths joined the protests, mounting mayhem brought a backlash. Unlike in the United States, however, in Northern Ireland, "the troubles" became a conflict of murder and terror that would last for decades.

QUESTIONS FOR ANALYSIS

- How did the Cold War affect the U.S. civil rights movement?
- How did the U.S. civil rights movement affect protest movements in other countries?

police and blacks in Watts, the largest African American district in Los Angeles, ignited the most destructive race riot in decades. For six days, blacks looted shops, firebombed white-owned businesses, and sniped at police officers and firefighters, leaving in their wake thirty-four dead, nine hundred injured, and four thousand arrested.

Watts proved to be just a prelude to a succession of "long hot summers." In 1966, rioting erupted in more than a score of northern ghettos, forcing whites to heed the squalor of the slums and the brutal behavior of police in the ghetto—problems the civil-rights movement had ignored. Frustrated by the allure of America's wealth portrayed on TV and by what seemed the empty promise of civil-rights laws, black mobs stoned passing motorists, ransacked stores, torched white-owned buildings, and hurled bricks at the troops sent to quell the disorder.

The following summer, black rage at oppressive conditions and impatience with liberal change erupted in 150 racial skirmishes and forty riots—the most intense and destructive period of racial violence in U.S. history. In Newark, New Jersey, twenty-seven people died and more than eleven hundred were injured. The following week, Detroit went up in smoke in the decade's worst riot. By the time the Michigan National Guard and U.S. army paratroopers quelled the riot, forty-three people had died, two thousand were injured, and seven thousand had been arrested. Then in 1968, following the assassination of Martin Luther King (discussed in Chapter 29), black uprisings flared in the ghettos of a hundred cities. The 1964–1968 riot toll included two hundred dead, seven thousand injured, forty thousand arrested, and at least $500 million in property destroyed—mostly white-owned stores and tenements that exemplified exploitation in the ghetto.

A frightened, bewildered nation asked why rioting occurred just when blacks achieved many of their goals. Militant blacks saw the uprisings as revolutionary violence to overthrow a racist, reactionary society. The Far Right thought them evidence of a communist plot. Conservatives described them as senseless outbursts by troublemakers. The administration's National Advisory Commission on Civil Disorders (known as the Kerner Commission) indicted white racism for fostering an "explosive mixture" of poverty, slum housing, poor education, and police brutality. The commission recommended increased federal spending to create new jobs for urban blacks, construct additional public housing, and end de facto (existing in practice, but not in law) school segregation in the North. Johnson and Congress, however, aware of the swelling white backlash, ignored the advice, and most whites approved their inaction.

"Black Power"

For many young African Americans, liberalism's response to racial inequality proved "too little, too late." The demand for **Black Power** sounded in 1966 paralleled the fury of the urban riots. More a cry of rage than a systematic doctrine, it sprang from decades of white intransigence, from poverty in its rawest form, and from the growing sense that whites never conceded to black demands except through coercion.

Derived from a long tradition of black nationalism, autonomy, and race pride, Black Power owed much to the charismatic leadership of Malcolm X. A former drug addict and street hustler, Malcolm X had converted to the Nation of Islam, or the Black Muslim faith, while in prison. Founded in Detroit in 1931 by Elijah Poole (who took the Islamic name Elijah Muhammad), the Black Muslims insisted that blacks practice self-discipline and self-respect,

MALCOLM X AND MUHAMMAD ALI The Black Muslim minister, Malcolm X, who preached a message of black nationalism, self-help, and racial separation, was a charismatic figure to many young black men, including boxer Cassius Clay, who joined the Nation of Islam in 1964 and then took the name Muhammad Ali. More than any other African American leader of his day, Malcolm X's celebration of the African heritage and black self-sufficiency pointed the way to a new black consciousness. (© Bettmann/Corbis)

> "If ballots won't work, bullets will."

and they rejected integration. Malcolm X accordingly urged African Americans to separate themselves from the "white devil" and to relish their African roots and their blackness. Blacks, he asserted, had to rely on armed self-defense and seize their freedom "by any means necessary." "If ballots won't work, bullets will," he said. Malcolm X's assassination by members of the Nation of Islam in February 1965, after he had broken with Elijah Muhammad, did not still his voice. *The Autobiography of Malcolm X* (1965) became the main text for the rising Black Power movement.

Two days after winning the world heavyweight championship in 1964, boxer Cassius Clay shocked the sports world by announcing his conversion to the Nation of Islam and his new name, Muhammad Ali. Refusing induction into the armed services on religious grounds, Ali was found guilty of draft evasion, stripped of his title, and exiled from boxing for three and a half years during his athletic prime. Inspired by the examples of Ali and Malcolm X—and bitter at the failure of the established civil-rights organizations to achieve a fundamental distribution of wealth and power—young, urban African Americans abandoned nonviolence and reform. In 1966, CORE and SNCC changed from interracial organizations committed to achieving integration nonviolently to all-black groups advocating racial separatism and Black Power "by any means necessary."

The Black Panther Party for Self-Defense, founded in Oakland, California, in 1966 by Huey P. Newton and Bobby Seale, urged blacks to become "panthers—striking by night and sparing no one." Despite sponsoring community centers and school breakfast programs, the Panthers attained national notoriety from their paramilitary style and shoot-outs with the police. A violent and often illegal campaign of repression by federal, state, and local authorities left some Black Panthers dead and more in prison, further splintering the black–white civil-rights alliance and contributing to the rightward turn in politics.

The Black Power movement failed to alleviate the poverty and racism afflicting African Americans, and the concept remained amorphous—ranging from notions of black capitalism to local control of schools to revolutionary schemes to overthrow the American system. But Black Power celebrated black pride and stressed the importance of black self-determination as no mass movement had done before. Scores of new community self-help groups and self-reliant black institutions exemplified it, as did the establishment of black studies programs at colleges, the mobilization of black voters to elect black candidates, and the encouragement of racial self-esteem—"black is beautiful." As never before, African Americans rejected skin bleaches, gave their children Islamic names, and gloried in soul music. "I may have lost hope," SCLC leader Jesse Jackson had students repeating with him, "but I am … somebody … I am … black … beautiful … proud … I must be respected." This message, and Black Power's critique of American society, resonated with other marginalized groups, and helped shape their protests.

> "I am … somebody… I am … black… beautiful… proud… I must be respected."

The Struggle Goes On

As a result of civil-rights activism, millions of blacks experienced significant upward mobility. In 1965, black students accounted for less than 5 percent of total college enrollment; by 1990, the figure had risen to 12 percent, close to their proportion in the general population. By 1990, some 46 percent of black workers held white-collar jobs. TV's *Cosby Show*, a late-1980s comedy in which Bill Cosby played a doctor married to a lawyer, portrayed this upwardly mobile world.

Outside this world lay the inner-city slums, inhabited by perhaps a third of the black population. Here, up to half the young people never finished high school, and the jobless rate soared as high as 60 percent, owing to suburbanization and deindustrialization. In 1980, the poverty rate among African Americans stood at 32 percent, three times the rate for non-Hispanic whites.

Cocaine and other drugs pervaded the inner cities. Some black children recruited as lookouts for drug dealers eventually became dealers themselves. With drugs came violence. In the 1980s, a young black male was six times as likely to be murdered as a young white male. Drug abuse affected all social levels, including yuppies and show-business celebrities, but drug use and trafficking particularly devastated the inner cities. Serious social problems among those left behind in the inner cities, as well as upward mobility and educational advances by African Americans, would continue into the twenty-first century (as discussed in Chapter 31).

To compensate for past racial discrimination in employment and education, some cities set aside a percentage of building contracts for minority businesses, industries adopted hiring goals and recruitment training program, and many educational institutions reserved slots for minority applicants. These so-called **affirmative action** programs faced court challenges, however. In *University of California Regents* v. *Bakke* (1978), the Supreme Court declared racial quotas unconstitutional, yet also held that universities might consider race as a factor in admission "to remedy disadvantages cast on minorities by past racial prejudice."

The Expanding Movement for Equality

Native Americans, Hispanic Americans, and Asian Americans were similarly affected by liberalism. They, too, were inspired by Kennedy's rhetoric, by Johnson's actions, and by the assertive outlook of Black Power. Each followed the black lead in challenging the status quo, demanding full and equal citizenship rights, and emphasizing group identity and pride. And like blacks, each group saw its younger members push for ever more radical action.

Native American Activism

In 1961, representatives of sixty-seven tribes drew up a Declaration of Purposes criticizing the termination policy of the 1950s (see Chapter 27), and in 1964 hundreds of Indians lobbied in Washington for inclusion in the War on Poverty (covered later in this chapter). Indians suffered the worst poverty and the highest disease and death rates of any American group. President Johnson responded by establishing the National Council on Indian Opportunity in 1965, which funneled more federal funds onto reservations than any previous program. Promising to erase "old attitudes of paternalism," Johnson advocated Indian self-determination, "the right of the First Americans to remain Indians while exercising their rights as Americans."

Militant Native Americans, meanwhile, began to organize. By 1968, younger Indian activists, calling themselves "Native Americans," demanded "Red Power." They protested the lack of protection for Indian land and water rights and the desecration of Indian sacred sites. They established reservation cultural programs to reawaken spiritual beliefs and teach native languages. The Navajo and Hopi protested strip-mining in the Southwest, the Taos Pueblo organized to reclaim the Blue Lake sacred site in northern New Mexico, and the Puyallup held "fish-ins" to assert old treaty rights to fish in the Columbia River and Puget Sound.

The most militant group, the **American Indian Movement** (AIM), founded in 1968 by Chippewas, Sioux, and Ojibwa living in Minnesota, sought to stop police harassment of Indians in urban "red ghettos." In November 1969, AIM occupied Alcatraz Island in San Francisco Bay and held it for nineteen months. As one participant glowed, "we got back our worth, our pride, our dignity, our humanity." AIM's militancy helped foster a new sense of identity among American Indians and aroused other Native Americans to be proud of their heritage. Their members "had a new look about them, not that hangdog reservation look I was used to," Mary Crow Dog remembered, and they "loosened a sort of earthquake inside me." Many of the eight hundred thousand who identified themselves as Indians in the 1970 census did so for the first time and by 1990 their number had soared to 1.7 million.

> "We got back our worth, our pride, our dignity, our humanity."

Hispanic Americans Organize

As earlier in American history, immigration swelled the ranks of minority groups in the second half of the twentieth century. Of enormous significance, President Johnson proposed and Congress enacted the **Immigration Act of 1965,** abolishing the national-origins quotas of the 1920s. Annual legal immigration began an increase from 250,000 to well over a million, and the vast majority of new immigrants came from Asia and Latin America. The Latino, or Hispanic American, population increased from 4.5 percent in 1970 to nearly 12 percent in 2000. Less than 1 percent of the U.S. population in 1960, Asian Americans (discussed in the next section) comprised more than 4 percent in 2000. During the 1960s, these groups contributed to the general spirit of activism.

Like Native Americans, Latinos—the fastest-growing minority—became impatient with their establishment organizations, which had been unable to better their dismal conditions: a median annual wage half the poverty level, a functional illiteracy rate of 40 percent among Mexican American adults, and de facto segregation common throughout the Southwest. As they turned to the more militant tactics of the civil-rights movement, Latinos found a charismatic leader in **César Estrada Chávez.**

Born on an Arizona farm first cultivated in the 1880s by his grandfather, Chávez grew up a migrant farm worker, joined the U.S. navy in World War II, and then devoted himself to gaining union recognition and improved working conditions for the mostly Mexican American farm laborers in California. A magnetic leader who, like Martin Luther King, blended religion with nonviolent resistance to fight for social change, Chávez led his followers in the Delano vineyards of the San Joaquin Valley to strike in 1965. He and United Farm Workers (UFW) cofounder Dolores Huerta organized consumer boycotts of table grapes to dramatize the farm workers' struggle, often referred to as *La Causa*.

Chavez and Huerta made *La Causa* part of the struggle of the entire Mexican American community and of the larger national civil-rights movement. For the first time, farm workers gained the right to unionize to secure better wages; by mid-1970, two-thirds of California grapes were grown under UFW contracts. Just as the UFW flag featured an Aztec eagle and the Virgin of Guadalupe, Chávez combined religion, labor militancy, and Mexican heritage to stimulate ethnic pride and politicization.

Also in the mid-1960s, young Hispanic activists began using the formerly pejorative terms **Chicano and Chicana** to express a militant collective identity. "Our main goal is to orient the Chicano to *think* Chicano so as to achieve equal status with other groups, not to emulate the Anglo." Rejecting assimilation, Chicano student organizations came together in 1967 in *El Movimiento Estudiantil Chicano de Aztlan (MEChA)*. MEChA demanded bilingual education and more Latino teachers in high schools as well as Chicano studies programs and organizations at colleges.

Similar zeal led poet Rodolfo "Corky" Gonzales to found the Crusade for Justice in Colorado in 1965 to fight police brutality and foster Chicano culture. It led Reies Lopez Tijerina to form the *Alianza Federal de Mercedes* in New Mexico to reclaim land usurped by whites in the 1848 Treaty of Guadalupe Hidalgo. It also led Jose Angel Gutierrez and others in Texas to create an alternative political party in 1967, *La Raza Unida*, to elect Latinos and instill cultural pride. Across the West, Hispanic American activists created the "brown is beautiful" vogue and the paramilitary Brown Berets, with conceptual roots in the Black Panthers.

Similarly inspired, Puerto Ricans in New York City founded the Young Lords. Modeled on the Black Panthers, the Young Lords published a newspaper, started drug treatment programs, and even hijacked ambulances and occupied a hospital to demand better medical services in the South Bronx.

Meanwhile, a steady influx of immigrants, both legal and illegal, continued to arrive in the United States. Where most had once come from Europe, some 45 percent now came from the Western Hemisphere and 30 percent from Asia. As in the past, economic need drew these newcomers. Mexico's chronic poverty forced many to seek jobs in the north. But life in the United States was

CÉSAR CHÁVEZ César Chávez, from a farm worker family, founded the United Farm Workers to help migrant Mexican farm hands, who worked long hours for meager pay. Utilizing nonviolent protests, consumer boycotts, and personal hunger strikes, Chávez and his followers won the enactment in 1975 of a California law requiring growers to bargain collectively with the elected representatives of the farm workers. *(© Bettmann/Corbis)*

often harsh. In 1980, some 26 percent of persons of Hispanic origin in the United States lived in poverty, twice the national rate. Despite adversity, Hispanic newcomers preserved their language and traditions, influencing U.S. culture in the process.

Millions of Hispanic immigrants lacked official documentation. Many sweated in the garment trades, cleaned houses, held low-paying service-sector jobs, and labored in agricultural fields. The **Immigration Reform and Control Act of 1986,** an update of the 1965 Immigration Act, outlawed the hiring of undocumented immigrants but offered legal status to aliens who had lived in the United States for five years.

Asian American Activism

Like their counterparts, young activists with roots in East Asia rejected the term *Oriental* in favor of *Asian American,* to signify a new ethnic consciousness. Formed at the University of California in 1968, the **Asian American Political Alliance** encouraged Asian Americans to claim their own cultural identity and, in racial solidarity with their "Asian brothers and sisters," to protest against the U.S. war in Vietnam.

Asian American students marched, sat in, and went on strike to gain courses on Asian American studies or to protest repressive dictatorships in their homeland. Others worked to improve housing and working conditions for Asian Americans in need.

The Redress and Reparations Movement agitated to force the government to make restitution for the wartime internment of Japanese Americans.

None of these movements for ethnic pride and power, in later decades, would sustain the fervent activism and media attention they attracted in the late 1960s. But by elevating the consciousness and nurturing the confidence of the younger generation, each contributed to the empowerment of its respective group and to the politics of identity that would continue to grow in importance.

Liberalism Ascendant, 1963–1968

Although a New Dealer in the 1930s, **Lyndon Baines Johnson** came to be distrusted by liberals as "a Machiavelli in a Stetson" and regarded as a usurper by Kennedy loyalists. He had become the

THE LBJ TREATMENT Not content unless he could wholly dominate friend as well as foe, Lyndon Johnson used his body as well as his voice to bend others to his will and gain his objectives. *(Lyndon B. Johnson Presidential Library)*

36th President of the United States through the assassination of a popular president in his home state. Though just nine years older than JFK, he seemed a relic of the past, a back-room wheeler-dealer, as crude as Kennedy was smooth.

Yet Johnson had substantial political assets. He had served in Washington almost continuously since 1932, accruing enormous experience and a close association with the Capitol Hill power brokers. He excelled at wooing allies, neutralizing opponents, forging coalitions, and achieving results.

Demonstrating his determination to prove himself to liberals, Johnson deftly handled the transition of power, won a landslide victory in 1964, and guided through Congress the greatest array of liberal legislation in U.S. history, surpassing the New Deal. Needing to outdo JFK, even FDR, LBJ had both great talents and glaring flaws. His swollen yet fragile ego could not abide the sniping of Kennedy loyalists—and the press. Wondering aloud, "Why don't people like me?" Johnson labored to make the American Dream a reality for everyone and to vanquish all foes at home and abroad. Ironically, in seeking consensus and adoration, Johnson divided the nation and left office repudiated.

Johnson Takes Over

Calling for quick passage of the tax-cut and civil-rights bills as a memorial to JFK, Johnson used his skills to win passage of the Civil Rights Act of 1964 and a $10 billion tax-reduction bill, which produced a surge in capital investment and personal consumption that further spurred economic growth and shrank the budget deficit. More boldly, Johnson declared "unconditional **war on poverty** in America."

> Johnson declared "unconditional war on poverty in America."

Largely invisible in an affluent America, according to Michael Harrington's *The Other America* (1962), some 40 million people lived in a "culture of poverty," lacking the education, medical care, and employment opportunities that most Americans took for granted. To be poor, Harrington asserted, "is to be an internal alien, to grow up in a culture that is radically different from the one that dominates the society."

LBJ championed a campaign to bring these "internal exiles" into the mainstream. Designed to offer a "hand up, not a handout," the Economic Opportunity Act established the Office of Economic Opportunity to fund and coordinate such programs as a job corps to train young people in marketable skills; VISTA (Volunteers in Service to America), a domestic peace corps; Project Head Start, to provide compensatory education for preschoolers from disadvantaged families; an assortment of public-works and training programs; and a Community Action Program to encourage the "maximum feasible participation" of the poor in decisions that affected them.

Summing up his goals in 1964, Johnson offered his vision of the **Great Society,** a place of "abundance and liberty for all. It demands an end to poverty and racial injustice," yet is more concerned with "the quality of goals than the quantity of goods." It serves not merely "the demands of commerce but the desire for beauty and hunger for community."

The 1964 Election

Johnson's Great Society horrified the "new conservatives," such as William F. Buckley and the college students of Young Americans for Freedom (YAF). The most persuasive criticism came from Arizona Senator **Barry Goldwater.** A western outsider fighting the power of Washington and a fervent anticommunist, Goldwater advocated as little federal governmental intervention in the economy as possible and opposed government efforts to expand and protect civil rights and liberties.

Johnson's jibe that civil-rights leaders would have to wear sneakers to keep up with him evoked no laughter from southern segregationists or from blue-collar workers in northern cities who dreaded the integration of their neighborhoods, schools, and workplaces. Their support of Alabama's segregationist governor George Wallace in the spring 1964 Democratic presidential primaries heralded a "white backlash" against the civil-rights movement.

Buoyed by this backlash, right-wing Republicans gained control of the GOP in 1964. They nominated Barry Goldwater for the presidency and adopted a platform totally opposed to liberalism. Determined to offer the nation "a choice not an echo," Goldwater lauded his opposition to civil-rights legislation, denounced the War on Poverty, and accused the Democrats of a "no-win" strategy in the Cold War, hinting that he might use nuclear weapons against Cuba and North Vietnam. His stance appealed most to those angered by the Cold War stalemate, by the erosion of traditional moral values, and by the increasing militancy of African Americans. But his charge that the Democrats had not pursued total victory in Vietnam allowed Johnson to appear the apostle of restraint: "We are not going to send American boys nine or ten thousand miles from home to do what Asian boys ought to be doing for themselves."

LBJ won a landslide victory, 43 million votes to Goldwater's 27 million. The GOP lost thirty-eight House and two Senate seats. Many proclaimed the death of Republican conservatism. But Goldwater's coalition of economic, social, and religious conservatives, and anti-integrationist whites, presaged the Right's future triumph. It transformed the Republicans from a moderate, eastern-dominated party to one decidedly conservative, southern, and western. It built a national base of financial support for conservative candidates; catalyzed the creation of new conservative publications and think-tanks; energized volunteers like Phyllis Schlafly to campaign for Goldwater and stay involved in politics; and mobilized future leaders of the party, like Ronald Reagan. But in the short run, the liberals controlled all three branches of government.

The Great Society

"Hurry, boys, hurry," LBJ urged his aides. "Get that legislation up to the hill and out. Eighteen months from now ol' Landslide Lyndon will be Lame-Duck Lyndon." Johnson flooded Congress with liberal proposals. The results were astounding, outpacing even the dazzling array of legislation enacted in the first two years of the New Deal (see Table 28.1).

> "Hurry, boys, hurry. Get that legislation up to the hill and out."

The Eighty-ninth Congress expanded the War on Poverty and passed the Voting Rights Act. It enacted **Medicare** to provide health insurance for the aged under social security and a **Medicaid** health plan for the poor. By 1975, the two programs would be serving 47 million people and account for a quarter of the nation's health-care expenditures. The legislators also appropriated funds for public education and housing and for aid to Appalachia and inner-city neighborhoods. They created new cabinet departments of transportation and of housing and urban development as well as the National Endowments for the Arts and the Humanities. The first president to send a special message on the environment to Congress, Johnson won the enactment of measures to control air and water pollution, protect endangered species, set aside millions of acres of wilderness, and preserve the natural beauty of the American landscape. As noted, Congress enacted the Immigration Act of 1965, abandoning the quota system enacted in the 1920s that had discriminated against Asians and southern and eastern Europeans and transforming America's racial and ethnic kaleidoscope.

The Great Society improved the lives of millions. The proportion of the poor in the population

TABLE 28.1 Major Great Society Programs

Law	Provisions	Purpose
Tax Reduction Act (1964)	Cuts by some $10 billion the taxes paid to use deficit spending to stimulate primarily by corporations and wealthy economic growth individuals.	To use deficit spending to stimulate economic growth.
Civil Rights Act (1964)	Bans discrimination in public accommodations, prohibits discrimination in any federally assisted program, outlaws discrimination in most employment, and enlarges federal powers to speed school desegregation.	To end racial discrimination on the basis of race, religion, or sex.
Economic Opportunity Act (1964)	Authorizes $1 billion for a War on Poverty and establishes the Office of Economic Opportunity to coordinate Head Start, Upward Bound, VISTA, the Job Corps, and similar programs.	To end poverty in the United States.
Elementary and Secondary Education Act (1965)	Provides more than $1 billion to public and parochial schools for textbooks, library materials, and special-education programs.	To aid "educationally deprived children."
Voting Rights Act (1965)	Suspends literacy tests and empowers "federal examiners" to register qualified voters in the South.	To end the disfranchisement of African Americans.
Medical Care Act (1965)	Creates a federally funded program of hospital and medical insurance for the elderly (Medicare), and authorizes federal funds to the states to provide free health care for welfare recipients (Medicaid).	To provide health insurance for senior citizens and medical care for the poor.
Housing and Urban Development Act (1965)	Appropriates nearly $8 billion for low- and middle-income housing and for rent supplements for low-income families, and creates the cabinet-level Department of Housing and Urban Development.	To improve housing for the poor and urban beautification.
Appalachian Regional Development Act (1965)	Targets $1 billion for highway construction, health centers, and resource development in Appalachia.	To stimulate economic growth in this depressed area.
Immigration Act (1965)	Ends the discriminatory system of national-origins quotas established in 1924.	To increase immigration to the U.S., especially from Asia and Latin America.
Higher Education Act (1965)	Appropriates $650 million for scholarships and low-interest loans to needy college students and for funds for grants to college libraries.	To promote higher education for less-wealthy students.
National Endowments for the Arts and the Humanities Act (1965)	Creates new federally funded endowments.	To promote artistic and cultural activities and development.
Demonstration Cities and Metropolitan Development Act (1966)	Provides extensive subsidies for housing, recreational facilities, welfare, and mass transit to selected "model cities," and covers up to 80 percent of the costs of slum clearance and rehabilitation.	To improve the quality of life in urban America.
Motor Vehicle Safety Act (1966)	Sets federal safety standards for the auto industry and a uniform grading system for tire manufacturers.	To reduce auto accidents.
Truth in Packaging Act (1966)	Broadens federal controls over the labeling and packaging of foods, drugs, cosmetics, and household supplies.	To protect consumers from misleading product claims.

dropped from 22 percent in 1960 to 13 percent in 1969, infant mortality declined, and African American family income rose from 54 percent to 61 percent of white family income. The percentage of blacks living below the poverty line plummeted from 40 percent to 20 percent. Great Society programs gave those on the bottom reason to hope and a sense of entitlement to a fair share of the American Dream. But because Johnson oversold the Great Society and Congress underfunded it, rising expectations outdistanced results.

For many in need, the Great Society remained more a dream than a reality. The war against poverty, Martin Luther King, Jr., asserted, was "shot down on the battlefields of Vietnam." The Asian war diverted LBJ's attention from liberal reforms and devoured tax dollars that might have gone to the Great Society. Yet the perceived liberality of federal spending and the "ungratefulness" of rioting blacks, as well as the intrusive rulings of the Supreme Court, alienated many middle- and working-class whites. The Democrats' loss of forty-seven

TABLE 28.2 Major Decisions of the Warren Court

Court Case	Ruling	Significance
Brown v. Board of Education of Topeka (1954)	Racially segregated public schools violate the constitutional principle of equal treatment for all.	Outlawed segregation in public education.
Watkins v. U.S. (1957)	Congress's investigatory power is limited to matters directly pertinent to pending legislation.	Prohibited HUAC and other congressional committees from going on witch-hunts.
Yates v. U.S. (1957)	The Smith Act prohibits only the advocacy of concrete revolutionary action and not the preaching of revolutionary doctrine.	Ended the legal persecution of the Communist Party.
Baker v. Carr (1962)	The federal courts possess jurisdiction over state apportionment systems to ensure that the votes of all citizens carry equal weight.	Reduced the power of rural voters.
Engel v. Vitale (1962)	Requiring children to recite a prayer in public schools violates the separation of church and state.	Ended praying, and Bible reading the next year, in public schools.
Gideon v. Wainwright (1963)	States are required to provide attorneys at public expense for indigent defendants in felony cases.	Expanded the constitutional rights of alleged criminals.
New York Times Co. v. Sullivan (1964)	Public figures must prove "actual malice" to win libel suits against the press.	Expanded the First Amendment freedoms of the press.
Miranda v. Arizona (1966)	The police must advise a suspect of his or her constitutional right to remain silent and to have a counsel present during interrogation.	Broadened the rights of criminal suspects.
Loving v. Virginia (1967)	State antimiscegenation laws, which prohibit marriage between persons of different races, are unconstitutional.	Ended bans on interracial marriage.
Katzenbach v. Morgan (1968)	Upheld federal legislation outlawing state requirements that a prospective voter must demonstrate literacy in English.	Allowed Congress great latitude to expand the civil rights of minorities.
Green v. County School Board of New Kent County (1968)	So-called freedom-of-choice plans violate the *Brown* ruling that segregation in education is unconstitutional.	Placed burden of proof on schools to propose workable plans to end segregation.

House seats in 1966 ended the sway of congressional liberalism.

The Liberalism of the Warren Court

The Supreme Court, led by Chief Justice Earl Warren, far more liberal than public opinion or Congress, supported an activist government to protect the disadvantaged and accused criminals and expanded individual rights to a greater extent than ever before in American history.

In landmark cases (see Table 28.2), the Court prohibited Bible reading and prayer in public schools, limited local power to censor books and films, and overturned state bans on contraceptives. It ordered states to apportion legislatures on the principle of "one person, one vote," increasing the representation of urban minorities.

The Court's upholding of the rights of the accused in criminal cases, at a time of soaring crime rates, particularly incensed many Americans. Criticism of the Supreme Court reached a climax in 1966 when it ruled in **Miranda v. Arizona** that police must advise suspects of their right to remain silent and to have counsel during questioning. In 1968, presidential candidates Richard Nixon and George Wallace would win favor by promising to appoint judges who emphasized "law and order" over individual liberties.

The Vietnam Crusade, 1961–1975

The activist liberals who boldly tried to uplift the downtrodden also went to war to contain communism in Vietnam. The nation's longest war, and most controversial, would shatter the liberal consensus and divide the United States as nothing had since the Civil War.

Origins and Causes

American involvement in Vietnam grew out of the containment policy to stop the spread of communism. First as a means of strengthening our anti-Soviet ally France, President Truman authorized U.S. aid for French efforts to reestablish its colonial rule in Indochina. After the outbreak of war in Korea, with all of Asia now viewed as a Cold War battleground, Truman ordered vastly increased assistance for the French army fighting the Vietminh, a broad-based Vietnamese nationalist coalition led by the communist Ho Chi Minh. By 1954, the United States was paying three-quarters of the French war costs in Vietnam.

But the French were losing. In early 1954, the Vietminh besieged twelve thousand French troops in the valley of Dienbienphu. France appealed for U.S. intervention, and some American officials toyed with the idea of a nuclear strike, which President Eisenhower flatly rejected. In May, the French surrendered at Dienbienphu. An international conference in Geneva arranged a cease-fire and divided Vietnam at the seventeenth parallel, pending elections in 1956 to choose the government of a unified nation.

Although unwilling to go to war, Eisenhower would not accept a communist takeover of Vietnam. In what became known as the **domino theory,** Eisenhower warned that, if Vietnam fell to the communists, then Thailand, Burma, Indonesia, and ultimately all of Asia would follow. The United States refused to sign the Geneva Peace Accords and in late 1954 created the Southeast Asia Treaty Organization (SEATO), a military alliance patterned on NATO (see Chapter 26).

In June 1954, the CIA installed Ngo Dinh Diem, a fiercely anticommunist Catholic, as premier and then president of an independent South Vietnam. CIA agents helped him eliminate political opposition and block the election to reunify Vietnam specified by the Geneva agreements. As Eisenhower later admitted,

"possibly 80 percent of the population would have voted for the communist Ho Chi Minh as their leader." Washington pinned its hopes on Diem to maintain a noncommunist South Vietnam with American dollars rather than American lives.

But the autocratic Diem's Catholicism alienated the predominantly Buddhist population, and his refusal to institute land reform and end corruption spurred opposition. In December 1960, opponents of Diem coalesced in the communist-led **National Liberation Front** (NLF). Backed by North Vietnam, the insurgency soon controlled half of South Vietnam.

Kennedy and Vietnam

Following the 1962 compromise settlement in Laos, President Kennedy, resolved not to give further ground in Southeast Asia, stepped up clandestine operations against the North, ordered massive shipments of weaponry to South Vietnam, and increased the number of American forces there from less than seven hundred in 1960 to more than sixteen thousand by late 1963 (see Figure 28.1). Like Eisenhower, he believed that letting "aggression" go unchecked

> "Possibly 80 percent of the population would have voted for the communist Ho Chi Minh as their leader."

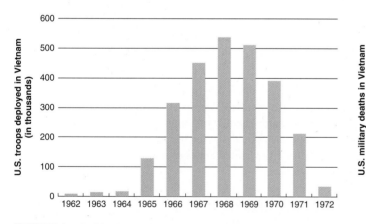

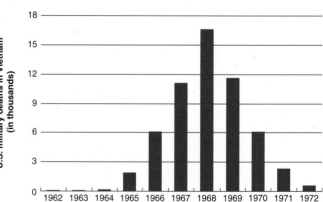

FIGURE 28.1 U.S. COMBAT IN VIETNAM After President Kennedy gradually increased the number of American advisers in Vietnam from less than a thousand to more than sixteen thousand, the continuing inability of South Vietnam to prevent the National Liberation Front, aided by North Vietnam, from winning led President Johnson to escalate the direct American involvement in the fighting—bringing a corresponding escalation of American combat fatalities. President Nixon then tried a policy of "Vietnamization," substituting American aid and weapons for American military personnel. It reduced American combat deaths but failed to defeat the North Vietnamese. © Cengage Learning. All rights reserved.

Source: Data from http://www.heritage.org/Research/NationalSecurity/cda06-02.cfm; and http://www.militaryfactory.com/vietnam/casualties.asp#13.

would lead to wider wars (the Munich analogy); thought that the communist takeover of one nation would lead to others going communist (the domino theory); and viewed international communism as a monolithic force, a single global entity controlled by Moscow and Beijing. He wanted to prove that the United States was not the "paper tiger" that Mao Zedong (Mao Tse-tung) mocked.

To counter Vietcong, or NLF gains in the countryside, the United States used both chemical defoliants, which destroyed vegetation and deprived the Vietcong of natural cover, and napalm bombs, whose petroleum jelly burned at 1,000 degrees and clung to whatever it touched, including human flesh. It also forcibly uprooted Vietnamese peasants and moved them into fortified villages, or "strategic hamlets," to prevent infiltration by the Vietcong. But South Vietnamese President Diem rejected American pressure to gain popular support through reform measures, instead crushing demonstrations by students and Buddhists. By mid-1963, Buddhist monks were setting themselves on fire to protest Diem's repression, and Diem's own generals were plotting a coup.

Frustrated American policymakers concluded that only a new government could prevent a Vietcong victory and secretly encouraged the coup to overthrow Diem. On November 1, South Vietnamese military leaders captured and murdered Diem and his brother, the head of the secret police. Although the United States promptly recognized the new government (the first of nine South Vietnamese regimes in the next five years), it too made little headway against the Vietcong. JFK now faced two unpalatable alternatives: increase the combat involvement of American forces or withdraw and seek a negotiated settlement.

What Kennedy would have done remains unknown. Less than a month after Diem's death, John Kennedy himself fell to an assassin's bullet. His admirers contend that by late 1963 he favored the withdrawal of American forces after the 1964 election. "It is their war ... it is their people and their government who have to win or lose the struggle," he proclaimed. Yet the president then restated the domino theory and promised that America would not withdraw from the conflict. Virtually all his closest advisers held that an American victory

ANTI-DIEM BUDDHIST PROTESTS After Diem's troops fired on Buddhists attempting to celebrate Buddha's 2,587th birthday, Buddhist monk Thich Quang Duc burned himself to death in downtown Saigon in June 1963. It was the first of several self-immolations in South Vietnam. Photographs and videotapes of these horrific protests, shown around the world, helped convince the Kennedy administration that Diem's leadership of South Vietnam could no longer be supported. *(AP Images)*

in Vietnam was essential to check communism in Asia. National Security Adviser McGeorge Bundy, Secretary of Defense Robert McNamara, and Secretary of State Dean Rusk would counsel Kennedy's successor accordingly.

Lyndon Johnson's Endless War

Now President Johnson had to choose between intervening decisively or withdrawing from a conflict that three previous presidents had insisted the communists must not win. Privately describing Vietnam as "a raggedy-ass fourth-rate country" undeserving of American blood and dollars, LBJ feared that an all-out American military effort might lead to World War III and foresaw that full-scale engagement in "that bitch of a war" would destroy "the woman I really loved—the Great Society." Yet Johnson also accepted the domino theory and Munich analogy and saw both the nation's and his own credibility as on the line. He worried that a pullout would make him appear cowardly, threaten his liberal agenda, and leave him vulnerable to conservative attack.

Trapped between unacceptable alternatives, feeling like "a catfish who had just grabbed a big juicy worm with a right sharp hook in the middle of it," Johnson escalated a Vietnamese civil war into America's war, hoping that U.S. firepower would force Ho Chi Minh to the bargaining table. But the North Vietnamese and NLF calculated that they could gain more by outlasting the United States than by negotiating. In 1964, Johnson took steps to impress North Vietnam with American resolve and to block his opponent, Barry Goldwater, from capitalizing on Vietnam in the presidential campaign. He ordered the Pentagon to prepare for air strikes against North Vietnam; appointed General Maxwell Taylor, an advocate of escalation, as ambassador to Saigon; and had his advisers draft a congressional resolution authorizing an escalation of American military action. In early August, North Vietnamese patrol boats allegedly clashed with two U.S. destroyers in the Gulf of Tonkin (see Map 28.3). Privately surmising that the "navy might have been shooting at whales out there," Johnson publicly announced that Americans had been victims of Hanoi's "open aggression on the high sea." Never admitting that the U.S. ships took part in covert raids against North Vietnam, Johnson ordered retaliatory air strikes on North Vietnamese naval bases and asked Congress to pass the prepared resolution giving him the authority to "take all necessary measures to repel any armed attack" on American forces "and to prevent further aggression." Assured that this meant no "extension of the present conflict," the Senate passed the Gulf of Tonkin Resolution 88 to 2, and the House 416 to 0.

Privately, LBJ called the resolution "grandma's nightshirt—it covered everything." Although it was initially designed to deflect Goldwater's charge that he was weak on communism, Johnson also considered the resolution a blank check to commit U.S. forces if that became necessary. Yet he assured the public during the 1964 campaign that he would neither deploy American troops to fight in Vietnam nor extend the war by bombing North Vietnam.

Both assurances were short-lived. Early in 1965, Johnson ordered "Operation Rolling Thunder," the sustained bombing of North Vietnam. It would lead to the dropping of eight hundred tons of bombs a day on North Vietnam between 1965 and 1968, three times the tonnage dropped by all the combatants in World War II. Yet it neither forced Hanoi to negotiate nor stopped the flow of soldiers and supplies coming from North Vietnam via the so-called Ho Chi Minh Trail (see Map 28.3).

Unable to turn the tide by bombing, Johnson committed U.S. combat troops. Adopting a "meat-grinder" or attrition strategy, Johnson sought to inflict unacceptable casualties on the communists to force them to the peace table. Johnson sent 485,000 troops (a greater military force than the U.S. had deployed in Korea) to Vietnam by the end of 1967 (see Figure 28.1). But superiority in numbers and weaponry did not defeat an enemy that could choose when and where to attack and then melt back into the jungle. Determined to battle until the United States lost the will to fight, Hanoi matched each American troop increase with its own. No end was in sight.

First among pacifists and socialists, then on college campuses, and lastly in the wider society, a growing number of Americans opposed the war. In March 1965, students and faculty at the University of Michigan staged the first teach-in to raise questions about U.S. intervention. Later that spring, twenty-five thousand people, mainly students, rallied in Washington to protest the escalation. In 1966, large-scale campus antiwar protests erupted. Students demonstrated against the draft and university research for the Pentagon. They proved only a prelude to 1967's massive Spring Mobilization to End the War in Vietnam protests in New York and San Francisco, which drew half a million participants, and the October demonstrations at the Pentagon by another hundred thousand.

MAP 28.3 **THE VIETNAM WAR, TO 1975** Wishing to guarantee an independent, noncommunist government in South Vietnam, Lyndon Johnson remarked in 1965, "We fight because we must fight if we are to live in a world where every country can shape its own destiny. To withdraw from one battlefield means only to prepare for the next." © Cengage Learning.

LBJ HAUNTED BY VIETNAM As each step up the escalation ladder led to the next, and then the next, President Johnson increasingly felt trapped—caught in a war that he could not win and that was destroying his dream of a Great Society. *(Courtesy Paul Szep/Library of Congress)*

Intellectuals and clergy joined the chorus of opposition to the war. Some decried the massive bombing of an underdeveloped nation; some doubted the United States could win at any reasonable cost; some feared the demise of the Great Society and liberalism. In 1967, prominent critics, including Senator Robert Kennedy and Martin Luther King, spurred hundreds of thousands to participate in antiwar protests.

Critics also noted that the war's toll fell most heavily on the poor. Owing to college deferments, the use of influence, and a military-assignment system that shunted the better-educated to desk jobs, lower-class youths were twice as likely to be drafted and, when drafted, twice as likely to see combat duty as middle-class youths. About 80 percent of the enlisted men who fought in Vietnam came from poor and working-class families; only two of the twelve hundred men in Harvard's class of 1970 served in Vietnam.

TV coverage of the war further eroded support. Scenes of children maimed by U.S. bombs and of dying Americans, replayed nightly, laid bare the horror of war and undercut the optimistic reports of government officials. Americans shuddered as they watched U.S. troops, supposedly winning the hearts and minds of the Vietnamese, burn villages

and leave thousands of civilians mutilated or dead.

Yet for every protestor shouting "Hell No, We Won't Go!" many more war supporters affixed bumper stickers reading "America, Love It or Leave It!" Until 1968, most Americans either supported the war or remained undecided. "I want to get out, but I don't want to give up" expressed a widespread view. They were not prepared to accept a communist victory over the United States.

Equally disturbing was how polarized the nation had grown. **"Hawks"** would accept little short of total victory, whereas **"doves"** insisted on negotiating, not fighting. Civility vanished. As Johnson termed his critics "nervous Nellies" and refused to de-escalate, demonstrators paraded past the White House chanting, "Hey, hey, LBJ, how many kids did you kill today?" By 1968, the president had become a virtual prisoner in the White House, unable to speak in public without being shouted down. So ended an era of hope and liberalism.

> "Hell No, We Won't Go!"

The Tet Offensive and a Shaken President

In January 1968, liberal Democratic senator **Eugene McCarthy** of Minnesota, a Vietnam War critic, announced he would challenge LBJ for the presidential nomination. Pundits scoffed that McCarthy had no chance of unseating Johnson, who had won the presidency in 1964 by the largest margin in U.S. history. The last time such an insurgency had been attempted, in 1912, even the wildly popular Teddy Roosevelt had failed. Yet McCarthy persisted, determined that at least one Democrat should enter the primaries on an antiwar platform.

Suddenly, on January 31—the first day of Tet, the Vietnamese New Year—America's hopes for victory in Vietnam sank, and with them LBJ's political fortunes. NLF and North Vietnamese forces mounted a huge offensive, attacking more than a hundred South Vietnamese cities and towns, and even the U.S. embassy in Saigon. U.S. and South Vietnamese troops repulsed the offensive, inflicting a major military defeat on the communists, who failed to unleash a general uprising against the government in Saigon or to hold any South Vietnamese city. With the Viet Cong largely decimated, the brunt of the fighting now had to be borne by North Vietnamese troops.

Victory, however, came at an enormous psychological cost. The dramatic initial reports of the media, highlighting communist success and the immense scope of the Tet offensive, undercut Johnson administration claims of imminent victory, of "light at the end of the tunnel." They deepened the growing mood of gloom about the war and intensified doubts that the United States could win at an acceptable cost. Public approval of the president's conduct of the war fell to just 26 percent in the immediate aftermath of Tet.

After Tet, moreover, McCarthy's criticism of the war won many new sympathizers. *Time, Newsweek,* and influential newspapers published editorials urging a negotiated settlement. The nation's premier newscaster, Walter Cronkite of CBS, observed that, at best, the war would end in a stalemate. "If I've lost Walter," LBJ sighed, "then it's over. I've lost Mr. Average Citizen." The number of Americans who described themselves as prowar "hawks" slipped from 62 percent in January to 41 percent in March, while the antiwar "doves" jumped from 22 percent to 42 percent.

Beleaguered, Johnson pondered a change in American policy. When the Joint Chiefs of Staff sought 206,000 additional troops, he turned to old friends for advice. Former secretary of state and venerable Cold Warrior Dean Acheson told him, "the Joint Chiefs of Staff don't know what they're talking about." Clark Clifford, once a hawk and now secretary of defense, concluded "that the military course we were pursuing was not only endless but hopeless."

Meanwhile, nearly five thousand college students had swarmed to New Hampshire to stuff envelopes and ring doorbells for Eugene McCarthy in the nation's first primary contest. "Clean for Gene," they cut their long hair and dressed conservatively so as not to alienate potential supporters. McCarthy astonished the experts by winning nearly half the popular vote in a state usually regarded as conservative.

After this upset, twice as many students converged on Wisconsin to canvass its more liberal voters. Expecting Johnson to lose, Senator **Robert Kennedy,** also promising to end the war, entered the Democratic contest. Projecting the family's glamour and magnetism, Kennedy was the one candidate who Johnson feared could deny him renomination. Indeed, millions viewed Kennedy as the rightful heir to the White House. Appealing to minorities, the poor, and working-class ethnic whites, Kennedy became, according to a columnist, "our first politician for the pariahs, our great national outsider."

On March 31, Johnson surprised a television audience by announcing a halt to the bombing in North Vietnam. Adding that he wanted to devote all his efforts to the search for peace, LBJ then announced startlingly, "I shall not seek, and I will not accept, the nomination of my party for another term as your president." Embittered by the personal abuse he had endured and reluctant to polarize the nation further, LBJ inaugurated peace negotiations and called it quits. Both physically and emotionally spent, LBJ lamented, "The only difference between the [John F.] Kennedy assassination and mine is that I am alive and it has been more torturous." Two days later, pounding the final nail into Johnson's political coffin, McCarthy trounced the president in the Wisconsin primary.

Ignored and often forgotten in retirement, Johnson died of a heart attack in January 1973—on the same day the Paris Peace Accords ended America's combat role in Vietnam. In many ways a tragic figure, he had carried out Vietnam policies shaped by his predecessors and received little acclaim for his enduring domestic achievements, especially in civil rights and reducing poverty. Although he often displayed high idealism and generosity of spirit, the enduring image of LBJ remained that of a crude, overbearing politician with an outsized ego that masked deep insecurities.

Nixon's War

Following his election in 1968, President Richard Nixon plotted a strategy of détente—reduced tensions—with the USSR and China that hinged on ending the Vietnam War. The war had sapped American military strength, worsened inflation, and devastated Lyndon Johnson. "I'm not going to end up like LBJ, holed up in the White House afraid to show my face on the street. I'm going to stop the war. Fast."

The Nixon Doctrine, announced in August 1969, redefined America's role in the Third World as that of a helpful partner rather than a military protector. It reflected the war weariness of both the electorate and U.S. troops in Vietnam. Johnson's decision to negotiate rather than escalate had left American troops with the sense that little mattered except survival. Morale plummeted. Discipline collapsed. Racial conflict became commonplace and drug use soared. The army reported hundreds of cases of "fragging"—enlisted men killing officers. By war's end, 20 percent of the Americans who served in Vietnam, nearly 500,000, had received less-than-honorable discharges.

The toll of atrocities against the Vietnamese also mounted. Instances of Americans dismembering enemy bodies, torturing captives, and murdering civilians came to light. In March 1968, an army unit led by an inexperienced lieutenant, William Calley, massacred several hundred defenseless civilians in My Lai. Soldiers gang-raped girls, lined up women and children in ditches and shot them, and then burned the village. Revelations of such incidents, and the increasing number of returned soldiers who

THE MY LAI MASSACRE Under the command of First Lieutenant William Calley, the men of Charlie Company entered the small village of My Lai in March 1968 to attack the Vietcong believed to be there. Instead, they found unarmed civilians, mostly women and children, and massacred them. The military kept the incident secret for a year, but when news of the incident surfaced late in 1969, it became symbolic of the war's brutality and the futility of the U.S. effort in the Vietnam War. *(Ron Haeberle/TimeLife Pictures/Getty Images)*

joined Vietnam Veterans Against the War, undercut the already-diminished support for the war.

Despite pressure to end the war, Nixon would not sacrifice America's prestige. Seeking "peace with honor," he acted on three fronts. First: "Vietnamization," which would replace American troops with South Vietnamese. By 1972, U.S. forces had been cut from half a million to thirty thousand. Second: bypassing South Vietnamese leaders, Nixon sent Kissinger to negotiate directly, and secretly, with North Vietnam's foreign minister, Le Duc Tho. Third: to force the communists to compromise despite the U.S. troop withdrawal, Nixon escalated the bombing of North Vietnam and secretly ordered air strikes on Cambodia and Laos. He told an aide,

I want the North Vietnamese to believe I've reached the point where I might do anything to stop the war. We'll just slip the word to them that "for God's sake, you know Nixon is obsessed about communism. We

can't restrain him when he's angry—and he has his hand on the nuclear button"—and Ho Chi Minh himself will be in Paris in two days begging for peace.

The secret B-52 raids neither made Hanoi beg for peace nor disrupted communist supply bases. They did, however, undermine the stability of Cambodia, and increase North Vietnam infiltration of troops into that tiny republic. Nixon ordered a joint U.S.-South Vietnamese incursion into Cambodia at the end of April 1970. The invaders seized large caches of arms and bought time for Vietnamization. But the costs were high. It ended Cambodia's neutrality, widened the war throughout Indochina, and provoked massive American protests, culminating in student deaths at Kent State University and Jackson State (discussed in Chapter 29).

In February 1971, Nixon had South Vietnamese troops invade Laos to destroy communist bases there. The South Vietnamese were routed. Emboldened, North Vietnam mounted a major

Images of Vietnam

(AP Images)

(AP Images)

It is often said that a picture is worth a thousand words. These photographs show a crying, naked Vietnamese girl running down a road, her body burned by napalm, and a South Vietnamese police chief summarily executing a prisoner he believed to be a Vietcong. These images appeared on the front pages of newspapers and on television broadcasts around the world within a day after they were taken. Subsequently, they were reproduced and refashioned in an array of media. Note how they could be used as a means of persuasion, of judgment on the war, of critical reflection.

QUESTIONS

1. What makes these images so powerful and such successful examples of visual culture?
2. What do they expose—and what goes unstated?
3. How might they have affected public opinion regarding the war?

campaign in April 1972—the Easter Offensive—their largest since 1968. Nixon retaliated by mining North Vietnam's harbors and unleashing B-52s on its major cities, vowing: "The bastards have never been bombed like they are going to be bombed this time."

America's Longest War Ends

The 1972 bombing helped break the impasse in the Paris peace talks, stalemated since 1968. Just days before the 1972 presidential election, Kissinger announced that "peace is at hand." The cease-fire agreement he had secretly negotiated with Le Duc Tho required the withdrawal of all U.S. troops, provided for the return of American prisoners of war, and allowed North Vietnamese troops to remain in South Vietnam.

Kissinger's negotiation sealed Nixon's reelection, but South Vietnam's President Thieu refused to sign a cease-fire permitting North Vietnamese troops to remain in the South. An angry Le Duc Tho then pressed Kissinger for additional concessions, and Nixon retaliated with massive B-52 raids. The 1972 Christmas bombing of Hanoi and Haiphong, the most destructive of the war, roused fierce domestic opposition but broke the deadlock.

The Paris Accords, signed in late January 1973, essentially restated the terms of the earlier truce. It ended hostilities between the United States and North Vietnam, but left unresolved the differences between North and South Vietnam, guaranteeing that Vietnam's future would yet be settled on the battlefield. After the "decent interval" that Kissinger and Nixon had insisted upon, North Vietnamese troops in the spring of 1975 overran South Vietnam, took control of Saigon, and forced American helicopters to airlift the last remaining officials out of the besieged U.S. embassy, (see Table 28.3).

America's longest war had ended in defeat. It had left fifty-eight thousand American dead and three hundred thousand wounded. The expenditure of at least $150 billion (more than $700 billion in 2009 dollars) had damaged the economy, diverted resources from reform, and triggered huge budget deficits and inflation. It shattered the liberal consensus and inflamed dissent. "No more Vietnams" decided many in the military: the U.S. should not fight abroad unless its national security was clearly at stake, there was demonstrable public support, and it had the necessary means to accomplish the goal.

Virtually all who survived, wrote one marine veteran, returned "as immigrants to a new world. For the culture we had known dissolved while we were in Vietnam, and the culture of combat we lived in so intensely … made us aliens when we returned." Beyond media attention on the psychological difficulties of readjusting to civilian life, which principally fostered an image of them as disturbed and dangerous, the nation paid little heed to its Vietnam veterans—reminders of a war that Americans wished to forget.

Even fewer gave much thought to the 2 million Vietnamese casualties, or to the suffering in Laos, or the price paid by Cambodia. In 1975, the fanatical Khmer Rouge (Cambodian communists), led by Pol Pot, took power and turned Cambodia into a genocidal "killing field," murdering some 2 million, an estimated third of the population.

"We've adjusted too well," complained Tim O'Brien, a veteran and novelist of the war. "Too many of us have lost touch with the horror of war. … It would seem that the memories of soldiers should serve, at least in a modest way, as a restraint on national bellicosity. But time and distance erode memory. We adjust, we lose the intensity. I fear that we are back where we started. I wish we were more troubled."

CONCLUSION

Kennedy's liberal rhetoric captivated the media and obscured a so-so domestic record. Stymied by the conservative coalition in Congress, Kennedy did more to stimulate hope than to achieve change. Others would force changes from the bottom up, and the next president, Lyndon Johnson, would persuade Congress to make a reality of the liberal ideal of an activist government promoting a fairer life for all Americans.

Fed up with the more legalistic, cautious strategy of the civil-rights movement in the past, young African Americans in the 1960s initiated a new direct action phase in black America's struggle for equal rights. Their activism, bubbling up from the local level, and Martin Luther King's stirring oratory and leadership, led to the landmark Civil Rights and Voting Rights Acts, which ended the legality of racial discrimination and black disfranchisement, provided greater equality of opportunity for African Americans, and nurtured the self-esteem of blacks. However, the laws left untouched the maladies of the urban black ghetto. There, unfulfilled expectations and frustrated hopes exploded into rioting, which helped trigger a white backlash that undermined support for the liberal agenda.

For Kennedy's successor, Lyndon Johnson, that agenda meant Great Society legislation promoting health, education, voting rights, urban renewal,

TABLE 28.3 The Vietnam War: A Chronology

Year	Event
1945	Ho Chi Minh announces Declaration of Independence from France.
1950	French-controlled Vietnam receives U.S. financial aid and military advisers.
1954	Dienbienphu falls to Ho's Vietminh. Geneva Accords end Indochina War and temporarily divide Vietnam at the seventeenth parallel. Ngo Dinh Diem becomes South Vietnam's premier.
1955	Diem establishes the Republic of Vietnam. U.S. advisers take over training of South Vietnamese army (ARVN).
1960	National Liberation Front (Vietcong) formed.
1961	President John Kennedy markedly increases military aid to South Vietnam.
1962	Strategic-hamlet program put in operation.
1963	Buddhist protests commence. ARVN coup overthrows and assassinates Diem. 16,000 U.S. military personnel in Vietnam.
1964	General William Westmoreland takes charge of U.S. Military Assistance Command in South Vietnam. Gulf of Tonkin incident and subsequent U.S. congressional resolution. United States bombs North Vietnam. 23,300 U.S. military personnel in Vietnam.
1965	First American combat troops arrive in South Vietnam, at Danang. 184,000 U.S. military personnel in Vietnam.
1966	B-52s attack North Vietnam for first time. Senate Foreign Relations Committee opens hearings on U.S. in Vietnam. 385,000 U.S. military personnel in Vietnam.
1967	Major antiwar demonstrations in New York and San Francisco; protest march on the Pentagon. 485,600 U.S. military personnel in Vietnam.
1968	North Vietnamese forces surround Khesanh. Tet offensive. My Lai massacre. President Lyndon Johnson announces partial bombing halt and decision not to run for reelection. Peace talks begin in Paris. General Creighton Abrams replaces Westmoreland as commander of American troops in Vietnam. 536,000 U.S. military personnel in Vietnam.
1969	United States begins bombing North Vietnamese bases in Cambodia. Provisional Revolutionary Government (PRG) formed by Vietcong. First U.S. troop withdrawal announced after American military personnel in Vietnam reach peak strength of 543,400 in April. Ho Chi Minh dies. Nationwide antiwar protests in October. 475,200 U.S. military personnel in Vietnam.
1970	United States and South Vietnamese forces join in Cambodian incursion. Student protests force 400 colleges and universities to close following Kent State killings. Cooper-Church amendment limits U.S. role in Cambodia. Senate repeals Gulf of Tonkin Resolution. 334,600 U.S. military personnel in Vietnam.
1971	United States provides air support for South Vietnamese invasion of Laos. Antiwar rally of 400,000 in Washington. Daniel Ellsberg releases Pentagon Papers to the *New York Times*.
1972	North Vietnam launches first ground offensive since 1968. U.S. bombing and mining of North Vietnamese ports. Last U.S. ground troops leave South Vietnam. Preliminary peace agreement reached; National Security Adviser Henry Kissinger announces that "peace is at hand." South Vietnam rejects peace treaty. United States bombs Hanoi and Haiphong. 24,200 U.S. military personnel in Vietnam.
1973	Peace agreement signed in Paris by North and South Vietnam, the Vietcong, and the United States. End of U.S. draft. Congress passes War Powers Act. First American POWs released in Hanoi. U.S. bombing in Southeast Asia ends. Fewer than 250 U.S. military personnel in Vietnam.
1974	South Vietnam announces new outbreak of war.
1975	North Vietnamese offensive captures Danang. Senate rejects President Gerald Ford's request for emergency aid for South Vietnam. South Vietnam surrenders following North Vietnam's capture of Saigon. Khmer Rouge takes control in Cambodia. Pro-Hanoi People's Democratic Republic established in Laos.

immigration reform, federal support for the arts and humanities, protection of the environment, and a war against poverty—the most sweeping liberal measures since the New Deal, and a significant enlargement in the role of the federal government in the lives of most Americans. Although the aggressiveness and violence of some blacks, and the Great Society's vast expansion of governmental powers and expenditures, helped shatter the liberal consensus, many liberal programs endured. Most Americans still supported Social Security and Medicare, favored a safety net of benefits for those truly in need, and did not want an unmanaged economy or a polluted environment.

Still, in the riot-torn streets of the "long hot summers," and, above all, the rice paddies of

Vietnam, the liberal consensus exploded. To prevent South Vietnam from being taken over by the communists, Kennedy significantly increased the number and fighting role of American advisers in Vietnam and gave the green light for a coup to overthrow Diem, the unpopular head of the government in Saigon. Inheriting a deteriorating limited war from Kennedy, LBJ also chose to escalate America's involvement, hoping to force North Vietnam to negotiate a compromise. Three years later, a half-million American troops were stationed in Vietnam, and the United States was dropping more bombs on Vietnam than had been dropped in World War II. Still, the United States was no closer to achieving its objective, and Richard Nixon would fare no better. Although the nation had not been so deeply divided since the Civil War, Nixon's determination to prevent the United States from appearing a "pitiful helpless giant," kept the war dragging on for four more years, with increasing American casualties and destruction in Indochina, until he accepted the limitations of U.S. power and bowed to the resolution of the North Vietnamese. Yet, the bitterness engendered by the war, and its unprecedented—and, for many, humiliating—defeat, would linger, and the liberal idealism articulated by King would remain a dream.

KEY TERMS

John F. Kennedy   (p. 858)

Cuban missile crisis   (p. 862)

Civil Rights Act of 1964   (p. 864)

Voting Rights Act   (p. 865)

Black Power   (p. 868)

affirmative action   (p. 869)

American Indian Movement   (p. 870)

Immigration Act of 1965   (p. 870)

César Estrada Chávez   (p. 870)

Chicano and *Chicana*   (p. 871)

Immigration Reform and Control Act of 1986   (p. 871)

Asian American Political Alliance   (p. 871)

Lyndon Baines Johnson   (p. 872)

war on poverty   (p. 872)

Great Society   (p. 873)

Barry Goldwater   (p. 873)

Medicare   (p. 873)

Medicaid   (p. 873)

Miranda v. *Arizona*   (p. 875)

domino theory   (p. 876)

National Liberation Front   (p. 876)

"hawks"   (p. 880)

"doves"   (p. 880)

Eugene McCarthy   (p. 880)

Robert Kennedy   (p. 881)

FOR FURTHER REFERENCE

Christian G. Appy, *Patriots: The Vietnam War Remembered from All Sides* (2003). A fascinating oral history of the war.

Michal Belknap, *The Supreme Court under Earl Warren, 1953–1969* (2005). The soundest brief treatment of the Warren Court.

Mark Philip Bradley and Marilyn B. Young, eds., *Making Sense of the Vietnam Wars: Local, National, and Transnational Perspective* (2008). A comprehensive and analytical collection.

Joseph E. Lowndes, *From the New Deal to the New Right: Race and the Southern Origins of Modern Conservatism* (2008). A wide-ranging explanation.

John Prados, *Vietnam: The History of an Unwinnable War, 1945–1975* (2009). An indispensable, comprehensive synthesis.

Barbara Ransby, *Ella Baker and the Black Freedom Movement: A Radical Democratic Vision* (2003). A political and intellectual biography of a key African American woman activist.

Sean J. Savage, *JFK, LBJ, and the Democratic Party* (2004). A solid study of the two presidents as party leaders.

Harvard Sitkoff, *King: Pilgrimage to the Mountaintop* (2008). A concise biography of the radical, and relevant, Martin Luther King, Jr.

Roberta Ulrich, *American Indian Nations from Termination to Restoration, 1953–2006* (2010). The origins and aftermaths of federal termination.

Randall B. Woods, *LBJ: Architect of American Ambition* (2006). A highly readable study.

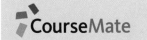 **CourseMate**

Visit the CourseMate website at **www.cengagebrain.com** for additional study tools and review materials for this chapter.

A Time of Upheaval, 1961–1980

GIRLS SAY YES

to boys who say NO

DOROTHY BURLAGE (*Courtesy of Dorothy Dawson Burlage*)

DOROTHY BURLAGE grew up in southeast Texas, a proper southern belle as well as a self-reliant "frontier woman." Her conservative Southern Baptist parents taught her to believe in the brotherhood of man and to conform to the conservative values of her old slaveholding community. At the University of Texas, she watched with awe as black students her age engaged in a civil-rights struggle she likened to a holy crusade.

She left her sorority, moved into the university's only desegregated dormitory, and joined the Christian Faith-and-Life Community, where she imbibed a heady brew of liberal Christian existentialism. Its commitment to nonviolent radical change propelled Burlage into the civil-rights movement's quest for the "beloved community." The young activists in SNCC became her political model, their ethos her moral beacon.

Burlage attended the founding conference of Students for a Democratic Society (SDS) in 1962. It exhilarated her to be with like-minded idealists from different backgrounds, eager to create a better world: "It was a rare moment in history and we were blessed to be given that opportunity." She gloried in peers who shared her values, reaffirmed her world view, and validated her activism. Burlage remained involved in SDS for the rest of the decade until, disillusioned by both the constant need to be "more radical and more willing to take risks to *prove* yourself" and the powerful conservative backlash, she ceased her activism and went back to school.

Commitment and then disengagement would characterize many of Dorothy's peers. The baby boomers in college spawned a tumultuous student movement and convulsive counterculture that gave the sixties its distinctive aura of upheaval. They exploded the well-kept world of the 1950s, when "nice" girls did not have sex or pursue careers, when African Americans feared to vote or assert themselves. They revived both the Left and Right. Then came 1968, the pivotal year. It had, *Time* magazine would later write, "the vibrations of earthquake about it. America shuddered. History cracked open. ... It reverberates still in the American mind."

Like an earthquake, for many Americans, the events of 1968 brought commitments and optimism crashing down. The decade that had begun with high hopes ended in deep disillusionment. One consequence was a widespread turning inward. Many in Dorothy's generation now became preoccupied with themselves—which again transformed the nation. Both an agent in and beneficiary of the era's transformation, Republican Richard Nixon would win the presidency in 1968 and then gain an overwhelming reelection victory in 1972. Presiding over the most radical changes in

THE JOAN BAEZ SISTERS AND DRAFT RESISTANCE By 1966, opposition to the draft had become a prominent aspect of the antiwar movement. Slogans such as "Girls say yes to boys who say no" popularized the protests against both the Vietnam War and universal military service for men. (*National Museum of American History, Smithsonian Institution, Gift of William Mears*)

American foreign policy since the start of the Cold War, Nixon ended U.S. involvement in Vietnam and inaugurated a period of détente, or reduced tensions, with China and the Soviet Union. In 1974, however, having flouted the very laws he had pledged to uphold, Nixon resigned in disgrace to avoid impeachment. His legacy was a public disrespect for politics seldom matched in U.S. history.

Despite the Watergate revelations, however, conservatism gained strength in the Ford and Carter administrations. As Americans tired of calls for equality and justice, and as jobs in the industrial sector withered, social activism declined and liberalism languished. Dorothy's and most of her peers' vibrant sense of American exceptionalism, innocence, and virtue perished, crushed by the disastrous war in Vietnam, unbridled dissent and disorder, the assassination of popular leaders, presidential lies and crimes, and the destruction—by rapidly rising energy costs and runaway inflation—of the long post–World War II economic boom.

FOCUS Questions

- In what ways did the student movement and counterculture shape the 1960s and 1970s?
- What were the major successes and failures of the Women's Liberation Movement?
- How did Richard Nixon's political strategy reflect the racial upheavals and radicalism of this era?
- What were the main causes and consequences of the Watergate scandal?
- What were the major failures of the Ford and Carter presidencies?

Coming Apart

By the 1960s, the number of American students pursuing higher education had risen from 1 million in 1940 to 8 million. More than half the U.S. population was then under age thirty. Their sheer numbers gave the young a collective identity and guaranteed that their actions would have impact. And not just in the United States. Major student demonstrations shook the governments of Japan, Korea, Turkey, and Venezuela in 1960, and many more would follow.

Most baby boomers followed conventional paths. They sought a secure place in the system, not its overthrow. They preferred beer to drugs and football to political demonstrations. They joined fraternities and sororities and majored in subjects that would equip them for the job market. Whether or not they went to college—and fewer than half did—the vast majority had their eyes fixed primarily on a good salary.

Many politically engaged young people mobilized on the right, joining organizations like Young Americans for Freedom (YAF), which by 1970 boasted fifty thousand members—far more than any other student group. Rather than John Kennedy, these youths idolized Barry Goldwater, who embodied the traditional values and muscular anticommunism they cherished. YAF would be the seedbed of a new generation of conservatives who later gained control of the GOP, yet it was overshadowed in the 1960s by young activists in the New Left.

Toward a New Left

Although a tiny minority of youth, an insurgent band of leftist students got the lion's share of attention. Most, comfortably middle-class, took economic security for granted, and felt "free" to criticize the shortcomings of the consumer society. Hopeful, they welcomed the idealism of the civil-rights movement, admired the mavericks and outsiders of the fifties, and answered the inspiring call of President Kennedy "to make a difference" and serve the nation.

In June 1962, some sixty students adopted the Port Huron Statement, a broad critique of American society and a call for more genuine human relationships. Proclaiming themselves "a new left," they organized the **Students for a Democratic Society** (SDS), which envisioned a nonviolent youth movement transforming the United States into a "participatory democracy" in which individuals would control the decisions that affected their lives. They pledged to revitalize American democracy and to end consumerism, militarism, and racism.

The generation of activists who found their agenda in the Port Huron Statement had their eyes opened by the police dogs in Birmingham, the assassination of President Kennedy, and the escalating war in Vietnam. Most never joined SDS but associated with what they vaguely called "the Movement" or "the New Left." Unlike the Leftists of the 1930s, they rejected Marxist ideology and emulated SNCC's style. Many became radicalized by the rigidity of campus administrators and mainstream liberalism's inability to achieve swift, fundamental change. Only a radical rejection of the liberal consensus, they presumed, could restructure society and create a genuinely democratic nation.

CHRONOLOGY 1961–1980

1964	Berkeley Free Speech Movement (FSM). The Beatles arrive in the United States.
1965	Ken Kesey and Merry Pranksters stage first "acid test."
1966	Abolition of automatic student deferments from the draft.
1967	March on the Pentagon. Israeli-Arab Six-Day War.
1968	Tet offensive. Martin Luther King, Jr., assassinated; race riots sweep nation. Students take over buildings at Columbia University. Robert F. Kennedy assassinated. Violence mars Democratic convention in Chicago. Vietnam peace talks open in Paris. Richard Nixon elected president.
1969	Apollo 11 lands first Americans on the moon. Nixon begins withdrawal of U.S. troops from Vietnam. Woodstock festival.
1970	United States invades Cambodia. Students killed at Kent State and Jackson State Universities. Beatles disband. Earth Day first celebrated.
1971	*Swann* v. *Charlotte-Mecklenburg Board of Education.* *New York Times* publishes *Pentagon Papers.* Nixon institutes wage-and-price freeze. South Vietnam invades Laos with the help of U.S. air support.
1972	Nixon visits China and the Soviet Union. SALT I agreement approved. Break-in at Democratic National Committee headquarters in Watergate complex. Nixon reelected president.
1973	Vietnam cease-fire agreement signed. Senate establishes special committee to investigate Watergate. President Salvador Allende ousted and murdered in Chile. Vice President Spiro Agnew resigns; Gerald Ford appointed vice president. *Roe* v. *Wade.* Yom Kippur War; OPEC begins embargo of oil to the West. Saturday Night Massacre.
1974	House Judiciary Committee votes to impeach Nixon. Nixon resigns; Ford becomes president.
1975	South Vietnamese government falls. Mayagüez incident.
1976	Jimmy Carter elected president.
1977	Panama Canal treaties ratified. Introduction of Apple II computer. Gay Pride parades in New York and San Francisco.
1978	Carter authorizes federal funds to relocate Love Canal residents.
1979	Menachem Begin and Anwar el-Sadat sign peace treaty at White House. Second round of OPEC price increases. Accident at Three Mile Island nuclear plant. Carter establishes full diplomatic relations with the People's Republic of China. Iran hostage crisis begins.

From Protest to Resistance

Returning from the Mississippi Freedom Summer to the Berkeley campus of the University of California in fall 1964, Mario Savio and other student activists tried to solicit funds and recruit volunteers near the campus gate, a spot traditionally open to political activities. Prodded by local conservatives, university administrators suddenly banned such practices; but when police arrested one of the activists, students surrounded the police car and kept it from moving. Savio then founded the **Berkeley Free Speech Movement** (FSM), a coalition of student groups insisting on the right to campus political activity. Likening the university to an impersonal machine, and its students to interchangeable machine parts, Savio insisted that "when the operation of the machine becomes so odious, makes you so sick to heart, you've got to put your bodies upon the gears and upon the wheels … and you've got to make the machine stop until we're free." More than a thousand students then sat-in on the administrative "gears." Their arrests led to more demonstrations and a strike by nearly 70 percent of the student body.

The conservative former movie star Ronald Reagan, running for governor in 1966, vowed to "clean up the mess at Berkeley," with its "Beatniks, radicals and filthy speech advocates" and its "sexual orgies so vile I cannot describe them." But the demands and tactics of the FSM reverberated on campuses nationwide. Students disenchanted with filing into impersonal buildings to endure lectures from remote professors initiated a wave of protests seeking greater involvement in university affairs. Their objectives changed the character of American higher education: curricular reform, the end of rules regulating dormitory life, and the admission of more minority students.

The escalation of the war in Vietnam, and the abolition of automatic student deferments from the draft in January 1966, transformed campus protests into a *mass* social movement. Initially buoyed with hope, activists set out to stop the war with peaceful protests. Popularizing the slogan "Make Love—Not War," SDS organized some two hundred new chapters and harassed campus recruiters for the Dow Chemical Company, the chief producer of flesh-burning napalm and the defoliant Agent Orange used on Vietnam forests. The futility of such protests alienated young antiwar protestors, and in 1967, SDS—urging a shift "From Protest to Resistance"—supported draft resistance and civil disobedience in selective service centers. By 1968, it claimed one hundred thousand members on three hundred campuses and attracted a half-million antiwar protesters to its spring Mobilization to End the War in Vietnam. With no end in sight, they chanted, "Burn cards, not people" (meaning draft cards) and "Hell no, we won't go!"

That spring, at least forty thousand students on a hundred campuses demonstrated against war and racism. In April, the SDS chapter at Columbia University demanded the university end all its military research projects, and the Students' Afro-American Society insisted it stop the construction of a new gymnasium, claiming that it encroached on the Harlem community. Shouting "Gym Crow must go," a thousand students barricaded themselves inside five campus buildings, declaring them "revolutionary communes" and holding them for six days. "Up against the wall, motherfucker," SDS's leader told the Columbia president. "This is a stickup."

Outraged by the brutality of the police who retook the buildings by storm, the moderate majority of Columbia students joined a sympathy boycott of classes that shut down the university for the rest of the semester. Similar scenarios recurred throughout the country, and elsewhere. Students in Czechoslovakia, France, Germany, Ireland, Italy, Japan, Mexico, and South Korea expressed their own revolutionary bombast. Their protests far exceeded in size and ferocity anything that occurred

MARIO SAVIO AT BERKELEY Speaking to students at the University of California at Berkeley in 1964, Mario Savio depicted the university as a faceless bureaucratic machine rather than a community of learning. Accordingly, he urged students to put their "bodies upon the gears" to stop the machine. The Free Speech Movement led by Mario Savio soon became the model for similar campus protests throughout the United States and the world. *(© Bettmann/Corbis)*

FLOWER POWER AT THE MARCH ON THE PENTAGON The year 1967 brought the start of truly significant nationwide protest against the Vietnam War. In October, an estimated 100,000 people attended an antiwar rally in Washington, and many sought to "invade" the Pentagon, the nerve center of the American war effort. *(© Bernie Boston)*

in the United States. In part, the turbulence of the young reflected the sheer numbers of the post-war baby boom in many nations, which produced a heightened sense of the power of youth, higher levels of expectations and impatience, and a huge number of university students attracted to noncon-formity and even rebellion. Satellite technology and new portable video cameras now made it easy to instantly transmit student uprisings in one nation to students around the globe.

The year 1969 saw the high point of the Movement with the New Mobilization, a series of huge antiwar demonstrations culminating in mid-November with a March Against Death. Three hundred thousand protestors descended on Washington to march in a candle-lit parade, carrying signs with the names of soldiers killed or villages destroyed in Vietnam. By 1972, antiwar sentiment would be nationwide. In contrast to the apolitical students of the 1950s, youth in the 1960s proved themselves able to challenge the authorities and inequities of American society.

Kent State and Jackson State

Although revulsion against the war continued to grow after Richard Nixon assumed office in 1969, his periodic announcements of troop with-drawals from Vietnam brought a lull in campus

demonstrations. On April 30, 1970, however, the U.S. invasion of Cambodia jolted a war-weary nation and reawakened student protest.

At Kent State University in Ohio, as elsewhere, antiwar students broke windows and torched the ROTC building. Nixon branded them "bums," his vice president compared them to Nazi storm troop-ers, and the Ohio governor slapped martial law on the university. Three thousand National Guardsmen in full battle gear rolled onto the campus in armored personnel carriers. On May 4, as six hundred Kent State students demonstrated, Guardsmen in Troop G, poorly trained in crowd control, opened fire on students retreating from tear gas, leaving four dead and eleven wounded. None had broken a law or was a campus radical.

Ten days later, Mississippi state patrolmen, responding to a campus protest, unleashed a bar-rage of gunfire at a women's dormitory at a black college, Jackson State, killing two students and wounding a dozen. Nationwide, students exploded in anger against the violence, the war, and the presi-dent. More than four hundred colleges and univer-sities, many of which had seen no previous unrest, shut down as students boycotted classes. The war had come home.

The nation was polarized. Most students blamed Nixon for widening the war, yet more Americans

"MY GOD, THEY'RE KILLING US" Following President Nixon's announcement of the military incursion into Cambodia, a formally neutral nation, many colleges exploded in anger. To quell the protests at Kent State University, where more than a thousand students clashed with local police, Ohio National Guardsmen fired on students, killing four. News of the shootings outraged many students nationwide, touching off yet another round of campus protests, which led hundreds of colleges to cancel final exams and shut down for the semester. *(John Filo)*

blamed the victims for the campus violence and criticized students for undermining U.S. foreign policy. Patriotism, class resentment against privileged college students, and a fear of social chaos underlay the condemnation of protesters. Many Kent townspeople shared the view of a local merchant that the guard had "made only one mistake— they should have fired sooner and longer." A local ditty promised, "The score is four, and next time more."

> The guard had "made only one mistake—they should have fired sooner and longer."

Legacy of Student Frenzy

The campus disorders after the invasion of Cambodia were the final spasm of a tumultuous, now fragmenting, movement. SDS shattered into desperate splinter groups, each seeking to prove itself more radical than the others. Endorsing terrorist violence, the "Weathermen" (Bob Dylan's "You Don't Need a Weatherman to Tell You Which Way the Wind Blows") launched the "Days of Rage" in Chicago, merely justifying the government's repression of the remnants of the antiwar movement. When a bomb planted by antiwar radicals destroyed a science building at the University of Wisconsin in summer 1970, killing a graduate student, most deplored the tactic. With the resumption of classes in the fall, the fad of "streaking"—racing across campus in the nude—more reminiscent of the 1920s than the 1960s, heralded a change in the student mood. By then, Nixon had significantly reduced the draft calls, and the entire conscription system was soon to be ended. Some antiwar activists turned to other causes, or to communes, careers, and parenthood.

The consequences of campus upheavals outlived the New Left. Student radicalism provoked

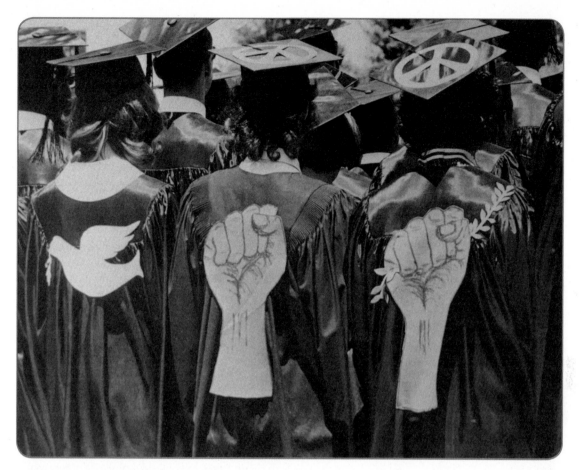

THE STUDENT MOOD AFTER KENT STATE While many older Americans supported the actions of the Ohio National Guard, students across the country boycotted classes and forced hundreds of campuses to shut down. Some continued to protest during graduation at the University of Massachusetts. *(© Bettmann/Corbis)*

a massive backlash from Americans who insisted that law and order was the basis of a civilized society. It spurred the resentment of millions of Americans, shattering the liberal consensus and propelling Republicans like Ronald Reagan to prominence. "If it takes a bloodbath, let's get it over with," he declared of militants in 1966. "No more appeasement!"

At the same time, the New Left helped mobilize campuses into a force that the government could not ignore, and it made continued U.S. involvement in Vietnam difficult. The Movement also liberalized many facets of campus life and made university governance less authoritarian: virtually ending dress codes and curfews, making ROTC an elective rather than a requirement, and forcing the increased recruitment of minority students and the proliferation of Black Studies programs. Such changes, however, fell short of the New Left vision of remaking society and politics. While masses of students could be mobilized in the short run for a particular cause, only a few made long-term commitments to Movement activism. The generation that the New Left had hoped would be the vanguard

of radical change preferred pot to politics, and rock to revolution.

The Countercultural Rebellion

The alienation and hunger for change that drew some youths into radical politics led others to cultural rebellion, to personal rather than political change, to discarding middle-class conformity, careerism, and sexual repression. A San Francisco journalist termed these young people **"hippies."** They disdained consumerism, preferring to make what they needed and share it with others. They donned simple garments and let their hair grow long. Love, cooperation, and immediate gratification became their mantra.

Many hippies joined communes and tribes that glorified personal liberation, helped bring ecology and alternative medicine into the mainstream, and disdained decorum. In urban areas such as San Francisco's Haight Ashbury or Chicago's Old

Town—"places where you could take a trip without a ticket"—communards experimented with drugs, mysticism, and uninhibited sexuality. Historian Theodore Roszack called them "a **'counter culture'** ... a culture so radically disaffiliated from the mainstream assumptions of our society that it scarcely looks to many as a culture at all, but takes on the alarming appearance of a barbarian intrusion."

Hippies and Drugs

Illustrative of the gap between the two cultures, one saw marijuana as a "killer weed," a menace to health and life, and the other thought it a harmless social relaxant. At least half the college students in the late sixties tried marijuana, and a minority used mind-altering drugs, particularly LSD. The high priest of LSD, Timothy Leary, preached "Tune in, turn on, drop out." On the West Coast, novelist Ken Kesey and his followers, the Merry Pranksters, conducted "acid tests" (distributing free tablets of LSD in orange juice) and created the "psychedelic" craze of Day-Glo-painted bodies gyrating to electrified rock music under flashing strobe lights.

Many youths distanced themselves from middle-class respectability, flaunting outrageous personal styles ("do your own thing") and shaggy beards; expressing contempt for consumerism by wearing surplus military clothing or torn jeans; and expanding the language to include *bummer, far-out,* and *groovy.* Typical of the generation that had been schooled in the deprivation and duty of the 1930s and 1940s, newly elected Governor Ronald Reagan of California responded by defining a hippie as one "who looked like Tarzan, walked like Jane, and smelled like Cheetah."

Musical Revolution

"This the dawning of the age of Aquarius," sang the cast of 1968's *Hair,* and the nation pulsed with music that both echoed and developed a separate generational identity, a distinct youth culture. In the early 1960s, the revived popularity of folk music mirrored youth's search for an "authentic" alternative to what they considered an artificial consumer culture. Expressing their idealism in protesting war and racism, Bob Dylan sang hopefully of changes "blowin' in the wind" and indignantly of changes that would "shake your windows and rattle your walls."

"Beatlemania" swept the country in 1964 (see Beyond America). The Beatles would soon be joined by Motown rhythm-and-blues black performers and eardrum-shattering acid rockers—extolling "sex, drugs, and rock-and-roll" for a generation at war.

In August 1969, 400,000 young people gathered for the **Woodstock festival** in New York's Catskill Mountains to celebrate their vision of freedom and harmony. For one long weekend, they reveled in rock music and openly shared drugs and sexual partners. One magazine claimed it "the model of how good we will all feel after the revolution." Many heralded Woodstock as the dawning of an era of love and peace—the Age of Aquarius.

> "Sex, drugs, and rock-and-roll."

Its luster had already dimmed. "Freedom's just another word for nothing left to lose," sang Janis

CHICANO MORATORIUM This march to protest the Vietnam War, held in East Los Angeles in 1970, brought together the Brown Power, Women's Liberation, and antiwar movements—all three of which drew ideological and tactical inspiration from the civil rights campaign of African Americans. *(Devra Weber)*

Joplin, one of a number of rock stars who would soon die of drug addiction. The pilgrimage of "flower children" to the Haight and to New York's East Village in the mid-sixties had brought in their wake a train of rapists and organized-crime dope peddlers. In August 1969, hippie Charles Manson and his "family" of runaways ritually murdered a pregnant movie actress and four of her friends, and the Rolling Stones hired the Hell's Angels motorcycle gang to guard them at their rock concert at the Altamont Raceway near San Francisco. While the Stones snarled "Street Fighting Man," the Hell's Angels terrorized spectators and stabbed and stomped a young black man to death. In 1970, the Beatles disbanded. John Lennon sang, "The dream is over."

> "The dream is over."

Advertisers awoke to the economic potential of the youth culture, using "revolution" to sell cars and jeans. Rock groups, commanding huge fees, became big business. Although the counterculture's quest for personal liberation undoubtedly sapped the forces of protest, it exerted a lasting influence on attitudes toward family life and sex. Self-fulfillment remained a popular goal, and the questioning of conventional values and authority became commonplace.

The Sexual Revolution

The counterculture's "if it feels good, do it" approach fit the hedonistic and permissive ethic of the 1960s, leading to a revolution in sexual norms. Although the AIDS epidemic and the graying of the baby boomers in the late 1980s chilled the ardor of promiscuity, liberalized sexual mores were more publicly accepted than ever before, making full gender equality and gay liberation realizable goals.

Many commentators linked the increase in sexual permissiveness to "the Pill"—an oral contraceptive that freed women from the threat of pregnancy. It became available in 1960, and by 1970, 10 million women were taking it. Still other women used the intrauterine device (IUD, later banned as unsafe) or the diaphragm. Many universities ended their rules on dormitory visits and living off campus, allowing more women to explore and enjoy their sexuality, but also increasing pressures from men for women to have sex lest they be labeled "frigid" and unliberated. Some states legalized abortion. In New York, one fetus was legally aborted for every two babies born in 1970. The Supreme Court's **Roe v. Wade** (1973) decision struck down all remaining state laws infringing on a woman's constitutional right to abortion during the first trimester (three months) of pregnancy.

The Supreme Court also threw out most laws restricting any "sexually explicit" art with "redeeming social importance." Mass culture exploited the new permissiveness. *Playboy* featured ever-more-explicit erotica, and women's periodicals encouraged readers to enjoy recreational sex. *The Joy of Sex* (1972)—a "Gourmet Guide to Love Making"—became a fixture in middle-class bedrooms. Hollywood filled movie screens with scenes of couples having sex; Broadway presented plays featuring full-frontal nudity and mock orgies; and even television presented dramas about, and frank discussions of, once-forbidden topics. Attitudinal changes brought behavioral changes, and vice versa. Cohabitation—living together without marriage—became thinkable to average middle-class Americans. Some marital counselors even touted "open marriage" (in which spouses are free to have sex with other partners) and "swinging" (sexual sharing with other couples) as cures for stale relationships. By the mid-1970s breakthroughs had clearly occurred—especially among college-educated young women—in attitudes toward premarital sex, homosexual relations between consenting adults, and abortion.

Influenced by changing norms of personal freedom and self-fulfillment, the institutions of marriage and family would be fundamentally altered. Freer social behavior and language spread throughout much of American society. But what some hailed as liberation others bemoaned as moral decay. Offended by open sexuality and its preferences, and by "topless" bars and X-rated theaters, many Americans applauded politicians who promised a war on immorality. The public association of the counterculture and the sexual revolution with student radicalism and ghetto riots swelled the tide of conservatism in the 1970s.

Feminism and a Values Revolution

The rising tempo of social activism also stirred a new spirit of self-awareness and dissatisfaction among educated women, catalyzing the Second wave of Feminism, which would outlast the other social movements and profoundly alter the economic and legal status of women, as well as attitudes about gender roles and sexual relationships.

A Second Feminist Wave

Several events fanned the embers of women's discontent into flames. Unprecedented numbers of women were going to college and employed outside

the home. In 1963, the report of John Kennedy's Presidential Commission on the Status of Women documented occupational inequities similar to those endured by minorities. Women received less pay than men for comparable work, and they made up only 7 percent of the nation's doctors and less than 4 percent of its lawyers. The women who served on the presidential commission successfully urged that the Civil Rights Act of 1964 prohibit gender-based as well as racial discrimination in employment.

Dismayed by the Equal Employment Opportunity Commission's failure to act on complaints of sex discrimination, a group of activists formed the **National Organization for Women** (NOW) in 1966. A civil-rights group for women, NOW labored "to bring women into full participation in the mainstream of American society." It lobbied for equal opportunity, filed lawsuits against gender discrimination, and mobilized public opinion against sexism.

NOW's prominence owed much to the publication of journalist Betty Friedan's critique of domesticity, *The Feminine Mystique* (1963). Friedan decried "the problem that has no name"—the discontent of educated, middle-class wives and mothers who, told that "they could desire no greater destiny than to glory in their own feminity," had subordinated their own aspirations to the needs of men. Friedan urged women, imprisoned in a "comfortable concentration camp," to escape by pursuing careers that would establish their own independent identity and would "fulfill their potentialities as human beings."

Still another catalyst for feminism came from the involvement of younger women in the civil-rights and anti–Vietnam War movements. These activists had acquired confidence in their own potential, an ideology to understand oppression, and experience in the strategy and tactics of organized protest. They also became conscious of their own second-class status, as they were sexually exploited and relegated to menial jobs by male activists. In the words of the civil rights movement's Casey Hayden: the "assumptions of male superiority are as widespread and deep-rooted and every much as crippling to the woman as the assumptions of white supremacy are to the Negro."

Although small in number, young women who shared such thoughts would soon create a women's liberation movement more critical of sexual inequality than NOW.

> The "assumptions of male superiority are as widespread and deep-rooted and every much as crippling to the woman as the assumptions of white supremacy are to the Negro."

Women's Liberation

In 1968, militant feminists adopted "consciousness-raising" as a recruitment device and a means of transforming women's perceptions of themselves and society. Tens of thousands of women assembled in supportive groups to share experiences and air grievances. They learned that others felt dissatisfaction similar to their own: "When I saw that what I always felt were my own personal hangups was as true for every other woman in that room as it was for me! Well, that's when my consciousness was raised." Women came to understand that their personal, individual problems were in fact shared problems with social causes and political solutions—"the personal is political." This new consciousness opened eyes and minds and begot a sense that "sisterhood is powerful."

Women's liberation groups employed a variety of publicity-generating, confrontational tactics. In 1968, radical feminists crowned a sheep Miss America to dramatize their belief that beauty pageants enslaved women "in high-heeled, low-status

THE "BRITISH INVASION" More than just a host of new rock bands from England, the so-called "British Invasion" liberated American fashion styles with mini skirts, hot pants, fishnet stockings, and then maxi skirts and pantsuits. With them came Vidal Sassoon haircuts and a new wave of film-making about uninhibited, permissive Britain. (*© Corbis. All Rights Reserved.*)

roles" and set up "freedom trash cans" in which women could discard girdles, make-up, and other "women-garbage." They demanded inclusion in the Boston Marathon, no longer accepting the excuse that "it is unhealthy for women to run long distances." Overcoming male condescension, they established health collectives and shelters for abused women, created day-care centers and rape crisis centers, founded abortion-counseling services and women's studies programs. Publishing nearly five hundred new feminist publications, they fought negative portrayals of women in the media and advertising. Terms like *male chauvinist pig* entered the vocabulary and those like *chicks* exited.

In August 1970, feminists joined in the largest women's rights demonstration ever. Commemorating the fiftieth anniversary of woman suffrage, the Women's Strike for Equality brought out tens of thousands of women to parade for the right to equal employment and safe, legal abortions. By then, the women's movement had already ended newspapers' practice of listing employment opportunities under separate "Male" and "Female" headings and pressured banks to issue credit to women in their own name.

In the 1970s, feminists focused especially on three issues: equal treatment in education and employment, access to abortion, and passage of the **Equal Rights Amendment** (ERA) barring discrimination on the basis of sex. In 1972, Title IX of the Education Amendments Act prohibited educational institutions that received federal funds from discriminating on the basis of sex. Women gained entry to the U.S. military academies in 1976; and at the state and local levels, they won laws expanding what constituted rape as well as greater protection for victims of domestic violence and more effective prosecution of abusers. Many single-sex colleges became coeducational. The percentage of female students in medical schools rose from 8 to 24 percent and in law schools from 5 percent to 40 percent in the 1970s. By century's end, women would constitute about 20 percent of all state and federal legislators.

The right to control their own sexuality and to make the decisions regarding having children became feminist rallying cries. In addition to using "the Pill," some women challenged demeaning obstetrical practices. Others explored alternatives to hospital births and popularized alternatives to radical mastectomy for breast cancer. And many, aware of the dangers of illegal abortions, pushed for their legalization, achieved in *Roe* v. *Wade*. Perhaps the most controversial ruling of the century, *Roe* v. *Wade* and the subsequent doubling of abortions, to 1.5 million by 1980, triggered an enormous backlash

from social conservatives and from Catholics and Protestants, many of whom believed abortion to be the moral equivalent of murder. Abortion opponents would seek a "right to life" amendment to the Constitution and simultaneously energize Phyllis Schlafly's "STOP ERA" campaign.

In 1972, both houses of Congress passed the ERA with little opposition and, within a year, twenty-eight of the necessary thirty-eight states approved the proposed amendment. Its ultimate adoption seemed self-evident. Then Schlafly, a Republican organizer and working woman herself, took up the fight. Her monthly newsletter, *The Phyllis Schlafly Report*, added antifeminism to its traditional attacks on communism and federal social programs. Her affirmation of traditional gender roles struck a responsive chord with many men as well as with working-class women who felt estranged from the largely upper-middle-class feminist movement. Schlafly charged that the ERA would force women into combat roles in the military, necessitate "unisex toilets," and promote lesbianism. Her relentless assault helped kill the amendment. Selling millions of records, country artist Tammy Wynette sang "Don't Liberate Me, Love Me."

While the number of women working outside the home leaped from under 20 million in 1960 to nearly 60 million by 1990 (see Figure 29.1), women's wages still lagged behind those of men, the workplace remained gender segregated, and

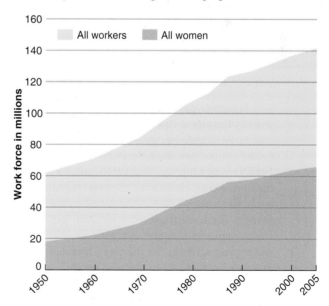

FIGURE 29.1 WOMEN IN THE WORK FORCE, 1950–2005 After 1960, the numbers of American women who were wage earners surged upward. Both the women's movement and economic pressures encouraged this trend. © Cengage Learning. All rights reserved. No distribution allowed without express authorization.

Source: *U.S. Department of Labor, Bureau of Labor Statistics* (www.bls.gov).

the "glass ceiling" that limited their ability to rise beyond a certain corporate level remained in place. As divorce and out-of-wedlock births became more common, the number of women heading families increased; by 1980, only 15 percent of American families with children had a father who worked and a mother who stayed at home. Children now constituted the bulk of the poor, and sociologists wrote about the "feminization of poverty."

Evidenced by the rising divorce rate in the 1970s, from one-third to one-half of the marriages occurring annually, complex issues of role-sharing befuddled middle-class families too. Women who worked still bore primary responsibility for their homes and family. Yet day-care centers for working women became commonplace; grown women were no longer "girls," gender-neutral terms (for example, *firefighter* in place of *fireman*) came into vogue, and the ideal male changed from swashbuckler to one more "in touch with his feelings." Few pined for the era when child care, housework, and volunteerism had defined "women's sphere." American women had learned, according to historian Gerda Lerner:

that they belong to a subordinate group; that they have suffered wrongs as a group; that their condition of subordination is not natural, but societally determined; that they must join with other women to remedy these wrongs; and finally, that they must and can provide an alternative vision of societal organization in which women as well as men will enjoy autonomy and self-determination.

Gay Liberation

Like feminists, gay men and women were emboldened by the new sexual openness to assert their values, and stimulated by the other protest movements in the sixties, **gay liberation** emerged publicly in 1969. During a routine raid by New York City police, the homosexual patrons of the Stonewall Inn, a gay bar in Greenwich Village, unexpectedly fought back fiercely. The furor triggered a surge of "gay pride," a new sense of identity and self-acceptance, and widespread activism. As the Gay Liberation Front asserted, "We are going to be who we are."

By 1973, some eight hundred openly gay groups campaigned for equal rights, for incorporating lesbianism into the women's movement, and for removing the stigma of immorality and depravity attached to being gay. That year, the American Psychiatric Association officially ended its classification of homosexuality as a mental disorder.

"We are going to be who we are."

In 1977, "Gay Pride" parades drew seventy-five thousand marchers in New York City and three hundred thousand in San Francisco. More taboos fell: Elaine Noble, an avowed lesbian, won a seat in the Massachusetts legislature in 1974, and Harvey Milk, an openly gay candidate, was elected to the San Francisco board of supervisors in 1977. In 1987, Massachusetts congressman Barney Frank publicly acknowledged his homosexuality. Many states and cities repealed laws against same-sex relations between consenting adults and, like the U.S. Civil Service Commission in 1975, barred job discrimination on the basis of sexual orientation.

Environmental Activism

Building on the concerns raised in the early sixties, environmentalists also carried the tide of reform into the 1970s. Following the first Earth Day in April 1970, which attracted some 20 million participants, large numbers of Americans began to focus on ecology and the interaction of humans with their environment. For the first time, the media began to highlight acid rain, global warming, nuclear waste disposal, and other human-caused environmental hazards. Well-publicized disasters greatly furthered concern. Cleveland's Cuyahoga River burst into flames, and Lake Erie "died," both contaminated by decades of toxic chemical dumping. A huge oil spill fouled the coast of Santa Barbara, and many Americans choked on the air they breathed while dead fish floated in local rivers and beaches closed owing to sewage contamination.

Environmental advocacy groups gained many fresh recruits. Older organizations such as the Sierra Club and the Audubon Society continued their efforts to preserve natural areas for habitat protection and the recreational and aesthetic pleasures of future generations. Newer groups such as Greenpeace and Friends of the Earth worked against threats to ecological balance. Founded in 1971 when Canadian activists protested a planned U.S. nuclear test on an island in the Bering Sea, Greenpeace established its U.S. branch a year later, working to preserve old-growth forests and protect the world's oceans. By 2000, it had 250,000 U.S. members. The Save the Whales campaign, launched by the Animal Welfare Institute in 1971, opposed the slaughter of the world's largest mammals by fleets of floating processing factories that made dog-and-cat food.

Environmentalists also targeted the nuclear-power industry, adopting techniques from the civil-rights and antiwar campaigns to protest at planned nuclear facilities. The movement crested in 1979 when a partial meltdown crippled the **Three Mile Island** nuclear-power plant in Pennsylvania. A movie released at the same time, *China Syndrome*, portrayed a fictitious but plausible nuclear-power disaster caused by a California earthquake. Deepening public concerns about nuclear power encouraged citizen groups like the Clamshell Alliance in New England to stop new atomic power plants from going online.

However, at a time of concern over an energy crisis, and of rising unemployment, Americans divided over environmental issues like construction of the Trans-Alaska Pipeline in 1973 and whether or not to abandon atomic power, offshore oil drilling, and restrictions on logging. A popular bumper sticker read: "If You're Hungry and Out of Work, Eat An Environmentalist." Yet other Americans sought a healthy lifestyle that promoted less consumption. Cigarette smoking declined. Organic food consumption increased. A jogging craze swept the middle class.

> "If You're Hungry and Out of Work, Eat An Environmentalist."

The "Me Decade"

Whatever political views Americans held, personal pursuits and self-fulfillment largely shaped 1970s American society. Journalist Tom Wolfe dubbed this turn from the public sphere the "Me Decade," and many citizens—reacting to defeat in Vietnam, an economic downturn, and the corruption of public officials—retreated inward, following the advice of Robert Ringer's best-seller *Looking Out for Number One*.

Highly individualistic pet causes flourished, as did new faiths. Some young people practiced Transcendental Meditation or joined the Reverend Sun Myung Moon's Unification Church. Others embraced the International Society for Krishna Consciousness, whose shaved-head, saffron-robed followers added an exotic note in airports and on college campuses. Several thousand rural communes arose as some counterculture veterans sought to escape the urban-corporate world, practice organic farming, revive old technologies, and live in harmony with nature. Most communes proved short-lived.

Journalists discovered the "Yuppie" (young urban professional), preoccupied—often obsessed—with physical fitness and consumer goods. Yuppies jogged and bicycled; ate pesticide-free natural foods; and in a process known as gentrification, purchased and restored rundown inner-city apartments, often displacing poor and elderly residents in the process. Self-indulgence appeared to be their

hallmark, and many identified with conservatism's priority on, above all, individual rights.

As baby boomers sang "We want the world, and we want it now!" the 1970s saw the rise of punk rock, an aggressively anti-establishment genre promoted by groups like the Sex Pistols. Tejano music spread from Texas to win national popularity thanks to performers such as Selena Quintanilla. Rap or hip-hop, whose free-form improvised recitations had roots in Jamaican reggae music and West African storytelling traditions, emerged from poor black New York City neighborhoods. And disco music spotlighted the desire to dance on one's own and to pursue individual rather than societal goals.

In the cultural arena, much but not all reflected the era's malaise. Along with films featuring the madness of the war in Vietnam and corruption in high places, blockbuster movies like *Star Wars* (1977) offered escapist fare. *Happy Days*, the top TV show of 1976–1977, evoked nostalgia for the 1950s. The TV series *Dallas*, chronicling the steamy affairs of a Texas oil family, captivated millions, as did numerous other hit programs featuring characters that defied traditional morality. And beginning in 1971 and gaining popularity throughout the decade, *All in the Family* featured a blue-collar working stiff, Archie Bunker, raging against "girls with skirts up to here" and "men with hair down to there," as well as just about everything else associated with the 1960s. Whether those who laughed were rejecting Archie's bigoted politics or endorsing his tirades against big government and social disorder may never be known. But the character his creator meant to be a cultural and political dinosaur actually forecast a shift to the right, a backlash against "the sixties."

A Divided Nation

By 1968, the combined stresses and strains in American society had produced the most tumultuous era in the United States since the Civil War. The tensions that year resulted in riots, fiery demonstrations, two stunning assassinations, Lyndon Johnson's retreat in Vietnam and from politics, and an election that heralded a realignment in American politics—the first since the New Deal—and the demise of liberalism.

Assassinations and Turmoil

Three days after the Wisconsin primary, a bullet from a sniper's high-powered rifle killed Martin Luther King, Jr., in Memphis, Tennessee, where he had gone to support striking sanitation workers. The presumed assassin, James Earl Ray, a white escaped convict, would confess, be found guilty, and then recant, leaving aspects of the killing unclear. As in the assassination of John F. Kennedy, it seemed unworthy that one misfit was alone responsible.

As the news spread, black ghettos burst into violence in more than a hundred cities. Twenty blocks of Chicago's West Side went up in flames, and Mayor Richard Daley ordered police to shoot to kill arsonists. In Washington, DC, under night skies illuminated by seven hundred fires, army units in combat gear set up machine-gun nests outside the Capitol and White House. It would take seventy-five thousand troops to quell the riots, which left forty-six dead, three thousand injured, and nearly twenty-seven thousand in jail.

Entering the race as the favorite of the party bosses and labor chieftains, LBJ's vice president, **Hubert Humphrey,** turned the contest for the nomination into a three-cornered scramble. **Eugene McCarthy** remained the candidate of the "new politics"—a moral crusade against war and injustice directed to affluent, educated liberals. **Robert Kennedy** campaigned as the tribune of the less privileged, the sole candidate who appealed to both the white ethnic working class and the minority poor. In early June, after his victory in the California primary, the brother of the murdered president was himself assassinated by a Palestinian refugee, Sirhan Sirhan, who loathed Kennedy's pro-Israel views.

The deaths of King and Kennedy frustrated untold Americans. The murders denied them a fundamental democratic right, the right to choose their own leaders. "I won't vote," a youth said. "Every good man we get, they kill." Although Kennedy's death cleared the way for Humphrey's nomination, increasing numbers of Democrats turned to third-party candidate George Wallace's thinly veiled appeal for white supremacy or to the GOP nominee Richard M. Nixon. The Republican, appealing to those disgusted with inner-city riots and antiwar demonstrations, promised to end the war in Vietnam with honor and to restore "law and order." Nixon also said he would heed "the voice of the great majority of Americans, the forgotten Americans, the non-shouters, the non-demonstrators, those who do not break the law, people who pay their taxes and go to work, who send their children to school, who go to their churches, … who love this country." Tapping the same wellsprings of anger and frustration, Wallace pitched his message to southern segregationists and blue-collar workers fed up with antiwar demonstrators and black militants. Wallace vowed, if elected, to crack down on "long-hair, pot-smoking, draft-card-burning youth."

> "I won't vote. Every good man we get, they kill."

In August 1968, violence outside the Democratic National Convention in Chicago reinforced the appeal of both Wallace and Nixon. Determined to avoid the rioting that wracked Chicago after King's assassination, Mayor Richard Daley had turned the city into a virtual fortress, denying demonstrators permits to march or engage in meaningful protest and giving police a green light to attack "the hippies, the **yippies,** and the flippies." On August 28, as a huge national television audience looked on and protesters chanted "The whole world is watching," Daley's bluecoats took off their badges and clubbed demonstrators, tossed tear gas at bystanders, and bloodied reporters and photographers. The police's brutal response—termed a "police riot" by the official commission that investigated—tore the Democrats apart and created an image of them as the party of dissent and disorder. Some 70 percent of Americans supported the police violence against the protestors. Hubert Humphrey, who for years had dreamed of becoming president, had received a nomination that appeared worthless.

Conservative Resurgence

Nixon capitalized on the tumult. Portraying himself as the candidate of the Silent Majority, he criticized the Supreme Court for safeguarding criminals and radicals; promised to crack down on "pot, pornography, protest, and permissiveness"; and asserted that "our schools are for education—not integration."

George Wallace, meanwhile, stoked the fury of the working class against "bearded anarchists, smart-aleck editorial writers, and pointy-headed professors looking down their noses at us." He vowed that "if any demonstrator ever lays down in front of my car, it'll be the last car he'll ever lie down in front of." Nearly 14 percent of the electorate—primarily young, lower-middle-class, small-town workers—cast their votes for Wallace.

In a narrow outcome with large consequences, Nixon and Humphrey split the rest of the vote almost evenly (see Map 29.1). But with Humphrey receiving just 38 percent of the white vote and not even close to half the labor vote, the long-dominant New Deal coalition was shattered. The election spelled clear-cut defeat for those who had dreamed of a society committed to social justice and economic equality. The liberal era had ended.

The 57 percent of the electorate who chose Nixon or Wallace would dominate American politics into the next century. While the Democratic Party fractured into a welter of contending groups, the Republicans attracted a new majority, many of whom lived in the suburbs and the Sunbelt—the southern states of the Old Confederacy, the desert

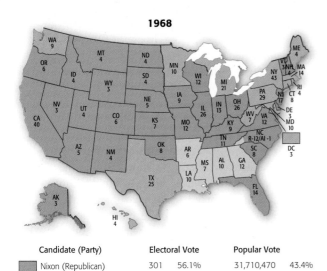

1968

Candidate (Party)	Electoral Vote		Popular Vote	
Nixon (Republican)	301	56.1%	31,710,470	43.4%
Humphrey (Democrat)	191	35.5%	30,898,055	42.3%
Wallace (American Independent)	46	8.4%	9,446,167	12.9%

MAP 29.1 THE ELECTION OF 1968 © Cengage Learning. All rights reserved. No distribution allowed without express authorization.

Southwest, and populous southern California—and who regarded the federal government as wasteful, blamed protestors and hippies for lawlessness, and objected to special efforts to assist minorities and those on welfare.

A Matter of Character

A Californian of Quaker roots, Richard Milhous Nixon was elected to Congress as a navy veteran in 1946. He won prominence for his role in the HUAC investigation of Alger Hiss (see Chapter 26) and advanced to the Senate in 1950 by accusing his Democratic opponent of disloyalty. He served two terms as Eisenhower's vice president but lost the presidential race to Kennedy in 1960 and a run for the California governorship in 1962. Ignoring what seemed a political death sentence, Nixon campaigned vigorously for GOP candidates in 1966 and won his party's nomination and the presidency in 1968.

Nixon yearned to be remembered as an international statesman, but domestic affairs kept intruding. He tried to reform the welfare system and solve complex economic problems. But the underside of Nixon's personality appealed to the darker recesses of the nation and intensified the fears and divisions among Americans.

Although highly intelligent, he displayed the rigid self-control of a man monitoring his own every move. When the private Nixon emerged, he was suspicious, insecure, seeking vengeance. His conviction that enemies lurked everywhere, waiting to destroy him, verged on paranoia. He sought

"THE WHOLE WORLD IS WATCHING" Photographs and televised pictures of Chicago police beating and gassing antiwar protesters and innocent bystanders at the Democratic convention in 1968 linked Democrats in the public mind with violence and mayhem. The scenes made Republican Richard Nixon a reassuring presence to those he would term "the silent majority." *(© Bettmann/Corbis)*

A Divided Nation 905

> "Get them on the ground ... stick our heels in, step on them hard ... crush them, show them no mercy."

to annihilate his Democratic opponents, to "get them on the ground ... stick our heels in, step on them hard ... crush them, show them no mercy."

The classic outsider, reared in pinched surroundings, physically awkward, unable to relate easily to others, Nixon remained fearful that he would never be accepted. At the beginning of his administration, however, his strengths stood out. He spoke of national reconciliation, took bold initiatives internationally, and dealt with domestic problems responsibly.

Symbolic of his positive start, the nation celebrated the first successful manned mission to the moon. In July 1969, the Apollo 11 lunar module, named *Eagle,* descended to the Sea of Tranquility. As millions watched on television, astronaut **Neil Armstrong** walked on the moon's surface and proclaimed, "That's one small step for man, one giant leap for mankind." Five more lunar expeditions followed, and in 1975 the space race essentially ended with the United States and the Soviet Union engaging in cooperative efforts to explore the rest of the universe.

"ONE GIANT LEAP FOR MANKIND" On July 20, 1969, American astronaut Neil Armstrong became the first human to set foot on the moon's surface. As a television camera beamed back pictures, Armstrong and Edwin "Buzz" Aldrin spent 21 hours on the moon, gathering samples, measuring temperatures, and planting a small American flag. *(NASA/Johnson Space Center)*

The first newly elected president since 1849 whose party controlled neither house of Congress, Nixon cooperated with the Democrats to increase social-security benefits, build subsidized housing, expand the Job Corps, and grant the vote to eighteen-year-olds. He especially sought measures to protect the environment and signed bills for cleaner air and water, for reducing toxic wastes, and for the further protection of endangered species and wilderness. He also approved legislation creating the Occupational Safety and Health Administration (OSHA), which enforced health and safety standards in the workplace, and the Environmental Protection Agency (EPA), which required federal agencies to prepare an environmental-impact analysis for all proposed projects.

Conservatives grumbled as government grew larger and more intrusive and as race-conscious employment policies, including affirmative-action quotas, were mandated for all federal contractors. Conservatives grew still angrier when Nixon unveiled the Family Assistance Plan (FAP) in 1969. A bold effort to overhaul the welfare system, FAP proposed a guaranteed minimum annual income for all Americans. Caught between liberals who thought the income inadequate and conservatives who disliked it on principle, FAP died in the Senate.

A Troubled Economy

Nixon inherited the fiscal consequences of President Johnson's effort to wage the Vietnam War and finance the Great Society by deficit financing—to have both "guns and butter." Facing a "whopping" budget deficit of $25 billion in 1969 and an inflation rate of 5 percent (see Figure 29.2), Nixon cut government spending and encouraged the Federal Reserve Board to raise interest rates. The result was a combination of inflation and recession that economists called "stagflation" and Democrats termed "Nixonomics."

Accelerating inflation lowered the standard of living of many families and sparked a wave of strikes as workers sought wage hikes to keep up with the cost of living. It encouraged the wealthy to invest in art and real estate rather than technology and factories. More plants shut down, industrial jobs dwindled, and many displaced workers lost their savings, their health and pension benefits, and their homes.

Throughout 1971, Nixon lurched from policy to policy. Declaring "I am now a Keynesian," he increased deficit spending to stimulate the private sector, which resulted in the largest budget deficit since World War II. Then, Nixon devalued

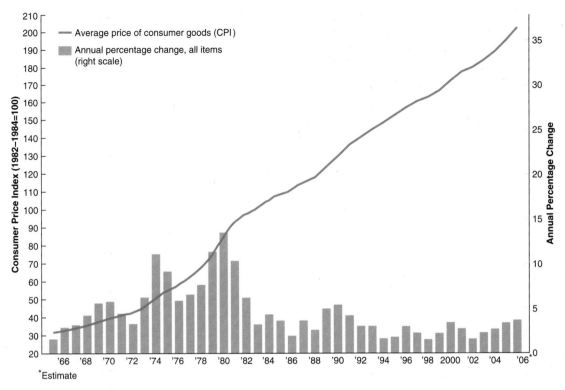

FIGURE 29.2 INFLATION, 1965–2006 Inflation, which had been moderate during the two decades following World War II, began to soar with the escalation of the war in Vietnam in the mid-1960s. In 1979 and 1980, the nation experienced double-digit inflation in two consecutive years for the first time since World War I.

the dollar to correct the balance-of-payment deficit. Finally, he froze wages, prices, and rents for ninety days, a short-term fix that worked until after the 1972 election. Then Nixon again reversed course, replacing controls with voluntary—and ineffective—guidelines. Inflation zoomed as the **Organization of Petroleum Exporting Countries** (OPEC), a group of Third World nations that had joined together to set production levels and prices, launched an embargo that raised the price of crude oil, and sluggish growth dogged the economy throughout the decade.

Law and Order

Despite his public appeals for unity, Nixon hoped to divide the American people in ways that would create a new Republican majority coalition. His "southern strategy" sought to attract Dixie's white Democrats into the GOP fold, while his stands on crime, drugs, and protestors wooed blue-collar laborers and suburbanites—voters whom political strategist Kevin Phillips described as "in motion between a Democratic past and a Republican future."

To combat the militants he despised, Nixon used the full resources of the federal government.

He had the IRS audit their tax returns, the Small Business Administration deny them loans, and the National Security Agency illegally wiretap them. The FBI worked with local officials to disrupt and immobilize the Black Panthers, the CIA illegally investigated and compiled dossiers on thousands of American citizens, and the Justice Department prosecuted antiwar activists and black radicals in highly publicized trials. Nixon's aides also drew up an "enemies list" of adversaries to be harassed by the government.

In 1970, Nixon widened his offensive against the antiwar movement by approving the Huston Plan, which would use the CIA and FBI in various illegal activities. The plan called for wiretapping and electronic surveillance, break-ins to gather or plant evidence of illegal activity, and a new agency to centralize domestic covert operations under White House supervision. But FBI chief J. Edgar Hoover opposed the plan as a threat to the bureau's independence. Blocked, Nixon secretly created his own White House unit to discredit his opposition and ensure executive secrecy. Nicknamed **"the plumbers"** because of their assignment to plug government leaks, the team was headed by former FBI agent G. Gordon Liddy and former CIA operative E. Howard Hunt.

The plumbers first targeted Daniel Ellsberg, a former Defense Department analyst who had given the press the **Pentagon Papers,** a secret chronicle of U.S. involvement in Vietnam. On June 13, the *New York Times* began publishing the *Pentagon Papers,* revealing a long history of White House lies to Congress, foreign leaders, and the American people. Although the papers contained nothing about his administration, Nixon, fearing that they would undermine trust in government and establish a precedent for publishing classified material, sought to bar their publication. The Supreme Court, however, ruled that publication of the *Pentagon Papers* was protected by the First Amendment. Livid, Nixon directed the Justice Department to indict Ellsberg for theft and ordered the plumbers to break into the office of Ellsberg's psychiatrist in search of information to discredit the man who had become a hero to the antiwar movement.

The Southern Strategy

Nixon especially courted whites upset by the drive for racial equality. The administration opposed extension of the Voting Rights Act of 1965, sought to cripple enforcement of the Fair Housing Act of 1968, pleaded for the postponement of desegregation in Mississippi's schools, and filed suits to prohibit busing children to desegregate schools.

The strategy of wooing angry and fearful whites also dictated Nixon's Supreme Court nominations. To reverse the Warren court's liberalism, he sought strict constructionists—judges who would not "meddle" in social issues or be "soft" on criminals. In 1969, he appointed Warren Burger as chief justice. Although the Senate then twice rejected southern conservatives nominated by Nixon, the president succeeded in appointing Harry Blackmun of Minnesota, Lewis Powell of Virginia, and William Rehnquist of Arizona. Along with Burger, they steered the Court in a centrist direction, ruling liberally in most cases involving abortion, desegregation, and the death penalty, while shifting to the right on civil liberties, community censorship, and police power.

As the 1970 congressional elections neared, Nixon's vice president, Spiro T. Agnew, assailed the Democrats as "sniveling hand-wringers" and the news media as "nattering nabobs of negativism." Liberals deplored Agnew's alarming alliterative allegations, but the 1970 elections proved a draw, with the GOP losing just nine House seats and winning two Senate seats.

> Agnew assailed the Democrats as "sniveling hand-wringers" and the news media as "nattering nabobs of negativism."

Successes Abroad, Crises at Home

Above all else, Nixon focused on foreign affairs. Considering himself a master of *realpolitik*—a pragmatic approach stressing national interest rather than ethical goals; he sought to check Soviet expansionism and to limit the nuclear-arms race and reduce superpower conflict. To achieve a new era of **détente**—reduced tensions—with the communist world, Nixon chose **Henry Kissinger,** a refugee from Hitler's Germany and professor of international relations, who shared Nixon's penchant for secrecy and for the concentration of decision-making power in the White House, as his chief foreign policy advisor.

In his second inaugural, Nixon pledged "to make the next four years the best four years in America's history." Ironically, they would rank among its sorriest. His vice president would resign in disgrace, his closest aides would go to jail, and he would serve barely a year and a half of his second term before resigning to avoid impeachment.

Détente

Having entered into negotiations to end the war in Vietnam (see Chapter 28), Nixon pursued détente with the Soviet Union and a turnabout in Chinese-American affairs. These developments, the most significant shift in U.S. foreign policy since the start of the Cold War, created a new relationship among the United States, the Soviet Union, and China.

Presidents from Truman to Johnson had refused to recognize the People's Republic of China, to allow its admission to the United Nations, and to permit American allies to trade with it. But by 1969, a widening Sino-Soviet split made the prospect of improved relations with both nations attractive to Nixon, who hoped to have "closer relations with each side than they did with each other." In June 1971, Kissinger began secret negotiations with Beijing, laying the groundwork for Nixon's historic February 1972 trip to China "to seek the normalization of relations." The first visit ever by a sitting American president to the largest nation in the world, it ended more than twenty years of Chinese-American hostility. Full diplomatic recognition followed in 1979.

Equally significant, Nixon went to Moscow in May 1972 to sign agreements with the Soviets on trade, technological cooperation, and the limitation of nuclear weapons. The **Strategic Arms Limitation Treaty** (SALT I) froze each side's offensive nuclear missiles for five years and committed both countries to strategic equality rather than nuclear superiority; and the Anti-Ballistic Missile (ABM) Treaty restricted the deployment by both sides of nationwide missile-defense systems. Although they did not end the arms race, the treaties moved both countries toward "peaceful coexistence" and, in an election year, enhanced Nixon's stature.

Shuttle Diplomacy

Not even better relations with China and the Soviet Union ensured global stability. In 1967, Israel, fearing an imminent Arab attack, launched a preemptive strike on its neighbors, routing them in six days and seizing Sinai and the Gaza Strip from Egypt, the West Bank and East Jerusalem from Jordan, and Syria's Golan Heights. Israel promised to give up the occupied lands in exchange for a negotiated peace, but the Arab states refused to negotiate with Israel or to recognize its right to exist. Palestinians, many of them refugees since the creation of Israel in 1948, turned to the Palestine Liberation Organization (PLO), which demanded Israel's destruction.

War exploded again in 1973 when Egypt and Syria attacked Israel on the Jewish high holy day of Yom Kippur. Only massive shipments of military supplies from the United States enabled a reeling Israel to stop the assault. In retaliation, the Arab states embargoed shipments of crude oil to the United States and its allies. The five-month embargo dramatized U.S. dependence on foreign energy sources and, following a spike in oil prices, sharply intensified inflation.

The dual shocks of the energy crisis at home and rising Soviet influence in the Arab world spurred Kissinger to engage in "shuttle diplomacy." Flying from one Middle East capital to another for two years, he negotiated a cease-fire, pressed Israel to cede some captured territory, and persuaded the Arabs to end the oil embargo. Although Kissinger's diplomacy left the Palestinian issue festering, it successfully excluded the Soviets from a major role in Middle Eastern affairs.

Nixon-Kissinger *realpolitik* based American aid on a nation's willingness to oppose communism, not on the nature of its government. Thus the Nixon administration liberally supplied arms and assistance to the shah of Iran, the white supremacist regime of South Africa, and President Ferdinand Marcos in the Philippines, as well as furnishing aid to antidemocratic regimes in Argentina, Brazil, South Korea, and Portuguese colonial authorities in Angola.

When Chileans elected a Marxist, Salvador Allende, president in 1970, Nixon secretly funded the CIA to support opponents of the leftist regime and cut off economic aid to Chile. In 1973, a military junta overthrew the Chilean government and killed Allende. Nixon quickly recognized the new dictatorship, and economic aid and investment again flowed to Chile.

The Election of 1972

Nixon's reelection appeared certain. He faced a deeply divided Democratic Party and counted on his diplomatic successes and the winding down of the Vietnam War to win over moderate voters. He expected his southern strategy and law-and-order posture to attract conservative voters. Nixon's only possible worry, another third-party candidacy by Wallace, vanished on May 15, 1972, when Wallace was shot during a campaign stop. Paralyzed from the waist down, Wallace withdrew from the race, leaving Nixon a monopoly on the white backlash.

The Senate's most outspoken dove, **George McGovern** of South Dakota, capitalizing on antiwar sentiment, blitzed the Democratic primaries. He gained additional support from new party rules requiring state delegations to include minority, female, and youthful delegates in approximate proportion to their numbers. Actress

NIXON AND MAO In February 1972, after a secret foray by Kissinger to Beijing, President Nixon stunned the world by going to the People's Republic of China, toasting his counterpart Mao Zedong, strolling through the Forbidden City, and walking along the Great Wall. *(© Bettmann/Corbis)*

California's delegation looked "like a couple of high schools, a grape boycott, a Black Panther rally, and four or five politicians who walked in the wrong door."

Shirley MacLaine approvingly described California's delegation as "looking like a couple of high schools, a grape boycott, a Black Panther rally, and four or five politicians who walked in the wrong door." A disapproving labor leader complained about "too much hair and not enough cigars at this convention," but McGovern won the nomination.

Perceptions of McGovern as inept and radical drove away all but the most committed supporters. McGovern dropped his vice-presidential running mate, Thomas Eagleton, when it became known that Eagleton had received electric-shock therapy for depression. Subsequently, several prominent Democrats publicly declined to run with him. McGovern's endorsement of decriminalization of marijuana, immediate withdrawal from Vietnam, and pardons for those who had fled the United States to avoid the draft exposed him to GOP ridicule as the candidate of the radical fringe.

Remembering his narrow loss to Kennedy in 1960 and too-slim victory in 1968, Nixon left no stone unturned. To do whatever was necessary to win, he appointed his attorney general, John Mitchell, to head the Committee to Re-Elect the President (CREEP). Millions of dollars in campaign contributions financed "dirty tricks" against Democrats and paid for an espionage unit, led by Liddy and Hunt, to spy on the opposition. In 1972, it received Mitchell's approval to wiretap telephones at the Democratic National Committee headquarters in Washington's Watergate apartment and office complex. However, a security guard foiled the break-in to install bugs in June 1972. Arrested were James McCord, a retired CIA officer and the security coordinator of CREEP, and several other Liddy and Hunt associates.

Dirty tricks went from a scandal to a constitutional crisis when Nixon abused the power of his office to cover up wrongdoing and hinder criminal investigations. Asserting that "no one in the White House staff, no one in this administration, presently employed, was involved in this bizarre incident," Nixon coached associates on what they should tell investigators, authorized the payment of hush money and hints of a presidential pardon to buy the silence of those

Nixon asserted that "no one in the White House staff, no one in this administration, presently employed, was involved in this bizarre incident."

arrested, and directed the CIA to halt the FBI's investigation on the pretext that it would damage national security.

With the McGovern campaign a shambles and Watergate seemingly contained, Nixon amassed nearly 61 percent of the popular vote and an overwhelming 520 electoral votes. Supported primarily by minorities and low-income voters, McGovern carried just Massachusetts and the District of Columbia. The election solidified the 1968 realignment. Nevertheless, the GOP gained only twelve seats in the House and lost two in the Senate, demonstrating the growing difficulty of unseating incumbents, the rise in ticket-splitting, and the decline of both party loyalty and voter turnout. Only 55.7 percent of eligible voters went to the polls (down from 63.8 percent in 1960).

The Watergate Upheaval

The scheme to conceal links between the White House and the accused Watergate burglars had succeeded during the 1972 campaign. But after the election, federal judge "Maximum John" Sirica, known for his tough treatment of criminals, used the threat of heavy sentences to pressure one burglar into confessing that the White House knew in advance of the break-in and that the defendants had committed perjury during the trial. Two *Washington Post* reporters, Carl Bernstein and Bob Woodward, following clues furnished by a secret informant named **"Deep Throat"**—identified in 2005 as Mark Felt, second in command at the FBI—wrote a succession of front-page stories tying the break-in to illegal contributions and "dirty tricks" by CREEP.

In February 1973, the Senate established the Special Committee on Presidential Campaign Activities to investigate, and stunning evidence of scandal revealed the existence of a White House "enemies list," the president's use of government agencies to harass opponents, and administration favoritism in return for illegal campaign donations. Both the president's special counsel and the acting head of the FBI testified to the involvement of the White House in the Watergate break-in, forcing Nixon to announce the resignation of his principal aides and the appointment of a special Watergate prosecutor with broad powers of investigation and subpoena. Then the most dramatic bombshell, the disclosure that Nixon taped every conversation in the Oval Office, meant there was an incontrovertible record of "what the president knew and when he knew it."

When the special prosecutor insisted on access to the tapes, Nixon ordered the attorney general to fire him. The attorney general and the number-two

HONK FOR IMPEACHMENT Although Richard Nixon continued to fight back, appealing to the majority that had reelected him that the Watergate investigation was a conspiracy of the liberal eastern establishment, in 1974 an increasing number of Americans no longer believed the President. On August 8, acknowledging only a "few mistakes of judgment," Nixon resigned his presidency to avoid certain impeachment. *(AP Images)*

man in the Justice Department refused and were dismissed in what became known as the "Saturday night massacre." More than 150,000 telegrams poured into the White House, and eighty-four members of Congress sponsored sixteen different bills of impeachment. The House Judiciary Committee began impeachment proceedings, and Congress went to the Supreme Court to demand access to the original tapes.

Adding to Nixon's woes, Vice President Agnew pleaded no contest—"the full equivalent to a plea of guilty," according to the trial judge—to charges of income tax evasion and solicitation of bribes, both as governor of Maryland and as vice president. Agnew left office in October 1973 with a fine and suspended sentence, and was replaced, under provisions of the Twenty-fifth Amendment, by House Minority Leader Gerald R. Ford of Michigan.

A President Disgraced

In late July 1974, the Supreme Court ruled unanimously in *United States* v. *Nixon* that the unedited tapes must be turned over to Congress. The tapes produced the "smoking gun," proving beyond

doubt that Nixon had ordered the cover-up, engaged in a criminal conspiracy to hinder the investigation of the break-in, and lied about his role for more than two years. The House Judiciary Committee adopted three articles of impeachment, charging Nixon with obstruction of justice, abusing the powers of the presidency by using federal agencies to harass citizens and deprive them of their rights, and contempt of Congress for refusing to obey a congressional subpoena for the tapes. Checkmated, Nixon surrendered the subpoenaed tapes.

In trying to explain Watergate, some historians point to the increasing expansion of presidential power, "the imperial presidency," stretching back several decades. Others argue that Nixon simply got caught and that his liberal foes forced him to pay a higher price for his misdeeds than had other presidents. Most focus on Nixon himself and his obsession to destroy his hated adversaries. Whatever the cause, Richard Nixon, certain the Senate would vote to convict him once impeached, became the first president to resign—and Gerald Ford took office as the nation's first chief executive who had not been elected either president or vice president.

A Troubled Nation and Presidency

In the aftermath of the Vietnam debacle and Richard Nixon's disgrace, presidents **Gerald Ford** and **Jimmy Carter** grappled with inflation, recession, and industrial stagnation. They faced humiliations abroad, and, for Carter, an especially maddening hostage crisis. The confident 1950s and early 1960s, when prosperous America had savored its role as the Free World's leader, now seemed remote. A nation convinced that it was immune to the historical forces that constrained other societies seemed prey to forces beyond its control—particularly significant foreign competition and an energy crisis.

Panic at the Pump

In 1973–1974, Americans sat in their cars and waited in long lines to buy gasoline at skyrocketing prices. Angry and frustrated, motorists fought each other and battled with police. At one service station with no gas to sell, a driver threatened the attendant, "You are going to give me gas or I will kill you." The nation had long taken cheap, abundant energy for granted, yet remained heavily dependent on the third of its oil it imported. This vulnerability became apparent when Arab nations, angered by Nixon's support of Israel during the 1973 war, cut off

> "You are going to give me gas or I will kill you."

the supply of oil to the West. Then, the seven Arab members of OPEC quadrupled the cost of a barrel of oil from $3 to $12 in 1976. OPEC would almost triple it again, to $34 in 1979, pushing the price of a gallon of gas over $1 for the first time, a price barrier many had thought unreachable (see Figure 29.3). Overall, consumer prices would more than double in the 1970s, with inflation soaring to 14 percent. It battered American families and turned hard-pressed taxpayers against the welfare programs adopted during past Democratic administrations.

Disturbing economic developments forced millions of Americans in the 1970s to, according to a magazine, "Learn to Live with Less": less energy and jobs, less possibilities and power. Unemployment ranged between 6 and 10 percent, nearly twice the usual postwar level, and the federal deficit soared from $8.7 billion in 1970 to $72.7 billion in 1980. Federal borrowing to cover the deficit increased the costs of all businesses that had to borrow, which worsened the rising price spiral and the galloping inflation rate that had resulted from President Johnson's attempt to fund both the Vietnam War and the Great Society without raising taxes. Moreover, in 1971 the dollar, long the strongest currency in the world, fell to its lowest level since 1949, and the United States posted its first trade deficit—importing more than it exported—in almost a century.

Most acutely, higher costs and greater foreign competition ravaged the manufacturing regions of the Midwest and Northeast, soon to be called the "Rust Belt." The automobile industry was especially hard hit by soaring gasoline prices that boosted sales of more fuel-efficient foreign imports, mainly from Japan. U.S. purchases of foreign cars grew from 2 million in 1970 to 4 million in 1989. Chrysler, the third largest automaker, was saved from bankruptcy only by a $1.2 billion federal loan guarantee. Facing severe production cutbacks, the Big Three carmakers eliminated the jobs of one in three autoworkers between 1978 and 1982.

Long-term sources of industrial decline included aging machinery, inefficient production methods, complacent management, and fierce competition from foreign companies paying lower wages, especially in the countries of the Pacific Rim. In 1979–1983, 11.5 million U.S. workers lost jobs because of plant closings and cutbacks. Although new employment opportunities opened in the so-called knowledge-based industries (and would lead to an uneven economic revival later in the century), many industrial workers lacked the skills to fill these jobs.

With the loss of industrial jobs, the union movement weakened. In 1960, 31 percent of U.S. workers belonged to unions; thirty years later, that figure had been virtually halved to 16 percent, with further

OPEC OIL EMBARGO To retaliate against the United States and its allies for aiding Israel in its 1973 war with Egypt and Syria, the Organization of Petroleum Exporting Countries, led by Saudi Arabia and other Arab nations, halted oil shipments to the United States, Western Europe, and Japan. Secretary of State Henry Kissinger could do little as the energy crisis rattled the world economy and shook the foundations of the American Dream. *(Drawing by Draper Hill © 1975, The Commercial Appeal, Memphis. Used with Permission)*

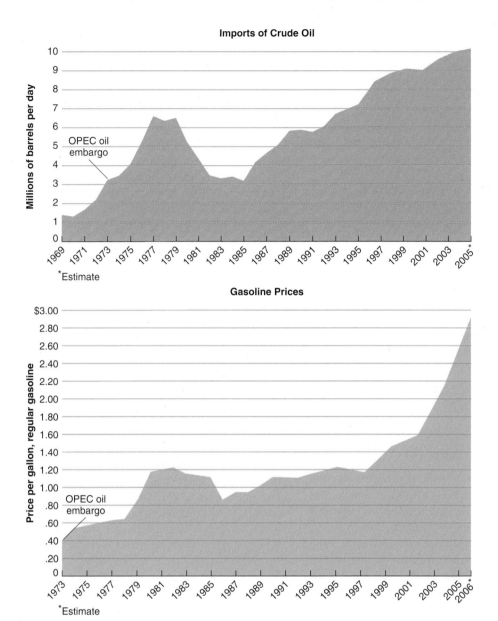

Imports of Crude Oil

Gasoline Prices

FIGURE 29.3 THE ENERGY CRISIS: CRUDE-OIL IMPORTS AND GASOLINE PRICES, 1969–2006 After surging in the 1970s, U.S. oil imports dipped in the early 1980s owing to a deep recession and fuel conservation, only to rise to unprecedented levels in the mid-1990s (top). Similarly, gasoline prices spiked in the 1970s and early 1980s, dipped a bit, leveled off in the 1990s, and then in 2000 began a steep upward climb that would continue through the decade. © Cengage Learning. All rights reserved. No distribution allowed without express authorization.

declines ahead. Some workers did join unions in these years, mainly teachers, public employees, and service workers, many of whom were female. Service-sector unionization, however, only slowed, but did not reverse, the overall decline of union membership.

Gerald Ford, Caretaker

Former Michigan congressman Gerald Ford became president after Nixon's resignation, August 9, 1974. Acknowledging he was "a Ford not a Lincoln," he urged Americans to move beyond the "long national nightmare" of Watergate. The honeymoon quickly ended, however, when Ford pardoned Nixon for "any and all crimes" committed while in office, meaning that Nixon would neither have to assume responsibility nor face prosecution for his actions.

Economic problems, particularly inflation, dogged Ford's presidency. In October 1974, Ford unveiled a program of voluntary price restraint dubbed "Whip Inflation Now" (WIN), but prices continued upward. When the Federal Reserve Board tried to cool the economy by raising interest rates, a severe recession resulted. Unemployment approached 11 percent by 1975. Then Ford tried

> A union official lamented "a nation of hamburger stands ... a country stripped of industrial capacity and meaningful work ... a service economy."

tax cuts to stimulate business activity. They made inflation worse and did little to promote employment. As oil and gas prices soared, Americans for the first time since World War II struggled to curb energy consumption. Congress set fuel-efficiency standards for automobiles in 1975 and imposed a national speed limit of fifty-five miles per hour.

National morale sank further in late April 1975 when the South Vietnamese government fell, and television chronicled desperate helicopter evacuations from the U.S. embassy in Saigon (soon renamed Ho Chi Minh City). A few weeks later, Cambodia seized a U.S. merchant ship, the *Mayagüez*. Ford ordered a military rescue, which freed the thirty-nine *Mayagüez* crew members but cost the lives of forty-one U.S. servicemen. As the nation entered the election year 1976—also the bicentennial of the Declaration of Independence—Americans found little reason for optimism.

Jimmy Carter, Outsider

Gerald Ford won the 1976 Republican nomination, turning back a strong challenge from former California governor Ronald Reagan, who opposed détente. Jimmy Carter—a Georgia peanut grower, graduate of the naval academy, and former governor—effectively used the media to bypass party machines and sweep the Democratic primaries by stressing his honesty, his evangelical Christian faith, and his status as a Washington outsider who would bring the virtue and morality of small-town America to government.

With his running mate, Minnesota senator Walter Mondale, Carter squeaked to victory with 51 percent of the vote. Underscoring his rejection of Nixon's "imperial presidency," Carter walked with his wife Rosalyn in the inaugural parade, and in an echo of Roosevelt's fireside radio chats, he delivered some TV speeches wearing a sweater and seated by a fireplace.

Despite the populist symbolism and huge Democratic majorities in Congress, Carter never shaped a liberal agenda. Lacking both Washington experience and the inclination to deal with the capitol's key political players, he distanced himself from congressional Democrats and could not break the legislative gridlock. At heart a fiscal conservative, he favored cutting federal spending. "Government cannot solve our problems," he asserted in

> "Government cannot solve our problems."

his second State of the Union address. "It cannot eliminate poverty, or provide a bountiful economy, or reduce inflation, or save our cities, or cure illiteracy, or provide energy." Accordingly, Carter left unresolved the major economic and social problems of the 1970s, especially, **"stagflation"**—economic stagnation combined with price inflation—which topped 20 percent in 1979.

Carter further disappointed liberals by pushing for deregulation—the removal of government controls on the airline, railroad, and trucking industries, as well as on oil and natural gas prices—and by failing to adopt an effective energy policy. Angered by rising gasoline prices and increasing dependence on foreign oil—more than 40 percent by 1980—Americans wanted energy self-sufficiency (see Going to the Source). Yet, on the central domestic policy issue of his time, Carter proposed a program that barely reduced oil consumption, grandiosely calling it the "moral equivalent of war"; most Americans sneered at it as MEOW. His failures contributed immensely to the destruction of what remained of the liberal coalition and enormously boosted the fortunes of political conservatism.

In Niagara Falls, New York, where for years the Hooker Chemical and Plastics Corporation had dumped tons of waste in a district known as Love Canal, Carter confronted a major environmental crisis. In 1953, Hooker had covered the landfill with earth and sold it to the city. Homes and schools sprang up, but residents complained of odors and strange substances oozing from the soil. In the late 1970s, tests confirmed that toxic chemicals, including deadly dioxin, were seeping into buildings, polluting the air, and discharging into the Niagara River. Medical researchers found elevated levels of cancer, miscarriages, and birth defects among Love Canal residents.

In 1978, President Carter authorized federal funds to relocate Love Canal families, and in 1980 he declared the situation a national emergency, freeing more federal money for relocation and clean-up. As his presidency ended, Carter signed legislation creating a federal "Superfund" to clean up the nation's most polluted sites. In addition, the **Alaska Lands Act** set aside more than 100 million acres of public land for parks, wildlife refuges, and national forests and added twenty-six rivers to the nation's Wild and Scenic River System. These two bills proved to be Carter's rare successes.

Carter's foreign-policy record proved mixed. He spoke out for human rights, pushed through a Panama Canal Treaty that transferred full control over the canal to Panama by 2000, and brought together Egyptian President Anwar Sadat and Israeli Premier Menachem Begin at Camp

Carter and Stockman on Energy

In his first presidential speech on energy, Jimmy Carter sought to win the support of the American people for conservation and for governmental solutions. In response, Congressman David Stockman (R-MI) argued against federal intervention and for allowing unfettered global markets to provide abundant energy.

Carter on energy: Our national energy plan is based on 10 fundamental principles. The first principle is that we can have an effective and comprehensive energy policy only if the Government takes responsibility for it and if the people understand the seriousness of the challenge and are willing to make sacrifices. . . .

The third principle is that we must reduce our vulnerability to potentially devastating embargoes. We can protect ourselves from uncertain supplies by reducing our demand for oil, by making the most of our abundant resources such as coal, and by developing a strategic petroleum reserve. . . .

The fifth principle is that we must be fair. Our solutions must ask equal sacrifices from every region, every class of people, and every interest group. Industry will have to do its part to conserve just as consumers will. The energy producers deserve fair treatment, but we will not let the oil companies profiteer.

The sixth principle, and the cornerstone of our policy, is to reduce demand through conservation. . . . Conservation is the quickest, cheapest, most practical source of energy. Conservation is the only way we can buy a barrel of oil for about $2. It costs about $13 to waste it.

The seventh principle is that prices should generally reflect the true replacement cost of energy. We are only cheating ourselves if we make energy artificially cheap and use more than we can really afford. . . .

The ninth principle is that we must conserve the fuels that are scarcest and make the most of those that are plentiful. We can't continue to use oil and gas for 75 percent of our consumption, as we do now, when they only make up 7 percent of our domestic reserves. We need to shift to plentiful coal, while taking care to protect the environment, and to apply stricter safety standards to nuclear energy.

The tenth and last principle is that we must start now to develop the new, unconventional sources of energy that we will rely on in the next century.

Stockman's response: At bottom, the notion that "home grown energy is better" implies a radical rejection of the global trading system and the law of comparative advantage [that some nations can more efficiently produce certain commodities, such as oil] on which it is premised. . . . The result would be substantial, unnecessary loss in national output, and an artificially high domestic-energy-cost structure which would reduce the competitiveness of our exports and increase the cost-advantage of imports. . . .

Overall, the planet's accessible natural hydrocarbon reserves readily exceed 20 trillion barrels. This is the equivalent of five centuries of consumption at current rates. . . . The case for fossil-fuel exhaustion simply cannot rest on physical scarcity or the stinginess of the planet.

. . . It is time to discard our medieval energy maps. There is no region filled with lurking dragons and other perils on the far side of the ocean. So rather than institute a politically imposed and bureaucratically managed and enforced regime of domestic-energy autarky [a policy based on authoritarian power], we need do little more than decontrol domestic energy prices, dismantle the energy bureaucracy, and allow the U.S. economy to equilibrate at the world level. Energy supply and demand will take care of itself . . . and by thus encouraging full integration of the U.S. economy into the world marketplace's search for the least-cost-development sequence of our planet's prodigious remaining energy resources, we will produce the highest possible level of domestic economic growth and welfare.

Source: Jimmy Carter, "The Energy Problem," April 18, 1977, Public Papers of the Presidents of the United States: Jimmy Carter, 1977–1981; and David Stockman, "The Wrong War? The Case Against a National Energy Policy," Public Interest, 53 (Fall 1978).

QUESTIONS

1. How do the two men differ on the causes and solution of the energy crisis?
2. Explain how the goals of Carter's energy proposals might conflict with his economic and environmental goals?

David—refusing to let them leave until they agreed to make peace. However, the other Arab states rejected the **Camp David Accords;** Israel continued to build Jewish settlements in the occupied territories; Islamic fundamentalists assassinated Sadat in 1981. Peace in the Middle East remained as elusive as ever.

Toward the Soviet Union, Carter first showed conciliation, but toughness ultimately won out. In 1979, Carter and the Soviet leader Leonid Brezhnev signed the SALT II treaty, limiting each side's nuclear arsenals. Senate ratification stalled when Cold Warriors who had never accepted détente attacked the treaty for allegedly favoring the Soviets. Support dissolved entirely in late December 1979 when the Soviets invaded Afghanistan. Carter revived registration for the military draft, boycotted the 1980 Summer Olympics in Moscow, and embargoed grain shipments to Russia.

Iran

The low point of Carter's presidency involved Iran. Protests against a repressive regime headed by the shah of Iran, a long-time American ally, who had come to power in 1953 with CIA help (see Chapter 26), swelled in 1979. In November, after Carter admitted the shah to the United States for cancer treatment, the Islamic militant supporters of Ayatollah Khomeini stormed the U.S. embassy in Tehran and seized sixty-six American hostages, demanding the return of the shah in exchange for the captured Americans. Thus began a 444-day ordeal that virtually paralyzed the Carter administration. Night after night, TV images of blindfolded hostages, anti-American mobs, and U.S. flags being burned rubbed American nerves raw. A botched rescue attempt in April 1980, in which several U.S. helicopters malfunctioned and eight GIs died, added to the nation's humiliation—and to the public's view of Carter as an ineffective bumbler. Not until January 20, 1981, the day Ronald Reagan took office as the new president, did the Iranian authorities release the hostages.

As with Herbert Hoover in the early 1930s, Americans turned against the remote figure in the White House. When Carter's approval rating sagged to 26 percent in mid-1979 (lower than Nixon's when he resigned as a result of Watergate), he retreated to Camp David, where he delivered a TV address blaming the American people's "crisis of confidence" for the nation's troubles. When a cabinet reshuffle was all that followed, most Americans thought the helpless Carter was the problem. The 1980 Democratic convention glumly renominated Carter, but defeat in November loomed. A

successful post-presidential career of public service would do much to restore Carter's reputation and bring him the Nobel Peace Prize in 2002. But in 1980, most Americans hungered for a new president and changed policies.

CONCLUSION

Baby boomers took material comfort and their own importance for granted. Longing for meaning in their lives, as well as personal liberty, they sought a more humane democracy, a less racist and consumerist society, and an end to the war in Vietnam. Failing to get what they wanted quickly, the New Left became increasingly radical and violent. Most of the young, however, were more interested in "sex, drugs, and rock-and-roll." Ultimately, the student movement and counterculture helped prod the United States into becoming a more tolerant, diverse, and permissive society. They helped pave the way for the environmental movement and spurred an end to America's longest war—which had cost the nation dearly in lives and dollars, in turning Americans against one another and in diverting society from pressing needs.

The youth rebellion, racial rioting, and the Tet offensive in Vietnam brought politics to a boil in 1968. The year of assassinations and turmoil cost Democrats the White House and triggered a conservative resurgence and major political realignment. Pursuing the national interest by *realpolitik,* President Richard Nixon and Henry Kissinger undertook secret negotiations with North Vietnam to end hostilities. At the same time, they opened the way for reduced tensions with China and the Soviet Union, enhancing the world outlook for peace, while also giving economic and military assistance to anticommunist dictatorships.

Equally vital to his political success, Nixon wooed whites upset by civil strife and by hippies and radicals. He emphasized law and order to attract the silent majority concerned with the upsurge of criminality and breakdown of traditional values, and he played upon middle-class resentment of rising taxes to pay for the federal largess going to minorities and the poor. Following a "southern strategy," he nominated conservatives for the Supreme Court, opposed extension of the Voting Rights Act and school busing for racial integration, and cracked down on militant blacks and young radicals.

In 1972, the secret schemes Nixon had put in place to spy upon and destroy those who opposed his Vietnam policies began to unravel. His obsession for secrecy and his paranoia about opponents brought his downfall. The arrest of the Watergate burglars and the subsequent attempted cover-up of

White House involvement led to revelations of a host of "dirty tricks" and criminal acts, the indictment of nearly fifty Nixon administration officials and the jailing of a score of his associates, and a House Judiciary Committee vote to impeach the president. To avoid certain conviction, a disgraced Nixon resigned on August 9, 1974. Neither his successor, Gerald Ford, nor Jimmy Carter restored confidence in the White House. The national government seemed helpless as the plague of inflation, energy crisis, recession, and deindustrialization swept the land. The deepening public disenchantment with politicians and disillusionment with government, which had led Dorothy Burlage and millions of others to turn inward, would last throughout the 1970s and into the next century.

KEY TERMS

Students for a Democratic Society   (p. 890)

Berkeley Free Speech Movement   (p. 891)

"hippies"   (p. 895)

counter culture   (p. 896)

Woodstock festival   (p. 896)

Roe v. Wade   (p. 897)

National Organization for Women   (p. 900)

Equal Rights Amendment   (p. 901)

gay liberation   (p. 902)

Three Mile Island   (p. 903)

Hubert Humphrey   (p. 904)

Eugene McCarthy   (p. 904)

Robert Kennedy   (p. 904)

yippies   (p. 904)

Neil Armstrong   (p. 906)

Organization of Petroleum Exporting Countries   (p. 907)

"the plumbers"   (p. 907)

Pentagon Papers   (p. 908)

détente   (p. 908)

Henry Kissinger   (p. 908)

Strategic Arms Limitation Treaty   (p. 908)

George McGovern   (p. 909)

"Deep Throat"   (p. 910)

Gerald Ford   (p. 912)

Jimmy Carter   (p. 912)

"stagflation"   (p. 914)

Alaska Lands Act   (p. 914)

Camp David Accords   (p. 916)

FOR FURTHER REFERENCE

Thomas Borstelmann, *The 1970s: A New Global History from Civil Rights to Economic Inequality* (2011). How and why the 1970s mattered.

Stephanie Coontz, *A Strange Stirring:* The Feminine Mystique *and American Women at the Dawn of the 1960s* (2011). The impact of Betty Friedan's work evaluated.

David Eisenbach, *Gay Power: An American Revolution* (2006). A solid account of this important struggle.

J. Brooks Flippen, *Nixon and the Environment* (2000). Makes a strong case for the commitment to environmental causes by Nixon appointees.

Matthew J. Lassiter, *The Silent Majority: Suburban Politics in the Sunbelt South* (2007). How class supplanted race as the driving force in Republican dominance.

Chana Kai Lee, *For Freedom's Sake: The Life of Fannie Lou Hamer* (2000). An eloquent biography of the civil rights activist.

Joseph E. Lowndes, *From the New Deal to the New Right: Race and the Southern Origins of Modern Conservatism* (2008). A thoughtful interpretation of the link between racism and conservatism.

Peter H. Irons, *Jim Crow's Children: The Broken Promise of the Brown Decision* (2004). The human dimensions of *Brown*'s aftermath movingly rendered.

Keith W. Olson, *Watergate: The Presidential Scandal That Shook America* (2003). A readable explanation of the Watergate scandal.

Daniel S. Pierce, *Real NASCAR: White Lightning, Red Clay, and Big Bill France* (2010). An entertaining history of southern stock-car racing into the 1970s.

Ruth Rosen, *The World Split Open: How the Modern Women's Movement Changed America* (2001). All that the title promises.

Dominic Sandbrook, *Mad as Hell: The Crisis of the 1970s and the Rise of the Populist Right* (2011). An engaging examination of the decade's populist impulses.

Sean Wilentz, *Bob Dylan in America* (2010). A fascinating personal account of Dylan's life and music.

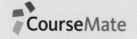

A Conservative Revival and the End of the Cold War, 1980–2000

END OF THE BERLIN WALL, NOVEMBER 1989 *(© Bettmann/Corbis)*

TENSION GRIPPED EAST BERLIN LATE IN 1989, amid rumors that "Die Mauer," the wall that divided the city, might soon be opened. In May, Soviet premier Mikhail Gorbachev had announced that Moscow would no longer uphold the pro-Soviet governments of Eastern Europe. One by one, these governments fell. On October 18, East Germany's communist regime collapsed.

Among the Cold War's physical reminders, the most notorious was the Berlin Wall, built by the Russians in 1961. Snaking around the city and ramming through its heart, this concrete barrier with its watchtowers and armed guards endured as a stark emblem of Cold War divisions. Nearly two hundred people had been shot trying to escape across the Wall. On the West Berlin side, colorful graffiti defied the Wall's grim expanse.

President Kennedy, visiting the Wall in 1963, had uttered his memorable proclamation, "Ich bin ein Berliner" ("I am a Berliner"). In 1987, President Ronald Reagan made the pilgrimage, demanding, "Mr. Gorbachev, tear down this wall!"

Now the end had come. As guards opened the gates, East Berliners joyously poured through and West Berliners greeted them with flowers, tears, and shouts of welcome. Long-divided families joyously reunited. In one of the first real-time global media events, TV cameras and communications satellites beamed the story worldwide.

The celebrations lasted for days. Russian cellist Mstislav Rostropovitch gave an impromptu concert at the Wall. The American Leonard Bernstein conducted a celebratory concert in Berlin. Even before the official demolition, ordinary Berliners attacked the Wall with picks and hammers. A hated Cold War symbol soon faded into history, as the Soviet Union itself disintegrated.

The Cold War's end looms large in this chapter. We begin, however, by continuing the story of the post-1960s conservative shift in American politics, which culminated in Ronald Reagan's election as president in 1980. We then examine U.S. politics and foreign affairs during Reagan's presidency, shaped by free-market ideology and a fierce anti-communism.

The Soviet Union's collapse and the Cold War's end allowed long-muted regional conflicts to surface. While U.S. leaders struggled with the long-running Israeli-Palestinian conflict and other post–Cold War trouble spots, a crisis erupted in the Middle East as Iraq invaded oil-rich Kuwait. Reagan's successor, George H.W. Bush, responded adroitly. Bush's domestic achievements, however, proved less impressive.

Democrat Bill Clinton won the 1992 presidential race, but Republican gains in 1994 made clear the conservative movement's continued strength. While Clinton moved to the right on domestic issues, events in the Balkans, the Middle East, and

PRESIDENT RONALD REAGAN AND SOVIET PREMIER MIKHAIL GORBACHEV IN MOSCOW, 1988 In Reagan's second presidential term, Cold War tensions eased dramatically. *(AP Images)*

elsewhere demanded attention as well. As Clinton's second term ended in scandal and a failed impeachment effort, a disputed 2000 presidential election restored the White House to Republican control. Ostentatious consumption, new communications technologies, and cultural conflict shaped American life at century's end. Despite challenges, liberalism remained a force, and the basic reforms rooted in FDR's New Deal and LBJ's Great Society remained in place.

FOCUS Questions

- What core beliefs guided Ronald Reagan's presidency?

- What were George H.W. Bush's principal achievements and failures as president?

- What domestic policy issues, political events, and economic trends most influenced Bill Clinton's presidency?

- How did the Clinton administration respond to political and economic developments abroad?

- What economic trends, technological innovations, and cultural trends shaped American life in the 1990s?

A Conservative Shift in Culture and Politics

Ronald Reagan won the presidency in 1980 riding the conservative tide that had been building for years. Domestically, Reagan and his congressional allies enacted tax cuts and deregulatory measures reflecting their free-market, small-government ideology. The Reagan era began with a recession and ended with a stock-market crash. In between, though, inflation eased and the overall economy improved. Reagan's policies produced mounting federal deficits, however, while economic inequities, inner-city problems, and stubborn unemployment persisted.

An avid Cold Warrior, Reagan boosted military spending and adopted a tough stance toward Russia. The administration's secretive efforts to overthrow a leftist regime in Latin America triggered a constitutional crisis in Reagan's second term. But a dramatic easing of Cold War tensions ended his presidency on a high note.

Roots of the Conservative Turn

Post-1945 U.S. conservatism, an unstable blend of antigovernment libertarianism, anticommunism, and nostalgia for a premodern past, found a champion in William F. Buckley, who launched the *National Review* magazine in 1955; founded Young Americans for Freedom (1960); and started a conservative TV talk show, *Firing Line,* in 1966. Barry Goldwater's 1964 presidential campaign, though unsuccessful, gave evidence of conservatism's latent strength.

While the 1960s' counterculture and antiwar protests drew media attention, many Americans deplored what they saw as the decade's radical excesses. As we saw in Chapter 29, Richard Nixon exploited this disaffection to win the White House in 1968. Think tanks like the Heritage Foundation (1973), founded by Colorado beer baron Joseph Coors, promoted the conservative cause.

In local communities in the fast-growing South and West (see Chapter 27, Map 27.1), conservatives came together and mobilized politically. Southern California's Orange County, recently transformed from citrus groves to suburban developments, illustrates this process. Orange County conservatives—mostly upwardly mobile, white evangelical Protestants—were intensely anticommunist, dismayed by 1960s' radicals, and suspicious of the "liberal elites" dominating the media and national politics. Recognizing their common agenda, these conservatives organized locally. Foreshadowing changes ahead nationally, Orange County helped elect Ronald Reagan governor of California in 1966 and in 1978 rallied behind Proposition 13, a state referendum mandating deep cuts in property taxes.

Conservatives mobilized around specific issues, especially abortion. As noted in Chapter 29, in the wake of *Roe* v. *Wade,* "right to life" activists pressed for a constitutional amendment outlawing abortion. Led by Roman Catholic and conservative Protestant activists, "pro-life" advocates rallied, signed petitions, and picketed abortion clinics and pregnancy-counseling centers.

Feeling the pressure, Congress in 1976 ended Medicaid funding for most abortions, effectively denying this procedure to the poor. Handing conservatives another victory, President Nixon in 1972 had vetoed a bill funding day-care centers, criticizing its "communal approach to child-rearing." The Equal Rights Amendment, denounced by Phyllis Schlafly and other conservatives, died in 1982—three states short of ratification.

To religious conservatives, gay and lesbian activism foretold society's moral collapse. "God... destroyed the cities of Sodom and Gomorrah because of this terrible sin," thundered TV evangelist

1980	Ronald Reagan elected president.
1981	Major cuts in taxes and domestic spending. Large increases in military budget.
1982	Equal Rights Amendment dies. CIA funds contra war against Nicaragua's Sandinistas. Central Park rally for nuclear weapons freeze.
1983	239 U.S. marines die in Beirut terrorist attack. U.S. deploys Pershing II and cruise missiles in Europe. Reagan proposes Strategic Defense Initiative (Star Wars). U.S. invasion of Grenada.
1984	Reagan defeats Walter Mondale to win second presidential term.
1984–1986	Congress bars military aid to contras.
1985	Rash of airline hijackings and other terrorist acts.
1986	Congress passes South African sanctions. Immigration Reform and Control Act.
1987	Congressional hearings on Iran-contra scandal. Stock-market crash.
1988	Reagan trip to Moscow. George H.W. Bush elected president.
1989	Massive Alaskan oil spill by *Exxon Valdez*. Supreme Court, in several 5-to-4 decisions, restricts civil-rights laws. China's rulers crush prodemocracy movement. Berlin Wall is torn down.
1990	Federal Clean Air Act strengthened. Americans with Disabilities Act passed. Iraq invades Kuwait. Recession (1990–1993). Germany reunified; Soviet troops start withdrawal from Eastern Europe.
1991	Persian Gulf War (Operation Desert Storm). Hearings on Clarence Thomas's Supreme Court nomination. Collapse of Soviet Union.
1992	Supreme Court in *Planned Parenthood* v. *Casey* approves abortion restrictions but upholds *Roe* v. *Wade*. President Bush commits U.S. troops in Somalia. Bill Clinton elected president.
1993	Congress approves NAFTA treaty. Economy expands, stock market surges (1993–2000). Clinton health-care reform plan fails (1993–1994). Eighty Branch Davidians die in fire as federal agents raid compound in Waco, Texas. World Trade Center bombing kills six.
1994	Christian Coalition gains control of Republican Party in several states. Yasir Arafat and Yitzhak Rabin sign Oslo Accords at White House. Clinton withdraws U.S. forces from Somalia. United States joins the World Trade Organization (WTO). Republicans proclaim "Contract with America" and win control of House and Senate; Newt Gingrich becomes Speaker.
1995	Oklahoma City federal building bombed. Dayton Accords achieve cease-fire in Bosnia; Clinton commits U.S. troops to enforce agreement.
1996	Welfare Reform Act. Clinton defeats Robert Dole to win second presidential term.
1997	Congressional battle over tobacco industry regulation.
1998	Clinton impeached by House of Representatives in sex scandal.
1999	Senate dismisses impeachment charges. Columbine High School shootings. U.S. and NATO forces intervene in Kosovo.
2000	George W. Bush wins presidency when Supreme Court ends Florida election dispute.

Jerry Falwell. In 1977, singer Anita Bryant led a successful campaign against a Miami ordinance protecting homosexuals' civil rights. "God created Adam and Eve, not Adam and Bruce," she pointed out. Soon after, *Good Housekeeping* magazine readers voted Bryant America's "most admired woman." Other cities, too, reversed earlier measures protecting gay rights.

In 1978, as the backlash intensified, a member of the San Francisco board of supervisors fatally shot gay activist and board member Harvey Milk and Milk's political ally, Mayor George Moscone. When the killer received a

> "God... destroyed the cities of Sodom and Gomorrah because of this terrible sin."

light sentence, riots erupted in the city. (Thirty years later, actor Sean Penn won an Academy Award for his starring role in a film celebrating Milk's career.)

The conservative movement gained strength from the political mobilization of evangelical Protestants, with their emphasis on strict morality, biblical authority, and a "born again" conversion experience. Evangelical denominations such as the Southern Baptist Convention grew explosively in the 1970s and 1980s, as did independent suburban megachurches. Meanwhile, liberal churches whose ministers had rallied behind the civil-rights and antiwar movements lost members.

Evangelicals had supported antislavery and other social reform before the Civil War. Their modern-day successors also preached reform, but of a conservative variety. Jerry Farwell's Moral Majority, founded in 1979 as a "pro-life, pro-family, pro-moral, and pro-America" crusade, supported conservative candidates. So did Pat Robertson, founder of the Christian Broadcasting Network. Tim LaHaye of San Diego, another politicized evangelical, was also active in mobilizing support for conservative causes. In 1981, LaHaye founded the Council for National Policy, a secretive political lobby.

While battling abortion, homosexuality, and pornography, often in alliance with conservative Catholics, evangelicals also attacked the Supreme Court's 1962 *Engel* v. *Vitale* decision banning organized prayer in public schools on First Amendment grounds. They advocated home schooling and private Christian schools to shield children from what they saw as the public schools' permissiveness and secularist (nonreligious) values.

Christian bookstores, religious radio stations, and TV evangelists fueled the revival. Falwell's *Old Time Gospel Hour*, Robertson's *700 Club*, and other luminaries of the so-called electronic church attracted a loyal following. In a world of change, evangelicals found certitude and a sense of community in their shared faith. In the process, they profoundly influenced late-twentieth-century American life.

Not all evangelicals were political conservatives. Most African American evangelicals remained in the Democratic Party. Some white evangelicals resisted the rightward political turn. In general, however, newly politicized evangelicals helped propel the conservative tide that carried Ronald Reagan to the White House in 1980.

Conservatism Triumphant: The 1980 Election

Reagan grew up in Dixon, Illinois, the son of an alcoholic father and a devout mother. In 1937, after a stint as a radio sports announcer, he went to Hollywood. His fifty-four films proved forgettable, but he gained political experience as president of the Screen Actors' Guild. A New Dealer in the 1930s, Reagan moved rightward in the 1950s, and in 1954 became the General Electric Company's corporate spokesperson. In a 1964 TV speech for Barry Goldwater, he lauded American individualism and the free-enterprise system. As governor of California (1967–1975), he espoused conservative ideas and denounced campus demonstrators, but also proved open to compromise.

In the 1980 Republican primaries, Reagan bested his principal opponent, George H.W. Bush (father of the later President George W. Bush), whom he then chose as his running mate. Belying his sixty-nine years, he campaigned vigorously against President Jimmy Carter, seeking a second term. In the election, Reagan garnered 51 percent of the vote to 41 percent for the Carter-Mondale ticket (see Map 30.1). (An independent candidate, liberal Republican John Anderson, collected most of the balance.)

Republicans gained eleven Senate seats, winning a majority for the first time since 1955, and narrowed the Democrats' majority in the House of Representatives. The Republican successes revealed the power of conservative political action committees (PACs) whose computerized mass mailings focused on emotional issues like abortion and gun control.

Benefiting from the continuing erosion of Democratic strength in the South fostered by

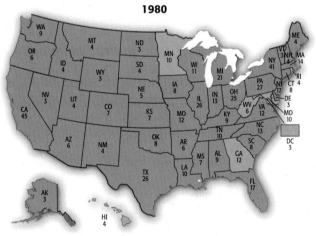

1980

Candidate (Party)	Electoral Vote		Popular Vote	
Reagan (Republican)	489	90.9%	43,642,639	50.5%
Carter (Democrat)	49	9.1%	35,480,948	41.0%
Anderson (Independent)			5,251,421	6.1%

MAP 30.1 THE ELECTION OF 1980 Jimmy Carter's unpopularity and Ronald Reagan's telegenic appeal combined to give Reagan a crushing electoral victory.

Richard Nixon, Reagan carried every southern state except Carter's Georgia. He also swept every state west of the Mississippi except Minnesota and Hawaii. More than half of white blue-collar workers, once solidly Democratic, voted Republican. Of FDR's New Deal coalition, only black voters remained solidly Democratic.

Jerry Falwell's pro-Reagan Moral Majority registered an estimated 2 million new voters in 1980 and 1984. The organization disbanded after 1984, but Pat Robertson's Christian Coalition took its place, mobilizing evangelicals to elect candidates to local office as a stepping stone to expanded national influence.

Population changes contributed to Reagan's success. While urban Democratic strongholds in the Northeast and Midwest lost population in the 1970s, Texas, California, Florida, and other more conservative Sunbelt states grew.

Voters frightened by stagflation welcomed Reagan's promise that tax cuts would bring recovery. His antigovernment rhetoric and dismissal of social-welfare programs like Johnson's War on Poverty resonated with white middle-class and blue-collar Americans. Like his one-time political hero Franklin Roosevelt, Reagan promised a new deal. But unlike FDR's, Reagan's new deal meant individualism, smaller government, lower taxes, and untrammeled free enterprise.

Reagan, a seasoned actor and public speaker, wrapped these themes into an appealing message of moral affirmation and support for "traditional values." At a time of national malaise, he exuded confidence. His unabashed patriotism, calls for military strength, and praise of America's greatness soothed the battered psyche of a nation traumatized by Vietnam and the frustrations of the seventies. Some found Reagan's core ideology negative and mean-spirited. But in 1980, most voters embraced his hopeful message.

Enacting the Conservative Economic and Political Agenda

While Reagan rhetorically endorsed the religious conservatives' cultural agenda, he mostly ignored it once in office. By contrast, he actively promoted his economic and political program, with broad—though far from universal—public support.

Reagan's economic plan, dubbed "Reaganomics" by the media, boiled down to the belief that the U.S. economy, if freed from taxes and regulations, would achieve wonders of productivity. Reagan proposed a 30 percent cut in federal income taxes over three years. Trimming this proposal slightly, Congress voted a 25 percent cut: 5 percent in 1981, 10 percent in 1982 and 1983.

RONALD AND NANCY REAGAN Just as FDR did with his radio "fireside chats," Ronald Reagan felt at home in front of the cameras and used television to connect and communicate with voters. *(© David H. Wells/CORBIS)*

To partially counterbalance the lost revenues, Congress slashed more than $40 billion from domestic spending. Economists still warned that the tax cut would produce huge federal deficits, but Reagan insisted that lower tax rates would stimulate economic growth, pushing up tax revenues. In the Republican primaries, George H.W. Bush had ridiculed Reagan's rosy predictions as "voodoo economics," but as vice president he tactfully remained silent.

Business deregulation had begun under Carter, but Reagan pushed it into new areas such as banking, the savings-and-loan industry, and communications. Transportation regulations aimed at improving air quality and fuel economy were trimmed back. Interior Secretary James Watt of Wyoming opened federal wilderness areas, forest lands, and coastal waters to oil, gas, and timber companies and cut back on environmental and endangered species protections. Watt earlier spearheaded the so-called Sagebrush Rebellion, a campaign by ranchers, farmers, and mineowners to shift federal lands in the West to state and county control (see Map 30.2). Environmental groups protested Watt's policies and demanded his ouster. After various public-relations gaffes, Watt resigned in 1983.

Reagan had little sympathy for organized labor. In 1981, when the Professional Air Traffic Controllers Organization (PATCO) went on strike, Reagan invoked the 1947 Taft-Hartley law against strikes by federal employees and ordered them back to work. When more than eleven thousand PATCO members defied the order, Reagan fired them and barred them permanently from federal employment. Reagan acted within the law, but his action struck many as unduly harsh.

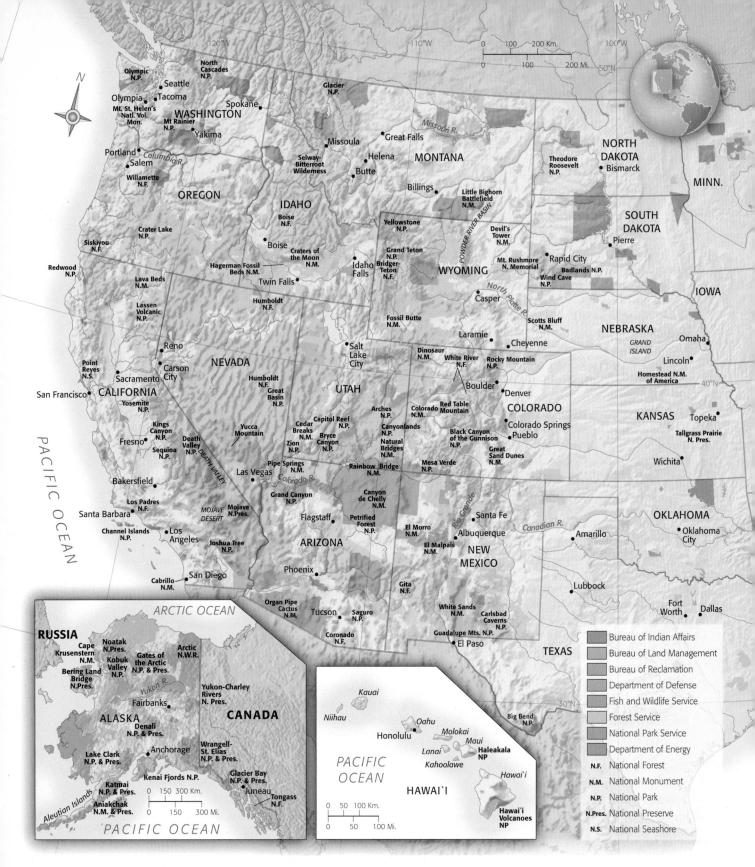

MAP 30.2 LANDOWNERSHIP IN THE WEST From national parks to hydroelectric facilities and military test sites, the federal government's vast holdings in the West influenced the politics of the region. © Cengage Learning. All rights reserved. No distribution allowed without express authorization.

Legend:
- Bureau of Indian Affairs
- Bureau of Land Management
- Bureau of Reclamation
- Department of Defense
- Fish and Wildlife Service
- Forest Service
- National Park Service
- Department of Energy
- N.F. National Forest
- N.M. National Monument
- N.P. National Park
- N.Pres. National Preserve
- N.S. National Seashore

To combat continuing inflation (see Chapter 29), the Federal Reserve Board pushed up interest rates. This medicine, coupled with falling oil prices, did lower inflation, but high interest rates also brought on a recession. By late 1982, unemployment stood at 10 percent. Reagan's cuts in social programs worsened the plight of the poor, including inner-city blacks and Hispanics. The Fed's policy also hurt U.S. exports. As foreign investors bought Treasury bonds to earn high U.S. interest rates, the dollar rose in value, making U.S. export goods more expensive. With U.S. imports of cars, TVs, and other goods from Japan and elsewhere soaring, the trade deficit surged to $111 billion in 1984.

Facing a recession and rising federal deficits, Reagan in 1982–1983 slowed military spending, approved emergency job programs, restored some spending on social programs, and authorized tax increases disguised as "revenue-enhancement measures." Nevertheless, the recession hurt Reagan's popularity, and Democrats made gains in the 1982 midterm elections.

By 1983, with the economy rebounding, the stock market surged. Money managers like Ivan Boesky, an apparent genius at stock transactions, became celebrities. E.F. Hutton and other brokerage firms lured new investors. Corporate mergers proliferated. Savings-and-loan (S&L) companies, newly deregulated and flush with deposits from eager investors, ladled out billions to developers planning shopping malls, condominiums, and retirement villages.

The Wall Street frenzy had an unsavory underside. In 1985, E.F. Hutton officials pled guilty to illegal fund manipulation. Ivan Boesky went to prison after a 1986 conviction for insider trading (profiting through advance knowledge of corporate actions). The high-flying S&L industry would collapse in 1988 (as detailed later in this chapter). The 1987 film *Wall Street* captured the decade's darker side. As protagonist Gordon Gekko, a hard-driving speculator played by Michael Douglas, puts it: "Greed, for lack of a better word, is good. Greed is right, greed works. Greed … captures the essence of the evolutionary spirit."

> "Greed, for lack of a better word, is good. Greed is right, greed works. Greed … captures the essence of the evolutionary spirit."

On October 19, 1987, the stock market crashed, reducing the paper value of the nation's stocks by 20 percent overnight. The market soon recovered, but the collapse had a sobering effect on giddy investors.

Even during the boom, systemic economic problems persisted. Federal budget deficits—the predictable consequence of Reagan's tax cuts and military spending spree—surpassed $200 billion in 1985 and 1986. Budget deficits, the trade deficit, widening economic disparities amid the boom times, and a savings-and-loan crisis related to deregulation must rank among Reagan's economic legacies.

Reagan also shaped the Supreme Court. His 1981 selection of Sandra Day O'Connor as the first woman Supreme Court justice won praise. He nudged the high court in a conservative direction in 1986 by elevating William Rehnquist, a Nixon appointee, to the chief justiceship upon Warren Burger's retirement, and nominating Antonin Scalia to replace him. Scalia would prove a leader of the Court's conservative wing, defending the powers of the executive branch, opposing abortion rights, and upholding the view that the "original intent" of the Constitution's eighteenth-century framers must guide any governmental responses to changing social realities.

When another vacancy opened in 1987, Reagan nominated Robert Bork, a judge and legal scholar whose abrasive personality and rigid views led the Senate to reject him. After a second failed nomination, Reagan's third choice, Anthony Kennedy, a conservative California jurist, won quick confirmation.

The Cold War Heats Up

The late 1970s' deterioration in U.S.–Soviet relations worsened during Reagan's first term. Addressing a convention of evangelicals, the president demonized the Soviet Union as an "evil empire." Anti-Soviet fury exploded in September 1983 when the Russians shot down a Korean passenger plane that strayed into their airspace, killing all 269 aboard.

Insisting that post-Vietnam America had grown dangerously weak, Reagan launched a military expansion. The Pentagon's budget nearly doubled, reaching more than $300 billion by 1985. The buildup included nuclear weapons. Secretary of State Alexander Haig spoke of using "nuclear warning shots" in a conventional war; other officials mused about the "winnability" of nuclear war. Despite protests across Europe, the administration deployed 572 nuclear missiles in Western Europe in 1983, fulfilling a NATO decision to match Soviet missiles in Eastern Europe. In an echo of the 1950s, the administration issued a nuclear-war defense plan whereby city-dwellers would flee to nearby small towns, and a Defense Department official proposed backyard shelters as adequate protection in a nuclear war.

ANTI-SANDINISTA CONTRAS ON PATROL IN NICARAGUA, 1987 Under Reagan, the CIA recruited, financed, and equipped an army to overthrow Nicaragua's leftist Sandinista regime. This support continued clandestinely despite congressional prohibitions, leading to the so-called Iran-contra scandal. *(© Bill Gentile/Corbis)*

Spooked by all the talk of nuclear war, many Americans rallied to a campaign for a multinational freeze on the manufacture and deployment of nuclear weapons. Antinuclear protesters packed New York's Central Park in June 1982. That November, voters in nine states, including California and Wisconsin, approved nuclear-freeze referenda.

To counter the freeze campaign, Reagan in March 1983 proposed the **Strategic Defense Initiative** (SDI), a computerized antimissile system involving space based lasers and other high-tech components. Critics quickly dubbed the scheme "Star Wars." Experts warned of monumental technical hurdles and the danger of further escalating the nuclear-arms race. Nevertheless, Reagan prevailed, and Congress authorized a costly SDI research program.

Fearing communist gains in Latin America, the administration backed El Salvador's military junta in its brutal suppression of a leftist insurgency supported by Fidel Castro's Cuba (see Map 30.3). In Nicaragua, Reagan vigorously opposed the Sandinista insurgents who overthrew dictator Anastasio Somoza in 1979. The Sandinistas, Reagan claimed, were turning Nicaragua into a communist state like Cuba. In 1982,

the CIA organized and financed an anti-Sandinista guerrilla army, called the contras, based in neighboring Honduras and Costa Rica. The contras, with links to the hated Somoza regime, conducted raids and sabotage in Nicaragua that killed many civilians.

Fearing another Vietnam, Congress late in 1982 voted a year-long halt in U.S. military aid to the contras, and in 1984 imposed a two-year ban. Ignoring these prohibitions, the White House secretly continued to funnel money to the contras, resulting in a major scandal in Reagan's second term.

Reagan's one success in Latin America involved the tiny island of Grenada, where a 1983 coup had installed a pro-Castro government. In October 1983, two thousand U.S. troops invaded Grenada and substituted a pro-U.S. government.

Extending its anticommunist campaign to Afghanistan, the Reagan administration (expanding a policy started by President Carter) secretly funneled funds and equipment to Islamic fighters, called *mujahadeen*, battling to expel Russian troops that had invaded Afghanistan in 1979 to prop up an unpopular pro-Russian regime. Ironically, young **Osama bin Laden,** a wealthy Saudi Arabian who would later become a deadly foe of America, was

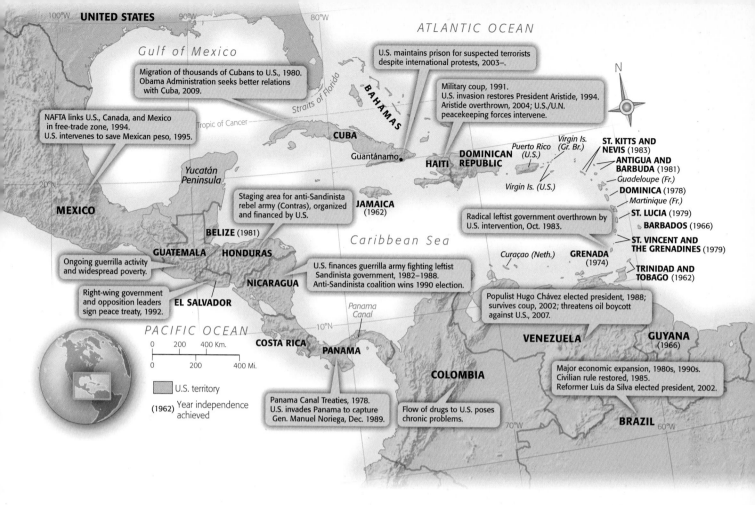

MAP 30.3 THE UNITED STATES IN CENTRAL AMERICA AND THE CARIBBEAN, 1978–2006 Plagued by poverty, population pressures, repressive regimes, and drug trafficking, this region has experienced turmoil and conflict—but also hopeful developments—in recent decades.

also financing the mujahadeen, putting him and the United States briefly on the same side.

Reagan's determination to make America "stand tall" again in the world had broad appeal, as did his tax cuts and celebration of the free-enterprise system. Americans also liked Reagan's upbeat style, typified by his jaunty response in March 1981 when a ricocheting bullet fired by a deranged young man struck him in the chest. Rushed to the hospital, Reagan insisted on walking in. "Please tell me you're all Republicans," he quipped to physicians. (The attack disabled Reagan's press secretary, James Brady, who later joined the campaign for stricter gun control.)

With the recession fading, Reagan and Vice President Bush were enthusiastically renominated at the 1984 Republican convention. Staged for TV, the convention

> "Please tell me you're all Republicans," the president quipped to physicians.

accented themes of patriotism, prosperity, and Reagan's personal charm.

In the Democratic primaries, civil-rights leader Jesse Jackson garnered 3.5 million votes and won five southern states. But former Vice President Walter Mondale captured the nomination with backing from party leaders, labor unions, and other traditional Democratic constituencies. His vice-presidential choice, New York congresswoman Geraldine Ferraro, became the first woman to run on a major-party presidential ticket.

Reagan's ideological and personal appeal, combined with prosperity and the continued support of "Reagan Democrats," proved decisive. Reagan and Bush won 59 percent of the popular vote and carried every state but Mondale's Minnesota plus the District of Columbia. The Republicans' post-1968 dominance of the White House—interrupted only by Jimmy Carter's single term—continued.

In 1985, frustrated by the Democrats' image as a "big government" and "tax-and-spend" party, Arkansas governor Bill Clinton, Tennessee senator Al Gore, and others formed the more centrist

A Conservative Shift in Culture and Politics

Democratic Leadership Council (DLC). Clinton would later use the DLC as a springboard for a presidential bid.

The Iran-Contra Scandal and a Thaw in U.S.–Soviet Relations

Reagan's second-term achievements included the 1986 Immigration Reform and Control Act (see Chapter 29) and a tax-reform law making the system less complicated. These were overshadowed, however, first by a major White House scandal and then by a dramatic easing of Cold War hostilities.

The so-called **Iran-contra scandal,** began obscurely in 1986 with reports that in 1985 the United States had shipped, via Israel, 508 anti-tank missiles to Iran, America's avowed enemy. Admitting the sale, Reagan claimed the goal had been to encourage "moderate elements" in Tehran and to gain the release of U.S. hostages held in Lebanon by pro-Iranian groups. In February 1987, a presidentially appointed investigative panel blamed Reagan's chief of staff, Donald Regan, who resigned.

Next came the revelation that Oliver North, a National Security Council aide, had secretly diverted profits from the Iran arms sales to the Nicaraguan contras despite Congress's ban on such aid. To hide this crime, North and his secretary had altered and destroyed incriminating documents.

In May 1987 congressional hearings on the scandal were opened. North, in his U.S. marine uniform, boasted of his patriotism, and National Security Adviser John Poindexter testified that he had deliberately concealed the scheme from President Reagan. The congressional investigative committee found no proof that Reagan knew of illegalities, but criticized the lax management and contempt for the law that pervaded the White House. In 1989, North was convicted of obstructing a congressional inquiry and destroying and falsifying official documents. (The conviction was later reversed on a technicality.) Although less damaging than Watergate, the Iran-contra scandal took its toll in public trust of government.

Attorney General Edwin Meese resigned in 1988 amid charges of using his influence to promote ventures from which he hoped to profit. In 1989 came revelations that former interior secretary James Watt and other prominent Republicans had collected hundreds of thousands of dollars for using their influence to help housing developers seeking federal subsidies. Reagan's popularity seemed unaffected; some dubbed him the Teflon president—nothing stuck to him.

> Reagan cheerfully argued that "the evil empire" was becoming more benign.

Improved U.S.–Soviet relations highlighted Reagan's second term. At meetings in Europe in 1985 and 1986, Reagan and Soviet premier Mikhail Gorbachev revived the stalled arms-control process. Beset by economic problems and by unrest in Eastern Europe, Gorbachev worked to reduce superpower tensions while restructuring Russia's economy, loosening Moscow's grip in Eastern Europe, and bringing more openness to Russia's government.

In 1987, in Washington, Reagan and Gorbachev signed the **Intermediate-range Nuclear Forces** (INF) **Treaty,** eliminating twenty-five hundred U.S. and Soviet missiles from Europe (see Table 30.1). This, in turn, led to Reagan's historic May 1988 visit to Moscow, where the two leaders strolled in Red Square.

Some Reaganites protested as their hero embraced the world's top communist. But Reagan cheerfully pointed to Gorbachev's reforms and argued that the "evil empire" was becoming more benign. Most Americans welcomed improved relations with Moscow.

The INF treaty and Reagan's trip to Moscow marked a significant thaw in the Cold War. While historians still debate the relative importance of Reagan's military buildup versus the Soviet Union's internal weaknesses in producing this outcome, the fact that one of America's most dedicated Cold Warriors presided over the early stages of the Cold War's end remains a striking irony of recent U.S. history.

Conflict and Terrorism in the Middle East and Beyond

Although the Cold War conflict eased, the Reagan administration faced serious challenges abroad. In 1980, and under strongman Saddam Hussein, Iraq invaded its neighbor Iran. The incoming Reagan administration, hoping to slow the spread of the anti-American Islamic fundamentalism fomented by Iran's Ayatollah Khomeini, backed Iraq in what became an eight-year war. (Two decades later, the United States would invade Iraq to overthrow Saddam Hussein, covered in Chapter 31.)

As the administration confronted the ongoing conflict among Israel, the Palestinians, and Israel's Arab foes, it faced conflicting interests. The United States gave its ally Israel large annual grants in military aid and other assistance, while also providing aid to Egypt and the Palestinians and importing oil from Saudi Arabia and other Arab states.

In June 1982, when extremists linked to the Palestinian Liberation Organization (PLO) shot and critically wounded Israel's ambassador to Great

TABLE 30.1 Milestones in Nuclear-Arms Control

Year	Event	Provisions
1963	Limited Test Ban Treaty	Prohibits atmospheric, underwater, and outer-space nuclear testing.
1967	Outer Space Treaty	Prohibits weapons of mass destruction and arms testing in space.
1968	Non-Proliferation Treaty	Promotes peaceful uses of nuclear energy; aims to stop the global spread of nuclear weapons.
1972	Strategic Arms Limitation Treaty (SALT I)	Limits for five years U.S. and Soviet deployment of strategic weapons systems.
	Anti-Ballistic Missile (ABM) Treaty	Restricts U.S. and Soviet testing and deployment of defensive systems. (Allowed to expire, 2002.)
1974	Threshold Test Ban Treaty	Establishes limits on size of underground tests.
1979	Strategic Arms Limitation Treaty (SALT II)	Limits strategic launch vehicles and delivery craft and restricts the development of new missiles. (The treaty was never ratified, but the United States and the Soviet Union observed its terms.)
1982	Strategic Arms Reduction Talks (START)	Sought a 50 percent reduction in U.S. and Soviet strategic nuclear weapons.
1988	Intermediate-range Nuclear Forces (INF)	Commits the United States and the Soviet Union to withdraw their intermediate-range nuclear missiles from Eastern and Western Europe and to destroy them.
1991	START Treaty	Provides for a 25 percent cut in U.S. and Soviet strategic nuclear weapons.
1996	Comprehensive Test Ban Treaty (CTBT)	Bans all nuclear weapons tests and explosions; 179 nations have ratified the CTBT. President Clinton signed the treaty, but the Senate rejected it in 1999.
2002	Treaty on Strategic Offensive Reduction	Requires deep cuts in number of U.S. and Soviet nuclear warheads by 2012.
2010	New START Treaty	Limits United States and Russia to 1,550 nuclear warheads, and re-establishes lapsed inspection and verification procedures. Ratified by the Senate, December 2010.

Britain, Israeli troops under Defense Minister Ariel Sharon attacked PLO bases in southern Lebanon and forced its leaders to evacuate the country. As part of this operation, a Lebanese Christian militia, with Sharon's approval, invaded two Palestinian refugee camps thought to harbor PLO terrorists, where they massacred hundreds of residents, including women and children. In September 1982, Reagan ordered two thousand marines to Lebanon as part of a multinational force to keep peace among the country's religious and political factions. On October 23, 1983, a Shiite Muslim crashed an explosives-filled truck into a U.S. barracks, killing 239 marines. Reagan had never made clear how the deployment served U.S. interests, and early in 1984 he withdrew the surviving marines.

In 1987, Palestinians launched an *intifada,* or uprising, against Israeli occupation of Gaza and the West Bank, territories occupied by Israel since the 1967 war. In response, Secretary of State George Shultz (who had replaced Alexander Haig) proposed negotiations leading to an independent Palestinian state. Israel refused to negotiate until the *intifada* ended, however, and the Palestinians rejected Shultz's proposals for not assuring Palestinian interests. Over U.S. objections, Jewish settlement continued in the occupied territories.

A deadly byproduct of the Middle East conflict was a series of bombings, assassinations, hijackings, and hostage-takings by anti-Israel and anti-American terrorists. At the 1972 Summer Olympics in Munich, Palestinian gunmen killed eleven Israeli athletes. In 1985, terrorists bombed the Vienna and Rome airports and hijacked a TWA flight en route from Athens to Rome, holding the crew and passengers hostage for seventeen days and killing one passenger, a U.S. sailor. That same year, armed men demanding the release of Palestinians held by Israel hijacked an Italian cruise ship, dumping a wheelchair-bound Jewish American passenger into the sea.

PAN AM FLIGHT 103 ENDS IN TRAGEDY The destruction of this plane by a concealed bomb over Scotland in 1988, with a heavy loss of life, was the deadliest of numerous terrorist incidents in these years. *(© Bettmann/Corbis)*

A 1986 bombing of a Berlin club popular with Americans killed two GIs. Accusing Libyan strongman Muammar al-Qaddafi of this and other attacks, Reagan ordered the bombing of Libyan military sites. But the attacks continued. In December 1988, a bomb detonated aboard Pan Am flight 103, en route from London to New York. It crashed near Lockerbie, Scotland, killing all 259 aboard, including many Americans. In 1991, U.S. and British authorities indicted two Libyan officials in the attack. In 1999, Qaddafi released the two for trial. A Scottish court acquitted one, but convicted the other and imposed a life sentence.

The stationing of U.S. troops in Saudi Arabia, site of Islam's holiest shrines, as well as expanding Jewish settlements in the Palestinian territories, fed the anger that fueled terrorist attacks. So did deep religious and political divisions. Hatred of Israel, and even denial of its right to exist, gripped parts of the Muslim world. Radical Islamic clerics called for *jihad* (holy war in defense of Islam) against a Christian (or secular) West that seemed increasingly dominant militarily, economically, and culturally.

The Reagan Years: A Summing Up

Despite nerve-wracking terrorist attacks, many Americans felt confident about the nation's prospects as Reagan's term ended. After Nixon's disgrace, Ford's caretaker presidency, and Carter's rocky tenure, Reagan's two terms restored a sense of stability to U.S. politics. Domestically, Reagan compiled a mixed record. Inflation eased, and the economy improved after 1982. But the federal deficit soared, and the antiregulatory spirit planted the seeds of future problems. Despite Reagan's antigovernment rhetoric, on his watch the federal budget and bureaucracy continued to grow. Reagan himself proved pragmatically ready to compromise when circumstances dictated.

Building on Nixon's strategy, Reagan exploited the anxieties of middle-class white voters. He dismissed 1960s-style social activism, criticized affirmative-action programs, and ridiculed the welfare system by recounting urban legends about Cadillac-driving "welfare queens."

To his critics, Reagan's celebration of individual freedom could readily morph into self-centered materialism. Apart from individualism, anticommunism, and content-free patriotism, they contended, Reagan offered no social vision or common goals around which all Americans could rally.

In 1988, former chief of staff Donald Regan, still smarting over his forced resignation, published a memoir that portrayed Reagan as little more than an automaton: "Every moment of every public appearance was scheduled, every word was scripted, every place where Reagan was expected to stand was chalked with toe marks."

Reagan's admirers praised him for reasserting the values of self-reliance, criticizing government excesses, and restoring national pride. The 1984

Summer Olympics in Los Angeles, they suggested, when exuberant American fans had waved flags and chanted "USA, USA," captured this revived confidence. Reagan's fierce anticommunism and military build-up, they contended, hastened America's Cold War victory. Alzheimer's disease darkened Reagan's post-presidential years, but aspiring Republican politicians still seek to recapture the Reagan magic.

Domestic Drift and a New World Order

George H.W. Bush was a patrician in politics. Son of a Connecticut senator, Yale graduate, and World War II bomber pilot, he entered the Texas oil business, served in Congress, and was a U.N. ambassador and CIA director before becoming Reagan's running mate in 1980. Elected president in 1988, Bush reacted decisively to a foreign crisis, but proved less impressive on domestic issues.

1988: The Conservative Momentum Continues

Easily winning the 1988 Republican presidential nomination, Bush in a Reagan-esque acceptance speech pledged, "Read my lips: no new taxes." As his running mate, he selected Indiana senator Dan Quayle, son of a newspaper publisher.

On the Democratic side, Jesse Jackson again did well in the primaries, but Massachusetts governor Michael Dukakis captured the nomination, choosing Texas senator Lloyd Bentsen to fill out the ticket.

> "Read my lips: no new taxes."

In the campaign, Bush emphasized prosperity and improved Soviet relations, while distancing himself from the Iran-contra scandal. A TV commercial aired by Bush supporters played on racist stereotypes in criticizing a Massachusetts prisoner-furlough program supported by Dukakis.

Dukakis emphasized his managerial skills, pointed to holes in the "Swiss-cheese" Reagan economy, and urged "Reagan Democrats" to return to the fold. But Dukakis's focus on competence rather than ideology offered no compelling political vision. Both candidates relied on sound bites and TV photo opportunities. Bush visited flag factories and military plants. Dukakis proved his toughness on defense by posing in a tank. Editorial writers deplored the "junk-food" campaign.

Bush won, carrying forty states and garnering 54 percent of the vote. Dukakis prevailed in only ten states plus the District of Columbia. The Democrats, however, retained control of Congress.

The Cold War Ends; Global Challenges Persist

The Soviet Union's collapse, heralded by the opening of the Berlin Wall, proceeded with breathtaking rapidity. East Germany's communist regime imploded. The Baltic republics annexed by Moscow in 1940—Estonia, Latvia, and Lithuania—declared independence. The other Soviet republics moved toward autonomy as well.

In July 1991, President Bush and Mikhail Gorbachev signed a treaty reducing their nuclear arsenals by 25 percent. Secretary of Defense Dick Cheney proposed a 25 percent reduction in U.S. military forces over five years. NATO announced major troop reductions.

That August, die-hard communists tried to overthrow Gorbachev. But thousands of Muscovites, rallied by Boris Yeltsin, president of the Russian Republic, protectively surrounded Moscow's parliament building, and the coup failed. Gorbachev, overwhelmed by forces he himself had unleashed, soon resigned, and Boris Yeltsin filled the power vacuum.

The Cold War was over. Speaking at Pearl Harbor on December 7, 1991, fifty years after the attack that propelled the United States into World War II, President Bush proclaimed: "[N]ow we stand triumphant—for a third time this century— this time in the wake of the Cold War. As in 1919 and 1945, we face no enemy menacing our security."

But even as Americans savored the moment, new problems arose, some of them a byproduct of the Cold War's end. As the Soviet Union fragmented, Secretary of State James Baker, a Bush family friend, worked to ensure the security of nuclear missiles based in Russia and in newly independent Ukraine, Belarus, and Kazakhstan, and to prevent rogue states or terrorists from acquiring nuclear materials or know-how from these countries.

For decades, the superpowers had backed client states and rebel insurgencies around the world. As the Cold War ended, some local disputes faded as well. In Nicaragua, Bush abandoned Reagan's proxy war against the leftist Sandinista government. In the Philippines, a former U.S. colony and long-time military ally, the United States closed two naval bases under pressure from the Philippines legislature.

Meanwhile, South Africa's policy of racial segregation—apartheid—provoked worldwide protests, supported by U.S. black leaders and campus activists. In 1986, over Reagan's veto, Congress had

MICHAEL DUKAKIS CAMPAIGNS FOR PRESIDENT IN 1984 To demonstrate his firmness on military preparedness, the Democratic candidate posed in a tank, but seemed dwarfed by the helmet and heavy machinery. *(AP Images)*

joined other nations in imposing economic sanctions against white-ruled South Africa, including a ban on U.S. corporate investment. Yielding to these pressures and to domestic anti-apartheid campaigners, the South African government in 1990 released black leader Nelson Mandela after years in prison. When South Africa scrapped its apartheid policy in 1991, President Bush lifted the sanctions. In 1994, Mandela was elected president and his party, the African National Congress, assumed power.

In 1989, Chinese troops brutally crushed a prodemocracy demonstration in Beijing's Tiananmen Square, killing several hundred students and workers. The Bush administration curtailed diplomatic contacts, but Bush, committed to expanding U.S. trade, did not break diplomatic relations or cancel trade agreements with Beijing.

The Persian Gulf War, 1991

On August 2, 1990, Iraq invaded neighboring Kuwait. Iraq's dictator, Saddam Hussein, viewed Kuwait's ruling sheiks as Western puppets and asserted Iraq's historic claims to Kuwait's vast oil fields.

The United States had backed Iraq in its war with Iran. But now, confronted by Iraq's invasion of a vital, oil-producing nation, Bush responded decisively, assembling a force of more than five hundred thousand U.S. troops. A multination coalition, including Persian Gulf states, contributed additional troops and logistics.

When Saddam ignored a UN resolution demanding Iraq's withdrawal by January 15, 1991, both houses of Congress endorsed military action. Most Democrats voted against war, however, favoring economic sanctions. Vietnam memories stirred as America debated another war.

Beginning January 16, U.S. bombers pounded Iraqi troops, supply depots, and command centers in Iraq's capital, Baghdad. In retaliation, Saddam fired Soviet-made Scud missiles against Tel Aviv and other Israeli cities, as well as against Riyadh, the capital of Saudi Arabia, which backed the U.S.-led war. As TV viewers watched distant explosions filmed through aircraft bombsights, and interceptor missiles streaking off to attack incoming Scuds, the war seemed unreal, almost like a video game.

On February 23, two hundred thousand U.S. troops moved across the desert toward Kuwait (see Map 30.4). Thousands of Iraqi soldiers fled or surrendered. U.S. forces destroyed thirty-seven hundred Iraqi tanks while losing only three. With Iraqi resistance crushed, President Bush declared a cease-fire, and Kuwait's ruling family returned to power. U.S. casualties numbered 148 dead—including thirty-five killed inadvertently by U.S. firepower—and 467 wounded. Iraqi military casualties were

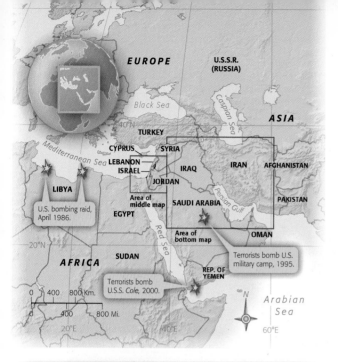

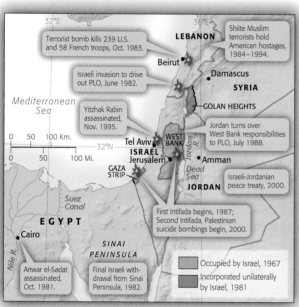

estimated at twenty-five thousand to sixty-five thousand.

For President Bush, the **Persian Gulf War** proved that Americans were prepared to use force to pursue national interests. "By God, we've kicked the Vietnam syndrome once and for all," he declared.

Bush and his top advisers rebuffed some who urged invading Iraq itself and overthrowing Saddam Hussein. Such an invasion, they feared, could lead to an extended occupation. The UN did impose "no-fly zones" on Iraqi aircraft, and a somewhat chastened Saddam granted UN inspectors access to his weapons-production facilities. Nevertheless, Saddam's army brutally suppressed antigovernment uprisings by Iraq's Shiite Muslims and ethnic Kurds.

Troubles at Home: Economic Woes, Racial Tensions, Environmental Threats

At home, a rare accomplishment for Bush was the **Americans with Disabilities Act** of 1990. Supported by Bush, this law barred discrimination against disabled persons in hiring or education. As in the earlier civil-rights movement, Congress acted following demonstrations and lobbying by the disabled and their advocates. Thanks to this law, job opportunities for handicapped persons increased and public schools enrolled more physically or developmentally impaired children.

Otherwise, the Bush years saw more problems than achievements on the home front. By the early 1990s, the impact of Reagan-era tax cuts and deregulation began to hit home. First came the collapse of the savings-and-loan (S&L) industry, provider of home loans and a modest but secure return to depositors. In the late 1970s, as inflation had pushed up interest rates, the S&Ls had offered higher interest to retain investors, even though the S&L's assets were mostly in fixed-rate mortgages. Following the Reagan tax cuts, money flowed into S&Ls with their attractive rates. Meanwhile, in the deregulatory fervor, Congress eased the rules governing S&Ls, enabling them to make loans on risky real-estate ventures. Amid a glut of commercial development, many of these investments went bad. In 1988–1990, nearly six hundred S&Ls failed, especially in the Southwest, wiping out depositors' savings.

MAP 30.4 THE MIDEAST CRISIS, 1980–2000 With terrorist attacks, the Iran-Iraq War, the Persian Gulf War, and the ongoing struggle between Israel and the Palestinians, the Middle East saw almost unending violence and conflict in these years. © Cengage Learning. All rights reserved. No distribution allowed without express authorization.

KUWAIT, 1991: DOCUMENTING THE PERSIAN GULF WAR Dressed in combat fatigues, U.S. press photographers and a TV cameraperson record images from the conflict for the homefront media. *(© Bettmann/Corbis)*

Because the government insures S&L deposits, the Bush administration in 1989 set up a program to repay depositors and sell hundreds of foreclosed office towers and apartment buildings in a depressed market. Estimates of the bailout's cost topped $400 billion.

Meanwhile, the federal deficits mounted, thanks in part to Reagan's tax cuts and military spending. In 1990, Bush agreed to a deficit-reduction plan involving spending cuts and tax increases. Bush's retreat from his "no new taxes" pledge angered voters. Despite this plan, the 1992 deficit neared $300 billion, thanks to the Persian Gulf War, S&L bailout, and soaring welfare and Medicare payments.

Making matters worse, another recession had struck in 1990. Retail sales slumped; housing starts fell. General Motors, battered by Japanese imports, laid off thousands of workers—a foretaste of worse to come. By 1992, the jobless rate exceeded 7 percent and the ranks of Americans living in poverty had risen alarmingly. If 1984 was "morning in America," wrote a columnist, quoting a Reagan campaign slogan, this was "the morning after."

The recession worsened inner-city poverty and despair. In April 1992, an outbreak of arson and looting in Watts, the predominantly black district of Los Angeles and scene of rioting in 1965 (see Chapter 28), left forty persons dead and millions in property damage. The immediate cause was outrage over a jury's acquittal of white police officers whose brutal beating of a black motorist had been captured on videotape.

Underlying the outbreak, too, was tension between local residents and Korean American shopkeepers. The black filmmaker Spike Lee anticipated such a scenario in his 1989 movie *Do the Right Thing*, set in a mainly black district of Brooklyn. In the film, a dispute between the Italian American owner of a pizza restaurant and a local black youth escalates into a full-scale riot that the police combat with heavy-handed brutality.

Environmental worries increased during Bush's presidency. In March 1989, a giant oil tanker, the *Exxon Valdez*, ran aground in Alaska's Prince William Sound, spilling more than 10 million gallons of oil. The accident fouled coastal habitats, killed thousands of sea otters and shore birds, and jeopardized Alaska's fisheries. Bush deplored the spill, but insisted that America's energy-hungry economy required ever more oil, coal, and natural gas.

That summer, air pollution in many U.S. cities exceeded federal standards. A 1991 Environmental Protection Agency study found that pollutants were eroding the atmosphere's ozone layer, which reduces cancer-causing solar radiation. Growing numbers of scientists also warned of global climate change related to increasing levels of carbon dioxide in the atmosphere and the role of human activity in causing it (see Chapter 31, Beyond America).

AFTERMATH OF THE *EXXON VALDEZ* DISASTER An oil-soaked cormorant after the 1989 oil spill in Alaska's Prince William Sound. *(CHRIS WILKINS/AFP/Getty Images)*

Squeezed between environmental concern and his party's free-market ideology and links to the energy industries, Bush signed a stricter Clean Air Act passed by the Democratic Congress in 1990, but otherwise backed oil exploration in Alaskan wilderness preserves, proposed to open protected wetlands to developers, and largely ignored a 1992 UN conference addressing environmental issues.

Of President Bush's two Supreme Court nominations, David Souter, a New Hampshire judge of moderate views, won easy confirmation. With Clarence Thomas, however, Bush continued Reagan's effort to push the court to the right. Bush nominated Thomas in 1991 to replace Thurgood Marshall, a black who as an NAACP lawyer had helped win the historic *Brown* school desegregation case (see Chapter 27). Thomas, an African American with limited judicial experience or qualifications, supported right-wing causes and, as head of the Equal Employment Opportunity Commission (EEOC) under Reagan, had opposed affirmative-action programs.

In the Senate confirmation hearings, a former EEOC staff member, Anita Hill, accused Thomas of sexual harassment. Thomas narrowly won confirmation, but Republican efforts to discredit Hill angered many women, and this may have played a role in the 1992 elections, when women candidates did particularly well.

On the Court, Thomas allied with other Republican-appointed justices who supported expanded executive power and a strict interpretation of the Constitution. Sometimes joined by moderates Sandra Day O'Connor or Anthony Kennedy, the conservative bloc narrowed the rights of arrested persons; curbed death-penalty appeals; cut back affirmative-action programs; and, in *Planned Parenthood* v. *Casey* (1992), upheld a Pennsylvania law imposing restrictions on abortion providers.

1992: America's Voters Choose a New Course

Given President Bush's popularity after the Persian Gulf War, many top Democrats opted out of the 1992 presidential race. But Arkansas Governor **William Jefferson (Bill) Clinton** took the plunge. Fending off reports of marital infidelity, Clinton won the nomination. As his running mate, he chose Tennessee senator **Albert (Al) Gore, Jr.**

President Bush quashed a primary challenge by conservative columnist Pat Buchanan, but at the Republican convention, underscoring the party's rightward turn, Buchanan and evangelist Pat Robertson gave hard-line speeches on divisive cultural issues. A third-party candidate, H. Ross Perot, founder of a Texas data-processing firm, insisted that the nation's economic problems could easily be solved by remedies that voters would ratify through electronic "town meetings." Perot's popularity neared 40 percent at one point, but his eccentricities and thin-skinned response to criticism cost him support.

While Bush promised more attention to domestic issues in a second term, Clinton hammered on the recession and the problems of the middle class. Clinton won 43 percent of the vote to Bush's 38 percent. Perot's 19 percent was the best for a third-party candidate since Teddy Roosevelt in 1912. Clinton did well in the South, carried Ohio and other swing states, and lured back many blue-collar and suburban "Reagan Democrats." The recession, Bush's lackluster domestic record, and the divisive Perot campaign all helped Clinton. With Democrats now in control of Congress and the White House, Clinton's presidential prospects looked promising.

Thirty-eight African Americans and seventeen Hispanics won congressional seats. The new Senate included six women and the House forty-seven. California became the first state with two women senators, Barbara Boxer and Dianne Feinstein. Illinois elected the first African American woman senator, Carol Moseley Braun.

Apart from the Persian Gulf War, President Bush's single term proved unmemorable. A *New*

York Times editorial, judging him "shrewd and energetic in foreign policy … , clumsy and irresolute at home," went on: "The domestic Bush flops like a fish, leaving the impression that he doesn't know what he thinks or doesn't much care, apart from the political gains to be extracted from an issue."

> "The domestic Bush flops like a fish."

Domestic and Global Issues at Century's End

Clinton's presidency soon met setbacks, notably the failure of an ambitious national health-care plan and the 1994 midterm election produced a Republican landslide. Energized congressional Republicans pursued their conservative agenda, including—with Clinton's cooperation—sweeping welfare reform.

Clinton preferred domestic issues, but world events intruded. Abroad, four key challenges loomed: instability in the former Soviet Union, Israeli–Palestinian relations, security threats posed by nuclear proliferation and Islamic terrorism, and U.S. trade and investment interests in an evolving global economy (covered in this chapter's last section).

Trade, Gay Rights, Health Care: Clinton's Mixed Record

Born in Arkansas in 1946, Bill Clinton was part of the baby-boom generation that admired Elvis and came of age in the era of JFK, Vietnam, and the Beatles. After college and a fellowship at Oxford University, he attended Yale Law School where he met his future wife, Hillary Rodham. Returning to Arkansas, he was elected governor at age thirty-two. Now, at forty-six, he was president.

As a founder of the New Democratic Coalition—moderates eager to shed the party's "ultraliberal" reputation—Clinton in his campaign stressed middle-class concerns and muted the party's traditional attention to the poor and social-justice issues. Seeking middle ground on abortion, he said it should be "safe, legal, and rare." He endorsed environmental protection; indeed, his running mate, Al Gore, in 1992 published an environmental manifesto, *Earth in the Balance* (see Going to the Source).

Clinton named women to head several cabinet departments and advisory panels. To fill a Supreme Court vacancy in 1993, he nominated Judge Ruth Bader Ginsberg. (When a second vacancy arose in 1994, Clinton chose moderate liberal Stephen G. Breyer.) In 1996, he named Madeleine K. Albright as secretary of state—the highest U.S. government office ever held by a woman.

To reduce the budget deficit and combat the recession, Clinton proposed military spending cuts, tax increases, and programs to stimulate job creation. Congress adopted the spending cuts and tax increases, but with the economy improving, shelved the stimulus package.

With Clinton's support, Congress in 1993 ratified the **North American Free Trade Agreement** (NAFTA), negotiated by the Bush administration. This pact admitted Mexico to the U.S.–Canadian free-trade zone created earlier. While Ross Perot and others warned that U.S. jobs would flee to Mexico, NAFTA backers, including most economists, predicted a net job gain as Mexican markets opened to U.S. products. (After twenty years the debate continues, with economists finding both positive and negative economic effects within the NAFTA trading bloc, including the United States.)

Other early Clinton initiatives faltered. Fulfilling a campaign pledge to gay-rights organizations, Clinton proposed to end the ban on gays in the military. When religious conservatives and some military leaders protested, he backed off and embraced a compromise summed up in the phrase "Don't ask, don't tell." The ban continued, but officers were barred from querying service members about their sexual orientation.

Health-care reform proved an even greater minefield. With Medicare costs exploding, and millions of citizens lacking health insurance, this issue stood high on Clinton's "to do" list. Working in secret, a task force headed by **Hillary Rodham Clinton** devised a plan for universal health insurance. Cost-containment provisions included health-care purchasing cooperatives, caps on insurance premiums, and limits on Medicare/Medicaid payments to physicians. Higher tobacco taxes would cover start-up expenses.

Lobbyists for physicians, insurance and tobacco companies, and other special interests rallied the opposition. By fall 1994, the ambitious plan was dead. But soaring costs and dissatisfaction with the status quo guaranteed that this issue would remain on the political agenda.

Jolted by these setbacks, Clinton in 1994 turned to issues with broad appeal: crime fighting and welfare reform. His anticrime bill included a ban on assault weapons and funds for more prisons and police officers. After partisan maneuvering, Congress enacted a bill similar to Clinton's proposal.

BILL AND HILLARY CLINTON CAMPAIGNING IN TEXAS, AUGUST 1992 Holding a future voter as microphones record the moment, Bill Clinton demonstrates the popular appeal that helped him win the presidency. Hillary Clinton would soon emerge as a powerful political figure in her own right. *(Bob Daemmrich Photography)*

Clinton's welfare-reform bill put a two-year limit on payments from the federal welfare program, Aid to Families with Dependent Children (AFDC). After that, able-bodied recipients would have to find work, in a public-service job if necessary. The bill included job training and child-care provisions, measures to force absent fathers ("deadbeat dads") to support their offspring, and procedures to bar unmarried welfare mothers who had more babies from automatically receiving increased payments. In 1995, having regained control of Congress, Republicans shaped their own, even tougher bill (discussed shortly).

The approaching midterm election found the administration mired in problems. Republican critics publicized the Clintons' earlier involvement in a murky Arkansas real-estate speculation. The 1993 suicide of an assistant White House counsel, a Clinton insider, attracted conspiracy theorists. In 1994, Paula Jones, an Arkansas state employee, sued Clinton for alleged sexual harassment during his governorship.

Radio commentator Rush Limbaugh won fans for his jeering attacks on the Clintons and liberals in general. The religious Right remained a potent political force. Pat Robertson's **Christian Coalition,** with hundreds of chapters nationwide, controlled several state Republican parties.

Favorable economic news helped Clinton somewhat. Nevertheless, although the inflation and unemployment rates were falling, an ominous 58 percent of Americans told pollsters in October 1994 that they felt no better off despite the economic upturn.

Conservative Resurgence and Welfare Reform: 1994–1996

Bill Clinton had run as a "new Democrat," but by 1994 Republicans tarred him as an old Democrat of the big-government, "tax-and-spend" variety, beholden to gays, feminists, and other "special interests." The failed health-care plan, they charged, simply perpetuated the New Deal/Great Society style of top-down reform.

Al Gore Reflects on Our Relation to Nature

In 1992, the year he was elected vice president, Al Gore published *Earth in the Balance: Ecology and the Human Spirit*. While this best-selling work mostly discussed specific environmental hazards and proposed remedies, Gore here reflects more broadly on modern society's relationship to the natural world.

Civilization has become astonishingly complex, but as it grows ever more elaborate, we feel increasingly distant from our roots in the earth. In one sense, civilization itself has been on a journey from its foundations in the world of nature to an ever more contrived, controlled, and manufactured world. . . . [T]he price has been high. At some point during this journey we lost our feeling of connectedness to the rest of nature. We now dare to wonder: Are we so unique and powerful as to be essentially separate from the earth?

Many of us act—and think—as if the answer is yes. It is now all too easy to regard the earth as a collection of "resources" having an intrinsic value no larger than their usefulness at the moment. Thanks in part to the scientific revolution, we organize our knowledge of the natural world into smaller and smaller segments and assume that the connection between these separate compartments aren't really important. In our fascination with the parts of nature, we forget to see the whole.

The ecological perspective begins with a view of the whole, an understanding of how the various parts of nature interact in patterns that tend toward balance and persist over time. But . . . we are part of the whole too, and looking at it ultimately means looking at ourselves. And if we do not see that the human part of nature has an increasingly powerful influence over the whole of nature—that we are, in effect, a natural force just like the winds and the tides—then we will not be able to see how dangerously we are threatening to push the earth out of balance. . . .

Even though it is sometimes hard to see their meaning, we have by now all witnessed surprising experiences that signal the damage from our assault on the environment. . . . But our response to these signals is puzzling. Why haven't we launched a massive effort to save our environment? . . . Why do some images startle us into immediate action . . . [while] other images, though sometimes equally dramatic, produce instead a kind of paralysis? . . .

Now that our relationship to the earth has changed so utterly, we have to see that change and understand its implications. . . . [T]he startling images of environmental destruction now occurring all over the world . . . are symptoms of an underlying problem broader in scope and more serious than any we have ever faced. Global warming, ozone depletion, the loss of living species, deforestation—they all have a common cause: the new relationship between human civilization and the earth's natural balance. . . .

[T]he faith that is so essential to restore the balance now missing in our relationship to the earth is the faith that we do have a future. We can believe in that future and work to achieve it and preserve it, or we can whirl blindly on, behaving as if one day there will be no children to inherit our legacy. The choice is ours; the earth is in the balance.

Source: *Excerpts from EARTH IN THE BALANCE by Al Gore. Copyright © 1992 by Senator Al Gore. Reprinted by permission of Houghton Mifflin Harcourt Publishing Company. All rights reserved.*

QUESTIONS

1. In Gore's view, how have science and technology altered the way we view nature?
2. Considering economic, political, and cultural factors, how would you answer Gore's rhetorical question: "Why haven't we launched a massive effort to save our environment?"

SECRETARY OF STATE MADELEINE ALBRIGHT WITH JAPANESE DEFENSE MINISTER FUMIO KYUMA, FEBRUARY 1997 Appointed by President Bill Clinton as the first woman secretary of state, Albright grappled with the complexities of a post–Cold War world. *(YoshikazuTsuno/Getty Images)*

> Clinton had run as a "new Democrat," but Republicans tarred him as an old Democrat of the big-government, "tax-and-spend" variety.

A network of conservative organizations, from the Christian Coalition to the National Rifle Association, sustained the rightward swing in U.S. politics. Direct-mail campaigns and conservative radio commentators tirelessly hammered such hot-button issues as abortion, gun control, gay rights, school prayer, "radical feminism," sex education, and an alleged erosion of "family values."

Georgia congressman **Newt Gingrich** mobilized the discontent. In September 1994, about three hundred Republican congressional candidates signed Gingrich's "Contract with America," pledging to support tax cuts, tougher crime laws, antipornography measures, a balanced-budget amendment, and other reforms. The Contract nationalized the midterm election, normally fought on local issues.

In November, voters gave the GOP control of both houses of Congress for the first time since 1954. In Texas, George W. Bush, son and namesake of the former president, defeated a popular Democratic governor. Evangelicals again turned out in large numbers, mostly to vote Republican.

In the Senate, North Carolina's reactionary Jesse Helms became chairman of the Foreign Relations Committee, and ninety-two-year-old Strom Thurmond of South Carolina, presidential candidate of the segregationist States' Rights Party in 1948, headed the Armed Services Committee. In the House of Representatives, a jubilant horde of 230 Republicans, seventy-three of them newly elected, chose Newt Gingrich as Speaker, made Rush Limbaugh an "honorary member," and set about enacting the Contract with America. A constitutional amendment requiring a balanced federal budget passed the House but narrowly failed in the Senate. House Republicans also targeted the Public Broadcasting System and the National Endowment for the Arts, suspected of a liberal bias. Fulfilling the antipornography pledge, Congress passed a Communications Decency Act strengthening the government's

ACTOR CHARLTON HESTON AT A NATIONAL RIFLE ASSOCIATION CONVENTION The NRA was one of a network of organizations that helped stimulate a powerful conservative backlash in the 1994 midterm election. *(© Bettmann/Corbis)*

censorship powers. (In 1997, the Supreme Court ruled it unconstitutional.)

The torrent of bills, hearings, and press releases recalled the heady days of the early New Deal. Now, however, the activist energy came from the conservative side of the political spectrum.

The architect of this revolution, Newt Gingrich, stumbled in 1995 when he accepted, then returned, a $4.5 million advance from a publishing house owned by Rupert Murdoch, a conservative media tycoon with interests in federal legislation. Gingrich's network of political action groups, dubbed "Newt, Inc.," funded by corporations and conservative foundations, also drew critical scrutiny.

Turning to welfare reform, congressional Republicans criticized the system on both economic and public-policy grounds. AFDC, with 14.2 million women and children on its rolls (see Figure 30.1), cost about $125 billion in 1994, including direct payments, food stamps, and Medicaid benefits, up sharply from 1989. Though dwarfed by the benefits enjoyed by the middle class through social security, Medicare, farm subsidies, and various tax loopholes, this was still a substantial sum. On public-policy grounds, the critics contended that the welfare system encouraged irresponsible social behavior and trapped recipients in a multi-generational cycle of dependence. Many linked the soaring rate of out-of-wedlock births to AFDC policies that paid mothers higher benefits for each child.

As a consensus emerged on the system's flaws, debate focused on how to change it. While Clinton favored federally funded child-care and job-training programs to ease the transition from welfare to work, Republicans argued that businesses, the states, and private agencies could best provide these services. Clinton vetoed two bills lacking the safeguards he thought essential.

At last, Clinton signed the **Welfare Reform Act of 1996.** Modifying sixty years of welfare policy, the law replaced AFDC with block grants to states to develop their own temporary-assistance programs within funding limits and guidelines restricting recipients to two years of continuous coverage, with a five-year lifetime total.

Advocates for the poor warned of the effects on inner-city children whose mothers lacked education or job skills, but many observers rated

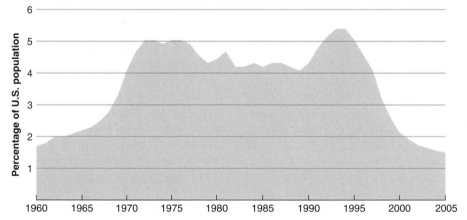

FIGURE 30.1 PERCENTAGE OF U.S. POPULATION ON WELFARE, 1960–2005 From just 1.7 percent in 1960, the percentage of Americans on welfare crept steadily upward until 1994. The post-1994 decline reflected both improved economic conditions and the impact of the Welfare Reform Act of 1996. © Cengage Learning. All rights reserved. No distribution allowed without express authorization.

Sources: Administration for Children and Families, Department of Health and Human Services; House Committee on Ways and Means, Subcommittee on Human Resources Report, February 26, 2006.

welfare reform at least a qualified success. From 1996 to 2005, the number of families on welfare fell by 57 percent (see Figure 30.1), and the out-of-wedlock birthrate leveled off. The percentage of unmarried mothers in the work force rose from around 48 percent in 1996 to around 65 percent in 2000, although many held low-paying, unskilled jobs, and changed jobs frequently. In 2009, as an economic recession hit home (see Chapter 31), the number of families receiving cash-assistance welfare benefits rose, as did the number receiving food stamps. The totals remained far below pre-1996 levels, however.

Clinton Confronts the Post–Cold War World

As we have seen, global crises persisted despit—and sometimes as a direct consequences of—the Cold War's end. In Yugoslavia, an unstable nation comprised of Serbia, Bosnia, Croatia, and other enclaves, the ruling communist party collapsed in 1990. As Yugoslavia broke apart, Serbian forces incited by Serbia's president Slobodan Milosevic launched a campaign of "ethnic cleansing" in neighboring Bosnia. Supported by Bosnia's ethnic Serbs, they killed or drove out Muslims and Croats. In August 1995, after UN peacekeepers failed to stop the killing, a joint U.S. and NATO operation launched air strikes against Bosnian Serb targets.

Later in 1995, the Clinton administration flew the leaders of Bosnia's warring factions to Dayton, Ohio, for talks. The resulting Dayton Accords imposed a cease-fire and created a governing framework for Bosnia. Clinton committed twenty thousand U.S. troops to a NATO operation to enforce the cease-fire.

In 1998, when Serbian forces attacked Muslims in Serbia's southern province, Kosovo, Clinton approved U.S. bombing of Serbian facilities in Kosovo and in Serbia itself, including Belgrade, the capital, as part of a NATO response. As Serb forces withdrew from Kosovo, U.S. troops joined a NATO occupying force, and refugees slowly returned. In 2001, a new Serbian government, eager for Western aid, delivered Slobodan Milosevic to a war-crimes tribunal at The Hague. The trial ended inconclusively with Milosevic's death in 2006.

In Russia, meanwhile, President Boris Yeltsin's position weakened amid hard times and corruption linked to Russia's hasty conversion to a free-market economy. Moscow's costly 1995 invasion of the breakaway Islamic republic of Chechnya further undermined Yeltsin.

Despite Yeltsin's fading popularity, the Clinton administration continued to support him, and used diplomacy, economic aid, and technical assistance to ensure the safe disposal of deactivated nuclear weapons throughout the former Soviet Union. In 1999, the administration backed Russia's admission to the Group of Seven (G-7), the world's leading industrialized nations. In the same year, however, over Russia's protests, the United States supported NATO's decision to admit three new members from the former Soviet bloc—Hungary, Poland, and the Czech Republic. With Yeltsin's resignation in December 1999, Prime Minister Vladimir Putin, a former agent of the KGB, the Soviet secret police, succeeded him as president, opening a new chapter in the tortured history of U.S.–Russian relations.

In the Israeli–Palestinian conflict, of vital U.S. concern, prospects brightened in 1993 when negotiators from the two sides meeting in Norway agreed on a framework for peace providing for a Palestinian state, the return of Israeli-held land in the West Bank and Gaza, and further talks on Palestinian refugees' claims and the final status of Jerusalem (see Map 30.4). In 1994, President Clinton presided as Israeli Prime Minister Yitzhak Rabin and the PLO's Yasir Arafat signed the agreement at the White House.

After hopeful beginnings, however, this initiative failed. In 1995, a young Israeli opposed to the Oslo Accords assassinated Rabin. Israel's next election brought to power Benjamin Netanyahu of the hard-line Likud Party. Suicide bombings in Israel by Palestinian extremists in 1996–1997 triggered retaliatory attacks. Under U.S. pressure, Netanyahu withdrew some Israeli forces from the West Bank. But as attacks continued, Netanyahu halted the withdrawal. By 2000, the West Bank and Gaza had an estimated two hundred thousand Jewish settlers, with accompanying checkpoints, security forces, and limited-access highways making existence difficult for Palestinians.

In July 2000, Clinton invited Arafat and Israel's new prime minister, Ehud Barak, of the more moderate Labour Party, for talks at Camp David. Barak made major concessions, reportedly including acceptance of a Palestinian state; Israeli withdrawal from most of the West Bank and all of Gaza; and the transfer of Jerusalem's Temple Mount, sacred to both Muslims and Jews, to a vaguely defined "religious authority." In return, the PLO would end hostilities and give up further claims on Israel.

Arafat rejected Barak's offer, however, and the summit failed. The Palestinians launched a new *intifada*, and in 2001 Israelis elected the hard-liner Ariel Sharon prime minister. As Clinton left office, the conflict raged on.

In 1997, when Iraq's Saddam Hussein barred UN inspectors from facilities suspected of research on chemical and nuclear weapons, Clinton dispatched ships, bombers, and troops to the Persian Gulf and sought support for a multinational military strike. But France, Russia, and various Arab states resisted, and the stand-off continued.

Other nations, too, posed threats of nuclear proliferation. Neither India nor Pakistan, at odds over the disputed region of Kashmir, had signed the 1968 Nuclear Nonproliferation Treaty (NPT). In 1988, India tested a "nuclear device" and Pakistan soon followed. Both the Bush and Clinton administrations imposed sanctions on the two countries, but the threat of nuclear confrontation in this volatile region remained urgent.

North Korea, despite having signed the NPT, used nuclear-weapons development and missile testing as a bargaining chip to secure economic aid from the United States and other nations. In 1994, facing UN economic sanctions and the loss of international assistance, North Korea pledged to halt its nuclear-weapons program. In 1999, wracked by famine, North Korea agreed to suspended missile testing in return for economic and diplomatic concessions. The secretive nation's nuclear intentions remained opaque and worrisome as Clinton's term ended.

Terrorism: "The War of the Future"

Attacks by anti-American Islamic extremists continued. A February 1993 bomb blast beneath one of the towers of New York's World Trade Center killed six persons and injured hundreds. Five Islamic militants were arrested, and three, including the alleged mastermind, a blind Egyptian cleric known for his hatred of America, were convicted of murder and given life sentences.

The terrorist threat extended to Africa. In 1992, President Bush committed twenty-six thousand U.S. troops to a UN humanitarian mission in Somalia, a predominantly Muslim East African nation beset by civil war and famine. As the warring factions battled, forty-four Americans were killed, including eighteen in Mogadishu, Somalia's capital. President Clinton withdrew the U.S. force in 1994. Later evidence implicated Osama bin Laden in the killings. Son of a wealthy Saudi contractor, bin Laden had been expelled from Saudi Arabia in 1991 and settled in Sudan, where he financed construction and agricultural projects but also plotted anti-Western terrorist activities.

On August 7, 1998, simultaneous bombings of the U.S. embassies in Nairobi; Kenya; and Dar es-Salaam, Tanzania, killed 220—including twelve Americans. U.S. intelligence again pinpointed bin Laden, by now organizing terrorist training camps in Afghanistan. Clinton ordered cruise-missile strikes on one of these Afghan camps as well as on a suspected chemical-weapons factory in Sudan allegedly financed by bin Laden. A U.S. grand jury charged bin Laden with complicity in the embassy attacks and the earlier killing of GIs in Somalia.

Declared Secretary of State Albright: "We are involved here in a long-term struggle …, This is, unfortunately, the war of the future." Underscoring Albright's grim assessment, on October 12, 2000, a bomb aboard a small boat in the harbor of Aden, Yemen, ripped a gaping hole in the U.S. destroyer *Cole*, killing seventeen sailors (see Map 30.4).

> Secretary of State Albright declared of terrorism, "We are involved here in a long-term struggle. ... This is, unfortunately, the war of the future."

Defining America's Role amid Global Changes

As the century ended, the peaceful post–Cold War era that many had anticipated seemed a cruel mirage. The Soviet adversary had collapsed, but crises flared around the world. Like firefighters battling many small blazes rather than a single conflagration, policy makers now wrestled with a baffling tangle of issues.

Some larger trends could be discerned. Economic and cultural **globalization** played an ever greater role. International trade and finance increasingly shaped America's foreign-policy interests. U.S. movies, popular music, and TV programs (including the sermons of televangelists) reached a worldwide audience in an age of communications satellites.

Along with globalization, however, came a widening chasm that divided the prosperous, comparatively stable industrialized world from societies marked by poverty, disease, illiteracy, and explosive population growth. This vast gulf helped spawn resentment, hatred, and terrorism.

Ancient ethnic hatreds re-ignited as the bipolar Cold War world fragmented. The lethal conflict in the former Yugoslavia was far from unique. Similar clashes erupted in many regions. In the African nation of Rwanda, as many as a million people perished in 1994 in genocidal violence between two hostile ethnic groups, the Hutu and the Tutsi.

Thousands more fled in panic, creating a refugee crisis. (The 2004 film, *Hotel Rwanda,* about a courageous Rwandan hotel manager who sheltered over a thousand Tutsi refugees, conveyed the horror of the genocide.) Traumatized by the Somalia fiasco, President Clinton did not intervene.

Religious fundamentalism intensified the global unrest. As Muslim fundamentalists denounced Western liberalism and secularism, a lethal minority—often drawn from an impoverished urban underclass—embraced violence as a religious duty. In India, violence erupted in 1992 when Hindu fundamentalists destroyed an ancient Muslim mosque they claimed had been built on an even more ancient Hindu shrine. Meanwhile, some ultra-religious Israeli Jews (supported by U.S. Christian fundamentalists) claimed a divine right to the West Bank and Jerusalem's Temple Mount, the basis of ancient biblical texts.

Confronting such complexities, some U.S. citizens simply gave up. In a 1997 poll, only 20 percent of Americans said they followed foreign news, down sharply from the 1980s, with the biggest drop among young people. TV coverage of events abroad fell by more than 50 percent from 1989 to 1995.

Newt Gingrich's 1994 Contract with America largely ignored foreign policy, and key Republican legislators pushed isolationist views. Jesse Helms, as chair of the Senate Foreign Relations Committee, denounced the United Nations and criticized environmental treaties. Congressional Republicans refused to pay $1 billion in past UN dues. Bending to such pressures (and to Pentagon objections), Clinton in 1998 declined to sign a multinational treaty banning land mines, even though these mines remain deadly for years, often killing or maiming children.

Nevertheless, opinion polls indicated that most Americans supported internationalist approaches to global problems and envisioned a positive role for America in the world. The U.S. part in negotiating the Dayton Accords that brought peace to Bosnia offered a noteworthy instance of this role. Another came in 1998 when former Democratic senator George Mitchell, appointed by President Clinton as a special envoy to Northern Ireland, helped to negotiate a peace treaty between Catholics favoring independence and Protestants advocating continued ties to Great Britain.

With the Cold War's end, some hoped that the United Nations, long hostage to the superpowers' conflict, could fulfill the role its supporters had envisioned in 1945. Indeed, by 2010, nearly one hundred thousand UN peacekeepers were deployed in fifteen world trouble spots. A complex network of UN agencies addressed global environmental,

THE *USS COLE* AFTER A SUICIDE BOMBING DURING A REFUELING STOP IN THE PORT OF ADEN, OCTOBER 2000 These years saw a rising level of terrorist attacks by anti-American militants based in the Middle East and in North Africa. *(AP Images)*

UN PEACEKEEPERS AT WORK: BOSNIA, 1995 As ethnic and religious violence engulfed Bosnia, members of a United Nations peacekeeping force distribute food to refugees. *(© Bettmann/Corbis)*

nutritional, public-health, and human-rights issues. The UN-sponsored International Court of Justice at The Hague adjudicated disputes between nations and tried perpetrators of mass violence in Bosnia, Rwanda, Liberia, and elsewhere.

Tobacco Wars, White House Scandal, Disputed Election, 1996–2000

Straddling the political center, Bill Clinton won reelection in 1996. Along with sending U.S. forces to Kosovo and the final stab at resolving the Israeli–Palestinian dispute, his second term saw a battle over tobacco-industry regulation and a sex scandal that led to his impeachment. A disputed presidential election in 2000 deepened the nation's divisions.

Clinton Battles Big Tobacco and Woos Political Moderates

Chastened by his party's defeat in the 1994 midterm election, President Clinton fought back. In a 1995 budget battle, Clinton outmaneuvered House Speaker Newt Gingrich, who annoyed voters by twice allowing a partial government shutdown.

Kansas senator Bob Dole, a partially disabled World War II veteran, won the 1996 Republican presidential nomination after General Colin Powell, the popular former chairman of the Joint Chiefs of Staff, declined to run. Fundraising scandals marred Clinton's reelection campaign. After an event at a Los Angeles Buddhist temple attended by Vice President Al Gore, priests and nuns sworn to poverty contributed over a hundred thousand dollars to the Democratic cause, apparently from Asian businessmen currying favor with the administration. But Dole ran a lackluster campaign, and Clinton won with 49 percent of the vote to Dole's 41 percent. (Ross Perot garnered 8 percent.) The Republicans retained control of Congress but proved more subdued than after their 1994 triumph.

Tobacco regulation, a major public-health issue, loomed large as Clinton's second term began. In 1997, facing lawsuits by former smokers and by states saddled with medical costs linked to smoking-related diseases, the tobacco industry agreed to pay some $368 billion in settlement. The agreement limited tobacco advertising, especially when directed at young people.

Because the agreement required government approval, the debate shifted to Washington. Legislators from tobacco states defended the industry, but the Clinton administration backed a bill imposing tougher penalties, higher cigarette taxes, and stronger antismoking measures. The bill's supporters documented the industry's manipulation of nicotine levels and targeting of children. The industry struck back with a $40 million lobbying campaign and heavy contributions to key politicians, killing the bill. The Republican Party, commented Arizona Republican senator John McCain, appeared to be "in the pocket of the tobacco companies." In 1998, the tobacco industry and most states reached a new settlement, scaled back to $206 billion.

Pursuing his middle-of-the-road strategy, Clinton in his January 1998 State of the Union address offered some initiatives to help the poor, such as enrolling the nation's 3 million uninsured children in Medicaid, but mostly highlighted proposals attractive to the middle class (college-tuition tax credits; extending Medicare to early retirees) and fiscal conservatives (reducing the national debt; shoring up social security). Some liberals dismissed the speech as "Progressivism Lite," but it had broad appeal.

Further, Clinton's economic policies contributed to the decade's prosperity and in 1998 produced the first federal budget surplus in nearly thirty years. Under normal circumstances, Clinton's record would have assured that his presidency, despite early missteps, would end in a glow of success.

Scandal Grips the White House

But conditions were not normal. Even as Clinton spoke, scandal swirled around his presidency. Adultery charges had long clung to Clinton, and now he faced Paula Jones's sexual-harassment suit, dating from his days as Arkansas governor.

Seeking to prove a pattern of sexual harassment, Jones's lawyers quizzed Clinton about rumors linking him to a young White House intern, Monica Lewinsky. Under oath, Clinton and Lewinsky denied everything. As the rumors became public, Hillary Clinton blamed "a vast right-wing conspiracy." Clinton settled Paula Jones's suit by paying her $850,000, but problems remained. In telephone conversations illegally taped by her "friend" Linda Tripp, Lewinsky had described a White House affair with Clinton. Tripp passed the tapes to Kenneth Starr, an independent counsel investigating the Clintons' Arkansas real-estate dealings. Fitting Tripp with a recording device, the FBI secured further Lewinsky evidence.

Starr's inquiry now shifted to whether Clinton had committed perjury in his Paula Jones testimony and persuaded Lewinsky to lie. In August, after a promise of immunity, Lewinsky admitted the affair to a grand jury. As the scandal unfolded in tabloid headlines, late-night television jokes, and Internet humor, Clinton in a brief TV address conceded "inappropriate" behavior but attacked Starr as politically motivated.

In a September 1998 report to the House Judiciary Committee, Starr recommended Clinton's impeachment for perjury, influencing others to commit perjury, and obstructing justice by coaching his secretary on his version of events. The Judiciary Committee, on a party-line vote, forwarded four articles of impeachment to the House of Representatives. In a similarly partisan vote, the House approved and sent to the Senate two articles of impeachment: perjury and obstruction of justice.

The public, however, sent the Republicans an ominous message: Clinton's approval ratings rose, and the Democrats gained five House seats in the 1998 midterm elections. Few believed the president's actions met the Constitution's "high crimes and misdemeanors" standard for removal from office. With the economy booming and Clinton's political program generally popular, voters appeared willing to tolerate his personal flaws. Further, many saw him as the target of Republican zealots.

The trial began in January 1999. With Chief Justice William Rehnquist presiding, House Republicans presented their case. White House lawyers dismissed the charges as a "witches' brew of speculation." On February 12, the Senate rejected both charges, and the trial ended. In November, Newt Gingrich, a leader of the impeachment effort but now embroiled in his own ethical and personal controversies, resigned as Speaker and left Congress.

While the impeachment failed, the scandal tarnished Clinton's reputation. Still facing legal liability as he left office in January 2001, the president admitted to perjury, paid a $25,000 fine, and lost his law license for five years.

2000: Divided Nation, Disputed Election

At their 2000 convention, the Democrats nominated Vice President Al Gore for the top job. He chose as his running mate Connecticut senator Joseph Lieberman, who had denounced Clinton's behavior in the Lewinsky affair.

In the Republican contest, Arizona's somewhat maverick senator John McCain, a Vietnam-era prisoner of war, made a strong bid. But Texas governor **George W. Bush,** with powerful backers, a familiar name, and a folksy manner, won the nomination. His running mate, Dick Cheney, had been defense secretary in the first Bush administration. The environmentally minded Green Party nominated consumer advocate Ralph Nader.

Both Gore and Bush courted the center while trying to hold their bases. For Bush, this included energy companies, religious conservatives, and so-called Reagan Democrats in the white middle class and blue-collar ranks. Gore's base included liberals, many academics and professionals, union members, environmentalists, feminists, and African Americans. The Hispanic vote remained divided.

Gore boasted of the nation's prosperity and pledged to extend health-care coverage and protect social security. In TV debates, Gore proved more informed and articulate, but some found him pompous. Perhaps unwisely, Gore kept Clinton at arm's length, despite the president's popularity.

Bush was widely seen as a lightweight, dependent on family influence. As Texas's former Democratic governor Ann Richards quipped, "George was born on third base and thought he had hit a home run." Calling himself a "compassionate conservative," Bush subtly reminded voters of Clinton's misdeeds by promising to restore dignity to the White House. Polls showed that most voters agreed with Gore on the issues, but preferred Bush as a person.

On election day, Gore won the popular vote by more than 500,000. But the all-important Electoral College outcome came down to Florida, where a handful of votes separated the two candidates (see Map 30.5).

THE FLORIDA ELECTION DISPUTE A Fort Lauderdale judge scrutinizes a partially punched-out ballot in late November 2000. *(© Bettmann/Corbis)*

Flaws in Florida's voting process quickly emerged. In Palm Beach County, a poorly designed ballot led several thousand Gore supporters to vote for Pat Buchanan, running on Ross Perot's Reform Party ticket. In counties with many black voters, antiquated voting machines rejected thousands of ballots in which the paper tabs, called "chads," were not fully punched out. When election officials began a hand count of rejected ballots, Bush's lawyers sued to prevent it.

On November 21, the Florida Supreme Court, with a preponderance of Democrats, unanimously ruled that the ongoing recount should constitute the official result. Bush's legal team appealed to the U.S. Supreme Court. Despite a long-established precedent leaving electoral disputes to the states, the justices accepted the case. On November 26, Florida's secretary of state, Katherine Harris, certified the original, contested Florida vote, awarding Bush the state. (Harris, a political ally of Florida governor Jeb Bush, the candidate's brother, had co-chaired George W. Bush's Florida campaign.)

After further legal maneuvering, the Supreme Court on December 12, by a 5-to-4 vote, halted the recount and let Harris's ruling stand. Gore conceded the next day. Five Supreme Court justices (all Republican appointees) had made George W. Bush president. Had the nearly 100,000 Floridians who voted for third-party candidate Ralph Nader not had that option, Gore would almost certainly have won the state and the presidency.

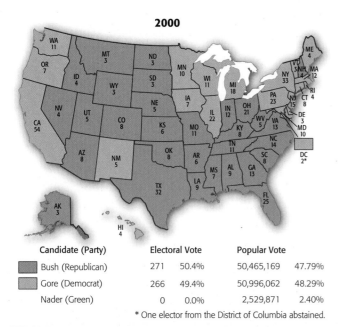

2000

Candidate (Party)	Electoral Vote		Popular Vote	
Bush (Republican)	271	50.4%	50,465,169	47.79%
Gore (Democrat)	266	49.4%	50,996,062	48.29%
Nader (Green)	0	0.0%	2,529,871	2.40%

* One elector from the District of Columbia abstained.

MAP 30.5 **THE ELECTION OF 2000** For the first time since 1888, the winner of the popular vote, Al Gore, failed to win the presidency. The Supreme Court's intervention in the disputed Florida outcome put George W. Bush in the White House. © Cengage Learning. All rights reserved. No distribution allowed without express authorization.

The election produced an evenly divided Senate, giving Vice President Cheney the deciding vote. Hillary Rodham Clinton, the first presidential spouse to pursue an independent political career, won election as senator from New York. The Republicans narrowly held the House of Representatives.

Economic and Cultural Trends at Century's End

The Clinton years saw sustained economic growth, increased productivity, falling unemployment, low inflation, and the first federal budget surplus in years. Economic globalization fueled U.S. economic growth, but when foreign economies faltered, the American economy stumbled as well.

As corporate profits surged and the stock market soared, America exuded a glow of abundance amid leisure-time diversions. But real wages lagged, many workers lacked the skills valued by the emerging knowledge-based economy, and the gap between the super wealthy and most Americans widened. A continuing AIDS epidemic, outbursts of mass violence, and acrimonious cultural disagreements also characterized American society as the twentieth century ended.

An Uneven Prosperity

From 1992 to 2000, the jobless rate fell from 7.5 percent to 4 percent. The gross domestic product, a key economic indicator, rose nearly 40 percent in the decade (see Figure 30.2). Leisure pursuits and consumer spending burgeoned. In 2000, Americans spent $105 billion on new cars and $107 billion on video, audio, and computer equipment. Attendance at the Disney theme parks in Florida and California neared 30 million in 2000. Crucial to the boom was a revolution in information technology (see Technology and Culture).

Wall Street stock prices far outran many companies' actual earnings prospects. From under 3,000 in 1991, the Dow Jones Industrial Average approached 12,000 by early 2001. By 1998, nearly half of U.S. families owned stock directly or through their pension plans. In 1996, Federal Reserve Board chairman Alan Greenspan warned of "irrational exuberance" in the stock market, but with little effect.

Information technology (IT) stocks fed the boom. The NASDAQ index, loaded with technology stocks, shot up from under 500 in 1991 to over 5,000 by early 2000. Some stock offerings by unknown IT start-up companies hit fantastic levels, turning young entrepreneurs into paper millionaires. Corporate mergers and acquisitions in the media industry proliferated. In 2000, communications giant Viacom swallowed CBS for $41 billion. In one super-merger, Internet company America Online (AOL) acquired Time-Warner (the product of earlier mergers) for $182 billion.

The prosperity was spotty, however. From 1979 to 1996, the share of the total national income going to the wealthiest 20 percent of Americans increased by 13 percent, while the share going to the poorest 20 percent *dropped* by 22 percent. Commented economist Richard Freeman in 1998: "The U.S. has the most unequal distribution of income among advanced countries—and the degree of inequality has increased more here than in any comparable country." This disparity would widen in the years ahead (see Chapter 31).

Adjusted for inflation, the buying power of the average worker's paycheck fell or remained flat from 1986 to 2000. As corporations maintained profits by downsizing, cost cutting, and exporting

Unemployment Rate, 1990–2011

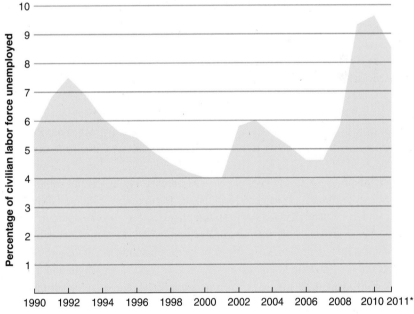

*First Quarter

FIGURE 30.2 UNEMPLOYMENT IN AMERICA, 1990–2011 The overall jobless rate fell during the boom years of the 1990s, though not all would-be workers benefited from the general prosperity. When recession hit in 2001 and more severely in 2008 (see Chapter 31), the unemployment rate spiked upward. © Cengage Learning. All rights reserved. No distribution allowed without express authorization.

Source: *Bureau of Labor Statistics, U.S. Department of Labor.*

The Personal Computer

Computers date from World War II, but in the early postwar decades only government agencies and large corporations could afford the giant mainframe computers manufactured by the International Business Machines (IBM) Corporation (see Chapter 27). Even the smaller models built by Seattle's Digital Equipment Corporation (DEC) were too bulky and expensive for individual use.

With the development of silicon chip transistors and integrated circuits in the late 1950s, the data that could be implanted on a single chip increased enormously. Computers could now be miniaturized. The personal computer (PC) did not spring from a single research project, however, but rather from many young hobbyists. In the late 1960s, for example, Seattle high schoolers Bill Gates and Paul Allen spent their spare time at the DEC plant, where company officials let them tinker in exchange for finding flaws (or "bugs") in the programs (called software) that enabled DEC's computers to perform useful functions. In 1972, Gates and Allen, still teenagers, formed Traf-O-Data, a programming company.

In 1974, an Albuquerque electronics firm, Micro Instrumentation Telemetry Systems (MITS), developed a $397 do-it-yourself computer kit using Intel chips. (They called their computer Altair, a star mentioned in TV's *Star Trek* series.) When *Popular Electronics* featured it on the magazine's January 1975 cover, orders poured in.

With limited memory and primitive programming, the Altair involved awkward levers rather than a keyboard. A practical PC would clearly require better design and better software. Paul Allen, by now working in Massachusetts, and Bill Gates, a Harvard freshman, offered to upgrade Altair's operating system by modifying BASIC, a program developed at Dartmouth College. MITS accepted, and Allen and Gates, changing their company name to Microsoft, moved to Albuquerque. MITS soon collapsed, and the Altair vanished, but the personal computer era was launched.

Early enthusiasts cultivated a countercultural lifestyle. As one later recalled, "[We had our] genetic coding in the 60s, in the anti-establishment…, anti-discipline attitudes." Hobbyists such as San Francisco's Homebrew Computer Club freely shared ideas, hardware, and software. As the PC's commercial potential became clear, however, a business ethic took hold. In 1976, Bill Gates, at age twenty-one, published "An Open Letter to Hobbyists," criticizing the free sharing (or "piracy") of software.

Meanwhile, in Cupertino, California, young Stephen Wozniak and Steven Jobs assembled a prototype small computer in a garage and sold models to friends. In 1976, Wozniak and Jobs marketed their first PC—Apple I—through a San Francisco electronics store. By 1980, sales hit $118 million. Radio Shack and other chain stores expanded their marketing reach. Giant IBM soon took notice, and in 1981 launched the IBM-PC, using Microsoft's operating system.

Whether users chose IBM's PC or Apple's Macintosh (introduced in 1984), personal computers now took off. The sizzling industry fueled the 1980s stock market boom. Youthful entrepreneurs launching start-up companies in northern California's "Silicon Valley" became overnight millionaires as investors bid up the prices of new stock offerings. (When recession hit in 2000, the bubble burst and many of those fortunes evaporated.)

Bulky typewriters, calculators, and adding machines—the information technologies of earlier eras—gathered dust as people shifted to computer-based word processing and data management. PCs transformed office routines in businesses, hospitals, and schools. Instead of typing letters, filing paper documents, running duplicating machines, and entering accounting records in ledger books, secretaries now sat at their PC stations. High-school typing classes gave way to computer instruction. In libraries, electronic databases replaced card catalogs. Computer games transformed kids' leisure activities. PCs' memory capacity continually increased, and the "mouse," developed at Stanford University in the 1960s, made computers easier to operate. By 2007, 251 million personal computers were in use in the United States, and more than a billion worldwide, and microcomputers were standard equipment in automobiles and appliances. Palm Pilot, the first handheld computer, made its debut in 1996.

The computer-based Internet, developed for the Defense Department, initially linked only military installations. By the 1990s, thanks to new software and a system called the World Wide Web, the Internet and e-mail were revolutionizing communications and information-sharing. In July 2009, Americans conducted 10.5 billion searches on Google, Yahoo!, and other search engines. Encyclopedias gathered dust on library shelves as researchers tracked down relevant sources online.

With the new technology came new worries. Would time spent at the PC screen (nearly 28 hours weekly for the average user in 2006) erode human contact? Would video games

THE YOUNG BILL GATES The computer programming company started by Gates and Paul Allen as teenagers grew into the multi-billion-dollar Microsoft Corporation. *(© Bettmann/Corbis)*

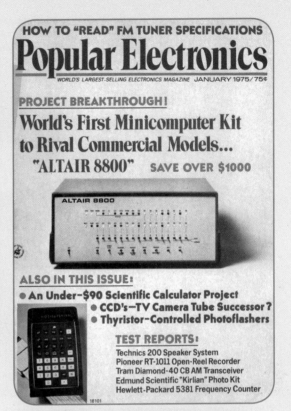

THE PROTOTYPE PERSONAL COMPUTER, THE ALTAIR 8800 The Altair, a name inspired by the TV series *Star Trek*, was operated by levers rather than from a keypad as in later PCs. When *Popular Electronics* featured it in 1975, orders poured in. *(Gernsback Publications, Inc./Picture Research Consultants & Archives)*

isolate the players from social interaction and blur the distinction between real and virtual? Would the slower spread of PCs among blue-collar families and inner-city minorities widen social-class distinctions? Congress and the courts wrestled with the problem of Internet pornography and sexual predators. Viruses and spam (unwanted mass mailings) frustrated computer users.

Privacy issues arose after the terrorist attacks of September 11, 2001. Congress authorized federal agents to investigate library patrons' Internet use, and President Bush approved federal spying on e-mail and telephone communications without court warrants (see Chapter 31).

While the debate flows on, new technologies and applications unfold at dizzying speed. Social networks such as MySpace, Facebook, and Twitter support an endless flow of electronic chatter. Countless bloggers comment freely on political and social developments. Miniaturized devices such as Apple's iPod (2001) allow users to download their favorite music and create their own playlists.

As microcomputer and cellphone technologies converged, wireless devices such as the BlackBerry smartphone (2002) and Apple's iPhone (2007) combined e-mail, mobile telephoning, text messaging, fax capability, Internet access, and media-download

capability. The social and economic impact of all this seemed almost incalculable. CD sales plummeted as music fans turned to online sources. Newspapers faced bankruptcy as readers got their news online. Bookstores struggled as customers purchased books online or bypassed print altogether thanks to Amazon's Kindle (2007), which enables users to download and read books on a handheld device.

From modest beginnings, the personal computer spawned a mind-boggling array of transformative communications technologies. The revolution launched in the 1970s—by a handful of teenagers—changed the world.

QUESTIONS FOR ANALYSIS

- What technological developments made the personal computer possible?
- What were the most important cultural and social effects of personal computers and the new communications technologies they spawned?

THE HUMMER, MACHO VEHICLE OF THE 1990s A civilian version of the Humvee, a military vehicle used in the Persian Gulf War, these gas-guzzling behemoths became status symbols during the economic boom of the 1990s. General Motors stopped production of the largest model in 2006 and shuttered the brand completely in 2010. (© Dick Reed/Corbis)

jobs overseas, workers faced uncertain times. The growing service sector included not only white-collar positions, but also low-paying jobs in fast-food outlets, custodial work, car washes, telemarketing, and so forth. Only 13.5 percent of the labor force was unionized in 2000, eroding this means by which workers had historically bettered their wages and job conditions. As unions grew weaker, protests by labor leaders failed to prevent Congress's ratification of the 1993 NAFTA treaty.

Job market success increasingly required special skills, posing problems for displaced industrial workers and those lacking advanced education. Overall employment statistics also obscured racial and ethnic variables. In 2000, the jobless rate for blacks and Hispanics remained significantly higher than the rate for whites. As shifting immigration patterns created an increasingly diverse American population (see Chapter 31), newcomers with needed skills found well-paying positions, but many took low-paying jobs with few benefits or long-term prospects. In short, while many Americans prospered during these boom years, millions more experienced minimal gains or none at all.

As the economy boomed and banks passed out credit cards like candy, consumer debt soared alarmingly. Unscrupulous finance companies offered would-be homeowners mortgages they could ill afford, often at low "teaser" rates that rose sharply after a year or two. The deregulation of business and banking that began in the late 1970s and continued through the Clinton years (and beyond) encouraged these dangerous trends. Credit buying and the deregulation mania gave the economy a glow of prosperity, but also laid the groundwork for unwelcome economic consequences (see Chapter 31).

America and the World Economy

As the NAFTA agreement showed, trade issues ranked high on Clinton's agenda. When the U.S. trade deficit hit $133 billion in 1993, including a $59 billion trade gap with Japan, Clinton, like his predecessor, pressured the Japanese to buy more U.S. goods.

Global economic considerations increasingly shaped U.S. foreign policy. Despite China's human rights abuses and one-party rule, Clinton welcomed Chinese president Jiang Zemin in 1997 and visited China in 1998. This reflected economic realities. In 2000, U.S. imports from China surpassed $100 billion, making it America's fourth largest trading partner, after Canada, Mexico, and Japan.

In 1997–1998, a banking and credit crisis threatened the booming export economies of Thailand,

South Korea, Indonesia, and other Asian nations and indirectly jeopardized the U.S. economy. The International Monetary Fund, a Washington-based agency to which the United States is the largest contributor, put together a $40 billion bailout package to stabilize the situation. As the crisis spread to Japan, the Clinton administration pressed that country to undertake economic reforms. U.S. prosperity and well-being increasingly depended on developments in a complex global economy.

Affluence and a Search for Heroes

As Wall Street and Silicon Valley spawned thousands of youthful millionaires, *Vanity Fair* magazine in 1997 described New York as "the champagne city, making the brash consumption of the 1980s look like the depression." Elegant restaurants offered absurdly expensive cigars and wines; exclusive shops sold $13,000 handbags. The sales of gas guzzling sport-utility vehicles (SUVs) soared. When a White House press secretary was asked in 2001 if people should reduce consumption to conserve energy, he replied, "[I]t should be the goal of policy makers to protect the American way of life—the American way of life is a blessèd one."

The boom encouraged a hard-edged "winner take all" mentality like that of the Gilded Age, when the rich turned their backs on the rest of society. In *Bowling Alone: The Collapse and Revival of American Community* (2000), political scientist Robert Putnam found diminished civic engagement; weakened interest in public affairs; and a more self-absorbed, individualistic society. *The Prayer of Jabez* (2000), a best-selling motivational book, cited a shepherd's prayer recorded in the Bible ("Bless me indeed, and enlarge my territory") as a key to success. "If Jabez had worked on Wall Street," wrote the author, "he might have prayed 'Lord, increase the value of my investment portfolio.'"

The mass culture offered escapist fare. The 1997 film *Titanic* grossed $600 million. The top-rated TV show of 1999–2000, *Who Wants to Be a Millionaire?*, celebrated raw greed. So-called reality shows like *Survivor* offered viewers a risk-free taste of challenges that contemporary American life itself often lacked, at least for the privileged.

THE McMANSION: DOMESTIC ARCHITECTURE AS CONSPICUOUS CONSUMPTION As some Americans grew rich in the boom years of the 1980s and 1990s, ostentatious and pretentious houses, nicknamed McMansions, sprang up across the country. *(Cal Warlick)*

Millions followed TV coverage of the 1995 trial of O.J. Simpson, a former football star accused of killing his former wife and her friend. The 1996 murder of a six-year-old Colorado girl whose parents had pushed her into child beauty pageants similarly mesmerized the public. The Clinton sex scandals often seemed little more than another media diversion in a sensation-hungry decade.

But the popular culture also offered evidence of more complex social crosscurrents. Some critics interpreted *Titanic,* which sided with its working-class hero in steerage against the rich snobs in first class, as a comment on America's widening class differences. One even called the movie "an exercise in class hatred." Dissatisfaction with a materialistic culture and money-driven politics, some suggested, found expression in bestselling books about past heroes and more heroic times, such as Stephen Ambrose's *Eisenhower* (1991); David McCullough's *Truman* (1993); and Tom Brokaw's *The Greatest Generation* (1998), about the GIs who fought in World War II.

The 2001 film *Pearl Harbor,* argued critic Frank Rich, reflected a longing "for what is missing in our national life: some cause larger than ourselves." Concluded Rich: "Even those Americans who are...foggy about World War II...know intuitively that it was fought over something more blessed than the right to guzzle gas."

The AIDS Epidemic Rages On; Outbursts of Violence Stir Concern

Beneath the prosperity, darker currents stirred. The AIDS crisis continued its deadly course. By 2000, U.S. deaths surpassed 458,000, with more new cases of AIDS and HIV, an infection that often precedes full-blown AIDS, diagnosed each year. Tony Kushner's play *Angels in America* (1991–1992), and the long-running rock musical *Rent* (1996), an update of the opera *La Bohème,* explored the human and cultural impact of AIDS. As knowledge about preventive measures spread and HIV treatments advanced, the U.S. crisis abated somewhat by the early twenty-first century—but the worldwide epidemic continued, with sub-Saharan Africa particularly hard hit.

A popular 1999 film, *American Beauty,* and TV's *The Sopranos,* an HBO series about a mobster and his family, explored a violent substratum in American life. True, overall crime rates fell nearly 20 percent between 1992 and 2000—a decline experts attributed to prosperity, a drop in the young male population, the waning crack cocaine epidemic, and tougher sentencing rules. (The prison population approached 2 million by 2000.) But violent outbursts punctuated the decade. Gun deaths exceeded

MATTHEW SHEPARD Shepard's brutal murder in Laramie, Wyoming, by two homophobic youths in October 1998 stirred nationwide protests. *(AP/Wide World Photos)*

twenty-eight thousand in 2000. In April 1999, two students at Columbine High School near Denver fatally shot twelve students and a teacher before committing suicide. After this massacre, President Clinton called for stricter gun-control laws, but the National Rifle Association fought such efforts.

The culture wars sometimes spurred violence. In 1998, two youths tortured and murdered a gay student at the University of Wyoming, Matthew Shepard, because of his sexual orientation. In the 1990s, at least five physicians who performed abortions or staff members at clinics providing this service were murdered, and other clinics were bombed.

On April 19, 1995, in the decade's worst incident of mass violence, explosives concealed in a truck demolished a federal office building in Oklahoma City, killing 168, including nineteen children in a day-care center. Police soon arrested Timothy McVeigh, a Gulf War veteran obsessed with conspiracy theories. McVeigh, convicted of murder, was executed in 2001. A co-conspirator, Terry Nichols, received a life sentence.

The **Oklahoma City bombing** came precisely two years after a government raid on the Waco, Texas, compound of the Branch Davidians, a heavily armed apocalyptic religious sect led by David Koresh. An earlier confrontation at Waco had left four government agents and six Davidians dead. The April 1993 raid ended tragically when fires inside the compound, probably set by Koresh and others, killed some eighty Davidians as federal tanks moved in. Timothy McVeigh boasted that his Oklahoma City attack represented retaliation for Waco.

GRIEVING A LOVED ONE Columbine High School students (from left) Darcy Craig, Molly Byrne, and Emily Dubin stop to pay their respects at a make-shift memorial set up in a park near the high school, Thursday, April 22, 1999. *(AP/World Wide Photos)*

Culture Wars: A Broader View

While the 1990s' culture wars typically did not descend into violence, they did involve fierce contests that some viewed as a struggle for the nation's soul. During the Cold War, the ideological menace had centered in Moscow. Now, many Americans projected the same black-and-white worldview onto the home-front culture and searched for the enemy within.

The struggle unfolded on many fronts, from tel-evangelists' programs, bookstore shelves, and radio talk shows to school-board protests and demonstrations at family-planning clinics. Some endorsed a constitutional amendment permitting prayer in public school classrooms; others criticized history textbooks as insufficiently patriotic or excessively multicultural. The Southern Baptist Convention, America's largest Protestant denomination, urged a boycott of Disney World for unofficially sponsoring "Gay Pride" days. In 1995, the Smithsonian Institution canceled a planned exhibit marking the fiftieth anniversary of the U.S. atomic bombing of Japan when politicians and veterans' organizations criticized it for graphically documenting the bombs' human toll and for presenting differing contemporary views of the bombings.

Politicized evangelical groups denounced the nation's alleged moral decline. In 1997, thousands of men representing a conservative Protestant movement called Promise Keepers rallied in Washington, DC, for a day of prayer, hymn singing, and pledges to reclaim leadership of their families. Activists complained about Republican politicians who courted their votes but ignored their agenda once in power.

Pat Robertson's *The New World Order* (1991) interpreted world history as a vast conspiracy that will soon end in the rule of the Antichrist. The best-selling *Left Behind* series of novels (1995–2004), coauthored by the conservative activist Tim LaHaye, described an approaching end time when satanic forces will take over America and the world.

But did the apocalyptic culture warriors speak for most Americans? Was the nation as polarized as the overheated rhetoric, amplified by the mass media, sometimes suggested? In *One Nation After All* (1998), sociologist Alan Wolfe found most contemporary Americans surprisingly tolerant of diverse views and lifestyles. "[T]here is little truth to the charge that middle-class Americans, divided by a culture war, have split into two hostile camps," Wolfe concluded. "Middle-class Americans, in their heart of hearts, are desperate that we once again become one nation."

CONCLUSION

What broad themes emerge from the turbulent American scene as the twentieth-century closed—so recent, yet already fading in memory? Certainly the conservative political and cultural turn, symbolized by Ronald Reagan's presidency, looms large. Indeed, some see Reagan as a "transformational president" comparable to Franklin D. Roosevelt. Reagan, a master politician who wrapped his ideological message in a sunny vision of America's past greatness and future promise, unquestionably dominates the era's political landscape.

Yet Reagan did not accomplish the conservative turn single-handedly. He benefited from currents in American public life decades in the making, including an initially muted but ultimately influential repudiation by conservative ideologists of New Deal liberalism in favor of small-government, free-market economic ideas. Underlying Reagan's success, too, was the resentment of blue-collar and middle-class whites against the civil-rights movement and Lyndon Johnson's social programs, a backlash against the antiwar activism and counterculture of the 1960s, and the political mobilization of religious conservatives.

The latter process is particularly interesting. Many of the trends that troubled religious conservatives—secularization, hedonism, the alleged erosion of "family values"—had little to do with politics. They were byproducts of long-term social changes and of contemporary mass culture and a consumption-driven economy driven by television, the movies, and the ceaseless marketing of consumer goods.

Yet from the 1970s onward, prominent leaders and organizations politicized evangelicals' cultural uneasiness, demonizing the Democratic Party as the source of the moral crisis, and the Republican Party as the savior. A great irony of the period is that while evangelicals flocked to the Republican banner, most GOP politicians, including Reagan, gave little more than lip service to their cultural and moral agenda. Instead, they used their power to enact an economic program—tax cuts that particularly benefited corporations and upper-income groups, business deregulation, cuts in social programs—that was quite contrary to the economic interests of their culturally conservative supporters, often drawn from society's blue-collar and lower-middle-class ranks.

Another striking characteristic of Reagan's presidency is his pragmatic willingness to shift positions in light of changing circumstances, despite his ideological commitments. This pragmatism, sometimes on display on domestic policy issues, emerged most dramatically in his welcoming response to the most important global development of his presidency: the transformations in Russia that presaged the end of the Cold War.

In assessing this period, it is tempting to overstate both the completeness of the "conservative revolution" and the pervasiveness of the culture wars. In fact, liberal resistance to the conservative economic agenda remained vigorous and articulate. The federal government that Reagan rhetorically belittled actually grew during his presidency, and the landmark achievements of the New-Deal/Great Society reforms remained in place. In the larger society, major changes, already under way, continued. Race relations, though far from utopian, were vastly different than a generation earlier. Women continued to enter many fields once largely closed to them. Acceptance of gays and lesbians advanced markedly despite the fulminations of cultural warriors.

Where does President Clinton fit in? Opportunistic, accommodating to shifting political currents, Clinton clearly moved the Democratic Party to a more centrist position than that of, say, George McGovern, the party's 1968 presidential candidate. Yet he resisted the harsher approaches of some welfare reformers; battled Big Tobacco's lobbying forces; and, though his health-care reform failed, placed the issue squarely on the national agenda.

From a longer perspective, the era's most notable trends may well be ones little related to political battles or culture wars. The computer revolution, climate change, the rise of a globalized economy, and social/political ferment in the Muslim world all seemed likely to shape America's future in profound ways.

KEY TERMS

Ronald Reagan (p. 920)

Strategic Defense
   Initiative (p. 926)

Osama bin Laden (p. 926)

Democratic Leadership
   Council (p. 928)

Iran-contra scandal (p. 928)

Intermediate-range Nuclear
   Forces Treaty (p. 928)

George H. W. Bush (p. 931)

Persian Gulf War (p. 933)

Americans with Disabilities
   Act (p. 933)

William Jefferson (Bill)
   Clinton (p. 935)

Albert (Al) Gore, Jr. (p. 935)

North American Free Trade
   Association (p. 936)

Hillary Rodham
   Clinton (p. 936)

Christian Coalition (p. 937)

Newt Gingrich (p. 939)

Welfare Reform Act of
   1996 (p. 940)

globalization (p. 942)

George W. Bush (p. 945)

Oklahoma City
   bombing (p. 952)

FOR FURTHER REFERENCE

Michael R. Beschloss and Strobe Talbott, *At the Highest Levels: The Inside Story of the End of the Cold War* (1994). A historian and a journalist-turned-diplomat trace the Cold War's demise.

Robert M. Collins, *Transforming America: Politics and Culture during the Reagan Years* (2007). A perceptive interpretive history linking political, cultural, and technological trends in an era of growing polarization.

David T. Courtwright, *No Right Turn: Conservative Politics in a Liberal America* (2010). A readable work stressing tensions between the conservative movement's economic and cultural camps and noting resistance to the conservative turn.

Jason DeParle, *American Dream: Three Women, Ten Kids, and a Nation's Drive to End Welfare* (2005). A *New York Times* reporter recounts the effects of the 1996 welfare-reform law on three mothers and their children.

Barry Hankins, *American Evangelicals: A Contemporary History of a Mainstream Religious Movement* (2008). An accessible work illuminating evangelicals' beliefs, diversity, and role in American life, both historically and in the contemporary era.

Cheryl Hudson and Gareth Davies, eds., *Ronald Reagan and the 1980s: Perceptions, Policies, Legacies* (2008). A balanced and judicious set of essays assessing Reagan's presidency from differing perspectives.

Susan Jeffords and Lauren Rabinowitz, eds., *Seeing Through the Media: The Persian Gulf War* (1994). Thought-provoking essays on how the media covered the war.

David Maraniss, *First in His Class: A Biography of Bill Clinton* (1995). Investigates the sources of Clinton's political drive and his intense need to be liked.

Lisa McGirr, *Suburban Warriors: The Origins of the New American Right* (2001). A historian's study of grassroots conservatism in pivotal Orange County, California.

Julian E. Zelizer, "Rethinking the History of American Conservatism," *Reviews in American History,* June 2010, pp. 368–392. A provocative essay emphasizing liberalism's persistence despite the conservative resurgence.

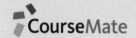

A Changing Nation Confronts Home-Front Crises and New Global Realities, **2001 to the Present**

IN THE SUMMER OF 2009, as a severe recession gripped the United States, a wave of home foreclosures swept the nation. As Dan Barry, a journalist for *The New York Times,* covered the story, he reported on a California company, the Real Estate Disposition Corporation, or REDC, that traveled from city to city, organizing foreclosure sales for banks overwhelmed with foreclosed properties. In Salt Lake City, REDC's mortgage sale was held in the Grand Ballroom of a local hotel. One story in particular caught Barry's attention, and he reported it in *The Times* on July 6, 2009.

ACTIVIST CALLS FOR FORECLOSURE RELIEF Beginning in 2007, a collapse in real estate prices drove millions of Americans to the brink of foreclosure. *(© James Leynse/Corbis)*

In 2002, a young businessman, Paul Furse, purchased a property carved from a former sheep ranch on West Rambouillet Drive in a section of Salt Lake City called South Jordan, overlooking a nearby Mormon Church with the Wasatch Mountains in the distance. Having some construction experience, Furse and his wife, with their four young children, decided to work with an architect to design and build their own home on the lot. They even recorded the construction process in a home video. The children, ranging in age from seven to fifteen, worked on the house afternoons and evenings, while also keeping up with their school assignments.

The family loved their home, built with their own labor, but Furse faced business reverses in a difficult economic environment and fell behind on his mortgage and construction-loan payments. "I could feel it slipping," the oldest daughter told reporter Dan Barry.

Now the foreclosed house stood empty, the furniture gone, the family-room fireplace cold, the wedding and family portraits removed from the walls. The Furse family rented a smaller house some distance from their dream home. As the auction in the hotel ballroom extended into the night, the Furse homestead at last came up and was quickly purchased by an eager buyer. Such stories were repeated many times over in America as a recession that began in the housing market in 2007–2008 gripped the entire economy.

This final chapter of *The Enduring Vision* looks at the events and trends shaping U.S. history today. While Americans adapted to new immigration patterns, a revolution in communications technologies, and unsettling economic changes,

BARACK OBAMA CAMPAIGNS IN SPRINGFIELD, ILLINOIS, AUGUST 2008 Obama drew enthusiastic crowds in his historic presidential campaign. *(© Tannen Maury/epa/Corbis)*

31

differences over cultural issues persisted and a conservative administration in Washington pursued its vision of the nation's future. Looming over the period were the shocking terrorist attacks of September 11, 2001, and the administration's response, including controversial security measures and a bitterly divisive conflict in Iraq. The historic election of an African American as president in 2008 rekindled hope in the nation's enduring capacity for renewal, yet even that euphoric moment was quickly caught up in continuing threats abroad compounded by a severe recession and political gridlock at home.

FOCUS Questions

- How effectively did the Bush administration respond to the September 11 attacks, internationally and domestically?

- What were the principal global challenges facing the United States in the early twenty-first century, and how did Washington (under both Republican and Democratic leadership) respond?

- What demographic and economic trends (in addition to the recession) have most shaped contemporary America?

- What were the causes of the recession that hit the United States in 2008, and what measures did the Obama administration take in response?

- What factors account for the political gridlock and rancorous tone of American politics in the years 2009–2012?

America Under Attack: September 11, 2001, and Its Aftermath

On September 11, 2001, a devastating attack horrified the nation. President George W. Bush mobilized a multinational coalition to invade Afghanistan, stronghold of al Qaeda, the organization responsible. Bush also secured new laws and reorganized federal agencies to tighten homeland security. Accusing Iraq's dictator Saddam Hussein of complicity in the 9/11 attacks, Bush launched an invasion of Iraq as well.

A New Administration, a Day of Horror

Assuming the presidency in January 2001, George W. Bush named General **Colin Powell** as secretary of state, making him the highest-ranking African American to serve in a presidential administration. **Condoleezza Rice,** a Russian specialist at Stanford University, also African American, became national security adviser. Other appointees, like Vice President **Richard (Dick) Cheney** and Secretary of Defense **Donald Rumsfeld,** were veterans of earlier Republican administrations with corporate ties. Ultraconservative John Ashcroft became attorney general.

Bush proposed education reforms, tax cuts favoring the wealthy, an energy bill shaped by the energy industries, and initiatives welcomed by his conservative Christian base. With Bush attentive mainly to his core supporters, his approval ratings fell. This changed dramatically on **September 11, 2001,** a day of horror that energized the administration and dominated Bush's remaining years in office.

On that morning, three commercial airliners hijacked by terrorists slammed into the Pentagon and the twin towers of New York's World Trade Center. As the blazing towers collapsed, 2,752 men and women met their deaths, including nearly 350 firefighters and 23 police officers. The Pentagon attack left 245 dead on the ground. A fourth plane crashed in Pennsylvania when heroic passengers overpowered the hijackers. Nearly 250 passengers and crew in the four planes perished. When investigators identified the nineteen hijackers as Muslims from the Middle East, President Bush urged Americans to distinguish between a few terrorists and the world's 1.2 billion Muslims, including some 6 million in the United States. Islamic leaders worldwide repudiated the attacks, although demonstrators in some Arab cities and Palestinian refugee camps celebrated.

As the nation mourned, political divisions faded. The World War II anthem "God Bless America" enjoyed renewed popularity. "United We Stand" proclaimed billboards and bumper stickers. The airline and hospitality industries reeled as jittery travelers canceled trips. Anxiety increased in October, when letters containing deadly anthrax spores appeared in the offices of NBC News, two senators, and a tabloid newspaper. Five persons, including two postal

> "United We Stand" proclaimed billboards and bumper stickers.

2001
Bush administration repudiates Kyoto protocol on emission standards.

Congress passes $1.35 trillion tax cut bill.

Stock market falls; wave of corporate bankruptcies and scandals.

Congress passes No Child Left Behind Act.

U.S. withdraws from ABM (Anti-Ballistic Missile) Treaty and pursues missile-defense system.

Terrorist attacks on World Trade Center, Pentagon (September 11).

U.S. and allied forces overthrow Taliban regime in Afghanistan.

Captured fighters and others imprisoned at Guantánamo Bay, Cuba.

USA-Patriot Act passed.

2002
McCain-Feingold Campaign Reform Act passed.

Department of Homeland Security created.

Bush authorizes warrantless spying by National Security Administration.

Republicans gain in midterm elections.

2003
U.S. and coalition forces invade Iraq (March 21).

North Korea withdraws from Nuclear Non-Proliferation Treaty.

Prescription-drug benefits added to Medicare.

2004
Revelation of abuses at Baghdad's Abu Ghraib prison.

George W. Bush wins second term, defeating John Kerry.

2005
Congress passes Energy Act.

Trade deficit and budget deficit hit record levels.

Bush names John Roberts and Samuel Alito to Supreme Court.

Hurricane Katrina devastates New Orleans.

Lobbyist Jack Abramoff indicted on multiple criminal charges.

2006
Tom DeLay resigns House seat.

Widespread criticism of government response to Hurricane Katrina.

Radical Hamas organization wins Palestinian elections.

Iran resumes nuclear enrichment program.

U.S. sells India nuclear fuel and reactor parts.

2006 (Cont.)
Administration's immigration-reform bill fails; arrests and deportation of illegal immigrants increase.

Democrats gain control of both houses in midterm elections.

Resignation of Defense Secretary Donald Rumsfeld.

2007
Bush sends more troops to Iraq; violence declines.

Real-estate market falls; recession begins.

2008
United States and Iraq set timetable for U.S. troop withdrawals.

Military situation in Afghanistan worsens.

Recession deepens; major banks fail; job losses increase.

Congress passes bank bailout legislation.

Barack Obama, America's first African American president, is elected; Democrats make gains.

Gaza rockets hit Israel; Israel responds with major military attack causing heavy civilian casualties.

2009
President Obama orders closing of Guantánamo prison.

Obama reverses Bush administration on vehicle emissions, stem-cell research.

Congress enacts broad economic stimulus package as recession worsens.

2010
Supreme Court's *Citizens United* v. *Federal Elections Commission* ruling opens door to unlimited campaign contributions.

Catastrophic BP oil spill in Gulf of Mexico.

Obama signs landmark health-care measure into law.

Dodd-Frank Act regulates abuses in financial-services and mortgage industries.

Republicans regain House of Representatives.

2011
Osama bin Laden killed by U.S. special forces in Pakistan.

Final withdrawal of U.S. combat forces from Iraq.

"Arab Spring" revolutions unseat dictators in Egypt, Tunisia, and Libya.

Budget showdown nearly leads to shutdown of government.

2012
Senate rejects House budget calling for changes to Medicare, cuts in federal spending.

U.S. Supreme Court upholds Affordable Care Act.

Barack Obama defeats Mitt Romney and wins reelection.

workers, died from anthrax-tainted mail. In 2008, a researcher at an army biological research laboratory committed suicide after the FBI identified him as the likely perpetrator.

Confronting al Qaeda in Afghanistan

President Bush declared the attacks an "act of war," and the Senate unanimously authorized Bush to use "all necessary and appropriate force" to retaliate and to prevent future terrorist attacks. The president's approval ratings neared 90 percent. On September 20, before a joint session of Congress, Bush blamed **al Qaeda** ("the base"), an organization headed by Osama bin Laden in Afghanistan. Bin Laden, already under indictment for the 1998 attack on U.S. embassies in Africa, had long denounced America for supporting Israel and for stationing "infidel" troops on Saudi soil.

Bush also targeted the Taliban, a Pakistan-based Muslim fundamentalist movement that had controlled Afghanistan since 1996. This U.S. effort enjoyed NATO backing and broad international

A DAY OF HORROR: SEPTEMBER 11, 2001 Smoke billows from the World Trade Center's north tower moments after a commercial aircraft hijacked by terrorists crashed into it. *(© Hubert Boesl/epa/Corbis)*

support. Pakistan's military government endorsed Bush's decision to invade, despite Taliban enclaves in Pakistan's border regions. On October 7, a U.S.-led coalition of forces launched the attack.

The Taliban soon surrendered Kabul, the Afghan capital (see Map 31.1), and by mid-December, the U.S.-led coalition claimed victory. Hundreds of captured prisoners were sent to the U.S. base in **Guantánamo Bay,** Cuba. With U.S. support, Afghan tribal leaders named an interim prime minister, Hamid Karzai. However, Osama bin Laden, Taliban leader Mullah Omar, and many al Qaeda loyalists escaped capture.

Tightening Home-Front Security

Congress late in 2001 created the Transportation Security Administration to oversee an expanded force of airport security personnel. Over the protests of civil liberties advocates, the Justice Department rounded up hundreds of Middle Easterners in the United States, some for minor visa violations, and held them without filing charges.

The **USA-Patriot Act,** the administration's sweeping antiterrorist bill passed by Congress in October 2001, granted the government authority to monitor telephone and e-mail communications. Civil libertarians and others protested this expansion of federal power. (Congress renewed the Patriot Act in 2005, adding some civil-liberties safeguards.)

The media soon reported missed clues before the 9/11 attack. Through the summer of 2001, President Bush's daily security briefings included warnings of an al Qaeda plot to hijack a U.S. airliner. In August 2001, the FBI bungled a Minnesota flight school's warning of a suspicious person seeking to enroll. (Later linked to the 9/11 plot, he was tried and given a life sentence.)

In November 2002, Congress created a new **Department of Homeland Security,** which absorbed the Federal Emergency Management Agency (FEMA) and other agencies.

In 2005, Bush appointed a Director of National Intelligence to coordinate the government's fifteen different intelligence agencies. Whether such

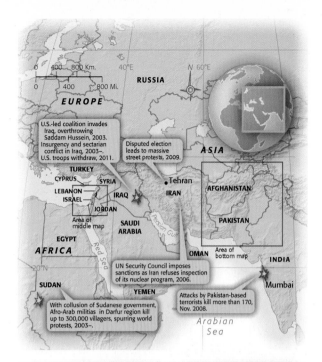

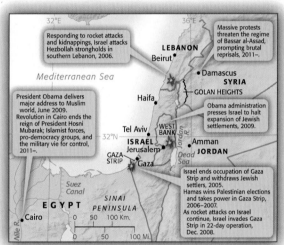

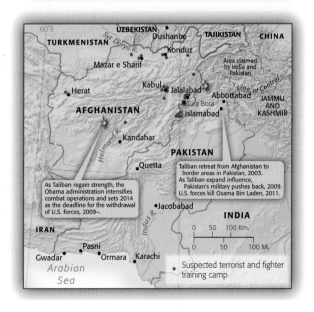

MAP 31.1 **AFGHANISTAN AND PAKISTAN** After the attacks of September 11, 2001, U.S. and NATO forces attacked the terrorist organization al Qaeda, based in Afghanistan. The country's radical Islamist Taliban regime was overthrown, but many fighters retreated to the mountains along the Afghanistan-Pakistan border. Afghanistan remained violent and unsettled, and al Qaeda leader Osama bin Laden was still at large. © Cengage Learning. All rights reserved. No distribution allowed without express authorization.

A GRIEVING NATION Rescuers remove a flag-draped body from the ruins of the World Trade Center. *(Don Tellock/Gamma/Zuma Press)*

bureaucratic reshufflings actually increased security remained unclear.

War in Iraq, 2003–2004

Although Afghanistan remained unstable and Osama bin Laden uncaptured, the administration's attention shifted elsewhere. In his January 2002 State of the Union address, President Bush especially targeted Iraq's ruler, Saddam Hussein, weakened but still in power following the 1991 Persian Gulf War. In coordinated speeches and interviews, Cheney, Rumsfeld, Rice, and other officials accused Saddam of complicity in the 9/11 attacks and of developing nuclear, chemical, and biological weapons.

This focus on Iraq was orchestrated by a close-knit group of Republican **neoconservatives,** including Cheney, Rumsfeld, and their key aides. (The term, meaning "new conservatives," originally applied to Democrats who switched to the Republican Party when the Democratic Party moved leftward in the 1960s.)

Throughout the Cold War, some hardliners rejected negotiation, advocating instead a policy of overwhelming U.S. military superiority and aggressive challenges to Soviet power. With the Soviet Union's collapse, neoconservatives continued to promote the aggressive projection of U.S. power worldwide. Any actual or potential threat to America's global interests, they insisted, must be resisted by all available means, including preemptive military action. For neoconservatives, the traditional foreign policy goal of resolving conflict by compromise conveyed weakness. The point was not to negotiate with adversaries, but to defeat them.

With George W. Bush's election, neoconservatives gained the opportunity to put their ideology into practice. Although Cheney, Rumsfeld, and their top aides were its real architects, Bush was its public spokesperson, clothing it with an aura of religious certitude. America must "rid the world of evil" he proclaimed after 9/11. "The liberty we prize," he added in his 2003 State of the Union address, "is not America's gift to the world, it is God's gift to humanity." The administration's proposed military intervention in Iraq proved controversial from the outset. Critics challenged the administration to prove its claims. A preemptive war would violate U.S. principles, they charged, and could drag on for years, outrage the Muslim world, and divert attention from Afghanistan. British prime minister Tony

Blair backed the administration, but other NATO allies, along with most Arab leaders, objected.

Nevertheless, in October 2002, Congress authorized President Bush to "defend the national security ... against the continuing threat posed by Iraq." While Republicans supported the resolution, Democrats were divided, with some fearful of opposing a resolution Bush called vital to American security. As Lyndon Johnson had cited the Gulf of Tonkin Resolution to justify his Vietnam War escalation, so President Bush used this resolution to justify invading Iraq.

Bolstered by the 2002 midterm elections, in which Republicans regained control of the Senate and increased their House majority, the administration pushed its Iraq invasion plans. In a February 2003 UN speech, Secretary of State Colin Powell, relying on CIA evidence, insisted that Saddam Hussein was developing weapons of mass destruction (WMDs).

On March 19, 2003, U.S. cruise missiles hit Baghdad. Two days later, U.S. and British troops invaded southern Iraq, populated by anti-Sadaam Shi'ite Muslims. Securing the region's oil fields, the invaders moved north (see Map 31.2). In early April, U.S. troops occupied Baghdad and toppled a large statue of Saddam. As the regime fell and Saddam fled, basic municipal services collapsed and widespread looting erupted.

On May 1, aboard the aircraft carrier *Abraham Lincoln* off San Diego, President Bush declared: "[M]ajor combat operations in Iraq have ended." A banner behind him proclaimed "Mission Accomplished." Bush named Paul Bremer, a Foreign Service officer, to administer affairs in Iraq. In December, Saddam was captured. After conviction by special tribunal of Iraqi judges of human-rights and genocidal abuses, he was hanged in December 2006. Iraq's Sunni Muslims, though a minority, long dominated Iraqi politics. Resenting their loss of power, they mobilized to expel the invaders. Radical Muslim fighters from outside Iraq added to the unrest. So did a young

> "[M]ajor combat operations in Iraq have ended," Bush declared.

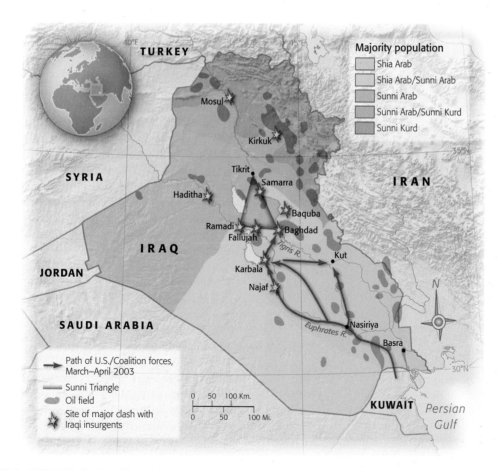

MAP 31.2 IRAQ With Saddam Hussein's overthrow by U.S.-led forces in 2003, violence erupted among Iraq's ethnic and religious groups, including the majority Shia Muslims concentrated in the southeast and the minority Sunni Muslims, who ruled the country under Saddam.

anti-American Shi'ite cleric, Moqtada al-Sadr, popular among Baghdad's poor.

Conditions worsened through 2004, with kidnappings, suicide bombings, and highway blasts caused by improvised explosive devices (IEDs). In June, Bremer transferred power to a provisional Iraqi government, but little changed. The campaign the Bush team had launched so confidently seemed bogged down. Secretary of State Powell, who privately opposed the war, resigned in November. Bush named Condoleezza Rice to replace him.

Politics and the Economy as a New Century Begins

While pursuing the post–9/11 "war on terror," the early Bush administration also proposed tax cuts and other measures reflecting its conservative ideology.

PRESIDENT GEORGE W. BUSH, MAY 1, 2003 Wearing a flight suit, a confident Bush prepares to fly to the aircraft carrier *USS Abraham Lincoln* anchored off San Diego, to proclaim victory in Iraq. (© *Reuters/Corbis*)

Meanwhile, the nation endured a recession and a cascade of bankruptcies and corporate scandals.

Economic Reverses and Corporate Scandals

George W. Bush's presidency began with a short but sharp recession. The high-flying Silicon Valley IT companies led the downturn. An estimated 250 such businesses collapsed in a few months. The market value of the surviving companies plummeted.

The recession soon spread. The stock market fell by 24 percent. Industrial production dropped; unemployment rose. The Bush administration, having inherited a budget surplus, now projected years of deficits. To stimulate recovery, the Federal Reserve Board cut interest rates to a forty-year low.

A wave of corporate bankruptcies and scandals in the energy and telecommunications fields further eroded investor confidence. Houston's Enron Corporation, with close ties to the administration, was an early casualty. A marketer of electric power that had moved into utilities and telecommunications, Enron in 2000 ranked seventh among America's corporations. The end came with brutal swiftness in 2001 when Enron filed for bankruptcy and admitted to falsifying profit reports. More than five thousand jobless Enron workers also lost their retirement funds, consisting mostly of Enron stock. Shortly before the collapse, the company's top officials sold their Enron stock, profiting handsomely. In 2006, a Houston jury convicted Enron founder Kenneth Lay and the company's CEO Jeffrey Skilling on multiple counts of fraud and conspiracy.

In 2002, America's second-largest telecommunications company, WorldCom, admitted to falsifying its annual reports, filed for bankruptcy, and fired seventeen thousand employees. WorldCom's CEO, convicted of securities fraud, received a twenty-five-year prison sentence. Also in 2002, the CEO of Tyco, an industrial-products company, was indicted for looting the company of $600 million, including $2 million for his wife's birthday party on a Mediterranean island. Along with a prison sentence, he was fined $70 million and ordered to repay Tyco $134 million.

> "I cannot think of a time when business ... has been held in less repute."

Declared a Wall Street investment banker: "I cannot think of a time when business ... has been held in less repute." The University of Maryland business school organized field trips to penitentiaries where imprisoned executives lectured students on honesty. Responding to public anger, Congress in July 2002 imposed stricter financial reporting rules on corporations and toughened criminal penalties for business fraud.

Recovery began in 2003, stimulated by consumer spending (much of it on credit) and a housing boom. But prosperity was spotty. While the average real income of the nation's richest 1 percent increased by more than 12 percent in 2004, that of the remaining 99 percent grew by only 1.5 percent. Observed economist Paul Krugman: "It's a great economy if you're a high-level corporate executive or someone who owns a lot of stock. For most other Americans, economic growth is a spectator sport." By mid-2006, even this uneven recovery faltered, and the jittery stock market again sank. The worst recession since the 1930s lay ahead.

The Republican Domestic Agenda

In February 2001, President Bush proposed $1.6 trillion in income-tax cuts over a ten-year period, with wealthy taxpayers receiving the highest percentage reduction. The cuts would stimulate investment,

SCANDAL IN CORPORATE AMERICA Jeffrey Skilling, former CEO of Houston's collapsed Enron Corporation, and later convicted of fraud, testifies before a congressional committee in February 2002. Other corporate scandals soon followed. *(AP Images/Dennis Cook)*

Bush argued. Democrats attacked the bill for favoring the rich and warned that such deep cuts would produce even larger federal deficits.

In May, Congress passed a $1.35 trillion tax cut somewhat less slanted toward the rich. Mounting budget deficits predictably followed, erasing the surplus Clinton had achieved. Nevertheless, the Republican-led Congress cut taxes further in 2003 and 2005.

The administration's 2001 energy bill emerged from secret meetings of oil and gas executives with Vice President Cheney (a former energy company head). Enron's Kenneth Lay, a major GOP contributor, played a key role. The bill eased environmental regulations on energy companies and provided tax incentives to expand coal, oil, nuclear power, and natural gas production, including drilling in Alaska's **Arctic National Wildlife Refuge** (ANWR), strongly opposed by environmentalists.

The bill Congress passed in 2005 included most of these provisions, though. Congress did reject drilling in ANWR and offered tax credits for purchasing hybrid vehicles and energy-efficient appliances and incentives for research on renewable and cleaner energy sources. Despite lobbying by environmental groups, Congress did not tighten vehicle fuel-efficiency requirements. Overall, the law pleased the energy companies that helped draft it.

Bush's education program, labeled **No Child Left Behind,** passed by Congress in 2001, required states to administer standardized reading and math tests in grades four and eight. Schools that failed to raise test scores even after required remedial programs faced the loss of federal funds and other penalties. Critics worried that teachers would focus too exclusively on the tested subjects. Others warned of federal intrusion in public education, traditionally a local matter. As test data accumulated, results proved mixed.

Reflecting Republicans' preference for private-sector solutions to social problems, the administration also supported school vouchers, by which children in poorly performing public schools could receive grants to enroll in private schools, mostly church-sponsored. While many supported the voucher idea, others, including the teachers' unions, criticized vouchers for draining tax dollars from the public schools and allowing private schools to "cherry pick" the most promising applicants. Congressional Democrats rejected Bush's call for a federally funded voucher program.

Some education reformers also supported charter schools, which gain exemption from many regulations governing public schools in exchange for agreeing to contracts mandating specific student achievement goals. By 2011, some 5,600 charter schools across the nation enrolled an estimated 2 million students.

MUSK OXEN IN ALASKA'S ARCTIC NATIONAL WILDLIFE REFUGE Proposals by the George W. Bush administration to permit oil drilling in the refuge stirred controversy. *(John Domines/Time Life Pictures/Getty Images)*

This attention to school reform suggested that the nation's public education system did, indeed, need strengthening—particularly in a globalizing economy and an information-based job market.

Rewarding his conservative religious base, Bush created an Office of Faith-Based and Community Initiatives to funnel tax dollars to church-run social programs. Grants went to antiabortion groups, organizations promoting teenage sexual abstinence, and evangelical prison ministries.

President Bush pleased abortion opponents by restricting stem-cell research. Stem cells are produced during an early stage of human embryo development, and fertility clinics often have "surplus" fertilized embryos. Because stem cells can develop into more specialized human cells, they are valuable for medical research. In 2001, Bush barred federal funding for research involving stem cells harvested from human embryos in the future.

Committed to a free-market ideology, Bush's appointees throughout the federal bureaucracy reduced regulatory oversight of business and finance and weakened environmental and consumer protection laws.

Campaign Finance Reform and the 2004 Election

Citizens who deplored the ever-growing role of money in politics targeted so-called soft-money contributions to political parties that then flowed on to specific candidates. In the 2000 election, soft-money contributions reached $400 million. Big contributors ranged from (mostly Republican) business lobbies, anti-abortion groups, and the National Rifle Association to (mostly Democratic) labor unions, trial lawyers, and teachers' unions.

In 2002, President Bush signed a campaign finance reform bill cosponsored by Arizona Republican senator John McCain and Wisconsin Democrat Russell Feingold. It banned soft-money contributions and restricted TV "issue ads" designed to influence elections. In a 2010 decision, however, discussed later in this chapter, the U.S. Supreme Court largely negated such efforts to limit the role of outside money in campaigns. As the 2004 election approached, Howard Dean, a former Vermont governor, emerged as the early frontrunner for the Democratic presidential nomination. Criticizing the Iraq War, Dean built a following via the Internet, especially on college campuses. His campaign faded, however, as senators **John Kerry** of Massachusetts and John Edwards of North Carolina gained momentum. Nevertheless, Dean tapped into growing opposition to the Iraq War and demonstrated the Internet's political potential.

Kerry won the nomination and chose Edwards as his running mate. Democratic strategists hoped Kerry's distinguished Vietnam War record would neutralize charges of Democratic weakness on defense while underscoring Bush's avoidance of service in Vietnam. Bush and Cheney, raising some

$150 million from corporations and wealthy individual donors, again headed the Republican ticket.

Although Kerry had voted for the Patriot Act and initially supported the Iraq War, he now accused Bush of misleading the nation and criticized parts of the Patriot Act as threats to civil liberties. He also called for stricter environmental laws, tougher fuel-efficiency standards, and support for renewable energy.

President Bush defended both the Iraq War and the Patriot Act. Citing Kerry's changing positions, Republicans accused him of "flip-flopping." Anti-Kerry TV commercials, funded by a shadowy group supposedly independent of the Republican campaign, questioned his Vietnam record.

Cultural issues such as abortion, the death penalty, gun control, and gay rights loomed large in the campaign. In 2004, San Francisco's mayor challenged California law by marrying same-sex couples, and the Massachusetts Supreme Court ruled that banning same-sex marriage violated the state constitution's equal rights clause. Outraged religious conservatives applauded Bush's call for a constitutional amendment banning gay marriage. Antigay marriage referenda, on the ballot in eleven states, passed in all eleven. Bush carried nine of the eleven, including Ohio, a key swing state.

Bush, a tax-cutting president seen as a leader in the "war on terror" and a defender of embattled conservative cultural values, eked out a razor-thin victory, garnering 50.7 percent of the popular vote. Republicans gained a net of four Senate seats and four House seats.

Democrats took heart from the fact that Kerry won 55 percent of voters under thirty, a growing cohort. In Illinois, a young African American Democratic state legislator, Barack Obama, won election to the U.S. Senate.

The election highlighted the Internet's political role. During the campaign and after, *MoveOn .org*, a website initially launched to oppose President Clinton's impeachment and later devoted to resisting the Iraq War, raised funds and mobilized e-mails and telephone calls on behalf of liberal candidates and causes. While conservative organizations had long built support through magazines, direct mail, and talk radio, liberals appeared to have the edge in Internet-based activism, especially among young people.

Conservative political and religious groups remained active. But so did progressive organizations such as People for the American Way, Planned Parenthood, and the Sierra Club. Even among evangelical Christians, support for Bush was not unanimous. Jim Wallis of the evangelical Sojourners movement espoused social justice and the search for peace in his books and *Sojourners* magazine.

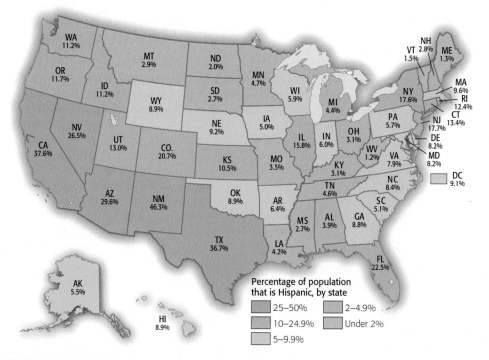

MAP 31.3 **DISTRIBUTION OF U.S. HISPANIC POPULATION BY STATE, 2000** Though concentrated in the Southwest and California, Hispanics represent a significant and growing minority in New York, Illinois, Florida, and other states. Nearly 60 pecent are of Mexican origin, and nearly 10 percent are from Puerto Rico (whose residents are U.S. citizens). The remaining 30 percent are from throughout the Caribbean, Central America, and South America. © Cengage Learning. All rights reserved. No distribution allowed without express authorization.

Source: U.S. Census Bureau, Census 2000, *The Hispanic Population.*

Debating Iraq and Confronting Other Global Challenges

As the Iraq conflict dragged on, home-front support eroded. Revelations of prisoner abuse, illegal spying on U.S. citizens, and distortions in the administration's case for invading Iraq sapped Bush's standing at home and abroad. The Israeli–Palestinian struggle, nuclear proliferation threats, and concern about climate change posed further challenges.

The Continuing Struggle in Iraq

As Bush's second term began, conditions in Iraq worsened. Sunni insurgents in Baghdad and in strongholds north of the capital battled to prevent a Shi'ite-dominated government. A November 2004 anti-insurgent operation in Fallujah involved approximately ten thousand U.S. and Iraqi forces. Typically, however, the insurgents returned after the troops withdrew. Followers of the radical Shi'ite cleric Moqtada al-Sadr attacked Sunnis, GIs, journalists, and foreign contractors alike. Muslim militants from elsewhere, attracted by the U.S. presence, added to the unrest.

Reconstruction lagged, and basic municipal services faltered. A subsidiary of the Halliburton Company, once headed by Vice President Cheney, with $3.6 billion in no-bid reconstruction contracts, faced accusations of fraud. Iraq's vital oil exports remained below prewar levels.

On the political front, Sunnis boycotted a January 2005 election, resulting in a Shi'ite-dominated National Assembly. Sunnis accused Shi'ite militias and Interior Ministry "death squads" of kidnapping and killing Sunni leaders and detonating car bombs in Sunni neighborhoods. In February 2006, suicide bombers destroyed a revered Shi'ite mosque in Samarrah dating to 944 C.E., triggering anti-Sunni reprisal attacks. (The Kurds in northern Iraq, hoping for an independent Kurdish state, remained aloof from the sectarian violence.)

As thousands of refugees fled Iraq or sheltered in makeshift camps, an Iraqi leader lamented: "If this is not civil war, then God knows what civil war is." As other coalition forces withdrew, the United States bore the brunt of the anti-insurgency fighting.

> "If this is not civil war, then God knows what civil war is."

Sagging Support at Home

Under these circumstances, U.S. public opinion turned against the war. In November 2005, Pennsylvania Democratic congressman Jack Murtha, a

CHAOS IN IRAQ: AFTERMATH OF THE DESTRUCTION OF THE IMAM ALI MOSQUE IN NAJAF, AUGUST 29, 2003 As Shi'ite Muslims crowded the mosque for Friday prayers, a car bomb killed at least 125 people, including a top Shi'ite religious leader, and destroyed one of Shia Islam's holiest shrines. The bombing underscored sectarian violence in Iraq following the U.S.-led invasion. *(AP Images)*

decorated Vietnam War veteran, urged immediate withdrawal from Iraq. Conservative writer William Buckley bluntly declared: "[T]he American objective in Iraq has failed." Michael Moore's anti-Bush satirical documentary *Fahrenheit 9/11* packed movie theaters in 2004. Singers including Bruce Springsteen, Neil Young, and the Dixie Chicks country trio expressed opposition to the administration's policies. On the other hand, conservative media voices such as radio personality Rush Limbaugh and commentators on Rupert Murdoch's Fox TV network supported the president, along with many evangelical religious leaders. In an already polarized cultural and political climate, the Iraq War further divided America.

Under critical scrutiny, the administration's arguments for invading Iraq crumbled. After the invasion, investigators found no WMDs. President Bush's claim in his 2003 State of the Union address that Iraq had imported uranium from Africa proved false, and Saddam's alleged role in the 9/11 attacks remained unproven. A Senate inquiry found that Vice President Cheney and other administration officials had pressured the CIA to link Saddam to al Qaeda while ignoring contradictory data.

Defense Secretary Rumsfeld's prewar assurances that a small U.S. force equipped with high-tech weaponry would achieve quick victory proved tragically wrong. When Army chief of staff General Eric Shineski told Congress in March 2003 that success in Iraq would require several hundred thousand troops, Rumsfeld derided this estimate. Although Shinesky's estimate proved accurate, Bush initially rejected calls for Rumsfeld's dismissal. "I am the decider, and I decide what is best," declared Bush in April 2006, "and what's best is for Don Rumsfeld to remain as secretary of defense."

Shocking evidence of prisoner mistreatment deepened home-front malaise. In 2004, photographs surfaced showing the abuse and sexual humiliation of Iraqis held by U.S. forces at Baghdad's Abu Ghraib prison. Further evidence soon revealed a broader pattern of prisoner abuse, approved at the highest level, including at Guantánamo, where more than five hundred prisoners from Afghanistan were held without trial. In a secret 2002 memo, a Justice Department lawyer argued that the Geneva Conventions protecting prisoners of war did not apply to persons the president designated as "enemy combatants." The only interrogations constituting torture, he wrote, were those causing "death, organ failure, or serious impairment of bodily functions." All else was permissible.

This "torture memo," approved by Bush's White House counsel, became public in 2004, unleashing more controversy. The International Red Cross and prisoner rights organizations denounced as torture interrogation techniques at Guantánamo, including "water boarding," in which the victim is nearly drowned. The army, however, called its interrogation techniques "safe, secure, and humane," and the administration claimed the right to hold the Guantánamo prisoners without trial as long as the open-ended "war on terrorism" continued. Evidence also surfaced that the CIA had secretly flown some detainees to an uncertain fate in Egyptian and Eastern European prisons.

In 2005, Congress passed legislation proposed by Senator John McCain forbidding "cruel, inhuman, and degrading" treatment of prisoners. McCain himself had been tortured as a POW in Vietnam. Bush signed the bill but issued a "signing statement," asserting, in effect, that he was not bound to obey it.

This was one of many such pronouncements by which the president "interpreted" bills he was signing, even though the Constitution gives presidents no authority to interpret laws as they choose. The *New York Times* editorialized in May 2006: "This president seems determined not to play by any rules other than the ones of his own making."

Americans also learned in 2005 that President Bush in 2002 had secretly authorized the National Security Agency (NSA), a government body created in 1952, to tap U.S. citizens' overseas phone calls and e-mails without securing a warrant as required by law. Evidence also surfaced that the NSA had tapped domestic as well as foreign phone calls and e-mails and that the FBI had targeted peace groups and journalists for surveillance. In defense of this warrantless surveillance, Bush and Attorney General Alberto Gonzales argued that the 2001 congressional resolution authorizing the president to use "all necessary and appropriate force" to prevent future attacks covered almost anything the administration chose to do. These invasions of privacy disturbed not only civil libertarians but many ordinary citizens as well.

In *Hamdi* v. *Rumsfeld* (2004), the Supreme Court addressed the Bush administration's claim that "enemy combatants" could be held indefinitely. This case involved a U.S. citizen captured in Iraq in 2001 and held thereafter without trial or legal counsel. Eight of the justices agreed that the government had violated Hamdi's Fifth Amendment right to due process. Four justices went further, declaring that all alleged enemy combatants, whether U.S. citizens or not, had the right to trial.

> "This president seems determined not to play by any rules other than the ones of his own making."

In response to criticism, the Bush administration set up special military tribunals, not bound by the customary rules of courtroom procedure, to try the Guantánamo prisoners. In 2006, the Supreme Court ruled that such tribunals violated both the Constitution and the Geneva Conventions.

In March 2006, *Time* magazine reported that in November 2005, U.S. marines killed twenty-four unarmed Iraqi men, women, and children after a roadside IED killed one of their unit. As this and other atrocities came to light, memories of the Vietnam era massacre at My Lai stirred uneasily. Amid a cascade of disturbing news, the reputation not only of the Bush administration but of America itself suffered.

By 2011, when combat operations in Iraq finally ended, as discussed later in this chapter, U.S. military deaths neared 4,500, with more than 33,000 wounded, many severely. Figures on Iraqi civilian dead, both from combat crossfire and sectarian violence, though difficult to tally precisely, clearly mounted into the tens of thousands.

Other International Crises Loom for Bush and His Successors

Despite the open wound of the Iraq War, other urgent global issues confronted the Bush administration, including the Israeli–Palestinian conflict, nuclear weapons proliferation, and climate change. These were long-term challenges, clearly extending beyond any single presidential administration.

On the Israeli–Palestinian front, the Bush administration accomplished little. As the Palestinian *intifada* (uprising) continued, Israeli Prime Minister Ariel Sharon demanded an end to the violence before resuming talks, while Palestinian leader Yasir Arafat insisted that protests would continue so long as Israel fostered Jewish settlements in Palestinian territory. In 2002, Israel began a security barrier, partially extending into the West Bank, to control access and discourage attacks.

The Bush administration proposed a so-called road map to peace in 2003, but it did not push the initiative. In 2005, Israel withdrew Jewish settlements from Gaza, but in January 2006 Palestinian elections gave victory to the radical Hamas organization, which condoned attacks on Israel and even denied Israel's right to exist. Taking control of Gaza, Hamas rejected a call by the United States, the European Union, Russia, and the UN, collectively called the Quartet, to renounce violence and recognize Israel.

Meanwhile, Hezbollah, a militant Lebanon-based Shi'ite organization supported by Iran and Syria, killed or kidnapped several Israeli soldiers and lobbed rockets into northern Israel. In retaliation, Israel invaded Lebanon in July 2006 and bombed not only Hezbollah bases but also bridges, highways, and Beirut's airport. The Israelis soon withdrew, leaving Hezbollah intact and claiming victory.

As Hamas militants in Gaza fired rockets into border towns, Israel in December 2008 launched a full-scale air and ground assault on Gaza, jammed with 1.5 million people. More than thirteen hundred Gazans died, including forty children at two UN schools. The Israelis withdrew after three weeks, leaving Hamas in power and the underlying conflict no nearer solution.

The danger of nuclear proliferation worsened in these years. Impoverished and isolated North Korea withdrew from the Nuclear Nonproliferation Treaty and in 2006 tested both a long-range missile and a nuclear weapon. Despite stop-and-start negotiations, North Korea exploded an even more powerful bomb in May 2009 and fired more missiles, alarming neighboring nations, as well as the United States.

Iran, meanwhile, pursued a uranium-enrichment program, allegedly for nuclear power development. Under UN pressure, Iran suspended this program in 2004 but resumed it in 2006 after the election of Mahmoud Ahmadinejad, a fanatically anti-American, anti-Israeli Islamic fundamentalist, as president. Secretary of State Rice worked with the UN and European allies to induce Iran to open its program to inspection or face economic sanctions, but the stand-off continued. An Iranian long-range missile test in May 2009 deepened uneasiness about its intentions. Citing these threats, the Bush administration pursued a land-based version of President Reagan's missile-defense system (see Chapter 30). Russian president Vladimir Putin vigorously opposed the administration's plans to build radar facilities in Poland and the Czech Republic as part of this missile-defense program.

In 2006, President Bush agreed to provide fuel and parts for India's nuclear power reactors even though India refused to sign the Nuclear Nonproliferation Treaty and barred UN inspectors from its nuclear weapons facilities. Critics warned that this would encourage other nations to pursue nuclear weapons programs. Meanwhile, political instability in Pakistan, a nuclear power, intensified fears of deepening nuclear dangers stalking the world.

On the list of urgent global challenges, environmental hazards and climate change loomed large as well. Three Mile Island, Love Canal, and the *Exxon Valdez* disaster (see Chapters 29 and 30) underscored modern technology's environmental risks.

A 1986 nuclear power plant explosion at Chernobyl in the Ukraine and a 1984 disaster in Bhopal, India, in which deadly gases from a U.S.-owned chemical plant killed seventeen hundred people, highlighted the global scope of these risks. Polluted water caused untold deaths in poor countries.

Environmental hazards included radioactive waste disposal. In 2002, President Bush designated Nevada's Yucca Mountain as the storage site for nuclear wastes that will remain deadly for thousands of years. But as Nevada politicians protested and scientists warned of seismic activity and water seepage in the area, the project stalled. Meanwhile, radioactive byproducts of dismantled weapons and aging nuclear power plants accumulated in temporary sites.

Above all, **climate change** loomed as a grave threat (see Beyond America). The United States, with less than 5 percent of the world's population, accounts for 25 percent of global energy consumption, primarily from fossil fuels widely viewed as contributing to climate change. The Bush administration downplayed the environmental impact of fossil-fuel consumption. Energy conservation might be a "sign of personal virtue," said Vice President Cheney, but had little place in shaping public policy. The administration rejected calls for stricter emissions standards, weakened enforcement of existing regulations, and marginalized government scientists who questioned its policies.

Despite America's important role, climate change remained a truly global issue, with India, China, and other developing economies generating massive greenhouse gas emissions as well. (As host of the 2008 Olympic Games, China did reduce Beijing's notorious air pollution, at least temporarily.)

A 1997 UN conference on global warming held in Kyoto, Japan, set strict emission targets for industrialized nations. President Clinton signed the **Kyoto Accords** but did not submit the document for Senate ratification, fearing defeat. President Bush repudiated the agreement on the grounds that it would hurt the U.S. economy and did not include developing nations such as China and India. The Kyoto Accords, revised to meet U.S. objections, went into effect in 2005, with only the United States, Australia, India, and China remaining aloof.

As late as November 2008, in its final months, the Bush administration opened thousands of acres near fragile national park sites in Utah to oil and gas exploration. Bush's environmental record, charged the head of the EPA under President Nixon, "represents a radical rollback of environmental policy going back … many, many years."

Social and Economic Trends in Contemporary America

As a new century began, long-term population shifts and changing immigration patterns, with other developments, brought significant changes to U.S. society. Upward mobility continued for some, but so did poverty and inequality. Economic changes benefited some but disadvantaged others, including inner-city residents and displaced industrial workers, widening the economic gap between those at the top and the rest of society.

An Increasingly Diverse People

Americans have long been a people on the move, and this mobility continues. California's population grew by nearly 7.5 million from 1990 to 2010, Maricopa County, Arizona (which includes Phoenix), by nearly 1.7 million. The South expanded rapidly in these years as well. Across the Midwest and Great Plains, by contrast, populations remained stable and even declined.

Household patterns changed as well. The proportion of "traditional" families headed by a married heterosexual couple fell from 74 percent in 1960 to under 50 percent in 2007. Commented *The New York Times*: "In modern America no type of family can really be recognized to the exclusion of all others."

Heavy immigration from Asia and Latin America reversed a long decline in the proportion of foreign-born persons in the population. From a low of about 5 percent in 1970, this figure stood at 12 percent in 2010 (see Figure 31.1). The 2010 U.S. population of 308.7 million was about 13 percent Hispanic, 12 percent black, 4 percent Asian, and 1 percent American Indian (see Figure 31.2). The nation's Hispanics—nearly 60 percent of Mexican origin, with Puerto Ricans, Cubans, and Salvadorans comprising most of the balance—are predicted to make up 25 percent of the population by 2050. (See Map 31.3.) Some 6 million Muslims, mainly from the Middle East and North Africa, add to the ethno-religious mix.

These demographic changes have far-reaching political, economic, and cultural implications and offer a preview of a dynamic future nation very different from that of yesterday or today.

Upward Mobility and Social Problems in a Multiethnic Society

African American median household income in 2007 approached $35,000. Although below the

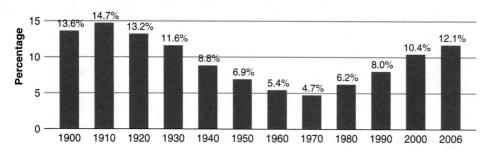

FIGURE 31.1A FOREIGN-BORN AS A PERCENTAGE OF U.S. POPULATION, 1900–2006 After gradually declining from a peak of nearly 15 percent in 1910 to under 5 percent in 1970, the proportion of the U.S. population that is foreign-born again began to rise, reaching more than 12 percent by 2006.

1880			1920			1960			1980			2007		
Country	No.	%	Country	No.	%	Country	No.	%	Country	No.	%	Country	No.	%
Germany	1,967	29	Germany	1,696	12	Italy	1,257	13	Mexico	2,199	16	Mexico	11,739	31
Ireland	1,855	28	Italy	1,610	12	Germany	900	10	Germany	849	6	China*	1,930	5
Gr. Britain	918	14	USSR	1,400	10	Canada	952	9.8	Canada	843	6	Philippines	1,701	4.5
Canada	717	11	Poland	1,140	8.2	Gr. Britain	765	7.9	Italy	832	5.9	India	1,502	4
Sweden	194	2.9	Canada	1,138	8.2	Poland	748	7.7	Gr. Britain	649	4.6	El Salvador	1,104	3

FIGURE 31.1B TOP COUNTRIES OF ORIGIN OF FOREIGN-BORN POPULATION, 1880–2007 (Totals in thousands; % is of foreign-born) This listing of the top countries of origin of the foreign-born population from 1880 to 2007 reveals significant shifts as well, first from northern Europe and the British Isles to southern and eastern Europe, and then to Asia and Latin America.

Includes Hong Kong, Taiwan, and Paracel Islands.

Source: *Bureau of Census, U.S. Department of Commerce.*

national median of around $50,700, this represented a substantial gain, in constant dollars, since 1990. (The recession that hit in 2008, discussed later in this chapter, reduced this figure to $32,584 by 2009.) College-educated blacks enjoyed significantly higher earnings, and 57 percent of black high school graduates in 2005 went on to college. TV's long-running *Cosby Show* (1984–1992), starring Bill Cosby as an obstetrician and his wife (Phylicia Rashad) as an attorney, offered a fictional version of this upwardly mobile group of African Americans.

But many inner-city blacks faced dismal job prospects, poor schools, and drug-related crime. Prison statistics for ill-educated young black males, often involving drug-related offenses, were similarly bleak.

Inner-city black women face risks of drug use, HIV/AIDS infection, and out-of-wedlock pregnancy. In 2010, 72 percent of black births were to unmarried

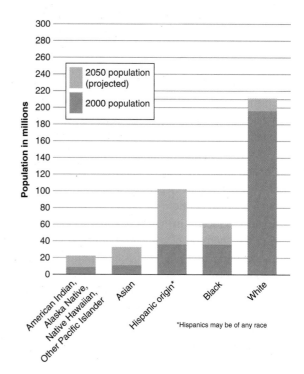

FIGURE 31.2 U.S. POPULATION BY RACE AND HISPANIC ORIGIN, 2000 AND 2050 (PROJECTED) By 2050, the Census Bureau projects, non-Hispanic whites will constitute only about half the total U.S. population.

Source: *U.S. Census Bureau, 2004.*

women, almost twice the percentage in 1970. Many of these unmarried mothers were teenagers, reducing their prospects for education and employment. (Out-of-wedlock births among other groups also rose, but at a far lower rate.)

Inner-city churches and community organizations addressed the multiple social problems of their neighborhoods. In 2006, a group of big-city mayors demanded action to curb the plague of illegal guns.

Among Native Americans, renewed tribal pride and activism continued, including lawsuits to enforce long-ignored Indian treaties. Tribal gambling casinos, approved by Congress in 1988, proliferated. By 2008, about four hundred casinos generated more than $18 billion in annual income. Some tribal leaders lamented the social problems casinos sometimes brought in their wake, but casino income did fund tribal schools, museums, job training, and substance-abuse programs.

The Hispanic population resisted sweeping generalizations. While Mexican Americans concentrated in the Southwest, many lived elsewhere. (See Map 31.4.) Cubans, Puerto Ricans, and Haitians (mostly of African origin), resided mainly in Florida, New York, New Jersey, and Illinois.

Hispanic households' median income neared $40,000 by 2008, and unemployment among Hispanics dropped from 9 percent in 1995 to 5.6 percent in 2007. However, in 2007, 21.5 percent lived in poverty, many in troubled inner-city neighborhoods. Religion and family loom large in Hispanic culture, but stressful social conditions took their toll. In 2007, more than five thousand Hispanics held elective public office, including Los Angeles mayor Antonio Villaraigosa. Ten million Hispanics streamed to the polls in 2008, making them an increasingly important constituency. In 2009, filling a Supreme Court vacancy, President Barack Obama successfully nominated Sonia Sotomayor, a U.S. district court judge of Puerto Rican descent. Of the nation's 13 million Asian Americans in 2007, 75 percent had arrived since 1980. Prizing education and supported by family networks, many followed a trajectory of academic achievement and upward mobility. Nearly 50 percent of adult Asian Americans hold college degrees, and among high school graduates, the college enrollment rate nears 90 percent.

By 2050, demographers predict, given baby-boom mortality and comparative fertility rates, non-Hispanic whites, while still a plurality, will simply be another minority. Adding further diversity, 14.6 percent of newly married couples in 2008 married outside their racial or ethnic group, up from 6.8 percent in 1980. Recognizing these realities, the Census Bureau now permits citizens to check more than one racial category, or none at all.

With the graying of the baby-boom generation (those born between 1946 and 1964), America is also aging. The proportion of Americans over sixty-five, about 13 percent in 2009, is projected to reach 20 percent by 2050—a statistic with profound implications for health care, Social Security and Medicare funding, and other economic and social issues.

The "New Economy" and Its Mixed Effects

In the early twentieth century, industrial production replaced agriculture as America's economic engine. The century's end saw an equally profound transformation: the rise of a professional and service-based economy (see Figure 31.3). Farming and manufacturing continued, of course, but with far fewer workers.

In the U.S. work force of 154 million in 2011, about 60 percent held white-collar jobs, ranging from sales clerks, office workers, and teachers to physicians, lawyers, engineers, computer programmers, and business executives. Service-sector employees in health care, custodial work, restaurants, and so forth accounted for another 16 percent. Only 23 percent worked in manual-labor fields that as recently as 1960 had dominated the labor market.

2008

Candidate (Party)	Electoral Vote		Popular Vote	
Obama (Democrat)	365	68%	69,498,459	52.9%
McCain (Republican)	173	32%	59,948,283	45.6%

MAP 31.4   THE ELECTION OF 2008 In a definitive result, Barack Obama defeated John McCain with nearly 53 percent of the popular vote and 68 percent of the electoral vote. Obama made deep inroads into traditional Republican strongholds, winning Indiana, Virginia, and North Carolina. © Cengage Learning. All rights reserved. No distribution allowed without express authorization.

AMERICANIZATION, TWENTY-FIRST-CENTURY STYLE Recent immigrants from Afghanistan join a fitness class in Fremont, California, in 2001. *(Monica Almeida/The New York Times/Redux)*

This transformation had mixed effects. Young people with education, skills, and contacts did well in the new electronics, programming, and telecommunications fields and in the corporate and financial services sectors. For others, supermarkets, car washes, fast-food outlets, and discount superstores provided entry-level jobs, but few long-term prospects.

As the computer-based information revolution continued (see Chapter 30, Technology and Culture), newspaper circulation fell significantly. Even major papers such as *The New York Times* faced hard times as Americans turned to TV or online news sources—which for some meant Jon Stewart's satirical *Daily Show* on TV's Comedy Central. The new technologies affected the music and book industries as well. CD sales fell dramatically as fans downloaded songs electronically to their laptops or iPods. Bound-book sales declined as readers turned to handheld devices. The bookstore chain Borders declared bankruptcy in 2011.

The economic transformation summed up by the term "globalization" complicated all these changes. Today's large corporations and financial institutions are all global in scope. Thanks to regional trading blocs such as NAFTA and multinational agreements administered by the **World Trade Organization** (WTO), the production and marketing of goods and the flow of capital now largely ignores national boundaries. The WTO, created in 1995 as successor to an earlier body set up in 1947, monitors and promotes trade among its 153 member nations.

The 2007 U.S. trade deficit approached $800 billion. This imbalance mainly reflected imports of oil, automobiles (mostly Japanese), and consumer goods from China. The 2007 trade deficit with China alone surged to $256 billion. Managing U.S.–Chinese economic relations proved particularly complex. U.S. manufacturers complained that China artificially manipulated its currency to make Chinese exports cheaper. However, big-box discounters, and their customers, welcomed cheap Chinese imports.

China's 2010 gross domestic product (GDP) of $8.7 trillion ranked second in the world, after the United States. Some economists predicted that China's GDP would surpass America's in twenty years. For China to sustain its growth and provide its people a higher living standard, the U.S. market was crucial. On exchange visits in 2005 and 2006, President Bush and China's leaders acknowledged their economic interdependence, while recognizing

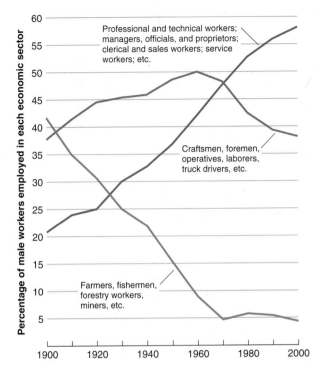

FIGURE 31.3 CHANGING PATTERNS OF WORK, 1900–2000
This chart illustrates the sweeping changes in the U.S. labor force in the twentieth century. The proportion of male workers in farming, fishing, forestry, and mining fell dramatically. The percentage of workers in industry and related occupations climbed until about 1960, and then began to decline. The service, technical, managerial, sales, clerical, and professional categories rose steadily throughout the century. © Cengage Learning.

Sources: *Historical Statistics of the United States, Colonial Times to 1970 (1975); Statistical Abstract of the United States, 2002; Caplow, Hicks, and Wattenberg,* The First Measured Century: An Illustrated Guide to Trends in America *(Washington, DC: The AEI Press, 2001).*

strains in the relationship, including China's repressive regime and poor human-rights record.

U.S. economic well-being increasingly depends on developments beyond the nation's borders. As imports replaced American-made products and manufacturers shifted operations overseas to cut labor costs, displaced workers faced unemployment or lower-wage service-sector jobs. Union membership by 2007 sank to only 12 percent of the labor force, leaving workers even more vulnerable.

The shifting fortunes of the U.S. auto industry typifies the pattern. After losing sales because of rising gasoline prices in the 1970s (see Chapter 30), American carmakers had returned to profitability with gas-guzzling SUVs and light trucks. But as gas prices again rose after 2000, car buyers turned to more fuel-efficient imports, particularly Japan's Toyota, Honda, and Nissan. By mid-2007, foreign carmakers had captured more than half the U.S. market—a historic first.

Foreign automakers set up U.S. production plants, mostly in the South and West, and mostly nonunion. By 2008, Toyota employed thirty-six thousand workers in fourteen U.S. plants and supported thousands more through its dealerships, parts suppliers, and advertising agencies.

At GM, a century-old icon of America's industrial might, annual losses spurted to nearly $39 billion in 2008. GM's stock price tumbled, and the company shed tens of thousands of jobs. Said one GM engineer: "This once was the premier company ... to work for. You were at the top of the heap, the major leagues. ... Today, you know this company is crumbling around you."

From 2005 through mid-2008, GM, Chrysler, and Ford eliminated nearly 150,000 jobs and closed thirty-five plants, causing pain across America. The 2008 recession (discussed later in this chapter) further battered the domestic auto companies, though a government bailout helped them weather the storm. Economists continued to defend globalization as beneficial for America overall, lowering consumer prices and opening world markets for U.S. exports. But for displaced workers, this was cold comfort. In addition to the impact on U.S. industrial workers, human-rights activists charged that corporations in a "race to the bottom" open factories in poor countries where workers, often young women, live in prison-like barracks and work long hours for low wages with no benefits. Such factories often are environmental polluters as well.

Amid economic worries and a "war on terror," post–9/11 popular culture reflected crosscurrents of anxiety and escapism. Rupert Murdoch's Fox TV network, while rallying support for Bush, also offered the top-rated *American Idol* program, in which amateur vocalists competed for audience votes. Such shows, along with long-running syndicated game shows *Jeopardy* and *Wheel of Fortune* and the contrived scenarios of so-called reality programs, provided distraction from the stress of contemporary life. A longing to obliterate shadowy enemies perhaps contributed to the success of fantasy movies such as *Spider-Man 3* (2007) and *The Incredible Hulk* (2008), in which comic-book superheroes battle menacing foes.

> "This once was the premier company ... to work for. You were at the top of the heap, the major leagues. ... Today, you know this company is crumbling around you."

THE CONTEMPORARY U.S. WORKPLACE: YOUNG WORKERS AT GOOGLE RELAX IN THE COMPANY GAME ROOM; AN ELDERLY WALMART EMPLOYEE WALKS THE AISLES While skilled workers in the information technology fields did well, unskilled and older workers often struggled to make ends meet in low-wage jobs with few benefits. *(© Catherine Karnow/CORBIS; © James Leynse/CORBIS)*

The Bush Era Ends

Along with the ongoing Iraq War, President Bush's second term brought multiple setbacks, including soaring federal deficits, a bungled attempt at immigration reform, and an inept response to a devastating hurricane. Two Supreme Court appointments extended Bush's conservative legacy, but lobbying scandals further eroded Bush's standing as his term ended.

Mounting Deficits, Immigration Controversies, Disaster in New Orleans

In 2003, Congress enacted Bush's proposal to pay part of seniors' prescription drug expenses under the federal Medicare program. Democrats charged that the plan mainly benefited drug firms and insurance companies and would worsen a deepening federal budget deficit.

George W. Bush, leader of a party historically committed to fiscal prudence, presided over spending levels unprecedented in U.S. history. The prescription drug benefit helped push the government's share of Medicare costs to $179 billion in 2007, more than five times the 1990 figure. Medicare and social security costs, plus Bush's tax cuts, the unfunded Iraq and Afghan wars, and interest payments on the national debt, produced yawning federal deficits from 2002 on. Congress members of both parties continued the time-honored practice of quietly inserting into spending bills pet projects known as "earmarks" that benefited their districts.

Foreign investors funded the mushrooming federal debt by purchasing U.S. government bonds. China, awash in dollars—thanks to its U.S. exports—held nearly $700 billion in U.S. government bonds by 2008.

In 2005, Bush proposed a partial privatization of social security, the New Deal pension program. Under Bush's plan, people could shift some of their social security funds to private investment accounts. Although the social security system faced budgetary strains as the baby-boom generation retired, Bush's scheme failed to win acceptance. Most citizens preferred a government program to the uncertainties of the market.

The administration stumbled again over immigration policy. Of the estimated 11 million undocumented immigrants in the United States, most from Mexico or elsewhere in Latin America, many worked in a low-wage "shadow economy" as farm laborers, janitors, motel cleaners, or nursing-home attendants or in food-processing plants. In 2005, the administration proposed a bill by which these workers could eventually gain legal status. The debate that erupted revealed deep divisions in U.S. public opinion. Supporters invoked America's tradition of welcoming newcomers. Undocumented immigrants, they argued, did the essential work shunned by others. Businesses employing immigrants supported the bill. But opponents denounced it as "amnesty" for lawbreakers. Deport them, they argued, and the law of supply-and-demand would push up wages for the jobs they held, attracting U.S.-born workers. Late in 2005, the House of Representatives, with strong Republican support, defied the administration by passing a tough immigration bill criminalizing illegal aliens and requiring their deportation; strengthening the U.S.–Mexican border; and making it a felony for anyone, including ministers, priests, and health-care providers, to help undocumented immigrants.

The reaction was swift. Religious leaders denounced the bill. Protesters, supported by Spanish-language radio and TV, marched in Los Angeles and other cities. The bill's supporters mobilized as well. Radio personality Rush Limbaugh angrily denounced the marches. In the Southwest, volunteers organized a vigilante-like "Minuteman Project" to patrol the border.

With the Hispanic vote in play (some called it "the sleeping giant of American politics"), politicians proceeded cautiously. In the Senate, a bipartisan bill funded tougher border controls, but also established procedures by which undocumented immigrants could secure citizenship. Defying the White House, a bloc of Senate Republicans defeated the compromise bill.

Abandoning immigration reform, the administration took a harsh line. In 2006, Bush signed a bill to build a 700-mile reinforced fence along the U.S.–Mexican border. Federal agents raided plants employing undocumented Hispanics. Humanitarian and civil-rights groups protested, noting the impact on children and disrupted families. A 2008 film, *The Visitor,* portrayed the human consequences of rigidly enforced deportation policies. In 2008, the Supreme Court struck down an administration effort to deny deportees legal representation.

The administration took another hit in August 2005, when **Hurricane Katrina** struck the Gulf Coast, taking as many as fourteen hundred lives, inflicting heavy property damage, disrupting shipping on the Mississippi River, and smashing oil refineries and offshore oil rigs. New Orleans suffered most. Much of the city lies below sea level, protected by levees. Over the years, developers drained surrounding marshland, destroying a buffer against storm surges. As New Orleans' levees

NEW ORLEANS IN THE AFTERMATH OF HURRICANE KATRINA, SEPTEMBER 1, 2005 Four days after the city's levees burst and flood waters devastated their homes, New Orleans residents await evacuation to the Superdome, which quickly became a scene of nightmarish conditions as thousands of desperate people crowded in. *(© Bettmann/Corbis/ Michael Ainsworth/Dallas Morning News/Corbis)*

burst, rampaging water flooded the lower wards, home to many poor blacks. Many drowned or died awaiting rescue. Others lost homes and possessions. The elderly, hospitalized, and nursing home residents suffered most. Thousands poured into New Orleans's Superdome, which soon became a squalid disaster zone.

Washington's response was appallingly inadequate. Despite a local FEMA official's urgent warnings, neither President Bush nor the Homeland Security director recognized the emergency. FEMA head Michael Brown, a political appointee with no disaster experience, proved hopelessly inept. Though praised by Bush ("Heck of a job, Brownie"), he soon resigned. The distribution of emergency relief funds involved massive fraud and ineptitude. FEMA spent $900 million on twenty-six thousand mobile homes, many of which sat unused. Despite

> Though praised by Bush ("Heck of a job, Brownie"), the FEMA head soon resigned.

the reorganization of the national security bureaucracy after 9/11, Hurricane Katrina revealed the same pattern of missed warnings, failed communication, and bumbling response.

Extending Republican Influence: From the Supreme Court to K Street

Supreme Court justice Sandra Day O'Connor, a key swing vote in close decisions, retired in 2005. To replace her, Bush nominated federal judge John Roberts, who had held posts in the Reagan administration. When Chief Justice Rehnquist died that September, Bush elevated Roberts to the chief justiceship. He won easy Senate confirmation while revealing little about his judicial philosophy.

To fill the second vacancy, Bush first nominated his White House counsel, a longtime Texas friend. Widely criticized as unqualified, she soon withdrew. Bush next nominated Samuel Alito, Jr., who, as a federal judge, had endorsed the sweeping view of executive powers asserted by the Bush administration to justify its post–9/11 actions at home and abroad. Alito won confirmation, 58 to 42.

With Roberts and Alito joining Scalia and Thomas as a bloc of reliably conservative justices, Justice Anthony Kennedy emerged as the swing vote. Prochoice advocates feared (and abortion opponents hoped) that the increasingly conservative high court would overturn *Roe* v. *Wade*, the 1973 abortion-rights ruling. Although the issue remained contentious, opinion polls showed broad support for *Roe* v. *Wade*, with about 55 percent endorsing legal abortions with certain restrictions and 24 percent favoring no legally imposed restrictions at all. In *Gonzales* v. *Carhart* (2007), the Supreme Court, on a 5 to 4 vote, upheld a 2003 congressional ban on late-term abortions. In the decision, however, the majority cited *Roe* v. *Wade* as a precedent, thus implicitly reaffirming that ruling.

As Supreme Court politics attracted notice, so did the influence of Washington lobbyists. (This term stems from the era when individuals representing special interests would crowd the lobbies of the Capitol and state legislatures.) Long a part of U.S. politics, lobbyists' influence increased during the ascendancy of Texas Republican Congressman Tom "the Hammer" DeLay, who became House majority leader in 2003. From 2000 to 2005, the ranks of registered Washington lobbyists more than doubled, to nearly thirty-three thousand, with many more unregistered ones. Implementing a plan dubbed "the K Street project" (after the Washington street where many lobbyists had offices), DeLay extracted campaign contributions from lobbyists and pressured them to hire Republican staffers—often members of legislators' families. This reflected a broader GOP effort, originating with White House political strategist Karl Rove, to create a permanent Republican majority.

An eruption of scandals in 2005 focused attention on lobbyists and money's role in politics. In September, DeLay resigned as majority leader, and soon left Congress altogether, after a grand jury indicted him for violating Texas election laws by engineering a redistricting scheme that benefited Republicans. In December, a federal grand jury indicted Jack Abramoff, a Washington lobbyist with ties to DeLay. Abramoff had collected millions from corporations trying to influence legislation, including $82 million from Indian tribes seeking to influence the award of casino licenses. Laundered through dummy organizations, this money paid for dinners, gifts, campaign donations, and golf junkets for Congress members—including some Democrats—while Abramoff siphoned off millions for himself.

Pleading guilty, Abramoff went to prison. Both he and DeLay had close White House connections, but President Bush denied any wrongdoing. As public disgust mounted, politicians scrambled to return tainted contributions and regulate lobbyists more strictly.

A Shifting Political Landscape: The 2006 Election and Beyond

In the 2006 midterm election, voters rendered a stinging verdict on the Bush administration and the Republican-led Congress. Even President Bush admitted that his party had taken a "thumping." Democrats gained thirty-two House seats, retaking control for the first time in twelve years. The Democrat Nancy Pelosi of San Francisco became Speaker of the House, the first woman to hold that post. Democrats also narrowly won control of the Senate, 51 to 49. The number of women senators rose to sixteen, a record high. Democrats won a majority of governorships, including Massachusetts, where Deval Patrick became only the second African American elected governor since Reconstruction.

The election results also signaled deep national discontent over the Iraq War. Consequently, President Bush fired Defense Secretary Rumsfeld and named Robert Gates his successor. A former CIA director, Gates had served on a blue-ribbon Iraq Study Group whose 2006 report criticized both the decision to invade Iraq and the administration's conduct of the war. Vice President Cheney's influence diminished as well, as Secretary of State Rice and other administration officials challenged the imprisonments without trial, harsh interrogation techniques, sweeping domestic surveillance, and other policies promoted by Cheney after 9/11.

Advised by General David Petraeus, the new commander in Iraq, Bush in 2007 ordered a temporary "surge" of troops to Iraq. With additional GIs patrolling Baghdad and other trouble spots, sectarian violence declined. An uneasy cease-fire by Shi'ite militias and cooperation by Sunni clan leaders helped as well. Assassinations, suicide bombings, and IED attacks continued, but U.S. military deaths in Iraq for 2008 fell sharply from previous years. In November 2008, the Iraqi parliament ratified an agreement with Washington for the complete withdrawal of U.S. combat forces by 2012.

In December 2008, Bush made a final visit to Baghdad. At a news conference with Prime Minister Nouri al-Maliki, an Iraqi journalist hurled his shoes at the president—a gesture of contempt in Arabic societies—while shouting, "This is for widows and orphans and all those killed in Iraq!" The president shrugged off the incident. "That's what happens in

JACK ABRAMOFF LEAVES THE FEDERAL COURTHOUSE IN WASHINGTON, DC, JANUARY 2006 The once-powerful lobbyist pled guilty to charges of conspiracy, tax evasion, and mail fraud in a scandal involving campaign contributions, gifts, and other perks designed to influence politicians' votes. *(AP Images/Gerald Herbert)*

free societies," he commented, "where people try to draw attention to themselves."

Despite encouraging developments, the situation, in General Petraeus's words, remained "fragile and reversible." Historically a patchwork of ethnic and religious groups ruled by successive invaders and then by British colonial administrators after World War I, Iraq had achieved independence only in 1932. Whether it could avoid fragmentation, sectarian turmoil, or renewed despotism remained unknown.

Despite Bush's claim that Saddam Hussein's overthrow justified the war, most Americans continued to view it as a disastrous mistake, diverting resources from the more vital conflict in Afghanistan. Reports of poor care in veterans' hospitals and massive fraud in the Iraq reconstruction program deepened public anger over the war.

Other controversies plagued Bush's final years in office. In March 2007, Vice President Cheney's chief of staff was convicted and imprisoned for perjury and obstruction of justice. The case arose from charges that Cheney's office had revealed to reporters the identity of a covert CIA agent, as part of a campaign to discredit her husband, a critic of the administration's prewar claims about Iraq's nuclear weapons program.

In August 2007, Attorney General Alberto Gonzales resigned amid an uproar over the hiring and firing of U.S. attorneys and Justice Department lawyers for blatantly political reasons rather than competence and experience. Gonzales's approval of the Justice Department's "torture memo" and of illegal FBI spying during his tenure as White House counsel added to the firestorm of criticism.

As Bush's presidency wound down, his approval ratings sank to around 25 percent—close to the lowest ever recorded for any president and a steep decline from their stratospheric levels after 9/11. What caused this reversal? Beyond the unpopular Iraq War and related issues of torture, unlimited detention, and violations of citizens' rights, many saw a go-it-alone approach that damaged America's standing worldwide. Critics also targeted the administration's dismissal of scientific evidence on the role of human activity in climate change, the politicization of federal agencies, the secretive power exercised by Vice President Cheney and a small circle of like-minded advisers, and the dominance of narrow partisanship and rigid ideology in shaping administration policies. To his opponents, Bush's black-and-white worldview, preference for snap decisions based on gut instincts, and reluctance to admit mistakes further limited his effectiveness.

The Economist, a respected London-based magazine that had endorsed Bush in 2000, reached a harsh judgment as his term ended: "He leaves the White House as one of the least popular and most divisive presidents in American history, ... [and] the most partisan ... in living memory. ... [G]ood policy repeatedly took a back seat to Mr. Bush's overweening political ambition. Both the country and, ultimately, the Republican Party are left the worse for it."

Many Americans continued to support Bush, of course. The Iraq invasion, tax cuts, educational reforms, and free-market suspicion of government regulation all had their admirers. Bush himself defended his record, insisting that even his most

> "He leaves the White House as one of the least popular and most divisive presidents in American history."

controversial post–9/11 actions aimed to protect the country from terrorists. In 2008, despite Bush's personal unpopularity, 46 percent of the electorate voted Republican. Citing Harry Truman's post-presidential popularity, Bush suggested rather wistfully that he, too, would be vindicated by history.

The Obama Presidency

The 2008 election represented a historic landmark in American history: the election of the first African American president, Barack Obama. Launched on a wave of hope and enthusiasm, the Obama administration pursued an ambitious agenda, headed by health-care reform. But a sharp political backlash, a stubborn recession, and chronic problems abroad portended challenges ahead.

Obama Wins in 2008

Among the 2008 Democratic presidential contenders, New York senator and former first lady **Hillary Clinton** emerged as the frontrunner; **Barack Obama,** a first-term black senator from Illinois, seemed an improbable long shot. Of an array of Republican hopefuls, Arizona senator **John McCain** outlasted the rest. A Vietnam War bomber pilot who spent six years in a Hanoi prison, McCain had built a reputation as a party maverick. As running mate, he chose Alaska governor Sarah Palin, an evangelical Christian with a populist touch who had bucked her state's Republican establishment to win the governorship after serving as a small-town mayor. After an initial buzz of excitement, Palin struck many as ill-informed and unqualified.

In the Democratic contest, Barack Obama won the Iowa primary and emerged as a formidable candidate, especially among young people attracted by his cool demeanor and inspiring speeches at rallies that attracted thousands. Energized by Internet websites, Obama backers phoned, put up posters, and rang doorbells. They also contributed millions to his campaign, far outstripping McCain's fundraising efforts. Winning the nomination after a grueling series of primaries against a determined Hillary Clinton, Obama chose as his running mate Delaware senator Joseph Biden.

McCain, downplaying his differences with the Bush administration, stressed his patriotism, called for victory in Iraq, and courted evangelical Christians despite his earlier criticism of some politicized preachers as "agents of intolerance." In TV debates, the seventy-two-year-old McCain sometimes seemed out of touch, especially on economic matters, while Obama exuded confidence.

Responding to divisive pronouncements by his black minister, Obama delivered a thoughtful address on race that won favorable comment (see Going to the Source). Obama hammered the Bush administration's failures and emphasized his themes of change, hope, and overcoming partisan divisions.

Obama captured 53 percent of the popular vote and a solid Electoral College majority, carrying not only such crucial swing states of Florida, Ohio, and Pennsylvania, but also Virginia and North Carolina, long Republican strongholds. Along with overwhelming black support, he won 67 percent of the Hispanic vote, a significant increase over John Kerry's 2004 total, and nearly 70 percent of the eighteen–to–twenty-four-year old vote. The Democrats widened their majorities in both houses of Congress.

Around the world, people savored the historic moment. Nearly 150 years after the Emancipation Proclamation, and half a century beyond the civil-rights struggles of the 1950s and 1960s, an African American had won the presidency. Obama himself marveled in his inaugural address that sixty years earlier, many Washington restaurants would have denied his father service.

Barack Obama was born in Hawaii in 1961, the son of a Kenyan university student and his white wife, an anthropologist from Kansas. The couple soon separated, and Obama was reared by his mother and grandparents. After college and Harvard Law School, he worked as a community organizer in Chicago, and in 1996 won election to the Illinois legislature. His wife Michelle, also a lawyer, traced her southern ancestry to slavery days.

In his inaugural address, delivered before a vast throng in Washington and a global radio and television audience, Obama rejected what he called the "worn out dogmas" that blocked bold responses to urgent problems. Implicitly targeting the Bush administration's excesses, he said: "We reject as false the choice between our safety and our ideals. … Those ideals still light the world, and we will not give them up for expedience's sake. … [O]ur power alone cannot protect us, nor does it entitle us to do as we please." "America's "patchwork heritage" of ethnicities and national origins, of "Christians and Muslims, Jews and Hindus and nonbelievers," was no liability, he declared, but a great asset as the nation sought to restore its battered reputation in an equally diverse world.

When Obama was unexpectedly awarded the Nobel Peace prize in October 2009, after only nine months in office, it was widely viewed as a recognition of his high aspirations and an expression of hope for the future.

Barack Obama Reflects on Race in America

In the 2008 presidential campaign, anti-Obama ads showed snippets from sermons by Rev. Jeremiah Wright, the black minister of Chicago's Trinity United Church of Christ, the church Obama had attended. Wright harshly criticized racism in America, and even America itself. Following are excerpts from a March 18 speech in which Obama addressed the issue.

I am the son of a black man from Kenya and a white woman from Kansas. ... I am married to a black American who carries within her the blood of slaves and slaveowners—an inheritance we pass on to our two precious daughters. I have brothers, sisters, nieces, nephews, uncles and cousins, of every race and every hue, scattered across three continents, and for as long as I live, I will never forget that in no other country on Earth is my story even possible. ...

[T]he issues that have surfaced over the last few weeks reflect the complexities of race in this country that we've never really worked through—a part of our union that we have yet to perfect. ... [M]any of the disparities that exist in the African-American community today can be directly traced to ... the brutal legacy of slavery and Jim Crow. ...

For the men and women of Reverend Wright's generation, the memories of humiliation and doubt and fear have not gone away; nor has the anger and the bitterness of those years. ... That anger is not always productive; indeed, all too often it distracts attention from solving real problems; ... and prevents the African-American community from forging the alliances it needs to bring about real change. But the anger is real ... and to simply wish it away ... only serves to widen the chasm of misunderstanding that exists between the races.

In fact, a similar anger exists within segments of the white community. Most working- and middle-class white Americans don't feel that they have been particularly privileged by their race. ... They've worked hard ... , many times only to see their jobs shipped overseas or their pension dumped after a lifetime of labor. They ... feel their dreams slipping away; in an era of stagnant wages and global competition, opportunity comes to be seen as a zero sum game, in which your dreams come at my expense ... [and] resentment [against blacks seen as benefiting from affirmative-action programs] builds over time. ...

Just as black anger often proved counterproductive, so have these white resentments distracted attention from the real culprits of the middle class squeeze—a corporate culture rife with inside dealing, questionable accounting practices, and short-term greed; a Washington dominated by lobbyists and special interests; economic policies that favor the few over the many. ... This is where we are right now. It's a racial stalemate we've been stuck in for years. ... But I have asserted a firm conviction ... that working together we can move beyond some of our old racial wounds. ...

The profound mistake of Reverend Wright's sermons is not that he spoke about racism in our society. It's that he spoke as if our society was static; as if no progress has been made; as if this country ... is still irrevocably bound to a tragic past. But what we know—what we have seen—is that America can change. That is the true genius of this nation. What we have already achieved gives us hope—the audacity to hope—for what we can and must achieve tomorrow ... Let us find that common stake we all have in one another, and let our politics reflect that spirit as well.

QUESTIONS

1. How does Obama explain the anger in Jeremiah Wright's sermons?

2. Do you agree with Obama's claim that the anger he finds among many middle-class and working-class white Americans has primarily economic causes? (Be specific in your answer.)

Early Initiatives at Home and Abroad

Obama named Hillary Clinton secretary of state, a post she would fill with great effectiveness. He ordered the Guantánamo prison closed (a policy that proved complicated to implement) and granted an interview to a popular Arabic-language television network. Obama's choice as attorney general, Eric Holder, declared in his Senate confirmation hearing that water boarding, the interrogation technique used on some Guantánamo prisoners, constituted torture and would be forbidden.

In a speech in Prague in April 2009, Obama pledged to work for a world free of nuclear weapons. North Korea's nuclear tests, Iran's secretive nuclear program, and the dangerous instability of nuclear-armed Pakistan underscored the urgency of this issue.

Obama also asked Congress to end the so-called "Don't ask, don't tell," policy requiring gays in the military to conceal their sexual orientation. After legal and political maneuvering, the policy was officially rescinded in 2011.

Obama lifted Bush's ban on stem-cell research and named Steven Chu, a Nobel laureate in physics and advocate of alternative energy sources, to lead the Department of Energy. To head the EPA, he chose an authority on environmental protection. Reversing Bush administration policy, Obama announced that by 2016 all new automobiles, light trucks, and SUVs would be required to meet the tougher fuel-efficiency standards already adopted by California and other states. Obama also urged redoubled work on alternative energy sources to reduce the nation's reliance on fossil fuels and to cut the emissions contributing to global climate change.

In April 2010, the nation faced another catastrophic oil spill when a drilling platform operated by the British-based BP energy company exploded and burned in the Gulf of Mexico, killing eleven workers and fouling large sections of the Gulf Coast's valuable fisheries industry. Obama (mindful of his predecessor's mishandling of the Katrina disaster) ordered the Coast Guard to monitor BP's clean-up efforts, imposed a temporary moratorium on deep-water drilling in the Gulf, and appointed a federal administrator to distribute damage claims from a fund established by BP.

Obama Wins a Close-Fought Victory on Health-Care Reform

Despite a gathering economic crisis, Obama pursued his top domestic goal: health-care reform to control costs while extending coverage to the uninsured. Securing cost-cutting pledges from the drug industry, health insurers, hospital associations, and other key players, Obama called on Congress to enact comprehensive health-care legislation.

Reform momentum soon slowed, however. Some critics resorted to scare tactics, conjuring visions of government "death panels" denying care to the elderly or terminally ill. As they had since President

PRESIDENT OBAMA SIGNS HEALTH CARE INTO ACTION The Patient Protection and Affordable Care Act of 2010 mandated health insurance for most Americans, provided subsidies to poor Americans who couldn't afford it, and guaranteed health coverage for all, even those with pre-existing conditions. *(© Bettmann/Corbis)*

Truman's day, opponents warned of "socialized medicine" and "a government-run health care system," even though Medicare, the federal health-insurance program for the elderly, enjoyed broad popularity. The pharmaceutical and health-insurance industries, profiting handsomely under the present system, opposed any cost-control regulations beyond what they had already voluntarily pledged.

Reform proponents, by contrast, pointed to the millions of uninsured Americans, the loss of coverage that often came with unemployment, insurance companies' denial of coverage to high-risk applicants, and the spiraling costs of U.S. health care in contrast to other nations with comparable or superior medical outcomes.

Despite Obama's call for bipartisan cooperation, party divisions hardened. Even Democrats were divided. Democrats from conservative districts favored a cautious, incremental approach. Democratic liberals, by contrast, supported a "public option," a government health-insurance program, supplementing the private system, that would serve the uninsured and provide a benchmark for cost control. The August 2009 death of Massachusetts Democratic senator Edward Kennedy, a champion of health-care reform, inspired advocates to redoubled efforts.

In March 2010, on strictly party lines, Congress passed and Obama signed a health-care reform law, the Patient Protection and Affordable Care Act. The law extended Medicare coverage to some 32 million uninsured Americans, with the costs to be covered by Medicare savings, higher Medicare rates to upper-income earners, and tax increases on the wealthiest Americans. The law also prohibited insurance companies from denying coverage because of preexiting conditions and extended coverage to dependent children up to age twenty-six.

Recession Strikes

Even as the acrimonious health-care debate unfolded, attention increasingly turned to a recession that had begun in 2007 in the real-estate market and quickly worsened. Beginning in the late 1990s, housing prices spiked upward, especially in California, Florida, the Southwest, and Northeast. The bubble burst in 2007. As real-estate prices tumbled, homebuilding and commercial developments stalled.

The crisis soon spread, worsened by lax governmental regulation. In 1999, Congress repealed the Glass-Steagall Act, a 1933 law designed to regulate bank practices and protect depositors. Introduced by Republicans, the repeal won bipartisan support and was signed by President Clinton. Freed of regulatory constraints, investment banks could now acquire unregulated financial services companies and indulge in various forms of financial chicanery. During the real-estate boom, unscrupulous lending companies extended mortgages to homebuyers who could ill afford them. With slogans like "No credit? No problem" and low initial rates that quickly jumped higher, predatory lenders lured first-time home buyers, many of them black and Hispanic. By 2008, nearly 30 percent of all mortgages were rated as "subprime." These risky mortgages were then sold to Wall Street investment banks or other financial institutions that bundled or "securitized" them into stock offerings purchased by pension funds, mutual funds, and foreign banks. Decades of deregulation, driven by free-market ideology, encouraged both predatory lending and the marketing of highly risky securities.

As the real-estate market weakened, homeowners facing exorbitant mortgage payments could neither sell their homes nor refinance their mortgages. Many defaulted, leaving behind empty, neglected houses and a sea of foreclosure signs. As homeowners defaulted, the value of the securities based on these mortgages collapsed. Wall Street banks and financial services companies found themselves holding securities, now relabeled "toxic assets," they could not sell, and whose actual market value no one knew.

Wall Street's largest banks faced disastrous losses, with some nearing insolvency. Giant Lehman Brothers collapsed in September 2008. Fearing further losses, the big banks stopped lending. As credit froze, the broader economy suffered. Business activity slowed; jittery consumers cut spending. The Dow Jones stock market average, after soaring above 14,000 in October 2007, sank to under 8,000 by March 2009, wiping out billions in investors' assets.

The recession hit home as Americans saw their savings, property values, and retirement funds shrivel and as companies announced layoffs. In 2008, 2.6 million workers lost their jobs, the highest rate of loss in sixty years. By September 2009, the unemployment rate stood at 9.8 percent. Even this figure did not include involuntary part-time workers or discouraged jobseekers who had stopped looking. In Michigan, home of the U.S. auto industry, the jobless rate passed 15 percent. Even the high-flying IT sector suffered, as mighty Microsoft and the giant chipmaker Intel announced layoffs. As the worst recession since the Great Depression bit deeper, college students worried about their prospects. For displaced workers and unskilled youth, an already tough job market looked even grimmer.

The recession struck an economy whose benefits were already very unevenly distributed. While some had profited handsomely from the Bush tax cuts, the soaring stock market, and the boom in financial services and electronics technologies, most Americans' real income remained flat through the Bush years.

HOMEOWNERS FACE A CRISIS AS RECESSION HITS As unemployment rose and retirement savings shrunk in value, many homeowners could not meet their mortgage payments. An enterprising real-estate agent in Coral Gables, Florida, organized a "Foreclosure Boat Tour" for potential buyers of foreclosed homes. *(Joe Raedle/Getty Images)*

The surge in consumer spending was largely financed with plastic. Total consumer debt in 2008, excluding mortgages, approached $2.6 trillion. After a decade when both Washington and American consumers had plunged deeply into debt, the chickens now came home to roost. In 2009, U.S. banks wrote off $83 billion in unpaid credit-card debt.

The Bush administration in its waning months tried to grapple with the crisis. In July 2008, despite his party's free-market beliefs, President Bush signed a bill that helped homeowners refinance their mortgages, tightened mortgage-lending regulations, and strengthened federal oversight of two privately owned but government-supported home-loan agencies—nicknamed Fannie Mae and Freddie Mac—that were deeply implicated in the crisis. In late in 2008, Congress appropriated $700 billion to provide more capital to the investment banks in hopes of stimulating the economy. But as the Treasury Department ladled out the billions, it imposed few rules on what the banks should do with the money, and most simply used it to stabilize their own balance sheets rather than making loans to promote recovery.

Revelations of the bloated earnings of the financiers who had caused the crisis deepened public anger. In 2004–2007, the CEO of Countrywide Finance, a giant subprime mortgage lender, made $270 million. As late as December 2008, after fourth-quarter losses of $15 billion, Merrill Lynch's CEO doled out millions in bonuses to top executives and spent $2.2 million redecorating his office. A familiar pattern of greed and excess in the upper reaches of American capitalism as millions faced desperate times was again unfolding.

In an era of globalization, the crisis quickly spread. Banks in Europe and Asia tightened credit as the U.S. securities in their portfolios lost value. With Obama in the White House, the recession he had inherited was now his problem. Treasury Secretary Timothy Geithner, formerly president of the Federal Reserve Bank of New York, and economist Lawrence Summers, named head of the White House National Economic Council, led Obama's recession-fighting team. (Ironically, both had supported the deregulatory legislation that helped lay the groundwork for the crisis.)

In February 2009, Obama signed a $787 billion economic-stimulus bill. It channeled $120 billion to states for highways, bridges, rapid transit, and other infrastructure projects; appropriated additional billions for school construction and energy-related projects; and cut taxes for middle- and lower-income Americans while restoring higher rates for upper-income earners. Ominously, despite Obama's pleas for bipartisanship, only three Senate Republicans voted for the bill.

Obama also insisted that future distributions from the Wall Street bailout package must ensure that banks actually channeled the funds into the credit market, to promote recovery. He also called for limits on executive compensation in return for federal money. When *The New York Times* revealed that Wall Street executives had pocketed $18.4 billion in bonuses in 2008 while their banks received government bailout money, Obama denounced the news as "outrageous."

While the administration granted a multi-billion-dollar emergency bailout to the ailing U.S. auto industry, Obama created a While House task force to oversee the industry's long-term restructuring. Chrysler filed for bankruptcy, though a takeover by the Italian automaker Fiat brightened its long-term prospects. As once mighty General Motors briefly entered bankruptcy in 2009, Americans realized the depth of the crisis facing this core domestic industry. After government assistance and a court-ordered reorganization, including losses to stock- and bondholders and concessions by unions, GM returned to profitability in 2010.

In July 2010, Obama signed a financial-services reform law, called the Dodd-Frank Act for its two principal sponsors, addressing abuses that had led to the economic meltdown. The law strengthened federal oversight of the financial-services industry and outlawed mortgage abuses and speculative bank practices that had proliferated during the mania for business deregulation.

Economists generally agreed that the Dodd-Frank law helped correct glaring abuses, and that Obama's economic recovery program, though less aggressive than it might have been, prevented the recession from becoming far worse. Further, the years 2010 and 2011 bought tantalizing signs of recovery, including a gradually reviving housing market and a stabilizing and then slowly improving employment picture. But millions of Americans still faced economic woes, and in a bitterly contentious political climate, Obama received little credit for his accomplishments and much of the blame for the slow pace of recovery. Leading Republicans fed this mood. As Senate minority leader Mitch McConnell of Kentucky candidly acknowledged in October 2010: "The single most important thing we want to achieve is for President Obama to be a one-term president."

A Tangle of Problems in Afghanistan, Pakistan, and Iran

Meanwhile, the war in Afghanistan ground on. A resurgent Taliban, allied with radical Islamist groups in Pakistan, increased attacks on U.S. troops, Afghan government forces, and the civilian

PRESIDENT OBAMA AND SENATOR MITCH McCONNELL Although the image shows the president and Senate majority whip shaking hands, political polarization, party-line votes, and harsh rhetoric marked relations between Obama and his Republican opponents in Congress. *(AP/Wide World Photos)*

population. With some 68,000 G.I.s deployed in that country, U.S. military fatalities by the end of 2011 neared two thousand, with nearly one thousand additional dead among the 38,000 NATO coalition forces. U.S. military wounded surpassed 14,000. As the Taliban regained control in parts of southern Afghanistan, they weakened the U.S.-backed government of President Hamid Karzai and destabilized neighboring Pakistan as well. Rampant government corruption, accusations of fraud in an August 2009 election, and Afghanistan's leading role in the cultivation of opium poppies (from which heroin is manufactured) further complicated the picture.

Declaring the Afghan struggle a "war of necessity" (in contrast to George W. Bush's misadventure in Iraq), Obama initially committed 30,000 more troops to the conflict. In 2011, however, as home-front support for the war eroded, particularly among his own party, Obama announced major troop withdrawals by the summer of 2012 and a complete withdrawal by 2014. As the Americans simultaneously combatted the Taliban and sought to open lines of communication with them while maintaining relations with an increasingly erratic Afghan government, the future in Afghanistan appeared deeply uncertain.

A clear Obama success came in May 2011, when U.S. special forces killed Osama bin Laden in a safe house near a major Pakistani military installation. Pakistani protests at not being consulted about this operation added to their grievances over U.S. drone aircraft raids that targeted militants in Pakistan's

U.S. SOLDIERS IN AFGHANISTAN DISCUSS TACTICS FOR COMBATING THE TALIBAN As home-front support for the conflict wavered, American diplomats and military leaders faced major challenges in defining and achieving U.S. objectives in this region of the world. *(© David Bathgate/Corbis)*

lawless borderlands, but sometimes killed civilians. As Washington accused elements of the Pakistani military of supporting Taliban-related groups, relations between the two countries worsened.

Meanwhile, Iran, still fiercely anti-American and anti-Israel, continued to pursue a nuclear-development program in secure underground facilities. Allegedly for peaceful purposes, the program increasingly seemed aimed at developing nuclear weapons. As the Western powers imposed ever-stricter sanctions and warned of military measures, Iran responded belligerently, even threatening to close the Straits of Hormus, a vital lifeline through which Iranian oil passed to the world market.

Washington Gridlock, Grassroots Anger, the 2010 Midterm Election

A conciliator by temperament, Obama took office confident that he and the Republican opposition could reach compromise on urgent national issues. This hope proved unrealistic. Taking advantage of a Senate rule requiring a "supermajority" of 60 percent on major bills, the Republicans thwarted Obama at every turn and spurned his conciliatory efforts. Even some Obama supporters perceived him as too deferential and too ready to give ground even before hard bargaining began. Remembering Obama the feisty, aggressive campaigner, they longed for a more feisty, aggressive president.

Adhering to their free-market ideology, the Republicans argued that tax cuts and fewer business regulations would stimulate recovery and end the recession. Insisting that the federal deficit posed the nation's most urgent problem, they demanded spending cuts in social programs to address it. The deficit was indeed a serious issue, compounded by rising social security and Medicare costs. Ironically, however, the deficit problem had been severely worsened by Bush-era tax cuts, by the unfunded prescription-drug benefit, and by the unfunded wars in Iraq and Afghanistan—conflicts for which U.S. taxpayers had made no sacrifices. Yet when Obama, in his quest for compromise, proposed modest tax increases for the very wealthiest Americans as part of a deficit-reduction package, the Republican leadership adamantly refused.

Among the electorate at large, an ugly mood spread. Some Americans formed the so-called Tea Party movement, inspired by the original Boston Tea Party of 1773 protesting British taxation. Venting their hostility to "Obamacare," taxes, big government, and federal assistance to mortgage holders who had lost their homes, they also demonized Obama personally, accusing him of being a socialist and even questioning his U.S. citizenship.

The 2010 midterm election reflected the sour national mood, worsened by the recession. The Republicans regained control of the House of Representatives, with many new Tea Party members even more rigidly anticompromise than their party leadership, ensuring continued gridlock. Several showdowns initiated by Tea Party members over raising the federal debt limit, normally a noncontroversial act to preserve the nation's credit, threatened government shutdowns.

Newly elected Republican governors and legislators in Ohio and Wisconsin pushed through harsh measures restricting the rights of public-employee unions, including teachers. (In both states, angry voters pushed back. Ohio voters repealed the antiunion law by referendum, and Wisconsin voters organized a recall campaign to force a special gubernatorial election.)

The 2010 election generated some $4 billion in campaign contributions—an all-time record for a mid-term election—much of it from outside corporate donors and other groups. Fueling this vast infusion of cash was a landmark 2010 Supreme Court decision, *Citizens United* v. *Federal Elections Commission*. This 5 to 4 ruling held that the First Amendment granted corporations, unions, or any other group the right to spend unlimited sums to influence elections. This decision effectively gutted the McCain-Feingold campaign-finance law and indeed threw into confusion a century of efforts to restrain the role of big money in politics. Encouraged by the electoral results, the Republican

leadership dug in still more firmly against any Obama proposals, even blocking White House nominees for public office that, under other conditions, would have been routinely approved. Congress refused, for example, to approve Obama's choice to head the new Consumer Financial Protection Bureau, authorized by the Dodd-Frank law to protect consumers from predatory mortgage lenders, credit-card issuers, and other financial-services providers. Opponents claimed the new agency lacked sufficient congressional oversight. In 2012, taking advantage of a congressional recess, Obama appointed Richard Cordray, Ohio's attorney general and a consumer advocate, to the post.

In the face of continual gridlock, public opinion turned against Congress. In an October 2011 *New York Times*/CBS News poll, only 9 percent of Americans approved of Congress's performance, the lowest figure ever recorded. By contrast, Obama's ratings, from a low of 41 percent in September 2011, began to trend upward, though his electoral prospects clearly depended on factors beyond his control—above all the state of the economy, both domestically, and in Europe, which was struggling with a serious debt crisis in Greece and other countries.

Deepening the political malaise was a growing realization that the economic disparities between the very wealthiest Americans and the rest of the

OCCUPY WALL STREET PROTEST This protest movement, with its signature slogan "We are the 99%," spread from New York City to scores of other cities in the summer of 2011. *(Mario Tama/Getty Images)*

9/11 MEMORIAL Dedicated on September 11, 2011, ten years after the terrorist attacks, this moving memorial to the victims includes deep reflecting pools where the World Trade Center towers once stood. *(© Bettmann/Corbis)*

population, including the vast middle class, had widened enormously in recent decades, reaching levels not seen since the 1920s. While overall U.S. median income, corrected for inflation, has declined since 1999, that of the top 1 percent has soared. Expressing this sense of inequity, an "Occupy Wall Street" movement began in October 2011 with hundreds of protesters occupying a park near Manhattan's financial district. The movement quickly spread to other U.S. cities and beyond. While conservatives defended such vast disparities as a natural outcome of a meritocratic, free-market system, others saw serious dangers to social harmony and to the sense of common purpose characteristic of the nation at its best.

As another presidential election loomed, President Obama used the January 2012 State of the Union address to highlight his campaign themes. Pointing to signs of economic improvement, he made job creation and economic fairness his highest priorities and insisted that the richest citizens should pay their fair share of taxes. America faced a choice, he said, between a society where "a shrinking number of people do really well while a growing number of Americans barely get by," and a society "where everyone gets a fair shot, everyone does their fair share, and everyone plays by the same rules."

Sharpening the contrast between his readiness to compromise and Republican obstructionism, the president again called for an end to partisan gridlock, "Our destiny is stretched together like those fifty stars and those thirteen stripes … ," Obama declared; "This nation is great because we built it together."

In the Republican response, Governor Mitch Daniels of Indiana insisted that his party was upholding the principles of free enterprise, frugal government, and "the dignity and capacity of the individual citizen," against Democratic big-government solutions. In contrast to the more libertarian wing of his party, however, Daniels insisted that the social safety net of social security and Medicare must be preserved and that the wealthiest American had a duty to pay their fair share toward resolving the deficit crisis.

The 2012 Presidential Election

Conservatism dominated the 2012 Republican presidential primaries. Several prominent moderate Republicans, including Mitch Daniels and former Florida governor Jeb Bush (brother of the

43rd president), decided not to run. Others, like Jon Huntsman, failed to gain traction and dropped out of the race early.

Ironically, it was Mitt Romney, the candidate with the weakest conservative credentials, who won the Republican nomination. As candidate for governor of Massachusetts in 2002, he supported *Roe v. Wade*; in office, he signed a landmark health care law that—like Obama's Affordable Care Act—mandated coverage and provided premium support for the poor. But in the Republican primaries in 2011 and 2012, he re-billed himself as "severely conservative," called for a huge tax cut and tough measures regarding illegal immigration, and opposed abortion rights and "Obamacare." This swing to the right helped Romney appeal to the Republican base.

Once he got to the general election, Romney pivoted again and adroitly moved to the center on key issues. In three televised debates, Romney embraced health-care reform on the state level and agreed with many of Obama's foreign policies, notably the president's use of economic sanctions against Iran and his promise to withdraw all U.S. troops from Afghanistan. Highlighting his success as a corporate CEO, Romney cast himself as the candidate best able to create jobs, forge bipartisan consensus, and balance a $1 trillion federal budget deficit. And Romney parried Obama's call to balance the budget with higher taxes on the wealthy by claiming that he could achieve the same result by closing unspecified tax loopholes.

At the start, Obama's reelection campaign faced strong headwinds. In 2011 and the first half of 2012, the unemployment rate hovered between 9 and 10 percent, while 4.1 million struggling homeowners received foreclosure notices. However, the "green shoots" of an economic recovery began to take hold. By the fall, Obama could point to improvements since he took office, such as a rebounded auto industry, net job growth, and falling unemployment (down to 7.8 percent by September). In a stroke of political good fortune, the recovery was especially strong in the swing state of Ohio. There, Democrats and labor unions were riding high after defeating a Republican effort in 2011 to strip collective bargaining rights from public-sector workers. The president's bailout of the automobile industry was popular in Ohio as well.

Obama's campaign also held a clear advantage with African Americans and the fast-growing Hispanic population. Since 2008, when two-thirds of Hispanics supported the president, about 4 million Hispanics were newly eligible to vote. In June 2012, Obama issued an executive order halting the deportation of thousands of young,

undocumented immigrants who were attending school or serving in the military. That same month, Obama's signature legislative accomplishment, the Affordable Care Act, was saved from destruction when the Supreme Court upheld it in a 5–4 decision.

President Obama also seemed to have the advantage on foreign policy. The so-called Arab Spring revolutions of 2011 unseated dictators in Tunisia and Egypt. American warplanes helped depose a long-time foe of the United States, Libyan ruler Muammar Gaddafi. Another U.S. antagonist, Bashar al-Assad of Syria, faced a massive internal insurgency and was hanging on to power by a thread. And the crisis over Iran's nuclear program abated somewhat when U.S. sanctions crippled that country's economy. In addition, Obama pulled U.S. troops out of Iraq, ordered the raid in May 2011 that killed Osama bin Laden, and called for a withdrawal of all American troops from Afghanistan by the end of 2014. And although

MITT ROMNEY. The sign on the podium reads "Protect and Strengthen Medicare." However, Romney's running mate, congressman Paul Ryan, proposed cuts to Medicaid and changes to Medicare, which would be converted into a voucher system for future retirees. (© *BRIAN BLANCO/epa/Corbis*)

Obama's increasing reliance on unmanned drones sparked criticism, his support for these deadly drone attacks remained popular among U.S. voters (including Mitt Romney, who supported them). Obama's decisive response to Hurricane Sandy, which devastated the New Jersey coast just eight days before the election, also burnished his credentials as Commander in Chief.

On election day, President Obama prevailed in Ohio and won a second term. Although narrower than 2008's victory, the 2012 result illustrated the extent to which politics had been transformed by changing demographics. About 45 percent of Obama's support came from minority voters. One of ten voters was Hispanic: 70 percent voted for the president. Obama won the youth vote by more than 20 percent.

Furthermore, Obama's support for reproductive rights and equal pay for women helped him sustain a Democratic advantage among female voters. (The 113th Congress included a record number of women elected to the House [77] and the Senate [20], including consumer advocate Elizabeth Warren, the first-ever female senator from Massachusetts.) Buoyed by these trends, Democrats maintained control of the Senate. Meanwhile, Romney's chief advantage was among older voters and white males—a shrinking share of the electorate. "A coalition of aging white men," wrote journalist Nicholas Kristof, "is a recipe for failure in a nation that increasingly looks like a rainbow."

But even as they fretted about their place in a changed political landscape, Republicans rejected the notion that Obama had received a mandate to rule without compromise. "The American people re-elected the president, and re-elected our majority in the House," said John Boehner, the Republican Speaker of the House. "If there is a mandate, it is a mandate for both parties to find common ground and take steps together to help our economy grow and create jobs, which is critical to solving our debt." As a budget crisis loomed, both sides now faced difficult choices with consequences for every American.

CONCLUSION

This most recent chapter in the American story we have traced in *The Enduring Vision* clearly had its shining moments, including the election of the nation's first African American president. Even Barack Obama's political opponents recognized the symbolic significance of his election. Yet this was also a stressful time. Beginning with the devastating attacks of September 11, 2001, and continuing through a controversial war in Iraq, a mortgage crisis and deep recession that upended the lives of millions of Americans, economic challenges from emerging economies, and a period of unusual political rancor, these were years of uncertainty and anxiety.

In such times, seeking a longer historical perspective beyond the daily headlines can offer reassurance. The United States has faced many uncertain times, but the nation also has a history of overcoming challenges and discovering sources of renewal. As President Obama declared in his 2008 inaugural address, "The time has come to reaffirm our enduring spirit, to choose our better history."

What, then, is the "enduring vision" of our title? There is, of course, no single vision, but many. That is part of America's meaning. Nor is this a vision of a foreordained national destiny unfolding effortlessly, but rather of successive generations' often-frustrating struggle to better their common life as a people. At their best, these shared aspirations are rooted in hope, not fear, in a sense of unity, not divisiveness. In 1980, Jesse de la Cruz, a Mexican American activist for California's migrant workers, summed up her philosophy: "Is America progressing toward the better? ... With us, there's a saying: *La esperanza muere al ultimo*. Hope dies last. You can't lose hope. If you lose hope, that's losing everything."

KEY TERMS

FOR FURTHER REFERENCE

Andrew J. Bacevich, *The Limits of Power: The End of American Exceptionalism* (2008). A professor of international relations and retired U.S. Army colonel examines the delusions he sees underlying America's post–Cold War foreign policy and military interventions.

Jason Burke, *The 9/11 Wars* (2011). A veteran British journalist offers a comprehensive history of the "war on terror" and its impact on the nations and peoples it affected.

Lloyd C. Gardner, *The Long Road to Baghdad: A History of U.S. Foreign Policy from 1970 to the Present* (2008). A diplomatic historian traces the shift from Cold War containment policy to a more aggressive approach, culminating in the Iraq War.

Jack L. Goldstein, *The Terror Presidency: Law and Judgment Inside the Bush Administration* (2007). A legal scholar's assessment of the Bush administration's legal and constitutional abuses in the name of national security.

Stefan Halper and Jonathan Clarke, *America Alone: The Neo-Conservatives and the Global Order* (2005). In-depth history of the origins of an influential ideological movement.

James Kloppenberg, *Reading Obama: Dreams, Hope, and the American Political Tradition* (2011). An intellectual historian traces the development of Obama's pragmatic ideology and its links to key strands of American political thought.

Paul Krugman, *The Return of Depression Economics and the Crisis of 2008* (2009). A Nobel-prize-winning economist compares the conditions leading to the Depression of the 1930s and those underlying the 2008 recession.

Robert Kuttner, *Obama's Challenge: America's Economic Crisis and the Power of a Transformative Presidency* (2008). Cautiously optimistic assessment of what President Obama and a Democratic Congress might achieve despite an economic recession.

Barack Obama, *Dreams from My Father: A Story of Race and Inheritance* (1995). The future president writes of his roots, shaping experiences, and race in America.

Lawrence N. Powell and Clarence L. Mohr, eds., "Through the Eye of Katrina: The Past as Prologue," *Journal of American History,* December 2007. A special issue placing the Katrina disaster in historical perspective.

Charlie Savage, *Takeover: The Return of the Imperial Presidency and the Subversion of American Democracy* (2008). A Pulitzer-prize-winning journalist examines the expansion of executive power in the Bush-Cheney era.

Joseph E. Stieglitz, *Freefall: America, Free Markets, and the Sinking of the World Economy* (2010). A leading economist offers an accessible factual and theoretical analysis of the 2008 recession, linking it to the upsurge of free-market ideology and business deregulation.

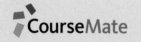

Visit the CourseMate website at **www.cengagebrain.com** for additional study tools and review materials for this chapter.

APPENDIX

DOCUMENTS

Declaration of Independence

IN CONGRESS, JULY 4, 1776
THE UNANIMOUS DECLARATION OF THE
THIRTEEN UNITED STATES OF AMERICA

When, in the course of human events, it becomes necessary for one people to dissolve the political bands which have connected them with another, and to assume, among the powers of the earth, the separate and equal station to which the laws of nature and of nature's God entitle them, a decent respect to the opinions of mankind requires that they should declare the causes which impel them to the separation.

We hold these truths to be self-evident: That all men are created equal; that they are endowed by their Creator with certain unalienable rights; that among these are life, liberty, and the pursuit of happiness; that, to secure these rights, governments are instituted among men, deriving their just powers from the consent of the governed; that whenever any form of government becomes destructive of these ends, it is the right of the people to alter or to abolish it, and to institute new government, laying its foundation on such principles, and organizing its powers in such form, as to them shall seem most likely to effect their safety and happiness. Prudence, indeed, will dictate that governments long established should not be changed for light and transient causes; and accordingly all experience hath shown that mankind are more disposed to suffer, while evils are sufferable, than to right themselves by abolishing the forms to which they are accustomed. But when a long train of abuses and usurpations, pursuing invariably the same object, evinces a design to reduce them under absolute despotism, it is their right, it is their duty, to throw off such government, and to provide new guards for their future security. Such has been the patient sufferance of these colonies; and such is now the necessity which constrains them to alter their former systems of government. The history of the present King of Great Britain is a history of repeated injuries and usurpations, all having in direct object the establishment of an absolute tyranny over these states. To prove this, let facts be submitted to a candid world.

He has refused his assent to laws, the most wholesome and necessary for the public good.

He has forbidden his governors to pass laws of immediate and pressing importance, unless suspended in their operation till his assent should be obtained; and, when so suspended, he has utterly neglected to attend to them.

He has refused to pass other laws for the accommodation of large districts of people, unless those people would relinquish the right of representation in the legislature, a right inestimable to them, and formidable to tyrants only.

He has called together legislative bodies at places unusual, uncomfortable, and distant from the depository of their public records, for the sole purpose of fatiguing them into compliance with his measures.

He has dissolved representative houses repeatedly, for opposing, with manly firmness, his invasions on the rights of the people.

He has refused for a long time, after such dissolutions, to cause others to be elected; whereby the legislative powers, incapable of annihilation, have returned to the people at large for their exercise; the state remaining, in the mean time, exposed to all the dangers of invasions from without and convulsions within.

He has endeavored to prevent the population of these states; for that purpose obstructing the laws of naturalization of foreigners; refusing to pass others to encourage their migration hither, and raising the conditions of new appropriation of lands.

He has obstructed the administration of justice, by refusing his assent to laws for establishing judiciary powers.

He has made judges dependent on his will alone, for the tenure of their offices, and the amount and payment of their salaries.

He has erected a multitude of new offices, and sent hither swarms of officers to harass our people and eat out their substance.

He has kept among us, in times of peace, standing armies, without the consent of our legislatures.

He has affected to render the military independent of, and superior to, the civil power.

He has combined with others to subject us to a jurisdiction foreign to our constitution, and unacknowledged by our laws, giving his assent to their acts of pretended legislation:

For quartering large bodies of armed troops among us;

For protecting them, by a mock trial, from punishment for any murders which they should commit on the inhabitants of these states;

For cutting off our trade with all parts of the world;

For imposing taxes on us without our consent;

For depriving us, in many cases, of the benefits of trial by jury;

For transporting us beyond seas, to be tried for pretended offenses;

For abolishing the free system of English laws in a neighboring province, establishing therein an arbitrary government, and enlarging its boundaries, so as to render it at once an example and fit instrument for introducing the same absolute rule into these colonies;

For taking away our charters, abolishing our most valuable laws, and altering fundamentally the forms of our governments;

For suspending our own legislatures, and declaring themselves invested with power to legislate for us in all cases whatsoever.

He has abdicated government here, by declaring us out of his protection and waging war against us.

He has plundered our seas, ravaged our coasts, burned our towns, and destroyed the lives of our people.

He is at this time transporting large armies of foreign mercenaries to complete the works of death, desolation, and tyranny already begun with circumstances of cruelty and perfidy scarcely paralleled in the most barbarous ages, and totally unworthy of the head of a civilized nation.

He has constrained our fellow-citizens, taken captive on the high seas, to bear arms against their country, to become the executioners of their friends and brethren, or to fall themselves by their hands.

He has excited domestic insurrection among us, and has endeavored to bring on the inhabitants of our frontiers the merciless Indian savages, whose known rule of warfare is an undistinguished destruction of all ages, sexes, and conditions.

In every stage of these oppressions we have petitioned for redress in the most humble terms; our repeated petitions have been answered only by repeated injury. A prince, whose character is thus marked by every act which may define a tyrant, is unfit to be the ruler of a free people.

Nor have we been wanting in our attentions to our British brethren. We have warned them, from time to time, of attempts by their legislature to extend an unwarrantable jurisdiction over us. We have reminded them of the circumstances of our emigration and settlement here. We have appealed to their native justice and magnanimity; and we have conjured them by the ties of our common kindred, to disavow these usurpations, which would inevitably interrupt our connections and correspondence. They, too, have been deaf to the voice of justice and of consanguinity. We must, therefore, acquiesce in the necessity which denounces our separation, and hold them, as we hold the rest of mankind, enemies in war, in peace friends.

We, therefore, the representatives of the United States of America, in General Congress assembled, appealing to the Supreme Judge of the world for the rectitude of our intentions, do, in the name and by the authority of the good people of these colonies, solemnly publish and declare, that these United Colonies are, and of right ought to be, FREE AND INDEPENDENT STATES; that they are absolved from all allegiance to the British crown, and that all political connection between them and the state of Great Britain is, and ought to be, totally dissolved; and that, as free and independent states, they have full power to levy war, conclude peace, contract alliances, establish commerce, and do all other acts and things which independent states may of right do. And for the support of this declaration, with a firm reliance on the protection of Divine Providence, we mutually pledge to each other our lives, our fortunes, and our sacred honor.

JOHN HANCOCK [President]
[and fifty-five others]

Constitution of the United States of America

Preamble

We the people of the United States, in order to form a more perfect union, establish justice, insure domestic tranquillity, provide for the common defense, promote the general welfare, and secure the blessings of liberty to ourselves and our posterity, do ordain and establish this CONSTITUTION for the United States of America.

Article I

SECTION 1. All legislative powers herein granted shall be vested in a Congress of the United States, which shall consist of a Senate and a House of Representatives.

SECTION 2. The House of Representatives shall be composed of members chosen every second year by the people of the several States, and the electors in each State shall have the qualifications requisite for electors of the most numerous branch of the State Legislature.

No person shall be a Representative who shall not have attained to the age of twenty-five years, and been seven years a citizen of the United States, and who shall not, when elected, be an inhabitant of that State in which he shall be chosen.

Representatives and direct taxes shall be apportioned among the several States which may be included within this Union, according to their respective numbers, *which shall be determined by adding to the whole number of free persons, including those bound to service for a term of years and excluding Indians not taxed, three-fifths of all other persons.* The actual enumeration shall be made within three years after the first meeting of the Congress of the United States, and within every subsequent term of ten years, in such manner as they shall by law direct. The number of Representatives shall not exceed one for every thirty thousand, but each State shall have at least one Representative; *and until such enumeration shall be made, the State of New Hampshire shall be entitled to choose three, Massachusetts eight, Rhode Island and Providence Plantations one, Connecticut five, New York six, New Jersey four, Pennsylvania eight, Delaware one, Maryland six, Virginia ten, North Carolina five, South Carolina five, and Georgia three.*

Note: Passages that are no longer in effect are printed in italic type.

When vacancies happen in the representation from any State, the Executive authority thereof shall issue writs of election to fill such vacancies.

The House of Representatives shall choose their Speaker and other officers; and shall have the sole power of impeachment.

SECTION 3. The Senate of the United States shall be composed of two Senators from each State, *chosen by the legislature thereof,* for six years; and each Senator shall have one vote.

Immediately after they shall be assembled in consequence of the first election, they shall be divided as equally as may be into three classes. The seats of the Senators of the first class shall be vacated at the expiration of the second year, of the second class at the expiration of the fourth year, and of the third class at the expiration of the sixth year, so that one-third maybe chosen every second year; *and if vacancies happen by resignation or otherwise, during the recess of the legislature of any State, the Executive thereof may make temporary appointments until the next meeting of the legislature, which shall then fill such vacancies.*

No person shall be a Senator who shall not have attained to the age of thirty years, and been nine years a citizen of the United States, and who shall not, when elected, be an inhabitant of that State for which he shall be chosen.

The Vice President of the United States shall be President of the Senate, but shall have no vote, unless they be equally divided.

The Senate shall choose their other officers, and also a President *pro tempore,* in the absence of the Vice President, or when he shall exercise the office of the President of the United States.

The Senate shall have the sole power to try all impeachments. When sitting for that purpose, they shall be on oath or affirmation. When the President of the United States is tried, the Chief Justice shall preside: and no person shall be convicted without the concurrence of two-thirds of the members present.

Judgment in cases of impeachment shall not extend further than to removal from the office, and disqualification to hold and enjoy any office of honor, trust or profit under the United States; but the party convicted shall nevertheless be liable and subject to indictment, trial, judgment and punishment, according to law.

SECTION 4. The times, places and manner of holding elections for Senators and Representatives shall be prescribed in each State by the legislature thereof; but the Congress may at any time by law make or alter such regulations, except as to the places of choosing Senators.

The Congress shall assemble at least once in every year, and such meeting *shall be on the first Monday in December, unless they shall by law appoint a different day.*

SECTION 5. Each house shall be the judge of the elections, returns and qualifications of its own members, and a majority of each shall constitute a quorum to do business; but a smaller number may adjourn from day to day, and maybe authorized to compel the attendance of absent members, in such manner, and under such penalties, as each house may provide.

Each house may determine the rules of its proceedings, punish its members for disorderly behavior, and with the concurrence of two-thirds, expel a member.

Each house shall keep a journal of its proceedings, and from time to time publish the same, excepting such parts as may in their judgment require secrecy; and the yeas and nays of the members of either house on any question shall, at the desire of one-fifth of those present, be entered on the journal.

Neither house, during the session of Congress, shall, without the consent of the other, adjourn for more than three days, nor to any other place than that in which the two houses shall be sitting.

SECTION 6. The Senators and Representatives shall receive a compensation for their services, to be ascertained by law and paid out of the treasury of the United States. They shall in all cases except treason, felony and breach of the peace, be privileged from arrest during their attendance at the session of their respective houses, and in going to and returning from the same; and for any speech or debate in either house, they shall not be questioned in any other place.

No Senator or Representative shall, during the time for which he was elected, be appointed to any civil office under the authority of the United States, which shall have been created, or the emoluments whereof shall have been increased, during such time; and no person holding any office under the United States shall be a member of either house during his continuance in office.

SECTION 7. All bills for raising revenue shall originate in the House of Representatives; but the Senate may propose or concur with amendments as on other bills.

Every bill which shall have passed the House of Representatives and the Senate, shall, before it become a law, be presented to the President of the United States; if he approve he shall sign it, but if not he shall return it with objections to that house in which it originated, who shall enter the objections at large on their journal, and proceed to reconsider it. If after such reconsideration two-thirds of that house shall agree to pass the bill, it shall be sent, together with the objections, to the other house, by which it shall likewise be reconsidered, and, if approved by two-thirds of that house, it shall become a law. But in all such cases the votes of both houses shall be determined by yeas and nays, and the names of the persons voting for and against the bill shall be entered on the journal of each house respectively. If any bill shall not be returned by the President within ten days (Sundays excepted) after it shall have been presented to him, the same shall be a law, in like manner as if he had signed it, unless the Congress by their adjournment prevent its return, in which case it shall not be a law.

Every order, resolution, or vote to which the concurrence of the Senate and House of Representatives may be necessary (except on a question of adjournment) shall be presented to the President of the United States; and before the same shall take effect, shall be approved by him, or being disapproved by him, shall be repassed by two-thirds of the Senate and House of Representatives, according to the rules and limitations prescribed in the case of a bill.

SECTION 8. The Congress shall have power

To lay and collect taxes, duties, imposts, and excises, to pay the debts and provide for the common defense and general welfare of the United States; but all duties, imposts and excises shall be uniform throughout the United States;

To borrow money on the credit of the United States;

To regulate commerce with foreign nations, and among the several States, and with the Indian tribes;

To establish an uniform rule of naturalization, and uniform laws on the subject of bankruptcies throughout the United States;

To coin money, regulate the value thereof, and of foreign coin, and fix the standard of weights and measures;

To provide for the punishment of counterfeiting the securities and current coin of the United States;

To establish post offices and post roads;

To promote the progress of science and useful arts by securing for limited times to authors and inventors the exclusive right to their respective writings and discoveries;

To constitute tribunals inferior to the Supreme Court;

To define and punish piracies and felonies committed on the high seas and offenses against the law of nations;

To declare war, grant letters of marque and reprisal, and make rules concerning captures on land and water;

To raise and support armies, but no appropriation of money to that use shall be for a longer term than two years;

To provide and maintain a navy;

To make rules for the government and regulation of the land and naval forces;

To provide for calling forth the militia to execute the laws of the Union, suppress insurrections, and repel invasions;

To provide for organizing, arming, and disciplining the militia, and for governing such part of them as may be employed in the service of the United States, reserving to the States respectively the appointment of the officers, and the authority of training the militia according to the discipline prescribed by Congress;

To exercise exclusive legislation in all cases whatsoever, over such district (not exceeding ten miles square) as may, by cession of particular States, and the acceptance of Congress, become the seat of government of the United States, and to exercise like authority over all places purchased by the consent of the legislature of the State, in which the same shall be, for erection of forts, magazines, arsenals, dock-yards, and other needful buildings;—and

To make all laws which shall be necessary and proper for carrying into execution the foregoing powers, and all other powers vested by this Constitution in the government of the United States, or in any department or officer thereof.

SECTION 9. *The migration or importation of such persons as any of the States now existing shall think proper to admit shall not be prohibited by the Congress prior to the year 1808; but a tax or duty may be imposed on such importation, not exceeding $10 for each person.*

The privilege of the writ of habeas corpus shall not be suspended, unless when in cases of rebellion or invasion the public safety may require it.

No bill of attainder or ex post facto law shall be passed.

No capitation, or other direct, tax shall be laid, unless in proportion to the census or enumeration herein before directed to be taken.

No tax or duty shall be laid on articles exported from any State.

No preference shall be given by any regulation of commerce or revenue to the ports of one State over those of another; nor shall vessels bound to, or from, one State, be obliged to enter, clear, or pay duties in another.

No money shall be drawn from the treasury, but in consequence of appropriations made by law; and a regular statement and account of the receipts and expenditures of all public money shall be published from time to time.

No title of nobility shall be granted by the United States: and no person holding any office of profit or trust under them, shall, without the consent of the Congress, accept of any present, emolument, office, or title, of any kind whatever, from any king, prince, or foreign state.

SECTION 10. No State shall enter into any treaty, alliance, or confederation; grant letters of marque and reprisal; coin money; emit bills of credit; make anything but gold and silver coin a tender in payment of debts; pass any bill of attainder, ex post facto law, or law impairing the obligation of contracts, or grant any title of nobility.

No State shall, without the consent of Congress, lay any imposts or duties on imports or exports, except what may be absolutely necessary for executing its inspection laws: and the net produce of all duties and imposts, laid by any State on imports or exports, shall be for the use of the treasury of the United States; and all such laws shall be subject to the revision and control of the Congress.

No State shall, without the consent of Congress, lay any duty of tonnage, keep troops or ships of war in time of peace, enter into any agreement or compact with another State, or with a foreign power, or engage in war, unless actually invaded, or in such imminent danger as will not admit of delay.

Article II

SECTION 1. The executive power shall be vested in a President of the United States of America. He shall hold his office during the term of four years, and, together with the Vice President, chosen for the same term, be elected as follows:

Each state shall appoint, in such manner as the legislature thereof may direct, a number of electors, equal to the whole number of Senators and Representatives to which the State may be entitled in the Congress; but no Senator or Representative, or person holding an office of trust or profit under the United States, shall be appointed an elector.

The electors shall meet in their respective States, and vote by ballot for two persons, of whom one at least shall not be an inhabitant of the same State with themselves. And they shall make a list of all the persons voted for, and of the number of votes for each; which list they shall sign and certify, and transmit sealed to the seat of government of the United States, directed to the President of the Senate. The President of the Senate shall, in the presence of the Senate and the House of Representatives, open all the certificates, and the votes shall then be counted. The person having the greatest number of votes shall be the President, if such number be a majority of the whole number of electors appointed; and if there be more than one who have such majority, and have an equal number of votes, then the House of Representatives shall immediately choose by ballot one of them for President; and if no person have a majority, then from the five highest on the list said house shall in like manner choose the President. But in choosing the President the votes shall be taken by States, the representation from each State having one vote; a quorum for this purpose shall consist of a member or members from two-thirds of the States, and a majority of all the States shall be necessary to a choice. In every case, after the choice of the President, the person having the greatest number of votes of the electors shall be the Vice President. But if there should remain two or more who have equal votes, the Senate shall choose from them by ballot the Vice President.

The Congress may determine the time of choosing the electors and the day on which they shall give their votes; which day shall be the same throughout the United States.

No person except a natural-born citizen, *or a citizen of the United States at the time of the adoption of this Constitution,* shall be eligible to the office of President; neither shall any person be eligible to that office who shall not have attained to the age of thirty-five years, and been fourteen years a resident within the United States.

In case of the removal of the President from office or of his death, resignation, or inability to discharge the powers and duties of the said office, the same shall devolve on the Vice President, and the Congress may by law provide for the case of removal, death, resignation, or inability, both of the President and Vice President, declaring what officer shall then act as President, and such officer shall act accordingly, until the disability be removed, or a President shall be elected.

The President shall, at stated times, receive for his services a compensation, which shall neither be increased nor diminished during the period for which he shall have been elected, and he shall not receive within that period any other emolument from the United States, or any of them.

Before he enter on the execution of his office, he shall take the following oath or affirmation:—"I do solemnly swear (or affirm) that I will faithfully execute the office of the President of the United States, and will to the best of my ability preserve, protect and defend the Constitution of the United States."

SECTION 2. The President shall be commander in chief of the army and navy of the United States, and of the militia of the several States, when called into the actual service of the United States; he may require the opinion, in writing, of the principal officer in each of the executive departments, upon any subject relating to the duties of their respective offices, and he shall have power to grant reprieves and pardons for offenses against the United States, except in cases of impeachment.

He shall have power, by and with the advice and consent of the Senate, to make treaties, provided two-thirds of the Senators present concur; and he shall nominate, and by and with the advice and consent of the Senate, shall appoint ambassadors, other public ministers and consuls, judges of the Supreme Court, and all other officers of the United States, whose appointments are not herein otherwise provided for, and which shall be established by law: but Congress may by law vest the appointment of such inferior officers, as they think proper, in the President alone, in the courts of law, or in the heads of departments.

The President shall have power to fill up all vacancies that may happen during the recess of the Senate, by granting commissions which shall expire at the end of their next session.

SECTION 3. He shall from time to time give to the Congress information of the state of the Union, and recommend to their consideration such measures as he shall judge necessary and expedient; he may, on extraordinary occasions, convene both houses, or either of them, and in case of disagreement between them, with respect to the time of adjournment, he may adjourn them to such time as he shall think proper; he shall receive ambassadors and other public ministers; he shall take care that the laws be faithfully executed, and shall commission all the officers of the United States.

SECTION 4. The President, Vice President and all civil officers of the United States shall be removed from office on impeachment for, and on conviction of, treason, bribery, or other high crimes and misdemeanors.

Article III

SECTION 1. The judicial power of the United States shall be vested in one Supreme Court, and in such inferior courts as the Congress may from time to time ordain and establish. The judges, both of the Supreme and inferior courts, shall hold their offices during good behavior, and shall, at stated times, receive for their services a compensation which shall not be diminished during their continuance in office.

SECTION 2. The judicial power shall extend to all cases, in law and equity, arising under this Constitution, the laws of the United States, and treaties made, or which shall be made, under their authority;—to all cases affecting ambassadors, other public ministers and consuls;—to all cases of admiralty and maritime jurisdiction;—to controversies to which the United States shall be a party;—to controversies between two or more States;—*between a State and citizens of another State;*—between citizens of different States;—between citizens of the same State claiming lands under grants of different States, and between a State, or the citizens thereof, and foreign states, citizens or subjects.

In all cases affecting ambassadors, other public ministers and consuls, and those in which a State shall be party, the Supreme Court shall have original jurisdiction. In all the other cases before mentioned, the Supreme Court shall have appellate jurisdiction, both as to law and fact, with such exceptions, and under such regulations, as the Congress shall make.

The trial of all crimes, except in cases of impeachment, shall be by jury; and such trial shall be held in the State where said crimes shall have been committed; but when not committed within any State, the trial shall be at such place or places as the Congress may by law have directed.

SECTION 3. Treason against the United States shall consist only in levying war against them, or in adhering to their enemies, giving them aid and comfort. No person shall be convicted of treason unless on the testimony of two witnesses to the same overt act, or on confession in open court.

The Congress shall have power to declare the punishment of treason, but no attainder of treason shall work corruption of blood, or forfeiture except during the life of the person attainted.

Article IV

SECTION 1. Full faith and credit shall be given in each State to the public acts, records, and judicial proceedings of every other State. And the Congress may by general laws prescribe the manner in which such acts, records, and proceedings shall be proved, and the effect thereof.

SECTION 2. The citizens of each State shall be entitled to all privileges and immunities of citizens in the several States.

A person charged in any State with treason, felony, or other crime, who shall flee from justice, and be found in another State, shall on demand of the executive authority of the State from which he fled, be delivered up, to be removed to the State having jurisdiction of the crime.

No person held to service or labor in one State, under the laws thereof, escaping into another, shall, in consequence of any law or regulation therein, be discharged from such service or labor, but shall be delivered up on claim of the party to whom such service or labor may be due.

SECTION 3. New States may be admitted by the Congress into this Union; but no new State shall be formed or erected within the jurisdiction of any other State; nor any State be formed by the junction of two or more States, or parts of States, without the consent of the legislatures of the States concerned as well as of the Congress.

The Congress shall have power to dispose of and make all needful rules and regulations respecting the territory or other property belonging to the United States; and nothing in this Constitution shall be so construed as to prejudice any claims of the United States, or of any particular State.

SECTION 4. The United States shall guarantee to every State in this Union a republican form of government, and shall protect each of them against invasion; and on application of the legislature, or of the executive (when the legislature cannot be convened), against domestic violence.

Article V

The Congress, whenever two-thirds of both houses shall deem it necessary, shall propose amendments to this Constitution, or, on the application of the legislatures of two-thirds of the several States, shall call a convention for proposing amendments, which, in either case, shall be valid to all intents and purposes, as part of this Constitution, when ratified by the legislatures of three-fourths of the several States, or by conventions in three-fourths thereof, as the one or the other mode of ratification may be proposed by the Congress; provided *that no amendments which may be made prior to the year one thousand eight hundred and eight shall in any manner affect the first and fourth clauses in the ninth section of the first article;* and that no State, without its consent, shall be deprived of its equal suffrage in the Senate.

Article VI

All debts contracted and engagements entered into, before the adoption of this Constitution, shall be as valid against the United States under this Constitution, as under the Confederation. This Constitution, and the laws of the United States which shall be made in pursuance thereof; and all treaties made, or which shall be made, under the authority of the United States, shall be the supreme law of the land; and the judges in every State shall be bound thereby, anything in the Constitution or laws of any State to the contrary notwithstanding.

The Senators and Representatives before mentioned, and the members of the several State legislatures, and all executive and judicial officers, both of the United States and of the several States, shall be bound by oath or affirmation to support this Constitution; but no religious test shall ever be required as a qualification to any office or public trust under the United States.

Article VII

The ratification of the conventions of nine States shall be sufficient for the establishment of this Constitution between the States so ratifying the same.

Done in Convention by the unanimous consent of the States present, the seventeenth day of September in the year of our Lord one thousand seven hundred and eighty-seven and of the Independence of the United States of America the twelfth. In witness whereof we have hereunto subscribed our names.

[Signed by]
Gº WASHINGTON
Presidt and Deputy from Virginia [and thirty-eight others]

Amendments to the Constitution

Amendment I*

Congress shall make no law respecting an establishment of religion, or prohibiting the free exercise thereof; or abridging the freedom of speech, or of the press; or the right of the people peaceably to assemble, and to petition the government for a redress of grievances.

Amendment II

A well-regulated militia being necessary to the security of a free State, the right of the people to keep and bear arms shall not be infringed.

Amendment III

No soldier shall, in time of peace, be quartered in any house without the consent of the owner, nor in time of war, but in a manner to be prescribed by law.

Amendment IV

The right of the people to be secure in their persons, houses, papers, and effects, against unreasonable searches and seizures, shall not be violated, and no warrants shall issue but upon probable cause, supported by oath or affirmation, and particularly describing the place to be searched, and the persons or things to be seized.

Amendment V

No person shall be held to answer for a capital, or otherwise infamous crime, unless on a presentment or indictment of a grand jury, except in cases arising in the land or naval forces, or in the militia, when in actual service in time of war or public danger; nor shall any person be subject for the same offense to be twice put in jeopardy of life or limb; nor shall be compelled in any criminal case to be a witness against himself, nor be deprived of life, liberty, or property, without due process of law; nor shall private property be taken for public use without just compensation.

Amendment VI

In all criminal prosecutions, the accused shall enjoy the right to a speedy and public trial, by an impartial jury of the State and district wherein the crime shall have been committed, which district shall have been previously ascertained by law, and to be informed of the nature and cause of the accusation; to be confronted with the witnesses against him; to have compulsory process for obtaining witnesses in his favor, and to have the assistance of counsel for his defense.

Amendment VII

In suits at common law, where the value in controversy shall exceed twenty dollars, the right of trial by jury shall be preserved, and no fact tried by a jury shall be otherwise reexamined in any court of the United States, than according to the rules of the common law.

Amendment VIII

Excessive bail shall not be required, nor excessive fines imposed, nor cruel and unusual punishments inflicted.

Amendment IX

The enumeration in the Constitution, of certain rights, shall not be construed to deny or disparage others retained by the people.

Amendment X

The powers not delegated to the United States by the Constitution, nor prohibited by it to the States, are reserved to the States respectively, or to the people.

*The first ten amendments (Bill of Rights) were adopted in 1791.

Amendment XI

[Adopted 1798]
The judicial power of the United States shall not be construed to extend to any suit in law or equity, commenced or prosecuted against one of the United States by citizens of another State, or by citizens or subjects of any foreign state.

Amendment XII

[Adopted 1804]
The electors shall meet in their respective States, and vote by ballot for President and Vice President, one of whom, at least, shall not be an inhabitant of the same State with themselves; they shall name in their ballots the person voted for as President, and in distinct ballots the person voted for as Vice President, and they shall make distinct lists of all persons voted for as President, and of all persons voted for as Vice President, and of the number of votes for each, which lists they shall sign and certify, and transmit sealed to the seat of government of the United States, directed to the President of the Senate;—the President of the Senate shall, in the presence of the Senate and House of Representatives, open all the certificates and the votes shall then be counted;—the person having the greatest number of votes for President shall be the President, if such number be a majority of the whole number of electors appointed; and if no person have such majority, then from the persons having the highest numbers not exceeding three on the list of those voted for as President, the House of Representatives shall choose immediately, by ballot, the President. But in choosing the President, the votes shall be taken by States, the representation from each State having one vote; a quorum for this purpose shall consist of a member or members from two-thirds of the States, and a majority of all the States shall be necessary to a choice. And if the House of Representatives shall not choose a President whenever the right of choice shall devolve upon them, before *the fourth day of March* next following, then the Vice President shall act as President, as in the case of the death or other constitutional disability of the President.

The person having the greatest number of votes as Vice President shall be the Vice President, if such a number be a majority of the whole number of electors appointed; and if no person have a majority, then from the two highest numbers on the list the Senate shall choose the Vice President; a quorum for the purpose shall consist of two-thirds of the whole number of Senators, and a majority of the whole number shall be necessary to a choice. But no person constitutionally ineligible to the office of President shall be eligible to that of Vice President of the United States.

Amendment XIII

[Adopted 1865]
SECTION 1. Neither slavery nor involuntary servitude, except as a punishment for crime whereof the party shall

have been duly convicted, shall exist within the United States, or any place subject to their jurisdiction.

SECTION 2. Congress shall have power to enforce this article by appropriate legislation.

Amendment XIV

[Adopted 1868]

SECTION 1. All persons born or naturalized in the United States, and subject to the jurisdiction thereof, are citizens of the United States and of the State wherein they reside. No State shall make or enforce any law which shall abridge the privileges or immunities of citizens of the United States; nor shall any State deprive any person of life, liberty, or property, without due process of law; nor deny to any person within its jurisdiction the equal protection of the laws.

SECTION 2. Representatives shall be apportioned among the several States according to their respective numbers, counting the whole number of persons in each State, excluding Indians not taxed. But when the right to vote at any election for the choice of Electors for President and Vice President of the United States, Representatives in Congress, the executive and judicial officers of a State, or the members of the legislature thereof, is denied to any of the male inhabitants of such State, being twenty-one years of age and citizens of the United States, or in any way abridged, except for participation in rebellion, or other crime, the basis of representation therein shall be reduced in the proportion which the number of such male citizens shall bear to the whole number of male citizens twenty-one years of age in such State.

SECTION 3. No person shall be a Senator or Representative in Congress or Elector of President and Vice President, or hold any office, civil or military, under the United States, or under any State, who, having previously taken an oath, as a member of Congress, or as an officer of the United States, or as a member of any State legislature, or as an executive or judicial officer of any State, to support the Constitution of the United States, shall have engaged in insurrection or rebellion against the same, or given aid and comfort to the enemies thereof. Congress may, by a vote of two-thirds of each house, remove such disability.

SECTION 4. The validity of the public debt of the United States, authorized by law, including debts incurred for payment of pensions and bounties for services in suppressing insurrection or rebellion, shall not be questioned. But neither the United States nor any State shall assume or pay any debt or obligation incurred in aid of insurrection or rebellion against the United States, or any claim for the loss or emancipation of any slave; but all such debts, obligations, and claims shall be held illegal and void.

SECTION 5. The Congress shall have the power to enforce, by appropriate legislation, the provisions of this article.

Amendment XV

[Adopted 1870]

SECTION 1. The right of citizens of the United States to vote shall not be denied or abridged by the United States or by any State on account of race, color, or previous condition of servitude.

SECTION 2. The Congress shall have power to enforce this article by appropriate legislation.

Amendment XVI

[Adopted 1913]

The Congress shall have power to lay and collect taxes on incomes, from whatever source derived, without apportionment among the several States, and without regard to any census or enumeration.

Amendment XVII

[Adopted 1913]

SECTION 1. The Senate of the United States shall be composed of two Senators from each State, elected by the people thereof, for six years; and each Senator shall have one vote. The electors in each State shall have the qualifications requisite for electors of [voters for] the most numerous branch of the State legislatures.

SECTION 2. When vacancies happen in the representation of any State in the Senate, the executive authority of such State shall issue writs of election to fill such vacancies: Provided, that the Legislature of any State may empower the executive thereof to make temporary appointments until the people fill the vacancies by election as the Legislature may direct.

SECTION 3. This amendment shall not be so construed as to affect the election or term of any Senator chosen before it becomes valid as part of the Constitution.

Amendment XVIII

[Adopted 1919; repealed 1933]

SECTION 1. *After one year from the ratification of this article the manufacture, sale, or transportation of intoxicating liquors within, the importation thereof into, or the exportation thereof from the United States and all territory subject to the jurisdiction thereof, for beverage purposes, is hereby prohibited.*

SECTION 2. *The Congress and the several States shall have concurrent power to enforce this article by appropriate legislation.*

SECTION 3. *This article shall be inoperative unless it shall have been ratified as an amendment to the Constitution by the legislatures of the several States, as provided by the Constitution, within seven years from the date of the submission thereof to the States by the Congress.*

Amendment XIX

[Adopted 1920]

SECTION 1. The right of citizens of the United States to vote shall not be denied or abridged by the United States or by any State on account of sex.

SECTION 2. The Congress shall have the power to enforce this article by appropriate legislation.

Amendment XX

[Adopted 1933]

SECTION 1. The terms of the President and Vice President shall end at noon on the 20th day of January, and the terms of Senators and Representatives at noon on the 3d day of January, of the years in which such terms would have ended if this article had not been ratified; and the terms of their successors shall then begin.

SECTION 2. The Congress shall assemble at least once in every year, and such meeting shall begin at noon on the 3d of January, unless they shall by law appoint a different day.

SECTION 3. If, at the time fixed for the beginning of the term of the President, the President-elect shall have died, the Vice President-elect shall become President. If a President shall not have been chosen before the time fixed for the beginning of his term, or if the President-elect shall have failed to qualify, then the Vice President-elect shall act as President until a President shall have qualified; and the Congress may by law provide for the case wherein neither a President-elect nor a Vice President-elect shall have qualified, declaring who shall then act as President, or the manner in which one who is to act shall be selected, and such persons shall act accordingly until a President or Vice President shall have qualified.

SECTION 4. The Congress may by law provide for the case of the death of any of the persons from whom the House of Representatives may choose a President whenever the right of choice shall have devolved upon them, and for the case of the death of any of the persons from whom the Senate may choose a Vice President whenever the right of choice shall have devolved upon them.

SECTION 5. Sections 1 and 2 shall take effect on the 15th day of October following the ratification of this article.

SECTION 6. This article shall be inoperative unless it shall have been ratified as an amendment to the Constitution by the Legislatures of three-fourths of the several States within seven years from the date of its submission.

Amendment XXI

[Adopted 1933]

SECTION 1. The eighteenth article of amendment to the Constitution of the United States is hereby repealed.

SECTION 2. The transportation or importation into any State, Territory, or Possession of the United States for delivery or use therein of intoxicating liquors, in violation of the laws thereof, is hereby prohibited.

SECTION 3. This article shall be inoperative unless it shall have been ratified as an amendment to the Constitution by conventions in the several States, as provided in the Constitution, within seven years from the date of submission thereof to the States by the Congress.

Amendment XXII

[Adopted 1951]

SECTION 1. No person shall be elected to the office of President more than twice, and no person who has held the office of President, or acted as President, for more than two years of a term to which some other person was elected President shall be elected to the office of President more than once. But this article shall not apply to any person holding the office of President when this article was proposed by the Congress, and shall not prevent any person who may be holding the office of President, or acting as President, during the term within which this article becomes operative from holding the office of President or acting as President during the remainder of such term.

SECTION 2. This article shall be inoperative unless it shall have been ratified as an amendment to the Constitution by the legislatures of three-fourths of the several States within seven years from the date of its submission to the States by the Congress.

Amendment XXIII

[Adopted 1961]

SECTION 1. The District constituting the seat of Government of the United States shall appoint in such manner as the Congress may direct:

A number of electors of President and Vice President equal to the whole number of Senators and Representatives in Congress to which the District would be entitled if it were a State, but in no event more than the least populous State; they shall be in addition to those appointed by the States, but they shall be considered for the purposes of the election of President and Vice President, to be electors appointed by a State; and they shall meet in the District and perform such duties as provided by the twelfth article of amendment.

SECTION 2. The Congress shall have the power to enforce this article by appropriate legislation.

Amendment XXIV

[Adopted 1964]

SECTION 1. The right of citizens of the United States to vote in any primary or other election for President or Vice President, for electors for President or Vice President, or for

Senator or Representative in Congress, shall not be denied or abridged by the United States or any State by reason of failure to pay any poll tax or other tax.

SECTION 2. The Congress shall have the power to enforce this article by appropriate legislation.

Amendment XXV

[Adopted 1967]
SECTION 1. In case of the removal of the President from office or of his death or resignation, the Vice President shall become President.

SECTION 2. Whenever there is a vacancy in the office of the Vice President, the President shall nominate a Vice President who shall take office upon confirmation by a majority vote of both Houses of Congress.

SECTION 3. Whenever the President transmits to the President pro tempore of the Senate and the Speaker of the House of Representatives his written declaration that he is unable to discharge the powers and duties of his office, and until he transmits to them a written declaration to the contrary, such powers and duties shall be discharged by the Vice President as Acting President.

SECTION 4. Whenever the Vice President and a majority of either the principal officers of the executive departments or of such other body as Congress may by law provide, transmit to the President pro tempore of the Senate and the Speaker of the House of Representatives their written declaration that the President is unable to discharge the powers and duties of his office, the Vice President shall immediately assume the powers and duties of the office as Acting President.

Thereafter, when the President transmits to the President pro tempore of the Senate and the Speaker of the House of Representatives his written declaration that no inability exists, he shall resume the powers and duties of his office unless the Vice President and a majority of either the principal officers of the executive department[s] or of such other body as Congress may by law provide, transmit within four days to the President pro tempore of the Senate and the Speaker of the House of Representatives their written declaration that the President is unable to discharge the powers and duties of his office. Thereupon Congress shall decide the issue, assembling within forty-eight hours for that purpose if not in session. If the Congress, within twenty-one days after receipt of the latter written declaration, or, if Congress is not in session, within twenty-one days after Congress is required to assemble, determines by two-thirds vote of both Houses that the President is unable to discharge the powers and duties of his office, the Vice President shall continue to discharge the same as Acting President; otherwise, the President shall resume the powers and duties of his office.

Amendment XXVI

[Adopted 1971]
SECTION 1. The right of citizens of the United States, who are eighteen years of age or older, to vote shall not be denied or abridged by the United States or by any State on account of age.

SECTION 2. The Congress shall have power to enforce this article by appropriate legislation.

Amendment XXVII[a]

[Adopted 1992]
No law, varying the compensation for services of the Senators and Representatives, shall take effect, until an election of Representatives shall have intervened.

---

[a]Originally proposed in 1789 by James Madison, this amendment failed to win ratification along with the other parts of what became the Bill of Rights. However, the proposed amendment contained no deadline for ratification, and over the years other state legislatures voted to add it to the Constitution; many such ratifications occurred during the 1980s and early 1990s as public frustration with Congress's performance mounted. In May 1992, the Archivist of the United States certified that, with the Michigan legislature's ratification, the article had been approved by three-fourths of the states and thus automatically became part of the Constitution.

THE AMERICAN LAND

ADMISSION OF STATES INTO THE UNION

STATE	DATE OF ADMISSION	STATE	DATE OF ADMISSION
1. Delaware	December 7, 1787	26. Michigan	January 26, 1837
2. Pennsylvania	December 12, 1787	27. Florida	March 3, 1845
3. New Jersey	December 18, 1787	28. Texas	December 29, 1845
4. Georgia	January 2, 1788	29. Iowa	December 28, 1846
5. Connecticut	January 9, 1788	30. Wisconsin	May 29, 1848
6. Massachusetts	February 6, 1788	31. California	September 9, 1850
7. Maryland	April 28, 1788	32. Minnesota	May 11, 1858
8. South Carolina	May 23, 1788	33. Oregon	February 14, 1859
9. New Hampshire	June 21, 1788	34. Kansas	January 29, 1861
10. Virginia	June 25, 1788	35. West Virginia	June 20, 1863
11. New York	July 26, 1788	36. Nevada	October 31, 1864
12. North Carolina	November 21, 1789	37. Nebraska	March 1, 1867
13. Rhode Island	May 29, 1790	38. Colorado	August 1, 1876
14. Vermont	March 4, 1791	39. North Dakota	November 2, 1889
15. Kentucky	June 1, 1792	40. South Dakota	November 2, 1889
16. Tennessee	June 1, 1796	41. Montana	November 8, 1889
17. Ohio	March 1, 1803	42. Washington	November 11, 1889
18. Louisiana	April 30, 1812	43. Idaho	July 3, 1890
19. Indiana	December 11, 1816	44. Wyoming	July 10, 1890
20. Mississippi	December 10, 1817	45. Utah	January 4, 1896
21. Illinois	December 3, 1818	46. Oklahoma	November 16, 1907
22. Alabama	December 14, 1819	47. New Mexico	January 6, 1912
23. Maine	March 15, 1820	48. Arizona	February 14, 1912
24. Missouri	August 10, 1821	49. Alaska	January 3, 1959
25. Arkansas	June 15, 1836	50. Hawaii	August 21, 1959

TERRITORIAL EXPANSION

TERRITORY	DATE ACQUIRED	SQUARE MILES	HOW ACQUIRED
Original states and territories	1783	888,685	Treaty of Paris
Louisiana Purchase	1803	827,192	Purchased from France
Florida	1819	72,003	Adams-Onís Treaty
Texas	1845	390,143	Annexation of independent country
Oregon	1846	285,580	Oregon Boundary Treaty
Mexican cession	1848	529,017	Treaty of Guadalupe Hidalgo
Gadsden Purchase	1853	29,640	Purchased from Mexico
Midway Islands	1867	2	Annexation of uninhabited islands
Alaska	1867	589,757	Purchased from Russia
Hawaii	1898	6,450	Annexation of independent country
Wake Island	1898	3	Annexation of uninhabited island
Puerto Rico	1899	3,435	Treaty of Paris
Guam	1899	212	Treaty of Paris
The Philippines	1899–1946	11 5,600	Treaty of Paris; granted independence
American Samoa	1900	76	Treaty with Germany and Great Britain
Panama Canal Zone	1904–1978	553	Hay-Bunau-Varilla Treaty
U.S. Virgin Islands	1917	133	Purchased from Denmark
Trust Territory of the Pacific Islands*	1947	717	United Nations Trusteeship

*A number of these islands have been granted independence: Federated States of Micronesia, 1990; Marshall Islands, 1991; Palau, 1994.

THE AMERICAN PEOPLE

POPULATION, PERCENTAGE CHANGE, AND RACIAL COMPOSITION FOR THE UNITED STATES, 1790–2010

| CENSUS | POPULATION OF UNITED STATES | INCREASE OVER PRECEDING CENSUS | | RACIAL COMPOSITION, PERCENT DISTRIBUTION* | | | |
		NUMBER	PERCENTAGE	WHITE	BLACK	LATINO	ASIAN
1790	3,929,214			80.7	19.3	NA	NA
1800	5,308,483	1,379,269	35.1	81.1	18.9	NA	NA
1810	7,239,881	1,931,398	36.4	81.0	19.0	NA	NA
1820	9,638,453	2,398,572	33.1	81.6	18.4	NA	NA
1830	12,866,020	3,227,567	33.5	81.9	18.1	NA	NA
1840	17,069,453	4,203,433	32.7	83.2	16.8	NA	NA
1850	23,191,876	6,122,423	35.9	84.3	15.7	NA	NA
1860	31,433,321	8,251,445	35.6	85.6	14.1	NA	NA
1870	39,818,449	8,375,128	26.6	86.2	13.5	NA	NA
1880	50,155,783	10,337,334	26.0	86.5	13.1	NA	NA
1890	62,947,714	12,791,931	25.5	87.5	11.9	NA	NA
1900	75,994,575	13,046,861	20.7	87.9	11.6	NA	0.3
1910	91,972,266	15,997,691	21.0	88.9	10.7	NA	0.3
1920	105,710,620	13,738,354	14.9	89.7	9.9	NA	0.3
1930	122,775,046	17,064,426	16.1	89.8	9.7	NA	0.4
1940	131,669,275	8,894,229	7.2	89.8	9.8	NA	0.4
1950	150,697,361	19,028,086	14.5	89.5	10.0	NA	0.4
1960†	179,323,175	28,625,814	19.0	88.6	10.5	NA	0.5
1970	203,235,298	23,912,123	13.3	87.6	11.1	NA	0.7
1980	226,504,825	23,269,527	11.4	85.9	11.8	6.4	1.5
1990	248,709,873	22,205,048	9.8	83.9	12.3	9.0	2.9
2000	281,421,906	32,712,033	82.2	82.2	12.2	11.7	3.8
2010	308,745,538	27,323,632	9.7	72.4	12.6	16.3	4.8

*Not every racial group included (e.g., no Native Americans). Data for 1980, 1990, 2000, and 2010 add up to more than 100% because those who identify themselves as "Latino" may be of any race.
†First year for which figures include Alaska and Hawaii.

Source: *Census Bureau, Historical Statistics of the United States, updated by relevant Statistical Abstract of the United States and http://factfinder.census.gov.*

POPULATION DENSITY AND DISTRIBUTION, 1790–2010

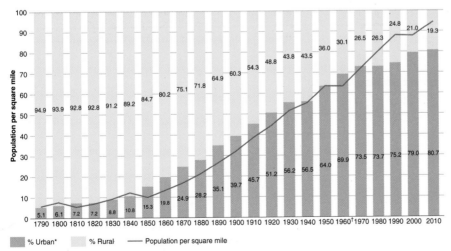

*The Bureau of the Census defines "urban" as communities of 2,500 or more inhabitants.
†First year for which figures include Alaska and Hawaii.

Source: *Census Bureau, Historical Statistics of the United States, updated by relevant Statistical Abstract of the United States.*

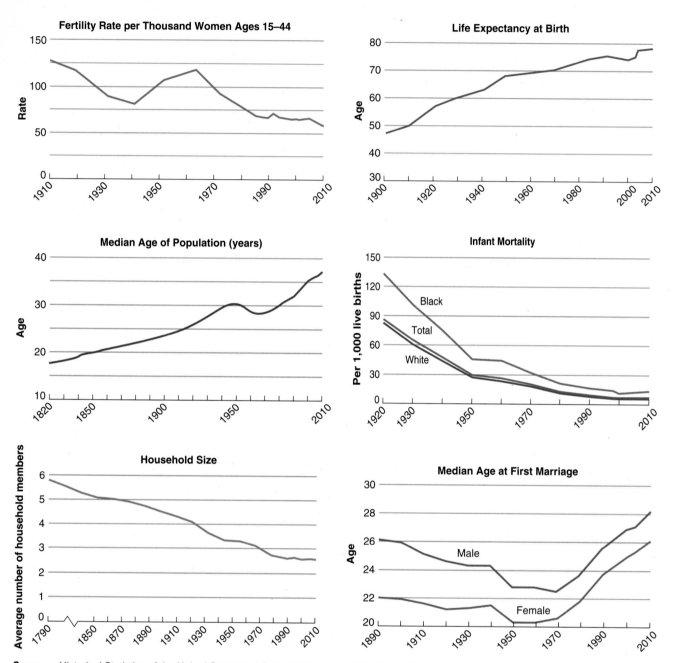

ESTIMATED IMMIGRATION TOTALS BY DECADE

	IMMIGRATION TOTALS BY DECADE		
YEARS	NUMBER	YEARS	NUMBER
1820–1830	151,824	1911–1920	5,735,811
1831–1840	599,125	1921–1930	4,107,209
1841–1850	1,713,251	1931–1940	528,431
1851–1860	2,598,214	1941–1950	1,035,039
1861–1870	2,314,824	1951–1960	2,515,479
1871–1880	2,812,191	1961–1970	3,321,677
1881–1890	5,246,613	1971–1980	4,493,314
1891–1900	3,687,546	1981–1990	7,338,062
1901–1910	8,795,386	1991–2000	9,095,417
		2001–2006	8,795,000
		2009	8,944,170

MAJOR SOURCES OF IMMIGRATION, 1820–2000

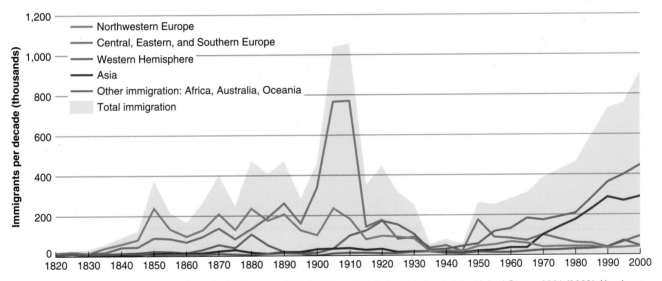

Sources: *Historical Statistics of the U.S., Colonial Times to 1970 (1975) and Statistical Abstract of the United States, 2001 (2002). Numbers do not include undocumented immigrants.* © Cengage Learning. All rights reserved. No distribution allowed without express authorization.

THE AMERICAN WORKER

YEAR	TOTAL NUMBER OF WORKERS	MALES AS PERCENT OF TOTAL WORKERS	FEMALES AS PERCENT OF TOTAL WORKERS	MARRIED WOMEN AS PERCENT OF FEMALE WORKERS	FEMALE WORKERS AS PERCENT OF FEMALE POPULATION	PERCENT OF LABOR FORCE UNEMPLOYED
1870	12,506,000	85	15	NA	NA	NA
1880	17,392,000	85	15	NA	NA	NA
1890	23,318,000	83	17	14	19	4(1894=18)
1900	29,073,000	82	18	15	21	5
1910	38,167,000	79	21	25	25	6
1920	41,614,000	79	21	23	24	5(1921=12)
1930	48,830,000	78	22	29	25	9(1933=25)
1940	53,011,000	76	24	36	27	15(1944=1)
1950	62,208,000	72	28	52	31	5.3
1960	69,628,000	67	33	55	38	5.5
1970	82,771,000	62	38	59	43	4.9
1980	106,940,000	58	42	55	52	7.1
1990	125,840,000	55	45	54	58	5.6
2000	135,208,000	53	47	55	60	4.0
2009*	154,142,000	53.3	46.7	51.7	59**	9.9

NA=Not Available

*Data not strictly comparable with earlier years. See 2008 *Statistical Abstract*, Table 569, note 2.
**Females 16 years of age and older.

Sources: *U.S Census Bureau; Statistical Abstract of the United States (2006, 2008); U.S. Department of Labor,"Women in the Labor Force," Report 1026, December 2010.*

THE AMERICAN GOVERNMENT

PRESIDENTIAL ELECTIONS, 1789–2012

YEAR	STATES IN THE UNION	CANDIDATES	PARTIES	ELECTORAL VOTE	POPULAR VOTE	PERCENTAGE OF POPULAR VOTE
1789	11	GEORGE WASHINGTON	No party designations	69		
		John Adams		34		
		Minor candidates		35		
1792	15	GEORGE WASHINGTON	No party designations	132		
		John Adams		77		
		George Clinton		50		
		Minor candidates		5		
1796	16	JOHN ADAMS	Federalist	71		
		Thomas Jefferson	Democratic-Republican	68		
		Thomas Pinckney	Federalist	59		
		Aaron Burr	Democratic-Republican	30		
		Minor candidates		48		
1800	16	THOMAS JEFFERSON	Democratic-Republican	73		
		Aaron Burr	Democratic-Republican	73		
		John Adams	Federalist	65		
		Charles C. Pinckney	Federalist	64		
		John Jay	Federalist	1		
1804	17	THOMAS JEFFERSON	Democratic-Republican	162		
		Charles C. Pinckney	Federalist	14		
1808	17	JAMES MADISON	Democratic-Republican	122		
		Charles C. Pinckney	Federalist	47		
		George Clinton	Democratic-Republican	6		
1812	18	JAMES MADISON	Democratic-Republican	128		
		DeWitt Clinton	Federalist	89		
1816	19	JAMES MONROE	Democratic-Republican	183		
		Rufus King	Federalist	34		
1820	24	JAMES MONROE	Democratic-Republican	231		
		John Quincy Adams	Independent Republican	1		
1824	24	JOHN QUINCY ADAMS	Democratic-Republican	84	108,740	30.5
		Andrew Jackson	Democratic-Republican	99	153,544	43.1
		William H. Crawford	Democratic-Republican	41	46,618	13.1
		Henry Clay	Democratic-Republican	37	47,136	13.2
1828	24	ANDREW JACKSON	Democratic	178	642,553	56.0
		John Quincy Adams	National Republican	83	500,897	44.0
1832	24	ANDREW JACKSON	Democratic	219	687,502	55.0
		Henry Clay	National Republican	49	530,189	42.4
		William Wirt	Anti-Masonic	7	33,108	2.6
		John Floyd	National Republican	11		

Because candidates receiving less than 1 percent of the popular vote are omitted, the percentage of popular vote may not total 100 percent. Before the Twelfth Amendment was passed in 1804, the Electoral College voted for two presidential candidates; the runner-up became vice president.

YEAR	STATES IN THE UNION	CANDIDATES	PARTIES	ELECTORAL VOTE	POPULAR VOTE	PERCENTAGE OF POPULAR VOTE
1836	26	MARTIN VAN BUREN	Democratic	170	765,483	50.9
		William H. Harrison	Whig	73		
		Hugh L. White	Whig	26		
		Daniel Webster	Whig	14		
		W. P. Mangum	Whig	11		
1840	26	WILLIAM H. HARRISON	Whig	234	1,274,624	53.1
		Martin Van Buren	Democratic	60	1,127,781	46.9
1844	26	JAMES K. POLK	Democratic	170	1,338,464	49.6
		Henry Clay	Whig	105	1,300,097	48.1
		James G. Birney	Liberty	0	62,300	2.3
1848	30	ZACHARY TAYLOR	Whig	163	1,360,967	47.4
		Lewis Cass	Democratic	127	1,222,342	42.5
		Martin Van Buren	Free Soil	0	291,263	10.1
1852	31	FRANKLIN PIERCE	Democratic	254	1,601,117	50.9
		Winfield Scott	Whig	42	1,385,453	44.1
		John P. Hale	Free Soil	0	155,825	5.0
1856	31	JAMES BUCHANAN	Democratic	174	1,832,955	45.3
		John C. Fremont	Republican	114	1,339,932	33.1
		Millard Fillmore	American	8	871,731	21.6
1860	33	ABRAHAM LINCOLN	Republican	114	1,339,932	33.1
		Stephen A. Douglas	Democratic	12	1,382,713	29.5
		John C. Breckinridge	Democratic	72	848,356	18.1
		John Bell	Constitutional Union	39	592,906	12.6
1864	36	ABRAHAM LINCOLN	Republican	212	2,206,938	55.0
		George B. McClellan	Democratic	21	1,803,787	45.0
1868	37	ULYSSES S. GRANT	Republican	214	3,013,421	52.7
		Horatio Seymour	Democratic	80	2,706,829	47.3
1872	37	ULYSSES S. GRANT	Republican	268	3,596,745	55.6
		Horace Greeley	Democratic	*	2,843,446	43.9
1876	38	RUTHERFORD B. HAYES	Republican	185	4,034,311	48.0
		Samuel J. Tilden	Democratic	184	4,288,546	51.0
		Peter Cooper	Greenback	0	75,973	1.0
1880	38	JAMES A. GARFIELD	Republican	214	4,453,295	48.5
		Winfield S. Hancock	Democratic	155	4,414,082	48.1
		James B. Weaver	Greenback-Labor	0	308,578	3.4
1884	38	GROVER CLEVELAND	Democratic	219	4,879,507	48.5
		James G. Blaine	Republican	182	4,850,293	48.2
		Benjamin F. Butler	Greenback-Labor	0	175,370	1.8
		John P. St. John	Prohibition	0	150,369	1.5
1888	38	BENJAMIN HARRISON	Republican	233	5,477,129	47.9
		Grover Cleveland	Democratic	168	5,537,857	48.6
		Clinton B. Fisk	Prohibition	0	249,506	2.2
		Anson J. Streeter	Union Labor	0	146,935	1.3

*When Greeley died shortly after the election, his supporters divided their votes among the minor candidates.

Because candidates receiving less than 1 percent of the popular vote are omitted, the percentage of popular vote may not total 100 percent.

YEAR	STATES IN THE UNION	CANDIDATES	PARTIES	ELECTORAL VOTE	POPULAR VOTE	PERCENTAGE OF POPULAR VOTE
1892	44	GROVER CLEVELAND	Democratic	277	5,555,426	46.1
		Benjamin Harrison	Republican	145	5,182,690	43.0
		James B. Weaver	People's	22	1,029,846	8.5
		John Bidwell	Prohibition	0	264,133	2.2
1896	45	WILLIAM McKINLEY	Republican	271	7,102,246	51.1
		William J. Bryan	Democratic	176	6,492,559	47.7
1900	45	WILLIAM McKINLEY	Republican	292	7,218,491	51.7
		William J. Bryan	Democratic	155	6,356,734	45.5
		John C. Wooley	Populist Prohibition	0	208,914	1.5
1904	45	THEODORE ROOSEVELT	Republican	336	7,628,461	57.4
		Alton B. Parker	Democratic	140	5,084,223	37.6
		Eugene V. Debs	Socialist	0	402,283	3.0
		Silas C. Swallow	Prohibition	0	258,536	1.9
1908	46	WILLIAM H. TAFT	Republican	321	7,675,320	51.6
		William J. Bryan	Democratic	162	6,412,294	43.1
		Eugene V. Debs	Socialist	0	420,793	2.8
		Eugene W. Chafin	Prohibition	0	253,840	1.7
1912	48	WOODROW WILSON	Democratic	435	6,296,547	41.9
		Theodore Roosevelt	Progressive	88	4,118,571	27.4
		William H. Taft	Republican	8	3,486,720	23.2
		Eugene V. Debs	Socialist	0	900,672	6.0
		Eugene W. Chafin	Prohibition	0	206,275	1.4
1916	48	WOODROW WILSON	Democratic	277	9,127,695	49.4
		Charles E. Hughes	Republican	254	8,533,507	46.2
		A. L. Benson	Socialist	0	585,113	3.2
		J. Frank Hanly	Prohibition	0	220,506	1.2
1920	48	WARREN G. HARDING	Republican	404	16,143,407	60.4
		James N. Cox	Democratic	127	9,130,328	34.2
		Eugene V. Debs	Socialist	0	919,799	3.4
		P. P. Christensen	Farmer-Labor	0	265,411	1.0
1924	48	CALVIN COOLIDGE	Republican	382	15,718,211	54.0
		John W. Davis	Democratic	136	8,385,283	28.8
		Robert M. La Follette	Progressive	13	4,831,289	16.6
1928	48	HERBERT C. HOOVER	Republican	444	21,391,993	58.2
		Alfred E. Smith	Democratic	87	15,016,169	40.9
1932	48	FRANKLIN D. ROOSEVELT	Democratic	472	22,809,638	57.4
		Herbert C. Hoover	Republican	59	15,758,901	39.7
		Norman Thomas	Socialist	0	881,951	2.2
1936	48	FRANKLIN D. ROOSEVELT	Democratic	523	27,752,869	60.8
		Alfred M. Landon	Republican	8	16,674,665	36.5
		William Lemke	Union	0	882,479	1.9

Because candidates receiving less than 1 percent of the popular vote are omitted, the percentage of popular vote may not total 100 percent.

YEAR	STATES IN THE UNION	CANDIDATES	PARTIES	ELECTORAL VOTE	POPULAR VOTE	PERCENTAGE OF POPULAR VOTE
1940	48	FRANKLIN D. ROOSEVELT	Democratic	449	27,307,819	54.8
		Wendell L. Willkie	Republican	82	22,321,018	44.8
1944	48	FRANKLIN D. ROOSEVELT	Democratic	432	25,606,585	53.5
		Thomas E. Dewey	Republican	99	22,014,745	46.0
1948	48	HARRY S TRUMAN	Democratic	303	24,105,812	49.5
		Thomas E. Dewey	Republican	189	21,970,065	45.1
		Strom Thurmond	States' Rights	39	1,169,063	2.4
		Henry A. Wallace	Progressive	0	1,157,172	2.4
1952	48	DWIGHT D. EISENHOWER	Republican	442	33,936,234	55.1
		Adlai E. Stevenson	Democratic	89	27,314,992	44.4
1956	48	DWIGHT D. EISENHOWER	Republican	457	35,590,472	57.6
		Adlai E. Stevenson	Democratic	73	26,022,752	42.1
1960	50	JOHN F. KENNEDY	Democratic	303	34,227,096	49.7
		Richard M. Nixon	Republican	219	34,108,546	49.5
		Harry F. Byrd	Independent	15	502,363	0.7
1964	50	LYNDON B. JOHNSON	Democratic	486	43,126,506	61.1
		Barry M. Goldwater	Republican	52	27,176,799	38.5
1968	50	RICHARD M. NIXON	Republican	301	31,770,237	43.4
		Hubert H. Humphrey	Democratic	191	31,270,533	42.7
		George C. Wallace	American Independent	46	9,906,141	13.5
1972	50	RICHARD M. NIXON	Republican	520	47,169,911	60.7
		George S. McGovern	Democratic	17	29,170,383	37.5
1976	50	JIMMY CARTER	Democratic	297	40,827,394	49.9
		Gerald R. Ford	Republican	240	39,145,977	47.9
1980	50	RONALD W. REAGAN	Republican	489	43,899,248	50.8
		Jimmy Carter	Democratic	49	35,481,435	6.6
		John B. Anderson	Independent	0	5,719,437	1.0
		Ed Clark	Libertarian	0	920,859	
1984	50	RONALD W. REAGAN	Republican	525	54,451,521	58.8
		Walter F. Mondale	Democratic	13	37,565,334	40.5
1988	50	GEORGE H. W. BUSH	Republican	426	47,946,422	54.0
		Michael S. Dukakis	Democratic	112	41,016,429	46.0
1992	50	WILLIAM J. CLINTON	Democratic	370	43,728,275	43.2
		George H. W. Bush	Republican	168	38,167,416	37.7
		H. Ross Perot	Independent	0	19,237,247	19.0
1996	50	WILLIAM J. CLINTON	Democratic	379	47,401,185	49.0
		Robert Dole	Republican	159	39,197,469	41.0
		H. Ross Perot	Independent	0	8,085,295	8.0
2000	50	GEORGE W. BUSH	Republican	271	50,456,169	47.9
		Albert Gore, Jr.	Democratic	267	50,996,116	48.4
		Ralph Nader	Green	0	2,783,728	2,7
2004	50	GEORGE W. BUSH	Republican	286	60,693,281	50.7
		John Kerry	Democratic	252	57,355,978	48.3
		Ralph Nader	Independent	0	405,623	0.3
2008	50	BARACK OBAMA	Democratic	365	66,882,230	53.0
		John McCain	Republican	173	58,343,671	46.0
		Ralph Nader	Independent	0	726,462	0.6
2012	50	BARACK OBAMA	Democratic	332*	59,721,138*	51.0*
		Mitt Romney	Republican	206*	57,095,342*	49.0*

Because candidates receiving less than 1 percent of the popular vote are omitted, the percentage of popular vote may not total 100 percent.

*Estimate; final numbers not available when text went to press.

THE AMERICAN ECONOMY

KEY ECONOMIC INDICATORS

Year	Gross National Product (GNP) and Gross Domestic Product (GDP)[a] (in $ billions)	Steel Production (in tons)	Corn Production (millions of bushels)	Automobiles Registered	New Housing Starts	Foreign Trade (in $ millions) Exports	Imports
1790	NA	NA	NA	NA	NA	20	23
1800	NA	NA	NA	NA	NA	71	91
1810	NA	NA	NA	NA	NA	67	85
1820	NA	NA	NA	NA	NA	70	74
1830	NA	NA	NA	NA	NA	74	71
1840	NA	NA	NA	NA	NA	132	107
1850	NA	NA	592[d]	NA	NA	152	178
1860	NA	13,000	839[e]	NA	NA	400	362
1870	7.4[b]	77,000	1,125	NA	NA	451	462
1880	11.2[c]	1,397,000	1,707	NA	NA	853	761
1890	13.1	4,779,000	1,650	NA	328,000	910	823
1900	18.7	11,227,000	2,662	89,000	189,000	1,499	930
1910	35.3	28,330,000	2,853	458,300	387,000(1918=118,000)	1,919	1,646
1920	91.5	46,183,000	3,071	8,131,500	247,000(1925=937,000)	8,664	5,784
1930	90.7	44,591,000	2,080	23,034,700	330,000(1933=93,000)	4,013	3,500
1940	100.0	66,983,000	2,457	27,465,800	603,000(1944=142,000)	4,030	7,433
1950	286.5	96,836,000	3,075	40,339,000	1,952,000	9,997	8,954
1960	506.5	99,282,000	4,314	61,682,300	1,365,000	19,659	1 5,093
1970	1,016.0	131,514,000	4,200	89,279,800	1,434,000	42,681	40,356
1980	2,819.5	111,835,000	6,600	121,601,00	1,292,000	220,626	244,871
1990	5,764.9	98,906,000	7,933	133,700,000	1,193,000	394,030	485,453
2000	9,963.1	112,242,000	9,968	1 33,600,000[f]	1,569,000	781,918	1,218,022
2009	14,265	56,000,000	13,200	134,080,000	554,000	1,578,945	1,958,009

NA = Not available

[a]In December 1991 the Bureau of Economic Analysis of the U.S. government began using gross domestic product rather than gross national product as the primary measure of U.S. production.

[b]Figure is average for 1869–1878.

[c]Figure is average for 1879–1888.

[d]Figure for 1849.

[e]Figure for 1859.

[f]Does not include sports utility vehicles (SUVs) and light trucks.

FEDERAL BUDGET OUTLAYS AND DEBT

YEAR	DEFENSE[c]	VETERANS BENEFITS[a]	INCOME SECURITY[a]	SOCIAL SECURITY[a]	HEALTH AND MEDICARE[a]	EDUCATION[a, d]	NET INTEREST PAYMENTS[a]	FEDERAL DEBT (DOLLARS)
1790	14.9	4.1[b]	NA	NA	NA	NA	55.0	75,463,000[c]
1800	55.7	0.6	NA	NA	NA	NA	31.3	82,976,000
1810	48.4(1814:79.7)	1.0	NA	NA	NA	NA	34.9	53,173,000
1820	38.4	17.6	NA	NA	NA	NA	28.1	91,016,000
1830	52.9	9.0	NA	NA	NA	NA	12.6	48,565,000
1840	54.3(1847:80.7)	10.7	NA	NA	NA	NA	0.7	3,573,000
1850	43.8	4.7	NA	NA	NA	NA	1.0	63,453,000
1860	44.2(1865:88.9)	1.7	NA	NA	NA	NA	5.0	64,844,000
1870	25.7	9.2	NA	NA	NA	NA	41.7	2,436,453,000
1880	19.3	21.2	NA	NA	NA	NA	35.8	2,090,909,000
1890	20.9(1899:48.6)	33.6	NA	NA	NA	NA	11.4	1,222,397,000
1900	36.6	27.0	NA	NA	NA	NA	7.7	1,263,417,000
1910	45.1 (1919:59.5)	23.2	NA	NA	NA	NA	3.1	1,146,940,000
1920	37.1	3.4	NA	NA	NA	NA	16.0	24,299,321,000
1930	25.3	6.6	NA	NA	NA	NA	19.9	16,185,310,000
1940	17.5(1945:89.4)	6.0	6.0	0.3	0.5	20.8	9.4	42,967,531,000
1950	32.2	20.3	9.6	1.8	0.6	0.6	11.3	256,853,000,000
1960	52.2	5.9	8.0	12.6	0.9	8.0	7.5	290,525,000,000
1970	41.8	4.4	8.0	15.5	6.2	4.4	7.3	308,921,000,000
1980	22.7	3.6	14.6	20.1	9.4	5.4	8.9	909,050,000,000
1990	23.9	2.3	11.7	19.8	12.4	3.1	14.7	3,266,073,000,000
2000	16.2	2.6	14.1	22.7	19.9	3.5	12.3	5,629,000,000,000
2010	19.1	3.0	18.9	24.0	2.8	13.5	197.0[e]	13,500,000,000,000

NA = Not available.

[a]Figures represent percentage of total federal spending for each category. Not included are transportation, commerce, housing, and various other categories.

[b]1789–1791 figure.

[c]1791 figure.

[d]Include straining, employment, and social services.

[e]Congressional Budget Office, "Federal Debt and Interest Costs," December 2010.

INDEX

Colorado: Native Americans' displacement in, 507–508; Union entered by, 518

Columbia Broadcasting System (CBS), 711

Columbia Phonograph Company, 682

Columbia Pictures, 712

Columbia River: dam on, 746

Columbine High School, shooting at, 952

Comedy shows, radio, 711

Commission on Training Camp Activities, 675

Committee on Public Information (CPI), 680

Committee to Re-Elect the President (CREEP), 910

Common Law (Holmes), 636

Communications Decency Act, 939–940

Communism. *See also* Anti-communism: containing, 805, 808; domino theory, 876; New Deal agencies suspected of, 751; Red scare of 1919–1920, 694–695

Communist Party, lynchings publicized by, 756

Competition: Great Depression and, 741; immigrant labor as, 627, 687; labor-related, 556, 627, 687, 751; Rockefeller and, 541; wage, 556, 751

Composers, 762

Compromise of 1877, 500

Computers: age of, 834 (illus); personal, and IT revolution, 948–949; WWII and, 779

Comstock, Anthony, 581

Comstock, Daniel, 761

Comstock, Henry, 522

Comstock Lode, 522

Concentration camps, WWII Nazi, 772

Coney Island, 643, 643 (illus), 644 (illus)

Confederate States of America: Amnesty Act and, 494; Native Americans siding with, 528; reconstruction and, 473, 475 (illus)

Confederate veterans, pensions of, 548

Confederation. *See also* Articles of Confederation

Conformity: 1950s consumerism and, 836; social critics of, 836, 840

Congress: African Americans in, 710; anti-trust efforts of, 542, 561, 656; Democratic control of 1936, 748; Department of Homeland Security and, 961; eightieth, 817–818; electoral commission created by, 498; first woman elected to, 684;

reconstruction and, 470; reconstruction by, 474–476, 475 (illus), 479, 480; War of 1812 voted for by (*See also* Continental Congress; National Congress of American Indians)

Congressional Union for Woman Suffrage, 648

Congress of Industrial Organizations, 755

Congress of Racial Equality (CORE), 789, 851

Connor, Eugene ("Bull"), 863

Conroy, Jack, 736

Conservation, 530–531; Cheney on, 971; Roosevelt (Theodore) and, 655, 656

Conservatives/conservatism: resurgence in 1994–1996, 904–905

Consolidation: railroad, 538–539; 1920s business, 700–702; 1950s business, 833; steel/iron, 541 (illus)

Conspicuous consumption, 590, 636

Constitution Hall, Anderson concert use of denied at, 749

Constitution of the United States, A3–A7. *See also* Amendments; specific amendments; amendments to, A7–A11; Civil Rights Act declared unconstitutional, 612; presidential power and, 969; progressivism and, 661–662; Reconstruction era, 495; segregation and, 847

Constitutions: New Deal and, 742, 747

Construction: dams, 741, 746; federal spending on highway, 836; highway, 824; New Deal, 746; 1950s, 840; 1929–1945 statistics on, 735, 735 (illus)

Consumer debt, 987

Consumer goods, 700, 702, 709–711

Consumerism: 1950s conformity and, 835–836; television and, 841–842

Consumer loans, 733, 733 (illus)

Consumer Protection, 654–655; Progressive Era bringing, 654–655

Consumption: electricity, 831; postwar economic boom and, 830

Containment: anticommunism and, 802–813, 803, 805, 808

Contract with America, Gingrich's, 943

Contras: in Nicaragua, 926 (illus); secret funding to, 926

Conventions: black majority in, 480

Converse, Frederick, 717

Conversion. *See also* Christianity

Convict laborers, 497, 549, 556, 558

Convict-lease system, 611

Cooke, Jay, 494

Coolidge, Calvin, 732

Coolidge, Calvin ("Silent Cal"), 695, 705; federal aid opposed by, 707; image-making of, 705; on outdoor recreation, 711

Coors, Joseph, 920

Copland, Aaron, 759

Coral Sea, battle of, 783

Cordray, Richard, 990

CORE. *see* Congress of Racial Equality (CORE)

Corn. *See also* Maize: Great Plains farming and, 518

Corporate America: Utopian vision of, 763–764

Corporate America, rise of, 536–542. *See also* Business; Business regulation

Corporate mergers, 947

Corporations, wage-cuts by, 734

Corruption. *See also* Scandals: Arthur as symbol of, 604; elections and, 602; Garfield and, 599; Gould/Union Pacific and, 538, 538 (illus); during Harding's presidency, 705; industrialization and, 538–539; Mugwumps and, 606, 625; progressivism literature/journalism on, 636–637; Puck on, 604, 605 (illus); Republican reconstruction, 481; by Tweed Ring, 493, 493 (illus), 497

Cortina, Juan, 520

COS. *see* Charity Organization Society (COS)

Cosby Show, 974

Cosmopolitan, 589

Cost accounting, 539, 540

Cost-analysis approach: applied to steel industry, 539; railroad industry, 538

Cotton Belt, 492 (map)

Cotton Club, 717

Cotton industry, 486; industrial South's, 548; strikes in, 756, 757 (illus)

Cotton mills, wages in, 550

Coughlin, Charles, 745, 747

Council of National Defense, 676

Council of Twelve Apostles, 519

"Councils of Defense," 685

Count Basie, 762

Countercultural revolution, 895–897; hippies and drugs, 896; music, 896–897; sexual revolution, 897

Country of the Pointed Firs, The (Jewett), 589

Countryside Finance, 987

Courtship, 715

Cowboys: cattle frontier and, 523–528; gauchos and, 526–527

Cox, George B., 602

Cox, James M., 695

Coxey, Jacob, 615, 615 (illus)

Cradle Will Rock, The (Blitzstein), 746

Crane, Stephen, 590

Credit: postwar South's crop-lien, 487; Public Credit Act, 495

Credit cards, 835

Crédit Mobilier, 493

Creel, George, 680

CREEP. *see* Committee to Re-Elect the President (CREEP)

Crime: organized, 725

Criticism: cultural, 716; social, 836, 840

Crocker, Charles, 555, 557

Crockett, Davy, 841

Croix de Guerre, 677

Croly, Herbert, 636, 681

Cronkite, Walter, on Vietnam, 881

Crop-lien economy, 487

Crops: rotation, 487

Crow Indians, 504, 505

Crum, Bartley, 820

Crusade for Justice, 871

Cuba: African American soldiers in, 626, 626 (illus); black troops in, 623; 1897 crisis over, 622–623, 624 (illus); Guantánamo Bay, 625, 961; missile crisis, 860–862; naval blockade of, 860–861; Platt Amendment and, 624

Cult of domesticity, 577

Culture. *See also* Popular culture; specific Native American cultures: African American music/dance and, 720–721, 721 (illus); after WWII, 841; celebrities in 1920s, 716–717; conflicts of, 588–595, 725–726; genteel, 589–591; Harlem Renaissance and, 720–721, 721 (illus); in jazz age, 715–721; middle class late 1800s society and, 577; national artistic, 589; Popular Front influence on, 758, 759; in 1930s, 758–764; saloon, 584, 585 (illus); 1920s mass, 709–715; television, 841–843, 843 (illus); woman's sphere assumptions and, 649–650; WWII, 788

Currency: major legislation on, 603, 604 (illus); paper/greenbacks, 603; Specie Resumption Act and, 495

Currency Act of 1900, 617

Curry, John Steuart (painter), 762

Curtis Act, 513, 513 (illus), 529

Custer, George Armstrong, 508

Customs, immigration, 571

CWA. *see* Civil Works Administration (CWA)

Cycle of indebtedness, 550

Czechoslovakia: Communist takeover of, 808; Nazi troops in, 770

D

Dairy farming, 734

Dakota Sioux, 505

Daley, Richard, 904

Dalrymple, Oliver, 528

Dams: New Deal construction of, 741, 746, 749; soil erosion and, 749

Danbury Hatters, 650

Dance/dancers: African American stereotyping and, 758; Ghost, 511, 514; sound films and, 761; Sun, 505

Darrow, Clarence, 723

Darwin, Charles, 526, 530, 562, 636, 723

Daugherty, Harry, 705

Daughters of the American Revolution, 749

Davis, Henry Winter, 471

Davis, John W., 708

Davis, Katherine Bement, 649

Davis, Miles, 841

Dawes Severalty Act, 510; Board of Indian Commissioners and, 512; reversal of, 757

Days of Rage (Chicago), 894

Dayton Accords, 941, 943

DC. *see* Direct current (DC)

Dean, Howard, 966

Dearborn Independent (newspaper), 722

"Death panels," 985

Deaths/death rate: 1900–1920, 642; in Afghanistan war, 988; dust bowl and, 744; from frequent pregnancies, 650; Gazan, 970; 1918 influenza pandemic, 688, 688 (illus); Iraq war, 970; Korean war, 813; Native American, 845; Philippine war, 626; September 11, 2001, 958; WWI forms of, 679; WWII, 782, 795, 796, 798

Debs, Eugene V., 561, 652, 658, 684, 685

Debt. *See also* Cycle of indebtedness; Federal deficit: personal, 835; southern cotton mills and, 550; WWI, 707

Declaration of Independence, A1–A2; anti-imperialists on, 625

Decolonization: Africa/Asia, 804, 804 (map), 806; Cold War and, 807

Deep Throat, 910

Defense budget: Eisenhower and, 825; FDR's, 770; under Truman, 811

Defense industry, 776–777, 786; 1950s economic boom and, 831–832

Defense spending, WWII, 777

DeForest, Lee, 760

Degas, Edward, 591

DeLay, Tom ("the Hammer"), 981

De Mille, Cecil B., 712

Demobilization, World War II, 814–818

Democracy: prohibition's failure and, 726; WWI propaganda and, 680–681

Democratic National Convention and, riots/police violence at, 904, 905 (illus)

Democrats/Democratic Party: African Americans forced to vote for, 611; Bryan nominated by, 656; Cleveland as, 605–606; coalition during New Deal, 748; during Coolidge presidency, 708; counterattacks by, 481–483; disputed election of 1876, 497–500, 499 (map); election of 1952 and, 822–823; FDR nomination by, 737; Gold standard, 654; House captured in 1910 by, 657; Ku Klux Klan arm of, 482, 482 (illus), 483, 498 (illus); League of Nations supported by, 694; racism of reconstruction-era, 484; reconstruction era, 495; silver advocates dominating, 616; South "redeemed" by, 496–497; South ruled by, late nineteenth-century, 601; Truman and, 783, 803; urban-immigrant wing of, 726; woman suffrage and, 649

Demographic changes, 971

Demonetization, 604, 604 (illus)

Dempsey, Jack, 714

Dennett, Mary Ware, 650

Dennis v. United States, 821

Department of Health, Education and Welfare, 824

Department stores, 577–578, 579 (illus), 702

Deportation: of Mexican farm laborers, 845, 846 (illus); of Russian-born immigrants, 695

Depressions, economic. *See also* Great Depression; Recession: 1873, 487; immigration and, 645, 645 (illus); industrialization and, 536; politics during 1890s, 613–618

De Priest, Oscar, 710

Deregulation: Carter/Reagan and, 925

Desegregation: of buses, 850; Central High School (Arkansas), 847, 848 (illus); lunch-counter sit-ins and, 851; South opposition to, 847–848; Sumner's bill for, 485; Truman and, 847

Desertification, land, 527

Desert Land Act, 517

Design: industrial, 762; postwar American, 772

Détente, 908–909

Marshall, Thurgood, 847, 935

Marshall Plan, 805, 808

Martí, José, 622

Marx, Karl, 563, 652

Marx Brothers, 758

Marxism, 563

Massachusetts. *See also* Massachusetts Bay

Massacre (film), 758

Mass culture: 1920s, 709–715; 1950s consumerism and, 835–836

Mass entertainment, 758; 1920s onset of, 711–712

Masses, The (magazine), 652, 685

Mass media, 715

Mass society, 709–715

Maxidiwiac ("Buffalo Bird Woman"), 503–504, 503 (illus)

"May Night by the Roadside," 717

McAdoo, William, 673, 676, 680, 708

McCain, John, 966, 983

McCain-Feingold campaign finance law, 990

McCarran Internal Security Act, 822

McCarthy, Eugene, 880–881, 904

McCarthy, Joseph, 802, 821, 822, 822 (illus); downfall of, 823; on television, 843

McCartney, Paul, 898

McCay, Winsor, 761

McClure's (magazine), 637

McConnell, Mitch, 988, 988 (illus)

McCoy, Joseph G., 524

McDonald's, 839

McGovern, George, 909–910

McGuire, Thomas B., 555

McKay, Claude, 720

McKinley, William F., 600, 622; assassination of, 653; election of, 616; tariff of, 606, 614, 616; war declared on Spain by, 620

McNamara, Robert, 862

McNary-Haugen Bill, 707

McPherson, Aimee Semple, 723

Mearn, Andrew, 634

Meat Inspection Act, 655

"Me Decade," 903

Media: German, 681; mass, 715; political use of, 706, 727, 727 (illus), 842–843

Medicaid, 873

Medicare, 873, 986

Medicine Lodge Treaty, 507

Medicines: higher education and, 579; patent, 654 (illus), 655

Meet the Beatles, 898

Mein Kampf (Hitler), 768

Mellon, Andrew, 705, 706, 732

Menarche, age of first, 852

Mencken, H. L., 716, 723

Menlo Park, New Jersey, Edison laboratory in, 543, 543 (illus)

Merchants: Chinese, 555; on tax reform, 642

Mergers: corporate, 538–539, 538 (illus), 700–702; labor movement and, 833

Merrill Lynch, 987

Metro-Goldwyn-Mayer, 712

Meuse-Argonne, WWI and, 677, 678 (map), 679, 680

Mexican-Americans: in armed forces, 792; in Texas labor camp, 843; Trans-Mississippi Western settlement and, 520–521; unemployment of, 756; workers, 721, 722, 722 (illus)

Mexican-American unions, Southwest migrant workers ignored by, 722

Mexican immigrants: deportation of farm-working, 845, 846 (illus); Operation Wetback and, 845; during 1953–1955 recession, 845

Mexico: Americans in Díaz's, 670; cattle-raising in, 526; "lost territories" of, WWI and, 674; Wilson and, 670–671; woman suffrage in, 718

MGM, 820

Micheaux, Oscar, 720

Microsoft, 986

Middle class: ideal womanhood of, 582; industrial labor from, 555; jazz age and, 715–716; labor strikes as shock to, 560; modernism and, 591; moral concerns of reformers from, 642–644; public education expansion sought by, 593–595; society/culture, 577; Victorian morality opposed by women of, 591–593

Middle-class women: in progressive movement, 632–633; Victorian morality opposed by, 591–593; woman suffrage and, 648

Middle colonies. *See also* specific colony

Middle East: decolonization in, 807; Eisenhower Doctrine on, 826

Middletown (Lynd/Lynd), 710

Midwest: new immigrants to, 570, 570 (map)

Mies van der Rohe, Ludwig, 773

Migrants/migration: within former Confederacy, 483–484; of freedmen, 499, 499 (illus); industrialization and, 568–571; Kansas, 499, 499 (illus), 517; to southern states, 479

Migrants/Migration: dust-bowl, 742; farm workers, 751; intellectual, 772–773

Migration, African American: to cities, 549, 645, 710; internal, 784, 790; WWI, 686–687, 686 (illus); WWII and, 784, 790

Milhaud, Darius, 773

Militarism, 652 (illus)

Military. *See also* Armed forces, U. S.; Soldiers, U.S.; Wars/warfare: build-up/expansion, 674, 675; defense industry and, 777; Haiti and, 768; Japanese bases of U. S., 809; labor strikes squashed by, 561; number serving in WWII, 784; reduction of, 931; research scholars dependent on, 826

Military aid: to Greece/Turkey, 805; to Serbia, 941

Military employment, 778, 778 (illus)

Military-industrial complex, 826

Military rule, during reconstruction, 482

Military tribunals, 970

Milosevic, Slobodan, 941

Mine Owners' Protective Association, 561

Miners: black, 549

Minimum wage, New Deal, 750, 753

Mining: frontier, 522–524; frontiers, 522, 522 (map); unions for, 561

Mining town, poverty in Kentucky, 844, 844 (illus)

Minnesota, settlement/Native Americans of, 505

Minor, Virginia, 478

Minority neighborhoods, interstate highway system destroying, 839

Minor v. Happersett, 478

Minstrel shows: vaudeville arising from, 587–588

Miranda v. Arizona, 875

Mises, Ludwig von, 772

Miss America Pageant, 714

Missile-defense program, Bush, G. W., 970

Missile development, 852

Missions/missionaries: in China, 667; economic expansion and, 667; paradox of, 621; women as global, 620–621, 620 (illus), 621 (illus)

Mississippi Freedom Democratic Party (MFDP), 864

Mississippi Freedom Summer Project of 1964, 864

Mississippi plan (1875), 497

Mississippi region: reconstruction era violence in, 497

Mississippi River, flood of, 707, 708, 708 (illus), 728

Mitchell, George, 943

Mitchell, John, 910

Quant, Mary, 898
Quicksand (Larsen), 720
Quinn, Anthony, 845
Quota system, immigration, 721

R

Rabbit Run (Updike), 841
Rabin, Yitzhak, 941
Race music, 852
Race/racism. See also Desegregation; Discrimination; Racial violence; Segregation; Segregation, racial: in advertising, 560, 560 (illus); African/Hispanic Americans resisting exploitation and, 756–757, 757 (illus); agrarian protest groups and, 608; antiprostitution laws and, 644; in armed forces, 787; atomic bombs of WWII and, 796; Christianity for "weaker races," 619; citizenship denied on basis of, 552; convict-lease system and, 611; draft and, 685; Great Plains settlers and, 517; Korean War racial integration, 813; mass culture of 1920s and, 714; missionaries and, 620–621; Nazi theories of, 770; New Deal and, 749; Obama on, 984; Philippines and, 626; postwar politics of, 847; progressivism and, 645–647, 648 (illus); reconstruction-era Democrat, 484; reform and, 644, 645, 661; social class barriers deepened by, 567; Southern Manifesto, 847, 849; 1890s rising, 521; Supreme Court and, 612; Wilson's presidency and, 647; woman suffrage and, 648–649; WWI and, 675, 687; WWII and, 788–790
Race relations: 1950s, 829–830
Race riots, 479; during Great Depression, 756; Red scare and, 694–695, 695 (illus); during WWII, 790
Racial violence: 1919–1920, 695
Racism: discrimination, 843
Radical Republicans, 472 (illus); black suffrage supported by, 470
Radio, 711, 712 (illus); Great Depression and, 758; political use of, 706, 727; standardization of, 711; WWII news programs on, 788
Radioactive fallout, 825
Radio Corporation of America (RCA), 711
Ragged Dick (Alger), 554
Ragtime, 588, 643
Railroad Administration, 676
Railroads/railroad industry: bonanza farms and, 525; conservation and,

531; consolidation of, 538–539; corruption and, 493; first transcontinental, 514–516; Grange movement and, 607; land grants for, 514, 516 (map); management innovations, 537–538; reform, 640; regulation, 654; Sedan-Mezières, 680; settlers and, 516–517; strikes in, 560–561; time zones established by, 516 (map); unions crushed by, 561; wage raises/reforms in, 640
Rainey, Gertrude ("Ma"), 714
Rainsford, William S., 582
Ramona (Jackson), 520
Ranching, Trans-Mississippi West, 525
Randolph, A. Philip, 789, 864
Rankin, Jeannette, 684, 776
Rationing, WWII and, 779
Rauschenbusch, Walter, 582
La Raza Unida, 871
RCA (Radio Corporation of America), 711
R&D. see Research and development (R&D)
Reader's Digest, 711
Reagan, Ronald, 823, 923 (illus), 930–931; Cold War and, 925–928; conservative domestic agenda of, 923, 925; 1980 election of, 922–923, 923 (map); Gorbachev and, 918 (illus), 919; as governor of California, 891; Latin America and, 926; Regan on public appearances of, 930; Sandinista insurgents opposed by, 926; shooting of, 927
Real Estate Disposition Corporation (REDC), 957
Real estate recession, 986
Realism: Catholic objection to, 761; film, 758; radio and, 763, 763 (illus)
Rebel Without a Cause, 854
Recall petition, 639
Recession: 1920, 700; 1953–1955, 845; FDR and, 751; during Obama administration, 986–988
Reconstruction, 468–501, 475 (illus), 476 (map); abandonment of, 496–500; African Americans after, 611–613; amendments, 478 (illus); Amnesty Act of, 494; congressional, 474–476, 476 (illus), 480; Constitution and, 495; ex-confederate counterattacks to, 481–483; governments, 478–483; Iraq, 968; land ownership and, 486–487; Liberal's Revolt during, 494; Lincoln's plan for, 470–471; Panic of 1873, 494; politics, 470–478; presidential, 472–473, 486; under Republican rule, 480–481;

sharecropping during, 487, 488–489, 488 (illus), 492 (illus); White League and, 497, 498 (illus)
Reconstruction Acts, 470; of 1867, 475, 476 (map); Johnson's veto of, 473; list/dates of, 475 (illus)
Reconstruction Finance Corporation (RFC), 734, 741
Recreation: immigrant children's, 583, 583 (illus); outdoor, 711
Recruitment. See also Draft: of African Americans for WWI, 676, 676 (illus); Red Army, 781, 782, 794
Red Cloud, chief, 509
Red Cross (illus), 690
Red Menace (film): anti-communism, 819
A Red Record (Wells-Barnett), 647
Red River valley, wheat boom/collapse in, 525, 528
Red River War, 508
Red scare: 1919–1920, 694–695; Red Menace (film), 819; second, 802, 817, 818
Reed, Donald, 714
Reed, Walter, 668
Reference library, legislation, 640
Reform Party, Perot's, 946
Reform/reformers. See also Activism; Labor unions; New Deal; specific enactments: campaign funding, 966–967; civil service, 604–605; education, 965; electoral, 640; global progressive, 634–635, 634 (illus), 635 (illus); housing, 635; late 1800s change in approach of, 581; local politics, 638–639; middle-class, 567; Native American, 510; poverty of late 1800s and, 580; Progressive Era, 633, 637; public education, 593–595; race/racism and, 644, 645, 661; racism and, 644, 645; sanitary, 574; separation of races and, 609; social gospel movement for, 638; Social gospel movement for, 582; tariff/banking, 659; utopian, 563; working class and, 580–583; WWI and, 685
Refugee camps: massacre at Palestine, 929
Refugees: Iraq, 968
Refugee(s): dust-bowl, 751; Jewish, 771
"Refusing to Give the Lady a Seat," 694, 694 (illus)
Regan, Donald, 928, 930
Regulation. See also Business regulation; Environmental regulation; Health regulations; Pricing controls: railroad, 654

Rehnquist, William, 945, 980

Religions. *See also* Puritans/Puritanism; specific religions: African American, 484; political parties of late 1800s and, 602; poverty and, 582; Sioux, 505

Religion(s): education and, 840–841; Fundamentalism in, 723; WWI opponents and, 684

Religious right (political wing), 967

Religious toleration. *See also* Act for Religious Toleration

Remington, Frederic, 527, 527 (illus), 529

Renaissance (in Europe). *See also* American Renaissance; Harlem Renaissance

Repeal: prohibition, 726

Report on the Lands of the Arid Regions of the United States (Powell), 531

Republican Party: 1896, 616–618; 1930, 734; in Congress of 1947–1948, 817–818; contributors to, 965; 1918 control by, 691; disputed election of 1876, 497–500; factions within 1880s, 599; FDR criticized by, 748; Hoover and, 727; neoconservatives, 962; Obama presidency and, 989–990; politics dominated by, 600, 613–614; post-Civil War South ruled by, 479, 480–481; 1920s, 705–706; South ruled by, 479, 480–481, 498 (illus); tariff support by, 600, 606

Republicans/Republicanism: black suffrage goal of, 477; FDR and, 774; freemen as backbone of, 479–480; as Insurgents, 656, 657; "Irreconcilables," 693; modern, 823; New Deal coalition of, 751; property rights and, 476; radical, 470, 472 (illus); reconstruction and, 473–474, 477, 495–496; "Reservationists," 693; in South Carolina legislature, 480, 480 (illus); 1870s retreat of, 495–496

Republic of Hawai'i, 619

Republic Steel Company, 755

Research and development (R&D), 832; Reagan's SDI, 926

Research scholars, military and, 826

Research university, 579

"Reservationists," 693

Reservations, Native American, 507, 511, 511 (map), 513 (illus); Protestant reform of abuses on, 508; WWII changes in, 790

Resettlement Administration, 747; FSA replacing, 751

Resistance. *See also* Civil rights movement; Protest; Revolts/rebellions: draft, 675, 684–685; nonviolent, 851

Resources, water, 655

Reuther, Walter, 754, 755, 755 (illus)

Revelle, Roger, 972

Revels, Hiram, 480

Revenue Act of 1942, 779

Revenue Act of 1935 (Wealth Tax Act), 745 (illus)

Revolts/rebellions. *See also* Protest; Resistance: African/Asian colony, 805; Boxer Rebellion, 667, 670; habeas corpus in cases of, 483; 1872 Liberal Republican, 496; Liberal's, 494

Revolution. *See also* American Revolution; Glorious Revolution: sexual, 715; television, 841–843, 843 (illus)

Rhapsody in Blue (Gershwin), 717

Rice, Condoleezza, 958, 962, 964, 981

Rice, Joseph Mayer, 594

Rice/rice industry: sharecropping applied to, 487

Rich, tax cuts favoring, 706, 732

Richards, Ann, 946

Richards, Ellen, 649

Rickey, Branch, 829

Riesman, David, 837

Rights. *See also* Civil rights; Civil Rights movement; Property rights; Women's Liberation; Women's rights; Women's suffrage: fishing, 619; limiting of sharecropper/tenant, 497; Native American, 757, v; workers', 754

Right wing (political), religious, 967

Riis, Jacob, 580, 634

Ringling Brothers, 712, 712 (illus)

Riots: antiblack, 646; Los Angeles "zoot suit," 791; race, 479, 694–695, 695 (illus), 756, 790

River, The (Lorenz), 747

Roaring Twenties, 699

Roberts, John, 980–981

Robeson, Paul, 720

Robinson, Bill, 758

Robinson, Edward G., 758

Robinson, Jackie, 829–830, 829 (illus), 846

Robinson, Jo Ann, 850

Rock-and-roll, 852

"Rock Around the Clock," 852

Rockefeller, John D., 541, 548, v; campaign contributions of, 616; University of Chicago and, 578

Rockwell, Norman, 711

Roentgen, Wilhelm, 544

Roe v. Wade, 897, 981

Rogers, Ginger, 761

Rolling Stones, 897, 899

Roman Catholics. *See also* Catholics/Catholicism

Rome-Berlin-Tokyo Axis (Axis), 771, 772, 774, 775, 777, 784, 788, 796, 797

Roosevelt, Eleanor, 731; activism of, 737, 738 (illus), 749; African Americans and, 749; Depression-era children's letters to, 754; NYA and, 749; shyness of, 737

Roosevelt, Franklin Delano, 618, 695, 730–731 (illus), 731; advisors/cabinet of, 737–738; Campobello incident and, 731, 731 (illus); "cash and carry" policy of, 774; death of, 794; Democratic coalition/reelection of, 748–749; economic intervention in WWII, 774; election of 1920 and, 695, 695 (illus); election of 1932 and, 736–737; election of 1936 and, 748–759; election of 1944 and, 784; "fireside chats" of, 743; "Good Neighbor" policy of, 768; Grand Alliance and, 783–784; "Hundred Days" measures of Congress under, 739, 739 (illus); Japanese internment and, 792; mobilization for war by, 774, 776–781; New Deal of, 691; polio of, 731; 1938–1939 pre WWII actions of, 770–771; racial directive of, 789; Recession confronted by, 750–751; Supreme Court and, 749; top political adviser, 737; vetoes by, 779; WWII goals of, 783

Roosevelt, Theodore, 529, 619, 662, 684; communing with Nature, 656, 657 (illus); Corollary to Monroe Doctrine, 669; environmental concern of, 655; Hoover compared to, 728; labor dispute approach of, 653; in Latin America/Asia, 668–670; on muckrakers, 637; Nobel Peace Prize awarded to, 670; Panama Canal and, 668, 668 (illus); path to presidency of, 653; physical fitness of, 653, 656; political skills of, 653–654; racial record of, 646–647; Taft and, 653–658, 668–670; as war hero, 623

Rosenberg, Julius/Ethel, 821, 821 (illus)

Rosie the Riveter, 786

Rostropovitch, Mstislav, 919

Roth, Philip, 841

Roughing It (Twain), 523

Rounders, 585

Rowe, Billy, 469

Rowe, Katie, 469, 469 (illus)

Rubber Soul, 898

Rubinstein, Arthur, 773

PACIFIC
OCEAN

49°N

WASHINGTON
1889

Columbia R.

OREGON COUNTRY
(By Agreement
with Britain, 1846)

OREGON
1859

IDAHO
1890

42°N

40°N

MONTANA
1889

Missouri R.

NORTH DAKOTA
1889

SOUTH DAKO
1889

WYOMING
1890

Great
Salt
Lake

NEVADA
1864

UTAH
1896

MEXICAN CESSION
(1848)

Colorado R.

COLORADO
1876

NEBRASKA
1867

LOUISI
PURCH
(From Franc

K

CALIFORNIA
1850

30°N

ARIZONA
1912

NEW MEXICO
1912

O

TEXAS
(Independent Repu
Annexed 1845)

GADSDEN PURCHASE
(From Mexico, 1853)

Rio Grande

TEXAS
1845

Nueces R.

PACIFIC OCEAN

HAWAI'I
1959

HAWAI'I
(Annexed 1898)

0 50 100 Km.

0 50 100 Mi.

160°W   155°W

20°N

170°E

50°N

PACIFIC OCEAN

170°W

RUSSIA

70°N

ALASKA
1959

CANADA

60°N

ALASKA PURCHASE
(From Russia, 1867)

0   200   400 Km.

0   250   400 Mi.

160°W   150°W   140°W

MEXICO

120°W   110°W   100°W   90°W

CANADA

Lake Superior

Lake Michigan

Lake Huron

Lake Ontario

Lake Erie

WISCONSIN
1848

MICHIGAN
1837

MINNESOTA

NEW YORK

MAINE
1820

VT.
1791

N.H.

MASS.

CONN.

R.I.

PENNSYLVANIA

ILLINOIS
1818

INDIANA
1816

OHIO
1803

MASON-DIXON LINE

NEW
JERSEY
1790

DELAWARE

MARYLAND

WEST
VIRGINIA
1863

KENTUCKY
1792

VIRGINIA

MISSOURI
1821

THE ORIGINAL UNITED STATES
(By Treaty with Britain, 1783)

MISSOURI
COMPROMISE LINE

2000

NORTH
CAROLINA

TENNESSEE
1796

Mississippi R.

ARKANSAS
1836

SOUTH
CAROLINA

GEORGIA

MISSISSIPPI
1817

ALABAMA
1819

(Seized from Spain,
1810, 1813)

LOUISIANA
1812

St. Lawrence R.

THIRTEEN COLONIES

THE ORIGINAL

ATLANTIC
OCEAN

N

Territorial Growth
of the
United States

1820 Date of states admission to the Union

● Geographic center of population by decade

0	150	300 Km.
0	150	300 Mi.

FLORIDA
(By Treaty with
Spain, 1819)

FLORIDA
1845

Gulf of Mexico

BAHAMAS

CUBA

HAITI

DOMINICAN
REPUBLIC

GREENLAND
(DENMARK)

ICELAND

ALASKA
(U.S.)

CANADA

UNITED STATES

40°N

Azores
(Port.)

80°N

60°N

ATLANTIC OCEAN

Bermuda
(U.K.)

WESTERN
SAHARA
(MOROCCO)

Midway Is.
(U.S.)

Hawaiian Is.
(U.S.)

MEXICO

BAHAMAS

DOMINICAN REP.

Virgin Is.
(U.S.)

CUBA

JAMAICA HAITI

BELIZE

HONDURAS   Puerto Rico
(U.S.)

GUATEMALA

EL SALVADOR   NICARAGUA

ST. KITTS AND NEVIS

ANTIGUA AND BARBUDA

DOMINICA

BARBADOS

ST. LUCIA

GRENADA   ST. VINCENT AND
THE GRENADINES

CAPE
VERDE

20°N

SE

GAMBIA

GUINEA-BISSAU

SI.
LE

PACIFIC OCEAN

COSTA RICA

PANAMA

TRINIDAD AND TOBAGO

VENEZUELA   GUYANA

COLOMBIA

FR. GUIANA
(FRANCE)

SURINAM

Equator

Galapagos Is.
(Ecuador)

ECUADOR

PERU

0°

SAMOA

French Polynesia
(France)

BRAZIL

BOLIVIA

TONGA

PARAGUAY

20°S

Easter Is.
(Chile)

CHILE

URUGUAY

ARGENTINA

40°S

0   1,000   2,000 Km.

0   1,000   2,000 Mi.

Falkland Is.
(U.K.)

60°S

160°W   140°W   120°W   100°W   80°W   60°W   40°W   20°W

80°S

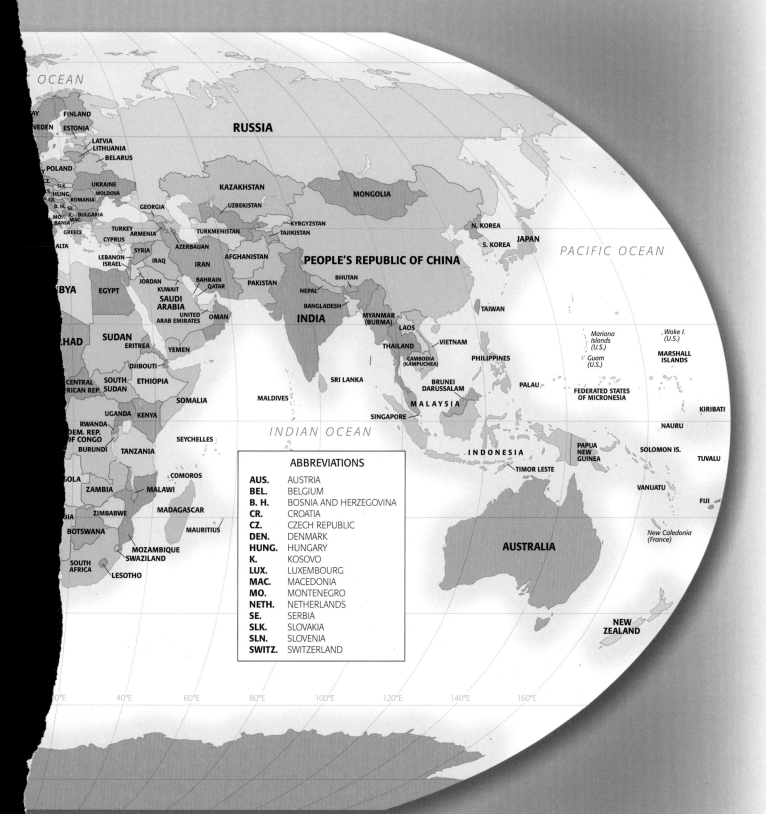